Fifteenth Edition

MW00987758

ANTHROPOLOGY

THE HUMAN CHALLENGE

WILLIAM A. HAVILAND
Professor Emeritus, University of Vermont

HARALD E. L. PRINS
Kansas State University

DANA WALRATH
University of Vermont

BUNNY McBRIDE
Kansas State University

CENGAGE
Learning

Australia • Brazil • Mexico • Singapore • United Kingdom • United States

CENGAGE
Learning·

Anthropology: The Human Challenge,
Fifteenth Edition
**William A. Haviland, Harald E. L. Prins,
Dana Walrath, Bunny McBride**

Product Director: Marta Lee-Perriard

Product Manager: Elizabeth Beiting-Lipps

Content Developer: Catherine Craddock and Stefanie Chase

Product Assistant: Chelsea Meredith

Content Project Manager: Cheri Palmer

Art Director: Michael Cook

Manufacturing Planner: Judy Inouye

Production Service and Compositor:
MPS Limited

Photo and Text Researchers:
Lumina Datamatics Ltd.

Copy Editor: Jennifer Gordon

Text Designer: Lisa Buckley

Cover Designer: Larry Didona

Cover Image: Global communication: almir 1968/iStock/Getty Images. / Satellite in outer space over earth: Ryan Etter/ Ikon Images/Getty Images. / Sipan, Tomb of the Lord of Sipan, Moche funeral site: Bruno Cossa/Grand Tour/Corbis. / Black hat dancer at Paro Tsechu: Blaine Harrington III/Corbis. / Tufted Capuchin: Ben Cranke/ Oxford Scientific/Getty Images. / Mitosis (transmission electron micrograph): Dr. Klaus Boller/Science Source. / Scientist examining DNA autoradiogram: Andrew Brookes/ Cultura Exclusive/Getty Images. / Zanibar, children playing draughts in street: Tuul and Bruno Morandi/The Image Bank/Getty Images. / Excavating a governor's tomb: Sandro Vannini/Corbis. / Man teaching girl calligraphy: Floresco Productions/Corbis.

Interior Design Images: iStockPhoto.com/ Patrick Ellis, iStockPhoto.com/Amoled, iStockPhoto.com/amdandy

© 2017, 2014 Cengage Learning

ALL RIGHTS RESERVED. No part of this work covered by the copyright herein may be reproduced or distributed in any form or by any means, except as permitted by U.S. copyright law, without the prior written permission of the copyright owner.

Unless otherwise noted, all content is © Cengage Learning.

For product information and technology assistance, contact us at
Cengage Learning Customer & Sales Support, 1-800-354-9706

For permission to use material from this text or product, submit all requests online at **cengage.com/permissions**
Further permissions questions can be e-mailed to
permissionrequest@cengage.com

Library of Congress Control Number: 2015960734
Student Edition:
ISBN: 978-1-305-58369-6

Loose-leaf Edition:
ISBN: 978-1-305-86335-4

Cengage Learning
20 Channel Center Street
Boston, MA 02210
USA

Cengage Learning is a leading provider of customized learning solutions with employees residing in nearly 40 different countries and sales in more than 125 countries around the world. Find your local representative at **www.cengage.com**

Cengage Learning products are represented in Canada by Nelson Education, Ltd.

To learn more about Cengage Learning Solutions, visit **www.cengage.com**

Purchase any of our products at your local college store or at our preferred online store **www.cengagebrain.com**

Printed in the United States of America
Print Number: 01   Print Year: 2016

DEDICATION

In loving memory of **Joshua Lieberman,**

who brought song, laughter, ease, and precision

to the center of being human.

Putting the World in Perspective

MERCATOR

Although all humans we know about are capable of producing accurate sketches of localities and regions with which they are familiar, **cartography** (the craft of mapmaking as we know it today) had its beginnings in 16th-century Europe, and its subsequent development is related to the expansion of Europeans to all parts of the globe. From the beginning, there have been two problems with maps: the technical one of how to depict on a two-dimensional, flat surface a three-dimensional spherical object, and the cultural one of whose worldview they reflect. In fact, the two issues are inseparable, for the particular projection one uses inevitably makes a statement about how one views one's own people and their place in the world. Indeed, maps often shape our perception of reality as much as they reflect it.

In cartography, a **projection** refers to the system of intersecting lines (of longitude and latitude) by which part or all of the globe is represented on a flat surface. There are more than a hundred different projections in use today, ranging from polar perspectives to interrupted "butterflies" to rectangles to heart shapes. Each projection causes distortion in size, shape, or distance in some way or another. A map that correctly shows the shape of a landmass will of necessity misrepresent the size. A map that is accurate along the equator will be deceptive at the poles.

Perhaps no projection has had more influence on the way we see the world than that of Gerhardus Mercator, who devised his map in 1569 as a navigational aid for mariners. So well suited was Mercator's map for this purpose that it continues to be used for navigational charts today. At the same time, the Mercator projection became a standard for depicting landmasses, something for which it was never intended. Although an accurate navigational tool, the Mercator projection greatly exaggerates the size of landmasses in higher latitudes, giving about two-thirds of the map's surface to the northern hemisphere. Thus the lands occupied by Europeans and European descendants appear far larger than those of other people. For example, North America (19 million square kilometers) appears almost twice the size of Africa (30 million

MOLLWEIDE

VAN DER GRINTEN

ROBINSON

square kilometers), whereas Europe is shown as equal in size to South America, which actually has nearly twice the landmass of Europe.

A map developed in 1805 by Karl B. Mollweide was one of the earlier *equal-area projections* of the world. Equal-area projections portray landmasses in correct relative size, but, as a result, distort the shape of continents more than other projections. They most often compress and warp lands in the higher latitudes and vertically stretch landmasses close to the equator. Other equal-area projections include the Lambert Cylindrical Equal-Area Projection (1772), the Hammer Equal-Area Projection (1892), and the Eckert Equal-Area Projection (1906).

The Van der Grinten Projection (1904) was a compromise aimed at minimizing both the distortions of size in the Mercator and the distortion of shape in equal-area maps such as the Mollweide. Although an improvement, the lands of the northern hemisphere are still emphasized at the expense of the southern. For example, in the Van der Grinten, the Commonwealth of Independent States (the former Soviet Union) and Canada are shown at more than twice their relative size.

The Robinson Projection, which was adopted by the National Geographic Society in 1988 to replace the Van der Grinten, is one of the best compromises to date between the distortions of size and shape. Although an improvement over the Van der Grinten, the Robinson Projection still depicts lands in the northern latitudes as proportionally larger at the same time that it depicts lands in the lower latitudes (representing most Third World nations) as proportionally smaller. Like European maps before it, the Robinson Projection places Europe at the center of the map with the Atlantic Ocean and the Americas to the left, emphasizing the cultural connection between Europe and North America, while neglecting the geographic closeness of northwestern North America to northeastern Asia.

The following pages show four maps that each convey quite different cultural messages. Included among them is the Gall-Peters Projection, an equal-area map that has been adopted as the official map of UNESCO (the United Nations Educational, Scientific, and Cultural Organization), and a map made in Japan, showing us how the world looks from the other side.

The Robinson Projection

The map below is based on the Robinson Projection, which is used today by the National Geographic Society and Rand McNally. Although the Robinson Projection distorts the relative size of landmasses, *it does so much* *less than most other projections*. Still, it places Europe at the center of the map. This particular view of the world has been used to identify the location of many of the cultures discussed in this text.

MI

NENETS

KHANTY

YUPIK ESKIMO

RUSSIAN

TUVAN

LOVAKIAN

ERB

SNIAN

CHECHEN

MONGOLIAN

ARMENIAN

UYGHUR

TURK

UZBEK

KURD

TAJIK

JAPANESE

SYRIAN

KUCHI

KOHISTANI

BAKHTIARI

WLAD 'ALI

BEDOUIN

NYINBA

TIBETAN

HAN CHINESE

PASHTUN

BAHRAINI

KAREN

MOSUO

TAIWANESE

SHAIVITE

NUER

TIGREAN

NAYAR

ANDAMAN

HANUNOO

TRUK

DINKA

AFAR

SOMALI

VEDDA

AZANDE

ACHOLI

KOTA AND KURUMBA

PINGELAP ISLANDER

MBUTI

TURKANA

MALDIVIAN

TODA AND BADAGA

ACEH

WAPE

NANDI

KAPAUKU

ENGA

UTU

KIKUYU

MINANGKABAU

TSEMBAGA

TUTSI

GUSII

MAASAI

TIRIKI

BUGIS

ARAPESH

SOLOMON ISLANDER

HADZA

BALINESE

TROBRIANDER

DOBU

SWAZI

ZULU

BASUTO

ABORIGINAL

MAORI

TASMANIAN

The Gall-Peters Projection

The map below is based on the Gall-Peters Projection, which has been adopted as the official map of UNESCO. Although it distorts the shape of continents (countries near the equator are vertically elongated by a ratio of 2 to 1), the Gall-Peters Projection does show all continents according to their correct relative size. Though Europe is still at the center, it is not shown as larger and more extensive than the Third World.

UNITED
STATES

CANADA

GREENLAND

UNITED STATES

MEXICO

BAHAMAS

HAITI

DOMINICAN REPUBLIC

CUBA

JAMAICA

NICARAGUA

BELIZE
GUATEMALA
EL SALVADOR
HONDURAS
COSTA RICA
PANAMA

VENEZUELA

FRENCH GUIANA

COLOMBIA

GUYANA
SURINAM

ECUADOR

BRAZIL

PERU

BOLIVIA

PARAGUAY

CHILE

ARGENTINA   URUGUAY

NEW ZEALAND

ANTARCTICA

The Turnabout Map

The way maps may reflect (and influence) our thinking is exemplified by the Turnabout Map, which places the South Pole at the top and the North Pole at the bottom. Words and phrases such as "on top," "over," and "above" tend to be equated by some people with superiority. Turning things upside-down may cause us to rethink the way North Americans regard themselves in relation to the people of Central America.

© 1982 by Jesse Levine Turnabout Map™—Dist. by Laguna Sales, Inc., 7040 Via Valverde, San Jose, CA 95135

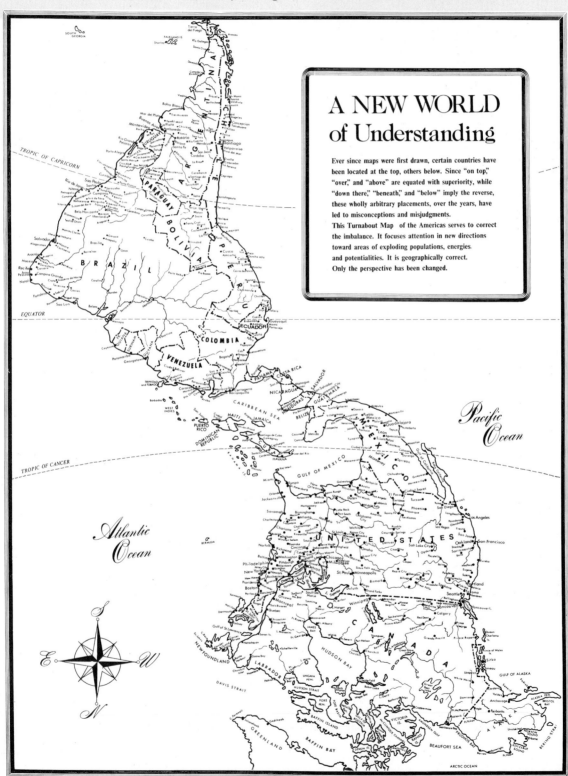

A NEW WORLD of Understanding

Ever since maps were first drawn, certain countries have been located at the top, others below. Since "on top," "over," and "above" are equated with superiority, while "down there," "beneath," and "below" imply the reverse, these wholly arbitrary placements, over the years, have led to misconceptions and misjudgments.

This Turnabout Map of the Americas serves to correct the imbalance. It focuses attention in new directions toward areas of exploding populations, energies and potentialities. It is geographically correct. Only the perspective has been changed.

Brief Contents

Features Contents

Contents

Chapter 7

Origins of the Genus *Homo*   167

Chapter 8

The Global Expansion of *Homo sapiens* and Their Technology   199

Chapter 9
The Neolithic Revolution: The Domestication of Plants and Animals   227

Chapter 10
The Emergence of Cities and States   251

Chapter 11
Modern Human Diversity— Race and Racism   275

Chapter 12
Human Adaptation to a Changing World   295

Chapter 13
Characteristics of Culture   323

Chapter 14
Ethnographic Research— Its History, Methods, and Theories   343

Chapter 15

Language and Communication 371

Chapter 16

Social Identity, Personality, and Gender 395

Chapter 17
Patterns of Subsistence   417

Chapter 18
Economic Systems   441

Preface

For the last edition of this textbook, we did some serious housecleaning—sorting through the contents "clear down to the bottom to determine what should be kept and what should be tossed to make room for new material that warrants a place in a limited space." Our efforts resulted in a book more thoroughly revised than any new edition since Bill Haviland took on coauthors at the turn of the century. For the current edition of *Anthropology: The Human Challenge*—the fifteenth—we continued our paring down efforts, reducing the overall narrative by 10 percent in order to give more space to stimulating visuals and other pedagogical enhancements. Once again, our own ongoing research fueled our efforts, as did vital feedback from students and anthropology professors who have used and reviewed previous editions. Once again, we scrutinized the archetypal examples of our discipline and weighed them against the latest innovative research methodologies, archaeological discoveries, genetic and other biological findings, linguistic insights, ethnographic descriptions, theoretical revelations, and significant examples of applied anthropology.

Our Mission

Most students enter an introductory anthropology class intrigued by the general subject but with little more than a vague sense of what it is all about. Thus, the first and most obvious task of our text is to provide a thorough introduction to the discipline—its foundations as a domain of knowledge and its major insights into the rich diversity of humans as a culture-making species. Recognizing the wide spectrum of students enrolled in entry-level anthropology courses, we cover the fundamentals of the discipline in an engaging, illustrative fashion—providing a broad platform on which teachers can expand the exploration of concepts and topics in ways that are meaningful to them and to their particular group of students.

In doing this, we draw from the research and ideas of a number of traditions of anthropological thought, exposing students to a mix of theoretical perspectives and methodologies. Such inclusiveness reflects our conviction that different approaches offer distinctly important insights about human biology, behavior, and beliefs.

If most students start out with only a vague sense of what anthropology is, they often have even less clearly defined (and potentially problematic) views concerning the position of their own species and cultures within the larger world. A second task for this text, then, is to encourage students to appreciate the richness and complexity of human diversity. Along with this goal is the aim of helping them to understand why there are so many differences and similarities in the human condition, past and present.

Debates regarding globalization and notions of progress; the "naturalness" of the mother, father, child(ren) nuclear family; new genetic technologies; and how gender roles relate to biological variation all benefit greatly from the distinct insights gained through anthropology's wide-ranging, holistic perspective. This aspect of the discipline is one of the most valuable gifts we can pass on to those who take our classes. If we as teachers (and textbook authors) do our jobs well, students will gain a wider and more open-minded outlook on the world and a critical but constructive perspective on human origins and on their own biology and culture today. To borrow a favorite line from the famous poet T. S. Eliot, "The end of all our exploring will be to arrive where we started and know the place for the first time" ("Little Gidding," *Four Quartets*).

We have written this text, in large part, to help students make sense of our increasingly complex world and to navigate through its interrelated biological and cultural networks with knowledge, empathy, and skill, whatever professional path they take. We see the book as a guide for people entering the often-bewildering maze of global crossroads in the 21st century.

A Distinctive Approach

Two key factors distinguish *Anthropology: The Human Challenge* from other introductory texts: our integrative presentation of the discipline's four fields and a trio of unifying themes that tie the book together.

Integration of the Four Fields

Unlike traditional texts that present anthropology's four fields—biological (physical) anthropology, archaeology, linguistics, and cultural or social anthropology—as if they were separate or independent, our book takes an integrative approach. This reflects the holistic character of the discipline, a domain of knowledge where members of our species are studied in their totality—as social creatures biologically evolved with the inherent capacity for learning and sharing culture by means of symbolic communication. This approach also reflects our collective experience as practicing anthropologists who recognize that we cannot fully understand humanity in all its fascinating complexity unless we see the systemic interplay among environmental, physiological, material, social, ideological, psychological, and symbolic factors, both past and present.

For analytical purposes, however, we discuss biological anthropology as distinct from archaeology, linguistics, and sociocultural anthropology. Accordingly, there are separate chapters that focus primarily on each field, but the links among them are shown repeatedly. Among many examples of this integrative approach, "Modern Human Diversity—Race and Racism" (Chapter 11) discusses the social context of race and recent cultural practices that have impacted the human genome. In addition, every chapter includes a Biocultural Connection feature to further illustrate the interplay of biological and cultural processes in shaping the human experience.

Unifying Themes

In our own teaching, we recognize the value of marking out unifying themes that help students see the big picture as they grapple with the vast array of material involved with the study of human beings. In *Anthropology: The Human Challenge* we employ three such themes:

1. *Systemic adaptation.* We emphasize that every culture, past and present, like the human species itself, is an integrated and dynamic system of adaptation that responds to a combination of internal and external factors, including influences of the environment.
2. *Biocultural connection.* We highlight the integration of human culture and biology in the steps humans take to meet the challenges of survival. The biocultural connection theme is interwoven throughout the text—as a thread in the main narrative and in boxed features that highlight this connection with a topical example for every chapter.
3. *Globalization.* We track the emergence of globalization and its disparate impact on various peoples and cultures around the world. European colonization was a global force for centuries, leaving a significant and often devastating footprint on the affected peoples in Asia, Africa, and the Americas. Decolonization began about 200 years ago and became a worldwide wave in the mid-1900s. However, since the 1960s, political and economic hegemony has taken a new and fast-paced form: globalization (in many ways a process that expands or builds on imperialism). Attention to both forms of global domination—colonialism and globalization—runs through *Anthropology: The Human Challenge*, culminating in the final chapter where we apply the concept of structural power to globalization, discussing it in terms of hard and soft power and linking it to structural violence.

Pedagogy

Anthropology: The Human Challenge features a range of learning aids, in addition to the three unifying themes described previously. Each pedagogical piece plays an important role in the learning process—from clarifying and enlivening the material to revealing relevancy and aiding recall.

Accessible Language and a Cross-Cultural Voice

In the writing of this text, we consciously cut through unnecessary jargon to speak directly to students. Manuscript reviewers have recognized this, noting that even the most difficult concepts are presented in straightforward and understandable prose for today's first- and second-year college students. Where technical terms are necessary, they appear in bold type with a clear definition in the narrative. The definition appears again in the running glossary at the bottom of our pages, as well as in a summary glossary at the end of the book.

To make the narrative more accessible to students, we deliver it in chewable bites—short paragraphs. Numerous subheads provide visual cues to help students track what has been read and what is coming next.

Accessibility involves not only clear writing enhanced by visual cues, but also an engaging voice or style. The voice of *Anthropology: The Human Challenge* is distinct among introductory texts in the discipline because it has been written from a cross-cultural perspective. We avoid the typical Western "we/they" voice in favor of a more inclusive one to make sure the narrative resonates with both Western and non-Western students and professors. Also, we highlight the theories and work of anthropologists from all over the world. Finally, we have drawn the text's cultural examples from industrial and postindustrial societies as well as nonindustrial ones.

Compelling Visuals

The Haviland et al. texts garner praise from students and faculty for having a rich array of visuals, including maps, photographs, and figures. This is important because humans—like all primates—are visually oriented, and a well-chosen image may serve to "fix" key information in a student's mind. Unlike some competing texts, nearly all of our visuals are in color, enhancing their appeal and impact.

Photographs

Our pages feature a hard-sought collection of arresting, content-rich photographs. Large in size, many of them come with substantial captions composed to help students do a "deep read" of the image. Each chapter features more than a dozen pictures, including our popular Visual Counterpoints—side-by-side photos that effectively compare and contrast biological or cultural features.

Maps

Map features include our "Putting the World in Perspective" map series, locator maps, and distribution maps that provide overviews of key issues such as pollution and energy consumption. Of special note are the Globalscape maps and stories, described in the boxed features section a bit further on.

Challenge Issues

Each chapter opens with a Challenge Issue and accompanying photograph, which together carry forward the book's theme of humankind's responses through time to the fundamental challenges of survival within the context of the particular chapter.

Student Learning Objectives, Knowledge Skills, and Chapter Checklists

Each chapter begins with a set of learning objectives presented just after the Challenge Issue and photograph. These objectives focus students on the main goals, identifying the knowledge skills they are expected to have mastered after studying each chapter. The main goals are incorporated in a closing Chapter

Checklist, which summarizes the chapter's content in an easy-to-follow format.

Thought-Provoking Questions

Each chapter closes with four Questions for Reflection, including one that relates back to the Challenge Issue introduced in the chapter's opening. Presented right after the Chapter Checklist, these questions ask students to apply the concepts they have learned by analyzing and evaluating situations. They are designed to stimulate and deepen thought, trigger class discussion, and link the material to the students' own lives.

In addition, every Biocultural Connection essay ends with a probing question designed to help students grapple with and firmly grasp that connection. Also, the Globalscape features conclude with a Global Twister question, which asks students to think more deeply about the issue presented in the essay.

Integrated Methods: Digging into Anthropology

New to this edition is our **Digging into Anthropology** feature, presented at the end of every chapter, just after the Questions for Reflection. These hands-on assignments present opportunities to delve into every chapter's content through mini fieldwork projects designed to integrate methodology throughout the book and encourage students to explore topics in their own culture.

Integrated Theory: Barrel Model of Culture

Past and present, every culture is an integrated and dynamic system of adaptation that responds to a combination of internal and external factors. A pedagogical device we refer to as the "barrel model" of culture illustrates this. Depicted in a simple but telling drawing (Figure 13.7), the barrel model shows the interrelatedness of social, ideological, and economic factors within a cultural system along with outside influences of environment, climate, and other societies. Throughout the book, we link examples to this point and this image.

Integrated Gender Coverage

In contrast to many introductory texts, *Anthropology: The Human Challenge* integrates coverage of gender throughout the book. Thus, material on gender-related issues is included in *every* chapter. As a result of this approach, gender-related material in this textbook far exceeds the single chapter that most books devote to the subject.

We have chosen to integrate this material because concepts and issues surrounding gender are almost always too complicated to remove from their context. Spreading this material through all of the chapters has a pedagogical purpose because it emphasizes how considerations of gender enter into virtually everything people do. Gender-related material ranges from discussions of gender roles in evolutionary discourse and studies of nonhuman primates to intersexuality, homosexual identity, same-sex marriage, and female genital mutilation. Through a steady drumbeat of such coverage, this edition avoids ghettoizing gender to a single chapter that is preceded and followed by resounding silence.

Glossary as You Go

The running glossary is designed to catch the student's eye, reinforcing the meaning of each newly introduced term. It is also useful for chapter review, enabling students to readily isolate the new terms from those introduced in earlier chapters. A complete glossary is also included at the back of the book. In the glossaries, each term is defined in clear, understandable language. As a result, less class time is required for going over terms, leaving instructors free to pursue other matters of interest.

Special Boxed Features

Our text includes five types of special boxed features. Every chapter contains a Biocultural Connection, along with two of the following three features: an Original Study, Anthropology Applied, or Anthropologist of Note. In addition, about half of the chapters include a Globalscape. These features are carefully placed and introduced within the main narrative to alert students to their importance and relevance. A complete listing of features is presented on page xiv.

Biocultural Connections

Appearing in every chapter, this signature feature of the Haviland et al. textbooks illustrates how cultural and biological processes interact to shape human biology, beliefs, and behavior. It reflects the integrated biocultural approach central to the field of anthropology today. All of the Biocultural Connections include a critical thinking question. For a quick peek at titles, see the listing of features on page xiv.

Original Studies

Written expressly for this text, or adapted from ethnographies and other original works by anthropologists, these studies present concrete examples that bring specific concepts to life and convey the passion of the authors. Each study sheds additional light on an important anthropological concept or subject area for the chapter in which it appears. Notably, each Original Study is carefully integrated within the flow of the chapter narrative, signaling students that its content is not extraneous or supplemental. Appearing in nineteen chapters, Original Studies cover a wide range of topics, evident from their titles (see page xv).

Anthropology Applied

Featured in sixteen chapters, these succinct and fascinating profiles illustrate anthropology's wide-ranging relevance in today's world and give students a glimpse into a variety of the careers anthropologists enjoy (see page xiv for a listing).

Anthropologists of Note

Profiling pioneering and contemporary anthropologists from many corners of the world, this feature puts the work of noted anthropologists in historical perspective and draws attention to the international nature of the discipline in terms of both subject matter and practitioners. This edition highlights more than eighteen distinct anthropologists from all four fields of the discipline (see page xiv for a list of the profiles).

Globalscapes

Appearing in fourteen chapters, this unique feature charts the global flow of people, goods, and services, as well as pollutants and pathogens. With a map, a story, and one or two photos highlighting a topic geared toward student interests, every Globalscape shows how the world is interconnected through human activity. Each one ends with a Global Twister—a question that encourages students to think critically about globalization. Check out the titles of Globalscapes on page xiv.

Highlights in the Fifteenth Edition

Anthropology: The Human Challenge has undergone a thorough updating. Definitions of key terms have been honed. Many new visuals and ethnographic examples have been added and others dropped. Nearly every chapter features a new opening photograph and related Challenge Issue. The much-used Questions for Reflection include at least one new question per chapter, and on the heels of those questions we have added a brand-new Digging into Anthropology feature with hands-on assignments that prompt deeper investigation through mini projects related to each chapter's contents.

As with earlier editions, we further chiseled the writing to make it all the more clear, lively, engaging, and streamlined. *On average, chapter narratives have been trimmed by about 10 percent.* Statistics and examples have been updated throughout—in the narrative, captions, and figures. In addition to numerous revisions of boxed features, some of these are completely new.

Finally, we have replaced footnotes with in-text parenthetical citations, making sources and dates more visible and freeing up space for larger visuals. The complete listing of citations appears in the bibliography at the end of the book.

Beyond these across-the-board changes, particular changes have been made within each chapter.

Chapter 1: The Essence of Anthropology

This opening chapter emphasizes the contemporary relevance of anthropology as it introduces students to the holistic perspective, philosophical underpinnings and defining methodological approaches that run across its distinct four fields. Students will come to understand anthropology in relation to other disciplines and as a living laboratory that allows for the testing of hypotheses without the influence of culture-bound notions. A new Challenge Issue, centered on the repurposing of free antimalarial mosquito nets as fishing nets, shows the interconnectedness of our world today as individuals must choose between disease prevention and the health benefits of increased fishing yields.

Our discussion of anthropology and globalization brings students to the current global refugee crisis through new material on the distinction between nation and state and a new Globalscape "Safe Harbor?" on the plight of Rohingya boat people. Similarly, the global flow of food and pesticides is highlighted with the new placement of the Biocultural Connection "Picturing Pesticides."

The diversity of anthropologists and the subjects and forms of work they undertake will draw students in as they see: the collaborative nature of contemporary anthropological research through archaeologist Anne Jensen's work in the Arctic; innovative ethnographic forms in the work of cultural anthropologist Gina Athena Ulysse; novel field sites as with cultural anthropologist Philippe Bourgois's fieldwork among homeless substance abusers; cutting-edge technology in the genetics work of forensic anthropologist Mercedes Doretti in the updated Anthropology Applied feature ("Forensic Anthropology: Voices for the Dead"); and even the collaboration between archaeologists and microbreweries with the work of biomolecular archaeologist Pat McGovern.

The new Digging into Anthropology feature, "Talking Trash: Hidden in the Middens," on archaeology and trash provides the opportunity for students to learn archaeological concepts through hands-on experience. This feature is enhanced by the chapter updates on William Rathje's Garbage Project that focus on trash production and disposal in large urban areas.

Chapter 2: Biology, Genetics, and Evolution

This chapter on biology, genetics, and evolution opens with a new Challenge Issue demonstrating the link between culture and science and the ways in which biotechnology has become vital to identity and security in the 21st century. To help students stay abreast of technological developments in genetics and their applications in the world (without overwhelming them), the details on DNA replication to protein synthesis have been significantly refined and streamlined.

Compelling photographs with content-rich captions illustrate basic concepts such as toxic mutagenic agents and complement the historical aspects of this chapter's content. Figure changes include updated cell division art, a new homeobox gene photo, a locator map of the Dadaab refugee camp, and an 18th-century illustration of a chimpanzee. The discussions of heredity and population genetics have been significantly condensed and clarified. A new Digging into Anthropology feature, "Making Meaning of Memes," asks students to apply the principles of genetics, heredity, and evolution to social media as they trace the appearance, dissemination, and mutation of memes.

Chapter 3: Living Primates

This photo-rich chapter introduces students to our closest relatives in the animal world—the other primates—and the impact we humans have on our cousins. It opens with a discussion of the influence of globalization on populations of living primates in the world today through a new Challenge Issue describing the capture and global trade of slow lorises, one of many primates prized as pets in some societies. The updated endangered primate map further drives home the urgency of primate conservation. Exploring the basic biology of all the living primates, this chapter emphasizes the place of humans *within* the group of primates and basic mammalian primate adaptation compared to that of reptiles. It engages with biological concepts such as homeotherms versus isotherms, k-selection versus r-selection, ancestral and derived characteristics, convergent evolution, preadaptation, adaptive radiation, and ecological niche. New figures on vertical clinging and leaping and brachiation help to illustrate these concepts; the figure on the relationships among the primates has been updated to take into account the new data regarding the gorilla genome.

A new Biocultural Connection, "Gibbons and Sopranos Both Need to Be Heard," demonstrates the close relationship of humans to our primate relatives by examining the similarities between gibbon vocalizations and soprano singing. The Anthropology Applied feature, "Saving Our Ape Cousins: Primatologists,

Community Action, and the African Wildlife Foundation," has been extensively updated, telling the stories of primate conservation efforts under way across the African continent with the African Wildlife Foundation. The brave and creative methods of primatologists are explored in the Digging into Anthropology feature, "Finding or Losing Your Inner Ape." Here, students are challenged to experience their daily lives with some primate quality either enhanced or restricted as a way to tease apart human and nonhuman behavior and biology.

Chapter 4: Primate Behavior

Filled with cutting-edge discoveries and theories about primate behavior, this chapter opens with a new Challenge Issue that considers eminent primatologist Frans de Waal's work on morality—previously regarded as a uniquely human attribute—among our primate cousins. We introduce students to the research and activism of primatologists such as Jane Goodall and explore the notion of primate culture as evidenced in their communicative abilities, their distinct group traditions, and their ability to grasp complex tasks such as toolmaking.

A new Biocultural Connection on the language capacities of Kanzi the bonobo explores primatologist Sue Savage-Rumbaugh's intriguing notion that his life has made him in effect bicultural. The new Digging into Anthropology feature asks students to engage with Kanzi's pictorial language through observation on their own use of emoji in daily communication. Jane Goodall and her work are the focus of both the Anthropologists of Note (along with primatologist Kinji Imanishi) and the updated and expanded Anthropology Applied features—including her activism to protect the rights of apes and to eliminate the use of chimps in biomedical research, reflecting the U.S. National Institutes of Health decision to end this practice entirely. The Globalscape spotlights gorilla hand ashtrays and Dian Fossey's efforts to protect gorillas and to conserve their habitats in Rwanda, Uganda, and the Democratic Republic of Congo.

Chapter 5: Field Methods in Archaeology and Paleoanthropology

This chapter, detailing the investigative methods utilized by paleoanthropologists and archaeologists in the field, also situates these methods in contemporary sociopolitical contexts. It opens with a tragic example that challenges all of us to find ways to preserve our shared cultural heritage. How can we protect archaeological sites from destructive actions—such as the devastation at the ancient city of Palmyra and the killing of the Syrian archaeologist who tried to protect these remains from ISIS—a group that considers the relics to be sacrilegious? We also explore other threats to archaeological sites—looters motivated by profit, disruption of

sites from normal activities, and the distinctive world-views at work when scientists and indigenous peoples differ in their approaches to ancient remains.

The chapter explores the importance of work conducted in the lab after excavation. The updated Biocultural Connection on Kennewick Man incorporates recent results from genetic investigation and a new photo. A new Anthropology Applied feature, "The Atari Burial Grounds," shows how field methods at dig sites are useful even for recently buried artifacts. The Original Study on excavations at El Pilar in Belize has been repositioned and significantly updated by Anabel Ford. Enhanced with new images and content-rich captions, including an archaeological comic by John Swogger, the chapter has also been significantly condensed to provide a more direct overview of field methods. The hands-on Digging into Anthropology feature challenges students to feel the earth in their hands as they carry out the field methods detailed in the chapter.

Chapter 6: From First Primates to First Bipeds

With this first of several human evolution chapters, we start by introducing paleoanthropology as a science of discovery: a discipline that reshapes its understanding of the past with each new finding. The Challenge Issue features the stunning announcement in October 2015 of the new species, *Homo naledi*, to illustrate the place of paleoanthropology in the news and our collective imaginations today. But the chapter opener also explains the challenges involved in viewing new discoveries and placing them in the progression from the first primates to the first bipeds to humans. We consider the debates among paleoanthropologists about how specimens might be identified as unique species, the role of dating in paleoanthropological interpretations, and the question of when the genus *Homo* appeared.

This chapter has been extensively revised for clarity, succinctness, and accuracy. We have reorganized headings to reflect these revisions while retaining comparisons between the earliest bipeds of the fossil record to humans and to chimps. New photographs of some of the early fossils—including Little Foot, Ida, and *Ardipithecus ramidus*—as well as updated figures indicating the new Plio-Pleistocene split and the evolutionary branching of gorillas further enrich the chapter. The chapter's Biocultural Connection on human birth demonstrates the relevance of paleoanthropological theories to contemporary medical practice. A new Anthropologists of Note feature examines the legacy of paleoanthropologists Louis and Mary Leakey through several generations of family members who continue to make significant contributions to paleoanthropology. The new Digging into Anthropology feature "Fool with Your Ancestors" asks students to engage with the infamous Piltdown hoax by imagining a false find that might gain credibility because it reifies prevailing beliefs.

Chapter 7: Origins of the Genus *Homo*

This exploration of the origins of the genus *Homo* opens with the challenge to consider just what it is that makes us human. Through the example of the use of fire, we introduce the theme that runs through this chapter: What is the relationship between the biological changes preserved in the fossil record and the evidence of culture preserved in the archaeological record? Significantly reorganized to avoid redundancies, flow naturally, and drive home the central points, this chapter gives careful attention to the primary theories in the field today. Chapter 7 prepares students to engage with theories of modern human origins that follow.

The chapter retains its presentation of the contributions of female paleoanthropologists, a discussion of gendered interpretations of the fossil record, and the work of paleoartists to flesh out the bones of our ancestors. It also includes major recent discoveries such as the *Homo naledi* fossils mentioned in the previous chapter; the 2015 discovery of the Lomekwi stone tools that predate Oldowan assemblages by 700,000 years; and new research on a Neandertal hyoid bone that impacts interpretation of their capacity for spoken language. A new Digging into Anthropology feature on language and communication closes the chapter.

Chapter 8: The Global Expansion of *Homo sapiens* and Their Technology

This chapter provides a comprehensive streamlined discussion of theories for modern human origins and the spread of *Homo sapiens* throughout the globe. It asks students to engage with the nature of the relationship between biological change and cultural change as we get closer to the present. When in our evolutionary history does associating behavior with physical appearance become untenable, as it would be today when examining living peoples? The chapter opens by exploring the Eurocentrism embedded in the focus on the art and artifact of Europe by shifting our focus to the Paleolithic art from Indonesia. It also challenges students to think about whether the creation of art was tied to a speciation event involving the spread of a new and improved sort of human across the globe. The chapter hones students' critical thinking skills by showing the distinction between genetic, cultural, and morphological data and the challenges inherent in reconciling these kinds of data with one another.

The chapter discusses in detail the place of genetic studies in mapping the spread of *Homo sapiens*, incorporates new material on the Denisovan and Neandertal genomes, and provides a look at recent genetic studies on the peopling of the Americas. A new Anthropologist of Note feature introduces students to the work of paleogeneticist Svante Pääbo, and this chapter's Globalscape on UNESCO World Heritage Sites has been updated to reflect the current list of endangered sites. A new Digging into Anthropology feature engages with the chapter's updated Biocultural Connection by asking students to examine the Paleolithic diet that has gained popularity in some contemporary societies.

Chapter 9: The Neolithic Revolution: The Domestication of Plants and Animals

This comprehensive chapter on the Neolithic revolution contains a suite of features demonstrating the relevance of the ancient domestication of plants and animals to contemporary life. It opens with a new Challenge Issue exploring the recent global enthusiasm for the crop quinoa, an ancient food of Andean peoples in South America. But worldwide demand for quinoa has destabilized the lifeways of the region in which this crop was originally domesticated. The Neolithic set into motion a pattern of competition for resources that now takes place on a global scale.

An updated section on the Irish potato famine illustrates the impact of British policy on the Irish, revealing the interplay of political, economic, and farming factors that resulted in tragic consequences. The chapter offers new content-rich captions—for a photo of bottle gourds used by Datooga women to carry and store liquids and for an ancient winery with pottery vessels at Areni-1 in Armenia—providing a view of the role of genetics in archaeology. We have repositioned the Anthropology Applied feature on pre-Columbian fish farming to add more naturally to the theme of resource competition.

The biological consequences of the Neolithic have been incorporated into the text with a fresh writing style including new art illustrating bone growth and Harris line formation. Further, the 2015 avian flu outbreak and subsequent mass slaughter of poultry have been incorporated into this chapter's Globalscape and into the table on diseases acquired from domesticated animals. A new Digging into Anthropology feature "Domestication Today" asks students to study their own pets for a view into what drives domestication of animals.

Chapter 10: The Emergence of Cities and States

With most of this world's 7 billion-plus inhabitants living in urban environments, this chapter on the emergence of cities and states demonstrates the vital role of archaeology to solving problems brought about by this dominant form of social organization. The chapter's opening Challenge Issue explores the relationship between centralized authority and war, using the destruction of archaeological treasures during the current civil war in Syria as an example. The chapter's new Globalscape "Illicit Antiquities" on the looting that has accompanied this war contains some surprising profiteers and archaeological heroes.

The chapter has been reorganized, particularly in "The Making of States" section, for better clarity and simplicity. The section on the interdependence of cities is updated to include the 2011 tsunami in Japan, a more detailed discussion of the Syrian civil war, the Ebola virus, as well as the role of social media and global interconnections through cyberspace and airspace. The chapter's case study of Tikal demonstrates the range of archeological methods used in the exploration of a complex site. A new visually rich Original Study, "Ani: Identities and Conflicts in and Around a Silk Road City" by Gregory Areshian, connects global politics past and present to the discipline of archaeology.

This chapter also engages deeply with social stratification—an outcome of cities and states that has a profound impact on human populations today. Through visuals and hands-on activities, students see elaborate cemeteries transformed into housing as the population of Cairo, Egypt, expands. "Mapping Class," the new Digging into Anthropology feature, asks students to bring an awareness of social stratification to their local communities as they create maps that note differences in characteristics—such as building density and materials, transportation, and access to services—according to class.

Chapter 11: Modern Human Diversity—Race and Racism

With the violence that has accompanied the rise of racism and interethnic violence globally, the anthropological perspective on human diversity is increasingly important. We have substantially revised this chapter to reflect the structural and physical violence against minorities globally and specific responses to this violence. Race and racism are presented in this chapter through present-day examples that engage students with familiar, modern iterations of these thought-provoking concepts. A new Challenge Issue describes the June 2015 Emanuel African Methodist Episcopal Church murders in Charleston, South Carolina, as a horrific example of racism's continued impact in our world. We explore the social and political realities of race and reinforce the absence of biologically distinct races throughout this chapter.

We have completely revamped and streamlined discussions on race and intelligence for improved pedagogy, and then we ask students to look for bias in the standardized tests and college entrance exams they have taken in the new Digging into Anthropology feature. We provide other contemporary examples of discussions of race and racism, including the 2015 Baltimore police brutality protests; racial identity as

evidenced through the story of Rachel Dolezal; and the Black Lives Matter movement that has grown in response to the violence. In the chapter's new Original Study, "Reflections on the AAA Die-In as a Symbolic Space of Social Death," Faye Harrison reflects on bringing the Black Lives Matter movement into the national anthropology meetings. The new Globalscape "Finding Home?" explores the movement of Korean-born adoptees who have returned to Korea in response to the racism and dissociation they have felt in the United States. The chapter's Biocultural Connection, "Beauty, Bigotry, and the Epicanthic Fold of the Beholder," has been updated to include global statistics on double eyelid plastic surgery.

We have expanded the chapter's examination of genocide, and its inherent connection with racism, with the inclusion of Gregory Stanton's eight phases of genocide and prevention, as well as the Rohingya Muslims' current risk of genocide. The term *genocide* has been added as a glossary term. The chapter provides appropriate approaches to the study of human diversity that avoid the false categories of race. It explores human variation through characteristics such as skin color, lactose digestion, blood type, and so on while debunking the notion of race-specific medicines.

Chapter 12: Human Adaptation to a Changing World

This chapter focuses on the biology of human adaptation and the profound influence of culture on all aspects of human biology. Updates for this edition integrate recent global developments and their impacts on human adaptation. A new Challenge Issue on the Great Pacific garbage patch illustrates how human action is altering the earth's habitability as pollution at a massive scale interferes with global food webs. By using evolutionary, ecological, critical, and biocultural medical anthropological approaches, the chapter grounds human adaptation in the realm of sickness and health. We have updated the case study of the prion disease kuru to show newly discovered biological responses to prion disease that may have a deep history in human endocannibalism.

We have added new glossary terms *epigenetics* and *resistant strain* as part of the discussion on human adaptation. Epigenetics is further explored in an updated section on new research on the intergenerational effects of traumatic experiences. A new Biocultural Connection explores the controversial topic of vaccination, while considering the effects of vaccination on human adaptation. Building on the discussion from the Challenge Issue, the new Digging into Anthropology feature closes the chapter by asking students to explore the operation of waste management systems in their own communities.

Chapter 13: Characteristics of Culture

This chapter addresses anthropology's core concept of *culture,* exploring the term and its significance for individuals and societies. It opens with a vibrant new Challenge Issue photo highlighting Kuchi nomads in Afghanistan, recognizable by their distinctive dress and pack camels. Five other new photos are part of this chapter's revision, including a satellite image illustrating the transformation of vast stretches of the Arabian Desert into rich agricultural land with water from non-renewable sources deep under ground.

The main narrative begins with a section on culture and adaptation, setting the foundation for a discussion of culture and its characteristics. Our recolored "barrel model" illustration shows the integrative and dynamic nature of culture and introduces the key concepts of cultural infrastructure, social structure, and superstructure. We present the Kapauku Papua of Western New Guinea as an example of culture as an integrated system and explore pluralistic societies and subcultures through an updated look at the Amish in North America.

The chapter includes discussions on culture, society, and the individual; ethnocentrism and cultural relativism; and cultural change in the age of globalization. Special features include the Biocultural Connection, "Modifying the Human Body," with an updated illustration, an Anthropologist of Note on Bronislaw Malinowski, and the Anthropology Applied feature, "New Houses for Apache Indians" by George Esber, who describes his role in designing culturally appropriate homes for a Native American community. The new Digging into Anthropology task, "Hometown Map," invites students to map aspects of their community utilizing the barrel model.

Chapter 14: Ethnographic Research— Its History, Methods, and Theories

Opening with a new Challenge Issue on fieldwork accompanied by a lively visual of a young anthropologist returning from a tortoise hunt with Ayoreo Indians in Paraguay, this chapter takes a distinct approach to discussing ethnographic research. It begins with a historical overview on the subject—from the colonial era and salvage ethnography to acculturation studies, advocacy anthropology, cyberethnography, and multi-sited ethnography in the era of globalization. Relaying this story, we touch on the work of numerous anthropologists, past and present.

The chapter continues with a detailed discussion on ethnographic research methods—from selecting a research question and site to doing preparatory research to engaging in participant observation. It chronicles the ethnographer's approach to gathering qualitative and quantitative data, delineates the challenges of fieldwork, and touches on the creation of an ethnography in written, film, or digital formats. Readers will also find an overview of anthropology's theoretical perspectives, along with discussions of the comparative method and the Human Relations Area Files. Moral dilemmas and ethical responsibilities encountered in anthropological research are also explored.

Boxed features include an Original Study on fieldwork in the Trobriand Islands, a Biocultural Connection feature on the environmental and economic conditions that impact attitudes about pigs, and an Anthropologists of Note feature highlighting Margaret Mead and Gregory Bateson's collaborative research in Papua New Guinea. The new Digging into Anthropology assignment calls on students to carry out a bit of multi-sited research with six individuals in their social network: two with whom they live, two with whom they interact at work or school, and two with whom they communicate via social media channels but rarely see.

Chapter 15: Language and Communication

This chapter begins with a dynamic new photograph of a busy Chinatown street in Thailand's capital city of Bangkok, where signs appear in multiple languages. It goes on to investigate the nature of language and the three branches of linguistic anthropology—descriptive linguistics, historical linguistics, and the study of language in its social and cultural settings (ethnolinguistics and sociolinguistics). Also found here are sections on paralanguage and tonal languages and a unique introductory exploration of talking drums and whistled speech. The sections on sociolinguistics and ethnolinguistics cover gendered speech, social dialects, code switching, and linguistic relativity, drawing on a range of examples from Lakota Indians in South Dakota to Aymara Indians in Bolivia and Hopi Indians in Arizona.

Our discussion on language loss and revival includes a look at modern technology used by linguistic anthropologists collaborating on field research with speakers of endangered Khoisan "click" languages in southern Africa. It also features the latest data on the digital divide and its impact on ethnic minority languages—plus an updated chart showing Internet language populations. A historical sketch about writing takes readers from traditional speech performatives and memory devices to Egyptian hieroglyphics to the conception and spread of the alphabet. A concluding section on literacy and modern telecommunication looks at issues of language in our globalized world.

New photos include Visual Counterpoint images contrasting social space across cultures. Boxed features include S. Neyooxet Greymorning's Anthropology Applied essay on language revitalization, Lyn White Mile's Original Study on her research with Chantek the orangutan, and a Biocultural Connection on the biology of human speech. "Body Talk," a new Digging into Anthropology task, asks students to investigate the relationship between language and culture by documenting the body language of six people from different cultures and experimenting with altering their own body language.

Chapter 16: Social Identity, Personality, and Gender

Looking at individual identity within a sociocultural context, this chapter surveys the concept of self, enculturation and the behavioral environment, social identity through personal naming, the development of personality, the concepts of group and modal personality, and the idea of national character. The new opening Challenge Issue features Khanty mothers and their fur-clad children on a reindeer sled at their winter camp in Siberia—one of several new photos in this chapter.

The section on culture and personality includes Margaret Mead's classic research on gender and personality, followed by an Anthropologist of Note essay on Ruth Benedict. Also featured in this section is a case study on childrearing and gender among traditional and nontraditional Ju/'hoansi and a revised overview of three childrearing patterns, including interdependence training among the Beng of West Africa. A section on group personality describes the Yanomami masculine ideal of *waiteri,* followed by discussions on the questions of national character and core values.

Our exploration of alternative gender models includes a highly personal Original Study about intersexuality. Ethnographic examples concerning transgender include the Bugis of Indonesia, who recognize five genders. "The Social Context of Sexual and Gender Identity" section provides new global statistics on state-sponsored homophobia. On its heels is the broad-ranging section, "Normal and Abnormal Personality in Social Context," which presents the extreme *sadhu* tradition in India and then discusses mental disorders and concepts of "normality" across time and cultures. The Biocultural Connection offers a cross-cultural view on psychosomatic symptoms and mental health, while a concluding section, "Personal Identity and Mental Health in Globalizing Society," drives home the need for medical pluralism with a variety of modalities fit for humanity in the worldwide dynamics of the 21st century. This chapter's Digging into Anthropology assignment, "Gender Across Generations," charges students to do intergenerational interviewing on the concepts of femininity and masculinity to gain insight on gender differentiation.

Chapter 17: Patterns of Subsistence

Here we investigate the various ways humans meet their basic needs and how societies adapt through culture to the environment, opening with a dramatic new photo of a peasant farmer practicing wet-rice cultivation on the steep slopes of China's Guangxi Province—one of half a dozen new visuals enlivening this chapter. The chapter narrative, significantly revised and reconfigured with several new headings, begins with a general discussion of adaptation, followed by a new section titled "Adaptation, Environment, and Ecosystem," which includes a case study on the Tsembaga who raise pigs in Papua New Guinea. On the heels of that comes a brief section on adaptation and culture areas, featuring a new map. Next come modes of subsistence and their characteristics. It begins with food foraging—including a section chronicling the impact of technology on foragers, with Mbuti Pygmies providing an ethnographic example. Moving on to food-producing societies, we discuss pastoralism, crop cultivation, and industrial food production, including a case study of Bakhtiari herders in Iran, a discussion on peasantry, and the $55 billion U.S. poultry business.

A section on adaptation and cultural evolution touches on the notion of progress, explores convergent and parallel evolution through ethnographic examples, and features the latest ethnohistorical research on ecosystemic collapse on Rapa Nui, commonly known as Easter Island. A new conclusion looks at population growth and the limits of progress.

The chapter's boxed features include an Original Study on slash-and-burn cultivation in the Amazon basin in Brazil, an Anthropology Applied piece about reviving ancient farming practices in Peru, and a Globalscape on the international poultry industry. "Global Dining," the topic of this chapter's Digging into Anthropology task, gives students an opportunity to see how they "embody" globalization by having them locate the sources of their groceries on a map.

Chapter 18: Economic Systems

Opening with a new Challenge Issue and photo highlighting an open city market in the highlands of Guatemala, this reworked chapter offers eight new photographs and captions, including a new Visual Counterpoint on harvesting and exporting tea. After a brief description of economic anthropology, illustrated by a case study on the yam complex in Trobriand culture, we discuss production and resources (natural, technological, labor). Considering labor resources and patterns, we look at gender, age, cooperative labor, and task specialization, drawing on ethnographic examples that include salt mining in Ethiopia.

A section on distribution and exchange explains various forms of reciprocity (including an illustrated description of the Kula ring), trade and barter, redistribution (with brief accounts of the Inca empire and the northwestern American Indian potlatch), and market exchange. The discussion on leveling mechanisms features an ethnographically rich photo of a contemporary Tlingit potlatch in Sitka, Alaska. After providing an overview on the history of money as a means of exchange, we conclude with a section on local economies and global capitalism, featuring discussions on the informal economy and the development and marketing of genetically modified seeds.

Boxed features include an Anthropology Applied piece on global ecotourism in Bolivia, a newly illustrated Biocultural Connection on chocolate, and an Anthropologist of Note about Tlingit anthropologist Rosita Worl's work with Sealaska, an indigenous collective that markets wood products and other goods. The new Digging into Anthropology task, "Luxury Foods and Hunger Wages," asks students to track down the source of a luxury food or drink, the ethnicities and wages of those who harvested it, and the profit margin of the company that markets it.

Chapter 19: Sex, Marriage, and Family

Exploring the connections between sexual reproductive practices, marriage, family, and household, this chapter opens with a gorgeous photo of a Muslim bride and her female relatives and friends displaying hands decorated with traditional henna design. Particulars addressed in the chapter include the incest taboo, endogamy and exogamy, dowry and bridewealth, cousin marriage, same-sex marriage, divorce, residence patterns, and nonfamily households. Up-to-date definitions of *marriage*, *family*, *nuclear family*, and *extended family* encompass current real-life situations around the world. Of the dozen visuals in this chapter, six are new.

The diverse ethnographic examples in this chapter come from many corners of the world. Opening paragraphs on the traditional sexual freedom of young people in the Trobriand Islands lead into a discussion on the regulation of sexual relations across cultures. A section on marriage and the regulation of sexual relations includes a recent example of Shariah law as it relates to women and adultery—along with a nuanced commentary about the relationship between such restrictive rules and the incidence of sexually transmitted diseases. Also featured is a short case study on sexual and marriage practices among the Nayar in India, which describes consanguineal and affinal kin.

A discussion on endogamy and exogamy includes a fresh look at cousin marriages among Pakistani immigrants in England. Immigration is also touched upon in the "Forms of Marriage" section, which notes the impact immigration is having on polygamy statistics in Europe and the United States, even as the practice declines in sub-Saharan Africa. Other ethnographic examples concern woman–woman marriage among the Nandi of Kenya, dowries in the Kyrgyz Republic, all-male households among the Mundurucu in Brazil's Amazon rainforest, and matrilocal residence among traditional Hopi Indians.

A closing section sketches the impact of global capitalism, electronic communication, and transnationalism on love relations. It includes revised subsections on adoption, new reproductive technologies, and migrant workforces. Boxed features include an Original Study on arranged marriages in India, a Biocultural Connection on marriage prohibitions in the United States, and an Anthropologist of Note on Claude Lévi-Strauss. The new Digging into Anthropology feature is titled "Sex Rules?" It involves making a list of six distinctive sets of sexual relationships, noting which are socially accepted or prohibited by law or faith and what the punishment is for breaking the prohibition. The second half of the exercise is comparison and analysis.

Chapter 20: Kinship and Descent

Beginning with a new photograph of a clan gathering in Scotland, this chapter marks out the various forms of descent groups and the role descent plays as an integrated feature in a cultural system. The narrative includes details and examples of lineages, clans, phratries, and moieties (highlighting Hopi Indian matriclans and Scottish highland patriclans, among others), followed by illustrated examples of a representative range of kinship systems and their kinship terminologies.

Along with an array of new and revised visuals, this chapter offers ethnographic examples from the Han Chinese, the Maori of New Zealand, and the Canela Indians of Brazil; it also takes a look at diasporic communities in today's globalized world. A section entitled "Making Relatives" explores fictive kin and ritual adoption, illustrating that in cultures everywhere, people have developed ideas about how someone becomes "one of us." We also present a discussion of kinship and new reproductive technologies, touching on the mind-boggling array of reproductive possibilities and how they are impacting humanity's conceptions of what it means to be biologically related.

Boxed features include an Anthropology Applied piece on resolving Native American tribal membership disputes, a thought-provoking Original Study on honor killings among Turkish immigrants in the Netherlands, and a freshly illustrated Biocultural Connection piece about ancient Maori mythical traditions that are now supported by genetic research. The Digging into Anthropology project, "What's in a Name?," invites students to glean the importance of kin terms by interviewing someone ("EGO") and mapping EGO's kin-group.

Chapter 21: Grouping by Gender, Age, Common Interest, and Social Status

Starting with a vibrant photograph of Afghan horsemen playing *buzkashi*, their country's fiercely competitive national sport, this chapter includes discussions on grouping by gender, age, common interest, and social status.

The gender grouping discussion features ethnographic material from the Mundurucu of Brazil, among others, while age grouping highlights the Tiriki and Maasai of East Africa. Common-interest grouping examples range from "pink vigilantes" in India to the African diaspora in the United States. A section on associations in the digital age provides new figures on the rapid and widespread changes in social networking platforms across the globe. The revised section on grouping by social status explores social class and caste. We give special attention to the traditional Hindu caste system in India and touch on customarily closed European social classes known as estates, as well as the history of racial segregation in South Africa and the United States. Indicators of social status are discussed, along with social mobility and various means of maintaining stratification.

Boxed features include an updated Globalscape profiling the impact of football on Côte d'Ivoire's ethnic conflicts, a Biocultural Connection about the African Burial Ground Project in New York City, an Original Study on the Jewish *eruv*, and an Anthropology Applied feature on policy research revealing institutionalized inequality. The new Digging into Anthropology assignment is designed to help students reflect on how their social media self and relationships may differ from their face-to-face self and relationships.

Chapter 22: Politics, Power, War, and Peace

This chapter opens with a new Challenge Issue and photo in which masses of people, besieged by Syria's civil war, are trying to escape the Yarmouk refugee neighborhood outside of Damascus. The main narrative begins by defining power and politics, followed by descriptions of uncentralized and centralized political systems and their characteristics—from bands and tribes to chiefdoms and states. Ethnographic examples include the Ju/'hoansi Bushmen, the Kapauku Papua, the Pashtun of Afghanistan and Pakistan, and the Kpelle of Liberia. We explain the distinction between state and nation, highlighting the Kurdish fight for independence. After discussing the concepts of authority and legitimacy, the narrative explores the link between politics and religion and gender—touching on the role religion may play in legitimizing the political order and leadership and taking a historical, cross-cultural look at the incidence of female leadership. Among the ethnographic examples we present is the dual-gender government system of the Igbo in Nigeria.

A section titled "Cultural Controls in Maintaining Order" investigates internalized control (such as self-control) and externalized control (such as sanctions), as well as witchcraft. The witchcraft discussion features new material on modern witch hunts, including a searing photo of a woman who fell victim to one. Under the heading "Holding Trials, Settling Disputes, and Punishing Crimes," we contrast traditional kin-based approaches to those of politically centralized societies. This includes descriptions of Inuit song duels in Canada and Kpelle trials by ordeal in Liberia, plus a discussion of restorative justice.

A section on violent conflict sketches the evolution of warfare and the impact of technology, including drones. It presents a brief new profile (with photo) of the self-proclaimed Islamic State and its *jihad*. Delving further into ideologies of aggression, it chronicles a Christian holy war in Uganda. Following discussions on genocide and contemporary armed conflicts, the narrative looks at approaches to peacemaking—diplomacy, treaty making, and the politics of nonviolent resistance, including brief profiles of movements led by Mohandas Gandhi in India and Aung San Suu Kyi in Myanmar. An updated Anthropology Applied box on dispute resolution has been relocated to this section. Other special features in this chapter include a Biocultural Connection on gender, sex, and human violence and an updated Globalscape on Somali pirates. "Politics and Purses," the Digging into Anthropology assignment for this chapter, takes students on a journey to locate links between money and power.

Chapter 23: Spirituality, Religion, and Shamanism

This chapter, rich with nine new visuals, opens with a colorful new photo and Challenge Issue highlighting a sacred Buddhist dance ritual in Bhutan. The main narrative begins with a discussion of superstructure and worldview. Noting the distinction between spirituality and religion, we discuss the anthropological approach to studying them and offer an updated chart and a map showing the numbers of religious adherents and the concentrations of major religions around the world. After introducing myths and their role in mapping cosmology, we discuss supernatural beings and spiritual forces—from gods and goddesses to ancestral spirits and the concepts of animism and animatism. This section features a new image of the dual-gender divinity, Ardhanaraishvara.

Next we mark out religious specialists. Our overview of priests and priestesses includes a Biocultural Connection on the masculinization of Taiwanese nuns and a discussion on spiritual lineages, comparing how authority is obtained and passed on among Tibetan Buddhists and three other religious groups. A comprehensive exploration of shamanism features our "shamanic complex" diagram, a description of shamanic healing among the Ju/'hoansi with a remarkable new photo, and an Anthropologist of Note on modern-day shamanic practitioner-teacher Michael Harner.

In a section on ritual performances, we discuss taboos and cleansing ceremonies, rites of passage (with ethnographic examples noting the phases of separation, transition, and incorporation), rites of intensification, magic (imitative and contagious), and divination (with a new Visual Counterpoint juxtaposing "bone throwing" diviners in South Africa with a *feng shui* master in Hong Kong). A section on witchcraft offers a brief cross-cultural overview, followed by a more detailed description of Navajo skin-walkers. Next come sacred sites—from shrines to mountains—and the pilgrimages (devotions in motion) they inspire. This includes a subsection on female saints (highlighting Marian devotions and Black Madonnas) and a discussion of desecration, past and present.

In a section on cultural dynamics, we explore religious and spiritual change, including revitalization movements and syncretic religions (especially Vodou in Haiti). Turning to religious pluralism and secularization, we give an overview of spirituality and religious practices today (including an Original Study on Shariah banking), driving home the point that the anthropological study of religion is crucial to gaining an understanding of today's world. This chapter's Digging into Anthropology, "Going Through a Phase," calls on students to observe a rite of passage, take note of its phases, and analyze why the event requires a ritual.

Chapter 24: The Arts

This chapter begins with a Challenge Issue about articulating ideas and emotions through various art forms, illustrated by a dramatic new photograph showing a crowd of Kayapo Indians staging a political protest in artful ceremonial paint and dress. The main narrative explores three key categories of art—visual, verbal, and musical. It features eight new photographs, including a new Visual Counterpoint juxtaposing ancient rock art and modern urban graffiti.

Describing the distinctly holistic approach anthropologists bring to the study of art, we note the range of cultural insights art discloses—from kinship structures to social values, religious beliefs, and political ideas. We also explain aesthetic and interpretive approaches to analyzing art, as applied to rock art in southern Africa and cross-cultural depictions of the Last Supper in the Bible. A revised verbal arts section presents several ethnographic examples, including the Abenaki creation myth and the culturally widespread "Father, Son, and Donkey" tale.

The section on music carries readers from flutes made of bones from 42,000 years ago to traditional and new age shamans drumming to evoke trances; from rapping and beatboxing to online music mashups; from laborers on the edge of the Sahara working to the beat of a drum to West African *griots* recounting personal histories through percussion and lyrics. We touch on the elements of music, including tonality, rhythm, and melody, and through music we explore the functions of art. Boxed features include a Biocultural Connection about the role of peyote in Huichol art, a newly illustrated Original Study on tattoos, a Globalscape on artful West African coffins, and a moving Anthropology Applied feature about a Penobscot Indian anthropologist recreating traditional regalia as part of a cultural and economic survival strategy. The new Digging into Anthropology assignment, "A Heart for Art," invites students to look into a public art performance in their own community and compare that to the Kayapo Indians' artful political protest featured in the chapter's opening photo and Challenge Issue.

Chapter 25: Processes of Cultural Change

A new opening photo showing a crowd of people stranded by a delayed train in India suggests the challenge of human dependency on major technological advances made since the invention of the steam engine. Globalization themes and terms are woven through this chapter, which includes definitions distinguishing *progress* from *modernization* and *rebellion* from *revolution*. Discussing mechanisms of change—primary and secondary innovation, diffusion, and cultural loss, as well as repressive change—we highlight the spearthrower (atlatl) and wheel-and-axle technology, as well as the dynamics that encourage or discourage innovative tendencies. Examples in the discussion on diffusion range from bagpipes in Bhutan to the spread of maize and the metric system.

A streamlined exploration of cultural change and loss covers acculturation and ethnocide—featuring an illustrated passage on Yanomami. After discussing directed change, we chronicle reactions to change—explaining syncretism through the story of Trobrianders transforming the British game of cricket and elaborating on revitalization movements with a description of cargo cults in Melanesia and the revival of sacred precolonial rituals such as sun worship in Bolivia. A discussion on rebellion and revolution highlights the Zapatista Maya Indian insurgency in southern Mexico and the Chinese communist revolution (including a new photo and caption concerning its long-term impact on women). Discussing processes of modernization, we consider self-determination among indigenous peoples with two contrasting examples: the Shuar Indians of Ecuador and a newly illustrated story of Sámi reindeer herders in northwest Russia and Scandinavia.

Boxed features include a Biocultural Connection on the emergence of new diseases, an Anthropologist of Note on Eric R. Wolf, and an Anthropology Applied about development anthropology and dams, with a fascinating satellite image of China's Three Gorges Dam. A new Digging into Anthropology, "Life Without Imports," asks students to analyze how their culture would change if they faced a political revolution that prohibited the consumption of foreign goods and information.

Chapter 26: Global Challenges, Local Responses, and the Role of Anthropology

Our final chapter opens with a new photo of an Internet café in China coupled with a revised Challenge Issue about cultural adaptations that have fueled population growth and globalization. The main narrative begins with a new passage describing the stunning globalizing effect of today's digital telecommunication technology—featuring a new illustration of satellites orbiting earth and raising the question of whether our species can successfully adapt to the dynamic ecosystem of the current geological epoch known as the Anthropocene. A section titled "Cultural Revolutions: From *Terra Incognita* to Google Earth" offers a 500-year overview of technological inventions that have transformed humanity's lifeways, expanded interconnections, and changed our perceptions about our place and destiny in the universe. It ends with the first full-view photograph taken of earth and speculations by some that a homogenous global culture is in the making.

A section on global integration processes marks out the emergence of international organizations. We then consider pluralistic societies, multiculturalism, and fragmentation, illustrating the push-and-pull aspects of today's world. A section on global migrations catalogues the number of internal and external migrants, including transnationals working in one country while remaining citizens of another, plus the millions of refugees forced outside their countries. Marking out challenges migrants face, we include a new section titled "Diasporas and Xenophobia," followed by "Migrants, Urbanization, and Slums," reporting on the 1 billion people worldwide now living in slums.

Next comes what may be most important section in this chapter, "Structural Power in the Age of Globalization," with comprehensive subsections on hard power (economic and military) and soft power (media) featuring updated and newly designed graphs. On its heels is a revised overview of the problems of structural violence—from poverty and income disparity; to hunger, obesity, and malnutrition; to pollution and global warming. This section features a new world map showing income inequality. Another world map depicts energy consumption. Discussing reactions to

globalization, we touch on religious fanaticism among Muslims and Christians, along with the human rights struggles of ethnic minorities and indigenous peoples. The chapter concludes with an encouraging look at anthropology's role in meeting the inequities and other challenges of globalization.

Special box features include a Biocultural Connection about the threat to Arctic cultures from outside contamination; an updated Globalscape about dumping toxic waste in poor countries; an Anthropology Applied piece on Ann Dunham (President Obama's mother), who was a pioneer in microfinancing; and an uplifting Anthropologist of Note profile about Paul Farmer and his global Partners In Health foundation. The new Digging into Anthropology feature, "How Are You Wired?," calls on students to analyze their use of telecommunication devices.

Supplements

Anthropology: The Human Challenge comes with a comprehensive supplements program to help instructors create an effective learning environment both inside and outside the classroom and to aid students in mastering the material.

Online Instructor's Manual, PowerPoint Slides, and Test Bank

The instructor's manual offers detailed chapter outlines, lecture suggestions, key terms, and student activities such as video exercises and Internet exercises. In addition, there are over seventy-five chapter test questions including multiple choice, true/false, fill in the blank, short answer, and essay.

Readings and Case Studies

Classic and Contemporary Readings in Physical Anthropology, edited by M. K. Sandford with Eileen M. Jackson

This highly accessible reader emphasizes science—its principles and methods—as well as the historical development of physical anthropology and the applications of new technology to the discipline. The editors provide an introduction to the reader as well as a brief overview of the article so students know what to look for. Each article also includes discussion questions and Internet resources.

Classic Readings in Cultural Anthropology, 4th edition, edited by Gary Ferraro

Now in its fourth edition, this reader includes historical and recent articles that have had a profound effect on the field of anthropology. Organized according to the major topic areas found in most cultural anthropology courses, this reader includes an introduction to the material as well as a brief overview of each article and discussion questions.

Globalization and Change in Fifteen Cultures: Born in One World, Living in Another, edited by George Spindler and Janice E. Stockard

In this volume, fifteen case studies describe cultural change in diverse settings around the world. The fifteen authors of the original case studies provide insight into the dynamics and meanings of change, as well as the effects of globalization at the local level.

Case Studies in Cultural Anthropology, edited by George Spindler and Janice E. Stockard

Select from more than sixty classic and contemporary ethnographies representing geographic and topical diversity. Newer case studies focus on cultural change and cultural continuity, reflecting the globalization of the world.

Case Studies on Contemporary Social Issues, edited by John A. Young

Framed around social issues, these contemporary case studies are globally comparative and represent the cutting-edge work of anthropologists today.

Case Studies in Archaeology, edited by Jeffrey Quilter

These engaging accounts of new archaeological techniques, issues, and solutions—as well as studies discussing the collection of material remains—range from site-specific excavations to types of archaeology practiced.

Acknowledgments

No textbook comes to fruition without extensive collaboration. Beyond the shared endeavors of our author team, this book owes its completion to a wide range of individuals, from colleagues in the discipline to those involved in development and production processes. Sincere thanks to colleagues who brought their expertise to bear—as sounding boards and in responding to questions concerning their specializations: Marta P. Alfonso-Durruty, Frans B. M. de Waal, John Hawks, Amber Campbell Hibbs, Adrie Kusserow, Heather Loyd, William Mitchell, Gillian E. Newell, Martin Ottenheimer, Svante Pääbo, Herbert Prins, and Michael Wesch. We are particularly grateful for the manuscript reviewers listed below, who provided detailed and thoughtful feedback that helped us to hone and re-hone our narrative.

We carefully considered and made use of the wide range of comments provided by these individuals. Our decisions on how to utilize their suggestions were influenced by our own perspectives on anthropology and teaching, combined with the priorities and page limits of this text. Thus, neither our reviewers nor any of the other anthropologists mentioned here should be held responsible for any shortcomings in this book. They should, however, be credited as contributors to many of the book's strengths: Julie Adkins, Brian Bates, Beau Bowers, Amanda Paskey, Warren Roberts, Joe Rubenstein, James Sewastynowicz, and Leanna Wolfe.

Thanks to colleagues who provided material for some of the Original Study, Biocultural Connection, and Anthropology Applied boxes: Gregory Areshian, Tavid Bingham, Michael Blakey, Nancy I. Cooper, Hillary Crane, Margo DeMello, Katherine Dettwyler, Clark L. Erickson, George S. Esber, Anabel Ford, S. Neyooxet Greymorning, Marvin Harris, Faye V. Harrison, Donna Hart, John Hawks, Michael M. Horowitz, Ann Kendall, Susan Lees, Roger Lewin, Charles C. Mann, Jonathan Marks, Bill Maurer, H. Lyn White Miles, Serena Nanda, Jennifer Sapiel Neptune, Martin Ottenheimer, Sherry Simpson, Jason Silverstein, Amanda Stronza, William Ury, Clementine van Eck, Annette B. Weiner, Dennis Werner, and R. K. Williamson.

We have debts of gratitude to office workers in our departments for their cheerful help in clerical matters: Karen Rundquist and research librarian extraordinaire Nancy Bianchi. Aram Bingham, Tavid Bingham, and Adrienne Rule tracked innumerable details with insight and good cheer. Also worthy of note here are the introductory anthropology teaching assistants at Kansas State University and the students from the University of Vermont College of Medicine and the Honors College who, through the years, have shed light for us on effective ways to reach new generations of students. And, finally, we recognize the introductory students themselves, who are at the heart of this educational endeavor and who continually provide feedback in formal and informal ways.

Our thanksgiving inventory would be incomplete without mentioning individuals at Wadsworth/Cengage Learning who helped conceive of this text and bring it to fruition. Of special note is our content development editor Catherine (Cat) Craddock, who came to us midstream when her predecessor Stefanie Chase took another post at Cengage. Both women brought joy, steadiness, and skill to our efforts. Thanks also to Gordon Lee, our former product manager, and his successor Elizabeth (Libby) Beiting-Lipps—Gordon for his integrity, brainstorming skills, and lively collaborative manner, and Libby for welcoming us so graciously to her already substantial workload. Additional gratitude to Michael Cook (art director), Cheri Palmer (content project manager), and Jennifer Levanduski (marketing director).

In addition to all of the above, we have had the invaluable aid of several most able freelancers, including our long-cherished copy editor Jennifer Gordon, thoroughly kind and kindly thorough; our stellar production coordinator Jill Traut of MPS Limited, who can keep more balls in the air than the best of jugglers; and our resilient veteran photo researcher Sarah Evertson. Thanksgiving as well to Larry Didona, cover designer; Lisa Buckley, text interior designer; GraphicWorld for new maps; Santosh Kumar for artwork; and lastly the composition team lead by Rakesh Pandey.

And finally, *as always,* we are indebted to family members and close friends who have put up with our hectic schedules during every textbook revision season—and provided us with good company when we managed to take a break.

About the Authors

Authors Bunny McBride, Dana Walrath, Harald Prins, and William Haviland.

All four members of this author team share overlapping research interests and a similar vision of what anthropology is (and should be) about. For example, all are true believers in the four-field approach to anthropology, and all have some involvement in applied work.

WILLIAM A. HAVILAND is professor emeritus at the University of Vermont, where he founded the Department of Anthropology and taught for thirty-two years. He holds a PhD in anthropology from the University of Pennsylvania.

He has carried out original research in archaeology in Guatemala and Vermont; ethnography in Maine and Vermont; and physical anthropology in Guatemala. This work has been the basis of numerous publications in various national and international books and journals, as well as in media intended for the general public. His books include *The Original Vermonters*, coauthored with Marjorie Power, and a technical monograph on ancient Maya settlement. He also served as consultant for the award-winning telecourse *Faces of Culture*, and he is coeditor of the series *Tikal Reports*, published by the University of Pennsylvania Museum of Archaeology and Anthropology.

Besides his teaching and writing, Dr. Haviland has given lectures for numerous professional as well as nonprofessional audiences in Canada, Mexico, Lesotho, South Africa, and Spain, as well as in the United States. A staunch supporter of indigenous rights, he served as expert witness for the Missisquoi Abenaki of Vermont in an important court case over aboriginal fishing rights.

Awards received by Dr. Haviland include being named University Scholar by the Graduate School of the University of Vermont in 1990; a Certificate of Appreciation from the Sovereign Republic of the Abenaki Nation of Missisquoi, St. Francis/Sokoki Band in 1996; and a Lifetime Achievement Award from the Center for Research on Vermont in 2006. Now retired from teaching, he continues his research, writing, and lecturing from the coast of Maine. He serves as a trustee for the Abbe Museum in Bar Harbor, focused on Maine's Native American history, culture, art, and archaeology. His most recent books are *At the Place of the Lobsters and Crabs* (2009) and *Canoe Indians of Down East Maine* (2012), along with the monograph *Excavations in Residential Areas of Tikal* (2015).

HARALD E. L. PRINS is a University Distinguished Professor of cultural anthropology at Kansas State University. Academically trained at half a dozen Dutch and U.S. universities, he previously taught at Radboud University (Netherlands), Bowdoin College and Colby College in Maine, and as a visiting professor at the University of Lund, Sweden. He has received numerous honors for his teaching, including the Conoco Award for Outstanding Undergraduate Teaching in 1993, Presidential Award in 1999, Coffman Chair of Distinguished Teaching Scholars in 2004, Carnegie Foundation Professor of the Year for Kansas in 2006, and the AAA/Oxford University Press Award for Excellence in Undergraduate Teaching of Anthropology in 2010.

His fieldwork focuses on indigenous peoples in the western hemisphere, and he has long served as an advocacy anthropologist on land claims and other native rights. In that capacity, Dr. Prins has been a lead expert witness in both the U.S. Senate and Canadian federal courts. He has refereed for forty academic book publishers and journals. His own numerous academic publications appear in nine languages, with books including *The Mi'kmaq: Resistance, Accommodation, and Cultural Survival* (Margaret Mead Award finalist).

Also trained in filmmaking, he served as president of the Society for Visual Anthropology and has

Courtesy of the authors

coproduced award-winning documentaries. He has been the visual anthropology editor of *American Anthropologist*, coprincipal investigator for the U.S. National Park Service, international observer in Paraguay's presidential elections, and a research associate at the National Museum of Natural History, Smithsonian Institution.

DANA WALRATH—an award-winning writer, artist, and anthropologist—is a faculty member at the University of Vermont College of Medicine. After earning her PhD in medical and biological anthropology from the University of Pennsylvania, she taught there and at Temple University. Dr. Walrath broke new ground in paleoanthropology through her work on the evolution of human childbirth. She has also written on a wide range of topics related to gender in paleoanthropology, the social production of sickness and health, sex differences, genetics, and evolutionary medicine. Her work has appeared in edited volumes and in journals such as *Current Anthropology, American Anthropologist, American Journal of Physical Anthropology*, and *Anthropology Now*. Her books include *Aliceheimer's*, a graphic memoir, and *Like Water on Stone*, a verse novel.

She developed a novel curriculum in medical education at the University of Vermont College of Medicine that brings humanism, anthropological theory and practice, narrative medicine, and professionalism skills to first-year medical students. Dr. Walrath also has an MFA in creative writing from Vermont College of Fine Arts and has exhibited her artwork in North America and Europe. Her recent work in the field of graphic medicine combines anthropology with memoir and visual art. Spanning a variety of disciplines, her work has been supported by diverse sources such as the National Science Foundation, the Templeton Foundation, the Centers for Disease Control, the Health Resources and Services Administration, the Vermont Studio Center, the Vermont Arts Council, and the National Endowment for the Arts. She spent 2012–2013 as a Fulbright Scholar at the American University of Armenia and the Institute of Ethnography and Archaeology of the National Academy of Sciences of Armenia. She is working on a second graphic memoir that combines her *Aliceheimer's* work with her fieldwork on aging and memory in Armenia and a graphic novel about the genetics of mental illness.

BUNNY MCBRIDE is an award-winning author specializing in cultural anthropology, indigenous peoples, international tourism, and nature conservation issues. Published in dozens of national and international print media, she has reported from Africa, Europe, China, and the Indian Ocean. Holding an MA from Columbia University and highly rated as a teacher, she has taught at the Salt Institute for Documentary Field Studies and at Principia College, where she was a visiting faculty member in the Anthropology Department on and off for many years. Since 1996 she has been an adjunct lecturer of anthropology at Kansas State University.

Among McBride's many publication credits are the books *Women of the Dawn; Molly Spotted Elk: A Penobscot in Paris*; and *Our Lives in Our Hands: Micmac Indian Basketmakers*. She has also contributed chapters in a dozen books and coauthored several books, including *Indians in Eden and The Audubon Field Guide to African Wildlife*. Working on a range of issues and projects with Maine Indian tribes since 1981, McBride received a commendation from the Maine state legislature for her research and writing on the history of Native American women. *Boston Globe Sunday Magazine* featured a long profile about her, and Maine Public Television made a documentary about her research and writing on Molly Spotted Elk.

In recent years, McBride has served as coprincipal investigator for a National Park Service ethnography project and curated several museum exhibits, including "Journeys West: The David & Peggy Rockefeller American Indian Art Collection" for the Abbe Museum in Bar Harbor, Maine. Her exhibit, "Indians & Rusticators," received a Leadership in History Award from the American Association for State and Local History (2012). As of 2016, she serves on the advisory panel for the Women's World Summit Foundation (based in Geneva, Switzerland) after ten years on the organization's board and three as its president.

Uriel Sinai/The New York Times/Redux

How do we make sense of the world? Who are we, and how are we connected to the person pictured here? Why might we look different from this person or speak a different language? Anthropologists approach such questions holistically, framing them in a broad, integrated context that considers human culture and biology, in all times and places, as inextricably intertwined. Consider David Abongo Owich pictured here catching baby catfish in Kenya's Lake Victoria with repurposed mosquito nets, provided by health organizations to regions with a high incidence of malaria, which is spread by mosquitoes. However, the free malarial nets are useful for trapping fish, so some choose to improve their diet rather than protect themselves from malaria. This has led to problems not only with the continued spread of the disease but with overfishing and water contamination from the insecticides in the nets. Historically, disease-specific interventions have often overlooked the needs and values of each particular human society. The anthropological perspective equips us to negotiate today's interconnected, globalized world, enabling us to contribute to practical solutions for the problems of contemporary life.

The Essence of Anthropology

The Anthropological Perspective

Anthropology is the study of humankind in all times and places. Of course, many disciplines focus on humans in some way. For example, anatomy and physiology concentrate on our species as biological organisms. Anthropology focuses on the interconnections and interdependence of all aspects of the human experience in all places, in the present and deep into the past, well before written history. This unique, broad **holistic perspective** equips anthropologists to address that elusive thing we call *human nature*.

Anthropologists welcome the contributions of researchers from other disciplines and, in return, offer their findings to these disciplines. Anthropologists may not know as much about the structure of the human eye as anatomists or as much about the perception of color as psychologists. As synthesizers, however, anthropologists seek to understand how anatomy and psychology relate to color-naming practices in different societies. Because they look for the broad basis of ideas and practices without limiting themselves to any single social or biological aspect, anthropologists acquire an expansive and inclusive overview of our species.

Embracing a holistic perspective allows anthropologists to guard against possible personal or cultural biases. As the old saying goes, people often see what they believe rather than what appears before their eyes. By maintaining a critical awareness of their own assumptions about human nature—checking and rechecking the ways their beliefs and actions might be shaping their research—anthropologists strive to gain objective knowledge about humans. With this in mind, anthropologists avoid the pitfalls of **ethnocentrism**, a belief that the ways of one's own culture are the best or only proper ones. Thus anthropologists have expanded our understanding of diversity in human thought, biology, and behavior, as well as our understanding of the many things humans have in common.

In this chapter you will learn to

- Describe the discipline of anthropology and make connections between each of its four fields.

- Compare anthropology to the sciences and the humanities.

- Identify the characteristics of anthropological field methods and the ethics of anthropological research.

- Explain the usefulness of anthropology in light of globalization.

anthropology The study of humankind in all times and places.

holistic perspective A fundamental principle of anthropology: The various parts of human culture and biology must be viewed in the broadest possible context in order to understand their interconnections and interdependence.

ethnocentrism The belief that the ways of one's own culture are the only proper ones.

Gina Ulysse

Figure 1.1 Anthropologist Gina Athena Ulysse
Anthropologists come from many corners of the world and contribute to the field in myriad ways. Dr. Gina Athena Ulysse, pictured here, was born in Pétion-Ville, Haiti, and immigrated to the United States with her family when she was a teenager. Now an associate professor of anthropology at Wesleyan University, she is a writer and spoken word scholar-artist. Her work explores Haitian history, identity, spirituality, and the lingering, dehumanizing effects of colonialism. Her performances incorporate spoken word and Vodou chant, blurring the lines between anthropology and art. She recently brought her performance back to Haiti while wearing the International Peace Belt, first created from coins that went out of circulation when the euro replaced most former European currencies. Today 115 of the world's 196 countries are represented on the belt. As a "living link between cultures and a symbol of peace and unity of all nations" (Artists for World Peace, 2015), the belt has traveled to over twenty-five countries on five continents.

as for one investigating tropical food gardens or traditional healing ceremonies. We might say anthropology is a discipline concerned with unbiased evaluation of diverse human systems, including one's own.

Although other social sciences have predominantly concentrated on contemporary peoples living in North American and European (Western) societies, anthropologists have historically focused on non-Western peoples and cultures. Anthropologists work with the understanding that to fully access the complexities of human ideas, behavior, and biology, *all humans*, wherever and whenever, must be studied. A cross-cultural and long-term evolutionary perspective distinguishes anthropology from other social sciences. This approach guards against theories that are **culture-bound**—based on assumptions about the world and reality that come from the researcher's own culture.

As a case in point, consider the fact that infants in the United States typically sleep apart from their parents. To people accustomed to multibedroom houses, cribs, and car seats, this may seem normal, but cross-cultural research shows that *co-sleeping,* of mother and baby in particular, is more common globally (Figure 1.2). Further, the practice of sleeping apart favored in the United States dates back only about 200 years (McKenna & McDade, 2005). Cultural norms are neither universal nor eternal.

Anthropologists come from many different backgrounds, and individuals practicing the discipline vary in their personal, national, ethnic, political, and religious beliefs (Figure 1.1). At the same time, they apply a rigorous methodology for researching from the perspective of the culture being studied, which requires them to check for the influences of their own biases. This is as true for an anthropologist analyzing the global banking industry

Consider also the medical practice of organ transplantation, which has become widespread since the first kidney transplant between twin brothers in Boston in 1954.

culture-bound A perspective that produces theories about the world and reality that are based on the assumptions and values from the researcher's own culture.

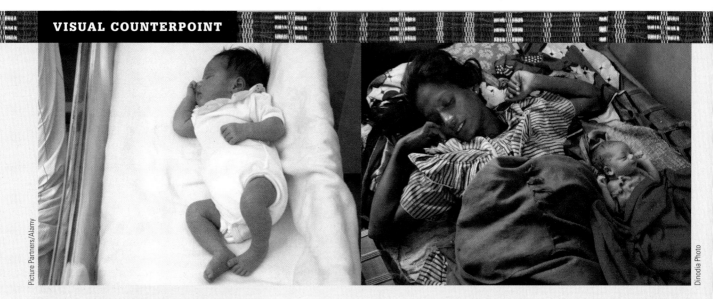

Picture Partners/Alamy

Dinodia Photo

VISUAL COUNTERPOINT

Figure 1.2 Sleeping Habits Across Cultures
A newborn baby in United States lies alone in a hospital cradle. A newborn Ho baby in Chakradharpur, India, sleeps nestled beside her mother. The patterns set in the first hours of life repeat in the coming weeks, months, and years. The U.S. pattern promotes the cultural norm of 8 isolated, uninterrupted hours of sleep at night throughout all phases of the life span. Cross-cultural research shows that co-sleeping and periods of wakefulness during the night are far more common. For U.S. infants sleeping alone in cribs, the consequences can be dire. They do not benefit from breastfeeding cues provided by someone sleeping nearby. Consequently, they are more susceptible to sudden infant death syndrome (SIDS), a phenomenon in which a baby, usually between 4 and 6 months old, stops breathing and dies while asleep. The highest rates of SIDS are found among infants in the United States (McKenna, Ball, & Gettler, 2007). That 50 to 70 million adults in the United States suffer from sleep disorders may also be a product of this cultural pattern (Institute of Medicine, 2006).

Today, transplants between unrelated individuals are common, so much so that organs are illegally trafficked, often across continents from the poor to the wealthy. A practice like organ transplantation can only exist if it fits with cultural beliefs about death and the human body. The dominant North American and European view—that the body is a machine that can be repaired much like a car—makes organ transplantation acceptable. However, in Japan the concept of brain death (that a person is "dead" when the individual's brain no longer functions, despite a still-beating heart) is hotly contested. Their idea of personhood does not incorporate a mind–body split, so Japanese people do not accept that a warm body is a corpse from which organs can be harvested. In addition, the idea of organs as anonymous "gifts" does not fit with the Japanese social pattern of reciprocal exchange. Consequently, organ transplants are rarely performed in Japan (Lock, 2001).

The findings of anthropologists have often challenged the conclusions of sociologists, psychologists, and economists. At the same time, anthropology is indispensable to those in other disciplines because it provides the only consistent check against culture-bound assertions. In a sense, anthropology is to these disciplines what the laboratory is to physics and chemistry: an essential testing ground for their theories.

Anthropology and Its Fields

Individual anthropologists tend to specialize in one of four fields or subdisciplines: cultural anthropology, linguistic anthropology, archaeology, and biological (physical) anthropology (Figure 1.3). Some anthropologists consider archaeology and linguistics to be part of a broader study of human cultures, but both subdisciplines have close ties to biological anthropology. For example, although linguistic anthropology focuses on the cultural aspects of language, it has deep connections to the evolution of human language and to the biological basis of speech and language studied within biological anthropology.

Researchers in each of anthropology's fields gather and analyze data to explore similarities and differences among humans, across time and space. Moreover, individuals within each of the four fields practice **applied anthropology**, using anthropological knowledge and methods to prevent or solve practical problems. Most applied anthropologists actively collaborate with the communities

applied anthropology The use of anthropological knowledge and methods to solve practical problems, often for a specific client.

Figure 1.3 The Four Fields of Anthropology
Note that the divisions among the fields are not sharp, indicating that their boundaries overlap. Also, all four fields include the practice of applied anthropology.

in which they work—setting goals, solving problems, and conducting research together. In this book, the Anthropology Applied features spotlight how anthropology contributes to solving a wide range of challenges.

An early example of the application of anthropological knowledge to a practical problem is the international public health movement that began in the 1920s. This marked the beginning of **medical anthropology**—a specialization that brings theoretical and applied approaches from cultural and biological anthropology to the study of human health and disease. The work of medical anthropologists sheds light on connections between human health and political and economic forces, both locally and globally. Examples of this

---

medical anthropology A specialization in anthropology that brings theoretical and applied approaches from cultural and biological anthropology to the study of human health and disease.

cultural anthropology The study of patterns in human behavior, thought, and emotions, focusing on humans as culture-producing and culture-reproducing creatures. Also known as *social* or *sociocultural anthropology*.

culture A society's shared and socially transmitted ideas, values, and perceptions, which are used to make sense of experience and generate behavior and are reflected in that behavior.

ethnography A detailed description of a particular culture primarily based on fieldwork.

fieldwork The term anthropologists use for on-location research.

participant observation In ethnography, the technique of learning a people's culture through social participation and personal observation within the community being studied, as well as interviews and discussion with individual members of the group over an extended period of time.

ethnology The study and analysis of different cultures from a comparative or historical point of view, utilizing ethnographic accounts and developing anthropological theories that help explain why certain important differences or similarities occur among groups.

---

specialization appear in many of the Biocultural Connection features in this text, including "Picturing Pesticides."

Cultural Anthropology

Cultural anthropology (also called *social* or *sociocultural anthropology*) is the study of patterns of human behavior, thought, and feelings. It focuses on humans as culture-producing and culture-reproducing creatures. To understand the work of cultural anthropologists, we must clarify the meaning of **culture**—a society's shared and socially transmitted ideas, values, and perceptions, which are used to make sense of experience and which generate behavior and are reflected in that behavior. These are the (often unconscious) standards by which societies—structured groups of people—operate. These standards are socially *learned*—not acquired through biological inheritance. Cultures may vary considerably from place to place, but no person is "more cultured" in the anthropological sense than any other.

Integral to all the anthropological fields, the concept of culture might be considered anthropology's distinguishing feature. After all, biological anthropologists are distinct from biologists *primarily* because they take culture into account. Cultural anthropologists may study the legal, medical, economic, political, or religious system of a given society, knowing that all aspects of culture interrelate as part of a unified whole. They may focus on divisions in a society—such as gender, age, or class. These same categories are also significant to archaeologists who study a society through its material remains, to linguistic anthropologists who examine ancient and modern languages, and to biological anthropologists who investigate the physical human body.

Cultural anthropology has two main components: ethnography and ethnology. An **ethnography**—a detailed description of a particular culture—is based on **fieldwork**, the term *all* anthropologists use for on-location research. Ethnographic fieldwork entails a combination of social participation and personal observation within the community being studied and interviews and discussions with individual members of a group. This methodology, commonly referred to as **participant observation** (Figure 1.4), provides the information used to make systematic comparisons of cultures all across the world. Known as **ethnology**, such cross-cultural research allows anthropologists to develop theories about differences and similarities among groups.

Ethnography

Through participant observation—eating a people's food, sleeping under their roof, learning how to speak and behave acceptably, and personally experiencing their habits and customs—the ethnographer seeks to understand a particular way of life. Being a participant observer does not mean that the anthropologist must join in battles to study a culture in which warfare is prominent; but by living among a warring people, the ethnographer can ascertain how warfare fits into the overall cultural framework.

Jeffrey Schonberg

Figure 1.4 Fieldwork among Urban Drug Users For over ten years, anthropologist Philippe Bourgois and photographer-ethnographer Jeff Schonberg spent time among heroin and crack users on the streets of San Francisco. Their research—including photographs, field notes, and audio recordings—explores the experience of homelessness, addiction, and marginalization. Their book, *Righteous Dopefiend: Homelessness, Addiction, and Poverty in Urban America*, and an accompanying traveling exhibit are based on their findings.

Ethnographers must take care not to place too much emphasis on one part of a culture at the expense of another. Only by discovering how *all* parts—social, political, economic, and religious practices and institutions—relate to one another can ethnographers begin to understand the cultural system. Ethnographers' essential tools are notebooks, pen/pencil, camera, recording devices, laptop computer, and, increasingly, smartphones. Most important of all, they need flexible social skills.

The popular image of ethnographic fieldwork is that it occurs among hunters, herders, or farmers who live in far-off, isolated places. To be sure, much ethnographic work continues to be done in remote villages in Asia, Africa, or Latin America, islands of the Pacific Ocean, and deserts of Australia. However, with the demise of colonialism in the mid-20th century, anthropologists now also focus on industrialized societies and urban neighborhoods.

Ethnographic fieldwork is no longer expert Western anthropologists studying people in "other" places; today it is a collaborative approach among anthropologists from all parts of the world and the varied communities in which they work. Anthropologists from around the globe employ the same research techniques developed in the study of non-Western peoples to explore diverse subjects such as religious movements, street gangs, refugee settlements, land rights, corporate bureaucracies, and health-care systems in Western cultures.

Ethnology

Largely descriptive in nature, *ethnography* provides raw data needed for *ethnology*—the branch of cultural anthropology that involves cross-cultural comparisons and theories that explain differences or similarities among groups. Cross-cultural comparisons can lead to insights about one's own beliefs and practices. Consider, for example, the amount of time spent on domestic chores by industrialized peoples and traditional food foragers—people who rely on wild plant and animal resources for subsistence. Anthropological research has shown that, despite access to "labor-saving" appliances such as dishwashers, washing machines, vacuum cleaners, and microwave ovens, urban dwellers in the United States who are not working outside their homes put 55 hours a week into their housework. In contrast, Aboriginal women in Australia devoted 20 hours a week to their chores (Bodley, 2008, p. 106). Nevertheless, consumer appliances have become important indicators of a high standard of living across the globe due to the widespread belief that they reduce housework and increase leisure time. Systematic comparisons allow ethnologists to generate scientific explanations of cultural features and social practices in all times and places.

Applied Cultural Anthropology

Today, cultural anthropologists contribute to applied anthropology in a variety of contexts ranging from business to education to healthcare to governmental interventions to humanitarian aid. For example, anthropologist Nancy Scheper-Hughes (2003) has taken her investigative work on the global problem of illegal organ trafficking and used it to help found Organs Watch, an organization dedicated to solving this human rights issue.

BIOCULTURAL CONNECTION

Picturing Pesticides

The toxic effects of pesticides have long been known. After all, these compounds are designed to kill bugs. However, it has not been as simple to document the toxic effects of pesticides on humans because those impacts may take years to become apparent.

Anthropologist Elizabeth Guillette, working in a Yaqui Indian community in Mexico, combined ethnographic observation, biological monitoring of pesticide levels in the blood, and neurobehavioral testing to document the impairment of child development by pesticides.[a] Working with colleagues from the Technological Institute of Sonora in Obregón, Mexico, Guillette compared children and families from two Yaqui communities: a valley farm whose residents were exposed to large doses of pesticides and a ranching village in the foothills nearby.

Guillette found that the frequency of pesticide use among the farming Yaqui was forty-five times per crop cycle with two crop cycles per year. In the farming valleys, she also noted that families tended to use household bug sprays on a daily basis, thus increasing their exposure to toxic pesticides. In the foothill ranches, she found that the only pesticides that the Yaqui were exposed to consisted of DDT sprayed by the government to control malaria. In these communities, indoor bugs were swatted or tolerated.

Pesticide exposure was linked to child health and development through two sets of measures. First, levels of pesticides in the blood of valley children at birth and throughout their childhood were examined and found to be far higher than in the children from the foothills. Further, Guillette found that the breast milk of nursing mothers from the valley farms revealed the presence of pesticides.

Second, children from the two communities were asked to perform a variety of normal childhood activities, such as jumping, memory games, playing catch, and drawing pictures. The children exposed to high doses of pesticides showed significantly poorer stamina, eye–hand coordination, large motor coordination, and drawing ability compared to the Yaqui children from the foothills. Notably, although the valley children exhibited no overt symptoms of pesticide poisoning, their delays and impairment in neurobehavioral abilities may be irreversible.

Though Guillette's study was thoroughly embedded in one ethnographic community, she emphasizes that the exposure to pesticides among the Yaqui farmers is typical of agricultural communities globally and has significance for changing human practices regarding the use of pesticides everywhere.

Biocultural Question

Given the documented developmental damage these pesticides have inflicted on children, should their sale and use be regulated globally? Are there potentially damaging toxins in use in your community?

---

[a]Guillette, E. A., Meza, M. M., Aquilar, M. G., Soto, A. D., & Garcia, I. E. (1998, June). An anthropological approach to the evaluation of preschool children exposed to pesticides in Mexico. *Environmental Health Perspectives 106* (6), 347–353

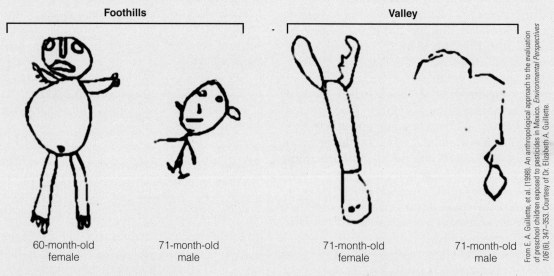

Foothills		Valley	
60-month-old female	71-month-old male	71-month-old female	71-month-old male

Compare the drawings typically done by Yaqui children heavily exposed to pesticides (*valley*) to those made by Yaqui children living in nearby areas who were relatively unexposed to pesticides (*foothills*).

From E. A. Guillette, et al. (1998). An anthropological approach to the evaluation of preschool children exposed to pesticides in Mexico. *Environmental Perspectives 106*(6), 347–353. Courtesy of Dr. Elizabeth A. Guillette.

Figure 1.5 Preserving Endangered Languages Linguistic anthropologist Greg Anderson (*right*) has devoted his career to documenting and saving indigenous languages. He founded and now heads the Living Tongues Institute for Endangered Languages and works throughout the globe to preserve languages that are dying out at a shocking rate of about one every two weeks. Here he is recording for the first time the language of Koro, spoken by some 1,000 people in India's remote northeastern state, Arunachal Pradesh. Situated near India's contested border with China, this region offers much for linguistic investigation.

Living Tongues Institute

Linguistic Anthropology

Perhaps the most distinctive feature of the human species is language. Although the sounds and gestures made by some other species—especially apes—may serve functions comparable to those of human language, no other animal has developed a system of symbolic communication as complex as that of humans. Language allows people to create, preserve, and transmit countless details of their culture from generation to generation.

Linguistic anthropology focuses on the structure and history of human languages and their relation to social and cultural contexts. It shares data, theories, and methods with the more general discipline of linguistics, but it also includes distinctly anthropological questions, such as, how does language influence or reflect culture? And how does language use differ among distinct members of a society?

In its early years, linguistic anthropology emphasized the documentation of languages of cultures under ethnographic study—particularly those whose future seemed precarious due to colonization, forced assimilation, population decimation, capitalist expansion, or other destructive forces. When the first Europeans began to colonize the world five centuries ago, an estimated 12,000 distinct languages existed. By the early 1900s—when anthropological research began to take off—many languages and peoples had already disappeared or were on the brink of extinction (Figure 1.5). Sadly, this trend continues, with predictions that nearly half of the world's remaining 6,000 languages will become extinct over the next hundred years (Crystal, 2002; Knight, Studdert-Kennedy, & Hurford, 2000).

Linguistic anthropology has three main branches: descriptive linguistics, historical linguistics, and language in relation to social and cultural settings. All three yield valuable information about how people communicate and how they understand the world around them.

Descriptive Linguistics

This branch of linguistic anthropology involves the painstaking work of dissecting a language by recording, delineating, and analyzing all of its features. This includes studying its structure (including grammar and syntax), its unique linguistic repertoire (figures of speech, word plays, and so on), and its relationship to other languages.

Historical Linguistics

Languages, like cultures, are alive, malleable, and changing. Online tools such as *Urban Dictionary* track the changes in North American slang, and traditional dictionaries include new words and usages each year. Historical linguists track these changes to increase understanding of the human past. By working out relationships among languages and examining their spatial distributions, these specialists may estimate how long the speakers of those languages have lived where they do. By identifying those words in related languages that have survived from an ancient ancestral tongue, historical linguists can suggest not only where but also *how* speakers of an ancestral language lived. Such work has shown, for example, how the Bantu family of languages spread from its origins in western Africa (in the region of today's Nigeria and Cameroon) to the majority of the continent. Over the course of several millennia, Bantu-speaking peoples came to inhabit most of sub-Saharan Africa, bringing the language, farming technology, and other aspects of their culture with them.

linguistic anthropology The study of human languages—looking at their structure, history, and relation to social and cultural contexts.

Language in Its Social and Cultural Settings

Some linguistic anthropologists study the social and cultural contexts of a language. The idea of *linguistic relativity* arose in the early 20th century, as European and American scholars began to master foreign languages with very different grammatical structures. Linguistic relativity is the idea that linguistic diversity reflects not just differences in sounds and grammar but also differences in ways of making sense of the world. For example, observing that the Hopi Indians of the American Southwest have no words for the concept of past, present, and future led early proponents of linguistic relativity to suggest the Hopi people had a unique conception of time (Whorf, 1946).

Complex ideas and practices integral to a culture's survival can also be reflected in language. For example, among the Nuer, a nomadic group that travels with grazing animals throughout South Sudan, a baby born with a visible deformity is not considered a human baby. Instead, it is called a baby hippopotamus. This name allows for the safe return of the "hippopotamus" to the river where it belongs. Such infants would not be able to survive in Nuer society, so linguistic practice is compatible with the compassionate choice the Nuer have had to make.

Some theorists have challenged the notion of linguistic relativity, arguing that biological universals underlie the human capacity for language and thought. Cognitive scientist Steven Pinker has even suggested that, at the biological level, thought is nonverbal (Pinker, 1994). Whatever the case, a holistic anthropological approach considers language to be dependent on both a shared biological basis and on specific cultural patterning.

Focusing on specific speech events, some linguistic anthropologists may research how factors such as age, gender, ethnicity, class, religion, occupation, or financial status affect speech (Hymes, 1974). Because members of any culture may use a variety of different registers and inflections, the ones they choose (often unconsciously) to use at a specific instance convey particular meanings. For example, linguistic anthropologists might examine whether U.S. women's tendency to end statements with an upward inflection, as though the statements were questions, reflects a pattern of male dominance in this society.

Linguistic anthropologists also focus on the socialization process through which individuals become part of a culture. Children take on this fundamental task as they develop, but it can be seen in adults as well. Adults may need to assimilate because of a geographic move or because of a new professional identity. First-year medical students, for example, amass 6,000 new vocabulary words and a series of linguistic conventions as they begin to take on the role of a physician.

Applied Linguistic Anthropology

Linguistic anthropologists put their research to use in a number of settings. Some, for example, collaborate with recently contacted cultural groups, small nations (or tribes), and ethnic minorities in preserving or reviving languages suppressed or lost during periods of oppression by dominant societies. Their work includes helping to create written forms of languages that previously existed only orally. This sort of applied linguistic anthropology represents a trend toward mutually useful collaboration that is characteristic of much anthropological research today.

Archaeology

Archaeology is the branch of anthropology that studies human cultures through the recovery and analysis of material remains and environmental data. Such material products include tools, pottery, hearths, and enclosures that remain as traces of past cultural practices, as well as human, plant, and marine remains, some dating back 2.5 million years. These traces and their arrangements reflect specific human ideas and behavior. For example, restricted concentrations of charcoal that include oxidized earth, bone fragments, and charred plant remains, located near pieces of fire-cracked rock and tools suitable for food preparation, indicate cooking. Such remains can reveal much about a people's diet and subsistence practices.

In addition to studying a single group of people at a specific place and time, archaeologists use material remains to investigate broad questions, including settlement or migration patterns across vast areas, such as the peopling of the Americas or the spread of the earliest humans from Africa. Together with skeletal remains, material remains help archaeologists reconstruct the biocultural context of past human lifeways and patterns. Archaeologists organize this material and use it to explain cultural variability and change through time. Although archaeologists tend to specialize in particular regions or time periods, a number of subspecializations exist.

Historical Archaeology

Compared to historians, who rely on written records, archaeologists can reach much further back in time for clues to human behavior. But to call a society "prehistoric" does not mean that these past peoples were less interested in their history or that they did not have ways of recording and transmitting information. It simply means that written records do not exist.

Archaeologists are not limited to the study of societies without written records; they may study those for which historic documents are available to supplement the material remains. **Historical archaeology**, the archaeological study of places for which written records exist, often provides data that differ considerably from the historical record. In most literate societies, written records are associated with governing elites rather than with farmers,

archaeology The study of cultures through the recovery and analysis of material remains and environmental data.

historical archaeology The archaeological study of places for which written records exist.

fishers, laborers, or slaves, and therefore they include biases of the ruling classes. In fact, in many historical contexts, "material culture may be the most objective source of information we have" (Deetz, 1977, p. 160).

Bioarchaeology

A number of archaeological specializations deal with preserving cultural practices in the remains of living things. **Bioarchaeology**, the study of human remains—bones, skulls, teeth, and sometimes hair, dried skin, or other tissue—emphasizes preservation of cultural and social processes in skeletons. For example, mummified skeletal remains from the Andean highlands in South America preserve not only this burial practice but also provide evidence of some of the earliest brain surgery ever documented. In addition, these bioarchaeological remains exhibit skull deformations that were used to distinguish nobility from other members of society.

Other specializations include *archaeological ethnobotany*, the study of how past peoples made use of indigenous plants; *biomolecular archaeology*, the analysis of traces of living organisms left in material remains (Figure 1.6); *zooarchaeology,* the tracking of animal remains recovered in excavations; and *marine archaeology,* the investigation of submerged sites or sailing vessels from hundreds or even thousands of years ago.

Contemporary Archaeology

Although most archaeologists concentrate on the past, some study material objects in contemporary settings, including garbage dumps. Just as a 3,000-year-old shell mound (*midden*) at the tip of South America offers significant clues about prehistoric communities living on mussels, fish, and other natural resources, modern garbage dumps provide evidence of everyday life in contemporary societies. For large cities like New York, the accumulation of daily garbage—such as newspapers, rubble, and plastic—is staggering. In just a few centuries, millions of inhabitants have dumped so much trash that this urban area has been physically raised 6 to 30 feet (Rathje & Murphy, 2001).

One of the earliest anthropological studies of modern garbage—University of Arizona's Garbage Project—began with a study of household waste of Tucson residents in 1973. When surveyed by questionnaire, only 15 percent of households reported consuming beer, and none reported more than eight cans a week. Analysis of garbage from the same area, however, showed that 80 percent of the households consumed beer, and 50 percent discarded more than eight cans per week (Rathje & Murphy, 2001). Thus, the Garbage Project has tested the validity of research survey techniques, upon which sociologists, economists, other social scientists, and policymakers rely. The tests show a significant difference between what people *say* they do and what the garbage analysis shows they *actually* do.

University of Pennsylvania Museum of Archaeology and Anthropology, Philadelphia

Figure 1.6 The Biomolecular Archaeology of Ancient Beverages Biomolecular archaeologist Dr. Patrick McGovern is known as the Indiana Jones of ancient beverages. By chemically analyzing the residue in ancient vessels, as well as replicating the crafting processes, "Dr. Pat" and his team at the University of Pennsylvania's Museum of Archaeology and Anthropology in Philadelphia recreate the drinks of long ago, including a honey-grape-saffron beer from the 2,700-year-old tomb of King Midas in Turkey and a chili-chocolate concoction found on 3,400-year-old pottery fragments in Honduras. Through collaboration with the craft brewery Dogfish Head, the beverages that delighted ancient tongues are now available for today's connoisseurs.

Applied Archaeology

The Garbage Project also shows applied archaeology in action. Its landfill excavation program, initiated in 1987, produced the first reliable data on what materials actually go into landfills and what happens to them there. Again, common beliefs turned out to be at odds with reality. For example, when buried in deep compost landfills, biodegradable materials such as newspapers take far longer to decay than anyone expected. The data gathered from the Garbage Project's landfill studies on hazardous wastes and rates of decay of various materials play a major role in landfill and waste disposal regulation and management today (Rathje & Murphy, 2001).

---

bioarchaeology The archaeological study of human remains—bones, skulls, teeth, and sometimes hair, dried skin, or other tissue—to determine the influences of culture and environment on human biological variation.

Cultural Resource Management

For many, archaeology evokes images of ancient pyramids and temples. Instead, much archaeological fieldwork is **cultural resource management**. Unlike traditional archaeological research, cultural resource management is a legally required part of any activity that might threaten important aspects of a country's prehistoric and historic heritage. Many countries, from Chile to China, use archaeological expertise to protect and manage their cultural heritage.

In the United States, for example, if a construction company plans to replace a highway bridge, it must first contract with archaeologists to identify and protect any significant prehistoric or historic resources that might be affected. And when archaeological investigation unearths Native American cultural items or human remains, federal laws come into play again. The Native American Graves Protection and Repatriation Act (NAGPRA), passed in 1990, provides a process for the return of these remains—especially human bones and burial gifts, such as copper jewelry, weapons, and ceramic bowls—to lineal descendants, culturally affiliated Indian tribes, and Native Hawaiian organizations.

In addition to working in all the capacities mentioned, archaeologists also help engineering firms prepare environmental impact statements. Some of these archaeologists operate out of universities and colleges, while others are on the staff of independent consulting firms. When state legislation sponsors any kind of archaeological work, it is referred to as *contract archaeology.*

Biological Anthropology

Biological anthropology, also called *physical anthropology,* focuses on humans as biological organisms. Traditionally, biological anthropologists concentrated on human evolution, primatology, growth and development, human adaptation, and forensics. Today, **molecular anthropology**, or the anthropological study of genes and genetic relationships, contributes significantly to our understanding of human evolution (*paleogenetics*), adaptation, and diversity. Comparisons among groups separated by time, geography, or the frequency of a particular gene can reveal

how humans have adapted and where they have migrated. As experts in the anatomy of human bones and tissues, biological anthropologists lend their knowledge about the body to applied areas such as gross anatomy laboratories, public health, and criminal investigations.

Paleoanthropology

Dealing with much greater timespans than other branches of anthropology, **paleoanthropology** is the study of the origins, predecessors, and early representatives of the present human species. Focusing on long-time biological changes (evolution), paleoanthropologists seek to understand how, when, and why we became the species we are today. In biological terms, we humans are *Homo sapiens,* a species in the larger order of primates, one of the many kinds of mammals. Because we share a common ancestry with other primates (monkeys and apes), paleoanthropologists look back to the earliest primates or even to the earliest mammals to reconstruct the complex path of human evolution. Paleoanthropology, unlike other evolutionary studies, takes a **biocultural** approach, focusing on the interaction of biology and culture.

Paleoanthropologists compare fossilized skeletons of our ancestors to other fossils and to the bones of living members of our species. Combining this knowledge with biochemical and genetic evidence, they strive to scientifically reconstruct human evolutionary history. With each new fossil discovery, paleoanthropologists have another piece to add to the puzzle.

Primatology

Studying the anatomy and behavior of other primates helps us understand what we share with our closest living relatives and what makes humans unique. Therefore, **primatology**, or the study of living and fossil primates, is a vital part of biological anthropology. Primates include the Asian and African apes, as well as monkeys, lemurs, lorises, and tarsiers.

Biologically, humans are members of the ape family—large-bodied, broad-shouldered primates without tails. Studies of apes in the wild show that their social lives include sharing learned behavior. Increasingly, primatologists designate the shared, learned behavior of nonhuman apes as *culture.* Primate studies offer scientifically grounded perspectives on the behavior of our ancestors and the abilities of our closest living relatives. As human activity encroaches on all parts of the world, many primate species are endangered. Primatologists, such as Jane Goodall (**Figure 1.7**), champion the rights of these remarkable animals and the preservation of their habitats.

Human Growth, Adaptation, and Variation

Some biological anthropologists specialize in the study of human growth and development. They examine biological mechanisms of growth as well as the impact of the environment on the growth process. For example, Franz Boas, a pioneer of American anthropology of the early 20th century (see the Anthropologists of Note feature) compared

cultural resource management A branch of archaeology concerned with survey and/or excavation of archaeological and historical remains that might be threatened by construction or development; also involved with policy surrounding protection of cultural resources.

biological anthropology The systematic study of humans as biological organisms; also known as *physical anthropology.*

molecular anthropology The anthropological study of genes and genetic relationships, which contributes significantly to our understanding of human evolution, adaptation, and diversity.

paleoanthropology The anthropological study of biological changes through time (evolution) to understand the origins and predecessors of the present human species.

biocultural An approach that focuses on the interaction of biology and culture.

primatology The study of living and fossil primates.

the heights of immigrants who spent their childhood in the "old country" (Europe) to the increased heights reached by their children who grew up in the United States. Today, biological anthropologists study the impact of disease, pollution, and poverty on growth. Comparisons between human and nonhuman primate growth patterns provide clues to the evolutionary history of humans. Detailed anthropological studies of the hormonal, genetic, and physiological bases of healthy growth in living humans also contribute significantly to the health of children today.

Studies of human adaptation focus on the capacity of humans to adapt to their environment, biologically and culturally. This branch of biological anthropology takes a comparative approach to humans living today in a variety of environments. Humans are the only primate group to inhabit the entire earth. Although cultural adaptations make it possible for people to live in some environmentally challenging places, biological adaptations also contribute to survival in extreme cold, heat, and high altitude.

Some of these biological adaptations are built into the genetic makeup of populations. The long period of human growth and development also provides ample opportunity for the environment to shape the human body. Such *developmental adaptations* account for permanent features of human variation such as the enlargement of the right ventricle of the heart among the Quechua Indians living at high altitude plains (Altiplano) of the Andes, a mountain range that extends along the western rim of South America. Humans also experience *physiological adaptations*, short-term changes in response to a particular environmental stimulus. For example, if a woman who normally lives at sea level flies to La Paz, Bolivia—a city at an altitude of 3,660 meters (nearly 12,000 feet)—her body will increase production of the red blood cells that carry oxygen. All of these kinds of biological adaptation contribute to present-day human variation.

AP Images/Jean-Marc Bouju

Figure 1.7 Primatologist Jane Goodall
Over fifty-five years ago, Jane Goodall began studying chimpanzees to shed light on the behavior of our distant ancestors. The knowledge she has amassed reveals striking similarities with our species. Goodall has devoted much of her career to championing the rights of our closest living relatives.

Genetic human differences include visible traits such as height, body build, and skin color, as well as biochemical factors such as blood type and susceptibility to certain diseases. Still, we remain members of a single species. Biological anthropology applies all the techniques of modern biology to achieve fuller understanding of human variation and its relationship to the different environments in which people have lived. Biological anthropologists' research on human variation has debunked false ideas of biologically defined races, a notion based on widespread misinterpretation of human variation.

Forensic Anthropology

The application of biological anthropology to legal settings is **forensic anthropology**. In addition to helping law enforcement identify murder victims and perpetrators, forensic anthropologists investigate human rights abuses such as genocide, terrorism, and war crimes. These specialists use genetic information and details of skeletal anatomy to establish the age, sex, population affiliation, and stature of the deceased. Forensic anthropologists can also determine whether a person was right-handed or left-handed, exhibited any physical abnormalities, or had experienced trauma. (See the Anthropology Applied feature in this chapter to read about the work of several forensic anthropologists and forensic archaeologists.)

forensic anthropology The examination of human biological and cultural remains for legal purposes.

Franz Boas (1858–1942) • Matilda Coxe Stephenson (1849–1915)

Franz Boas on a sailing ship, about 1925.

Franz Boas was not the first to teach anthropology in the United States, but it was Boas and his students, with their insistence on scientific rigor, who integrated anthropology courses into college and university curricula. Born and raised in Germany where he studied physics, mathematics, and geography, Boas did his first ethnographic research among the Inuit (Eskimos) in Arctic Canada in 1883 and 1884. After a brief academic career in Berlin, he came to the United States where he worked in museums and conducted ethnographic research among the Kwakiutl (Kwakwaka'wakw) Indians in the Canadian Pacific. In 1896, he became a professor at Columbia University in New York City. He authored an incredible number of publications, founded professional organizations and journals, and taught two generations of great anthropologists, including numerous women and ethnic minorities.

As a Jewish immigrant, Boas recognized the dangers of ethnocentrism and especially racism. Through ethnographic fieldwork and comparative analysis, he demonstrated that white supremacy theories and other schemes ranking non-European peoples and cultures as inferior were biased, ill informed, and unscientific. Throughout his long and illustrious academic career, he promoted anthropology not only as a human science but also as an instrument to combat racism and prejudice in the world.

Among the founders of North American anthropology were a number of women, including **Matilda Coxe Stevenson**, who did fieldwork among the Zuni Indians of Arizona. In 1885, she founded the Women's Anthropological Society in Washington, DC, the first professional association for women scientists. Three years later, hired by the Smithsonian's Bureau of American Ethnology, she became one of the first women in the world to receive a full-time scientific position. Along with several other pioneering female anthropologists in North America, she was highly influential among women's rights advocates in the late 1800s. The tradition of women building careers in anthropology continues. In fact, since World War II more than half the presidents of the more than 10,000-member American Anthropological Association have been women.

Matilda Coxe Stevenson in New Mexico, about 1900.

Recording observations on film as well as in notebooks, Stevenson and Boas were also pioneers in visual anthropology. Stevenson used an early box camera to document Pueblo Indian religious ceremonies and material culture, while Boas photographed Inuit and Kwakiutl Indians from the early 1890s for cultural as well as physical anthropological documentation. Today, their early photographs are greatly valued not only by anthropologists and historians, but also by indigenous peoples themselves.

Anthropology, Science, and the Humanities

Anthropology has been called the most humane of the sciences and the most scientific of the humanities—a designation that most anthropologists accept with pride.

Given their intense involvement with people of all times and places, anthropologists have amassed considerable information about human failure and success, weakness and greatness—the real stuff of the humanities. Anthropologists remain committed to the proposition that one cannot fully understand another culture by simply observing it; one must *experience* it. A commitment to fieldwork and the systematic collection of data also demonstrate the scientific side of anthropology. Anthropology is an **empirical** social science based on observations or information about humans taken in through the senses and verified by others, rather than on intuition or faith. However, anthropology is distinguished from other sciences by the diverse ways in which its scientific research is conducted.

Science, a carefully honed way of producing knowledge, aims to reveal and explain the underlying logic and structural processes of our world. A creative scientific endeavor seeks testable explanations for observed phenomena, ideally in terms of the workings of unchanging principles or laws. Two basic ingredients are essential for this: imagination and skepticism. Imagination, though having the potential to lead us astray, helps us recognize unexpected ways phenomena might be ordered and to think of old things in new ways. Without it, there can be no science. Skepticism allows us to distinguish fact (an observation independently verified by others) from fancy, to test our speculations, and to prevent our imaginations from running wild. In their search for explanations, scientists do not assume things are always as they appear on the surface. After all, what could be more obvious than the earth staying still while the sun travels around it every day?

Like other scientists, anthropologists often begin their research with a **hypothesis** (a tentative explanation or hunch) about possible relationships between certain observed facts or events. By gathering various kinds of data that seem to ground such suggested explanations in evidence, anthropologists come up with a **theory**, an explanation supported by a reliable body of data. Theories guide us in our explorations and may result in new knowledge. Efforts to demonstrate connections between *known* facts or events may yield *unexpected* facts, events, or relationships. Newly discovered facts may provide evidence that certain explanations, however popular or firmly believed to be true, are unfounded. Without supporting evidence, hypotheses must be dropped. Moreover, no scientific theory—no matter how widely accepted by the international community of scholars—is beyond challenge. In other words, anthropology relies on empirical evidence.

It is important to distinguish between scientific theories—which are always open to challenges born of new evidence or insights—and doctrine. A **doctrine**, or dogma, is an opinion or belief formally handed down by an authority as true and indisputable. For instance, those who accept a creationist doctrine of human origins as recounted in sacred texts or myths do so on the basis of religious authority, conceding that such views may be contrary to genetic, geological, biological, or other explanations. Such doctrines cannot be tested or proved: They are accepted as matters of faith.

Although the scientific approach may seem straightforward, its application is not always easy. For instance, once a hypothesis has been proposed, the person who suggested it is strongly motivated to verify it, and this can cause one to unwittingly overlook negative evidence. Scientists might not see that their hypotheses or interpretations are culture-bound. But by using the anthropological principle that culture shapes our thoughts, scientists can think outside the "culture box," framing their hypotheses and interpretations without bias. By encompassing both humanism and science, the discipline of anthropology can draw on its internal diversity to overcome the limits culture can impose on scientific inquiry.

Doing Anthropology in the Field

Because anthropologists are keenly aware that their personal and cultural backgrounds may shape their research questions or even affect their actual observations, they rely heavily on a technique that has been successful in other disciplines: They immerse themselves in the data to the fullest extent possible. In the process, anthropologists become so familiar with even the smallest details that they can begin to recognize underlying patterns that might otherwise have been overlooked. This enables anthropologists to frame meaningful hypotheses, which then may be subjected to further testing or validation in the field.

Although fieldwork was introduced earlier in this chapter in connection with cultural anthropology, it is characteristic of *all* the anthropological subdisciplines. Archaeologists and paleoanthropologists excavate sites in the field. A biological anthropologist interested in the effects of globalization on nutrition and growth will live with a community of people to study this question. A primatologist might live with a group of chimpanzees or baboons just as a linguist will study the language of a community by living with that group. Such immersion challenges anthropologists to be constantly aware of ways that cultural factors influence research questions. Anthropological researchers self-monitor through constantly checking their own biases and assumptions as they work; they present these self-reflections along with their observations, a practice known as *reflexivity*.

Unlike many other social scientists, anthropologists usually do not go into the field armed with prefigured questionnaires. Though they will have completed background research and devised tentative hypotheses, anthropologists recognize that maintaining an open mind can lead to the best discoveries. As fieldwork proceeds, anthropologists sort out their observations, sometimes

---

empirical An approach based on observations of the world rather than on intuition or faith.

hypothesis A tentative explanation of the relationships between certain phenomena.

theory A coherent statement that provides an explanatory framework for understanding; an explanation or interpretation supported by a reliable body of data.

doctrine An assertion of opinion or belief formally handed down by an authority as true and indisputable.

Forensic Anthropology: Voices for the Dead

The work of Clyde C. Snow, Mercedes Doretti, and Michael Blakey

Forensic anthropology is the analysis of skeletal remains for legal purposes. Law enforcement authorities call upon forensic anthropologists to use skeletal remains to identify murder victims, missing persons, or people who have died in disasters such as plane crashes. Forensic anthropologists have also contributed substantially to the investigation of human rights abuses by

The excavation of mass graves by the Guatemalan Foundation for Forensic Anthropology (Fernando Moscoso Moller, director) documents the human rights abuses committed during Guatemala's bloody civil war, a conflict that left 200,000 people dead and another 40,000 missing. In 2009, in a mass grave in the Quiche region, Diego Lux Tzunux uses his cell phone to photograph the skeletal remains believed to belong to his brother Manuel who disappeared in 1980. Genetic analyses allow forensic anthropologists to confirm the identity of individuals so that family members can know the fate of their loved ones. The analysis of skeletal remains provides evidence of the torture and massacre sustained by these individuals.

by formulating and testing limited or low-level hypotheses or by intuition. Anthropologists work closely with the community so that the research process becomes a collaborative effort. If the results fail to fit together in a consistent manner, researchers know they must inquire further. Anthropologists establish validity, or the reliability of the research conclusions, through the replication of observations and/or experiments by other researchers. It then becomes obvious if one's colleagues have gotten it right.

In anthropology, having others validate one's work can be challenging. Access to a particular research site may be impeded by difficulties of travel, obtaining permits, insufficient funding, and social, political, and economic turmoil. As well, sites, people, and cultures change over time. For these reasons, one researcher cannot easily confirm the reliability or completeness of another's account. As a result, anthropologists bear a special responsibility for accurate reporting. They must clearly explain details of the research: Why was the specific location selected as a research site? What were the research objectives? What were local conditions during fieldwork? Which local individuals provided key information and insights? How were the data collected and recorded? How did the researchers check their own biases? Without this information, it is difficult for others to judge the validity of the account and the soundness of the researcher's conclusions.

identifying victims and documenting the cause of death.

Among the best-known forensic anthropologists is Clyde C. Snow, who studied the remains of General Custer and his men from the 1876 battle at Little Big Horn and identified the remains of the Nazi war criminal Josef Mengele in Brazil. In 1984, Snow was instrumental in establishing the first forensic team devoted to documenting human rights abuses around the world: the Argentine Forensic Anthropology Team (EAAF in Spanish). At the time, the newly elected civilian government asked Snow's team to help identify remains of the *desaparecidos* or "disappeared ones"—the 9,000 or more people who were eliminated by death squads during seven years of military rule. Besides providing factual accounts of the fate of victims to their surviving kin and refuting the assertions of revisionists that the massacres never happened, the work of Snow and his Argentinean associates was crucial in convicting several military officers of kidnapping, torture, and murder.

Since Snow's pioneering work, forensic anthropologists have become increasingly involved in investigating human rights abuses globally. Mercedes Doretti, an Argentinean who worked with Snow to establish the EAAF, is a good example of today's forensic anthropologist.[a] In 2003, she began investigating mishandled and misidentified human remains in Mexico, including murdered women, migrant workers, and victims of gang violence.

Because of obstructive government officials, corrupt medical professionals, and incomplete or inaccurate records, Doretti could not rely on official documentation and had to conduct her own investigations. She continues to work closely with victims' families, emphasizing respect and compassion, and has created forensic DNA banks in Mexico, Honduras, and El Salvador to help with identifying remains.[b]

Forensic anthropologists specializing in skeletal remains commonly work closely with forensic archaeologists. Their relationship is like that between a forensic pathologist, who examines a corpse to establish time and manner of death, and a crime scene investigator, who searches the site for clues. While the forensic anthropologist deals with the human remains—often only bones and teeth—the forensic archaeologist controls the site, recording the position of relevant finds and recovering any clues associated with the remains.

For example, in 1995, the United Nations commissioned a team to investigate mass murder in Rwanda; the team included archaeologists from the U.S. National Park Service's Midwest Archaeological Center. They performed the standard archaeological procedures of mapping the site; determining its boundaries; photographing and recording all surface finds; and excavating, photographing, and recording buried skeletons and associated materials in mass graves.[c]

In 1991, in another part of the world, construction workers in New York City discovered an African burial ground from the 17th and 18th centuries. Directed by Michael Blakey, the African Burial Ground Project's researchers used a bioarchaeological rather than a strictly forensic approach to examine the complete cultural and historical context and lifeways of the people buried there. The more than 400 individuals, many of them children, were worked so far beyond their ability to endure that their spines were fractured—incontrovertible evidence of the horror of slavery in this busy North American port.

Thus, several kinds of anthropologists analyze human remains for a variety of purposes. Their work contributes to the documentation and correction of violence committed by humans of the past and present. In doing so, they shape a more just future.

---

[a]"Mercedes Doretti: Forensic Anthropologist." (2007, January 28). *MacArthur Foundation*. http://www.macfound.org/fellows/820/ (retrieved July 1, 2015)

[b]Borrell, B. (2012, October 8). Forensic anthropologist uses DNA to solve real-life murder mysteries in Latin America. *Scientific American*. http://www.scientificamerican .com/article/qa-forensic-anthropologist -mercedes-doretti/ (retrieved July 1, 2015)

[c]Haglund, W. D., Conner, M., & Scott, D. D. (2001). The archaeology of contemporary mass graves. *Historical Archaeology* 35 (1), 57–69.

On a personal level, fieldwork requires researchers to step out of their cultural comfort zone into a world that is unfamiliar and sometimes unsettling. Anthropologists in the field are likely to face a host of challenges—physical, social, mental, political, and ethical. They may have to adjust to unfamiliar food, climate, and hygiene conditions. They often struggle with emotional and psychological challenges such as loneliness, feeling like perpetual outsiders, being socially awkward in their new cultural setting, and having to be alert around the clock because anything that is happening or being said may be significant to their research. Political challenges include the possibility of unwittingly letting themselves be used by community factions or being viewed with suspicion by government authorities who may see them as spies. And there are ethical dilemmas: What does one do if faced with a troubling cultural practice such as female circumcision? How do anthropologists deal with demands for food, supplies, or medicine? Is it acceptable to deceive people to gain vital information?

At the same time, fieldwork often leads to meaningful personal, professional, and social rewards—from lasting friendships to vital knowledge and insights concerning the human condition. The following Original Study featuring archaeologist Anne Jensen and the Inupiat Eskimo community of Barrow, Alaska, conveys some of the meaning and impact of anthropological research in a context of mutual cooperation and respect.

Whispers from the Ice BY SHERRY SIMPSON

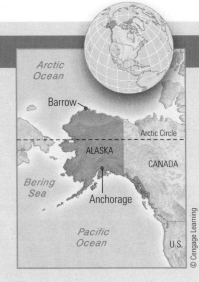

People grew excited when a summer rainstorm softened the bluff known as Ukkuqsi, sloughing off huge chunks of earth containing remains of historic and prehistoric houses, part of the old village that predates the modern community of Barrow. Left protruding from the slope was a human head. Archaeologist Anne Jensen happened to be in Barrow buying strapping tape when the body appeared. Her firm, SJS Archaeological Services, Inc., was closing a field season at nearby Point Franklin, and Jensen offered the team's help in a kind of archaeological triage to remove the body before it eroded completely from the earth.

The North Slope Borough hired her and Glenn Sheehan, both associated with Pennsylvania's Bryn Mawr College, to conduct the work. The National Science Foundation, which supported the three-year Point Franklin Project, agreed to fund the autopsy and subsequent analysis of the body and artifacts. The Ukkuqsi excavation quickly became a community event. In remarkably sunny and calm weather, volunteers troweled and picked through the thawing soil, finding trade beads, animal bones, and other items. Teenage boys worked alongside grandmothers. The smell of sea mammal oil, sweet at first then corrupt, mingled with ancient organic odors of decomposed vegetation. One man searched the beach for artifacts that had eroded from the bluff, discovering such treasures as two feather parkas. Elder Silas Negovanna, originally of Wainwright, visited several times, "more or less out of curiosity to see what they have in mind," he said. George Leavitt, who lives in a house on the bluff, stopped by one day while carrying home groceries and suggested a way to spray water to thaw the soil without washing away valuable artifacts. Tour groups added the excavation to their rounds.

"This community has a great interest in archaeology up here just because it's so recent to their experience," says oral historian Karen Brewster, a tall young woman who interviews elders as part of her work with the North Slope Borough's division of Inupiat History, Language, and Culture. "The site's right in town, and everybody was really fascinated by it."

Slowly, as the workers scraped and shoveled, the earth surrendered its historical hoard: carved wooden bowls, ladles, and such clothing as a mitten made from polar bear hide, bird-skin parkas, and mukluks. The items spanned prehistoric times, dated in Barrow to before explorers first arrived in 1826.

The work prompted visiting elders to recall when they or their parents lived in traditional sod houses and relied wholly on the land and sea for sustenance. Some remembered sliding down the hill as children, before the sea gnawed away the slope. Others described the site's use as a lookout for whales or ships. For the archaeologists, having elders stand beside them and identify items and historical context is like hearing the past whispering in their ears. Elders often know from experience, or from stories, the answers to the scientists' questions about how items were used or made. "In this instance, usually the only puzzled people are the archaeologists," jokes archaeologist Sheehan.

A modern town of 4,000, Barrow exists in a cultural continuum, where history is not detached or remote but still pulses through contemporary life. People live, hunt, and fish where their ancestors did, but they can also buy fresh vegetables at the store and jet to other places. Elementary school classes include computer and Inupiat language studies. Caribou skins, still ruddy with blood, and black brant carcasses hang near late-model cars outside homes equipped with television antennas. A man uses power tools to work on his whaling boat. And those who appear from the earth are not just bodies, but relatives. "We're not a people frozen in time," says Jana Harcharek, an Inupiat Eskimo who teaches Inupiat and nurtures her culture among young people. "There will always be that connection between us [and our ancestors]. They're not a separate entity."

The past drew still closer as the archaeologists neared the body. After several days of digging through thawed soil, they used water supplied by the local fire station's tanker truck to melt through permafrost until they reached the remains, about 3 feet below the surface. A shell of clear ice encased the body, which rested in what appeared to be a former meat cellar. With the low-pressure play of water from the tanker, the archaeologists teased the icy casket from the frozen earth, exposing a tiny foot. Only then did they realize they had uncovered a child. "That was kind of sad, because she was about my daughter's size," says archaeologist Jensen.

The girl was curled up beneath a baleen toboggan and part of a covering that Inupiat elder Bertha Leavitt identified as a kayak skin by its stitching. The child, who appeared to be 5 or 6, remained remarkably intact after her dark passage through time. Her face was cloaked by a covering that puzzled some onlookers. It didn't look like human hair, or even fur, but something with a feathery residue. Finally, they concluded it was a hood from a feather parka made of bird skins. The rest of her body was delineated muscle that had freeze-dried into a dark brick-red color. Her hands rested on her knees, which were drawn up to her chin. Frost particles coated the bends of her arms and legs.

"We decided we needed to go talk to the elders and see what they wanted, to get some kind of feeling as to whether they wanted to bury her right away, or whether they were willing to allow some studies in a respectful manner—studies that would be of some use to residents of the North Slope," Jensen says. Working with community elders is not a radical idea to Jensen or Sheehan, whose previous work in the Arctic has earned them high regard from local officials who appreciate their sensitivity. The researchers feel obligated not only to follow community wishes, but to invite villagers to sites and to share all information through public presentations. In fact, Jensen is reluctant to discuss findings with the press before the townspeople themselves hear it.

Here two Inupiat stand above another buried ancestor called Uncle Foot who surfaced along the eroding seawall in Barrow. Because Uncle Foot was so close to the shoreline, his remains were ultimately lost to the sea.

"It seems like it's a matter of simple common courtesy," she says. Such consideration can only help researchers, she points out. "If people don't get along with you, they're not going to talk to you, and they're liable to throw you out on your ear." In the past, scientists were not terribly sensitive about such matters, generally regarding human remains—and sometimes living natives—as artifacts themselves. Once, the girl's body would have been hauled off to the catacombs of some university or museum, and relics would have disappeared into exhibit drawers in what Sheehan describes as "hit-and-run archaeology."

"Grave robbers" is how Inupiat Jana Harcharek refers to early Arctic researchers. "They took human remains and their burial goods. It's pretty gruesome. But, of course, at the time they thought they were doing science a big favor. Thank goodness attitudes have changed."

Today, not only scientists but municipal officials confer with the Barrow Elders Council when local people find skeletons from traditional platform burials out on the tundra, or when bodies appear in the house mounds. The elders appreciate such consultations, says Samuel Simmonds, a tall, dignified man known for his carving. A retired Presbyterian minister, he presided at burial ceremonies of the famous "frozen family," ancient Inupiats discovered in Barrow [in 1982]. "They were part of us, we know that," he says simply, as if the connection between old bones and bodies and living relatives is self-evident. In the case of the newly discovered body, he says, "We were concerned that it was reburied in a respectful manner. They were nice enough to come over and ask us."

The elders also wanted to restrict media attention and prevent photographs of the body except for a few showing her position at the site. They approved a limited autopsy to help answer questions about the body's sex, age, and state of health. She was placed in an orange plastic body bag in a stainless steel morgue with the temperature turned down to below freezing.

With the help of staff at the Indian Health Service Hospital, Jensen sent the girl's still-frozen body to Anchorage's Providence Hospital. There she assisted with an autopsy performed by Dr. Michael Zimmerman of New York City's Mount Sinai Hospital. Zimmerman, an expert on prehistoric frozen bodies, had autopsied Barrow's frozen family in 1982 and was on his way to work on the prehistoric man recently discovered in the Alps.

The findings suggest the girl's life was very hard. She ultimately died of starvation, but also had emphysema caused by a rare congenital disease—the lack of an enzyme that protects the lungs. She probably was sickly and needed extra care all her brief life. The autopsy also found soot in her lungs from the family's sea mammal oil lamps, and she had osteoporosis, which was caused by a diet exclusively of meat from marine mammals. The girl's stomach was empty, but her intestinal tract contained dirt and animal fur. That remains a mystery and raises questions about the condition of the rest of the family. "It's not likely that she would be hungry and everyone else well fed," Jensen says.

That the girl appears to have been placed deliberately in the cellar provokes further questions about precontact burial practices, which the researchers hope Barrow elders can help answer. Historic accounts indicate the dead often were wrapped in skins and laid out on the tundra on wooden platforms, rather than buried in the frozen earth. But perhaps the entire family was starving and too weak to remove the dead girl from the house, Jensen speculates. "We probably won't ever be able to say, 'This is the way it was,'" she adds. "For that you need a time machine."

The scientific team reported to the elders that radiocarbon dating places the girl's death in about AD 1200. If correct—for dating is technically tricky in the Arctic—the date would set the girl's life about 100 years before her people formed settled whaling villages, Sheehan says.

Following the autopsy and the body's return to Barrow . . . , one last request by the elders was honored. The little girl, wrapped in her feather parka, was placed in a casket and buried in a small Christian ceremony next to the grave of the other prehistoric bodies. Hundreds of years after her death, an Inupiat daughter was welcomed back into the midst of her community.

The "rescue" of the little girl's body from the raw forces of time and nature means researchers and the Inupiat people will continue to learn still more about the region's culture. Sheehan and Jensen returned to Barrow in winter 1994 to explain their findings to townspeople. "We expect to learn just as much from them," Sheehan said before the trip. A North Slope Cultural Center . . . will store and display artifacts from the dig sites.

Laboratory tests and analyses also will contribute information. The archaeologists hope measurements of heavy metals in the girl's body will allow comparisons with modern-day pollution contaminating the sea mammals that Inupiat eat today. The soot damage in her lungs might offer health implications for Third World people who rely on oil lamps, dung fires, and charcoal for heat and light. Genetic tests could illuminate early population movements of Inupiats.

The project also serves as a model for good relations between archaeologists and Native people. "The larger overall message from this work is that scientists and communities don't have to be at odds," Sheehan says. "In fact, there are mutual interests that we all have. Scientists have obligations to communities. And when more scientists realize that, and when more communities hold scientists to those standards, then everybody will be happier."

Source: Simpson, S. (1995, April). Whispers from the ice. *Alaska*, 23–28.

Questions of Ethics

Anthropologists deal with private and sensitive matters, including information that individuals would prefer not to have generally known about them. In the early years of the discipline, many anthropologists documented traditional cultures they assumed would disappear due to disease, warfare, or changes imposed by colonialism, growing state power, or international market expansion. Some worked as government administrators or consultants gathering data used to formulate policies concerning indigenous peoples. Others helped predict the behavior of enemies during wartime.

How does one write about important but delicate issues and at the same time protect the privacy of the individuals who have shared their stories? The kinds of research carried out by anthropologists, and the settings within which they work, raise important moral questions about potential uses and abuses of our knowledge. Who will utilize our findings and for what purposes? Who decides what research questions are asked? Who, if anyone, will benefit from the research? For example, in the case of research on an ethnic or religious minority whose values may be at odds with the dominant society, will government bureaucracies or industrial corporations use anthropological data to suppress that group? And what of traditional communities around the world? Who is to decide what changes should, or should not, be introduced for community development? And who defines "development"—the community, a national government, or an international agency like the World Bank?

After the colonial era ended in the 1960s, and in reaction to controversial research practices by some anthropologists in or near violent conflict areas, anthropologists began formulating a code of ethics to ensure that their research would not harm the groups being studied. This code outlines a range of moral responsibilities and obligations. It includes this core principle: Anthropologists must do everything in their power to ensure that their research does not harm the safety, dignity, or privacy of the people with whom they work, conduct research, or perform other professional activities.

Recently, some of the debates regarding this code have focused on potential ethical breaches that might occur if anthropologists work for corporations or undertake classified contract work for the military. Although the American Anthropological Association (AAA) has no legal authority, it issues policy statements on ethics questions as they come up. For example, the AAA recommended that research notes from medical settings should be protected and not subject to court subpoena. This honors the ethical imperative to protect the privacy of individuals who have shared their personal health issues with anthropologists.

Figure 1.8 A Coltan Miner in Congo
These are the hands of a miner holding coltan, a tarlike mineral mined in eastern Congo. Refined, coltan turns into a heat-resistant powder capable of storing energy. As the key component of capacitors in small electronic devices, it is highly valued on the global market. Coltan mines, enriching the warring Congolese factions that control them, are hellholes for the thousands of people, including children, who work the mines. Bought, transported, and processed by foreign merchants and corporations, small bits of this mineral eventually end up in cell phones and laptop computers worldwide.

© Mark Craemer

Emerging technologies have ethical implications that impact anthropological inquiry. For example, the ability to sequence and patent particular genes has led to debates about who has the right to hold a patent—the individuals from whom the particular genes were obtained or the researcher who studies the genes? Similarly, do ancient remains belong to the scientist, to the people living in the region under scientific investigation, or to whoever happens to have possession of them? Global market forces have converted these remains into expensive collectibles, resulting in a systematic looting of archaeological and fossil sites.

While seeking answers to these questions, anthropologists recognize that they have special obligations to three sets of people: those whom they study, those who fund the research, and those in the profession who rely on published findings to increase our collective knowledge. Because fieldwork requires trust between researchers and the community in which they work, the anthropologist's first responsibility is to the people who have shared their stories and their community. Everything possible must be done to protect their physical, social, and psychological welfare and to honor their dignity and privacy. This task is frequently complex. For example, telling the story of a people gives information both to relief agencies who might help them and to others who might take advantage of them.

Maintaining one's own culture is an internationally recognized basic human right, and any connection with outsiders can endanger the cultural integrity of the community being studied. To overcome some of these ethical challenges, anthropologists frequently collaborate with and contribute to the communities in which they are working, inviting the people being studied to have some say about if and how their stories are told. In research involving ancient human remains, collaboration with local people not only preserves the remains from market forces but also honors the connections of indigenous people to the places and remains under study.

Anthropology and Globalization

A holistic perspective and a long-term commitment to understanding the human species in all its variety equip anthropologists to grapple with a challenge that has overriding importance for each of us today: **globalization**. This concept refers to worldwide interconnectedness, evidenced in rapid global movement of natural resources, trade goods, human labor, finance capital, information, and infectious diseases (Figure 1.8). Although worldwide travel, trade relations, and information flow have existed for several centuries, the pace and magnitude of these long-distance exchanges have picked up enormously in recent decades; the Internet, in particular, has greatly expanded information exchange capacities.

---

globalization Worldwide interconnectedness, evidenced in rapid global movement of natural resources, trade goods, human labor, finance capital, information, and infectious diseases.

The powerful forces driving globalization are technological innovations, cost differences among countries, faster knowledge transfers, and increased trade and financial integration worldwide. Globalization touches almost everybody's life on the planet, and it is as much about economics as it is about politics. Further, globalization changes human relations and ideas, as well as our natural environments; even geographically remote communities are quickly becoming interdependent—and often vulnerable—through globalization.

Anthropologists witness the impact of globalization on human communities in all corners of the world. They try to explain how individuals and organizations respond to the massive changes confronting them. A two-edged sword, globalization may generate economic growth and prosperity, but it may also undermine long-established institutions. Generally, globalization has brought significant gains to more educated groups in wealthier countries, while at the same time contributing to the erosion of traditional cultures.

Through such upheaval and disruption, globalization contributes to rising levels of ethnic and religious conflict throughout the world. Anthropology's important distinction between the commonly misunderstood terms *nation* and *state* can help clarify the source of this political turmoil. A **nation** is a socially organized group of people who putatively share a common origin, language, and cultural heritage, whereas a **state** is a politically organized territory with institutions that are internationally recognized. Unlike nations, most modern states are recent phenomena, their borders having been drawn by colonial powers or other authorities. Because of this, states and nations rarely coincide—nations being split among different states, and states typically being controlled by members of one nation. The ruling nation uses its control to gain access to the land, resources, and labor of other nationalities within the state.

Most armed conflicts and human rights abuses of today have roots in this nation/state distinction. The Rohingya, an ethnic Muslim minority, provide a case in point. They are a distinct nation of between 1 and 1.5 million people living in Myanmar, with an additional several hundred thousand having fled to neighboring states. In 2012, Myanmar saw thousands of Rohingya Muslims, who were not recognized by the government as citizens, killed or displaced by the Buddhist majority. See the Globalscape feature for a closer look at the continuing effects of this conflict.

nation A people who share a collective identity based on a common culture, language, territorial base, and history.

state A political institution established to manage and defend a complex, socially stratified society occupying a defined territory.

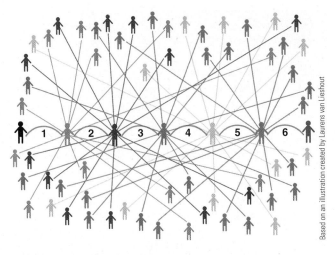

Based on an illustration created by Laurens van Lieshout

Figure 1.9 Six Degrees of Separation
The phrase "six degrees of separation," diagrammed here, refers to the idea that everyone is on average approximately six steps away, by way of introduction, from any other person on earth. Thus, a chain of "a friend of a friend" statements can be made to connect any two people in six steps or fewer. Originally coined by Hungarian writer Frigyes Karinthy in his 1929 short story "Chains," it was popularized by the 1993 film *Six Degrees of Separation*, created from the play by American John Guare. It became all the more popular after four college students invented the trivia game Six Degrees of Kevin Bacon, in which the goal is to link any actor to film star Kevin Bacon through no more than six performance connections.

Because all of us now live in a global village, we can no longer afford the luxury of ignoring our neighbors, no matter how distant they may seem. In this age of globalization, anthropology not only provides humanity with useful insights concerning diversity, it may also assist us in avoiding or overcoming problems born of that diversity. In countless social arenas, from schools to businesses to hospitals, anthropologists have done cross-cultural research that makes it possible for educators, businesspeople, doctors, and humanitarians to do their work more effectively.

As illustrated by many examples in this textbook, ignorance or ethnocentric (mis)information about other societies, beliefs, and practices can cause or fuel serious problems throughout the world. This is especially true in an age when human interactions and interdependence have been transformed by global information exchange and transportation advances. There are only six degrees of separation between each of us and any other person on earth (Figure 1.9). Anthropology offers a way of looking at and understanding the world's peoples—insights that are nothing less than basic skills for survival in an increasingly globalized world.

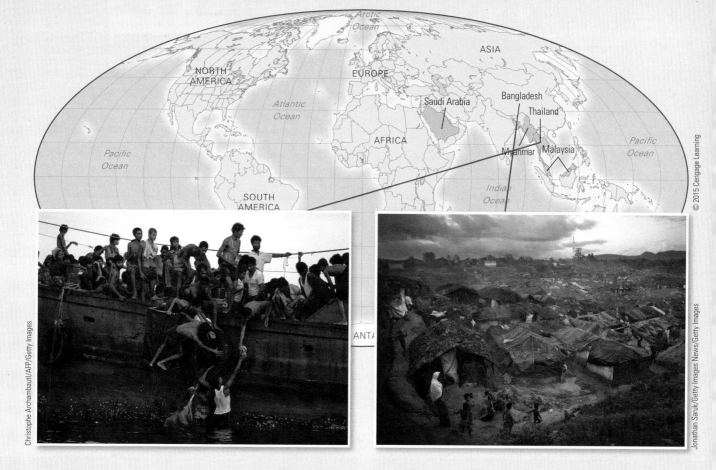

Safe Harbor?

A shabby wooden boat, packed with passengers, sits off the coast of Thailand in May 2015. The people on board are exhausted, weeping, and dressed in ragged, dirty clothing. They call out to the Thai officials for help—they have been at sea for months, robbed and abandoned by their captain and crew, and they are starving. Some have died already, their bodies thrown overboard into the sparkling Andaman Sea. The survivors seek a harbor, shelter, food, and water. The Thai military drops provisions into the water near the boat. Then, denying the migrants permission to land, it accompanies them back out to sea once again.

According to the United Nations High Commissioner for Refugees, Myanmar has 810,000 stateless inhabitants, who do not have the basic rights of citizenship, and nearly 600,000 other internally displaced individuals.[a] After a brutal pogrom in 2012, tens of thousands of stateless Rohingya Muslims fled Myanmar to Bangladesh, desperate to escape institutional discrimination and poor living conditions at home. Many other Rohingya languished in squalid refugee camps in Bangladesh, where they fell victim to traffickers who promised them safe passage through Thailand and a waiting job in Malaysia in exchange for large sums of money. Often, before their journey was done, the fee increased and the employment prospects vanished. Many never realized the promise of a better life.

When the Thai government cracked down on the smuggling routes of these traffickers, Myanmar's neighbors suddenly found thousands of migrants landing on their shores. Although these countries had been quietly accepting Rohingya refugees for years, they began closing their doors, leaving thousands of migrants stranded at sea. At the height of this crisis, Saudi Arabia, a distant country whose state religion is Islam, offered refugees protection and free residency permits. But otherwise, because they lacked state citizenship, the Rohingya Muslims had no government to appeal to, no embassy to petition, and nowhere to go but further adrift at sea while the world wondered what would become of them.

Global Twister

How can minority nations, like the Rohingya, be protected within states that contain multiple distinct groups? In the case of Saudi Arabia, religious unity was the motivation for state protection of the Rohingya refugees. Is that a good way for a state to be defined? Does your state treat all the nations it contains equally?

[a]UNHCR: The UN Refugee Agency. (2015a). Myanmar. *UNHCR.org.* http://www.unhcr.org/pages/49e4877d6.html (retrieved September 29, 2015)

CHAPTER CHECKLIST

What is anthropology?

✓ Anthropology is the objective and systematic study of humankind in all times and places.

✓ Anthropology contains four major fields: cultural anthropology, linguistic anthropology, archaeology, and biological anthropology.

✓ Individuals practice applied anthropology in each of anthropology's fields; applied anthropology uses anthropological knowledge to solve practical problems.

What do anthropologists do in each of its four fields?

✓ Cultural anthropologists study humans in terms of their cultures, the often-unconscious standards by which social groups operate.

✓ Linguistic anthropologists study human languages and may deal with the description of a language, with the history of languages, or with how languages are used in particular social settings.

✓ Archaeologists study human cultures through the recovery and analysis of material and biological remains and environmental data.

✓ Biological anthropologists focus on humans as physical organisms; they particularly emphasize tracing the evolutionary development of the human animal and studying biological variation within the species today.

How is anthropology different from other disciplines?

✓ Anthropology has long emphasized the study of non-Western societies and a holistic approach, which aims to formulate theoretically valid explanations and interpretations of human diversity based on detailed studies of all aspects of human biology, behavior, and beliefs in all known societies, past and present.

✓ The humanities, social sciences, and the natural sciences come together in anthropology to create a genuinely humanistic science. Anthropology's link with the humanities can be seen in its concern with people's beliefs, values, languages, arts, and literature—oral as well as written—but above all in its attempt to convey the experience of living in different cultures.

How do anthropologists conduct research?

✓ Fieldwork, characteristic of all the anthropological subdisciplines, includes complete immersion in research settings ranging from archaeological and paleoanthropological survey and excavation, to living with a group of primates in their natural habitat, to biological data gathered while living with a group. Ethnographic participant observation with a particular culture or subculture is the classic field method of cultural anthropology.

✓ After the fieldwork of archaeologists and physical anthropologists, researchers conduct laboratory analyses of excavated remains or biological samples collected in the field.

✓ The comparative method is key to all branches of anthropology. Anthropologists make broad comparisons among peoples and cultures—past and present. They also compare related species and fossil groups.

✓ Ethnology, the comparative branch of cultural anthropologists, uses a range of ethnographic accounts to construct theories about cultures from a comparative or historical point of view. Ethnologists often focus on a particular aspect of culture, such as religious or economic practices.

How do anthropologists face the ethical challenges that emerge through conducting anthropological research?

✓ Anthropologists must stay aware of the potential uses and abuses of anthropological knowledge and the ways it is obtained.

✓ The anthropological code of ethics, first formalized in 1971 and continually revised, outlines the moral and ethical responsibilities of anthropologists to the people whom they study, to those who fund the research, and to the profession as a whole.

What can anthropology contribute to our understanding of globalization?

✓ A long tradition of studying the connections among diverse peoples over time gives anthropology a theoretical framework to study globalization in a world increasingly linked through technological advancements.

✓ Anthropology equips global citizens to challenge ethnocentrism and to understand human diversity.

✓ Anthropology has essential insights to offer the modern world, particularly when understanding our neighbors in the global village has become a matter of survival for all.

QUESTIONS FOR REFLECTION

1. In this chapter's opening Challenge Issue, you learned about the repurposing of nets intended to combat malaria. Would you support the distribution of these nets? What would you do if you had to choose between plentiful food and protection from malaria? Do you make any similar choices in your own life?

2. Anthropology embraces a holistic approach to explain all aspects of human beliefs, behavior, and biology. How might anthropology challenge your personal perspective on the following questions: Where did we come from? Why do we act in certain ways? What makes us the way we are?

3. Globalization can be described as a two-edged sword. How does it foster growth and destruction simultaneously?

4. This chapter contains several examples of applied anthropology. Can you think of a practical problem in the world today that would benefit from anthropological knowledge and methods?

DIGGING INTO ANTHROPOLOGY

Talking Trash: Hidden in the Middens

Archaeologists have long focused on *middens*, a refuse or garbage disposal area in archaeological sites. The trash ancient peoples have left behind provides many clues about their lifeways. What did they eat? What sorts of tools did they use? What kind of work did they do? What did they do for fun? Modern garbage is just as interesting. What's more, the information we can glean from recovered trash can be combined with theories generated from other sources. For example, how does trash from an individual's kitchen compare to what people say about their diets? Do those who believe in the notion of recycling truly follow it in practice?

Go through your own trash and use it to generate some questions that you might ask others. Then find trashcans in two distinct residential settings and ask their owners if you can examine them. Before investigating, ask for their responses to the questions you have devised. Compare and contrast what you have found. Plastic gloves and a big plastic garbage bag on which to lay the trash are a must!

Dpa Picture Alliance/Alamy

CHALLENGE ISSUE

In the 21st century, human biology and technology have become intricately intertwined. Because biological traits are held to be reliable markers of personal identity, some security devices now rely on biology, such as fingerprint scanners and palm vein readers. DNA is perhaps the final frontier in this progression. Many people now seek personal genealogy reporting and DNA sequencing in their quest for self-knowledge. Genetics has much to contribute to an anthropological understanding of humans past and present. But is DNA the essence of who we are? Because DNA's functioning is similar to how computers process and run programs, some researchers are experimenting with the idea of using DNA as a long-term storage device for digital information. Commonalities between biology and technology account for the industrial and academic success in merging the two spheres, while also suggesting there are dangers inherent in interpreting ourselves as mechanical objects. How might our inclination to understand ourselves programmatically fall short? What are the social consequences of seeing ourselves as organisms determined by our DNA, or by any other aspect of biology?

Biology, Genetics, and Evolution

Evolution and Creation Stories

Many cultures have a myth to explain the appearance of humans on earth. The Bible's Book of Genesis provides one such example. The Nez Perce, American Indians native to eastern Oregon and Idaho, provide us with a vastly different story. For the Nez Perce, human beings are the creation of Coyote, a trickster-transformer. Coyote chased the giant beaver monster Wishpoosh over the earth, leaving a trail to form the Columbia River. When Coyote caught Wishpoosh, he killed him, dragged his body to the riverbank, and cut it into pieces, each body part transforming into one of the various peoples of this region. The Nez Perce were made from Wishpoosh's head, thus conferring on them great intelligence and horsemanship (Clark, 1966).

Creation stories depict the relationship between humans and the rest of the natural world, sometimes reflecting a deep connection among people, other animals, and the earth. In the Nez Perce creation story, groups of people derive from specific body parts—each possessing a special talent and relationship with a particular animal. By contrast, the story of creation in Genesis—shared by Jews, Christians, and Muslims—emphasizes human uniqueness and the concept of time. Creation takes place as a series of actions over the course of six days. God's final act of creation is to fashion the first human in his own image before the seventh day of rest.

Like creation stories, evolution—the major organizing principle of the biological sciences—accounts for the diversity of life on earth. Evolution provides mechanisms for change and explanations for how the innumerable organisms, both in the past and today, came into being. Evolution differs from creation stories in that it uses testable hypotheses to explain the diversity of life in a consistent scientific language. Scientists have deciphered the molecular basis of evolution and the mechanisms through which evolutionary forces work on populations of organisms. But scientific thought does not come out of a vacuum. As you will see, historical and cultural processes contribute to scientific thought.

In this chapter you will learn to

- Compare the theory of evolution with creation stories.

- Identify the place of humans in the classification of all living things.

- Explain the molecular basis of evolution and the four evolutionary processes: mutation, gene flow, genetic drift, and adaptation.

- Describe how evolutionary processes account for the diversity of life on earth.

- Contrast how evolutionary processes work at the individual and population level.

- Explain how humans have adapted to their environments.

- Describe how new species come into being.

explorers exploited foreign lands, their approach to the natural world changed. The discovery of new life forms challenged the previously held notion of fixed, unchanging life on earth. The invention of instruments, such as the microscope to study the interior of cells, also led to a new appreciation of life's diversity. Thus, in the mid-18th century, Swedish scientist Carolus Linnaeus (also known as Carl von Linné) developed the *Systema Naturae*, or system of nature, to classify the diversity of living things collected and shipped to Europe from throughout the globe. Linnaeus categorized the living things into a tiered system known as a *taxonomy* on the basis of internal and external visual similarities.

Noting the similarity among humans, monkeys, and apes, Linnaeus classified them together as **primates** (Figure 2.1), one of several kinds of **mammal**, which are animals having body hair or fur who suckle or nurse their young. **Species**, the smallest working units in biological classificatory systems, are reproductively isolated populations or groups of populations capable of interbreeding to produce fertile offspring. Species are subdivisions of larger, more inclusive groups, called **genera** (singular, **genus**). Humans, for example, are classified in the genus *Homo* and the species *sapiens*.

Linnaeus based his classificatory system on the following criteria:

1. *Body structure:* A Guernsey cow and a Holstein cow are the same species because they have identical body structure. A cow and a horse do not.
2. *Body function:* Cows and horses give birth to live young. Although they are different species, they are closer than either cows or horses are to chickens, which lay eggs and have no mammary glands.
3. *Sequence of bodily growth:* At the time of birth—or hatching out of the egg—young cows and chickens possess body plans basically like that of their parents. They are therefore more closely related to each

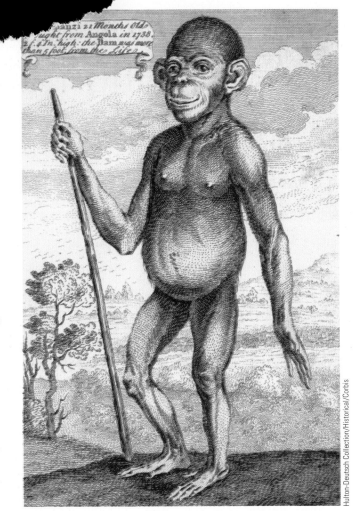

Figure 2.1 Chimp or Human?
Initial scientific struggles to classify great apes—and to identify and weigh the significance of the similarities and differences between them and humans—are reflected in early European renderings of apes, including this 18th-century image of a chimpanzee portrayed as a biped equipped with a walking stick.

Hulton-Deutsch Collection/Historical/Corbis

other than either one is to the frog, whose tadpoles undergo a series of changes before attaining the basic adult form.

Modern **taxonomy** (from the Greek for "naming divisions"), or the science of classification, retains the structure of the Linnaean system but takes genetics as well as body structure, function, and growth into account to construct the relationships among living things. Molecular comparisons aimed at parasites, bacteria, and viruses allow scientists to trace the origins of particular diseases, such as swine flu, Ebola, or HIV (human immunodeficiency virus). An emphasis on genetics has led to a reworking of taxonomic designation in the human family, among other families, as is described in Table 2.1.

primate The group of mammals that includes lemurs, lorises, tarsiers, monkeys, apes, and humans.

mammal The class of vertebrate animals distinguished by bodies covered with hair or fur, self-regulating temperature, and in females, milk-producing mammary glands.

species The smallest working unit in biological classificatory systems; reproductively isolated populations or groups of populations capable of interbreeding to produce fertile offspring.

genus (genera) In the system of classification, a group of like species.

taxonomy The science of classification.

TABLE 2.1

The Classification of Humans

Taxonomic Category	Category to Which Humans Belong	Biological Features Used to Define and Place Humans in This Category
Kingdom	Animalia	Humans are animals. We do not make our own food (as plants do) but depend upon intake of food.
Phylum	Chordata	Humans are chordates. We have a *notochord* (a rodlike structure of cartilage) and nerve chord running along the back of the body as well as gill slits in the embryonic stage of our life cycle.
Subphylum*	Vertebrata	Humans are vertebrates, possessing an internal backbone with a segmented spinal column.
Class	Mammalia	Humans are mammals: warm-blooded animals covered with fur and possessing mammary glands for nourishing their young after birth.
Order	Primates	Humans are primates: a kind of mammal with a generalized anatomy, a relatively large brain, and grasping hands and feet.
Suborder	Anthropoidea	Humans are anthropoids: social, daylight-active primates.
Superfamily	Hominoid	Humans are hominoids with broad, flexible shoulders and no tail. Chimps, bonobos, gorillas, orangutans, gibbons, and siamangs are also hominoids.
Family/Subfamily	Hominid/ Hominin	Humans are hominids. We are hominoids from Africa, genetically more closely related to chimps, bonobos, and gorillas than to hominoids from Asia. Some scientists use "hominid" to refer only to humans and their ancestors. Others include chimps and gorillas in this category, using the subfamily "hominin" to distinguish humans and their ancestors from chimps and gorillas and their ancestors. The two taxonomies differ according to emphasis on genetic versus morphological similarities.
Genus Species	*Homo sapiens*	Humans have large brains and rely on cultural adaptations to survive. Genus and species names are always italicized.

© Cengage Learning

*Most categories can be expanded or narrowed by adding the prefix "sub" or "super." A family could thus be part of a superfamily and in turn contain two or more subfamilies.

Cross-species comparisons describe anatomical features of similar function as **analogous**, while anatomical features that have evolved from a common ancestral feature are called **homologous** (Figure 2.2). For example, the arm and hand of a human and the wing of a bat evolved from the front leg of a common ancestor. Although they have acquired different functions, they are homologous structures. During their early embryonic development, homologous structures arise in a similar fashion and pass through similar stages before differentiating. The wings of birds and butterflies look similar and have a similar function (flying): These are analogous structures because they do not follow the same developmental sequence.

When constructing evolutionary relationships, only homologies matter. Comparison and analysis have allowed scientists to group species into genera and into even larger groups such as families, orders, classes, phyla (plural of *phylum*), and kingdoms. Characteristics shared by all the organisms in the group define each taxonomic level.

The Discovery of Evolution

Just as European seafaring and exploitation brought about an awareness of the diversity of life across the globe, industrialization in Europe brought about an awareness of change in life forms through time. As workers cut away earth to lay railway tracks and excavated limestone for buildings, they uncovered fossils that would revolutionize scientific thought.

At first, religious doctrine was used to interpret fossilized remains of elephants and giant saber-toothed tigers in Europe. The early 19th-century theory of *catastrophism,* championed by French paleontologist Georges Cuvier, invoked the Great Flood described in Genesis to account for the disappearance of these species on European lands.

analogous In biology, a term referring to structures of different organisms that are superficially similar due to similar function but that do not share a common developmental pathway or structure.

homologous In biology, a term referring to structures of two different organisms that arise in similar fashion and pass through similar stages during embryonic development, although they may have different functions.

Mark Carwardine/Photolibrary/Getty Images

Darrell Gulin/Photodisc/Getty Images

Figure 2.2 **Homologous and Analogous**

Bats and butterflies both use their wings to fly. But any resemblance of the insect wing to the analogous structures in a bird or a mammal derives solely from their similar function. The course of insect wing development as well as its structure differs from that of the bat. But compare your own hand to the bat wing and you will see an excellent example of homology. Look closely at the bones supporting the wing, and you can see that they are the same bones found in the human arm and hand. Homologous structures have the same embryonic origins but ultimately take on different functions. Humans can only dream about using our arms and hand bones for flight. Still, our grasping hands have made us the species that we are today.

Another French scientist, Jean-Baptiste Lamarck, was among the first to suggest a mechanism to account for biodiversity that did not rely upon scriptures. His theory of the *inheritance of acquired characteristics* proposed that behavior brought about changes in organisms' forms, such as the famed giraffe that gained its long neck by stretching to reach leaves on the highest treetop branches and passed this acquired trait onto its offspring. Lamarck was the first to connect the structure of organisms with the environments they inhabit. While the mechanism Lamarck proposed for change over time works well for qualities inherited via culture, it falls short as an explanation of basic biological inheritance. Nevertheless, recent studies of how external environmental factors can switch genes on and off—an area known as *epigenetics*—demonstrate a place for Lamarckian theory in biological inheritance.

At about the same time that Lamarck formulated his ideas, British geologist Sir Charles Lyell proposed a nonreligious theory to account for variations in the earth's surface. His theory, *uniformitarianism,* maintained that immediately observable changes in the earth's surface from erosion and other natural processes could be explained if those variations had taken place over extremely long periods of time. Lyell's theory was incompatible with religious doctrine because the length of time required for uniformitarianism far exceeded the biblical

assertion that the earth is only 6,000 years old. But by the start of the 19th century, many naturalists had come to accept the idea that the earth was much older and that life had evolved, even though they were not clear about how it happened. It remained for Charles Darwin (1809–1882) to formulate a theory that has withstood the test of time.

Darwin began the study of medicine at the University of Edinburgh in Scotland. Finding himself unfit for this profession, he went to Christ's College, Cambridge, to study theology. He then left school to accompany Captain Robert FitzRoy as a naturalist aboard the *Beagle,* a British Royal Navy sloop, embarking on an expedition to various poorly mapped parts of the world. The voyage lasted almost five years, taking the young scientist along the coasts of South America, to the Galapagos Islands, across the Pacific to Australia, and then across the Indian and Atlantic oceans back to South America before returning to England in 1836 (Figure 2.3).

Observing the tremendous diversity of living creatures as well as the fossils of extinct animals, Darwin noted that species varied according to the environments they inhabited. The observations he made on this voyage, his readings of Lyell's geological theories, and discussions he had with Captain FitzRoy all contributed to Darwin's most famous book, *On the Origin of Species*. Published in 1859, twenty years after he returned from his voyage, this book

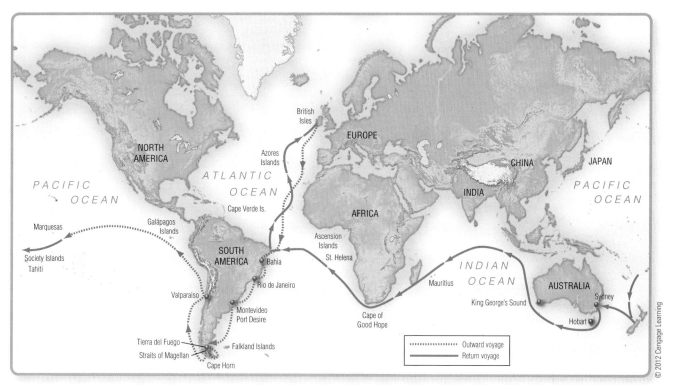

Figure 2.3 The Voyage of the *Beagle*
During his journey of almost five years, Darwin was exposed to the diversity of plant and animal life, as well as to the varied environments across the globe. He also saw the horror of New World slavery in action for the first time. Together, these observations planted the seeds for his evolutionary theory.

accounts for change within species and for the emergence of new species in purely naturalistic terms.

Darwin added observations from English farm life and intellectual thought to observations he made while on the *Beagle*. He paid particular attention to domesticated animals and farmers' "artificial selection," a practice of breeding stock to select for specific traits. Darwin's theoretical breakthrough derived from an essay by economist Thomas Malthus (1766–1834), which warned of the potential consequences of increased human population, particularly of the poor. Malthus observed that animal populations, unlike human populations, remained stable: An overproduction of offspring would be followed by a large proportion of the animal offspring not surviving to maturity.

Darwin combined his observations into the theory of **natural selection** as follows: All species display a range of variation, and all have the ability to expand beyond their means of subsistence. It follows that, in their "struggle for existence," organisms with variations that help them to survive in particular environments will reproduce with greater success than those without such variations. Thus, over time, the most advantageous variations become the most frequent and the species evolves. In retrospect, the idea seemed so obvious that Thomas Henry Huxley, one of the era's most prominent scientists,

remarked, "How extremely stupid of me not to have thought of that" (quoted in Durant, 2000, p. 11).

However straightforward the idea of evolution by natural selection may appear, the theory was (and continues to be) a source of considerable controversy. Two problems plagued Darwin's theory throughout his career: First, how did variation initially arise? Second, what was the mechanism of heredity by which traits could be passed from one generation to the next?

Heredity

Ironically, some of the information Darwin needed was available by 1866. Gregor Mendel (1822–1884), a Roman Catholic monk, developed the basic laws of heredity while working in the monastery gardens in Brno (Brünn), a city in today's Czech Republic. Mendel, who was raised on a farm, possessed two particular talents: a flair for mathematics and a passion for gardening.

natural selection The evolutionary process through which factors in the environment exert pressure, favoring some individuals over others to produce the next generation.

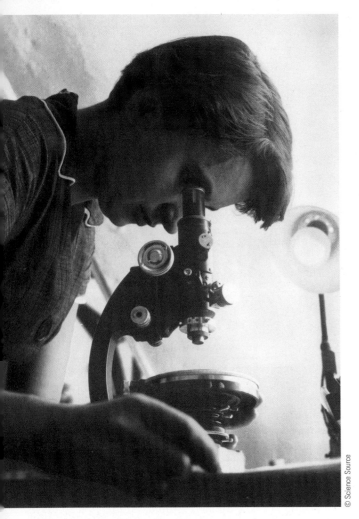

© Science Source

Figure 2.4 Rosalind Franklin and the Structure of DNA
British scientist Rosalind Franklin's pioneering work in x-ray crystallography played a vital role in unlocking the secret of the genetic code in 1953. Without her permission, Franklin's colleague Maurice Wilkins showed one of her images to James Watson. In his book *The Double Helix* (1968), Watson wrote, "The instant I saw the picture my mouth fell open and my pulse began to race." While her research was published simultaneously in the prestigious journal *Nature* in 1953—alongside that of James Watson, Francis Crick, and Maurice Wilkins—her untimely death from cancer meant that only the gentlemen received the Nobel Prize for the double-helix model of DNA in 1962.

gene The portion of a DNA molecule that directs the synthesis of specific proteins.

law of segregation The Mendelian principle that variants of genes for a particular trait retain their separate identities through the generations.

law of independent assortment The Mendelian principle that genes controlling different traits are inherited independently of one another.

chromosome In the cell nucleus, the structure visible during cellular division containing long strands of DNA combined with a protein.

DNA (deoxyribonucleic acid) The genetic material consisting of a complex molecule whose base structure directs the synthesis of proteins.

As with all farmers of his time, Mendel had an intuitive understanding of biological inheritance. He went a step further, though, in that he recognized the need for theoretical explanations. At age 34, he began careful breeding experiments in the monastery garden, starting with pea plants.

Over eight years, Mendel cultivated more than 30,000 plants, controlling their pollination, observing the results, and figuring out the mathematics behind it all. This allowed him to unravel the basic laws of heredity. He published his findings in the *Proceedings of the Natural History Society of Brünn* in 1866. However, because this German-language publication was not widely read, it took decades before scientists elsewhere recognized the significance of Mendel's discoveries.

By 1900, cell biology had advanced to the point where rediscovery of Mendel's laws was inevitable, and in that year three European botanists, working independently of one another, rediscovered not only the laws but also Mendel's original paper. With this rediscovery, the science of genetics began. Today, a comprehensive understanding of heredity, molecular genetics, and population genetics supports Darwinian evolutionary theory.

The Transmission of Genes

We define a **gene** as a portion of a DNA molecule containing a sequence of base pairs that encodes a particular protein. But when biologists coined the term from the Greek word for "birth" at the turn of the 20th century, the molecular basis of the gene was still fifty years away from discovery. Mendel had perceived the presence and activity of genes when he discovered that inheritance was *particulate*, rather than *blending*. In other words, the units controlling the expression of visible traits come in pairs, one from each parent, and retain their separate identities over the generations rather than blending into a combination of parental traits in offspring. This was the basis of Mendel's **law of segregation**. Another finding—Mendel's **law of independent assortment**—states that different traits (under the control of distinct genes) are inherited randomly and independently of one another.

Mendel based his laws on statistical frequencies of observed characteristics, such as color and texture in generations of plants. When scientists discovered the **chromosome**, the cellular structure containing the genetic information, at the start of the 20th century, they provided a visible vehicle for transmission of the traits proposed in Mendel's laws.

Then in 1953, James Watson and Francis Crick discovered the mechanism for inheritance based on the structure of **DNA (deoxyribonucleic acid)**—long strands that form chromosomes. (Rosalind Franklin, shown in Figure 2.4, was a largely unknown contributor to this scientific breakthrough.) DNA is a complex molecule with an unusual *double-helix* shape, rather like two strands of a rope twisted around each other with ladder-like steps between the two strands (Figure 2.5). Alternating sugar and phosphate molecules form the backbone of these strands connected to each other by pairs from among the four genetic "base" molecules: adenine, thymine, guanine, and cytosine (usually written as A, T, G, and C). Connections between the backbone strands occur between so-called complementary pairs of bases (A to T and G to C). This arrangement confers upon genes the unique property of replication—being able to make exact copies of themselves.

Genes and Alleles

A sequence of chemical bases on a molecule of DNA (a gene) constitutes a recipe for making proteins. As science writer Matt Ridley puts it, "Proteins . . . do almost every

chemical, structural, and regulatory thing that is done in the body: they generate energy, fight infection, digest food, form hair, carry oxygen, and so on" (Ridley, 1999, p. 40). Almost everything in the body is made of or by proteins, which makes the genes responsible for such proteins all the more important.

An alternate form of any given gene is known as an **allele**, whereas the term *gene* just refers to the location on a chromosome that codes for a particular protein. For example, the gene for a human blood type in the A-B-O system refers to a specific portion of a DNA molecule on chromosome 9 that is 1,062 letters long (a medium-sized gene). This particular gene specifies the production of an **enzyme**, a kind of protein that initiates and directs a chemical reaction. Occurring in two forms (the A allele and B allele), this enzyme causes specific molecules involved in immune responses to attach to the surface of red blood cells. Alleles correspond to that particular blood type. Figure 2.6 displays a **karyotype**, the array of chromosomes found inside a single cell. Genes provide the recipe for the many proteins that keep us alive and healthy.

The human **genome**—the complete structure sequence of human DNA—contains 3 billion chemical bases, with about 20,000 genes, a number similar to that found in most mammals. Of the 3 billion bases, humans and mice are about 90 percent identical. Both species have three times as many genes as does the fruit fly, but surprisingly humans and mice have half the number of genes found in the rice plant! At the same time, those 20,000 or so human genes account for only a small fraction of the entire genome, indicating that scientists still have far more to learn about how genes work. Frequently, genes themselves are split by long stretches of DNA that are not part of the known protein code; for example, the 1,062 bases of the A-B-O blood-group gene are interrupted by five such stretches. In the course of protein production, these stretches of DNA are metaphorically snipped out and left on the cutting-room floor.

How is the DNA recipe converted into a protein? Through a series of intervening steps, each three-base sequence of a gene, called a **codon**, specifies production of a particular amino acid, strings of which build proteins. Because DNA cannot leave the cell's nucleus

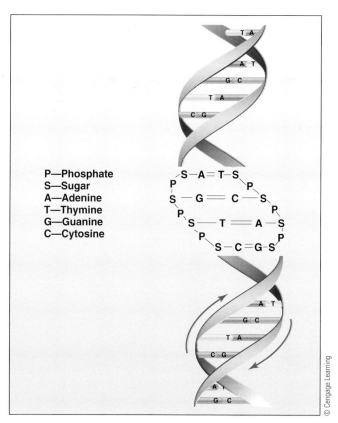

P—Phosphate
S—Sugar
A—Adenine
T—Thymine
G—Guanine
C—Cytosine

© Cengage Learning

Figure 2.5 The Structure of DNA
This diagrammatic representation of a portion of DNA (deoxyribonucleic acid) illustrates its twisted, ladder-like structure. Alternating sugar and phosphate groups form the structural sides of the ladder. The connecting "rungs" are formed by pairings between complementary bases—adenine with thymine and guanine with cytosine.

allele An alternate form of a single gene.
enzyme A protein that initiates and directs chemical reactions.
karyotype The array of chromosomes found inside a single cell.
genome The complete structure sequence of DNA for a species.
codon The three-base sequence of a gene that specifies a particular amino acid for inclusion in a protein.

Karyotype with a Few Genetic Loci

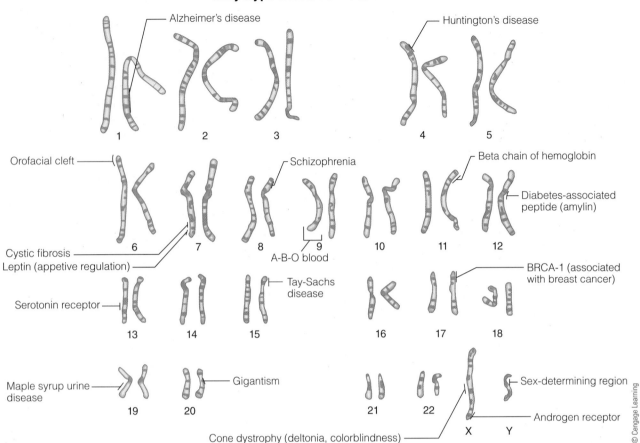

Figure 2.6 A Human Karyotype

An array of chromosomes from the nucleus of one cell is called a karyotype. The twenty-three pairs of chromosomes humans possess include twenty-two pairs of body chromosomes plus one pair of sex chromosomes, for a total of forty-six chromosomes. Notice the characteristic shape and relative size of each of the chromosomes and the locations of certain genes associated with various diseases and conditions identified by the Human Genome Project. A glance at the overall karyotype indicates a normal number of chromosomes and that this individual is genetically male. The female phenotype is determined by the presence of two X chromosomes. Offspring inherit an X chromosome from their mothers but either an X or a Y from their fathers, resulting in approximately equal numbers of male and female offspring in subsequent generations. Although the Y chromosome is critical for differentiation into a male phenotype, compared to other chromosomes, the Y is tiny and carries little genetic information.

(Figure 2.7), the directions for a specific protein are first converted into **RNA (ribonucleic acid)** in a process called **transcription**. RNA is single stranded and differs from DNA in the structure of its sugar-phosphate backbone and in the presence of the base uracil (U) rather than thymine. Next, the RNA travels to a **ribosome**, the cellular structure where **translation** of the directions found in the codons occurs, producing proteins (Figure 2.8).

There are twenty amino acids, which are strung together in different amounts and sequences to produce an almost infinite number of different proteins. This is the **genetic code**, and it is the same for every living thing, whether a worm a plant, or a person. In addition to the genetic information stored in the chromosomes of the nucleus, complex organisms also possess cellular structures called *mitochondria*, each of which has a single circular chromosome. On the other end of the spectrum, simple living things without nucleated cells, such as the retrovirus that causes AIDS, contain their genetic information only as RNA.

RNA (ribonucleic acid) Single-stranded molecules similar to DNA but with uracil substituted for the base thymine; transcribes and carries instructions from DNA within the nucleus to the ribosomes, where it directs protein synthesis. Some simple life forms contain RNA only.

transcription The process of conversion of instructions from DNA into RNA.

ribosome The structure in the cell where translation occurs.

translation In genetics, the process of conversion of RNA instructions into proteins.

genetic code The set of rules by which codons (sequences of three bases) in genetic material specify amino acids in protein synthesis.

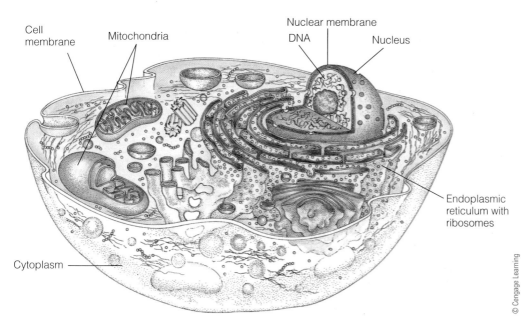

Cell membrane
Mitochondria
Nuclear membrane
DNA
Nucleus
Endoplasmic reticulum with ribosomes
Cytoplasm

© Cengage Learning

Figure 2.7 A Nucleated Cell
The figure shows the three-dimensional structure of a nucleated cell. DNA is located in the nucleus. Because DNA cannot leave the nucleus, genes must first be transcribed into RNA, which carries genetic information to the ribosomes, where protein synthesis occurs. Note also the mitochondria, which contain their own circular chromosomes and mitochondrial DNA.

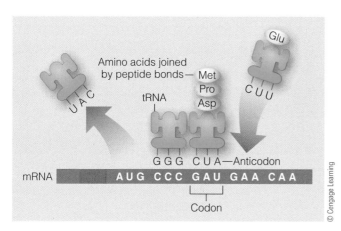

Glu
Amino acids joined by peptide bonds — Met Pro Asp
tRNA
C U U
U A C
G G G   C U A—Anticodon
mRNA   AUG CCC GAU GAA CAA
Codon

© Cengage Learning

Figure 2.8 From DNA into Proteins
Codons of DNA (a sequence of three bases) are transcribed into the complementary codons of a kind of RNA called messenger RNA (mRNA) in order to leave the nucleus. In the ribosomes, these codons are translated into proteins by transfer RNA (tRNA), which strings the amino acids together into the specified chains. Can you think of the bases that would have been found in the DNA that correspond to the section of mRNA pictured here?

Mistakes can occur in the replication process, adding or subtracting repeats of the four bases: A, C, G, and T. This happens with some frequency and differently in every individual. As these "mistakes" accumulate over time, people develop their unique DNA fingerprint.

Cell Division

To grow and maintain good health, the body cells of an organism must divide and produce new cells. Cell division begins when chromosomal DNA replicates and each chromosome becomes a **sister chromatid,**

two copies of the original chromosome that are joined in the shape of an X. To do this, the DNA "unzips" between the base pairs—adenine from thymine and guanine from cytosine—and then each base on each now-single strand attracts its complementary base, reconstituting the second half of a double helix. Then, the sister chromatids separate, and a new cell membrane surrounds each new chromosome set and becomes the nucleus that directs the activities of a new cell. This kind of cell division is called **mitosis**. Barring errors in this replication process, cells divide mitotically to form daughter cells that are exact genetic copies of the parent cell.

Like most animals, humans reproduce sexually. The "popularity" of sex from an evolutionary perspective derives from the genetic variation that it provides. All animals contain two versions of each chromosome, having inherited one from each parent. In humans this involves twenty-three pairs of chromosomes. Sexual reproduction can bring favorable alleles together, purge the genome of harmful ones, and allow beneficial alleles to spread without being held back by disadvantageous variants of other genes.

Although human societies have always regulated sexual reproduction in some ways, the science of genetics has had a tremendous impact on social aspects of reproduction. Among wealthier parents-to-be, prenatal genetic testing has become increasingly common. Such testing aims to eliminate conditions not favored within a society. For example, in India, where sons are historically preferred,

sister chromatid One-half of the X shape of a chromosome visible after replication. Each half is a copy of the original chromosome.

mitosis A kind of cell division that produces daughter cells that are genetic copies of the parent cell.

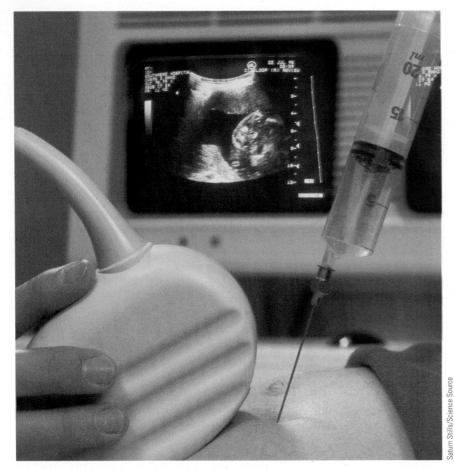

Figure 2.9 Prenatal Genetic Testing by Amniocentesis
Prenatal genetic testing is conducted most frequently by amniocentesis, a technique that began in the 1960s. The procedure involves a medical practitioner drawing fluid containing cells from a developing embryo from the womb of a pregnant woman. Lab technicians then analyze the chromosomes and specific genes for abnormalities. Cultural anthropologists have shown that a biological fact (such as an extra 21st chromosome or Down syndrome) is open to diverse interpretations and reproductive choices by "potential parents" (Rapp, 1999). New reproductive technologies have far-reaching social consequences. Genetic testing may lead to the labeling of certain people as undesirable, pitting women's reproductive rights against the rights of those with disabilities.

prenatal genetic testing has led to selective abortion of female fetuses (Figure 2.9) (Arnold, Kishor, & Roy, 2002).

No aspect of human reproduction or genetics is simply biological. Social and political processes impact the interpretation and use of genetic technology. The technology, in turn, shapes social definitions of family, identity, and the types of citizens preferred by a given society. This chapter's Biocultural Connection describes how DNA testing has made its way into the lives of African refugees seeking reunification with their families in the United States.

Sexual reproduction increases genetic diversity, which in turn contributes to adaptation among sexually reproducing species. Sexual reproduction involves the merging of two cells, one from each parent, to make a new individual. If two regular body cells, each containing twenty-three pairs of chromosomes, were to merge, the lethal result would be a new individual with forty-six pairs of chromosomes. Instead, sexual reproduction involves joining specialized sex cells (eggs and sperm) produced by a different kind of cell division, called **meiosis**.

Meiosis begins like mitosis, with the replication and doubling of the original chromosomes through the formation of sister chromatids. Cells then proceed to divide into four new cells, each having half the number of chromosomes compared to the parent cell (Figure 2.10). Human eggs and sperm have only twenty-three single chromosomes (half of a pair), whereas body cells have twenty-three pairs, or forty-six chromosomes.

Meiosis has important implications for genetics. Because paired chromosomes are separated, the daughter cells will not be identical. Two of the four new cells will have half of each pair of chromosomes, and the other two will have the second half of the original chromosome pair. In addition, corresponding portions of one chromosome may "cross over" to the other one, somewhat scrambling the genetic material compared to the original chromosomes.

Sometimes, the original pair is **homozygous**, possessing identical alleles for a specific gene. For example, if both chromosomes of the original pair for the gene for A-B-O blood type possess the allele for type A blood, then all new cells will have the A allele. But if the original pair is **heterozygous**, with the A allele on one chromosome and the B allele on the other, then half of the new cells will contain only the B allele; the offspring have a 50–50 chance of getting either one.

What happens when a child inherits the allele for type O blood from one parent and that for type A from the other? Will the child have blood of type A, O, or

Saturn Stills/Science Source

meiosis A kind of cell division that produces the sex cells, each of which has half the number of chromosomes found in other cells of the organism.

homozygous A term referring to a chromosome pair that bears identical alleles for a single gene.

heterozygous A term referring to a chromosome pair that bears different alleles for a single gene.

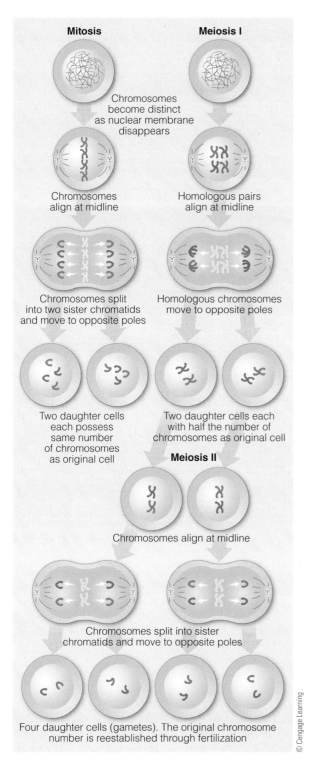

Figure 2.10 Cell Division: Mitosis and Meiosis in Humans
Each chromosome consists of two sister chromatids, which are exact copies of each other. During mitosis, these sister chromatids separate into two identical daughter cells. In meiosis, the cell division responsible for the formation of gametes, the first division halves the chromosome number. The second meiotic division is essentially like mitosis and involves the separation of sister chromatids. Chromosomes in red came from one parent; those in blue came from the other. Meiosis results in four daughter cells that are not identical.

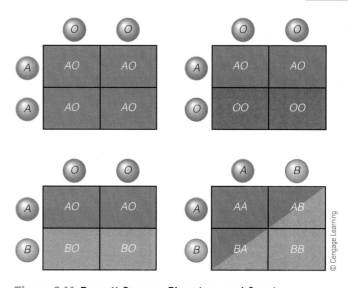

Figure 2.11 Punnett Squares, Phenotype, and Genotype
These four Punnett squares (named for British geneticist Reginald Punnett) illustrate some of the possible phenotypes and genotypes of offspring within the A-B-O system. The alleles of one parent are listed on the left-hand side of the square, while the other parent's alleles are listed across the top. The potential genotypes of offspring are listed in the colored squares by letter. Offspring phenotypes are indicated by color: Blue indicates the type A phenotype; orange indicates the B phenotype. Individuals with one A and one B allele have the AB phenotype and make both blood antigens, a protein on the surface of the red blood cell. Individuals with the O phenotype (magenta) have two O alleles.

some mixture of the two? Figure 2.11 illustrates some of the possible outcomes. Many of these questions were answered by Mendel's original experiments.

Mendel discovered that certain alleles can mask the presence of others; one allele is **dominant**, whereas the other is **recessive**. Actually, it is the traits that are dominant or recessive rather than the alleles themselves; we refer to dominant and recessive alleles for the sake of convenience. Thus, one can say that the allele for type A blood is dominant to the type O allele. A heterozygous individual, with one A and one O allele, will have type A blood. The heterozygous (AO) individual will have exactly the same observed physical characteristic, or **phenotype**, as the homozygous (AA) individual, even though the two have a different genetic composition, or **genotype**. Only

dominant In genetics, a term to describe the ability of an allele for a trait to mask the presence of another allele.

recessive In genetics, a term to describe an allele for a trait whose expression is masked by the presence of a dominant allele.

phenotype The observable characteristic of an organism that may or may not reflect a particular genotype due to the variable expression of dominant and recessive alleles.

genotype The alleles an individual possesses for a particular trait.

Bonds Beyond Blood: DNA Testing and Refugee Family Unification *By Jason Silverstein*

In February 2008, the U.S. government began to assess the use of DNA testing as documentary proof of familial relationship among asylum seekers from Africa attempting reunification with family members already in the United States. The pilot study began with 500 residents of the Dadaab refugee camp in Nairobi, Kenya, where an estimated 465,000

Covering 50 square kilometers in northeastern Kenya, the Dadaab refugee camp is the largest in the world. As of May 2015, the camp was host to 350,000 (down from 465,000 at its height) people seeking sanctuary from political persecution and starvation brought about by civil war and drought in their homelands. Here, Somali refugees pray during Eid al-Fitr, marking the end of the Muslim holy month of Ramadan.

Jonathan Ernst/Reuters /Landov

the homozygous recessive genotype (OO) will show the phenotype of type O blood.

The dominance of one allele does not mean that the recessive one is lost or in some way blended. A type A heterozygous parent (AO) will produce sex cells containing both A and O alleles. (This is an example of Mendel's law of segregation, that alleles retain their separate identities.) Recessive alleles can be handed down for generations before they show up in the phenotype when matched with another recessive allele in the process of sexual reproduction. The dominant allele masks the expression of the recessive allele.

Because all of the traits Mendel studied in garden peas showed this dominant–recessive relationship, it was believed for some years that this was the only relationship possible. Later studies show that, in some cases, neither allele is dominant; they are both *codominant*. Codominance in human heredity can be seen in the inheritance of blood-type alleles A and B. Heterozygous individuals have a phenotype of AB because neither allele can dominate the other.

Blood types illustrate another complexity of heredity. Although we each have at most two alleles for any given gene—only one allele can appear on each of the two homologous chromosomes—the number of possible alleles for that gene found in a population is not limited to two. For example, over 100 alleles

refugees currently live in a space designed for 90,000. DNA testing was later expanded to include 3,000 refugees in Ethiopia, Uganda, Ghana, Guinea, and Côte d'Ivoire.

The pilot program operated on the assumption of "guilty until proven family." Anything other than DNA proof of relationship was recorded as fraud. Refusal to test was recorded as fraud. On a petition with multiple family members, if one person refused, did not show up for, or failed the test, then the entire petition was recorded as fraud. Shockingly, the "anchor" (the person with whom the applicants desired to reunite) was never tested. Only the relationships between individuals on the application were tested. By the time the pilot phase ended, these policies resulted in the classification of 80 percent of family reunification claims as fraudulent, and the U.S. government suspended the reunification program. As DNA testing increasingly becomes the standard by which border security officials investigate kinship claims, what makes a family legitimate will be determined by the social prescriptions of the receiving community.

The definition of *family* is not necessarily portable across borders. Refugees are forced to conform their qualifications of family and, thus, their very life stories to the social norms of the receiving community. We should not confuse the neutrality of DNA as hereditary material with the neutrality of those who collect, process, and interpret it. Far from value-neutral technology, DNA testing for family reunification reveals an allegiance to a particular social universe and often conceals the reality of the refugees' lived experience.

One especially lucid example of this claim is provided by a refugee case manager who remarked that polygamous families (those with more than one spouse) are never resettled (in other words, would never pass the family-relatedness test). Given the testing protocol of the pilot project (testing the genetic relationship between applicants and not between the applicant and the anchor), one readily can imagine that a mother as a primary applicant may not share DNA with her child.

Family is not simply genetic or socially prescribed; it is also existentially evolved, especially for refugees who have spent years if not decades in camps. An interviewer with the United Nations High Commissioner for Refugees related stories about parents who did not want to distinguish between their biological and adopted, often war-orphaned, children. Given that the verification interview takes place in front of the children, avoiding this distinction may have little to do with what

security officials cruelly call fraud or abuse. As one case manager starkly put it, the DNA testing methodology overlooks that those who survive often do not survive unscathed.

Biocultural Question

When DNA testing is used by authorities for identification purposes, what rifts open between the truth of one's life and what can be extracted from one's blood? What should we be searching for when we want to know who a person truly is?

Adapted from Silverstein, J. (2012). Bonds beyond blood: DNA testing and refugee family resettlement. *Anthropology News* 53 (4), 11.

---

exist for **hemoglobin**, the blood protein that carries oxygen.

Polygenetic Inheritance

So far, we have described traits of organisms that are determined by just one gene. However, multiple genes control most physical traits, such as body build, skin color, or susceptibility to disease. In such cases, we speak of **polygenetic inheritance**, in which the respective alleles of two or more genes influence phenotype. For example, several individuals may have the exact same height, but because there is no single height gene that determines an individual's size, it is impossible to neatly unravel the genetic underpinnings of 160 centimeters (5 feet 3 inches). Characteristics subject to polygenetic inheritance exhibit a continuous range of variation in their phenotypic expression that does not correspond to simple Mendelian rules. As biological anthropologist Jonathan Marks demonstrates in the following Original Study, the relationship between genetics and continuous traits remains misunderstood.

---

hemoglobin The protein that carries oxygen in red blood cells.
polygenetic inheritance Two or more genes contributing to the phenotypic expression of a single characteristic.

ORIGINAL STUDY

Ninety-Eight Percent Alike: What Our Similarity to Apes Tells Us about Our Understanding of Genetics

BY JONATHAN MARKS

It's not too hard to tell Jane Goodall from a chimpanzee. Goodall is the one with long legs and short arms, a prominent forehead, and whites in her eyes. She's the one with a significant amount of hair only on her head, not all over her body. She's the one who walks, talks, and wears clothing.

A few decades ago, however, the nascent field of molecular genetics recognized an apparent paradox: However easy it may be to tell Jane Goodall from a chimpanzee on the basis of physical characteristics, it is considerably harder to tell them apart according to their genes.

More recently, geneticists have been able to determine with precision that humans and chimpanzees are over 98 percent identical genetically, and that figure has become one of the most well-known factoids in popular scientific literature. It has been invoked to argue that we are simply a third kind of chimpanzee, together with the common chimp and the rarer bonobo; to claim human rights for nonhuman apes; and to explain the roots of male aggression.

Using the figure in those ways, however, ignores the context necessary to make sense of it. Actually, our amazing genetic similarity to chimpanzees is a scientific fact constructed from two rather more mundane facts: our familiarity with apes and our unfamiliarity with genetic comparisons.

To begin with, it is unfair to juxtapose differences between the bodies of people and apes with similarities in their genes. After all, we have been comparing bodies of humans and chimpanzees for 300 years, and we have been comparing DNA sequences for less than [35] years.

Now that we are familiar with chimpanzees, we quickly see how different they look from us. But when chimpanzees were a novelty, in the 18th century, scholars were struck by the overwhelming similarity of human and ape bodies. And why not? Bone for bone, muscle for muscle, organ for organ, the bodies of humans and apes differ only in subtle ways. And yet, it is impossible to say just how physically similar they are. Forty percent? Sixty percent? Ninety-eight percent? Three-dimensional beings that develop over their lifetimes don't lend themselves to a simple scale of similarity.

Genetics brings something different to the comparison. A DNA sequence is a one-dimensional entity, a long series of A, G, C, and T subunits. Align two sequences from different species and you can simply tabulate their similarities; if they match 98 out of 100 times, then the species are 98 percent genetically identical.

But is that more or less than their bodies match? We have no easy way to tell, for making sense of the question "How similar are humans and chimps?" requires a frame of reference. In other words, we should be asking: "How similar are humans and chimps, compared to what?" Let's try and answer the question. How similar are humans and chimps, compared to, say, sea urchins? Humans and chimpanzees have limbs, skeletons, bilateral symmetry, a central nervous system; each bone, muscle, and organ matches. For all intents and purposes, humans and chimpanzees aren't 98 percent identical, they're 100 percent identical.

On the other hand, when we compare the DNA of humans and chimps, what does the percentage of similarity mean? We conceptualize it on a linear scale, on which 100 percent is perfectly identical, and 0 percent is totally different. But the structure of DNA gives the scale a statistical idiosyncrasy.

Because DNA is a linear array of those four bases—A, G, C, and T—only four possibilities exist at any specific point in a DNA sequence. The laws of chance tell us that two random sequences from species that have no ancestry in common will match at about one in every four sites.

Moreover, the genetic comparison is misleading because it ignores qualitative differences among genomes. Genetic evolution involves much more than simply replacing one base with another. Thus, even among such close relatives as humans and chimpanzees, we find that a chimp's genome is estimated to be about 10 percent larger than a human's; that one human chromosome contains a fusion of two small chimpanzee chromosomes; and that the tips of each chimpanzee chromosome contain a DNA sequence that is not present in humans.

In other words, the pattern we encounter genetically is actually quite close to the pattern we encounter anatomically. In spite of the shock the figure of 98 percent may give us, humans are obviously identifiably different from, as well as very similar to, chimpanzees. The apparent paradox is simply a result of how mundane apes have become and how exotic DNA still is.

Source: Marks, J. (2000, May 12). 98% alike (What our similarity to apes tells us about our understanding of genetics). *Chronicle of Higher Education*, B7. Copyright © 2000 by Chronicle of Higher Education. Reprinted with permission of the author.

Evolutionary Forces and Populations

At the level of an individual, genetic traits are transmitted from parent to offspring, enabling a prediction about the chances that any given individual will display some phenotypic characteristic. At the level of a group, the study of genetics takes on additional significance. It reveals how evolutionary processes account for the diversity of life on earth.

A key concept in genetics is that of the **population**, or a group of individuals within which breeding takes place. **Gene pool** refers to all the genetic variants possessed by members of a population. Over generations, the relative proportions of alleles in a population change (biological evolution) according to the varying reproductive success of individuals within that population. In other words, at the level of population genetics, **evolution** can be defined as changes in allele frequencies in populations. This is also known as *microevolution*. Four evolutionary forces—mutation, genetic drift, gene flow, and natural selection—create and pattern biological diversity.

Mutation

Mutation, the ultimate source of evolutionary change, constantly introduces new genetic variation. Mutation occurs randomly. Although some mutations may be harmful or beneficial to individuals, most mutations are neutral. But in an evolutionary sense, random mutation is inherently positive: It provides the variation upon which the other evolutionary forces work. New body plans—such as walking on two legs compared to knuckle-walking like our closest relatives, chimpanzees and gorillas—ultimately derive from a series of genetic mutations. A random mutation might create a new allele that modifies a protein, making possible a novel biological task. Without the variation brought in through mutations, populations could not change over time in response to changing environments.

Mutations may arise whenever copying mistakes are made during cell division. This may involve a change in a single base of a DNA sequence or, at the other extreme, relocation of large segments of DNA, including entire chromosomes. As you read this page, the DNA in each cell of your body is being damaged (Culotta & Koshland, 1994). Fortunately, DNA repair enzymes constantly scan DNA for mistakes, slicing out damaged segments and patching up gaps. Moreover, for sexually reproducing species like humans, the only mutations of any evolutionary consequence are those occurring in sex cells because these cells form future generations.

New mutations arise continuously because no species has perfect DNA repair; thus all species continue to evolve. Environmental factors may increase the rate at which mutations occur (**Figure 2.12**). These factors include certain dyes, antibiotics, and chemicals used in food preservation. Radiation, whether of industrial or solar origin, represents another important cause of mutations. Even stress can increase mutation rates (Chicurel, 2001). Ultimately, mutations confer versatility at the population level, making it possible for an evolving species to adapt more quickly to environmental changes. Remember, however, that mutations occur randomly and thus do not arise out of need for some new adaptation.

Genetic Drift

Genetic drift refers to chance fluctuations of allele frequencies in the gene pool of a population. Changes at the population level derive from random events at the level of individual survival. For example, a squirrel in good health and with a number of advantageous traits may be killed in a forest fire, while another nearby squirrel with less adaptive traits might escape the fire and reproduce. In a large population, such accidents of nature are unimportant; the accidents that preserve individuals with certain alleles will be balanced out by the accidents that destroy them. However, in small populations, such averaging out may not be possible.

Because today's global human population size is large, we might suppose that human beings are unaffected by genetic drift. But a chance event like a rockslide that kills five people from a town with a population of 1,000 could significantly alter the frequencies of alleles in the local gene pool. Whenever biological variation is observed, whether in the distant past or present, it is always possible that chance events of genetic drift are responsible for it.

A **founder effect** is a specific kind of genetic drift that may occur when an existing population splits up into two or more new ones, especially if only a small number of individuals are the founders of a new population. In such cases, the gene frequencies of the smaller population tend not to contain the full range of variation present in the larger one. An interesting example of founder effects can be seen on the Pacific Ocean island of Pingelap in Micronesia, where 5 percent of the

---

population In biology, a group of similar individuals that can and do interbreed.

gene pool All the genetic variants possessed by members of a population.

evolution The changes in allele frequencies in populations; also known as *microevolution*.

mutation The chance alteration of genetic material that produces new variation.

genetic drift The chance fluctuations of allele frequencies in the gene pool of a population.

founder effect A particular form of genetic drift deriving from a small founding population not possessing all the alleles present in the original population.

Figure 2.12 Pollution and Mutation
These eight children, each missing a hand, were among ninety children born with missing terminal limbs over a twenty-year period in Moscow, Russia. Their family homes were all clustered in polluted industrialized sections of the city, and the missing limbs are the result of prenatal exposure to toxins. These children and their families certainly face many obstacles as a result of this birth defect. Yet from an evolutionary perspective, the mutations leading to limb loss will have no consequences unless they appear in the reproductive cells and are transmitted to future generations.

population is completely colorblind, a condition known as *achromatopsia*. This is not the "normal" red–green colorblindness that affects 8 to 20 percent of males in most populations, but rather a complete inability to see color. The high frequency of achromatopsia began around 1775, after a typhoon swept through the island, reducing its total population to only twenty individuals. Among the survivors was a single individual who was

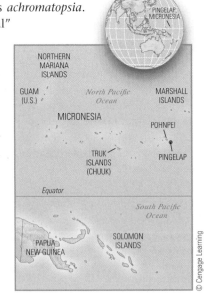

heterozygous for this condition. After a few generations, this gene became fully embedded in the expanding population. Today, a full 30 percent of the island's inhabitants are carriers of the colorblind gene, compared to a mere .003 percent seen in the United States (Sacks, 1998).

Gene Flow

Gene flow, or the introduction of new alleles from nearby populations, brings new genetic variation into a population: Interbreeding allows "road tested" genes to flow into and out of populations. Migration of individuals or groups into the territory occupied by others may lead to gene flow. Geographic factors also affect gene flow. For example, if a river separates two populations of small mammals, preventing interbreeding, these populations will begin to accrue random genetic differences due to their isolation (genetic drift). If the river changes course and the two populations can again interbreed freely, new alleles that may have been present in only one population will now be present in both populations due to gene flow.

Among humans, social factors—such as mating rules, intergroup conflict, and our ability to travel great distances—affect gene flow. For example, the last 500 years have seen the introduction of alleles into Central and

gene flow The introduction of alleles from the gene pool of one population into that of another.

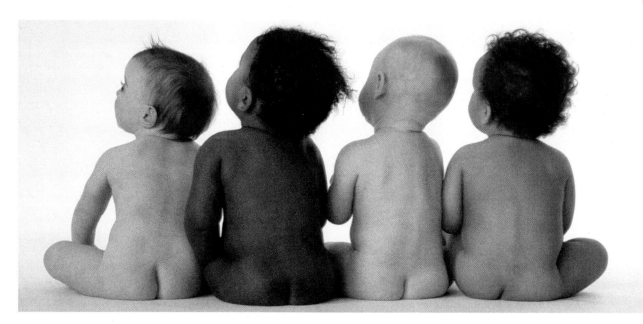

Camille Tokerud/The Image Bank/Getty Images

Figure 2.13 Birth Weight and Stabilizing Selection
Across the globe, newborn babies weigh on average between 5 and 8 pounds. Stabilizing selection seems to be operating here to keep infant size well matched to the size of the human birth canal for successful childbirth. Natural selection can promote stability as well as change.

South American populations from both the Spanish and Portuguese colonists and the Africans imported as slaves. More recent migrations of people from East Asia and the rest of the world have added to this mix. Throughout the history of human life on earth, gene flow has prevented populations from developing into separate species.

Natural Selection

Although gene flow and genetic drift may produce changes in the allele frequency of a population, that change would not necessarily make the population better adapted to its biological and social environment. Natural selection, the evolutionary force described by Darwin, accounts for **adaptation**—a series of beneficial adjustments to a particular environment. As we will explore throughout this text, humans can adapt to their environment through culture as well as biology. When biological adaptation occurs at a genetic level, natural selection is at work. In the process, the frequency of genetic variants for harmful or nonadaptive traits within the population reduces while the frequency of genetic variants for adaptive traits increases. Over time, changes in the genetic structure of the population can result in formation of new species.

Popular writing often reduces natural selection to the notion of the "survival of the fittest," a phrase coined by 19th-century British philosopher Herbert Spencer. The phrase implies that disease, predation, and starvation eliminate the physically weak from the population. Obviously, the survival of the fittest has some bearing on natural selection. But at times, "less fit" individuals survive

and even do quite well, but do not reproduce. They may be incapable of attracting mates, or they may be sterile, or they may produce offspring that do not survive after birth. While they may survive to relatively old ages, they do not pass on their genes to succeeding generations.

Ultimately, all natural selection is measured in terms of **reproductive success**—mating and production of viable offspring who will in turn carry on one's genes. In some human societies, a woman's social worth is assessed in terms of reproductive success or her ability to bear children. In these contexts, infertility becomes a human rights issue.

Despite the importance of adaptation and natural selection in shaping living organisms, many traits have no adaptive function. All male mammals, for example, possess nipples, even though they serve no useful purpose. For female mammals, however, nipples are essential to reproductive success. The two sexes are not separate entities, shaped independently by natural selection, but are variants upon a single body plan, elaborated during embryonic development.

Natural selection often promotes stability instead of change. **Stabilizing selection** occurs in populations that are already well adapted or where change would be disadvantageous (Figure 2.13). In these cases, natural selection will favor the retention of allele frequencies more or less as

adaptation A series of beneficial adjustments to a particular environment.

reproductive success The relative production of fertile offspring by individual members of a population.

stabilizing selection Natural selection acting to promote stability rather than change in a population's gene pool.

Figure 2.14

Disproportionate Features
This x-ray showing the unusually large size of a kiwi egg illustrates that evolution does not continue by preplanned design but rather by a process of tinkering with preexisting body forms. In a similar fashion, the wings of flying insects developed from structures that were originally used for paddling around in water and were later repurposed as they became large relative to body size.

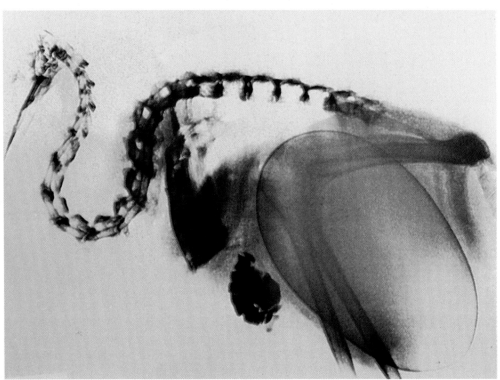

Otorohanga Zoological Society, Inc.

they are. Evolution tends not to proceed in a steady, stately progression over vast periods of time. Instead, the life history of most species consists of relative stability or gradual change punctuated by shorter periods of more rapid change (or extinction) when altered conditions require new adaptations or when a new mutation produces an opportunity to adapt to some other available environment. Determining when and whether enough changes have accumulated within a population to constitute a distinct species is a classic biological and philosophical problem.

Further, traits that seem nonadaptive in the present may be coopted for later use, and traits that appear adaptive might have come about due to unrelated changes in the pattern of growth and development. For instance, the unusually large size of a kiwi's egg enhances the survivability of kiwi chicks, in that they are particularly large and capable when hatched (Figure 2.14). Nevertheless, the largeness of kiwi eggs probably did not evolve because the size is adaptive. Instead, kiwis evolved from an ancestor that was the size of an ostrich, and in birds, egg size reduces at a slower rate than does body size. Therefore, the outsized eggs of kiwi birds seem to be no more than a developmental byproduct of a reduction in body size (Gould, 1991b).

Natural selection differs from the concept of design as it acts only upon the existing store of genetic variation; it cannot create something entirely new. Variation protects populations from dying out or species from going extinct when environments change. Natural selection is a process of tinkering, balancing beneficial and harmful effects of a specific allele in a specific environment, as the following case study of sickle-cell anemia illustrates.

The Case of Sickle-Cell Anemia

Sickle-cell anemia is a painful disease in which oxygen-carrying red blood cells change shape (sickle), clogging the finest parts of the circulatory system (Figure 2.15). In the early part of the 20th century, geneticists in Chicago first observed that the disease disproportionately impacted African Americans. Further investigation found that populations living in a clearly defined area of Central Africa had the sickle-cell allele at surprisingly high frequencies. Geneticists wanted to understand why such a harmful hereditary disability persisted in these populations. According to the theory of natural selection, alleles that are harmful tend to disappear from a group because individuals who are homozygous for the abnormality generally die—are "selected out"—before they reproduce. Why, then, has this seemingly harmful condition persisted in populations from tropical Africa?

The answer to this mystery began to emerge when researchers noticed that a particularly deadly form of malaria (falciparum malaria) was prevalent in the same areas that had high rates of sickle-cell anemia (Figure 2.16).

sickle-cell anemia An inherited form of anemia produced by a mutation in the hemoglobin protein that causes the red blood cells to assume a sickle shape.

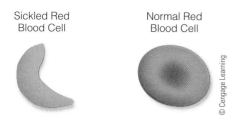

Figure 2.15 Sickle and Normal Red Blood Cells
Sickle-cell anemia is caused by a genetic mutation in a single base of the hemoglobin gene, resulting in abnormal hemoglobin, called hemoglobin S or Hb^S. (The normal hemoglobin allele is called Hb^A, not to be confused with blood type A.) Those afflicted by the disease are homozygous for the Hb^S allele, and all their red blood cells "sickle." Codominance is observable with the sickle and normal alleles. Heterozygotes (genotype Hb^A Hb^S) make 50 percent normal hemoglobin and 50 percent sickle hemoglobin. Shown here is a sickled red blood cell compared to a normal red blood cell.

This form of malaria causes many deaths or, in those who survive, high fevers that interfere with individuals' reproductive abilities. Moreover, researchers discovered hemoglobin abnormalities among people living in parts of the Arabian Peninsula, Greece, Algeria, Syria, and India, all regions where malaria is (or was) common. In fact, selection due to environmental malaria favored heterozygous individuals with normal and sickling hemoglobin. The loss of alleles for abnormal hemoglobin caused by death from sickle-cell anemia was countered by the loss of alleles for normal hemoglobin, as those homozygous for normal hemoglobin were more likely to die from malaria.

The mutation that causes hemoglobin to sickle consists of a change in a single base of DNA, so it can arise readily by chance (**Figure 2.17**). The resulting mutant allele codes for an amino acid substitution in the beta chain of the hemoglobin protein that causes red blood cells to take on a characteristic sickle shape. In homozygous individuals with two sickle-hemoglobin alleles, collapse and clumping of the abnormal red blood cells block the capillaries and create tissue damage. Afflicted individuals commonly die before reaching adulthood. Except under low oxygen or other stressful conditions, heterozygous individuals suffer no ill effects. In regions with malaria, the heterozygous condition improves individuals' resilience to malaria and hence their reproductive success relative to the "normal" homozygous condition.

This example demonstrates how adaptations tend to be specific; the abnormal hemoglobin was adaptive only in environments in which the malarial parasite flourished. When individuals adapted to malarial regions relocated to regions relatively free of malaria, the abnormal

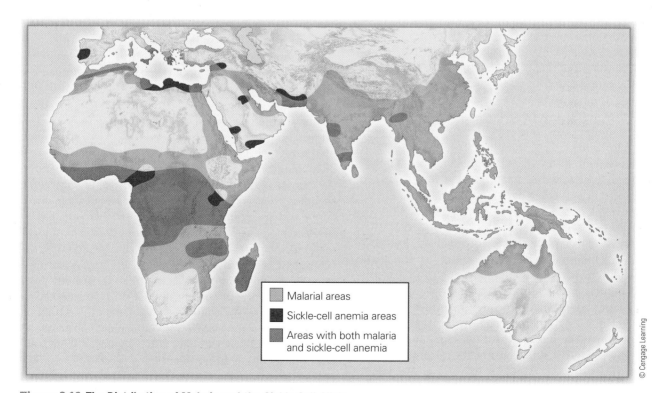

Malarial areas

Sickle-cell anemia areas

Areas with both malaria and sickle-cell anemia

Figure 2.16 The Distribution of Malaria and the Sickle-Cell Allele
In regions with a high incidence of falciparum malaria, people native to these areas have a higher than normal rate of the allele that causes sickle-cell anemia. Researchers have surmised that natural selection preserved the allele for the sickle-cell trait to protect individuals from the devastating effects of malaria.

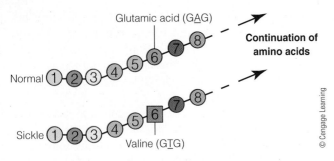

Figure 2.17 Simple Mutation, Dramatic Consequences
Mutation of a single base of DNA can result in a radically different protein. Pictured here are codons 1 through 8 for the beta chain of hemoglobin, the protein that carries oxygen in red blood cells, and the amino acids these codons specify. The normal allele (*top*) and the sickle-cell allele (*bottom*) differ only by the substitution of the base thymine for adenine in the codon in position 6, which in turn substitutes valine for glutamic acid. This simple mutation makes the red blood cells bend into a sickle shape, clogging the capillary beds and causing great pain, which is what occurs with sickle-cell anemia. Sickling occurs because the amino acid valine, compared to glutamic acid in the normal allele, gives the hemoglobin molecule different properties. The beta chain is 146 amino acids long, and a simple mutation can have dramatic and tragic consequences.

hemoglobin became comparatively disadvantageous. Although the rates of sickle-cell trait remain relatively high among African Americans—about 8 percent have the sickling trait—this has significantly declined from the 22 percent estimated among the first Africans who were sold as slaves. A similar decline in the sickle-cell allele would occur over the course of several generations in malarial zones if that deadly disease were brought under control.

This example also illustrates the role culture plays in biological adaptation. In Africa, the severe form of malaria was not a significant problem until humans abandoned food foraging for farming a few thousand years ago. To farm, people had to clear areas of the natural forest cover. In the forest, decaying vegetation on the forest floor gave the ground an absorbent quality so that the heavy rainfall rapidly soaked into the soil. But once stripped of its natural vegetation, the soil lost this quality. In addition, without the forest canopy to break the force of rainfall, heavy rains compacted the soil further. The stagnant puddles that subsequently formed provided the perfect breeding environment for the type of mosquito that hosts the malarial parasite. These mosquitoes then began to flourish and transmit the malarial parasite to humans.

Thus, humans unwittingly created the kind of environment that made a disadvantageous trait—the abnormal hemoglobin associated with sickle-cell anemia—advantageous. Although the biological process of evolution accounts for frequency of the sickle-cell allele, cultural processes shape the environment to which humans adapt.

Adaptation and Physical Variation

Anthropologists study biological diversity by referring to **cline**, or the continuous gradation over space in the form or frequency of a trait. The spatial distribution or cline for the sickle-cell allele allowed anthropologists to identify the adaptive function of this gene in a malarial environment. Clinal analysis of a continuous trait such as body shape, which is controlled by a series of genes, allows anthropologists to interpret human global variation in body build as an adaptation to climate.

Generally, people long native to regions with cold climates tend to have greater body bulk (not to be equated with fat) relative to their extremities (arms and legs) than do people native to regions with hot climates, who tend to be relatively tall and slender. In hot, open country people benefit from a long, slender body that can get rid of excess heat quickly. A small slender body can also promote heat loss due to a high surface area to volume ratio. A person with larger body bulk and relatively short extremities may suffer more from summer heat, but this person will conserve needed body heat under cold conditions because a bulky body has less surface area relative to volume.

Climate can also contribute to human variation through its impact on the process of growth and development (developmental adaptation). For example, some of the biological mechanisms for withstanding cold or dissipating heat have been shown to vary depending upon the climate that individuals experience as children. People spending their youth in very cold climates develop circulatory system modifications that allow them to remain comfortable at temperatures that those from warmer climates cannot tolerate. Similarly, hot climates promote development of a higher density of sweat glands, creating a more efficient system for sweating to keep the body cool.

Cultural processes complicate studies of biological adaptation to climate. For example, a poor diet during childhood affects the growth process and ultimately impacts adult body shape and size. Clothing also complicates these studies. In fact, culture rather than biology accounts for much of the way people adapt to cold. For instance, to cope with bitter cold Arctic climates, the Inuit peoples of northern Canada (and other Eskimos) created artificial tropical environments for themselves inside their clothing. Such cultural adaptations allow humans to inhabit the entire globe.

cline The gradual change in the frequency of an allele or trait over space.

Macroevolution and the Process of Speciation

While *microevolution* refers to changes in the allele frequencies of populations, **macroevolution** focuses on **speciation**—the formation of new species—and on the evolutionary relationships among groups of species. The microevolutionary forces of mutation, genetic drift, gene flow, and natural selection can lead to macroevolutionary change as species diverge.

As defined earlier in the chapter, *species*—a population or group of populations capable of interbreeding and producing viable, fertile offspring—are reproductively isolated. The bullfrogs in one farmer's pond are the same species as those in a neighboring pond, even though the two populations may never actually interbreed; in theory, they could interbreed if brought together. But isolated populations may be in the process of evolving into different species, and it is hard to tell exactly when they become distinct.

Factors, known as *isolating mechanisms*, can separate breeding populations and lead to the appearance of new species. Because isolation prevents gene flow, changes that affect the gene pool of one population cannot be introduced into the gene pool of another. Random mutation may introduce new alleles in one of the isolated populations but not in the other. Genetic drift and natural selection may affect the two populations in different ways. Over time, as the two populations continue to differ from each other, speciation occurs in a branching fashion known as **cladogenesis**. Speciation can also happen without branching, as a single population accumulates sufficient new mutations over time to be considered a separate species. This process known as **anagenesis** (Figure 2.18) appears in the fossil record when a group of organisms takes on a different appearance over time.

Speciation can occur at various rates. Scholars generally consider speciation through natural selection to occur at a slow rate as organisms become better adapted to their environments. Sometimes, however, speciation can occur quite rapidly. For example, a genetic mutation such as one involving a key *regulatory gene*, a gene that turns other genes off and on, can lead to formation of a new body plan. Such genetic accidents may involve material that is broken off, transposed, or transferred from one chromosome to another.

Genes that regulate the growth and development of an organism may have a major effect on its adult form. Scientists have discovered certain key genes called *homeobox genes* that are responsible for large-scale effects on the growth and development of an organism (Figure 2.19). If a new body plan happens to be adaptive, natural selection will maintain this new form for long periods of time rather than promoting change.

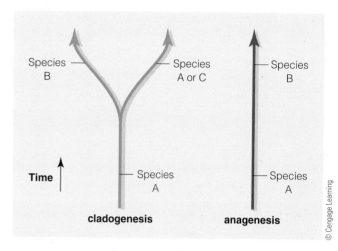

Figure 2.18 Mechanisms of Speciation
Cladogenesis occurs as different populations of an ancestral species become reproductively isolated. Through genetic drift and differential selection, the number of descendant species increases. Speciation by anagenesis can take place as small differences in traits that (by chance) are advantageous in a particular environment accumulate in a species' gene pool, eventually transforming an old species into a new one. Genetic drift may also contribute to anagenesis.

© Cengage Learning

Paleontologists Stephen Jay Gould and Niles Eldredge have proposed that speciation occurs in a pattern of **punctuated equilibrium**, or the alternation between periods of rapid speciation and times of stability. Often this model of evolutionary change is contrasted with speciation through adaptation, sometimes referred to as *Darwinian gradualism*. A close look at the genetics and the fossil record indicates that evolutionary change occurs via both mechanisms. Genetic mechanisms underlie both rapid and gradual changes because mutations can have small or large effects.

It is particularly interesting to see how molecular genetics supports Darwinian evolution. For example, the tailoring of beak shape and size to diet among finches on the Galapagos Islands, in the Pacific Ocean west of Ecuador, constituted Darwin's classic example of natural

---

macroevolution Evolution above the species level or leading to the formation of new species.

speciation The process of forming new species.

cladogenesis Speciation through a branching mechanism whereby an ancestral population gives rise to two or more descendant populations.

anagenesis A sustained directional shift in a population's average characteristics that leads to speciation.

punctuated equilibrium A model of macroevolutionary change that suggests evolution occurs via long periods of stability or stasis punctuated by periods of rapid change.

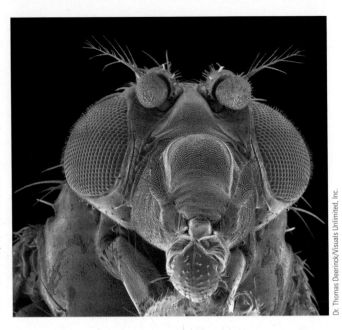

Science VU/Dr. F. Rudolph Turner/Visuals Unlimited, Inc

Dr. Thomas Deerinck/Visuals Unlimited, Inc.

Figure 2.19 **Homeobox Genes and New Body Plans**
Sometimes mutation in a single gene can cause reorganization of an organism's body plan. Here the antennepedia homeobox gene has caused this fruit fly to develop in places that would normally be antennae. Another homeobox gene, antennapedia, causes legs to develop in the place of antennae on the heads of fruit flies.

selection (Figure 2.20). Recently, scientists identified two proteins along with the underlying genes that control beak shape and size in birds (Lamichhaney et al. 2015). It is all the more impressive that Darwin was able to make his inferences about natural selection without the benefit of molecular genetics.

In biological terms, evolution accounts for all that humans share as well as the broad array of human diversity. Evolution is also responsible for the creation of

new species over time. Primatologist Frans de Waal has said, "Evolution is a magnificent idea that has won over essentially everyone in the world willing to listen to scientific arguments" (de Waal, 2001b, p. 77). We will return to the topic of human evolution in chapters that follow, but first we will look at the other living primates to understand the kinds of animals they are, what they have in common with humans, and what distinguishes the various forms.

(a) Ground finch
  Main food: seeds
  Beak: heavy

(b) Tree finch
  Main food: leaves, buds,
  blossoms, fruits
  Beak: thick, short

(c) Tree finch (called
  woodpecker finch)
  Main food: insects
  Beak: stout, straight

(d) Ground finch (known
  as warbler finch)
  Main food: insects
  Beak: slender

© 2010 Cengage Learning Inc.

Figure 2.20 **Adaptation and Darwin's Finches**
Scientists have begun to unravel the genetic mechanisms controlling the shape and size of beaks of the finches studied by Darwin on the Galapagos Islands. Darwin noted how beak shape and size were related to each species' diet and used the birds to illustrate adaptation to a particular ecological niche. Finches with blunt crushing beaks are seedeaters while others with long probing beaks pick between cactus thorns for food or use their beaks to reach insects.

CHAPTER CHECKLIST

How does evolutionary theory differ from creation stories?

✓ Scientific theories are based on testable hypotheses.

✓ Scientific theories provide mechanisms to account for the diversity of life on earth.

How are living things classified, and how did this system come about?

✓ The science of taxonomy classifies living organisms into a series of progressively more inclusive categories on the basis of visual similarities and developmental patterns.

✓ Carolus Linnaeus devised the *Systema Naturae*, the first comprehensive system to classify species on the basis of similarities in body structure, body function, and sequence of bodily growth.

✓ Modern taxonomy incorporates genetic characteristics into the basic Linnaean system.

✓ Species, the smallest working units in biological classificatory systems, are reproductively isolated populations or groups of populations capable of interbreeding to produce fertile offspring.

What is evolution, and when was this central biological theory formulated?

✓ Charles Darwin formulated his theory of evolution in 1859, based on differential reproductive success among members of a population that become adapted to their environment through natural selection.

✓ Four evolutionary forces—mutation, genetic drift, gene flow, and natural selection—affect the genetic structures of populations. Evolution at the level of population genetics (also known as microevolution) is change in allele frequencies.

✓ Macroevolution focuses on the formation of new species (speciation) and on the evolutionary relationships among groups.

What is the molecular basis of evolution?

✓ Genes, the units of heredity, are segments of molecules of DNA (deoxyribonucleic acid). The entire structure sequence of DNA is known as the genome.

✓ DNA resembles two strands of rope twisted around each other with ladder-like rungs made of complementary bases connecting the two strands.

✓ The sequence of bases along the DNA molecule directs the production of proteins. Proteins constitute specific identifiable traits such as blood type.

✓ Different versions or alternate forms of a gene for a given trait are called alleles. The total number of different alleles of the various genes in a population is its gene pool.

How do cells and organisms reproduce?

✓ DNA molecules can replicate so that new daughter cells will be exact genetic copies of the parent cell.

✓ DNA molecules are located on chromosomes, structures found in the nucleus of each cell. Chromosomes consist of two sister chromatids.

✓ Each species has a characteristic number of chromosomes, found in pairs in sexually reproducing organisms. Humans have twenty-three pairs of chromosomes.

✓ Mitosis is the kind of cell division that results in two identical daughter cells.

✓ Meiosis results in four sex cells, each containing half the number of chromosomes of the parent cell. Fertilization, the union of an egg and a sperm cell, reestablishes the normal number.

How do different traits get inherited across generations?

✓ Individuals inherit traits independently from each parent.

✓ Dominant alleles are able to mask the presence of recessive alleles. *Codominant* alleles are both expressed when present.

✓ *Phenotype* refers to the physical characteristics of an organism. *Genotype* refers to its genetic composition. Two organisms may have different genotypes but the same phenotype.

How do the four evolutionary forces contribute to the diversity of life on earth?

✓ Mutation provides the ultimate source of genetic variation.

✓ Genetic drift refers to the effects of random events on the gene pools of populations.

✓ Gene flow, the introduction of new variants of genes from nearby populations, distributes new variation to all populations and prevents speciation.

✓ Natural selection reduces the frequency of alleles for harmful or maladaptive traits within a population and increases the frequency of alleles for adaptive traits.

What are some examples of human adaptation through natural selection?

✓ The sickle-cell trait, caused by the inheritance of an abnormal form of hemoglobin, is an adaptation to life in regions in which malaria is common.

✓ People native to cold climates tend to have greater body bulk relative to their extremities while individuals from hot climates tend to be relatively tall and slender.

How are new species formed?

✓ Speciation can occur in a branching fashion (cladogenesis) or without branching (anagenesis) as a population accumulates sufficient new mutations over time to be considered a separate species.

✓ Microevolutionary forces can lead to macroevolutionary change, but the tempo of evolutionary change varies.

✓ Mutations in regulatory genes can bring about rapid change. According to the punctuated equilibrium model, macroevolution is characterized by long spans of relative stability interspersed with periods of rapid change.

QUESTIONS FOR REFLECTION

1. Have genetics and DNA become a part of your everyday experience? If so, how? Has genetics challenged your conception of what it means to be human? How much of your life, or of the lives of people around you, is dictated by the structure of DNA?

2. Scientific fact and theory can challenge other belief systems. Is it possible for scientific models of human evolution and religious stories of creation to coexist? How do you personally reconcile science and religion?

3. The four evolutionary forces—mutation, genetic drift, gene flow, and natural selection—all affect biological variation. Some are at work in individuals while others function at the population level. Compare and contrast these evolutionary forces, outlining their contributions to biological variation.

4. The frequency of the sickle-cell allele in populations provides a classic example of adaptation on a genetic level. Describe the benefits of this deadly allele. Are mutations good or bad?

DIGGING INTO ANTHROPOLOGY

Making Meaning of Memes

Memes going viral on the Internet might seem to have little connection to biology and genetics. But they share a common ancestry. Evolutionary biologist Richard Dawkins coined the term *meme* to refer to an abstract unit of cultural transmission, analogous to the role of the gene in biology (Dawkins, 1976). Arguing that cultural information is subject to many of the same evolutionary forces as biological attributes, Dawkins's idea gave rise to the field of memetics, drawing in scholars from a variety of disciplines. A meme can be virtually anything that self-replicates (spreads from person to person), including phrases, songs, gestures, fashion trends, viral videos, rituals, religious traditions, cuisine, technologies, and so on.

Choose a contemporary meme and investigate its hereditary history, considering how the evolutionary forces discussed in this chapter have played into its cultural pathway. When and how has it mutated? What other meme "alleles" has it competed with for reproductive success? How has it adapted to different cultural environments? On the other hand, how does the meme fail to conform with genetic hereditary processes?

Reuters/Corbis

CHALLENGE ISSUE

For generations, the big-eyed and sweet-faced slow loris has been a part of the traditional mythology and medicine of the peoples of Southeast Asia. Traditional hunters trap the night-active slow loris with a forked stick and use its various parts to treat ailments from broken bones to asthma to sexually transmitted disease. Today, Internet videos of these adorable primates, garnering millions of hits, have spread loris mythology throughout the world. This fame has been devastating, as it has created an immense demand for slow lorises as pets and tourist attractions; all species of this unique primate are now endangered. Their sharp teeth and specialized arm glands, which secrete a stinky liquid that gets mixed with their saliva, have led some to label the slow lorises venomous. In order to make them safe for human interaction as pets, their teeth are painfully wrenched out; many do not survive the procedure and ensuing captivity. Despite international protections designating slow loris trade illegal, up to 90 percent of the creatures have been wiped out (Nekaris et al., 2010). And slow lorises are not alone. Many other primates—including all the great apes, our closest relatives—are endangered, due primarily to human activity. If the difference between our primate relatives and us is our greater intelligence and complex language, it is time to use both these gifts to protect them. We humans face the challenge of speaking out and working to ensure other primates do not become extinct.

Living Primates

In October 1960, young Jane Goodall sent word to her mentor in Kenya, British paleoanthropologist Louis Leakey, that she had observed two chimps turning sticks into tools for fishing termites out of their nesting mounds. Leakey replied, "Now we must redefine 'tool,' redefine 'man,' or accept chimpanzees as humans" (Jane Goodall Institute, 2015).

Field studies of primates by Western scientists have always contained a degree of *anthropocentrism* and a focus on what nonhuman primates can tell us about ourselves. Indeed, that is the purpose of this chapter. A close look at the biology and behavior of primates lets us gain a deeper understanding of those characteristics we share with them as well as those that make us distinctively human. Studying behavior, communication, and tool use among our primate cousins today helps us unravel the old nature–nurture question: How much of human behavior is biologically determined and how much of it derives from culture?

Today, we are the only primate to inhabit the entire globe. As human population size rises to unsustainable levels, many primate groups are hovering on the brink of extinction. Figure 3.1 shows the natural global distribution of living and fossil primates. It also indicates where critically endangered primate species are struggling to survive. In this light, the purpose of this chapter is not just to learn more about ourselves, but also to learn how to protect our primate cousins and the planet we share.

In this chapter you will learn to

- Identify the key methods of primatologists and the ethics they uphold.

- Situate primates in the animal kingdom and compare them to other mammals and reptiles.

- Construct evolutionary relationships among the primates.

- Recognize the basic features of primate anatomy and behavior.

- Distinguish the characteristics of the five natural groups of primates.

- Identify critical issues and methods in primate conservation.

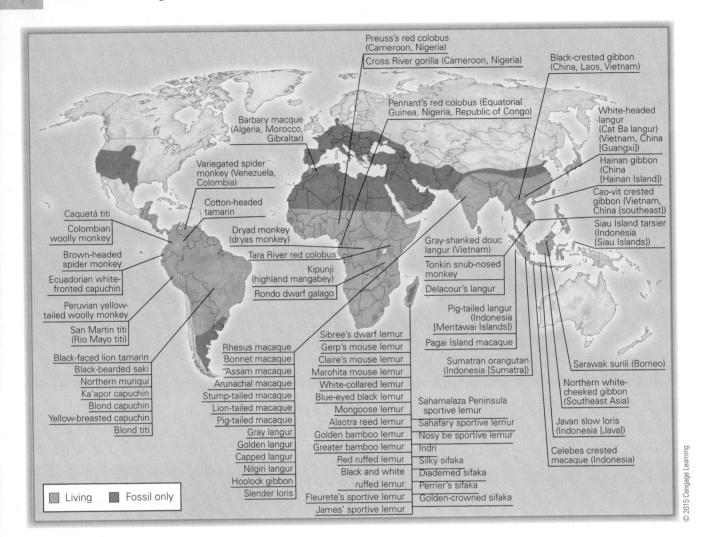

Figure 3.1 The Global Distribution of Living and Fossil Nonhuman Primates
In the past, when more of the world was covered by tropical forests, the range of primates was far greater than it is now. Today, human activity threatens our primate cousins throughout the globe. The figure also shows the location of today's critically endangered (very high risk of extinction) primate species.

© 2015 Cengage Learning

Methods and Ethics in Primatology

Just as anthropologists employ diverse methods to study humans, so do primatologists when they study the biology, behavior, and evolutionary history of our closest living relatives. Some primatologists concentrate on the comparative anatomy of ancient skeletons, while others trace evolutionary relationships by studying the comparative physiology and genetics of living species. Primatologists study the biology and behavior of living primates in their natural habitats as well as in zoos, primate research colonies, and learning laboratories.

The most famous primatologist is Jane Goodall, a world-renowned British researcher who has devoted her career to in-depth observation of chimpanzees in their natural habitat. While documenting the range and nuance of chimpanzee behavior, she has also championed

conservation of primate habitats and humane treatment of primates in captivity.

The philosophy of conservation and preservation has led to innovations in research methods. Primatologists have developed a number of noninvasive methods that allow the study of primates in the field with minimal physical disruption. Primatologists gather hair, feces, and other body secretions left by the primates in the environment for later analysis in the laboratory. These analyses provide invaluable information about characteristics such as dietary habits or genetic relationships.

Work with captive animals has allowed primatologists to document the humanity of our primate cousins and their amazing linguistic and conceptual abilities. Some primatologists have devoted their careers to teaching captive primates to communicate through pictures on a computer screen or American Sign Language. Of course, even compassionate captivity imposes stress on primates. Still, the knowledge gained through these studies will ultimately contribute to primate conservation and survival.

At first glance, it might seem inherently more humane to work with animals in the field, instead of captivity. But even field studies raise important ethical issues. Primatologists must maintain an awareness of how their presence affects the behavior of the group. For example, does becoming tolerant of human observers make the primates more vulnerable? Primates habituated to humans commonly range beyond established wilderness preserves and come in close contact with other humans, who may be more interested in hunting than observing. Contact between primates and humans can also expose endangered primates to infectious diseases carried by humans.

Whether working with primates in captivity or in the field, primatologists seriously consider the well-being of the primates they study. U.S. primatologist Michele Goldsmith explores these issues in depth in this chapter's Original Study.

Gorilla Ecotourism: Ethical Considerations for Conservation

ORIGINAL STUDY

BY MICHELE L. GOLDSMITH

For the past two decades, I have been studying and writing about the impact of ecotourism on mountain gorillas living in Bwindi Impenetrable National Park, Uganda. As a biological anthropologist and conservationist, my main focus has been on habituation, which is a necessary prerequisite for tourism, and how it influences gorilla behavior and well-being. *Habituation* refers to the acceptance by wild animals of a human observer as a neutral element in their environment. Although information from habituated primates has been instrumental in providing a wealth of information for research and conservation, little attention has been given to the costs these animals bear when their fear of humans is removed.

The first impacts of habituation occur during the process of acclimation. Habituators follow the animals from a distance and, over time, slowly get closer and closer. Many factors contribute to the speed and success of the process, such as the terrain (open areas versus thick forest), prior exposure to humans, hunting pressure, and so on. The process can be stressful for the gorillas and even dangerous for the habituators. During the habituation process, a group of western lowland gorillas exhibited fear in their vocalizations, increased their aggressive behavior, and changed their daily ranging pattern.[a] Such fear and stress can lead to loss of reproductive function and to a weakened immune system. Aggressive behavior has resulted in habituators being charged by silverback males with some humans being hit and bitten.

Once fully habituated, gorillas may then experience unforeseen consequences. For example, gorillas that have lost their fear of humans are especially vulnerable to hunting. Five Bwindi gorillas habituated for research were found dead, having been killed by poachers so they could capture a young infant gorilla. In addition, humans have also brought great instability and warfare to areas where gorilla populations live. Sudden evacuation of research and tourist sites leaves behind habituated gorillas that become easy targets for the poacher's gun.

With regard to long-term changes in ecology and behavior, my research has shown that the diet, nesting, and ranging patterns of habituated gorilla groups are different from other "wild" gorillas in the same study area. The Nkuringo group, habituated in 1998 for tourism that started in 2004, lives near the edge of the protected Bwindi Impenetrable National Park. These gorillas spend close to 90 percent of their time outside the park, in and

Primatologist Michele Goldsmith making observations of gorillas in the field.

Michele L. Goldsmith/Photograph © Katherine Hope

around human-inhabited areas and farms. These behavioral changes have many costs to the gorillas, such as increased contact with humans and human waste, conflict with farmers that could result in injury, increased exposure to hunting given that these areas are mostly open fields, and increased risk of disease transmission.[b]

Another effect on behavior may be an artificial increase in group size. For example, a group of some forty-four animals now exists in the Virungas, where the average group size is usually ten individuals. Furthermore, it is thought that, due to their fear of humans, "wild" adult male gorillas that would normally challenge other dominant males are either deterred from presenting a challenge or are less successful in their challenge against habituated groups.

Perhaps the biggest threat to habituated great apes is disease.[c] There are over nineteen viruses and eighteen parasites that are known to infect both great apes and humans. These diseases have been responsible for between sixty-three and eighty-seven ape deaths in habituated groups (both research and tourist groups) in the Virungas, Bwindi, Mahale, Tai, and Gombe. As for the gorillas in Bwindi, it has been shown that parasites such as *Cryptosporidium* and *Giardia* are most prevalent in habituated groups living near humans along the border of the park.

Is gorilla tourism sustainable? Early gorilla tourism in the 1980s did appear to be a salvation because it helped to halt poaching and provide value to the living animal that was lacking. However, now the balance seems to have

tipped. As of 2011, *61 percent* of the entire mountain gorilla population *is now habituated* for either research (17%) or tourism (44%). We know habituated gorillas are more susceptible to stress, experience changes in their behavior, and are more vulnerable to human disease. The fear remains that one deadly, highly infectious disease could travel quickly through the small isolated populations and leave few survivors. *What is most important is not habituating more groups but better managing of the already habituated groups.* Ethical considerations are crucial as we continue to put gorilla populations at risk.[d] Habituation, especially for tourism, may not be an ape's salvation.

Written expressly for this text.

[a]Blom, A., Cipolletta, C., Brunsting, A. M. H., & Prins, H. T. (2004). Behavioral responses of gorillas to habituation in the Dzanga-Ndoki National Park, Central African Republic. *International Journal of Primatology 25* (1), 179–196.

[b]Goldsmith, M. L., Glick, J., & Ngabirano, E. (2006). Gorillas living on the edge: Literally and figuratively. In N. E. Newton-Fisher, H. Notman, J. D. Paterson, & V. Reynolds (Eds.), *Primates of western Uganda* (pp. 405–422). New York: Springer.

[c]Woodford, M. H., Butynski, T. M., & Karesh W. B. (2002). Habituating the great apes: The disease risks. *Oryx 36* (2), 153–160.

[d]Goldsmith, M. L. (2005). Habituating primates for field study: Ethical considerations for great apes. In T. Turner (Ed.), *Biological anthropology and ethics: From repatriation to genetic identity* (pp. 49–64). New York: SUNY Press.

Primates as Mammals

Primates, humans included, are one of several different kinds of mammal, a class that includes rodents, carnivores, and ungulates (hoofed mammals) among others. Other primates include lemurs, lorises, tarsiers, monkeys, and apes. Humans—together with chimpanzees, bonobos, gorillas, orangutans, gibbons, and siamangs—form the hominoids, colloquially known as apes, a superfamily within the primate order. Biologically speaking, as hominoids, humans are apes.

Primates, like other mammals, are intelligent, having more in the way of brains than reptiles or other vertebrates. Increased brainpower and the mammalian pattern of growth and development form the biological basis of the flexible behaviors typical of mammals.

In most species, the egg is retained within the womb of the female until the embryo achieves an advanced state of growth, and the young are born live. Once born, the young receive milk from their mothers' mammary glands, the physical feature from which the class Mammalia gets its name (**Figure 3.2**). During this period of infant dependency, young mammals learn the survival skills they will need as adults. Primates in general, and apes in particular, have a long period of infant and childhood dependency in which the young learn the ways of their social group.

The first mammals—small often **nocturnal** (active at night) creatures—evolved from reptiles over 200 million years ago (mya). With the mass extinction of many reptiles, including the dinosaurs, some 65 million years ago, mammals had a greater choice of **ecological niche**, or functional position within a habitat. A species' niche incorporates factors such as diet, activity, terrain, vegetation, predators, prey, and climate. New niches opened as the earth cooled during this time period, permitting mammals to fill them. This led to a mammalian **adaptive radiation**, which is the rapid diversification of an evolving population following a change in the environment.

nocturnal Active at night and at rest during the day.

ecological niche A species' way of life considered in the full context of its environment including factors such as diet, activity, terrain, vegetation, predators, prey, and climate.

adaptive radiation The rapid diversification of an evolving population as it adapts to a variety of available niches.

Figure 3.2 Nursing Chimp
A glance at this female chimp and her infant attests to all that we share with our closest living relatives, whose bodies have the same basic form as our own. We are equipped to read their body language and facial expressions, perhaps recalling our own experiences just from looking at them. For all mammals, nursing young is an important part of rearing relatively few offspring at a time. Ape mothers tend to nurse their offspring for four or five years. The practice of bottle-feeding infants in North America and Europe is a massive departure from the ape pattern. Despite the documented health benefits for mothers (such as lowered breast cancer rates) and children (strengthened immune systems), cultural norms sometimes present obstacles to breast-feeding. In the United States, for example, only 27 percent of mothers breast-feed their year old or 12-month-old infants. By contrast, across the globe, women nurse their children on average for about three years.

By chance, mammals were **preadapted**—possessing the biological equipment to take advantage of the new opportunities available to them through the mass extinction and climate change. As a **homeotherm**, a mammal has the ability to maintain a constant body temperature. A mammal can be active at a wide range of environmental temperatures, whereas a reptile, as an **isotherm**, which

takes its body temperature from the surrounding environment, becomes progressively sluggish as the surrounding temperature drops.

However, mammals require a high-calorie diet to maintain a constant body temperature. To meet this need, mammals developed superior senses of smell and hearing relative to reptiles. Mammals and reptiles also differ in their patterns of caring for their young. Mammals are **k-selected** (from *Kapazität*, the German word for "capacity"), meaning they produce relatively few offspring at a time and provide them with considerable parental care. In contrast, reptiles are **r-selected** (from the word *rate*), which means they produce many young at a time and invest little effort caring for them after they are born.

Although some mammals are relatively more k- or r-selected, all mammals have higher nutritional requirements compared to reptiles due to their pattern of parental investment and their maintenance of a constant body temperature. They also tend to be more active than other members of the animal kingdom. Mammals are able to sustain their high activity level because of a relatively constant body temperature, an efficient respiratory system featuring a separation between the nasal (nose) and mouth cavities (allowing them to breathe while they eat), a diaphragm to assist in drawing in and letting out breath, and an efficient four-chambered heart that prevents mixing of oxygenated and deoxygenated blood.

Mammals' limbs are positioned beneath the body, rather than out to the sides. This arrangement allows for direct support and easy, flexible movement. Their joints permit growth in the young while simultaneously providing strong, hard joint surfaces that will stand up to the stresses of sustained activity. Mammals stop growing when they reach adulthood, whereas reptiles continue to grow throughout their life span.

Mammals and reptiles also differ in terms of their teeth. Reptilian teeth are pointed, year peglike, and nearly identical in shape. Mammalian teeth are specialized for particular purposes: incisors for nipping, gnawing, and cutting; canines for ripping, tearing, killing, and fighting; premolars for either slicing and tearing or crushing and grinding (depending on the kind of animal); and molars for crushing and grinding (Figure 3.3). This enables mammals to eat a wide variety of foods—an advantage, given that they require more food than reptiles to sustain their high activity level. The specialization of mammal teeth

preadapted Possessing characteristics that, by chance, are advantageous in future environmental conditions.

homeotherm An animal that maintains a relatively constant body temperature despite environmental fluctuations.

isotherm An animal whose body temperature rises or falls depending on the temperature of the surrounding environment.

k-selected Reproduction involving the production of relatively few offspring with high parental investment in each.

r-selected Reproduction involving the production of large numbers of offspring with relatively low parental investment in each.

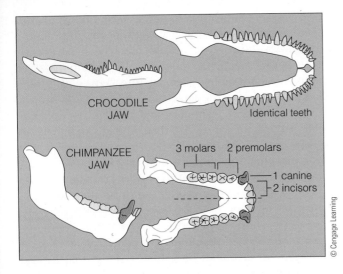

Figure 3.3 Comparison of Reptilian and Mammalian Teeth
The crocodile jaw, like the jaw of all reptiles, contains a series of nearly identical teeth. If a tooth breaks or falls out, a new tooth will emerge in its place. Mammals, by contrast, possess precise numbers of specialized teeth, each with a particular shape characteristic of the group, as indicated on the chimpanzee jaw: Incisors in front are shown in blue, canines behind in red, followed by two premolars and three molars in yellow (the last being the wisdom teeth in humans).

also allows scientists to identify species and evolutionary relationships through dental comparisons. But mammals pay a price for their dental specialization: Reptiles can repeatedly replace teeth throughout their life, whereas mammals are limited to two sets. The first set serves immature animals and is replaced by the permanent adult teeth.

The earliest primate-like creatures emerged when a milder climate returned, favoring the spread of dense tropical and subtropical forests over much of the earth. The adaptive radiation of mammals included the evolutionary development of **arboreal** (tree-living) mammals from which primates evolved. The relatively small size of the earliest primates allowed them to use tree branches not accessible to larger competitors and predators. Arboreal life opened up an abundant new food supply. Primates could gather leaves, flowers, fruits, insects, birds' eggs, and even nesting birds, rather than waiting for them to fall to the ground. Natural selection favored those who judged depth correctly and gripped the branches tightly. The animals that survived life in the trees passed on their genes to succeeding generations.

arboreal Living in the trees.

diurnal Active during the day and at rest at night.

derived Characteristics appearing in a later species that did not occur in ancestral populations.

ancestral Characteristics appearing in a later species that also occurred in ancient populations.

convergent evolution In biological evolution, a process by which unrelated populations develop similarities to one another due to similar function rather than shared ancestry.

Unlike their nocturnal ancestors, most primate species today are **diurnal**—active in the day. Being active in the day increased mammals' reliance on their sight, which led to greater learning capacity in the primate brain. Unlike reptiles, who process visual information with neurons in the retina, mammals process visual information in the brain, permitting integration with information received through other senses such as sound, touch, taste, and smell. The transition to diurnal life in the trees involved important biological adjustments that helped shape the biology and behavior of humans today.

Primate Taxonomy

Taxonomies reflect scientists' understanding of the natural world. But because scientific knowledge of evolutionary relationships among living things shifts over time, these classificatory systems are continually under construction. With new scientific discoveries, taxonomic categories have to be redrawn. This can cause disagreement among scientists because new taxonomies reflect perspectives on evolutionary relationships.

When creating a taxonomic grouping, scientists pay particular attention to a group's unique features that appear more recently in evolutionary history, calling these features **derived**. By contrast, **ancestral** characteristics occur not only in the present-day species but also in ancient forms. For example, bilateral symmetry—a body plan in which the right and left sides of the body are mirror images of each other—is an ancestral trait in humans. Because bilateral symmetry characterizes all vertebrates including fish, reptiles, birds, and mammals, it does not contribute to the reconstruction of evolutionary relationships among primates. Instead, scientists look at recently evolved derived features in order to construct evolutionary relationships.

Convergent evolution—in which two or more distant forms develop similarities to one another due to similar function rather than shared ancestry—complicates taxonomic analysis. Classic examples of convergence are discussed in Chapter 2, such as the wings of birds and butterflies, which resemble each other because these structures serve similar functions. Convergent evolution occurs when an environment exerts similar pressures on distantly related organisms, causing these species to resemble each other. It can be challenging to distinguish physical similarities produced by convergent evolution from those resulting from shared ancestry.

Convergence of homologous structures can occur among more closely related groups, such as when an identical structure present within several distinct, distantly related species takes on a similar form. Hind-leg dominance in lemurs—a primate group found on Madagascar, a large, isolated island off the coast of Africa—and in humans provides an example of convergence. Most primates possess hind limbs that are either shorter or of the same length as the forelimbs. Though lemurs and humans are distantly related, the pattern of locomotion in both species relies on longer hind limbs. Humans walk on two legs, while lemurs use their long legs to push off and propel themselves from tree to tree. Hind-leg dominance appeared separately in these two groups and does not indicate a close evolutionary relationship. Only shared *derived* features establish relationships among groups of species.

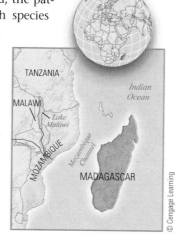

There are two hot spots in the taxonomic classification of primates: one at the level of dividing the primate order into two suborders and the other at the level of the human family and subfamily. In both cases, the older classificatory systems, dating back to the time of Linnaeus, developed from shared visible physical characteristics. By contrast, the newer taxonomic systems depend upon genetic analyses. Molecular evidence has confirmed the close relationship between humans and other primates. Genetic comparisons have also challenged evolutionary relationships inferred from physical characteristics. Laboratory methods involving genetic comparisons range from scanning species' entire genomes to comparing the precise sequences of base pairs in DNA, RNA, or amino acids in proteins.

Scientists studying taxonomy use data derived from both genetics and from morphology (body form and structure). They refer to the overall similarity of body plans within taxonomic groupings as a **grade**. The examination of shared sequences of DNA and RNA allows researchers to establish a **clade**, a taxonomic grouping that contains a single common ancestor and all of its descendants. Genetic analyses allow for precise quantification, but what the numbers mean is not always clear (recall the Original Study, "Ninety-Eight Percent Alike: What Our Similarity to Apes Tells Us about Our Understanding of Genetics" from Chapter 2).

The Linnaean system divides primates into two suborders: **prosimian** (Prosimii from Latin for "before monkeys"), which include lemurs, lorises, and tarsiers, and **anthropoid** (Anthropoidea from Greek for "human-like"), which include monkeys, apes, and humans. Some refer to prosimians as the "lower primates" because they resemble the earliest fossil primates. Most prosimians are cat-sized or smaller, although some larger forms existed in the past. Prosimians also retain certain ancestral features common among nonprimate mammals that the anthropoids have lost over time, such as claws and moist, naked skin on their noses.

In Asia and Africa, all prosimians are nocturnal and arboreal creatures—again, like the fossil primates. However, a variety of diurnal ground-dwelling prosimians inhabit the island of Madagascar. In the rest of the world, only anthropoids are diurnal. Anthropoids are sometimes referred to as "higher primates" because they appeared later in evolutionary history and because of a lingering belief that the group including humans is more "evolved." From a contemporary biological perspective, no species is more evolved than any other.

Molecular evidence led scientists to propose a new primate taxonomy (Table 3.1). Researchers discovered a close genetic relationship between the tarsiers—nocturnal tree-dwellers who resemble lemurs and lorises—and monkeys and apes (Goodman et al., 1994). The taxonomic scheme reflecting this genetic relationship places lemurs and lorises in the subdivision **strepsirrhine** (Strepsirrhini, from the Greek for "turned nose"). In turn, the subdivision **haplorrhine** (Haplorrhini, Greek for "simple nose") contains the tarsiers, monkeys, and apes, separating tarsiers from monkeys and apes at the infraorder level. Although the newer taxonomic scheme accurately reflects genetic relationships, comparisons among grades, or general levels of organization, in the older prosimian and anthropoid classification make more sense when examining morphology and lifeways.

The older taxonomic scheme divides the anthropoid primates into two infraorders: **platyrrhine** (Platyrrhini, Greek for "flat-nosed"), or New World monkeys, and **catarrhine** (Catarrhini, Greek for "drooping nose"), consisting of the superfamilies Cercopithecoidea (Old World monkeys) and Hominoidea (apes). Although "New World" and "Old World" reflect a Eurocentric vision of history (the Americas were considered new only to European explorers and not to the indigenous peoples already living there), these terms have evolutionary and geologic relevance with respect to primates, as we will see in later chapters. Old World monkeys and apes, including humans, have a 40-million-year shared evolutionary history in Africa distinct from the course taken by anthropoid primates in the tropical Americas. "Old World" in this context represents the origins of anthropoid primates.

grade A general level of biological organization seen among a group of species; useful for constructing evolutionary relationships.

clade A taxonomic grouping that contains a single common ancestor and all of its descendants.

prosimian The suborder of primates that includes lemurs, lorises, and tarsiers.

anthropoid The suborder of primates that includes New World monkeys, Old World monkeys, and apes (including humans).

strepsirrhine The subdivision within the primate order based on shared genetic characteristics; includes lemurs and lorises.

haplorrhine The subdivision within the primate order based on shared genetic characteristics; includes tarsiers, New World monkeys, Old World monkeys, and apes (including humans).

platyrrhine The primate infraorder that includes New World monkeys.

catarrhine The primate infraorder that includes Old World monkeys, apes, and humans.

TABLE 3.1

Two Alternative Taxonomies for the Primate Order: Differing Placement of Tarsiers

Suborder	Infraorder	Superfamily (Family)	Location
I.			
Prosimii (lower primates)	Lemuriformes Lorisiformes	Lemuroidea (lemurs, indriids, and aye-ayes) Lorisoidea (lorises) Tarsioidea (tarsiers)	Madagascar Asia and Africa Asia
Anthropoidea (higher primates)	Platyrrhini (New World monkeys) Catarrhini	Ceboidea Cercopithecoidea (Old World monkeys) Hominoidea (apes and humans)	Tropical Americas Africa and Asia Africa and Asia (humans worldwide)
II.			
Strepsirrhini	Lemuriformes Lorisiformes	Lemuroidea (lemurs, indriids, and aye-ayes) Lorisoidea (lorises)	Madagascar Asia and Africa
Haplorrhini	Tarsiiformes Platyrrhini (New World monkeys) Catarrhini	Tarsioidea (tarsiers) Ceboidea Cercopithecoidea (Old World monkeys) Hominoidea (apes and humans)	Asia Tropical Americas Africa and Asia Africa and Asia (humans worldwide)

© Cengage Learning

In human evolution, taxonomic controversy derives from relationships established by the molecular evidence among the hominoids. Members of the **hominoid** or ape superfamily—gibbons, siamangs, orangutans, gorillas, chimpanzees, bonobos, and humans—share physical characteristics such as broad shoulders and an absent tail. The human characteristics of bipedalism (walking on two legs) and culture led scientists to think that all the other apes were more closely related to one another than any of them were to humans. As a result they classified humans and their ancestors into the **hominid** family to distinguish them from the other apes.

Advances in molecular analysis of blood proteins and DNA later demonstrated a closer relationship between humans and the African apes (chimps, bonobos, and gorillas) compared to the Asian apes (orangutans and the smaller siamangs and gibbons). Some scientists then proposed that African apes should be included in the hominid family, with humans and their ancestors distinguished from the other African hominoids at the taxonomic level of subfamily, as a **hominin** (Figure 3.4).

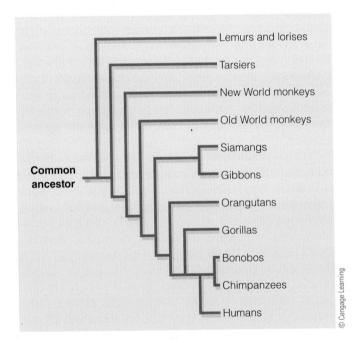

Figure 3.4 Relationships among the Primates
Molecular evidence establishes these relationships among various primate groups. This evidence shows that tarsiers are more closely related to monkeys and apes than to the lemurs and lorises that they resemble physically. Present thinking is that the split between the human and African ape lines took place between 5 and 8 million years ago.

© Cengage Learning

hominoid The taxonomic superfamily within the Old World primates that includes gibbons, siamangs, orangutans, gorillas, chimpanzees, bonobos, and humans.

hominid The African hominoid family that includes humans and their ancestors. Some scientists—recognizing the close relationship of humans, chimps, bonobos, and gorillas—use the term *hominid* to refer to all African hominoids. They then divide the hominid family into two subfamilies: the Paninae (chimps, bonobos, and gorillas) and the Homininae (humans and their ancestors).

hominin The taxonomic subfamily or tribe within the primates that includes humans and our ancestors.

Although scientists today agree about the close relationship among humans, chimpanzees, bonobos, and gorillas, they disagree about whether to use the term *hominid* or *hominin* to describe the taxonomic grouping of humans and their ancestors. Museum displays and much of the popular press tend to retain the old term *hominid*, emphasizing the visible differences between humans and the other African apes. Scientists and publications using *hominin* (such as *National Geographic*) emphasize the importance of genetics in establishing relationships among species. More than name games, these word choices reflect theoretical relationships among closely related species.

The DNA sequences of humans and African apes are 98 percent identical, but the organization of DNA into chromosomes differs between humans and other great apes. Bonobos and chimps, like gorillas and orangutans, possess an extra pair of chromosomes compared to humans; in humans, however, two medium-sized chromosomes have fused together to form chromosome 2. Chromosomes are numbered according to their size as they are viewed microscopically, so that chromosome 2 is the second largest of the human chromosomes (recall Figure 2.7). Of the other pairs, eighteen are virtually identical between humans and the African apes, whereas the remaining ones have been reshuffled.

Overall, there are fewer differences between humans and other African apes compared to those found between gibbons (with twenty-two pairs of chromosomes) and siamangs (twenty-five pairs of chromosomes). In captivity, these two closely related species have produced live hybrid offspring. Most studies suggest a closer relationship between the two species in the genus *Pan* (chimps and bonobos) and humans than either has to gorillas. The complete DNA sequencing of the western lowland gorilla suggests that this species split from chimps and humans close to 10 million years ago (Scally et al., 2012). Chimps and bonobos are, of course, more closely related to each other than either is to gorillas or humans.

Primate Characteristics

The living primates, including humans, share a number of features. For instance, in baseball, a pitcher can strike out a batter due to the primate characteristics of grasping, throwing, and seeing in three dimensions. Many primate characteristics developed from life in the trees, their arboreal niche. For animals that preyed upon the insects living on the fruit and flowers of trees and shrubs, dexterous hands and keen vision would have been enormously adaptive.

Primate Teeth

The primate diet—shoots, leaves, insects, and fruits—did not require the specialization of teeth seen in other mammals. In most primates (humans included), on each side of each jaw, in front, are two straight-edged, chisel-like broad teeth called incisors (**Figure 3.5**). There is often a large, flaring, fanglike canine tooth behind each incisor. Canines are used for defense as well as tearing and shredding food.

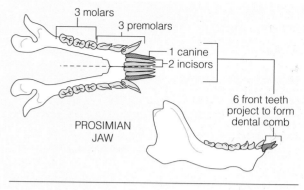

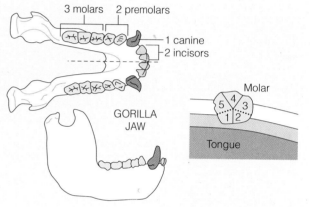

Figure 3.5 **Primate Dentition**

Because the exact number and shape of the teeth differ among primate groups, teeth are frequently used to identify evolutionary relationships and group membership. Prosimians (*top*), with a dental formula of 2-1-3-3, possess two incisors, one canine, three premolars, and three molars on each side of their upper and lower jaws. Also, lower canines and incisors project forward, forming a "dental comb," which is used for grooming. A dental formula of 2-1-2-3, typical of Old World monkeys and apes, can be seen in the gorilla jaw (*bottom*). Note the large projecting canines. On one of the molars, the cusps are numbered to illustrate the Y5 pattern found in hominoids.

Behind the canines, the premolars and molars (the "cheek teeth") grind and chew food. Molars erupt through the gums over the course of a young primate's growth and development (6-year molars, 12-year molars, and wisdom teeth in humans). Thus, different kinds of teeth served the functions of grasping, cutting, and grinding. The exact number of premolars and molars and the shape of individual teeth differ among primate groups (Table 3.2).

The course of primate evolution includes a trend toward a reduction in the number and size of the teeth. The ancestral **dental formula**, or pattern of tooth type and number in mammals, consists of three incisors, one canine, five premolars, and three molars (expressed as

dental formula The number of each tooth type (incisors, canines, premolars, and molars) on one-half of each jaw. Unlike other mammals, primates possess equal numbers on their upper and lower jaws, making the dental formula for the species a single series of numbers.

TABLE 3.2

Primate Anatomical Variation and Specialization

Primate Group	Skull and Face	Dental Formula and Specializations	Locomotor Pattern and Morphology	Tail and Other Skeletal Specializations
Earliest fossil primates	Eye not fully surrounded by bone	2-1-4-3		
Prosimians	Complete ring of bone surrounding eye Upper lip bound down to the gum Long snout	2-1-3-3 Dental comb for grooming	Hind-leg dominance for vertical clinging and leaping	Tail present
Anthropoids	Forward-facing eyes fully enclosed in bone Free upper lip Shorter snout			
New World monkeys		2-1-3-3	Quadrupedal	Prehensile (grasping) tail in some
Old World monkeys		2-1-2-3 Four-cusped molars	Quadrupedal	Tail present
Apes		2-1-2-3 Y5 molars on lower jaw	Suspensory hanging apparatus	No tail

© Cengage Learning

3-1-5-3) on each side of the jaw, top and bottom, for a total of forty-eight teeth. In the early stages of primate evolution, one incisor and one premolar were lost on each side of each jaw, resulting in a dental pattern of 2-1-4-3. This change differentiated primates from other mammals.

Over the millennia, as the first and second premolars became smaller and eventually disappeared altogether, the third and fourth premolars grew larger and added a second pointed projection, or cusp, thus becoming "bicuspid." In humans, all eight premolars are bicuspid, but in other Old World anthropoids, the lower first premolar is not bicuspid. Instead, it is a specialized, single-cusped tooth with a sharp edge to act with the upper canine as a shearing mechanism. The molars, meanwhile, evolved from a three-cusp pattern to one with four and even five cusps. The five-cusp pattern is characteristic of the lower molars of living and extinct hominoids. Because the grooves separating the five cusps of hominoid lower molars look like the letter Y, hominoid lower molars are said to have a Y5 pattern. Humans have departed somewhat from the Y5 pattern as tooth and jaw size reduced such that the second and third molars generally have only four cusps. Four- and five-cusp molars economically combined the functions of grasping, cutting, and grinding in one tooth.

The evolutionary trend for human dentition has generally been toward economy, with fewer, smaller, more efficient teeth doing more work. With thirty-two teeth (a 2-1-2-3 dental formula shared with the Old World

monkeys and apes), we possess fewer teeth than some primates. However, this trend does not indicate that species with more teeth are less evolved; it only shows that their evolution followed a different path.

The canines of most primates develop into long dagger-like teeth that enable them to rip open tough husks of fruit and other foods (Figure 3.6). In many species, males possess larger canine teeth than females. This sex difference is an example of **sexual dimorphism**—differences between the sexes in the shape or size of a feature. Adult males frequently use these large canines for social communication. If an adult male gorilla, baboon, or mandrill raises his upper lip to display his large, sharp canines, a youngster becomes submissive. The oversized roots of smaller human canines suggest larger canines in our ancestry.

Primate Sensory Organs

Adaptation to arboreal life involved changes in primates' sensory organs. The sense of smell, vital for the earliest ground-dwelling, nocturnal mammals, enabled them to sniff out their food and detect hidden predators in the dark. But for active tree life during daylight, good vision provides advantages for judging the location of the next branch or tasty morsel. Accordingly, the sense of smell declined in primates over time, while vision became highly developed.

Travel through the trees demands judgments concerning depth, direction, distance, and the spatial relationships between objects such as vines or branches. Monkeys, apes, and humans achieved this through binocular stereoscopic color vision (Figure 3.7), the ability to see the world in the three dimensions of height, width, and depth. **Binocular vision** (in which two eyes sit next

sexual dimorphism Within a single species, differences between males and females in the shape or size of a feature not directly related to reproduction, such as body size or canine tooth shape and size.

binocular vision Vision with increased depth perception from two eyes set next to each other, allowing their visual fields to overlap.

to each other on the same plane so that their visual fields overlap) and nerve connections that run from each eye to both sides of the brain confer complete depth perception characteristic of three-dimensional or **stereoscopic vision**. This arrangement allows nerve cells to integrate the images derived from each eye. Increased brain size in the visual area in primates, and a greater complexity at nerve connections, also contribute to stereoscopic color vision.

Visual acuity varies throughout the primate order in terms of both color and spatial perception. Prosimians, most of whom are nocturnal (like the slow loris from the beginning of this chapter), lack color vision. The eyes of lemurs and lorises (but not tarsiers) are capable of reflecting light off the retina, the surface where nerve fibers gather images in the back of the eye, intensifying the limited light in the forest at night. In addition, prosimian vision is binocular without the benefits of stereoscopy. Their eyes look out from either side of their muzzle or snout. Though there is some overlap of visual fields, their nerve fibers do not cross from each eye to both halves of the brain.

By contrast, monkeys, apes, and humans possess both color and stereoscopic vision. The ability to distinguish colors allows anthropoid primates to choose ripe red fruits

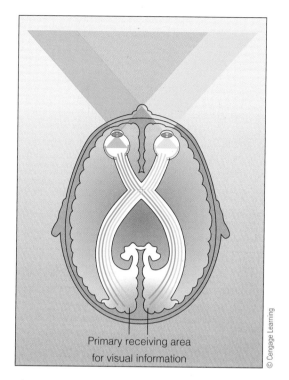

Primary receiving area
for visual information

© Cengage Learning

Figure 3.7 Primate Vision
Monkeys, apes, and humans possess binocular stereoscopic vision. Binocular vision refers to overlapping visual fields due to forward-facing eyes. Three-dimensional or stereoscopic vision comes from binocular vision and the transmission of information from each eye to both sides of the brain.

or tender, immature green leaves due to their coloration. This markedly improves their diet compared to most other mammals. In addition to color vision, anthropoid primates possess a unique structure called the *fovea centralis*, or central pit, in the retina of each eye. Like a camera lens, this feature enables the animal to focus on a particular object for acutely clear perception without sacrificing visual contact with the object's surroundings.

The primates' emphasis on visual acuity came at the expense of their sense of smell. Smells are processed in the forebrain, and in animals that depend greatly on the sense of smell, the forebrain projects into the snout. A large protruding snout, however, interferes with stereoscopic vision. As primates became diurnal tree-dwelling animals in search of insects, they no longer needed to live "nose to the ground," sniffing the earth in search of food. The anthropoids in particular have the least-developed sense of smell of all land animals. Though our sense of smell allows humans to distinguish perfumes, and even to distinguish family members from strangers, our brains have come to emphasize vision rather than smell. Prosimians, by contrast,

D. Hurst/Alamy

Figure 3.6 Powerful Canines
Though the massive canine teeth of some male primates are serious weapons, they are more often used to communicate rather than to draw blood. By raising his lip to flash his canines, this mandrill will get the young members of his group in line right away. Over the course of human evolution, overall canine size decreased, as did differences in canine size between males and females.

stereoscopic vision Complete three-dimensional vision, or depth perception, from binocular vision and nerve connections that run from each eye to both sides of the brain, allowing nerve cells to integrate the images derived from each eye.

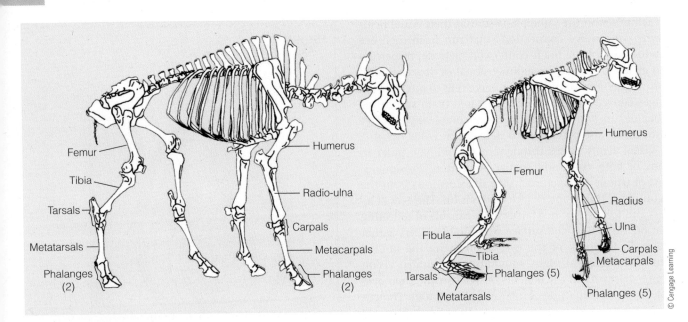

© Cengage Learning

Figure 3.8 Skeletal Comparisons of Gorilla and Bison
All primates possess the same ancestral vertebrate limb pattern seen in reptiles and amphibians, consisting of a single upper long bone, two lower long bones, and five radiating digits (fingers and toes), as seen in this gorilla skeleton (*right*). Other mammals such as bison (*left*) have a modified version of this pattern. In the course of evolution, bison have lost all but two of their digits, which form their hooves. The second long bone in the lower part of the limb is reduced. Note also the joining of the skull and vertebral column in these skeletons. In bison (as in most mammals) the skull projects forward from the vertebral column, but in semi-erect gorillas, the vertebral column is further beneath the skull.

still rely more on smell than on vision, and they possess numerous scent glands for marking objects in their territories.

Arboreal primates also have an acute sense of touch. An effective feeling and grasping mechanism helps prevent them from falling while speeding through the trees. The early mammals from which primates evolved possessed tiny touch-sensitive hairs at the tips of their hands and feet. In primates, sensitive pads backed up by nails on the tips of the animals' fingers and toes replaced these hairs.

The Primate Brain

These changes in sensory organs correspond to changes in the primate brain. An increase in brain size, particularly in the cerebral hemispheres—the areas supporting conscious thought—occurred in the course of primate evolution. In monkeys, apes, and humans, the cerebral hemispheres completely cover the cerebellum, the part of the brain that coordinates muscles and maintains body balance.

This development led to the flexibility seen in primate behavior. Instead of relying on reflexes controlled by the cerebellum, primates constantly react to a variety of features in the environment. Messages from the hands and feet, eyes and ears, and from the sensors of balance, movement, heat, touch, and pain are simultaneously relayed to the cerebral cortex. The cortex had to evolve considerably

in order to receive, analyze, and coordinate these impressions and transmit the appropriate response back down to the motor nerves. This enlarged, responsive cerebral cortex provides the biological basis for flexible behavior patterns found in all primates, including humans.

If the evolution of visual acuity and daytime activity led to larger primate brains, it is also likely that hunting insects in the trees played a part in brain enlargement. This would have required great agility and muscular coordination, favoring development of the brain centers. Interestingly, many higher mental faculties developed in an area alongside the motor centers of the brain. Another hypothesis that may account for primate brain enlargement involves the use of hands as tactile instruments to replace the teeth and jaws or snout. The hands assumed some of the grasping, tearing, and dividing functions of the jaws, again requiring development of the brain centers for more complete coordination.

The Primate Skeleton

The skeleton gives an animal with an internal backbone, or a **vertebrate**, its basic shape, supports the soft tissues, and helps protect vital internal organs (Figure 3.8). In primates, for example, the skull protects the brain and eyes. A number of factors distinguish the shape of the primate skull from those of most other mammals: changes in dentition, changes in the sensory organs of sight and smell, and increased brain size.

The primate braincase, or **cranium**, tends to be high and vaulted. Anthropoid primates possess a solid bony

vertebrate An animal with a backbone, including fish, amphibians, reptiles, birds, and mammals.

cranium The braincase of the skull.

Figure 3.9 Brachiation
All apes or hominoids possess a suspensory hanging apparatus that allows them to hang from the branches of the forest canopy. But only gibbons and siamangs are masters of brachiation—swinging from branch to branch. These hominoids can also walk bipedally for brief periods of time when they need their arms free for carrying, but they cannot sustain bipedal locomotion for more than 50 to 100 meters (about the same in yards). Hominoid anatomy, the human line excepted, is better adapted to knuckle-walking and hanging in the trees.

partition between the eye and the temple, which protects their eyes from the contraction of the chewing muscles immediately next to them. The **foramen magnum** (Latin for "big opening") is the large opening at the base of the skull; the spinal cord passes through this opening to connect to the brain. The foramen magnum provides important clues about evolutionary relationships. In most mammals, as in dogs and horses, this opening faces directly backward, with the skull projecting forward from the vertebral column. In humans, by contrast, the vertebral column joins the skull toward the center of its base, thereby placing the skull in the balanced position required for habitual upright posture. Other primates, though they frequently cling, sit, or hang with their body upright, are not as fully committed to upright posture as humans, so their foramen magnum is situated further back.

In anthropoid primates, the snout or muzzle portion of the skull reduces in size as they rely more upon vision. The smaller snout interferes less with stereoscopic vision and enables the eyes to take a frontal position. As a result, primates have flatter faces than some other mammals.

Below the primate skull and the neck is the **clavicle**, or collarbone, a bone found in ancestral mammals but lost in some mammals such as cats. The size of the clavicle varies across the primate order according to pattern of locomotion. Quadrupedal primates like monkeys with narrow, sturdy bodies possess smaller clavicles. Apes, by contrast, have broad clavicles that orient the arms at the side rather than at the front of the body, forming part of this group's **suspensory hanging apparatus** (see Table 3.2). The clavicle also supports the **scapula** (shoulder blade) and muscles required for flexible yet powerful arm movement—permitting large-bodied apes to hang suspended below tree branches and to move through **brachiation**, or swinging from branch to branch (Figure 3.9).

The limbs of the primate skeleton follow the basic ancestral plan seen in the earliest vertebrates. Other animals possess limbs specialized to optimize their pattern of locomotion. In each primate arm or leg, the upper portion of the limb has a single long bone, the lower portion has two long bones, and the hands or feet have five radiating digits

(phalanges). The structural characteristics of the primate foot and hand make them excellent **prehensile** (grasping) devices for use in moving from branch to branch: The digits are extremely flexible, the big toe is fully **opposable** to the other digits (in all but humans and their immediate ancestors), and the thumb is opposable to the other digits.

The flexible vertebrate limb pattern in primates was a valuable asset to evolving humans. Grasping hands, for example, contributed to our own ancestors' manufacture and use of tools, a pathway that led to the revolutionary ability to adapt through culture. By comparing humans to other primates, we see that many of the characteristics we consider distinctly human are, in fact, variants of typical primate traits. We humans look the way we do because we are primates, and the differences between us and our primate cousins—especially the apes—are more differences of degree than of kind.

Living Primates

Except for a few species of Old World monkeys who live in temperate climates and humans who inhabit the entire globe, living primates inhabit warm areas of the world. We will briefly explore the diversity of the five natural groupings of living primates: lemurs and lorises, tarsiers, New World monkeys, Old World monkeys, and apes. We will examine each group's distinctive habitat, biological features, and behavior.

---

foramen magnum A large opening in the skull; the spinal cord passes through this opening to connect to the brain.

clavicle The collarbone connecting the sternum (breastbone) with the scapula (shoulder blade).

suspensory hanging apparatus The broad powerful shoulder joints and muscles found in all the hominoids, allowing these large-bodied primates to hang suspended below the tree branches.

scapula The shoulder blade.

brachiation Moving from branch to branch using the arms, with the body hanging suspended below.

prehensile Having the ability to grasp.

opposable Having the ability to bring the thumb or big toe in contact with the tips of the other digits on the same hand or foot in order to grasp objects.

blickwinkel/Huetter/Alamy

Figure 3.10 Lemurs
Over the course of their evolutionary history, primates came to rely more on their vision than
their sense of smell. Prosimians, the earliest group of primates to appear, maintain their primary
reliance on smell. On the island of Madagascar, home to many species of diurnal ground-dwelling
lemurs, such as these ring-tailed lemurs, the prosimians mark their territory and communicate
through smelly messages left for others with a squirt from the glands located on their wrists.

Lemurs and Lorises

Lemurs live only on the large island of Madagascar (off the
east coast of Africa), whereas lorises range from Africa to
southern and eastern Asia. Lemurs encountered no competition from anthropoid primates until humans arrived
on Madagascar; they are diurnal (active during the day)
and, in some cases, ground-dwelling (Figure 3.10). By
contrast, lorises, like the slow loris from the beginning of
the chapter, are nocturnal and arboreal.

All these animals are small, with none larger than a
good-sized dog. In general body outline, they resemble
rodents and insectivores, with short pointed snouts, large
pointed ears, and big eyes. Lemurs and lorises resemble
nonprimate mammals in that the upper lip is bound down
to the gums, limiting their range of facial expression. The
split, moist, naked skin on the nose around the nostrils
facilitates a keen sense of smell. Most also have a long tail;
the ring-tailed lemur's is similar to that of a raccoon.

Lemurs and lorises have typical primate "hands,"
although they use them simultaneously rather than one
at a time. Their fingers and toes are particularly strong

with sensitive pads and flattened nails located at their
tips. They retain a claw on their second toe, sometimes
called a grooming claw, which they use for scratching and
cleaning. Lemurs and lorises possess another unique structure for grooming: a dental comb made up of the lower
incisors and canines, which projects forward from the jaw
and can be run through the fur. Behind the incisors and
canines, lemurs and lorises have three premolars and molars, resulting in a dental formula of 2-1-3-3.

Lemurs and lorises have scent glands at their wrists,
under their arms, and sometimes in their anal region that
they use for communication. Individuals leave smelly
messages for one another by rubbing their scent glands
on tree branches or other fixtures of the environment.
Through such olfactory clues, lemurs and lorises can recognize distinct individuals within their own group as well
as pinpoint their location and physical state. They also
use scent to mark their territory, thus communicating
to members of other groups. In the case of the slow loris
from the beginning of the chapter, these scent glands
produce a liquid that, when mixed with saliva, potentially
causes an allergic reaction in predators. Whether this is a

© 2017 Cengage Learning

Figure 3.11 Vertical Clinging and Leaping
Some primates, including lemurs and tarsiers, use a mode of arboreal locomotion called vertical clinging and leaping. These primates use their elongated back legs to propel themselves from one vertical branch to another. They do a "180" in the air and land facing the second vertical branch or support. This allows the primates to move quickly through the forest while keeping their bodies upright.

defense mechanism, a deterrent, or simply a byproduct of the lorises' scent communication is still being studied.

With hind legs longer than their front legs, lemurs and lorises keep their forelimbs in a palms-down position when they move on all fours. Some species can also move from tree to tree by **vertical clinging and leaping** (Figure 3.11). With their distinctive mix of characteristics, lemurs and lorises appear to occupy a place between the anthropoid primates and insectivores, the mammalian order that includes moles and shrews.

Tarsiers

Outwardly, tarsiers resemble lemurs and lorises (Figure 3.12). Molecular evidence, however, indicates a closer relationship to monkeys, apes, and humans. In the structure of the nose and lips, and the part of the brain governing vision, tarsiers most resemble monkeys. The head, eyes, and ears of these kitten-sized arboreal creatures are huge in proportion to the body. They have the remarkable ability to turn their heads 180 degrees so they can see where they have been as well as where they are going. Their digits end in platelike adhesive discs.

Tarsiers are mainly nocturnal insect-eaters, occupying a niche similar to that of the earliest ancestral primates. They are named for the elongated tarsal, or foot bone, that gives them the leverage to jump 6 feet or more. Like some lemurs, tarsiers possess longer hind limbs than front limbs, which they use for vertical clinging and leaping.

New World Monkeys

New World monkeys live in tropical forests from southern Mexico to northern Argentina. In outward body plan,

Nature Picture Library/Corbis

Figure 3.12 Tarsiers
With their large eyes, tarsiers are well adapted for nocturnal life. If humans possessed eyes proportionally the same size as tarsiers relative to the size of our faces, our eyes would be as big as oranges. To humans, these little primates seem remarkably quiet, but scientists have discovered that in fact tarsiers communicate using pure ultrasound, which is inaudible to us. Their hearing range is similar to that of bats and far surpasses the hearing of all other primates. In their nocturnal habit and outward appearance, tarsiers resemble lemurs and lorises. Genetically, however, they are more closed related to monkeys and apes, causing scientists to rework the suborder divisions in primate taxonomy to reflect this evolutionary relationship.

vertical clinging and leaping Using the back legs to propel oneself from a vertical branch while rotating 180 degrees, enabling one to land facing a second vertical branch.

they closely resemble Old World monkeys (discussed soon), except that New World monkeys possess flat noses with widely separated, outward-flaring nostrils. Their infraorder name Platyrrhini (from the Greek for "flat-nosed") comes from this characteristic.

There are five different families of New World monkeys, and they range in size from less than a pound to over 30 pounds. New World monkeys have long tails. All members of one group, the family Atelidae, possess prehensile or grasping tails that they use as a fifth limb (Figure 3.13). The naked skin on the underside of their tail resembles the sensitive skin found at the tips of our fingers and is even covered with whorls like fingerprints.

Because of primatology's emphasis on human origins, researchers have tended to study Old World species more extensively than New World species. The arboreal habitat of New World monkeys also makes it more difficult for researchers to observe them. In recent decades, however, primatologists have conducted numerous long-range field studies on a variety of species of New World monkeys.

For example, anthropologist Karen Strier has studied the woolly spider monkey, or muriqui, in the state of Minas Gerais, Brazil, for over three decades. Her field studies progressed from examining muriqui diet, social structure, and **demographic** information (population characteristics, such as the number of individuals of each age and sex) to tracking the reproductive cycles and health of these large, peaceful forest-dwellers. She pioneered a noninvasive method to measure reproductive hormone levels and the presence of parasites through analysis of the feces of individual animals—catching feces (in a gloved hand) the moment it drops from the trees or quickly retrieving it from the ground. Through analysis of these samples, Strier was able to document correlations between diet and fertility.

Strier also documented a reduced parasite load in muriquis that consumed certain plants—apparently for their medicinal or therapeutic value. Amazonian peoples have been known to use some of these plants for the same reason. As these human populations have become increasingly removed from their traditional lifeways due to globalization and modernization, the muriqui remain a valuable resource to reclaim knowledge of the forest. According to Strier, "While traditional peoples of the Amazon have survived long enough to impart some of their knowledge of forest plants, the indigenous human societies of the Atlantic forest are long gone. The muriqui and other monkeys may provide humans with their best guides to the forest's medicinal values" (Strier, 1993, p. 42). Field studies like Strier's not only have contributed to our understanding of the behavior and biology of New World monkeys but have also played a

Figure 3.13 New World Spider Monkey
Grasping hands and three-dimensional vision enable primates like this South American spider monkey to lead an active life in the trees. In some New World monkey species, a grasping or prehensile tail makes tree life even easier. The naked skin on the underside of the tail resembles the sensitive skin found at the tips of our fingers and is even covered with whorls like fingerprints. This sensory skin allows New World monkeys to use their tails as a fifth limb.

demographic A population characteristic such as the number of individuals of each age and sex.

Ingo Arndt/Getty Images/Minden Pictures

© Cengage Learning

Platyrrhines walk on all fours with their palms down and scamper along tree branches in search of fruit, which they eat sitting upright. Although New World monkeys spend much of their time in the trees, they rarely hang suspended below the branches or swing from limb to limb by their arms and have not developed the extremely long forelimbs and broad shoulders characteristic of the apes.

Old World Monkeys

Old World monkeys, which are divided from the apes at the taxonomic level of superfamily, may live on the ground or in trees, using a quadrupedal (four-footed) pattern of locomotion on the ground or a palms-down position in the trees. Old World or catarrhine (from the Greek for "sharp-nosed") primates resemble New World monkeys in their basic body plan, but their noses are distinctive, with closely spaced, downward-pointing nostrils. Two subfamilies, the Cercopithecinae and the Colobinae, contain eleven and ten genera, respectively. Old World monkeys occupy a broader range of habitats compared to New World monkeys, which occupy only tropical forests.

Figure 3.14 The Proboscis Monkey
Although all Old World monkeys share certain features like a narrow body plan, a nonprehensile tail, and a 2-1-2-3 dental formula, some have unusual specializations. The proboscis monkey, found in the mangrove swamps of Borneo, is known for its unusual protruding nose, which provides a chamber for extra resonance for its vocalizations. When a monkey is alarmed, the nose fills with blood so that the resonating chamber becomes even more enlarged.

major role in bringing back a number of species from the brink of extinction.

New World monkeys—unlike Old World monkeys, apes, and humans—possess a 2-1-3-3 dental formula (three, rather than two, premolars on each side of each jaw). This is not as much a functional distinction as it is a difference in evolutionary path. The common ancestor of Old World anthropoids and New World anthropoids possessed this 2-1-3-3 dental pattern. In the New World species this pattern remained, while in the Old World species a molar was lost.

Some Old World monkeys such as mandrills (pictured in Figure 3.6) have brightly colored faces and genitals. Others, like proboscis monkeys (Figure 3.14), have long, droopy noses. They all possess a 2-1-2-3 dental formula (two, rather than three, premolars on each side of each jaw) and tails that are never prehensile. They may be either arboreal or terrestrial, using a quadrupedal pattern of locomotion on the ground or in the trees in a palms-down position. They have narrow bodies with hind limbs and forelimbs of equal length, a reduced clavicle (collarbone), and relatively fixed and sturdy shoulder, elbow, and wrist joints.

BIOCULTURAL CONNECTION

Gibbons and Sopranos Both Need to Be Heard

What does this white-handed gibbon have in common with an opera singer? They are both primates, of course, and it is possible they can both be a little flashy. But more than that, they sometimes use their voices in similar ways. Until recently, scientists believed that humans' unique vocal anatomy was responsible for our power of speech. But Takeshi Nishimura and his colleagues at the Primate Research Institute at Japan's Kyoto University found that the gibbons they studied used vocal techniques similar to those of opera singers, particularly sopranos. This indicates that it is not just the gibbons' vocal anatomy, but how they use it, that produces their resonant calls.[a] Both gibbons and singers need to be heard over great distances or above other sounds, and both have tapped into the power of harmonics to do so.

When we listen to music or other sounds, what we hear as one "note" is actually made up of different harmonics, with the strongest—the pitch itself—being the fundamental frequency. What do the other harmonics sound like? The easiest way to hear them, perhaps, is to listen to a bell—the bigger, the better— and to try to pick out the shimmery sounds surrounding the main tone the bell is producing. By

manipulating these other harmonics using their vocal tracts and other parts of their anatomies, both gibbons and sopranos can create a sound that carries—either to friends on the other side of the jungle or over the sounds of an exuberant orchestra without any artificial amplification.

Scientists have known that gibbons and humans have similar vocal physiology, but what surprised Nishimura and his colleagues is the similar way in which gibbons and singers manipulate their sound. To begin, in the case of both primates, a stream of air vibrates the vocal folds in the larynx (voice box), producing a sound. As the sound travels toward the mouth, there are a number of ways in which it can be finessed. The most important similarity the researchers found between gibbons and sopranos is in how they shape their vocal tracts (the tubes connecting the mouth to the lungs). When the vocal tract is shaped to match the pitch the vocal folds are producing, the sound becomes a lot stronger and more resonant.[b] This is very different from what we think of as shouting, as it is incredibly efficient and is not as tiring for the voice.

To try out your own resonant voice, think about what your throat and lungs do when you cry. Does the back of your throat

(your soft palate) seem to stretch? Do your hooty "boo hoos" sound loud and clear, making your nose or your cheeks tingle? That's resonance you're feeling, and it means that when you cry, your body wants others to know about it! No wonder both gibbons and opera singers can command such attention with their striking vocal acrobatics.

Biocultural Question

What biological factors might influence how we use our voices? How about cultural factors? Which of these factors might we share with gibbons or other primates?

[a]Eichenseher, T. (2012, August 25). Gibbons and opera singers use the same voice tools. *National Geographic*. http://news.nationalgeographic.com /news/2012/08/120823-gibbon-song -opera-singer-helium-science-environment/ (retrieved October 27, 2015)
[b]Lougheed, K. (2012, August 23). Helium reveals gibbon's soprano skill: Ape uses operatic techniques to be heard across the forest. *Nature*. http://www.nature.com /news/helium-reveals-gibbon-s-soprano -skill-1.11257 (retrieved October 26, 2015)

Arboreal species of Old World monkeys include the mantled guereza (*Colobus guereza*) monkey, a species known to have been hunted by chimpanzees. Other Old World monkeys are equally at home on the ground and in the trees. These include the macaques—some nineteen species that range from tropical Africa and Asia to Gibraltar on the southern coast of Spain to Japan. At the northern-most portions of their range, these primates inhabit temperate rather than strictly tropical environments.

Baboons, a kind of Old World monkey, have been of particular interest to paleoanthropologists because they live in environments similar to those inhabited by some of our earliest ancestors. Largely terrestrial, baboons have abandoned trees (except for sleeping and refuge) and live in the savannahs, deserts, and highlands of Africa. Somewhat dog-faced, they have long muzzles and a fierce look. They eat leaves, seeds, insects, lizards, and small mammals. Baboons live in large, well-organized troops composed of related females and adult males that have transferred out of other troops.

Other Old World species also have much to tell us. For example, over the past several decades, primatologists have documented primate social learning and innovation in colonies of macaques in Japan. Similarly, field studies of vervet monkeys in eastern and southern Africa have revealed that these Old World monkeys possess sophisticated communication abilities. Fascinating discoveries by primatologists studying all over the world contribute not only to the disciplines of primatology, evolutionary biology, and ecology, but also to our deepening understanding of ourselves. We will look more extensively at the behavior of baboons and a variety of other Old World species, particularly the apes, in the following chapter.

Small and Great Apes

Our closest cousins in the animal world, the apes (gibbons, siamangs, orangutans, gorillas, bonobos, and chimps) are large, wide-bodied primates with no tails. As members of the hominoid superfamily, apes and humans possess a

Anup Shah/Nature Picture Library

Chris Stock/Lebrecht Music and Arts Photo Library/Alamy

Gibbons and opera singers use their vocal tracts in similar ways in order to efficiently project sound across great distances with little strain.

shoulder anatomy specialized for hanging suspended below tree branches. Among apes only small, lithe gibbons and siamangs swing from branch to branch in the pattern known as brachiation. At the opposite extreme are gorillas who generally climb trees by gripping the trunk and branches with their prehensile hands and feet. Although small gorillas may swing between branches, larger individuals limit their swinging to leaning outward from a limb to reach for fruit. Gorillas spend most of their time on the ground. All apes except humans and their immediate ancestors possess arms that are longer than their legs.

When moving on the ground, African apes "knuckle-walk" on the backs of their hands, resting their weight on the middle joints of the fingers. They can stand erect when reaching for fruit or peering over tall grass. The semi-erect posture is natural in apes when on the ground because the curvature of their vertebral column places their high center of gravity in front of their hip joint. Thus, they are both top heavy and front heavy. Though apes can

walk on two legs (bipedally) for short periods of time, they cannot sustain this for more than several minutes.

Standing about a meter high (39 inches), gibbons and siamangs, the small ape species native to Southeast Asia and Malaysia, have compact, slim bodies with extraordinarily long arms compared to their legs. Masters of brachiation, they can also run erect, holding their arms out for balance. Gibbon and siamang males and females are similar in size, living in social groups of two adults and their offspring. Although humans and gibbons are distantly related, they share some surprising vocal capabilities, as discussed in this chapter's Biocultural Connection.

Orangutans found in Borneo and Sumatra are divided into two distinct species. Considerably taller and much heavier than gibbons and siamangs, orangutans possess the bulk that is characteristic of the great apes. With close-set eyes and facial prominence, orangutans appear quite human. The people of Sumatra gave orangutans their name "person of the forest," using the Malay term

Jay Ullal

Figure 3.15 Go Fish
This male orangutan was photographed off Kaja Island in the middle of the Gohong River in Borneo. A resident of a preserve where captive animals are rehabituated into the wild, the young male copied this hunting behavior by watching humans spear fishing along the same river. Although so far the orangutan has been unable to nab a fish with his spear tip, his intent is clear. This rare photograph, along with the first photograph of a swimming orangutan, appears in the beautiful book titled *Thinkers of the Jungle*, by Gerd Schuster, Willie Smits, and photographer Jay Ullal.

orang, which means "person." On the ground, orangutans walk with their forelimbs in a fists-sideways or a palms-down position. They are, however, more arboreal than the African apes (Figure 3.15).

Although sociable by nature, the orangutans of Borneo spend most of their time alone (except in the case of females with young) because they have to forage over a wide area to obtain sufficient food. By contrast, in the swamps of Sumatra an abundance of fruits and insects sustains groups of adults and permits coordinated group travel. Thus, habitats shape their social life.

Gorillas, found in equatorial Africa, are the largest of the apes; an adult male can weigh over 450 pounds, with females about half that size (Figure 3.16). Scientists distinguish between two gorilla species: *Gorilla gorilla* (western) and *Gorilla beringei* (eastern). A thick coat of glossy black hair covers gorilla bodies, and mature males have a silvery gray upper back. With a strikingly

human look about the face, gorillas, like humans, focus on things in their field of vision by directing the eyes rather than moving the head.

Gorillas are mostly ground-dwellers, but the lighter females and young may sleep in trees in carefully constructed nests. Because of their weight, adult males spend less time in trees but raise and lower themselves among tree branches when searching for fruit. Gorillas knuckle-walk, using all four limbs with the fingers of the hands flexed, placing the knuckles instead of the palm on the ground. They stand erect to reach for fruit, to see something more easily, or to threaten perceived sources of danger with their famous chest-beating displays. Although known for these displays (which protect the members of their troop), adult male silverback gorillas are the gentle giants of the forest. Mild-mannered and tolerant, gorillas' behavioral repertoire includes bluffing aggression. As vegetarians, gorillas devote a major

Figure 3.16 Gorillas and Sexual Dimorphism
Primates and many other species exhibit sexual dimorphism, or differences between males and females not related directly to reproduction. Compare these adult gorillas—the male (*right*) and the two females (*left*). Not only is the male gorilla nearly twice the size of the females, but their faces have a different shape. Notice how the females' faces are more like the faces of the young gorillas in the front of the photo. From the earliest embryological stage to adolescence, male and female sex hormones control the process of growth and development so that the male and female adult phenotypes differ in a variety of ways. Scientists have proposed that high levels of sexual dimorphism characterize primate groups in which male–male competition is high.

portion of each day to eating volumes of plant matter to sustain their massive size.

In the past, chimpanzees (see Figure 3.2) and bonobos (Figure 3.17), two closely related species of the genus *Pan*, were thought to be the same species. Bonobos live only in the rainforests of the Democratic Republic of Congo. The common chimpanzee, by contrast, widely inhabits the forested portions of sub-Saharan Africa. Probably the best known of the apes, chimpanzees and bonobos have long been favorites in zoos and circuses. When bonobos were recognized as a distinct species in 1929, they were commonly called "pygmy chimpanzees." *Bonobo* replaced this term because not only does their size range overlap with that of chimpanzees, but—as we will explore in the next chapter—behavior rather than size constitutes the most striking difference between the two groups.

Although chimpanzees and bonobos are thought of as particularly quick and clever, all four great apes are equally intelligent, despite some differences in cognitive styles. More arboreal than gorillas but less so than orangutans, chimpanzees and bonobos forage on the ground much of the day, knuckle-walking like gorillas. At sunset, they return to the trees where they build their nests.

Primate Conservation

This survey of living primates illustrates the diversity of our closest living relatives. To ensure that they will continue to share the planet with us, primate conservation

has become an issue of vital importance. Nearly 50 percent of the known primate species and subspecies face extinction in the next few years.

Threats to Primates

In Asia the statistics are alarming, with more than 70 percent of species threatened and at least 80 percent at risk in Indonesia and Vietnam. This includes all of the great apes, as well as such formerly widespread and adaptable species as rhesus macaques. In the wild these animals are endangered by habitat destruction caused by economic development (farming, lumbering, cattle ranching, rubber tapping), as well as by hunters and trappers who pursue them for food, trophies, research, or as exotic pets.

Primatologists have long known the devastating effects of habitat destruction through the traditional practice of slash-and-burn agriculture. However, primate habitats are at far greater risk from contemporary hazards. War impacts primate habitats significantly, and the effects linger long after the battles. Hunters may use the automatic weapons left behind from human conflicts in their pursuit of bushmeat (wild game). Also, because monkeys and apes are so closely related to humans, some scientists regard them as essential for biomedical research. Although captive breeding provides most of the primates used in laboratories, an active trade in live primates still threatens their native extinction. Globalization also exerts a profound impact on local conditions, which we saw in this chapter's introduction with the popularity of slow loris "pets" due to Internet stardom.

Steve Bloom Images/Alamy

Figure 3.17 A Bonobo
Over a decade of civil war in the Democratic Republic of Congo, the natural habitat of bonobos, and the aftermath of the genocide in neighboring Rwanda have drastically threatened the survival of bonobos, a species known for harmonious social life. These violent times have prompted the hunting of bonobos to feed starving people and the illegal capture of baby bonobos as pets. Primatologists and local conservationists have turned from observational fieldwork to economic development projects aimed at restoring the stability in the region required for the continued survival of bonobos and mountain gorillas.

Conservation Strategies

Because of their vulnerability, the conservation of primates is urgent. Traditional conservation efforts have emphasized habitat preservation above all else, but primatologists have expanded their efforts to include educating local communities and discouraging the hunting of primates for food and medical purposes. Some primatologists even help implement alternative economic strategies for local peoples so that human and primate populations can return to the successful coexistence that prevailed before colonialism and globalization destabilized traditional homelands. This chapter's Anthropology Applied looks at these economic development efforts in the Democratic Republic of Congo.

In direct conservation efforts, primatologists work to maintain some populations in the wild, either by establishing preserves in areas the animals already occupy or by moving populations to suitable habitats. These approaches require constant monitoring and management to ensure that sufficient space and resources remain available. As humans encroach on primate habitats, translocation of primates to protected areas is a viable strategy for primate conservation, and primatologists provide invaluable field studies to guide these relocations.

One example is the work of U.S. primatologist Shirley Strum, who has been studying a troop of free-ranging baboons in Kenya for decades. When the troop began raiding crops and garbage on newly established farms, she was instrumental in successfully moving this troop and two other local troops—130 animals in all—to more sparsely inhabited country 150 miles away. Knowing their habits, Strum was able to trap, tranquilize, and transport the animals to their new home

Figure 3.18 The Golden Lion Tamarin
Because of their exceptional beauty, golden lion tamarin monkeys (or golden marmosets) have been kept as pets since colonial times. More recently, they have also been threatened by development given that they reside in the tropical forest habitats around the popular tourist destination of Rio de Janeiro, Brazil. A major conservation effort was initiated in the 1980s to save these monkeys; it included planting wildlife corridors to connect the remaining forest patches and releasing animals bred in captivity into these newly created environments. Today, live wild births have increased steadily, and the golden lion tamarin population is recovering from the threat of extinction.

© Martin Bennett/Alamy

while preserving the baboons' vital social relationships. Strum's careful work allowed for a smooth transition. With social relations intact, the baboons did not abandon their new homes nor did they block the transfer of new males, with their all-important knowledge of local resources, into the troop. The success of her effort, which had never been tried with baboons, proves that translocation is a realistic technique for saving endangered primate species. However, this conservation effort depends first on available land, where preserves can be established to provide habitats for endangered primates.

A second strategy has been developed to help primates that have been illegally trapped—either for market as pets or for biomedical research. This approach involves returning these recovered animals to their natural habitats. Researchers have established orphanages in which specially trained human substitute mothers support the young primates so that they can gain enough social skills to return to living with their own species.

A third strategy for preventing primate extinction is to maintain breeding colonies in captivity. These colonies encourage psychological and physical well-being, as well

as reproductive success. Primates in zoos and laboratories do not successfully reproduce when deprived of amenities such as opportunities for climbing, materials for nest building, access to other primates for socializing, and places for privacy. Although such features contribute to the success of breeding colonies in captivity, ensuring the survival of our primate cousins in suitable natural habitats is a far greater challenge that humans must meet in the years to come.

Intense primate conservation efforts are beginning to pay off. For example, in recent years, the population size of the mountain gorilla (*Gorilla beringei beringei*) has increased despite the political chaos of the Democratic Republic of Congo. Western lowland gorilla populations (*Gorilla gorilla*) are also on the rise. Similarly, tamarin monkey populations in Brazil (Figure 3.18) have stabilized despite being on the brink of extinction thirty-five years ago, demonstrating the effectiveness of the conservation initiatives put into place. According to primatologist Sylvia Atsalis, "The presence alone of scientists has been shown to protect primates, acting as a deterrent to habitat destruction and hunting. . . . The more people we can send, the more we can help to protect endangered primates" (quoted in Kaplan, 2008).

Saving Our Ape Cousins: Primatologists, Community Action, and the African Wildlife Foundation

The African Wildlife Foundation (AWF) was founded in 1961 with the mission of protecting Africa's wildlife and habitats. In the early 2000s, the AWF, under the leadership of Belgian primatologist Jef Dupain, initiated projects to support the continued survival of bonobos and mountain gorillas in the Democratic Republic of Congo (DRC), as well as to assist local human populations devastated by a decade of civil war in Congo and the massive influx of refugees from neighboring Rwanda. Primatological fieldwork in the region had thrived in sites established during the 1970s, but in the mid-1990s, war and genocide led to the forced removal of primatologists. Although many left the region, Dupain stayed, in part to monitor the kind of bushmeat being bought and sold in the markets in Kinshasa.

With the human population desperate and starving and the poachers armed with automatic weapons, the park rangers charged with protecting the great apes were outnumbered, and many primates perished. A fragile peace was achieved in the region in 2003, and AWF initiatives have been reestablished, including involving local communities in agricultural practices to protect the Congo River and its tributaries and to preserve their precious animal populations.

One AWF program—the African Conservation Schools program—refurbishes or rebuilds local schools to encourage a community focus on conservation. For example,

the Ilima School is in the heart of bonobo territory in the DRC, and its community is now committed to environmental education and preservation. Another example is the old Manyara Ranch Primary School in Tanzania, which had been situated in the middle of an active wildlife corridor; the new location of the rebuilt school avoids having animals and students disrupt each other's activities.[a]

AWF initiatives also include encouraging a variety of alternative economic practices in communities bordering existing wildlife preserves. For example, around the

Virunga National Park, a UNESCO World Heritage site and home to the endangered mountain gorilla, Congolese Enterprise Officer Wellard Makambo monitors beekeeping and a mushroom farm collective, run by Congolese women. He also advises members of a conflict resolution team dealing with the gorillas that have left the wildlife preserve so that they can raid human crops. Local communities require reassurance and restitution, while gorillas need to be returned safely to the park.[b]

Today, Africa's great apes and other wildlife continue to be devastated by human

In addition to the projects mentioned in this feature, the African Wildlife Foundation has ongoing projects in all the countries marked in orange.

© 2015 Cengage Learning

AFP/Getty Images

A quarter of the world's mountain gorillas (some 210 of them) live in Virunga National Park. The International Gorilla Conservation Program, a collaboration between the African Wildlife Foundation, the World Wildlife Fund, and Flora and Fauna International, supports their continued survival. Saving orphaned gorillas who have lost their parents to poaching or trafficking, is critical to these efforts. Here a Virunga warden, Patrick Karabaranga, plays with one of these orphans.

activity, including the bushmeat trade and illegal trafficking. In 2014 in the Dja Faunal Reserve in Cameroon, home to chimpanzees and western lowland gorillas, the AWF found that poaching greatly surpassed the level of sustainability. About 3,000 African great apes are lost every year to trafficking alone—sold as exotic pets or for entertainment.[c] Because demand is high for young apes, an entire group of chimpanzees, perhaps ten individuals, might be killed so a trafficker can obtain one infant.

In 2013, the AWF established the African Apes Initiative, directed by Dupain. The aim of the program is to preserve populations of African apes by focusing on those habitats that are most endangered. In the DRC, where rich rainforests along the tributaries of the mighty Congo River are bonobos' only natural habitat, Dupain and the AWF helped establish the Lomako-Yokokala Faunal Reserve. In Niokolo-Koba

National Park in Senegal and the Dja Faunal Reserve (both UNESCO World Heritage Sites), the AWF trains and outfits rangers, who use software called CyberTracker on handheld computers to record and track both wildlife and poachers. In the Dja Reserve in 2014, rangers arrested 35 poachers and destroyed 200 hunting camps, all the while at risk from aggressive poachers' guns and machetes.[d]

Although the battle is ongoing, the AWF, through its anti-poaching measures and economic development projects has already had measurable positive impacts on mountain gorilla populations. Ever expanding the scope and methods of its projects, the AWF plays a crucial role in the struggle for the continued survival of all Africa's great apes.

[a]"A new beginning." (2015, April 29). African Wildlife Foundation. https://www.awf.org/blog/new-beginning (retrieved October 6, 2015); "Manyara Ranch Primary School." (2015). African Wildlife Foundation. http://www.awf.org/projects/manyara-ranch-primary-school (retrieved October 6, 2015)

[b]"20 years of IGCP: Lessons learned in mountain gorilla conservation." (2011). International Gorilla Conservation Programme. http://www.igcp.org/wp-content/themes/igcp/docs/pdf/IGCPLessonsLearned_English_web.pdf (retrieved October 27, 2015)

[c]"AWF testifies on trafficking of Africa's great apes." (2014, October 20). African Wildlife Foundation. https://www.awf.org/news/awf-testifies-trafficking-africas-great-apes (retrieved October 6, 2015)

[d]"Group to trek through Cameroon's Dja Reserve." (2015, April 23). The Outdoor Wire. http://www.theoutdoorwire.com/story/142976853179bz8qvb05h (retrieved October 27, 2015)

CHAPTER CHECKLIST

How do primatologists conduct field research?

✓ Researchers rely on observation and collection of feces and hair samples left behind in order to minimize contact that could endanger primate populations.

✓ Conservation efforts are combined with research to ensure the future study of wild populations.

✓ Animals in captivity have provided opportunities to interact with and discover the communicative capabilities of many primates.

How does mammal biology compare to reptilian biology?

✓ As homeotherms, mammals can survive in a wider variety of climates than isothermic reptiles, but mammals require more calories to survive.

✓ Mammals are k-selected, rather than r-selected, meaning that parents spend much more time rearing fewer offspring.

✓ Mammals possess various types of specialized teeth that are replaced only once over a lifetime. Reptile teeth are all nearly identical with unlimited replacement.

How does taxonomy apply to primates, and what issues does it pose?

✓ Taxonomists use shared derived characteristics to establish evolutionary relationships.

✓ The Linnaean system focuses on the measure of anatomical similarity known as a grade. By this system, primates consist of two subfamilies called Prosimii and Anthropoidea. Anthropoids are divided into the infraorders Platyrrhini and Catarrhini.

✓ A new taxonomic scheme based on quantifying genetic similarities proposes a regrouping of primates into two suborders: Strepsirrhini and Haplorrhini. It also distinguishes the hominin subfamily of hominids (humans and their ancestors) from the other African apes.

What features distinguish primates from other mammals?

✓ Primates have a long period of childhood dependency and are large-brained, which enables both learned and adaptive behavior.

✓ Primates developed binocular stereoscopic color vision as they became both diurnal and arboreal. Primate teeth reflect the diversity of food sources available among the trees.

✓ The fovea centralis is unique to primates and allows focusing the eye without sacrificing peripheral vision. Enhanced visual acuity has come at the expense of sense of smell.

✓ The primate foramen magnum is closer to the base of the skull, allowing an upright posture.

✓ Primate digits have sensitive pads, usually accompanied by flattened nails. Most species have opposable thumbs and big toes.

What features characterize the five natural groups of primates?

✓ Lemurs and lorises have large ears, big eyes, pointed snouts that limit facial expression, a claw on their second toe used for grooming, and several scent glands for communication. As a group, they retain more ancestral primate characteristics.

✓ Tarsiers are tiny arboreal creatures with oversized eyes and heads and elongated foot bones that allow for far jumps. They are genetically closer to monkeys and apes, though as nocturnal insect-eaters, they resemble early ancestral primates.

✓ New World monkeys are flat-nosed tree-dwellers that walk on all fours and rarely hang from trees by their arms. One subgroup possesses a long prehensile tail that is used as an extra limb.

✓ Old World monkeys are alternately terrestrial and arboreal and have downward-pointing nostrils and nonprehensile tails. They walk on all fours with palms down, and many species exhibit sophisticated social organization, communication, and learning abilities.

✓ Having no tails, apes are all adapted to hanging by their arms and in some species to brachiate. Their clavicles position their arms at the sides of the body. They are able to stand erect due to the curvature of their vertebrae. African apes knuckle-walk when on the ground, and all apes but humans have forelimbs that are longer than their legs.

What pressures do primate populations currently face?

✓ Habitat destruction caused by economic development and globalization has led to the endangered status of many primate species, especially the great apes.

✓ Primates in war-torn regions are particularly threatened by the presence of automatic weapons and disruption to conservation efforts.

✓ Relocation, reintroduction, and captive colony strategies have met with success in recent years, and some populations are rebounding due to such conservation efforts.

QUESTIONS FOR REFLECTION

1. Has learning more about the numerous similarities between us and our primate cousins, from slow lorises to chimpanzees to gorillas, motivated you personally to meet the challenge of preventing their extinction? What human factors are causing endangerment of primates? How can governments and organizations work to prevent their extinction? How can individuals?

2. What are the main differences between mammals and reptiles? Do we share any ancestral features with reptiles? What aspects of mammalian primate biology do you see reflected in yourself or in people you know?

3. Considering some of the trends seen among the primates, such as increased brain size or fewer teeth, why is it incorrect to say that some primates are more evolved than others? What is wrong with the statement that humans are more evolved than chimpanzees?

4. Two systems exist for dividing the primate order into suborders because of difficulties with classifying tarsiers. Should classification systems be based on genetic relationships or based on the biological concept of grade? Is the continued use of the older terminology an instance of unwillingness to change or a difference in philosophy? How do the issues brought up by the tarsier problem translate to the hominoids?

DIGGING INTO ANTHROPOLOGY

Finding or Losing Your Inner Ape

For many years, primatologists have known that chimpanzees sleep in treetop nests that they fashion daily by lashing branches together. But to really understand the purpose and inner workings of these nests, biological anthropologist Fiona Stewart took her participant observation into the trees. She spent six nights sleeping in abandoned chimps' nests at a field site in western Tanzania (Stewart & Pruetz, 2013). By "aping" the chimps' behavior, she was able to collect data and make observations on factors such as threats from predators, sleep disturbances, bug bites, and temperatures.

Using her method as an inspiration, take one basic facet of ape biology behavior into "the field" and make observations as to how it works or doesn't work in practice. What would happen, for example, if you taped your opposable thumbs to your hand and needed to take a shower? This simulates the non-ape condition. What if you no longer had spoken language but wanted to communicate with a loved one? You might rely on other facets of language at which apes excel. Choose to either lose an ape capacity or to rely on one as you go out into the world. Record your observations.

Lisa Newbern

CHALLENGE ISSUE

Not that long ago, scientists thought only humans used tools, were self-aware, and developed culture—all of which we have now observed in other species. Increasingly, it seems many of the characteristics historically thought to be unique to humans occur to different degrees in our primate cousins, especially the apes. Take, for instance, the question of morality. Dutch primatologist Frans de Waal has spent decades observing and documenting the building blocks of morality in chimps and bonobos—including empathy, a sense of fairness, and altruism. Some primatologists have documented chimpanzees' and other primates' capacity for violence, but de Waal challenges this "veneer theory"—that primate morality, including human morality, is a thin veneer over a brutal nature. Bonobos in particular are often observed comforting—through embraces, touches, and sexual contact—individuals who have suffered the loss of a family member or other hardship. Even very young bonobos, thought to lack the complex reasoning necessary for picturing themselves "in another's shoes," will comfort hurting individuals, a response de Waal argues is based on what they are feeling (Davies, 2013). Apes even manifest guilt, as in the case of Lody the bonobo, who hung his head and hugged himself in shame after accidentally biting off a veterinarian's finger—an incident Lody remembered fifteen years later, when he ran to the visiting vet to inspect her incomplete hand (Dye, 2013). More and more, primatologists like de Waal are finding that the capacity for morality and other "human" traits are not exclusive to our species.

Primate Behavior

Research into primate behavior has repeatedly shown the behavioral sophistication of our closest living relatives. Primates use tools, learn, and can be dishonest, just as humans can. Although the young Jane Goodall was criticized for naming the chimpanzees she studied, social interactions, particularly among the apes, demonstrate that they recognize one another as individuals and adjust their behavior accordingly. (Many other long-lived social mammals, such as elephants and dolphins, do the same.) Certainly, biology plays a role in such primate behaviors, but often, as with humans, social traditions also determine behavior. Nevertheless, some broad biological factors underlie the social traditions of primates.

Primates take more time to reach adulthood compared to most other mammals. During this lengthy period of growth and development, they learn the behaviors of their social group. Observations of primates in their natural habitats over the past decades have shown that social interaction, organization, learning, reproduction, care of the young, and communication among our primate relatives resemble human behavior. As we study primate behavior to learn about ourselves, who we are as a species today, and how we got here, it becomes clear that many of our differences reflect only the degree of expression of shared characteristics.

Primates as Models for Human Evolution

As we will explore in the human evolution chapters, the human line split from a common ancestor we share with the African apes. Although this split occurred millions of years ago, paleoanthropologists in the mid-20th century were hopeful that observations made among the living apes might shed light on the lifeways of the fossil species they were discovering. To that end, Louis Leakey sent Jane Goodall to study chimpanzees in Gombe Stream Chimpanzee Reserve (now a national park) on the eastern shores of Lake Tanganyika in Tanzania, as well as

In this chapter you will learn to

- Identify the range of variation of primate behavior and the theories that account for it.

- Distinguish different forms of primate social organization.

- Examine the biological basis of primate behavior, with particular emphasis on the primate life cycle, social learning, and the environment.

- Explore the cultural influences on theories of primate behavior.

- Distinguish the diverse behavioral patterns of our closest relatives— orangutans, gorillas, chimpanzees, and bonobos—with particular emphasis on sexual behavior, cooperation, hunting, and tool use.

- Describe the linguistic capacities of the great apes.

- Define *primate culture* in the context of human evolution.

- Explore the moral questions surrounding the use of chimpanzees in biomedical research.

supported the fieldwork of U.S. primatologist Dian Fossey, studying mountain gorillas in Rwanda, and German primatologist Biruté Galdikas, studying orangutans in Borneo.

But as forest-dwellers, each of these ape species inhabited an environment that differed considerably from the grassy savannahs inhabited by the earliest human ancestors known at that time. Instead, paleoanthropologists turned to baboons: Old World monkeys native to the savannah environments of eastern Africa where the richest fossil evidence of our ancestors had been found.

Although baboons differ considerably from our two-legged ancestors, their survival strategies provide some clues as to how early humans adapted to the savannah environment. Fully ground-dwelling members of the genus *Papio*, baboons are among the largest of the Old World monkeys. Troops of baboons can be seen sitting together on the dry savannah earth to forage for corms (thick, nutritious underground parts of plants), keeping a watchful eye out for predators. At the first sign of danger, alarm calls by members of the troop will signal all the individuals to retreat to safety.

Baboons live in groups that vary dramatically in size, from less than ten individuals to hundreds. In some species the groups are multi-male multi-female, while others are made up of a series of *polygynous* groups—one male with several females that he dominates (Figure 4.1). Sexual dimorphism—anatomical differences between males and females—is high in baboons, and males can use their physical advantages to overpower females easily.

Figure 4.1 Baboon Social Learning
The behavior of baboons, a type of Old World monkey, has been particularly well studied. There are several distinct species of baboon, each with its own social rules. Troops of hamadryas baboons, the sacred baboons of ancient Egypt pictured here, consist of a series of smaller groups made up of a single male and several females over which he dominates. Female hamadryas baboons, if transferred to a troop of olive baboons, where females are not as submissive, maintain the passive behaviors learned in their original troop. But a female olive baboon placed in the hamadryas troop quickly learns submissive behaviors in order to survive.

But the degree to which males choose to do so varies from group to group.

When constructing their theories, paleoanthropologists did not expect our ancestors to possess a tail or **ischail callosity**—a hardened, nerveless pad on the buttocks that allows baboons to sit for long periods of time. Tails are strictly a monkey characteristic, not an ape one, and among the hominoids only gibbons and siamangs possess ischial callosities. Instead, paleoanthropologists were looking for examples of *convergence*—behaviors that might appear in large-bodied, dimorphic primates living in large multi-male multi-female groups in a savannah environment. Paleoanthropology's "baboon hypothesis" led to many excellent long-term field studies that have yielded fascinating data on baboons' social organization, omnivorous diet, communication, mating patterns and other reproductive strategies. As with most primate field studies, the evolutionary questions remain in the background while the rich repertoire of primate behavior takes center stage.

While the savannah environment has certainly been important in human evolution, recent fossil discoveries and analyses have led paleoanthropologists back into the forest, where the earliest two-legged ancestors lived. Researchers now also focus on human origins and the transition from a forested environment to the savannah. Recent field studies of chimpanzees in more savannah-like environments, explored in this chapter, have yielded fascinating results.

Primate Social Organization

As social animals, primates live and travel in groups, which vary in size and composition from species to species. Different environmental and biological factors have been linked to the groups' sizes, and different primate species exhibit various organizational forms (Figure 4.2). For example, gibbons live in small nuclear family units consisting of a pair of bonded adults and their offspring, whereas orangutans tend to lead more solitary existences, with males and females coming together only to mate. Young orangutans stay with their mothers until they reach adulthood. The northern muriqui monkeys of Brazil live in a peaceful, egalitarian society with no hierarchy (Strier, 2015).

In contrast to the polygynous organization of some baboon species, a very few New World species are *polyandrous* with a single female and her young living in groups with multiple males. Twins are common in these species, and the males help with parenting.

Chimps and bonobos live in large multi-male multi-female groups. Among them, the largest social organizational unit in primatology is a **community**, usually composed of fifty or more individuals who collectively inhabit a large geographic area. Rarely do all of these animals congregate. Instead, they travel individually or in small subgroups. In the course of their travels, subgroups may join and forage together, but eventually these

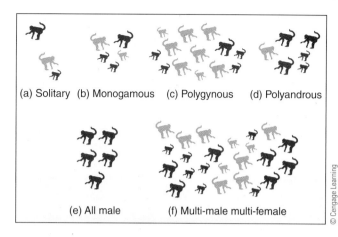

(a) Solitary   (b) Monogamous   (c) Polygynous   (d) Polyandrous

(e) All male   (f) Multi-male multi-female

© Cengage Learning

Figure 4.2 Primate Social Organization
Primate social organization ranges from (a) solitary to (b) monogamous to (c) polygynous (single male with many females and their young) to (d) the rare polyandrous (single female with multiple males and her young) to (e) all male to (f) multimale multi-female groups of various sizes and ages. In this illustration, females are rust-colored, and males are dark brown.

subgroups will break up again into smaller units. Typically, when individuals split off from a subgroup, others join, so the composition of subunits shifts frequently.

Gorilla groups are "families" of five to thirty individuals led by a mature silverback male and including younger (black-backed) males, females, and the young. Occasionally, field studies reveal variation in the typical pattern—some gorilla groups in Uganda and Rwanda contain multiple silverback males. Still, in one of these multi-male groups studied in Rwanda, a single dominant male fathered all but one of ten juveniles (Gibbons, 2001b).

The dominant male gorilla usually prevents subordinate males from mating with the group's females. He will force young, sexually mature males, who take on the characteristic silver color when they are sexually mature (about 11 to 13 years of age), to leave their **natal group**—the community they have known since birth. After some time as a solitary male in the forest, a young silverback may find the opportunity to start his own social group by winning outside females. Occasionally, these solitary males will form an all-male group. In the natal group, if the dominant male is weakening with age, one of his sons may remain with the group to succeed to his father's position. Alternatively, an outside male may take over the group. With the dominant male in control, gorillas rarely fight over food, territory, or sex, but they will fiercely defend the group.

ischial callosity A hardened, nerveless pad on the buttocks that allows baboons and other primates to sit for long periods of time.

community In primatology, a unit of primate social organization composed of fifty or more individuals who collectively inhabit a large geographic area.

natal group The group or the community an animal has inhabited since birth.

In many primate species, including humans, adolescence marks the time when individuals change their relationship with the group they have known since birth. This change often takes the form of migration to new social groups. In many species, females constitute the core of the social system. For example, offspring tend to remain with the group to which their mother, rather than their father, belongs. Among gorillas, male adolescents leave their natal groups more frequently than females. However, among chimpanzees and bonobos, adolescent females are often the ones to migrate.

Among Tanzanian chimpanzee communities studied, about half the females leave the community they have known since birth to join another group (Moore, 1998). Other females may also temporarily leave their group to mate with males of another group. Among bonobos, adolescent females appear to always transfer to another group where they promptly establish bonds with those females. Although biological factors such as hormonal influence on sexual maturity play a role in adolescent migration, the variation across species and within the chimpanzees indicates that differences may also derive from the learned social traditions of the group.

Home Range

Primates usually move within a circumscribed area, or **home range**, which varies in size depending on the group and on ecological factors such as food availability. Ranges often change seasonally, and the number of miles traveled daily by a group varies. Some areas, known as *core areas,* are used more often than others and typically contain water, food sources, resting places, and sleeping trees. The ranges of different groups may overlap, as among bonobos, where 65 percent of one community's range may overlap with that of another. By contrast, chimpanzee territories, at least in some regions, are exclusively occupied and will be defended from intrusion (Figure 4.3).

Gorillas do not defend their home range against incursions of others of their kind, although they will defend their group if it is threatened. In the lowlands of Central Africa, it is not uncommon to find several families feeding in close proximity to one another. In encounters with other communities of their species, bonobos will defend their immediate space through vocalizations and displays but rarely through fighting. Usually, they settle down and feed side by side, often grooming, playing, and engaging in sexual activity between groups as well. Female bonobos will even prevent war with neighboring groups, rushing ahead of the males to greet the enemy with an orgy instead of violence (de Waal, 2014).

home range The geographic area within which a group of primates usually moves.

dominance hierarchy An observed ranking system in primate societies, ordering individuals from high (alpha) to low standing corresponding to predictable behavioral interactions including domination.

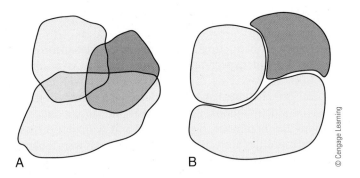

A   B

Figure 4.3 Home Range and Territory
As illustrated in A, home ranges can overlap. When members of the same species meet one another in the shared parts of the range, there might be some tension, deference, or peaceful mingling. Some groups maintain clear territories (B) that are strictly defended from any intrusion by members of the same species.

Chimpanzees, by contrast, have been observed patrolling their territories to ward off potential trespassers. Moreover, Jane Goodall (see Anthropologists of Note) has recorded the destruction of one chimpanzee community by another invading group. This sort of deadly inter-community interaction has never been observed among bonobos. Some have interpreted the apparent territorial behavior as an expression of the supposedly violent nature of chimpanzees. However, others have suggested that the violence Goodall witnessed was a response to overcrowding that resulted from human activity.

Social Hierarchy

In the past, primatologists believed that a male **dominance hierarchy**, in which some animals outrank and dominate others, formed the basis of primate social structures. They noted that physical strength and size play a role in determining an animal's rank. By this measure, males generally outrank females. However, the male-biased cultures of many early primatologists may have contributed to this theoretical perspective, with its emphasis on domination through superior size and strength. Male dominance hierarchies seemed "natural" to these initial researchers.

Over the last fifty years, detailed field studies, including cutting-edge research by female primatologists such as Goodall, have illuminated the nuances of primate social behavior, the relative harmony of primate social life, and the importance of female primates. High-ranking female chimpanzees may dominate low-ranking males. And among bonobos, female rank determines the social order of the group far more than male rank. Although strength and size do contribute to a bonobo's social position, other factors also come into play, including the rank of the bonobo's mother, a factor largely determined through her cooperative social behavior and how effectively each individual creates alliances with others.

Anup Shah/Minden Pictures

Figure 4.4 G–G Rubbing
The two female bonobos pictured here are engaging in genital–genital, or G–G, rubbing. This is one of the many sexual practices bonobos use to reduce tension and resolve social conflicts. Among bonobos, primatologists have observed every possible combination of ages and sexes engaging in a remarkable array of sexual activities that goes far beyond male–female mating for purposes of biological reproduction.

For males, drive or motivation to achieve high status also influences rank. For example, in the Gombe community studied by Goodall, one male chimp had the idea to incorporate noisy kerosene cans into his charging displays, thereby intimidating all the other males. As a result, he rose from relatively low status to the number one (alpha) position.

On the whole, bonobo females form stronger bonds with one another compared to chimpanzee females. Moreover, the strength of the bond between bonobo mother and son interferes with bonds among males. Bonobo males defer to females in feeding, and alpha females have been observed chasing alpha males; such males may even yield to low-ranking females, particularly when groups of females form alliances. Furthermore, allied females will band together to force an aggressive male out of the community. Allied bonobo females cooperate despite not being genetically related. Female dominance prevails among bonobos instead of the male dominance characteristic of chimps.

Western primatologists' focus on social rank and attack behavior may be a legacy of the individualistic,

competitive nature of the societies in which evolutionary theory originated. Those cultures have often concentrated on the struggle and competition of natural selection instead of coexistence within a fixed social order. By contrast, the early Japanese primatologist Kinji Imanishi developed a holistic ecosystem-based theory of evolution and initiated long-term field studies of bonobos that have ultimately demonstrated the importance of cooperation rather than competition. In social species that cooperate and depend upon one another, **reconciliation**—a friendly reunion between former opponents not long after a conflict—has more evolutionary import than the fight that preceded it (Aureli & de Waal, 2000; de Waal, 2000).

Reconciliation takes varied forms. Female bonobos reconcile by rubbing their clitorises and swollen genitals together (Figure 4.4). Chimpanzees reconcile with a hug

reconciliation In primatology, a friendly reunion between former opponents not long after a conflict.

Jane Goodall (b. 1934) • Kinji Imanishi (1902–1992)

In July 1960, **Jane Goodall** arrived with her mother at Lake Tanganyika at the Gombe Stream, in what is now Tanzania, East Africa. Goodall was the first of three women Kenyan anthropologist Louis Leakey sent to study the great apes in the wild (the others were Dian Fossey and Biruté Galdikas, who studied gorillas and orangutans, respectively); Goodall's task was to begin a long-term study of chimpanzees. Little did she realize that, fifty-five years later, she would still be at Gombe.

Born in London, Goodall grew up and was schooled in Bournemouth, England. As a child, she dreamed of living in Africa, so when an invitation arrived to visit a friend in Kenya, she jumped at the opportunity. While in Kenya, she met Leakey, who gave her a job as an assistant secretary. Before long, she was on her way to Gombe. Within a year, the outside world began to hear extraordinary things about this pioneering woman and her research: tales of toolmaking apes, cooperative hunts by chimpanzees, and what seemed like exotic chimpanzee rain dances. By the mid-1960s, her work had earned her a doctorate from Cambridge University, and Gombe was on its way to becoming one of the most dynamic field stations for the study of animal behavior anywhere in the world.

Although Goodall is still very much involved with chimpanzees, she now spends a good deal of time lecturing, writing, and overseeing the work of other researchers. She is passionately committed to primate conservation and is dedicated to halting illegal trafficking in chimps as well as fighting for the humane treatment of captive chimps. In a 2015 interview with *The Globe and Mail's* Ivan Semeniuk, Goodall, who travels 300 days out of the year, says there is still so much to do, and now that she is over 80, she must speed up rather than slow down. Always looking ahead, Goodall says, "All my efforts would be in vain, all the efforts of everybody who's trying to conserve and protect would be useless, if we're not raising new generations to be better stewards than we've been."[a]

Jane Goodall in the field with chimpanzees at Gombe.

Kay & Karl Ammann/Bruce Coleman INC./Alamy

and mouth-to-mouth kiss. The reconciliation techniques of other primates and other mammalian species, including dolphins and hyenas, have been observed in the wild. Although some attribute reconciliation behavior to simple biology, de Waal carried out a series of experiments demonstrating that primates *learn* these social skills (de Waal, 2001a). He took two species of Old World monkey, the aggressive rhesus macaque and the mellower stump-tailed macaque, and housed some of them together for five months. At the end of this period, rhesus macaques that had learned reconciliation from the stump-tailed macaques continued to practice these behaviors when living strictly with rhesus macaques.

Chimps, as de Waal observed, take reconciliation a step further: Some individuals, generally older females, take on the role of mediator. Recognizing a dispute between two other individuals (by noticing, for example, that two chimpanzees are sitting near one another but avoiding eye contact), this mediator will groom one of the combatants for a bit. When she gets up to groom the other combatant, the first fighter follows and grooms her. She eventually leaves the two fighters grooming each other.

I was walking along a path in a valley, and there was a grasshopper on a leaf in a shrubbery. Until that moment I had happily caught insects, killed them with chloroform, impaled them on pins, and looked up their names, but I realized I knew nothing at all about how this grasshopper lived in the wild.[b]

In his most important work, *The World of Living Things*, first published in 1941, Imanishi developed a comprehensive theory about the natural world rooted in Japanese cultural beliefs and practices. Imanishi's work challenged Western evolutionary theory in several ways. Rather than focusing on the biology of individual organisms, Imanishi used a holistic approach suggesting that naturalists examine "specia" (a species society) to which individuals belong as the unit of analysis. Instead of focusing on time, Imanishi emphasized space in his approach to the natural world, noting how the space each living thing occupied was connected to others around it in a fixed social order. He highlighted the harmony of all living things rather than conflict and competition among individuals of a single species.

Imanishi's research techniques, now standard worldwide, developed directly from his theories: long-term field study of primates in their natural societies using methods from ethnography. With his students, Imanishi conducted pioneering field studies of African apes and Japanese and Tibetan macaques. Japanese primatologists were the first to document the importance of kinship, the complexity of primate societies, patterns of social learning, and the unique character of each primate social group. Because of the work by Imanishi and his students, we now think about the distinct cultures of primate societies.

Kinji Imanishi initiated the earliest field studies of bonobos in the 1940s. While his field methods have been influential, today, cigarettes are not involved.

[a]"Jane Goodall on why retirement isn't factoring in to her future plans." (2015, April 17). Jane Goodall interviewed by Ivan Semeniuk. *The Globe and Mail*. http://www.theglobeandmail.com/news/news-video/video-jane-goodall-on-why-retirement-isnt-factoring-in-to-her-future-plans/article24004092/ (retrieved October 9, 2015)
[b]Kawakatsu, H. (1999). Imanishi's view of the world. *Journal of Japanese Trade and Industry* 18 (2), 15; Matsuzawa, T., & McGrew, W. C. (2008, July 22). Kinji Imanishi and 60 years of Japanese primatology. *Current Biology* 18 (14), R587–R591.

Long before Louis Leakey sent the first Western primatologists into the field, **Kinji Imanishi**—naturalist, explorer, and mountain climber—profoundly influenced primatology in Japan and throughout the world. Although fully aware of Western methods and theories, he developed a radically different approach to the scientific study of the natural world. Imanishi dates his transformation to a youthful encounter with a grasshopper:

Individual Interaction and Bonding

Grooming, the ritual cleaning of another animal to remove parasites and other matter from its skin or coat, has social as well as practical benefits (Figure 4.5). The grooming animal deftly parts the hair of the one being groomed and removes foreign objects, often eating them. Besides being hygienic, grooming can signify friendliness, closeness, appeasement, reconciliation, or even submission. Bonobos and chimpanzees have favorite grooming partners.

Interestingly, different chimp communities have different styles of grooming. In one East African group, for example, two chimps groom each other face-to-face, with one hand, while clasping their partner's free hand. In another group 90 miles distant, the handclasp does not occur. In East Africa, all communities incorporate leaves in their grooming, but in West Africa they do not.

grooming The ritual cleaning of another animal's coat to remove parasites and other matter.

Gunter Ziesler/Photolibrary/Getty Images

Figure 4.5 Primate Grooming
Grooming is an important activity among all Old World monkeys and apes, as shown here in a group of chimps grooming one another in a pattern known as the *domino effect*. Such activity is important for strengthening bonds among individual members of the group.

Besides grooming, other behaviors demonstrate group sociability. For instance, primatologists have witnessed embracing, touching, and the joyous welcoming of other members of the ape community. These important behavioral traits undoubtedly existed among human ancestors.

Gorillas, though gentle and tolerant, tend toward aloofness and independence. Restraint characterizes interaction among adults, with friendship and closeness typifying only the relationships between adults and infants. Among bonobos, chimpanzees, gorillas, and orangutans, as among most other primates, the mother–infant bond is the strongest and longest lasting. It may endure for many years—commonly for the lifetime of the mother. Gorilla infants share their mothers' nests but have also been seen sharing nests with mature childless females. Bonobo, chimpanzee, and gorilla males pay attention to juveniles, thus contributing to their socialization. Bonobo males even carry infants occasionally. Their interest in youngsters does not

elicit the nervous reaction from the mothers that it does among chimps; chimp mothers may be reacting to the occasional infanticide on the part of chimpanzee males, a behavior never observed among bonobos.

Sexual Behavior

Most mammals mate only during specified annual or biannual breeding seasons. Although some primates have a fixed breeding season tied to a simultaneous increase in body fat or to the consumption of specific plant foods, many primate species can breed throughout the year. Among the African apes, as with humans, there is no fixed breeding season. In chimps, frequent sexual activity—initiated by either the male or the female—occurs during **estrus**, the period when the female is receptive to impregnation (Figure 4.6). In chimpanzees the skin around the genitals swells during estrus as a visible sign to potential mates. Bonobo females, by contrast, always appear fertile due to their constant genital swelling and interest in sex. Gorillas appear to show less interest in sex than either chimps or bonobos.

estrus In some primate females, the time of sexual receptivity during which ovulation is visibly displayed.

Figure 4.6 Gelada Estrus
Because geladas, a kind of Old World monkey, spend far more time sitting than standing upright, it is not as practical to signal ovulation through genital swelling. Instead, this species signals estrus through the reddening of a patch of furless skin on their chests. This way it is easy for other members of the group to see that they are fertile even while they are foraging.

Michel Gunther/Science Source

When in estrus, a chimpanzee female engages in a lot of sexual activity, sometimes copulating as many as fifty times in one day with a dozen different partners. For the most part, females mate with males of their own group. Dominant males often try to monopolize females in full estrus, although this cannot succeed without cooperation from the female. Sometimes an individual female and a lower-ranking male will form a temporary bond, leaving the group together for a few "private" days during the female's fertile period. Interestingly, the relationship between reproductive success and social rank differs for males and females. In the chimpanzee community studied by Goodall, low- or mid-level males sired about half the infants. Although high female rank is linked with successful reproduction, social success for males—achieving alpha status—does not translate neatly into the evolutionary currency of reproductive success.

Blickwinkel/Mcphoto/Vlz/ Alamy

Anup Shah/Minden Pictures

Figure 4.7 Mature and Adolescent-Looking Orangutans
The orangutan on the left has developed the physical bulk and secondary sex characteristics typical of adult males of his species. The orangutan on the right has retained his slight adolescent physique even though his primary sex characteristics are fully mature, allowing him to father offspring. Surprisingly, these two individuals might be close to the same age.

Bonobos (like humans) do not limit their sexual behavior to times of female fertility. The constant genital swelling of female bonobos, in effect, conceals **ovulation**, or the moment when an egg released into the womb is receptive for fertilization. The absence of genital swelling conceals ovulation in humans. For both humans and bonobos, concealed ovulation plays a role in separating sexual activity for social and pleasurable reasons from the biological task of reproduction. In fact, among bonobos (as among humans) sexuality goes far beyond male–female mating for purposes of biological reproduction.

Among bonobos, primatologists have observed virtually every possible combination of ages and sexes engaging in sexual activities, including oral sex, tongue kissing, and massaging each other's genitals (de Waal, 2001a). Male bonobos may mount each other, or one may rub his scrotum against another's. Researchers have also observed bonobos "penis fencing"—hanging face-to-face from a branch and rubbing their erect penises together as if crossing swords. Among females, genital rubbing is particularly common. Most of this sex functions to reduce tensions and resolve social conflicts. Bonobo sexual activity is very frequent, but also very brief, lasting only 8 to 10 seconds.

Field studies by primatologists have documented a variety of sexual behaviors among other species as well. For example, some male orangutans become sexually mature but retain the appearance of adolescents (**Figure 4.7**).

ovulation The moment when an egg released from an ovary into the womb is receptive for fertilization.

Scientists initially interpreted this arrested development as a sign of stress. However, primatologists showed this to be a reproductive strategy that allows these arrested males to father offspring without posing a threat to nearby males who have all the secondary sex characteristics of adulthood (Maggioncalda & Sapolsky, 2009). But adult females tend to not be sexually receptive to these undeveloped males. Thus, the arrested males will often forcibly copulate with females in order to pass on their genes. Interestingly, should the dominant male die or move on, these other males will then physically mature and change their behavior.

Are these forced copulations by orangutans equivalent to rape among humans? Or is this behavior a natural part of orangutan sexuality to which human standards should not be applied? Likewise, individuals uncomfortable with sexual diversity among humans might see the sexual behavior of bonobos as deviant. As we study the sexual behavior of primates, we must be acutely aware of how we might be imposing our own cultural notions onto the behaviors of our closest living relatives.

Consider, for example, the traditional approach to gorilla sexuality solely in terms of male control. Primatologists described the dominant silverback as having exclusive breeding rights with the females, although sometimes the alpha male tolerated the presence of a young adult male, allowing him occasional access to a low-ranking female. Today, when we consider the female gorilla's perspective, we find an explanation for why males leave the home group by the time they become silverbacks. Young males then can entice partners away from the group in order to have reproductive success. Females recognize the future potential in an incipient silverback and the possibility of forming a new group and thus will mate with these young adult males. Today's scientists recognize the importance of female choice in reproduction.

The vast majority of primate species are not **monogamous**—in primatology, a term that means bonded exclusively to a single sexual partner. Still, many smaller species of New World monkeys, a few island-dwelling populations of leaf-eating Old World monkeys, and all of the smaller apes (gibbons and siamangs) appear to mate for life with a single individual of the opposite sex. These monogamous species have a lower degree of sexual dimorphism than our closest primate relatives (the great apes) or our own ancient ancestors.

Evolutionary biologists, dating back to Charles Darwin himself, have proposed that sexual dimorphism (for example, larger male size in apes, beautiful feathers in peacocks) relates to competition among males for access to females. In such models, while significant evolutionary change happened to males, females evolved by just tagging along, what Canadian primatologist Linda Fedigan has called the "coat-tails theory" of evolution (Fedigan, 1992). She points out that evolutionary theories about sexual dimorphism and reproductive behaviors are particularly

susceptible to becoming "gendered." That is, the gender norms of the scientists can easily creep their way (subconsciously, of course) into the theories they are creating. Darwin's era, despite the reign of Queen Victoria, was firmly patriarchal, and male–male competition prevailed in British society. Women of Darwin's time and class were denied basic rights such as voting. Inheritance laws favored first-born male heirs. Feminist analyses such as Fedigan's have contributed substantially to the developing discipline of primatology.

Primate field studies have revealed that male–male competition is just one of many factors playing a role in primate reproduction. Male–male competition can be reduced, as it is in orangutans, through arrested development. In baboons, a very sexually dimorphic species, the female chooses her mate just as often as the choice is determined through male–male competition. Females frequently choose to mate with lower-ranking males that show strong male–female **affiliative** actions (tending to promote social cohesion) and good parental behavior (Sapolsky, 2002).

Among baboons, paternal involvement has been shown to have distinct advantages for offspring, including more rapid growth in baboon infants that receive attention from their fathers. In addition, adult males will also intercede on their offspring's behalf when the young ones are involved in fights. For female baboons, choosing a good mate based on affiliative qualities can optimize reproductive success.

Reproduction and Care of Young

The average female monkey or ape spends most of her adult life either pregnant or nursing her young. Apes generally nurse each of their young for about four to five years. After weaning her infant, she will come into estrus periodically until she becomes pregnant again.

Among primates, as among some other mammals, females generally give birth to one infant at a time. Natural selection may have favored single births among arboreal primates because primate infants (humans included), possessing a highly developed grasping ability, must be transported about while holding onto their mother. More than one clinging infant would interfere with her movement through the trees. Only the smaller nocturnal prosimians, the primates closest to the ancestral condition, typically bear more than one infant at a time. Among the anthropoids, only the true marmoset, a kind of New World monkey, has a pattern of habitual twinning. Other species like humans will twin occasionally. In marmosets, both parents share infant care, with fathers doing most

monogamous In primatology, mating for life with a single individual of the opposite sex.

affiliative Behaving in a manner that tends to promote social cohesion.

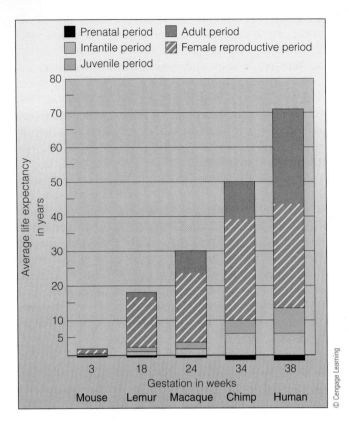

© Cengage Learning

Figure 4.8 The Primate Life Cycle
A long life cycle, including a long period of childhood
dependency, is characteristic of the primates. In biological
terms, infancy ends when young mammals are weaned, and
adulthood is defined as sexual maturation. In many species,
such as mice, animals become sexually mature as soon as
they are weaned. Among primates, a juvenile period for social
learning occurs between infancy and adulthood. For humans,
the biological definitions of *infancy* and *adulthood* are modified
according to cultural norms.

of the carrying. Polyandry also occurs among marmosets,
presumably as an adaptation to carrying multiple young.

Primates bear few young but devote much time and
effort to the care of each offspring. Compared to other
mammals, such as mice, which pass from birth to adulthood in mere weeks, primates spend a long time growing
up. Generally, the more closely related to humans a primate species is, the longer its period of infant and childhood dependency (**Figure 4.8**). A lemur depends upon its
mother for only a few months after birth, whereas an ape
is dependent for four or five years. A chimpanzee in the
wild cannot survive if its mother dies before it reaches the
age of 4 at the very least. The larger social group, rather
than just the mother, sustains juvenile primates. The
young use this period to learn and refine a variety of behaviors. If the mother of a juvenile primate dies, an older
member of the group may adopt the youngster. Among
bonobos, a juvenile who has lost his or her mother has
very little social standing.

The long interval between primate births, particularly among the apes, results in small population size. A
female chimpanzee, for example, does not reach sexual
maturity until about age 10, and once she produces her
first live offspring, five or six years pass before she will
bear another. So, assuming that none of her offspring die
before adulthood, a female chimpanzee must survive for
at least twenty or twenty-one years just to maintain the
chimpanzee population. In reality, chimpanzee infants
and juveniles do die sometimes, and not all females
live full reproductive lives. This accounts for the lower
population size of apes compared to monkeys. Likewise,
humans' short intervals between births account for our
ever-increasing population.

Despite the effect on population size, a long slow period of growth and development, particularly among the
hominoids, provides opportunities. Young monkeys and
apes are born without built-in responses dictating specific
behavior in complex situations. Like young humans, they
learn how to strategically interact with others and even to
manipulate them for their own benefit—by trial and error,
observation, imitation, and practice. Young primates learn
to modify their behavior based on the reactions of other
members of the group. Each individual has a unique physical appearance and personality. Youngsters learn to match
their interactive behaviors to each individual's social position and temperament. Anatomical features common to all
monkeys and apes, such as a free upper lip (unlike lemurs
and cats, for example), allow for communicative facial expressions. Much of this learning takes place through play.

For primate infants and juveniles, play does more than
pass the hours. Young primates play to learn about their
environment, to learn social skills, and to test a variety
of behaviors. Chimpanzee infants mimic the food-getting
activities of adults, "attack" dozing adults, and "harass"
adolescents. Observers have watched young gorillas do
somersaults, wrestle, and play organized games, such as
jostling for position on a hillside or following and mimicking a single youngster. One juvenile, becoming annoyed at
repeated harassment by an infant, picked it up, climbed a
tree, and deposited it on a branch from which it was unable
to get down; eventually, its mother came to retrieve it.

Communication and Learning

Primates, like many animals, vocalize. They have a great
range of calls, often used together with movements of
the face or body to convey a message. By studying the
reactions of animals that hear the calls, primatologists
have distinguished a number of specific calls, such as
warnings, threat calls, defense calls, and gathering calls.
Chimps use various calls to announce the arrival of individuals or calls (called "pant-hoots") to inquire. But most

DLILLC/ Documentary/Corbis

Figure 4.9 Universal Hominoid Expressions
Many ape nonverbal communications are easily recognized
by humans, as we share the same gestures. This capacity
allows us to communicate across cultures and across
species. Among humans, this capacity also makes
miscommunication more likely when visual cues are missing
or do not match the accompanying words.

vocalizations—like facial expressions, gestures, and
postures—communicate an emotional state, such as distress,
fear, or excitement, rather than information (Figure 4.9).
For example, chimps will smack their lips or clack their
teeth to express pleasure with sociable body contact. Together, these facilitate group protection, coordination of
group efforts, and social interaction in general.

To what degree are various forms of communication universal and to what degree are they specific to a given group?
On the group-specificity side, primatologists have recently
documented dialects that emerge when specific social groups
within a species are isolated in their habitats. Social factors,
genetic drift, and habitat acoustics could all contribute to the
appearance of these dialects (de la Torre & Snowden, 2009).

Smiles, kisses, and embraces have long been understood to be universal among humans and our closest
relatives. But recently, additional universals have been
documented. For example, athletes who are blind use
the same gestures to express submission or victory as
sighted athletes, although they have never seen such
gestures themselves (Figure 4.10) (Tracy & Matsumoto,
2008). This raises interesting questions about the extent
to which primate communications are biologically hardwired or learned.

Visual communication can also take place through objects, such as the bonobos' use of trail markers. When foraging during the day, the community breaks up into smaller
groups. Those in the lead will indicate their direction by deliberately stomping down the vegetation or ripping off large
leaves and placing them at the intersections of trails or where
downed trees obscure the path. Thus, the bonobos know
where to come together at the end of the day (Recer, 1998).

Primate calls can also communicate specific threats.
For example, researchers documented how the alarm
calls of vervet monkeys communicate several levels of

**Figure 4.10 Gestures
of the Blind**
Athletes who have been
blind since birth use the
same body gestures to
express victory and defeat
as sighted athletes.
Because they do this
without ever having seen an
"end zone" celebration, this
indicates that these body
gestures are hardwired into
humans and presumably
derive from our primate
heritage.

Bob Willingham

Humans and Bonobos: A Bicultural Conversation

Linguists have long argued that humans are uniquely capable of using language. However, the research done by U.S. primatologist Sue Savage-Rumbaugh and her colleagues since the 1970s challenges this idea.

It began with a bonobo named Kanzi, who, as an infant, tagged along while his mother Matata had language lessons involving pictures called lexigrams.[a] Though Kanzi showed no interest in the lessons, later he spontaneously began to use lexigrams himself. Rather than give Kanzi school-like lessons, Savage-Rumbaugh decided upon a more organic approach, encouraging him to express himself based on his social and physical environment. She built a familial relationship with Kanzi, living with him, going for hikes with him, and playing games.

The Great Ape Trust, photo courtesy of Sue Savage-Rumbaugh

Kanzi the bonobo uses lexigrams to communicate with primatologist Sue Savage-Rumbaugh at the Great Ape Trust of Iowa.

information to elicit specific responses from others in the group (Seyfarth, Cheney, & Marler, 1980). The calls designated different types of predators (birds of prey, big cats, snakes) and where the threat might arise. Further, the researchers have documented how young vervets learn the appropriate use of the calls. If a young individual utters the correct call, adults will repeat it, triggering appropriate escape behavior (heading into the trees to get away from a cat or into brush to be safe from an eagle). But if an infant utters the cry for an eagle in response to a leaf falling from the sky or for a nonthreatening bird, no adult calls will ensue.

From an evolutionary perspective, behaviors such as these vervet alarm calls puzzle scientists. Biologists assume the forces of natural selection work on behavioral traits just as they do on genetic traits. It seems reasonable that individuals in a group of vervet monkeys capable of

warning one another of predators would have a significant survival advantage over those without this capability. However, evolutionary biologists would also expect the animals to act in their own self-interest, with survival of self being paramount. By giving an alarm call, an individual calls attention to itself, thereby becoming an obvious target for the predator. How, then, could **altruism**, or concern for the welfare of others, evolve so that individuals place themselves at risk for the good of the group? Biologists suggest net gain is important. Consider being given a choice between receiving $10 million, with the stipulation that you give $6 million to your neighbor, or receiving $10. While taking the $10 million and netting $4 million benefits your neighbor to a much greater degree, it is ultimately a selfish act (Nunney, 1998).

Natural selection of beneficial social traits was probably an important influence on human evolution because some degree of cooperative social behavior among primates became important for food-getting, defense, and mate attraction. Indeed, U.S. anthropologist Christopher Boehm argues, "If human nature were merely selfish, vigilant punishment of

altruism Concern for the welfare of others expressed as increased risk undertaken by individuals for the good of the group.

Kanzi appeared to value this relationship greatly after Matata left the research facility; the first day she was gone, he used his lexigrams more than 300 times, asking Savage-Rumbaugh for comfort and for help finding his mother.

Eventually, Kanzi was using hundreds of symbols—representing objects, activities, and even abstract concepts like now. Savage-Rumbaugh also claims Kanzi can understand almost 3,000 English words, an assertion she has tested repeatedly by giving Kanzi specific and unusual instructions—such as putting pine needles in the refrigerator—via a headset or sitting motionless and with her face masked, conditions that prevent him from interpreting her facial expressions or gestures.[b] He is nearly always successful. His sister Panbanisha has made similar achievements in learning to communicate with lexigrams and understand spoken English.

In addition to being able to communicate with their human family, Savage-Rumbaugh claims Kanzi and Panbanisha are *bicultural*—able to view the world in a manner similar both to bonobos who do not use language, like Matata, and to humans. Panbanisha's son Nyota and Kanzi's son Teco—ape and human-reared offspring of language-competent apes—provide an additional unique opportunity for Savage-Rumbaugh and her colleagues to investigate the concept of human–ape biculturalism.

For instance, infant Teco, like a human baby, did not cling with his feet. He also demonstrates more ability to consciously control his tongue and breathing.[c] Savage-Rumbaugh sees this as evidence of neural changes preceding physical changes, in part due to the shared culture enabled by better communication. In a 2012 interview with *Harper's*, Savage-Rumbaugh describes her findings:

If one wants to determine how we became human, one has to look at the cultural transitions from quadrupedal to bipedal, from clinging to not clinging, from foraging to carrying food and storing, from inhabiting only warm climates to inhabiting all climates, from fear of fire to control of fire, and so on. These are things we do not because we are human, but because our culture defines them as productive ways of living.[d]

Research like Savage-Rumbaugh's—and bonobos like Kanzi—remind us of how much humans and apes have to learn from each other.

Biocultural Question

Compare the way that Kanzi and Panbanisha acquired language to how a human child learns language. Do you agree with Savage-Rumbaugh that these bonobos are bicultural? Are you bicultural in any ways? Is this reflected in your language?

[a]Hamilton, J. (2006, July 8). A voluble visit with two talking apes. National Public Radio. July 8, 2006. http://www.npr.org/2006/07/08/5503685/a-voluble-visit-with-two-talking-apes (retrieved October 9, 2015)

[b]Raffaele, P. (2006, November). Speaking bonobo. *Smithsonian Magazine*. http://www.smithsonianmag.com/science-nature/speaking-bonobo-134931541/?no-ist=&page=1 (retrieved October 9, 2015)

[c]Hale, B. (2012, August 6). A Q&A with Sue Savage-Rumbaugh. *Harper's Magazine*. http://harpers.org/blog/2012/08/a-qa-with-sue-savage-rumbaugh/ (retrieved October 9, 2015)

[d]Ibid.

deviants would be expected, whereas the elaborate prosocial prescriptions that favor altruism would come as a surprise" (Boehm, 2000, p. 7).

With primate survival dependent on social cooperation, evolutionary forces favor the development of strong communication skills. Decades-long experiments with captive apes reveal remarkable communicative abilities. In some cases bonobos and chimpanzees have been taught to communicate using symbols, as in the case of Kanzi, a bonobo who uses a visual keyboard (see this chapter's Biocultural Connection). Other chimpanzees, gorillas, and orangutans have been taught American Sign Language.

Controversy surrounds this research in part because it challenges notions of human uniqueness. Nevertheless, it has become evident that apes are quite capable of understanding language and can even use rudimentary grammar. They generate original utterances, ask questions, distinguish naming something from asking for it, develop original ways to tell lies, coordinate their actions, and spontaneously teach language to others. Even though they cannot literally "speak," it is now clear that all of the great ape species can develop language skills to the level of a 2- to 3-year-old human (Lestel, 1998; Miles, 1993). At the same time, chimps can outperform college students at a computer-based memory game (Inoue & Matsuzawa, 2007). Over the course of evolution, human brains have lost some visual-spatial skill to make space for language.

Numerous examples of inventive behavior that gets passed on to the group through imitation have been observed among monkeys and apes. The snow monkeys or macaques of the research colony on Koshima

© Cengage Learning

Age Fotostock/Superstock

Figure 4.11 Macaque Social Learning

In the same way that young Imo got her troop to begin washing sweet potatoes in saltwater, at the Kyoto University Primate Research Institute's field station on Koshima Island another young female macaque recently taught other macaques to bathe in hot springs. In the Nagano Mountains of Japan, this macaque, named Mukubili, began bathing in the springs. Others followed her, and now this is an activity practiced by all members of the group.

grain could be separated from sand if it was placed in water. The sand sank and the grain floated clean, making it much easier to eat. She also began washing the sweet potatoes that primatologists provided—first in fresh water but later in the ocean, presumably because of the pleasant saltwater taste. In each case, only the young animals imitated the innovations; Imo's mother was the lone older macaque to embrace them right away. Similarly, a female macaque named Mukubili at a field site in the Nagano Mountains initiated the practice of bathing in hot springs, a behavior other members of the group happily adopted (Figure 4.11).

Researchers noted another example of innovation in food manipulation among captive chimpanzees in the zoo of Madrid, Spain. It began when a 5-year-old female rubbed apples against a sharp corner of a concrete wall in order to lick the mashed pieces and juice left on the wall. From this youngster, the practice of "smearing" spread to her peers, and within five years most group members were performing the operation frequently and consistently. The innovation has become standardized and durable, having transcended two generations in the group (Fernández-Carriba & Loeches, 2001).

Freely living chimpanzees in West Africa provide another dramatic example of learning: These chimps have developed a way to crack open hard-shelled oil-palm nuts—the hardest nuts in the world. For this they use tools: an anvil stone with a level surface on which to place the nut and a good-sized hammerstone to crack it. Not just any stone will do; it must be the right shape and weight, and the anvil may require leveling by placing smaller stones beneath one or more edges. Nor does random banging away do the job. The nut must be hit at the right speed and trajectory or it simply flies off into the forest. Lastly, the apes must avoid mashing their fingers rather than the nut. According to fieldworkers, the expertise of the chimps far exceeds that of any human who tries cracking these tough nuts.

Youngsters learn this process by staying near to adults who are cracking nuts, where their mothers share some of the food. This teaches them about the edibility of the

Island, Japan, are famous for this. In the 1950s and early 1960s, one particularly bright young female macaque named Imo (Japanese primatologists always considered it appropriate to name individual animals) started several innovative behaviors in her troop. She figured out that

nuts but not how to get at what is edible. This they learn by observing and "aping" (copying) the adults. At first, they play with a nut or stone alone; later they begin to randomly combine objects. They soon learn, however, that placing nuts on anvils and hitting them with a hand or foot gets them nowhere.

Only after three years of futile effort do they begin to coordinate all the actions and objects. Even then, and only after a great deal of practice by the age of 6 or 7 years, do they become proficient. They practice this skill for over a thousand days. Evidently, social motivation accounts for their perseverance when after at least three years of failure no reward reinforces their effort. At first, a desire to act like their mothers motivates them; only later does the desire to feed on the tasty nutmeat take over (de Waal, 2001a).

Use of Objects as Tools

Young primates learn how to make and use tools from adults in the group. A **tool** may be defined as an object used to facilitate some task or activity. The nut cracking just discussed—involving both hands, two tools, and exact coordination—is the most complex tool-use task observed by researchers in the wild. But other examples of tool use among apes in the wild abound. Chimpanzees, bonobos, and orangutans all make and use tools.

Tool use and toolmaking capacities are distinct traits. Tool use—for example, pounding something with a convenient stone—requires far less acumen than toolmaking, which involves deliberate modification of some material for an intended use. Otters that use unmodified stones to crack open clams may be tool users, but they are not toolmakers. Not only do chimpanzees modify objects to make them suitable for particular purposes, but they also modify these objects in regular and set patterns. They pick up and even prepare objects for future use at some other location, and they can use objects as tools to solve new problems.

Chimps have been observed using stalks of grass, twigs that they have stripped of leaves, and sticks up to 3 feet (.9 meters) long that they have smoothed down to "fish" for termites (Figure 4.12). They insert the modified stick

Martin Harvey/Photolibrary/Getty Images

Figure 4.12 Fishing for Termites
Chimps use a variety of tools in the wild. Here a chimp uses a long stick stripped of its side branches to fish for termites—the first chimp tool use described by Jane Goodall in the 1960s. Chimps will select a stick when still quite far from the termite mound and modify its shape on the way to the snacking spot.

tool An object used to facilitate some task or activity. Although toolmaking involves intentional modification of the material of which it is made, tool use may involve objects either modified for some particular purpose or completely unmodified.

into a termite nest, wait a few minutes, pull the stick out, and eat the insects clinging to it, all of which requires considerable dexterity. Chimpanzees are equally deliberate in their own nest building, testing vines and branches for sturdiness before settling down in a tree. Chimps will move to another site if the conditions are not adequate.

Other examples of tool use among chimpanzees include leaves used as wipes or sponges to get drinking water out of a hollow. In aggressive or defensive displays, chimps use large sticks and stones as clubs or missiles. Chimps use twigs as toothpicks to clean teeth as well as to extract loose baby teeth. They use these dental tools on themselves as well as on one another (McGrew, 2000).

In the wild, bonobos have not been observed making and using tools to the extent seen in chimpanzees. However, their use of trail markers may be considered a form of tool use. Further, a captive bonobo has been observed learning how to make stone tools that are remarkably like the earliest tools our own ancestors made, providing further evidence of their toolmaking capacities.

That chimpanzees use plants for medicinal purposes illustrates their selectivity with raw materials, a skill required to tool manufacture. Chimps that appear ill have been observed seeking out specific plants of the genus *Aspilia*. They eat the leaves one at a time without chewing them, instead letting them soften in their mouths for a long time before swallowing. Primatologists have discovered the leaves pass through the chimps' digestive systems relatively intact, scraping parasites off the intestinal walls in the process.

Although gorillas (like bonobos and chimps) build nests, they have not been observed to make and use other tools in the wild. This likely stems from the fact that they have no particular need for tools to obtain their easily obtained diet of leaves and nettles.

Hunting

Prior to the 1980s, most primates were thought to be vegetarian, with humans alone considered meat-eating hunters. Since then, detailed field studies have revealed that many primates are omnivores who eat a broad range of foods. Though some do have specialized adaptations—such as a complex stomach and shearing teeth to aid in the digestion of leaves or an extra-long small intestine to slow the passage of juicy fruits to maximize their absorption—the diets of monkeys and apes are extremely varied. Goodall's fieldwork among chimpanzees at Gombe demonstrates that these apes supplement their primary diet of fruits and other plant foods with insects and meat. Even more surprising, she found that in addition to killing small invertebrate animals for food, chimpanzees also hunt and eat monkeys. Chimps grab adult red colobus monkeys and flail them to death. Since Goodall's pioneering work, other primatologists have documented

hunting behavior in baboons and capuchin monkeys, among others.

Chimpanzee females sometimes hunt, but males do so far more frequently. The hunters spend hours watching, following, and chasing intended prey. Moreover, instead of the usual primate practice of each animal finding its own food, hunting frequently involves teamwork to trap and kill prey, particularly when hunting baboons. Once a potential victim has been isolated from its troop, three or more adult chimps will carefully position themselves to block escape routes while another pursues the prey. Following the kill, most who participated get a share of the meat, either by grabbing a piece as chance affords or by begging for it.

Chimpanzees frequently kill animals weighing up to 25 pounds and eat much more meat than previously believed. Annually, hunting parties of chimps at Gombe kill about 20 percent of the population of colobus monkeys that share their habitat, many of them babies, often by shaking them out of 30-foot (about 9 meters) treetops. Chimps may capture and kill as many as seven victims in a raid. These hunts usually take place during the dry season when plant foods are less available. On average, each chimp at Gombe eats about one-fourth of a pound of meat per day during the dry season. For female chimps, a supply of protein-rich food helps support the increased nutritional requirements of pregnancy and lactation.

In West Africa, somewhat different chimpanzee hunting practices have been observed. At Tai National Park in Côte d'Ivoire, for instance, chimpanzees engage in highly coordinated team efforts to chase monkeys hiding in very tall trees in the dense tropical forest. Individuals who especially distinguish themselves in a successful hunt are rewarded with more meat.

Bonobos also supplement their diet with meat obtained by hunting, although among bonobos, females predominantly hunt. These female hunters regularly share carcasses with other females but are less likely to share with males. Even when the most dominant male throws a tantrum nearby, he may still be denied a share of meat. Female bonobos behave in much the same way when it comes to sharing other foods such as fruits.

Although it has long been assumed that male chimpanzees were the primary hunters, U.S. primatologist Jill Pruetz and her colleagues researching in Fongoli, Senegal, have documented habitual hunting by groups

© Cengage Learning

of young female and male chimpanzees using spears. The chimps took spears they had sharpened with their teeth and jabbed them repeatedly into the hollow parts of trees where small animals, including primates, might be hiding. Although the male chimpanzees in Fongoli still do the majority of the killing, the researchers found that females did most of the tool-assisted hunting (Pruetz et al., 2015).

© Cengage Learning

That young chimpanzees, one adolescent female in particular, are the most frequent spear hunters indicates that this innovation appeared in the group quite recently. Just as the young female Japanese macaques mentioned previously were the innovators in those groups, this young female chimp seems to be leading this behavior in Senegal. The savannah conditions of the Fongoli Reserve make these observations particularly interesting in terms of human evolutionary studies: Paleoanthropologists have suggested that among our ancestors out on the savannah, males hunted while females gathered. The Fongoli observation undermines this theory.

The Question of Culture

The more we learn of the behavior of our nearest primate relatives, the more we become aware of their learned, socially shared practices and knowledge. Do chimpanzees, bonobos, and other apes have culture? The answer appears to be yes. Detailed studies of ape behavior reveal varied use of tools and patterns of social engagement that seem to derive from the traditions of a specific group rather than from a biologically determined script. A young individual's ability to learn a social group's complex, flexible patterns of behavior is something the other apes share with humans.

If we agree that these other primates possess culture, does this demand rethinking how humans behave toward them, such as stopping the use of monkeys and apes in biomedical research and ending animal trafficking? Jane Goodall argues vehemently for this change. She emphasizes that cultural processes determine the place of animals within biomedical research, and she advocates eliminating the cultural distinction between humans and our closest relatives. (See this chapter's Anthropology Applied feature for more on Goodall's advocacy work.) Governments have begun responding to her calls as seen by the 2008 approval by the Spanish Parliament of the

"Declaration on Great Apes," which extends some human rights to gorillas, chimpanzees, bonobos, and orangutans (O'Carroll, 2008). In 2015, two laboratory chimpanzees in New York State were briefly given a writ of *habeas corpus*, which appeared to legally grant them personhood. The judge later amended the court order to remove the phrase, but the high-profile case garnered much public attention (Grimm, 2015).

In December 2010 the U.S. National Institutes of Health (NIH) commissioned the U.S. Institute of Medicine to study whether there was a need for chimps in biomedical and behavioral research. The answer was such an unequivocal no that the NIH will no longer fund any new projects involving research chimpanzees. The NIH also committed to reviewing all existing studies and dismantling any that do not meet the stringent criteria outlined in the Institute of Medicine's report. By 2012, the NIH decided to retire most government-owned chimpanzees to sanctuaries. In 2015, research using chimpanzees stopped altogether.

Despite this progress, powerful social barriers still work against the well-being of our animal relatives. In Western societies there has been an unfortunate tendency to erect what paleontologist Stephen Jay Gould refers to as "golden barriers" that set us apart from the rest of the animal kingdom (quoted in de Waal, 2001a). Sadly, this mindset blinds us to the fact that a continuum exists between us (humans) and them (animals), which in turn may lead us to more easily justify primate trafficking and cruelty (see this chapter's Globalscape). We have already seen that the physical differences between humans and apes are largely differences of degree, rather than kind. It now appears that the same is true with respect to behavior. As British primatologist Richard Wrangham put it,

> Like humans, [chimpanzees] laugh, make up after a quarrel, support each other in times of trouble, medicate themselves with chemical and physical remedies, stop each other from eating poisonous foods, collaborate in the hunt, help each other over physical obstacles, raid neighboring groups, lose their tempers, get excited by dramatic weather, invent ways to show off, have family traditions and group traditions, make tools, devise plans, deceive, play tricks, grieve, are cruel and are kind. (quoted in Mydans, 2001, p. 5)

This is not to say that we are "just" another ape; obviously, degree does make a difference. Nevertheless, the continuities between our primate kin and us reflect a common evolutionary heritage, giving us the responsibility to help our cousins today. The biology and behavior of the other living primates, like the contemporary study of genetics, provide valuable insight into human origins. We next turn to the methods scientists use in the study of the human past, allowing us to recover data directly from fossilized bones and preserved cultural remains.

Chimpanzees in Biomedical Research: Jane Goodall and the Fight to End the Practice

Biological similarities among humans, apes, and Old World monkeys have led to the extensive use of nonhuman primate species in biomedical research aimed at preventing or curing disease in humans. Some biomedical research disturbs animals minimally. For example, DNA can be extracted from the hair naturally shed by living primates, allowing for cross-species comparisons of disease genes. Other biomedical research is far more invasive. For example, to document the infectious nature of kuru, a disease closely related to mad cow disease, extract from the brains of sick humans is injected into the brains of living chimpanzees, who develop the classic features of kuru—uncontrollable spasticity, seizures, dementia, and ultimately death.

These research animals are subjected to procedures that would be considered morally reprehensible if done on humans. Jane Goodall makes a convincing case for ending the practice of invasive research:

> Surely it should be a matter of moral responsibility that we humans, differing from other animals mainly by virtue of our more highly developed intellect and, with it, our greater capacity for understanding and compassion, ensure that the medical progress slowly detaches its roots from the manure of non-human animal suffering and despair. Particularly when this involves the servitude of our closest relatives.[a]

Mickey, pictured here, was one of the hundreds of chimps who spent decades of her life alone in a concrete-and-steel windowless cage in a private research facility in New Mexico run by Frederick Coulston. After years of testing the effects of various infectious diseases, cosmetics, drugs, and pesticides on chimps like Mickey, the Coulston laboratory finally closed in 2002 when government research funding was withdrawn due to repeated violations of the Animal Welfare Act. But after years of abuse and neglect, research chimpanzees lack the skills to participate in chimpanzee social life. Furthermore, research animals have often been infected with

Courtesy of Save the Chimps, the world's largest sanctuary for rescued chimpanzees; www.savethechimps.org

The toll of a life spent in the Coulston research facility is evident in Mickey, who has since been rescued by Save the Chimps.

deadly diseases such as HIV or hepatitis and cannot be released into the wild. Fortunately, Mickey and the other research chimps were given sanctuary through Save the Chimps, one of several organizations that rescue research animals.

Goodall, a UN Messenger of Peace, has remained vocal about this issue throughout her career. In 2011, after over 200 government-owned chimps were slated to be sent to the Southwest National Primate Research Center in Texas to be available for invasive research, Goodall and 1,000 scientists and doctors sent a letter to the director of the National Institutes of Health (NIH) demanding an end this practice. In 2013, the NIH decided to retire all but 50 of its chimps. In a gratified yet poignant statement, Goodall praised the decision while calling for the nation to remember the 50 chimps who remained.[b]

The biological similarities of humans and other primates leading to such research practices derive from a long, shared evolutionary history. By comparison, the cultural rules that have allowed our closest relatives to be the subjects of biomedical research are relatively recent. In November 2015, Dr. Goodall's call was heard: the head of the U.S. NIH announced that the fifty chimpanzees reserved for potential research studies would all be eligible for retirement.

[a]Goodall, J. (1990). *Through a window: My thirty years with the chimpanzees of Gombe.* Boston: Houghton Mifflin.

[b]Sweeney, S. (2013, June 26). NIH director accepts recommendations to retire research chimpanzees. Jane Goodall Institute. http://www.janegoodall.org/media/news/nih-director-accepts-recommendations-retire-research-chimpanzees (retrieved October 9, 2015)

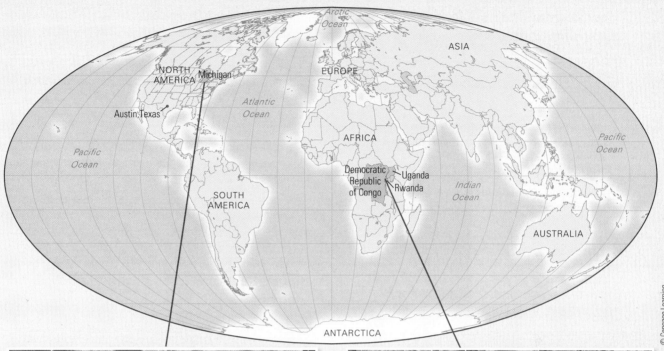

Gorilla Hand Ashtrays?

Ashley, a 20-year-old from Austin, Texas, once tweeted: "Guy at this party talking about gorilla hand ashtrays! What?" The unnamed guy was talking about one of the many real threats to gorillas in the wild. With no natural enemies, human actions alone are responsible for the shrinking population of gorillas in their natural habitats in Rwanda, Uganda, and the Democratic Republic of Congo. Despite conservation work begun by the late primatologist Dian Fossey, who pioneered field studies of the gorillas in the 1970s, ashtrays made from gorilla hands and gorilla heads remain coveted souvenirs for unsavory tourists. A poacher can sell these body parts and the remaining bushmeat for a handsome profit.

Today, not only do logging and mining in gorilla habitats destroy these forests, but new roads make it easier for poachers to access the gorillas. Local governments of Rwanda and Uganda, in partnership with the Fossey Fund and the Bush Meat Project, have organized poaching patrols and community partnerships to protect the endangered gorillas. Thousands of miles away, Ashley and her friends can also help by recycling their cell phones. The mineral coltan (shown in Chapter 1, Figure 1.8) that is found in cell phones is mined primarily from gorilla habitats in the Democratic Republic of Congo. Recycling, as pictured here in a Michigan cell phone recycling plant, will reduce the amount of new coltan needed.

Global Twister

Encouraging recycling of cell phones and discouraging poaching both will help protect gorilla populations. How would you go about convincing average cell phone users or poachers to change their habits or livelihoods to protect endangered gorillas?

© Cengage Learning

Jim West/Alamy

© Population Media, www.populationmedia.org

CHAPTER CHECKLIST

How does primate social organization differ among species?

✓ Chimps and bonobos compose communities of up to fifty members split among subgroups that change as individuals join and leave.

✓ Gorillas group into "families" led by a silver-backed male who tends to have exclusive mating rights. Upon maturity, younger males are forced to leave their natal group and may go on to form their own family or join an all-male group.

✓ Baboons live in troops of varying size that may comprise several smaller single-male multi-female (polygynous) groups.

✓ Gibbons and a few other species are monogamous and live with only their nuclear families.

How does primate biology reflect behavioral and environmental factors?

✓ Natural selection has favored single births among tree-dwelling primates whose young must cling to their mothers for transport. The long period until maturity provides opportunity for learning social behaviors, communication, and practical skills.

✓ Bonobo genitals maintain a constant state of swelling, which conceals ovulation and reflects their frequent and regular sexual activity. Sexual interactions are an important component of bonobo social organization and often mark reconciliation.

✓ A free upper lip allows apes a greater range of facial expression than that present in other primates, which contributes to their advanced communicative abilities.

✓ Baboons and some other species possess ischial callosities, permitting them to sit for long durations—an important feature for ground-dwellers. Primatologists have proposed that sexual dimorphism varies among primate species according to the degree of male–male competition.

What are some possible cultural influences on theories about primate behavior?

✓ Primatologists from male-biased cultures supposed that male-dominated hierarchies were the natural order of other primate social structures. However, female dominance is prevalent among some species, such as bonobos.

✓ A host of characteristics—including size, the rank of one's mother, motivation, and alliances—contribute to an individual's rank within primate groups.

✓ Western social norms may skew perceptions of the importance of social hierarchy and male–male competition in primatology. Cooperation and reconciliation are vitally important aspects of primate behavior.

✓ Females' choices in selection of mates based on affiliative and paternal behavioral qualities are important evolutionary forces among many primates.

How do the behavioral patterns and linguistic capabilities of the great apes compare?

✓ Apes combine vocalizations, gesturing, and facial expressions to communicate a variety of messages directly. Survival for many species depends on strong communication skills and effective social cooperation.

✓ Individuals in captivity have been taught to communicate using visual symbols and have learned American Sign Language. Innovation and adoption of new skills by whole groups is widespread.

✓ Chimps and bonobos are known for making tools whereas gorillas do not. Furthermore, chimps know to use certain plants for medicinal purposes and regularly hunt monkeys and other smaller animals, even using prepared spears.

What ethical concerns arise from the use of primates in biomedical research?

✓ The use of primates in biomedical research was traditionally derived from a firm distinction between the other primates and us.

✓ Recognition of primate culture contradicts the suppositions of human uniqueness.

✓ As our closest relatives, apes deserve the same rights we extend to fellow humans.

✓ Recent laws in several countries have begun to ban the use of apes in biomedical research.

QUESTIONS FOR REFLECTION

1. Does human morality differ from the building blocks of morality observed in some ape species? What facets of your own morality do you feel you were born with? What facets have you learned?

2. What kinds of communication systems have been observed in primates? How do these differ from human language? How are they the same?

3. Given the variation seen in the specific behaviors of chimp, bonobo, and gorilla groups, is it fair to say that these primates possess culture?

4. Many primate species are endangered today due to human action. What features of ape biology also contribute to apes' limited population size? Do these biological limitations pertain to humans? Why or why not?

DIGGING INTO ANTHROPOLOGY

Picture This

Kanzi the bonobo uses pictograms to communicate. Humans use pictures to communicate as well—from prehistoric paintings to ancient and modern hieroglyphic writing to current societies using complex text-based written languages. For instance, a generic figure of a person may denote a restroom. A red circle with a slash through it indicates something is forbidden. Many people today also incorporate emoji into their daily text messaging and other written communications. In fact, John McWhorter, a linguist at Columbia University, calls emoji an expressive human way to converse and even to convey tone in a medium that does not allow for many words (Haber, 2015).

How much do picture communications impact your life? Have you ever had a pictures-only conversation on a phone or online? Could you communicate using only pictures? For one day, make note of all the times picture communication is part of your day, from wordless street signs to food and clothing labels to computer icons to emoticons. Do the results surprise you?

REUTERS/Social Media

CHALLENGE ISSUE

Even in ideal circumstances, paleoanthropological and archaeological fieldwork is demanding and delicate. Scientific efforts can be further complicated when local groups contest the rights to ancient remains. In an extreme example, in May 2015 militants from the group known as ISIL (Islamic State of Iraq and the Levant) or ISIS (Islamic State of Iraq and Syria) captured the ancient city of Palmyra, located in the heart of present-day Syria. As the center of the Palmyrene empire, which extended from lands in present-day Turkey to Egypt in the 3rd century, the city was known for its blend of Greco-Roman and Persian styles of art and architecture. The site had already been extensively looted and vandalized amid the chaos of the Syrian civil war, ongoing since 2012, but its capture by ISIL marked a drastic and irreversible fate for the city. ISIL announced a policy of destruction of statues and shrines built for ancient deities, pictured here, which these militant religious fundamentalists consider sacrilegious. Even more tragically, in August 2015 the group executed Syrian archaeologist Khaled al-Asaad when he refused to help them locate ancient treasures that ISIL wanted to sell to fund their activities. Al-Asaad had helped organize efforts to relocate many artifacts for safekeeping and was a lifelong scholar of the UNESCO World Heritage protected site. Investigating and preserving ancient remains challenge us to collectively solve the complex question of who owns the past and how we can best protect precious remains. Archaeologists maintain that for the benefit of local peoples and the global community alike, these questions must be answered with an eye to long-term preservation, cooperation, and peace.

Field Methods in Archaeology and Paleoanthropology

Paleoanthropologists and archaeologists reconstruct the biology and behavior of humans and their ancestors using a remarkable array of techniques. They share a focus on **prehistory**, a conventional term used to refer to the period of time before written records. For some people, the term *prehistoric* might conjure up images of "primitive" cavemen and cavewomen, but it does not imply a lack of history or any inferiority—merely a lack of *written* history. The next several chapters of this book will consider that ancient past; this chapter prepares for that exploration by presenting the methods archaeologists and paleoanthropologists use to give us our understanding of human prehistory.

Most of us are familiar with some kind of archaeological material: a coin dug out of the earth, a fragment of an ancient pot, a spear point used by an ancient hunter. Archaeology consists of far more than finding and cataloguing such cultural treasures. Instead, archaeologists use material and ecological remains to reconstruct the culture and worldview of past human societies. Archaeologists examine every recoverable detail from past societies, including all kinds of structures: temples, hearths, garbage dumps, bones, and plant remains. Although it may appear that archaeologists are digging up *things*, they are really digging up human biology, behavior, and beliefs.

Similarly, paleoanthropologists who study the physical remains of our ancestors and other ancient primates do more than find and catalogue old bones. Paleoanthropologists recover, describe, and organize these remains to see what they can tell us about human biological evolution.

prehistory A conventional term used to refer to the period of time before the appearance of written records.

In This Chapter You Will Learn To

- Define the site identification and excavation methods of archaeologists and paleoanthropologists.

- Describe the best excavation practices with particular emphasis on collaboration among diverse scientists and community members.

- Explain how archaeologists and paleoanthropologists employ a variety of laboratory techniques in their investigations once an excavation is complete.

- Distinguish among various absolute and relative dating methods.

- Describe geologic time, continental drift, and molecular clocks and their role in reconstructing the past.

Recovering Cultural and Biological Remains

Archaeologists and paleoanthropologists face a dilemma. The only way to thoroughly investigate our past is to excavate sites where cultural and biological remains are found. Unfortunately, excavation results in a site's destruction. Thus, anthropologists precisely record the location and context of everything recovered, no matter how small, as they excavate. Without these records, the knowledge that can be derived from such remains diminishes dramatically. As anthropologist Brian Fagan has put it, "The fundamental premise of excavation is that all digging is destructive, even that done by experts. The archaeologist's primary responsibility, therefore, is to record a site for posterity as it is dug because there are no second chances" (Fagan, 1995, p. 19).

Archaeologists excavate to recover an **artifact**, any object fashioned or altered by humans—a flint scraper, a basket, an axe, the ruins of a house or its walls. An artifact expresses a facet of human culture. Artifacts, as products or representations of human behavior and beliefs, help archaeologists define **material culture**, or durable aspects of culture such as tools, structures, and art. Archaeologists also integrate an **ecofact**, the natural remains of plants and animals found in the archaeological record, to help them interpret much about associated artifacts. A further distinction is made between these categories and a **feature**, which is a nonportable element of human activity such as a hearth or a ditch or an architectural element such as a wall. Archaeologists take into account how the artifacts and physical remains make their way into the ground. What people do with the things they have made, how they dispose of them, and how they lose them reflect important aspects of human culture.

Cultural and physical remains represent distinct kinds of data, but the most comprehensive interpretation of the human past requires the integration of ancient human biology and culture. Often paleoanthropologists and archaeologists work together to systematically excavate and analyze fragmentary remains, placing scraps of bone, shattered pottery, and scattered campsites into broad interpretive contexts.

The Nature of Fossils

Some of the oldest biological remains have survived through the process of fossilization. Broadly defined, a **fossil** is any mineralized trace or impression of an organism that has been preserved in the earth's crust from a past geologic time. Fossilization typically involves the hard parts of an organism like bones, teeth, shells, horns, and the woody tissues of plants. Although the soft parts of an organism are rarely fossilized, casts or impressions of footprints, brains, and even whole bodies are sometimes found. Because dead animals quickly attract meat-eating scavengers and bacteria that cause decomposition, they rarely survive long enough to become fossilized. Entirely preserved fossil skeletons dating from before the cultural practice of burial about 100,000 years ago are exceedingly rare (Figure 5.1).

For an organism to become a fossil, it must be covered by some protective substance soon after death. Preservation of an organism or part of an organism can take place

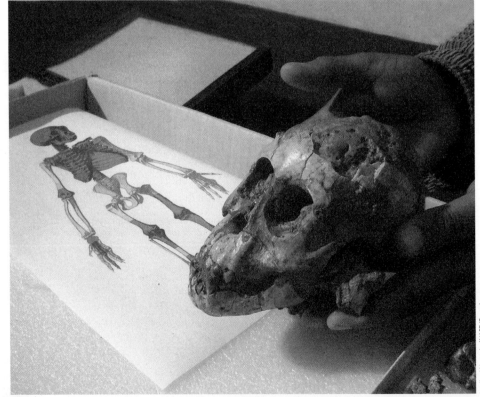

Figure 5.1 Lucy's Baby
In September 2006, researchers announced the discovery of a spectacular new fossil—the skeleton of a young child dated to 3.3 million years ago. The fossil was first discovered in the Dikika area of northern Ethiopia in 2000. Since then, researchers worked on careful recovery and analysis of the fossilized remains so that when the announcement was made in 2006, a great deal was already known about the specimen. Their analyses have determined that this child, a little girl about 3 years old who likely died in a flash flood, was a member of the same species as the famous Lucy specimen (see Chapter 6). Due to the importance of this find, scientists have referred to this child as "Lucy's Baby" though the child lived about 150,000 years before Lucy.

Lealisa Westerhoff/AFP/Getty images

Jean Louis Pradels/Maxppp/Landov

Figure 5.2 **The Ice Man Ötzi**
In rare circumstances, human bodies are so well preserved that they could be mistaken for recent corpses. Such is the case of Ötzi, the 5,200-year-old Ice Man, exposed by the melting of an alpine glacier in the Tyrolean Alps in 1991. Both the Italian and the Austrian governments felt they had legitimate claims on this rare find, and they mounted legal, geographic, and taphonomic arguments for housing the body. These arguments continued as the specimen, just released from the ice, began to thaw.

in a number of ways that do not necessarily lead to fossilization. The whole animal may be frozen in ice (Figure 5.2), like the famous mammoths found in Siberia, safe from predators, weathering, and bacteria. Natural resins exuding from evergreen trees may enclose an organism allowing it to later become hardened and fossilized as a golden translucent material known as *amber*. Specimens of spiders and insects dating back millions of years have been preserved in the Baltic Sea area in northeastern Europe, which is rich in resin-producing evergreens such as pine, spruce, and fir trees.

Lake bottoms and sea basins provide optimal conditions for preservation because sediment can quickly cover the organism. An entire organism may also be mummified or preserved in tar pits, peat, oil, or asphalt bogs, in which the chemical environment prevents the growth of decay-producing bacteria.

However, fossils generally consist of scattered teeth and fragments of bones found embedded in rock deposits. Most have been altered in some way in the process of becoming fossilized. **Taphonomy** (from the Greek for "grave"), the study of the biologic and geologic processes by which dead organisms become fossils, provides systematic understanding of the fossilization process vital for the scientific interpretations of the fossils themselves.

Fossilization occurs most frequently among marine animals and other creatures living near water. As the remains of organisms accumulate on the floor of shallow seas, rivers, or lakes, they become covered by sediment and silt, or sand. These materials gradually harden into shale and limestone, forming a protective shell around the skeleton of the organism. The internal cavities of bones or teeth and other parts of the skeleton fill in with mineral deposits from the sediment immediately surrounding the specimen. Then the external walls of the bone decay and are replaced by calcium carbonate or silica.

Unless protected in some way, the bones of a land-dweller are generally scattered and exposed to the deteriorating influence of the elements, predators, and scavengers.

artifact Any object fashioned or altered by humans.

material culture The durable aspects of culture, such as tools, structures, and art.

ecofact The natural remains of plants and animals found in the archaeological record.

feature A nonportable element such as a hearth or a ditch or an architectural element such as a wall that is preserved in the archaeological record.

fossil The mineralized remains of past life forms.

taphonomy The study of how bones and other materials come to be preserved in the earth as fossils.

Figure 5.3 **Sima de los Huesos**
To excavate the ancient Stone Age site Sima de los Huesos or "Pit of Bones," Spanish paleoanthropologist Juan Luis Arsuaga and his team spend nearly an hour each day traveling underground through a narrow passage to a small enclosed space, rich with human remains. Here, the fossils are excavated with great care and transported back to the laboratory, where the long process of interpretation and analysis begins. Arsuaga's team has proposed that the high number of individuals recovered from this single cave site indicates ritual surrounding death—a placement of the dead as in an ossuary rather than a burial. If true, this site, dated to sometime between 350,000 and 600,000 years ago, would provide some very early evidence of ritualistic treatment of the dead.

Occasionally, terrestrial animals living near lakes or rivers become fossilized if they die next to or in the water. A land-dweller may also become fossilized if it happens to die in a cave (Figure 5.3), or if some other meat-eating animal drags its remains to a site protected from erosion and decay. In caves, conditions are often excellent for fossilization, as minerals contained in water dripping from the ceiling may harden over bones left on the cave floor.

Burial of the Dead

The cultural practice of burial that began (regularly) about 100,000 years ago has increased the preservation of complete fossil skeletons. The human fossil record from before this time consists primarily of fragmentary remains with an occasional complete skeleton. The fossil record for many other primates is even poorer because organic materials decay rapidly in the tropical forests where they lived. The records are more complete for primates (such as evolving humans) that lived on the grassy plains or in savannah environments, where conditions were more favorable to the formation of fossils. Several localities in Ethiopia, Kenya, and Tanzania in East Africa, found near ancient lakes and streams and often encased between layers of volcanic ash, yield numerous fossils important for our understanding of human evolution.

Searching for Artifacts and Fossils

Where are artifacts and fossils found? Places containing archaeological remains of previous human activity are known as *sites*. Many kinds of sites exist, and sometimes it

© Javier Trueba/Science Photo Library

is difficult to define their boundaries, for remains may be strewn over large areas. Sites are even found under water (Figure 5.4). Some examples of sites identified by archaeologists and paleoanthropologists are hunting campsites, from which hunters went out to hunt game; kill sites, in which game was killed and butchered; village sites, in which domestic activities took place; and cemeteries, in which the dead, and sometimes their belongings, were buried.

As we go back in time, the association of skeletal and cultural remains becomes less likely. No cultural remains older than 2.6 million years have been discovered, perhaps because the earliest tools used by our ancestors were likely made of organic materials (such as the termite-fishing sticks used by chimpanzees) and so are much less likely to be preserved.

Site Identification

Although archaeologists still may discover sites for exploration by chance, modern survey techniques allow researchers to investigate, map, and plot large geographic areas for excavation. A survey can be made from the ground, but using remote sensing techniques is more common today. Archaeologists have used aerial photographs to find sites since the 1920s. They are still widely used today along with a variety of innovations in the geographical and geological sciences such as geographic information systems (GIS), ground-penetrating radar (GPR), and unmanned aerial vehicles (UAVs).

High-resolution aerial photographs, including satellite imagery, resulted in the astonishing discovery of over 500 miles of prehistoric roadways connecting numerous sites in the Four Corners region of the United States (where Arizona, New Mexico, Colorado, and Utah meet). This discovery led to a new understanding of prehistoric Pueblo Indian economic, social, and political organization. Evidently, large centers in this region governed a number of smaller satellite communities, mobilized labor for large public works, and allowed for the distribution of goods over substantial distances.

In open country, archaeologists can easily identify more obvious sites, such as the human-made mounds or *tells* of the Middle East, that rise as swells from the ground. Otherwise, a **soil mark**—a stain that shows up on the surface of recently plowed fields—can indicate a potential site. Soil marks led archaeologists to many of the Bronze Age burial mounds in Hertfordshire and Cambridgeshire, England. The mounds hardly rose out of the ground, yet each was circled at its core by chalky soil marks. In forested regions, changes in vegetation can provide evidence of a site. For example, the topsoil of ancient storage and refuse pits is often richer in organic matter than that of the surrounding areas, and so it grows distinctive vegetation. At Tikal, an ancient Maya site in Guatemala, breadnut trees usually grow near the remains of ancient houses, guiding archaeologists to these sites for exploration.

Archaeologists also use documents, maps, and folklore in the search for sites. For example, Homer's ancient Greek epic poem the *Iliad* helped lead Heinrich Schliemann, the famous

Figure 5.4 Underwater Archaeology
Here a diver recovers antique amphorae (the traditional containers for transporting wine, olives, olive oil, grain, and other commodities) from the site of a shipwreck in the Mediterranean Sea near the village of Kas, Turkey. The shipwreck dates back to the time of the Trojan War (over 3,000 years ago). Underwater archaeologists—led in this expedition by George Bass from the Institute of Nautical Archaeology of Texas A&M University collaborating with the Bodrum Museum of Underwater Archaeology in Bodrum, Turkey—reconstruct facets of the past, including ancient trade routes and shipbuilding techniques, through the analysis of such remains.

and controversial 19th-century German archaeologist, to the discovery of Troy. (As was typical of that time, Schliemann's excavation methods destroyed much of the actual remains.) Place names and local lore often indicate the presence of an archaeological site in an area. Archaeologists therefore often depend upon collaboration with local people who are familiar with the history of the land, or who even have ancestral connections to the physical and cultural remains being studied, as seen in this chapter's Original Study.

soil mark A stain that shows up on the surface of recently plowed fields revealing an archaeological site.

Action Archaeology and the Community at El Pilar BY ANABEL FORD

ORIGINAL STUDY

Resource management and conservation are palpable themes of the 21st century. Nowhere is this more keenly felt than in the tropics, seemingly our last terrestrial frontier. The Maya forest, one of the world's most biodiverse areas, is experiencing change at a rapid rate. Over the next decades this area's population will double, threatening the integrity of the tropical ecosystems with contemporary development strategies that are at odds with the rich biodiversity of the region.

Curiously, in the past the Maya forest was home to a major civilization with at least three to nine times the current population of the region. The prosperity of the Classic Maya civilization has been touted for the remarkable quality of their unique hieroglyphic writing; the beauty of their art expressed in stone, ceramics, and plaster; and the precision of their mathematics and astronomy. What was the secret of Maya conservation and prosperity? How can archaeology shed light on the conservation possibilities for the future? These are the questions I address in my research at El Pilar.

I began my work as an archaeologist in the Maya forest in 1972. Eschewing the monumental civic centers that draw tourist and scholar alike, I was interested in the everyday life of the Maya through the study of their cultural ecology—the multifaceted relationships of humans and their environment. Certainly, the glamorous archaeological centers intrigued me; they were testaments to the wealth of the Maya civilization. Yet, it seemed to me that an understanding of the ancient Maya landscape would tell us more about the relationship of the Maya and their forest than yet another major temple. After all, the Maya were an agrarian civilization.

The ancient Maya agricultural system must be the key to their growth and accomplishments. With more than a century of exploration of the temple centers, we know that the civic centers were made for the ceremonial use of the ruling elite, that the temples would hold tombs of the royals, and that they would include dedications of some of the most astounding artworks of the ancient world. Centers, too, would present stone stele erected in commemoration of regal accomplishments with hieroglyphic writing that is increasingly understood as codification of the Maya language. These facts about the Maya point to successful development founded in their land-use strategies that supported the increasing populations, underwrote the affluent elite glamour, and allowed for the construction and maintenance of major civic centers over two millennia. The Maya farmers were at the bottom of this astounding expansion, and that is where I thought there could be real discoveries.

Because agriculture figures so importantly in preindustrial agrarian societies, such as the Maya, we would expect that the majority of the settlements would be farming ones. But how can we understand the farming techniques and strategies? Our appreciation of the traditional land-use methods has been subverted with technology and a European ecological imperialism that inhibits a full understanding of other land-use systems.

During the conquest of the Maya area, Spaniards felt there was nothing to eat in the forest; presented with a staggering cornucopia of fruits and vegetables that could fill pages, they asserted they were starving because there was no grain or cattle. Today, we use European terms that are in many ways inappropriate in describing the agricultural lands of traditional systems. The word *arable* specifically means "plowable" and is derived from the Latin word *arare*, or "to plow." In common usage, *arable* is equated with *cultivable* and is considered in those terms by the United Nations Food and Agriculture Organization, as well as by E. O. Wilson in his treatise *The Future of Life*. But by doing so, the connotation eliminates land-use and management practices that have a subtler impact on the environment. *Fallow* is loosely used to indicate abandoned fields, but really *fallow* means "unseeded plowed field." To European eyes, plowing was equivalent to cultivating, but in the New World cultivating was done by hand and depended on natural rainfall. Thus, cultivating embraced a much broader meaning that included selected fields of crops, tree succession, diverse home gardens and orchards, and managed forest gardens. In fact, it meant the entire landscape mosaic.

It is important to remember that the Maya, like all Native Americans prior to the tumultuous conquest 500 years ago, lived in the Stone Age. Their land management did not need metal tools and worked without domesticated animals. This was not a hindrance, as it would seem today, but a fact that focused land use and intensification in other realms. Farmers were called upon to use their local skill and knowledge to provide for daily needs. And, as with all Native Americans, this skill would involve the landscape and most particularly the plants and their relationship to animal habitat.

Reports of yields of grain from the Mesoamerican maize fields, or *milpas*, suggest that they were more than two to three times as productive as the fertile fields of the Seine River near Paris of the 16th century, the time of the conquest. The Maya farmed in cooperation with the natural environment. Like the Japanese rice farmer Masanobu Fukuoka describes in his book *One Straw Revolution*, Maya farmers today use their knowledge of the insects to ensure pollination, their understanding of animals to promote propagation, their appreciation of water to determine planting, and their observations of change and nuance to increase their yields. This is not at all like current agricultural development models that rely on increasingly complex techniques to raise production, disregarding nature in the process.

My focus on the patterns of the ancient Maya settlements has provided me with important answers to questions of how the Maya achieved their success. The answers lie in finding where the everyday Maya lived, when they lived there, and what they did there. Although popular notions would have you think that the Maya were a seething sea of humanity displacing the forest for their cities, I have discovered patterns on the landscape indicating that at their height in the Late Classic from 600 to 900 CE, the Maya occupied less than two-thirds of the landscape. More than 80 percent of the settlements were concentrated into less than 40 percent of the area, whereas another 40 percent of the region was largely unoccupied. This diversity of land-use intensity created a patchwork of stages—what traditional farmers see as a cycle from forest to field and from field to orchard and from orchard back to forest again. The result in the Maya forest garden was an economic landscape that supported the ancient Maya, fueled wealth in the colonial and independence eras with lumber, and underwrote capitalism with the natural gum chicle. Today, more than 90 percent of the dominant trees of the forest are of economic value. The Maya constructed this valuable forest over the millennia.

El Pilar team members (left to right) archaeologists Clarke Wernecke, Anabel Ford, Rudy Larios, master forest gardener Carmen Cruz, and master story teller Teo Williams.

© Rolox Awards for Excellence, Susan Gray

Despite my interest in daily life in the forest, monumental buildings became a part of my work. While conducting a settlement survey in the forest, I uncovered and mapped El Pilar, a major ancient Maya urban center with enormous temples towering more than 22 meters high and plaza expanses greater than soccer fields. The whole center of civic buildings covers more than 50 hectares. El Pilar is the largest center in the Belize River area and is located only 47 kilometers from Tikal, which has become a tourist destination, presenting an opportunity to explore new ways to tell the Maya story. My observation that the ancient Maya evolved a sustainable economy in the tropics of Mesoamerica guided my approach to developing El Pilar.

Astride the imaginary line separating Belize from Guatemala, El Pilar has been the focus of a bold conservation design for an international peace park on a long-troubled border. The vision for El Pilar is founded on the preservation of cultural heritage in the context of the natural environment. With a collaborative and interdisciplinary team of local villagers, government administrators, and international scientists, we have established the El Pilar Archaeological Reserve for Maya Flora and Fauna. Since 1993, the innovations of the El Pilar program have forged new ground in testing novel strategies for community participation in the conservation development of the El Pilar Archaeological Reserve. This program touches major administrative themes of global importance: tourism, natural resources, foreign affairs, agriculture, rural development, and education. Yet the program's impact goes further. Working with traditional forest gardeners affects agriculture, rural enterprise, and capacity building. There are few areas untouched by the program's inclusive sweep, and more arenas can contribute to its evolution.

At El Pilar, I practice what I call "action archaeology," a pioneering conservation model that explores solutions of the past to draw out those that benefit contemporary populations. For example, the co-evolution of Maya society and the environment provide clues about sustainability in this region today. At El Pilar we have advanced programs that will simulate Maya forest gardens as an alternative to conventional resource-diminishing plow-and-pasture farming methods. Working with the traditional farmers, we have established model gardens that will help to transfer knowledge to the younger generation and carry on important embedded conservation strategies. The forest survives and demonstrates resilience to impacts brought on by human expansion. The ancient Maya lived with this forest for millennia, and the El Pilar program argues there are lessons to be learned from that past.

The El Pilar program recognizes the privilege it has enjoyed in forging an innovative community participatory process, in creating a unique management planning design, and in developing a new tourism destination. The success of local outreach at El Pilar can best be seen in the growth of the community organizations such as the El Pilar Forest Garden Network and Amigos de El Pilar. With groups based in both Belize and Guatemala working together, the El Pilar program can help build an inclusive relationship between the community and the reserve that is mutually beneficial. The development of this dynamic relationship lies at the heart of the El Pilar philosophy—resilient and with the potential to educate communities, reform local-level resource management, and inform conservation designs for the Maya forest.

Written expressly for this text, 2005. Anabel Ford is the director of the Mesoamerican Research Center, University of California, Santa Barbara, and president of the nonprofit Exploring Solutions Past: The Maya Forest Alliance. www.marc.ucsb.edu /elpilar/. Reprinted by permission of Professor Anabel Ford.

Patrick Dieudonne/Robert Harding Picture Library Ltd/Alamy

Figure 5.5 Village of Skara Brae
The gradual action of wind and storms blowing away sand eventually exposed the village of
stone huts dug into the ground at Skara Brae on Scotland's Orkney Islands. The structures were
occupied around 5,000 years ago, making them some of the best-preserved remnants of this era.

Sometimes natural processes, such as soil erosion or droughts, expose sites (Figure 5.5). For example, in eastern North America, erosion along coastlines and riverbanks may expose a prehistoric refuse mound known as a **midden**. Alternatively, human actions unrelated to anthropological investigations may reveal physical and cultural remains. For instance, limestone quarrying at a variety of sites in South Africa early in the 20th century led to the discovery of the earliest human-like fossils from millions of years ago (see Chapter 6). Disturbances of the earth on a smaller scale, such as plowing, may turn up bones, fragments of pots, and other archaeological objects.

Cultural Resource Management

Because construction projects frequently uncover archaeological remains, in many countries, including the United States, such projects require government approval in order to ensure the identification and protection of those finds (Figure 5.6). *Cultural resource management*, introduced in Chapter 1, is routinely included in the environmental review process for federally funded or licensed construction projects in North America, as it is in Europe. For example, in the United States, if the transportation department of a state government plans to replace a highway bridge, the state must first contract with archaeologists to identify and protect any significant resources that might be affected by this new construction.

Since passage of the Historic Preservation Act of 1966, the National Environmental Policy Act of 1969, the Archaeological and Historical Preservation Act of 1974, and the Archaeological Resources Protection Act of 1979, cultural resource management has been required for any construction project that is partially funded or licensed by the U.S. government. As a result, the practice of cultural resource management has flourished. Many archaeologists are employed by U.S. government agencies such as the Army Corps of Engineers, the National Park Service, the Forest Service, and the Natural Resource

midden A refuse or garbage disposal area in an archaeological site.

The U.S. National Park Service

Figure 5.6 African Burial Ground

In 1991, construction workers in New York's Lower Manhattan—at the site of a proposed 34-story, $276-million U.S. federal office building—discovered skeletal remains. This chance find led to one of the most important archaeological sites of colonial America: a massive African burial ground, covering nearly 6 acres. Activists, politicians, and anthropologists worked together to protect and ultimately excavate the site. The investigations documented the extreme physical hardships endured by these earliest American slaves—men women, and children—as well as the contributions they made to the economic and cultural development of colonial America. The excavations also showed how the slaves maintained some cultural continuity with their African homeland against great odds. After completing analyses of the skeletal remains of over 400 of the estimated 20,000 people buried there, the remains were respectfully reinterred in a commemorative ceremony, "Rites of Ancestral Return." Today, instead of an office building, a memorial and a historical exhibit mark the site.

Conservation Service, assisting in the preservation, restoration, and salvage of archaeological resources. Canada and the United Kingdom have programs very similar to those of the United States. From Chile to China, various governments use archaeological expertise to manage their cultural heritage.

When cultural resource management work or other archaeological investigation unearths Native American cultural items or human remains in the United States, federal laws come into the picture again. The Native American Graves Protection and Repatriation Act (**NAGPRA**), passed in 1990 by the U.S. Congress, outlines a process for the return of these remains to lineal descendants, culturally affiliated Indian tribes, and Native Hawaiian organizations. NAGPRA has become central to the work of anthropologists who study Paleo-Indian and more recent indigenous cultures in the United States.

In addition to working in all the capacities mentioned, archaeologists also consult for engineering firms to help them prepare environmental impact statements. Some of these archaeologists operate out of museums, universities,

NAGPRA The Native American Graves Protection and Repatriation Act, a federal law that outlines a process for the return of remains to related native peoples.

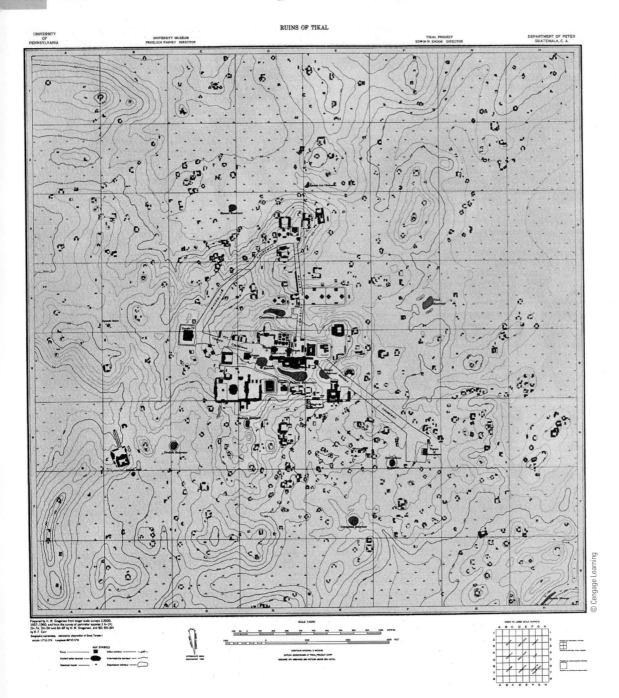

Figure 5.7 The Grid System

At large sites covering several square miles, archaeologists construct a giant grid, as shown in this map of the center of the ancient Maya city of Tikal in Guatemala. Each square of the grid is one-quarter of a square kilometer; excavators number individual structures according to the square in which they are found.

and colleges, while others work for independent consulting firms. When state legislation sponsors any kind of archaeological work, it is referred to as *contract archaeology*.

grid system A system for recording data in three dimensions for an archaeological excavation.

Excavation

Once investigators identify a site likely to contribute to their research agenda, they plan out an excavation designed to meet research goals. To begin the excavation, the team clears the land and plots the area as a **grid system** (Figure 5.7), dividing the site surface into squares of equal size and numbering and marking each square with stakes. This way, every object found can be located precisely in the square from which it came. Remember, context is everything!

Each grid system has a starting point, such as a large rock, the edge of a stone wall, or an iron rod sunk into the ground located precisely in three dimensions. This point is the reference or **datum point**. At large sites covering several square miles, the plotting may be done in terms of individual structures, numbered according to the squares that make up a giant grid. With great care, archaeological teams dig each square of the grid separately, using trowels to scrape the soil and screens to sift all the loose soils, to recover even the smallest artifacts such as flint chips or beads. Another technique, called **flotation**, consists of immersing soil in water causing the particles to separate. Some will float and others will sink to the bottom, allowing for easy retrieval of fine objects, such as fish scales or very small bones.

If the site is **stratified**—that is, if the remains lie in layers one upon the other—archaeologists will dig each layer, or stratum, separately. Each layer represents a particular span of time and period of settlement. Thus, it will contain artifacts deposited at the same time and belonging to the same culture (**Figure 5.8**). Cultural change can be traced through the order in which artifacts were deposited—deeper layers reveal older artifacts. If no stratification is present, then the archaeologist digs by arbitrary levels. Each square must be dug so that its edges and profiles are straight; walls between squares are often left standing to serve as visual correlates of the grid system.

Paleoanthropologists working on older sites, without the benefit of archaeological layers, must employy

geological expertise because interpretation of a fossil depends utterly on its place in the sequence of rocks that contain it. The geological context provides the dates that place specimens in the human evolutionary sequence. More recent archaeological sites can be dated more reliably. Hence, paleoanthropological expeditions today generally are made up of teams of specialists in various fields in addition to physical anthropology so that all the necessary expertise is available.

Excavation of Bones

Removing a fossil from its burial place without damage requires surgical skill and caution. To remove newly discovered bones, the paleoanthropologist begins uncovering the specimen using pick and shovel for initial excavation, then small camel-hair brushes and dental picks to remove loose and easily detachable debris surrounding the bones. Once the researchers uncover the entire specimen (a process that may take days of intensive patient labor), they cover the bones with shellac and tissue paper to prevent cracking and damage during further excavation and handling.

The excavation team prepares both the fossil and the earth immediately surrounding it, or the *matrix*, for removal as a single block. They cut the bones and matrix out of the earth but do not remove them. Next the team adds more shellac to the entire block to harden it. They cover the bones with burlap bandages dipped in plaster. Then they enclose the block in more plaster and burlap bandages, perhaps splinted with tree branches, and allow it to dry overnight. After it has hardened, the excavators carefully remove the entire block from the earth, now ready for packing and transport to a laboratory. Before leaving the discovery area, the investigator makes a thorough sketch map of the terrain and pinpoints the find on geological maps to aid future investigators.

The State of Preservation of Archaeological and Fossil Evidence

The results of an excavation depend greatly on the condition of the remains. Inorganic materials such as stone and metal are more resistant to decay than organic ones such as wood and bone. Sometimes the anthropologist discovers an *assemblage*—a collection of artifacts—made of durable inorganic materials, such as stone tools, and

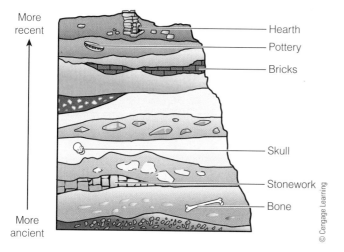

Figure 5.8 An Archaeological Profile
Archaeologists create profiles or vertical representations of the sites they excavate. In stratified sites where archaeological remains lie in stacked layers, with older layers deeper or lower down and more recent layers above them, profiles are especially informative. Geologic processes will result in strata of different depths in different places. Interpretation of the site depends upon careful mapping of each stratum using the grid system.

datum point The starting point or reference for a grid system.

flotation An archaeological technique employed to recover very tiny objects by immersion of soil samples in water to separate heavy from light particles.

stratified In archaeology, a term describing sites where the remains lie in layers, one upon another.

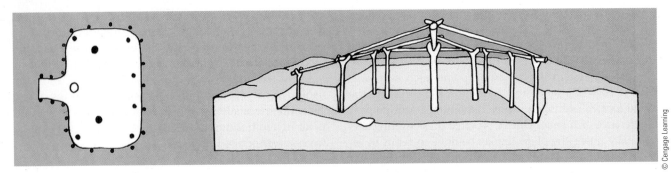

Figure 5.9 Reconstruction from Traces of Organic Remains
Although the wooden posts of a house have long since decayed, their positions may still be marked by discoloration of the soil. The plan shown on the left—of an ancient post-hole pattern and depression at a prehistoric settlement in Snaketown, Arizona—permits the hypothetical house reconstruction on the right.

traces of organic ones long since decomposed, such as woodwork (Figure 5.9), textiles, or food.

Climate, local geological conditions, and cultural practices also play a role in the state of preservation. For example, much of our knowledge of ancient Egyptians stems from their belief that eternal life could be achieved only if the dead were buried with their worldly possessions. Hence, the tombs of the rulers of dynastic Egypt often contain wooden furniture, textiles, flowers, written scrolls on paper made from papyrus reeds, or even the skeletons of other humans they owned. Of course, these ancient Egyptian burial practices selectively preserved more information about the elite members of society than the average individual. But even the earliest Egyptian burials, consisting of shallow pits in the sand, often yield well-preserved corpses due to rapid desiccation, or complete drying out, in the warm desert climate (Figure 5.10).

The dryness of certain caves also promotes the preservation of **coprolite** (derived from the Greek word for "dung"), which is the scientific term for fossilized human or animal excrement. Coprolites provide information on prehistoric diet and health. From the analysis of elements

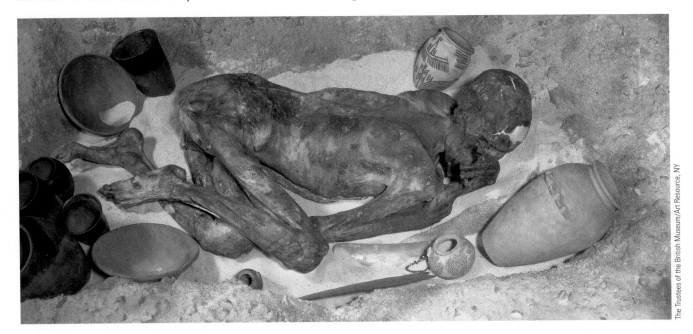

Figure 5.10 Preservation and Environment
The preservation of archaeological remains is dependent upon the environment. Even before the invention of mummification technologies, buried bodies were very well preserved in Egypt because they dried so quickly in the extremely arid environment. For the same reason, the artifacts alongside such remains may appear barely touched by time, seemingly as fresh as they were when deposited in the tombs as long as 5,000 years ago.

coprolite Fossilized excrement material providing evidence of the diet and health of past organisms.

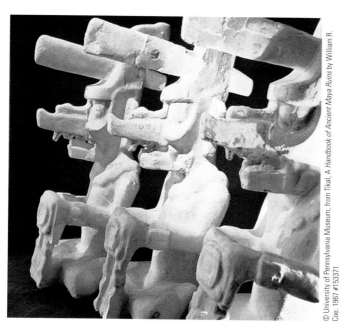

Figure 5.11 Reconstructing Decayed Wood Carvings
At the Maya site of Tikal, these intricately carved figures, originally made of wood, were recovered from a king's tomb by pouring plaster into a cavity in the soil that was left when the original organic material decayed.

© University of Pennsylvania Museum, from Tikal, A *Handbook of Ancient Maya Ruins* by William R. Coe. 1967 #153371

preserved in coprolites—such as seeds, insect skeletons, and tiny bones from fish or amphibians—archaeologists and paleoanthropologists can directly determine diets from the past. This information, in turn, can shed light on overall health. Coprolites also allow scientists a rare chance to examine genetic material from ancient human ancestors.

Certain climates can obliterate all evidence of organic remains. In the tropical rainforests of Mesoamerica (the region encompassing central and southern Mexico and northern Central America), rain and humidity quickly destroyed almost all traces of woodwork, textiles, or basketry from ancient Maya sites. Fortunately, impressions of these artifacts can sometimes be preserved in plaster (**Figure 5.11**), and stone carvings and pottery figurines may depict some objects made of wood or plant fibers. Thus, even in the face of substantial decay of organic substances, archaeologists can still learn about these remains.

Sorting Out the Evidence

Excavation records include a scale map of all the features, the stratification of each excavated square, a description of the exact location and depth of every artifact or bone unearthed, and photographs and scale drawings of the objects. Such detailed records allow the researchers to piece together the archaeological and biological evidence so as to arrive at a plausible reconstruction of a culture. Although researchers conducting an excavation may focus only on certain kinds of remains, they must record every aspect of the site. Future researchers may need a piece of

information to answer a question that no one thought of at the time of the initial investigation. In other words, archaeological sites are nonrenewable resources. Even the most meticulous excavation results in a permanent disturbance of the arrangement of artifacts.

Sometimes sites are illegally looted, which can result in loss not only of the artifacts themselves but of the site (**Figure 5.12**). Although looting has long been a threat to the archaeological record, today it is a high-tech endeavor. Avid collectors and fans of archaeological sites unwittingly aid looting through sharing site and artifact location information on the Internet, which has also provided a market for artifacts.

Meticulous care does not end with excavation. Archaeologists and paleoanthropologists apply a variety of laboratory methods to studying the artifact or fossil, once freed from the surrounding matrix. Generally, archaeologists and paleoanthropologists plan on at least 3 hours of laboratory work for each hour of fieldwork.

In the lab, archaeologists first clean and catalogue all artifacts before beginning any analyses. Then archaeologists will determine each artifact's function from its shape and traces of manufacture and wear. For example, Russian archaeologist S. A. Semenov, who devoted many years to the study of prehistoric technology, described a flint tool used as a scraper. He determined, by examining the wear patterns of the tool under a microscope, that the prehistoric individuals who used it would alternate the direction of their scraping to avoid straining the muscles of the hand. From the work of Semenov and others, we now know that right-handed individuals made most stone tools preserved in the archaeological record, a fact that has implications for brain structure. Relationships among populations can also be discerned from material remains (**Figure 5.13**).

Paleoanthropologists, bioarchaeologists, and forensic anthropologists use a variety of investigative techniques to examine bones and teeth. For example, the examination of dental specimens under the microscope might reveal markings on teeth that provide clues about diet. Paleoanthropologists often make an imprint or **endocast** of the inside of a skull to determine the size and shape of ancient brains.

Just as DNA fingerprinting might be used in forensic investigations, paleoanthropologists apply advances in genetic technology to ancient human remains. By extracting genetic material from skeletal remains, they can make DNA comparisons among the specimen, other fossils, and living people. Small fragments of DNA are amplified or copied repeatedly using **polymerase chain reaction (PCR)** technology to provide a sufficient amount of material to perform these analyses. However, unless DNA is

endocast A cast of the inside of a skull; used to help determine the size and shape of the brain.

polymerase chain reaction (PCR) A technique for amplifying or creating multiple copies of fragments of DNA so that it can be studied in the laboratory.

Figure 5.12 Looting
When looters harvest artifacts to sell illegally, they simply pull them from the ground or the air, as was the case with the 1,000-year-old Khmer warrior statue, looted from Koh Ker, Cambodia, in 2012. Only the feet and pedestal were left while the rest of the warrior was smuggled out of the country before eventually being voluntarily returned to Cambodia. Looters steal far more than the artifacts themselves. They also steal all the information that could have been gleaned from a proper excavation of the site. Even if police ultimately recover the artifacts from the thieves, or from the collectors who purchase such artifacts illegally, lack of context and precise location of the artifacts in relation to every other detail of the site severely limits the opportunity to reconstruct lifeways of past peoples. Further, looters often completely destroy the sites they loot, erasing evidence of their crime along with any details archaeologists might have salvaged.

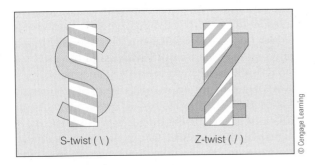

S-twist (\ )   Z-twist (/)

Figure 5.13 Actions in Objects
In northern New England, prehistoric pottery was often decorated by impressing the damp clay with a cord-wrapped stick. Examination of cord impressions reveals that coastal people made cordage by twisting fibers to the left (Z-twist), whereas those living inland did the opposite (S-twist). The nonfunctional differences reflect motor habits so deeply ingrained as to seem completely natural to the cordage makers. From this, we may infer two distinctively different populations.

preserved in a stable material such as amber, it will decay over time. Therefore, analyses of DNA extracted from specimens older than about 50,000 years become increasingly unreliable due to the decay of DNA.

The bioarchaeologist combines the biological anthropologist's expertise in skeletal biology with the archaeological reconstruction of human cultures. Examination of human skeletal material provides important insights into ancient peoples' diets, gender roles, social status, and patterns of activity. For example, analysis of human skeletons reveals that elite members of society had access to more nutritious foods and that the less well-nourished lower classes did not reach their full growth potential. In fully preserved adult skeletons, the sex of the deceased individual can be determined with a high degree of accuracy, allowing for comparisons of male and female life expectancy, mortality, and health status (Figure 5.14). These analyses can help establish the social roles of men and women in past societies.

New biomedical technology also plays a role in the investigation of remains from both the past and the present. For example, CT (computed tomography) scans have added new information in forensic, bioarchaeological, and paleoanthropological investigations. Recent and ancient remains are now routinely scanned, yielding considerable information about the structural details of bones. Although a CT scan cannot substitute for an autopsy in forensic contexts, it may facilitate identification in situations like mass disasters. In addition, it can provide evidence of past trauma that might otherwise remain hidden in an investigation aimed at determining an immediate cause of death (Leth, 2007).

In archaeological contexts, CT technology has been particularly useful for determining whether damage to remains took place during excavation or whether it preceded death. For example, after the remains of Egyptian pharaoh Tutankhamun ("King Tut") were scanned, scientists uniformly agreed that the young king did not die of a head injury as previously thought; some suggested that a broken femur may have been the cause of his death almost 3,300 years ago (Handwerk, 2005). To minimize handling, scientists scan these rare specimens only once, allowing future researchers to study the digital images instead of the remains.

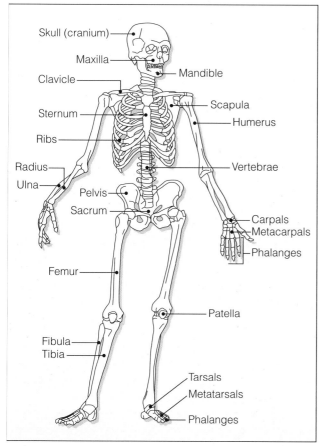

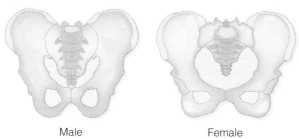

Male   Female

© Cengage Learning

Figure 5.14 The Human Skeleton
Learning the basic skeleton will be useful in the chapters ahead as we trace the history of human evolution. In addition, bear in mind that the complete male and female skeletons differ, on average, in some consistent ways that allow skeletal biologists to identify the sex of the deceased individual. Some of these differences relate to the fact that generally males outsize females. But the successful adaptation of the human female pelvis to childbirth makes it the most dimorphic bone of the body and the best way for researchers to determine the sex of skeletal remains. Notice the typically more open space on the interior of the female pelvis corresponding to the birth canal. In males, bones project into this space.

Digital technologies have also helped resolve conflicts involving the rights to skeletal remains, as scientists can continue to study imaged specimens after repatriation to the communities that claim them. Still, many aboriginal groups question the practice of digitizing remains of their people

without permission. For example, the University of Vienna in Austria has been challenged by representatives of the Ju/'hoansi people of southern Africa because the remains that the Austrian ethnological museum holds were not donated; rather, they were taken early in the century by Rudolf Pöch, an Austrian medical doctor and anthropologist, as was common practice at that time. Roger Chennells, the South African legal advisor for the Ju/'hoansi, states their position: "We have not been consulted, and we do not support any photographic archiving of our people's remains—we are opposed to it" (quoted in Scully, 2008, p. 1155).

By the standards of the 1990 Native American Graves Protection and Repatriation Act (NAGPRA), the Ju/'hoansi would have legal decision-making authority over the fate of these remains; but the equivalent of NAGPRA has not yet been codified in international law. Even with NAGPRA in place, scientists and native peoples approach the handling of remains quite differently, as seen with Kennewick Man, a 8,900–9,000-year-old skeleton that was dislodged by the Columbia River in the state of Washington in 1996, the subject of this chapter's Biocultural Connection.

Dating the Past

With accurate and detailed records of their excavations in hand, archaeologists and paleoanthropologists can begin to investigate a crucial research issue: the question of age. As we have seen, analysis and interpretation of cultural and physical remains hinges upon accurate calculation of the age of the artifacts or specimens. How then, do scientists reliably date the materials retrieved from excavations?

Remains can be dated by noting their position in the earth, by measuring the amounts of certain chemicals contained in fossil bones and artifacts, or through association with other plant, animal, or cultural remains. These techniques, known as **relative dating**, do not establish precise dates for remains. Instead, they establish the relationship among a series of remains by using geologic principles to place remains in chronological order. **Absolute or chronometric dating** (from the Latin for "measuring time") provides actual dates calculated in years "before the present" (BP). Relying upon advances in chemistry and physics, these methods use properties such as rates of decay of radioactive elements present in

relative dating In archaeology and paleoanthropology, designating an event, object, or fossil as being older or younger than another by noting the position in the earth, by measuring the amount of chemicals contained in fossil bones and artifacts, or by identifying its association with other plant, animal, or cultural remains.

absolute or chronometric dating In archaeology and paleoanthropology, dating archaeological or fossil materials in units of absolute time using scientific properties such as rates of decay of radioactive elements.

BIOCULTURAL CONNECTION

Kennewick Man

The "Ancient One" and "Kennewick Man" both refer to the 8,900–9,000-year-old skeletal remains that were found in 1996 below the surface of Lake Wallula, part of the Columbia River, in Kennewick, Washington. This discovery has been the center of continuing controversy since it was made. Who owns these human remains? Who can determine what shall be done with them? How do the biological characteristics preserved in these remains play a role in determining their fate?

Because the skeleton was found in an area for which the U.S. Army Corps of Engineers is responsible, this federal agency first took possession of the remains. At first, Kennewick Man was assumed to be a 19th-century specimen of European origin. Once the remains were carbon dated to the much earlier time period, five nearby American Indian groups claimed them under NAGPRA. Kennewick Man was found within their ancestral homeland, so they argued that they were "culturally affiliated" with the individual they refer to as "Ancient One." Viewing these human bones as belonging to an ancestor, they wished to return them to the earth in a respectful ceremony.

Fearing the loss of a unique scientific specimen, a group of scientists, including archaeologists and biological anthropologists, filed a lawsuit in federal court to prevent reburial before the bones were researched and analyzed. Their legal challenge was based on the notion that cultural affiliation is a very difficult concept when it concerns such ancient human remains, which are among the oldest ever discovered in the western hemisphere. The scientists focused on the fact that the region's Native American peoples could not prove they are direct lineal descendants. They further cited anatomical differences between the skeleton and modern aboriginal peoples, suggesting that Kennewick Man may have been more closely related to Polynesian or East Asian populations.

In 2004 federal court rulings permitted initial scientific investigations. Just as these investigations were wrapping up in July 2005, the Senate Indian Affairs Committee heard testimony on a proposal by Arizona Senator John McCain to expand NAGPRA so that remains such as these would be once again prohibited from study. Congress adjourned without this bill becoming law, and the remains have been studied continually since then.

Finally, in July 2015, a Danish team reported the first results from a detailed DNA analysis of the remains in the journal *Nature*.[a] These findings confirm that Kennewick Man is in fact more closely related to Indian tribes of the Pacific northwest than to any other modern population. The study, which determined relationships based on the frequency of shared alleles in the genome, also revealed a link between Kennewick Man and Central and South American native peoples. This revelation suggests that the northwestern tribes represent a lineage that split from the people who would eventually migrate into the southern continent.

Ironically, science was required to validate the Native Americans' original claim—a claim that would have prevented the research from happening at all. Since the announcement, the coalition of tribes has redoubled on their efforts for repatriation.

Now that scientists have had the opportunity to learn more about Kennewick Man, they might be more willing to let him go. Although the initial hypotheses, based on craniometric data, had failed to adequately identify the skeleton, genetic tests had also been attempted without success early on. Some researchers wonder how much more we could discover from such remains with more time and advanced technology.

Biocultural Question

If the skeletons of your ancestors were the subject of scientific study, how would you react? How far back in time should rights, like those granted by NAGPRA, extend?

[a]Rasmussen, M., et al. (2015, July 23). The ancestry and affiliations of Kennewick Man. *Nature* 523 (7561), 455–458.

---

the remains themselves or in the surrounding soil. By comparing dated remains across a variety of sites, anthropologists can establish timelines for major events such as evolutionary adaptations, migrations, and technological developments.

Each of the many relative and absolute dating techniques has certain weaknesses. Ideally, archaeologists and paleoanthropologists utilize as many methods as appropriate, given the materials available and funds at their disposal. This redundancy significantly reduces the risk of error. Table 5.1 describes several of the most common dating techniques.

Relative Dating

Stratigraphy is probably the most reliable relative dating method (recall Figure 5.8). Based on the simple principle that the oldest layer, or stratum, was deposited first (it is the deepest) whereas the newest layer was deposited last (in undisturbed situations, it lies at the top), stratigraphy establishes a reliable sequence of age at a given site. Thus, even in the absence of precise dates, one knows the *relative* age of objects in one stratum compared with the ages of those in other strata. However, defining the stratigraphy of a given site can be complicated by geologic activities

stratigraphy In archaeology and paleoanthropology, the most reliable method of relative dating by means of strata.

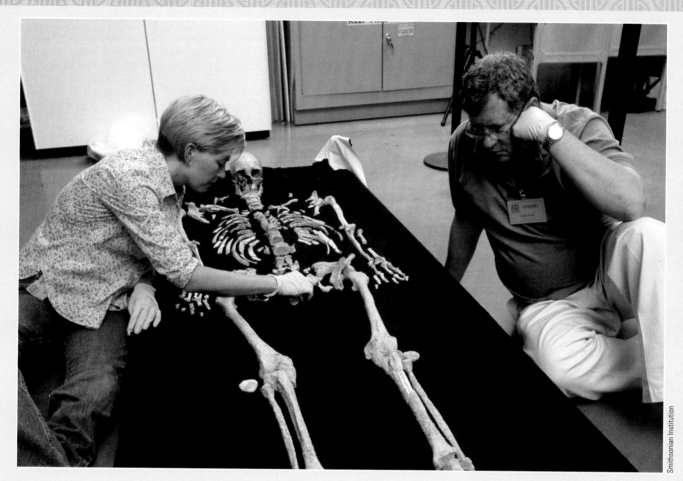

The names for this prehistoric skeleton, Kennewick Man and Ancient One, exemplify the conflict between scientists and American Indians. For researchers, the skeleton is a specimen for study, but for Native Americans, it is a member of the family. Doug Owsley (*right*) is the forensic anthropologist from the Smithsonian Institution who has been leading the research team that includes forensic anthropologist Kari Bruwelheide (*left*).

such as earthquakes that shift the position of stratigraphic layers or human activity, as seen in Figure 5.15.

Archaeologists also use the relative dating technique of **fluorine dating**, based on the fact that the amount of fluorine deposited in bones is proportional to the amount of time they have been in the earth. The oldest bones contain the greatest amount of fluorine and vice versa. The fluorine test can help date bones that cannot be ascribed with certainty to any particular stratum. The variation in the amount of naturally occurring fluorine from region to region limits the validity of this method for cross-site comparisons of fluorine values. Fluorine dating was vital for exposing the infamous Piltdown hoax in England, in which a human skull and orangutan jaw were placed together in the earth as false evidence for an early human ancestor (see Chapter 6).

Relative dating can also be done by **seriation**, a method of establishing sequences of plant, animal, or even cultural remains. With seriation, the order of appearance of a succession (or series) of plants, animals, or artifacts provides relative dates for a site based on a series established in another area. An example of seriation based on cultural artifacts is the Stone–Bronze–Iron Age series used by prehistorians. Within a given region, sites containing artifacts

fluorine dating In archaeology or paleoanthropology, a technique for relative dating based on the fact that the amount of fluorine in bones is proportional to their age.

seriation In archaeology and paleoanthropology, a technique for relative dating based on putting groups of objects into a sequence in relation to one another.

TABLE 5.1

Absolute and Relative Dating Methods Used by Archaeologists and Paleoanthropologists

Dating Method	Time Period	Process and Use	Drawbacks
Stratigraphy	Relative only	Based on the law of superposition, which states that lower layers or strata are older than higher strata; establishing the age of biological and cultural remains based on the layer in which they are found	Site specific; natural forces, such as earthquakes, and human activity, such as burials, disturb stratigraphic relationships
Fluorine analysis	Relative only	Comparing the amount of fluorine from surrounding soil absorbed by specimens after deposition; older remains will have absorbed more fluorine	Site specific
Faunal and floral series	Relative only	Sequencing remains into relative chronological order based on an evolutionary order established in another region with reliable absolute dates; called palynology when done with pollen grains	Dependent upon known relationships established elsewhere
Seriation	Relative only	Sequencing cultural remains into relative chronological order based on stylistic features	Dependent on known relationships established elsewhere
Dendrochronology	About 3,000 years before present (BP) maximum	Comparing tree growth rings preserved in a site with a tree of known age	Requires ancient trees of known age, limited time depth
Radiocarbon	Accurate < 50,000 BP	Comparing the ratio of radioactive carbon 14 (^{14}C), with a half-life of 5,730 years, to stable carbon (^{12}C) in organic material; after organisms die, only the ^{14}C decays (half of it every 5,730 years), so the ratio between ^{14}C and ^{12}C determines an actual date since death	Increasingly inaccurate when assessing remains from more than 50,000 years ago
Potassium argon (K-Ar)	> 200,000 BP	Using volcanic ash, comparing the amount of radioactive potassium (^{40}K), with a half-life of 1.25 billion years, to stable argon (^{40}Ar)	Requires volcanic ash; requires cross-checking due to contamination from atmospheric argon
Amino acid racemization	40,000–180,000 BP	Comparing the ratio of right- and left-sided proteins in a three-dimensional structure; decay after death causes these proteins to change	Amino acids leached out variably from soil cause error
Thermoluminescence	Possibly up to 200,000 BP	Measuring the amount of light given off due to radioactivity when the specimen is heated to high temperatures	Technique developed for recent materials such as Greek pottery; not clear how accurate the dates are for older remains
Electron spin resonance	Possibly up to about 200,000 BP	Measuring the resonance of trapped electrons in a magnetic field	Works with tooth enamel, not yet developed for bone; problems with accuracy
Fission track	Wide range of times	Measuring the tracks left in crystals by uranium as it decays; good cross-check for K-Ar technique	Useful for dating crystals only
Paleomagnetic reversals	Wide range of times	Measuring the orientation of magnetic particles in stones and linking them to whether the earth's magnetic field pulled toward the north or south during their formation	Large periods of normal or reversed magnetic orientation require dating by some other method; some smaller events are known to interrupt the sequence
Uranium series	40,000–180,000	Measuring the amount of uranium decaying in cave sites	Large error range

© Cengage Learning

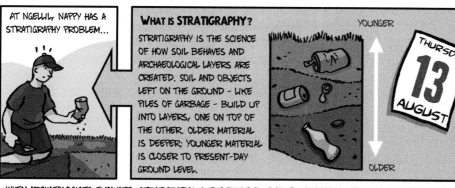

Figure 5.15 Making it Public
Archaeologist John Swogger has started to use comics to make archaeology, its methods, and its results accessible to the public, such as this one that documents a recent expedition to the Pacific island of Palau. How can you account for the presence of a beer can in a lower stratigraphic layer? What dating techniques are at work in this excavation?

the earliest African fossils in human evolution, paleoanthropologists have developed faunal series in regions where accurate chronometric dates can be established. They then use these series to establish relative sequences in other regions. Similar series have been established for plants, particularly using grains of pollen. With this approach, known as **palynology**, the kind of pollen found in any geologic stratum indicates the kind of vegetation that existed at the time that stratum was deposited. Hence, palynology also helps to reconstruct the environments in which prehistoric peoples lived.

Chronometric Dating

Some archaeological sites yield written records that provide archaeologists with a fascinating account of dates and times (Figure 5.16). But precise dates usually derive from a variety of absolute or chronometric dating methods. These techniques apply chemistry and physics to calculate the ages of physical and cultural remains, though each one is limited to a particular timespan and carries a certain margin of error.

One of the most widely used methods of absolute dating is **radiocarbon dating**. This method uses the fact that while they are alive, all organisms absorb radioactive carbon (known as carbon 14

made of iron are generally more recent than sites containing only stone tools. In well-investigated cultural areas, archaeologists have developed series for particular styles of pottery.

Scientists make similar inferences with animal or faunal series. For example, very early North American Indian sites have yielded the remains of mastodons and mammoths—animals now extinct. These remains allow scientists to date these sites to a time before these animals died out, roughly 10,000 years ago. For dating some of

or ^{14}C) as well as ordinary carbon 12 (^{12}C) in proportions identical to those found in the atmosphere. Absorption of carbon 14 (^{14}C) ceases at the time of death, and the ratio

---

palynology In archaeology and paleoanthropology, a technique of relative dating based on changes in fossil pollen over time.

radiocarbon dating In archaeology and paleoanthropology, a technique of chronometric dating based on measuring the amount of radioactive carbon (^{14}C) left in organic materials found in archaeological sites.

© University of Pennsylvania Museum CX 61-4-123

Figure 5.16 Maya Calendric Glyphs
Some ancient societies devised precise ways of recording dates that archaeologists have been able to correlate with our own calendar. Here is the tomb of an important ruler, Siyaj Chan K'awiil II, at the ancient Maya city of Tikal. The glyphs painted on the wall give the date of the burial in the Maya calendar, which is the same as March 18 of the year 457 AD in the Gregorian calendar.

between the two forms of carbon begins to change as the unstable radioactive element carbon 14 begins to "decay." Each radioactive element decays, or transforms into a stable nonradioactive form, at a specific rate. The amount of time it takes for one-half of the radioactive material to decay is expressed as the "half-life." For carbon 14, it takes 5,730 years for half of a given quantity of carbon 14 to decay to stable nitrogen 14. In another 5,730 years (11,460 years total), half of the remaining amount will also decay to nitrogen 14 so that only one-quarter of the original amount

of carbon 14 will be present. Thus, the age of an organic substance such as charcoal, wood, shell, or bone can be measured through determining the changing proportion of carbon 14 relative to the amount of stable carbon.

Though scientists can measure the amount of radioactive carbon left in even a few milligrams of organic substance from a recent specimen, the miniscule amount of carbon 14 present in remains from the distant past limits accurate detection. The radiocarbon method can adequately date organic materials up to about 50,000 years old, but dating older material is far less reliable.

Because there is always a certain amount of error involved, radiocarbon dates (like all chronometric dating methods) are not as absolute as is sometimes thought. This is why any stated date always has a plus-or-minus (±) factor attached to it corresponding to one standard deviation above and below the mean value. For example, a radiocarbon date of 5,200 ± 120 years ago means that there is a two out of three chance (or a 67 percent chance) that the true date falls somewhere between 5,080 and 5,320 years ago.

A more accurate, though more limited, method of absolute dating is **dendrochronology** (derived from *dendron*, a Greek word meaning "tree"). Originally devised for dating Pueblo Indian sites in southwestern North America, this method is based on the fact that in the right kind of climate, trees add one (and only one) new growth ring to their trunks every year. The rings vary in thickness, depending upon the amount of rainfall received in a year, so that tree ring growth registers climatic fluctuation. By taking a sample of wood, such as a beam from a Pueblo Indian house, and comparing its pattern of rings with those in the trunk of a nearby tree of known age, archaeologists can date the archaeological material.

Dendrochronology is applicable only to wooden objects. Furthermore, it works only in regions that contain living trees of great age, such as giant sequoias and bristlecone pines. Radiocarbon dating of wood from bristlecone pines dated by dendrochronology allows scientists to correct the carbon 14 dates and bring them into agreement with calendar dates.

Potassium-argon dating, another commonly used method of absolute dating, is based on a technique similar to that of radiocarbon analysis. Following intense heating, as from a volcanic eruption, radioactive potassium decays at a known rate to form argon; any previously existing argon will have been released by the heating of the molten lava. The half-life of radioactive potassium is 1.3 billion years. Measuring the ratio of potassium to argon in a given rock accurately dates deposits back millions of years.

Potassium-argon analysis can indicate the age of fossils and artifacts found encased between layers of volcanic ash (as at Olduvai and other sites in East Africa). But as with radiocarbon dates, potassium-argon dates are always stated with a plus-or-minus margin of error attached. Further, potassium-argon dating loses precision with materials younger than about 200,000 years.

---

dendrochronology In archaeology and paleoanthropology, a technique of chronometric dating based on the number of rings of growth found in tree trunks.

potassium-argon dating In archaeology and paleoanthropology, a technique of chronometric dating that measures the ratio of radioactive potassium to argon in volcanic debris associated with human remains.

Neither the radiocarbon nor the potassium-argon methods work well during the time period extending from about 50,000 years ago to about 200,000 years ago. Because this same time period happens to be very important in human evolutionary history, scientists have attempted to develop complementary methods for this critical period.

One such method, *amino acid racemization*, is based on the fact that amino acids trapped in organic materials gradually change, or racemize, after death, from left-handed forms to right-handed forms. Thus, the ratio of left- to right-handed forms should indicate the specimen's age. Unfortunately, in substances like bone, moisture and acids in the soil can leach out the amino acids, thereby introducing a serious source of error. However, ostrich eggshells have proved immune to this problem; the amino acids are so effectively locked up in a tight mineral matrix that they are preserved for thousands of years. Because ostrich eggs were widely used as food and the shells as containers in Africa and the Middle East, they provide a powerful means of dating sites of the later parts of the Old Stone Age (Paleolithic), between 40,000 and 180,000 years ago.

Electron spin resonance, which measures the number of trapped electrons in bone, and *thermoluminescence*, which measures the amount of light emitted from a specimen when heated to high temperatures, are two additional methods that have been developed to fill in prehistoric time gaps. Dates derived from these two methods have been vital for reconstructing human origins.

A few other chronometric techniques rely on the element uranium. *Fission track dating*, for example, counts radiation damage tracks on mineral crystals. Like amino acid racemization, all these methods have problems: They are complicated and tend to be expensive, many can be carried out only on specific kinds of materials, and some are so new that their reliability is not yet unequivocally established. It is for these reasons that they have not been as widely used as radiocarbon and potassium-argon dating techniques.

Paleomagnetic reversals contribute another interesting dimension to absolute dating methodologies by providing a way to cross-check dates (Figure 5.17). This method is based on the shifting magnetic pole of the earth—the same force that controls the orientation of a compass needle.

Today, a compass points to the north because we are in a period defined as the geomagnetic "normal." Over the past several million years, there have been extended periods of time during which the magnetic field of the earth pulled toward the South Pole. Geologists call these periods *geomagnetic reversals*. Iron particles in stones will be oriented into positions determined by the dominant magnetic pole at the time of the stone's formation, allowing scientists to derive broad ranges of dates for huge layers of rock. Human evolutionary history contains a geomagnetic reversal starting 5.2 million years ago that ended 3.4 million years ago, followed by a normal period until 2.6 million years ago; then a second reversal began, lasting until about 700,000 years ago when the present normal period began. This paleomagnetic

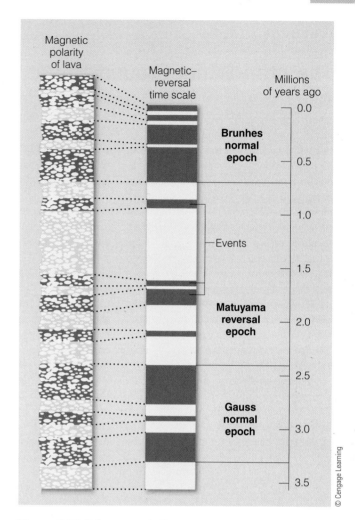

Figure 5.17 Paleomagnetic Reversals
Scientists have documented a geomagnetic polarity time scale in which the changes in the earth's magnetic force—to north or south—have been calibrated. This geomagnetic time scale provides scientists with opportunities to cross-check other dating methods.

sequence can be used to date sites to either normal or reversed periods and can be correlated with a variety of other dating methods to cross-check their accuracy.

Concepts and Methods for the Most Distant Past

As this chapter's Anthropology Applied feature demonstrates, archaeological expertise can still be valuable for recovery of very recent remains, where dating is not an issue. But context and dating are vital for the interpretation of older fossils and cultural remains. Because mammalian primate evolution extends so far back in time, paleoanthropologists reconstruct our evolutionary history in conjunction with information about the geologic history of the earth, which is 4.6 billion years old.

ANTHROPOLOGY APPLIED

The Atari Burial Grounds

Many archaeological expeditions are inspired by myths or legends. Usually such tales date back further than the 1980s, but for defunct videogame maker Atari, overzealous business practices, a cult following, and some solid detective work led to one of the most curious excavations of recent times. Self-identified "punk archaeologists" William Caraher, Raiford Guins, Andrew Reinhard, Richard Rothaus, and Bret Weber, who led the excavation of the Atari burial grounds, saw this excavation as part spectacle, part public service for the town that housed the dump. For them it was also a way to comment on the intersection of archaeological practice and popular culture while recovering and researching the recent past.[a]

Atari had been the undisputed king of the videogame world in the 70s and early 80s, thanks to popular home and arcade titles such as Pong and Yars' Revenge. With the success of the 1982 film *E.T. the Extra-Terrestrial*, the Atari company seized the opportunity to create a videogame adaptation of the movie. Atari paid handsomely for the rights to pursue this venture and then rushed the design of the game in order to allow for massive production of cartridges for their home console before that year's holiday season. *E.T.* had been one of the highest-grossing films of all time, so Atari initially manufactured around 4 million copies of the game in expectation of similar commercial success.

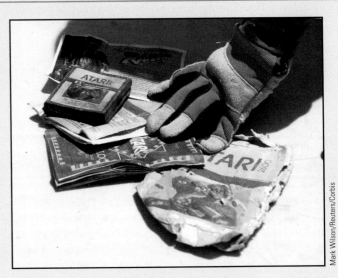

One of the E.T. the Extraterrestrial Atari videogames recovered from the landfill in Alamogordo, New Mexico, has made its way into the Smithsonian Institution collections as an artifact that reflects a moment in the cultural history of the United States: the gaming crash of 1982–1985.

Mark Wilson/Reuters/Corbis

Continental Drift and Geologic Time

The geologic time scale is unfamiliar because few people deal with hundreds of millions of anything, let alone years, on a regular basis. To understand this type of scale, U.S. astronomer Carl Sagan correlated the geologic time scale for the history of the earth to a single calendar year. In this "cosmic calendar," the earth itself originates on January 1, the first organisms appear approximately 9 months later around September 25, followed by the earliest vertebrates around December 20, mammals on December 25, primates on December 29, hominoids at 10:15 am on New Year's Eve, bipeds at 9:30 pm, with our species appearing in the last minutes before midnight. Human evolutionary history begins with the December 25 appearance of the mammals in the Mesozoic era, roughly 245 million years ago (mya). **Figure 5.18** plots out the more recent events in mammalian primate evolution that take place during the final week of Sagan's cosmic calendar.

By 190 million years ago—the end of what geologists call the Triassic period—true mammals were on the scene. Mammals from the Triassic, Jurassic (135–190 mya), and Cretaceous (65–135 mya) periods are largely known from hundreds of fossils, especially teeth and jaw parts. Because teeth are the hardest, most durable structures, they often outlast other parts of an animal's skeleton. Fortunately, investigators often are able to infer a good deal about the total animal on the basis of only a few teeth found in the earth.

Over such vast amounts of time, the earth itself has changed considerably. During the past 200 million years, the position of the continents has shifted through a process called **continental drift** or the rearrangement of adjacent landmasses, accounted for by the theory of plate tectonics. According to this theory, the continents, embedded in platelike segments of the earth, move their positions as the edges of the underlying plates are created or destroyed (**Figure 5.19**). Plate movements are also responsible for geologic phenomena such as earthquakes, volcanic activity, and mountain formation. Continental drift impacted the distribution of fossil primates (recall Figure 3.1) and played a role in the earliest stages of human evolutionary history.

continental drift According to the theory of plate tectonics, the movement of continents embedded in underlying plates on the earth's surface in relation to one another over the history of life on the planet.

Though the release was highly anticipated, gamers quickly discovered a slow and frustrating game that fell far short of expectations. Many were returned, and retailers canceled orders leading to an overstock of around 3 million cartridges in Atari warehouses. Faced with competition from other vendors and market saturation for its other products, Atari reported losses of $583 million in 1983 and was subsequently dismantled and sold off over the next year.

Truckloads of Atari equipment were reported buried in a landfill in Alamogordo, New Mexico, in the fall of 1983. Though the company stated that it was disposing of broken and inoperable materials, the recent disappointment of the E.T. game fueled rumors that Atari was burying millions of copies of that title in an act of shame. In the years to come, E.T. would often be panned as the "worst game ever made," responsible for the brief implosion of the entire gaming industry that followed.

The mythic status of E.T. as a cautionary tale of hubris in the videogame industry led to an interest in excavating the landfill. In 2013, Canadian filmmakers secured permission to dig up the refuse and produce a documentary on the subject, with the aim of discovering the true fate of the reviled game.[b] With the help of the punk archaeologists and videogame historians, the effort uncovered over a thousand Atari cartridges, including some copies of E.T. the Extra-Terrestrial. Former Atari managers later revealed that over 700,000 cartridges had been buried in Alamogordo, although many other Atari games were represented in larger proportions. There had been no specific effort to "send E.T. home."

The archaeologists recorded and catalogued their findings for the New Mexico Museum of Space History for display and auction on behalf of the City of Alamogordo, which retains ownership of all landfill materials. Even the Smithsonian Institution has kept one of the recovered copies of E.T., citing its significance in marking "the end of an era for videogame manufacturing."[c]

[a]Caraher, W., Guins, R., Reinhard, A., Rothaus, R., & Weber, B. (2014, August 7). Why we dug Atari. *The Atlantic*. http://www.theatlantic.com/technology/archive/2014/08/why-we-dug-atari/375702/ (retrieved October 30, 2015); Muckle, R. (2014, September/October). Punk archaeology and excavating video games in New Mexico. *Anthropology News* 55 (9-10), 4–5.

[b]*Atari: Game over: The long road here.* (2014, November 20). Directed by Zak Penn. 66 min. Fuel Entertainment.

[c]Robarge, D. (2014, December 15). From landfill to Smithsonian collections: "E.T. the Extraterrestrial" Atari 2600. *Smithsonian*. http://americanhistory.si.edu/blog/landfill-smithsonian-collections-et-extra-terrestrial-atari-2600-game (retrieved October 30, 2015)

The Molecular Clock

In the 1960s, molecular biochemist Allan Wilson from New Zealand and his U.S. graduate student Vince Sarich (Figure 5.20) developed the revolutionary concept of a **molecular clock**. Although not a dating method per se, such clocks help detect when the branching of related species from a common ancestor took place in the distant past. They can establish a series of relationships among closely related species that reinforce absolute or relative dates established at specific fossil localities. However, because the molecular clock depends on mutation rates that vary between species, scientists are constantly refining as more data are uncovered.

For the first molecular clock, Sarich and Wilson used a technique that had been around since the beginning of the 20th century: comparison of the blood proteins of living groups (Sarich & Wilson, 1967). Today, this technique has been expanded to include comparisons in bases of DNA. With Wilson as his mentor, Sarich worked on serum albumin, a protein from the fluid portion of the blood (like the albumin that forms egg whites) that can be precipitated out of solution. *Precipitation* refers to the chemical transformation of a substance dissolved in a liquid back into its solid form. One of the forces that will cause such precipitation is contact of this protein with antibodies directed against it. Antibodies are proteins produced by organisms as part of an immune response to an infection. The technique relies on the notion that the stronger the biochemical reaction between the protein and the antibody (the more precipitate), the closer the evolutionary relationship. The antibodies and proteins of closely related species resemble one another more than the antibodies and proteins of distant species.

Sarich made immunological comparisons between a variety of species and suggested that he could establish dates for evolutionary events by calculating a molecular rate of change over time. By assuming a constant rate of change in the protein structure of each species, Sarich used these results to predict times of divergence between related groups. Each molecular clock needs to be set, or calibrated, by the dates associated with a known event, such as the divergence between prosimian and anthropoid primates or a major change in the continental plates, as established by absolute dating methods.

Using this technique, Sarich proposed a sequence of divergence for the living hominoids showing that human,

molecular clock The technique that dates of divergences among related species can be calculated through an examination of the genetic mutations that have accrued since the divergence.

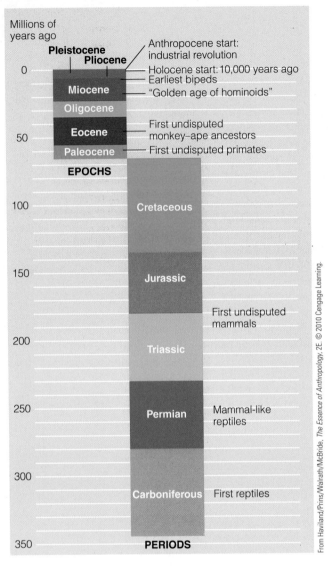

Figure 5.18 Milestones of Mammalian Primate Evolution
This timeline highlights some major milestones in the course of mammalian primate evolution that ultimately led to humans and their ancestors. The Paleocene, Eocene, Oligocene, and Miocene epochs are subsets of the Tertiary period. The Quaternary period begins with the Pleistocene and continues today. It includes the Holocene epoch that began at the end of the last Ice Age around 12,000 years ago. In 2000, the Dutch Nobel Prize–winning atmospheric chemist Paul Crutzen used the term *Anthropocene* to describe the world since the industrial revolution because of the profound geologic changes human activity imposes on the earth. Geologic societies around the globe are currently debating the inclusion of Anthropocene as a formal geologic unit.

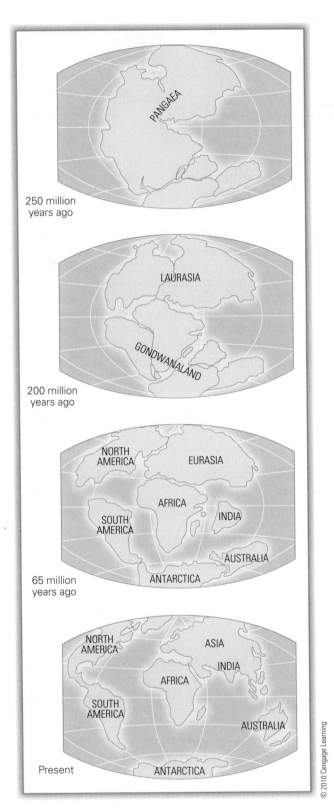

Figure 5.19 Continental Drift
Continental drift is illustrated here during several geologic periods. At the time of the extinction of the dinosaurs 65 million years ago, continental drift caused the seas to open up, creating isolating barriers between major landmasses. About 23 million years ago, at the start of the time period known as the Miocene epoch, African and Eurasian landmasses reconnected, and the Indian subcontinent joined Asia.

chimp, and gorilla lines split roughly 5 million years ago (mya). He boldly stated that it was impossible to have a separate human line before 7 million years ago, "no matter what it looked like." Before this work, anthropologists had thought that the great apes—chimpanzees and bonobos, gorillas, and orangutans—were more closely related to one another than any of them were to humans. This work was the first proof

Figure 5.20 Wilson and Sarich
Allan Wilson (*right*) developed the notion of a molecular clock with his graduate student Vince Sarich (*left*) and published the groundbreaking paper "Immunological Time Scale for Human Evolution" in the journal *Science* in 1967. The molecular clock proposes that evolutionary events such as the split between humans and apes can be dated through an examination of the number of genetic mutations that accumulated since two species diverged from a common ancestor. A biochemist by training, Wilson's "hybrid science" was both innovative and controversial within anthropology.

Roger Ressmeyer/Encyclopedia/Corbis

that human origins are firmly in Africa and that humans, chimps and bonobos, and gorillas are more closely related to one another than any of them are to the orangutans. A discovery in the laboratory, like the molecular clock, can drastically change the interpretation of the fossil evidence.

The Sciences of Discovery

The previous discussion demonstrates that anthropologists participate in an unusual kind of science. Paleoanthropology and archaeology are sciences of discovery. As new fossil discoveries and artifacts come to light, interpretations inevitably change, improving our understanding of human evolutionary and cultural history. Today, discoveries can occur in the laboratory as easily as on the site of an excavation. Molecular studies provide new lines of evidence in much the same way that a fossil or pottery

figurine provides new data as it is unearthed. Just like detectives at an investigation, scientists use each new clue to refine our collective understanding of the past.

Archaeological and fossil evidence is imperfect. Chance circumstances of preservation have determined what has and what has not survived the consequences of time. Thus, scientists reconstruct the biology and culture of our ancestors on the basis of fragmentary and, at times, unrepresentative samples of physical and cultural remains. Chance also impacts the discovery of prehistoric remains. Vestiges may come to light due to factors ranging from changing sea level to a local government's decision to build a highway.

Ancient cultural processes have also shaped the archaeological and fossil record. We know more about the past due to the cultural practice of deliberate burial. We also know more about the elite segments of past societies because they have left more material culture behind. However, as archaeologists have shifted their focus from gathering treasures to the reconstruction of human behavior, they have gained a more complete picture of ancient societies. Similarly, paleoanthropologists no longer simply catalogue fossils; they interpret data about our ancestors in order to reconstruct the biological processes responsible for who we are today. The challenge of reconstructing our past will be met by a continual process of re-examination and modification as anthropologists discover evidence in the earth, among living people, and in the laboratory leading to new understandings of human origins.

CHAPTER CHECKLIST

How do archaeologists and paleoanthropologists identify sites for excavation?

✓ Aerial photographs and other surveying tools reveal environmental clues such as soil markings. Survey may be combined with documents, folklore, and found artifacts in order to locate important sites.

✓ Many excavations take place where natural forces such as erosion or drought leave sites exposed.

✓ Chance discoveries, like those from mining or construction, have led to the recovery of significant historical remains.

What excavation practices are preferred?

✓ Excavators map the land into a grid system to precisely record the location of found objects, and they choose a fixed landmark to use as the reference (datum point) of the grid. Photographs and scale drawings supplement the written excavation data.

✓ The destructive nature of excavation demands that researchers record information on all found objects including those irrelevant to their original purpose.

✓ Where stratification is present, layers corresponding to distinct time periods are dug carefully, one at a time. If searching for smaller objects, the excavation team may utilize the flotation technique to separate particles of varying density.

✓ For bone excavation, the earth matrix containing the specimen is cut out and hardened using shellac and plaster bandages. Then the entire block is removed and shipped to a laboratory for the final stages of extraction.

How do scientists continue excavation analysis in the lab?

✓ Close examination of wear patterns on artifacts can lead to understanding of early human behaviors. Similarly, markings on teeth suggest dietary habits, and endocasts reveal brain size and shape.

✓ Bioarchaeologists use anatomical data to reconstruct cultures of the past.

✓ Technology such as CT scanning minimizes handling and potential damage to specimens; three-dimensional digital images permit the continued scientific study of remains that must be repatriated.

✓ DNA samples can be extracted from more recent skeletal remains.

What are the important dating methods, and how do they differ?

✓ Relative dating techniques establish the age of remains by association with the surrounding earth or other nearby remains. Researchers may combine several techniques to create accurate timelines of the past. Relative dating methods include stratigraphy, the fluorine method, and seriation.

✓ Most absolute dating techniques rely on rates of decay of radioactive elements present in remains in order to estimate a numerical age. Absolute methods include techniques such as radiocarbon dating, potassium-argon dating, amino acid racemization, and, in the case of wooden remains, dendrochronology.

How do geologic phenomena contribute to our understanding of human history?

✓ Knowledge of geomagnetic reversals can be used to date ancient remains by examining the position of iron particles in stone artifacts.

✓ Continental drift has impacted the course of human evolution by separating populations that then diverged to become distinct species.

What is the molecular clock, and what does it reveal about human evolution?

✓ Scientists used molecular clocks to determine that humans, chimps, bonobos, and gorillas split into different evolutionary branches between 5 and 7 million years ago in Africa. All African hominoids are more closely related to one another than any is to the orangutan.

✓ The evolutionary proximities of living species can be estimated by comparing their blood proteins. Assuming these proteins have changed at a constant rate over time, scientists estimate when the last common ancestor of two species lived.

QUESTIONS FOR REFLECTION

1. Who owns the past? How much does politics affect the answer to that question? What should archaeologists do when groups that claim rights to cultural heritage intend to destroy it?

2. The cultural practice of burial of the dead altered the fossil record and provided valuable insight into the beliefs and practices of past cultures. The same is true today. What beliefs are reflected in the traditions for treatment of the dead in your culture?

3. Controversy has surrounded Kennewick Man since this skeleton was discovered on the banks of the Columbia River in Washington in 1996. Did scientists deserve the opportunity to study the remains at the expense of Native American wishes? What should happen next?

4. How can an interpretation of physical or cultural remains change depending upon the date assigned to the remains? Why are metaphors used in the context of geologic time?

DIGGING INTO ANTHROPOLOGY

Digging Anthropology

This chapter talks about the actual digging that paleoanthropologists and archaeologists perform, so it's time for you to do some digging yourself! Assemble a team and mimic the processes described here as best you can. First is site identification: Locate a place that might be interesting to dig like a backyard, beach, or riverbank and acquire permission as necessary. Make a map of the area, choose a datum point, and draw out a grid. Then you can gather your tools: A trowel will suffice to get going, though you may want some of the other archaeological tools such as a sifting screen, shovel, or brushes depending upon conditions and availability. Once you find a remnant of human activity, record it, protect it, and take it back to your "lab" for cleanup, cataloguing, and analysis. See if you can use techniques like stratigraphy to date your finds!

Gallo Images/Getty Images

CHALLENGE ISSUE

What makes us human? Where and when did our first ancestors appear? Paleoanthropologists answer these questions by studying our primate relatives, the fossil record, and geology. They use this fragmentary evidence to reconstruct a coherent trajectory of our evolutionary history. Each new discovery impacts this narrative, often stirring up controversy. Take, for example, the announcement at the Cradle of Human Kind Visitor Center in Gauteng, South Africa, in September 2015, of a new member of the genus *Homo* discovered in the nearby Rising Star Cave. The enthusiasm of University Vice Chancellor Adam Habib, South African Deputy President Cyril Ramaphosa, and Professor Lee Berger is palpable as they reveal *Homo naledi*. Berger and his team argue that these fossils, from at least fifteen distinct individuals, display human features and appear to have been deliberately buried. However, others disagree, saying that the hasty excavation and laboratory work led to inaccurate dating. Still others contend that the fossils resemble established species of the genus *Homo*, or even that they are closer to earlier bipeds. Paleoanthropologists debate each new discovery constantly updating their interpretations of our evolutionary history.

From First Primates to First Bipeds

6

In geologic terms, humans appeared in the world recently, although not as recently as some new strains of bacteria. Our form—like that of any organism—came about only as a consequence of a whole string of accidental happenings in the past. The history of any species contains many such occurrences. This chapter begins our focus on human origins, starting with our earliest primate ancestors. Much of who we are, as culture-bearing biological organisms, derives from our mammalian primate heritage.

Primate Origins

Early primates began to emerge during a time of great global change at the start of the Paleocene epoch 65 million years ago (mya). Evidence suggests that a meteor or some other extraterrestrial body slammed into the earth where the Yucatan Peninsula of Mexico is now, cooling global temperatures to such an extent as to cause the extinction of the dinosaurs (as well as numerous other species). For 100 million years, dinosaurs had dominated most terrestrial environments suitable for vertebrate animals and would probably have continued to do so without such a climate change. Although mammals appeared at about the same time as reptiles, they were small, inconspicuous creatures. With the demise of the dinosaurs, new opportunities became available, allowing mammals to begin their great adaptive radiation into a variety of species, including our own ancestors, the earliest primates (Figure 6.1).

Newly evolved grasses, shrubs, and other flowering plants proliferated enormously during this same time period. This diversification, along with a milder climate, favored the spread of tropical and subtropical forests over the earth. The spread of these huge belts of forest set the stage for the expansion of some mammals into the trees. Forests provided our early ancestors with the ecological niches in which they would flourish. See Figure 6.2 for a full timeline of primate evolution.

In this chapter you will learn to

- Identify the course of primate evolution and its major geologic events.

- Recognize the anatomy of bipedalism and how paleoanthropologists identify the hominin line and distinct species in the fossil record.

- Discuss how cultural biases interfered with scientific recognition of the African origins of humans.

- Describe paleoanthropology in action: how paleoanthropologists construct the trajectory of human origins from fragmentary remains.

- Compare the earliest bipeds to one another and to chimps and humans.

- Identify two types of australopithecines: the gracile and the robust.

- Describe the earliest appearance of the genus *Homo* in the fossil record.

Figure 6.1 Extinction of the Dinosaurs

Although popular media depict the coexistence of humans and dinosaurs, in reality the extinction of the dinosaurs occurred 65 million years ago, while the first bipeds ancestral to humans appeared between 5 and 8 million years ago. The climate changes beginning 65 million years ago allowed for the adaptive radiation of mammals and a diversification of plant life. The appearance of the true seed plants (the angiosperms) provided not only highly nutritious fruit seeds and flowers but also a host of habitats for numerous edible insects and worms—just the sorts of food required by mammals with their higher metabolism. For species like mammals to continue to survive, a wide diversity of plants, insects, and even single-celled organisms needs to be maintained. In ecosystems these organisms are dependent upon one another.

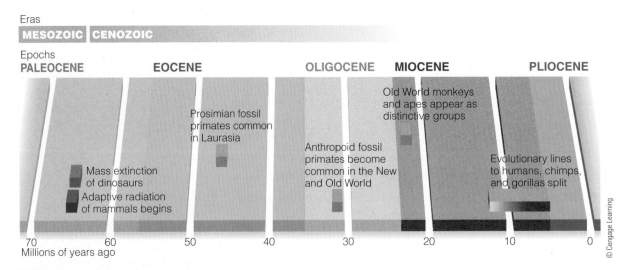

Figure 6.2 Timeline of Primate Evolution

This timeline depicts some of the major events of primate evolution.

One explanation for primate evolution, the **arboreal hypothesis**, proposes that life in the trees was responsible for enhanced visual acuity and manual dexterity in primates. Misjudgments and errors of coordination led to falls that injured or killed the individuals poorly adapted to arboreal life. Natural selection would favor those that judged depth correctly and gripped the branches strongly. Early primates that took to the trees were probably in some measure preadapted by virtue of behavioral flexibility, better vision, and more dexterous fingers than their contemporaries.

Primatologist Matt Cartmill's **visual predation hypothesis** suggests that primate visual and grasping abilities were also promoted through the activity of hunting for insects by sight (Cartmill, 1974). The relatively small size of the early primates allowed them to make use of the smaller branches of trees; larger, heavier competitors and most predators could not follow. The move to the smaller branches also gave them access to an abundant food supply; the primates were able to gather insects, leaves, flowers, and fruits directly rather than waiting for them to fall to the ground.

The first "true" primates appeared by about 55 million years ago at the start of the Eocene epoch. During this time period, an abrupt warming trend caused the extinction of many older mammalian forms, which were replaced by recognizable forerunners of some of today's mammals, including the prosimians. Over fifty prosimian fossil genera have been found in Africa, North America, Europe, and Asia, where the warm, wet conditions of the Eocene sustained extensive rainforests (Figure 6.3). Relative to ancestral primate-like mammals, these early primate families had enlarged braincases, slightly reduced snouts, and a somewhat forward position of the eye orbits, which, though not completely walled in, were surrounded by a complete bony ring called a *postorbital bar* (Figure 6.4).

Near the end of the Eocene, temperatures took a sudden dive, triggering the formation of an icecap over previously forested Antarctica. The result was a marked reduction in the range of suitable environments for primates. The formation of icecaps also led to lower sea levels, perhaps changing opportunities for migration of primates. In North America, now well isolated from Eurasia, primates became extinct, and elsewhere their range seems to have been reduced considerably.

Oligocene Anthropoids

During the Oligocene epoch, about 23 to 34 million years ago (mya), the anthropoid primates diversified and expanded their range. We have fossil evidence of at least sixty genera from two different families from places like Egypt's Fayum region, along with newly discovered localities in Algeria (North Africa) and Oman (Arabian Peninsula). All quadrupeds, some have the ancestral dental formula (2-1-3-3) seen in New World

Natural History Museum, University of Oslo, Norway

Figure 6.3 Ida
The fossil record indicates that Eocene primates, ancestors of today's prosimians and anthropoids, were abundant, diverse, and widespread. One of these fossil finds is the spectacularly well-preserved 47-million-year-old specimen nicknamed "Ida," which received a lot of media attention in 2009 when two sections of her remains were reunited after almost thirty years in separate private collections. Nevertheless, scientists continue to debate whether Ida is a true anthropoid, a distinction that would place her on the line leading to humans.

monkeys and prosimians, whereas others have the derived dental formula shared by Old World monkeys and apes: two incisors, one canine, two premolars, and three molars (2-1-2-3) on each side of the jaw. Their smaller eye orbits (which indicate that these specimens were diurnal) have a complete wall, another feature of anthropoid primates.

arboreal hypothesis An explanation for primate evolution that proposes that life in the trees was responsible for enhanced visual acuity and manual dexterity in primates.

visual predation hypothesis An explanation for primate evolution that proposes that hunting behavior in tree-dwelling primates was responsible for their enhanced visual acuity and manual dexterity.

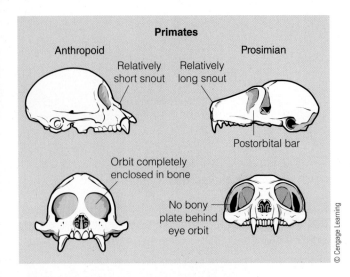

Primates

Anthropoid

Prosimian

Relatively short snout

Relatively long snout

Postorbital bar

Orbit completely enclosed in bone

No bony plate behind eye orbit

© Cengage Learning

Figure 6.4 Prosimian and Anthropoid Skulls
Ancestral features seen in Eocene and Oligocene primates are still seen in prosimians today. Like modern lemurs, these fossil prosimians have a postorbital bar, a bony ring around the eye socket that is open in the back. Anthropoid primates have orbits completely enclosed in bone. Note also the difference in the relative size of the snout in these two groups. Paleoanthropologists make these kinds of comparisons as they reconstruct our evolutionary history.

Many of these Oligocene species possess a mixture of monkey and ape features. Of particular interest is the genus *Aegyptopithecus* (pronounced "e-GYPT-o-PITH-ee-kus"; Greek for "Egyptian ape"), an Oligocene anthropoid that has sometimes been called a monkey with an ape's teeth. Its lower molars have the five cusps of an ape, and the upper canine and lower first premolar exhibit the sort of shearing surfaces found in monkeys and apes. Its skull has forward-facing eye sockets completely protected by a bony wall. The endocast of its skull indicates that it had a larger visual cortex than that found in prosimians. Relative to its body size, the brain of *Aegyptopithecus* was smaller than that of more recent anthropoids. Still, this primate seems to have had a larger brain than any prosimian, past or present. Possessed of a monkey-like skull and body, and fingers and toes capable of powerful grasping, it evidently moved about quadrupedally in a manner similar to a monkey.

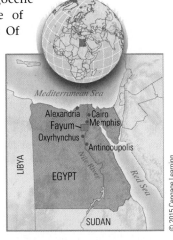

Mediterranean Sea

Alexandria · Cairo
Fayum · Memphis
Oxyrhynchus
· Antinooupolis

LIBYA

EGYPT

Nile River

Red Sea

SUDAN

© 2015 Cengage Learning

Although no bigger than a modern house cat, *Aegyptopithecus* was, nonetheless, one of the larger Oligocene primates. Primatologists consider the larger *Aegyptopithecus* fossils to be males, noting that these specimens also possess more formidable canine teeth and deeper mandibles (lower jaws) compared to the smaller females. This inference is based on modern anthropoids, where such sexual dimorphism correlates with social systems with high competition among males.

New World Monkeys

The earliest evidence of primates in Central and South America dates from the Oligocene epoch. Scientists hypothesize that these primates came to South America from Africa by means of giant floating clumps of vegetation of the sort that originate even today in the great rivers of West and Central Africa. In the Oligocene, the distance between the two continents, though still formidable, was far less than it is today. Favorable winds and currents could have carried New World monkey ancestors on these floating islands of vegetation to South America quickly enough for them to survive.

Miocene Apes and Human Origins

True apes first appeared in the fossil record during the Miocene epoch, 5 to 23 million years ago. It was also during this time period that the African and Eurasian landmasses made direct contact. For most of the preceding 100 million years, the Tethys Sea—a continuous body of water that joined what are now the Mediterranean Sea and the Black Sea to the Indian Ocean—created a barrier to migration between Africa and Eurasia. Once joined through what is now the Middle East and Gibraltar, Old World primates, such as the apes, could extend their range from Africa into Eurasia. Miocene ape fossil remains have been found everywhere from the caves of China, to the forests of France, to East Africa, where scientists have recovered the oldest fossil remains of bipeds. So varied and ubiquitous were the fossil apes of this period that the Miocene has been called the golden age of the hominoids. The word *hominoid* comes from the Latin roots *homo* and *homin* (meaning "human being") and the suffix *oïdes* ("resembling").

In addition to the Old World anthropoid dental formula of 2-1-2-3, hominoids can be characterized by the derived characteristics of Y5 molars, lack of a tail, and broad flexible shoulder joints. One of the Miocene apes is the direct ancestor of the human line; exactly which one remains a question. An examination of the history of the contenders for direct human ancestor among the Miocene apes demonstrates how reconstruction of evolutionary relationships involves much more than simply bones. Scientists interpret fossil finds by drawing on existing beliefs and knowledge. With new discoveries, interpretations change.

The first Miocene ape fossil remains were found in Africa in the 1930s and 1940s by the British archaeologist A. T. Hopwood and the renowned British Kenyan paleoanthropologist Louis Leakey (see Anthropologists of Note).

The Leakeys

No account of 20th-century anthropology is complete without noting the contributions of the Leakey family. Few figures in the history of the science discovered so many key fossils, received so much public acclaim, or stirred up as much controversy as **Louis Leakey** (1903–1972) and his second wife **Mary Leakey** (1913–1996). Their legacy has continued through two more generations of family members as well as a multitude of students and collaborators.

Born in Kenya of missionary parents, Louis received his early education from an English governess and subsequently was sent to England for a university education. He returned to Kenya in the 1920s to begin his career. In 1931, Louis and his research assistant from England, Mary Nicol (whom he married in 1936), began working in their spare time at Olduvai Gorge in Tanzania, where German paleontologist Hans Reck had found a contentious ancient human skeleton in 1913. Numerous animal fossils as well as crude stone tools were lying scattered on the ground and eroding out of the walls of the gorge, but the Leakeys did not find human biological remains there, despite repeated expeditions over many years.

Their patience and persistence were not rewarded until 1959, when Mary found the first fossil, an *Australopithecus boisei* skull. A year later, their 19-year-old son **Jonathan** (b. 1940) found the first specimens that would be termed *Homo habilis*, and Olduvai began to be known as one of the most important sources of fossils relevant to human evolution in all of Africa. While Louis reconstructed, described, and interpreted the fossil material, Mary made the definitive study of the Oldowan tools, a very early stone tool industry.

The Leakeys' important discoveries were not limited to those at Olduvai. In the early 1930s they found the first fossils of Miocene apes in Africa at Rusinga Island in Lake Victoria as well as a number of skulls showing a mixture of derived and ancestral features at Kanjera in western Kenya. In 1948, at Fort Ternan, Kenya, the Leakeys found the remains of a late Miocene ape with features that seemed appropriate for an ancestor of the bipeds. After Louis's death, Paul Abell, a member of an expedition led by Mary Leakey, found the first fossilized footprints of early bipeds at Laetoli, Tanzania.

The Leakey tradition continues—with son **Richard** (b. 1944), Richard's wife **Meave** (b. 1942), and their daughter (Louis and Mary's granddaughter) **Louise** (b. 1972). Richard was at the forefront of paleoanthropology in the 1970s when he led expeditions that uncovered the Nariokotome Boy, the Kenyan Black Skull, as well as several important early *Homo* skulls. Although Richard has since retreated from fieldwork to focus on conservation and political activism, Meave and Louise continue the study of human origins in the Turkana Basin of Kenya, where they made their stunning *Kenyanthropus platyops* discovery, among others.

Louis Leakey supported a good deal of important work by others. He made it possible for Jane Goodall to begin her landmark field studies of chimpanzees and later he was instrumental in setting up Dian Fossey's similar studies of gorillas and Biruté Galdikas's studies of orangutans. He also set into motion the fellowship program responsible for the training of numerous paleoanthropologists from Africa.

Louis had a flamboyant personality and a way of interpreting fossil materials that frequently did not stand up to careful scrutiny, but this did not stop him from publicly presenting his views as if they were the gospel truth; it was this aspect of the Leakeys' work that generated controversy. Nonetheless, the research of the Leakey family has contributed greatly to our much fuller understanding of human origins.

Not only did Louis and Mary Leakey contribute substantially to paleoanthropology through numerous archaeological fossil finds, but they also created a lineage of paleoanthropologists. Here they are in the 1950s.

Robert Sisson/National Geographic Creative

These fossils turned up on one of the many islands in Lake Victoria, the 27,000-square-mile lake where Kenya, Tanzania, and Uganda meet. Impressed with the chimp-like appearance of these fossil remains, Hopwood suggested that the new species be named *Proconsul*, combining the Latin root for "before" (*pro*) with the stage name of a chimpanzee who was performing in London at the time.

Dated to the early Miocene (17 to 21 mya), *Proconsul* exhibited some of the classic hominoid features, like the characteristic pattern of Y5 grooves in the lower molar teeth and the lack of a tail. However, the adaptations of the upper body seen in later apes (including humans), such as a skeletal structure adapted for hanging suspended below tree branches, were absent. In other words, *Proconsul* had some apelike features as well as some features of four-footed Old World monkeys (Figure 6.5). This mixture of ape and monkey features makes *Proconsul* a contender for a missing link between monkeys and apes, although at least seven fossil hominoid groups besides *Proconsul* have been found in East Africa from the early to middle Miocene.

Before these African fossil discoveries, European scientists in the early 20th century concentrated on the various species of European ape—all members of the genus *Dryopithecus* (pronounced "DRY-o-PITH-ee-kus"). They believed that humans evolved where "civilization" developed and that these apes could be the missing link to humans. Moreover, investigators initially did not consider that humans were more closely related to the African apes than they were to the other intelligent great ape—the Asian orangutan. Chimps, bonobos, gorillas, and orangutans were thought to be more closely related to one another than any of them were to humans.

The construction of evolutionary relationships still relied upon visual similarities among species, much as it did in the mid-1700s when Linnaeus developed the taxonomic scheme that grouped humans with other primates. Chimps, bonobos, gorillas, and orangutans all possess the same basic body plan, adapted to hanging by their arms from branches or knuckle-walking on the ground. Humans and their ancestors had an altogether different form of locomotion—walking upright on two legs (Figure 6.6). On an anatomical basis, the first Miocene ape to become bipedal could have come from any part of the vast range of Old World Miocene apes.

Today, scientists agree that genetic evidence firmly establishes that the human line diverged from those leading to chimpanzees between 5 and 8 million years ago with gorillas diverging somewhat earlier. Although any fossil discoveries in Africa from this critical time period have the potential to be the missing link between humans and the other African ape species, controversy surrounds the interpretation of many of these fossil finds. Still, scientists

Figure 6.6 Bipedal Apes?
While an ape like this bonobo can walk upright on two legs for a minute or two, no ape can sustain this form of locomotion for long periods of time. The shift to bipedalism involved structural changes in the skeleton that apes do not possess.

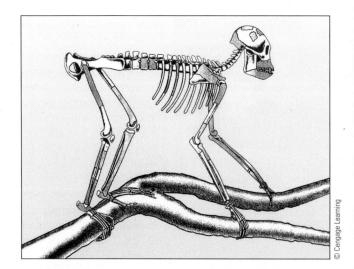

© Cengage Learning

Figure 6.5 A Reconstructed Skeleton of *Proconsul*
Note the apelike absence of a tail but limb and body proportions similar to monkeys. *Proconsul*, however, was capable of greater rotation of forelimbs than monkeys.

agree on the basic evolutionary relationships among the Old World anthropoid primates (Figure 6.7).

For example, in 2007 scientists announced a new 10-million-year-old ape species discovered in Ethiopia as ancestral to gorillas (Suwa et al., 2007). Named *Chorora-pithecus abyssinicus*—after Chorora, the local area where the fossil was found, and Abyssinia, the historical Arab name of Ethiopia—the scientists who found the nine fossil teeth claim that this specimen indicates that the gorilla lineage had become distinct from the human and chimp lines 2 to 4 million years before those lines split. Other scientists have required more fossil evidence before pushing back the timing of the split.

Some fossil discoveries have begun to fill in the critical period of 5 to 8 million years ago. In the summer of 2002, a team of international researchers in Chad unearthed a well-preserved skull dated to between 6 and 7 million years ago (Figure 6.8). Calling their find *Sahelanthropus*

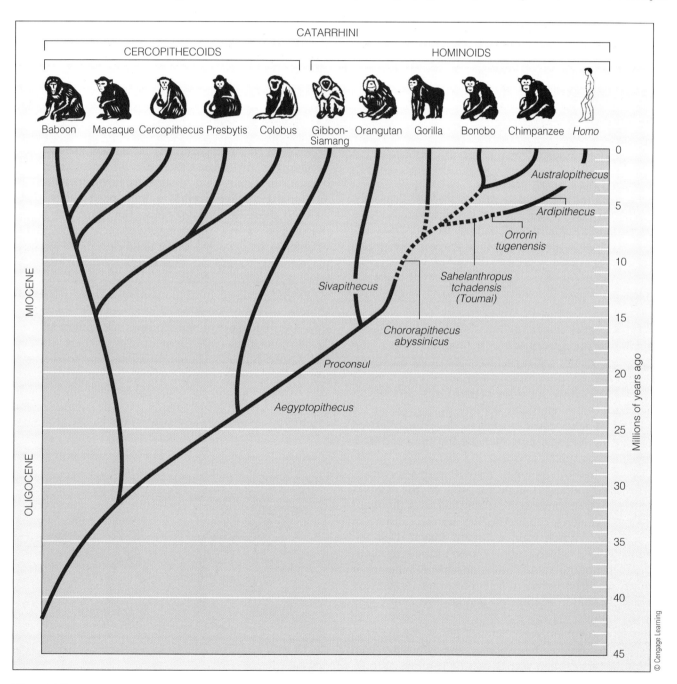

Figure 6.7 Relationships among the Old World Anthropoids
Although debate continues over details, this chart represents a reasonable reconstruction of evolutionary relationships among the Old World anthropoid primates. Note that except for humans, chimps, and bonobos, these groups listed contain two or more species. (Extinct evolutionary lines are not shown.)

© Michael Brunet

Figure 6.8 *Sahelanthropus tchadensis*
The spectacular skull from Chad nicknamed "Toumai" ("hope for life" in the region's Goran language) has been proposed as the earliest direct human ancestor. Although the 6- to 7-million-year-old specimen is beautifully preserved and has some derived features, some paleoanthropologists do not believe that the skull alone establishes bipedalism, the hallmark of the human line.

tchadensis ("Sahel human of Chad," referring to the Sahel, a belt of semi-arid land bordering the southern edge of the Sahara Desert), the researchers suggested that this specimen represented the earliest known ancestor of humans (Brunet et al., 2002). Inclusion of any fossil specimen in the human evolutionary line depends upon evidence for **bipedalism** (also called *bipedality*), the shared derived characteristic distinguishing humans and their ancestors from the other African apes.

Some paleoanthropologists argue that this specimen, nicknamed "Toumai" ("hope for life" in the region's Goran-language), cannot be established as a hominin from its skull alone, considering the degree of distortion present. The research team maintains that derived features, such as a reduced canine tooth, indicate its status as a member of the human evolutionary line. Whether or not this specimen proves to be a direct human ancestor, as the only skull from this time period, it remains a very important find.

In 2001, 6-million-year-old fossils discovered in Kenya were also reported as human ancestors. Officially given the species name *Orrorin tugenensis* (*Orrorin* meaning "original man" and *tugenensis* meaning "from the Tugen Hills")

but nicknamed "Millennium Man," controversy also surrounds these specimens (Senut et al., 2001).

The evidence for *Orrorin* consists of bone fragments from the arm and thigh, a finger bone, some jaw fragments, and teeth from at least five individuals. The thighbones demonstrate possible but not definite bipedalism. Unfortunately, the distal, or far ends, of the thighbone that would prove this are not fully preserved. The humerus (upper arm) appears to be more like that of humans, but arm bones cannot confirm bipedalism. Surprisingly, many other unexpected fragments can provide strong evidence of bipedalism, as we will explore next.

The Anatomy of Bipedalism

Anatomical changes accompany bipedalism literally from head to toe. An isolated skull may be one indicator of bipedalism (**Figure 6.9**) because balancing the head in an upright posture requires a skull position relatively centered above the spinal column. The spinal cord leaves the skull at its base through the foramen magnum (see Chapter 3). In a knuckle-walker like a chimp, the foramen magnum sits toward the back of the skull, whereas in a biped it is toward the front.

Extending down from the skull of a biped, the spinal column makes a series of convex and concave curves that together maintain the body in an upright posture by positioning the body's center of gravity above the legs rather than forward. The curves correspond to the neck (cervical), chest (thoracic), lower back (lumbar), and pelvic (sacral) regions of the spine, respectively. In a chimp, the shape of the spine follows a single arching curve (**Figure 6.10**). Interestingly, at birth the spines of human

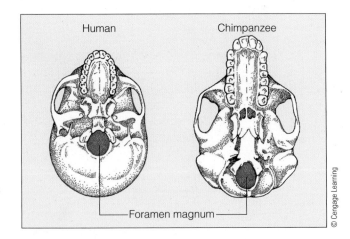

© Cengage Learning

Figure 6.9 **The Foramen Magnum**
Bipedalism can be inferred from the position of the foramen magnum, the large opening at the base of the skull. Note its relatively forward position on the human skull (*left*) compared to the chimpanzee skull.

bipedalism A special form of locomotion, distinguishing humans and their ancestors from the African great apes, in which the organism walks upright on two feet; also called *bipedality*.

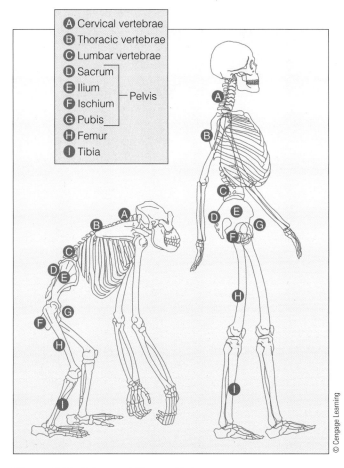

Figure 6.10 Chimp and Human Skeletons
Differences between skeletons of chimps and humans reflect their habitual mode of locomotion. Notice the curves in the spinal column of the human as well as the basin-shaped pelvis.

A Cervical vertebrae
B Thoracic vertebrae
C Lumbar vertebrae
D Sacrum ⎤
E Ilium   ⎥
F Ischium ⎬ Pelvis
G Pubis ⎦
H Femur
I Tibia

© Cengage Learning

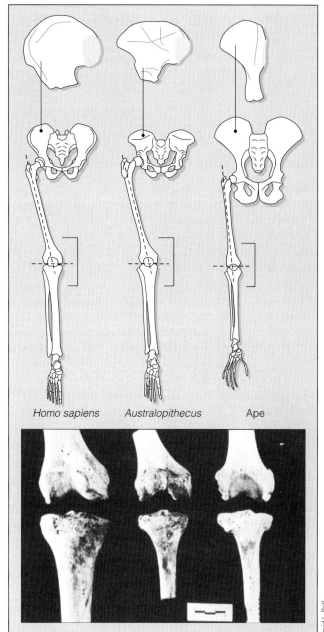

Homo sapiens   Australopithecus   Ape

David L. Brill

Figure 6.11 Lower Limb Comparisons
The upper hip bones and lower limbs of (*from left*) *Homo sapiens*, *Australopithecus* (an ancestral hominin species), and an ape can be used to determine means of locomotion. The striking similarities between the human and australopithecine bones are indicative of bipedal locomotion.

babies have a single arching curve as seen in adult apes. As humans mature, the curves characteristic of bipedalism appear: the cervical curve at about 3 months and the lumbar curve at around 12 months—a time when many babies begin to walk.

The shape of the pelvis also differs considerably between bipeds and other apes. Instead of an elongated shape following the arch of the spine as seen in the chimp, the biped has a wider and foreshortened pelvis that provides structural support for the upright body. With a wide bipedal pelvis, the lower limbs would be oriented away from the body's center of gravity if the thighbones (femora) did not angle in toward each other from the hip to the knee, a phenomenon termed "kneeing in." (Notice how your own knees and feet can touch when standing whereas your hip joints remain widely spaced.) This angling does not continue past the knee to the shinbones (tibia), which are oriented vertically (**Figure 6.11**).

Other characteristics of bipeds are their stable arched feet and the absent opposable big toe. The position of the ape big toe is **abducted** (sticking out away from the midline) while the human big toe is **adducted** (pulled in

toward the midline). In general, humans and their ancestors possess shorter toes than the other apes.

These anatomical features allow paleoanthropologists to diagnose bipedal locomotion even in fragmentary

abduction Movement away from the midline of the body or away from the center of the hand or foot.

adduction Movement toward the midline of the body or toward the center of the hand or foot.

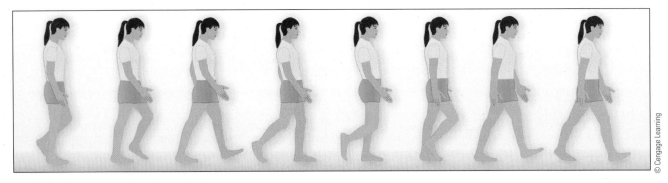

Figure 6.12 Bipedal Gait
The bipedal gait in some regards is really *serial monopedalism*, or movement by means of one foot at a time through a series of controlled falls. While the body is supported in a one-legged stance, a biped takes a stride by swinging the other leg forward. The heel of the foot is the first part of the swinging leg to hit the ground. Then as the biped continues to move forward, the individual rolls from the heel toward the toe, pushing or "toeing off" into the next swing phase of the stride.

remains such as the top of the shinbone or the base of a skull. Bipedal locomotion can also be established through fossilized footprints, which preserve the characteristic stride used by humans and their ancestors (**Figure 6.12**). Once bipedalism establishes a fossil specimen as a hominin, paleoanthropologists turn to other features, such as the skull or teeth, to reconstruct relationships among the various fossil hominin groups.

The most dramatic confirmation of our ancestors' walking ability comes from Laetoli, Tanzania, where two (perhaps three) individuals walked across newly fallen volcanic ash 3.6 million years ago (**Figure 6.13**). Because it was damp, the ash took the impressions of their feet, and these were sealed beneath subsequent ash falls until discovered in the late 1970s by a team led by British paleoanthropologist Mary Leakey (see Anthropologists of Note).

Ardipithecus

A dramatic paleoanthropological discovery was announced in the fall of 2009: a remarkably complete skeleton of a putative human ancestor dated to 4.4 million years ago (**Figure 6.14**). Only half a dozen partially complete fossil skeletons on the human line older than 1 million years have ever been discovered, and this one is the oldest. Nicknamed "Ardi" for the new genus **Ardipithecus**, these fossil remains, unearthed between 1992 and 1995, have dramatically changed what we know about the earliest bipeds (White et al., 2009). The genus actually contains two species, *A. ramidus* and the older *A. kadabba,* whose less complete remains date to between 5.2 and 5.8 million years ago.

Ardipithecus One of the earliest genera of bipeds that lived in East Africa. *Ardipithecus* is actually divided into two species: the older, *A. kadabba*, which dates to between 5.2 and 5.8 million years ago, and the younger, *A. ramidus*, which dates to around 4.4 million years ago.

Figure 6.13 Laetoli Footprints
The Laetoli Footprints are some of the earliest evidence of hominoid bipedalism in the fossil record. Because the footprints were preserved in volcanic ash, paleoanthropologists can date when these steps were taken at the Laetoli site in Tanzania. Mary Leakey led the team of paleoanthropologists that discovered this 24 meters (80 feet) long trail of footprints.

David Brill Photography

Figure 6.14 *Ardipithecus ramidus*
Paleonthropological analyses of the Ardi remains discovered in the early 1990s established that she was a forest-dwelling human ancestor. For over fifteen years, an international team of forty-seven scientists conducted painstaking excavation, reconstruction, and analysis to create a complete picture of the lifeways of this new species. Here (*left to right*) are three members of that team: Gen Suwa from Japan, Berhane Asfaw from Ethiopia, and Tim White from the United States. Through this process Ardi has become personified. A series of research papers in the prestigious journal *Science*, along with a Discovery Channel documentary about how the scientists went about their work, reveal not only the importance of the find but how Ardi has captured our collective imagination.

(Once the name of a genus has been established, it can be abbreviated with the first letter followed by the complete species name.) The discovery of *A. ramidus* shows that some of the earliest bipeds inhabited a forested environment much like that of contemporary chimpanzees, bonobos, and gorillas; the remains were found in deposits along Ethiopia's Awash River accompanied by fossils of forest animals. Ardi's name comes from the local Afar language, in which *Ardi* means "floor" and *ramid* means "root."

As is often the case with fossil discoveries, paleoanthropologists debate Ardi's exact place on the human line. Many paleoanthropologists expected the earliest bipeds to resemble something halfway between humans and chimps. Indeed, at 120 centimeters (47 inches) tall and a weight of about 50 kilograms (110 pounds), Ardi was about the size of a female chimpanzee, with corresponding brain size and tooth enamel thickness as well. But despite possessing a chimps' grasping big toe, Ardi's overall body plan is closer to that of some early Miocene apes. Ardi was suited to traveling across the tops of branches with the palms of her hands and feet facing downward, as well as walking between the trees on the ground in an upright position. The other African apes, as we saw in previous chapters, knuckle-walk on the forest floor and hang suspended below the branches. Nevertheless, some scientists suggest *Ardipithecus* is a side branch on the human evolutionary tree rather than our direct ancestor.

Australopithecus

By the early 20th century, fossils of more recent Pliocene bipeds had already been uncovered in East Africa and South Africa (**Figure 6.15**). The name for this genus, **Australopithecus**, was coined in 1924 when a partial skull and natural brain cast of a young individual was brought to the attention of anatomist Raymond Dart of the University of Witwatersrand in Johannesburg, South Africa. Found by workers in a limestone quarry in the South African town of Taung, the specimen (dubbed "Taung Child") was unlike any creature Dart had seen before. Recognizing an intriguing mixture of ape and human characteristics, Dart proposed a new taxonomic category for the specimen—*Australopithecus africanus* or "southern ape of Africa"—suggesting that it represented an extinct species that was ancestral to humans (**Figure 6.16**).

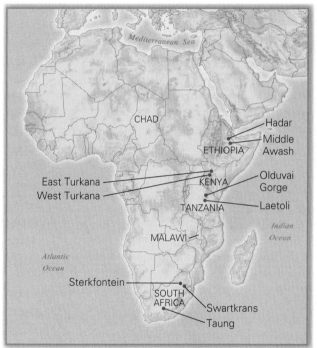

© Cengage Learning

Figure 6.15 **Map of *Australopithecus* Sites**
Australopithecine fossils have been found in South Africa, Malawi, Tanzania, Kenya, Ethiopia, and Chad. In the Miocene, the Eurasian and African continents made contact at the eastern and western ends of what is now the Mediterranean Sea. As these landmasses met, rifting also occurred, gradually raising the elevation of the eastern third of Africa. The drier climates that resulted may have played a role in human evolution in the distant past. This rifting also gives us excellent geologic conditions for finding fossils today.

Australopithecus The genus including several species of early bipeds from South Africa and East Africa living between about 1.1 and 4.3 million years ago, one of whom was directly ancestral to humans.

Pascal Goetgheluck/Science Source

Figure 6.16 The Taung Child
Discovered in South Africa in 1924, the Taung Child was the first fossil specimen placed in the genus *Australopithecus*. Though Raymond Dart correctly diagnosed the Taung Child's bipedal mode of locomotion as well as its importance in human evolution, scientists immediately rejected Dart's claims that this small-brained biped with a human-like face was a direct ancestor to humans.

Although the anatomy of the base of the skull indicated that the Taung Child was probably a biped, the scientific community was not ready to accept the notion of a small-brained African ancestor to humans. Dart's original paper describing the Taung Child was published in the February 1925 edition of the prestigious journal *Nature*. The next month's issue was filled with venomous critiques rejecting Dart's proposal that this specimen represented a human ancestor. Criticisms of Dart ranged from biased to fussy to sound. Some scholars chastised Dart for incorrectly combining Latin and Greek in the genus and species name he coined. Other critics more justifiably questioned the wisdom of making inferences about the appearance of an adult of the species based only on the fossilized remains of a young individual. However, ethnocentric bias was the biggest obstacle to Dart's proposed human ancestor. Paleoanthropologists of the early 20th century assumed that human ancestors had possessed large brains for millions of years and expected to find evidence of them in Europe or Asia. No researchers at the time believed that human evolution had occurred in Africa; this expectation was partially due to the infamous Piltdown Man.

In 1912, British amateur archaeologist Charles Dawson claimed to have uncovered a specimen consisting of a human-like skull with an apelike jaw at the Piltdown gravels of Sussex, England. Working with paleontologist Arthur Smith Woodard, Dawson had reconstructed the cranium from fragments and immodestly named it *Eoanthropus dawsoni* or "Dawson's Dawn Man" (Figure 6.17). The bones of some extinct animal species had also been discovered at Piltdown, lending credibility to the claim that Dawson's skull represented an ancient human ancestor. Until the 1950s, the Piltdown remains were widely accepted as the missing link between apes and humans; today, they are known as one of the biggest hoaxes in the history of science.

There were several reasons for widespread acceptance of Piltdown Man. As Darwin's theory of evolution by natural selection gained acceptance in the early 20th century, intense interest developed in finding traces of prehistoric human ancestors. On the basis of his knowledge of embryology and the comparative anatomy of living apes and humans, Darwin even suggested in his 1871 book *The Descent of Man* that early humans had, among other things, a large brain and an apelike face and jaw.

Although the tools made by prehistoric peoples were commonly found in Europe, their bones were not. A few fossilized skeletons had come to light in France and Germany, but they did not resemble the predicted missing link, nor had any human fossils ever been discovered in England. Given this state of affairs, the Piltdown finds could not have come at a better time: a long-awaited missing link, and with the bonus that it was found on English soil.

Fortunately, the self-correcting nature of science prevailed. While a handful of scholars questioned Piltdown Man's authenticity early on, it took the application of the newly developed fluorine dating (described in Chapter 5) by British physical anthropologist Kenneth Oakley and colleagues in 1953 to conclusively expose the hoax. The forgery consisted of a 600-year-old human skull and a recent jaw from an orangutan that had been chemically treated to appear fossil-like. These findings fully vindicated Dart and the Taung Child.

The Pliocene Environment and Hominin Diversity

The tremendous geologic changes of the Miocene epoch continued into the Pliocene. The steady movement of geologic plates supporting the African and Eurasian continents resulted in a collision of the two landmasses at either end of what now is the Mediterranean Sea. This contact allowed for the spread of species between the continents.

The same tectonic movements led to the creation of the Great Rift Valley system, a separation between geologic plates extending from the Middle East through the Red Sea and East Africa into South Africa. **Rifting** created the steady increase in the elevation of the eastern third of the African continent, which experienced a cooler and drier climate and a transformation of vegetation from forest to dry grassy **savannah**. Rifting also contributed to the volcanic activity in the region, which has provided opportunities for accurate dating of fossil specimens.

rifting In geology, the process by which a rift, or a long narrow zone of faulting, results when two geologic plates separate.
savannah Semi-arid plains environment with few scattered trees.

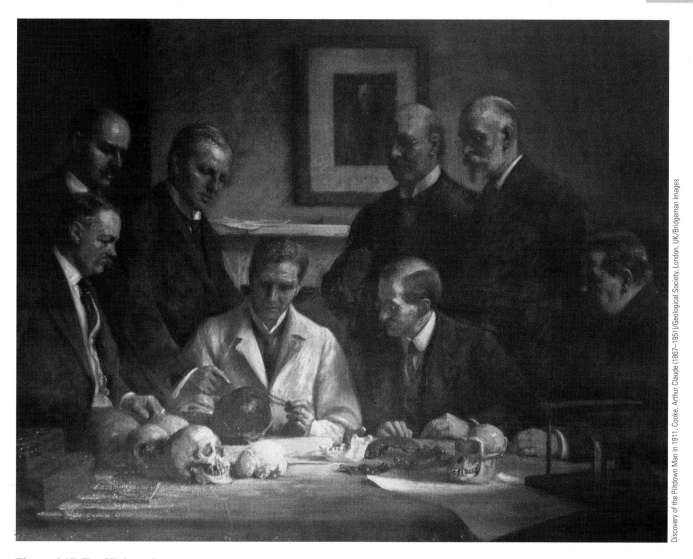

Figure 6.17 **The Piltdown Gang**
The Piltdown Man was widely accepted as ancestral to humans, largely because it fit with conventional expectations that the missing link would have a large brain and an apelike face. No one knows with certainty how many of the Piltdown gang—scientists supporting this specimen as the missing link—were actually involved in the forgery. Sir Arthur Conan Doyle, the author of the Sherlock Holmes detective stories, has been implicated.

Diverse Australopithecine Species

Since Dart's original find, hundreds of other fossil bipeds have been discovered, first in South Africa and later in Tanzania, Malawi, Kenya, Ethiopia, and Chad. As they were discovered, scientists defined a variety of different genera and species, but over time researchers have determined that the single genus *Australopithecus* includes most of these species. Anthropologists recognize possibly as many as ten species of the genus (Table 6.1). In addition, some other groups of fossil bipeds from the Pliocene epoch (1.6 to around 5 mya) have been discovered, including the earliest representatives of the genus *Homo*. Because

the East African sites are the most reliably dated, we will look at these fossils first, followed by the South African australopithecines, and then we close the chapter with a late-appearing grade of australopithecine that coexisted with the genus *Homo*.

East Africa

The oldest australopithecine species known so far consists of some jaw and limb bones from Kenya that date to between 3.9 and 4.2 million years ago (see *Australopithecus anamensis* in Table 6.1). Meave and Louise Leakey (daughter-in- law and granddaughter, respectively, of Louis and Mary, see Anthropologists of Note) discovered

TABLE 6.1

Species of *Australopithecus* and Other Pliocene Fossil Hominins*

Species	Location	Dates	Notable Features/Fossil Specimens
Ardipithecus ramidus	Ethiopia	4.4 mya†	Fossil remains of over thirty-five individuals including Ardi (another species, *Ardipithecus kadabba*, dates to 5.4–5.8 mya)
Australopithecus anamensis	Kenya	3.9–4.2 mya	Oldest australopithecine
Australopithecus deyiremeda	Ethiopia	3.3–3.5 mya	Newly proposed relative of A. afarensis with slightly more robust jaws
Kenyanthropus platyops	Kenya	3.2–3.5 mya	Contemporary with australopithecines, believed by some to be a member of that genus
Australopithecus afarensis	East Africa	2.9–3.9 mya	Lucy, Lucy's Child, the Laetoli footprints
Australopithecus bahrelghazali	Chad	3–3.5 mya	Only australopithecine from Central Africa
Australopithecus africanus	South Africa	2.3–3 mya	First discovered, gracile, well represented in fossil record (Taung)
Australopithecus aethiopicus	Kenya	2.5 mya	Oldest robust australopithecine (Black Skull)
Australopithecus garhi	Ethiopia	2.5 mya	Later East African australopithecine with human-like dentition
Australopithecus boisei	Kenya	1.2–2.3 mya	Later robust form coexisted with early *Homo* (Zinj)
Australopithecus robustus	South Africa	1–2 mya	Coexisted with early Homo
Australopithecus sediba	South Africa	1.97–1.98 mya	May be ancestral to early *Homo* and a descendant of A. africanus
Homo naledi	South Africa	?	Possibly a transitional species between australopithecines and *Homo* if dated to between 2–2.5 mya

* Paleoanthropologists differ in the number of species they recognize; some believe that the species represent separate genera.

† Million years ago.

these fossils in 1995, giving them a name meaning "ape-man of the lake." The jaw of *anamensis* shows particularities in the teeth such as a true *sectorial*: a lower premolar tooth shaped to hone the upper canine as seen in apes. In humans and more recent ancestors, the premolar has a characteristic bicuspid shape and does not sharpen the canine each time the jaws come together. As in other australopithecines and humans, thick enamel coats the molar teeth. The limb bone fragments indicate bipedalism.

The next australopithecine species defined in the fossil record, *Australopithecus afarensis*, is also one of the best known due to the Laetoli footprints from Tanzania, the famous Lucy specimen (Figure 6.18), and the recent discovery of the 3.3-million-year-old remains of a young child called "Lucy's Baby" (recall Figure 5.1). Lucy consists of bones from almost all parts of a single 3.2-million-year-old skeleton discovered in 1974 in the Afar Triangle of Ethiopia (hence the name *afarensis*). Standing only 3½ feet tall, this adult female was named after the Beatles song "Lucy in the Sky with Diamonds," which the paleoanthropologists listened to as they celebrated her discovery. In 1975, the same team also discovered the "First Family"—a collection of *afarensis* bones from at least thirteen individuals, ranging in age from infancy to adulthood, who died together as a result of some single calamity.

Fossil localities in Ethiopia and Tanzania have yielded at least sixty individuals from *Australopithecus afarensis*. Potassium-argon techniques securely date the specimens from Ethiopia's Afar region to between 2.9 and 3.9 million years ago, and material from Laetoli, in Tanzania, to 3.6 million years ago. Altogether, A. *afarensis* appears to be a sexually dimorphic bipedal species with estimates of body size and weight ranging between 1.1 and 1.6 meters (3½–5 feet) and 29 and 45 kilograms (64–100 pounds), respectively.

Assuming that larger mature fossil specimens were males and smaller specimens females, males were about one and a half times the size of females. This falls between the lesser degree of dimorphism present in modern chimpanzees and the greater amount seen in gorillas and orangutans. Some research suggests that A. *afarensis'* sexual dimorphism was closer to chimpanzees and modern humans (Larsen, 2003). A. *afarensis* males possess canine teeth significantly larger than those of females, though canine size is reduced compared to that of chimps (Figure 6.19).

Nearly 40 percent complete, the Lucy specimen has provided invaluable information about the shape of the pelvis and torso of early human ancestors. From the waist up, A. *afarensis* resembles an ape and from the waist

Figure 6.18 Lucy

Safely back in Ethiopia since 2013, after the six-year traveling exhibit that was organized and curated by the Ethiopian government and the Houston Museum of Natural History, Lucy retains her powerful draw. Some paleoanthropologists had warned that placing the 3.2-million-year-old fragile ancient skeleton on public display was far too risky. The Smithsonian Institution and the Cleveland Museum of Natural History declined to host the show for this reason. Others felt that the benefits outweighed the risks. During the trip, Lucy's remains were CT scanned so that future generations of scientists could study them without actually handling the fragile bones. In addition, the revenues from the tour were used to help modernize Ethiopia's museums. Did the tour raise public awareness of human origins and the vital role of Africa—in particular, Ethiopia—in our evolutionary history? Certainly, President Barack Obama's visit to Lucy in Ethiopia in the summer of 2015 brought attention to her and to our species' African origins. Lucy also has become the best sort of diplomat—a symbol of human unity, through whom we can all trace our ancestry.

Saul Loeb/AFP/Getty Images

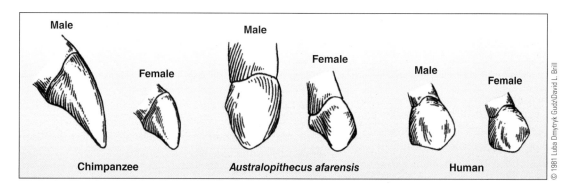

© 1981 Luba Dmytryk Gudz/David L. Brill

Figure 6.19 Sexual Dimorphism in Canine Teeth

In addition to the different levels of sexual dimorphism of canine teeth seen in chimps, australopithecines, and humans, respectively, also note the more dagger-like shape of the chimp canines compared to the hominins.

Figure 6.20 Comparisons of Trunk Skeletons of Modern Human, *A. afarensis*, and Chimp

In its pelvis, the australopithecine resembles the modern human, but its rib cage shows the pyramidal configuration of the ape.

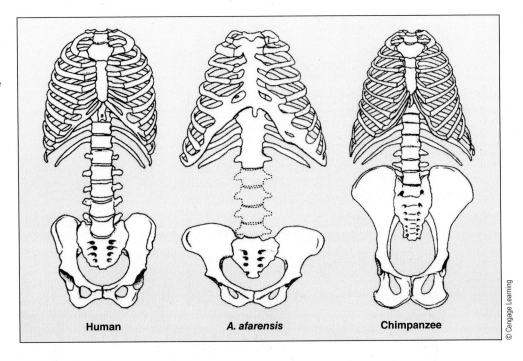

Human   **A. afarensis**   **Chimpanzee**

© Cengage Learning

down, a human (Figure 6.20). In addition, because her forearm bones are relatively shorter than those of apes, it is believed that, like humans, Lucy's upper limbs were lighter and her center of gravity lower in the body than in other apes. Still, Lucy and other early australopithecines possessed arms that were long in proportion to their legs when compared to the proportions seen in humans.

Though she lived about 150,000 years before her namesake, Lucy's Baby will add considerably to our knowledge about the biology and behavior of *A. afarensis* (Alemseged et al., 2006). These well-preserved remains of a child, thought to have died in a flash flood, include a

hyoid bone (located in the throat region) that will allow scientists to reconstruct australopithecine patterns of vocalization. Although the lower limbs clearly indicate bipedalism, the specimen's scapula and long curved finger bones are more apelike.

The curvature of the fingers and toes and the somewhat elevated position of the shoulder joint seen in adult specimens indicate that *A. afarensis* was better adapted to tree climbing than were more recent human ancestors. In the following Original Study, U.S. paleoanthropologist John Hawks discusses the kinds of evidence used to reconstruct a behavior such as tree climbing in our ancestors.

ORIGINAL STUDY

Ankles of the Australopithecines *BY JOHN HAWKS*

Recent University of Michigan PhD Jeremy DeSilva gets some nice press about his work demonstrating that fossil hominins didn't climb like chimpanzees.

"Frankly, I thought I was going to find that early humans would be quite capable, but their ankle morphology was decidedly maladaptive for the kind of climbing I was seeing in chimps," DeSilva told LiveScience. "It kind of reinvented in my mind what they were doing and how they could have survived in an African savannah without the ability to go up in the trees."[a]

This is a good example of the comparative method in paleoanthropology. We can't observe the behavior of

extinct species; we can only observe the behavior of their living relatives. We can observe the anatomy of fossil specimens, but testing hypotheses about their behavior requires us to understand the relationship between anatomy and behavior in living species. We've known about the anatomy of fossil hominin ankles for a long time, but it's not so obvious how the anatomical differences between them and chimpanzee ankles relates to behavior.

DeSilva studied the tibiae and anklebones of early hominins and concludes "that if hominins included tree climbing as part of their locomotor repertoire, then they were performing this activity in a manner decidedly unlike modern chimpanzees."

© Kristen Mosher/Danita Delimont. All rights reserved.

The amount of dorsiflexion in chimpanzees' feet allows them to climb trees with the feet in a position that is impossible for humans. Comparisons like this with living species allow paleoanthropologists to reconstruct the pattern of locomotion in fossil groups.

DeSilva's conclusion is straightforward and easy to illustrate. Chimpanzees climb vertical tree trunks pretty much like a logger does. A logger slings a strap around the trunk and leans back on it. Friction from the strap holds him up as he moves his feet upward; spikes on his boots hold him while he moves the strap.

Of course, chimpanzees don't have spikes on their feet, and they don't use a strap. Instead, their arms are long enough to wrap around the trunk, and they can wedge a foot against the trunk by flexing their ankle upward—dorsiflexing it—or grip the trunk by bending the ankle sideways—inverting the foot—around it....

You might wonder, yeah so what? Isn't it obvious that chimpanzees climb this way?

Well, it wasn't so obvious which features of the ankle might adapt chimpanzees to this style of climbing. By watching the chimpanzees (and other apes), DeSilva was able to determine the average amount (and range) of dorsiflexion and inversion of the feet while climbing, and could also assess the extent to which dorsiflexion is accomplished

at the ankle joint (as opposed to the midfoot). In this case, the observations were pretty obvious—chimpanzees were habitually flexing their ankles in ways that would damage a human ankle. Then, by examining the bony limits on human ankle flexibility, DeSilva showed that fossil hominins shared the same constraints on ankle movement as recent people. They couldn't have climbed like chimpanzees.

Human Climbing

I would say that the ankle-joint observations match the rest of the skeleton. It seems pretty obvious that *Australopithecus afarensis* and later hominins couldn't possibly have climbed in the chimpanzee-like manner described in DeSilva's paper because the hominins' arms were too short. If a logger tried to climb with his arms instead of a strap, even spikes on his feet would be relatively ineffective holding him up. Dorsiflexion would be hopeless—the normal component of force against the tree trunk would be insufficient to prevent slipping.

Humans who *aren't* loggers use a different strategy to climb vertical tree trunks—they put a large fraction of the surface area of their legs directly in contact with the trunk. Wrapping legs around and pressing them together gives the necessary friction to hold the body up.

If you're like me, you'll remember this climbing strategy ruefully from gym class, where "rope climbing" is the lowest common denominator of fitness tests. The sad fact is that many otherwise-normal humans fall on the wrong side of the line between mass and muscle power. Straining my groin muscles to the max, I still could never pull my way up a rope.

There's nothing magical about getting a human to climb. Ladders, after all, are relatively easy for the large fraction of the population who can't climb a rope or tree trunk. The trick with a ladder is that friction is organized in a more effective way for our ankle mechanics and arm length. But you don't need to schlep a ladder, if you can manage a little extra arm strength and a low enough body mass.

Early Hominin Climbing

Australopithecines were light in mass, and from what we can tell, they had strong arms. So they had what it takes for humans today to climb trees effectively—not like chimpanzees, but like humans. Up to *A. afarensis*, every early hominin we know about lived in an environment that was at least partially wooded.

...DeSilva hypothesizes a trade-off between climbing ability and effective bipedality, so that early hominins could not have effectively adapted to both. I don't think a chimpanzee-like ankle would have been any use with arms as short as australopithecines'. So I don't see the necessity of a trade-off in ankle morphology. *A. afarensis*—long before any evidence of stone tool manufacture—had very non-apelike arms, hands, and thumbs.

But there's one significant question that DeSilva omits discussing—the foot bones of a South African australopithecine: StW 573 [see Figure 6.23]. Clarke and Tobias[b] describe the foot of StW 573 as having a big toe that is abducted (sticks out) from the foot, intermediate between the chimpanzee and human condition. They conclude:

[W]e now have the best available evidence that the earliest South African australopithecine, while bipedal, was equipped to include arboreal, climbing activities in its locomotor repertoire. Its foot has departed to only a small degree from that of the chimpanzee. It is becoming clear that *Australopithecus* was not an obligate terrestrial biped, but rather a facultative biped and climber. (p. 524)

DeSilva studied the talus (an ankle bone), not the toe. StW 573 has a talus, and although it is not in DeSilva's sample, it probably would place very close to the other hominins in his comparison. Even Clarke and Tobias described its talus as humanlike—their argument for an intermediate form was based mostly on the toe.

But still, it's hard to believe that australopithecines would retain a chimpanzee-like big toe, if they couldn't use that big toe by inverting or dorsiflexing their foot in any significant way. By all other accounts, an abducted hallux (big toe) would only impede effective bipedality. It is of no use at all for a humanlike pattern of climbing. The only remaining utility would be for small-branch grasping, but small branches would seem unlikely as a support for hominin arboreality.

One possibility is that Clarke and Tobias were simply mistaken. That appears to be the explanation favored by Harcourt-Smith and Aiello[c] and McHenry and Jones,[d] who concluded that all known hominin feet appear to lack any "ape-like ability to oppose the big toe." They also point to the Laetoli footprint trails, most observers of which agree that the big toe was adducted, not abducted.

I tend to favor that explanation—australopithecines simply didn't have a grasping foot. But they may not have shared the medial longitudinal arch, at least not in the human configuration, and without it one might doubt that their gait featured as strong a toe-off as that of later humans. Who knows?

Adapted from Hawks, J. (2009, April 14). Ankles of the australopithecines. *John Hawks Weblog*. http://johnhawks.net/weblog/reviews/early_hominids/anatomy/desilva-2009-chimpanzee-climbing-talus.html (retrieved October 11, 2015). Copyright © 2009 John Hawks, all rights reserved. Reprinted by permission of the author.

---

[a] DeSilva, J. M. (2009). Functional morphology of the ankle and the likelihood of climbing in early hominins. *Proceedings of the National Academy of Sciences USA 106* (16), 6567–6572.

[b] Clarke, R. J., & Tobias, P. V. (1995). Sterkfontein member 2 foot bones of the oldest South African hominid. *Science 269* (5223), 521–524.

[c] Harcourt-Smith, W. E. H., & Aiello, L. C. (2004). Fossils, feet and the evolution of human bipedal locomotion. *Journal of Anatomy 204* (5), 403–416.

[d] McHenry, H. M., & Jones, A. L. (2006). Hallucial convergence in early hominids. *Journal of Human Evolution 50* (5), 534–539.

At the other end of the body, skull bones are vital for the reconstruction of evolutionary relationships. They allow paleoanthropologists to learn about the cognitive capacities of ancestral species. For example, the brow of an *A. afarensis* skull slopes backward to a relatively low height and has the ridge that helps give apes such massive-looking foreheads. Other ape features include large jaws relative to the size of the skull, no chin, and a small brain. Even the semicircular canal, a part of the ear crucial to maintenance of balance, is apelike. Cranial capacity, commonly used as an index of brain size for *A. afarensis*, averages about 420 cubic centimeters (cc), roughly equivalent to the size of a chimpanzee and about one-third the size of living humans. In addition to absolute brain size, the ratio of brain to body size contributes to intelligence. Unfortunately, with such a wide range of adult weights, this ratio cannot be determined for australopithecines.

Australopithecine teeth constitute one of the primary means for distinguishing among closely related groups. In *A. afarensis*, unlike humans, the teeth are all quite large, particularly the molars. The premolar is no longer fully sectorial as in *A. anamensis*, but most other features of the teeth represent a more ancestral rather than derived condition. For example, instead of the dental arch seen in humans, australopithecines possess more parallel tooth rows (the ancestral ape condition). The canines project slightly, and a slight gap known as a **diastema** remains between the upper incisors and canines as found in the apes (**Figure 6.21**).

To further complicate the diversity seen in *A. afarensis*, in 2001 Meave and Louise Leakey announced the discovery of an almost complete cranium, parts of two upper jaws, and assorted teeth from a site in northern Kenya, dated to between 3.2 and 3.5 million years ago (Leakey et al., 2001). Contemporaneous with early East African *Australopithecus*, the Leakeys see this as a different genus and named it **Kenyanthropus platyops** ("flat-faced

diastema A space between the canines and other teeth allowing the large projecting canines to fit within the jaw.

Kenyanthropus platyops A proposed genus and species of biped contemporaneous with early australopithecines; may not be a separate genus.

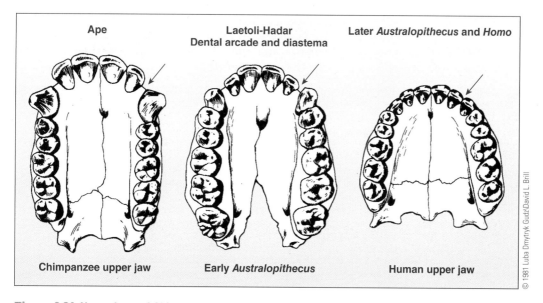

Ape

Laetoli-Hadar
Dental arcade and diastema

Later *Australopithecus* and *Homo*

Chimpanzee upper jaw

Early *Australopithecus*

Human upper jaw

© 1981 Luba Dmytryk Gudz/David L. Brill

Figure 6.21 **Upper Jaws of Chimps, Australopithecines, and Humans**
Note the differences in the arched dental arcade and the spacing between the canines and the adjoining teeth. Only the earliest australopithecines possess a diastema (a large gap between the upper canine and incisor), which is found in chimpanzees.

man of Kenya"). Unlike early australopithecines, *Kenyanthropus* has a small braincase and small molars set in a large, human-like, flat face. The Leakeys regard the fossils as ancestral to the genus *Homo*. Other paleoanthropologists disagree, suggesting that the Leakeys' interpretation rests on a questionable reconstruction of badly broken fossil specimens (White, 2003).

Central Africa

The first Central African australopithecine species, dated to the same time period as *Kenyanthropus platyops*, was discovered in Chad. Named *Australopithecus bahrelghazali* for a nearby riverbed, the specimen consists of a jaw and several teeth dated to between 3 and 3.5 million years ago. With time, perhaps more discoveries from this region (also home to the Toumai specimen discussed previously) will give a fuller understanding of the role of *A. bahrelghazali* in human evolution.

South Africa

Throughout the 20th century and into the present, a variety of sites in South Africa have yielded australopithecine fossils (Figure 6.22). These include numerous fossils found beginning in the 1930s at Sterkfontein and Makapansgat, in addition to Dart's original find from Taung. Absence of the clear stratigraphy and volcanic ash of East African sites makes these discoveries far more difficult to date and interpret. However, cutting-edge dating techniques have been applied to one unusually complete skeleton known as "Little Foot" (Figure 6.23),

dating it to 3.67 million years ago. Paleomagnetism and a faunal series established in East Africa have helped to place other fossils, like the Taung Child, to between 2.3

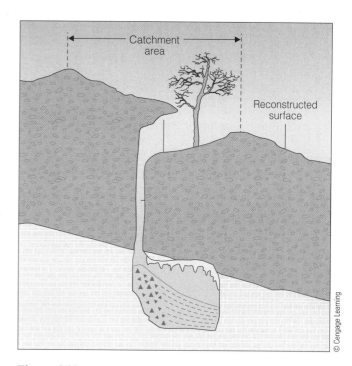

© Cengage Learning

Figure 6.22 **South African Limestone Cave Sites**
Many of the fossil sites in South Africa were limestone caverns connected to the surface by a shaft. Over time, dirt, bones, and other matter that fell down the shaft accumulated inside the cavern, becoming fossilized. In the Pliocene, trees that grew from earth next to the shaft's opening provided a sheltered location that may have been used by predators for eating without being bothered by scavengers.

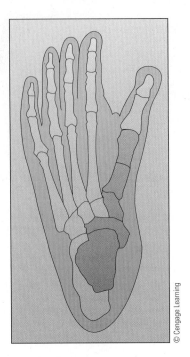

© Cengage Learning

Figure 6.23 Gracile Australopithecine Foot
Note the length and flexibility of the first toe (*at right*) in this drawing of the foot bones of the Sterkfontein, South Africa, specimen (StW 573) referred to in this chapter's Original Study, also known as "Little Foot." In 2015 scientists applied a new radioisotopic dating technique to the remains and pushed back their age to 3.67 million years. It took fifteen years just to excavate Little Foot after its discovery in 1994, proving just how difficult and sensitive interpretation of the fossil record can be.

and 3 million years ago. Paleoanthropologists usually classify all these specimens as *A. africanus*, also known as **gracile australopithecines**.

Researchers debate the presence of human qualities such as an enlarged brain in gracile australopithecines. At the moment, the weight of the evidence favors mental capabilities for all gracile australopithecines as being comparable to those of modern great apes (chimps, bonobos, gorillas, orangutans). Using patterns of tooth eruption in young australopithecines such as Taung, some paleoanthropologists further suggest that the

gracile australopithecine One member of the genus *Australopithecus* possessing a more lightly built chewing apparatus; probably had a diet that included more meat than that of the robust australopithecines; best represented by the South African species *A. africanus*.

robust australopithecine One member of the genus *Australopithecus*, living from 1 to 2.5 million years ago in East Africa and South Africa; known for the rugged nature of its chewing apparatus (large back teeth, large chewing muscles, and a bony ridge on the skull top to allow for these large muscles).

sagittal crest A crest running from front to back on the top of the skull along the midline to provide a surface of bone for the attachment of the large temporal muscles for chewing.

developmental pattern of australopithecines was more humanlike than apelike. Our current understanding of genetics and the macroevolutionary process indicates that a developmental shift likely underlies a change in body plan such as the emergence of bipedalism among the African hominoids.

Hominins of the Early Pleistocene

Other South African sites have yielded fossils from the early Pleistocene (beginning around 2.5 mya) whose skulls and teeth looked quite different from the gracile australopithecines described previously. Relative to the size of their braincases, these South African fossils, known as *Australopithecus robustus*, possess massive (robust) teeth, jaws, and chewing muscles that distinguish them from the slightly smaller gracile forms.

Robust Australopithecines

Over the course of evolution, several distinct groups of **robust australopithecines** have appeared not only in South Africa but throughout East Africa as well. The first remains were found at Kromdraai and Swartkrans in the 1930s in deposits that, unfortunately, cannot be securely dated. Current thinking puts them between 1 and 2 million years ago. Usually referred to as *A. robustus* (see Table 6.1), this species possessed a characteristic robust chewing apparatus including a **sagittal crest** (more pronounced in males) running from front to back along the top of the skull (**Figure 6.24**). This feature provides sufficient area on a relatively small braincase for attachment of the huge temporal muscles required to operate powerful jaws and maintain a diet based on uncooked plant foods. Also present in famously herbivorous modern gorillas, the sagittal crest provides an example of convergent evolution.

The first East African robust australopithecine was discovered by Mary Leakey in the summer of 1959, the centennial year of the publication of Darwin's *On the Origin of Species*. She found it in Olduvai Gorge, a massive fossil-rich gash in the earth, near Ngorongoro Crater, on the Serengeti Plain of Tanzania. About 40 kilometers (25 miles) long and 91 meters (300 feet) deep, Olduvai Gorge cuts through Pleistocene geologic strata revealing close to 2 million years of the earth's history.

Louis Leakey reconstructed his wife Mary's discovery and gave it the name *Zinjanthropus boisei* (Zinj, an old Arabic name for East Africa that means literally "Land of the Blacks," *boisei* after the benefactor who funded their expedition). At first, the stone tools found in association

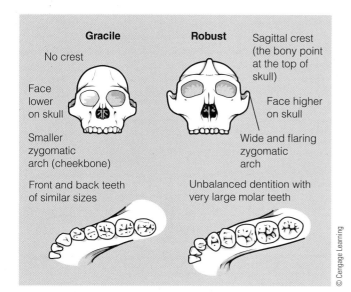

Figure 6.24 Gracile and Robust Australopithecines
The differences between gracile and robust australopithecines relate primarily to their chewing apparatus. Robust species have extremely large back teeth, large chewing muscles, and a bony ridge (sagittal crest) on the top of their skulls for the attachment of large temporal muscles. The front and back teeth of gracile species are balanced in size, and their chewing muscles (reflected in a less massive skull) are more like those seen in the later genus *Homo*. If you place your hands on the sides of your skull above your ears while opening and closing your jaw, you can feel where your temporal muscles attach to your skull. Glide your hands toward the top of your skull while still moving your jaw to feel where these muscles end in humans.

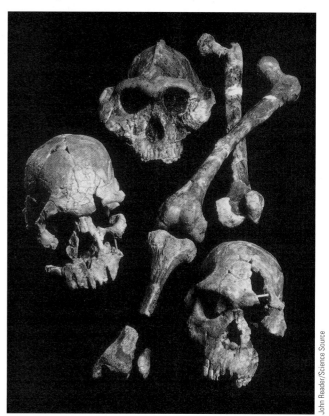

Figure 6.25 Robust Australopithecines and the Genus *Homo*
The robust australopithecines and the earliest members of genus *Homo* inhabited the earth at the same time. These particular skulls and leg bones were all found along the eastern shores of Lake Turkana in Kenya and are dated to between 1.7 and 1.9 million years ago. Many paleoanthropologists classify the two specimens with rounded skulls as members of the species *Homo habilis*. The robust australopithecine at the top of the photograph has the bony ridge (sagittal crest) along the top of its skull. Note that the dates for each of these species expands beyond the dates found at one particular site.

with this specimen led Louis Leakey to suggest that this ancient fossil seemed more human than *Australopithecus* and extremely close to modern humans in evolutionary development. Further study, however, revealed that *Zinjanthropus*, the remains of which consisted of a skull and a few limb bones, was an East African species of robust australopithecine, *Australopithecus boisei* (see Table 6.1). Potassium-argon dating places these fossils at about 1.75 million years old.

Since the time of Mary Leakey's original *A. boisei* find, numerous other fossils of this robust species have been found at Olduvai, as well as north and east of Lake Turkana in Kenya (**Figure 6.25**). These robust fossils date from between 1 and 2.5 million years ago. Like robust australopithecines from South Africa, East African robust forms possessed enormous molars and premolars. Despite a large mandible and palate, the anterior teeth (canines and incisors) were often crowded, owing to the room needed for the massive molars. The heavy skull, more massive even than seen in the robust forms from South Africa, has a sagittal crest and prominent brow ridge. Cranial capacity ranges from about 500 to 530 cubic

centimeters. Body size, too, is somewhat larger; estimates for the weight of the South African robust forms range between 32 and 40 kilograms (70 and 88 pounds), while the East African robusts probably weighed between 34 and 49 kilograms (75 and 108 pounds).

Because the earliest robust skull from East Africa, the Black Skull from Kenya, dated to 2.5 million years ago (see *A. aethiopicus* in Table 6.1), retains a number of ancestral features shared with earlier East African australopithecines, some suggest that it evolved from *A. afarensis*, giving rise to the later robust East African forms. Paleoanthropologists debate whether the South African robust australopithecines represent a southern offshoot of the East African line or convergent evolution from a South African ancestor. In either case, the later robust australopithecines developed molars and

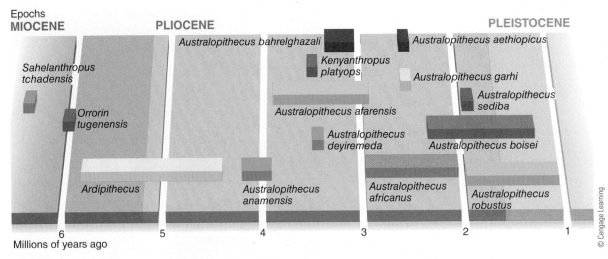

Figure 6.26 Timeline of Australopithecines and Other Ancestral Plio-Pleistocene Hominins
This timeline shows the fossil bipeds who were not members of the genus *Homo* and the scientific names by which they have been known, arranged according to when they lived. The genus *Homo* first appeared in the fossil record 2.5 million years ago and coexisted with the gracile species *A. garhi* and *A. sediba*. There is also overlap between *Homo* and the robust australopithecine species *A. aethiopicus, A. boisei,* and *A. robustus.* Whether the different species names are warranted is a matter of debate.

premolars that are both absolutely and relatively larger than those of earlier australopithecines, who possessed front and back teeth more in proportion to those seen in the genus *Homo*.

Many anthropologists believe that the late australopithecines avoided competition with early members of the genus *Homo*, their contemporaries, by becoming specialized consumers of plant foods. In the course of evolution, the **law of competitive exclusion** dictates that when two closely related species compete for the same niche, one will outcompete the other, bringing about the loser's extinction. Their lengthy coexistence from about 1 to 2.5 million years ago suggests that early *Homo* and late *Australopithecus* did not compete for the same niche (Figure 6.26).

Australopithecines and the Genus *Homo*

A variety of bipeds inhabited Africa about 2.5 million years ago. In 1999, more fossil discoveries from the Afar region of Ethiopia added *Australopithecus garhi* to the mix

(Figure 6.27). Though the teeth were large, this australopithecine possessed an arched dental arcade and a ratio between front and back teeth more like humans and South African gracile australopithecines than like robust groups. For this reason, some have proposed that *A. garhi* (named from the Afar word for "surprise") is ancestral to the genus *Homo*, though the question of which australopithecine was ancestral to humans remains particularly controversial.

In 2010, scientists announced a newly discovered gracile australopithecine named ***Australopithecus sediba***. First discovered in 2008 in South Africa by paleoanthropologist Lee Berger's then 9-year-old son Matthew, who was exploring while his father excavated a formal site nearby, this find consists of at least four partial skeletons, one of which is a well-preserved adolescent male. Best of all, *A. sediba* can be precisely dated to between 1.97 and 1.98 million years ago by paleomagnetism and uranium dating (Pickering et al., 2011). A variety of derived traits in the hand, forearm, and pelvis have led Berger's team to suggest that *A. sediba* is a transitional species between *A. africanus* and early *Homo* (Figure 6.28). Others argue that these specimens are part of the wide variation present in *A. africanus*. They also protest that *A. sediba* could not be ancestral to early *Homo* because the two groups seem to have coexisted.

A variety of scenarios have been proposed, each one giving a different australopithecine group the starring role as the immediate human ancestor (Figure 6.29). Paleoanthropologists use the dates of the specimens as well as derived features to link the contending

law of competitive exclusion When two closely related species compete for the same niche, one will outcompete the other, bringing about the latter's extinction.

Australopithecus sediba A recently identified species of South African gracile australopithecine dated precisely to between 1.97 and 1.98 million years ago, with derived *Homo*-like characteristics in the hands and pelvis.

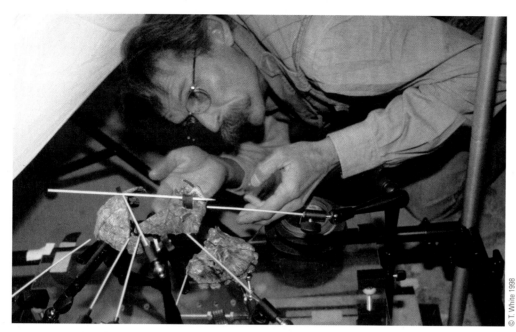

© T. White 1998

Figure 6.27
Reconstruction of Fossil Specimens
Photographer David Brill, a specialist in images of fossils and paleoanthropology, positions the upper jaw and the other skull fragments of *Australopithecus garhi* so that the fragments are aligned as they would be in a complete skull.

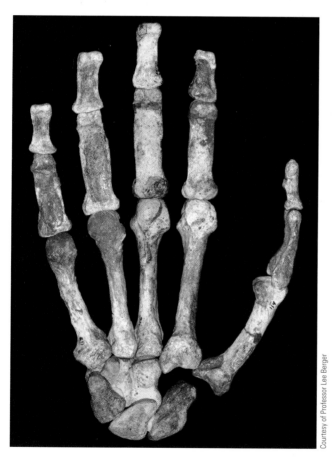

Courtesy of Professor Lee Berger

Figure 6.28 Exquisite Hands
Derived features of the hand and forearm, which *Australopithecus sediba* shares with humans, have led some scientists to suggest that this is the ancestral hominin that gave rise to the human line. From the analysis of the well-preserved bones, it appears that these ancient hominins were anatomically capable of a "precision grip," a feature characteristic of humans. The *A. sediba* pelvis also has evidence of derived morphology that would contribute to a more efficient stride.

australopithecines to *Homo*. Pelvic shape and forearm anatomy make the case for *A. sediba*. An arched dental arcade is the evidence promoted for *A. garhi*. The flat face and perhaps larger cranial capacity of *Kenyanthropus platyops* is also proposed as the link to *Homo*. In any case, paleoanthropologists agree that the robust australopithecines, though successful in their time, ultimately represent an evolutionary side branch.

Environment, Diet, and the Origins of the Human Line

How did evolutionary processes transform an early ape into a hominin? Besides investigating the fossil evidence, paleoanthropologists use scientific reconstructions of environmental conditions and inferences made from data on living nonhuman primates and humans to construct their hypotheses about this transformation.

For many years, the emergence of the savannah environment in East Africa has dominated the human evolutionary narrative. Although the evidence from *Ardipithecus* shows that the earliest members of the human line were forest-dwellers, over time the size of tropical forests decreased or, more commonly, broke up into mosaics where patches of forest were interspersed with savannah or other types of open country. The forebears of the human line likely lived in places with access to both trees and open savannah.

As the forests thinned, these early ancestors had to adapt to a new, more exposed environment. Traditional ape-type foods found in trees became less available,

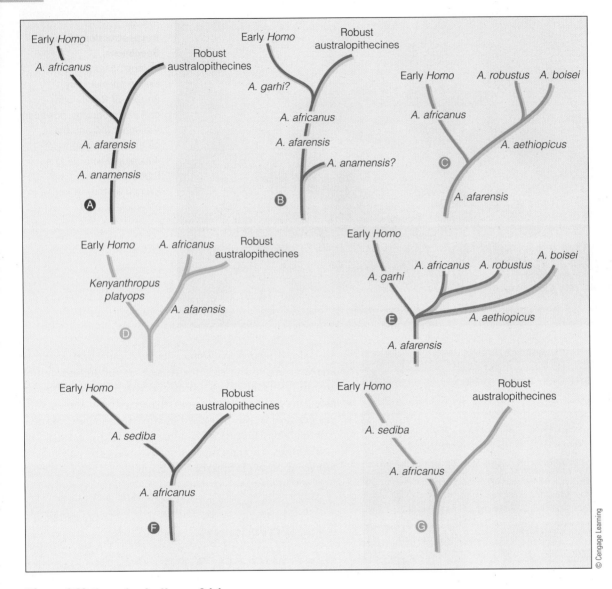

Figure 6.29 Scenarios for Human Origins
Paleoanthropologists debate the relationships among the various Pliocene groups and the question of which group is ancestral to the genus *Homo*. These diagrams present several alternative hypotheses. Most agree, however, that the robust australopithecines represent an evolutionary side branch and that *Ardipithecus ramidus* is ancestral to the australopithecines. Recent points of contention include whether *Australopithecus sediba* might be directly ancestral to the genus *Homo* and the place of the new species *Homo naledi*.

especially in seasons of reduced rainfall (Figure 6.30). Therefore, it became more and more necessary to forage on the ground for foods such as seeds, grasses, and roots. With reduced canine teeth, early bipeds were relatively defenseless against numerous carnivorous predators. The South African fossil evidence supports the notion that predators were a problem for early hominins. Most of the fossil specimens were dropped into rock fissures by predators such as leopards or, as in the case of the Taung Child, by an eagle.

Many investigators have argued that the hands of early bipeds took over the weapon functions of reduced canine teeth. Hands enabled them to threaten predators

by throwing stones and using wooden objects as clubs. Many of the other hominoids use their hands in this fashion. In australopithecines the use of clubs and throwing stones may have set the stage for the much later manufacture of more efficient weapons from bone, wood, and stone.

Although the hands of the later australopithecines were suitable for toolmaking, no evidence exists that any of them actually *made* stone tools. Still, using brain size as a measure, *Australopithecus* certainly had no less intelligence and dexterity than do modern great apes, all of whom make use of tools as described in Chapter 4. Most likely, the ability to make and use simple tools dates back

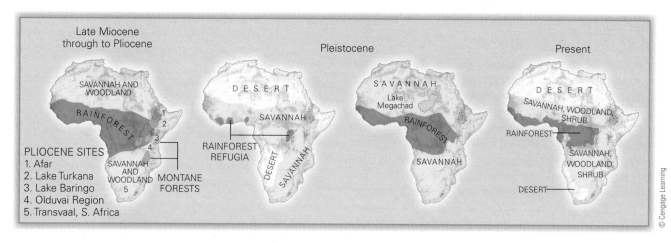

Figure 6.30 Climate Change and Vegetation Zones
Since the late Miocene, the vegetation zones of Africa have changed considerably. Cooler, drier periods during the Pliocene reduced forested areas to far less than what exist today. The loss of forest likely created selective pressures that favored bipedalism.

to the last common ancestor of the Asian and African apes, before the appearance of the first bipeds.

Unfortunately, these simple tools would not be preserved well in the fossil record, and certainly not for over a million years. Although we cannot be sure about this, in addition to clubs and objects thrown for defense, sturdy sticks may have been used to dig edible roots, and convenient stones may have been used (as some chimpanzees do) to crack open nuts. In fact, some animal bones from australopithecine sites in South Africa show microscopic wear patterns suggesting their use to dig edible roots from the ground. We may also allow the possibility that, like chimpanzees, females used tools more often to get and process food, while males more typically used tools as weapons. The female chimpanzees hunting with spears in Fongoli as described in Chapter 4 call into question these distinct roles for the sexes.

Humans Stand on Their Own Two Feet

There are serious drawbacks to bipedalism as a pattern of locomotion. For example, paleoanthropologists have suggested that bipedalism makes an animal more visible to predators, exposes its soft underbelly or gut, and interferes with the ability to instantly change direction while running. They also emphasize that bipedalism does not result in particularly fast running: Quadrupedal chimpanzees and baboons, for example, run 30 to 34 percent faster than we average bipeds. For 100-meter distances, our best athletes today may attain speeds of 34 to 37 kilometers per hour (21 to 23 miles per hour), while the larger African carnivores from which bipeds might need to run

can attain speeds up to 60 to 70 kilometers per hour (37 to 43 miles per hour). Also, the consequences of a leg or foot injury are more serious for a biped, whereas a quadruped can do amazingly well on three legs. Because each of these negatives would have placed our early ancestors at risk from predators, paleoanthropologists ask what made bipedal locomotion worth paying such a high price. What selective pressures favored bipedalism despite these disadvantages?

Bipedalism does appear to offer some advantage when it comes to endurance running, so humans do have an advantage over quadrupeds for distance running. One older theory proposed that bipedal locomotion allowed males to obtain food on the savannah and transport it back to females, who were restricted from doing so by the dependence of their offspring. The fact that female apes, not to mention women among food-foraging peoples, routinely combine infant care with foraging for food negates this theory. Indeed, among most food foragers, it is the women who commonly supply the bulk of the food eaten by both sexes.

Moreover, this model presumed pair bonding (one male attached to one female), a form of social organization atypical of terrestrial primates displaying the degree of sexual dimorphism that was characteristic of *Australopithecus*. Nor is pair bonding really characteristic of *Homo sapiens*. In a substantial majority of recent human societies, including those in which people forage for their food, some form of polygamy—marriage to two or more individuals at the same time—is not only permitted but preferred. And even in the supposedly monogamous United States, many individuals marry (and hence mate with) two or more others (the only requirement is that the person not be married to more than one mate at the same time).

In the end, the idea of males provisioning stay-at-home moms appears to be more culture-bound than based on the fossil evidence. A more accurate version of the theory emphasizes that any individual biped—whether male or female—has the ability to gather food from the ground for transport back to a tree or other place of safety for consumption. The biped does not have to remain out in the open, exposed and vulnerable, to do all of its eating. Paleoanthropologists, like all anthropologists, must exercise caution to avoid infusing theories about the fossil record with their own cultural beliefs. See the Biocultural Connection for another example of the influence of contemporary gender roles on paleoanthropological theories.

Besides making it possible to carry nourishment, bipedalism could have facilitated the food quest in other ways. With their hands free and body upright, the animals could reach otherwise unobtainable foodstuff on thorny trees too flimsy and too spiny to climb (Kaplan, 2007; Thorpe, Holder, & Crompton, 2007). Furthermore, they could gather other small food quickly using both hands in alternation. And in times of scarcity, being able to see farther, with the head in an upright position, would have helped them locate food and water sources.

Food may not have been the only thing transported by early bipeds. As we saw in Chapters 3 and 4, from birth primate infants must cling by themselves to their mothers, who use all their limbs in locomotion. Injuries caused by falling from the mother account for a significant proportion of infant mortality among apes. Thus, the ability to carry infants would have significantly contributed to the survival of offspring, and the ancestors of *Australopithecus* would have been capable of doing just this.

Although it appeared before our ancestors lived on the savannah, bipedalism likely served as a means to cope with heat stress out in the open as the forested environments shrank. In addition to bipedalism, our relative nakedness constitutes one of the most obvious differences between humans and other living hominoids. Humans have only a sparse layer of body hair over most of the body with a very dense cover of hair limited primarily to the head. Peter Wheeler, a British physiologist, has suggested that bipedalism and the human pattern of body hair growth are both adaptations to the heat stress of the savannah environment (Wheeler, 1993). Building upon the earlier "radiator" theory of paleoanthropologist Dean Falk (1990), Wheeler developed this hypothesis through comparative anatomy, experimental studies, and the observation that humans are the only apes to inhabit the savannah environment today.

Many other animals, however, inhabit the savannah, and each of them possesses some mechanism for coping with heat stress. Some animals, like many of the carnivores, limit their heavy activity to dawn or dusk when the sun is low in the sky or to the cooler nights. Some, like antelope, have evolved to tolerate high body temperatures that would kill humans due to overheating of the brain tissue. They accomplish this by cooling their blood in their muzzles through evaporation before it enters the vessels leading to the delicate tissues of the brain.

According to Wheeler, the interesting thing about humans and other primates is that

> We can't uncouple brain temperature from the rest of the body, the way an antelope does, so we've got to prevent any damaging elevations in body temperature. And of course the problem is even more acute for an ape, because in general, the larger and more complex the brain, the more easily it is damaged. So, there were incredible selective pressures on early hominids favoring adaptations that would reduce thermal stress-pressures that may have favored bipedalism. (quoted in Folger, 1993, pp. 34–35)

Wheeler has studied this notion by comparing the exposure to solar radiation for an early biped, like Lucy, in upright and quadrupedal stances. He found that the bipedal stance reduced exposure to solar radiation by 60 percent, indicating that a biped would require less water to stay cool in a savannah environment compared to a quadruped.

Wheeler further suggests that bipedalism made the human body hair pattern possible. Fur can keep out solar radiation as well as retain heat. A biped, with reduced exposure to the sun everywhere except the head, would benefit from hair loss on the body surface to increase the efficiency of sweating to cool down. On the head, hair serves as a shield, blocking solar radiation.

Some object to this scenario, citing that when bipedalism developed, savannah was not as extensive in Africa as it is today. In both East Africa and South Africa, environments included closed and open bush and woodlands. Moreover, fossil flora and fauna found with *Ardipithecus* and the possible human ancestors from the Miocene are typical of a moist, closed, wooded habitat.

However, the presence of bipedalism in the fossil record without a savannah environment does not indicate that bipedalism was not adaptive to these conditions. It merely indicates that bipedalism appeared without any particular adaptive benefits at first, likely through a random macromutation. Bipedalism provided a body plan preadapted to the heat stress of the savannah environment.

Recall that in the early 20th century, larger brains were thought to have permitted the evolution of bipedalism. We now know not only that bipedalism preceded the evolution of larger brains by several million years, but that bipedalism may have *preadapted* human ancestors for brain expansion. According to Wheeler,

> The brain is one of the most metabolically active tissues in the body. . . . In the case of humans it accounts for something like 20 percent of total energy consumption. So you've got an organ producing a lot of heat that you've got to dump. Once we'd become bipedal and naked and achieved this ability to dump heat, that may have allowed the expansion of the brain that took place later in human evolution. It didn't cause it, but you can't have a large brain unless you can cool it. (quoted in Folger, 1993, pp. 34–35)

Evolution and Human Birth

Because biology and culture have always shaped human experience, it can be a challenge to separate the influences of each of these factors on human practices. For example, in the 1950s paleoanthropologists developed the theory that human childbirth is particularly difficult compared to birth in other mammals. This theory was based in part on the observation of a "tight fit" between the human mother's birth canal and the baby's head, though several other primates also possess similarly tight fits between the newborn's head or shoulders and the birth canal. Nevertheless, changes in the birth canal associated with bipedalism coupled with the evolution of large brains were held responsible for difficult birth in humans.

At the same historical moment, childbirth practices in the United States were changing. In one generation from the 1920s to the 1950s, birth shifted from the home to the hospital. In the process childbirth transformed from something a woman normally accomplished at home, perhaps with the help of a midwife or relatives, into the high-tech delivery of a neonate (the medical term for a newborn) with the assistance of medically trained personnel. Women in the 1950s were generally fully anesthetized during the birth process. Paleoanthropological theories mirrored the cultural norms, providing a scientific explanation for the change in U.S. childbirth practices.

As a scientific theory, the idea of difficult human birth stands on shaky ground. No fossil neonates have ever been recovered, and only a handful of complete pelves (the bones forming the birth canal) exist. Instead, scientists must examine the birth process in living humans and nonhuman primates to reconstruct the evolution of the human birth pattern.

Cultural beliefs and practices, however, shape every aspect of birth. Cultural factors determine where a birth occurs, the actions of the individuals present, and beliefs about the nature of the experience. When paleoanthropologists of the 1950s and 1960s asserted that human childbirth is more difficult than birth in other mammals, they were drawing upon their own cultural beliefs that childbirth is dangerous and should occur in a hospital.

A quick look at global neonatal mortality statistics indicates that in countries such as the Netherlands and Sweden, healthy women give birth successfully outside of hospitals, as they did throughout human evolutionary history. In other countries, deaths related to childbirth reflect malnutrition, infectious disease, and the low social status of women, rather than an inherently faulty biology.

Album/Art Resource, NY

Tlazolteotl, the earth mother goddess of the Aztecs, is depicted here giving birth in a squatting position, which is favored by women throughout the world. For hospital births, women generally have to work against gravity to bring a child into the world because they tend to be placed on their backs with their legs in stirrups for the benefit of attending physicians.

Biocultural Question

Though well-nourished healthy women successfully birth their babies outside of hospital settings, caesarean section (C-section) rates have been rising in industrialized societies. In the United States one in three deliveries is by C-section, and in many Latin American countries more than half of all deliveries are by caesarean. What cultural factors have led to this practice? Would your personal approach to birth change with the knowledge that humans have successfully adapted to childbirth?

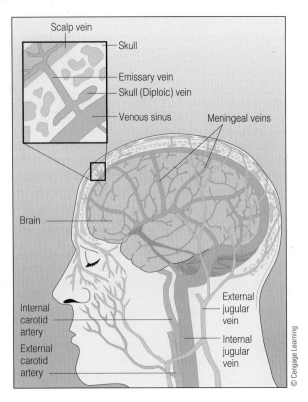

Figure 6.31 Cooling Hot-Headed Hominins
Instead of returning directly to the heart, in humans blood from the face and scalp may be directed into the braincase and then to the heart. Already cooled at the surface of the skin, blood is able to carry heat away from the brain.

Consistent with Wheeler's hypothesis is the fact that the system for drainage of the blood from the cranium of the earlier australopithecines is significantly different from that of the genus *Homo* (Figure 6.31).

Though paleoanthropologists cannot resolve every detail of the course of human evolution from the available data, over time the narrative they have constructed has improved. Today, we know that bipedalism preceded brain expansion by several million years. Bipedalism likely occurred as a sudden shift in body plan; then stabilizing selection took over, and little change took place for at least a few million years. Change again occurred about 2.5 million years ago, resulting in the branching out of new forms, including several robust species as well as the first appearance of the genus *Homo*. From about 2.3 million years ago until robust australopithecines became extinct around 1 million years ago, however, the robust forms underwent relatively little alteration. By contrast, after its appearance 2.5 million years ago, *Homo* began a steady course of brain expansion that continued over the next 2.3 million years until brain size reached its current state. With the appearance of this new larger-brained hominin, the first stone tools appear in the archaeological record.

Early Representatives of the Genus *Homo*

Just as the Leakeys thought, Olduvai Gorge with its stone tool assemblages was a good place to search for human ancestors. Part of today's Olduvai Gorge was once a lake. Almost 2 million years ago, numerous wild animals including a variety of bipeds inhabited its shores. In 1959—when the Leakeys found the bones of the first specimen of robust *Australopithecus boisei* in association with some of these tools and the bones of birds, reptiles, antelopes, and pigs—they thought they had found the remains of one of the toolmakers. Fossils unearthed a few months later and a few feet below this first discovery led them to change their mind. These fossil remains consisted of more than one individual, including a few cranial bones, a lower jaw, a clavicle, some finger bones (Figure 6.32), and the nearly

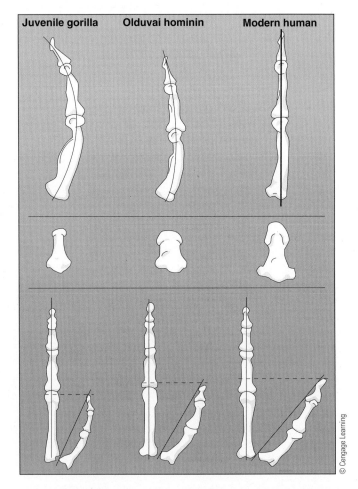

Figure 6.32 Comparative Anatomy of *Homo habilis* Hand Bones
A comparison of hand bones from a juvenile gorilla, *Homo habilis* from Olduvai, and a modern human highlights important differences in the structure of fingers and thumbs. In the top row are fingers, and in the second row are terminal (end) thumb bones. Although the terminal finger bones of the Olduvai specimen are more human, its lower finger bones are more curved and powerful. The bottom row compares thumb length and angle relative to the index finger.

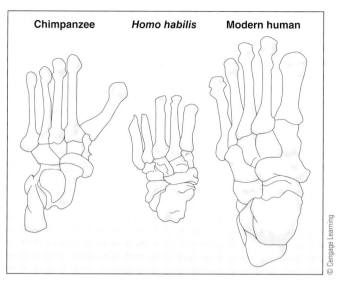

Figure 6.33 **Comparative Anatomy of *Homo habilis* Foot Bones** A partial foot skeleton of *Homo habilis* (*center*) is compared with the same bones of a chimpanzee (*left*) and a modern human (*right*). Note how *H. habilis'* bone at the base of the great toe is in line with the others, as it is in modern humans, making for effective walking but poor grasping.

complete left foot of an adult (Figure 6.33). Skull and jaw fragments indicated that these specimens represented a larger-brained biped without the specialized chewing apparatus of the robust australopithecines.

The Leakeys and colleagues named their find *Homo habilis* (Latin for "handy human") and suggested that tool-wielding *H. habilis* may have eaten the animals and possibly the *Australopithecus boisei*. Of course, we do not really know whether *A. boisei* from Olduvai Gorge met its end in this way, but we do know that cut marks from a stone tool are present on a jawbone from a 2.4-million-year-old australopithecine from South Africa (Pickering, White, & Toth, 2000). This was done, presumably, to remove the mandible, but for what purpose we do not know. In any event, it does lend credibility to the idea of *A. boisei* on occasion being dismembered by *H. habilis*.

Subsequent work at Olduvai has unearthed not only more skull fragments but other parts of the skeleton of *H. habilis* as well. Since the late 1960s, sites in South Africa, Ethiopia, and Kenya have yielded fossils of the genus *Homo* contemporaneous with those from Olduvai.

The eastern shores of Lake Turkana, on the border between Kenya and Ethiopia, have been particularly rich with fossils from earliest *Homo*. Richard Leakey (see Anthropologists of Note) discovered one well-known fossil, known as KNM ER 1470, at Koobi Fora. (The letters KNM stand for Kenya National Museum; the ER, for East Rudolf, the name for Lake Turkana during the colonial era in Kenya.) The deposits in which it was found are about 1.9 million years old; these deposits, like those at Olduvai,

also contain crude stone tools. The KNM ER 1470 skull is more modern in appearance than any *Australopithecus* skull and has a cranial capacity of 752 cubic centimeters (cc). However, the large teeth and face of this specimen resemble the earlier australopithecines.

This same site has provided another well-preserved skull from the same time period (KNM ER 1813); it possesses a cranial capacity of less than 600 cc but has the derived characteristics of a smaller, less projecting face and teeth (both of these specimens are shown in Figure 6.25). Though specimens attributed to *H. habilis* generally have cranial capacities greater than 600 cc, the cranial capacity of any individual is also in proportion to its body size. Therefore, many paleoanthropologists interpret KNM ER 1813 and ER 1470 as a female and male of a very sexually dimorphic species, with the smaller cranial capacity of KNM ER 1813 a reflection of her smaller body size (Figure 6.34).

Lumpers or Splitters?

Other paleoanthropologists do not agree with placing specimens as diverse as KNM ER 1813 and KNM ER 1470 in the single taxonomic group of *H. habilis*. Instead they feel that the diversity represented in these specimens warrants separating the fossils like the larger-brained KNM ER 1470 into a distinct coexisting group called *Homo rudolfensis*. Whether one chooses to call these or any other contemporary fossils *Homo rudolfensis* or *Homo habilis* is more than a name game. Fossil names indicate researchers' perspectives about evolutionary relationships among groups. Giving specimens separate species names signifies that they are part of a reproductively isolated group.

Some paleoanthropologists approach the fossil record with the perspective that making such detailed biological determinations is arbitrary and that variability exists within any group. Arguing that it is impossible to prove whether a collection of ancient bones and teeth represents a distinct species, these paleoanthropologists tend to be "lumpers," placing similar-looking fossil specimens together in more inclusive groups. For example, gorillas show a degree of sexual dimorphism similar to that which lumpers attribute to *H. habilis*.

"Splitters," by contrast, accentuate the variation in the fossil record, interpreting minor differences in the shape of skeletons or skulls as evidence of distinct biological species with corresponding cultural capacities. The late great South African paleoanthropologist Philip Tobias

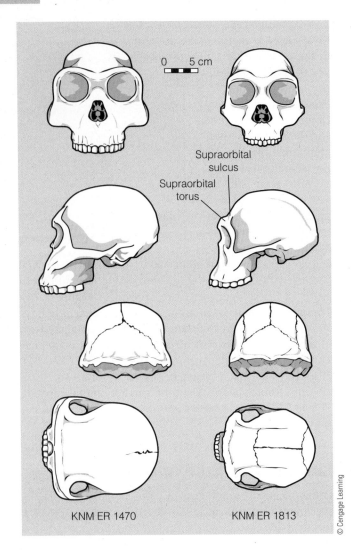

Supraorbital sulcus

Supraorbital torus

KNM ER 1470   KNM ER 1813

© Cengage Learning

Figure 6.34 One Diverse Species?
The KNM ER 1470 skull—one of the most complete skulls of *Homo habilis*—is close to 2 million years old and is probably a male; it contrasts with the considerably smaller KNM ER 1813 skull, probably a female. Some paleoanthropologists feel this variation is too great to place these specimens in the same species.

once quipped about the variable shape of the bony ridge above ancient eyes: "Splitters will create a new species at the drop of a brow ridge."

Splitting has the advantage of specificity while lumping has the advantage of simplicity. We will use a lumping approach throughout our discussion of the genus *Homo*.

Differences Between Early *Homo* and *Australopithecus*

By 2.4 million years ago, the evolution of the genus *Homo* was diverging from that of *Australopithecus*. In terms of body size, early *Homo* differs little from *Australopithecus*. Although early *Homo* had teeth that are large by modern standards—or even by those of a half-million years ago—they are smaller in relation to the size of the skull than those of any australopithecine. Early *Homo* also had undergone an enlargement of the brain indicating that early *Homo*'s mental abilities probably exceeded those of *Australopithecus*. Early *Homo* likely possessed a marked increase in ability to learn and to process information compared with australopithecines.

The later robust australopithecines from East Africa and South Africa that coexisted with early *Homo* evolved into specialized "grinding machines" with massive jaws and back teeth for processing plant foods. Robust australopithecine brain size did not change, nor is there firm evidence that they made stone tools. Thus, in the period between 1 and 2.5 million years ago, two kinds of bipeds were headed in very different evolutionary directions: the robust australopithecines, specializing in consuming plant foods and ultimately becoming extinct, and the genus *Homo*, with expanding cranial capacity, a varied diet that included meat, and the earliest evidence for stone toolmaking.

Without stone tools, early *Homo* could eat few animals (only those that could be skinned by tooth or nail); therefore, their diet was somewhat limited in terms of animal protein. But on the arid savannah, it is hard for a primate with a human-like digestive system to satisfy its protein requirements from just the available plant resources. Moreover, failure to do so has serious consequences: stunted growth, malnutrition, starvation, and death. Leaves and legumes (nitrogen-fixing plants, familiar modern examples being beans and peas) provide the best plant sources of protein; unfortunately, substances in the leaves and legumes cause proteins to pass right through the gut without being absorbed unless they are cooked.

Chimpanzees have a similar problem when out on the savannah. Even with canine teeth far larger and sharper than ours or those of early *Homo*, chimpanzees frequently have trouble tearing through the skin of other animals. In savannah environments, chimps spend about a third of their time foraging for insects (ants and termites), eggs, and small vertebrate animals. Such animal foods not only are easily digestible, but they provide high-quality proteins that contain all the essential amino acids, the building blocks of protein. No single plant food can provide this nutritional balance. Only a combination of plants can supply the range of amino acids provided by meat alone.

Lacking long, sharp teeth for shearing meat, our earliest ancestors likely foraged for insects, but sharp tools for butchering made it possible to efficiently eat meat. The initial use of tools by early *Homo* may be related to adapting to an environment that, since the Miocene, we know was changing from forests to grasslands. The physical changes that adapted bipeds for spending increasing amounts of time on the increasingly grassy terrain may have encouraged toolmaking.

Thus, with the appearance of the genus *Homo*, a feedback loop between biological characteristics and cultural innovations began to play a major role in our evolutionary history. This set the hominin line on a steady course of increasing brain size and a reliance on culture as the means of adaptation, as we explore in detail in the next chapter. Time will tell where exactly *Homo naledi* from the chapter opener lies in our evolutionary history.

CHAPTER CHECKLIST

What was the course of primate evolution, and how was it affected by geologic events?

✓ Early primates began to emerge after the extinction of dinosaurs 65 million years ago, when a meteor hit the earth and dramatically cooled global temperatures. The new climate led to the growth of forests over the earth, creating an ideal environment for early arboreal primates.

✓ A warming trend 55 million years ago caused the extinction of many earlier mammals and led to the evolution of the first true primates, including the prosimians.

✓ Primates became extinct in North America at the end of the Eocene era, when the earth cooled and icecaps formed over Antarctica.

✓ By 33 million years ago, during the Oligocene epoch, a diverse array of Old World anthropoid primates existed, possessing a mixture of ape and monkey features. The earliest evidence of New World monkeys also dates from the Oligocene epoch.

What are the distinguishing features of bipedalism, and how do paleoanthropologists use fossil evidence to identify hominins?

✓ Bipedalism is the characteristic that separates humans and their ancestors from the other African apes.

✓ Distinguishing features of bipedalism include a skull centered above the spinal column; a series of convex and concave curves in the spine; a wide pelvis; femora that "knee in"; stable arched feet and an adducted big toe; and shorter toes than other apes. These anatomical features allow scientists to determine bipedalism in fossils, even from fragmentary remains.

✓ Bipedal locomotion is the process of shifting the body's weight from one foot to the other as the nonsupporting foot swings forward. Scientists can use fossilized footprints to determine bipedal locomotion.

✓ After bipedalism is determined in a fossil, scientists turn to other characteristics, such as skull and teeth, to reconstruct relationships among fossil groups.

How did cultural biases interfere with the recognition of Africa as the place of origin of the human species?

✓ During the Miocene epoch, 5 to 23 million years ago, the African and Eurasian landmasses made direct contact, and the first hominoids appeared.

✓ During the later Miocene 5 to 14 million years ago, the fossil record in Africa became scarce because the rainforest environment did not permit the preservation of fossils.

✓ Western scientists tended to focus on European apes as the possible missing link to humans, believing that humans had evolved where Western civilization had developed.

✓ Western scientists were eager to label the Piltdown remains, found in England, as evidence of a missing link in human ancestry due to its location on British soil and its large cranial capacity. The remains were later revealed to be a hoax.

✓ These biases impeded the acceptance of the small-brained bipedal Taung Child from South Africa as one of our ancestors when it was first discovered. Ultimately, the self-correcting nature of science prevailed, and today scientists agree that the human line originated in Africa as a small-brained biped.

How do the earliest bipeds compare to one another? How do they compare to chimps? To humans?

✓ The earliest bipeds belonged to the genus *Ardipithecus*, which contains the species *Ardipithecus ramidus* and the older *Ardipithecus kadabba*. Though bipedal, the remarkably complete specimen Ardi physically resembles a chimp and inhabited forested environments.

✓ Most bipeds from the Pliocene epoch belong to the genus *Australopithecus*, which includes possibly as many as ten known species.

✓ *Australopithecus afarensis* resembles an ape from the waist up and a human from the waist down and was better adapted to life in the trees than more recent human ancestors.

✓ Australopithecines probably used tools in ways similar to modern chimpanzees.

✓ Bipedalism would have allowed australopithecines, like humans, to carry their offspring in their arms, reducing the risk of infant mortality for chimps whose young must cling to the mother for safety.

What are the distinguishing characteristics of gracile and robust australopithecines?

✓ Gracile australopithecines had about the same mental capacity as modern great apes. Their teeth were smaller than those of robust australopithecines, and they likely ate meat.

✓ Robust australopithecines were larger and possessed massive teeth, jaws, and chewing muscles that were attached to a sagittal crest, making them adapted for plant consumption.

What is the earliest appearance of the genus *Homo* in the fossil record?

✓ The earliest specimen from the genus *Homo* is the stone toolmaking species *Homo habilis*, discovered by the Leakeys in Olduvai Gorge. Since then, similar fossils have been discovered throughout Kenya, Ethiopia, and South Africa.

✓ Early *Homo* had smaller teeth and a larger brain than early *Australopithecus*. Its body was about the same size.

QUESTIONS FOR REFLECTION

1. How much evidence is necessary to allow designation of a new species in the fossil record? Consider the biological definition of species and compare this with arguments made for and against speciation among ancient remains. Does the naming game help or hinder our understanding of human evolution?

2. Although we often consider human intelligence as the quality that separates us from the other apes, bipedalism was the first feature to define the human evolutionary line. Does this surprise you? Does our early evolutionary history make us seem more like the other animals? Does this challenge your notions of what it means to be human?

3. Describe the anatomy of bipedalism, providing examples from head to toe of how bipedalism can be "diagnosed" from a single bone. Do you think evidence from a single bone is enough to determine whether an organism from the past was bipedal? What evidence would you use to support a case for tool use in early bipeds?

4. How do paleoanthropologists decide whether a fossil specimen from the distant past is male or female? Do our cultural ideas about males and females in the present affect the interpretation of behavior in human evolutionary history?

DIGGING INTO ANTHROPOLOGY

Fool with Your Ancestors

The Piltdown hoax was one of the longest and most significant frauds ever perpetrated in the history of science. It escaped detection for so long because it played into scientists' expectations and because there was a gap in the fossil record. Today, still, the scarcity of fossil evidence during the period of 5 to 8 million years ago prevents paleoanthropologists from definitively identifying the link between humans and the other great apes. This is the perfect opportunity to plot your own conspiracy! Design a fossil specimen that plays on current expectations about this period in human evolution to fill in the gap. Where should it be found? How old should it be to fit in with the other fossils you have learned about? What blend of derived and ancestral features will you give it? Write up an analysis of your fossil that explains why it is the undisputed missing link between humans and our last common ancestor with the other great apes.

The Natural History Museum, London/The Image Works

CHALLENGE ISSUE

What is it that makes us human? Intelligence undeniably plays a role. Perhaps nothing dramatizes humanity's emergence more powerfully than the harnessing of fire long ago. Captured in folklore—such as Prometheus in Greek mythology or Maui in the legends of New Zealand's Maori people or here in this reconstruction of life at Zhoukoudian Cave in China about 500,000 years ago—fire changed what early humans could eat and where they could live. Control of fire—like the emergence of toolmaking traditions, human language, and the ability to travel long distances and survive in cold environments—was connected to changes in human biology, specifically an increase in brain size. The emergence of the genus *Homo* separated our ancestors from the australopithecines and set the course for the eventual arrival of the species that we are today. How do we know that this change happened? How quickly did the evolution of the genus *Homo* take place? What distinct species form our lineage? And, finally, the most challenging question: What is the relationship between brain size (and the cultural innovations it allowed) and species designation?

Origins of the Genus *Homo*

In the quest for the origin of modern humans, paleoanthropologists confront mysteries by drawing from scant evidence that can be misleading and contradictory. Some of the mystery stems from the kind of evolutionary change that was set in motion with the appearance of the genus **Homo**. The earliest proposed members of genus *Homo* were recently discovered in sediments in Afar, Ethiopia, and date to about 2.8 million years ago (mya) (DiMaggio et al., 2015; Villmoare et al., 2015). The new South African *Homo naledi* fossils introduced in the previous chapter may date to a similar time range (Berger et al, 2015). Around this time, the brain size of our ancestors began to grow. Simultaneously, these first members of the genus *Homo* improved their cultural manipulation of the physical world through use of stone tools. Over time, they increasingly relied on cultural adaptation as a rapid and effective way to adjust to the environment.

The evolution of the human brain was imperative for human survival and the evolution of human culture. Over the course of the next 2.5 million or so years, increasing brain size and specialization of function permitted the development of language, planning, new technologies, and artistic expression. With the evolution of a brain that made versatile behavior possible, members of the genus *Homo* became biocultural beings.

U.S. biological anthropologist Misia Landau describes the narrative of human evolutionary history as a heroic epic (Landau, 1991). The hero, or evolving human, faces natural challenges that cannot be overcome from a strictly biological standpoint. When endowed with the gift of intelligence, the hero meets these challenges and becomes fully human. In this narrative, cultural capabilities increasingly separate humans from other evolving animals. But, as we have seen in earlier chapters, recent advances in primatology are undercutting this notion of human uniqueness.

Homo The genus of bipeds that appeared about 2.5 million years ago, characterized by increased brain size compared to earlier bipeds. The genus is divided into various species based on features such as brain size, skull shape, and cultural capabilities.

In this chapter you will learn to

- Describe the cultural capacity of various members of the genus *Homo* and how these capacities relate to anatomy preserved in fossils.

- Situate humans' place in the animal kingdom and recognize the cultural biases that have influenced the development of scientific theories about human evolution.

- Describe the debates surrounding relationships among fossil groups of the genus *Homo*.

- Identify the features that characterize the distinct eras of toolmaking.

- Discuss the controversy surrounding Neandertals' place in human evolution.

The mechanics of biological and cultural change differ. Cultural equipment and techniques can develop rapidly with innovations occurring during an individual's lifetime. By contrast, biological change requires many generations because it depends upon heritable traits. When a new type of stone tool appears, paleoanthropologists investigate whether the cultural change corresponds to a major biological change, such as the appearance of a new species. Debate within paleoanthropology often features the relationship between biological and cultural change.

The Discovery of the First Stone Toolmaker

Paleoanthropologists Louis and Mary Leakey began their search for human origins at Olduvai Gorge, Tanzania, because of the presence of crude stone tools unearthed there, which date back almost 2 million years to very early in the Pleistocene epoch. These tools define the **Oldowan tool tradition** and consist of implements made using a system of manufacture called the **percussion method** (Figure 7.1).

The toolmaker using the percussion method would obtain sharp-edged flakes from a stone (often a large, water-worn cobble) either by using another stone as a hammer (a hammerstone) or by striking the cobble against a large rock (anvil) to remove the flakes. Microscopic wear patterns show that these flakes were used for cutting meat, reeds, sedges, grasses, and wood. Small indentations on their surfaces suggest that the leftover cores were transformed into choppers for breaking open bones and perhaps for defense. The appearance of early stone tools marks the beginning of the **Lower Paleolithic**, the first part of the Old Stone Age.

From the time these tools were discovered, paleoanthropologists have regarded the Oldowan stone tool tradition as the oldest. But in May 2015, at three sites named Lomekwi in West Turkana, Kenya, researchers discovered even older tools. The **Lomekwian tool tradition** dates

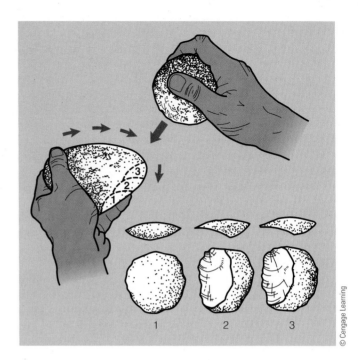

Figure 7.1 The Percussion Method
Early *Homo* in Africa invented the percussion method of stone tool manufacture by 2.5 million years ago. This technological breakthrough, which is associated with a significant increase in brain size, made it possible to butcher meat from scavenged carcasses.

to 3.3 million years ago, predating the earliest Oldowan tools by 700,000 years. This major discovery has reshaped how anthropologists view the beginning of the Old Stone Age or Lower Paleolithic (Harmand et al., 2015). These earliest stone tools mark the beginning of the hominin archaeological record. Lower Paleolithic tools have also been found in Gona, Ethiopia, known for assemblages dated to 2.6 million years ago, as well as sites near Gona in the Afar Triangle of Ethiopia and in the vicinity of Lake Turkana in northwestern Kenya.

Paleoanthropologists apply a methodology of **experimental archaeology**: the systematic recreation of ancient lifeways in order to test hypotheses, interpretations, and assumptions about the past. For example, researchers use raw materials to make stone tools themselves in an effort to understand the process of toolmaking. The process of fashioning tools allows researchers to analyze which skills

Oldowan tool tradition An early stone tool industry, beginning between 2.5 and 2.6 million years ago.

percussion method A technique of stone tool manufacture performed by striking the raw material with a hammerstone or by striking raw material against a stone anvil to remove flakes.

Lower Paleolithic The first part of the Old Stone Age beginning with the earliest Lomekwian tools spanning from about 200,000 or 250,000 years ago to 3.3 million years ago.

Lomekwian tool tradition The earliest stone tools dated to 3.3 million years ago, discovered in 2015 in Kenya.

experimental archaeology The recreation of ancient lifeways by modern paleoanthropologists in order to test hypotheses, interpretations, and assumptions about the past.

toolmaking requires. To consistently and efficiently produce well-formed, sharp-edged flakes from raw materials with the least effort, the toolmaker had to have in mind an abstract idea of the tool to be made, as well as a specific set of steps to transform the raw material into the finished product (Ambrose, 2001). The toolmaker also would have to know which kinds of stone have the flaking properties that allow the transformation to take place and where such stone could be found.

Tool fabrication sometimes required the transport of raw materials over great distances. The planning for the anticipated future trips undoubtedly was associated with changes in brain structure. These changes mark the beginning of the genus *Homo*. As described in the previous chapter, **Homo habilis** was the name given to the oldest members of the genus when first discovered in 1959. With larger brains and stone tools preserved in the archaeological record, paleoanthropologists began to piece together a picture of the life of early *Homo* (**Figure 7.2**). The relationship between the newly discovered *Homo naledi* fossils and *Homo habilis* will depend upon dating as well as whether tools are ultimately associated with these remains.

Dr Clive Bromhall/Oxford Scientific/Getty Images

Figure 7.2 Lower Paleolithic Toolmaking
Although hominoids have not been observed making stone tools in the wild, we have seen them use stones as tools as this chimpanzee who cracks palm nuts open between hammer and anvil-like stones. Recall too, that they make tools out of other materials such as the sticks that were shaped and transported for termiting. How do we translate this into evidence of our ancestors' cognitive capacities? Experimental archaeologists examine such phenomena by learning ancient toolmaking techniques and analyzing the exact processes involved. They perform the same behaviors and create the same artifacts so that they can understand which skills these lifeways required. This knowledge is indispensible for the interpretation of the material remains. Experimental archaeologists often master the entire range of ancient stone tool techniques described in this chapter in order to make comparisons among the various industries. Although not preserved in the archaeological record, we can safely assume that various perishable tools, used by hominoids in the wild, were also used by our ancestors.

Sex, Gender, and the Behavior of Early *Homo*

Until the 1960s, paleoanthropologists' depictions of the lifeways of early *Homo* concentrated on "man the hunter," a tough guy with a killer instinct, wielding tools on a savannah teeming with meat, while female members of the species stayed at home tending their young. Similarly, until the 1960s, most cultural anthropologists doing fieldwork among foragers stressed the role of male hunters and underreported the significance of female gatherers in providing food for the community. Western notions of **gender**, the cultural elaborations and meanings assigned to the biological differentiation between the sexes, played a substantial role in creating these biases.

As anthropologists became aware of their own biases, they began to set the record straight, documenting the vital role of "woman the gatherer" in provisioning the social group in foraging cultures, past and present. (See this chapter's Biocultural Connection for the specific contributions of female paleoanthropologists.) The division of labor among contemporary food foragers, like all gender relations, does not conform to fixed boundaries defined by biologically based sex differences. Instead, it is influenced by cultural and environmental factors. Uncovering such biases is as important as any new discovery for interpreting the fossil record (**Figure 7.3**).

Homo habilis "Handy human." The first fossil members of the genus *Homo* appearing about 2.5 million years ago, with larger brains and smaller faces than australopithecines.

gender The cultural elaborations and meanings assigned to the biological differentiation between the sexes.

Cavemen, Jackson, Peter (1922–2003)/Private Collection/© Look and Learn/Bridgeman Images

Figure 7.3 Gender Bias
In this reconstruction, the artist portrays separate roles for males and females. Do the roles depicted here derive from biological differences between the sexes or culturally established gender differences?

Studies of extant primates allow paleoanthropologists to appropriately incorporate gender into their theories. Evidence from chimpanzees and bonobos casts further doubt on a strictly sex-based division of labor in human evolutionary history. As described in Chapter 4, female chimpanzees have been observed participating in hunting expeditions, with the female chimps utilizing spears more often than the males. Meat from a successful hunt is shared within the group whether a male or a female chimpanzee provides it. Among bonobos, females hunt regularly and share meat as well as plant foods with one another. In other words, patterns of food sharing and hunting behaviors in these apes are variable, supporting the notion that

marrow The fatty nutritious tissue inside of long bones where blood cells are produced.

tertiary scavenger In a food chain, the third in line to get something from a carcass after a predator killed the prey.

culture plays a role in establishing these behaviors. No evidence exists to explain how procured foods may have been shared among our ancestors.

Hunters or Scavengers?

The elimination of biases in paleoanthropological interpretations helped to reveal that early members of the genus *Homo* were not hunters of large game. Oldowan tools and broken animal bones tell us that both *H. habilis* and large carnivorous animals were active at these locations. Marks on the bones—made by slicing, scraping, and chopping with stone tools—are present along with marks of gnawing teeth. Sometimes the gnawing marks overlie the butcher marks, indicating that other carnivores were attracted to the bones after *Homo* was done with them. In other cases, the butcher marks overlie the tooth marks of carnivores, indicating that the animals got there first.

Further, there is evidence that only parts of kills were transported away from the original location where they were obtained, suggesting that they were stolen from the kill of some other animal. The stone tools, too, were made of raw material procured at distances of up to 60 kilometers (about 37 miles) from where they were used to process pieces of carcasses. Finally, the incredible density of bones at some of the sites and patterns of weathering indicate that the sites were used repeatedly for perhaps five to fifteen years.

By contrast, contemporary hunting species typically bring whole carcasses back to camp or form a camp around a large animal in order to fully process it. After processing, nothing edible remains—neither meat nor **marrow** (the fatty nutritious tissue inside long bones where blood cells are produced). The bones themselves are broken up not just to get at the marrow but to fabricate tools and other objects of bone. The scavenging process may have required fabrication of carrying devices like net bags and trail markers like those (described in Chapter 4) used by modern bonobos.

Microscopic analysis of cut marks on bones reveals that the earliest members of the genus *Homo* were actually **tertiary scavengers**—that is, third in line to get something from a carcass after a predator killed the prey. After scavengers (such as hyenas and vultures) swarmed a recently killed carcass, our tool-wielding ancestors would reach the prey, breaking open the shafts of long bones to get at the rich marrow inside. A small amount of marrow is a concentrated source of both protein and fat. Furthermore, as the Original Study shows, evolving humans were probably prey themselves, and this selective pressure imposed by predators played a role in brain expansion (Hart & Sussman, 2005). *Homo habilis* likely continued to sleep in trees or rocky cliffs, in order to be safe from predators.

Sex, Gender, and Female Paleoanthropologists

Until the 1970s, a deep-seated bias of men's privileged status in Western society permeated the study of human evolution. Beyond the obvious labeling of fossils as particular types of "men," irrespective of the sex of the individual represented, males were portrayed as the active players in human evolution. Males were seen as providers and innovators, using their wits to become increasingly effective suppliers of food and protectors of passive females. Females were depicted as spending their time preparing food, caring for offspring, and performing other domestic tasks. Central to this biased view was the idea of "man the hunter," constantly honing his wits through the pursuit and killing of animals (Lovejoy, 1981). The men's hunt was considered the pivotal humanizing activity in evolution.

We now acknowledge that such ideas are culture-bound, reflecting the expectations of Western culture in the late 19th and early 20th centuries. This recognition came in the 1970s as a direct consequence of many highly capable women entering the profession of paleoanthropology.

Up until the 1960s, there were few women in any field of physical anthropology, but with graduate programs expanding and attitudes changing about the role of women in society, more and more women began earning doctorates. One of these was Adrienne Zihlman, who earned her doctorate at the University of California, Berkeley, in 1967. Zihlman authored a number of important papers critical of "man the hunter" scenarios.[a] She was not the first to do so; as early as 1971, Sally Linton wrote a preliminary paper on "woman the gatherer" and the male bias in anthropology.[b] But it was Zihlman who, from 1976 on, elaborated on the importance of female activities for human evolution. Others have joined in that effort, including Zihlman's graduate school companion and professional colleague Nancy Tanner.

The work of Zihlman and her female peers was crucial in forcing a reexamination of existing "man the hunter" scenarios. Over time, anthropologists have recognized the importance of scavenging in early human evolution as well as the value of gathering and other activities considered to be female behaviors.

There is still plenty to learn about human evolution, but thanks to these women we now know that it was not a case of females being "uplifted" through their association with progressively evolving males. Rather, the two sexes evolved together, with each making its own important contributions to the process.

Biocultural Question

Can you think of any examples of how gender norms are influencing theories about the biological basis of male and female behavior today?

---

[a] Tanner, N., & Zihlman. A. (1976). Women in evolution. Part I: Innovation and selection in human origins. *Signs 1* (3), 585–608.
[b] Slocum, S. (1975). Woman the gatherer: Male bias in anthropology. In R. R. Reiter (Ed.), *Toward an anthropology of women*. New York: Monthly Review Press.

ORIGINAL STUDY

Humans as Prey BY DONNA HART

There's little doubt that humans, particularly those in Western cultures, think of themselves as the dominant form of life on earth. And we seldom question whether that view holds true for our species' distant past.... We swagger like the toughest kids on the block as we spread our technology over the landscape and irrevocably change it for other species.

... The vision of our utter superiority may even hold true for the last 500 years, but that's just the proverbial blink of an eye when compared to the 7 million years that our hominid ancestors wandered the planet.

"Where did we come from?" and "What were the first humans like?" are questions that have been asked since Darwin first proposed his theory of evolution. One commonly accepted answer is that our early ancestors were killers of other species and of their own kind, prone to violence and even cannibalism. In fact, a club-swinging "Man the Hunter" is the stereotype of early humans that permeates literature, film, and even much scientific writing....

Even the great paleontologist Louis S. B. Leakey endorsed it when he emphatically declared that we were not "cat food." Another legendary figure in the annals of paleontology, Raymond A. Dart, launched the killer-ape-man scenario in the mid-20th century....

Dart had interpreted the finds in South African caves of fossilized bones from savannah herbivores together with damaged hominid skulls as evidence that our ancestors had been hunters. The fact that the skulls were battered in a peculiar fashion led to Dart's firm conviction that violence and cannibalism on the part of killer ape-men formed the stem from which our own species eventually flowered. In his 1953 article "The Predatory Transition from Ape to Man," Dart wrote that early hominids were "carnivorous creatures, that seized living quarries by violence, battered them to death, tore apart their broken bodies, [and] dismembered them limb from limb,...greedily devouring livid writhing flesh."

But what is the evidence for Man the Hunter? Could smallish, upright creatures with relatively tiny canine teeth and flat nails instead of claws, and with no tools or weapons in the earliest millennia, really have been deadly predators? Is it possible that our ancestors lacked the spirit of cooperation and desire for social harmony? We have only two reliable sources to consult for clues: the fossilized remains of the human family tree and the behaviors and ecological relationships of our living primate relatives.

When we investigate those two sources, a different view of humankind emerges. First, consider the hominid fossils that have been discovered. Dart's first and most famous find, the cranium of an *Australopithecus* child who died over 2 million years ago (called the "Taung Child" after the quarry in which the fossil was unearthed), has been reassessed by Lee Berger and Ron Clarke of the University of the Witwatersrand, in light of recent research on eagle predation. The same marks that occur on the Taung cranium are found on the remains of similarly sized African monkeys eaten today by crowned hawk eagles, known to clutch the monkeys' heads with their sharp talons.

C. K. Brain, a South African paleontologist like Dart, started the process of relabeling Man the Hunter as Man the Hunted when he slid the lower fangs of a fossil leopard into perfectly matched punctures in the skull of another australopithecine who lived between 1 million and 2 million years ago. The paradigm change initiated by Brain continues to stimulate reassessment of hominid fossils.

The idea that our direct ancestor *Homo erectus* practiced cannibalism was based on the gruesome disfigurement of faces and brain-stem areas in a cache of skulls a half-million years old, found in the Zhoukoudian cave, in China. How else to explain these strange manipulations except as relics of Man the Hunter? But studies over the past few years by Noel T. Boaz and Russell L. Ciochon—of the Ross University School of Medicine and the University of Iowa, respectively—show that extinct giant hyenas could have left the marks as they crunched their way into the brains of their hominid prey.

The list of our ancestors' fossils showing evidence of predation continues to grow. A 1.75-million-year-old hominid skull unearthed in the Republic of Georgia shows punctures from the fangs of a saber-toothed cat. Another skull, about 900,000 years old, found in Kenya, exhibits carnivore bite marks on the brow ridge....Those and other fossils provide rock-hard proof that a host of large, fierce animals preyed on human ancestors.

It is equally clear that, outside the West, no small amount of predation occurs today on modern humans. Although we are not likely to see these facts in American newspaper headlines, each year 3,000 people in sub-Saharan Africa are eaten by crocodiles, and 1,500 Tibetans are killed by bears about the size of grizzlies. In one Indian state between 1988 and 1998, over 200 people were attacked by leopards; 612 people were killed by tigers in the Sundarbans delta of India and Bangladesh between 1975 and 1985. The carnivore zoologist Hans Kruuk, of the University of Aberdeen, studied death records in eastern Europe and concluded that wolf predation on humans is still a fact of life in the region, as it was until the 19th century in western European countries like France and Holland.

The fact that humans and their ancestors are and were tasty meals for a wide range of predators is further supported by research on nonhuman primate species still in existence. My study of predation found that 178 species of predatory animals included primates in their diets. The predators ranged from tiny but fierce birds to 500-pound crocodiles, with a little of almost everything in between: tigers, lions, leopards, jaguars, jackals, hyenas, genets, civets, mongooses, Komodo dragons, pythons, eagles, hawks, owls, and even toucans.

Our closest genetic relatives, chimpanzees and gorillas, are prey to humans and other species. Who would have thought that gorillas, weighing as much as 400 pounds, would end up as cat food? Yet Michael Fay, a researcher with the Wildlife Conservation Society and the National Geographic Society, has found the remnants of a gorilla in leopard feces in the Central African Republic. Despite their obvious intelligence and strength, chimpanzees often fall victim to leopards and lions. In the Tai Forest in the Ivory Coast, Christophe Boesch, of the Max Planck Institute, found that over 5 percent of the chimp population in his study was consumed by leopards annually. Takahiro Tsukahara reported, in a 1993 article, that 6 percent of the chimpanzees in the Mahale Mountains National Park of Tanzania may fall victim to lions.

The theory of Man the Hunter as our archetypal ancestor isn't supported by archaeological evidence, either. Lewis R. Binford, one of the most influential figures in archaeology during the last half of the 20th century, dissented from the hunting theory on the ground that reconstructions of early humans as hunters were based on a priori positions and not on the archaeological record. Artifacts that would verify controlled fire and weapons, in particular, are lacking until relatively recent dates.

And, of course, there's also the problem of how a small hominid could subdue a large herbivore....Large-scale, systematic hunting of big herbivores for meat may not have occurred any earlier than 60,000 years ago—over 6 million years after the first hominids evolved.

What I am suggesting, then, is a less powerful, more ignominious beginning for our species. Consider this alternate image: smallish beings (adult females maybe weighing 60 pounds, with males a bit heavier), not overly analytical because their brain-to-body ratio was rather small, possessing the ability to stand and move upright, who basically spent millions of years as meat walking around on two legs. Rather than Man the Hunter, we may need to visualize ourselves as more like Giant Hyena Chow, or Protein on the Go.

Our species began as just one of many that had to be careful, to depend on other group members, and to communicate danger. We were quite simply small beasts within a large and complex ecosystem.

Is Man the Hunter a cultural construction of the West? Belief in a sinful, violent ancestor does fit nicely with

Just as a leopard will bring its prey up into the trees for a quiet repast today, giant cats of the past likely feasted upon out ancestors in this fashion. In fact, the fossil record includes australopithecine skulls pierced with holes just where a cat's giant canine teeth would be.

Christian views of original sin and the necessity to be saved from our own awful, yet natural, desires. Other religions don't necessarily emphasize the ancient savage in the human past; indeed, modern-day hunter-gatherers, who have to live as part of nature, hold animistic beliefs in which humans are a part of the web of life, not superior creatures who dominate or ravage nature and one another.

Think of Man the Hunted, and you put a different face on our past....We needed to live in groups (like most other primates) and work together to avoid predators. Thus an urge to cooperate can clearly be seen as a functional tool rather than a Pollyannaish nicety, and deadly competition among individuals or nations may be highly aberrant behavior, not hardwired survival techniques. The same is true of our destructive domination of the earth by technological toys gone mad.

Raymond Dart declared that "the loathsome cruelty of mankind to man . . . is explicable only in terms of his carnivorous, and cannibalistic origin." But if our origin was not carnivorous and cannibalistic, we have no excuse for loathsome behavior. Our earliest evolutionary history is not pushing us to be awful bullies. Instead, our millions of years as prey suggest that we should be able to take our heritage of cooperation and interdependency to make a brighter future for ourselves and our planet.

Adapted from Hart, D. (2006, April 21). Humans as prey. *Chronicle of Higher Education.* http://chronicle.com/article/Humans-as-Prey/23846 (retrieved October 14, 2015). Reprinted by permission of Donna Hart.

Whether as hunters or as the hunted, brain expansion and tool use played a significant role in genus *Homo*'s evolution. Advanced preparation for meat processing—implied by the storing of stone tools and the raw materials for making them—show considerable foresight and cooperation among our ancestors.

Brain Size and Diet

From its appearance around 2.8 million years ago, the genus *Homo* began a course of brain expansion that continued until about 200,000 years ago when brain size reached the proportion of contemporary people. The cranial capacity of the largely plant-eating robust australopithecines ranged from 310 to 530 cubic centimeters (cc). The cranial capacity of *Australopithecus sediba* was not large although they possessed some more *Homo*-like skeletal features. The cranial capacity of the earliest known meat-eater, *Homo habilis* from East Africa, ranged from 580 to 752 cc; in contrast, *Homo erectus*, who eventually used fire and hunted and scavenged for meat, possessed a cranial capacity of 775 to 1,225 cc.

Larger brains required parallel improvements in diet. The energy demands of the nerve tissue of which the brain is made are higher than the demands of other types of tissue in the human body. The brain accounts for just 2 percent of body weight, but it accounts for about 20 to 25 percent of energy consumed at resting metabolic rate in modern human adults. A vegetarian diet can meet the brain's energy demands, but plant food contains less energy compared to the same amount of meat. Large plant-eating animals, such as gorillas, spend all day munching on plants to maintain their large bodies. Consequently, meat-eating bipeds of both sexes may have had more leisure time to explore and manipulate their environment.

The archaeological record provides a tangible account of our ancestors' growing cultural abilities that correspond with expansion of the brain. Toolmaking, which puts a premium on manual dexterity, precision, and fine manipulation (Figure 7.4), indicates specialization of the brain. From the time genus *Homo* first appeared, increasing brain size and cultural development each presumably acted to promote the other.

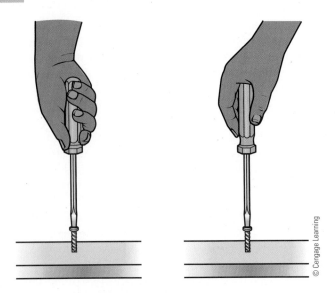

© Cengage Learning

Figure 7.4 **Power Versus Precision Grip**
A power grip (*left*) utilizes more of the hand whereas the precision grip (*right*) relies on the fingers for control, requiring corresponding organizational changes in the brain. Though *Australopithecus sediba* possessed a small brain, their hand anatomy indicates they could execute a precision grip.

The behaviors made possible by larger brains conferred advantages that increased reproductive success. In this way, natural selection of increased learning ability led to the evolution of larger and more complex brains up until about 200,000 years ago when brain size reached current levels. Bipedalism set the stage for the evolution of large brains and human culture. It freed the hands for activities such as toolmaking and carrying of resources or infants and opened opportunities for more major changes.

Homo erectus

In 1887, long before *Australopithecus* or early *Homo* were discovered, the Dutch physician Eugène Dubois set out to find the missing link between humans and apes. The presence of human-like orangutans in the Dutch East Indies (now Indonesia) led him to join the colonial service as an army surgeon and start his search there. Dubois found a few fossilized teeth, a skullcap, and a thighbone at Trinil on the island of Java, which seemed to him part ape, part human. The flat skull with its low forehead and enormous brow ridges resembled that of an ape, but at about 775 cubic centimeters it possessed a much larger cranial capacity, even though small by modern human standards. The femur was clearly human-like, and its

proportions indicated the creature was a biped. Believing that his specimens represented a bipedal missing link, Dubois named his find *Pithecanthropus erectus* (from the Greek *pithekos* meaning "ape," *anthropus* meaning "man") or "erect ape-man." Dubois used the genus name proposed in a paper by the German zoologist Ernst Haeckel, a strong supporter of Darwin's theory of evolution, who also supported the idea of an intermediate species between apes and humans.

As with the Taung Child australopithecine discovered in the 1920s, many scientists criticized Dubois's claim, suggesting that the skull (resembling an ape) and femur (resembling a human) came from different individuals. The controversy surrounding these specimens eventually led Dubois to store the fossil specimens under the floorboards of his dining room. Eventually, the discovery of more fossils provided enough evidence to support his claim. In the 1950s, the Trinil skullcap and similar specimens from Indonesia and China were assigned to the species ***Homo erectus***.

Fossils of *Homo erectus*

Remains of *Homo erectus* have been found in different places on three continents (Figure 7.5). "Lumpers," as discussed in the last chapter, emphasize that several shared characteristics connect varied *H. erectus* remains. However, others known as "splitters" prefer to divide *H. erectus* into multiple distinct groups because of differences between populations in the fossil evidence. "Splitters" limit the species *H. erectus* to specimens from Asia, whereas *Homo ergaster* is used for African specimens from the early Pleistocene period (Table 7.1).

Regardless of species designation, the fossil evidence indicates that beginning 1.8 million years ago these larger-brained members of the genus *Homo* lived in Africa and had spread to Eurasia. Fossils dating to 1.8 million years ago have been recovered from Dmanisi, Georgia, as well as from Mojokerto, on Java in Indonesia. A recently discovered and securely dated jaw from the Atapuerca site in Spain places the genus *Homo* in western Europe 1.2 million years ago (Carbonell et al., 2008). Additional specimens have been found at sites all over Europe and Asia.

Physical Characteristics of *Homo erectus*

Skull features are the best way to identify *H. erectus*. Cranial capacity ranges from 525 to 1,250 cc (average about 1,000 cc) with the smaller-brained specimens limited to early in its evolutionary history. Cranial capacity overlaps with both the nearly 2-million-year-old KNM ER 1470 skull from East Africa (752 cc) and the 1,000 to 2,000 cc range (average 1,300 cc) for modern human

Homo erectus "Upright human." A species within the genus *Homo* first appearing just after 2 million years ago in Africa and ultimately spreading throughout the Old World.

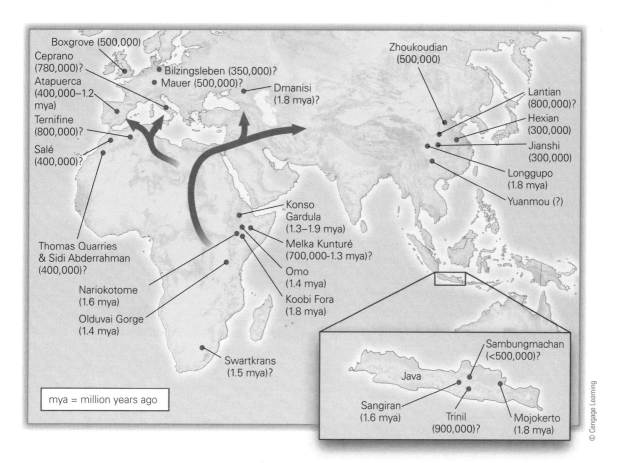

Figure 7.5 Map of *Homo erectus* Sites
Homo erectus sites are shown here with their dates. The arrows indicate the proposed routes
by which *Homo* spread from Africa to Eurasia. The question marks indicate the uncertain dating
for particular sites. "Splitters" give some of these fossils different names.

TABLE 7.1	

Alternate Species Designations for *Homo erectus* Fossils from Eurasia and Africa

Name	Explanation
Homo ergaster	Some paleoanthropologists contend that large-brained successors to *H. habilis* from Africa and Asia are too different to be the same species. Therefore, they use *H. ergaster* for the African specimens, saving *H. erectus* for the Asian fossils. Some paleoanthropologists place the recent discoveries from Dmanisi into this taxon.
Homo antecessor	This name was coined by "splitters" for the earliest *Homo* fossils from western Europe discovered in Spain; *antecessor* is Latin for "explorer" or "pioneer."
Homo heidelbergensis	Originally coined for the Mauer jaw (Mauer is not far from Heidelberg, Germany), this name is now used by some as a designation for all European fossils from about 500,000 years ago until the appearance of the Neandertals.

skulls (Figure 7.6). The cranium itself has a low vault (height of the dome of the skull top), and the head is long and narrow. When viewed from behind, the skull's width is greater than its height, with the greatest width at the base. In comparison, the skulls of modern humans are higher than they are wide, with the widest dimension in the region above the ears.

H. erectus possessed a massive brow ridge (Figure 7.7). When viewed from above, a marked constriction or "pinching in" of the skull can be seen just behind the brow ridge.

H. erectus skulls also possess a sloping forehead and a receding chin. Powerful jaws with large teeth, a protruding mouth, and huge neck muscles added to *H. erectus'* generally rugged appearance. Though large, the face, teeth, and jaws of this species are actually smaller than those of *H. habilis*.

Apart from its skull, *H. erectus'* skeleton differs only subtly from that of modern humans. Its bodily proportions resemble ours but with more robust muscles. Stature increased from the smaller australopithecines and earliest members of the genus *Homo*. Sexual dimorphism in body

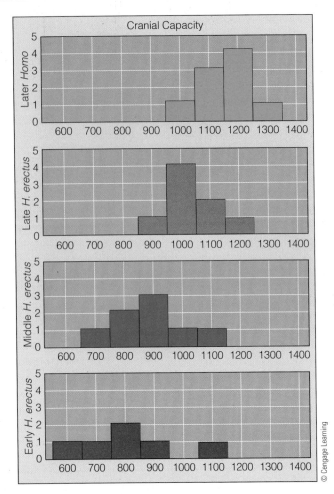

Figure 7.6 Ranges of Cranial Capacity
Cranial capacity (measured in cubic centimeters) in *Homo erectus* increased over time. The cranial capacity of late *Homo erectus* overlaps with the range seen in contemporary humans.

size appears to have decreased in *H. erectus* compared to earlier bipeds, possibly due to an increase in female size as an adaptation to childbirth. The discovery of a capacious female *Homo erectus* pelvis in Gona, Ethiopia, supports this notion (Simpson et al., 2008), although the large pelvis of *Australopithecus sediba* indicates that this trait might predate brain enlargement (Kibii et al., 2011).

Relationship among *Homo habilis, Homo erectus,* and Other Proposed Fossil Groups

The smaller teeth and larger brains of *Homo erectus* mark the continuation of a trend first seen in *Homo habilis*. Nevertheless, some skeletal resemblance to *H. habilis* remains, such as the shape of the thighbone, the long low vault

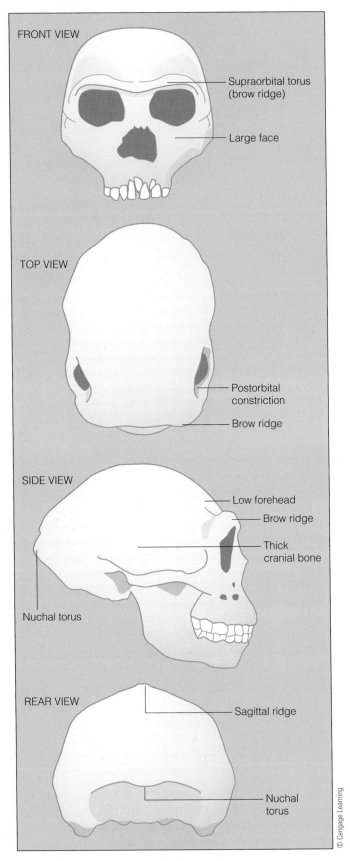

Figure 7.7 The Skull of *Homo erectus*
Note the enormous brow ridge of the *Homo erectus* skull, along with the sloping forehead and receding chin.

and marked constriction of the skull behind the eyes, and the smaller brain size of early *H. erectus* fossils.

Presumably *H. erectus* evolved from *H. habilis* abruptly, around 1.8 to 1.9 million years ago. Although Asian *H. erectus* possesses thicker bones and more pronounced brow ridges compared to African *H. erectus*, detailed anatomical comparisons indicate levels of variation approximating those seen in humans today (Rightmire, 1998). The mix of African and Asian characteristics in the 1.8-million-year-old specimens from Dmanisi, in the Caucasus—a region along the overland route between Africa and Eurasia—supports the notion of a single species.

The recent discovery of the small-brained 1.9-million-year-old "gracile" *Australopithecus sediba*, coexisting with these early members of the genus *Homo*, complicates matters. The discoverers proposed that derived aspects of its skeleton, such as a precision grip and a large pelvis, make *A. sediba* a viable contender for our direct ancestor. Despite complexities, the most recent fossils possess more derived appearances, and the oldest fossils (up to 1.8 million years old) display features reminiscent of earlier *H. habilis*.

Homo erectus from Africa

Fossils now assigned to *H. erectus* were discovered in Africa as long ago as 1933, but the better-known finds have been made since 1960, at Olduvai Gorge and at Lake Turkana, Kenya. These include the most complete *H. erectus* skeleton ever found, the Nariokotome Boy, an adolescent who died 1.6 million years ago (Figure 7.8). Paleoanthropologists infer the specimen's age from his teeth (the 12-year molars are fully erupted) and the stage of maturity of the bones. With a height of about 5 feet 3 inches at adolescence, the Nariokotome Boy could have attained a stature of about 6 feet by adulthood. A trail of *H. erectus* footprints along Lake Turkana, like those from Laetoli, support the estimates of *H. erectus* body mass (weight) and stature made from more fragmentary remains (Bennett et al., 2009).

Homo erectus Entering Eurasia

The Dmanisi site in the Caucasus Mountains of Georgia preserves evidence of *H. erectus'* movement from Africa into Eurasia. Dmanisi was first excavated as an archaeological site because of its historic importance as a crossroads for the caravan routes of ancient Armenia, Persia, and Byzantium, but when Oldowan stone tools were found in 1984, the hunt for fossil specimens began as well. Since then, paleoanthropologists have recovered some remarkable remains that, due to past volcanic activity in the region, can be accurately dated to 1.8 million years ago.

In 1999, researchers discovered two well-preserved skulls, one with a partial face. The genus *Homo's* early habitation of this region is supported at Dmanisi with archaeological, anatomical, and geological evidence. Since the Pleistocene, rising sea levels have made it impossible for paleoanthropologists to document coastal routes for the spread of *Homo* from Africa to Eurasia, making the evidence from Georgia the only direct verification of evolving humans' dispersion from Africa to Europe and to Asia.

Homo erectus from Indonesia

The skullcap and thighbone discovered by Dubois in Java are now considered typical Asian *H. erectus*. In the 1930s, German Dutch paleoanthropologist G. H. R. von Koenigswald discovered a number of additional *H. erectus* fossils at Sangiran, Java (see Figure 7.5). Von Koenigswald found a particular small skull that potassium-argon dating later assigned to the early Pleistocene, indicating that it was older than Dubois's Trinil skullcap, which dates to approximately 500,000 to 700,000 years ago.

Since 1960, Java has been a hot spot for additional fossils, accounting for the remains of around forty individuals. From 500,000 to 1.8 million years ago, *H. erectus* continuously populated Southeast Asia. *H. erectus* spread to Java at a time when lower sea levels resulted in a continuous landmass between most of Indonesia and the Asian continent.

Homo erectus from China

In the mid-1920s a combination of chance and a good understanding of anatomy led to the discovery of a fossil-rich *H. erectus* site in China. Davidson Black, a Canadian anatomist teaching at Peking Union Medical College, made the discovery. After purchasing a few ancient human-like teeth from a Beijing drugstore (which claimed the teeth had medicinal value), Black set out for the nearby countryside, where the drugstore's proprietor indicated the teeth had been found. At a place called Dragon Bone Hill in Zhoukoudian, 48 kilometers (30 miles) from Beijing (see Figure 7.5), Black began excavating in hopes of discovering the "owner" of the teeth. On the day before closing camp at the end of his first year of excavation, he found one molar tooth. Subsequently, Chinese paleoanthropologist W. C. Pei, who worked closely with Black, found a skull encased in limestone.

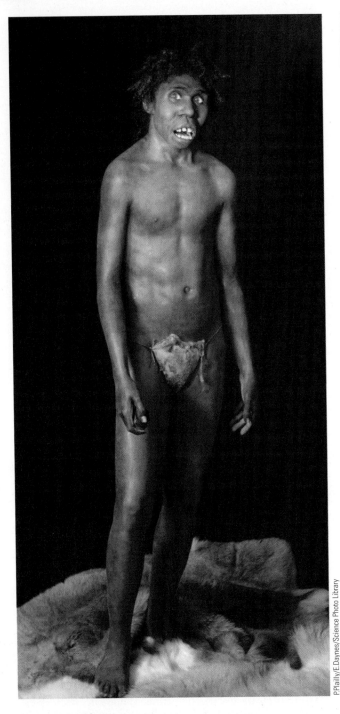

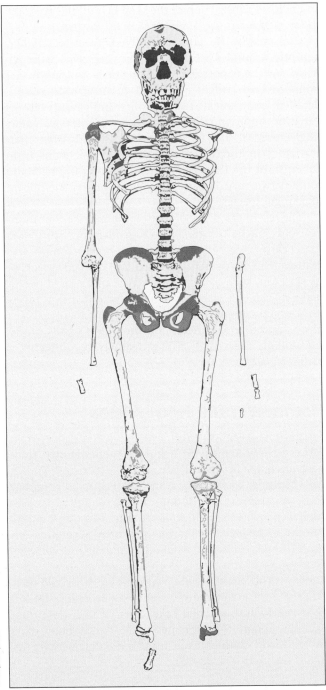

Figure 7.8 Nariokotome Boy

One of the oldest and certainly most complete *Homo erectus* fossils is the Nariokotome Boy from Lake Turkana, Kenya. Scientists have determined the age of this specimen by the degree to which the bones have finished growing and by the emergence of molar teeth. The shape of the pelvis indicates that the specimen is male, because it lacks the adaptations of the female pelvis to accommodate childbirth. But even though these remains come from a tall adolescent boy, this pelvis has been used to reconstruct theories about the evolution of human birth. This reconstruction by the Daynès Studio, Paris, France (see Élisabeth Daynès at work in Figure 7.17 later in this chapter) puts flesh on these ancient bones. When you look at this reconstruction, do you see elements of artistic license? Of bias? Do you see elements that surprise you?

Between 1929 and 1934, when he died from silicosis—a lung disease caused by exposure to silica particles in the excavation site's cave—Black labored along with Pei and French Jesuit paleontologist Pierre Teilhard de Chardin in the fossil-rich deposits of Zhoukoudian, uncovering fragment after fragment of ancient remains. Black named these fossils *Sinanthropus pekinensis,* or "Chinese human of Peking" (Beijing), called "Peking Man" at the time. Paleoanthropologists later identified these fossils as an East Asian representative of *H. erectus.*

After Black's death, the Rockefeller Foundation sent German anatomist and paleoanthropologist Franz Weidenreich to China to continue the work. By 1938, he and his colleagues had recovered the remains of more than forty individuals, over half of them women and children, from the limestone deposits of Zhoukoudian (Figure 7.9). Although many of the fossils were fragments—teeth, jawbones, and incomplete skulls—Weidenreich reconstructed a spectacular composite specimen.

However, World War II (1939–1945) halted the digging, and the original Zhoukoudian specimens were lost during the Japanese military occupation of China. Weidenreich and his team carefully packed and placed the fossils with U.S. Marines, but in the chaos of war, these precious fossils disappeared. In 2012, an international team of paleoanthropologists began searching for the missing fossils, guided by information from retired Marine Richard Bowen, who was stationed at the camp where the fossils were last seen. The potential location of the remains was pinpointed to a parking lot in the industrial city of Qinhuangdao. Paleoanthropologists are working with Chinese Cultural Heritage authorities to excavate the remains.

Fortunately, Weidenreich had made superb casts of most of the Zhoukoudian fossil specimens and sent them to the United States before leaving the site. After the war, other specimens of *H. erectus* were discovered in China, at Zhoukoudian and several other sites. The oldest skull is about 700,000 to 800,000 years old and comes from Lantian in central China. A fragment of a lower jaw from a cave in south-central China (Longgupo) is as old as the oldest Indonesian fossils. Like some of their Indonesian contemporaries, this Chinese fossil resembles African *H. habilis.* Although the two populations overlap in time, the majority of the Chinese fossils are slightly younger than those from Indonesia. Not surprisingly, Chinese *H. erectus* is less ancestral in appearance with smaller teeth, a short jaw, and an average cranial capacity of about 1,000 cc, compared to 900 cc for Indonesian *H. erectus,* indicating a more derived status.

Homo erectus from Western Europe

Although the genus *Homo* seems to have shown up on the Eurasian landmass 1.8 million years ago (at Dmanisi, Georgia), the fossil evidence from *western* Europe begins about 1.2 million years ago. Discoveries at the Sima del Elefante ("Elephant's Pit") site and Grand Dolina site in the Sierra de Atapuerca region of north-central Spain yielded fragments of four individuals dating to 1.2 million years ago. A skull from Ceprano in Italy is thought to be approximately the same age if not older. Again, whether these specimens are placed into the inclusive but varied species *H. erectus* or into several separate species differs according to the approach taken by paleoanthropologists (see Table 7.1).

Some other fossils attributable to *H. erectus*—such as a robust shinbone from Boxgrove, England, and a large lower jaw from Mauer, Germany—are close to half a million years old. The Mauer jaw came from a skull that was wide at the base, typical of *H. erectus,* and resembles material from North Africa from the same time period.

ullstein bild/Getty Images

Figure 7.9 Missing Peking Man
Here are some of the workers who assisted Franz Weidenreich with the original cave excavation where the Peking Man *Homo erectus* fossils were found near the village of Zhoukoudian. Weidenriech tried to ship the fossils to the United States as the violence of World War II reached China, but the specimens disappeared. After the war, scientists returned to Zhoukoudian and continued excavating. Today, Zhoukoudian has a museum to display the bones and artifacts, and the cave series is a UNESCO World Heritage Site.

This observation and the fact that the earliest evidence of the genus *Homo* in western Europe comes from Spain and Italy suggest continued gene flow between this region and northern Africa (Balter, 2001b). At the time, a mere 6 or 7 kilometers (about 4 miles) separated Gibraltar from Morocco (compared to 13 kilometers or about 8 miles today), and islands dotted the straits from Tunisia to Sicily. The only direct land connection between Africa and Eurasia runs through the Middle East and into Turkey and the Caucasus. Our ancestors may also have come across the southern Red Sea.

The Culture of *Homo erectus*

With its larger brain, *Homo erectus* surpassed its predecessors in cultural ability. *H. erectus* refined stone toolmaking technology and began to use fire for light, protection, warmth, and cooking. Indirect evidence indicates that the organizational and planning abilities of *H. erectus*, or at least the later ones, exceeded those of their predecessors.

Acheulean Tool Tradition

Implements of the **Acheulean tool tradition** accompany *H. erectus* remains in Africa, Europe, and Southwest Asia. Named for the stone tools first identified at St. Acheul, France, the signature piece of this tradition is the hand-axe: a teardrop-shaped tool pointed at one end with a sharp cutting edge all around (Figure 7.10).

The earliest hand-axes, from East Africa, date to about 1.6 million years ago. Those found in Europe are no older than about 500,000 years. Hand-axes appeared at the same time that archaeological sites in Europe became dramatically more common, suggesting an influx of individuals bringing Acheulean technology with them. Because the genus *Homo* spread into Asia before the invention of the first hand-axes, different forms of tools developed in East Asia.

Evidence from Olduvai Gorge indicates that the Acheulean grew out of the Oldowan and Lomekwian traditions: In lower strata, chopper tools were found along with remains of *H. habilis*; above these, the first crude hand-axes intermingle with chopper tools; and higher strata contain more finished-looking Acheulean hand-axes along with *H. erectus* remains.

Early Acheulean tools represent a significant step beyond the generalized cutting, chopping, and scraping

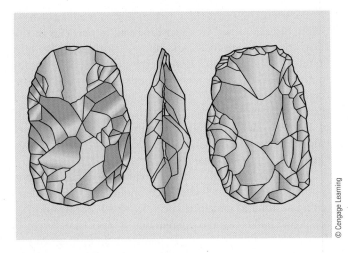

Figure 7.10 Acheulean Hand-Axe
The toolmaker imposed a standardized arbitrary form on the naturally occurring raw material to make this Acheulean hand-axe. The crafter made many separate strikes to create the sharp edge visible in profile.

© Cengage Learning

Oldowan tools, whose shapes were dictated by the original form, size, and mechanical properties of raw materials. The shapes of later Acheulean tools were more standardized, apparently reflecting preconceived designs imposed upon a diverse range of raw materials (Ambrose, 2001). Overall, Acheulean toolmakers could produce sharper points and more regular and larger cutting edges from the same amount of stone.

Besides hand-axes, *H. erectus* used tools that functioned as cleavers (hand-axes with straight, sharp edges where the point would otherwise be), picks and knives (variants of the hand-axe form), and flake tools. Many flake tools were byproducts of hand-axe and cleaver manufacture. Their sharp edges made them useful tools themselves, and many were retouched to make points, scrapers, and borers.

Toolkits took on regional variations during this period as well. In northern and eastern Europe, the archaeological record contains fewer hand-axes than in Africa and Southwest Asia. People there used simple flaked choppers, a wide variety of unstandardized flakes, and supplementary tools made of bone, antler, and wood. In East Asia, by contrast, people developed a variety of choppers, scrapers, points, and burins (chisel-like tools) different from those in Southwest Asia, Europe, and Africa.

Besides direct percussion, anvil (striking the raw material against a stationary stone) and bipolar percussion (holding the raw material against an anvil, but striking it at the same time with a hammerstone) methods were used in tool manufacture. Tens of thousands of stone tools have been found with *H. erectus* remains at Zhoukoudian, but stone implements are not at all common in Southeast

Acheulean tool tradition The prevalent style of the stone tools that are associated with *Homo erectus* remains; represented by the hand-axe.

The 700,000-year-old Kao Poh Nam rock shelter in Thailand provides possible evidence for deliberate, controlled use of fire. Here, a roughly circular arrangement of fire-cracked basalt cobbles was discovered along with artifacts and animal bones. Basalt rocks, not native to the rock shelter area, were likely carried in by *H. erectus*. The hearth is associated with bones, showing clear evidence of cut marks from butchering as well as burning.

Evidence from Swartkrans in South Africa may indicate the earliest use of fire by *H. erectus*. Here, deposits dated to between 1 and 1.3 million years ago contain bones that had been heated to much hotter temperatures than natural fires could produce. Heating the bones to such high temperatures would have made any meat on them inedible, suggesting that *H. Erectus* used the Swartkrans fires to ward off predators.

H. erectus may have also used fire to frighten away cave-dwelling predators so the fire users could live in the caves themselves. Of course, fire also provided warmth and light in these otherwise cold and dark habitations. Earlier bipeds likely used caves as part of their temperature-regulation strategy (Barrett et al., 2004), and the controlled use of fire expands this ability considerably.

Fire may have assisted in the quest for food as well. In the long, cold winters of places like central Europe and China, food was scarce. Edible plants were unavailable, and large herds of animals dispersed and migrated. Our ancestors may have searched for frozen carcasses of animals too large to hunt like woolly mammoths, woolly rhinoceroses, and bison that died naturally in the late fall and winter.

Using fire to thaw carcasses may have led to the idea of cooking food. Some paleoanthropologists suggest that the cooking of food altered the forces of natural selection by favoring further reduction in tooth size and supportive facial structure. The heavy jaws and large, sharp teeth required for chewing tough raw foods grew less necessary. Alternatively, the reduction of tooth size and supporting structure may have occurred outside the context of adaptation. The genetic changes responsible for increasing brain size may have caused a reduction in tooth size as a secondary effect. The discovery of a genetic mutation, shared by all humans but absent in apes, that acts to prevent growth of powerful jaw muscles supports this hypothesis. Without heavy jaw muscles attached to the outside of the braincase, a significant constraint to brain growth was removed. In other words, humans may have developed large brains as byproduct of jaw-size reduction (Stedman et al., 2004).

Figure 7.11 Bamboo Construction
In regions where bamboo is readily available for the fabrication of effective tools, stone tool industries might not have developed. Here, contemporary Chinese construction workers erect a bamboo scaffold, demonstrating this material's strength and versatility.

Asia. Here, favored materials likely were ones that do not preserve well, such as bamboo (Figure 7.11) and other local woods, which can make excellent knives, scrapers, and other tools.

Use of Fire

Homo erectus brings the first evidence of ancestral populations living outside the Old World tropics. Controlled use of fire allowed early humans to inhabit regions where winter temperatures regularly dropped below temperate climate levels—as they must have in northern China, the mountain highlands of Central Asia, and most of Europe. Members of the genus *Homo* spread to these colder regions some 780,000 years ago.

Cooking, however, does more than soften food. It detoxifies a number of poisonous plants; alters digestion-inhibiting substances so that important vitamins, minerals, and proteins can be absorbed while in the gut; and makes high-energy complex carbohydrates like starch digestible. Cooking increased the available nutritional resources and made humans more secure.

The partial predigestion of food by cooking also may have allowed a reduction in the size of the digestive tract. To establish this biological change, paleoanthropologists turn to comparative anatomy of the living hominoids. Despite many similarities in form to apes, contemporary humans possess substantially smaller digestive tracts. This reduced gut takes less energy to operate, making it easier to serve the energy demands of a larger brain.

Like tools, fire gave people more control over their environment. Fire modified the natural succession of day and night, perhaps encouraging *H. erectus* to stay up after dark to review the day's events and plan the next day's activities. The existence of populations in temperate climates implies planning because survival depended upon the ability to anticipate the needs of the winter season by advance preparation for the cold.

Studies of modern humans indicate that most people remain reasonably comfortable down to 10 degrees Celsius (50 degrees Fahrenheit) with minimal clothing as long as they keep active. Clothing does not fossilize, so we have no direct evidence of the kind of clothing *H. erectus* wore. We know only that colder climates required more sophisticated clothing. In short, our ancestors' use of fire allowed them to dramatically increase their geographic range and dietary options.

Hunting

Sites such as 400,000-year-old Torralba in Spain provide evidence that *Homo erectus* developed organized hunts of large animals. The ancient swamp at Torralba contains dismembered scattered remains of several elephants, horses, red deer, wild oxen, and rhinoceroses. No natural geologic process can explain these animals being accidently caught and dying in a swamp, and there is no evidence that other carnivorous animals pursued them there. However, the bones are closely associated with a few thousand stone tools of various forms, indicating that the genus *Homo* surely was involved.

It appears that the animals were driven into the swamp so that they could be easily killed. The remains of charcoal and carbon, widely but thinly scattered in the vicinity, raise the possibility that grassfires were used to drive the animals into the swamp. This evidence indicates that genus *Homo* had come a long way from mere opportunistic scavenging, as this type of elaborate, large-scale kill involves organizational and communicative skills.

Other Evidence of Complex Thought

Other evidence of *H. erectus'* capabilities comes from the small island of Flores in Indonesia. Flores lies east of a deep-water strait that acted as a barrier to animals to and from Southeast Asia throughout the Pleistocene. Getting to Flores required crossing open water: at minimum, 25 kilometers from Bali to Sumbawa, and 19 kilometers farther to Flores. The presence of 800,000-year-old stone tools on Flores indicates that somehow our ancestors navigated across the deep, fast-moving water.

Flores is also the site where the "hobbit" species, *Homo florensis*, was discovered in 2003. Tiny in stature and possessing many ancestral characteristics, the Flores fossils date from 13,000 to 73,000 years ago. Some paleoanthropologists propose that this dwarf species evolved directly from *H. erectus*, who arrived on the island with stone tools. Over generations, *H. florensis* then reduced in size, a phenomenon that can occur in isolated island populations.

Increased standardization and refinement of Acheulean hand-axes over time also provides evidence for a developing symbolic life. Deliberately marked objects of stone, bone, and ivory appear in Acheulean contexts at several sites in Europe. These include several objects from Bilzingsleben, Germany, including a mastodon bone with a series of deliberately engraved regular lines. Similarly, some of the oldest known rock carvings are associated with Acheulean tools in a cave in Bhimbetka, in Madhya Pradesh, India. These artifacts have no obvious utility or model in the natural world and appear to be purely artistic. Archaeologists argue that the use of such symbolic images requires some sort of spoken language, both to assign meaning to the images and to maintain the tradition they seem to represent.

The Question of Language

Although we have no definitive evidence of *Homo erectus'* linguistic abilities, indications of a developing symbolic life, planning for seasonal changes, and coordinating hunting activities imply improving linguistic competence. The observation that right-handed individuals made the majority of stone tools also supports the theory of increased specialization and lateralization of the evolving brain. In other primates and most mammals, the right and left sides of the brain duplicate each other's function; these animals use the right and left sides of their bodies equally and interchangeably. In humans, the emergence of handedness seems closely linked both developmentally (at about the age of 1 year) and evolutionarily with the appearance of language. Thus, evidence of handedness in Lower Paleolithic tools indicates that the kind of brain specialization required for language was well under way (Figure 7.12).

The fossil record provides evidence for evolving humans' linguistic capability. The vocal tract and brain of *H. erectus* are intermediate between those of *H. sapiens* and earlier *Australopithecus*. The **hypoglossal canal**—the passageway through the skull that accommodates the nerve that controls tongue movement, which is vital for spoken language—has taken on the characteristic large size seen in contemporary humans in fossil skulls dated to 500,000 years ago (Figure 7.13).

Possibly, a changeover from reliance on gestural to spoken language was a driving force in these evolutionary changes. Reductions of tooth and jaw size may also have contributed, with improved abilities to articulate speech sounds. From an evolutionary standpoint, spoken language provides some advantages over gestures. Individuals do not have to stop whatever they are doing with their hands to "talk," which would be especially useful to a species increasingly dependent on tool use. Spoken language also allows communication in the dark, past opaque objects, or among people whose gaze is concentrated on something else (potential prey, for example).

With *H. erectus*, we find a clearer manifestation of the interplay among cultural, physical, and environmental

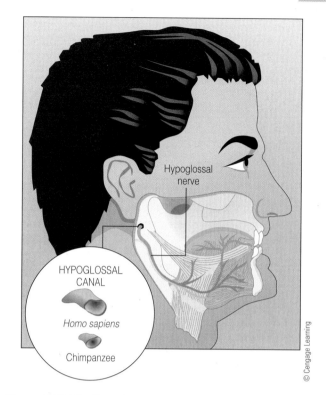

Figure 7.13 The Hypoglossal Canal
The size of the hypoglossal canal is much larger in humans than in chimpanzees. The nerve that passes through this canal controls tongue movement, which is vital to spoken language. All members of the genus *Homo* after about 500,000 years ago have an enlarged hypoglossal canal.

factors than ever before. However slowly, social organization, technology, and communication developed in tandem with an increase in brain size and complexity. In fact, the cranial capacity of late *H. erectus* is 31 percent greater than the mean for early *H. erectus*.

Archaic *Homo sapiens* and the Appearance of Modern-Sized Brains

Fossils from a number of sites in Africa, Asia, and Europe indicate that cranial capacity reached modern proportions between 200,000 and 400,000 years ago. Most fossil finds consist of parts of one or very few individuals. The fossils from Sierra de Atapuerca in northern Spain provide the only evidence of a substantial Paleolithic population (Figure 7.14). Dated to about 400,000 years ago (Parés et al., 2000), the remains of at least twenty-eight individuals of both sexes and of various ages were deliberately dumped

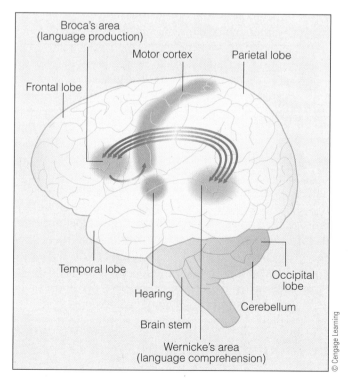

Figure 7.12 Language Areas of the Brain
Language areas in the left side of the brain. The right side of the human brain has different specialized functions.

hypoglossal canal The opening in the skull that accommodates the tongue-controlling hypoglossal nerve.

Javier Trueba/MSF/Science Source

Figure 7.14 Sima de los Huesos
These fossils from Sima de los Huesos ("Pit of the Bones"), Sierra de Atapuerca, Spain, are the best collection of *Homo* fossils from a single site. The scientists who discovered them place them in the species *Homo antecessor*, despite cranial capacities overlapping with the average size of contemporary humans. These fossils fit into the complex period of our evolutionary history when brain size and cultural capability began to separate members of genus *Homo* from earlier ancestral species.

the dead at Atapuerca may have involved some ritual activity that presaged burial of the dead, which became common after 100,000 years ago. Cranial capacity varied within this population from 1,125 to 1,390 cc, overlapping the upper end of the range for *H. erectus* and the average size of *H. sapiens* (1,300 cc). The bones display a mix of features—some typical of *H. erectus*, others of *H. sapiens*—including some incipient characteristics of the later appearing Neandertal.

Other remains from Africa and Europe from the same time range have shown a combination of *H. erectus* and *H. sapiens* features. Some—such as skulls from Ndutu (Tanzania), Swanscombe (England), and Steinheim (Germany)—have been classified as *H. sapiens*, while others—from Arago (France), Bilzingsleben (Germany), Petralona (Greece), and several African sites—have been classified as *H. erectus*. Yet all have cranial capacities that fit within the range exhibited by the Sima de los Huesos skulls, which are classified as *H. antecessor* (see Table 7.1).

Comparisons of these transitional skulls to those of living people or to *H. erectus* reflect their intermediate nature. The Swanscombe and Steinheim skulls are large and robust, with maximum breadth lower on the skull, prominent brow ridges, large faces, and big teeth. Similarly, the face of the Petralona skull from Greece resembles the later European Neandertals, while the back of the skull looks like *H. erectus*. Conversely, a skull from Salé in Morocco, which had a rather small brain for *H. sapiens* (930–960 cc), looks surprisingly modern from the back. Various jaws from France and Morocco seem to combine features of *H. erectus* with those of the Neandertals. Similarly, skulls from several sites in China exhibit the same mix of *H. erectus* and *H. sapiens* characteristics.

"Lumpers" suggest that the terms "late *H. erectus*" or "early *H. sapiens*" (or any other proposed species names within the genus *Homo*) serve no useful purpose and merely obscure the transitional status of these intermediate species. They tend to place these fossils in the **archaic *Homo sapiens*** category, a group that reflects both their large brain size and the ancestral features on the skull. "Splitters" use discrete names for specimens from this period to account for some of the geographic and morphologic variation these fossils exhibit. Both approaches reflect their respective opinions about evolutionary relationships among fossil groups.

(after defleshing their skulls) by their contemporaries into a deep cave shaft known today as Sima de los Huesos ("Pit of the Bones"). The recent *Homo naledi* discoveries in South African caves similarly suggest some sort of specialized treatment of the dead.

The presence of animal bones in the same pit with humans raises the possibility that early humans simply used the site as a dump. Alternatively, the treatment of

archaic *Homo sapiens* A loosely defined group within the genus *Homo* that "lumpers" assign to fossils with the combination of large brain size and ancestral features on the skull.

Levalloisian technique Toolmaking technique by which three or four long triangular flakes are detached from a specially prepared core; developed by members of the genus *Homo* transitional from *H. erectus* to *H. sapiens*.

Levalloisian Technique

With the appearance of large-brained members of the genus *Homo*, the pace of cultural change accelerated. These ancestors invented a new method of flake manufacture—the **Levalloisian technique**, named for the French site where such tools were first excavated. Sites in Africa, Europe, Southwest Asia, and even China have yielded flake tools produced by this technique along with Acheulean tools. In China, the technique could represent a case of independent invention, or it could indicate the spread of ideas from one part of the inhabited world to another.

The Levalloisian technique involves first preparing a core by removing small flakes over the stone's surface. Next the toolmaker sets up a platform by striking a crosswise blow at one end of the stone's core (**Figure 7.15**). Striking the platform removes three or four long flakes, whose size and shape have been predetermined by the preceding preparation, leaving a core nodule that looks like a tortoise shell from which large preshaped flake tools can be removed. In contrast to the methods used previously, this faster technique produces a longer (and sharper) edge for the same amount of flint.

Other Cultural Innovations

As the Levalloisian technique developed, our ancestors also invented hafting—the fastening of small stone bifaces and flakes to handles of wood (**Figure 7.16**). Hafting led to the development of knives and more complex spears.

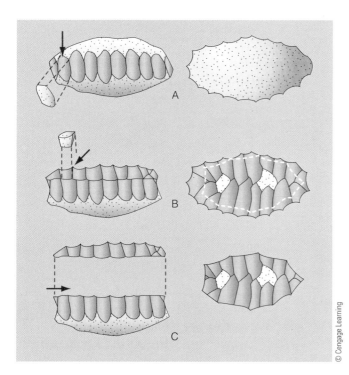

Figure 7.15 The Levalloisian Technique
These drawings show side (*left*) and top (*right*) views of the steps in the Levalloisian technique. Arrows indicate where the toolmaker strikes the core with another stone in order to shape it. Drawing A shows the preparatory flaking of the stone core; B, the same on the top surface of that core (the dotted line indicates what will ultimately become a tool; and C, the final step of detaching a flake tool of a size and shape predetermined by the preceding steps.

© Cengage Learning

© PhotoDisc/Getty Images

Figure 7.16 Hafting
The practice of hafting, the fastening of small stone bifaces and flakes to handles of wood, was a major technological advance appearing in the archaeological record at about the same time as the invention of the Levalloisian technique.

These new tools involved three components: a handle or shaft, a stone insert, and the materials to bind them. Hafting involved planned sequences of actions that could be performed at different times and places.

With this new technology, regional stylistic and technological variants marked the archaeological record, suggesting the emergence of distinct cultural traditions. At the same time, the proportions of raw materials procured from faraway sources increased. In contrast to Acheulean tools that were rarely more than 20 kilometers (12 miles) away from their source, Levalloisian tools have been found up to 320 kilometers (200 miles) away (Ambrose, 2001).

The use of yellow and red ochre as pigments, a development first identified in Africa, became especially common by 130,000 years ago. The use of ochre may signal a rise in ritual activity, similar to the deliberate placement of the human remains in the Sima de los Huesos, Atapuerca. The use of red ochre in ancient burials may relate to its similarity to the color of blood, as a powerful symbol of life.

Philippe Plailly & Atelier Daynès/Science Source

Figure 7.17 Fleshing Out the Bones
Paleoartists like Élisabeth Daynès work closely with paleoanthropologists to transform fossils and other kinds of data into a form we can see. Layering muscle, nerves, skin, and hair onto fossil casts, they produce striking yet faithful renderings of ancient individuals. The shape, size, and markings of bones let paleoartists see where soft tissues once lay. Narratives that scientists have created about our ancestors allow paleoartists to bring in features such as facial expression, body language, body hair, and skin color. Paleoartists themselves embody the essential human traits that make their craft possible: enlarged brains, sophisticated symbolic thought, imagination, and dexterous hands for wielding tools. But what about the culture and the beliefs of the paleoartists? What do you see when you compare this image to Figure 7.20?

The Neandertals

To many outside the field of anthropology, the **Neandertal** is the quintessential caveman, portrayed by imaginative cartoonists as a slant-headed, stooped, dim-witted individual clad in animal skins, carrying a big club as he plodded across the prehistoric landscape, perhaps dragging an unwilling female or a dead saber-toothed tiger. Novels and films have perpetuated the Neandertal stereotype.

Has the popular image of Neandertals as brutish and incapable of spoken language, much less abstract or innovative thinking, influenced interpretations of fossil and archaeological evidence? Neandertals remain one of the most contentious issues in paleoanthropology. Did they represent an inferior side branch of human evolution that went extinct

following the appearance of modern humans? Alternatively, are descendants of Neandertals walking the earth today?

Neandertals were an extremely muscular people living from approximately 30,000 to 125,000 years ago in Europe and in Southwest and Central Asia. Today genetic evidence extends their range both forward and back in time. Possessing brains larger than the modern average, Neandertal faces differed from those of later humans (**Figure 7.17**). Their large noses and teeth projected forward. They had prominent bony brow ridges over their eyes. A bunlike bony mass for attachment of powerful neck muscles protruded from the back of their skull. These features, not in line with classic forms of Western beauty, probably contributed to the conception of Neandertals as brutes.

One of the first Neandertals was found in a cave in the Neander Valley (*tal* means "valley" in German; *thal* was the old German spelling) near Düsseldorf, Germany, in 1856. This was well before scientific theories to account for human evolution had gained acceptance. (Darwin published

Neandertal A distinct fossil group within the genus *Homo* inhabiting Europe and Southwest Asia from approximately 30,000 to 125,000 years ago; today's genetic evidence extends their range both forward and back in time.

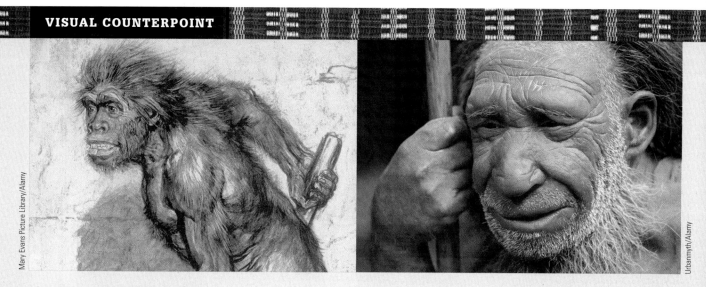

Figure 7.18 Neandertal Depictions

When Neandertals are portrayed as brutes as they were in this sketch from the early 20th century (*left*), based on the La Chapelle-aux-Saints skeleton, it is difficult to welcome them into our human ancestry. But when reconstructions portray them in a positive light, Neandertal ancestry seems more palatable. The image on the right is from the Neanderthal Museum in Mettmann, Germany. One can picture such an individual fitting with the reconstruction of Neandertal lifeways from the Shanidar site located in the Kurdistan region of today's Iraq. Excavated between 1957 and 1961, this site includes evidence of deliberate burial of nine individuals. Ochre and pollen associated with the skeletons led to the nickname the "original flower people" for the Shanidar remains. Although some have claimed that the pollen is a modern contaminant, analysis of the bones reveals a rich cultural system. One of the buried individuals, an older male, had survived for years after severe injuries that required amputating the lower half of one arm as well as a wound to his eye socket that would have left him partially blind. (The humerus or upper arm bone had withered—a gradual response to amputation of the lower arm.) Such evidence demonstrates the caregiving capacities of his community to nurse him through these injuries and help him survive for years afterward.

On the Origins of Species three years later in 1859.) Initially, experts did not know what to make of this discovery.

Examination of the fossil skull, a few ribs, and some limb bones revealed that the individual was a human being, but it did not look "normal." Some believed the bones were those of a sickly and deformed contemporary. Others thought the skeleton belonged to a soldier who had succumbed to "water on the brain" during the Napoleonic Wars earlier that century. One prominent anatomist believed the remains were those of an idiot suffering from malnutrition, whose violent temper got him into many fights, flattening his forehead and making his brow ridges bumpy. Similarly, an analysis of a skeleton found in 1908 near La Chapelle-aux-Saints in France mistakenly concluded that the specimen's brain was apelike and that he walked like an ape (Figure 7.18).

The evidence indicates that Neandertals were nowhere near as brutish and apelike as originally portrayed. Some researchers contend that Neandertals' intelligence was no different than modern humans'. Many now view them as the archaic *H. sapiens* of Europe and Southwest and Central Asia, ancestral to the more derived, anatomically modern populations of these regions of the last 30,000 years.

For example, paleoanthropologist C. Loring Brace observed that "classic" Neandertal features (Figure 7.19) are commonly present in 10,000-year-old skulls from Denmark and Norway (Ferrie, 1997).

Nevertheless, Neandertals differ from more recent human populations. Wear patterns on their large front teeth indicate that they may have been used for tasks other than chewing. In many specimens, front teeth were worn down to the root stub by 35 to 40 years of age. Neandertals' large noses probably helped to warm, moisten, and clean the dry, dusty frigid air of the glacial climate, preventing damage to the lungs and brain as seen in modern cold-adapted people. At the back of the skull, the occipital bony bun allowed for attachment of the powerful neck muscles and counteracted the weight of a heavy face.

All Neandertal fossils indicate that both sexes were muscular beings, equipped to take on rigorous physical activity. Relative to body mass, the limbs were short (as they are in modern humans native to especially cold climates) with extremely robust, dense bones. Their arms were exceptionally powerful, and pronounced attachments on their hand bones attest to a remarkably strong grip. Science writer

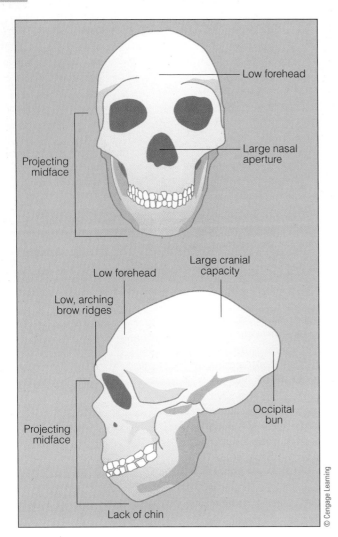

Figure 7.19 Neandertal Skulls
Features of the skull seen in "classic" Neandertals.

James Shreeve has suggested that a healthy Neandertal could lift an average North American football player over his head and throw him through the goalposts (Shreeve, 1995). Their massive, dense foot and leg bones suggest high levels of strength and endurance.

Because brain size is related to overall body mass, heavy robust Neandertal bodies account for the large average size of the Neandertal brain (1,400 cc versus 1,300 cc for modern humans). Paleoanthropologists have shifted to debating whether change in the *shape*, rather than just the size, of the brain and skull is associated with change in cultural capabilities, in part because the size of the Neandertal brain is at the high end of the human range.

Interpretations of Neandertal fossils have changed dramatically over time and are still surrounded by controversy. Those who propose that the Neandertal line went extinct emphasize Neandertals' biological differences and cultural inferiority. Those who include Neandertals in our direct ancestry emphasize sophisticated Neandertal culture and account for biological differences as regional adaptations to an extremely cold climate and the retention of ancestral traits in a somewhat isolated population (Figure 7.20). The recent discovery of a fossilized hyoid bone, which is key for making speech sounds, supports the sophistication of Neandertals. Analysis of the Neandertal hyoid suggests that it functioned similarly to how it functions in us today (D'Anastasio et al., 2013).

Javanese, African, and Chinese Archaic *Homo sapiens*

While large-brained Neandertals inhabited Europe and Southwest Asia, variants of archaic *H. sapiens* inhabited other parts of the world. Appearing much more like modern humans, these archaic *H. Sapiens* lacked the extreme midfacial projection and massive muscle attachments on the back of the skull characteristic of Neandertals.

Eleven skulls found near the Solo River in Ngandong, Java, are a prime example. These skulls indicated modern-sized brains ranging from 1,013 to 1,252 cc, while retaining features of earlier Javanese *H. erectus*. When their dating was recently revised (to between 27,000 and 53,000 years ago), some researchers concluded that this proved a late survival of *H. erectus* in Asia, contemporary with *H. sapiens*. But the Ngandong skulls are actually representatives of archaic *H. sapiens,* with modern-sized brains in ancient-looking skulls.

Fossils from various parts of Africa and China show a similar combination of ancient and modern traits. Neandertals could represent an extreme form of archaic *H. sapiens,* whereas elsewhere the archaics living in the same regions looked either like robust versions of the early modern populations or like somewhat more derived versions of the *H. erectus* populations that preceded them. All appeared to have modern-sized brains, with their skulls retaining some ancestral features.

Exciting recent discoveries in southern Siberia bring a new group of archaic *Homo sapiens*, the **Denisovan**, into the mix. Named for the cave in which they were discovered, the fossil evidence for Denisovans consists of a finger bone, a toe bone, and two molar teeth dated to between 30,000 and 80,000 years ago. Though limited, these relatively recent remains were well enough preserved to allow for genetic analyses (Reich et al., 2010, 2012). Interestingly, recently sequenced mitochondrial DNA from the Sima de los Huesos site in Spain resembles that of the Denisovans (Meyer et al., 2014).

Denisovans made blade tools and burins, more sophisticated stone tools characteristic of later peoples, as well

Denisovan A newly discovered group of archaic *Homo sapiens* from southern Siberia dated to between 30,000 and 50,000 years ago.

University of Michigan Photo Services

Figure 7.20 Wolpoff Versus Neandertal
As this face-off between paleoanthropologist Milford Wolpoff and his reconstruction of a
Neandertal shows, there are not very many differences between the two.

as pendants made from the teeth of a variety of animals.
Genetic analyses indicate that the Denisovans were local
descendants of *Homo erectus*, who possibly interbred with
the Neandertals inhabiting this region for a period of
time, and with other waves of *Homo sapiens* arriving later.
Features of both the Neandertal and Denisovan genomes
are present in modern humans.

Middle Paleolithic Culture

Environmental adaptations by *Homo* from the **Middle
Paleolithic**, or middle part of the Old Stone Age, were
both biological and cultural, but the capacity for cultural
adaptation was predictably superior to what it had been
in earlier members of the genus *Homo*. Their modern
brain size gave them greater cultural capabilities than
their ancestors. Such a brain played a role in technological innovations, considerably sophisticated conceptual
thought, and, almost surely, communication through
spoken language.

The Mousterian Tool Tradition

The **Mousterian tool tradition** and similar techniques
of Europe, Southwest Asia, and North Africa, dating to
between 40,000 and 125,000 years ago, are the best-
known toolmaking industries (Figure 7.21). Comparable
traditions are found in China and Japan, where they likely
arose independently from local toolmaking traditions.

These traditions indicate significant technological
advancement over preceding industries. For example,
an Acheulean flint worker could get 40 centimeters (16
inches) of working edge from a kilogram (2.2 pound)
core, while a Mousterian could get nearly 200 centimeters (6 feet) from the same core. All people—Neandertals
and other members of the genus *Homo* of the Middle

Middle Paleolithic The middle part of the Old Stone Age characterized
by the development of the Mousterian tool tradition and the earlier
Levalloisian traditions.

Mousterian tool tradition The tool industry of the Neandertals and
their contemporaries of Europe, Southwest Asia, and North Africa from
40,000 to 125,000 years ago.

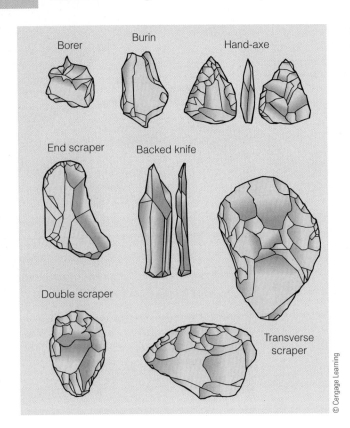

Borer

Burin

Hand-axe

End scraper

Backed knife

Double scraper

Transverse scraper

© Cengage Learning

Figure 7.21 The Mousterian Toolkit
The Mousterian tool tradition's wide range of tool types with specific functions resulted in finer workmanship.

Paleolithic who possessed more anatomically modern skulls, in Europe, North Africa, and Southwest Asia—used Mousterian tools.

The Mousterian tradition is named after the Le Moustier Neandertal cave site in southern France. The development of Mousterian tools likely was rooted in the older Acheulean tradition, but these tools are generally lighter and smaller than those of earlier industries. Previously just two or three flakes could be obtained from an entire core, but Mousterian toolmakers obtained many smaller flakes, which they skillfully retouched and sharpened. Toolkits also contained a greater variety of tool types: hand-axes, flakes, scrapers, borers, notched flakes for shaving wood, and many kinds of points that could be attached to wooden shafts to make spears. This variety of tools facilitated more effective use of food resources and enhanced the quality of clothing and shelter.

As population size steadily increased, early people started living in colder climates. And once there, these members of genus *Homo* had little choice but to adapt as climates turned even colder. A series of cultural adaptations made population expansion into previously uninhabited colder regions possible. The rare and seasonal availability of vegetable foods under such cold conditions made meat a critical staple. In particular, animal fats, rather than carbohydrates, become the chief source of energy. Energy-rich animal fat in the diets of cold climate meat-eaters provided the extra energy

needed for hunting and keeping the body warm. An abundance of associated animal bones found with cut marks underlines the importance of meat to Mousterian toolmakers. Frequently, the remains consist almost entirely of very large game—wild cattle (including the European bison known as aurochs), wild horses, and even mammoths and woolly rhinoceroses.

The Anthropology Applied feature shows that stone tools continue to be important for humans today. Clearly, the Neandertals were not mere casual or opportunistic hunters; rather, they engaged in carefully planned, organized hunts of very large and potentially dangerous game. The standardization of Mousterian hunting implements compared to household tools also reflects the importance of hunting for these ancient peoples.

At the same time, the complexity of the toolkit needed for survival in a cold climate may have decreased the users' mobility. Deeper deposits at Mousterian sites compared to earlier Lower Paleolithic sites suggest longer habitation in the same place. Such sites contain evidence of long production sequences, resharpening and discarding of tools, and large-scale butchering and cooking of game. Pebble paving, simple wall construction, and the digging of post holes and artificial pits show how the inhabitants worked to improve living conditions in caves and rock shelters. This evidence suggests that Mousterian sites were much more than stopovers in an ongoing quest for food.

In addition, there are indications that Neandertal social organization even developed some forms of healthcare to provide for physically disabled members of the group. For the first time, the remains of old people, many exhibiting treatment for trauma and healed wounds without infection, are well represented in the fossil record. The partially blind man with a withered upper arm from Shanidar in Iraq, described in Figure 7.18, provides one particularly dramatic example. Remains of another individual found at Krapina in Croatia suggest the possible surgical amputation of a hand. In La Chapelle, France, fossil remains indicate prolonged survival of a man badly crippled by arthritis. The earliest example of medical treatment comes from a 200,000-year-old site in France, where a toothless man was able to survive, probably because others in his group processed or prechewed food for him to swallow. Whether this indicates true compassionate care by these early people is not clear. However, it does show that cultural factors enabled individuals to provide care to others.

The Symbolic Life of Neandertals

Neandertals seem to have had a rich symbolic life. Several sites contain clear evidence that Neandertals buried their dead. The difficulty of digging an adult-sized grave without access to metal shovels suggests that burial was a tremendously important social activity. Moreover, intentional positioning of dead bodies indicates the symbolic significance of this action.

Stone Tools for Modern Surgeons

When Harvard University anthropologist Irven DeVore needed to have some minor melanomas removed from his face, he did not leave it up to the surgeon to supply the scalpels. Instead, he had graduate student John Shea create a scalpel. Making a blade of obsidian (a naturally occurring volcanic "glass") with the same techniques people used to create blades during the Upper Paleolithic, Shea hafted the obsidian in a wooden handle, using melted pine resin as glue and then lashing it with sinew. After the procedure, the surgeon reported that the obsidian scalpel was superior to metal ones.[a]

DeVore was not the first to undergo surgery with stone scalpels. In 1975, Don Crabtree, then at Idaho State University, prepared the scalpels used in his own heart surgery. In 1980, Payson Sheets at the University of Colorado created obsidian scalpels that were used successfully in eye surgery. And in 1986, David Pokotylo of the Museum of Anthropology at the University of British Columbia underwent reconstructive surgery on his hand with blades he made himself (the hafting was done by his museum colleague, Len McFarlane).

The reason for the use of scalpels modeled on ancient stone tools is that anthropologists realized obsidian's almost total superiority to normally used scalpel materials: It is 210 to 1,050 times sharper than surgical steel, 100 to 500 times sharper than a razor blade, and three times sharper than a diamond blade (which not only costs much more but cannot be made with more than 3 millimeters of cutting edge).

Obsidian blades are easier to cut with and do less damage in the process. Under a microscope, incisions made with the sharpest steel blades show torn, ragged edges and are littered with bits of displaced flesh.[b] Surgeons have better control with obsidian, and the incisions heal faster with less scarring and pain.

The superiority of obsidian scalpels led Sheets to form a corporation in partnership with eye surgeon Firmon Hardenbergh. Together, they developed a means of producing cores of uniform size from molten glass, as well as a machine to detach blades from the cores.

---

[a] Shreeve, J. (1995). *The Neandertal enigma: Solving the mystery of modern human origins* (p. 134). New York: William Morrow.

[b] Sheets, P. D. (1993). Dawn of a New Stone Age in eye surgery. In R. J. Sharer & W. Ashmore (Eds.), *Archaeology: Discovering our past.* Palo Alto, CA: Mayfield.

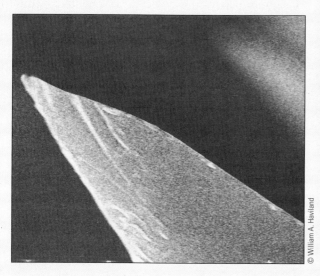 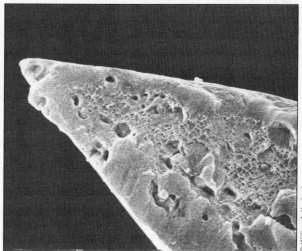

These electron micrographs of the tips of an obsidian blade (*left*) and a modern steel scalpel (*right*) illustrate the superiority of the obsidian.

To date, at least seventeen sites in Europe, South Africa, and Southwest Asia include Middle Paleolithic burials. Luckily for anthropologists, this is one reason for the relative abundance of reasonably complete Neandertal skeletons. At Kebara Cave in Israel, around 60,000 years ago, a Neandertal male between 25 and 35 years of age was placed in a pit on his back, with his arms folded over his chest and abdomen (Figure 7.22). Sometime later, after complete decay of attaching ligaments, the grave was reopened and the skull removed (a practice that, interestingly, is sometimes seen in burials in the same region roughly 50,000 years later). Similarly, the rich Krapina site in Croatia contains the remains of at least seventy individuals. Scientists have come to recognize cut marks on the bones as deliberate defleshing of the skeletons that are consistent with later ceremonial practices.

Shanidar Cave in today's Iraq provides evidence of a burial accompanied by what may have been a funeral

© Cengage Learning

Figure 7.22 Kebara Burial
The position of the body remains and the careful removal of the skull, without the lower jaw, indicate that the individual from Kebara Cave in Israel was deliberately buried there about 60,000 years ago.

ceremony. Pollen analysis of the soil around a skeleton found buried in a pit indicates that flowers had been placed below the body and in a wreath about the head. Because the key pollen types came from insect-pollinated flowers, few if any of the pollen grains found could have been blown into the pit through the air. These flowers were varieties valued historically for their medicinal properties.

Other evidence for symbolic behavior in Mousterian culture comes from the use of naturally occurring pigments: manganese dioxide and red and yellow ochre. Recovered chunks of these pigments reveal clear evidence of scraping to produce powder and of facets, like those that appear on a used crayon. A notable example is a carved and shaped section of a mammoth tooth to which a Mousterian artist also applied color about 50,000 years ago. This mammoth tooth may have been made for culturally symbolic purposes; it is similar to ceremonial objects made of bone and ivory dated to the later Upper Paleolithic and to the wooden *churingas* made by Aborigines in Australia.

The mammoth tooth, which was once smeared with red ochre, has a highly polished surface, suggesting it was handled a lot. Microscopic examination reveals that it was not shaped for any utilitarian purpose because it

lacks a working edge. Such objects imply, as archaeologist Alexander Marshack has observed, "that the Neandertals did in fact have conceptual models and maps as well as problem-solving capacities comparable to, if not equal to, those found among anatomically modern humans" (Marshack, 1989, p. 22).

The recent discovery of a painting "toolkit" in a South African cave pushes this behavior back to 100,000 years ago—and also to a region outside the Neandertal range. The toolkit shows that ancient artists made paint by mixing pigments that had been ground with stone together with bone marrow and charcoal (as binders) and a liquid, most likely water (Henshilwood et al., 2011). The next chapter will discuss in detail whether a new species was responsible for this or whether the paint manufacturing was just a part of Mousterian culture.

Evidence of Neandertals' symbolic activity raises the possibility of the presence and use of musical instruments, such as a proposed bone flute from a Mousterian site in Slovenia in southern Europe (Figure 7.23). This object, consisting of a hollow bone with perforations, has sparked controversy. Some see it as nothing more than a bone that a cave bear chewed on—producing the perforations. Its discoverer, French archaeologist Marcel Otte, on the other hand, sees it as a flute.

Unfortunately, the object is fragmentary, with five holes surviving: four on one side and one on the opposite side. The regular spacing of the four holes, fitting perfectly to the fingers of a human hand, and the location of the fifth hole at the base of the opposite side, at the natural location of the thumb, all lend credence to the flute hypothesis. Although there are also signs of gnawing by animals, these are superimposed over traces of human activity (Otte, 2000). Were it found in an Upper Paleolithic context, like a flute discovered in the Hohle Fels Cave in southwestern Germany, it would probably be accepted as a flute without argument. But the early date of Otte's flute indicates a Neandertal made it, which ties it to the larger controversy about Neandertals' cultural abilities and their place in human evolutionary history.

Speech and Language in the Middle Paleolithic

The Neandertals and other Middle Paleolithic *Homo* had modern-sized brains and sophisticated Mousterian toolkits, or tools that were even more advanced such as the Denisovan tools. Based on this evidence, we could surmise that they had some form of language. As paleoanthropologist Stanley Ambrose points out, the Mousterian toolkit's composite tools required the assembly of parts in different configurations to produce functionally different tools. He likens this ordered assembly of parts into tools to grammatical language "because hierarchical assemblies of sounds produce meaningful phrases and sentences, and

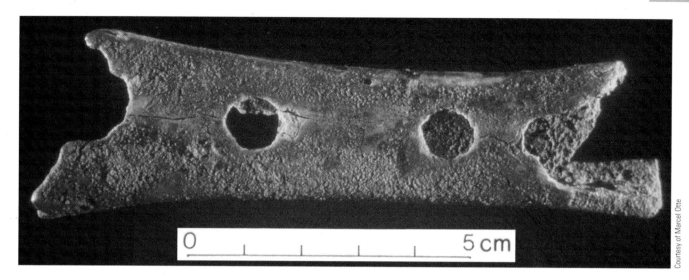

Courtesy of Marcel Otte

Figure 7.23 **The First Musical Instrument?**
There is a strong possibility that this object, found in trash left by Neandertals, is the remains of a flute made of bone.

changing word order changes meaning" (Ambrose, 2001, p. 1751). According to Ambrose, "a composite tool may be analogous to a sentence, but explaining how to make one is the equivalent of a recipe or a short story" (p. 1751). In addition, the evidence of manufactured objects with symbolic significance supports the presence of language in Middle Paleolithic *Homo*.

Beyond archaeological evidence like tools, specific anatomical features can be examined to determine whether this language was spoken or gestural. Some have argued that the Neandertals lacked the physical features necessary for speech. For example, a faulty reconstruction of the angle at the base of the Neandertal skull from the early 20th century was interpreted to indicate that the larynx was too high in the throat to support humanlike speech. Further, the hyoid bone associated with the muscles of speech in the larynx is preserved from the skeleton from the Kebara Cave burial in Israel. Its shape is identical to that of contemporary humans, indicating that the vocal tract was adequate for speech.

With respect to the brain, paleoneurologists agree that Neandertals had the neural development necessary for spoken language, arguing that the changes associated with language began even before the appearance of archaic *Homo sapiens*. Consistent, too, is an expanded thoracic vertebral canal (the thorax is the upper part of the body), a feature Neandertals share with modern humans but not with early *Homo erectus* (or any other primate). This feature suggests the increased breath control required for producing long phrases or single expirations of breath, punctuated with quick inhalations at meaningful linguistic breaks. Another argument—that a relatively flat base in Neandertal skulls would have prevented speech—has no merit, as some modern adults show as much flattening without having any difficulty speaking. When the anatomical evidence is considered in its totality, there is no compelling reason to deny Neandertals the ability to speak.

The discovery of a "language gene" by Swedish paleogeneticist Svante Pääbo and colleagues at the Max Planck Institute for Evolutionary Anthropology in Leipzig, Germany, adds an interesting new dimension to the study of the evolution of language (Lai et al., 2001). The gene, called FOXP2, was identified through the analysis of a family with a severe speech and language disorder over several generations. Pääbo hypothesized that genetic changes control the ability to make fine movements of the mouth and larynx necessary for spoken language. The identification of this gene in humans allowed scientists to compare its structure to other mammalian species.

The human FOXP2 gene differs from versions of the gene found in the chimpanzee, gorilla, orangutan, rhesus macaque, and mouse. We can identify these genetic differences among living species, but applying this knowledge to earlier members of the genus *Homo* is far more difficult. We do not know precisely when in human evolution the human form of the FOXP2 gene appeared or whether this gene was associated with the formation of a new *Homo* species.

In light of these genetic discoveries, it is also interesting to consider the work done on language capacity in the great apes. For example, Sue Savage-Rumbaugh's work with Kanzi the bonobo documented his ability to understand hundreds of spoken words and associate them with lexigrams (pictures of words) on a computer display (Savage-Rumbaugh & Lewin, 1994). Kanzi could understand the words but was unable to create the sounds himself, showing that speech and language are not identical.

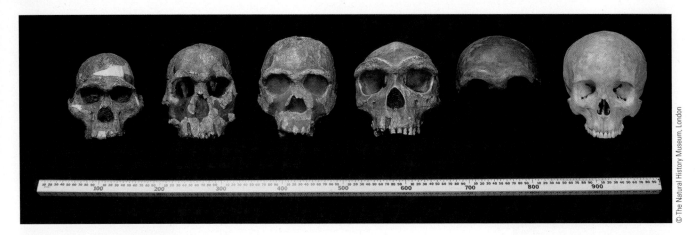

© The Natural History Museum, London

Figure 7.24 Comparing Crania
The African archaic *Homo sapiens* from Kabwe, Zambia (*fourth from the left*) is pictured here with a variety of earlier hominins as well as Kabwe's contemporaries and later members of the genus *Homo*. The Kabwe specimen is likely to have died from a dental infection that spread to the brain of this individual. To the right of the Kabwe specimen is his contemporary, the original cranium discovered in the Neander Valley, Germany, in 1856 (the only one without a face), followed by a recent *Homo sapiens* cranium. The other fossils, from the left, are a gracile australopithecine; *Homo habilis* (KNM ER 1470) discovered at Koobi Fora, Kenya; *Homo erectus* also from Koobi Fora. Increasing cranial capacity over time is evident from this series, as is the fact that Neandertal brains and that of Kabwe are in the modern human range. Even without the Neandertal face, some of the differences in the shape of the skull are evident, compared to *H. sapiens*. The African archaic *H. sapiens* is also quite different from the contemporary skeleton.

Culture, Skulls, and Modern Human Origins

For Middle Paleolithic *Homo*, cultural adaptive abilities relate to the fact that brain size was comparable to that of people living today (**Figure 7.24**). Archaeological evidence indicates that the increased cranial capacity enabled *Homo*'s development of sophisticated technology and considerably complex conceptual thought. During this same time period, large-brained individuals with anatomically modern skull shape began to appear. The earliest specimens with this skull shape—a more vertical forehead, diminished brow ridge, and a chin—appeared first in Africa and later in Asia and Europe. Whether the derived features in the skull indicate the appearance of a new species with improved cultural capabilities is hotly debated.

The transition from the Middle Paleolithic to the Upper Paleolithic occurred around 40,000 years ago. The Upper Paleolithic is known not only for a veritable explosion of tool industries, but also for clear artistic expression preserved in representative sculptures, paintings, and engravings (see Chapter 8). But the earliest anatomically modern humans, like the Neandertals and other archaic forms, used tools of the Middle Paleolithic traditions.

The relationship between the cultural developments of the Upper Paleolithic and the underlying biological differences between anatomically modern humans and archaic forms remains one of the most contentious debates in paleoanthropology. Discussions concerning the fate of the Neandertals and their cultural abilities are integral to this debate. Whether or not a new kind of human—anatomically modern with correspondingly superior intellectual and creative abilities—is responsible for the cultural explosion of the Upper Paleolithic will be a focus of Chapter 8.

CHAPTER CHECKLIST

What are the characteristics of the genus *Homo*?

✓ Genus *Homo* first appeared in East Africa and is characterized by increasing cranial capacity and the earliest stone tools.

✓ "Lumpers" identify the first species as *Homo habilis*, whereas "splitters" consider these fossils too varied to comprise a single species.

✓ *Homo erectus* appeared first in Africa around 1.9 million years ago and began spreading throughout the Old World.

✓ Cranial capacity in the genus *Homo* increased steadily from about 2.5 million years ago until about 200,000 years ago when it reached modern proportions. Other trends include reduced size of jaws and teeth, reduced sexual dimorphism, and increase in overall body size.

How and when did stone tool industries develop for the genus *Homo*?

✓ The first evidence of stone tools is dated to about 3.3 million years ago at Lake Turkana in Kenya. The Lower Paleolithic or Lower Stone Age began with these early tools of the Lomekwian tradition followed by the Oldowan tradition associated with *Homo habilis*. Ancient toolmakers used the percussion method of manufacture for these tools.

✓ *Homo erectus* originated the Acheulean tradition and exercised superior, more standardized craftsmanship compared to the preceding Lomekwian and Oldowan traditions.

✓ The Levalloisian tradition of stone tool manufacture and its practice of hafting coincided with cranial capacity reaching modern proportions between 200,000 and 400,000 years ago.

✓ The Neandertal timespan coincides with the Mousterian tool era, although all the members of the genus *Homo* living at that time employed these methods. Together the Levalloisian and the Mousterian traditions constitute the Middle Paleolithic. It surpassed the Lower Paleolithic in variety and refinement, signifying our ancestors' developing reliance on cultural adaptation for survival.

What is the relationship between biological and cultural change among early *Homo*?

✓ Brain size increased over the course of about 2.5 million years after the appearance of *H. habilis*, becoming the biological foundation for the cultural adaptation on which humans would rely for survival.

✓ As brain size reached modern proportions, the one-to-one correspondence between cultural innovation and larger brains no longer held.

✓ Meat eating satisfied the high-energy demands of larger brains and perhaps afforded leisure time for the development of culture and planning.

✓ Soft, cooked foods may have relaxed selection for large teeth and powerful jaws, permitting the cranium of *H. erectus* to expand significantly.

✓ Increased overall size and decreased sexual dimorphism may have contributed to successful adaptation to bearing large-brained young.

✓ Fossil evidence indicates that early *Homo* was a scavenger rather than a hunter of big game, as the biases of Western tradition had suggested. Early tools were used to butcher scavenged carcasses in order to extract as much nutrition as possible.

How do we describe the history and lifeways of *Homo erectus*?

✓ *H. erectus* appeared 1.8 million years ago, dispersing from Africa into Eurasia and Indonesia. A large cranial capacity, brow ridges, and a protruding mouth are some of the features that distinguish the *H. erectus* skull.

✓ Regional variation in fossils that are otherwise considered *H. erectus* has led some scientists to create alternate species designations.

✓ Evidence of controlled use of fire dates to 1.3 million years ago. This skill presumably enabled *H. erectus* to expand into colder regions of Eurasia as well as to scavenge for and thaw frozen meat. Fire also provided the enormous nutritional benefits of cooked food.

✓ Evidence of handedness in tool manufacture and an enlarged hypoglossal canal support claims of late *H. erectus*' speech and language abilities.

How do Neandertals compare to other members of *Homo*?

✓ Neandertal brains were larger than the modern average size, though their bulging facial features and muscular statures made them susceptible to derision by early Western scientists, especially before the theory of evolution was introduced.

✓ Aided by their implements and cognitive abilities, Neandertals could hunt large game effectively and relied upon these kills during the winter when vegetation was scarce.

✓ Neandertals practiced ritual burial and cared for ill and disabled members of their groups.

✓ Genetic, paleoneurological, anatomical, and artifact evidence all suggest Neandertals were capable of and used language, just as with other members of the genus *Homo* (generally classified as archaic *Homo sapiens*) who were living at that time.

QUESTIONS FOR REFLECTION

1. Members of the genus *Homo* draw upon integrated biological and cultural capabilities to face the challenges of existence. How do these factors play into the designation of species in the fossil record? How is the use of fire by ancestral species present in the fossil record both biologically and culturally?

2. Paleoanthropologists can be characterized as lumpers or splitters depending upon their approach to the identification of species in the fossil record. Which of these approaches do you prefer and why?

3. In his 1871 book *Descent of Man, and Selection in Relation to Sex*, Charles Darwin stated, "Thus man has ultimately become superior to woman. It is indeed fortunate that the law of equal transmission of characters prevails with mammals. Otherwise it is probable that man would have become as superior in mental endowment to woman as the peacock is in ornamental plumage to the peahen." How were the cultural norms of Darwin's time reflected in his statement? Can 21st-century paleoanthropologists speak about differences between the sexes in an evolutionary context without introducing their own cultural biases?

4. Though language itself does not "fossilize," the archaeological and fossil records provide some evidence of the linguistic capabilities of our ancestors. Using the evidence available, what sort of linguistic abilities do you think early *Homo* possessed?

DIGGING INTO ANTHROPOLOGY

Talk Without Speaking

Although paleoanthropologists debate when and how spoken language appeared in our evolutionary history, language makes us human. Can you imagine how difficult it would be to get through your daily life without spoken communication or a sophisticated gestural language such as American Sign Language? Next time you get together with friends, try performing a communal activity using only gestures for 1 hour. It could be preparing a meal, playing a friendly game, or just deciding what activity to do on the weekend. Before you begin, write down your thoughts about when you believe human language appeared. After you are done with the hour without speaking, record your observations on how you communicated without spoken language. Has this activity changed your impressions of who among our early ancestors used spoken language?

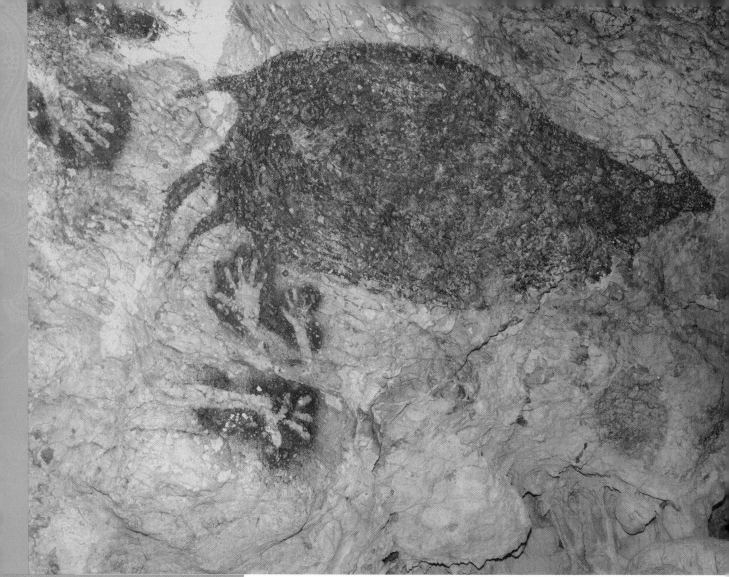

Fadil Aziz/Alcibbum Photograph/Alcibbum Photography/Corbis

CHALLENGE ISSUE

Does our capacity to make art make us human? It had long been thought that the earliest art coincided with the appearance of anatomically modern humans in Europe. The hand stencils and figurative art depicting a *babirusa* (pig-deer) from a cave on the Indonesian island of Sulawesi challenge this notion. When discovered in the 1950s, this art was estimated to be no more than 12,000 years old. But in 2014, scientists pushed back the dates to 35,400 to 39,900 years old, making them the oldest known representatives of their kind. Do the similarities between the Sulawesi and European cave art indicate that our ancestors brought artistic capabilities with them when they spread out of Africa? Or did this art develop independently? Some paleoanthropologists argue that a biological shift accounted for the imagination, symbolism, and cultural sophistication necessary to craft such works. Alternatively, local artists may have been capable of such creations, without needing an influx of new and improved humans. These ancient paintings challenge us to consider whether a biological change was at the root of the creative expression that unites all humankind.

The Global Expansion of *Homo sapiens* and Their Technology

8

In 1868, at the back of a rock shelter near the banks of the bucolic Vézère River, in a region of France now known for its delicious truffle mushrooms, the remains of eight ancient people were discovered. These **Cro-Magnon** people, named after the rock shelter in which they were found (Figure 8.1), resembled contemporary Europeans more than Neandertals and were associated with tools of the **Upper Paleolithic**, the last part of the Old Stone Age. The Cro-Magnon name was extended to thirteen other specimens recovered between 1872 and 1902 in the caves of southwestern France and, since then, to Upper Paleolithic skeletons discovered in other parts of Europe.

The Upper Paleolithic tools associated with Cro-Magnons and the impressive works of art that abound in the caves of this region made scientists and laypeople alike of that time consider them to be particularly clever. By contrast, the prevailing stereotypes of Neandertals characterized them as dim-witted and brutish. Thus, Cro-Magnons, an anatomically modern people with a superior culture, could sweep into Europe and replace a primitive local population.

These early discussions of human origins ethnocentrically focused on the European fossil evidence instead of incorporating evidence from throughout the globe. Today, fossil evidence for early anatomical modernity in Africa, evidence of regional continuity from Asia, new dating of earlier art such as that from Sulawesi, and the cave art at El Castillo in Spain (Pike et al., 2012) have reshaped our understanding of human evolution. Scientific innovations, such as the advent of reliable dating techniques and current breakthroughs in genetics including the recent studies of the Denisovans, allow paleoanthropologists to develop more comprehensive theories for the origins of modern humans.

Cro-Magnon A European people of the Upper Paleolithic after about 36,000 years ago.
Upper Paleolithic The last part (10,000 to 40,000 years ago) of the Old Stone Age, featuring tool industries characterized by long, slim blades and an explosion of creative symbolic forms.

In this chapter you will learn to

- Describe the cultural and technological developments of the Upper Paleolithic era.
- Compare the multiregional continuity and recent African origins hypotheses for modern human origins.
- Identify the emerging diversity of human cultures during the Upper Paleolithic.
- Recognize the legacy of Upper Paleolithic peoples in modern times.
- Describe the evidence of symbolic thought and the expanding role of art in ancient peoples.
- Explain how humans came to inhabit the entire globe.
- Summarize the major biological and cultural features of human evolution.

Figure 8.1 Cro-Magnon
With a high forehead, the Cro-Magnon skull is more like contemporary Europeans compared to the prominent brow ridge and sloping forehead seen in the Neandertal skull. Whether differences in skull shape rather than differences in age account for their cultural distinctions is hotly debated. The more recent Cro-Magnon skull even preserves evidence of continuity in diet with local contemporary French people because it exhibits signs of a fungal infection, perhaps caused by eating tainted mushrooms. Mushrooms are a delicacy in this region to this day.

Upper Paleolithic Peoples: The First Modern Humans

What do we mean by *modernity*? Two characteristics paleoanthropologists look at are skull shape and cultural practices, but it is still a difficult designation to make. Although Cro-Magnons resemble later populations of modern Europeans—in braincase shape, high broad forehead, narrow nasal openings, and common presence of chins—their faces were on average shorter and broader than those of modern Europeans, their brow ridges were a bit more prominent, and their teeth and jaws were as large as those of Neandertals. Some (a skull from the original Cro-Magnon site, for instance) even display the distinctive occipital bun of the Neandertals on the back of the skull. Similarly, early Upper Paleolithic skulls from Brno, Mladec, and Predmosti in the Czech Republic retain heavy brow ridges and Neandertal-like muscle attachments on the back of the skull.

Average brain size actually peaked in Neandertals at 10 percent larger than the contemporary human average. The reduction to today's average size correlates with a reduction in brawn, as bodies have become less massive overall. Living humans, in general, have faces and jaws smaller than those of Neandertals, but there are exceptions. For example, U.S. paleoanthropologists Milford Wolpoff and Rachel Caspari have pointed out that any definition of modernity that excludes Neandertals also excludes substantial numbers of recent and living Aborigines in Australia, although they are, quite obviously, a contemporary people (Figure 8.2). The fact is, no multidimensional diagnosis of anatomical modernity includes all living humans while excluding archaic populations (Wolpoff & Caspari, 1997).

Defining modernity in terms of culture also raises questions. The appearance of modern-sized brains in archaic *Homo* was related to increased reliance on cultural adaptation, but the Upper Paleolithic was a time of great technological innovation and creativity. Upper Paleolithic toolkits contain a preponderance of blade tools, with flint flakes at least twice as long as they are wide. The earliest blade tools come from sites in Africa, but these tools do not make up the majority of the tool types until well into the Upper Paleolithic.

Technological improvements may have reduced the intensity of selective pressures that had previously favored especially massive robust bodies, jaws, and teeth. A marked reduction in overall muscularity accompanied the new emphasis on elongated tools with greater mechanical advantages, more effective techniques of hafting, a switch from thrusting to throwing spears, and the development of net hunting. A climate shift from the extreme cold that prevailed in Eurasia during the last Ice Age to milder conditions may have diminished selective pressure for short stature as an adaptation to conserve body heat.

The Human Origins Debate

On a biological level, the great human origins debate distills down to the question of whether one, some, or all populations of the archaic groups played a role in the evolution of modern *Homo sapiens*. Those supporting the multiregional hypothesis argue for a simultaneous local transition from *Homo erectus* to modern *Homo sapiens* throughout the parts of the world inhabited by members of the genus *Homo*. By contrast, those supporting a theory of recent African origins argue that all contemporary peoples derive from one single population of archaic *Homo sapiens* from Africa. This model proposes that the improved cultural capabilities of anatomically modern humans allowed this group to replace other archaic forms as they began to migrate out of Africa sometime after 100,000 years ago. We next explore both theories in detail.

The Multiregional Hypothesis

Shared regional characteristics among African, Chinese, and Southeast Asian fossils of archaic *Homo sapiens* imply

David Gray/Reuters/Corbis

Figure 8.2 A Problematic Definition

Living people today such as Aborigines in Australia do not meet the definition of anatomical modernity proposed in the recent African origins model. Some paleoanthropologists suggest that this proves the definition itself is problematic. All living people are clearly full-fledged members of the species *Homo sapiens.*

genetic continuity within these respective populations, from *H. erectus* through to modern *H. sapiens*. For example, in China, Pleistocene fossils from the genus *Homo* consistently have small forward-facing cheeks and flatter faces than their contemporaries elsewhere, as is still true today. In Southeast Asia and Australia, by contrast, skulls are consistently robust, with huge cheeks and forward projection of the jaws. As new molecular research techniques have developed, scientists have amassed genetic data to support the physical evidence.

In this model, gene flow among populations keeps the human species unified throughout the Pleistocene. No speciation events remove ancestral populations such as Asian *H. erectus*, Denisovans, or Neandertals from the line leading to *H. sapiens*. Although proponents of the **multiregional hypothesis** accept the idea of continuity from the earliest European fossils through the Neandertals to living people, many other paleoanthropologists reject the idea that Neandertals were involved in the ancestry of modern Europeans.

The Recent African Origins Hypothesis

The **recent African origins hypothesis** (also called the *Eve hypothesis* or the *out of Africa hypothesis*) states that anatomically modern humans descended from one specific population of *Homo sapiens*, replacing not just the Neandertals but other populations of archaic *H. sapiens* as our ancestors spread out from their original homeland. This idea did not originate from fossil evidence but from a relatively new technique pioneered in the 1980s that uses mitochondrial DNA (mtDNA) to reconstruct family trees (Figure 8.3).

multiregional hypothesis The hypothesis that modern humans originated through a process of simultaneous local transition from *Homo erectus* to *Homo sapiens* throughout the inhabited world.

recent African origins hypothesis The hypothesis that modern humans are all derived from one single population of archaic *Homo sapiens* who migrated out of Africa after 100,000 years ago, replacing all other archaic forms due to their superior cultural capabilities; also called the *Eve hypothesis* and the *out of Africa hypothesis.*

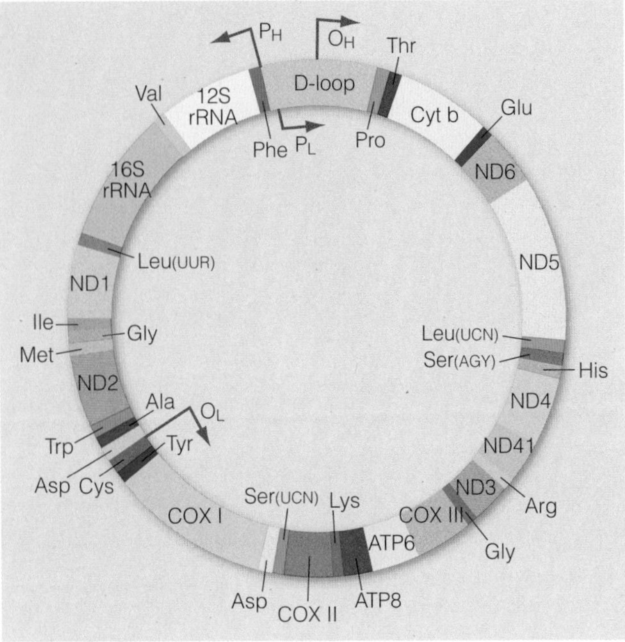

Figure 8.3 Mitochondrial DNA
The 16,569 bases in mitochondrial DNA (mtDNA) are organized into circular chromosomes present in large numbers in every cell. The human mtDNA sequence has been entirely sequenced, with functional genes identified. Because mtDNA is maternally inherited and not subject to recombination, it can be used to establish evolutionary relationships. However, population size impacts the preservation of variation in the mtDNA genome and complicates using contemporary mtDNA variation to calibrate a molecular clock.

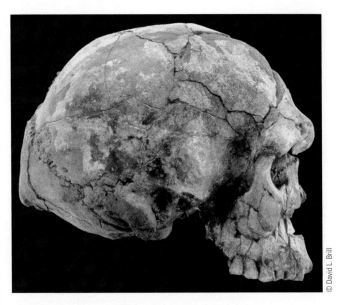

© David L. Brill

Figure 8.4 African Evidence for Anatomical Modernity
The recently discovered well-preserved specimens from Herto, Ethiopia, provide the best fossil evidence in support of the recent African origins hypothesis. Though these fossils unquestionably possess an anatomically modern appearance, they are still relatively robust. In addition, it is not clear whether the higher skull and forehead indicate superior cultural abilities.

Unlike nuclear DNA (in the cell nucleus), mtDNA is located in the mitochondria, the cellular structures that produce the energy needed to keep cells alive. Because sperm contribute virtually no mtDNA to the fertilized egg, mtDNA is inherited from one's mother and is not subject to recombination through meiosis and fertilization with each succeeding generation as is nuclear DNA. Therefore, changes in mtDNA over time occur only through mutation.

By comparing the mtDNA of living individuals from diverse geographic populations, anthropologists and molecular biologists seek to determine when and where modern *Homo sapiens* originated. As widely reported in the popular press, preliminary results suggest that the mitochondrial DNA of all living humans could be traced back to a "mitochondrial Eve" who lived in Africa about 200,000 years ago. If so, all other populations of archaic *H. sapiens*, as well as non-African *H. erectus*, would have to be ruled out of the ancestry of modern humans.

For many years, the recent African origins theory has been weakened by the lack of good fossil evidence from Africa. In 2003, however, skulls of two adults and one child, discovered in Ethiopia in 1997 (see Anthropologists of Note), were described as anatomically modern (**Figure 8.4**) and

were reconstructed and dated to 160,000 years ago (White et al., 2003). The discoverers of these fossils called them *Homo sapiens idaltu* (meaning "elder" in the local Afar language). Although conceding that the skulls are robust, they believe that these skulls have conclusively proved the recent African origins hypothesis, relegating Neandertals to a side branch of human evolution.

Reconciling the Evidence

For many years, the recent African origins hypothesis has been the majority position among Western paleoanthropologists, but it does not prevail throughout the international scientific community. Some Chinese paleoanthropologists, for example, generally favor the multiregional hypothesis because it fits well with the fossil discoveries from Asia and Australia. By contrast, the recent African origins hypothesis depends more upon the interpretation of fossils and cultural remains from Europe, Africa, and Southwest Asia.

Recent sequencing of the entire human genome for a variety of contemporary populations—as well as for fossil hominins including Cro-Magnons, Neandertals, and Denisovans—has added substantially to the evidence. Genetic studies show that features unique to the Neandertal genome remain in contemporary humans, particularly those of regions inhabited by Neandertals in the past.

ANTHROPOLOGISTS OF NOTE

Berhane Asfaw (b. 1953) • Svante Pääbo (b. 1955)

Born in Addis Ababa, Ethiopia, in 1953, **Berhane Asfaw** is a world-renowned paleoanthropologist leading major expeditions in Ethiopia. He is coleader of the international Middle Awash Research Project—the research team responsible for the discovery of spectacular ancestral fossils dating from the entire 6-million-year course of human evolutionary history, including *Ardipithecus ramidus, Australopithecus afarensis, Australopithecus garhi, Homo erectus,* and, most recently, the *Homo sapiens idaltu* fossils from Herto, Ethiopia.

Paleogeneticist Svante Pääbo has orchestrated some of the first studies of the genome of Neandertals and other ancient hominins.

Berhane Asfaw has been involved with most of the major recent finds in Ethiopia and has trained a generation of African paleoanthropologists.

At the June 2003 press conference, organized by Teshome Toga, Ethiopia's minister of culture, Asfaw described the Herto specimens as the oldest anatomically modern humans, likening Ethiopia to the Garden of Eden. This conference marked a shift in the Ethiopian government's stance toward the paleoanthropological research spanning Asfaw's career. Previous discoveries in the Middle Awash were also very important, but the government did not participate in or support this research.

Asfaw entered the discipline of paleoanthropology through a program administered by the Leakey Foundation providing fellowships for Africans to pursue graduate studies in Europe and the United States. Since this program's inception in the late 1970s, the Leakey Foundation has awarded sixty-eight fellowships totaling $1.2 million to Kenyans, Ethiopians, and Tanzanians to pursue graduate education in paleoanthropology.

Asfaw, mentored by U.S. paleoanthropologist Desmond Clark at the University of California, Berkeley, was among the earliest fellows in this program. They first met in 1979 when Asfaw was a senior studying geology in Addis Ababa. Asfaw obtained his doctorate in 1988 and returned to Ethiopia, where he had few Ethiopian anthropological colleagues, and the government had halted fossil exploration. Since that time, Asfaw has recruited and mentored many Ethiopian scholars and now has about a dozen on his team. Local scientists can protect the antiquities, safeguard fossil specimens, and mobilize government support. Asfaw's leadership in paleoanthropology has played a key role in helping the government recognize how important prehistory is for Ethiopia.

Svante Pääbo, named in 2007 by *Time* magazine as one of the 100 most influential people in the world, has revolutionized our understanding of paleogenetics and human evolution. Born and raised in Sweden, he is the son of an Estonian refugee and a Swedish Nobel Prize winner in biochemistry. As a boy, he was fascinated by Egyptian archaeology, and that interest led to his study of Egyptology at Uppsala University before he switched to medicine. Pursuing a doctorate in molecular genetics, he applied DNA cloning technologies to ancient human remains and demonstrated DNA survival in a 2,400-year-old Egyptian mummy.

After completing his doctorate in 1986, Pääbo joined the genetics laboratory at the University of California, Berkeley, headed by Allan Wilson, who had invented the molecular clock (see Chapter 5). This lab used the newly invented polymerase chain reaction (PCR) technique. Focusing on evolutionary genetics, Pääbo developed a method to analyze the DNA from ancient remains, which is often damaged and contaminated.

Pääbo accepted an academic position in Germany in 1990 and soon achieved scientific success: sequencing Neandertal DNA, determining the small percentage of genetic difference between humans and chimpanzees, and linking the FOXP2 gene to language. In 1997, he became the founding director of the Evolutionary Genetics Department at the Max Planck Institute for Evolutionary Anthropology. Based on high-throughput DNA sequencing technology, his team sequenced the draft genome of a Neandertal, based on DNA traced from 45,000-year-old fossils, and discovered genetic evidence of interbreeding between archaic and anatomically modern humans. News of his scientific overview of the genome (published in 2009 with fifty-three coauthors) created a sensation worldwide.

In 2012, Pääbo's team extracted DNA from a small human fossil excavated in a Siberian cave, which they determined was almost 80,000 years old. After mapping its genome, the team concluded that the fossil represented an unknown sister group of the Neandertals, now named Denisovans. This discovery demonstrates interbreeding between ancestors of modern *Homo sapiens* and Neandertals, as well as Denisovans, between 30,000 and 100,000 years ago.

Pääbo's pioneering work challenges contemporary evolutionary theory in several ways: It reveals that a small percentage of human DNA in living populations is derived from these two archaic human groups; it advances our understanding of prehistoric population movements; it challenges the recent African origins hypothesis; and, finally, it shows that the divisions between human groups are not natural but are cultural.

Further, some contemporary Melanesians share 4 to 6 percent of their DNA with Denisovans, as we discuss in a moment. As we will see, paleoanthropologists on both sides of the modern human origins debate marshal genetic, anatomical, and cultural evidence to both support and critique each hypothesis.

The Genetic Evidence

Though genetic evidence had been the cornerstone of the recent African origins hypothesis, reanalysis of the original mitochondrial DNA data set showed that Africa was not the sole source of mtDNA in modern humans. In addition, because both hypotheses of human origins recognize African roots of the human line, though at different times, the genetic evidence could simply indicate African origins of the genus *Homo* instead of the more recent species *Homo sapiens*. Assuming a different rate of molecular change will lead to different conclusions.

DNA analyses contain other problematic assumptions. For example, these models assume a steady rate of mutation, although mutation can be notoriously uneven. They also rely upon the assumption that selective pressures do not impact mtDNA, when in fact variants have been implicated in epilepsy and in a disease of the eye.

Another issue is that DNA is seen as traveling exclusively *from* Africa, when it is known that, over the past 10,000 years, there has been plenty of movement of humans *into* Africa as well. Studies of DNA carried on the Y chromosome (the sex chromosome inherited exclusively in the male line) provide some evidence of this reverse migration among some African populations. These data all confirm the importance of gene flow in human evolutionary history. Where the hypotheses differ is in terms of whether this gene flow occurred over the course of 200,000 years or 2 million years.

Starting in 1997, molecular paleoanthropologists under the direction of Swedish paleogeneticist Svante Pääbo of the Max Planck Institute (see Anthropologists of Note) began to study the mitochondrial DNA of fossil specimens, starting with the extraction of mtDNA from the original German Neandertal remains. Today, this work has expanded to nuclear DNA including mapping the entire Neandertal genome in 2010 (Green et al., 2010), as well as that of the ancient Denisovans (Max Planck Institute for Evolutionary Anthropology, 2014) and Cro-Magnons. Now scientists can quantify how much of a genome the ancient peoples share with contemporary peoples.

For example, living Eurasian peoples share between 2 and 4 percent of their genetic identity with Neandertals, and contemporary Melanesians share 4 to 6 percent with ancient Denisovans. Other evidence of gene flow among ancient populations comes from fossils, such as the genome sequenced from a 45,000-year-old thighbone discovered in Siberia that contains some of the same Neandertal strands identified in contemporary populations (Fu et al.,

2014). Both of these observations support regional continuity, although the case might seem to be less strong in Neandertals. The lower percentage of genetic identity, however, does not necessarily exclude a group from human ancestry. The amount of isolation and the inflow of new genes have an impact on the precise percentages of retained ancient molecular features. The Denisovan features may be better preserved in more isolated island populations compared to the Eurasian mainland, which was inhabited by Neandertals and where gene flow occurred more readily.

Further evidence from Australia illustrates that specific gene sequences can "go extinct" though the species itself does not. In this case, a mitochondrial DNA sequence present in a skeleton from Australia that is 40,000 to 62,000 years old (and that everyone agrees is anatomically modern) does not appear in recent native Australians (Gibbons, 2001a). In short, the genetic evidence that was once the mainstay of the recent African origins hypothesis has now come to demonstrate the gene flow among populations that has always been central to the multiregional continuity hypothesis. Many scientists propose a blending of multiregional continuity and the recent African origins hypotheses.

The Anatomical Evidence

Though the recent fossil discoveries certainly provide evidence of the earliest anatomically modern specimens in Africa, they do not resolve the relationship between biological change in the shape of the skull and cultural change as preserved in the archaeological record (**Figure 8.5**). The changes in the archaeological record and the appearance of anatomically modern skulls are separated by some 100,000 years. The evidence from Southwest Asia is particularly interesting in this regard. Here, at a variety of sites dated to between 50,000 and 100,000 years ago, there are fossils described as both anatomically modern and Neandertal, and they are associated with Mousterian technology.

Nevertheless, recent African origins proponents argue that anatomically modern peoples coexisted for a time with other archaic populations until the superior cultural capacities of the "moderns" resulted in extinction of the archaic peoples. Especially clear evidence of this is said to exist in Europe, where Neandertals and moderns are believed to have coexisted in close proximity between 30,000 and 40,000 years ago. However, defining fossils as either Neandertals or moderns illustrates the difficulty with defining a distinct biological species, given the variation found in humans.

If we think in terms of varied populations, as seen in living humans today, we find that features reminiscent of modern humans can be discerned in some of the later Neandertals. A specimen from Saint-Césaire in France, for example, has a higher forehead and a notable chin. A number of other Neandertals, too, show incipient chin development as well as reduced facial protrusion and smaller brow ridges. Conversely, the earliest anatomically modern human skulls from Europe often exhibit features reminiscent

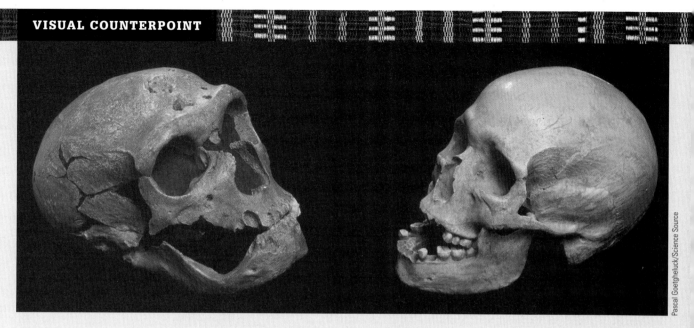

Pascal Goetgheluck/Science Source

Figure 8.5 Neandertals Compared to Recent *Homo sapiens*
A comparison of the Neandertal (*left*) and the contemporary *Homo sapiens* (*right*) shows that although both possess large brains, there are distinctive differences in the shape of the skull. The Neandertal has a large face, pronounced brow ridges, and a low, sloping forehead, whereas the contemporary *H. sapiens* has a high forehead and a chin. The back of the Neandertal, though not visible from this angle, is robust (as seen in the Herto skull pictured in Figure 8.4). In what other ways is Herto like these two specimens? How do these three skulls compare to the Cro-Magnon skull pictured in Figure 8.1?

of Neandertals (see Chapter 7). In addition, some typical Neandertal features such as the occipital bun are found in diverse living populations today such as Bushmen from southern Africa, Finns and Sámi from Scandinavia, and Aborigines from Australia. Accordingly, we might view the population of this region between 30,000 and 40,000 years ago as a varied one, with some individuals retaining a stronger Neandertal phenotype and others exhibiting the prominence of more modern characteristics (Figure 8.6). If all these groups were members of the same species, gene flow would be expected, and individuals would express a mosaic of traits. The genetic evidence supports such blending of biological traits, which accords with archaeological evidence that the intellectual abilities of late Neandertals were no different from those of early moderns.

The Cultural Evidence

Neandertals and anatomically modern humans alike used Mousterian toolkits during the Middle Paleolithic. At the time of the Upper Paleolithic transition, the Neandertals of Europe developed their own Upper Paleolithic technology (the Châtelperronian) comparable to the industries used by anatomically modern *Homo sapiens*. Around 40,000 years ago, a new Upper Paleolithic technology known as the **Aurignacian tradition**—named after Aurignac, France,

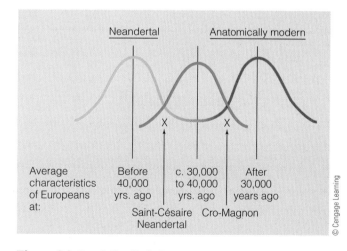

© Cengage Learning

Figure 8.6 Population Variation
This graph portrays a shift in average characteristics of an otherwise varied population over time from Neandertal to more modern features. Between 30,000 and 40,000 years ago, we would expect to find individuals with characteristics such as those of the Saint-Césaire Neandertal and the almost (but not quite) modern Cro-Magnon. Before and after this period of transition, both Neandertals and moderns had more classic features.

Aurignacian tradition Toolmaking tradition in Europe at the beginning of the Upper Paleolithic.

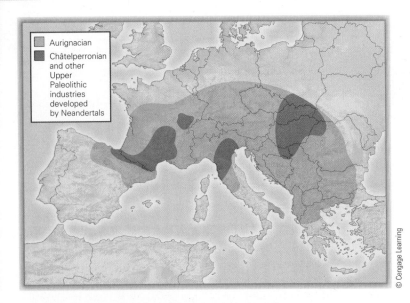

Figure 8.7 Aurignacian and Châtelperronian Traditions
Between 30,000 and 36,500 years ago, Upper Paleolithic industries—developed from the Mousterian tradition by European Neandertals—coexisted with the Aurignacian industry, which is usually associated with anatomically modern humans.

where tools of this sort were first discovered—appeared in Europe (**Figure 8.7**). Paleoanthropologists generally consider anatomically modern humans who spread into Europe from Southwest Asia to be the makers of Aurignacian tools. However, Neandertal remains were found

in association with an Aurignacian split-bone point at the central European site of Vindija, Croatia (Karavanić & Smith, 2000).

Some have argued that the Upper Paleolithic technology of the Neandertals was a crude imitation of the true technological advancements practiced by anatomically modern humans. In some respects, however, Neandertals outdid their anatomically modern contemporaries, as in the use of red ochre, a substance less frequently used by Aurignacian peoples than by their late Neandertal neighbors. This cannot be a case of borrowing ideas and techniques from Aurignacians because these developments clearly predate the Aurignacian (Zilhão, 2000).

Coexistence and Cultural Continuity

Neandertals and anatomically modern humans also coexisted in Southwest Asia long before the cultural innovations of the Upper Paleolithic (**Figure 8.8**). Here neither the skeletal nor the archaeological evidence supports cultural difference between the fossil groups or absolute biological difference. Although Neandertal skeletons are clearly present at sites such as the caves of Kebara and Shanidar in Israel and

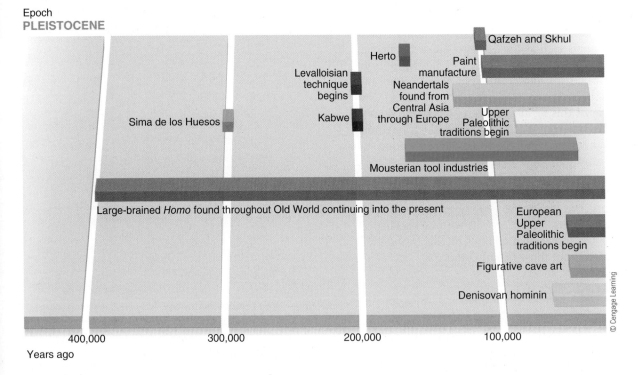

Figure 8.8 The Cultural Milestones in Human Evolution
Around 400,000 years ago, large-brained members of the genus *Homo* began to be found throughout Africa and Eurasia; corresponding cultural changes are evident as well. Analyses of DNA recovered from the Asian Denisovan hominins and late Neandertals indicate a deeper time depth for these "sibling" fossil groups whose lines diverged around 640,000 ago. Of course, large-brained members of the genus *Homo* continue into the present—all members of the unified species *Homo sapiens.*

Iraq, respectively, skeletons from some older sites have been described as anatomically modern. At the cave site of Qafzeh near Nazareth in Israel, for example, 90,000-year-old skeletons show none of the Neandertal hallmarks, although their faces and bodies are large and heavily built by today's standards. A statistical study comparing skull measurements determined that those from Qafzeh fell between the anatomically modern and the Neandertal norms, with slightly more similarity to the Neandertal (Brace, 2000).

Skeletons from Skhul, a site on Mount Carmel of the same period, were also part of a population whose continuous range of variation included individuals with markedly Neandertal characteristics. Individuals living at Skhul and Qafzeh were making and using the same Mousterian tools as those at Kebara and Shanidar, a fact that undercuts the notion of biologically distinct groups with different cultural abilities. Indeed, recent genetic studies also support the notion that these were not biologically distinct groups.

The examination of sites continuously inhabited throughout the Upper Pleistocene provides no significant evidence for behavioral differences between the Middle Paleolithic and early Upper Paleolithic at these sites. For example, the Upper Paleolithic peoples who used Kebara Cave continued to live in exactly the same way as their Neandertal predecessors: They procured the same foods, processed them similarly, used comparable hearths, and disposed of their trash in the same way. The only evident difference is that the Neandertals did not use small stones or cobbles to bank their fires for warmth as did their Upper Paleolithic successors.

Nevertheless, by 28,000 years ago, many of the extreme anatomical features seen in archaic groups like Neandertals seem to disappear from the European and Southwest and Central Asian fossil record. Instead, people with higher foreheads, smoother brow ridges, and distinct chins seemed to have Eurasia more or less to themselves. However, an examination of the full range of individual human variation across the globe and into the present reveals contemporary humans with skulls not meeting the anatomical definition of modernity proposed in the standard evolutionary arguments (recall Figure 8.2). Similarly, living people today possess many Neandertal features such as the occipital buns mentioned earlier. Human populations both now and during the Upper Paleolithic contain considerable physical variability.

Just how much gene flow took place among ancient human populations cannot be known precisely, but the sudden appearance of novel traits in one region later than their appearance elsewhere provides evidence of its occurrence. For example, some Upper Paleolithic remains from North Africa exhibit the kind of midfacial flatness previously seen only in East Asian fossils; similarly, various Cro-Magnon fossils from Europe show the short upper jaws, horizontally oriented cheekbones, and rectangular eye orbits previously seen in East Asians. Conversely, the round orbits, large frontal sinuses, and thin cranial bones seen in some archaic *H. sapiens* skulls from China represent the first appearance there of traits that have greater antiquity in Europe. The movement of these physical traits has a complex genetic basis that depends upon gene flow among populations.

Humans have a remarkable tendency to swap genes between populations, even in the face of cultural barriers. So do our primate cousins who tend to produce hybrids when two subspecies (and sometimes even species) come into contact either naturally or when bred in captivity. Moreover, without such gene flow, evolution inevitably would have resulted in the appearance of multiple species of modern humans, something that clearly has not happened. In fact, the low level of genetic differentiation among modern human populations can be explained easily as a consequence of high levels of gene flow.

Race and Human Evolution

The Neandertal question involves far more than simple interpretation of the fossil evidence. It raises fundamental issues about the relationship between biological and cultural variation. Can a series of biological features indicate particular cultural abilities?

As we examined the fossil record throughout this chapter and others, we made inferences about the cultural capabilities of our ancestors based on biological features in combination with archaeological features. The increased brain size of *Homo habilis* around 2.5 million years ago supported the notion that these ancestors were capable of more complex cultural activities than australopithecines, including the manufacture of stone tools. When we get closer to the present, can we make the same kinds of assumptions? Can we say that only the anatomically modern humans, with high foreheads and reduced brow ridges, and not archaic *Homo sapiens*, even with their modern-sized brains, were capable of making sophisticated tools and representational art?

Supporters of the multiregional hypothesis argue that we cannot. They suggest that using a series of biological features to represent a type of human being (Neandertals) with certain cultural capacities (inferior) is like making assumptions about cultural capabilities of living humans based on their appearance. In living peoples, such an assumption involves stereotyping or even racism. Supporters of the recent African origins hypothesis counter that because their theory embraces African human origins, it could hardly be considered prejudicial.

Although paleoanthropologists all acknowledge African origins for the first bipeds and the genus *Homo*, considerable disagreement exists with regard to the interpretation of the relationship between biological change and cultural change as we approach the present. The fossil

Upper Paleolithic Tools

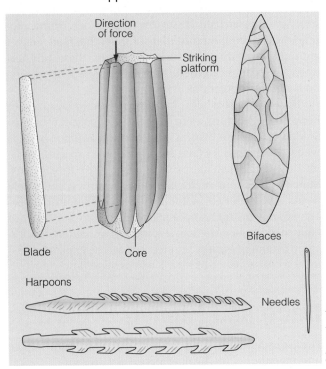

Figure 8.9 Upper Paleolithic Industries
The techniques of the Upper Paleolithic allowed for the manufacture of a wide variety of tools including the efficient production of blade tools from carefully prepared cores. In addition, pressure-flaking techniques allowed toolmakers to work with bone and antler, as well as stone, to produce excellently shaped harpoons and eyed needles and to craft finely wrought leaf-shaped bifaces characteristic of the Solutrean industry of Europe.

and archaeological evidence from the Middle Paleolithic does not indicate a simple one-to-one correspondence between cultural innovations and a biological change preserved in the shape of the skull.

Upper Paleolithic Technology

In the Upper Paleolithic new techniques of core preparation allowed for more intensive production of highly standardized blades and permitted the proliferation of this tool type. The toolmaker formed a cylindrical core, struck the blade off near the edge of the core, and repeated this procedure, going around the core in one direction until finishing near its center (Figure 8.9). The procedure is analogous to peeling long leaves off an artichoke. With this **blade technique**, an Upper Paleolithic flint-knapper could get 23 meters (75 feet) of working edge from a 1-kilogram (2-pound) core; a Mousterian knapper could get only 1.8 meters (6 feet) from the same-sized core.

Other efficient techniques of tool manufacture also came into common use at this time. One such method is **pressure flaking**, in which a bone, antler, or wooden tool is used to press rather than strike off small flakes as the final step in stone tool manufacture (Figure 8.10). The advantage of this technique is that the toolmaker has greater control over the final shape of the tool than is possible with percussion flaking alone. The Solutrean laurel leaf bifaces found in Spain and France are examples of this technique. The longest of these tools is 33 centimeters (13 inches) in length but less than a centimeter (about a quarter of an inch) thick. Through pressure flaking, tools could be worked with great precision into a variety of final forms, and worn tools could be effectively resharpened over and over until they were too small for further use.

Although invented in the Middle Paleolithic, the **burin**, a tool with a chisel-like edge, became more common in the Upper Paleolithic. Burins facilitated the working of bone, horn, antler, and ivory into useful things such as fishhooks, harpoons, and eyed needles. These implements made life easier for *Homo sapiens*, especially in colder northern regions where the ability to stitch together animal hides was particularly important for warmth.

Figure 8.10 Pressure Flaking
Flint-knapper Willy Kemps, like others engaged in experimental archaeology, has mastered ancient toolmaking techniques such as pressure flaking, as well as an understanding of the raw materials used at various sites. Here, he uses a moose-antler tool to press rather than strike small flakes off the edges of a core. This technique allows flint-knappers past and present to create tools far more intricate than those of the Mousterian, as you can see from his finished products.

blade technique A method of stone tool manufacture in which long, parallel-sided flakes are struck off the edges of a specially prepared core.

pressure flaking A technique of stone tool manufacture in which a bone, antler, or wooden tool is used to press, rather than strike off, small flakes from a piece of flint or similar stone.

burin A stone tool with chisel-like edges used for working bone, horn, antler, and ivory.

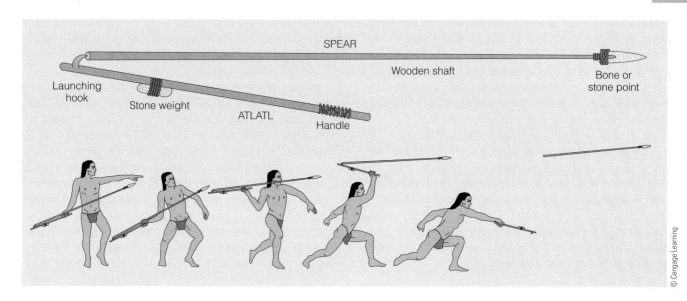

Figure 8.11 Spear-Throwers

Spear-throwers (atlatls) allowed Upper Paleolithic individuals to throw spears at animals from a safe distance while still maintaining reasonable speed and accuracy. Upper Paleolithic artists frequently combined artistic expression with practical function, ornamenting their spear-throwers with animal figures.

The spear-thrower, also known by its Aztec (Nahuatl) name *atlatl*, appeared at this time as well. Atlatls are devices made of wood, horn, or bone, one end of which is gripped in the hunter's hand while the other end has a hole or hook where the end of the spear is placed. It is held so as to effectively extend the length of the hunter's arm, thereby increasing the velocity and thrust of the spear when thrown, allowing it to pierce thick hides of game. The greater thrust made possible through the use of a spear-thrower greatly added to the efficiency of the spear as a hunting tool (**Figure 8.11**). Ancient toolmakers often carved elaborate animal images into the handles for their spear-throwers (**Figure 8.12**).

With handheld spears, hunters had to get close to their prey to make the kill. Because many of the animals they hunted were large and fierce, this was a dangerous business. The need to get within close striking range and the improbability of an instant kill exposed the hunter to considerable risk. But with the spear-thrower, the effective killing distance was increased; experiments demonstrate that the effective killing distance of a spear when used with a spear-thrower is between 18 and 27 meters (60 to 88 feet) and significantly less without.

Hunters can safely shorten the killing distance when their kill is assured. The use of poison on spear tips, as employed by contemporary hunters such as the Hadza of Tanzania, decreases the risk to a hunter at shorter range. The archaeological record provides evidence of this innovation with the invention of tiny, sharp, stone blades that could possibly serve as dart tips and provide a vehicle for poison delivery. The earliest examples of these "microliths" began during the Upper Paleolithic

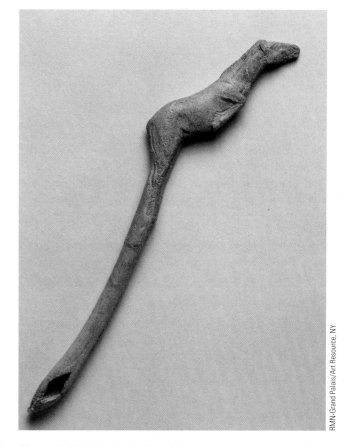

Figure 8.12 Early Production Art

Some atlatl handles appear to have been relatively mass produced, with identical animal figures such as this 15,000-year-old horse appearing in the archaeological record multiple times. This could be the signature of an individual toolmaker or of a specific cultural group, or it might relate to the hunting of a particular animal.

in Africa but did not become widespread until the Mesolithic or Middle Stone Age, as will be described in detail in Chapter 9.

Another important innovation, net hunting, appeared sometime between 22,000 and 29,000 years ago. Knotted nets, made from the fibers of wild plants such as hemp or nettle, left their impression on the clay floors of huts when people walked on them. When the huts later burned, these impressions, baked into the earth, provide evidence that suggests such nets existed. Their use accounts for the high number of hare, fox, and other small mammal and bird bones at archaeological sites. Like historically known and contemporary net hunters, such as the Mbuti of the Congo, everyone—men, women, and children—probably participated, frightening animals with loud noises to drive them to where hunters were stationed with their nets. This method lets hunters amass large amounts of meat without the requirement of great speed or strength.

The invention of the bow and arrow, which appeared first in Africa and arrived in Europe at the end of the Upper Paleolithic, marked another innovation in hunting techniques. The bow improves safety as well as stealth by increasing the distance between hunter and prey. Beyond 24 meters (79 feet), the accuracy and penetration of a spear thrown with a spear-thrower diminishes considerably whereas even a poor bow will shoot an arrow farther, with greater accuracy and penetrating power. A good bow, effective even at nearly 91 meters (300 feet), dramatically reduced the hunter's risk of being seriously injured by an animal fighting for survival as well as the chance of startling an animal and triggering its flight.

Upper Paleolithic industries allowed past peoples to adapt specifically to the various environments in which they were living. Boneyards containing thousands of animal skeletons indicate just how proficient people had become at securing food. For example, at Solutré in France, over a period of many years, Upper Paleolithic hunters killed 10,000 horses; at Predmosti in the Czech Republic, they were responsible for the deaths of 1,000 mammoths. The favored big game of European hunters, however, was reindeer, which they killed in even greater numbers.

Upper Paleolithic Art

Although tools and weapons demonstrate the ingenuity of Upper Paleolithic peoples, artistic expression provides the best evidence of their creativity. Some have argued that this artistry was made possible by a newly evolved biological ability to manipulate symbols and make images. However, the modern-sized brains of archaic *Homo sapiens* and increasingly compelling evidence of the presence of language or behaviors involving symbolism—such as burials—undercut this notion. Like agriculture, which

came later (see Chapter 9), the artistic explosion may have been no more than a consequence of innovations made by a people who already had possessed that capacity for tens of thousands of years.

In fact, just as many of the distinctive tools that were commonly used in Upper Paleolithic times first appear in the Middle Paleolithic, so too do objects of art. In Southwest Asia, a crude figurine made of volcanic tuff may be as ancient as 250,000 years old. Although some scholars contest whether this was carved, others believe that it indicates that people had the ability to carve all sorts of things from wood, a substance easier to fashion than volcanic tuff but rarely preserved for long periods of time. But with the Upper Paleolithic transition, the archaeological record becomes quite rich with figurative art that has no apparent utilitarian function. Most notable among these are the various Venus figurines found throughout Eurasia (**Figure 8.13**).

Middle Paleolithic archaeological contexts in various parts of the world also included ochre "crayons" used by ancient peoples to decorate or mark. In southern Africa, for example, regular use of yellow and red ochre goes back 130,000 years, with some evidence as old as 200,000 years. Systematic production of paint took place by 100,000 years ago, as seen in the South African paint factory mentioned in Chapter 7. In that site, the Blombos Cave, archaeologists discovered large abalone shells and specialized stones used for grinding ochre pigment. They also found the shoulder bone of a seal from which marrow, a key ingredient in paint, had been removed. Ancient artists had apparently blended the pigment with the marrow, charcoal, and water to make paint. Associated artifacts at this site include large crosshatched chunks of ochre as well as beads smeared with ochre dating to 77,000 years ago.

Ancient people may well have used these pigmented paints on their bodies, as well as objects such as beads and the 50,000-year-old mammoth-tooth *churinga* described in Chapter 7. Recall as well the use of ochre in burials in Mousterian contexts. The timeline in **Figure 8.14** shows some of the cultural events of the Upper Paleolithic and the years leading into it.

Music

Evidence that music played a role in the lives of Upper Paleolithic peoples is documented through the presence of bone flutes and whistles in various sites, the most recently discovered dated to 35,000 years old. But again, such instruments may have their origin in Middle Paleolithic prototypes, such as the probable Neandertal flute discussed in Chapter 7. Although we cannot know just where and when it happened, some genius discovered that bows could do more than kill prey; they could make music as well. Because the bow and arrow first appeared during the Upper Paleolithic, the musical bow likely got its start then as well. The oldest of the stringed instruments, the

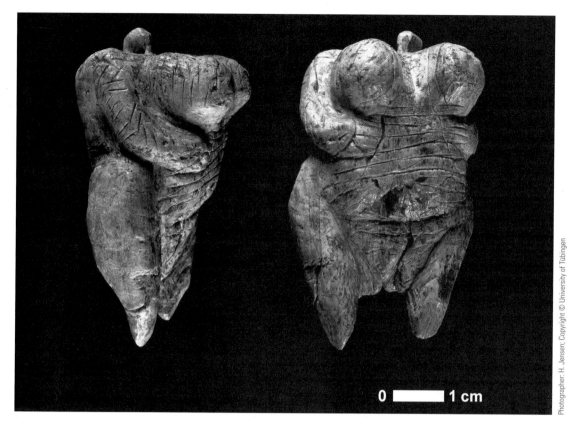

Photographer: H. Jensen; Copyright © University of Tübingen

0 ▬▬▬ 1 cm

Figure 8.13 **The Hohle Fels Cave Venus**
This tiny 35,000-year-old Venus figurine (about the size and weight of a small cluster of grapes) was discovered in the archaeologically rich Hohle Fels Cave in southwestern Germany in 2008. Because it was associated with the earliest presence of undisputed *Homo sapiens* in Europe, the piece changed paleoanthropological interpretations of the origins of figurative art. Prior to this discovery, the earliest figurative art had included only representations of animals; human figurines did not appear until about 30,000 years ago. The exaggerated breasts and vulva and stylized markings on this carving, as on similar prehistoric statuettes known as Venus figurines, indicate the importance of female fertility to our ancestors. Some suggest that these figurines demonstrate that our ancestors may have worshiped the power of females to give birth.

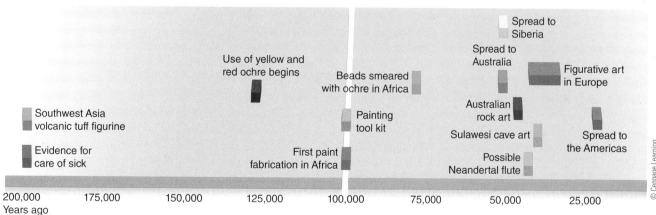

Epoch
PLEISTOCENE

Spread to Siberia

Spread to Australia

Use of yellow and red ochre begins

Beads smeared with ochre in Africa

Figurative art in Europe

Southwest Asia volcanic tuff figurine

Painting tool kit

Australian rock art

Evidence for care of sick

First paint fabrication in Africa

Sulawesi cave art

Spread to the Americas

Possible Neandertal flute

200,000   175,000   150,000   125,000   100,000   75,000   50,000   25,000
Years ago

© Cengage Learning

Figure 8.14 **Cultural Innovations of the Upper Paleolithic**
This timeline indicates the dates for some cultural innovations associated with the Upper Paleolithic. Evidence supports the presence of other innovations, such as deliberate burial and music during this time period.

Figure 8.15 Entoptic Phenomena in Cave Art
These rock art paintings from the Kimberley Region of western Australia depict things seen by dancers communicating with Wandjina (creation spirits) while in states of trance. Simple geometric designs such as zigzags, notches, dots, and spirals (as on the cave ceiling) as well as human and animal figures are common in these paintings.

musical bow ultimately made possible the rich array of such instruments in use today.

Cave or Rock Art

Some of the earliest evidence of cave art comes from Australia and dates back at least 45,000 years. This consists entirely of geometric patterns and repetitive motifs. The cave art from Sulawesi described in the chapter opener is nearly as old. Figurative pictures go back 40,000 years in Europe while both engravings and paintings of the same age come from rock shelters and outcrops in southern Africa. The 100,000-year-old paint factory in South Africa provides evidence that pictorial art may have appeared there even earlier. Bushmen peoples have continued to make various forms of rock art into the present. Scenes feature both humans and animals, depicted with extraordinary skill, often in association with geometric and other abstract motifs. Some sites reveal that ancient peoples had the seemingly irresistible urge to add to existing rock paintings, whereas others used new sites for creating what today we call graffiti.

The continuation of this rock art tradition, unbroken into the present, has allowed scientists to discover what this art means. Living peoples maintain a close connection between art and shamanism, with many scenes depicting visions seen in states of trance. Distortions in the art, usually of human figures, represent sensations felt by individuals in a state of trance, whereas the geometric designs depict illusions that originate in the central nervous system in altered states of consciousness. This **entoptic phenomenon**—a vision of luminous grids, dots, zigzags, and other designs that seem to shimmer, pulsate, rotate, and expand—occurs as one enters a state of trance (**Figure 8.15**). Sufferers of migraines experience similar hallucinations. Entoptic phenomena are typical of the Australian cave art mentioned previously.

entoptic phenomenon A vision of bright pulsating forms that is generated by the central nervous system and seen in states of trance.

Figure 8.16 Grotte de Chauvet
Ancestral humans painted these images of bison, panthers, and rhinoceroses some 32,000 years ago in the Chauvet Cave in France. These ancient paintings reflect a fundamental need to communicate, to record, and to share observations. Yet the ability to make these ancient paintings, like contemporary human culture, is rooted in the biology of the human hand, eye, and brain. Because these forms of expression appear in the Upper Paleolithic, is that evidence of a new species with such capabilities? Or is it simply a demonstration of cultural progression seen throughout the course of human evolutionary history? Do you think that our earlier ancestors made art that did not survive in the archaeological record?

Animals and Birds, Chauvet-Pont-d'Arc Cave, Ardeche (cave painting), Paleolithic/The Bridgeman Art Library

In many recent cultures, geometric designs are used as symbolic expressions of genealogical patterns, records of origins, and the afterlife. The animals depicted in this art, often with startling realism, are not the ones most often eaten. Rather, they are powerful beasts like the eland (a large African antelope); this power is important to shamans—individuals skilled at manipulating supernatural forces and spirits for human benefit—who try to harness it for their rainmaking, healing, and other rituals.

The most famous Upper Paleolithic art is that of Europe, largely because most researchers of prehistoric art are themselves of European background. Though the earliest of this art took the form of sculpture and engravings—often portraying such animals as reindeer, horses, bears, and ibexes—figurative art abounds in the spectacular paintings on the walls of 200 or so caves in southern France and northern Spain. With the exception of the 39,000-year-old site at El Castillo, Spain, the oldest of these are from about 32,000 years ago (Figure 8.16). Visually accurate portrayals of Ice Age mammals—including bison, aurochs, horses, mammoths, and stags—were often painted one on top of another.

Although well represented in other media like rock art, humans are not commonly portrayed in cave paintings; nor are scenes of events. Instead, the animals depicted are often abstracted from nature and rendered two-dimensionally—no small achievement for these early artists. Sometimes the artists made use of bulges and other features of the rock to impart a more three-dimensional feeling. Frequently, the paintings are in hard-to-get-at places although suitable surfaces in more accessible locations remain untouched. In some caves, the lamps by which the artists worked have been found; these are spoon-shaped objects of sandstone in which animal fat was burned. Experimentation has shown that such lamps would have provided adequate illumination over several hours.

The experimental work of French archaeologist Michel Lorblanchet in 1990 unraveled the techniques used by Upper Paleolithic peoples to create their cave paintings (described in the Original Study authored by science writer Roger Lewin). Interestingly, they turn out to be the same techniques used by the Aborigine rock painters in Australia and the artists in Sulawesi, Indonesia.

ORIGINAL STUDY

Paleolithic Paint Job BY ROGER LEWIN

Lorblanchet's recent bid to recreate one of the most important Ice Age images in Europe was an affair of the heart as much as the head. "I tried to abandon my skin of a modern citizen, tried to experience the feeling of the artist, to enter the dialogue between the rock and the man," he explains. Every day for a week in the fall of 1990 he drove the 20 miles from his home in the medieval village of Cajarc into the hills above the river Lot. There, in a small, practically inaccessible cave, he transformed himself into an Upper Paleolithic painter.

And not just any Upper Paleolithic painter, but the one who 18,400 years ago crafted the dotted horses inside the famous cave of Pech Merle.

You can still see the original horses in Pech Merle's vast underground geologic splendor. You enter through a narrow passageway and soon find yourself gazing across a grand cavern to where the painting seems to hang in the gloom. "Outside, the landscape is very different from the one the Upper Paleolithic people saw," says Lorblanchet. "But in here, the landscape is the same as it was more than 18,000 years ago. You see what the Upper Paleolithic people experienced." No matter where you look in this cavern, the eye is drawn back to the panel of horses.

The two horses face away from each other, rumps slightly overlapping, their outlines sketched in black. The animal on the right seems to come alive as it merges with a crook in the edge of the panel, the perfect natural shape for a horse's head. But the impression of naturalism quickly fades as the eye falls on the painting's dark dots. There are more than 200 of them, deliberately distributed within and below the bodies and arcing around the right-hand horse's head and mane. More cryptic still are a smattering of red dots and half-circles and the floating outline of a fish. The surrealism is completed by six disembodied human hands stenciled above and below the animals.

Lorblanchet began thinking about recreating the horses after a research trip to Australia over a decade ago. Not only is Australia a treasure trove of rock art, but its aboriginal people are still creating it. "In Queensland I learned how people painted by spitting pigment onto the rock," he recalls. "They spat paint and used their hand, a piece of cloth, or a feather as a screen to create different lines and other effects. Elsewhere in Australia people used chewed twigs as paintbrushes, but in Queensland the spitting technique worked best." The rock surfaces there were too uneven for extensive brushwork, he adds—just as they are in Quercy.

When Lorblanchet returned home he looked at the Quercy paintings with a new eye. Sure enough, he began seeing the telltale signs of spit-painting—lines with edges that were sharply demarcated on one side and fuzzy on the other, as if they had been airbrushed—instead of the brushstrokes he and others had assumed were there. Could you produce lines that were crisp on both edges with the same technique, he wondered, and perhaps dots too? Archeologists had long recognized that hand stencils, which are common in prehistoric art, were produced by spitting paint around a hand held to the wall. But no one had thought that entire animal images could be created this way. Before he could test his ideas, however, Lorblanchet had to find a suitable rock face—the original horses were painted on a roughly vertical panel 13 feet across and 6 feet high. With the help of a speleologist [cave scientist], he eventually found a rock face in a remote cave high in the hills and set to work.

Following the aboriginal practices he had witnessed, Lorblanchet first made a light outline sketch of the horses with a charred stick. Then he prepared black pigment for the painting. "My intention had been to use manganese dioxide, as the Pech Merle painter did," says Lorblanchet, referring to one of the minerals ground up for paint by the early artists. "But I was advised that manganese is somewhat toxic, so I used wood charcoal instead." (Charcoal was used as pigment by Paleolithic painters in other caves, so Lorblanchet felt he could justify his concession to safety.) To turn the charcoal into paint, Lorblanchet ground it with a limestone block, put the powder in his mouth, and diluted it to the right consistency with saliva and water. For red pigment he used ochre from the local iron-rich clay.

He started with the dark mane of the right-hand horse. "I spat a series of dots and fused them together to represent tufts of hair," he says, unselfconsciously reproducing the spitting action as he talks. "Then I painted the horse's back by blowing the pigment below my hand held so"—he holds his hand flat against the rock with his thumb tucked in to form a straight line—"and used it like a stencil to produce a sharp upper edge and a diffused

An upper Paleolithic artist painted this spotted horse in the French cave of Pech Merle. Note the same hand motif as is seen at El Castillo.

BPK, Berlin/Wolfgang Ruppert/Art Resource, NY

the upper hind leg, by spitting into the gap between parallel hands.

The belly demanded more ingenuity; he spat paint into a V-shape formed by his two splayed hands, rubbed it into a curved swath to shape the belly's outline, then finger-painted short protruding lines to suggest the animals' shaggy hair. Neatly outlined dots, he found, could not be made by blowing a thin jet of charcoal onto the wall. He had to spit pigment through a hole made in an animal skin. "I spent seven hours a day for a week," he says. "Puff . . . puff . . . puff. . . . It was exhausting, particularly because there was carbon monoxide in the cave. But you experience something special, painting like that. You feel you are breathing the image onto the rock—projecting your spirit from the deepest part of your body onto the rock surface."

Was that what the Paleolithic painter felt when creating this image? "Yes, I know it doesn't sound very scientific," Lorblanchet says of his highly personal style of investigation, "but the intellectual games of the structuralists haven't got us very far, have they? Studying rock art shouldn't be an intellectual game. It is about understanding humanity. That's why I believe the experimental approach is valid in this case."

lower edge. You get an illusion of the animal's rounded flank this way."

He experimented as he went. "You see the angular rump?" he says, pointing to the original painting. "I reproduced that by holding my hand perpendicular to the rock, with my palm slightly bent, and I spat along the edge formed by my hand and the rock." He found he could produce sharp lines, such as those in the tail and in

Excerpted from Lewin, R. (1993). Paleolithic paint job. *Discover 14* (7), 64–70. Copyright ©1993 The Walt Disney Co. Reprinted with permission of *Discover Magazine*.

Theories to account for the early European cave art often depend on conjectural and subjective interpretations. Some have argued that it is art for art's sake, but if that is so, why were animals often painted over one another, and why were they placed in inaccessible places? The latter might suggest that they served ceremonial purposes and that the caves were religious sanctuaries.

One suggestion is that the animals were drawn to ensure success in the hunt; another is that their depiction was seen as a way to promote fertility and increase the size of the herds on which humans depended. In Altamira Cave in northern Spain, for example, the art shows a pervasive concern for the sexual reproduction of the bison.

In cave art generally, though, the animals painted are not those most frequently hunted. Furthermore, cave art rarely includes depictions of animals being hunted, killed, copulating, birthing, or with exaggerated sexual parts, as is shown in the Venus figurines (Conard, 2009).

Another suggestion is that initiation rites, such as those marking the transition to adulthood, took place in the painted galleries. In support of this idea, footprints, most of which are small, have been found in the clay floors of several caves, and in one they even circle a modeled clay bison. As well, it appears that the small hands of ancient children created some of the finger "flutings," unpigmented grooves made into the soft surface of the cave walls (Sharpe & Van Gelder, 2006). The presence of children in the caves suggests that elders were transmitting knowledge to the new generation through painted animals and the countless "signs" and abstract designs that accompany much Upper Paleolithic art. Some have interpreted these markings as tallies of animals killed or as a reckoning of time according to a lunar calendar.

The abstract designs, including those such as the spots on the Pech Merle horses, suggest yet another possibility. For the most part, these are just like the entoptic designs that are so consistently present in the rock art of southern Africa and western Australia. Furthermore, the rock art of southern Africa shows the same painting of new images over older ones, as well as the same sort of fixation on large, powerful animals instead of the ones most often eaten. Thus, the cave art of Europe may well represent the same depictions of trance experiences, painted after the fact. Consistent with this interpretation, the isolation of the caves and the shimmering light on the cave walls themselves are conducive to the sort of sensory distortion that can induce trance.

Ornamental Art

Artistic expression, whatever its purpose may have been, was not confined to rock surfaces and portable objects. Upper Paleolithic peoples also ornamented their bodies with necklaces, rings, bracelets, and anklets made of perforated animal teeth, shells, and beads of bone, stone, and ivory. Clothing, too, was adorned with beads. Quite a lot of art was probably also executed in more delicate materials such as wood, bark, and animal skins, which have not been preserved. Thus, the rarity of Upper Paleolithic art in some parts of the inhabited world may be because some materials did not survive in the archaeological record, not because they never existed.

Gender and Art

As shown in Figure 8.13, the Upper Paleolithic also includes numerous portrayals of voluptuous women with body parts often described as exaggerated. Many appear to be pregnant, and some are shown in birthing postures. These so-called Venus figures have been found at sites from southwestern France to Siberia. Made of stone, ivory, antler, or baked clay, they differ little in style from place to place, testifying to the sharing of ideas over vast distances. Although some have interpreted the Venuses as objects associated with a fertility cult, others suggest that they may have been exchanged to cement alliances between groups.

Art historian LeRoy McDermott has suggested that the Venus figurines are "ordinary women's views of their own bodies" and the earliest examples of self-representation (McDermott, 1996). He suggests that the distortions and exaggerations of the female form visible in the Venus figurines derive from the ancient artist looking down over her own pregnant body. Paleolithic archaeologist Margaret Conkey opened the door to such interpretations through her work combining gender theory and feminist theory with the science of archaeology.

With a particular interest in the Upper Paleolithic art of Europe, Conkey has spent decades challenging the traditional notion that Paleolithic art was made by male artists as an expression of spiritual beliefs related to hunting activities. She emphasizes that many reconstructions of behavior in the past rely upon contemporary gender norms to fill in blanks left in the archaeological record. Conkey, believing that today's stereotypes may be distorting our view of the past, seeks clues about the role of gender in the archaeological research she conducts (Gero & Conkey, 1991).

In this regard, note that current scientists may describe Venus figurines largely in sexual terms rather than in terms of fertility and birth. For example, in a commentary that accompanied the description of the figurine from Hohle Fels Cave, British archaeologist Paul Mellars states: "The figure is explicitly—and blatantly—that of a woman, with an exaggeration of sexual characteristics (large, projecting breasts, a greatly enlarged and explicit vulva, and bloated belly and thighs) that by twenty-first-century standards could be seen as bordering on the pornographic" (Mellars, 2009, p. 176). Mellars's reaction to the Venus figurine reflects present-day attitudes toward the nude female form rather than the intent of an ancient artist.

Human biology provides us with some clues. Breasts and belly enlarge during pregnancy; the tissues around the vulva enlarge and stretch dramatically during the birth process. Breasts swell further with milk after a birth. These physiological changes were likely as awe inspiring to Paleolithic peoples as were hunting experiences, and Mellars's interpretation of the figurine as "pornographic" derives from the gender norms of his particular culture. Contemporary peoples with a different worldview would not react to the art in these terms.

Other Aspects of Upper Paleolithic Culture

Upper Paleolithic peoples lived not only in caves and rock shelters but also in structures built out in the open. In Ukraine, for example, remains of sizable settlements have been found in which huts were built on frameworks of intricately stacked mammoth bones (Figure 8.17). Where the ground was frozen, cobblestones were heated and placed in the earth to sink in, thereby providing sturdy, dry floors. Instead of shallow depressions or flat surfaces that radiated little heat, their hearths were stone-lined pits

© Goran Burenhult

Figure 8.17 **Upper Paleolithic Mammoth Bone Dwelling**
Pictured is a reconstructed dwelling made from interlocked and lashed mammoth bones. These dwellings are typically round in form with a central hearth or several scattered hearths. Pits with bones and butchering areas and flint-knapping areas often surround the dwellings. They tend to be strategically built along old river terraces near migration pathways that grazing animals would take between steppes and rivers. Although most of these dwellings date to between 14,000 and 20,000 years ago, one from the Moldova site dates back to 44,000 years ago and is associated with typical Neandertal tools. Others argue that the Moldova site represents the remains of a hunting blind.

that conserved heat for extended periods and made for more efficient cooking.

For the outdoors, Upper Paleolithic peoples had the same sort of tailored clothing worn in historic times by Arctic and sub-Arctic peoples. Further, they engaged in long-distance trade, as indicated, for example, by the presence of seashells and amber from the Baltic Sea in northern Europe at sites several hundred kilometers from the sources of these materials. Although Middle Paleolithic peoples also made use of rare and distant materials, these practices became far more regular in the Upper Paleolithic.

The Spread of Upper Paleolithic Peoples

Upper Paleolithic peoples expanded into regions previously uninhabited by their archaic forebears. Colonization of southern Siberia dates back about 280,000 years. Upper Paleolithic peoples reached the northeastern part of that region about 10,000 years later. Although reaching this region did not involve crossing large bodies of water, inhabiting Greater Australia and the Americas did require such voyages.

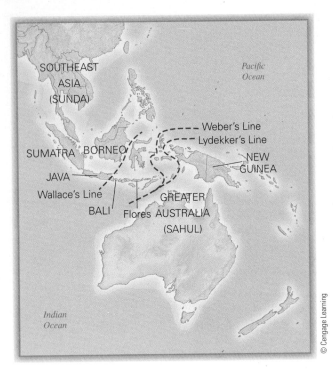

Figure 8.18 Sea Level and the Coastlines of Sunda and Sahul Habitation of Australia and New Guinea (joined together with Tasmania as a single landmass called Sahul) was dependent upon travel across the open ocean even at times of maximum glaciation when sea levels were low. This figure shows the coastlines of Sahul and Sunda (Southeast Asia plus the islands of Java, Sumatra, Borneo, and Bali) now and in the past. As sea levels rose with melting glaciers, sites of early human habitation were submerged. Wallace's Trench, a particularly deep part of the ocean, always separated Sunda and Sahul.

The Sahul

Between 50,000 and 60,000 years ago, people managed to reach Australia, New Guinea, and Tasmania, then connected to one another in a single landmass called the **Sahul**. To do this, they had to use some kind of watercraft because the Sahul was separated from the islands of Java, Sumatra, Borneo, and Bali, which are geologically a part of the Asian landmass. At times of maximum glaciation and low sea levels, these islands were joined to one another in a single landmass called **Sunda**, but a deep ocean trench—called the Wallace Trench, after Alfred Russel Wallace who discovered natural selection at the same time as Charles Darwin and who conducted fieldwork in the area—always separated Sunda and Sahul (Figure 8.18).

Sahul The greater Australian landmass including Australia, New Guinea, and Tasmania. At times of maximum glaciation and low sea levels, these areas were continuous.

Sunda The combined landmass of the contemporary islands of Java, Sumatra, Borneo, and Bali that was continuous with mainland Southeast Asia at times of low sea levels corresponding to maximum glaciation.

Anthropologist Joseph Birdsell (1977) has suggested several routes of island hopping and seafaring to make the crossing between these landmasses. Each of these routes involves crossing open water without land visible on the horizon. The earliest known site in New Guinea dates to 40,000 years ago. Sites in Australia are sometimes dated to even earlier, but these dates are especially contentious because they involve the critical question of the relationship between anatomical modernity and the presence of human-like culture.

Early dates for habitation of the Sahul indicate that archaic *Homo* rather than anatomically modern forms possessed the cultural capacity for oceanic navigation. Evidence from a recent genetic analysis of a hair sample taken from an Australian Aborigine over a century ago indicates direct dispersal from Africa for some people (Rasmussen et al., 2011). Once in Australia, these populations used ochre to create sophisticated rock art, as we discussed earlier. One painting in the Arnhem Land plateau depicts a species of giant bird thought to have gone extinct around 40,000 years ago.

Interestingly, considerable physical variation is seen in Australian fossil specimens from this period. Some specimens have the high forehead characteristic of anatomical modernity whereas others possess traits providing excellent evidence of continuity between living Aborigines and the earlier *Homo erectus* and archaic *Homo sapiens* fossils from Indonesia. Willandra Lakes—a region of southeastern Australia, far from where the earliest archaeological evidence of human habitation of the continent was found—is particularly rich with fossils. The variation present in these fossils illustrates the problems inherent with making a one-to-one correspondence between the skull of a certain shape and cultural capabilities.

Other evidence for sophisticated ritual activity in early Australia is provided by the burial of a man at least 40,000 years ago from Lake Mungo in the Willandra Lakes region. His body was positioned with his fingers intertwined around one another in the region of his penis, and red ochre had been scattered over the body. It may be that this pigment had more than symbolic value; for example, its iron salts have antiseptic and deodorizing properties, and there are recorded instances in which red ochre is associated with prolonging life and is used medicinally to treat particular conditions or infections. One historically known Aborigine society is reported to have used ochre to heal wounds, scars, and burns and to use it for those in pain, covering the body with the substance and placing it in the sun to promote sweating. Recently, the Australian National University returned the 40,000-year-old remains to the Mutthi Mutthi Aborigines (Pearlman, 2015). The Mutthi Mutthi, who have ancient ties to the lands where these remains were discovered, had objected to their removal, which had been done without their consent. See this chapter's Globalscape to learn about the importance of Willandra Lakes to global and local heritage today.

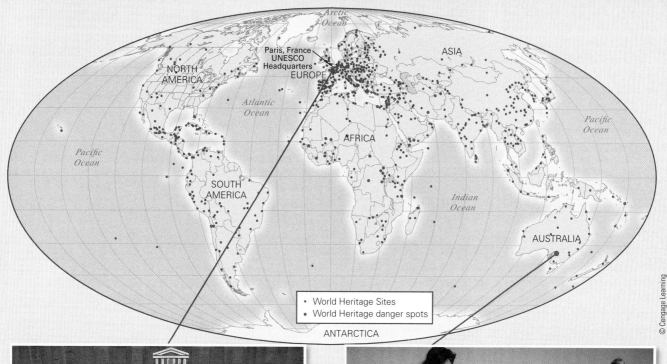

- World Heritage Sites
- World Heritage danger spots

© Cengage Learning

AP Images/Thibault Camus, File

Michael Amendolia/In Pictures/Corbis News/Corbis

Whose Lakes Are These?

Paleoanthropologists regularly travel to early fossil sites and to museums where original fossil specimens are housed. Increasingly, these same destinations are popular with tourists. Making sites accessible to everyone while protecting the sites requires considerable skill and knowledge. But most importantly, long before the advent of paleoanthropology or paleotourism, these sites were and are the homelands of living people.

Aboriginal people have lived along the shores of the Willandra Lakes region of Australia for at least 50,000 years. They have passed down their stories and cultural traditions even as the lakes dried up and a spectacular crescent-shaped, wind-formed dune (called a *lunette*) remained. The Mungo lunette has particular cultural significance to three Aboriginal tribal groups. Several major fossil finds from the region include cremated remains as well as an ochred burial, both dated to at least 40,000 years ago. Nearly 460

fossilized footprints dated to between 19,000 and 23,000 years ago were made by people of all ages who lived in the region when the Willandra Lakes were still full of water. How can a place of local and global significance be appropriately preserved and honored?

Since 1972, UNESCO's World Heritage List has been an important part of maintaining places like Willandra Lakes, which was itself inscribed as a World Heritage Site in 1981. Individual states apply to UNESCO for site designation, and if approved they receive financial and political support for maintaining the site. When designated sites are threatened by natural disaster, war, pollution, or poorly managed tourism, they are placed on a danger list, indicated with a red dot on the map above, forcing local governments to institute measures to protect the sites in order to continue receiving UNESCO support.

Each year approximately 30 new World Heritage Sites are designated. In 2015 the list included 1,031 locations: 197 natural preserves, 802 cultural sites, and 32 mixed sites. Fossil and archaeological sites are well represented on the World Heritage List. The Willandra Lakes site is recognized for both natural and cultural value.

Although important to the world community, Willandra Lakes has particular meaning to the Aborigines. Aunty Beryl Carmichael, an elder of the Ngiyaampaa people, explains that this land is integrated with her culture:

> Because when the old people would tell the stories, they'd just refer to them as "marrathal warkan," which means long, long time ago, when time first began for our people, as people on this land after creation.
>
> We have various sites around our country, we call them the birthing places of all our stories. And of course, the stories are embedded with the lore that governs this whole land. The air, the land, the environment, the universe, the stars.[a]

Not only are Aunty Beryl's stories and the land around Willandra Lakes critical for the Ngiyaampaa and other Aboriginal groups, but their survival ultimately contributes to all of us.

The following lists the sites considered endangered at the June 2015 meeting of the World Heritage Committee with the date they were first designated endangered. Committee members included representatives from countries throughout the globe including Algeria, Colombia, Croatia, Finland, Germany, India, Jamaica, Japan, Kazakhstan, Lebanon, Malaysia, Peru, Philippines, Poland, Portugal, Qatar, South Korea, Senegal, Serbia, Turkey, and Vietnam.

Afghanistan
Cultural Landscape and Archaeological Remains of the Bamiyan Valley (2003)
Minaret and Archaeological Remains of Jam (2002)

Belize
Belize Barrier Reef Reserve System (2009)

Bolivia
City of Potosí (2014)

Central African Republic
Manovo-Gounda St. Floris National Park (1997)

Chile
Humberstone and Santa Laura Saltpeter Works (2005)

Colombia
Los Katíos National Park (2009)

Côte d'Ivoire
Comoé National Park (2003)
Mount Nimba Strict Nature Reserve (1992)

Democratic Republic of the Congo
Garamba National Park (1996)
Kahuzi-Biega National Park (1997)
Okapi Wildlife Reserve (1997)
Salonga National Park (1999)
Virunga National Park (1994)

Egypt
Abu Mena (2001)

Ethiopia
Simien National Park (1996)

Georgia
Bagrati Cathedral and Gelati Monastery (2010)
Historical Monuments of Mtskheta (2009)

Guinea
Mount Nimba Strict Nature Reserve (1992)

Honduras
Río Plátano Biosphere Reserve (2011)

Indonesia
Tropical Rainforest Heritage of Sumatra (2011)

Iraq
Ashur (Qal'at Sherqat) (2003)
Hatra (2015)
Samarra Archaeological City (2007)

Jerusalem (site proposed by Jordan)
Old City of Jerusalem and Its Walls (1982)

Madagascar
Rainforests of the Atsinanana (2010)

Mali
Timbuktu (2012)
Tomb of Askia (2012)

Niger
Air and Ténéré Natural Reserves (1992)

Palestine
Birthplace of Jesus: Church of the Nativity and the Pilgrimage Route, Bethlehem (2012)
Palestine: Land of Olives and Vines – Cultural Landscape of Southern Jerusalem, Battir (2014)

Panama
Fortifications on the Caribbean Side of Panama: Portobelo-San Lorenzo (2012)

Peru
Chan Chan Archaeological Zone (1986)

Senegal
Niokolo-Koba National Park (2007)

Serbia
Medieval Monuments in Kosovo (2006)

Solomon Islands
East Rennell (2013)

Syrian Arab Republic
Ancient City of Aleppo (2013)
Ancient City of Bosra (2013)
Ancient City of Damascus (2013)
Ancient Villages of Northern Syria (2013)
Crac des Chevaliers and Qal'at Salah El-Din (2013)
Site of Palmyra (2013)

Tanzania, United Republic of
Ruins of Kilwa Kisiwani and Ruins of Songo Mnara (2004)

Uganda
Tombs of Buganda Kings at Kasubi (2010)

United Kingdom
Liverpool–Maritime Mercantile City (2012)

United States of America
Everglades National Park (2010)

Venezuela
Coro and Its Port (2005)

Yemen
Historic Town of Zabid (2000)
Old City of Sana'a (2015)
Old Walled City of Shibam (2015)

Global Twister

The listing of endangered sites brings global pressure on a state to find ways to protect the natural and cultural heritage contained within its boundaries. Given the recent destruction of some designated World Heritage Sites, how can we enhance this global social pressure?

---

[a] "Why the stories are told: Told by Aunty Beryl Carmichael." (2015). http://tom33.global2.vic.edu.au/literacy/ (retrieved November 22, 2015); see also "Aunty Beryl talks about the Dreaming." (2015). *The making of modern Australia.* http://www.abc.net.au/tv/makingaustralia/educationextras/episode-four/clip-three.htm (retrieved November 21, 2015)

As in many parts of the world, paleoanthropologists conducting research on human evolution in Australia are essentially constructing a view of history that conflicts with the beliefs of Aborigines. The story of human evolution is utterly dependent on Western conceptions of time, relationships established through genetics, and a definition of what it means to be human. All of these theories are at odds with Aboriginal beliefs about human origins. Still, while conducting their research on human evolution, paleoanthropologists working in Australia have advocated and supported the Aboriginal culture.

The Americas

Although scientists concur that American Indian ancestry can be traced ultimately back to Asian origins, just when people arrived in the Americas has been a matter of lively debate. This debate draws upon geographical, cultural, and biological evidence.

The conventional wisdom has long been that the first people migrated into North America over dry land that connected Siberia to Alaska. This land bridge was a consequence of the buildup of great continental glaciers. As the ice masses grew, there was a worldwide lowering of sea levels, causing an emergence of land in places like the Bering Strait where seas today are shallow. Thus, Alaska became, in effect, an eastward extension of Siberia (Figure 8.19). Climatic patterns of the Ice Age kept this land bridge, known as Beringia or the Bering Land Bridge, relatively ice free and covered instead with lichens and mosses that could support herds of grazing animals. It is possible that Upper Paleolithic peoples could have come to the Americas simply by following herd animals. The latest genetic evidence indicates movement took place back and forth across Beringia.

According to geologists, conditions were right for ancient humans and herd animals to traverse Beringia between 11,000 and 25,000 years ago. Though this land bridge was also open between 40,000 and 75,000 years ago, there is no evidence that conclusively confirms human migration at these earlier dates. As with the Sahul, early dates open the possibility of spread to the Americas by archaic *Homo*.

Although ancient Siberians did indeed spread eastward, it is now clear that massive glaciers blocked their way until 13,000 years ago at the earliest (Marshall, 2001). By then, people were already living farther south in the Americas. Thus, the question of how people first came to this hemisphere has been reopened. One possibility is that, like the first Australians, the first Americans may have come by boat or rafts, perhaps traveling between islands or ice-free pockets of coastline, from as far away as the Japanese islands and down North America's northwestern coast. Hints of such voyages are provided by a handful of North American skeletons (such as Kennewick

Figure 8.19 Land Bridge to the Americas
The Arctic conditions and glaciers in northeastern Asia and northwestern North America provided both opportunities and challenges for ancient peoples spreading to the Americas. On the one hand the Arctic climate provided a land bridge (Beringia) between the continents, but on the other hand the harsh environment posed considerable difficulties to humans. Ancient peoples may have also come to the Americas by sea. Once in North America, glaciers spanning a good portion of the continent determined the areas open to habitation.

Man) that bear a physical resemblance to the aboriginal Ainu people of northern Japan and their forebears. Unfortunately, because sea levels were lower than they are today, coastal sites used by early voyagers would now be under water.

Securely dated objects from Monte Verde, a site in south-central Chile, place people in southern South America by 14,500 years ago, if not earlier. Assuming the first populations spread from Siberia to Alaska, linguist Johanna Nichols suggests that the first people to arrive in North America did so by 20,000 years ago. She bases this estimate on the time it took various other languages to spread from their homelands—including Eskimo languages in the Arctic and Athabaskan languages from interior western Canada to New Mexico and Arizona (e.g. Navajo). Nichols's conclusion is that it would have taken at least 7,000 years for people to reach south-central Chile (Nichols, 2008).

A genetic study using mitochondrial and nuclear DNA indicates that the American Indian Upper Paleolithic peoples separated from Asian peoples prior to 40,000 years ago and occupied Beringia for about 20,000 years with little population growth (Kitchen, Miyamoto, & Mulligan, 2008). Population size expanded again as these peoples crossed Beringia between 15,000 and 17,000 years ago but then took different paths. One group traveled down the Pacific Coast and the other down the center of the continent. Although the dates generated in this study are as early as others have suggested, these findings support the notion that distinct language groups made separate migrations.

Another study suggests back and forth exchanges between Siberia and North America (Tamm et al., 2007). Yet a third study suggests three waves of migration across Beringia (Reich et al., 2012). The most recent genetic studies contradict one another. One proposes a single migration no earlier than 23,000 years ago, after which this population split into distinct North and South American groups (Raghavan et al., 2015). The other research suggests at least two sets of America-founding populations and emphasizes the close relationship between some Amazonians and Australasians to a common ancestral group in Asia (Skoglund et al., 2015).

As is the case with all investigations of the distant past, the narrative of how the Americas were peopled is under construction. Genetic data must be cross-checked with morphological data, linguistic data, and with the archaeological evidence. Each new discovery in the field or in the lab contributes to this chronicle. Careful verifications among various kinds of data allow for the eventual refinement of the account.

Although the earliest technologies in the Americas remain poorly known, they gave rise in North America, about 12,000 years ago, to the distinctive fluted spear points of **Paleoindian** hunters of big game, such as mammoths, mastodons, caribou, and now extinct forms of bison. Fluted points are finely made, with large channel flakes removed from one or both surfaces. This thinned section was inserted into the notched end of a spear shaft for a sturdy haft. Fluted points are found from the Atlantic seaboard to the Pacific Coast and from Alaska down into Panama. The efficiency of the hunters who made and used these points may have hastened the extinction of the mammoth and other large Pleistocene mammals. By driving large numbers of animals over cliffs, they killed many more than they could possibly use, thus wasting huge amounts of meat.

The bow and arrow was also widely used in the Americas, though it appeared there much later than it did in Africa and Eurasia. This does not mean, however, that the first Americans were all big game hunters. Other Paleoindians, including those who inhabited Monte Verde in Chile, far distant from Beringia, provide evidence of a very different way of life. These people foraged for plants and seafood and consumed a variety of smaller mammals. In each place, subsistence practices synchronized with the environment and other aspects of the local culture.

Major Paleolithic Trends

As we look at the larger picture, since the time the genus *Homo* appeared, evolving humans came to rely increasingly on cultural, as opposed to biological, adaptation. To handle environmental challenges, evolving humans developed appropriate tools, clothes, shelter, use of fire, and so forth. This was true whether human populations lived in regions that were hot or cold, wet or dry, forested or grassy. Though culture is ultimately based on what might loosely be called brainpower or, more formally, **cognitive capacity**, it is not genetic. Cultural innovations may be taught and can easily be transferred among individuals and groups.

Scientists have recently documented key differences in the proteins involved in brain metabolism in humans compared to other species that may account for some of this brainpower. Unfortunately, these metabolic changes are also associated with schizophrenia, indicating that there may have been some downsides to the process. This study suggests that the cultural practice of cooking freed the body to devote more energy to brain metabolism. Although cooking was certainly an innovation of ancient *Homo*, the varied low-fat diet and high exercise of our ancestors were in general healthier than the dietary patterns prevailing in many parts of the world today. See this chapter's Biocultural Connection for a discussion of how a return to the diets and lifestyles of our forebears may improve human health.

Certain trends stand out from the information anthropologists have gathered about the Old Stone Age in most parts of the world. One was toward increasingly more sophisticated, varied, and specialized toolkits. Tools became progressively lighter and smaller, resulting in the conservation of raw materials and a better ratio between length of cutting edge and weight of stone. Tools also became specialized according to region and function. Instead of crude all-purpose tools, more effective particularized devices were made to deal with the differing conditions of savannah, forest, and shore.

As humans came to rely increasingly on culture as a means to meet the challenges of existence, they were able to inhabit new environments. With more efficient tool technology, population size could increase, allowing humans to spill over into more diverse environments.

Paleoindian The people who were the earliest inhabitants of the Americas.

cognitive capacity A broad concept including intelligence, educability, concept formation, self-awareness, self-evaluation, attention span, sensitivity in discrimination, and creativity.

BIOCULTURAL CONNECTION

Paleolithic Prescriptions for Diseases of Today

Throughout most of our evolutionary history, humans led more physically active lives and ate a more varied low-fat diet than we do now. Our ancestors did not drink alcohol or smoke. They spent their days scavenging or hunting for animal protein while gathering vegetable foods, with some insects thrown in for good measure. They stayed fit through traveling great distances each day over the savannah and beyond.

Though we hail increased life expectancy as one of modern civilization's greatest accomplishments, this phenomenon—brought about in part by the discovery of antibiotics during the middle of the twentieth century—is quite recent. Anthropologists Mark Nathan Cohen and George Armelagos suggest that the downward trajectory for human health began when we left behind our Paleolithic lifeways and began farming instead of hunting and gathering, and then settled into permanent villages some 10,000 years ago.[a] The chronic diseases that linger—such as diabetes, heart disease, substance abuse, and high blood pressure—have their roots in this shift.

The prevalence of these "diseases of civilization" has increased rapidly over the past century. Anthropologists Melvin Konner and Marjorie Shostak and physician Boyd Eaton have suggested that our Paleolithic ancestors left us with a prescription for a cure. They propose that as "stone-agers in a fast lane," people's health will improve by returning to the lifestyle to which their bodies are adapted.[b] Such Paleolithic prescriptions are an example of evolutionary medicine—a branch of medical anthropology that uses evolutionary principles to contribute to human health.

Evolutionary medicine bases its prescriptions on the idea that rate of cultural change exceeds the rate of biological change. Our food-forager physiology was shaped over millions of years, whereas the cultural changes leading to contemporary lifestyles have occurred rapidly. For example, tobacco was domesticated in the Americas only a few thousand years ago and was widely used as both a narcotic and an insecticide. Alcoholic beverages—which depend on the domestication of a variety of plant species such as hops, barley, and corn—also could not have arisen without village life, as the fermentation process requires time and watertight containers. However, the high-starch diets and sedentary lifestyle of village life contribute to diabetes and heart disease.

Our evolutionary history offers clues about the diet and lifestyle to which our bodies evolved. By returning to our ancient lifeways, we can make the diseases of civilization a thing of the past.

Biocultural Question

Can you imagine what sort of Paleolithic prescriptions our evolutionary history would contribute for modern behaviors, such as childrearing practices, sleeping, and work patterns? Are there any ways that your culture or personal lifestyle is well aligned with past lifeways?

[a] Cohen, M. N., & Armelagos, G. J. (Eds.). (1984). *Paleopathology at the origins of agriculture.* Orlando: Academic Press.
[b] Eaton, S. B., Konner, M., & Shostak, M. (1988). Stone-agers in the fast lane: Chronic degenerative diseases in evolutionary perspective. *American Journal of Medicine* 84 (4), 739–749.

Improved cultural abilities may also have created a feedback loop with biological change. Tools and practices that allowed a decreased size and weight of face and teeth encouraged development of larger and more complex brains, and ultimately a reduction in body size and robustness. This dependence on intelligence rather than bulk is the linchpin of humans' increased reliance on cultural rather than physical adaptation. The development of conceptual thought can be seen in symbolic artifacts and signs of ritual activity throughout the world.

Through Paleolithic times, at least in the colder parts of the world, hunting became more important, and people became more proficient at it. Humans' intelligence enabled them to develop composite tools as well as the social organization and cooperation so important for survival and population growth. As discussed in the next chapter, this trend was reversed during the Mesolithic, when hunting lost its preeminence, and the gathering of wild plants and seafood became increasingly important.

As human populations grew and spread, cultural differences between regions also became more marked. Although some indications of cultural contact and intercommunication are evident in the development of long-distance trade networks, tool assemblages developed in response to the specific challenges and resources of specific environments.

As Paleolithic peoples eventually spread over all the continents of the world, including Australia and the Americas, changes in climate and environment called for new kinds of adaptations. In forest environments, people needed tools for working wood; on the open savannah and plains, humans began to use the bow and arrow to hunt the game they could not stalk closely; the people in settlements that grew up around lakes and along rivers and coasts developed harpoons and hooks; in the sub-Arctic regions, they needed tools to work the heavy skins of seals and caribou. Because culture is first and foremost a mechanism by which humans adapt, throughout the globe regional differentiations allowed Upper Paleolithic humans to face the challenges of their distinct environments.

CHAPTER CHECKLIST

What evidence supports the recent African origins hypothesis for modern human origins? What are its assumptions?

✓ Evidence to support the recent African origins hypothesis originally came from the study of mitochondrial DNA of modern humans, which was extrapolated to the past based on an assumed rate of constant change.

✓ The earliest anatomically modern fossils have been found in Africa dating to 200,000 years ago, relatively near in time to the estimation of when "Eve" should have existed.

✓ Issues with the recent African origins hypothesis include the movement of people into Africa, other geographical sources of mtDNA, and variable rates of molecular change.

✓ The recent African origins hypothesis supposes a strong connection between modern anatomy and cultural capacity that is inconsistent with findings on Neandertal culture.

What evidence supports the multiregional hypothesis for human origins? What are its assumptions?

✓ Modern humans retain certain anatomical characteristics of the *Homo erectus* fossils from the same region. This supports the idea that archaic humans all over the world simultaneously evolved into *Homo sapiens,* and that gene flow kept humans connected as a single species.

✓ Distinguishing between various archaic and anatomically modern fossils poses a great challenge because many specimens and modern humans exhibit a mix of features.

✓ The anatomical variety of both archaic and modern humans and evidence of high levels of gene flow throughout human history support the multiregional hypothesis.

✓ Recent cultural innovations have no correspondence to changes in human appearance.

✓ Comparison of genomes of ancient peoples such as the Neandertals and the Denisovans with living human groups demonstrates genetic continuity.

What were the major technological developments of the Upper Paleolithic era?

✓ Throughout the globe, blade tools became widespread along with an explosion of expressive arts.

Spear-throwing, the bow and arrow, and net hunting originated in this period. Hunting became a less dangerous and more effective manner of acquiring food.

✓ Pressure flaking gave toolmakers greater control over the shape of the tool while the blade technique yielded greater efficiency.

✓ In Europe Mousterian toolkits gave way to the earliest Upper Paleolithic industries—the Châtelperronian and Aurignacian traditions—shared by Neandertals and anatomically modern humans. Cultural distinctions between the two groups in Europe do not clearly indicate either as superior.

How did the role of art in human societies evolve over this period?

✓ Starting 40,000 years ago, figurative art proliferated, including carved figurines, flutes, and cave painting that most frequently depicted large mammals and abstract patterns seen perhaps in trance states.

✓ Evidence of paint manufacture goes back to 100,000 years ago when pigments were used as part of burial rituals and likely as body decoration. Figurative art that was not preserved in the archaeological record was also likely to have been created.

✓ Art began to be used in rituals and decorations, reflecting visions seen in altered states of consciousness known as entoptic phenomena.

✓ Interpretation of the artistic legacy of the Paleolithic remains subject to the biases of current social norms, as in the case of the Venus figurines.

How did humans spread throughout the globe during the Upper Paleolithic period?

✓ Spreading throughout the entire globe, Upper Paleolithic people built dwellings and tailored warm clothing that permitted habitation in harsh climates.

✓ Humans arrived in Australia around 50,000 years ago by crossing wide bodies of open water. Original migration to North America may also have occurred by sea, with continued exchange happening while the Bering Land Bridge existed.

✓ Given their vast geographic distribution, disparate societies developed distinct art, technology, lifestyle, and anatomy.

QUESTIONS FOR REFLECTION

1. What does it mean to be modern, biologically or culturally? How should we define *human*? Can creative artwork, like that pictured in this chapter's Challenge Issue, be considered indicative of distinctly human biology?

2. How do you feel about the possibility of having Neandertals as part of your personal ancestry? How might you relate the Neandertal debates to stereotyping or racism in contemporary society?

3. Why do you think that most of the studies of prehistoric art have tended to focus on Europe? Do you think this focus reflects ethnocentrism or bias about the definition of art in Western cultures?

4. Do you think that gender has played a role in anthropological interpretations of the behavior of our ancestors and the way that paleoanthropologists and archaeologists conduct their research? Do you believe that feminism has a role to play in the interpretation of the past?

DIGGING INTO ANTHROPOLOGY

Putting Paleolithic Prescriptions into Practice

In the late 2000s, the so-called caveman diet or Paleo diet became popular in some Western societies. Marketed as a life-extending, fat-burning panacea, it is a commercialized component of evolutionary medicine as described in this chapter's Biocultural Connection. The diet's adherents argue that cultural change has outpaced biological evolution with respect to diet, and they seek to commune with our Paleolithic ancestors and perhaps avoid some of the health consequences that plague us today. Detractors cite the underestimation of human adaptability and uncertainties about the precise nature of ancient diets. Whatever the nutritional facts, the controversy brings up the interesting anthropological question: What exactly did ancient humans eat? Create your own "caveman diet" by researching the edible plants and animals native to the region where you live. Given your knowledge of Upper Paleolithic technology, what game would humans have been capable of hunting or trapping? How could the different foods have been prepared? Then compare your results to the mainstream diet of your community. Which items have persisted and which are new? If you're feeling ambitious, you can gather classmates for a Paleolithic dinner party!

Laurent Giraudou/Sygma/Corbis

With the start of the Neolithic some 10,000 years ago—when some humans shifted to farming and domesticating animals as they settled into village life—competition for critical resources intensified. Today, that competition takes place on a global scale and places untenable pressures on the world's natural resources. Consider quinoa, a staple for Andean people of South America from the ancient Incas to modern-day villagers for 7,000 years. In the 1990s, this highly nutritious crop became popular worldwide, and consumer demand soared. But the impact on local quinoa farmers has been complicated: High demand raised the price, bringing local farmers a larger profit but making quinoa too expensive for their own consumption. In response, the Bolivian government now subsidizes quinoa for students and pregnant women. Quinoa's new popularity has also taken a toll on the land, as producers have turned to modern farming methods to meet the high demand. In such a resource competition, global demand often supersedes the needs of local inhabitants, but ultimately, for all of us to win, we need strategies to ensure a planet in balance.

The Neolithic Revolution: The Domestication of Plants and Animals

Throughout the Paleolithic, people depended exclusively on wild sources of food for their survival. They hunted and trapped wild animals, fished and gathered shellfish, eggs, berries, nuts, roots, and other plant foods. They relied on their wits, tools, and muscles to acquire what nature provided. When favorite foods became scarce, they adjusted by trying new potential foods or incorporating less desirable ones into their diets.

Over time, some peoples began to produce foods, tending specific plants and animals instead of using them in the form nature had provided. For some groups, tending rice, wheat, sheep, pigs, or beans led to a more sedentary existence. Settlement, in turn, allowed individuals to devote their energies to tasks other than the quest for food. Over the course of thousands of years, daily life changed. With good reason, the **Neolithic** era (literally, the New Stone Age) has been called revolutionary in human history.

The Mesolithic Roots of Farming and Pastoralism

As seen in the previous chapter, by the Upper Paleolithic, a period during which glaciers covered much of the northern hemisphere, humans had spread throughout the globe. By 12,000 years ago these glaciers had receded, changing human habitats globally. Sea levels rose, flooding land that had been dry during periods of glaciation, such as the Bering Strait, parts of the North Sea (recall Figure 8.19), and an extensive land area that had joined the eastern islands of Indonesia to mainland Asia (recall Figure 8.18).

Neolithic The New Stone Age; a prehistoric period beginning about 10,000 years ago in which peoples possessed stone-based technologies and depended on domesticated plants and/or animals for subsistence.

In this chapter you will learn to

- Identify the Mesolithic roots of farming and pastoralism.

- Describe the mechanisms of and evidence for plant and animal domestication.

- Compare theories about the reasons for this shift in lifeways.

- Identify the various centers of domestication globally.

- Examine the effects of food production on populations.

- Summarize the health consequences of the Neolithic revolution.

- Compare the cultural changes of the Neolithic to hunter-gatherer lifeways and to hierarchical notions of progress.

In some northern regions, warmer climates allowed forests to replace the barren tundra. In the process, some herd animals—upon which northern Paleolithic peoples had depended for much of their food, clothing, and shelter—disappeared from many areas. Some, like the caribou and musk ox, moved to colder climates; others, like the mammoths, died out completely. Without these large wild herds, cooperative hunts became less productive. Diets shifted to abundant plant foods as well as fish and other foods in and around lakes, bays, and rivers. In Europe, Asia, and Africa, anthropologists call this transitional period between the Upper Paleolithic and the Neolithic the **Mesolithic**, or Middle Stone Age. In the Americas, comparable cultures are referred to as **Archaic cultures**.

New technologies accompanied the changed postglacial environment. Toolmakers started manufacturing ground-stone tools, shaped and sharpened by grinding the tool against sandstone, often using sand as an additional abrasive. Once shaped and sharpened, these stones were set into wooden or antler handles to make effective axes and *adzes* (cutting tools with a sharp blade set at right angles to a handle). Though these tools take longer to make than those of chipped stone, they break less often with heavy-duty usage. Mesolithic peoples used these tools to clear trees or create dugout canoes and skin-covered boats. Archaeological evidence shows that Mesolithic foraging took place on the open water—coastal areas, rivers, and lakes—as well as on land.

The **microlith**—a small, hard, sharp blade—tradition flourished in the Mesolithic. Microlithic ("small stone") tools existed in central Africa by about 40,000 years ago, but they did not become common elsewhere until the Mesolithic. Ancient toolmakers could mass produce microliths from sections of blades and then attach them to an arrow or another tool shaft by using melted resin (from pine trees) as a binder.

Microliths provided Mesolithic people with an important advantage: The small size of the microlith enabled them to devise a wider array of composite tools made out of stone and wood or bone. For sickles, harpoons, arrows, knives, and daggers, they fit microliths into slots in wood, bone, or antler handles. In turn, these forms led to more sophisticated tools and weapons, such as bows to propel arrows.

Mesolithic The Middle Stone Age of Europe, Asia, and Africa beginning about 12,000 years ago.

Archaic cultures The term used to refer to Mesolithic cultures in the Americas.

microlith A small blade of flint or similar stone, which when hafted (sometimes several of them) into a wooden handle would make a tool that was widespread in the Mesolithic.

Natufian culture A Mesolithic culture from the lands that are now Israel, Palestine, Lebanon, and western Syria, between about 10,200 and 12,500 years ago.

Neolithic revolution The domestication of plants and animals by peoples with stone-based technologies beginning about 10,000 years ago and leading to radical transformations in cultural systems; sometimes referred to as the *Neolithic transition*.

A somewhat more settled lifestyle characterized the Mesolithic. People subsisting on wild game, seafood, and plants in the milder forested environments of the north did not need to follow migratory herds over large geographic areas. In the warmer parts of the world, where wild plant foods were more readily available, collection already had complemented hunting in the Upper Paleolithic. Thus, in areas like Southwest Asia, the Mesolithic was less of a changed way of life than was true in Europe. Here, the important **Natufian culture** flourished.

The Natufians lived between 10,200 and 12,500 years ago along the eastern coast of the Mediterranean Sea in caves, rock shelters, and small villages with stone- and mud-walled houses. They are named after Wadi en-Natuf, a ravine near Jerusalem, in Palestine's West Bank, where the remains of this culture were first found. Natufians buried their dead in communal cemeteries, usually in shallow pits without any other objects or decorations. One of their villages, Jericho in the Jordan River Valley, was settled between 10,000 and 11,000 years ago and contained a small shrine. Basin-shaped depressions in the rocks found outside homes and plastered pits beneath the floors of the houses indicate the Natufians stored plant foods. Natufians also used sickles—small stone blades set in straight handles of wood or bone. The sickles were originally used to harvest sedge for baskets but later were used to cut grain.

The Neolithic Revolution

Polished stone tool industries give the Neolithic, or New Stone Age, its name (Figure 9.1). However, it was the transition from a foraging economy based on hunting, gathering, and fishing to one based on food production that made this period revolutionary. Food foragers and village-dwellers alike used these Neolithic tools. This switch to food production, known as the **Neolithic revolution** (or *Neolithic transition*), spread over many centuries—even millennia—and grew directly from the preceding Mesolithic. Although this transition has been particularly well studied in Southwest Asia, archaeological evidence for food production also exists from other parts of the world, such as East Asia, Mesoamerica, and the Andes at similar or somewhat younger dates. Human groups throughout the globe independently, but more or less simultaneously, invented food production.

Figure 9.1 Tools of the Neolithic
The Neolithic gets its name from the polished stone tools that appeared during this period. Archaeologists have also recovered hafted sickles, mortars, and pestles as well as grain storage pits at some of the earliest Natufian settlements. The polished stone axes and hammerheads pictured here would have been hafted to handles made of wood. The handle would pass through the hole created in the tool or fitted up to the side of the polished stone and then secured with sinew and various glues.

Early Neolithic food production included both **horticulture**, the cultivation of crops in food gardens carried out with simple hand tools such as digging sticks and stone- or bone-bladed hoes, and **pastoralism**, breeding and managing migratory herds of domesticated grazing animals, such as goats, sheep, cattle, llamas, and camels.

Innovation—any new idea, method, or device that gains widespread acceptance in society—provides the ultimate source of all cultural change. **Primary innovation** refers to the creation, invention, or discovery by chance of a completely new idea, method, or device. For example, take the discovery that clay permanently hardens when exposed to high temperatures. Presumably, accidental firing of clay took place around numerous ancient campfires. This chance occurrence became a primary innovation when someone perceived its potential use. This perception allowed our ancestors to begin to make figurines of fired clay some 35,000 years ago.

A **secondary innovation** involves a deliberate application or modification of an existing idea, method, or

device. For example, during Neolithic times, ancient peoples applied the knowledge about fired clay to make pottery containers and cooking vessels. The earliest pottery vessels, radiocarbon dated to between 15,430 and 18,300 years ago, come from Yuchanyan Cave, located in southwestern China's Hunan Province.

What Is Domestication?

Domestication takes place as humans modify, intentionally or unintentionally, the genetic makeup of a population of wild plants or animals, sometimes to the extent that members of the population cannot survive or cannot reproduce without human assistance. Domestication resembles the interdependence between different species frequently seen in the natural world, where one species depends on another (that feeds upon it) for its protection and reproductive success. For example, certain ants native to the American tropics grow fungi in their nests, and these fungi provide the ants with most of their nutrition. Like human farmers, the ants add manure to stimulate fungal growth and eliminate competing weeds, both mechanically and through use of antibiotic herbicides. The fungi are protected and ensured reproductive success while providing the ants with a steady food supply.

In plant–human interactions, domestication ensures the plants' reproductive success while providing humans with food. Selective breeding eliminates thorns, toxins, and bad-tasting chemical compounds, which in the wild had served to ensure a plant species' survival, at the same time producing larger, tastier edible parts attractive to humans. U.S. environmentalist Michael Pollan suggests that domesticated plant species successfully exploit human desires so

---

horticulture The cultivation of crops in food gardens, carried out with simple hand tools such as digging sticks and hoes.

pastoralism The breeding and managing of migratory herds of domesticated grazing animals, such as goats, sheep, cattle, llamas, and camels.

innovation Any new idea, method, or device that gains widespread acceptance in society.

primary innovation The creation, invention, or chance discovery of a completely new idea, method, or device.

secondary innovation The deliberate application or modification of an existing idea, method, or device.

domestication An evolutionary process whereby humans modify, intentionally or unintentionally, the genetic makeup of a population of wild plants or animals, sometimes to the extent that members of the population cannot survive or cannot reproduce without human assistance.

that they are able to outcompete other plant species; he has even proposed that agriculture is something the grasses did to people as a way to conquer trees (Pollan, 2001).

Evidence of Early Plant Domestication

Paleobotanists can often tell the fossil of a wild plant species from a domesticated one by studying the shape and size of various plant structures. Domesticated plants differ from their wild ancestors in ways favored by humans. These features include increased size, at least of edible parts (Figure 9.2); reduction or loss of natural means of seed dispersal; reduction or loss of protective devices such as husks or distasteful chemical compounds; loss of delayed seed germination (important to wild plants for survival in times of drought or other temporarily adverse conditions); and development of simultaneous ripening of the seed or fruit.

For example, wild cereals have very fragile stems, whereas domesticated ones have tough stems. Under natural conditions, plants with fragile stems scatter their seeds readily, whereas those with tough stems do not. At harvest time, the grain stalks with soft stems would shatter at the touch of a sickle, short handled tools with semicircular blades, scattering the seeds to the wind. Inevitably, though unintentionally, most of the seeds that people were able to harvest would have come from the tough plants. Early domesticators probably also tended to select seeds from plants having few husks or none at all—eventually breeding them out—because husking prior to pounding the grains into meal or flour required extra labor.

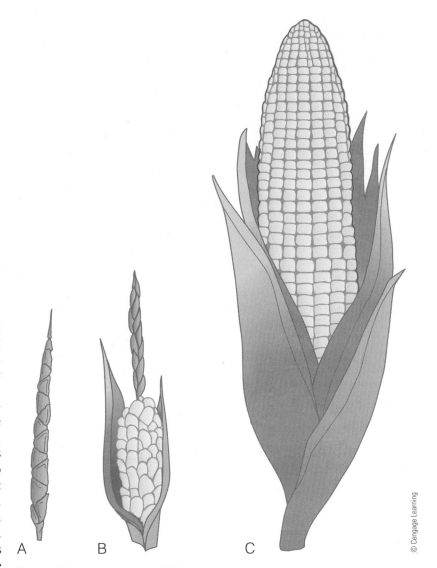

A   B   C

Figure 9.2 Domestication of Maize
Increased size of edible parts is a common feature of domestication. The large ear of corn or maize (C) that we know today is a far cry from the tiny ears (about an inch long) characteristic of 5,500-year-old maize (B). Maize may have arisen when a simple gene mutation transformed male tassel spikes of the wild grass called teosinte (A) into the small, earliest versions of the female maize ear. Teosinte, a wild grass from highland Mexico, is far less productive than maize and does not taste good. Like most plants that were domesticated, it was not a favored food for foraging peoples. Domestication transformed it into something highly desirable.

© Cengage Learning

Evidence of Early Animal Domestication

Domestication produced changes in the skeletal structure of some animals. For example, the horns of wild goats and sheep differ from those of their domesticated counterparts. Some domesticated sheep have no horns at all. Similarly, the overall size of an animal or portions of it can change with domestication as seen in the smaller canine teeth of domesticated pigs compared to the tusks found in wild boar.

The age and sex ratios of butchered animals at an archaeological site can indicate the presence of animal domestication. For example, archaeologists found differences in the age and sex ratios of goats at a 10,000-year-old site in the Zagros Mountains of Iran compared to those of wild herds. A sharp rise in the number of young male goats killed indicates that people were slaughtering the young males for food and leather and were saving the females for breeding. Although such herd management does not prove that the goats were fully domesticated, it indicates a step in that direction (Zeder & Hesse, 2000). Similarly, archaeological sites in the Andean highlands, dating to around 6,300 years ago, contain evidence that llamas were penned up, indicating the beginning of domestication.

Why Humans Became Food Producers

Although it might seem that a sudden flash of insight about the human ability to control plants and animals underlies the rise of domestication, the evidence points us in different directions. Contemporary foragers, for example, choose to forgo food production, even though they know full well the role of seeds in plant growth and that plants grow better under certain conditions than others. In fact, U.S. environmental historian Jared Diamond aptly describes contemporary food foragers as "walking encyclopedias of natural history with individual names for as many as a thousand or more plant and animal species, and with detailed knowledge of those species' biological characteristics, distribution, and potential uses" (Diamond, 1997, p. 143). Food foragers frequently apply such expertise to actively manage the resources on which they depend. For example, indigenous peoples living in northern Australia deliberately alter the runoff from creeks to flood extensive tracts of land, converting them into fields of wild grain. Indigenous Australians choose to continue to forage while also managing the land.

Food foragers may avoid food production simply because of the hard work it involves. In fact, available ethnographic data indicate that farmers, by and large, work far longer hours compared to most food foragers. Also, food production does not necessarily provide a more secure means of subsistence compared to food foraging. Low species diversity makes highly productive seed crops unstable from an ecological perspective. Without constant human attention, their productivity suffers.

Noting that food foragers have more time for play and relaxation than food producers, U.S. anthropologist Marshall Sahlins has labeled hunter-gatherers the original "affluent society" (Sahlins, 1972). Nevertheless, as food-producing peoples (including postindustrial societies) have deprived hunter-gatherers of more and more of the land base necessary for their way of life, this lifeway has become more difficult. The competition for resources ushered in during the Neolithic favors those cultures that develop concepts of land ownership.

Given the relative ease and balance of foraging, we may well ask why any human group abandoned food foraging in favor of food production. Several theories exist. The desiccation or oasis theory, first championed by Australian archaeologist V. Gordon Childe in the mid-20th century, suggests environmental causes. Glacial cover over Europe and Asia caused a shift in rain patterns from Europe to North Africa and Southwest Asia so that when the glaciers retreated northward, so did the rain. As a result, North Africa and Southwest Asia became drier, and people were forced to congregate at oases for water.

Relative food scarcity in such an environment drove people to collect the wild grasses and seeds growing around the oases, congregating in a part of Southwest Asia and Northeast Africa known as the Fertile Crescent (Figure 9.3). Eventually, they began to cultivate the grasses to provide enough food for the community. According to this theory, animal domestication began because the oases attracted hungry animals, such as wild goats, sheep, and cattle,

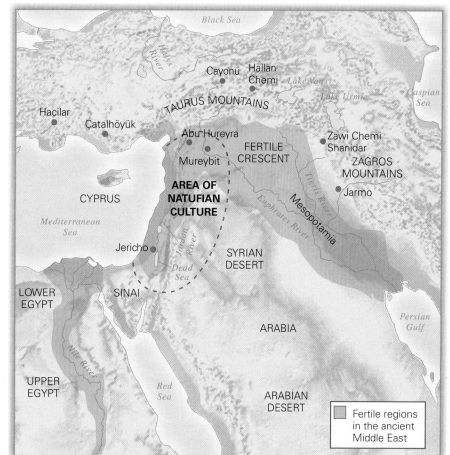

Figure 9.3 The Fertile Crescent
This area of Southwest Asia and North Africa shows the Fertile Crescent, the site of the beginning of domestication. Though originally defined not to include the Nile River Valley, many scholars today consider this region part of the Fertile Crescent. Domestication took place in all the river valleys and coastal areas (indicated in green) that were adjacent to deserts.

which came to graze on the stubble of the grain fields and to drink. Finding that these animals were often too thin to kill for food, people began to fatten them up.

The Fertile Crescent

Archaeological evidence indicates that the earliest plant domestication took place gradually in the Fertile Crescent, the long arc-shaped sweep of river valleys and coastal plains extending from the Upper Nile (Sudan) to the Lower Tigris (Iraq). People living at a site (Abu Hureyra) east of Aleppo, Syria, domesticated rye (a cereal) as early as 13,000 years ago, although wild plants and animals continued to be their major food sources (Hillman et al., 2001). Over the next several millennia they became full-fledged farmers, cultivating rye and wheat. By 10,300 years ago, crop cultivation spread to others in the region.

The Natufians, whose culture we touched on earlier in this chapter, provide an excellent case study for the processes by which culture and the environment interact. These Southwest Asian people lived at a time of dramatically changing climates. With the end of the last glaciation, temperatures not only became significantly warmer but markedly seasonal as well. Between 6,000 and 12,000 years ago, the region experienced the most extreme seasonality in its history, with dry summers significantly longer and hotter than today. As a consequence, many shallow lakes dried up, leaving just three in the Jordan River Valley.

At the same time, the region's plant cover changed dramatically. Among plants, annuals, including wild cereal grains and legumes (such as peas, lentils, and chickpeas), adapt well to environmental instability and seasonal dryness. Because they complete their life cycle in a single year, annuals can evolve very quickly under unstable conditions. Moreover, they store their reproductive abilities for the next wet season in abundant seeds, which can remain dormant for prolonged periods.

The Natufians, who lived where these conditions were especially severe, adapted by modifying their subsistence practices in two ways: First, they probably burned the landscape regularly to promote browsing by red deer and grazing by gazelles, the main focus of their hunting activities. Second, they placed greater emphasis on the collection and storage of wild seeds from the annual plants that they used for food through the dry season. The importance of stored foods, coupled with the scarcity of reliable water sources, promoted more sedentary living patterns, reflected in the substantial villages of late Natufian times. The Natufians' sickles for harvesting grain and the grinding stones they possessed for processing a variety of wild foods eased their shift to a reliance on seed.

The use of sickles to harvest grain turned out to have important if unexpected consequences. In the course of harvesting, the easily dispersed seeds fell at the harvest site, whereas those that clung to the stems came back to the settlement where people processed and stored them. The periodic burning of vegetation carried out to attract the deer and gazelle herds may have also affected the development of new genetic variation, because heat augments mutation rates. Also, fire removes individuals from a population, which changes the genetic structure of a population drastically and quickly.

Inevitably, some seeds from nondispersing variants were carried back to settlements and germinated, growing on dump heaps and other disturbed sites (latrines, areas cleared of trees, or burned-over terrain). Certain variants known as *colonizers* do particularly well in disturbed habitats, making them ideal candidates for domestication. Sedentism itself disturbs habitats as resources closer to settlements become depleted over time. Thus, variants of plants particularly susceptible to human manipulation had more opportunities to flourish where people were living. Under such circumstances, humans began to actively promote the growth of these plants, even by deliberately sowing them. Ultimately, people realized they could play a more active role in the process by purposefully breeding the strains they preferred. With this, domestication shifted from an unintentional to an intentional process.

The development of animal domestication in Southwest Asia seems to have proceeded along somewhat similar lines in the hilly country of southeastern Turkey, northern Iraq, and the Zagros Mountains of Iran. This region of rich environmental diversity contained large herds of wild sheep and goats. From the floodplains of the valley of the Tigris and Euphrates rivers, for example, travel to the north or east takes one into high country through three other ecological zones: first steppe; then oak and pistachio woodlands; and finally high plateau country with grass, scrub, or desert vegetation. Valleys that run at right angles to the mountain ranges afford relatively easy access across these zones. Today, a number of peoples in the region still graze their herds of sheep and goats on the low steppe in the winter and move to high pastures on the plateaus in the summer.

Food foragers inhabited these regions prior to the domestication of plants and animals. Each ecological zone contained distinct plant species, and because of the variation in altitude, plant foods matured at different times in different zones. These ancient peoples hunted a variety of animal species for meat and hides. The bones of hoofed animals—deer, gazelles, wild goats, and wild sheep—dominate the human refuse piles from these periods. Most of these hoofed animals naturally move back and forth from low winter pastures to high summer pastures. People followed the animals in their seasonal migrations, eating and storing other wild foods as they passed through different zones: palm dates in the lowlands; acorns, almonds, and pistachios higher up; apples and pears higher still; wild grains maturing at different times in different areas; and woodland animals in the forested region between summer and winter grazing lands.

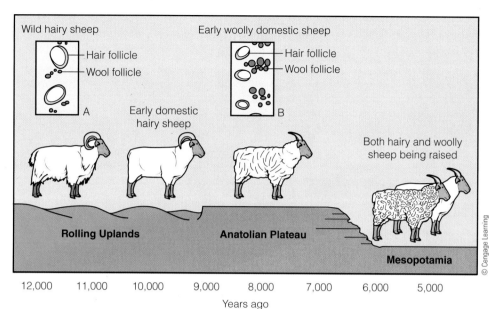

Figure 9.4 The Domestication of Sheep
Domestication of sheep resulted in evolutionary changes that created more wool. Inset A shows a section of the skin of wild sheep, as seen through a microscope, with the arrangement of hair and wool follicles. Inset B shows how this arrangement changed with domestication so that the sheep produced more wool.

The archaeological record indicates that, at first, the people of the Southwest Asia highlands hunted animals of all ages and sexes. But, beginning about 11,000 years ago, the percentage of immature sheep consumed increased to about 50 percent of the total. At the same time, people ate fewer of the female animals. (Feasting on male lambs increases yields by sparing the females for breeding.) This marks the beginning of human management of sheep.

The human management of flocks shielded sheep from the effects of natural selection, allowing the variants preferred by humans to have increased reproductive success. Variants attractive to humans did not arise out of need but randomly, as mutations do. But then humans selectively bred the varieties they favored. In such a way, those features characteristic of domestic sheep—such as greater fat and meat production, excess wool, and so on—began to develop (Figure 9.4). By 9,000 years ago, the shape and size of the bones of domestic sheep had become distinguishable from those of wild sheep. At about the same time and by similar means, humans domesticated pigs in southeastern Turkey and the lower Jordan River Valley.

Some researchers link animal domestication to the development of fixed territories and settlements. They suggest that resource ownership promotes postponing the short-term gain of killing prey for the long-term gain of continued access to animals in the future (Alvard & Kuznar, 2001). Eventually, ancient peoples introduced animal species domesticated in one area to regions outside their natural habitat. However, not all scientists believe domestication occurred in this way, with humans directing the process. Evolutionary anthropologist Brian Hare, featured in this chapter's Biocultural Connection, turns the theory around, arguing instead that animals (specifically, dogs) took advantage of new survival opportunities created by human settlements in the villages of the Neolithic.

The notion that dogs might have played a more active role in creating their own evolutionary relationship with humans underscores the fact that domestication took place as a series of interactions between species. Unaware of the long-term and revolutionary cultural consequences of their actions, the animal domesticators and domesticates alike sought only to maximize their available food sources. But as the domestication process continued, humans throughout the globe realized that the productivity of the domestic species increased relative to the wild species. Thus, these species became increasingly more important to subsistence, resulting in further domestication and further increases in productivity.

Other Centers of Domestication

In addition to Southwest Asia, the domestication of plants and sometimes animals took place simultaneously in the Indus Valley of South Asia, parts of the Americas (Mexico, Central America, the Andean highlands, the tropical forests of South America, and eastern North America), northern China, and Africa (Figure 9.5). In China, domestication of rice was under way along the middle Yangtze River by about 11,000 years ago. It took another 4,000 years, however, for domestic rice to dominate wild rice and become the dietary staple.

Similarly, decorations on pottery dated to between 5,000 and 8,800 years ago document rice as the earliest domesticated species of Southeast Asia. Other domesticates, particularly root crops such as yams and taro, dominate this region. Farming of root crops, or **vegeculture**,

---

vegeculture The cultivation of domesticated root crops such as yams, manioc, and taro together in a single field, generally by planting cuttings instead of seeds.

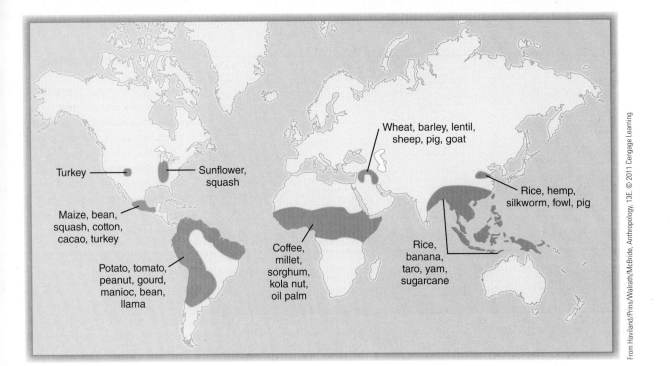

From Haviland/Prins/Walrath/McBride, Anthropology, 13E. © 2011 Cengage Learning

Figure 9.5 Early Plant and Animal Domestication
Domestication of plants and animals took place in widely scattered areas more or less simultaneously. The figure indicates some of the domesticates typical to each area such as wheat and sheep in Southwest Asia; sorghum and millet in Central Africa; rice and pigs in China; taro and bananas in Southeast Asia; maize and cacao in Mesoamerica; potatoes and llamas in South America; and squash and sunflowers in North America. Although the domesticated plants and animals appeared independently in distinct regions, humans today use all of them throughout the globe.

typically involves growing many different species together in a single field. Because this approximates the complexity of the natural vegetation, vegeculture tends to be more stable than seed crop cultivation. Propagation or breeding of new plants usually occurs through vegetative means—planting cuttings—rather than planting seeds.

In the Americas, the domestication of plants began about as early as it did in these other regions. Evidence for one species of domestic squash appears as early as 10,000 years ago in the coastal forests of Ecuador, the same time that another species independently appeared in an arid region of highland Mexico. The ecological diversity of the highland valleys of Mexico, like the hill country of Southwest Asia, provided an excellent environment for domestication (Figure 9.6). Movement of people through a variety of ecological zones as they changed altitude brought plant and animal species into new habitats, providing opportunities for "colonizing" species and humans alike.

Domestication in the Andean highlands of Peru, another environmentally diverse region, emphasized root crops, the most familiar being thousands of varieties of potatoes. Local farmers also domesticated plants for purposes other than eating, such as bottle gourds (Figure 9.7) and cotton. For livestock, South Americans domesticated guinea pigs, llamas, alpacas, and ducks. Common domesticates in the Mexican highlands included dogs, turkeys, and bees. American Indians living north of Mexico developed some of their own indigenous domesticates, including local varieties of squash and sunflowers.

CULTIGENS		PERCENTAGE			
		Hunting	Horticulture	Wild plant use	Years ago
					3,000
Squash Chili Amaranth Avocado	Cotton Maize Beans Gourds Sapote	29%		31%	3,500
					4,000
					4,500
Squash Chili Amaranth Avocado	Maize Beans Gourds Sapote	25%	50%		5,000
					5,500
Squash Chili Amaranth Avocado	Maize Beans Gourds Sapote	34%	52%		6,000
					6,500
					7,000
Squash Chili Amaranth Avocado		54%	40%		7,500
					8,000
					8,500

© Cengage Learning

Figure 9.6 Patterns of Neolithic Domestication in Mesoamerica
Subsistence trends in Mexico's Tehuacan Valley show that here, as elsewhere, dependence on horticulture came about gradually, over a prolonged period of time.

John Warburton-Lee Photography/Alamy

Figure 9.7 Domesticates for More than Food
Domesticated plants include a variety of species with various practical uses. Here two Datooga women from the Ngorongoro Highlands of Tanzania carry a large bottle gourd, a perfect vessel for carrying and storing liquids. The Datooga use bottle gourds to ferment and transport their local honey beer, a drink similar to mead. The inner chambers of bottle gourds also make them the perfect structure for a variety of musical instruments. Do any domesticated plants play a utilitarian role in your daily life?

Ultimately, American Indians domesticated over 300 food crops, including two of the four most important ones in the world today: potatoes and maize (the other two are wheat and rice). In fact, America's indigenous peoples first cultivated 60 percent of the crops grown in modern times; they not only developed the largest array of nutritious foods but also are the primary contributors to the world's varied cuisines. After all, where would Italian cuisine be without tomatoes? Thai cooking without peanuts? Northern European cooking without potatoes? It is no mistake that American Indians have been called the world's greatest farmers.

The domestication of plant species brought about the development of horticultural societies. Using neither irrigation nor plows, small communities of food-gardeners worked together with simple hand tools. Horticulturists typically cultivate a variety of crops in small gardens they have cleared by hand. Indians in the Amazon rainforest used sophisticated farming methods that left behind rich dark soil (Mann, 2002; Petersen, Neves, & Heckenberger, 2001). Reviving these ancient soil-enrichment techniques could contribute to better global management of rainforests and climate today.

Although plant domestication took place independently across the globe, at the same time people everywhere developed the same categories of foods: starchy grains (or root crops) accompanied by one or more legumes. For example, people in Southwest Asia combined wheat and barley with peas, chickpeas, and lentils, and people in Mexico combined maize with various kinds of beans. Together, the amino acids (building blocks of proteins) in these starch and legume combinations provide humans with sufficient protein. The starchy grains eaten at every meal in the form of bread, some sort of food wrapper (like a *tortilla*), or a gruel or thickening agent in a stew along with one or more legumes form the core of the diet. Each culture combines these rather bland sources of carbohydrates and proteins with flavor-giving substances that help the food go down.

In Mexico, for example, the chili pepper serves as the flavor enhancer par excellence (Figure 9.8). In other cuisines, bits of meat or fat, spices, dairy products, or mushrooms add the flavor. U.S. anthropologist Sidney Mintz (1985), who specializes in food, refers to this as the *core-fringe-legume pattern* (CFLP), noting its stability until the recent worldwide spread of processed sugars and high-fat foods.

Dogs Get Right to the Point

Some dog breeds have a receptive vocabulary; that is, they can understand hundreds of words. How can they do this? In turn, do their soulful eyes, head tipped to the side, or wagging tail really speak of unconditional love? What if they could speak themselves? Would they say something different from what their bodies seem to tell us?

Poet Billy Collins reveals in the poem "The Revenant" what one cranky dog, just put to sleep by his owner, came back to tell him:

I never liked you—not one bit.

When I licked your face, I thought of biting off your nose.[a]

Likewise, evolutionary anthropologist Brian Hare suggests that we view dog behavior, cognition, and communication through an anthropocentric lens.[b] He warns that these biases are in play when we speak of *Canis lupus familiaris*, a subspecies of wolf, as humankind's "best friend."

Hare came to this topic while researching chimpanzee cognition. Chimps, like the other great apes, can master human language at the level of a 2- to 3-year-old, and they can follow one another's gaze and figure out what might be in another chimp's line of sight.

Dogs and humans are unique among mammals in their ability to interpret and act upon the meaning of pointing.

However, they struggle to comprehend the gesture of pointing.

Instead of relegating pointing to another area of human uniqueness, Hare thought

of his own pet dogs, which, like all dogs, grasped this gesture immediately. Hare set about researching how and why dogs and humans, seemingly the lone species among

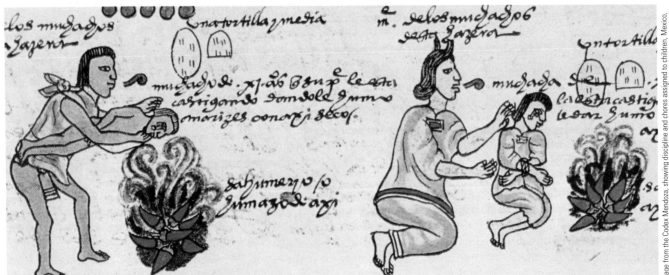

Figure 9.8 The Many Uses of Chili Peppers
Mexicans have used chili peppers for millennia. Chili peppers enhance the flavors of food and aid in digestion by helping with the breakdown of cellulose in diets heavy in plant foods. Chili peppers have other uses as well: This illustration from a 16th-century Aztec manuscript shows parents disciplining their children with smoke from chili peppers. Chili smoke was also used as a chemical weapon in warfare.

mammals, understand the meaning of pointing. He conducted pointing experiments using a "shell game" scenario, with dogs, chimps, wolves, and humans of all ages. Even puppies, like babies, understand pointing, which indicates that this ability is encoded in their genome and not a learned behavior. And like babies, they rely on social cues to interpret the meaning of a pointing finger.

The notion of a domesticated species, such as the dog, of course implies that one species has effectively altered the genetic makeup of another. To avoid anthropocentrism, Hare has used a dog's-eye view to think about domestication. Instead of seeing humans as the leaders in the process, he proposes that dogs domesticated themselves as humans began to live in discrete settlements during the Neolithic. Ancestral dogs, like wolves today, were probably partly scavengers and so came to orient to human habitations because of edible discarded material left by people. He suggests that those wolves that were the least timid about humans had a selective advantage in the "human cohabitation" niche and eventually evolved into domesticated dogs.

Social acceptance of dogs by humans, and vice versa, has led to many interesting and human-like behavioral adaptations in dogs. A dog "kissing" its owner's face may seem like love but really has its antecedents in the spitting up of prechewed food by wolves for their pack mates upon their return to the den. Although human owners do not spit up food for their dogs, they reward their dog's "love" through edible treats. Natural selection often produces such win–win scenarios among species—it's just that when humans are involved, we call it domestication!

This reconstruction of the history of the canine–human partnership provides an interesting context to those who have had to clean up after their dog has upset the household trash bin. As the sequel to such an escapade, when dog owners scold their dogs, dogs may show what we interpret as shame: head down, tail between the legs, body turned aside or walking away. Hare's experiments show that dogs will perform this behavior when scolded *even when they haven't broken any rule.* Their sensitivity to social judgment is so attuned that they can be in effect coerced into expressing what humans interpret as guilt when they are actually innocent. Evolutionary processes have favored dogs that could best manipulate humans.

Pointing has particular significance to a phenomenon in human psychology termed *joint attention*, which means that two individuals share awareness that both are visually fixing on a common visual target. The connection of joint attention exists when a dog explores an area to which a human points or when one person "points out" a path to another. But most importantly, joint attention lies at the heart of social awareness: Without it, we cannot function in groups. Interestingly, people with autism, who characteristically struggle with social cues and responses, also have a deficiency with pointing.

But not dogs. In the end they know just how to control us. The revenant dog from Billy Collins's poem gets the last laugh when he tells his owner about heaven:

. . . that everyone here can read and write,

the dogs in poetry, the cats and the others in prose.[c]

Biocultural Question

Can you think of other examples of how we may impose human norms of behavior onto other species? How is this the same or different from imposing notions specific to one culture onto another?

[a] Collins, B. (2005). The revenant. In *The trouble with poetry*. New York: Random House. Reprinted by permission of the Chris Calhoun Literary Agency.

[b] Hare, B., et al. (2002). The domestication of social cognition in dogs. *Science 298* (5598). 1634–1636.

[c] Collins, 2005.

Food Production and Population Size

Human population size has grown steadily since the Neolithic. The exact relationship between population growth and food production resembles the old chicken and egg question: Does population growth create the pressures that result in innovations, such as food production, or is population growth a consequence of food production? As already noted, domestication inevitably leads to higher yields, and higher yields make it possible to feed more people, although at the cost of more work.

Across human populations, increased dependence on farming and increased fertility seem to go hand in hand: Farming populations tend to have higher rates of fertility compared to hunter-gatherers. Hunter-gatherer mothers have their children about four to five years apart while some contemporary farming populations not practicing any form of birth control have another baby every year and a half (Figure 9.9). A complex interplay between human biology and culture lies at the heart of this difference. Some researchers suggest that the availability of soft foods for infants brought about by farming promoted population growth. In humans, frequent breast-feeding has a dampening effect on mothers' ovulation, inhibiting pregnancy in mothers who breast-feed exclusively. Because breast-feeding frequency declines when soft foods are introduced, fertility tends to increase.

However, many other pathways can also lead to fertility changes. For example, farming cultures tend to value numerous children as assets to help out with the many household chores. Further, higher fertility rates among farmers might derive from higher mortality rates due to infectious diseases brought about by the sedentary lifestyles and narrow diets characteristic of the Neolithic. High infant mortality, in turn, could raise the cultural value placed on fertility.

In the past, biases contributed to oversimplified anthropological explanations of fertility differences among peoples. Early anthropologists viewed the hunter-gatherer

VISUAL COUNTERPOINT

Dennis MacDonald/PhotoEdit

Gerald Cubitt

Figure 9.9 Diet and Fertility
The higher fertility of the Amish, a religious farming culture in North America, compared to that of the Ju/'hoansi hunter-gatherers from the Kalahari Desert was originally attributed to nutritional stress among the hunter-gatherers. We now know that childrearing beliefs and practices account for these differences. The Ju/'hoansi fertility pattern derives from the belief that a crying baby should be breast-fed, an action that biologically suppresses fertility. In farming populations, families view children as assets to help work the farm, and infant feeding practices reinforce high fertility rates. Children are weaned at young ages and transitioned to soft foods, a practice that promotes the next pregnancy. All human activity includes a complex interplay between human biology and culture.

lifestyle as inferior and interpreted the differences in fertility to be the consequence of nutritional stress among the hunter-gatherers. This theory was based in part on the observation that humans and many other mammals require a certain percentage of body fat to reproduce successfully (Frisch, 2002).

However, detailed studies among the !Kung or Ju/'hoansi (pronounced "zhutwasi") of the Kalahari Desert in southern Africa disproved this nutritional theory. The low fertility among the Ju/'hoansi ultimately derives from cultural beliefs about the right way to handle a baby: The Ju/'hoansi mother responds rapidly to her baby, breast-feeding whenever the infant shows any signs of

© Cengage Learning

fussing, day or night. On a biological level, the Ju/'hoansi pattern of breast-feeding in short, very frequent bouts suppresses ovulation, or the release of a new egg into the womb for fertilization (Konner & Worthman, 1980). Biology and culture interact in all aspects of the human experience.

The Spread of Food Production

Paradoxically, although domestication increases productivity, it also increases instability. As humans increasingly focus on varieties with the highest yields, other varieties become less valued and ultimately ignored. As a result, farmers depend on a rather narrow choice of resources, compared to the wide range utilized by food foragers. Today, modern agriculturists rely on a mere dozen species for about 80 percent of the world's annual tonnage of all crops.

This dependence on fewer varieties means that when a crop fails, for whatever reason, farmers have less to fall

Figure 9.10 **The Great Hunger**

During Ireland's Great Hunger (An Gorta Mór), starving Irish flocked to the ports such as Dublin from all over the country with the hope of escaping certain death by gaining ship passage to North America. Today, at the Custom House Quay in Dublin's Docklands where one of the first ships set sail in 1846, Dublin sculptor Rowan Gillespie's *Famine* commemorates the personal and national grief associated with this tragic time. Because political and economic discrimination were at the root of the starvation, displacement, and death (1 million people died) that selectively impacted poor Irish and not their English landlords, some have referred to this famine as genocide.

back on compared to food foragers. Furthermore, the common farming practice of planting crops together in one locality increases the likelihood of failure because proximity promotes the spread of disease among neighboring plants. Moreover, by relying on seeds from the most productive plants of a species to establish next year's crop, farmers favor genetic uniformity over diversity. In turn, some virus, bacterium, or fungus could wipe out vast fields of genetically identical organisms all at once as in the terrible Irish potato famine of 1845–1850 (Figure 9.10).

At that time in Ireland, the majority of the population was impoverished and dependent on potatoes for survival. Common people paid rent on small plots of land to landlords, who in turn rented large swaths of land from rich London landholders. Because British laws ensured that wheat and other crops earned a higher price than potatoes, Irish farmers were forced to sell these crops to make their rents, leaving potatoes as the main food staple for the Irish. When the potato blight hit, relief from the British government was slow and inadequate. A million Irish died of starvation and disease, and another 2 million abandoned their homes to migrate to the United States and elsewhere. The population of Ireland dropped from 8 million to 5 million as a result of the famine. The disaster that is now known as the Great Hunger (An Gorta Mór) developed from this interplay of economic and farming factors.

Farming's inherent biological instability and vulnerability to political maneuvering guaranteed that it would spread from its origins to neighboring regions through human migration. From Southwest Asia, for instance, farming expanded to the north and west, eventually spreading through all of Europe, as well as westward into North Africa and eastward to India. Domesticated variants also spread westward from China and Southeast Asia. Those who brought crops to new locations brought other things as well, including languages, beliefs, and new alleles for human gene pools. For instance, the descendants of some Irish people displaced by the famine, now living in many parts of the globe, have been shown to have a genetic propensity toward high levels of iron (hemochromatosis). Although the condition generally causes severe health problems, it may actually have improved people's chances of survival during that time of starvation, resulting in a high concentration of survivors who possessed the gene (Duffy, 2013). Besides genetic variation, **diffusion**, the spread of ideas, customs, or practices from one culture to another, leads to further innovations as cultures meet.

Diffusion occurred with the migration of Bantu-speaking people from the Niger River basin in West Africa to the southeast. Migration brought diffusion of crops, including pearl millet, watermelon, black-eyed peas, African yams, oil palms, and kola nuts (the source of modern cola drinks). These plants were first domesticated in West Africa but began spreading eastward by 5,000 years ago. Between 2,000 and 3,000 years ago, Bantu speakers with their crops reached the continent's east coast and a few centuries later reached its southern tip.

The Culture of Neolithic Settlements

Excavations of Neolithic settlements have revealed much about the daily activities of their former inhabitants. Archaeologists can reconstruct the business of making a living from structures, artifacts, and even food debris found at these sites. Jericho, an early farming community located near the Jordan River in the West Bank of Palestine provides an excellent case in point.

Jericho: An Early Farming Community

Excavations at the Neolithic settlement that later grew to become the city of Jericho have revealed the remains of a sizable farming community inhabited as early as 10,350 years ago. Here, in the Jordan River Valley, crops could be grown almost continuously due to the rich soils of an Ice Age lake that had dried up some 3,000 years earlier. In addition, waterborne deposits originating in the highlands to the west regularly renewed the fertility of the soil.

diffusion The spread of certain ideas, customs, or practices from one culture to another.

To protect their settlement against floods and associated mudflows, as well as invaders, the people of Jericho built massive walls of stone around the settlement. Within these walls (1.8 meters or 6 feet wide and 3.6 meters or 12 feet high) as well as behind a large rock-cut ditch (8.2 meters or 27 feet wide by 2.7 meters or 9 feet deep) an estimated 400 to 900 people lived in houses of mud brick with plastered floors arranged around courtyards.

Jericho's inhabitants also built a stone tower inside one corner of the wall, near the spring (Figure 9.11). Archaeologists estimate that it would have taken 100 people 104 days to build this tower. The village also included storage facilities as well as ceremonial structures, all made of mud brick. A village cemetery reflects the sedentary life of these early people. Common features in art, ritual, use of prestige goods, and burial practices indicate close contact between the farmers of Jericho and other villages in the vicinity. Marine shells, as well as obsidian and turquoise from nearby Sinai, discovered inside the walls document regional trade.

Neolithic Material Culture

Life in Neolithic villages included various innovations in toolmaking, pottery, housing, clothing, and even the digging of water wells. These aspects of material culture illustrate the dramatic social changes that took place during the Neolithic.

Toolmaking

Early harvesting tools consisted of razor-sharp flint blades inserted into handles of wood or bone. Later toolmakers added grinding and polishing the hardest stones to this toolmaking technique. Sickles, forks, hoes, and simple plows replaced basic digging sticks. Later, when domesticated animals became available for use as draft animals, these early farmers redesigned their plows. Villagers used mortars and pestles to grind and crush grain. Along with the development of diverse technologies, individuals acquired specialized skills for creating a variety of crafts including leatherwork, weavings, and pottery.

Pottery

In the Neolithic, people developed different forms of pottery for transporting and storing food, water, and various material possessions (Figure 9.12). Impervious to damage by insects, rodents, and dampness, pottery vessels can store small grains, seeds, and other materials. Moreover, villagers could cook their food in pottery vessels over the fire instead of cooking by dropping fire-heated stones directly into the food. Neolithic peoples used pottery for pipes, ladles, lamps, water containers, and other purposes; some cultures even used large pottery vessels for disposal of the dead. Significantly, pottery containers remain important for much of humanity today.

Widespread use of pottery made of clay and fired in very hot ovens indicates a sedentary community. Pottery abounds in all but a few of the earliest Neolithic settlements. Its fragility and weight make it less practical for use by nomads and hunters, who more typically use woven bags, baskets, and containers made of animal hide. Nevertheless, some modern nomads make and use pottery, just as some farmers today do not. In fact, food foragers in East Asia were making pottery vessels more than 15,000 years ago, long before pottery appeared in the emerging agricultural culture of Southwest Asia.

The manufacture of pottery requires skill and technological sophistication. Potters must know how to remove impurities from clay, how to shape it into desired forms, and how to dry it in a way that does not cause cracking. Proper firing requires potters to know how to heat clay so that it hardens and resists future disintegration from moisture without cracking or even exploding as it heats and later cools down.

Nathan Benn/Ottochrome/Corbis

Figure 9.11 The Tower of Jericho
The Natufian settlement of Jericho, located near the Jordan River in Palestine's West Bank, demonstrates that these ancient people had impressive social coordination, allowing them to build substantial structures. The defensive walls and the famous tower that stretched upward over 9 meters (28 feet) referenced in the Bible and gospel songs provide an example of cultural continuity in this region and beyond. The tower may have been part of a calendric ritual as the tower is built such that the shadows of mountains hit it first and then spread across the town at the sunset of the summer solstice (Barkai & Liran, 2008).

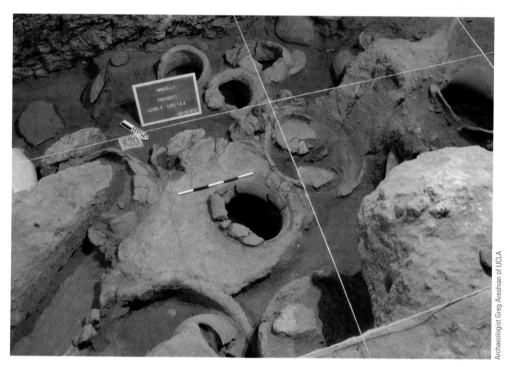

Figure 9.12 The First Vintners Archaeologists have recovered evidence of a winery dating back 6,100 years in the Areni-1 cave complex in southern Armenia. Indicators of wine production include a large hard-packed clay vat with elevated edges in which the wine fermented and jars in which the wine was stored. Ancient vintners used the old-fashioned method of trampling grapes with their feet. The same cave complex has also yielded the world's oldest shoe!

Archaeologist Greg Areshian of UCLA

Neolithic peoples decorated their pottery. Some engraved designs on the vessel before firing while others shaped special rims, legs, bases, and other details separately and fastened them to the finished pot. Painted and engraved decorations account for literally thousands of unique designs found among the pottery remains of ancient cultures.

Housing

Food production and the new sedentary lifestyle brought about another technological development—house building. Because most food foragers move around frequently, cave shelters, pits dug in the earth, and simple lean-tos made of hides, bark, and wooden poles serve the purpose of keeping the weather out. In the Neolithic, however, dwellings became more complex in design and more diverse in type. Some were constructed of wood, while others included more elaborate shelters made of stone, sun-dried brick, or branches plastered together with mud or clay.

Although permanent housing and food production tend to go hand in hand, some cultures created substantial housing without producing their food. For example, on the northwestern coast of North America, people lived in sturdy houses made of heavy planks hewn from cedar logs, yet their food consisted entirely of wild plants and animals, especially salmon and sea mammals.

Clothing

Neolithic peoples were the first to wear clothing made of woven textiles. The raw materials and technology necessary for the production of such clothing came from several sources: flax and cotton from farming; wool from domesticated sheep, llamas, or goats; and silk from

silkworms. Human invention contributed the spindle for spinning and the loom for weaving.

Social Structure

Archaeologists can draw certain inferences concerning the organization of Neolithic societies. Although archaeological sites contain indications of ceremonial and spiritual activity, village life seemed to lack central organization and hierarchy. Burials, for example, reveal an absence of social differentiation. Only rarely did early Neolithic peoples use stone slabs to construct or cover graves or include elaborate objects with the dead. Evidently, very few persons had attained the kind of exalted status that required an elaborate funeral. The smallness of most villages and the absence of extravagant buildings suggest that the inhabitants knew one another very well and were even related, so most of their relationships were probably highly personal ones, with equal emotional significance. Still, Neolithic peoples sometimes organized themselves to carry out impressive communal works preserved in the archaeological record, such as the site of Stonehenge in England (Figure 9.13).

Although there is some evidence of specialized social roles, in general Neolithic social structure had minimal division of

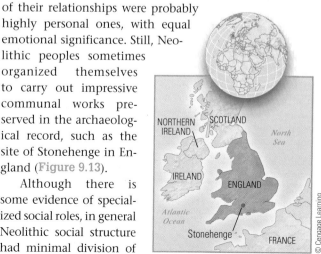

Celtic Collection, Homer Sykes/Alamy

Figure 9.13 **Druids at Stonehenge**
Sometimes Neolithic peoples organized themselves to carry out large projects, such as
constructing Stonehenge, the famous ceremonial and astronomical center built in England
some 4,500 years ago. Used as a burial ground long before the massive stone circle
was erected, Stonehenge reflects the builders' understanding of the forces of nature and
their impact upon food production. For instance, the openings of the stone circles aligns
precisely with the sunset of the winter solstice and the sunrise on the summer solstice.
This careful alignment indicates that Neolithic peoples were paying close attention to
the movement of the sun and to the seasonal growing cycle. Today, people such as the
Wiltshire Druids pictured here, still gather at Stonehenge for rituals associated with the
summer solstice.

labor. In such an **egalitarian society**, everyone has
about the same rank and shares equally in the basic resources that support income, status, and power. Villages
seem to have consisted of several households, each providing for most of its own needs. Kinship groups probably
met the organizational needs of society beyond the household level.

egalitarian society A society in which people have about the same rank
and share equally in the basic resources that support income, status,
and power.
Mesoamerica The region extending from central Mexico to the northern
regions of Central America.

Neolithic Cultures
in the Americas

In the Americas, the Neolithic revolution had its own
shape and timing. For example, Neolithic farming villages
were common in Southwest Asia between 8,000 and 9,000
years ago. But in **Mesoamerica**, the region from central Mexico to the northern regions of Central America,
as well as in the Andean highlands similar villages did
not appear until about 4,500 years ago. Pottery, which
developed in Southwest Asia shortly after plant and animal domestication, also did not emerge in the Americas
until about 4,500 years ago. Early Neolithic peoples in

the Americas did not use the potter's wheel. Instead, they manufactured elaborate pottery by hand. Looms and the hand spindle appeared in the Americas about 3,000 years ago. All of these developments in Mesoamerica and the Andean highlands occurred wholly independently from similar processes in Eurasia and Africa, with different crops, animals, and technologies.

Outside Mesoamerica and the Andean highlands, hunting, fishing, and gathering wild plant foods remained important to the economy of Neolithic peoples in the Americas. They applied some impressive technological innovations as seen in this chapter's Anthropology Applied feature. Diverse cultures of the Americas followed their own rich trajectories until European explorers brought disease and European domination.

The Neolithic and Human Biology

The shift to food production impacted human biology. Biological anthropologists studying human skeletons from Neolithic burial grounds have found evidence for somewhat less mechanical stress on peoples' bodies and teeth. Although exceptions exist, the teeth of Neolithic peoples generally show less wear, their bones are less robust, and compared to the skeletons of Paleolithic and Mesolithic peoples, they had less osteoarthritis (the result of stressed joint surfaces).

On the other hand, other skeletal features provide clear evidence for a marked deterioration in health and mortality. Skeletons from Neolithic villages show evidence of severe and chronic nutritional stress (Figure 9.14 and Figure 9.15) as well as pathologies related to infectious and deficiency diseases.

Dental decay increased during the Neolithic due to high-starch diets. Scientists have documented dental drilling of teeth in a 9,000-year-old Neolithic site in Pakistan (Coppa et al., 2006). Dental decay similarly increases in contemporary populations who switch from a varied hunter-gatherer diet to a high-starch diet.

Domestication and a sedentary lifestyle promote overpopulation relative to the resource base. As a result, even minor environmental fluctuations can lead to widespread hunger and malnutrition. Evidence of stress and disease increased proportionally

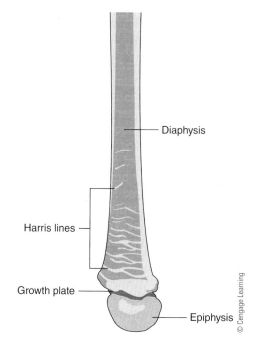

Figure 9.14 Long Bone Growth
During childhood, our long bones grow from areas made of cartilage called growth plates, located between a bony area at the joint known as an *epiphysis* and the long part of the bone, a *diaphysis*. Harris lines (first described by Dr. Harris in 1927), also called growth-arrest lines, form if growth is stopped due to temporary stress and then resumes.

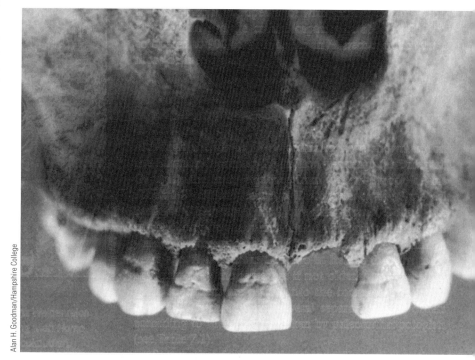

Figure 9.15 Enamel Hypoplasia
These teeth have less that the normal amount of enamel, which is indicative of arrested growth caused by famine or disease. These teeth are from an adult who lived in an ancient farming community in Arizona.

Pre-Columbian Fish Farming in the Amazon

by Clark L. Erickson

Two themes have long dominated the popular image of the Amazon: (1) the Myth of the Pristine Environment and (2) the Myth of the Noble Savage.... Today we know that much of what has been traditionally recognized as Wilderness in the Amazon is the indirect result of massive depopulation after the arrival of Europeans. The introduction of Old World diseases, slavery, missionization, resettlement, and warfare removed most of the native peoples from the land within 100 years....

Our work documents how native peoples of the Amazon (past and present) transformed, shaped, and in some cases, constructed areas often misidentified as pristine "wilderness." Our approach, called historical ecology or the archaeology of landscapes, assumes that all landscapes have long complex histories. High biodiversity today indicates past human activities such as opening up the forest, burning, and gardening. Since 1990, we have studied the vast networks of earthworks in the Bolivian Amazon built before the arrival of Europeans, including causeways of earth, artificial canals for canoe traffic, raised fields for growing crops in the savannahs, and settlement mounds of urban scale.

In 1995, the local governor invited us to begin archaeological investigations in Baures, a remote region of seasonally flooded savannahs, wetlands, and forest islands in northeast Bolivia. He loaned us his Cessna and pilot for an initial aerial survey. As the plane circled the landscape, we saw a complex web of straight roads, canals,

and moated earthwork enclosures below. During the dry season of 1996, I surveyed the area accompanied by a group of local hunters.

One artificial feature, referred to as a zigzag earthwork, particularly intrigued me. Low earthen walls zigzag across the savannahs between forest islands.... As we mapped them, I noted that there were small funnel-like openings where the earthworks changed direction...and realized that these matched the description of fish weirs of Amazonian peoples reported in the ethnographic and historical literature. Fish weirs—fences made of wood, brush, basketry, or stones with small openings that extend across bodies of water with baskets or nets placed in the openings—trap

migrating fish. While most fish weirs are simple ephemeral structures, in Baures permanent earthen weirs associated with small artificial ponds cover more than 500 square kilometers. Today receding floodwaters fill these ponds with fish for the dry season. I believe that before the arrival of Europeans, Amazonians used the weirs to store live fish until needed.

The native peoples of Baures shaped the environment into a productive landscape capable of providing sufficient protein to sustain large populations.... Archaeology provides the only means of documenting this important lost knowledge. As politicians, conservationists, and aid agencies seek sustainable solutions to both develop and conserve the Amazon, archaeologists can play a key role by providing time-tested models of land use.

Adapted from Erickson, C. L. (2001). Pre-Columbian farm fishing in the Amazon. *Expedition* 43 (3), 7–8.

Working with archaeologist Clark Erickson, artist Dan Brinkmeier of the Field Museum of Natural History has reconstructed the appearance of the ancient Baures fishing weirs.

with population density and the reliance on intensive agriculture. Further, the crowded conditions in settlements led to competition for resources with other villages, increasing the mortality rate due to warfare.

Neolithic peoples depended on crops selected for their higher productivity and storability rather than for nutritional balance. Moreover, as populations grew in size, they became increasingly vulnerable to periodic failures of domesticated crops. Thus, Neolithic peoples experienced worsened health and higher mortality compared to their Paleolithic forebears. Some have asserted that the switch from food foraging to food production was the worst mistake that humans ever made! It may be responsible for some of the greatest health challenges that humans face today (Cohen & Armelagos, 1984).

A sedentary, settled lifestyle brings problems such as the accumulation of garbage and human waste. Small groups of people, who move about from one campsite to another, leave their waste behind. Moreover, transmission of airborne diseases increases where people are gathered into villages. As we saw in Chapter 2, farming practices also created the ideal environment for the species of mosquito that spreads malaria.

The close association between humans and their domestic animals even facilitates the transmission of some animal diseases to people. A host of life-threatening diseases—including smallpox, chicken pox, and in fact all of the infectious diseases of childhood, overcome by medical science only in the latter half of the 20th century—came to humans through contact with domestic animals (Table 9.1). The concentration of domesticates in factory farms continues to threaten human health at large, as is evident from the 2009 swine flu pandemic (see this chapter's Globalscape) and the 2015 outbreak of avian flu in U.S. poultry farms.

TABLE 9.1

Diseases Acquired from Domesticated Animals

Disease	Animal with Most Closely Related Pathogen
Measles	Cattle (rinderpest)
Tuberculosis	Cattle
Smallpox	Cattle (cowpox) or other livestock with related pox viruses
Influenza	Pigs, ducks
Pertussis (whooping cough)	Pigs, dogs
Avian flu	Fowl (chickens and turkeys)

Close contact with animals provides a situation in which variants of animal pathogens may establish themselves in humans. Crowded factory farms and global agricultural trade further complicate the situation, as was the case with the 2009 pandemic of the swine flu variant, H1N1, and the 2015 avian flu outbreak.

The Neolithic and the Idea of Progress

Although the overall health of Neolithic peoples suffered as a consequence of this cultural shift, many view the transition from food foraging to food production as a great step upward on a ladder of progress. In part, this interpretation derives from one of the more widely held beliefs of Western culture—that human lifeways have progressed steadily over time. To be sure, farming allowed people to live together in substantial sedentary communities and to reorganize the workload in ways that permitted craft specialization. However, this does not represent a universal concept of progress but a set of cultural beliefs about the nature of progress. Each culture defines progress (if it does so at all) in its own terms.

Whatever the benefits of food production, Neolithic humans paid a substantial price for the development of **agriculture**—intensive crop cultivation, employing plows, fertilizers, and/or irrigation. As anthropologists Mark Cohen and George Armelagos put it, we see, "an overall decline in the quality—and probably in the length—of human life associated with the adoption of agriculture" (Cohen & Armelagos, 1984, p. 594).

Rather than imposing ethnocentric notions of progress on the archaeological record, anthropologists view the advent of food production as part of the diversification of cultures, something that began in the Paleolithic. Although some societies continued to practice various forms of hunting, gathering, and fishing, others became horticultural. The resource competition that began in the Neolithic has pushed hunter-gatherers into increasingly marginalized territories over time.

Some horticultural societies developed agriculture. Technologically more complex than horticultural societies, agriculturalists may use a wooden or metal plow pulled by one or more harnessed draft animals, such as horses, oxen, or water buffalos, to produce food on larger plots of land. Pastoralism arose in environments that were too dry, too grassy, too steep, too cold, or too hot for effective horticulture or intensive agriculture. Pastoralists breed and manage migratory herds of domesticated grazing and browsing animals, such as goats, sheep, cattle, llamas, or camels. For example, without plows, early Neolithic peoples could not farm the heavy grass cover of the Russian steppe, but they could graze their animals there. Thus, a number of peoples living in the arid grasslands and deserts that stretch from northwestern Africa into Central Asia kept large herds of domestic animals, relying on their neighbors for plant foods. Finally, some societies went on to develop civilizations—the subject of the next chapter.

agriculture Intensive crop cultivation, employing plows, fertilizers, and/or irrigation.

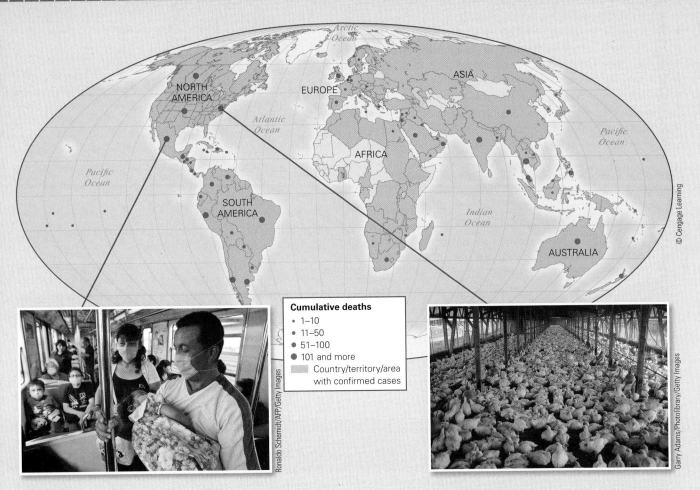

Cumulative deaths
- 1–10
- 11–50
- 51–100
- 101 and more
- Country/territory/area with confirmed cases

Factory Farming Fiasco?

In April 2009 protective masks and gloves were a common sight in Mexico City as the news of the swine flu pandemic appeared in the United States and Mexico. On June 11, 2009, the World Health Organization (WHO) made the pandemic official, and by July cases had been reported in three-quarters of the states and territories monitored by the WHO. Scientists across the world examined the genetic makeup of the virus to determine its origins.

From the outset of the pandemic, many signs have pointed to a pig farming operation in Veracruz, Mexico, called Granjas Caroll, which is a subsidiary of Smithfield Foods, the world's largest pork producer. However, U.S. genetic analyses led scientists to a different conclusion: "the virus may have originated in a U.S. pig that traveled to Asia as part of the hog trade. The virus may have infected a human there, who then traveled back to North America, where the virus perfected human-to-human spread, maybe even moving from the United States to Mexico."[a]

While scientists examine the genetic evidence for swine flu, a look at factory farming shows how these practices facilitate the proliferation of disease. For example, the pig population of North Carolina is about 10 million, and most of these pigs are crowded onto farms of over 5,000 animals. These pigs travel across the country as part of farming operations. A pig born in North Carolina may travel to the heartland of the United States to fatten up before a final trip to the slaughterhouses in California. Because pigs are shipped to several locations before slaughter, there are many opportunities for viruses to pass between species. The crowded conditions in factory farms also mean that if a virus enters a farm, it quickly can infect many individuals.

Farmers, health professionals, and government agencies are naturally worried about viruses spreading from animals to humans. Millions of animals are sometimes killed as a preventative measure. The 2015 avian flu outbreak precipitated the slaughter of over 6.5 million chickens and turkeys in the United States to prevent the spread of the disease. This kind of mass slaughter brings its own problems—the loss of many healthy animals, the waste of resources that had been used in their care, and the problem of how, and where, to dispose of the carcasses. Health risks of global food distribution have long been a concern, and the swine and avian flu outbreaks elevate these concerns to a new level.

Global Twister

Do you think preemptive mass slaughter is a tenable long-term way to address the problem of interspecies spread of disease? How else might this issue be addressed?

---

[a] Cohen, J. (2009). Out of Mexico? Scientists ponder swine flu's origin. *Science 324* (5928), 700–702.

CHAPTER CHECKLIST

What is the Mesolithic?

✓ Between the Paleolithic and Neolithic, the Mesolithic (Archaic in the Americas) was a time of warming after the last glacial period; it included rising sea levels, changes in vegetation, and the disappearance of herd animals from many areas.

✓ The Mesolithic was characterized by a shift from the hunting of big game to the hunting of smaller game and gathering of a broad spectrum of plants and aquatic resources.

✓ Because of an increased reliance on seafood and plants, some people developed more sedentary lifeways.

✓ Toolkits included microliths—small, hard, sharp blades of flint or similar stone that could be mass produced and hafted; larger blades were also used to produce implements like sickles.

✓ Archaic cultures of the Americas are comparable to the Old World Mesolithic.

What is the Neolithic revolution, and how did it come about?

✓ A shift to food production through the domestication of plants and animals constitutes most of the change of this period. Settlement in permanent villages accompanied food production, although some Neolithic peoples who depended on domesticated animals did not become sedentary. The use of polished stone tools by all peoples of this period gives the Neolithic its name.

✓ Hard stone was ground and polished for tools. Sickles, forks, hoes, and plows replaced simple digging sticks. Axes and adzes made of polished stone were far stronger and less likely to chip compared to earlier tools.

✓ Village life allowed for a reorganization of the workload, letting some individuals pursue specialized tasks.

✓ The change to food production took place independently and more or less simultaneously in various regions of the world: Southwest and Southeast Asia, highland Mexico and Peru, South America's Amazon forest, eastern North America, China, and Africa. Common food complexes were based on starchy grains and/or roots that were consumed with protein-containing legumes plus flavor enhancers.

✓ Southwest Asia contains the earliest known Neolithic sites consisting of small villages of mud huts with individual storage pits and clay ovens along with evidence of food production and trade.

✓ At ancient Jericho, remains of tools, houses, and clothing indicate Neolithic people first occupied the oasis between 10,000 to 11,000 years ago. At its height, Neolithic Jericho had a population of 400 to 900 people.

Comparable villages developed independently in Mexico and Peru by about 4,500 years ago.

What is domestication, and how can we recognize it?

✓ A domesticated plant or animal is one that has become genetically modified as an intended or unintended consequence of human manipulation.

✓ Analysis of plant remains at a site, examining the size and shape of various parts of the plant, usually indicates whether its occupants were food producers.

✓ Domestication produces skeletal changes in some animals. Age and sex imbalances in herd animals may also indicate manipulation by human domesticators.

✓ Domesticated crops are more productive but also more vulnerable. Food production requires more labor compared to hunting and gathering.

How did the Neolithic revolution impact social structure?

✓ Human population sizes have increased steadily since the Neolithic. Scholars debate whether pressure from increasing population size led to innovations or whether innovations allowed population size to grow.

✓ Periodic crop failures forced Neolithic peoples to move into new regions, spreading farming from one region to another, as occurred with migrations from Southwest Asia into Europe.

✓ Trade specializations came about due to the increased yields of food production. This included the extensive manufacture and use of pottery, the building of permanent houses, and the weaving of textiles.

✓ Social organization was relatively egalitarian as seen in the uniformity of housing and absence of socially differentiated burials.

✓ Neolithic peoples sometimes organized themselves to create monumental structures related to their belief systems.

What were the biological consequences of the Neolithic revolution?

✓ New diets, living arrangements, and farming practices led to increased incidence of disease and higher mortality rates. Increased fertility, however, more than offset mortality.

✓ Many infectious diseases originated in the Neolithic because of close contact between humans and animal domesticates.

✓ Increased competition for resources began in the Neolithic. Hunter-gatherers have become increasingly marginalized over time due to this competition.

QUESTIONS FOR REFLECTION

1. The changed lifeways of the Neolithic included the domestication of plants and animals as well as settlement into villages. This new way of life created a competition for resources. How is this competition manifest in the world today? Does it impact your life personally?

2. Why do you think some people of the past remained food foragers instead of becoming food producers? To what degree was the process of domestication conscious and deliberate? Were humans always directing this process?

3. Why are the changes of the Neolithic sometimes mistakenly associated with progress? Why have the social forms that originated in the Neolithic come to dominate the earth?

4. Although the archaeological record indicates some differences in the timing of domestication of plants and animals in different parts of the world, why is it incorrect to say that one region is more advanced than another?

DIGGING INTO ANTHROPOLOGY

Domestication Today

During the Neolithic age, humans began the transition from hunting and foraging to domesticating plants and animals, a trend that continues to this day. In some languages—including Norwegian, Spanish, and Mandarin—the words for *domesticating* and *taming* are the same. However, many other languages, like English and Japanese, use two separate words with different meanings. "Domesticating" refers to the human cultivation or breeding of species to bring out desirable physical or behavioral traits, while "taming" refers to an individual animal that has become, contrary to its natural inclination, tolerant of human interaction.

Do you have a pet? If it's a cat, a dog, a sheep, or even a goldfish, your pet is a member of a species that has been domesticated, as opposed to a wild animal forced to live in captivity, as is the case with many exotic pets. For one day, make a note of every interaction you have with your pet. What does your pet depend on you to provide? What do you provide for your pet in addition to meeting its basic needs? What does your pet provide for you?

In addition, think about the following: What challenges would a domesticated animal like a cat or dog face if it had to live in the wild? What challenges would its wild relatives—say, a bobcat or a wolf—face in captivity?

Tauseef Mustafa/Afp/Getty Images

CHALLENGE ISSUE

With the emergence of cities and states, human societies began to develop organized central governments and concentrated power that made it possible to build monumental structures and urban infrastructure. But cities and states also ushered in problems, many of which we still face today, such as large-scale warfare. Today, this pernicious aspect of civilization plagues Aleppo, Syria, one of the world's oldest continuously inhabited cities. Fighting within Aleppo's walled Old City led to a massive fire that destroyed its ancient marketplace. Aleppo residents viewed this market as the "soul" of their city. This loss compounds the profound human suffering—with over 300,000 lives lost, over 6 million displaced within Syria, and over 4 million forced to flee the country altogether—as civil war obliterates heritage and cultural identity. Syria's cultural loss also includes the destruction of the minaret of the Umayyad Mosque in Damascus, a Crusader castle, the Roman city of Palmyra, and countless artifacts and artworks that have been stolen. Securing our collective future and preserving our heritage require that we ensure that war is not an inevitable consequence of today's social organization.

The Emergence of Cities and States

10

A walk down a busy street in a city like New York or Tokyo shows us many facets of life in contemporary urban society. People going to and from offices and stores fill crowded sidewalks. Heavy traffic of cars, buses, bicycles, and trucks periodically comes to a standstill. A brief two-block stretch may contain a grocery store; shops selling clothing, cell phones, or electronics; a restaurant; a newsstand; a gasoline station; and a movie theater. Other neighborhoods may feature a museum, a police station, a school, a hospital, or a place of worship.

Each of these services or places of business depends on others from outside this two-block radius. A butcher shop, for instance, depends on slaughterhouses and ranches. A clothing store could not exist without designers; farmers who produce cotton, silk, and wool; and workers who manufacture synthetic fibers. Restaurants rely on refrigerated trucking and vegetable and dairy farmers. Hospitals need insurance companies, pharmaceutical companies, and medical equipment industries to function. All depend on the public utilities—the telephone, gas, water, and electric companies, not to mention the Internet. Interdependence defines modern cities.

Interdependence in a big city makes a variety of products readily available. But interdependence also creates vulnerability. If labor strikes, bad weather, or acts of violence cause one service to stop functioning, other services can deteriorate. At the same time, cities are resilient. When one service breaks down, others take over its functions. For instance, as wars damage basic infrastructure, people develop alternative systems to cope with everything from basic tasks such as procuring food and water to communication within global political systems (Figure 10.1). People coping with the aftermath of natural disasters such as Hurricane Katrina in the southern United States in 2005, the massive *tsunamis* that hit Japan in 2011 and the Philippines in 2013, or the devastating earthquake that struck Nepal in 2015 must also find such alternatives.

In this chapter you will learn to

- Define *civilization*, *cities*, and *states*, and identify their global origins.

- Identify the elements of archaeological exploration of ancient civilizations through a case study of the Maya city of Tikal.

- Examine the four major cultural changes that mark the transition from the Neolithic period to life in urban centers.

- Compare theories for the development of states.

- Identify the problems that accompany the development of cities and states.

Qais Usyan/AFP/Getty Images

Figure 10.1 Urban Growth amid Destruction
Decades of violence have severely compromised the infrastructure of Afghanistan, yet the size
of Kabul, the fifth fastest-growing city in the world, has swelled to over 4 million people. Streets
consist of rubble, and building facades stand as empty shells. Here children go to a public
spigot to get their family's daily water supply.

With the Internet and globalization, the interdependence of goods and services transcends far beyond city limits. Social media such as Facebook and Twitter allow instantaneous communication about geopolitical events and can mobilize global support. Harrowing images from crises and conflicts such as the Syrian civil war, downed airplanes, or the West African Ebola outbreak zip through cyberspace to connect us but also cause some to recoil. However, this intricate interconnected fabric of life did not always exist, and the concentrated availability of diverse goods developed only very recently in human history.

Defining Civilization

The word *civilization* comes from the Latin *civis*, meaning "an inhabitant of a city," and *civitas*, "the urban community in which one dwells." In everyday usage, the word

civilization connotes refinement and progress and may imply ethnocentric judgment. Anthropologists, however, avoid these culture-bound notions. In anthropology, **civilization** refers to a society in which large numbers of people live in cities, are socially stratified, and are governed by a ruling elite working through centrally organized political systems called states.

Neolithic villages grew into the world's first cities between 4,500 and 6,000 years ago, first in Mesopotamia (modern-day Iraq and Syria), then in Egypt's Nile Valley and the Indus Valley, today's India and Pakistan (Figure 10.2). In China, around the ancient city of Hsia, civilization was under way by 5,000 years ago. Independent of these developments in Eurasia and Africa, the first American Indian cities appeared in Peru around 4,000 years ago and in Mesoamerica about 3,000 years ago.

What characterized these first cities? Why are they called the birthplaces of civilization? The most obvious feature of cities—and of civilization—is their large size and population. But cities are more than overgrown villages. Consider the case of Çatalhöyük, a compact 9,500-year-old settlement in south-central Turkey that, though well

civilization In anthropology, a society in which large numbers of people live in cities, are socially stratified, and are governed by a ruling elite working through centrally organized political systems called states.

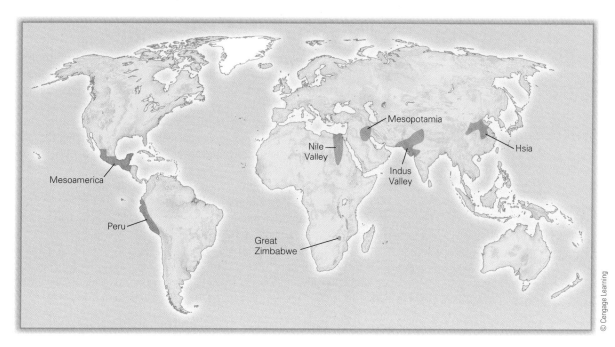

Figure 10.2 Map of Early Civilizations
The major early civilizations sprang from Neolithic villages in various parts of the world. Those of the Americas developed wholly independently of those in Africa and Eurasia. Chinese civilization seems to have developed independently of Southwest Asia, including the Nile and Indus civilizations. Although the Bantu city of Great Zimbabwe dates to later than all of these, it likewise was a major civilization that arose independently.

populated, was not a true city (Balter, 1998, 1999, 2001a; Hodder, 2006; Kunzig, 1999). The tightly packed houses for its more than 5,000 inhabitants left no room for streets. People traversed the tops of neighboring houses and dropped through a hole in the roof to get into their own home. Although house walls were covered with paintings and bas-reliefs, the houses were structurally similar to one another. People grew some crops, wove fabric from hemp, and tended livestock but also collected significant amounts of food from wild plants and animals, never intensifying their agricultural practices. Çatalhöyük contains no evidence of public architecture and only minimal evidence of a division of labor or a centralized authority.

Archaeological evidence from early urban hubs, by contrast, demonstrates organized planning by a central authority, technological intensification, and social stratification. For example, flood control and protection were vital components of the great ancient cities of the Indus Valley,

located in today's India and Pakistan. Mohenjo-Daro, an urban center with a population of at least 20,000 at its peak some 4,500 years ago, was built on an artificial mound, safe from floodwaters. City streets were laid out in a grid pattern with sophisticated drainage systems for individual homes, indicating further centralized planning.

Ancient peoples incorporated their worldview into the cities they built. For example, the great Mesoamerican city Teotihuacan, founded 2,200 years ago near present-day Mexico City, translated the solar calendar into a unified spatial pattern. Ancient city planners oriented the Street of the Dead—a grand north-south axis originating at the Pyramid of the Moon and bordered by the Pyramid of the Sun and the royal palace compound—to an astronomical marker, east of true north. They even channeled the Rio San Juan to conform to the city's grid (Figure 10.3). Thousands of apartment compounds and a grid of narrow streets surrounded this core, maintaining the east-of-north orientation throughout the city. Archaeologists estimate that over 100,000 people

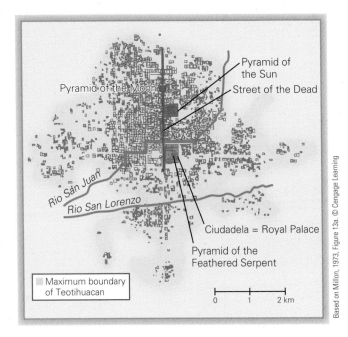

Based on Millon, 1973, Figure 13a. © Cengage Learning

Figure 10.3 Ancient City Planning
The founders of Teotihuacan imposed an audacious plan on several square kilometers of landscape in central Mexico. At the center is the Street of the Dead, originating at the Pyramid of the Moon (*near top*) and running past the Pyramid of the Sun, and, south of Rio San Juan, the palace compound. Note the gridded layout of surrounding apartment compounds and the channeled Rio San Juan. Teotihuacan's principal avenue, the Street of the Dead (*left*), was unequaled in scale until the construction of such modern-day avenues as the Champs-Élysées in Paris. Archaeologists estimate that 100,000 people lived in this city in various neighborhoods according to their social position. This major avenue was home to the elite.

inhabited Teotihuacan until its sudden collapse, possibly in the 7th century.

Teotihuacan contains clear evidence of both social and economic diversity. Variation in size and quality of apartment rooms indicates at least six levels of society. Those at the top of the social scale lived on or near the Street of the Dead. The Pyramid of the Sun, built along this avenue above a cave, was seen as a portal to the underworld and as the home of deities associated with death. Teotihuacan artisans worked on exotic goods and raw materials imported from distant regions, and at least two neighborhoods housed people with foreign affiliations: one for those from Oaxaca, the other (the "merchant's quarter") for those from the Gulf and Maya lowlands. Farmers, whose labor in fields (some of them irrigated) supplied the food to fellow city-dwellers, also resided in the city.

Far more than expanded villages, Mohenjo-Daro and Teotihuacan, like other early cities throughout the globe, exemplify a new way of life. The following case study provides a glimpse into another of the world's ancient cities and reveals how archaeologists went about studying this city—from the first exploratory surveys, to excavations, to theories proposed about its development.

Tikal: A Case Study

The ancient city of Tikal, situated in Guatemala in Central America about 300 kilometers (186 miles) north of Guatemala City, was one of the largest lowland Maya centers in existence. The Maya settled here 3,000 years ago, on a broad limestone terrace in a rainforest. By correlating the Maya calendar precisely with our own, archaeologists know that the civilization at Tikal flourished until 1,100 years ago.

At its height, Tikal covered about 120 square kilometers (46 square miles). The Great Plaza, a large paved area surrounded by about 300 major structures and thousands of houses, stood at Tikal's center (Figure 10.4). Starting from a small, dispersed population, Tikal grew to at least 45,000 people. By 1,550 years ago, its population density had reached 600 to 700 people per square kilometer, three

© Cengage Learning

times that of the surrounding region. Archaeologists explored Tikal under the joint auspices of the University of Pennsylvania Museum and the Guatemalan government from 1956 through the 1960s. At the time, it was the most ambitious archaeological project undertaken in the western hemisphere.

At first, archaeologists investigated only the major temple and palace structures near the Great Plaza, Tikal's epicenter. They later turned their attention to the hundreds of dwellings that surrounded larger buildings. Imagine trying to get a realistic view of life in a major city such as Chicago or Beijing by looking only at their monumental public buildings. Similarly, archaeologists realized that accurately reconstructing daily life at Tikal required exploring the full range of ruins. Through excavating small structures, archaeologists could estimate Tikal's population size and density, reconstruct everyday life and social organization, and test the conventional assumption that the subsistence practices of the Maya could not sustain large population concentrations (Haviland, 2002, 2014).

Surveying and Excavating the Site

Mapping crews surveyed 6 square kilometers (2.3 square miles) of forested land surrounding the Great Plaza to guide the small-structure excavation process. The dense rainforest canopy prevented the use of aerial photography for this mapping. Trees obscured all but the highest temples, and many of the small ruins remained practically invisible even on the ground (Figure 10.5). Four years of mapping revealed that ancient Tikal extended far beyond the original area surveyed. Continued surveying fully defined the city's boundaries and overall size.

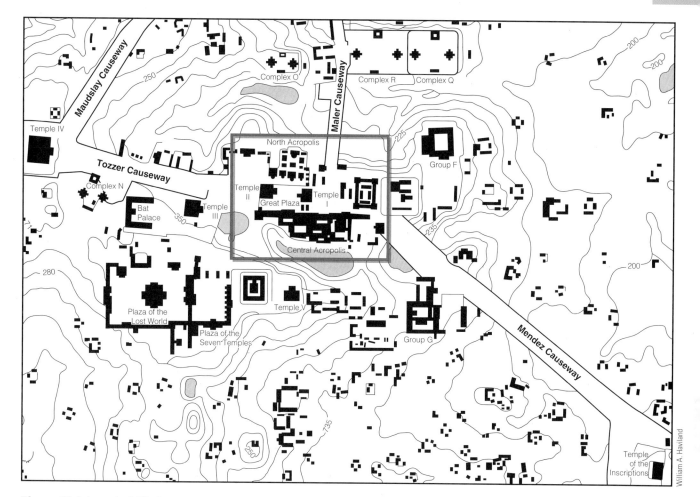

Figure 10.4 Layout of Tikal

Tikal spreads far beyond the Great Plaza and the monumental buildings that have been excavated and are mapped here. Archaeologists used surveying techniques, test pits, and other strategies to define the city's boundaries and to understand the full spectrum of lifeways that took place there. The red outline in the center of the map delineates the royal court, royal burial ground, and central marketplace. In addition to what is pictured here, Tikal extends several kilometers outward in every direction.

Evidence from the Excavation

Archaeologists reconstructed daily life in Tikal as well as the relationship between Tikal and other regions from the evidence they recovered. For example, granite, quartzite, hematite, pyrite, jade, slate, and obsidian imported either as raw materials or finished products demonstrated trade in nonperishable items. Marine materials came from Caribbean and Pacific coastal areas. In turn, Tikal residents exported chert (a flint-like stone used to manufacture tools) both in its raw form and as finished objects. Tikal's location between two river systems may have facilitated an overland trade route. There was also trade in perishable goods such as textiles, feathers, salt, and cacao.

Archaeologists found specialized woodworking, pottery, obsidian, and shell workshops at Tikal. Skillful carvings on stone monuments suggest the presence of occupational specialists, as did the fine artwork glazed into ceramic vessels. Textile workers, dental workers, makers of barkcloth "paper," scribes, masons, astronomers, and other occupational specialists also left traces of their work.

Tikal's scale required some form of bureaucratic organization. Maya glyphs (Figure 10.6) record that the government was headed by a hereditary ruling dynasty with sufficient power to organize massive public works, including a system of defensive ditches and embankments on the northern and southern edges of the city. The longest of these ran for a distance of perhaps 19 to 28 kilometers (6 to 17 miles). The Maya built numerous temples and public buildings.

Maya astrological experts tracked the dynasties and their conquests using a nonrepeating "long count" calendar system that tallied the number of days that had passed since a mythical creation date corresponding to August 11, 3114 BCE. According to Maya mythology, we live in the fourth world, the first three creations having been failed attempts by the gods. Doomsday predictions surrounded the end of the most recent long count on December 21, 2012. That same year, archaeologists uncovered a series of glyphs at a site near Tikal

Figure 10.5 Site Survey at Tikal
At many archaeological sites, archaeologists use aerial photography to survey and map out the basic structures before excavation. The dense tree cover at Tikal, where only the tips of the highest temples pierce the forest canopy, prevented this method, and archaeologists instead turned to ground survey techniques. Those familiar with the original *Star Wars* movie will be interested to know that the aerial views of the rebel camp (the Massassi Outpost on the fourth moon of Yavin) were filmed at Tikal.

Figure 10.6 Stone Documents
Carved monuments like this were commissioned by Tikal's rulers to commemorate important events in their regions. Archaeologists have deciphered the written language of glyphs chiseled into the stone. This monument portrays the reign of a king who ruled around 785 C.E. Only a specialist could have accomplished such skilled stone carvings. The glyphs also provide indirect evidence of writing specialists or scribes who may have kept records on perishable materials such as barkcloth paper. (For a translation of the inscription on the monument's left side, see Figure 10.13.)

indicating that the astronomically accurate Maya calendars extend far into the future (Saturno et al., 2012).

Religion at Tikal may have contributed to coping with agricultural uncertainty. During the long dry months, residents depended on rainwater collected in reservoirs during the rainy season. The ancient Maya may have perceived Tikal, with a high elevation relative to surrounding terrain, as a "power place," especially suited for making contact with supernatural forces and beings who brought the rain (Figure 10.7).

Maya priests could have influenced deities in times of drought and honored them in times of plenty. Priests—experts on the Maya calendar—also determined the most favorable time to plant crops. People resided in or near the city so that they could receive blessings and guidance from the priestly class. In turn, artisans, craftspeople, and other occupational specialists served the needs of elite priests and the ruling dynasty.

As population increased, new methods of food production sustained Tikal's residents. Fruit trees and other crops were grown around Maya houses in soils enriched by human waste. The Maya also constructed raised fields in areas that flooded during the rainy season that, with careful maintenance and fertilization, could be cultivated intensively, year after year. Converting low areas into reservoirs and constructing channels to carry runoff from plazas and other architecture into these reservoirs, the Tikal Maya maximized the collection of water for the dry season.

After sustaining population growth for several hundred years, the pressure for food and land reached a critical point and growth stopped. At the same time, warfare with other cities took its toll on Tikal. Abandoned houses, nutritional problems visible in skeletons recovered from burials, and construction of defensive ditches

Figure 10.7 Modern Maya at Tikal
Archaeologists have proposed that Tikal emerged as an important religious center due to its relative altitude in the region. This higher altitude may have created the perception of power and access to supernatural forces. Today, Tikal remains an important religious center for local Maya, who gather in front of the acropolis for a traditional ceremony.

and embankments are evidence of warfare. Following this violent outbreak, the strong central authority directed activities as before, for another 250 years or so.

As the case study, the excavations at Tikal demonstrate the splendor, the social organization, the belief systems, and the trading and agricultural practices of the ancient Maya civilization. New discoveries continue to enrich what we know about the Maya and other Mesoamerican civilizations (Figure 10.8).

Cities and Cultural Change

A person who grew up in a rural North American village today and moved to Philadelphia, Montreal, or Los Angeles would experience a very different way of life. The same would be true for a Neolithic village-dweller who moved into a Mesopotamian city 5,500 years ago. Because cultures are dynamic, integrated systems of adaptation that respond to external and internal factors, a shift to life in urban centers also includes changes in social structure

and ideology. Four basic changes mark the transition from Neolithic village life to life in the first urban centers: agricultural innovation, diversification of labor, central government, and social stratification.

Agricultural Innovation

New farming methods distinguished early civilizations from Neolithic villages. The ancient Sumerians, for example, built an extensive system of dikes, canals, and reservoirs to irrigate their farmlands and manage larger herds of animals. Irrigation improved crop yield and allowed farmers, freed from seasonal rain cycles, to harvest more crops in one year. Increased crop yields, in turn, contributed to higher population densities.

Diversification of Labor

Diversified labor also characterized early civilizations. In Neolithic villages without irrigation or plow farming, every family member participated in raising crops. Higher

Figure 10.8 Uncovering Hidden History
In the jungles of Honduras lie the remains of a society, dating from 800 to 1400 CE. Although this society seems to have had Maya influence—including paved roads, large buildings, and ball courts—archaeologists have found little evidence of Maya-like social hierarchy. Instead, these remains may have been associated with communities lacking strong institutionalized power. In studying these settlements, some of which are largely untouched, scientists employ both technologically advanced and more traditional methods. Aerial lidar (light and radar) mapping technology allows scientists to discern geographic features despite the jungle cover, including where humans have shaped the land. Traditional methods include documenting caches of artifacts discovered in the jungle, as U.S. archaeologist Chris Begley does here, as well as speaking with the contemporary indigenous Pech people about their ancestors.

crop yields and increased population permitted a sizable number of people to pursue nonagricultural activities on a full-time basis.

Ancient public records document various specialized workers. For example, an early Mesopotamian document from the old Babylonian city of Lagash (modern-day Tell al-Hiba, Iraq) lists the artisans and tradespeople paid from crop surpluses stored in the temple granaries. These lists included coppersmiths, silversmiths, sculptors, merchants, potters, tanners, engravers, butchers, carpenters, spinners, barbers, cabinetmakers, bakers, clerks, and brewers.

Bronze Age In the Old World, the period marked by the production of tools and ornaments of bronze; began about 5,000 years ago in China, the Mediterranean, and South Asia and about 500 years earlier in Southwest Asia.

Specialization allowed experts to invent new ways of making and doing things. In Eurasia and Africa, civilization ushered in the **Bronze Age**, a period marked by the production of tools, ornaments, and weapons made of this metal alloy. Copper and tin (the metals from which bronze is made) were smelted, or separated from their ores, then purified and cast to make plows, swords, axes, shields, spears, and other objects (Figure 10.9). Later, such tools were made from smelted iron. In wars, slings, stone knives, and spears could not stand up against metal spears, arrowheads, swords, helmets, and armor.

The indigenous civilizations of the Americas used metals such as copper, silver, and gold for ceremonial and ornamental objects, relying on stone for many of their everyday tools. The ready availability of obsidian (a glass formed by volcanic activity), its extreme sharpness (many

Stuart Hay, ANU

Figure 10.9 **3D Printing and the Conical Spear-Butt of Navan** In the early 20th century, a small, conical Bronze Age artifact was unearthed in Ireland. Archaeologists at the time classified the object as part of the butt of a spear. A century later, Australian archaeologist Billy Ó Foghlú had a different idea. He used modern 3D printing technology to create a mold and then cast a bronze replica of the artifact. He suspected it was not part of a weapon but rather a piece of a musical instrument. When Ó Foghlú employed the spear-butt instead as the mouthpiece for a 2-meter replica horn, the sound came alive, and the artifact's true purpose became clear. Here Ó Foghlú is playing a modern horn, a skill that informed his experimental archaeology.

times sharper than the finest steel), and the ease with which toolmakers can work it made it perfectly suited to their needs. Obsidian tools provide some of the sharpest cutting edges ever made (recall Chapter 7's Anthropology Applied, "Stone Tools for Modern Surgeons").

Extensive trade systems developed so that people could procure the raw materials they needed. Boats provided faster and less costly access to trade centers, compared to overland transport. A one-way trip from the ancient Egyptian cities along the Nile River to various Mediterranean ports took far less time by rowboat compared to the overland route. With a sailboat, it was even faster.

Egyptian kings, or pharaohs, sent expeditions in various directions for prized resources: to Nubia (northern Sudan) for gold; to the Sinai Peninsula for copper; to Arabia for spices and perfumes; to Asia for lapis lazuli (a blue semiprecious stone) and other jewels; to Lebanon for

cedar, wine, and funerary oils; and to Central Africa for ivory, ebony, ostrich feathers, leopard skins, cattle, and the captives they enslaved.

Chinese and Persian artifacts unearthed in Great Zimbabwe (Figure 10.10) in southern Africa indicate that these trading networks extended throughout the Old World by the 11th century. This city of 12,000 to 20,000 inhabitants served as the center of a Bantu state. Increased contact with foreign peoples through trade spread innovations and bodies of knowledge such as geometry and astronomy. Great Zimbabwe flourished more recently than many of the earliest cities mentioned in this chapter. Still it deserves special mention as it documents the presence of city-states in sub-Saharan Africa that predate European colonization.

Central Government

A governing elite emerged in early civilizations. The size and complexity of cities required a strong central authority to ensure that different interest groups, such as farmers or craft specialists, provided their respective services without infringing on one another. Governments of the past protected cities from their enemies by constructing fortifications and raising an army. They levied taxes and appointed tax collectors so that construction workers, the army, and other public expenses could be paid. They saw to it that merchants, carpenters, or farmers who made legal claims received justice and assured ordinary people that any harm done to one person by another would be justly handled. They arranged for storage of surplus food for times of scarcity and supervised public works such as extensive irrigation systems and fortifications.

Evidence of Centralized Authority

Evidence of centralized authority in ancient civilizations comes from law codes, temple records, monuments, and royal chronicles. The city structures themselves can show definitive signs of city planning as with the precise astronomical layout of the Mesoamerican city of Teotihuacan described earlier. Monumental buildings, temples, palaces, and large sculptures characterize ancient civilizations. For example, the Great Pyramid for the tomb of Khufu, an Egyptian pharaoh, is 236 meters (755 feet) long and 147 meters (481 feet) high; it contains about 2.3 million stone blocks, each with an average weight of 2.5 tons. The Greek historian Herodotus who visited Egypt long after the Great Pyramid was completed, reported that it took 100,000 men twenty years to build this tomb. Such gigantic structures could be built only because a powerful central authority was able to harness the considerable labor force, engineering skills, and raw materials necessary for their construction.

Writing or some form of recorded information indicates the existence of centralized authority. With writing, governors could disseminate information and store, systematize, and deploy written records for political,

© Robert Holmes/Corbis

Figure 10.10 Great Zimbabwe
The elliptical granite walls, held together without any mortar at Great Zimbabwe in southern
Zimbabwe, Africa, attest to the skill of the people who built these structures. When European
explorers, unwilling to accept the notion of civilization in sub-Saharan Africa, discovered
these magnificent ruins, they wrongly attributed them to white non-Africans. This false notion
persisted until archaeologists demonstrated that these structures were part of a city with
12,000 to 20,000 inhabitants that served as the center of a medieval Bantu state.

religious, and economic purposes. Of course, the development of writing went hand in hand with the development
of specialized laborers: scribes responsible for physically
creating the centralized authorities' records.

Scholars attribute the development of writing in Mesopotamia to recordkeeping of state affairs. Writing allowed
early governments to track accounts of their food surplus,
tribute records, and other business receipts. Some of the
earliest documents appear to be just such records—lists
of vegetables and animals bought and sold, tax lists, and
storehouse inventories.

Before 5,500 years ago, records consisted of "tokens,"
ceramic pieces shaped to indicate different commercial
objects. A cone shape could represent a measure of grain,
or a cylinder could be an animal. Over time, tokens came
to represent different animals, as well as processed foods
(such as oil, trussed ducks, or bread) and manufactured
or imported goods (such as textiles and metal) (Lawler,
2001). Ultimately, clay tablets with impressed marks representing objects replaced these tokens.

By 5,000 years ago, a new writing technique emerged
in the Mesopotamian city of Uruk in today's Iraq. Writers
used a reed *stylus* to make wedge-shaped markings on a
tablet of damp clay. Originally, each marking stood for a
word. Because most words in this language were monosyl-
labic, over time the markings came to stand for syllables,
and cuneiform writing developed (Figure 10.11).

Writing was independently invented in different parts
of the world (Figure 10.12). Traditionally, the earliest
writing was linked to Mesopotamia. However, in 2003,
archaeologists working in the Henan Province of central
China discovered signs carved into 8,600-year-old tortoise
shells; these markings resemble later-written characters
and predate the Mesopotamian evidence by about 2,000
years (Li et al., 2003).

In the Americas, writing systems came into use
among various Mesoamerican peoples, but the Maya had
a particularly sophisticated one designed to track the
elaborate celebrations of the accomplishments of their
rulers (Figure 10.13). Maya royalty glorified themselves

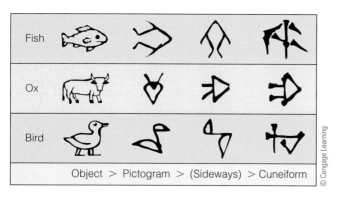

Figure 10.11 Cuneiform

Cuneiform writing developed from representational drawings of objects. Over time the drawings became simplified and more abstract, as well as being wedge-shaped so that they could be cut into a clay tablet with a stylus.

by recording their dynastic genealogies, important conquests, and marriages; by using grandiose titles to refer to themselves; and by associating their actions with important astronomical events. Like the recordkeeping of ancient Mesopotamia, this writing system helped maintain political power.

The Earliest Governments

A king and his advisors typically headed the earliest city governments, although a few ancient queens also ruled. Among these, Hammurabi, the Babylonian king who lived in Mesopotamia between 3,700 and 3,950 years ago, stands out as truly remarkable for the efficient government organization and highly developed legal system characterizing his reign. From Babylon, the capital of his empire, he issued a set of laws now known as the Code of Hammurabi, notable for its thorough detail and standardization. In 1901, a French archaeological team first discovered this code, entirely inscribed in stone with cuneiform writing. It prescribed the correct form for legal procedures and determined penalties for perjury and false accusation. It contained laws applying to property rights, loans and debts, family rights, and even damages paid for malpractice by a physician. It defined fixed rates to be charged in various trades and branches of commerce, and it instituted mechanisms to protect vulnerable people—the poor, women, children, and slaves—from injustice.

Officials ordered that the code be publicly displayed on huge stone slabs so that all members of society knew their rights and responsibilities. Distinct social classes were clearly reflected in the law ("rule of law" does not necessarily mean "equality before the law"). For example, if an aristocrat put out the eye of a fellow aristocrat, the law required that his own eye be put out in turn, hence the saying "an eye for an eye." However, if the aristocrat put out the eye of a slave, he simply owed the slave's owner half of the slave's value.

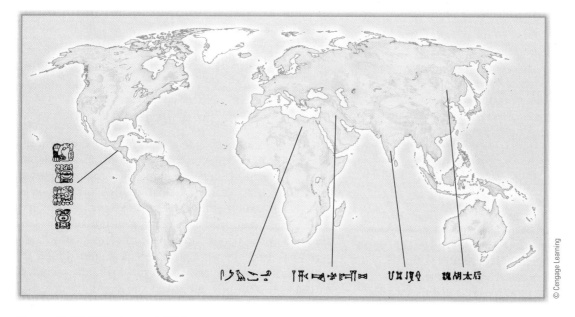

Figure 10.12 Birthplaces of Writing

The transience of spoken words contrasts with the relative permanence of written records. Throughout human history, writing has been independently invented at least five times.

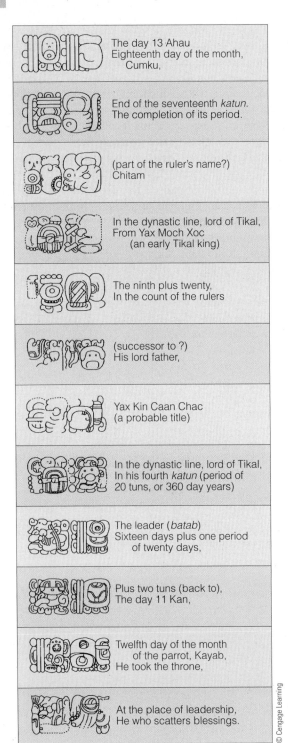

	The day 13 Ahau Eighteenth day of the month, Cumku,
	End of the seventeenth *katun*. The completion of its period.
	(part of the ruler's name?) Chitam
	In the dynastic line, lord of Tikal, From Yax Moch Xoc (an early Tikal king)
	The ninth plus twenty, In the count of the rulers
	(successor to ?) His lord father,
	Yax Kin Caan Chac (a probable title)
	In the dynastic line, lord of Tikal, In his fourth *katun* (period of 20 tuns, or 360 day years)
	The leader (*batab*) Sixteen days plus one period of twenty days,
	Plus two tuns (back to), The day 11 Kan,
	Twelfth day of the month of the parrot, Kayab, He took the throne,
	At the place of leadership, He who scatters blessings.

© Cengage Learning

Figure 10.13 Maya Writing
The translation of the text on the monument in Figure 10.6 gives some indication of the importance of dynastic genealogy to Maya rulers. The "scattering" mentioned may refer to bloodletting as part of the ceremonies associated with the end of one twenty-year period, or *katun*, and the beginning of the next. Archaeologists cracked the meaning of these glyphs over the course of many decades of intense study. The base 20 numerical system of bars and dots was the first breakthrough followed by the realization that the symbols represented syllables instead of an alphabet.

Although some civilizations flourished under a single ruler with extraordinary governing abilities, other civilizations prospered with a widespread governing bureaucracy that was efficient at every level. The government of the Inca empire is one such example. The Inca civilization of Peru and its surrounding territories reached its peak 500 years ago, just before the arrival of the Spanish invaders. Known for the monumental structures at Machu Picchu, built high in the Andes Mountains at an altitude of almost 2,500 meters (8,000 feet), this empire stretched 4,000 kilometers (2,500 miles) from north to south and 800 kilometers (500 miles) from east to west. Its population, numbering in the millions, consisted of many different ethnic groups. An emperor, regarded as the divine son of the Sun God, headed the government. Below him came the royal family, the aristocracy, imperial administrators, and lower nobility. Below them were the masses of artisans, craftspeople, and farmers. Governmental agriculture and tax officials closely supervised farming activities such as planting, irrigation, and harvesting. Teams of professional relay runners could carry messages up to 400 kilometers (250 miles) in a single day over a network of roads and bridges that remains impressive even today.

Despite the complexity of their civilization, the Inca had no known form of conventional writing. Instead, they used an ingenious coding system of colored strings with knots known as *quipu* or *khipu* (the Quechua word for "knot") to keep public records and historical chronicles. A smallpox epidemic brought to the Americas by Europeans devastated the Incas as well as other indigenous American peoples.

Social Stratification

The fourth cultural change characteristic of civilization is **social stratification**, or the emergence of social classes, a series of ranked social categories according to characteristics such as wealth, occupation, or kin-group. With social stratification, symbols of special status and privilege appeared, ranking people according to the kind of work they did or the family into which they were born. Social proximity to the head of government conferred high status. Although specialists—metalworkers, tanners, traders, or the like—generally outranked farmers, the people who engaged in these kinds of economic activities were either members of the lower classes or outcasts. Merchants of the past could sometimes buy their way into a higher class. With time, the possession of wealth and the influence it

Figure 10.14 Terra Cotta Warriors
Grave goods frequently indicate the status of deceased individuals in stratified societies. For example, China's first emperor Qin Shi Huang was buried in 210-209 BCE with 7,000 life-sized terra cotta figures of warriors complete with chariots and horses. In fact, an entire necropolis or "dead city" was built for the emperor, which, according to some historians, required 700,000 workers to complete.

could buy became their own prerequisite for high status, as seen in some contemporary cultures.

How do archaeologists know that different social classes existed in ancient civilizations? As described earlier, laws and other written documents, as well as archaeological features including dwelling size and location, can reflect social stratification. Burial customs also provide evidence. Graves excavated at early Neolithic sites consist mostly of simple pits dug in the ground. They contained few, if any, **grave goods**—utensils, figurines, and personal possessions, symbolically placed in the grave for the deceased person's use in the afterlife (Figure 10.14).

The graves excavated in civilizations vary widely in size, mode of burial, and the number and variety of grave goods. This reflects a stratified society, divided into social classes. The graves of important people contain not only various artifacts made from precious materials, but sometimes, as in some early Egyptian burials, the remains of servants evidently killed to serve their master in the afterlife.

Skeletons provide other evidence of stratification. Age at death, nutritional stress during childhood, as well as presence of certain diseases can be determined from skeletal remains. In stratified societies of the past, the dominant groups usually lived longer, ate better, and enjoyed an easier life than lower-ranking members of society, just as they do today.

The Making of States

From Africa to China to the South American Andes, ancient civilizations created magnificent palaces high above the ground, sculptures beautifully rendered using techniques that continue into the present, and vast,

social stratification The emergence of social classes—a series of ranked social categories according to characteristics such as wealth, occupation, or kin group.

grave goods Items such as utensils, figurines, and personal possessions, symbolically placed in the grave for the deceased person's use in the afterlife.

awe-inspiring engineering projects. To some, these impressive accomplishments indicate the superiority of civilization compared to other cultural forms, particularly when civilizations have come to dominate alternative social systems. But domination reflects aggression, size, and power—not cultural superiority. In other words, the emergence of centralized governments, characteristic of civilizations, has allowed some peoples to dominate others and for civilizations to flourish. Throughout millennia, civilization, domination, trade, and warfare have gone hand in hand, as this chapter's Original Study on Ani, the ancient Armenian city, illustrates.

ORIGINAL STUDY

Ani: Identities and Conflicts in and Around a Silk Road City BY GREGORY ARESHIAN

Kaleidoscopic events in the conflict-torn Middle East regularly appear on the radar screen of more than a billion people around the globe. Confused by the avalanche of news, casual observers may open a map of that region, which will show borders of twenty countries. Britain, France, and the Soviet Russia drew these artificial borders after World War I, between 1918 and 1923, according to their imperialistic interests. These borders—imposed without consideration for local geography and the existing political, religious, and ethnic boundaries throughout the region, which is currently home to more than 450 million people—created a multitude of conflicts that have persisted into the present.

The religious, ethnic, and cultural divisions that fuel today's conflicts began thousands of years ago. Over the centuries, political elites and peoples of the region struggled for power and domination, but they also negotiated solutions to their problems and forged alliances. Substantial periods of sociopolitical stability created conditions for local and regional growth and prosperity.

Historic memories preserved in religious, ethnic, and nationalistic narratives sometimes serve to justify and intensify today's conflicts. Archaeological sites along with major events of the past occupy prominent places in those stories. Multidisciplinary studies of such locations, based on comprehensive and holistic anthropological approaches, tell us not only about essential activities of past societies but also reveal the symbolic impact of major archaeological sites on current perceptions. The role of archaeologists is to disentangle fact and fiction in these sites.

The history of the majestic ruins of the city of Ani, the capital of Armenia in the 10th and 11th centuries CE under the Bagratuni royal dynasty, provides an excellent case in point. The city continued to prosper through all the political ups and downs of the domination by the Turko-Persian empire of the Great Seljuqs and the Mongol empire in the

Middle East until the middle of the 14th century CE. Today it is located in Turkey, on the closed border with Armenia.

Ani became the capital in 961 CE when Armenia acted as an important buffer zone between the world of Christendom in the west and the world of Islam in the east and south. The Byzantine empire, then at the zenith of its international power, backed the Bagratuni dynasty during the city's first period of sociocultural development, which lasted from 961 to 1064 CE. During that time, Ani was designed and developed as a royal city, a major urban center in contrast to the predominantly rural environment of castles, farming villages, and small towns where the Armenian landed nobility resided; the city was also a contrast to the monasteries of the Armenian Apostolic Church (part of Eastern Christianity and distinct from the Catholicism of western Europe and the Eastern Greek Orthodoxy of the Byzantine empire). The cityscape of Ani was highly innovative and organically connected to its landscape.

Ani is located at the center of a large plateau within the Caucasus Mountains. The city's core occupies a triangular promontory formed by two merging canyons. Only in the north is the promontory easily accessible from the plateau. There, a double line of walls, still standing to the height of 15 meters (49 feet) and made impregnable by thirty enormous towers of the inner line of defense, runs from the edge of one canyon to another. The design of the cityscape

- ■ Cilicia (Little Armenia)   ■ Lesser Armenia
- □ Greater Armenia   -- Bagratuni Kingdom

© Cengage Learning

because of the strength of its fortifications. When seized, its population suffered massacres, enslavement, and deportation. But in the second period of Seljuq, Georgian, and Mongol domination, the city became a major hub of international commerce in the Silk Road network connecting Eurasia from the Pacific to central Europe, stimulating the transcontinental exchange of goods, ideas, technologies, religions, and knowledge. Ani's importance for trade forestalled major destruction of the city by conquerors, who expected to benefit from its economic capacity.

Ani's prosperity peaked a third time when the city received a privileged status in the Mongol Ilkhanid empire. The Silk Road transcontinental system collapsed during the second half of the 14th to early 15th century and was replaced by the maritime global trade network of the Portuguese, Dutch, Spanish, and later British. With the demise of the Silk Road, Ani was abandoned, and its population emigrated to Crimea, Constantinople (modern Istanbul), and central Europe.

During the next few centuries, western European, Russian, and Armenian travelers visited and marveled at the splendid ruins of Ani. In 1892, a diverse team of scholars from major academic institutions of the Russian empire—historians, archaeologists, architects, and philologists—began large-scale excavations and studies of Ani, which, at that time, was completely within the borders of the empire. With some interruptions, the fieldwork continued until 1917. After the collapse of the Ottoman empire, the short-lived Republic of Armenia included Ani. When the Republic of Armenia was divided between the newly formed Republic of Turkey and the Soviet empire in 1921, approximately 85 percent of the archaeological site of Ani was left on the Turkish side of the border.

For nearly the century that has elapsed since the establishment of the current border, the fate of Ani has been heartbreaking. After the formation of the Republic of Turkey during the 1920s—a state that did not recognize the ethnic diversity of its population and the historical-cultural heritage of minorities—the archaeological site of Ani was subjected to complete neglect and even destruction. Some of its outstanding components, such as the Khtskonq Monastery and the Tignis Castle, were blown up with explosives. In the absence of supervision and protection, parts of the fortification walls and several monumental buildings were gradually demolished by inhabitants of surrounding villages who used the beautifully dressed stones of medieval structures for their current construction needs. Rare visitors to Ani would read plaques installed by Turkey's Ministry of Culture, explaining the meaning of specific buildings and presenting the history of the site without mentioning the Armenian heritage.

Some positive changes have begun in the last two decades, especially since 2002, when a new government of Turkey came to power. The looting of the site was stopped and conservation work has begun in different

projected the superior power of the capital and struck anyone who was approaching Ani with its urban image.

Besides its defenses in the north, most of Ani's monumental buildings (cathedrals and palaces) were aligned along the edges of canyons, unlike other medieval cities of Europe and the Middle East where major buildings were concentrated in the centers of cities, riverbanks, or coastlines. The walls of monumental buildings at Ani (including the fortifications) were built of smoothly dressed blocks of tuff stone of orange, rose, bisque, chestnut, light and dark gray, black, and other colors, creating an amazing palette-like tapestry throughout the whole city. Even fortification walls were decorated with masonry of different colors depicting Armenian Christian crosses and carpet-like designs. Sculptured dragons and bulls conveyed the identity of the city as a stronghold of Christianity and commerce. Multiple cathedrals and churches, each with a unique architectural design, gave Ani the name "the city of one thousand and one churches" in medieval Armenian and European histories, or "the city of five hundred churches" in Arabic histories.

The second major period in the history of Ani spanned from 1064 to the middle of the 14th century CE. In 1064, the army of the empire of Great Seljuqs captured Ani, which started a period of political volatility in the region. Ani was besieged multiple times, often unsuccessfully

The Church of the Redeemer, like so many of the buildings in Ani, an ancient capital of Armenia, have been deliberately destroyed and looted.

is a forgotten archaeological treasure, rarely visited by tourists and even scholars.

To Armenians, Ani represents the ultimate achievement of their culture and national heritage. But, short of taking a trip through Turkey, to visit Ani today citizens of the Republic of Armenia can only gaze at this medieval marvel through the barbed wire at the still-closed border between the two countries.

One can hope that the movement of the Turkish society toward multiculturalism continues and that the mutual mistrust between the Armenians and Turks abates. Ani may then become open, along with the Armenian–Turkish border, and welcomed again as an essential part of Armenian cultural heritage. In that bright future, Ani will become the shared cultural treasure of Turkey, Armenia, and humankind around the globe.

Written expressly for this text.

parts of the ancient city. Some of that work—such as on the Grand Cathedral of the Virgin Mary and on the Cathedral of the Savior—is satisfactory; in other cases it caused more damage than conservation. Yet, Ani today

As this study shows, the legacy of past empires consists of far more than archaeological ruins. Archaeological remains and their state of preservation reflect the tarnished history of relationships among empires that no longer exist. Accurately reconstructing and understanding the past through the excavation and preservation of ancient remains ultimately contributes to improved relations among living peoples.

Ecological Theories

In ecological theories, environmental factors drive the development of states. Among these, the **hydraulic theory**, or *irrigation theory*, holds that civilizations developed when Neolithic peoples realized the best farming occurred in the fertile soils of river valleys, provided they could control the periodic flooding. The centralized effort to control the irrigation process blossomed into the first

governing body, elite social class, and civilization. Others suggest that in regions of ecological diversity, procuring scarce resources requires trade networks controlled by a central authority. In Mexico, for example, trade networks distributed chili peppers grown in the highlands, cotton and beans from intermediate elevations, and salt from the coasts to people throughout the region.

Environmental barriers such as mountains, deserts, seas, or even other human populations might also be factors in state formation (Carneiro, 1970). As these hemmed in populations grow, without space into which to expand, they begin to compete for increasingly scarce resources. Internally, this may lead to social stratification, in which an elite class controls important resources to which lower classes have limited access. Externally, this leads to warfare and even conquest, which, to be successful, requires elaborate organization under a centralized authority (Figure 10.15). See this chapter's Globalscape for an example of warfare's current impact on archaeology.

Each of these ecological theories has limitations. Across the globe and through time, anthropologists find cultures that do not fit these models. For example, North American Indians possessed trade networks that extended from Labrador in northeastern Canada to the Gulf of Mexico and the Yellowstone region of the Rocky Mountains and even to the Pacific—all without centralized

hydraulic theory In archaeology, the theory that explains civilization's emergence as the result of the construction of elaborate irrigation systems, the functioning of which required full-time managers whose control blossomed into the first governing body and elite social class; also known as *irrigation theory*.

AP Images/Nabil al-Jurani

Figure 10.15 Policing Ancient Cities
To build a monument such as the Great Ziggurat of Ur, a temple in the ancient Mesopotamian city located in present-day Iraq, a centralized authority needed to be able to mobilize the laborers to build the structures and to amass defensive armies. In the present, centralized authorities such as the U.S. government and its military turn to archaeologists in times of war to protect cultural resources. The Archaeological Institute of America initiated an innovative program to educate U.S. Marines before their deployment. At U.S. Marine Corp Camp Lejeune in North Carolina, a mandatory class for both officers and enlisted men and women heading to Iraq included topics such as Mesopotamia's role in the development of writing, schools, libraries, law codes, calendars, and astronomy. Archaeologists taught soldiers basic archaeological techniques including effective strategies to protect sites against looters. Similar courses appropriate to each region are planned to accompany future U.S. military deployments.

control. And in many of the cultures that do not fit the theories of ecological determinism, neighboring cultures learned to coexist rather than pursuing warfare to the point of complete conquest.

Action Theory

Environmental theories often fail to recognize the capacity of ambitious, charismatic leaders to shape the course of human history. **Action theory**, on the other hand, acknowledges the relationship of society to the environment, but it also recognizes that forceful leaders strive to advance their positions through self-serving actions (Marcus & Flannery, 1996). In so doing, they may create change.

In the case of Maya history, for example, local leaders, who once relied on personal *charisma* for the economic and political support needed to sustain them in their positions, may have seized upon religion to solidify their power. Through religion they developed an ideology that endowed them and their descendants with supernatural ancestry and gave them privileged access to the gods on which their

followers depended. In this case, certain individuals could monopolize power and emerge as divine kings, using their power to subjugate any rivals. In the case of the Maya, the combination of existing cultural and ecological factors opened the way for the emergence of political dynasties. Thus, explanations of civilization's emergence tend to involve multiple causes, rather than just one.

Civilization and Its Discontents

Many people view civilization as a great step up on the so-called ladder of progress. But whatever its benefits, civilization certainly produced new problems. Among them is the challenge of waste disposal and its consequences.

---

action theory The theory that self-serving actions by forceful leaders play a role in civilization's emergence.

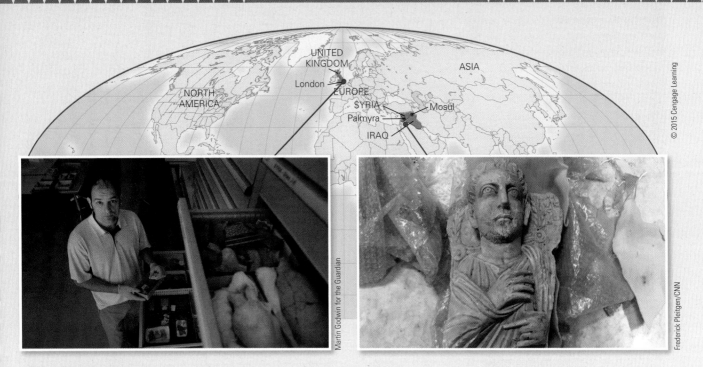

Martin Godwin for the Guardian

Frederick Pleitgen/CNN

© 2015 Cengage Learning

Illicit Antiquities?

In an antiquities shop in London, one might find a 3,000-year-old coin or a cylinder seal from ancient Mesopotamia, the land that is present-day Syria and Iraq. How did it get to London? Archaeologists have turned to another kind of digging to find the answer. Sometimes by posing as collectors in London or by serving as preservation experts to museum staff in this war-torn region, they are uncovering a network of profitable smuggling that ultimately benefits the Islamic State (ISIS or ISIL). British archaeologist Mark Altaweel, pictured here with the collection at the University College London's Institute of Archaeology, has done both.

With the intent of creating a fundamentalist Islamic state throughout the Middle East, ISIS has quickly taken over large swaths of land from Syria's Mediterranean coast to eastern Iraq. This territory contains innumerable ancient sites (Iraq alone claims over 10,000) and artifacts, which are now threatened. Between them, Iraq and Syria are home to ten UNESCO World Heritage Cultural Sites, including Palmyra. In 2015, ISIS's intentional detonation of the 1st-century Temple of Baalshamin in Palmyra forever deprived Syrians and the world of one of the best-preserved temples, at one of our most important archaeological sites. Syrian archaeologists had rescued hundreds of Roman busts before ISIS took control of the city—destroying parts of the site, looting, and beheading the director of antiquities at Palmyra, Khaled al-Asaad. Earlier in 2015, ISIS released a video of its members using sledgehammers to destroy ancient Assyrian statues from a museum in Mosul, Iraq. Looting adds yet another layer of destruction: ISIS permits locals to loot and then levies a *khums* tax on the money gained through the illegal sale of these artifacts.[a]

Some sources indicate that illegal trafficking in antiquities brings in tens of millions of dollars to ISIS's coffers, with artifacts being smuggled into Lebanon, Turkey, and Jordan before being sold to international buyers. Some of these looted artifacts have been found on sale in London antique shops.[b] These illegally exported artifacts may actually be the lucky ones. War has always been perilous for archeological and historical treasures. The Parthenon of Athens owes its ruinous condition to fighting between the Venetians and the Ottomans in the 17th century. Along with killing multitudes, Allied fire bombings reduced the historic city of Dresden, Germany, to rubble during World War II. Tens of thousands of artifacts were looted from the National Museum in Baghdad after the U.S. invasion of Iraq in 2003, 15,000 of which have never been recovered.

In an August 2015 interview in the *New York Times,* Syria's director general of antiquities, Maamoun Abdulkarim, said he was the "saddest director general in the world." He noted that Syria's antiquities and ancient sites are not the property of any political group, but for all Syrians, adding, "It's for you also—for American people, for European people, for Japanese people. It's all your heritage."[c] What remains to be seen is whether the world will be able to protect this precious heritage from those who would do it harm.

Global Twister

If artifacts from ancient civilizations from throughout the world represent our shared global heritage, how can such treasures be kept safe from destruction, looting, and retribution?

[a] Al-Azm, A., Al-Kuntar, S., & Daniels, B. I. (2014, September 2). ISIS' antiquities sideline. *New York Times*. http://www.nytimes.com/2014/09/03/opinion/isis-antiquities-sideline.html?_r=0 (retrieved November 3, 2015)

[b] Shabi, R. (2015, July 3). Looted in Syria—and sold in London: The British antiques shops dealing in artefacts smuggled by Isis. *The Guardian*. http://www.theguardian.com/world/2015/jul/03/antiquities-looted-by-isis-end-up-in-london-shops (retrieved November 3, 2015)

[c] Barnard, A. (2015, August 24). ISIS speeds up destruction of antiquities in Syria. *New York Times*. http://www.nytimes.com/2015/08/25/world/isis-accelerates-destruction-of-antiquities-in-syria.html?_r=0 (retrieved November 3, 2015)

In fact, waste disposal probably began to be a difficulty in settled farming communities even before civilizations emerged. As villages grew into cities, the crowded conditions and the buildup of garbage and sewage created optimal environments for infectious diseases such as plague, typhoid, and cholera. As a result, early cities were disease-ridden places with relatively high death rates.

Genetic adaptation to urban disease has influenced the course of history globally. Among northern Europeans, for example, the mutation of a gene on chromosome 7 makes carriers resistant to cholera, typhoid, and other bacterial diarrheas, all of which spread easily in urban environments. Because of the mortality caused by these diseases, selection favored spread of this allele among northern Europeans. But, as with sickle-cell anemia, protection comes at a price: cystic fibrosis, a usually fatal disease present in people who are homozygous for the altered gene.

Other acute infectious diseases accompanied the rise of towns and cities. In a small population, diseases such as chicken pox, influenza, measles, mumps, pertussis, polio, rubella, and smallpox will kill or immunize so high a proportion of the population that the virus cannot continue to propagate. The continued existence of such diseases depends upon the presence of a large population, as is found in cities.

City environments also promote tuberculosis (TB). The bacterium that causes TB cannot survive in the presence of sunlight and fresh air. Before people began working and living in dark, crowded urban centers, if an infected individual coughed and released the TB bacterium into the air, sunlight would prevent the spread of infection. TB, like many other sicknesses, can be called a disease of civilization.

Figure 10.16 Favelas

Over 10 million Brazilians live in *favelas*—impoverished, crowded urban neighborhoods where multigenerational homes are stacked practically on top of one another. Under these conditions, particularly when sanitation and ventilation are poor, diseases like TB, leprosy, and dengue fever can thrive.

Hans Lippert/imagebroker/Alamy

Social Stratification and Disease

Civilization affects disease in another powerful way. Social stratification impacts who gets sick as much as any bacterium, past and present. For example, Ashkenazi Jews of eastern Europe were forced into urban ghettos over several centuries, becoming especially vulnerable to the TB thriving in crowded, dark, confined neighborhoods (**Figure 10.16**). As with the genetic response to malaria (the sickle-cell allele) and bacterial diarrheas (the cystic fibrosis gene), TB triggered a genetic response in the form of the Tay-Sachs allele, which protects heterozygous individuals from TB.

Unfortunately, homozygotes for the Tay-Sachs allele develop a lethal, degenerative condition that remains common among Ashkenazi Jews. Without the selective pressure of TB, the frequency of the Tay-Sachs allele would never have increased. Similarly, without the strict social rules confining poor Jews to the ghettos (compounded by social and religious rules about marriage), the frequency of the Tay-Sachs allele would never have increased.

Today, not only are poor individuals more likely to become infected with TB, they are also less likely to be able to afford the medicines to treat this disease. For people in poor countries and for disadvantaged people in wealthier countries, tuberculosis, like AIDS, can be an incurable, fatal, infectious disease. Global health specialists have stated that both TB and HIV thrive on poverty (Bates et al., 2004). The poor of the world have borne a higher disease burden since the development of stratified societies characteristic of cities and states.

Colonialism and Disease

When Europeans with immunity to so-called Old World diseases came to the Americas for the first time, they brought these devastating diseases with them. Millions of Native Americans—who had never been exposed to

Perilous Pigs: The Introduction of Swine-Borne Disease to the Americas *BY CHARLES C. MANN*

On May 30, 1539, Hernando de Soto landed his private army near Tampa Bay, in Florida....Half warrior, half venture capitalist, Soto had grown very rich very young by becoming a market leader in the nascent trade for Indian slaves. The profits had helped to fund Pizarro's seizure of the Incan empire, which had made Soto wealthier still. Looking quite literally for new worlds to conquer, he persuaded the Spanish Crown to let him loose in North America....He came to Florida with 200 horses, 600 soldiers, and 300 pigs.

From today's perspective, it is difficult to imagine the ethical system that would justify Soto's actions. For four years his force, looking for gold, wandered through what is now Florida, Georgia, North and South Carolina, Tennessee, Alabama, Mississippi, Arkansas, and Texas, wrecking almost everything it touched. The inhabitants often fought back vigorously, but they had never before encountered an army with horses and guns.... Soto's men managed to rape, torture, enslave, and kill countless Indians. But the worst thing the Spaniards did, some researchers say, was entirely without malice—bring the pigs....

According to Charles Hudson, an anthropologist at the University of Georgia, ...the

AP Photo/Eric Gay

De Soto's pigs brought disease to America with devastating consequences for the millions of Native Americans who died from swine-borne sickness. Today the descendants of these pigs still leave destruction in their wake, through habitat destruction and destabilization of the ecosystem. Without any natural predators, their population has grown out of control. Aerial hunting, from the perch of a helicopter, has become a means to keep their numbers in check.

Spaniards approached a cluster of small cities, each protected by earthen walls, sizeable moats, and deadeye archers. In his usual fashion, Soto brazenly marched in, stole food, and marched out.

After Soto left, no Europeans visited this part of the Mississippi Valley for more than a century. Early in 1682 whites appeared again, this time Frenchmen in canoes...Area[s] where Soto had found

influenza, smallpox, typhus, and measles—died as a result. The microbes causing these diseases and the human populations upon which they depend developed in tandem over thousands of years of urban life in Eurasia, and before that in village life with a variety of domesticated animal species. Thus, anyone who survived had acquired immunity in the process. (See this chapter's Biocultural Connection for more on the death and disease Europeans brought with them when they colonized the Americas.) Very few diseases traveled back to Europe from the Americas. Instead, these colonizers brought back the riches that they had pillaged.

Anthropology and Cities of the Future

Only recently have public health measures reduced the risk of living in cities. Had it not been for a constant influx of rural peoples, cities might not have persisted. Europe's urban population, for example, did not become self-sustaining until early in the 20th century.

Besides health problems, many early cities faced social problems strikingly similar to those found in contemporary cities all over the world. Dense population and the

cities cheek by jowl...[were] deserted [without an] Indian village for 200 miles. About fifty settlements existed in this strip of the Mississippi when Soto showed up, according to Ann Ramenofsky, an anthropologist at the University of New Mexico.... Soto "had a privileged glimpse" of an Indian world, Hudson says. "The window opened and slammed shut. When the French came in and the record opened up again, it was a transformed reality. A civilization crumbled. The question is, how did this happen?"

The question is even more complex than it may seem. Disaster of this magnitude suggests epidemic disease. In the view of Ramenofsky and Patricia Galloway, an anthropologist at the University of Texas, the source of the contagion was very likely not Soto's army but its ambulatory meat locker: his 300 pigs. Soto's force itself was too small to be an effective biological weapon. Sicknesses like measles and smallpox would have burned through his 600 soldiers long before they reached the Mississippi. But the same would not have held true for the pigs, which multiplied rapidly and were able to transmit their diseases to wildlife in the surrounding forest. When human beings and domesticated animals live close together, they trade microbes with abandon. Over time mutation spawns new diseases: Avian influenza becomes human influenza, bovine rinderpest becomes measles.

Unlike Europeans, Indians did not live in close quarters with animals—they domesticated only the dog, the llama, the alpaca, the guinea pig, and, here and there, the turkey and the Muscovy duck....[W]hat scientists call zoonotic disease was little known in the Americas. Swine alone can disseminate anthrax, brucellosis, leptospirosis, taeniasis, trichinosis, and tuberculosis. Pigs breed exuberantly and can transmit diseases to deer and turkeys. Only a few of Soto's pigs would have had to wander off to infect the forest.

Indeed, the calamity wrought by Soto apparently extended across the whole Southeast. The Coosa city-states, in western Georgia, and the Caddoan-speaking civilization, centered on the Texas–Arkansas border, disintegrated soon after Soto appeared. The Caddo had had a taste for monumental architecture: public plazas, ceremonial platforms, mausoleums. After Soto's army left, notes Timothy K. Perttula, an archaeological consultant in Austin, Texas, the Caddo stopped building community centers and began digging community cemeteries....[After] Soto's.. . visit, Perttula believes, the Caddoan population fell from about 200,000 to about 8,500—a drop of nearly 96 percent.... "That's one reason whites think of Indians as nomadic hunters," says Russell Thornton, an anthropologist at the University of California at Los Angeles. "Everything else—all the heavily populated urbanized societies—was wiped out."

How could a few pigs truly wreak this much destruction?...One reason is that Indians were fresh territory for many plagues, not just one. Smallpox, typhoid, bubonic plague, influenza, mumps, measles, whooping cough—all rained down on the Americas in the century after Columbus....

To Elizabeth Fenn, the smallpox historian, the squabble over numbers obscures a central fact. Whether 1 million or 10 million or 100 million died,...the pall of sorrow that engulfed the hemisphere was immeasurable. Languages, prayers, hopes, habits, and dreams—entire ways of life hissed away like steam.... In the long run, Fenn says, the consequential finding is not that many people died but that many people once lived. The Americas were filled with a stunningly diverse assortment of peoples who had knocked about the continents for millennia. "You have to wonder," Fenn says. "What were all those people up to in all that time?"

Biocultural Question

Does the history of the decimation of American Indians through infectious disease have any parallels in the contemporary globalized world? Do infectious diseases impact all peoples equally?

Adapted from Mann, C. C. (2005). *1491: New revelations of the Americas before Columbus.* New York: Knopf.

---

inequalities of class systems and oppressive centralized governments created internal stress. The poor saw that the wealthy had all the things they themselves lacked. It was not just a question of luxury items; the poor did not have enough food or space in which to live with comfort, dignity, and health (Figure 10.17).

Abundant archaeological evidence also documents warfare in early civilizations. Cities were fortified. Ancient documents list battles, raids, and wars between groups. Cylinder seals, paintings, and sculptures depict battle scenes, victorious kings, and captured prisoners of war. Increasing population and the accompanying scarcity of fertile farmland

often led to boundary disputes and quarrels between states or between so-called tribal peoples and a state. When war broke out, people crowded into walled cities for protection.

Many of the problems associated with the first civilizations such as waste disposal, pollution-related health problems, crowding, social inequities, and warfare continue to challenge humanity today. Through the study of past civilizations and through comparison of contemporary societies, we now stand a chance of understanding these problems. Such understanding represents a central part of anthropologists' mission and can contribute to the ability of our species to transcend human-made problems.

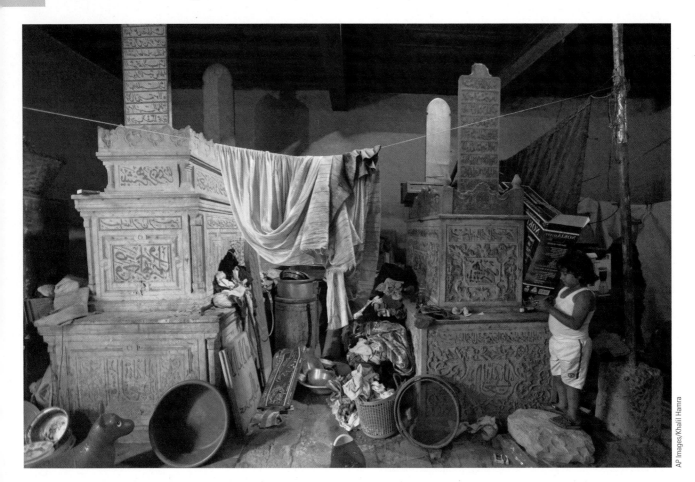

AP Images/Khalil Hamra

Figure 10.17 "City of the Dead"
One of Cairo's poorest neighborhoods, the "City of the Dead" is actually a cemetery. Thousands of poor Egyptian families use centuries-old mausoleums, built for some of Cairo's wealthy inhabitants, as makeshift homes. For the poor, a gravestone might serve as a table or a bed. Children play among the graves. Because the land on which these families live is officially a cemetery, this neighborhood lacks basic services such as running water and a sewer system.

CHAPTER CHECKLIST

When did the first cities and states develop, and how did this occur?

✓ The world's first cities grew out of Neolithic villages between 4,500 and 6,000 years ago—first in Mesopotamia, then in Egypt and the Indus Valley. In China, the process was under way by 5,000 years ago. Somewhat later, and completely independently, similar changes took place in Mesoamerica and the central Andes.

✓ Four basic cultural changes mark the transition from Neolithic village life to life in civilized urban centers: agricultural innovation, diversification of labor, emergence of centralized government, and social stratification.

What characteristics distinguished the four cultural changes leading to the development of urban centers?

✓ Agricultural innovation involved the development of new farming methods such as irrigation that increased crop yields. Agricultural innovations brought about other changes such as increased population size.

✓ Diversification of labor intensified as a result of population growth in cities. Some people could provide sufficient food for everyone so that others could devote themselves to specialization as artisans and craftspeople. Specialization led to the development of new technologies and the beginnings of extensive trade systems.

✓ The emergence of a central government provided an authority to deal with the complex problems associated with cities and permitted elites to mobilize workers to erect monumental structures. With the invention of writing, governments began keeping records and boasting of their own power and glory.

✓ Symbols of status and privilege appeared with the emergence of social classes, as individuals were ranked according to wealth they accumulated or controlled. Burial customs, grave goods, dwelling size, and records in documents and art provide evidence of social stratification.

Why did cities and states develop?

✓ Ecological theories emphasize the interrelation of the actions of ancient peoples with their environment. According to these theories, civilizations developed as centralized governments began to control irrigation systems, trade networks, and scarce resources.

✓ These theories omit the importance of the beliefs and values of cultures of the past as well as the actions of forceful, dynamic leaders. Action theories argue that leaders' efforts to promote their own interests may play a role in social change.

What problems beset early cities?

✓ Poor sanitation in early cities, coupled with large numbers of people living in close proximity, created environments in which infectious diseases were rampant.

✓ Early urban centers also faced social problems strikingly similar to those persisting in the world today. Dense populations, class systems, and strong centralized governments created internal stress.

✓ Warfare was common; cities were fortified, and armies served to protect and expand the state.

✓ European city-dwellers had already adapted to urban diseases that decimated both urban and rural Native American populations when the Europeans invaded the Americas.

QUESTIONS FOR REFLECTION

1. Since the origins of cities and states, humans have engaged in large-scale elaborate warfare, both between states and within them. War also leads to social upheaval, as in the case of the millions of Syrians who have been displaced by ongoing civil war. How do you think today's societies should address this issue?

2. What are some of the ways that differences in social stratification are expressed where you live? Does your community have any traditions surrounding death that serve to restate the social differentiation of individuals? Are there local traditions that serve to redistribute the wealth so that it is shared more evenly?

3. With today's global communication and economic networks, will it be possible to shift away from social systems involving centralized governments, or is a global, centralized authority inevitable?

4. With many archaeological discoveries, there is a value placed on "firsts," such as the earliest writing, the first city, or the earliest government. Given the history of the independent emergence of cities and states throughout the world, do you think that scholars should place more value on these events just because they are older?

DIGGING INTO ANTHROPOLOGY

Mapping Class

Archaeological exploration involves making detailed maps of each site. Mapmakers note the position, scale, density, and construction materials of buildings, roadways, monuments, and other substructures such as natural resources. Through these details, archaeologists can infer the presence of social stratification in communities.

Make a hand-drawn map of your community or use an existing satellite map. Compare the roadways, position, scale, and density of the buildings, and the construction materials used. Consider which neighborhoods have the best access to stores, transportation, public buildings, and open spaces or parks. How do your findings relate to class structures in your community?

Anadolu Agency/Getty Images

In June 2015, a gunman opened fire on those attending a prayer service at Emanuel African Methodist Episcopal Church in Charleston, South Carolina. Nine people, all black, died in what the white shooter later revealed was his attempt to incite a race war. The historic church had been associated with civil rights activism for a century. The 21-year-old gunman's online presence showed his preoccupation with white supremacy, neo-Nazism, and apartheid. Prior to this tragedy, a series of highly publicized incidents of police brutality against blacks in the United States spurred the Black Lives Matter movement and sparked a national discussion about race and injustice. Racism and hatred are fueled by false beliefs that precise biological features divide our species into discrete types. Obvious physical differences among humans exist, but biological evidence demonstrates unequivocally that separate races, or subspecies, do not. In fact, far more genetic diversity exists within a single so-called racial category than between any two. However, racism and its vocabulary continually surface throughout the world, whether in wage disparities, media commentary, or security profiling. Although distinct biological races do not exist, the social and political reality of race impacts, if not determines, the human experience in some societies, including the United States.

Modern Human Diversity—Race and Racism

From male to female, short to tall, light to dark, we can categorize biological variation in a number of ways, but in the end we are all members of the same species. Minute variations of our DNA give each of us a unique genetic fingerprint, yet this variation remains within the bounds of being genetically human. Any visible differences among modern humans exist within the framework of biological features shared throughout the species, and as a species, humans vary. Although we use the terms *black, white,* and *race* in this chapter, their reality is purely cultural.

Human genetic variation generally follows a continuous pattern of distribution across the globe. Biologically, some of this variation derives from interaction with the environment through the evolutionary process of natural selection. Random genetic drift accounts for the remainder. But the significance we give our biological variation is anything but random because cultures determine the way we perceive variation—in fact, whether we perceive it at all. In cultures where skin color bears no relationship to social status, people pay little attention to this physical characteristic. But people in countries such as the United States, Brazil, and South Africa notice skin color immediately because it remains a significant social and political category. The study of biological diversity, therefore, requires an awareness of the cultural dimensions that shape the questions asked about diversity as well as an understanding of the history of this knowledge use.

When European scholars first began their systematic study of human variation in the 18th and 19th centuries, they used small biological differences among human groups to divide them hierarchically so as to identify "better types" of humans. Today, this hierarchical approach has been appropriately abandoned. Before exploring how we study contemporary biological variation today, let's examine the effects of social ideas about race and racial hierarchy on the interpretation of biological variation, past and present.

In this chapter you will learn to

- Examine the history of human classification.

- Describe how the biological concept of race cannot be applied to humans.

- Recognize the conflation of biological race into cultural race in theories that attempt to link race to behavior and intelligence.

- Recognize some biological consequences of racism.

- Discuss physical anthropological approaches to the study of human biological variation.

- Describe the role of adaptation in human variation in skin color.

- Examine the interaction between biological and cultural components of how humans adapt.

The History of Human Classification

Some early European scholars tried to systematically classify *Homo sapiens* into subspecies, or races, based on geographic location and phenotypic features such as skin color, body size, head shape, and hair texture. The 18th-century Swedish naturalist Carolus Linnaeus (see Chapter 2) divided humans into subspecies based on geographic location and classified all Europeans as white, Africans as black, American Indians as red, and Asians as yellow.

The German physician Johann Blumenbach (1752–1840) introduced a significant and pernicious change in the hierarchy of human types. Considering the skull of a woman from the Caucasus Mountains (located between the Black and Caspian Seas of southeastern Europe and southwestern Asia) to be the most beautiful in his collection, Blumenbach saw it as a reflection of nature's ideal form: the circle. Surely, he reasoned, this "perfect" specimen resembled God's original creation. Moreover, he thought that the living inhabitants of the Caucasus region were the most beautiful in the world. Based on these criteria, he concluded that this high mountain range, which included lands mentioned in the Bible, was the place of human origins.

Blumenbach also concluded that all light-skinned peoples in Europe and adjacent parts of western Asia and northern Africa belonged to the same "variety." On this basis, he dropped the label "European" and replaced it with "Caucasian." Although he continued to distinguish American Indians as a separate variety, he regrouped dark-skinned Africans as "Ethiopian" and split those Asians not considered Caucasian into two separate groups: "Mongolian" (referring to most inhabitants of Asia, including China and Japan) and "Malay" (indigenous Australians, Pacific Islanders, and others).

Convinced that Caucasians were closest to the original ideal humans supposedly created in God's image, Blumenbach ranked them as superior. The other "varieties," he argued, were the result of "degeneration"; by moving away from their place of origin and adapting to different environments and climates, they had degenerated physically and morally into what many Europeans came to think of as inferior races. Political leaders have used this notion of superior and inferior races to justify brutalities ranging from repression to slavery to mass murder to genocide.

The tragic story of Ota Benga, a Twa Pygmy man who in the early 1900s was caged in a New York zoo with an orangutan, painfully illustrates the disastrous impact of racial dogma (Figure 11.1). Captured in a raid in Congo, Ota Benga came into the possession of North American businessman Samuel Verner, who was looking for exotic "savages" for exhibition in the United States. In 1904, Ota and other Twa were shipped across the Atlantic and exhibited at the St. Louis World's Fair. About 23 years old at the

Figure 11.1 Ota Benga
The placement of Ota Benga on display in the Bronx Zoo illustrates the depths of racism in the early 20th century. Here is Ota Benga posing for the camera when he was part of the African Exhibit at the St. Louis World's Fair. Ota's sharpened teeth (a cultural practice among his people) were seen as evidence of his supposedly cannibal nature.

Missouri Historical Society

time, Ota was 150 centimeters (4 feet 11 inches) tall and weighed 47 kilograms (103 pounds). Throngs of visitors came to see displays of indigenous peoples from around the globe, in their traditional dress, in replica villages, doing their customary activities. The fair was a success for the organizers, and all the Twa Pygmies survived to be shipped back to their homeland. Verner returned to Congo, and with Ota's help collected artifacts that he intended to sell to the American Museum of Natural History in New York City.

In the summer of 1906, Ota came back to the United States with Verner, who soon went bankrupt and lost his entire collection. Left stranded, Ota was placed in the care of the museum and then taken to the Bronx Zoo and exhibited in the monkey house, with an orangutan as company. After intensive protest, zoo officials released Ota from his cage and during the day let him roam free in the park, where visitors often harassed him. Ota (usually referred to as a "boy") was then turned over to an orphanage for African American children. In 1916, upon hearing that he would never return to his homeland, he took a revolver and shot himself through the heart (Bradford & Blume, 1992).

The racist display at the Bronx Zoo a century ago was by no means unique. Ota Benga's tragic life was the manifestation of a powerful ideology in which one small part of humanity sought to justify its claims of biological and cultural superiority. This ideology had particular resonance in North America, where people of European descent colonized lands originally inhabited by Native Americans and then went on to exploit African slaves and (later) Asians imported as a source of cheap labor.

According to U.S. anthropologist Audrey Smedley, the earliest settlers who came over from England had already refined this ideology of dehumanization and the practice of slavery in their dealings with the Irish (Smedley, 2007). They even imported Irish slaves and indentured servants and also enslaved American Indians.

Although the Emancipation Proclamation ended slavery in 1863 in the United States, dismantling its pseudoscientific bases is taking much longer. Racism is often fueled by folk beliefs about biological differences with destructive consequences, as we saw at the beginning of this chapter. In the early 20th century, when scholars began to challenge the concept of racial hierarchies, German American anthropologist Franz Boas (1858–1942) was among the strongest critics. An immigrant to the United States, founder of North America's four-field anthropology, and president of the American Association for the Advancement of Science, Boas criticized false claims of racial superiority in an important speech titled "Race Problems in America," published in the prestigious journal *Science* in 1909.

Ashley Montagu (1905–1999), a British student of Boas and one of the best-known anthropologists of his time, devoted much of his career to combating scientific racism. His book, *Man's Most Dangerous Myth: The Fallacy of Race*, published in 1942, took the lead in debunking the concept of clearly bounded races as a "social myth." The book has since gone through many editions, the last in 2008. Montagu's once controversial ideas have now become mainstream, and his text remains one of the most comprehensive treatments of the subject. The anthropological perspective on race is especially relevant to social justice movements calling for societal change or paradigm shifts, such as the 1960s civil rights era or recent Black Lives Matter activism in the United States.

Race as a Biological Concept

To understand why the racial approach to human variation has been so unproductive, and even injurious, we must first understand race in strictly biological terms. Biologists define **race** as a subspecies, or a population of a species differing geographically, morphologically, or genetically from other populations of the same species. As simple and straightforward as such a definition may seem, three factors complicate its use. First, it is arbitrary; no scientific criteria exist on how many differences it takes to make a

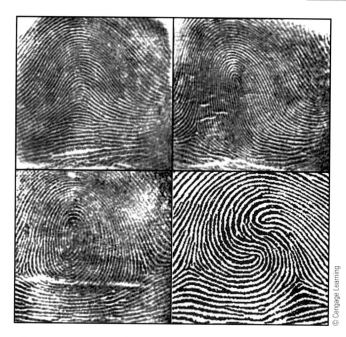

Figure 11.2 An Alternative Grouping
Fingerprint patterns of loops, whorls, and arches are genetically determined. Grouping people on this basis would place the Bushmen of southern Africa as "arches" (*upper left*). Most Europeans, sub-Saharan Africans, and East Asians would be grouped together as "loops" (*upper right*). Australian Aborigines and the people of Mongolia would be together as "whorls" (*lower left*). As with other attempts to divide humans into discrete categories, fingerprint-based racialization is complicated by tremendous variation within each group as well as blending between them, exemplified by the double loop whorl (*lower right*).

race. For example, if one researcher emphasizes skin color while another emphasizes fingerprint differences, they will not classify people in the same way (**Figure 11.2**).

Second, no single race has exclusive possession of any particular variant of any gene or genes. In human terms, the frequency of a trait like the type O blood group, for example, may be high in one population and low in another, but it is present in both. In other words, populations are genetically "open," meaning that genes flow between them. The only reproductive barriers that exist for humans are the cultural rules some societies impose regarding appropriate mates. As President Obama's family illustrates (a Luo father from western Kenya and a white mother born in Kansas, who, incidentally, was an anthropologist), these social barriers change over time.

A third problem is that the vast majority of genetic variation exists within a so-called racial group. In the 1970s, right on the heels of the civil rights movement, U.S. evolutionary biologist Richard Lewontin demonstrated that a

race In biology, the taxonomic category of a subspecies that is not applicable to humans because the division of humans into discrete types does not represent the true nature of human biological variation. In some societies, race is an important cultural category.

mere 7 percent of human genetic variation exists among racial groups (1972). As the science writer James Shreeve puts it, "most of what separates me genetically from a typical African or Eskimo also separates me from another average American of European ancestry" (Shreeve, 1994, p. 60).

Despite this finding, people in the United States remain fascinated by the role of genetics in racial difference. From the search for race-specific genes and treatments to booming genealogy businesses, the scientific facts of hundreds of thousands of years of gene flow makes separating our species into races based on a few visible characteristics impossible.

In July 2012, a genealogy business, Ancestry.com, released a report indicating that President Obama's mother, like so many white Americans, was descended from an African slave ancestor (Ancestry.com, 2012). This news made a splash, particularly because the ancestor was a man named John Punch, one of the first African slaves to be documented in this country (Thompson, 2012). The hype and folk appeal of such genealogical analyses belie the ultimate biological truth: We are all related (Figure 11.3). This chapter's Globalscape explores the complexity of our relatedness in the context of international adoption.

Figure 11.3 The Science and Business of Family Trees
Have you ever wondered if you were descended from Genghis Khan, Helen of Troy, or Ramses II? Today, the business of "recreational ancestry" allows people to trace their mitochondrial DNA (mtDNA) back thousands of years. What exactly do these ancestry traces discover? Because mtDNA is only passed from mother to child, you have one "match" from each generation (your mother, your mother's mother, and so on). As you trace your mtDNA through the roots of your family tree, the percentage of your ancestors who do not factor into the analysis increases. Going back through many generations, your mtDNA trace connects you to just a single person out of hundreds, thousands, or millions who led directly to your existence. Biologically, this connection means very little. In fact, mathematically, we are all both inbred and related. But, as evidenced by the success of the ancestry business, the folk concept of kinship remains a psychologically significant part of human existence in many societies. Can you see any folk beliefs reflected in this advertisement for one of the several large recreational ancestry companies?

Conflating Biology into the Cultural Category of Race

Although biologically separate human races do not exist, race remains a significant cultural category. Human groups frequently insert a false notion of biological difference into the cultural category of race to make it appear more factual and objective. In various ways, cultures define religious, linguistic, and ethnic groups as races, thereby confusing linguistic and cultural traits with physical traits.

For example, people in many Latin American countries classify one another into groups as Indian, *mestizo* (mixed), and *Ladino* (Spanish-speaking mixed). But despite the biological connotations of these terms, the criteria used for assigning individuals to these categories are determined by whether they wear shoes, sandals, or go barefoot; speak Spanish or an indigenous language; live in a thatched hut or a European-style house; and so forth. By speaking Spanish, wearing Western-style clothes, and living in a house in a non-Indian neighborhood, indigenous people shed their tribal identity and acquire a national identity as citizens of the country.

Similarly, the ever-changing racial categories used by the U.S. Census Bureau both reflect and reinforce the conflation of the biological and the cultural. The 2010 list includes large catchall political categories such as white and black but asks for specific tribal affiliations of American Indians or Alaskan Natives, a designation that comes much closer to a population in the biological sense. The Census Bureau asks people to identify Hispanic ethnicity, independent of the category of race, but considers Arabs and Christians of Middle Eastern ancestry as white (Caucasian) despite the political import of Arab and Muslim identity. To accommodate these ambiguities, the Census Bureau lets people check off multiple categories.

That the purported race of individuals can vary over the course of their lifetime speaks to the fact that cultural forces are what designate membership in a particular racial category (Hahn, 1992). Consider, for example, Rachel Dolezal, a civil rights activist and former official for the National Association for the Advancement of Colored People. In 2015 she gained national attention when her white parents stated she was "passing" as a black woman. Dolezal's detractors accused her of cultural appropriation, while her supporters argued that she identified as black, regardless of biology. The controversy sparked a national conversation about racial identity.

The U.S. Census Bureau gathers health statistics by racial categories for the purposes of correcting health disparities among social groups. Unfortunately, the false biological concept of race gets inferred in these analyses. As a result, the increased risk of dying from a heart attack for African Americans compared to whites is falsely attributed to biological differences rather than to healthcare disparities or other social factors. In 2005, amid controversy,

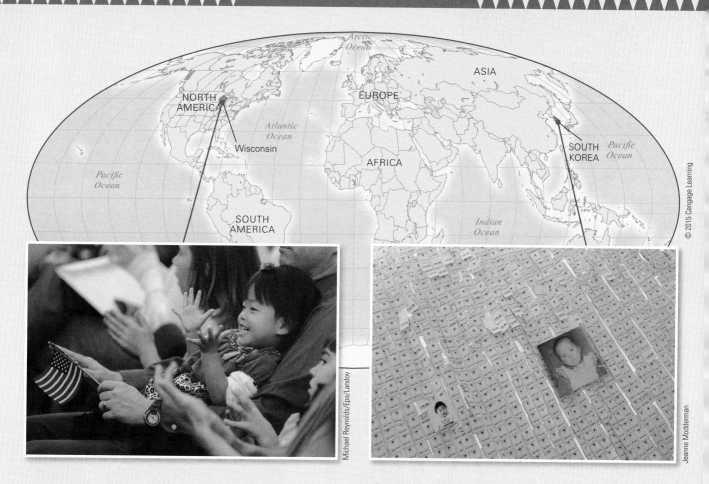

© 2015 Cengage Learning

Michael Reynolds/Epa/Landov

Jeanne Modderman

Finding Home?

Since the 1960s, over 200,000 South Korean children have been adopted by foreign parents, most of them in the United States. The vast majority of these children were born to unwed women, who face social, professional, and financial hardship because of their culture's opposition to single motherhood. In America, adoptive parents were often seen, and saw themselves, as the babies' rescuers, starting with Bertha and Harry Holt, who, in 1955, adopted eight children orphaned by the Korean War. They went on to found Holt International Children's Services.

The South Korean government eased the international adoption process as much as possible. However, many adoptive parents were unable to understand the social challenges, including racism, that their children faced growing up in the United States. In a 2015 interview, Laura Klunder, born in South Korea and adopted by a family in Wisconsin, told the *New York Times* that her parents, although loving, had difficulty dealing with the racism she encountered regularly at school. She said, "My parents told me they didn't see color. They couldn't engage on that level."[a] In addition, although many adoptees face similar difficulties, they are predominantly culturally American and face different challenges trying to connect with the culture of their native land.

Nevertheless, since the late 1990s, the Global Overseas Adoptees' Link (GOA'L), has been helping international adoptees

from South Korea return to live and work there. In 2010, one repatriated adoptee named Leanne (who also calls herself Girl #4708)—along with other adoptees, unwed mothers, and friends—created an art installation of thousands and thousands of price tags, some with photos, representing the 200,000 Korean children given up for adoption.[b] Today, a large number of adoptees, including Laura Klunder, have returned to their birth country. Hundreds now live in the vibrant, modern city of Seoul, where they are slowly assimilating into their birth culture.

Global Twister

Some adoptee organizations are against international adoptions. Why do you think they feel this way? How does international adoption affect adoptees, their birth families, their adoptive families, and their governments? What are the challenges? The benefits?

---

[a] Jones, M. (2015, January 14). Why a generation of adoptees is returning to South Korea. *New York Times Magazine*. http://www .nytimes.com/2015/01/18/magazine/why-a-generation-of-adoptees -is-returning-to-south-korea.html?_r=3 (retrieved November 5, 2015)
[b] Girl #4708. (2010, June 15). A collection of one. *Hello Korea! Adoptee repatriation adventure.* https://gyopo.wordpress.com/2010 /06/16/a-collection-of-one/ (retrieved November 5, 2015)

the U.S. Food and Drug Administration approved the first drug marked toward a single racial group. The drug, now called BiDil, was said to treat congestive heart failure in self-identified African Americans, the only patients to have participated in most of its studies. Although effective treatment for an underserved population is beneficial, the idea of race-specific divisions in the human genome is scientifically unsound. In addition, this kind of commercial marketing does nothing to address the social and political roots that determine the vast majority of health disparities.

Against a backdrop of prejudice, the conflation of the biological with the cultural has historically provided a "scientific" justification for the exclusion of whole categories of people from certain roles or positions in society. Before the civil rights era brought equal legal rights to all U.S. citizens, some states using the "one drop rule," also known as hypodescent, would assign individuals with mixed ethnicity or socioeconomic class to the subordinate group in the hierarchy. Similarly, the historical casta system in Mexico used intermarriage between various groups to position people within the hierarchical order (Figure 11.4).

Because of the colonial association of lighter skin with greater power and higher social status, people whose history includes domination by lighter-skinned Europeans

Figure 11.4 *Castas*

In colonial Mexico, sixteen different *castas* were designated, giving specific labels to individuals who were various combinations of Spanish, Indian, and African ancestry. These paintings of *castas* are traditionally arranged from light to dark as a series and reflect an effort to impose hierarchy despite the fluid social system in place. In the United States, descriptors such as *quadroon*, *octoroon*, *sambo*, and *mulatto* attempted to quantify the amount of mixture among races, and the hierarchy was more rigid; the "one drop rule" would ascribe individuals to a subordinate position within the hierarchy if they had even one drop of blood from a "lower" ranking group.

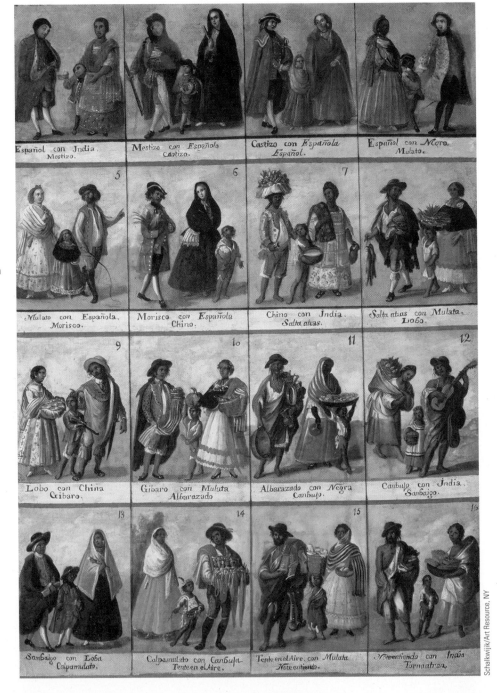

Schalkwijk/Art Resource, NY

have sometimes valued this phenotype. In Haiti, for example, the "color question" has been the dominant force in social and political life. Skin texture, facial features, hair color, and socioeconomic class collectively play a role in the ranking. According to Haitian anthropologist Michel-Rolph Trouillot, "a rich black *becomes* a mulatto, a poor mulatto *becomes* black" (Trouillot, 1996, p. 160).

The Nazis in Germany elevated a racialized worldview to state policy, with particularly evil consequences. Adolf Hitler's agenda was reinforced in part by the American eugenics movement of the early 20th century, with a 1916 book by Madison Grant, *The Passing of the Great Race*, as his bible. The Nuremberg race laws of 1935 codified the superiority of the Aryan race and the inferiority of the Gypsies and Jews as "alien races." The Nazi doctrine justified, on supposed biological grounds, political repression and extermination. In all, 11 million people (Jews, Gypsies, homosexuals, and other so-called inferior people, as well as political opponents of the Nazi regime) were deliberately put to death or died from starvation, disease, and exposure in labor camps.

Tragically, human history contains many atrocities on the scale of the Nazi Holocaust (from the Greek word for "wholly burnt" or "sacrificed by fire"). **Genocide**, a systematic program of extermination of one group by another, has a long history that predates World War II and continues today. From the massacre of 1.5 million Armenians during World War I to the massacre of nearly a million Tutsis by Hutus in Rwanda in 1994, an estimated 83 million people have died from genocides in the 20th century (M. White, 2003). Today, millions of people are still at risk, including the Rohingya Muslims of Myanmar (discussed in Chapter 1) and Christians and Yazidis of Syria and Iraq, whom the international group Genocide Watch designated as "emergencies" in 2015. All genocides contain eight recognizable stages: classification, symbolization, dehumanization, organization, polarization, preparation, extermination, and denial (Stanton, 1998). This structural understanding provides a framework to prevent genocide at each of these stages; although the actual killing may subside, genocide continues until denial ends (**Figure 11.5**).

AP Images/Mark Lennihan

Figure 11.5 Victims of Genocide

In April 2015, activists marched in New York City to demand that the U.S. government acknowledge the systematic extermination of 1.5 million Armenians, a hundred years ago, by the government of the Ottoman empire—today's Turkey—as genocide. More than events of the distant past, this genocide, like those committed against Native Americans and Africans brought to the Americas as slaves, continues to be stuck in genocide's final stage: denial. In the country that you call home, can you see legacies of genocide that have never been corrected? Can you imagine any circumstances under which you believe it is appropriate for a government to choose to ignore genocide in any of its phases?

The Social Significance of Race: Racism

Scientific facts, unfortunately, have been slow to change what people think about race. **Racism**, a doctrine of superiority by which one group justifies the dehumanization and degradation of others based on their distinctive physical characteristics, persists as a major political problem. Indeed, politicians have often exploited this concept as a means of mobilizing support, demonizing opponents, and eliminating rivals. Racial conflicts result from social stereotypes, not scientific facts. In this chapter's Original Study, U.S. anthropologist Faye V. Harrison discusses racism in the fabric of American society.

genocide The physical extermination of one people by another, either as a deliberate act or as the accidental outcome of activities carried out by one people with little regard for their impact on others.

racism A doctrine of superiority by which one group justifies the dehumanization and degradation of others based on their distinctive physical characteristics.

ORIGINAL STUDY

Reflections on the AAA Die-In as a Symbolic Space of Social Death BY FAYE V. HARRISON

At the American Anthropology Association annual meeting in Washington, DC, anthropologists participate in a "die-in" to show their solidarity with the Black Lives Matter movement.

Like hundreds of others, I participated in the December 5th [2014] die-in at the American Anthropological Association meeting in Washington, DC. Under the leadership of the Association of Black Anthropologists and galvanized through the ABA's alliance-building with other kindred-thinking AAA sections, the main lobby of the Marriott Hotel was converted into a symbolic space of social death for four and a half minutes. Darren Wilson and his fellow Ferguson, Missouri, police officers left the lifeless body of teenager Michael Brown in the middle of the street for four and half hours before it was covered up and taken away. Four and a half hours of exposure to the elements; four and a half hours of utter disrespect for the loss of the young man's life and disrespect for the family and community that would grieve the killing of yet another son on blood-stained ground. A blood-stained landscape of social and real-life death links Fruitvale Station in Oakland, California, to Ferguson, Missouri, and countless other sites across the nation and the world, where the lives of blacks and other people of color are being targeted for harassment, arrest, incarceration, and, in the worst case scenario, elimination and disposal....

A tragic pattern prevails across the land; it represents an escalation of extrajudicial executions targeting black and other dark(ened) bodies,...They are guilty of driving, walking, talking back, and, in the case of Jordan Davis in Jacksonville, Florida, even of listening to loud music while Black. The widely shared presumption is that these targeted individuals were dangerous threats to law and order and to personal security, particularly white people's safety and undisturbed peace. The controlling image or stereotype of the violently aggressive thug has been indiscriminately projected upon black bodies, particularly those performing black masculinities. The refusal of grand juries to indict and, in the case of trials, of juries to convict the rightful perpetrators of this violence reflects the extent to which black lives are devalued and infra-humanized in this society. It is for this reason that protesters all across the country and even our allies in other national settings are carrying signs asserting that "Black Lives Matter!" and exhorting "Don't Shoot!"

These poignant declarations resonate with those being made in public protests against the undeclared war on black youth in Brazil, where the pacification of poor neighborhoods, to make way for the World Cup and Olympics, is intensifying the already existent racially marked violence of police and privately commissioned militias—death squads—that participate in the ethnic/social cleansing of urban and rural space....

Our declarations of "Black Lives Matter" also resonate with the human rights protests all across Mexico, where 43 students, many if not all from poor indigenous backgrounds, disappeared from a teachers college in Iguala, Guerrero, in September [2014]. They were abducted by police and handed over to a drug gang that murdered them, if rumors and initial forensic evidence are accurate....

On November 25, 2014, the International Union of Anthropological and Ethnological Sciences (IUAES), of which I am currently president, published a brief statement in solidarity with Mexican and Latin American protesters, who include anthropologists, on the opinion page of the newspaper *La Jornada*. Like Ferguson, Mo., this is a tragic case of youth from oppressed communities being targeted by repressive social control practices.... As an anthropologist, a concerned citizen, and a mother, my mapping of human rights violations zooms in on my own backyard as well as in more distant zones of power disparities.

The four and a half minutes we all lay in complete silence on the lobby floor were quite intense. I filled my mind with meditative thoughts of Michael Brown, Trayvon Martin, and their parents, who channeled their profound grief and sorrow into internationally visible activism. I also saw the faces of my own three sons, now men. I remembered when I delivered the eldest during an unexpectedly difficult and protracted labor. Anxieties mounted within me about the challenges I would face of raising a Black male child in a racist society in which a threatening otherness would be attributed to him. I suspected that much of the discrimination he was likely to face would be much more subtle than what his father and grandfathers had known. But what I feared most and couldn't get out of mind was the specter of brutal police force and the potential hate crimes to which he might be subjected. I wondered whether, as a parent and a member

Marco Hill Photography

of a wider family and community, I would be sufficiently able to protect him and to guide him into full adulthood. I meditated and prayed that I would be able to meet the challenges and demands of Black motherhood.

As I labored with all my might to give birth to my baby boy, my man child who would be born into an unfulfilled promise land, . . . contrary to the expectations born of civil rights era optimism. Years later I would come to know that so much of the research anthropologists have done on the neoliberal landscapes of the past three decades have illuminated the troubling effects of structural racism's persistence and remaking in its entanglements with other dimensions of social inequality and conflict—class, gender, sexuality, and generation or age. However, the current conjuncture, articulated now as the Age of Ferguson, has severely challenged the optimism that many antiracist liberals and leftists have long embodied about the extent to which our society has changed for the better and is capable of changing at a positively discernible pace.

The depth, intensity, and pervasiveness of anti-blackness in the fabric of U.S. society compel us to rethink our models of and for social transformation. Those who subscribe to more pessimistic perspectives . . . urge us to relinquish our political naïveté in favor of more critically realistic views of what is, what is possible, and what should be done about them. Whether optimist, pessimist, or somewhere in between, perhaps we can agree that the "Black Lives Matter," "Don't Shoot," and "I Can't Breathe" demonstrations proliferating across the country clearly belie the widespread postracial pretensions and conceit that have denied grievances against racism the legitimacy as well as the political and policy attention they rightfully deserve.

The four and a half minutes were over. After getting up from the floor, I interacted with the two women who were nearest to me. One remarked on how intense those few minutes of silence had been for her. I agreed, as I wiped away tears streaming from my eyes. After exchanging our feelings and reactions, we gave each other a big group hug and expressed sincere thanks and appreciation for having experienced the die-in with colleagues whose knowledge, sensibilities, and politics we respected. That night at the AAA Business meeting, . . . a motion from the Section Assembly was passed without any opposition. The motion called for the association's making a public statement on Ferguson and Staten Island, appointing a task force to determine what anthropologists can do to address racialized policing, and urging the U.S. Department of Justice to investigate extrajudicial violence and killing. Many of us left the AAA meeting feeling that anthropologists can and will find meaningful ways to play a part in the struggle, as it will continue to unfold in the years to come. *La lucha continúa. A luta continua.* The struggle continues.

Adapted from Harrison, F. V. (2014, December 14). Reflections on the AAA die-in as a symbolic space of social death. *Savage Minds: Notes and Queries in Anthropology.* http://savageminds.org/2014/12/12/reflections-on-the-aaa-die-in-as-a-symbolic-space-of-social-death/ (retrieved November 6, 2015)

Race and Behavior

To date, no inborn behavioral characteristic can be attributed to any single group of people (which nonscientists might call a race) that cannot be explained in terms of cultural practices. If the Chinese happen to exhibit exceptional visual-spatial skills, it is probably because learning to read Chinese characters requires a visual-spatial mastery that Western alphabets do not (Chan & Vernon, 1988). All such behavioral differences or characteristics can be explained in terms of culture.

In the same vein, high crime rates, alcoholism, and drug use among certain groups can be explained with reference to culture rather than biology. Individuals alienated and demoralized by poverty, injustice, and unequal opportunity tend to abandon the dominant culture's traditional paths to success because these paths are blocked. In a racialized society, poverty and all its ill consequences affect some groups of people, like African Americans in the United States, much more severely than others (Figure 11.6).

Slowly, some of this systemic racism, a form of **structural violence**—physical and/or psychological harm caused by impersonal, exploitative, and unjust social, political, and economic systems—has been rectified.

For example, in 2010, the U.S. Congress passed the Fair Sentencing Act, legislation aimed at redressing many years of harsh penalties associated with crack cocaine use; crack is primarily associated with African Americans, as compared to the more expensive and equally potent powdered form of cocaine more often associated with white drug users. Before this legislation, white drug users would have to possess 100 times the amount of powdered cocaine to receive the same sentence as their African American crack-using counterparts (NACDL, 2010).

Race and Intelligence

Scholars and others who believe in the false notion of distinct human biological races have asked whether some races are inherently more intelligent than others. To address this issue requires, first, clarification of the term *intelligence*. Deciding what abilities or talents actually

structural violence Physical and/or psychological harm (including repression, environmental destruction, poverty, hunger, illness, and premature death) caused by impersonal, exploitative, and unjust social, political, and economic systems.

AP Images/Jose Luis Magana

Figure 11.6 The Legacy of Slavery

In recent years, incidents like the death of Freddie Gray at the hands of the Baltimore Police Department have illustrated the need for continued discussion of race relations in the United States. Any such discussion must include the history of slavery and of legal segregation in the South, as well as other forms of structural violence (such as real estate practices, employment practices, prison policies, and educational systems) that favor the white race at the expense of minorities. These social, political, and historical facts have far greater influence on U.S. race relations than minute genetic differences.

races. In the United States, systematic comparisons of intelligence between whites and blacks began in the early 20th century and were frequently combined with data gathered by physical anthropologists about skull shape and size. These kinds of studies continue into the present accompanied by discussions of immutable genetic origins for the difference in IQ scores between Americans of African, Asian, and European descent. An understanding of heredity and genetics undermines any such theory.

As Mendel discovered with his pea plants back in the late 19th century, genes are inherited independently of one another. Whatever the alleles that may be associated with intelligence, they bear no relationship to the ones for skin pigmentation or to any other aspect of human variation. Further, the expression of genes always occurs in an environment, and among humans, culture shapes all aspects of the environment.

Undoubtedly, social environment contributes substantially to intelligence. This should not surprise us, as environmental factors influence other genetically determined traits. Height in humans, for example, has a genetic basis, but it also depends upon both nutrition and health status (severe illness in childhood arrests growth, and renewed growth never makes up for this loss). Scientists have not yet teased apart the exact relative contributions of genetic and environmental factors on intelligence, height, or any other continuous trait. Although the burgeoning field of epigenetics has begun to unravel these interactions, the work is meaningful only in the context of individuals and discrete populations, not in the biologically false category of race (Marks, 2008b; Rose, 2009).

Research on the importance of the environment in the expression of intelligence further exposes the problems with generalizations about IQ and race. For example, IQ scores of groups of people throughout the world have risen by 3 points per decade since World War II (Flynn, 2012). In addition, the relationship between class and IQ has been amply established (Deary, 2001), as has the association between race and class in racialized societies like the United States (American Psychological Association, 2015). All these observations lead to three conclusions. First, there is a bias in IQ testing based on social class. Second, the assertion that IQ is biologically fixed and immutable is clearly false. Third, ranking human beings with respect to their intelligence scores in terms of racial difference is doubly false.

make up what we call intelligence remains contentious, even though some psychologists insist that it is a single quantifiable thing measured by IQ tests. Many more psychologists consider intelligence to be the product of the interaction of different sorts of cognitive abilities: verbal, mathematical/logical, spatial, linguistic, musical, bodily/kinesthetic, social, and personal (Jacoby & Glauberman, 1995). Each of these kinds of intelligence seems unrelated to the others in that individuals possess unique combinations of strengths in each of these areas. Just as humans inherit height, blood type, skin color, and so forth independently, it seems likely that to the degree that intelligence is heritable, each of these kinds of intelligence would be inherited independently.

Furthermore, scholars have shown the limits of IQ tests as a fully valid measure of inborn intelligence. An IQ test measures *performance* (something that one does) rather than *genetic disposition* (something that individuals are born with). Performance reflects past experiences (embedded in culture and the environment) and present motivational state, as well as innate ability.

Despite these limits, since their invention a century ago, some researchers have used IQ tests to try to prove that significant differences in intelligence exist among human

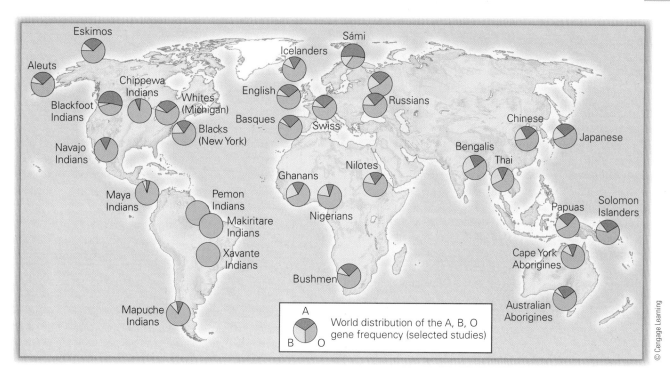

Figure 11.7 Blood Types
Frequencies of the three alleles for the A, B, and O blood groups for selected samples around the world illustrate the polytypic nature of *Homo sapiens*. The frequency of the alleles differs among "populations." Which of the groups here best represent populations (a group of individuals within which breeding takes place) in the biological sense?

Over the past 2.5 million years, all populations of the genus *Homo* have adapted primarily through culture—actively inventing solutions to the problems of existence rather than relying only on biological adaptation. With this in mind, we would expect a comparable degree of intelligence in all present-day human populations. The only way individual human beings will develop their innate abilities and skills to the fullest is by making sure that everyone has access to the necessary resources and opportunities to do so.

Studying Human Biological Diversity

How then can we study human biological variation? What are the scientifically appropriate ways to divide humans into groups? Considering the problems, confusion, and horrendous consequences, anthropologists have abandoned the race concept as being of no utility in understanding human biological variation. Instead, they study *clines,* which are the gradual changes in the distribution and significance of a single, specific, genetically based characteristic or continuous trait in a population. When expressed across an environmental gradient, clines reflect adaptation.

The physical characteristics of both populations and individuals derive from the interaction between genes and environments. For characteristics controlled by a single gene, different versions of that gene, known as alleles (see Chapter 2), also mediate variation. Such traits are called **polymorphic** (meaning "many shapes"). Our blood types—determined by the alleles for types A, B, and O blood—are an example of polymorphism and may appear in any of four distinct phenotypic forms (A, B, O, and AB).

When polymorphisms are distributed into geographically dispersed populations, biologists describe this feature as **polytypic** ("many types"); that is, uneven distribution of genetic variability among populations. For example, consider the polytypic distribution of the polymorphism for blood type (four distinct phenotypic groups: A, B, O, or AB). Some Native American populations possess the highest frequency of the O allele, especially some populations indigenous to South America. Certain European populations have the highest frequencies of the allele for type A blood (although the highest frequency is found among the Blackfoot Indians of the northern Plains in North America). Some Asian populations have the highest frequencies of the B allele (Figure 11.7). Even though single traits may be grouped within specific populations,

polymorphic A term to describe species with alternative forms (alleles) of particular genes.

polytypic A term to describe the expression of genetic variants in different frequencies in different populations of a species.

Beauty, Bigotry, and the Epicanthic Fold of the Beholder

Appearance matters. In the United States—a society that once used skin color to determine social status and still emphasizes the superiority of specific physical traits—the desire to acquire these characteristics through plastic surgery comes as no surprise.

Plastic surgery began in the United States during World War I, as medical doctors developed procedures to reconstruct disfigured soldiers. Soon doctors found other applications for these new techniques. Physical traits associated with ethnic groups lower on the social hierarchy provided new work for the fledgling medical specialty. Rhinoplasty, or the nose job, was originally a surgical procedure used to treat the "deformity" referred to in scientific literature as "Jewish nose." Doctors considered this a medical condition that affected the well-being of patients and demanded intervention. The modern plastic surgery literature still refers to various aspects of human variation as "deformities" that cause psychological and physical impairment to patients.

For immigrant groups, including European Jews who endured significant psychological scarring as a result of discrimination and racism, cosmetic surgery provided one means of gaining acceptance

into this new culture promising the American dream. Cosmetic procedures offered a way to adapt to the stressor of discrimination. As a result, the United States, with its history of racism and discrimination, inherited a significant market for dealing in certain phenotypic traits. In this sense, plastic surgery continues the work of the eugenics movement by eliminating undesirable phenotypes.

Of course, plastic surgeons maintain that individual pursuit of beauty and a natural desire to look one's best motivate their practice and insist that it has nothing to do with race. Yet, roughly 30 percent of all cosmetic procedures occur in minority populations—a relatively high proportion. Many of these procedures, especially ones that alter features strongly identified with a particular ethnic group, have been criticized as a means of "occidentalizing" ethnic populations.

In response to the controversy, plastic surgeons published *Ethnic Considerations in Facial Aesthetic Surgery*[a] with the goal of outlining a "universal standard of beauty" while making considerations for each ethnic group. This difficult task quickly unraveled as the authors' so-called universal aesthetics were revealed to be simply Western standards recast in a politically correct form.

Double eyelid surgery, a procedure that removes the epicanthic fold common in people with East Asian ancestry, is at the center of the debate. The procedure to give the eyes a rounder look occurs among East Asians almost exclusively. It is the third most common cosmetic procedure—after breast augmentation and nose reshaping.

In South Korea, plastic surgery is common, socially acceptable, and encouraged. In Seoul's Improvement Quarter, between 400 and 500 clinics and hospitals offer nips and tucks from nose jobs to jaw tapering within a single square mile. Here, double eyelid surgery is the most common procedure; former president Roh Moo-hyun underwent the procedure in 2005 while in office. The procedure was first popularized after the Korean War, when the United States offered free reconstructive surgery to war victims. Double eyelid surgery quickly caught on with Koreans who wanted to look more "Western," including prostitutes hoping to attract American soldiers.[b]

A doctor writing in 1954 in the *American Journal of Ophthalmology* described a Chinese American patient who reported that people consistently mocked the shape of his eyes and told him that

when a greater number of traits are considered, no specific human "types" exist. Instead, evolutionary forces work independently on each of these traits.

Anthropologists have not been immune to making false assumptions about physical appearance and biological traits. Some early U.S. biological anthropologists proposed that a flat facial profile, extensive fatty deposits around the cheeks, and an **epicanthic fold** (a fold of skin at the corner of the eye) were adaptations to a cold climate; however, these anthropologists had grouped together too many traits. These features—although common in populations native to the cold regions of East and Central Asia as well as Arctic North America—do not appear in all cold-adapted populations. Although head shape might

have some relationship to climate, any feature might also be present in a population due to genetic drift.

Further, in a racialized society like the United States, phenotypic characteristics are imbued with cultural meaning. Indeed, the epicanthic fold is such a defining feature of identity that many Asian Americans, as well as Asians themselves, choose to undergo cosmetic surgery to attain the phenotype of the dominant culture, as described in this chapter's Biocultural Connection. In contrast to the shape of facial features, skin color—the trait so often used to separate people into groups—provides an excellent example of the role of natural selection in human variation.

Culture and Biological Diversity

Cultural adaptation is vital for the human species, but cultural forces also impose their own selective pressures. For

epicanthic fold A fold of skin at the inner corner of the eye; common in Asian populations.

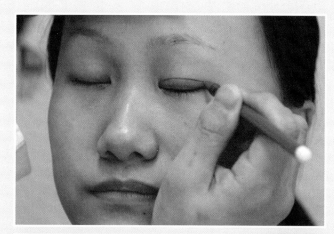

A plastic surgeon explains to a patient how double eyelid surgery could remove the epicanthic fold (*top*), giving her eyes a rounder and more Western look.

because he looked sleepy, his business must be sleepy too. After double eyelid surgery, he related that he was treated more respectfully and that his business became more successful.[c] This account illustrates how years of persecution become internalized, only to morph into an expression of aesthetic preference.

Regardless of its cultural consequences, cosmetic surgery—whether chosen for its aesthetic properties or for the perceived social advantages of fitting in with a specific culture—demonstrates the high value still attached to certain phenotypic traits. Yet the very ability to manipulate these traits illustrates both their superficiality and the fundamental flaws in the concept of discrete biological races. Ethnic plastic surgery—at best a harmless pursuit to look good and more likely the insidious indication of racism's grip on society—shows us that the cost of beauty, or at least an idea of it, can be high indeed.

Biocultural Question

Where would you draw the line for determining when plastic surgery is medically required and when it is an elective procedure? Are there any aspects of your own appearance about which you have internalized a negative perception due to the social value of this characteristic?

[a] Matory, W. E., Jr. (Ed.). (1998). *Ethnic considerations in facial aesthetic surgery.* Philadelphia: Lippincott-Raven.

[b] *Marx, P.* (2015, March 23). About face. *New Yorker.* http://www.newyorker.com /magazine/2015/03/23/about-face (retrieved November 5, 2015)

[c] Kaw, E. (1993). Medicalization of racial features: Asian American women and cosmetic surgery. *Medical Anthropology Quarterly* 7 (1), 74–89.

Nir Elias/Reuters/Landov

example, take the reproductive fitness of individuals with diabetes—a disease with a known genetic predisposition. Ready medication in North America and Europe makes people with diabetes as biologically fit as anyone else. However, without access to the needed medication, a situation all too common globally, diabetes results in death. In fact, one's financial status, place of birth, religion, and so on affect one's access to medication; however unintentional it may be, culture determines biological fitness.

Culture can also contribute directly to the development of disease. For example, type 2 diabetes, very common among overweight individuals who get little exercise—a combination that describes 61 percent of people from the United States today—disproportionately affects the poor. Further, people in other places who have adopted the Western high-sugar diet and low activity pattern have seen their incidence of diabetes and obesity skyrocket.

For years, scientists attributed a tendency toward diabetes among Native Americans to their **thrifty genotype**, which is a genotype that may permit efficient storage of fat to draw on in times of food shortage. Researchers believe the thrifty genotype characterized all humans until about 6,000 years ago (Allen & Cheer, 1996). In times of scarcity, individuals with the thrifty genotype conserve glucose (a simple sugar) for use in the brain and red blood cells (as opposed to other tissues such as muscle), as well as nitrogen (vital for growth and health). Regular access to glucose particularly through the lactose in milk led to selection for the nonthrifty genotype as protection against Type 2 diabetes.

thrifty genotype A human genotype that may permit the efficient storage of fat to draw on in times of food shortage and conservation of glucose and nitrogen.

Figure 11.8 Diabetes among Native Americans
Forced reservation life has had deadly consequences for Native Americans. For example, this ethnocide, or the loss and destruction of traditional cultural practices, created skyrocketing rates of obesity and diabetes as the high carbohydrate and low activity pattern of mainstream U.S. culture replaced traditional American Indian lifeways. Here we see young women of the Salt River Maricopa-Pima tribes preserving their traditional dances at the Cupa Days Festival on the Pala Indian Reservation. Restoring cultural traditions, such as consuming "slow release" foods like prickly pears and walking in the desert, can contribute substantially to improved heath.

Recently, U.S. conservation biologist Gary Nabhan and U.S. anthropologist Laurie Monti have enriched the discussion of diabetes among American Indians by focusing on diet and activity instead of a genetic difference (Figure 11.8). They show that native "slow release" foods such as the prickly pear lower the glucose levels of Native Americans prone to diabetes (Nabhan, 2004). The research has chronicled the ability of these foods to sustain people during long treks into the desert. These "treatments," unlike biomedical shots and pills, predate the appearance of the disease and also empower and preserve native cultures. Each culture developed as a complete adaptive system so it stands to reason that biological variation and cultural variation would be linked.

And what of cultures with traditions of dairying? This cultural practice acted as an agent of biological selection for lactose tolerance: the ability to digest **lactose**, the primary constituent of fresh milk. This ability depends on the capacity to make a particular enzyme, **lactase**. Most mammals as well as most human populations do not continue to produce lactase into adulthood. Adults with lactose intolerance

(85 percent of adults globally) suffer from gas pains and diarrhea when they consume milk or milk products. Only populations with a long tradition of dairying (as seen in northern and eastern Europe, eastern Africa, Central Asia, and the Middle East) tend to retain lactase into adulthood. With fresh milk contributing significantly to their diets, selection in the past favored those individuals with the allele that confers the ability to assimilate lactose, selecting out those without this allele.

The synchronicity between genetic and cultural adaptations goes awry when underlying biological variation is ignored. For example, because North American and European societies associate milk with health, powdered milk used to be a staple of economic aid to other countries. But for populations who do not retain lactase into adulthood, milk consumption causes diarrhea, abdominal cramping, and even bone degeneration. In fact, the humanitarian aid shipment of powdered milk to 2 million people left homeless in the wake of an earthquake in Chile in 1960 caused widespread sickness. Since this tragedy, relief workers have learned to account for the relativity of "healthy" cultural practices.

Beans, Enzymes, and Adaptation to Malaria

In Chapter 2 we explored one biological adaptation to the deadly malarial parasite through the sickle-cell allele. Here we examine cultural adaptations to malaria through the local cuisine. Dietary and biological adaptations to malaria converge with the interaction between the fava bean and an enzyme in certain red blood cells.

The broad, flat fava bean (*Vicia faba*) is a dietary staple in malaria-endemic areas along the Mediterranean coast (Figure 11.9). An enzyme (G6PD or 6-phosphate dehydrogenase) serves to chemically transform one sugar, glucose-6 phosphate, to another sugar—in the process releasing an energy-rich molecule. The malaria parasite lives in red blood cells off of energy produced via G6PD. Individuals with a mutation in the G6PD gene, so-called G6PD deficiency, produce energy by an alternate pathway not involving this enzyme that the parasite cannot use. Furthermore, G6PD-deficient red blood cells seem to turn over more

lactose A sugar that is the primary constituent of fresh milk.

lactase An enzyme in the small intestine that enables humans to assimilate lactose (milk sugar).

has prompted a rich folklore around this simple food, including the ancient Greek belief that fava beans contain the souls of the dead.

Unfortunately, apprehension about fava beans has sometimes generalized to fear about many excellent sources of protein such as peanuts, lentils, chickpeas, soybeans, and nuts. Language accounts for this unnecessary deprivation. The Arabic name for fava beans is *foul* (pronounced "fool"), soybeans are called *foul-al-Soya,* and peanuts are *foul-al-Soudani;* in other words, the plants are linked linguistically even though they are unrelated biologically (Babiker et al., 1996).

Skin Color: A Case Study in Adaptation

Many people equate race with skin color. Before modern methods of transportation—from the earliest sailing ships to today's jets—variation in skin color across the globe followed a discrete pattern (**Figure 11.10** and **Figure 11.11**). Several factors impact variation in skin color: the transparency or thickness of the skin; a copper-colored pigment called carotene; reflected color from the blood vessels (responsible for the rosy color of lightly pigmented people); and the amount of **melanin** (from *melas,* a Greek word meaning "black")—a dark pigment in the skin's outer layer. People with dark skin have more melanin-producing cells than those with light skin, but everyone (except those with albinism) has a measure of melanin. Exposure to sunlight increases melanin production, causing skin color to deepen.

Melanin protects skin against damaging ultraviolet (UV) solar radiation, conferring less susceptibility to skin cancers and sunburn on dark-skinned peoples compared to those with less melanin. Dark skin also helps to prevent the destruction of certain vitamins under intense exposure to sunlight. Because the highest concentrations of dark-skinned people tend to be found in the tropical regions of the world, natural selection has seemed to favor heavily pigmented skin as a protection against exposure where ultraviolet radiation is most constant.

The inheritance of skin color involves several genes (rather than variants of a single gene), each with several alleles, thus creating a continuous range of expression for this trait. In addition, the geographic distribution of skin color tends to be continuous. In northern latitudes, light skin has an adaptive advantage related to the skin's important biological function as the manufacturer of vitamin D through a chemical reaction dependent upon sunlight. Vitamin D maintains the balance of calcium in the body essential for healthy bones and balance in the nervous system. In northern climates with little sunshine,

Figure 11.9 Fava Beans at Market
Fava beans, a dietary staple in the countries around the Mediterranean Sea, also provide some protection against malaria. However, in individuals with G6PD deficiency, the protective aspects of fava beans turn deadly. This dual role has led to a rich folklore surrounding fava beans.

Charles O. Cecil/Alamy

quickly, thus allowing less time for the parasite to grow and multiply. Although a different form of G6PD deficiency is also found in some sub-Saharan African populations, the form found in Mediterranean populations is at odds with an adaptation embedded in the cuisine of the region.

Enzymes naturally occurring in fava beans also contain substances that interfere with the development of the malarial parasite. In cultures around the Mediterranean Sea where malaria is common, fava beans are incorporated into the diet through foods eaten at the height of the malaria season. However, if an individual with G6PD deficiency eats fava beans, the substances toxic to the parasite become toxic to humans. With G6PD deficiency, fava bean consumption leads to hemolytic crisis (Latin for "breaking of red blood cells") and a series of chemical reactions that release free radicals and hydrogen peroxide into the bloodstream. This condition, known as favism,

melanin A dark pigment produced in the outer layer of the skin that protects against damaging ultraviolet solar radiation.

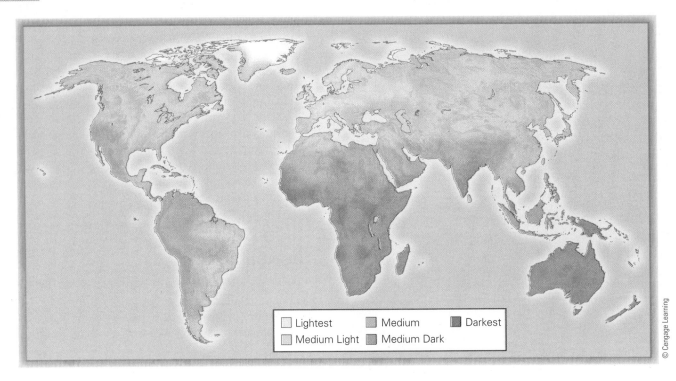

Figure 11.10 **Global Distribution of Skin Pigmentation**
This map illustrates the distribution of dark and light human skin pigmentation before 1492.
The earliest members of the genus *Homo*, who inhabited the tropics, likely had dark skin, which
protected them from UV radiation. In the tropics and at high altitudes, darker skin has selective
advantages. As humans spread to regions with less UV exposure, some pigmentation was lost.

Figure 11.11 **Distribution of Type B Blood in Europe**
The east-west gradient in the frequency of type B blood in Europe contrasts with the north-south gradient in skin color shown in Figure 11.10. Just as the clines for skin color and blood type must be considered independently, so too must whatever genes are involved in the complex of abilities known as intelligence.

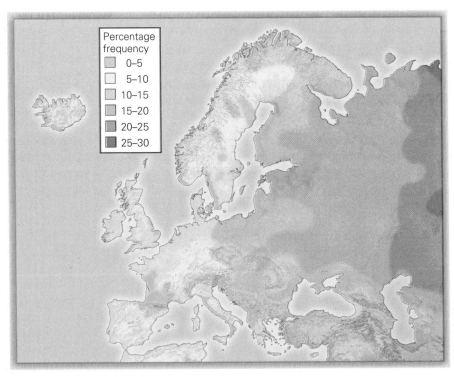

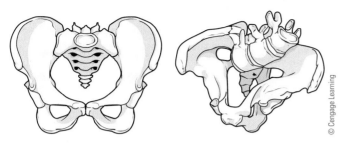

© Cengage Learning

Figure 11.12 When Skin Color Counts
Bone diseases such as osteomalacia and rickets caused by vitamin D deficiency can deform the birth canal of the pelvis to the degree that it can interfere with successful childbirth. Because sunshine is vital to the body's production of vitamin D, this disease was very common in the past among the poor in northern industrial cities because they had limited exposure to sunlight. Dietary supplements have reduced the impact of bone diseases, although these diseases continue to be a problem in cultures that require women and girls to dress so that they are completely veiled from the sun.

light skin allows enough sunlight to penetrate the skin and stimulate the formation of vitamin D. Dark pigmentation interferes with this process in environments with limited sunlight.

Cultural practices can contribute to avoiding the severe consequences of vitamin D deficiency (Figure 11.12). In the middle of the 20th century, parents in northern Europe and northern North America fed their children a daily spoonful of cod liver oil, rich in vitamin D, during the dark winter months. Today, pasteurized milk is fortified with vitamin D.

Race and Human Evolution

Throughout this chapter we have explored the fallacy of the biological category of race when applied to the human species. Generalizations cannot be made about types of humans because no discrete types of humans exist. By contrast, the paleoanthropological analysis of the fossil record explored in previous chapters includes defining specific types of ancestors based on biological and cultural capacities that go hand in hand.

The increased brain size of *Homo habilis* noted around 2.5 million years

ago supports the notion that these ancestors were capable of more complex cultural activities than australopithecines, including the manufacture of stone tools. Closer to the present, the same assumptions do not hold. At some point in our evolutionary history, we became a single, unified global species. Bearing this in mind, let's frame the modern human origins debate in terms of the content of this chapter.

The modern human origins controversy hinges on the question of whether cultural abilities and intelligence can be inferred from details of skull and skeletal shape and size. Supporters of the multiregional hypothesis argue that they cannot. These theorists suggest that using a series of biological features to represent a type of human being (Neandertals) with certain cultural capacities (inferior) is like making assumptions about the cultural capabilities of living humans based on their appearance. In living people, such assumptions are considered stereotypes or racism (Figure 11.13). On the other side of the debate, by arguing that ancient groups like Neandertals represent a distinct

David Hancock/Alamy

Figure 11.13 Unique Variations and Yet the Same
Aboriginal Australians challenge us to think long and hard about race and human origins. Their relatively dark pigmented skin reflects their tropical origins yet aspects of their skull shape lie outside the definition of "anatomical modernity" used by some paleoanthropologists. In Australia, those populations that spread south of the tropics (where, as in northern latitudes, ultraviolet radiation is less intense) underwent some reduction of pigmentation. But for all that, their skin color is still far darker than that of Europeans or East Asians (recall Figure 11.10). Most of today's Southeast Asian population spread there from southern China following the invention of farming. This expansion of lighter-skinned populations effectively "swamped" the original populations of this region, except in a few out-of-the-way places like the Andaman Islands, in the Bay of Bengal between India and Thailand. The bottom line is that we are all human, and population variation does not fit into perfectly discrete types even in recent human evolutionary history.

species, supporters of the recent African origins hypothesis (Eve hypothesis or out of Africa hypothesis) bypass the potential prejudice inherent in these assumptions. Both theories embrace African human origins, and in doing so they confront the issue of skin color—the physical feature with extreme political significance today.

Given what we know about the adaptive significance of human skin color, and the fact that, until about 800,000 years ago, members of the genus *Homo* were almost exclusively creatures of the tropics, lightly pigmented skins are likely a recent development in human history. Conversely, and consistent with humanity's African origins, darkly pigmented skins likely are quite ancient. Human skin, more liberally endowed with sweat glands and lacking heavy body hair compared to other primates, effectively eliminates excess body heat in a hot climate. This would have been especially advantageous to our ancestors on the savannah, who could have avoided confrontations with large carnivorous animals by carrying out most of their activities in the heat of the day. For the most part, tropical predators rest during this period, hunting primarily from dusk until

early morning. Without much hair to cover their bodies, selection would have favored dark skin in our earliest human ancestors. Thus, all humans have a black ancestry, no matter how white some of them may appear to be today.

One should not conclude that its relative newness makes lightly pigmented skin better or more highly evolved than heavily pigmented skin. Lightly pigmented peoples possess the enzyme tyrosinase, which converts the amino acid tyrosine into the compound that forms melanin, in sufficient quantity to make them very black. But they also possess genes that inactivate or inhibit it. Darker skin better suits the conditions of life in the tropics or at high altitudes, although with cultural adaptations like protective clothing, hats, and more recently invented sunscreen lotions, lightly pigmented people can survive there. Conversely, the availability of supplementary sources of vitamin D allows more heavily pigmented people to do quite well far away from the tropics. In both cases, culture has rendered skin color differences largely irrelevant from a purely biological perspective. With time and effort, skin color may eventually lose its social significance as well.

CHAPTER CHECKLIST

Does the biological concept of race apply to human variation?

✓ Humans are a single, highly variable species inhabiting the entire globe. Though biological processes are responsible for human variation, the biological concept of race or subspecies cannot be applied to human diversity. No discrete racial types exist.

✓ Scientists of the past placed humans into discrete races and then ordered them hierarchically. This work was discredited beginning in the early 20th century.

✓ Individual traits appear in continuous gradations (clines) from one population to another without sharp breaks. Traits are inherited independently, and populations are genetically open.

✓ The vast majority of human variation exists within single populations rather than across different populations.

How does the race concept function within societies?

✓ In many countries such as the United States, Haiti, Brazil, and South Africa, the sociopolitical category of race significantly impacts social identity and opportunity.

✓ Racial conflicts result from social stereotypes and not scientific facts.

✓ Racists of the past and present frequently invoke a false notion of biological difference to support unjust social practices.

✓ Behavioral characteristics attributed to race can be explained in terms of experience as well as a hierarchical social order affecting the opportunities and challenges faced by different groups of people, rather than biology.

What are the flaws with studies that attempt to link race and intelligence?

✓ These studies imply a biological basis and do not take into account that biological race does not exist.

✓ The inherited components of intelligence cannot be separated from those that are culturally acquired.

✓ There is still no consensus on what intelligence is, but it is generally agreed that intelligence is made up of several different talents and abilities, each of which would be separately inherited.

✓ The cultural and environmental specificity of IQ testing makes it invalid for broad comparisons.

Why does human skin color vary across the globe?

✓ Skin color, which is subject to tremendous variation, is a function of several factors: transparency or thickness of the skin, distribution of blood vessels, and amount of carotene and melanin in the skin.

✓ Exposure to sunlight increases the amount of melanin, darkening the skin.

✓ The cline of global variation in skin color derives from a balance between selective pressures: synthesis of vitamin D through the skin and protection from solar ultraviolet radiation.

✓ Today cultural factors lessen the impact of selective pressures on skin color. Its social significance remains strong in some cultures.

✓ All humans have African ancestry no matter how white they might appear today.

How have human cultures shaped human biology?

✓ Cultural practices shape human environments, which in turn can act on gene pools.

✓ Peoples with a dairying tradition possess the ability to digest milk sugars (lactose) into adulthood.

✓ Foods and activity patterns comprise a complete adaptive system.

✓ Western-style lifeways, which are characterized by diets high in sugar and low levels of activity, make the incidence of obesity and diabetes particularly high in populations with dietary traditions of "slow release" foods and high activity.

✓ Cultural and biological adaptations at times work at cross-purposes as seen with the example of G6PD deficiency and fava beans as adaptations to malaria.

QUESTIONS FOR REFLECTION

1. As a species, humans are extremely diverse, yet our biological diversity cannot be partitioned into discrete types, subspecies, or races. Nonetheless, race functions as a social and political category in some societies. How did so-called biological race and very real sociopolitical race play out in the 2015 Charleston, South Carolina, mass shooting? What are the beliefs about biological diversity and race in your community today?

2. Although we can see and scientifically explain population differences in skin color, why is it invalid to use the biological concept of subspecies or race when referring to humans? Can you imagine another species of animal, plant, or microorganism for which the subspecies concept makes sense?

3. Globally, health statistics are gathered by country. In addition, some countries such as the United States gather health statistics by so-called racial categories. How are these two endeavors different and similar? Should health statistics be gathered by group? How does structural violence impact the distribution of sickness and health? Provide examples from your community.

4. How do you define the concept of intelligence? Do you think scientists will ever be able to discover the genetic basis of intelligence?

DIGGING INTO ANTHROPOLOGY

Digging for Bias in Standardized Tests

When intelligence testing was invented in the early 20th century, racism was so deeply embedded in U.S. society that these tests were immediately used to make false claims of biological differences. Princeton psychologist Carl Brigham (1923, 1930), one of the original inventors and champions of these tests, began his career as a eugenicist, making claims about the lower intelligence of blacks and Europeans of Mediterranean origins. Though he later renounced that work, Brigham still believed in the cultural neutrality of intelligence testing. Between 1923 and 1926, he invented the Scholastic Aptitude Test, or SAT, a test that has become the standard for college entrance. Given what you have learned about language, experience, structural violence, and intelligence testing, explore whether culturally neutral intelligence testing has become reality. Find a sample IQ test, SAT, or similar "standardized" test and see if you find any incidences of culture-bound bias in the questions. Think about how members of diverse cultures might answer each question differently. How might the general practice of testing serve to maintain a racialized, resource-based status quo?

Jay Directo/AFP/Getty Images

CHALLENGE ISSUE

Human population growth requires increased resources—for food, clothing, and shelter. And what happens to the waste associated with all this consumption? Humans, especially those from industrialized societies, produce a staggering amount of garbage. When not disposed of properly, this trash can be destructive and even dangerous. A recent UN study found that world urban centers produce 8 to 10 billion tons of waste annually and that much of it ends up in the ocean (UN Environment Programme, 2015). The Great Pacific garbage patch, also called the Pacific trash vortex, is a vast floating dump where tides have pushed refuse together in the northern Pacific Ocean; it occupies as much space as the state of Texas or the country of Turkey. Marine debris on this scale threatens the stability of global food webs—preventing organisms like photosynthetic algae and plankton from creating nutrients and providing foundational food sources for all marine life. Continuing population growth intensifies the global trash problem. Our ability to meet the challenges of ever-increasing consumption and waste production will determine the earth's long-term health and ultimately our very existence.

Human Adaptation to a Changing World

12

Past, present, and future, the interaction of biology and culture has made humans the richly varied species that we are today. Together, biology and culture shape every aspect of the human condition from sickness to health and from birth to death. Indeed, a joke among anthropologists is that if you do not know the answer to an exam question about biology and culture, the answer is either "both" or "malaria" because answering "malaria" is just like answering "both."

Recall that farming practices (culture) of the past created the perfect environment for the malarial parasite. The genetic response (biology) to this environmental change was increased frequency of the sickle-cell allele. Today, contemporary global inequalities (culture) contribute to malaria's death toll (biology) in poorer subtropical countries. If malaria were a problem plaguing North America or Europe, would most citizens of these countries still be without adequate treatment or cure?

Similarly, African Americans have learned to distrust public health initiatives for genetic counseling to reduce the frequency of sickle-cell anemia in the United States (Tapper, 1999; Washington, 2006). This lack of trust derives from a legacy of institutionalized racism, manifested as mistreatment in the name of "science" in examples such as the Tuskegee Syphilis Study, carried out by the U.S. Public Health Service in Macon County, Alabama, from 1932 to 1972. Scientists withheld syphilis medication from a group of poor African American men without their knowledge, so that they could learn more about the biology of syphilis in the "Negro" (Figure 12.1).

Today, this could not happen. Any kind of biological research on human subjects without informed consent is illegal in the United States and in many other countries. Nevertheless, cultural forces continue to translate to poorer health outcomes for blacks compared to whites in countries like the United States. When examining a seemingly biological phenomenon like disease, we must determine the cultural factors involved as well—from how the phenomenon is represented in different social groups (reflected in the Tuskegee case by the false notion that syphilis would differ based on skin color) to how biological research is conducted.

In this chapter you will learn to

- Recognize old and new pressures to human survival across the globe.

- Describe human biological adaptations to high altitude, cold, and heat.

- Identify patterns of human growth and how the process allows humans to adapt.

- Explain the challenges that we have created for ourselves and how their effects fall upon distinct yet interconnected communities.

- Describe modern humans' variety of coping methods and treatments for health issues.

- Define disease versus illness and discuss cultural attitudes about both.

- Investigate the multiple causes of health problems from a medical anthropological perspective.

Figure 12.1 The Tuskegee Experiments
The Tuskegee Syphilis Study denied appropriate medical treatment to African American men in order to study the supposed differences in the biology of the disease in the "Negro." This human experimentation was not only false from a biological perspective but represented an egregious ethical breach in research conduct. Public outcry about this experiment led to regulations that protect all human subjects in biomedical research. Today, laws in the United States and in many other countries require informed consent of study participants for all research on human subjects.

The integration of biology and culture is the hallmark of anthropology. Throughout this book, we have emphasized biocultural connections in examples ranging from infant feeding and sleeping practices to the relationship between poverty and tuberculosis to medical procedures such as organ transplantation. In this chapter, we take a deeper look at this connection and examine some of the theoretical approaches biological and medical anthropologists use to examine the interaction of biology and culture. Humans have adapted to the natural environment with refined biological mechanisms, but these mechanisms can fall short in a globalizing world. Before looking at the challenges we face from changes in environments today, we will explore the biological mechanisms people have used over millennia to adapt to three environmental extremes: high altitude, cold, and heat.

genetic adaptation A discrete genetic change built into the allele frequency of a population or the microevolutionary change brought about by natural selection.

developmental adaptation A permanent phenotypic variation derived from interaction between genes and the environment during the period of growth and development.

Human Adaptation to Natural Environmental Stressors

Studies of human adaptation traditionally focus on humans' capacity to adapt or adjust to their environment through biological and cultural mechanisms. Darwin's theory of natural selection accounts for a **genetic adaptation**—a discrete genetic change built into the allele frequency of a population, such as the various adaptations to malaria that we have examined. Genetic adaptation also provides the mechanism for understanding that adaptations, evident in population variation of continuous phenotypic traits (such as skin color or body build), depend upon multiple interacting genes. Even without knowing the precise genetic bases to these adaptations, scientists can study them through comparative measurement of the associated phenotypic variation. Differential reproductive success always accounts for differences in allele frequency.

Beyond genetics, humans possess two additional biological mechanisms that drive adaptation. The first of these, **developmental adaptation**, also produces permanent phenotypic variation through environmental shaping of individual gene expression (Figure 12.2). Humans' extended period of growth and development allows the environment to exert its effects on individuals for a prolonged time period. The specific permanent phenotypic changes brought about through environmental interaction are not directly passed on to future generations. Even after most physical growth ceases, our genomes interact with the environment, producing discrete biological changes.

Epigenetics, the study of changes in gene function due to how cells read the genetic code, can also impact phenotype. Without any change in DNA sequence, epigenetics accounts for how the environment or the life cycle might shape the expression of specific genes. Factors ranging from naturally demanding physical conditions to human-made stressors, such as a traumatic experience, can turn specific genes off and on. Sometimes these changes are heritable, allowing epigenetics to shape future generations, as demonstrated in recent studies on the intergenerational transmission of the trauma of war and genocide (Yehuda & Bierer, 2008; Yehuda et al., 2015).

The anthropological focus on growth and development has a long history dating back to the work of Franz Boas, the founder of American four-field anthropology. Boas is credited with discovering the features of the human growth curve (Figure 12.3), demonstrating that human growth rate varies in typical patterns until adulthood, when physical growth ceases. Humans experience a period of very rapid growth after birth through infancy, followed by a gradually slowing rate of growth during childhood. At adolescence, the rate increases again during the adolescent growth spurt. Growth in height or stature results from the addition of new cells throughout the body, but particularly in the bones, where there are specific growth plates (Figure 12.4).

In addition to describing the long-term human growth pattern, anthropologists have demonstrated that within periods of growth, there are series of alternating bursts and relative quiet. When challenged by malnutrition, physical growth slows, favoring survival over height in adulthood. This adaptive mechanism may have negative consequences for subsequent generations as individuals who were malnourished as children often show reduced reproductive success as adults.

Jodi Cobb/National Geographic Stock

Figure 12.2 Twins
Diana Bozza and her identical twin Deborah Faraday share 100 percent genetic identity. Yet only Deborah suffered from early onset Alzheimer's disease. Pictured here is Diana comforting Deborah several years ago at an assisted living facility in Front Royal, Virginia. Diagnosed in 2004, Deborah was completely disabled while Diana has no symptoms of Alzheimer's. Deborah passed away from the disease in 2013. Though identical twins share 100 percent of their genetic material, their phenotypes can be distinct because of interactions between these genes and the environment over the course of each individual's distinct life.

Boas also demonstrated differences in the growth of immigrant children in the United States compared to their parents. This work was the earliest documentation of the variable effects of different environments on the growth process. Presumably, immigrant children resemble their parents genetically; therefore, size differences between immigrant children and their parents could be attributed to the environment alone. This kind of difference, known as a **secular trend**, allows anthropologists to make inferences about environmental effects on growth and development.

The human body's various systems have their own trajectory of growth and development shaped by both environmental and genetic factors (Figure 12.5). For example, age at **menarche** (first menstruation) varies tremendously across the globe. Over the past sixty years, a downward secular trend in age at menarche has become

epigenetics The study of changes in organisms that are caused by modification of gene function and expression rather than by modification of the DNA sequence.

secular trend A physical difference among related people from distinct generations that allows anthropologists to make inferences about environmental effects on growth and development.

menarche The first occurrence of menstruation in the human female.

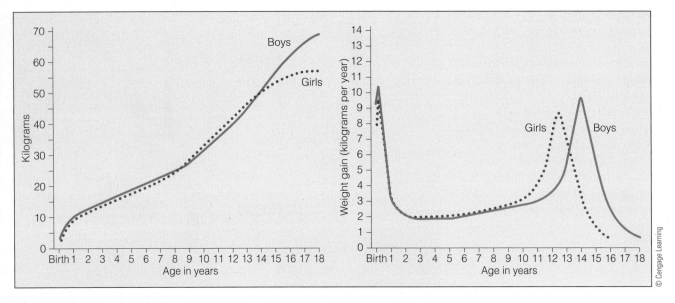

Figure 12.3 Human Growth Curves
Franz Boas defined the features of the human growth curve. The graph on the left depicts distance, or the amount of growth attained over time, and the graph on the right shows the velocity, or rate of growth over time. These charts are widely used throughout the globe to determine the health status of children.

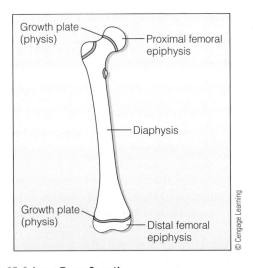

Figure 12.4 Long Bone Growth
Each long bone has specific regions (*in red*) of cartilage where growth occurs; these are called growth plates. This allows the harder bony tissue of the diaphysis to support the body and for the epiphyses to function within the joint while an individual is developing. This thighbone, or femur, has four distinct areas of growth. In an x-ray of a child who is still growing, the cartilage does not appear white like bone. Each bone has a particular sequence of maturation that is regulated by hormones. Growth stops when the epiphyses fuse with the rest of the bone, a process regulated by estrogens in both males and females. In males, the clavicle or collarbone is one of the last bones to fuse. In females, the pubic bone of the pelvis is one of the last bones to fuse.

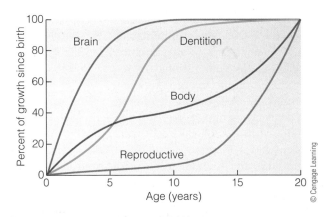

Figure 12.5 Development Trajectories
The various systems of the human body each follow their own trajectory of growth. Brain growth is most rapid in the first five years of life but continues at a slower pace into young adulthood. Children's immune systems also undergo rapid development early in life. Humans acquire most of their permanent dentition by the time their reproductive systems start to mature at adolescence; their 12-year molars have emerged, and only the wisdom teeth have not yet erupted. The pace of growth for the reproductive system and the body both increase rapidly at adolescence.

evident in North America. Whether this secular trend is attributable to healthy or problematic stimuli (such as childhood obesity or hormones in the environment) has yet to be determined. Genetic differences from population to population account for some variation, and environmental effects account for the remainder. The Bundi of New Guinea have the oldest average age (18) at menarche.

Friedrich Stark/Alamy

Figure 12.6 Nutrition and Fertility
The theory that human females require a minimum percentage of body fat in order to attain menarche accounts for some of the global variation in the age at which this occurs. Around the world, many women stay incredibly lean through a combination of hard labor and limited food availability, a condition that limits their fertility. Further, sufficient body fat maintains menstrual cycles throughout adulthood. Thus, female bodies regulate their potential pregnancies in times of limited food because successful pregnancy and breast-feeding require extra nutrition. In postindustrial societies, loss of periods, or amenorrhea, is common among athletes and among women with anorexia nervosa, a disorder in which individuals starve themselves.

By comparison, U.S. girls reach menarche on average at 12.4 years (Worthman, 1999).

An important theory accounting for sexual maturity ties age at menarche to the percentage of body fat possessed by growing individuals as a regulator of hormonal production (Frisch, 2002). Most female bodies require a minimum ratio of 17 percent body fat to lean mass for menarche to occur (Figure 12.6). This body fat helps with the conversion of androgens (the male hormones) to the female hormonal counterpart, estrogens. Highly active lean women, whether from athletics or some kind of labor, may experience a delayed menarche or a secondary loss of menstruation. Starvation and extreme obesity can both have the same effect.

Hormones impact fertility into adulthood, but teasing apart the role of biology and culture is complex.

For example, let's look at androgen hormone levels and women in high-powered careers. These women tend to have a more cylindrical shape, which could be because their bodies produce relatively more androgen than hourglass-shaped women, which may also account for lower fertility. Higher androgen levels may also represent a biological response to specific work environments that ultimately impede fertility for women in high-powered careers (Cashdan, 2008). Similarly, diminishing estrogen level after **menopause** (the cessation of menstrual cycles) causes female body fat distribution patterns to shift to a more male pattern.

---

menopause The cessation of menstruation cycles.

Peter T. Ellison (b. 1951)

The work of biological anthropologist **Peter Ellison** focuses on reproductive biology and human health across cultures. In the 1970s, Ellison first read Darwin's *Origin of Species* as a college student at St. John's College in Annapolis, Maryland. He found Darwin's text transformative and went to the University of Vermont to study biology; later he earned a doctorate in biological anthropology from Harvard, where he now runs a comprehensive program in reproductive ecology.

Ellison pioneered techniques for hormonal analysis from saliva, which he has used to monitor individuals' response to various environmental stressors. This noninvasive technique has allowed Ellison to conduct hormonal studies throughout the world and to correlate hormonal levels with social events. The research utilized long-term field sites in Congo, Poland, Japan, Nepal, and Paraguay, making it a truly global study. Ellison documented hormonal variations around biological events, such as egg implantation and breast-feeding, as well as cultural factors such as farm work or foraging.

Dr. Ellison is especially interested in the ways in which behavior and social stimuli affect reproductive physiology. In Western societies, he has explored hormonal levels of males and females in response to stimuli, such as winning a championship or taking a stressful exam. He has also studied the relationship between cancer development and exercise and stress. In his book *On Fertile Ground*, Ellison illustrates how evolutionary forces have shaped human reproductive physiology into a system capable of precise responses to environmental stimuli.

Peter Ellison (*left*) and colleague Peter Gray discuss how male testosterone levels differ between married and single men and among men of different cultures.

Human hormonal systems are highly sensitive to various environmental stimuli. U.S. biological anthropologist Peter Ellison works extensively on the connections between hormones and the environment—a subspecialty defined as *reproductive ecology* (see the Anthropologist of Note).

Although genetic and developmental adaptations become permanent parts of an adult's phenotype, **physiological adaptation** comes and goes in response to a specific environmental stimulus. Along with cultural

adaptations, these various biological mechanisms make humans the only primate species able to inhabit the entire globe. Over the course of our evolutionary history, most environmental stressors were climatic and geographic. Today, humans face a series of new environmental stressors of their own making.

Adaptation to High Altitude

High altitude differs from other natural environmental stressors because it is the least amenable to cultural adaptation. Humans can heat the cold and cool the heat, but the reduced availability of oxygen at high altitude poses more of a challenge. At a cellular level, high altitude results in reduced oxygen availability, or **hypoxia**

physiological adaptation A short-term physiological change in response to a specific environmental stimulus. An immediate short-term response is not very efficient and is gradually replaced by a longer-term response; see *acclimatization*.

hypoxia The reduced availability of oxygen in the atmosphere causing diminished oxygen at the cellular level.

(from the Greek *hypo*, for "low" or "under" and the word *oxygen*). Before the inventions of oxygen masks and pressurized cabins in airplanes, there was no way to culturally modify the conditions of high altitude. When people speak of the air being "thinner" at high altitude, they are referring to the concentration (partial pressure) of oxygen available to the lungs and the circulatory system. At high altitudes, the partial pressure of oxygen is sufficiently reduced so that most lowlanders experience severe oxygen deprivation (Figure 12.7).

Populations that have lived at high altitudes for generations, such as the Quechua Indians of the highlands of Peru and the Sherpa of the Himalayas, possess a remarkable ability to tolerate oxygen deprivation. Some of these abilities are encoded in the genetic makeup of these populations, allowing them to live and work at altitudes as high as 20,000 feet above sea level. In addition, developmental and physiological adaptations to the lower partial pressure of oxygen in the environment have rendered their body tissues resistant to oxygen deprivation (Figure 12.8).

Jim Rogash/Getty Images Sport/Getty Images

Figure 12.8 Born to Run
East African runners, like Caroline Rotich from Kenya, have won most major marathons over the past several decades. Adaptation to the hot, dry, yet mountainous region leads to a long, lean build (a product of the heat adaptation) and increased oxygen-carrying capacity. Although runners worldwide tend to be long and lean, many athletes now train at high altitudes so that when race day comes, their red blood cell count and hemoglobin levels allow them to carry more oxygen.

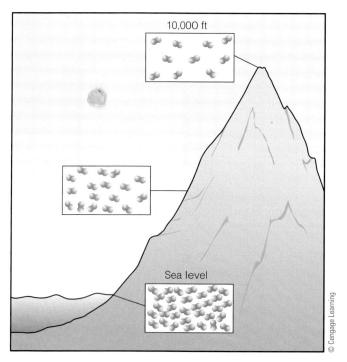

© Cengage Learning

Figure 12.7 Atmospheric Pressure
The amount of atmosphere above us determines the amount of pressure being exerted on oxygen molecules in the air. At sea level, the pressure of the atmosphere packs oxygen molecules more tightly together compared to the density of oxygen molecules at higher altitudes. This in turn impacts the ease at which oxygen can enter the lungs when we breathe. At high altitudes where it is more difficult for oxygen to enter the lungs naturally, mountain climbers will sometimes carry bottled oxygen for extra assistance.

Typical lowlanders can make both short- and long-term physiological adjustments to high altitude. In general, short-term changes help an individual avoid immediate crisis but are not efficient and are difficult to sustain. Long-term responses take over as the individual's physiological responses attain equilibrium with the environment. This process is known as **acclimatization**. Most lowlanders

acclimatization A long-term physiological adjustment made in order to attain equilibrium with a specific environmental stimulus.

stepping off an airplane in Cuzco, Peru, for example, will experience increased respiratory rate, cardiac output, blood pressure, and expanded arteries—all responses that cannot be maintained indefinitely. Instead, lowlanders acclimatize as their bodies begin to produce more red blood cells and hemoglobin to carry more oxygen. Because of differences in genetic makeup, individuals' physiological responses begin at varying altitudes.

Developmental adaptations are seen in individuals who grow up and develop at high altitude. Among the highland Quechua, for example, both the chest cavity and the right ventricle of the heart (which pushes blood to the lungs) are enlarged compared to lowland Quechua. This may have genetic underpinnings in that all Quechua experience a long period of growth and development compared to the average person in the United States.

Growth and development begin with reproduction, and high altitude has a considerable impact on this process. For populations that have not adapted to high altitude, successful reproduction requires some cultural interventions. For example, take the case of fertility among Spanish colonialists in the city of Potosi high in the Andes Mountains of Bolivia in South America. Founded as a silver mining town in 1545, during the first fifty-four years of this city's existence, no Spanish child was born who survived childhood. Indigenous populations did not have this problem. In response, Spanish women began the cultural practice of retreating to lower altitude for their pregnancy and the first year of their child's life (Piantadosi, 2003).

Cold stress is also a problem at high altitudes. A stocky body and short limbs help individuals conserve heat, in contrast to long, lanky bodies. We dissipate heat through the surface of our bodies. A stocky build has a lower surface area to volume ratio compared to longer builds. Small body size also results in a higher surface area to volume. These phenomena have been formalized into two rules named after the naturalists who made such observations in mammals. **Bergmann's rule** refers to the tendency for the bodies of mammals living in cold climates to be more massive than members of the same species living in warm climates (Figure 12.9). **Allen's rule** refers to the tendency of mammals living in cold climates to have shorter appendages (arms and legs) than members of the same species living in warm climates (Figure 12.10).

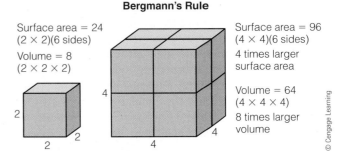

Figure 12.9 Bergmann's Rule
Bergmann's rule refers to the observation that as overall body size increases, the amount of surface area increases less rapidly than the amount of volume. This accounts for the tendency for mammals living in cold climates to be more massive than members of the same species living in warmer climates. This allows for the conservation of heat in cold climates and its dissipation in warm climates.

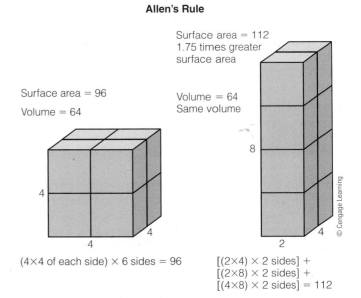

Figure 12.10 Allen's Rule
Allen's rule refers to the observation that in two bodies that have the same volume, the one that is long and lean rather than short and squat will have a greater surface area. This accounts for the tendency for mammals living in cold climates to have shorter appendages (arms and legs) than the same species living in warmer climates. Heat can be dissipated through long limbs or conserved through short ones.

Adaptation to Cold

Cold stress can exist without high altitude, as it does in the Arctic. In addition to the patterns of body and limb shape and size, other cold responses are evident in Arctic

Bergmann's rule The tendency for the bodies of mammals living in cold climates to be shorter and rounder than members of the same species living in warm climates.

Allen's rule The tendency for the bodies of mammals living in cold climates to have shorter appendages (arms and legs) than members of the same species living in warm climates.

Figure 12.11 Whale Hunting
Arctic populations acclimatize to frigid conditions through a variety of biological and cultural adaptations. Often biology and culture interact. The high-energy, readily available whale blubber diet, integral to Inuit cultural systems, also stimulates the body to burn this energy at a high metabolic rate. A high metabolic rate, in turn, helps the body stay warm in very cold climates.

Andrew Stewart/AGE Fotostock

populations. In extreme cold, the body needs to balance heat between its core and the limbs, which need enough heat to prevent frostbite. Humans balance this through a cyclic expansion and contraction of the blood vessels of their limbs called the **hunting response**. Blood vessels oscillate between closing down to prevent heat loss and opening up to warm the hands and feet. With initial exposure to extreme cold, blood vessels immediately constrict and alternate between open (warm) and shut (cold) so the temperature of the skin varies dramatically. Gradually, the oscillations become smaller and more rapid, allowing a

hunter the dexterity required for tying knots or positioning arrows.

Arctic peoples such as the Inuit also deal with cold through a high **metabolic rate**: the rate at which the body burns energy. A protein- and fat-rich diet (seal and whale blubber are common foods; see Figure 12.11) may

hunting response A cyclic expansion and contraction of the blood vessels of the limbs that balances releasing enough heat to prevent frostbite with maintaining heat in the body core.

metabolic rate The rate at which bodies burn energy (food) to function.

Figure 12.12 Cross-Section of Human Skin

Skin—a sensitive, functional, and highly diffuse organ of the human body—responds exquisitely to the environment. As described in Chapter 11, vitamin D is synthesized here as UVB rays penetrate the outer layer of skin. The potentially more harmful UVA rays can penetrate deeper into the skin and do not drive vitamin D production. In addition, skin regulates our adaptive response to heat through sweating. Blood vessels carry heat to the surface of the body. Water released through the sweat glands onto the surface of the skin through pores will evaporate and dissipate this body heat. Individuals who spend their growth and development in hotter climates possess more sweat glands as a developmental adaptation to heat. In addition, body build impacts heat dissipation. More skin or surface area allows an individual to dissipate heat more easily because of the increased number of sweat glands distributed on the skin.

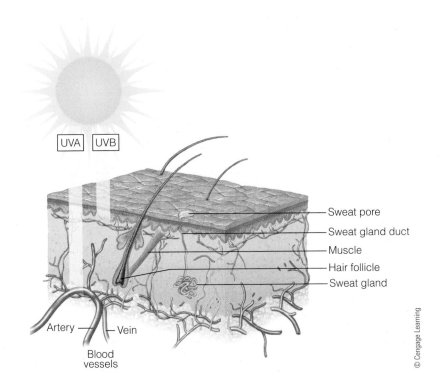

UVA UVB

Sweat pore
Sweat gland duct
Muscle
Hair follicle
Sweat gland

Artery — Vein

Blood
vessels

© Cengage Learning

help heighten metabolic rate, but genetic factors are likely also a factor.

Shivering generates heat and provides a short-term physiological response to cold, but it cannot be maintained for long periods of time. Instead, an individual's acclimatization to the cold involves adjustments to diet, activity pattern, metabolic rate, and the circulatory system.

Adaptation to Heat

Sweating is the human body's primary physiological mechanism for coping with extreme heat. The water released from sweat glands during sweating cools the body, but it must be replaced by drinking more, because exposure to heat can be fatal without water (**Figure 12.12**). Bergmann's and Allen's rules also apply to heat adaptation, because sweat glands, spread over a greater surface area on tall, thin bodies, facilitate water evaporation and heat loss. The more surface area a body has, the more surface area for the sweat glands. Long, slender bodies dissipate heat best. In hot and humid environments like rainforests, water evaporation poses a challenge. Here, human populations have adapted to minimize heat production through a diminished overall size while keeping a slender, lean build.

Human-Made Stressors of a Changing World

Traditionally, humans have modified natural stressors like heat and cold through cultural means such as housing, diet, and clothing. But in today's globalizing world, the impact of culture is much more complex. Today, cultural processes can *add* new stressors such as pollution, global warming, and exhaustion of natural resources. Indeed, as noted in Chapter 5, scholars added **Anthropocene** to the geological epochs to reflect the profound human modification of the earth since the industrial revolution.

Biological adaptation to these human-made stressors cannot keep pace with the rapid rate at which humans are changing the earth, as it takes many generations for beneficial alleles and phenotypes to become established in a population's genome. Until human cultures cooperate to collectively address these global challenges, unnatural stressors will inevitably lead to sickness and suffering. An integrated, holistic anthropological perspective has much to contribute to alleviating if not eliminating these human-made stressors.

The Development of Medical Anthropology

Medical anthropology, a specialization that cuts across all four fields of anthropology, contributes significantly

Anthropocene A geological epoch defined by massive environmental changes brought on by humans since the industrial revolution.

Figure 12.13 **Healing Symbols and Actions**
Shamans and biomedical doctors both rely upon symbols to heal their patients. The physician's white coat is a powerful symbol of medical knowledge and authority that communicates to patients just as clearly as does the feather headdress of a Tuva shaman from the mountains of southern Siberia. Tuva healing practices include direct contact with the individual who is sick as well as actions such as climbing to a mountaintop to burn cedar, shown here. Can you imagine the symbolic purpose of climbing to great heights? What do you think is the biomedical equivalent of the mountaintop? Here a pediatrician hugs her patient after giving him a shot. Imagine the trust involved in letting someone stab you with a sharp object and inject a foreign material into your body. How does the doctor have the authority to do this? Interestingly, medical schools in the United States frequently incorporate a "white coat" ceremony into medical education, conferring the power of the white coat onto new doctors.

to understandings of sickness and health in the 21st century. Medical anthropologists study the **medical system**—a patterned sets of ideas and practices relating to illness. Medical systems are cultural, similar to any other social institution. Medical anthropologists examine healing traditions and practices cross-culturally and the qualities all medical systems have in common. For example, the terms used by French cultural anthropologist Claude Lévi-Strauss to describe the healing powers of *shamans* (the name for indigenous healers from Siberia and now applied to traditional healers in many cultures) also refer to medical practices in Europe and North America. In both situations, the healer has access to a world of restricted knowledge (spiritual or scientific) from which average community members are excluded (Figure 12.13).

Medical anthropologists use scientific models drawn from biological anthropology, such as evolutionary theory and ecology, to understand and improve human health. They also focus on the connections between human health and political and economic forces, both globally and locally. A broad anthropological understanding of the origins of sickness is vital for alleviating human

suffering—especially in a globalized world where germs, cures, and pollution travel widely and rapidly.

Medical anthropology recognizes poverty as one major determinant of sickness. Anthropologists throughout the globe have demonstrated this connection and worked to improve health through social justice. This perspective now has support from the World Bank, a global financial lending institution for developing countries, with Korean American medical anthropologist and physician Jim Yong Kim as its president. Kim, the cofounder (with U.S. physician-anthropologist Paul Farmer) of Partners In Health, has spent his career improving human health through the eradication of poverty.

Science, Illness, and Disease

From the latest vaccine to cutting-edge cancer treatments, scientific research is often at the frontline of curing or eradicating sickness. But medical anthropology reveals

---

medical system A patterned set of ideas and practices relating to illness.

that medicine consists of far more than science. The earliest research on cross-cultural medicine was carried out by physician-anthropologists—individuals trained as both medical doctors and as anthropologists who participated in the international public health movement emerging early in the 20th century. While delivering the medical care that had developed in Europe and North America, these physician-anthropologists also studied the health beliefs and practices of the cultures they were sent to help; they returned with these accounts translated into Western biomedical terms.

Initially, Western biomedical approaches were considered culture-free depictions of human biology and were therefore used as an interpretive framework for examining the medical beliefs and practices of other cultures. Implicit in this work was the notion that supposedly objective Western approaches were superior. However, cultural anthropologists' fieldwork has shown that medical categories, like other aspects of a people's unique worldview, reflect the value system of their particular culture. For example, the Subanun people of Mindanao, the southernmost large island of the Philippines, give fungal infections of the skin different names depending on whether the infection is openly visible or hidden under clothes.

In the 1970s the place of biological and cultural knowledge in medical anthropology was dramatically reorganized. The admission of the People's Republic of China to the United Nations in 1971 played a significant role in this theoretical shift. Improved diplomatic relations and cultural exchange between mainland China and Western powers revealed a professional medical system in the East that rivaled Western biomedicine scientifically and technically. For example, the practice of open-heart surgery in China, using only acupuncture needles as an anesthetic, challenged anthropological assumptions of Western biomedical superiority. Scholars began proposing that *biomedicine* is a cultural system worthy of anthropological study, just like the medical systems in other cultures.

To effectively compare medical systems and health cross-culturally, medical anthropologists draw a theoretical distinction between the terms *disease* and *illness*. **Disease** refers to a specific physical or biological abnormality. **Illness** refers to the meanings and elaborations given to particular physical states. Disease and illness do not necessarily overlap. Illness could exist without a disease, or a disease may occur in the absence of illness.

In cultures with scientific medical systems, a key component of the social process of illness involves delineating human suffering by its biology. Occasionally, the labeling of an illness as a disease occurs even though the biology is poorly understood. For example, consider the contrasting ways alcoholism is viewed in the United States. Society tends to not sympathize with a person labeled a drunk, a partier, a barfly, or a boozer. By contrast, a person struggling with the disease of alcoholism receives cultural help from physicians, support from groups such as Alcoholics Anonymous, and perhaps even health insurance financing of medical treatments. The biology of alcoholism as a disease is still poorly understood, but by calling it a disease, it becomes a socially sanctioned and recognized illness within the U.S. medical system. See this chapter's Globalscape for an innovative method of reducing stigma and improving health through a focus on social aspects of sickness.

Schistosomiasis, a type of infection that comes from a parasitic flatworm called a blood fluke, provides an excellent example of disease existing without illness. Scientists have fully documented this parasite's life cycle, which alternates between water snails and human as hosts. The adult worms can live for years inside human intestines or urinary tracts and then spread to freshwater snails through human waste. Inside the snails, the parasite develops and then releases thousands of tiny creatures into freshwater. If humans swim, wade, or otherwise interact with this infested water, the parasite can bore its way through the skin, traveling back to the intestine or bladder where the life cycle continues.

The idea of parasites boring through the skin and living permanently inside the bladder or intestine may be revolting. But to people living where schistosomiasis is **endemic**—the public health term for a disease that is widespread in the population—this disease state is normal, and they typically seek no treatment. In other words, schistosomiasis is not considered an illness. Individuals may know about expensive effective biomedical treatments, but with a high likelihood of reinfection and low accessibility to drugs, they tend not to seek treatment. Over time, evolutionary forces generally lead to a tolerance between parasite and host that allows infected individuals to live normal lives.

Cultural perspectives are sometimes at odds with international public health goals, which are mostly based on Western biomedical understandings of disease. Medical anthropologists working on global public health issues are careful to not impose personal interpretations and meanings as they work to improve the health of others. In the Original Study, U.S. biological anthropologist Katherine Dettwyler explains how her work on childhood growth and health in Mali challenged her to rethink Down syndrome.

---

disease A specific physical or biological abnormality.

illness The meanings and elaborations given to a particular physical state.

endemic The public health term for a disease that is widespread in a population.

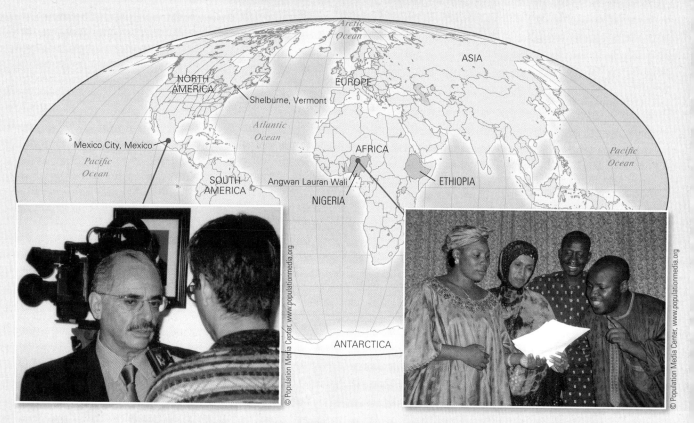

Map showing: Arctic Ocean, NORTH AMERICA, Shelburne, Vermont, Atlantic Ocean, Mexico City, Mexico, Pacific Ocean, SOUTH AMERICA, EUROPE, ASIA, AFRICA, Angwan Lauran Wali, NIGERIA, ETHIOPIA, Pacific Ocean, ANTARCTICA

© Population Media Center, www.populationmedia.org

© Population Media Center, www.populationmedia.org

From Soap Opera to Clinic?

In Angwan Lauran Wali, Nigeria, Hajara Nasiru listened to a radio soap opera, *Gugar Goge* ("Tell It to Me Straight"), and learned something that changed her life.[a] Created in Nigeria using a methodology developed originally in Mexico, the radio drama tells the story of 12-year-old Kande, who is forced to marry a man more than twice her age. She soon becomes pregnant, and after a prolonged labor, her baby dies. Kande develops an obstetric fistula (a hole between either the rectum and vagina or the bladder and vagina) leading to incontinence, infection, and nerve damage. Her husband abandons her, but a neighbor brings her to the hospital in the nearby city of Zaria. After the fistula is repaired, Kande is able to return to her father's home in full health.

Like Kande, Hajara married young (at 15), and by the age of 25 she had experienced eight labors, lost five children, and developed a fistula with her last labor. After living with debilitating discomfort for nine weeks, she invited her husband to also listen to the soap opera. *Gugar Goge* gave Hajara and her husband the information they needed. The show informed them that the fistula could be repaired and that Hajara need not suffer.

This radio drama is one of many created by local branches of the Population Media Center (PMC), a U.S.-based international nongovernmental organization, headquartered in Shelburne, Vermont, which uses "entertainment-education for social change." Mexican television producer Miguel Sabido, pictured above, developed PMC's methodology and created *telenovelas* that prompted dramatic social change across Mexico during the 1970s. One of Sabido's programs resulted in an eightfold increase in adult education, and another led to a 50 percent increase in contraceptive use.

The Population Media Center is bringing Sabido's methodology to the world, through work with local radio and television broadcasters, appropriate government ministries, and nongovernmental organizations. Their goal is to design and implement a comprehensive media strategy geared at family and reproductive health issues. This process takes place collaboratively, with local constituents identifying and addressing various health issues. These health issues get broad attention when transformed into a professionally produced radio drama such as *Gugar Goge*.

In addition to individual success stories like Hajara's, the success of these efforts can be measured quantitatively at the countrywide level. For example, radio programs broadcast in Ethiopia in two different languages between 2002 and 2004 changed the country's reproductive health behavior. The percentage of married women using contraception increased from 23 percent to 79 percent, and the birth rates decreased. Reducing fertility is a vital step a society must make to achieve better overall health. In exit interviews at family planning clinics, one-fourth of the 14,000 people surveyed cited the radio drama as their reason for coming.

Global Twister

Would the Sabido method work in your community? Is it already at work? What health issues would you like to see embedded in soap operas?

---

[a] Population Media Center. (2015). PMC in Nigeria. *PopulationMediaCenter.org*. https://www.populationmedia.org/location/nigeria/ (retrieved November 10, 2015)

ORIGINAL STUDY

Dancing Skeletons: Life and Death in West Africa BY KATHERINE DETTWYLER

I stood in the doorway, gasping for air, propping my arms against the door frame on either side to hold me up. I sucked in great breaths of cool, clean air and rested my gaze on the distant hills, trying to compose myself. Ominous black thunderclouds were massed on the horizon and moved rapidly toward the schoolhouse....

The morning had begun pleasantly enough, with villagers waiting patiently under the huge mango tree in the center of the village. But before long, the approaching storm made it clear that we would have to move inside. The only building large enough to hold the crowd was the one-room schoolhouse, located on the outskirts of the village....

Inside the schoolhouse, chaos reigned. It was 20 degrees hotter, ten times as noisy, and as dark as gloom. What little light there was from outside entered through the open doorway and two small windows. The entire population of the village crowded onto the rows of benches, or stood three deep around the periphery of the room. Babies cried until their mothers pulled them around front where they could nurse, children chattered, and adults seized the opportunity to converse with friends and neighbors. It was one big party, a day off from working in the fields, with a cooling rain thrown in for good measure. I had to shout the measurements out to Heather, to make myself heard over the cacophony of noise....

A middle-aged man dressed in a threadbare pair of Levis shoved a crying child forward. I knelt down to encourage the little boy to step up onto the scales and saw that his leg was wrapped in dirty bandages. He hesitated before lifting his foot and whimpered as he put his weight onto it....

"What's the matter with his leg?" I asked his father.

"He hurt it in a bicycle accident," he said.

I rolled my eyes at Heather. "Let me guess. He was riding on the back fender, without wearing long pants, or shoes, and he got his leg tangled in the spokes." Moussa translated this aside into Bambara, and the man acknowledged that was exactly what had happened....

The festering wound encompassed the boy's ankle and part of his foot, deep enough to see bone at the bottom. His entire lower leg and foot were swollen and putrid; it was obvious that gangrene had a firm hold....

"You have to take him to the hospital in Sikasso immediately," I explained.

"But we can't afford to," he balked.

"You can't afford not to," I cried in exasperation, turning to Moussa. "He doesn't understand," I said to Moussa. "Please explain to him that the boy is certain to die of gangrene poisoning if he doesn't get to a doctor right away. It may be too late already, but I don't think so. He may just lose his leg." Moussa's eyes widened with alarm. Even he hadn't realized how serious the boy's wounds were. As the father took in what Moussa was saying, his face crumpled.... Father and son were last seen leaving Merediela, the boy perched precariously on the back of a worn-out donkey hastily borrowed from a neighbor, while the father trotted alongside, shoulders drooping, urging the donkey to greater speed....

Lunch back at the animatrice's compound provided another opportunity for learning about infant feeding beliefs in rural Mali, through criticism of my own child feeding practices. This time it was a chicken that had given its life for our culinary benefit. As we ate, without even thinking, I reached into the center pile of chicken meat and pulled pieces of meat off the bone. Then I placed them over in Miranda's section of the communal food bowl and encouraged her to eat.

"Why are you giving her chicken?" Bakary asked.

"I want to make sure she gets enough to eat," I replied. "She didn't eat very much porridge for breakfast because she doesn't like millet."

"But she's just a child. She doesn't need good food. You've been working hard all morning, and she's just been lying around. Besides, if she wanted to eat, she would," he argued.

"It's true that I've been working hard," I admitted, "but she's still growing. Growing children need much more food, proportionately, than adults. And if I didn't encourage her to eat, she might not eat until we get back to Bamako."

Bakary shook his head. "In Dogo," he explained, "people believe that good food is wasted on children. They don't appreciate its good taste or the way it makes you feel. Also, they haven't worked hard to produce the food. They have their whole lives to work for good food for themselves, when they get older. Old people deserve the best food because they're going to die soon."...

...In rural southern Mali, "good food" (which included all the high protein/high calorie foods) was reserved for elders and other adults. Children subsisted almost entirely on the carbohydrate staples, flavored with a little sauce. My actions in giving Miranda my share of the chicken were viewed as bizarre and misguided. I was wasting good food on a mere child, and depriving myself....

In N'tenkoni the next morning, we were given use of the men's sacred meeting hut for our measuring session. A round hut about 20 feet in diameter, it had a huge center pole made from the trunk of a tree that held up the thatched roof. Because it had two large doorways, it was light and airy and would provide protection in the event of another thunderstorm....

There was some initial confusion caused by the fact that people outside couldn't really see what we were doing, and everyone tried to crowd in at once. That was straightened out by the chief, however, and measuring proceeded apace, men, women, children, men, women, children. One family at a time filed into the hut through one door, had their measurements taken, and departed through the other door. It was cool and pleasant inside the hut, in contrast to the hot sun and glare outside. Miranda sat off to one side, reading a book, glancing up from time to time, but generally bored by the whole thing.

"Mommy, look!" she exclaimed in mid-morning. "Isn't that an *angel*?" she asked, using our family's code word for a child with Down syndrome. Down syndrome children are often (though not always!) sweet, happy, and affectionate kids, and many families of children with Down syndrome consider them to be special gifts from God and refer to them as angels. I turned and followed the direction of Miranda's gaze. A little girl had just entered the hut, part of a large family with many children. She had a small round head, and all the facial characteristics of a child with Down syndrome—Oriental-shaped eyes with epicanthic folds, a small flat nose, and small ears. There was no mistaking the diagnosis. Her name was Abi, and she was about 4 years old, the same age as Peter.

I knelt in front of the little girl. "Hi there, sweetie," I said in English. "Can I have a hug?" I held out my arms, and she willingly stepped forward and gave me a big hug.

I looked up at her mother. "Do you know that there's something 'different' about this child?" I asked, choosing my words carefully.

"Well, she doesn't talk," said her mother, hesitantly, looking at her husband for confirmation. "That's right," he said. "She's never said a word."

"But she's been healthy?" I asked.

"Yes," the father replied. "She's like the other kids, except she doesn't talk. She's always happy. She never cries. We know she can hear because she does what we tell her to. Why are you so interested in her?"

"Because I know what's the matter with her. I have a son like this." Excitedly, I pulled a picture of Peter out of my bag and showed it to them. They couldn't see any resemblance, though. The difference in skin color swamped the similarities in facial features. But then, Malians think all white people look alike. And it's not true that all kids with Down syndrome look the same. They're "different in the same way," but they look most like their parents and siblings.

"Have you ever met any other children like this?" I inquired, bursting with curiosity about how rural Malian culture dealt with a condition as infrequent as Down syndrome. Children with Down syndrome are rare to begin with, occurring about once in every 700 births. In a community where thirty or forty children are born each year at the most, a child with Down syndrome might be born only once in twenty years. And many of them would not survive long enough for anyone to be able to tell that they were different. Physical defects along the midline of the body (heart, trachea, intestines) are common among kids with Down syndrome; without immediate surgery and neonatal

intensive care, many would not survive. Such surgery is routine in American children's hospitals, but nonexistent in rural Mali. For the child without any major physical defects, there are still the perils of rural Malian life to survive: malaria, measles, diarrhea, diphtheria, and polio. Some, like Peter, have poor immune systems, making them even more susceptible to childhood diseases. The odds against finding a child with Down syndrome, surviving and healthy in a rural Malian village, are overwhelming.

Not surprisingly, the parents knew of no other children like Abi. They asked if I knew of any medicine that could cure her. "No," I explained, "this condition can't be cured. But she will learn to talk, just give her time. Talk to her a lot. Try to get her to repeat things you say. And give her lots of love and attention. It may take her longer to learn some things, but keep trying. In my country, some people say these children are special gifts from God." There was no way I could explain cells and chromosomes and nondisjunction to them, even with Moussa's help. And how, I thought to myself, would that have helped them anyway? They just accepted her as she was.

We chatted for a few more minutes, and I measured the whole family, including Abi, who was, of course, short for her age. I gave her one last hug and a balloon and sent her out the door after her siblings....

I walked out of the hut,... trying to get my emotions under control. Finally I gave in, hugged my knees close to my chest, and sobbed. I cried for Abi—what a courageous heart she must have; just think what she might have achieved given all the modern infant stimulation programs available in the West. I cried for Peter—another courageous heart; just think of what he might achieve given the chance to live in a culture that simply accepted him, rather than stereotyping and pigeonholing him, constraining him because people didn't think he was capable of more. I cried for myself—not very courageous at all; my heart felt as though it would burst with longing for Peter, my own sweet angel.

There was clearly some truth to the old adage that ignorance is bliss. Maybe pregnant women in Mali had to worry about evil spirits lurking in the latrine at night, but they didn't spend their pregnancies worrying about chromosomal abnormalities, the moral implications of amniocentesis, or the heart-wrenching exercise of trying to evaluate handicaps, deciding which ones made life not worth living. Women in the United States might have the freedom to choose not to give birth to children with handicaps, but women in Mali had freedom from worrying about it. Children in the United States had the freedom to attend special programs to help them overcome their handicaps, but children in Mali had freedom from the biggest handicap of all—other people's prejudice.

I had cried myself dry. I splashed my face with cool water from the bucket inside the kitchen and returned to the task at hand.

Adapted from Dettwyler, K. A. (1994). *Dancing skeletons: Life and death in West Africa* (ch. 8). Long Grove, IL: Waveland Press, Inc. All rights reserved.

Although diseases are generally described in scientifically derived biological terms, the medical anthropological framework admits that these notions are not universal. Each culture's medical system provides a map of how to think about sickness and health and defines specific terms and mechanisms for thinking about, preventing, and managing illness.

Evolutionary Medicine

Evolutionary medicine—an approach to human sickness and health combining principles of evolutionary theory and human evolutionary history—draws from both scientific medicine and anthropology. Initially, it may seem dominated by human biological mechanisms, but evolutionary medicine emphasizes the biocultural integration characteristic of anthropology. Humans give cultural meaning to biological processes, and cultural practices impact human biology.

It is difficult to prove conclusively that specific ideas and theories from evolutionary medicine positively impact human health. Scientists work to amass a sufficient body of knowledge that support their theories, and when appropriate, test hypotheses experimentally. Frequently, treatments derived from evolutionary medicine lead to alterations in cultural practices and to a return to more natural states of human biology. As described in Chapter 8's Biocultural Connection on Paleolithic prescriptions, evolutionary medicine contributes to current attitudes about the diseases of civilization.

U.S. biological anthropologist James McKenna's work provides an excellent example of evolutionary medicine. McKenna has suggested that human infants have evolved to sleep with adults who provide breathing cues to the sleeping infant, protecting the child from sudden infant death syndrome (SIDS) (McKenna, Ball, & Gettler, 2007). McKenna used cross-cultural data of sleeping patterns and rates of SIDS to support his claim.

A series of experiments documented differences between the brainwave patterns of pairs of mothers and infants sleeping together versus pairs sleeping in separate rooms. These results fit McKenna's theory and challenge the cultural practice of solitary sleeping that predominates in North America. Evolutionary medicine suggests that cultural practices in industrial and postindustrial societies promote a variety of other biomedically defined diseases, ranging from psychological disorders to hepatitis (inflammation of the liver).

---

evolutionary medicine An approach to human sickness and health combining principles of evolutionary theory and human evolutionary history.

Symptoms as Defense Mechanisms

Scientists have documented that the human body mounts a series of physiological responses when faced with infection from a bacterium or virus. For example, a young individual learns to recognize an illness as a cold or flu by observing responses of the body, like fever, runny nose, sore throat, or vomiting.

Think of how you may have learned about sickness as a young child. A caregiver or parent might have touched your forehead or neck with the back of the hand to gauge your temperature. Maybe you had a thermometer placed under your arm, in your mouth, or in your ear to check you for fever. If any of these methods revealed a temperature defined as above normal, a medicine might have been given to lower the fever.

Evolutionary medicine proposes that many symptoms biomedicine treat are products of nature, developed over millennia. Some of these symptoms, such as fever, perhaps should be tolerated rather than suppressed, so the body can heal itself. An elevated temperature is part of the body's response to infectious particles, and reducing fever may provide a favorable environment for bacteria or viruses. Additionally, vomiting, coughing, and diarrhea may be adaptive because they remove harmful substances and organisms from the body. In other words, the cultural prescription to lower a fever or suppress a cough might actually prolong the disease.

Similarly, nausea and vomiting during early pregnancy may also represent an adaptive mechanism to avoid toxins during this most sensitive phase of fetal development. Many plants, particularly from the broccoli and cabbage families, naturally contain toxins developed through evolution to prevent them from being eaten by animals. Eating these plants during the first weeks of pregnancy can make the developing embryo vulnerable to mutation at the vital period during which it is rapidly creating new cells and differentiating into specific body parts. The pregnant woman's heightened sense of smell and susceptibility to nausea serve as natural defenses for her to avoid these foods.

Evolution and Infectious Disease

Evolutionary medicine provides key insights on infectious disease, especially in a globalizing world where people, viruses, and bacteria move freely. In biomedicine, infectious disease is viewed as conflict between humans and microorganisms; patients and doctors "fight" infectious diseases, and microorganisms possess one very clear advantage (**Figure 12.14**): The very short life cycles of viruses, bacteria, fungi, and parasites give them an evolutionary advantage over humans, because microorganisms' random mutations can quickly pose new threats to human health. This notion is particularly important when it comes to using antibiotics to fight infectious disease.

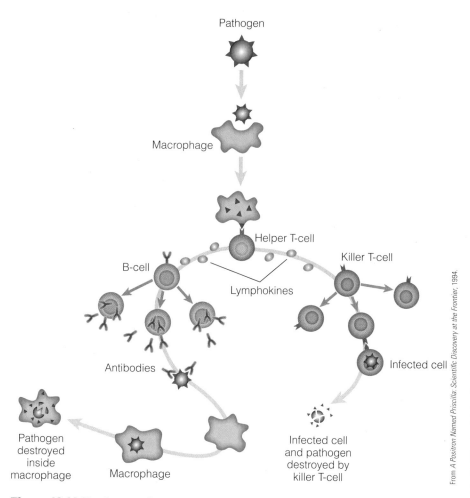

Pathogen

Macrophage

Helper T-cell

B-cell

Killer T-cell

Lymphokines

Antibodies

Infected cell

Pathogen
destroyed
inside
macrophage

Macrophage

Infected cell
and pathogen
destroyed by
killer T-cell

From *A Positron Named Priscilla: Scientific Discovery at the Frontier*, 1994.

Figure 12.14 The Immune System
Biomedical descriptions of the human immune system concentrate on "invading" pathogens, "triggering" the immune response, and "killer T-cells" that destroy the pathogens, as shown in this image introducing the fundamentals of the immune response. Medical anthropologist Emily Martin (1994, 1999) has shown that scientific depictions of infectious disease draw upon violent imagery common to the culture of the United States. Biomedical treatments involve taking antibiotics to kill "invading" organisms adding additional weapons to the "natural" human defenses. An evolutionary perspective suggests that the quick life cycle of microorganisms makes this "battle" a losing proposition for humans.

Evolutionary process provides a long-term natural mechanism for fighting infectious disease: Individuals who survive the infection possess genes that provide them with immunity. A group of sex workers in Kenya who have avoided the HIV infection despite constant exposure represent an interesting example of population-based resistance to disease (Fowke et al., 1996; Songok et al., 2012). Such examples may represent a process of hosts and microbes adjusting to one another through evolution. In order to survive, microbes cannot eliminate all their hosts, and so over time a balance is struck as a population becomes better able to resist and a microbe becomes less virulent.

Luckily, treatments, just like diseases, can also flow freely across the globe. For example, Brazil's internationally recognized HIV/AIDS program provides a model for prevention, education, and treatment that other nations can utilize. Brazil became the first country to guarantee free antiretroviral access to all its citizens in 1996, with policies that encouraged scientific innovation and reduced financial barriers to treatment. At the same time, Brazilian public health officials developed counseling and prevention programs in collaboration with community groups and religious organizations. A candid public education campaign on disease transmission—targeted at the fastest-growing groups affected by HIV, heterosexual women and young people—also contributed to the program's success.

In 2004, Brazil continued its innovations with the South to South Initiative providing assistance to HIV and AIDS programs in the African countries of Mozambique and Angola. These African countries have replicated the Brazilian approach of providing free antiretroviral agents and collaborating with civil and religious groups to develop appropriate counseling, education, and prevention programs (D'Adesky, 2004).

Vaccines, a well-known method for fighting infectious disease, stimulate the body to mount its own immune response to protect against later exposure to real infectious

Antibiotics kill many bacteria, but resistant strains are becoming more common. A **resistant strain** is a genetic variant of a specific bacterium that is not killed by antibiotics. If a resistant strain appears in an infected individual, antibiotic treatment removes all the nonresistant strains and in turn opens the door for the resistant strain to thrive. Without competition from the bacterium's original form, this mutant can proliferate easily and spread to other individuals.

Complex lengthy treatment regimes, often with multiple drugs, must be followed exactly to avoid the development of resistant strains. These treatments are prohibitively expensive in many parts of the world, and so diseases often spread from country to country as infectious microbes do not observe national boundaries. A truly global perspective is necessary to effectively understand and control any infectious process.

resistant strain A genetic variant of a specific bacterium that is not killed by antibiotics.

The Vaccine Debate Goes Viral

BY TAVID BINGHAM

In January 2016, founder and CEO of social media giant Facebook did something that millions of Facebook users do every day—he shared a picture of his child. But something about the picture's content and caption ignited a fierce debate over a biocultural practice with controversial disparate opinions. The image showed Zuckerberg and his young daughter Maxima seated in what appears to be a waiting room with the caption "Doctor's visit—time for vaccines!" Within a few days of posting, the picture had drawn over 3.2 million likes and more than 88,000 comments—many condemning and berating Zuckerberg for exposing his child to potentially harmful vaccines, while many others applauded and supported him for protecting his child's health and, by extension, the health of other children.

There is significant scientific evidence indicating the effectiveness of vaccines at preparing the body to fight off invading viruses and bacteria, thereby preventing the contraction and transmission of infectious disease. But the anti-vaccine movement is propelled to some degree by the idea that vaccines can have adverse health effects that outweigh the potential protection they might provide. Some believe that the exposure that immunizations inflict on the body can weaken the immune system. One national survey conducted in the United States found that one-quarter of parents feared that shots would diminish their children's ability to fight off illnesses in the long term.[a] Others fear unwanted side effects brought about by the body's response to the vaccine.

The modern anti-vaccine movement was fueled by one particular study published in *The Lancet*, a respected British medical journal, which claimed that the vaccine for measles, mumps, and rubella (the MMR vaccine) was linked with autism. This claim—though now retracted by the journal and most of its authors—garnered extensive media attention and gave anti-vaccine advocates a piece of frightening scientific evidence to back up to their cause.[b] MMR is an extremely common vaccination in the United States, where the first dosage is usually given between the ages of 12 and 15 months.

---

agents. Vaccinations have been responsible for major global reduction of disease, as in the case of smallpox. In addition, historical records show that people in Asia, Africa, Europe, and colonists in North America practiced a form of vaccination for this deadly disease through what were known as "pox parties." In modern times, some parents have revived this tradition by deliberately exposing their children to chicken pox rather than vaccines.

Despite medical reports to the contrary, some parents believe that vaccinations lead to other health problems. The vaccine to eradicate smallpox—a disease that killed 300 million people in the 20th century alone—is clearly beneficial, but it is harder to convince parents of the need for vaccines for less fatal childhood diseases. But opting out can have grim consequences: The rates of pertussis (whooping cough) have reached epidemic proportions in some parts of the United States. The pertussis problem has become so severe that a booster for it is now routinely added to tetanus shots.

Vaccinations, like all medical procedures, change the social fabric. The vaccine for chicken pox in the United States provides an interesting case in point. Before this vaccination became standard care, most American children experienced chicken pox as a rite of childhood. Parents watched their children become covered with ugly pox that eventually disappeared. The parents' experience models a concept that intense sickness can be followed by full recovery, which, in and of itself, can provide some comfort. Chicken pox is fatal only in extremely rare cases. See this chapter's Biocultural Connection for more discussion of the ways in which parents in the United States view vaccines.

Infectious disease and our efforts to stop it always occur in the context of the human-made environment. Since the Neolithic revolution, humans have increasingly altered the environment, resulting in an increased variety of infectious diseases. In this regard, evolutionary medicine shares much with political ecology—a discipline closely related to medical anthropology.

The Political Ecology of Disease

Ecological perspectives consider organisms in the context of their environment. Because human environments are shaped not only by local culture but by global political and economic systems, these features must all be considered in a comprehensive examination of human disease. Simply describing disease in terms of biological processes ignores deeper reasons that some individuals are more likely than others to become sick. A strictly biological approach also leaves out individual, community, and national differences in the resources available to cope with disease and illness. Prion diseases provide excellent

The transmission of viral infections like measles in public places, such as schools, is often at the center of the vaccine debate. One particularly high-profile example came in January 2015, with an outbreak of more than 70 cases of measles linked to Disneyland visitors in southern California. This news led to public outrage from pro-vaccine advocates. Partly in reaction to the Disneyland outbreak, later that year California Governor Jerry Brown signed controversial legislation requiring nearly all public school-children to have certain immunizations. At the time, California became one of just three states—Mississippi and West Virginia being the others—with such a strict vaccination law. The bill removed a previous exemption from vaccines for schoolchildren based on personal or religious beliefs, an exemption that about 13,000 families had used in the previous year.[c]

Although there is plenty of misinformation and sometimes provocative media attention to controversial vaccines, it is important to understand that all immunizations carry certain risks. The Centers for Disease Control publishes periodic Vaccine Information Statements (VISs) to inform the public about every type of vaccination, with specific VISs describing the recommended vaccines for children at each stage of development. These VISs also note the risks associated with a given vaccine and describe the specific circumstance in which particular individuals should not receive certain vaccines for medical reasons.

Written expressly for this text, 2016.

Biocultural Question

How do you feel about individuals being able to refuse vaccinations on the basis of personal or religious beliefs? What are the implications to public health of allowing individuals to opt out of vaccinations for contagious diseases?

[a] Gellin B. G., Maibach E. W., & Marcuse E. K. (2000, November). Do parents understand immunizations? A national telephone survey. *Pediatrics 106* (5), 1097–1102.

[b] Wakefield, A. J., et al. (1998). RETRACTED: Ileal-lymphoid-nodular hyperplasia, non-specific colitis, and pervasive developmental disorder in children. *Lancet 351* (9103), 637–641.

[c] CBS News/AP. (2015, June 30). California governor signs strict new vaccination law. *CBS News.* http://www.cbsnews.com /news/california-governor-signs-strict-new -vaccination-law/ (retrieved February 3, 2016)

illustrations of the ways in which both local and global factors impact the social distribution of disease.

Prion Diseases

In 1997 U.S. physician-scientist Stanley Prusiner won the Nobel Prize in medicine for discovering an entirely new disease agent called a **prion**—a protein lacking any genetic material that behaves as an infectious particle. Prions can cause the reorganization and destruction of other proteins, which may destroy brain tissue and the nervous system, resulting in neurodegenerative disease.

This discovery provided a biological mechanism for understanding mad cow disease, a serious problem in postindustrial societies, but more information is required to truly grasp how this disease spreads. Prions tainted the beef supply of several European and North American countries through the cultural practice of grinding up sheep carcasses and adding them to the commercial feed of beef cattle. Postindustrial farmers were aware that these sheep had a condition known as *scrapie*, but it had not yet been identified as infectious. Through the wide distribution of tainted feed, prion disease spread from sheep to cows, and then to humans who consumed tainted beef. Today, some countries ban the importation of beef from neighboring countries with documented prion disease. Such bans have a tremendous negative impact on local economies.

This type of disease was a major concern for the Fore (pronounced "foray") people of Papua New Guinea during the middle of the 20th century. The Fore gave the name *kuru* to the prion disease that killed many women and children in their communities. Local and global cultural processes had affected both the transmission of kuru and the measures taken to prevent its spread long before prion biology was understood. Kuru did not fit neatly into any known biomedical categories. Notably, the disease seemed to be limited to families of related individuals, but kinship records did not reveal a pattern of genetic transmission.

U.S. physician D. Carleton Gajdusek led an international team of health workers to assist the Fore with the devastation. The medical team turned to the notion of infectious disease, even though kuru's slow progression seemed to weigh

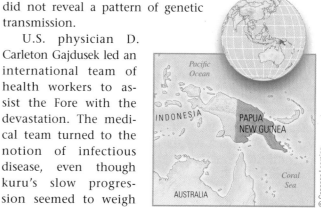

prion An infectious protein lacking any genetic material but capable of causing the reorganization and destruction of other proteins.

against an infectious cause. Material derived from infected individuals was injected into chimpanzees (recall Chapter 4's discussion of the ethics of this practice) to see whether they developed the disease. After 18 months, injected chimpanzees succumbed to the classic symptoms of kuru, and their autopsied brains indicated the same pathologies seen in humans with kuru. At this point, the disease was defined as infectious (garnering Gajdusek a Nobel Prize), but because prions were not yet discovered, scientists defined the infectious agent as an unidentified "slow virus."

Scientists knew that kuru was infectious, but it was still unclear why only some individuals were susceptible. The explanation requires a wider anthropological perspective, as Australian American medical anthropologist Shirley Lindenbaum explains in her book *Kuru Sorcery* (2013). Lindenbaum demonstrates that kuru is related to cultural practices regarding death and the way global factors impacted local practices.

Culturally, Fore women are responsible for preparing the bodies of their loved ones for the afterlife, putting women at greater risk for exposure to kuru. Lindenbaum discovered that women and children were at risk due to a combination of these local practices and global economic forces. In Fore society, men were responsible for raising pigs and slaughtering and distributing meat. The middle of the 20th century was a challenging time of transition for the Fore people. Colonial rule by Australia had changed the fabric of society, threatening traditional subsistence patterns and resulting in a shortage of protein from their traditional food source, pigs. Fore men preferentially distributed the limited amount of pig meat available to other men.

Fore women told Lindenbaum that due to starvation, they were required to consume their own dead (*endocannibalism*). Fore women preferred eating those who had died in a relatively "meaty" state from kuru compared to individuals wasted away from malnutrition. This practice was abandoned as the Fore subsistence pattern recovered, and the biological mechanisms of kuru transmission were revealed.

The story of kuru continues into the present with potential benefits for all of humanity. Scientists have discovered a genetic adaptation to prion disease dispersed widely among the people of Papua New Guinea, presumably in response to a long history of endocannibalism and prion epidemics in the distant past (Asante et al., 2015; Lindenbaum, 2013). As well, researchers have identified a newly evolved variant of the prion protein gene in one elderly Fore woman who, many decades ago, had eaten her kin, that died from kuru. Laboratory mice bred to express this gene have immunity to kuru and other prion diseases, leading some to speculate that this gene might even be protective against Alzheimer's and other dementias.

Medical Pluralism

As seen in the above example, the Fore medical system had its own explanations for the causes of kuru, primarily involving sorcery, that were compatible with biomedical explanations for the mechanisms of disease. Such blending of medical systems is common throughout the globe today. **Medical pluralism** refers to the practice of multiple medical systems, each with its own techniques and beliefs, in a single society. Individuals generally can reconcile conflicting medical systems and incorporate diverse elements from a variety of systems to ease their suffering.

Although Western biomedicine has contributed some spectacular treatments and cures for a variety of diseases, many of its practices and values are singularly associated with the European and North American societies in which they developed. The international public health movement attempts to bring biomedical successes into practice in the rest of the world. But to do so successfully, local cultural practices and beliefs must be taken into account. From kuru to organ transplantation, we see that contemporary sicknesses cannot be considered in isolation; the political and economic impact of diseases and their treatment must be considered holistically.

Globalization, Health, and Structural Violence

For most diseases, wealth means health. In 1948, the newly founded World Health Organization defined *health* as "a state of complete physical, mental and social well-being and not merely the absence of disease or infirmity," a definition that has never been amended (World Health Organization, 1948). While the international public health community works to improve health throughout the globe, heavily armed states, large corporations, and very wealthy elites work to rearrange emerging world systems to their competitive advantage. Power relationships that undermine the well-being of others represent the *structural violence* discussed in Chapter 11.

Health disparity, or the difference in the health status between the wealthy elite and the poor in stratified societies, is nothing new. Globalization has expanded and intensified structural violence, leading to enormous health disparities among individuals, communities, and even states (Figure 12.15). Medical anthropologists examine how structural violence leads to unequal access to treatment, and higher likelihood of disease through malnutrition, crowded conditions, and toxins.

Population Size and Health

Population size was extraordinarily small in early human evolutionary history compared to what it is today. With human population size at over 7.3 billion and still

---

medical pluralism The practice of multiple medical systems, each with its own techniques and beliefs, in a single society.

health disparity A difference in the health status between the wealthy elite and the poor in stratified societies.

climbing, we are reaching the earth's carrying capacity (Figure 12.16). India and China alone have well over 1 billion inhabitants each, and population growth continues rapidly. The scale of hunger, poverty, and pollution, and the many problems associated with these issues, will persist and grow along with increasing population.

Controversially, government-sponsored programs to limit population growth have posed new problems. For example, China's much-publicized "one child" policy, introduced in 1979 to control its soaring growth, led to spikes in sex-selective abortions, female infanticide, and female infant mortality due to abandonment and neglect. The resulting imbalance in China's male and female populations is referred to as the "missing girl gap." One study reported that China's male-to-female ratio has become so imbalanced that 111 million men would not be able to find a wife. Millions of rural couples also circumvented regulations

Figure 12.15 Illegal Trade in Organs

The illegal trade in organs for transplantation spans the globe, with poor individuals and states bearing the burden. Here in Sultanpur, Pakistan, 25-year-old Iqbal Zafar and three other villagers show the surgical scars that remain after having sold a kidney on the black market in order to pay off their debts. Until the Pakistani law that was passed in 2010 curbing these practices, a poor donor would receive just a fraction of the $5,000 to $6,000 that a rich individual paid to the Pakistani hospital that provided the transplant facilities. Many of the organ recipients had traveled to Pakistan as medical tourists in order to obtain the kidneys. On the other hand, the impoverished donors often received little to no postoperative care, a situation that could lead to grave health consequences.

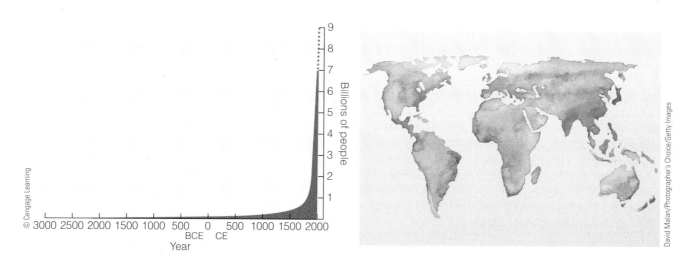

Figure 12.16 World Population

Human population size grew at a relatively steady pace until the industrial revolution, when a geometric pattern of growth began. Since that time, human population size has been doubling at an alarming rate. The earth's natural resources will not be able to accommodate the ever-increasing human population if the rates of consumption seen in Western industrialized nations, particularly in the United States, persist. Notice, as well, that human populations are not distributed evenly across the globe; the highest concentrations (*indicated by red tones*) are in urban centers and regions with fertile land. Climatic extremes and lack of natural resources like water characterize the sparsely populated areas, such as the Sahara Desert and Greenland.

Figure 12.17 Extremes of Malnutrition
The scientific definition of malnutrition includes undernutrition as well as excess consumption of foods, healthy or otherwise. Malnutrition leading to obesity is increasingly common among poorer people in industrialized countries. Obesity and Type 2 diabetes, previously degenerative diseases of adulthood only, now occur at alarming rates among children in the United States. Starvation is more common in poor countries or in those enduring political and economic upheaval, such as the child here from Yemen.

by not registering births—resulting in millions of young people who do not officially exist (Bongaarts, 1998). Government regulations softened slightly in the 1990s, when it became legal for rural couples to pay a fee and have a second child if their first was a girl, and in October 2015, the Chinese government announced an end to the controversial policy (Buckley, 2015; Pei, 2015). Now families are allowed two children.

Poverty and Health

With an ever-expanding population, a shocking number of people worldwide face hunger on a regular basis, leading to various health problems including premature death. Poor countries and poorer citizens of wealthier countries are disproportionately malnourished. About 1 billion people in the world are undernourished. Some 7.6 million children age 5 and under die every year due to hunger, and those who survive often suffer from physical and mental impairment (World Health Organization, 2014).

In wealthy industrialized countries, obesity, a particular version of malnourishment, is increasingly common (Figure 12.17). Obesity primarily affects poor people who are not physically active and who cannot afford more expensive healthy foods. The high-sugar and fat content of mass-marketed foods and "super-sized" portions underlie this dramatic change. Obesity also greatly increases the risk of diabetes, heart disease, and stroke. High rates of obesity among American youth have led U.S. public health officials to project that the current generation of adults may be the first generation to outlive their children due to a cause other than war.

Environmental Impact and Health

The disenfranchised experience a disproportionate share of famine and must also contend with the lion's share of contaminants and pollution (Figure 12.18). The industries of wealthier communities and states create the majority of the pollutants affecting the earth today. They often ship their waste elsewhere for processing by those with limited resources who feel the direct biological impact from these pollutants.

Natural forces also contribute to the global inequities. For example, deforestation and human industrial activity have increased emissions of greenhouse gases and resulted in global warming. As the carbon emissions from wealthy nations warm the climate globally, the impact will be more severe for individuals in tropical areas, which tend to be more affected by poverty. Experts predict that global warming will allow tropical diseases to expand their geographic range and increase the incidence of respiratory diseases due to additional smog caused by warmer temperatures. Solving the global warming problem requires the development of new tools to anticipate environmental consequences that play out over decades. Population control and conservative use of natural resources are necessary to meet this challenge.

Global warming is only one of a host of problems today that will impact human gene pools. Considering the consequences that seemingly benign innovations like dairying or farming (as discussed in Chapter 9) have on human biology, we may question many modern practices, such as increased exposure to radiation through x-rays, nuclear accidents, production of radioactive waste, and ozone depletion.

Figure 12.18 Ship-Breakers
For wages of about a dollar a day, workers at the ship-breaking yards of Bangladesh risk their health if not their lives as they toil in conditions of extreme heat, humidity, and exposure to a wide variety of toxins. Here, the large rusty tankers that have transported everything from crude oil to passengers throughout the globe are broken apart for recycling in an area that was pristine beach just decades ago. Workers dismember these ships by hand and are often barefoot; they have very little in the way of protective gear. Explosions and other accidents kill on average one worker a week. The long-term effects of toxins from the ships set other disease processes in motion. Some individuals might possess genotypes that can better process the toxins (comparable to the 90-year-old who has smoked two packs of cigarettes a day for over seventy years). And over time a population might become better able to tolerate these poisons through the process of biological adaptation. But in this case, a cultural solution—environmental regulation of the ship-breaking process—would protect these workers and our oceans and beaches and is a requirement for our collective human survival. As well, our global health requires addressing the social justice issues inherent in poor countries taking on the health burden of privileges enjoyed by the wealthy.

© Ian Berry/Magnum Photos

In addition to radiation exposure, humans also face increased exposure to other mutagenic agents, including a wide variety of chemicals like pesticides (recall the Biocultural Connection from Chapter 1). In the United States alone, there have been tens of thousands of poisoning cases and thousands of cases of cancer related to the manufacture and use of pesticides. Pesticides are linked to the deaths of millions of birds (which would have been happily gobbling down bugs), fish, and honeybees (bees facilitate efficient pollination of many crops). In all, pesticides are responsible for billions of dollars of environmental and public health damage in the United States each year. Even more so, they disproportionately affect populations around the world who have not generated the pollutants in the first place. Take, for example, the flow of industrial and agricultural chemicals via air and water currents to Arctic regions. Icy temperatures allow these toxins to enter the food chain. As a result toxins generated in temperate climates end up in the bodies of Arctic peoples who do not produce the toxins but who eat primarily foods that they hunt and fish.

Hormone-disrupting chemicals are another issue raising serious concerns because of their interference with the reproductive process. For example, in 1938 a synthetic estrogen known as DES (diethylstilbestrol) was developed and prescribed for various ailments ranging from acne to prostate cancer. In 1971 researchers realized that DES causes vaginal cancer in young women. Subsequent studies have shown that DES causes problems with the male reproductive system and can produce deformities of the female reproductive tract of individuals exposed to DES in utero. DES mimics the natural hormone, binding with appropriate receptors in and on cells, and thereby turns on biological activity associated with the hormone (Colborn, Dumanoski, & Myers, 1996).

DES is not the only chemical that disrupts hormones. Scientists have identified at least fifty-one chemicals, many of them in common use with comparable effects, and even this could be the tip of the iceberg. Some of these chemicals interfere with other parts of the endocrine system, such as thyroid and testosterone metabolism. Others are supposedly benign and inert substances such as plastics widely used in laboratories and chemicals added to polystyrene and polyvinyl chloride (PVCs) to make them more stable and less breakable. These plastics are widely used in plumbing, food processing, and food packaging.

Many detergents and personal care products, contraceptive creams, giant jugs used to bottle drinking water, and plastic linings in cans contain hormone-disrupting chemicals. Plastics line about 85 percent of food cans in the United States. After years of using plastics in microwave ovens, the harmful health consequences of compounds released from plastic wrap and plastic containers during microwaving have come to light. Most concerning is bisphenol-A (BPA)—a chemical widely used in the manufacturing of water bottles and other hard plastics. Researchers have documented BPA's association with higher rates of chronic diseases, like heart disease and diabetes, and disruptions to a variety of other reproductive and metabolic processes. BPA is most threatening to infants and fetuses.

Scientific confirmation of BPA's dangers has led governments to start taking action; for example, the Canadian government has declared BPA to be a toxic compound. However, eliminating this compound's use by the food industry may be easier than attempting to remove it from the environment. Billions of pounds of BPA have been produced each year, and in turn have been dumped into landfills and bodies of water. As with other cultural advances like the Neolithic revolution and the development of civilization, each invention creates new challenges for humans.

The Future of *Homo sapiens*

One major challenge we face in managing the environmental and health risks of new cultural practices is that serious consequences often do not appear until years or even decades later. Over time, cultural systems absorb these practices, which grow to command huge influential financial

interests. Today, cultural practices, probably as never before, impact human gene pools. The long-term effects on the human species remain to be seen, but as with disease today, poor people and people of color bear a disproportionate burden for these practices.

Globalization also spreads the values of wealthy consumers from industrialized countries to the inhabitants of poorer and developing countries, influencing their expectations and dreams. Luxurious standards of living require a disproportionate share of the earth's limited resources. Instead of globalizing a standard of living that the world's natural resources cannot meet, it is time for all of humanity to use today's global connections to learn how to live within the planet's carrying capacity (Figure 12.19).

Figure 12.19 Global Desires
Global media disseminate advertisements for luxury items and services smack into the lives of people ill equipped to afford them. How does this disjunction between life and the media disrupt individuals and communities? Are there limits to global communications for our common good? How can communication technology serve all humans equally?

Over the course of human evolutionary history, human ancestors spread from the African continent to inhabit the entire globe. From cities, to deserts, to mountaintops, to grassy plains, to rich tropical forests, human cultures in various environments became distinct from one another. Human groups devised specific beliefs and practices to meet the unique challenges of their surroundings. A secure future for our species requires a dramatic change in worldview so that we see humanity as *part of* the world, rather than as *master over* it.

Along with our collective stewardship of the earth, our future depends on recognition and respect for the world's various ethnic groups. Our continued survival depends on our ability to cultivate positive social connections among all kinds of people and recognize the ways we impact one another in an increasingly globalized world. Together, we can use the adaptive faculty of culture, the hallmark of our species, to ensure our continued survival.

CHAPTER CHECKLIST

What biological mechanisms allow humans to adapt to a variety of environments?

✓ Genetic adaptations such as shorter limbs and stocky build (in colder climates) and long, linear builds (in hotter climates) developed in regions where continuous experience over generations allowed for reproductive selection of such traits.

✓ Responses of individuals to their environments drive developmental adaptations over the growth stages of life. This process shapes gene expression in the way that best suits individuals to their specific environment.

✓ Developmental adaptations become permanent parts of an individual's phenotype but are not encoded directly into the genome and therefore do not get passed on directly to the next generation. Examples of such non-hereditary traits include stunted growth due to malnutrition and increased number of sweat glands in hot environments.

✓ Physiological adaptation allows the body to temporarily adjust to environmental stressors, such as low partial pressure of oxygen at high altitude or extremes of temperature.

✓ Individuals first experience short-term physiological responses that cannot be sustained indefinitely. Acclimatization refers to reversible long-term adaptations modifying ongoing bodily processes, such as metabolism rates or hemoglobin production.

✓ Human biological adaption cannot keep pace with environmental changes impacting global environments today.

What are medical systems, and how do they vary across cultures?

✓ Medical systems are a society's patterned set of ideas and practices relating to illness. Medical anthropologists study them cross-culturally, including Western biomedicine.

✓ Global medical systems all include a healer figure who possesses specialized, restricted knowledge from which others are excluded.

✓ Where multiple medical systems coexist (medical pluralism), individuals freely use what works from the various systems.

✓ Medical systems define whether a given physiological state (a disease) will be defined as an illness. For example, in regions where schistosomiasis is endemic, it may not be considered an illness. Without access to costly medicine or clean water, people tolerate moderate parasite loads.

What health hazards are attributable to the global political economy and population size?

✓ Privileged states, corporations, and individuals maintain systems that exercise structural violence upon the poor worldwide, resulting in unequal distribution of diseases.

✓ Hunger and obesity both impact poor communities and cause chronic health problems and early mortality.

✓ Wealthier communities create environmental contaminants such as carcinogenic pesticides and plastics or byproducts that tend to affect poor populations disproportionately.

✓ The effects of global warming, largely caused by pollution from rich nations' industries, will increase the incidence of tropical disease.

✓ With a rising global human population of over 7 billion, we will soon reach the earth's carrying capacity. Wealthy nations use a disproportionate amount of resources.

How have humans responded to the widening array of health threats?

✓ Evolutionary medicine emphasizes the importance of the human body's natural responses to disease and a return to cultural practices more in sync with our evolutionary history to improve health.

✓ Western scientific medicine has effectively introduced pharmaceutical and procedural innovation to fight pathogens, but it often ignores deeper causes of sickness and the levels of resource availability in other communities.

✓ Analysis of the political and economic causes of sickness has led to successful treatment and prevention of diseases such as AIDS, kuru, and mad cow disease.

✓ Recognition of the political and economic causes of disease can lead to cooperation on global health issues and contribute to mitigating suffering worldwide.

QUESTIONS FOR REFLECTION

1. In what ways do you and your community contribute to the growth of garbage vortexes that have developed over vast areas of the earth's oceans? What strategies can the world implement to limit these oceanic wastelands?

2. The anthropological distinction between illness and disease provides a way to separate biological states from cultural elaborations given to those biological states. Can you think of some examples of illness without disease and disease without illness?

3. What do you think of the notion of letting a fever run its course instead of taking a medicine to lower it? How do prescriptions suggested by evolutionary medicine fit with your own medical beliefs and practices?

4. Do you see examples of structural violence in your community that make some individuals more vulnerable to disease than others? How is this violence manifested?

DIGGING INTO ANTHROPOLOGY

Pick Through the Trash Story

Mismanagement of garbage is one of many pressing issues that humans need to address to ensure the earth's health. Access to waste disposal may be greater in the developed world, but communities in these areas also produce far more garbage per capita. Do some investigating in your town, community, or school to find out just how much trash is generated where you live. Visit the local dump or your school's waste management facility and ask for some information about how much trash is generated. How much is recycled? Where does trash passing through this facility eventually end up? A landfill? An incinerator? What problems does the waste management system confront? Write down what you find out and describe the strengths and weaknesses of your local facility.

Scott Olson/GettyImages

CHALLENGE ISSUE

Born naked and speechless, humans are naturally incapable of surviving without culture—a socially learned adaptive system designed to help us meet the challenges of survival. Each culture is distinct, expressing its unique qualities in numerous ways, including the way we speak, what we eat, the clothes we wear, and with whom we live. Although culture goes far beyond what meets the eye, it is inscribed everywhere we look. Here we see a family of Kuchi ("migrant") herders in northeast Afghanistan. Many Kuchi have recently settled down, but about 1.5 million are still fully nomadic, with livelihoods dependent upon goats and sheep. Using camels and donkeys to carry their belongings, this family follows age-old migration routes across mountains and valleys. Because mobility is key to their adaptation to an arid environment, nearly everything they own is portable. Kuchis come from different ethnic groups. The cultural identity of each group is marked by language and by the particular fabrics, forms, and colors of their belongings. They exchange their surplus animal products—meat, hides, wool, hair, *ghee* (butter), and *quroot* (dried yogurt)—for wheat, sugar, salt, metal and plastic goods, and other trade items. Ecological adaptation and symbolic expression of group identity are among the many interrelated functions of culture.

Characteristics of Culture

An introductory anthropology course presents what may seem like an endless variety of human societies, each with its own distinctive way of life, manners, beliefs, arts, and so on. Yet for all this diversity, these societies have one thing in common: Each is a group of human beings cooperating to ensure their collective survival and well-being.

Group living and cooperation are impossible unless individuals know how others are likely to behave in any given situation. Thus some degree of predictable behavior is required of each person within the society. In humans, it is culture that sets the limits of behavior and guides it along predictable paths that are generally acceptable to those who fall within the culture. The culturally specified ways in which we learn to act so that we conform to the social expectations in our community did not develop randomly. Among the major forces guiding how each culture has developed in its own distinctive way is the process of adaptation.

Culture and Adaptation

From generation to generation, humans, like all animals, have continuously faced the challenge of adapting to their environment, its conditions and its resources, as well as to changes over time. The term **adaptation** refers to a gradual process by which organisms adjust to the conditions of the locality in which they live. As discussed in previous chapters, organisms have generally adapted biologically as the frequency of advantageous anatomical and physiological features increases in a population through the process of natural selection.

Humans have increasingly come to depend on **cultural adaptation**, a complex of ideas, technologies, and activities that enables them to survive and even thrive in their environment. Biology has not provided people with built-in fur coats to protect them in cold climates, but it has given us the

adaptation A series of beneficial adjustments to a particular environment.

cultural adaptation A complex of ideas, technologies, and activities that enables people to survive and even thrive in their environment.

In this chapter you will learn to

- Explain culture as a dynamic form of adaptation.

- Distinguish culture from society and ethnicity.

- Identify characteristics common to all cultures.

- Describe the connection between culture, society, and individuals.

- Define and critique *ethnocentrism*.

ability to make our own coats, build fires, and construct shelters to shield ourselves against the cold. We may not be able to run as fast as a cheetah, but we are able to invent and build vehicles that can carry us faster and farther than any other creature.

Through culture and its many constructions, the human species has secured not just its survival but its expansion as well—at great cost to other species and, increasingly, to the planet at large. And by manipulating environments through cultural means, people have been able to move into a vast range of geographic zones, from the searing Sahara Desert in Africa to the rainiest place on earth in northeast India (Figure 13.1).

This is not to say that everything human beings do is *because* it is adaptive to a particular environment. For one thing, people do not just react to an environment as given; rather, they react to it as they perceive it, and different groups of people may perceive the same environment in radically different ways. People also react to things other than the environment: their own biological traits, their beliefs and attitudes, and the short- and long-term consequences of their behavior for themselves and other people and life forms that share their habitats.

Although humans maintain cultures to deal with problems, some cultural practices have proved to be maladaptive, inadequate, or ill fitting, sometimes creating

Moss Chapple/ZUMA Press/Newscom

Figure 13.1 A Living Bridge

This bridge in Meghalaya, India, is made of the roots of living strangler fig trees (*Ficus elastica*). Meghalaya ("Abode of the Clouds") may be the wettest place on earth, receiving an average rainfall of about 40 feet a year. Nearly all of the rain comes during the summer monsoon season, turning rivers and streams into raging torrents. The tangled roots of strangler figs help keep riverbanks from washing away, and the Khasi people living in this region train the roots into living bridges. Shaping a bridge is an epic project that cannot be accomplished in a single lifetime. From one generation to the next, individuals pass on the knowledge of how to guide and connect the hanging roots so they grow into a strong bridge. Dozens of these bridges form part of an essential and complex network of forest paths connecting the valleys of Meghalaya. Some of them are many centuries old.

new problems such as toxic water and air caused by certain industrial practices. A further complication is the relativity of any particular adaptation: What is adaptive in one setting may be seriously maladaptive in another. For example, the hygiene practices of food-foraging peoples—their habits of garbage and human waste disposal—are appropriate to contexts of biodegradable materials, low population densities, and a degree of residential mobility. But these same practices may become serious health hazards in the context of large, fully sedentary populations lacking space to dump (in)disposable waste, including plastic and chemicals. Today, with about 4 billion people living in cities, waste management is turning into a huge challenge in many parts of the world.

Similarly, behavior that is adaptive in the short run may be maladaptive over a longer period of time. For instance, the development of irrigation in ancient Mesopotamia (southern Iraq) made it possible for people to increase food production, but it also caused a gradual accumulation of salt in the soil, which contributed to the downfall of that civilization about 4,000 years ago. A comparable scenario exists in Saudi Arabia today (Figure 13.2).

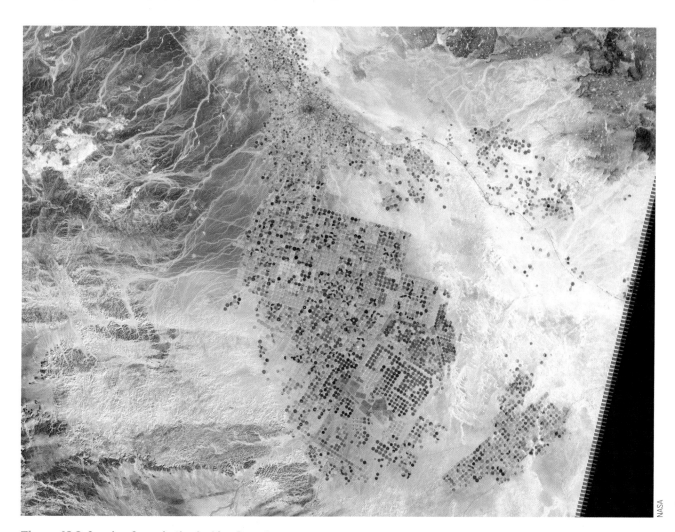

Figure 13.2 Growing Crops in the Arabian Desert
Landsat, a satellite constellation jointly managed by NASA Earth Observatory and the U.S. Geological Survey, captured this image of an expanding patch of green farmland in the middle of the vast Arabian Desert. The colors pink and yellow indicate dry, barren surfaces (mostly desert). Located in the basin of Wadi as-Sirhan and close to Rub' al Khali, the largest sand desert in the world, this area is inhabited by the Dawasir tribe. Over the past twenty-five years, this dry desert landscape has transformed into one of the richest agricultural districts in Saudi Arabia. Farms here depend entirely on fossil water pumped from huge aquifers deep below the desert surface. These underground lakes were formed during short, heavy rainfall periods between 2,000 and 6,000 years ago. A nonrenewable source, people have accessed this water by drilling wells through sedimentary rock, about 1,000 meters (3,300 feet) beneath the surface. Hydrologists believe it will only be economical to pump it for about fifty years. By then, the underground oil fields as well as aquifers may have been exhausted.

In many parts of the world today, the development of prime farmland for purposes other than food production increases dependency on food raised in less than optimal environments. Marginal farmlands can produce high yields with costly technology. However, over time, these yields will not be sustainable due to loss of topsoil, increasing salinity of soil, and silting of irrigation works, not to mention the high cost of fresh water and fossil fuel. Among countless examples is the vast expansion of almond orchards in California during a time when the state is experiencing an extended extreme drought. Critics note that this crop, which consumes 10 percent of the state's entire water supply, is unsustainable and increases the threat of turning California's Central Valley into a dust bowl.

For any culture to be successful across generations, it must foster collective human behavior that does not destroy its natural environment. In response to this challenge, our species has developed a great variety of cultures, each with its own unique features befitting the particular needs of societies located in different habitats in all corners of the globe. So, what do we mean by *culture*?

The Concept and Characteristics of Culture

Anthropologists conceived the modern concept of culture toward the end of the 19th century. Reaching deeper than observable behavior, **culture** is a society's shared and socially transmitted ideas, values, and perceptions, which are used to make sense of experience and generate behavior and are reflected in that behavior.

Through the comparative study of many human cultures, past and present, anthropologists have gained an understanding of the basic characteristics evident in all of them: Every culture is socially learned, shared, based on symbols, integrated, and dynamic. A careful study of these characteristics helps us to see the importance and the function of culture itself.

Culture Is Learned

All culture is socially learned rather than biologically inherited. One learns one's own culture by growing up with it, and the process whereby culture is passed on from one generation to the next is called **enculturation**.

culture A society's shared and socially transmitted ideas, values, and perceptions, which are used to make sense of experience and generate behavior, and are reflected in that behavior.

enculturation The process by which a society's culture is passed on from one generation to the next and individuals become members of their society.

Most animals eat and drink whenever the urge arises. Humans, however, are enculturated to do most of their eating and drinking at certain culturally prescribed times and feel hungry as those times approach. Eating times vary from culture to culture, as does what is eaten and how and where it is acquired, prepared, and consumed. Also, humans rely on food for more than nutrition. When used to celebrate rituals and religious activities, food "establishes relationships of give and take, of cooperation, of sharing, of an emotional bond that is universal" (Caroulis, 1996, p. 16).

Through enculturation every person learns socially appropriate ways of satisfying the basic biologically determined needs of all humans: food, sleep, shelter, companionship, self-defense, and sexual gratification. It is important to distinguish between the needs themselves, which are not learned, and the learned ways in which they are satisfied—for each culture determines in its own way how these needs will be met. For instance, Sinhalese children growing up in fishing families on the tropical island country of Sri Lanka surely have different ideas about what constitutes a great meal and a comfortable way to sleep than do the offspring of semi-nomadic Kazakh herders living in the high steppe grasslands of Central Asia (Figure 13.3).

All mammals exhibit learned behavior to some degree. Several species may even be said to have elementary culture, in that local populations share patterns of behavior that, as among humans, each generation learns from the one before and that differ from one population to another. It is important to note that not all learned behavior is cultural. For instance, a pigeon may learn tricks, but this behavior is the result of conditioning by repeated training, not the product of enculturation.

Beyond our species, examples of socially learned behavior are particularly evident among other primates. Chimpanzees, for example, will take a twig, strip it of all leaves, and smooth it down to fashion a "fishing" tool, which they use to extract termites from the insects' dirt mounds. Such toolmaking, which juveniles learn from their elders, is unquestionably a rudimentary form of cultural behavior once thought to be exclusively human. Research shows that in both nature and in captivity, primates in general and apes in particular "possess a near-human intelligence, generally including the use of sounds in representational ways, a rich awareness of the aims and objectives of others, the ability to engage in tactical deception, and the faculty to use symbols in communication with humans and each other" (Reynolds, 1994, p. 4).

Our increasing awareness of such traits in our primate relatives has spawned movements to extend human rights to apes—rights such as freedom from living in fear, respect for dignity, and not being subjected to incarceration (caging), exploitation (medical experimentation), or other mistreatment (Hays, 2015; O'Carroll, 2008).

David Edwards/National Geographic Creative

Figure 13.3 Learning Culture
Here we see a Kazakh father and son on a hunting expedition with a golden eagle in the Altai
Mountains of Mongolia, Central Asia. For centuries, Kazakhs have trained these birds of prey—
equipped with powerful talons and a wingspan of well over 2 meters (over 7 feet)—to partner
with them in hunting rabbit, fox, mountain goat, and even wolf, primarily for meat and hides.
Eagle hunting is a male tradition. Boys learn from their fathers and uncles how to capture,
raise, train, and handle an eagle from fledgling to maturity. This education includes learning
how to gallop with this huge raptor on their arm and when to release the mighty bird to
pursue the prey.

Culture Is Shared

As a shared set of ideas, values, perceptions, and standards of behavior, culture is the common denominator
that makes the actions of individuals intelligible to other
members of their society. Culture enables individuals in
a society to predict how fellow members are most likely
to behave in a given circumstance, and it informs them
how to react accordingly. A **society** is an organized group
or groups of interdependent people who generally share
a common territory, language, and culture and who act
together for collective survival and well-being. The ways
in which these people depend upon one another can be
seen in features such as their economic, communication,
and defense systems. They are also bound together by a
general sense of common identity.

Because culture and society are such closely related
concepts, anthropologists study both. Obviously, there

can be no culture without a society. Conversely, there are
no known human societies that do not exhibit culture.
Without culture, human society quickly falls apart. This
cannot be said for all animal species. Ants and bees, for
example, instinctively cooperate in a manner that clearly
indicates a remarkable degree of social organization, yet
this instinctual behavior is not a culture.

Although members of a society share a culture, it is
important to realize that no two people share the exact
same version of their culture. At the very least, there is
some distinction between the roles of children and elders,
men and women. This stems from the fact that there are
obvious differences between human infants, adults, and

society An organized group or groups of interdependent people who
generally share a common territory, language, and culture and who act
together for collective survival and well-being.

highly aged individuals, as well as between female and male reproductive anatomy and physiology. Every society gives cultural meaning to biological sex differences by explaining them in a particular way and specifying what their significance is in terms of social roles and expected patterns of behavior.

Because each culture does this in its own way, there can be tremendous variation from one society to another. Anthropologists use the term **gender** to refer to the cultural elaborations and meanings assigned to the biological differentiation between the sexes. So, although one's sex is biologically determined, one's gender is culturally constructed within the context of one's particular society.

Apart from sexual differences directly related to reproduction, biologically based reasons for contrasting gender roles have largely disappeared in modern industrialized and postindustrial societies. A major factor in this change is technology, which evens up the capabilities of men and women in many tasks requiring muscular strength—such as moving heavy automobile engines in assembly lines equipped with hydraulic lifts. Nevertheless, all cultures exhibit at least some role differentiation related to biology—some far more so than others.

In addition to cultural variation associated with gender, there is also variation related to age. In any society, children are not expected to behave as adults, and the reverse is equally true. But then, who is a child and who is an adult? Again, although age differences are natural, cultures give their own meaning and timetable to the human life cycle. In North America, for example, individuals are generally not regarded as adults until the age of 18. In many other cultures, adulthood begins earlier—often around age 12, an age closer to the biological changes of adolescence.

Subcultures: Groups Within a Larger Society

Besides age and gender differentiation, there may be cultural variation between subgroups in complex societies that share an overarching culture. These may be occupational groups in societies with an extensive division of labor, or social classes in a stratified society, or ethnic groups in pluralistic societies. When such a

group exists within a society—functioning by its own distinctive set of ideas, values, and behavior patterns while still sharing some common standards—we call it a **subculture**.

Amish communities are one example of a subculture in North America. Specifically, they are an **ethnic group**—people who collectively and publicly identify themselves as a distinct group based on various cultural features such as shared ancestry and common origin, language, customs, and traditional beliefs. The Amish originated in western Europe during the Protestant revolutions about 500 years ago. Today, members of this group number more than 200,000 and live mainly in the United States—in Pennsylvania, Ohio, Illinois, Indiana, and Wisconsin—as well as in Ontario, Canada.

These rural pacifists base their lives on their traditional Anabaptist beliefs, which hold that only adult baptism is valid and that "true Christians" (as they define them) should not hold government office, bear arms, or use force. They prohibit marriage outside their faith, which calls for obedience to radical Christian teachings, including rejection of material wealth and social separation from the "evils" of the "outside" world.

Resisting government attempts to force their children to attend regular public schools, Amish communities insist that education take place near home and that teachers be committed to Amish ideals. Among themselves, they usually speak a German dialect known as Pennsylvania Dutch (from *Deutsch*, meaning "German"). They use formal German for religious purposes, although children learn English in school. Valuing simplicity, hard work, and a high degree of neighborly cooperation (Figure 13.4), they dress in distinctive plain garb and even today rely on the horse for transportation as well as agricultural work. In sum, the Amish share the same **ethnicity**. This term, rooted in the Greek word *ethnikos* ("nation") and related to *ethnos* ("custom"), refers to the set of cultural ideas held by an ethnic group.

Because economic challenges make it impossible for most to subsist solely on farming, some Amish work outside their communities. Many more market homemade goods to tourists and other outsiders. Their economic separation from mainstream society has declined somewhat, but their cultural separation has not (Kraybill, 2001). They remain a reclusive community, more distrustful than ever of the dominant North American culture surrounding them and mingling as little as possible with non-Amish people.

The Amish are but one example of the way a subculture may develop and be dealt with by the larger culture within which it functions. Different as they are, the Amish actually put into practice many values that other North Americans often respect in the abstract: thrift, hard work, independence, a close family life. The degree of tolerance accorded to them, in contrast to some other ethnic groups, is also due in part to their European origin; they

---

gender The cultural elaborations and meanings assigned to the biological differentiation between the sexes.

subculture A distinctive set of ideas, values, and behavior patterns by which a group within a complex society operates, while still sharing common standards with that larger society.

ethnic group People who collectively and publicly identify themselves as a distinct group based on shared cultural features such as common origin, language, customs, and traditional beliefs.

ethnicity The term for the set of cultural ideas held by an ethnic group.

J. Irwin/ClassicStock/Alamy

Figure 13.4 Amish Barn Raising
The Amish people have held onto their traditional agrarian way of life in the midst of industrialized North American society. Their strong community spirit—reinforced by close social ties between family and neighbors, common language, traditional customs, and shared religious beliefs that set them apart from non-Amish people—is also expressed in a traditional barn raising, a large collective construction project.

are defined as being of the same "white race" as those who historically comprise dominant mainstream society.

Amish subculture in North America developed gradually in response to how members of this strict Protestant sect have adapted to survive within the wider North American society while holding tightly to the conservative rural lifeways of their European ancestors. In contrast, North American Indian subcultures are distinctive ways of life rooted in traditions of formerly independent societies. Native Americans endured invasion of their own territories and colonization by European settlers and were brought under the control of federal governments in the United States, Canada, and Mexico.

Although all American Indian groups have experienced enormous changes due to colonization, many have retained traditions significantly different from those of the dominant Euramerican culture surrounding them. This makes it difficult to determine whether they persevere as distinct cultures as opposed to subcultures. In this

sense, *culture* and *subculture* represent opposite ends of a continuum, with no clear dividing line between them. The Anthropology Applied feature on the next page examines the intersection of culture and subculture with an example concerning Apache Indian housing.

Pluralism

Our discussion raises the issue of a multi-ethnic or **pluralistic society** in which two or more ethnic groups or nationalities are politically organized into one territorial state but maintain their cultural differences. Pluralistic societies emerged after the first politically centralized states arose 5,000 years ago. With the rise of the state, it

pluralistic society A complex society in which two or more ethnic groups or nationalities are politically organized into one territorial state but maintain their cultural differences.

New Houses for Apache Indians

By George S. Esber

The United States, in common with other industrialized countries of the world, contains a number of more or less separate subcultures. Those who live by the standards of one particular subculture have their closest relationships with one another, receiving constant reassurance that their perceptions of the world are the only correct ones and coming to take it for granted that the whole culture is as they see it. As a consequence, members of one subculture frequently have trouble understanding the needs and aspirations of other such groups. For this reason anthropologists, with their special understanding of cultural differences, are frequently employed as go-betweens in situations requiring interaction between peoples of differing cultural traditions.

As an example, while I was still a graduate student in anthropology, one of my professors asked me to work with architects and the Tonto Apache Indians in Arizona to research housing needs for a new tribal community. Although the architects knew about cross-cultural differences in the use of space, they had no idea how to get relevant information from the Indian people. For their part, the Apaches had no explicit awareness of their needs, for these were based on unconscious patterns of behavior. For that matter, few people are consciously aware of the space needs for their own social patterns of behavior.

My task was to persuade the architects to hold back on their planning long enough for me to gather, through participant observation and a review of written records, the data from which Apache housing needs could be abstracted. At the same time, I had to overcome Apache anxieties over an outsider coming into their midst to learn about matters as personal as their daily lives as they are acted out, in and around their homes. With these hurdles overcome, I was able to identify and successfully communicate to the architects those features of Apache life having importance for home and community design. At the same time, discussions of my findings with the Apaches enhanced their own awareness of their unique needs.

As a result of my work, the Apaches moved into houses that had been designed with *their* participation, for *their* specific needs. Among my findings was the realization that the Apaches preferred to ease into social interactions rather than to shake hands and begin interacting immediately, as is more typical of the Anglo pattern. Apache etiquette requires that people be in full view of one another so each can assess the behavior of others from a distance prior to engaging in social interaction with them. This requires a large, open living space. At the same time, hosts feel compelled to offer food to guests as a prelude to further social interaction. Thus, cooking and dining areas cannot be separated from living space. Nor is standard middle-class Anglo kitchen equipment suitable because the need for handling large quantities among extended families requires large pots and pans, which in turn calls for extra-large sinks and cupboards. Built with such ideas in mind, the new houses accommodated long-standing native traditions.

On a return visit to the Tonto Apache reservation in 2010, I found that the original houses were fine, but many more units had been squeezed in to accommodate growing needs on a restricted land base. A recent acquisition of new lands, which more than doubled the size of the tiny reservation, offers new possibilities. The Tonto Apache opened a casino in 2007. Its success has resulted in significant changes—from impoverishment to being one of the biggest employers in the area.

Adapted from Esber, G. S. (1987). Designing Apache houses with Apaches. In R. M. Wulff & S. J. Fiske (Eds.), *Anthropological praxis: Translating knowledge into action.* Boulder, CO: Westview. 2007 & 2010 updates by Esber. Reprinted by permission of George S. Esber.

became possible to bring about the political unification of two or more formerly independent societies, each with its own culture, thereby creating a more complex order that transcends the theoretical one culture–one society linkage.

As mentioned in Chapter 1, anthropology makes an important distinction between state and nation. *States* are politically organized territories that are internationally recognized, whereas *nations* are socially organized bodies of people who share ethnicity—a common origin, language, and cultural heritage. For example, the Kurds constitute a nation, but their homeland is divided among several states: Iran, Iraq, Turkey, and Syria. The international boundaries among these states were drawn up after World War I (1914–1918) with little regard for the region's indigenous ethnic groups or nations. Similar state-formation processes have taken place throughout the world, especially in Asia and Africa, often destabilizing inherently fragile political conditions in these countries (Figure 13.5).

Pluralistic societies, which are common in the world today, all face the same challenge: They are composed of groups that, by virtue of their high degree of cultural variation, are all essentially operating by different sets of rules. Because social living requires predictable behavior, it may be difficult for the members of any one subgroup to accurately interpret and follow the different standards by which the others operate.

Ethnocentrism—defined in Chapter 1 as the belief that the cultural ways of one's own culture are superior—is

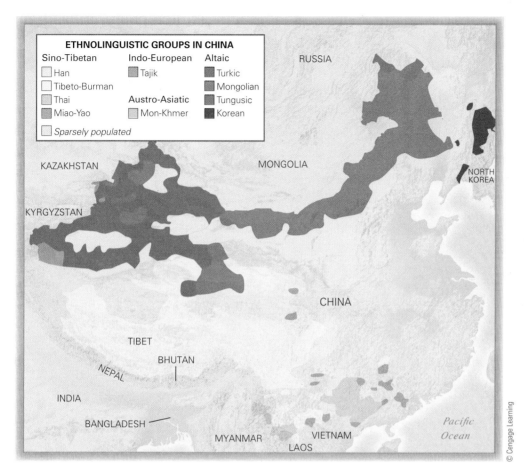

ETHNOLINGUISTIC GROUPS IN CHINA

Sino-Tibetan	Indo-European	Altaic
☐ Han	☐ Tajik	☐ Turkic
☐ Tibeto-Burman		☐ Mongolian
☐ Thai	**Austro-Asiatic**	☐ Tungusic
☐ Miao-Yao	☐ Mon-Khmer	☐ Korean
☐ *Sparsely populated*		

© Cengage Learning

Figure 13.5 **Ethnolinguistic Groups in China**
China is the largest country in the world, with a population of more than 1 billion people. A pluralistic society, it has fifty-five officially recognized nationalities. By far the largest nationality, or ethnic group, is the Han, comprising about 90 percent of the population. However, there are many ethnic minorities speaking radically different languages and having different cultural traditions. For example, the Uyghur (pictured in Figure 13.6), numbering over 8 million, are a Turkic-speaking people in Xinjiang Province in northwestern China. Unlike most Han, who are Buddhists, most Uyghur are Sunni Muslims. Historically dominating the Chinese state, the Han typically see themselves as the "real" Chinese and ignore the ethnic minorities or view them with contempt. This ethnocentrism is also reflected in names historically used for these groups.

prevalent around the world and contributes to cross-cultural misunderstanding and distrust among different subgroups within a pluralistic society. There are many current examples of troubled pluralistic societies, including Afghanistan and Nigeria, where central governments face major challenges in maintaining peace and lawful order. In countries where one ethnic group is substantially larger than others, such as the Han in China, greater numbers may be used to political and economic advantage at the expense of minority groups (Figure 13.6).

Culture Is Based on Symbols

Nearly all human behavior involves symbols. A **symbol** is a sound, gesture, mark, or other sign that is linked to something else and represents it in a meaningful way.

Because often there is no inherent or necessary relationship between a thing and its representation, symbols are arbitrary, acquiring specific meanings when people agree on usage in their communications.

Symbols—ranging from national flags to wedding rings, money, and words—enter into every aspect of culture, from social life and religion to politics and economics. We are all familiar with the fervor and devotion that a religious symbol can elicit from a believer. An Islamic crescent moon, Christian cross, or a Jewish Star of David—as well as the sun among Inca, a mountain among Kikuyus, or any other object of worship—may bring to mind years

symbol A sound, gesture, mark, or other sign that is arbitrarily linked to something else and represents it in a meaningful way.

Figure 13.6 The Uyghur Minority in China
The Uyghur, a Turkic-speaking Muslim ethnic minority in China, live in the country's northwestern province of Xinjiang. Politically dominated by China's Han ethnic majority, who comprise 90 percent of the population, Uyghurs are proud of their cultural identity and strive to hold onto their distinctive traditional heritage—as is evident in this photo of a Uyghur family group eating together on carpets woven with traditional Uyghur designs.

of struggle and persecution or may stand for a whole philosophy or religion.

The most important symbolic aspect of culture is language—using words to represent objects and ideas. Through language humans are able to transmit culture from one generation to the next. In particular, language makes it possible to learn from cumulative, shared experience. Without it, one could not inform others about events, emotions, and other experiences. Language is so important that one of the four main subfields of anthropology is dedicated to its study.

Culture Is Integrated

The breadth and depth of every culture is remarkable. It includes what people do for a living, the tools they use, the ways they work together, how they transform their environments and construct their dwellings, what they eat and drink, how they worship, what they believe is right or wrong, what they celebrate, what gifts they

exchange, who they marry, how they raise their children, and how they deal with misfortune, sickness, death, and so on. Because these and all other aspects of a culture must be reasonably well integrated in order to function properly, anthropologists seldom focus on one cultural feature in isolation. Instead, they view each in terms of its larger context and carefully examine its connections to related features.

For purposes of comparison and analysis, anthropologists conceptualize a culture as a structured system made up of distinctive parts that function together as an organized whole. Although they may sharply identify each part as a clearly defined unit with its own characteristics and distinctive place within the larger system, anthropologists recognize that social reality is complex and subject to change, and that divisions among cultural units are seldom clear-cut. Broadly speaking, a society's cultural features fall within three categories: social structure, infrastructure, and superstructure, as depicted in our "barrel model" (Figure 13.7).

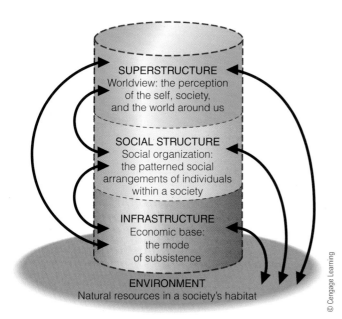

Figure 13.7 **The Barrel Model of Culture**
Every culture is an integrated and dynamic system of adaptation that responds to a combination of internal factors (economic, social, ideological) and external factors (environmental, climatic). Within a cultural system, there are functional relationships among the economic base (infrastructure), the social organization (social structure), and the ideology (superstructure). A change in one leads to a change in the others.

The Barrel Model of Culture

To ensure a community's biological continuity, a culture must provide a social structure for reproduction and mutual support. **Social structure** concerns rule-governed relationships—with all their rights and obligations—that hold members of a society together. Households, families, associations, and power relations, including politics, are all part of social structure. It establishes group cohesion and enables people to consistently satisfy their basic needs, including food and shelter for themselves and their dependents, by means of work.

There is a direct relationship between a group's social structure and its economic foundation, which includes subsistence practices and the tools and other material equipment used to make a living. Because subsistence practices involve tapping into available resources to satisfy a society's basic needs, this aspect of culture is known as **infrastructure**. It comprises strategies for the production and distribution of goods and services considered necessary for life.

Supported by this economic foundation, a society is held together by a shared sense of identity and worldview. This **superstructure** is composed of a collection of ideas, beliefs, and values, including religion, by which members of a society make sense of reality. Worldview, also known as ideology, comprises a people's overarching ideas about themselves and the world around them, and it gives meaning and direction to their lives.

Influencing and reinforcing one another—continually adapting to changing demographic, technological, political, economic, and ideological factors—the interconnected features in these three interdependent structures together form part of a cultural system.

Kapauku Culture as an Integrated System

The integration of economic, social, and ideological aspects of a culture can be illustrated by the Kapauku Papua, an indigenous mountain people of Western New Guinea. Dominated by males, Kapauku economy traditionally relies on plant cultivation, along with pig breeding, hunting, and fishing. Although plant cultivation provides most of the people's food, men achieve political power and positions of legal authority through pig breeding.

Among the Kapauku, living in an area now claimed by Indonesia, pig breeding is a complex business. Raising a lot of pigs requires a lot of food to feed them. The primary fodder is sweet potatoes, grown in garden plots. Gardening and tending to the pigs are tasks that fall exclusively in the domain of women's work. Thus, to raise many pigs a man needs numerous women in the household. As a result, multiple wives are not only permitted but are highly desired in Kapauku society. For each wife, however, a man must pay a bride-price, and this can be expensive. Furthermore, wives have to be compensated for their care of the pigs. Put simply, it takes pigs, by which wealth is measured, to get wives, without whom pigs cannot be raised in the first place. This requires considerable entrepreneurship, an ability that produces leaders in Kapauku society (Figure 13.8).

The interrelatedness of these elements with various other features of Kapauku culture is even more complicated. For example, one condition that encourages men to marry several women is a surplus of adult females, sometimes caused by loss of males through warfare. Among the Kapauku, recurring warfare has long been viewed as a

social structure The rule-governed relationships—with all their rights and obligations—that hold members of a society together. This includes households, families, associations, and power relations, including politics.

infrastructure The economic foundation of a society, including its subsistence practices and the tools and other material equipment used to make a living.

superstructure A society's shared sense of identity and worldview. The collective body of ideas, beliefs, and values by which members of a society make sense of the world—its shape, challenges, and opportunities—and understand their place in it. This includes religion and national ideology.

© Jurka Rona

Figure 13.8 Kapauku Papua Village, Western New Guinea
Kapauku economy relies on plant cultivation, hunting, fishing, and especially pig breeding. Women are responsible for raising the pigs and their main fodder, sweet potatoes. Only men with numerous wives manage to acquire many pigs needed for wealth and prestige. As a result, multiple wives are not only permitted, but are highly desired in Kapauku society.

necessary evil. By their rules of war, men may be killed but women may not. This system works to promote the imbalanced sex ratio that fosters the practice of having more than one wife. Having multiple wives tends to work best if all of them come to live in their husband's village. With this arrangement, the men of a village are typically blood relatives of one another, which enhances their ability to cooperate in warfare.

Considering all these factors, it makes sense that Kapauku typically trace ancestry through fathers, which, coupled with near-constant warfare, tends to promote male dominance. So it is not surprising to find that only men hold positions of leadership in Kapauku, as they appropriate the products of women's labor to enhance their political stature. Such male dominance is by no means characteristic of all human societies. Rather, as with the Kapauku, it arises only under particular sets of circumstances that, if changed, will alter the way in which men and women relate to each other.

Culture Is Dynamic

Cultures are dynamic systems that respond to motions and actions within and around them. When one element within the system shifts or changes, the entire system strives to adjust, just as it does when an outside force applies pressure. To function adequately, a culture must be flexible enough to allow such adjustments in the face of unstable or changing circumstances.

All cultures are, of necessity, dynamic, but some are far less so than others. When a culture is too rigid or static and fails to provide its members with the means required for long-term survival under changing conditions, it is not likely to endure. On the other hand, some cultures are so fluid and open to change that they may lose their distinctive character. The Amish mentioned earlier in this chapter typically resist change as much as possible but are constantly making balanced decisions to adjust when absolutely necessary. North Americans in general, however, have created a culture in which change has become a positive ideal, reflecting rapid and ongoing transformations in their society's demography, technology, economy, and so on.

Every culture is dynamically constructed and, not unlike a thermostat regulating room temperature, able to cope with recurrent strains and tensions, even dangerous disruptions and deadly conflicts. Sharing a culture, members of a society are capable of dealing with crises, solving their conflicts, and restoring order. Sometimes, however, the pressures are so great that the cultural features in the system are no longer adequate or acceptable, and the established order is changed.

Functions of Culture

Polish-born British anthropologist Bronislaw Malinowski argued that people everywhere share certain biological and psychological needs and that the ultimate function of all cultural institutions is to fulfill these needs (see Anthropologist of Note). Others have marked out different criteria, but the idea is basically the same: A culture cannot endure if it does not deal effectively with basic challenges. It has to equip members of a society with strategies for the production and distribution of goods and services considered necessary for life. To ensure that the group endures, it must also offer a social structure for reproduction and mutual support. Further, it has to provide ways and means to pass on knowledge

Bronislaw Malinowski (1884–1942)

Bronislaw Malinowski in the Trobriand Islands about 1916.

Courtesy Phoebe Apperson Hearst Museum of Anthropology

Bronislaw Malinowski, born in Poland, earned his doctorate in anthropology at the London School of Economics and later, as a professor there, played a vital role in making it an important center of anthropology. Renowned as a pioneer in participant observation, he stated that the ethnographer's goal is "to grasp the native's point of view . . . to realize *his* vision of *his* world."[a]

Writing about culture, Malinowski argued that people everywhere share certain biological and psychological needs and that the ultimate function of all cultural institutions is to fulfill those needs. Everyone, for example, needs to feel secure in relation to the physical universe. Therefore, when science and technology are inadequate to explain certain natural phenomena—such as eclipses or earthquakes—people develop religion and magic to account for those phenomena and to establish a feeling of security.

The quantity and quality of data called for by Malinowski's research approach set new scientific standards for anthropological fieldwork. He argued that it was necessary to settle into the community being studied for an extended period of time in order to fully explain its culture. He demonstrated this approach with his research in the Trobriand Islands of the southern Pacific Ocean between 1915 and 1918. Never before had such intensive fieldwork been done nor had such theoretical insights been gained into the functioning of another culture.

[a] Malinowski, B. (1961). *Argonauts of the western Pacific* (p. 25). New York: Dutton.

and enculturate new members so they can contribute to their community as well-functioning adults. Moreover, it must facilitate social interaction and provide ways to avoid or resolve conflicts both within their group and with outsiders.

Because a culture must support all aspects of life, as indicated in our barrel model, it must also meet the psychological and emotional needs of its members. This last function is met, in part, simply by the measure of predictability that each culture, as a shared design for thought and action, brings to everyday life. Of course, it involves much more than that, including a worldview that helps individuals understand their place in the world and face major changes and challenges. For example, every culture provides its members with certain customary ideas and rituals that enable them to think creatively about the meaning of life and death. Many cultures even make it possible for people to imagine an afterlife. Invited to suspend disbelief and engage in such imaginings, people find the means to deal with the grief of losing a loved one and to face their own demise with certain expectations.

In sum, for a culture to function properly, its various parts must be consistent with one another. But consistency is not the same as harmony. In fact, there is friction and potential for conflict within every culture—among individuals, factions, and competing institutions. Even on the most basic level of a society, individuals rarely experience the enculturation process in exactly the same way, nor do they perceive their reality in precisely identical fashion. Moreover, forces both inside and outside the society will change the cultural conditions.

Culture, Society, and the Individual

Ultimately, a society is no more than a union of individuals, all of whom have their own special needs and interests. To survive, it must succeed in balancing the immediate self-interest of its individual members with the needs and demands of the collective well-being of society as a whole. To accomplish this, a society offers rewards for adherence to its culturally prescribed standards. In most cases, these rewards assume the form of social approval. For example, in most state societies today, people who hold a good job, take care of family, pay taxes, and do volunteer work in the neighborhood may be spoken of as "model citizens" in the community.

To ensure the survival of the group, each person must learn to postpone certain immediate personal satisfactions. Yet the needs of the individual cannot be overlooked entirely or emotional stress and growing resentment may erupt in the form of protest, disruption, and even violence.

Consider, for example, the matter of sexual expression, which, like anything that people do, is shaped by culture. Sexuality is important in every society for it helps to strengthen cooperative bonds among members, ensuring the perpetuation of the social group itself. Yet sex can be disruptive to social living. Without clear rules about who has sexual access to whom, competition for sexual privileges can destroy the cooperative bonds on which human survival depends. In addition, uncontrolled sexual activity can result in reproductive rates that cause a society's population to outstrip its resources. Hence, as it shapes sexual behavior, every culture must balance the needs of society against individual sexual needs and desires so that frustration does not build up to the point of being disruptive in itself.

Cultures vary widely in the way they regulate sexual behavior. On one end of the spectrum, societies such as the Amish in North America or the Salafis in Saudi Arabia have taken an extremely restrictive approach, specifying no sex outside of marriage. On the other end are societies such as the Norwegians who generally accept premarital sex and often choose to have children outside marriage, or even more extreme, the Canela Indians in Brazil, whose social codes guarantee that, sooner or later, everyone in a given village has had sex with just about everyone of the opposite sex. Yet, even as permissive as the latter situation may sound, there are nonetheless strict rules as to how the system operates (Crocker & Crocker, 2004).

In all life issues, cultures must strike a balance between the needs and desires of individuals and those of society as a whole. Although some societies require a greater degree of cultural uniformity than others, every organized social group imposes pressure on its members to conform to certain cultural models, or standards, of acceptable public behavior, speech, and so on. These standards are commonly accepted and adhered to, and each society has institutions in place with a repertoire of cultural mechanisms to promote or enforce conformity. In many traditional societies, religious institutions play a major role in doing this, whereas in other places political forces may impose conformity, such as in a communist state. In capitalist societies, economic market pressures impose conformity

in numerous ways, including standards of beauty (see the Biocultural Connection).

Culture and Change

Cultures have always changed over time, but never as rapidly, radically, or massively as today. Change takes place in response to events such as population growth, technological innovation, climatological shifts, intrusion of foreigners, or modifications of ideas and behavior within a society.

Not all change is cultural. As living creatures, we typically experience multiple changes in the course of a lifetime that are part of the human life cycle. The longest confirmed human lifespan on record is 121 years, but very few individuals come close to reaching such advanced age. The average life span is much lower, although it has lengthened considerably in the past few decades. Currently, the global average life expectancy is about 73 years for females and 68 for males. In many countries, the life expectancy is at least 20 years less, and in others it is at least 10 years more. For example, the overall average in Angola is 51 years, compared to 84 years in Japan.

Changes in culture may result from technological innovation, foreign invasion, new trade goods, population growth, ecological shifts, and numerous other factors.

Although cultures must have some flexibility to remain adaptive, some changes cause unexpected and sometimes disastrous results. For example, consider the relationship between culture and the droughts that periodically afflict so many people living in African countries just south of the Sahara Desert. The lives of some 14 million nomadic herders native to this region are centered on cattle and other grazing animals. For thousands of years, these nomads have migrated seasonally to provide their herds with pasture and water, utilizing vast areas of arid lands in ways that allowed them to survive severe droughts many times in the past. Today, however, government officials actively discourage nomadism because it involves moving back and forth across relatively new and remote international boundaries that are often impossible to guard, making it difficult to track the people and their animals for purposes of taxation and other government controls.

Viewing the nomads as evading their authority, officials have established policies to keep migratory herders from ranging through their traditional grazing territories and to convert them into sedentary villagers. Simultaneously, governments have aimed to press pastoralists into a market economy by giving them incentives to raise many more animals than required for their own needs so that the surplus can be sold to augment the tax base. Combined, these policies have led to overgrazing, erosion, and a lack of reserve pasture during recurring droughts. Thus, droughts today are far more disastrous than in the past

Modifying the Human Body

Each healthy human individual, like any other biological organism, is genetically programmed to develop to its full potential. This includes reaching a certain maximum height as a fully mature adult. What that height is, however, varies according to population group. Dutch adult males, for example, average well over a foot taller than Mbuti men, who do not generally grow taller than 150 centimeters (5 feet). Whether we actually become as tall as our genes would allow, however, is influenced by multiple factors, including nutrition and disease.

In many cultures, being tall is viewed positively, especially for men. To make up for any perceived flaw in height, there is not much men can do to appear taller beyond wearing shoes with thick soles. But, in other areas, there are many alternatives to increase attractiveness and improve social status. Playing on this desire, and fueling it, the fashion industry creates and markets ever-changing styles of shoes, dresses, hairstyles, makeup, perfume, nail polish, hats, and whatever else to beautify the human body.

For thousands of years, people across the world have also engaged in modifying the human body itself—with tattoos, piercings, circumcision, footbinding, and even altering skull shape. In addition, modern medical technology has provided a vast new range of surgical procedures aimed at this goal.

With medicine as big business, many surgeons have joined forces with the beauty industry in what U.S. anthropologist Laura Nader calls "standardizing" bodies. Focusing on women's bodies, she notes "images of the body appear natural within their specific cultural milieus."[a] For example, breast implants are not seen as odd within the cultural milieu of the United States, and female circumcision and infibulation (also known as female genital mutilation or FGM) are not considered odd among people in several African countries.

Many feminist writers "differentiate [FGM] from breast implantation by arguing that American women *choose* to have breast implants whereas in Africa women are subject to indoctrination,"[b] given they undergo circumcision as young girls. But is a woman's decision to have breast implants, in fact, the result of indoctrination by the beauty-industrial complex?

This multibillion-dollar industry, notes Nader, "segments the female body and manufactures commodities of and for the body."[c] Among millions of women getting "caught in the official beauty ideology" are those in the United States who have breast implantation. On average, they are 36 years old with two children. Designated as the beauty industry's "insecure consumers," these women are "recast as patients" with an illness defined as hypertrophy (small breasts). Psychological health can be restored by cosmetic surgery correcting this so-called deformity in the female body.

The doctors who perform these operations are often regarded as therapists and artists as well as surgeons. One pioneering breast implant surgeon "took as his ideal female figure that of ancient Greek statues, which he carefully measured, noticing the exact size and shape of the breasts, their vertical and horizontal locations."[d] In response to beauty marketing, the business of plastic surgery is booming, and breast implantation is spreading across the globe.

Biocultural Question

Have you or anyone close to you made body alterations? If so, were these changes prompted by an "official beauty ideology" or something else?

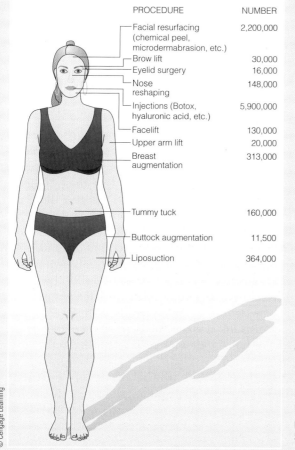

PROCEDURE	NUMBER
Facial resurfacing (chemical peel, microdermabrasion, etc.)	2,200,000
Brow lift	30,000
Eyelid surgery	16,000
Nose reshaping	148,000
Injections (Botox, hyaluronic acid, etc.)	5,900,000
Facelift	130,000
Upper arm lift	20,000
Breast augmentation	313,000
Tummy tuck	160,000
Buttock augmentation	11,500
Liposuction	364,000

© Cengage Learning

Selected Surgical and Nonsurgical Cosmetic Procedures in the United States, 2013

In 2013, the total number of procedures—including the selected cosmetic procedures pictured here—was about 11.5 million, comprised of 2 million cosmetic surgeries and 9.5 million nonsurgical procedures (chemical peels, laser treatments, Botox injections, and so on) at a total cost of about $12 billion. Ninety-one percent of all procedures were done on women, with breast augmentation the most popular. Although just 5 percent of the world's population resides in the United States, the country accounts for 15 percent of breast procedures performed worldwide. Since 2013, Brazil has edged out the United States for the greatest number of surgical cosmetic procedures performed in one country. However, per capita, South Korea has the highest rate of procedures, with the United States ranked fourth.

[a] Nader, L. (1997). Controlling processes: Tracing the dynamics of power. *Current Anthropology 38* (5), 715.

[b] Ibid., 716.

[c] Ibid. See also Coco, L. E. (1994). Silicone breast implants in America: A choice of the "official breast"? In L. Nader (Ed.), *Essays on controlling processes* (pp. 103–132). *Kroeber Anthropological Society Papers* (no. 77). Berkeley: University of California Press; and Claeson, B. (1994). The privatization of justice: An ethnography of control. In L. Nader (Ed.), *Essays on controlling processes* (pp. 32–64). *Kroeber Anthropological Society Papers* (no. 77). Berkeley: University of California Press.

[d] Nader, 1997, p. 716.

Mike Goldwater/Alamy

Figure 13.9 Consequences of Cultural Change
Climate and politics have conspired to create drastic cultural change among migratory herders,
such as this man in Niger. Here, as in other semi-arid regions of sub-Saharan Africa, severe
drought combined with restrictions on grazing lands have resulted in the death of many animals
and turned others into "bones on hoofs." Such catastrophes have forced many herders in these
regions to give up their old lifeways entirely.

because when they occur, they jeopardize the nomads'
very existence (Figure 13.9).

The market economy that led nomads to increase their
herds beyond sustainability is a factor in a wide range of
cultural changes. Many nomads, including thousands of
Kuchi herder families in Afghanistan (pictured at the start
of the chapter), settle down as farmers or move to cities for
cash-earning work opportunities. Across the globe, swift and
often radical cultural change is driven by capitalism and its
demand for market growth. Many welcome these changes,
but others are disturbed by the loss of their traditional way of
life and feel powerless to stop, let alone reverse, the process.

Ethnocentrism, Cultural Relativism, and Evaluation of Cultures

People in almost all cultures tend to be ethnocentric and
see their own way of life as the best of all possible worlds.
This is reflected in the way individual societies refer to
themselves. Typically, a society's traditional name for

itself translates roughly into "true human beings." In contrast, their name for outsiders commonly translates into
various versions of "subhumans," including "monkeys,"
"dogs," "weird-looking people," "funny talkers," and so
forth. When it comes to ethnocentrism, it is easy to find
examples (Figure 13.10).

Anthropologists have been actively engaged in reducing
ethnocentrism ever since they started to study and actually
live among foreign peoples with radically different cultures,
thus learning by personal experience that these "others"
were no less human than anyone else. Resisting the common urge to rank cultures as higher and lower (better and
worse), anthropologists have instead aimed to understand
individual cultures and the general concept of culture. To
do so, they have examined each culture on its own terms,
discerning whether or not the culture satisfies the needs
and expectations of the people themselves. If a people practiced human sacrifice or capital punishment, for example,
anthropologists asked about the circumstances that made
the taking of human life acceptable according to that particular group's values.

This brings us to the concept of **cultural
relativism**—the idea that one must suspend judgment
of other peoples' practices in order to understand those
practices in their own cultural context. Only through such
an approach can one gain a meaningful view of the values
and beliefs that underlie the behaviors and institutions of

cultural relativism The idea that one must suspend judgment of other
people's practices in order to understand them in their own cultural terms.

Figure 13.10   Perpetrating Ethnocentrism

Many people consider their own nation to be superior to others, framing their pride by proclaiming to be a "master race," "divine nation," or "chosen people" and viewing their homeland as sacred. Such nationalist ideology is associated with militant ethnocentrism and dislike, fear, or even hatred of foreigners, immigrants, and ethnic minorities. For instance, most Russians now agree with the Nationalist slogan "Russia for the Russians," and almost half believe their nation has a natural right to dominate as an empire. Russian Nationalists (*right*) are rightwing extremists, protesting the immigration of Tajiks, Turks, and other foreign laborers settling in Russia. Many thousands participate in anti-immigrant marches in Moscow and other major cities. In their extremism, they are matched by the Minutemen Civil Defense Corps in the United States. Active nationwide, these vigilantes view fellow whites as the only "true" Americans and are strongly anti-immigrant. The left photo shows the Minutemen in Palominas, Arizona, erecting a U.S.–Mexico border fence on private ranchland.

other peoples and societies, as well as clearer insights into the underlying beliefs and practices of one's own society.

Cultural relativism is not only a guard against ethnocentrism, but it is an essential research tool. However, employing it for research does not mean suspending judgment forever, nor does it require that anthropologists defend a people's right to engage in any cultural practice, no matter how destructive. All that is necessary is that we avoid *premature* judgments until we have a full understanding of the culture in which we are interested. Only then may anthropologists adopt a critical stance and in an informed way consider the advantages and disadvantages of particular beliefs and behaviors for a society and its members.

A valid question to ask in evaluating a culture is: *How well does it satisfy the biological, social, and psychological needs of those whose behavior it guides?* Specific indicators to answer this question are found in the nutritional status and general physical and mental health of its population; the average life expectancy; the group's relationship to its resource base; the prevalence of poverty; the stability and tranquility of domestic life; and the incidence of violence, crime, and delinquency. When traditional ways of coping no longer seem to work and people feel helpless to shape their lives in their own societies, symptoms of cultural breakdown become prominent (Figure 13.11).

Figure 13.11   Signs of Cultural Dissatisfaction

High rates of crime and delinquency are signs that a culture is not adequately satisfying a people's needs and expectations. This photo, taken inside the Men's Central Jail in Los Angeles, California, can be seen as such evidence. The United States has the highest incarceration rate in the world—about 700 prisoners per 100,000 inhabitants. From a global perspective, the United States incarcerates nearly 25 percent of the world's prisoners—more than 2.3 million people ("Jailhouse nation," 2015). The incarceration rate in "the land of the free" has risen sevenfold since the 1970s and is now five times the rate of Great Britain, nine times that of Germany, and fourteen times that of Japan.

In short, a culture may be understood as a complex maintenance system constructed to ensure the continued well-being of a group of people. It may be deemed successful as long as it secures the survival of a society in a way that satisfies its members.

What complicates matters is that any society is made up of groups with different interests, raising the possibility that some people's interests may be better served than those of others. For this reason, anthropologists must always ask *whose* needs and *whose* survival are best served by the culture in question. For example, in a male-dominated culture such as that of the Kapauku, discussed earlier in this chapter, a tribesman's pathway to success may come at the expense of his wife or wives because women carry the burden of tending the food gardens and herding the pigs—the basis of a man's wealth and prestige. Only by looking at the overall situation can a reasonably objective judgment be made as to how well a culture is working.

Our species today is challenged by rapid changes all across the globe, much of it triggered by powerful technology and dramatic population growth. In our current age of globalization, we must widen our scope and develop a truly worldwide perspective that enables us to appreciate cultures as increasingly open and interactive systems.

CHAPTER CHECKLIST

What is cultural adaptation?

✓ Cultural adaptation—a complex of ideas, activities, and technologies that enables people to survive and even thrive in their environment—has enabled humans to survive and expand into a wide variety of environments.

✓ Cultures have always changed over time, although rarely as rapidly or massively as many are today. Sometimes what is adaptive in one set of circumstances or over the short run is maladaptive over time.

What is culture, and what characteristics are common to all cultures?

✓ Culture is a society's shared and socially transmitted ideas, values, and perceptions, which are used to make sense of experience and generate behavior and are reflected in that behavior.

✓ Although every culture involves a group's shared values, ideas, and behavior, this does not mean that everything within a culture is uniform. For instance, in all cultures people's roles vary according to age and gender. (Anthropologists use the term *gender* to refer to the cultural elaborations and meanings assigned to the biological differences between sexes.) And in some societies there are other subcultural variations.

✓ A subculture (for example, the Amish) shares certain overarching assumptions of the larger culture collectively shared by members of a complex society, while observing its own set of distinct rules.

✓ Pluralistic societies are complex societies in which two or more ethnic groups or nationalities are politically organized into one territorial state but maintain their cultural differences.

✓ In addition to being shared, all cultures are learned, with individual members learning the accepted norms of social behavior through the process of enculturation. Also, every culture is based on symbols—transmitted through the communication of ideas, emotions, and desires—especially language. And culture is integrated, so that all aspects function as an integrated whole (albeit not without tension, friction, and even conflict). Finally, cultures are dynamic—constructed to adjust to recurrent pressures, crises, and change.

✓ As illustrated in the barrel model, all aspects of a culture fall into one of three broad, interrelated categories: infrastructure (the subsistence practices or economic system), social structure (the rule-governed relationships between a society's members), and superstructure (the collectively shared ideology or worldview).

✓ Cultural change takes place in response to events such as population growth, technological innovation, environmental crisis, intrusion of outsiders, or modification of values and behavior within a society. Although cultures must change to adapt to new circumstances, sometimes the unforeseen consequences of change are disastrous for a society.

What are the connections between individuals, their culture, and their society?

✓ As a union of individuals, a society must strike a balance between the self-interest of its members and with the needs and demands of the collective well-being of the group. To accomplish this, a society rewards adherence to its culturally prescribed standards in the form of social approval.

✓ However, individual needs cannot be entirely overlooked in a society. Doing so can foster stress and growing resentment, which may erupt in violence and lead to cultural breakdown.

What are ethnocentrism and cultural relativism, and what is the measure of a society's success?

✓ Ethnocentrism is the belief that one's own culture is superior to all others. To avoid making ethnocentric judgments, anthropologists adopt the approach of cultural relativism, which requires suspending judgment long enough to understand each culture in its own terms.

✓ The least biased measure of a culture's success may be based on answering this question: How well does a particular culture satisfy the physical and psychological needs of those whose behavior it guides? The following indicators provide answers: nutritional status and general physical and mental health of its population; the average life expectancy; the group's relationship to its resource base; the prevalence of poverty; the stability and tranquility of domestic life; and the incidence of violence, crime, and delinquency.

QUESTIONS FOR REFLECTION

1. Considering how the forces of globalization threaten the lifeways of Kuchi nomads and other traditional cultures around the world, do you view the disappearance of such cultures as unavoidable? Do you think tradition and ethnic identity are worth holding on to?

2. Many modern societies are complex and pluralistic. Are you familiar with any subcultures or different ethnic groups in your own society? Could you make friends with or even marry someone from another subculture or ethnicity? What kind of cultural differences or problems would you be likely to encounter, and how would you deal with ethnocentrism?

3. An often overlooked first step for developing an understanding of another culture is having knowledge and respect for one's own cultural traditions. Do you know the origins of the worldview commonly held by most people in your community? How do you think that developed over time, and what makes it so accepted or popular in your group today?

4. Today, more than 7.3 billion people inhabit the earth. That number is currently increasing by nearly 80 million a year—the population size of Iran or Germany. With finite natural resources and hugely escalating piles of waste, do you think technological inventions alone are sufficient to secure health and happiness for humanity on our ever-more crowded planet?

DIGGING INTO ANTHROPOLOGY

Hometown Map

The barrel model offers a simple framework to imagine what a culture looks like from an analytical point of view. Become a participant observer in your own culture. Walking, driving, or riding through your home area, make notes about its geographic location, natural or urban landscape, roads and railways, public spaces and offices, business and private buildings, economic activities, political organization, family life, ethnic makeup, and social interactions. Conclude your study with notes about your home area's religious institutions. At the end of your tour, dig into anthropology by fitting the elements you have described into the three layers of the barrel model and explaining how they may be interconnected as a whole—your hometown.

© Harald E. L. Prins

CHALLENGE ISSUE

Anthropologists take on the challenge of studying and describing cultures and finding scientific explanations for their differences and similarities. Why do people think, feel, and act in certain ways—and find it wrong or impossible to do otherwise? Answers must come from fact-based knowledge about cultural diversity—knowledge that is not culture-bound and is widely recognized as significant. Over the years, anthropology has generated such knowledge through various theories and research methods. In particular, anthropologists obtain information through long-term, full-immersion fieldwork based on participant observation. Here we see U.S. anthropologist Lucas Bessire (in the tan cap) and a dozen Ayoreo Indians returning to their village after a successful hunting expedition that yielded thirty-five tortoises. Weighing in at about 30 kilograms (9 pounds) and roasted in their shells over an open fire, tortoises are part of the Ayoreo's traditional diet. Bessire's vehicle, known among the Ayoreo as the "giant armadillo," has come in handy for community emergencies and for research that includes documenting the Ayoreo Indian community and its rapidly changing environment in the Gran Chaco of Paraguay. Non-Indian farmers and agribusinesses are rapidly deforesting this dry woodland habitat, destroying its wildlife and the indigenous cultures traditionally depending on this ecosystem.

Ethnographic Research—Its History, Methods, and Theories

As briefly discussed in Chapter 1, cultural anthropology has two main scholarly components: ethnography and ethnology. *Ethnography* is a detailed description of a particular culture primarily based on firsthand observation and interaction. *Ethnology* is the study and analysis of different cultures from a comparative or historical point of view, utilizing ethnographic accounts and developing anthropological theories that help explain why certain important differences or similarities occur among groups.

Historically, anthropology focused on non-Western traditional peoples whose languages were not written down—people whose communication was often direct and face-to-face and whose knowledge about the past was based primarily on oral tradition. Even in societies where writing exists, little of interest to anthropologists is detailed in writing. Thus, anthropologists have made a point of going to these places in person to observe and experience peoples and their cultures firsthand. This is called *fieldwork*.

Today, anthropological fieldwork takes place not only in small-scale communities in remote corners of the world, but also in modern urban neighborhoods in industrial or postindustrial societies. Anthropologists can be found doing fieldwork in a wide range of places and within a host of diverse groups and institutions, including global corporations, nongovernmental organizations (NGOs), mining towns, tourist resorts, migrant labor communities, slums, prisons, and refugee camps.

In our rapidly changing and increasingly interconnected world, where longstanding cultural boundaries between societies are being erased, new social networks and cultural constructs have emerged, made possible by long-distance mass transportation and communication technologies. To better describe, explain, and understand these complex but fascinating dynamics in a globalizing world, anthropologists today are adjusting their theoretical frameworks and research methods and approaches.

In this chapter you will learn to

- Explain why fieldwork is essential to ethnography.

- Situate historical changes in research questions and applications within their economic, social, and political contexts.

- Describe ethnographic research—its challenges and methods.

- Discuss the relationship between methods and theory.

- Contrast key theoretical perspectives in anthropology.

- Recognize the ethical responsibilities of anthropological research.

Our research questions are often influenced by the environmental, economic, political, military, or ideological concerns of a particular period. What we observe and consider significant is shaped or modified by a worldview, and our explanations or interpretations are framed in theories that gain and lose currency depending on ideological and political-economical forces beyond our individual control. Taking this into consideration, this chapter presents a historical overview of anthropology, its research methods and theories—underscoring the idea that ethnographic research does not happen in a timeless vacuum.

History of Ethnographic Research and Its Uses

Anthropology emerged as a formal discipline during the heyday of **colonialism** (1870s–1930s), a system by which a dominant society politically claims and controls a foreign territory primarily for purposes of settling and economic exploitation. Many European anthropologists focused on the study of traditional peoples and cultures in their colonies overseas. For instance, French anthropologists conducted most of their research in North and West Africa and Southeast Asia; British anthropologists studied in southern and eastern Africa; Dutch anthropologists researched the region that has become Indonesia, Western New Guinea, and Suriname; and Belgian anthropologists traveled to Congo in Africa. Anthropologists in North America focused primarily on their own countries' indigenous communities—usually residing in remote Arctic villages, or on tracts of land known as Indian reservations or First Nation Reserves.

At one time it was common practice to compare peoples still pursuing traditional lifeways—based on hunting, fishing, gathering, or small-scale farming or herding—with the prehistoric ancestors of Europeans and to categorize the cultures of these traditional peoples as "primitive." Anthropologists have long abandoned such ethnocentric terminology, but many others still think and speak of these traditional cultures as "backward" or "undeveloped." This misconception helped state societies, commercial enterprises, and other powerful outside groups justify expanding their activities and invading the lands belonging to these peoples, often exerting overwhelming pressure on them to change their ancestral ways.

---

colonialism System by which a dominant society politically claims and controls a foreign territory primarily for purposes of settling and economic exploitation.
urgent anthropology Ethnographic research that documents endangered cultures; also known as *salvage ethnography*.

Salvage Ethnography or Urgent Anthropology

Within this disturbing and often violent historical context, thousands of traditional communities worldwide have struggled to survive. In fact, many of these threatened peoples have become physically extinct. Others survived but were forced to surrender their territories and lifeways. Anthropologists have seldom been able to prevent such tragic events, but many have tried to make a record of these cultural groups. This important practice of documenting endangered cultures was initially called *salvage ethnography* and later became known as **urgent anthropology**, and it continues to this day (Figure 14.1).

By the late 1800s, many European and North American museums were sponsoring anthropological expeditions to collect cultural artifacts and other material remains (including skulls and bones), as well as vocabularies, myths, and other data. Anthropologists also began taking ethnographic photographs, and by the 1890s some began shooting documentary films or recording speech, songs, and music.

The first generation of anthropologists often began their careers working for museums, but those coming later were academically trained in the emerging discipline and became active in newly founded anthropology departments. In North America, most did their fieldwork on tribal reservations where indigenous communities were falling apart in the face of disease, poverty, and despair brought on by pressures of forced cultural change. These anthropologists interviewed elders still able to recall the ancestral way of life prior to the disruptions forced upon them. The researchers also collected oral histories, traditions, myths, legends, and other information, as well as old artifacts for research, preservation, and public display.

Anthropological theories have come and gone during the past few hundred years or so, but the plight of indigenous peoples struggling for cultural survival endures. Researchers can and still do contribute to cultural preservation efforts.

Acculturation Studies

In the 1930s, anthropologists began researching *culture contact*, studying how traditional cultures change when coming in contact with expanding capitalist societies. For several centuries, such contact primarily took place in the context of colonialism.

In contrast to Africa and Asia, where the natives vastly outnumbered the colonists, European settlers in the Americas, Australia, and New Zealand expanded their territories, decimating and overwhelming the indigenous inhabitants. These settler societies became politically independent, turning the colonies into new states. Several—such as Canada, Brazil, and the United States—recognized that the indigenous peoples had rights to land and set aside tracts where they could live, but not as independent nations. Surviving

Figure 14.1 Endangered Culture
Until recently, Ayoreo Indian bands lived largely isolated in the Gran Chaco, a vast wilderness in South America's heartland. One by one, these migratory foragers have been forced to "come out" due to outside encroachment on their habitat. Today, most dispossessed Ayoreo Indians find themselves in different stages of acculturation. This photo shows Ayoreo women of Zapocó in Bolivia's forest. Dressed in Western hand-me-downs and surrounded by plastic from the modern society that is pressing in on them, they weave natural plant fibers into traditionally patterned bags to sell for cash, while men make money by cutting trees for logging companies.

on reservations, these indigenous peoples, or tribal nations, are bureaucratically controlled as *internal colonies*.

Government-sponsored programs designed to compel tribal communities or ethnic minorities to abandon their ancestral languages and cultural traditions for those of the controlling society have ripped apart the unique cultural fabric of one group after another. These programs left many indigenous families impoverished, demoralized, and desperate. In the United States, this asymmetrical culture contact became known as *acculturation*. This is the massive cultural change that occurs in a society when it experiences intensive firsthand contact with a more powerful society— in particular, with an industrialized or capitalist society. In the course of the 20th century, numerous anthropologists carried out acculturation studies in Asia, Africa, Australia, Oceania, the Americas, and even in parts of Europe, thereby greatly contributing to our knowledge of complex and often disturbing processes of cultural change.

Applied Anthropology

Anthropologists were not the only ones interested in acculturation. In fact, business corporations, religious institutions, and government agencies responsible for the administration of colonies or tribal reservations actively promoted cultural change.

The British and Dutch governments, for example, had a vested interest in maintaining order over enormous colonies overseas, ruling foreign populations many times larger than their own. For practical purposes, these governments imposed a colonial system of *indirect rule* in which they depended on tribal chiefs, princes, kings, emirs, sultans, maharajas, or whatever their titles. These indigenous rulers, supported by the colonial regimes, managed the peoples under their authority by means of customary law. In the United States and Canada, a similar political system of indirect rule was established in which indigenous communities residing on tribal reservations were (and still are) governed by their own leaders largely according to their own rules, albeit under the surveillance of federal authorities.

Whatever the political condition of indigenous peoples—whether they reside on reservations, in colonies, or under some other form of authority exercised by a foreign controlling state—the practical value of anthropology became increasingly evident in the course of time. In identifying the disintegrating effects of asymmetrical culture contact, acculturation studies gave birth to *applied anthropology*—the use of anthropological knowledge and

Figure 14.2 Postage Stamp Honoring Gonzalo Aguirre Beltrán
First trained as a medical doctor, Gonzalo Aguirre Beltrán (1908–1996) became one of Mexico's most important anthropologists. He pioneered research on Afro-Mexicans and studied land tenure conflict among Mexican Indian communities in the 1930s. Influenced by acculturation theories developed by Melville Herskovits of Northwestern University and Robert Redfield of the University of Chicago, he headed the Instituto Nacional Indigenista (National Indigenous Institute) in the 1950s and 1960s. As an influential government official, he converted acculturation theory into state-sponsored policies integrating and assimilating millions of indigenous Mexican Indians into a national culture embracing ethnic diversity in a democratic state society.

methods to solve practical problems in communities confronting new challenges.

In 1937 the British government set up an anthropological research institute in what is now Zambia to study the impact of international markets on Central Africa's traditional societies. Over the next decade, anthropologists worked on a number of problem-oriented studies throughout Africa, including the disruptive effects of the mining industry and labor migration on domestic economies and cultures.

Facing similar issues in North America, the U.S. Bureau of Indian Affairs (BIA), which oversees federally recognized tribes on Indian reservations, established an applied anthropology branch in the mid-1930s. Beyond studying the problems of acculturation, the handful of applied anthropologists hired by the BIA were to identify culturally appropriate ways for the U.S. government to introduce social and economic development programs to reduce poverty, promote literacy, and solve a host of other problems on the reservations.

The international Society for Applied Anthropology, founded in 1941, aimed to promote scientific investigation of the principles controlling human relations and their practical application. Applied anthropology developed into an important part of the discipline and continued to grow even after colonized countries in Asia and Africa became self-governing states in the mid-1900s.

In Mexico—perhaps more than anywhere else in the world—anthropology has gained considerable prestige as a discipline, and its practitioners have been appointed to high political positions. The reasons for this are complex, but one factor stands out: Mexico, a former Spanish colony, is a large multi-ethnic democracy inhabited by millions of indigenous peoples who form the demographic majority in many regions. Converting acculturation theory into state-sponsored policies, influential government officials such as anthropologist Gonzalo Aguirre Beltrán sought to integrate myriad indigenous communities into a Mexican state that embraces ethnic diversity in a national culture (Aguirre Beltrán, 1974; Weaver, 2002) (Figure 14.2).

Today, many academically trained anthropologists specialize in applied research. They conduct research for a variety of local, regional, national, and international institutions, in particular nongovernmental organizations (NGOs), and are active worldwide.

Studying Cultures at a Distance

The study of anthropology shifted focus with the beginning of World War II and then the Cold War, during which capitalist countries (led by the United States) and communist countries (led by Russia) waged a war of political and economic hostility and conflict. Many anthropologists began studying modern state societies rather than limiting their research to small-scale traditional communities.

Aiming to discover basic personality traits, or psychological profiles, shared by the majority of the people in modern state societies, several U.S. and British anthropologists became involved in a wartime government program of national character studies. Officials believed such studies would help them to better understand and deal with the newly declared enemy states of Japan and Germany (in World War II) and later Russia and others.

During wartime, on-location ethnographic fieldwork was impossible in enemy societies and challenging at best in most other foreign countries. Some anthropologists developed innovative techniques for studying "culture at a distance." Their methods included the analysis of newspapers, literature, photographs, and popular films. They also collected information through structured interviews with immigrants and refugees from the enemy nations, as well as foreigners from other countries (Mead & Métraux, 1953).

To portray the national character of peoples inhabiting distant countries, anthropologists investigated a variety of topics including childrearing practices, in conjunction with examining print or film materials for recurrent cultural themes and values. This cultural knowledge was also used for propaganda and psychological warfare. Some of the insights from these long-distance anthropological studies were found to be useful in dealing with formerly colonized populations in so-called developing or Third World countries.

Studying Contemporary State Societies

Although there were theoretical flaws in the national character studies and methodological problems in studying cultures at a distance, anthropological research on contemporary state societies was more than just a war-related endeavor. Even when anthropologists devoted themselves primarily to researching non-Western small-scale communities, they recognized that a generalized understanding of human relations, ideas, and behavior depends upon knowledge of *all* cultures and peoples, including those in complex, large-scale industrial societies organized in political states. And, prior to the Second World War, several anthropologists were already researching in their own countries in settings ranging from factories to farming communities to suburban neighborhoods.

One early anthropologist doing research on the home front was Hortense Powdermaker. Born in Philadelphia, Powdermaker went to London to study under Polish anthropologist Bronislaw Malinowski and did her first major ethnographic fieldwork among Melanesians in the South Pacific. When she returned to the United States, she researched a racially segregated town in Mississippi in the 1930s (Powdermaker, 1939). During the next decade, she focused on combating U.S. dominant society's racism against African Americans and other ethnic minorities. While in the South, Powdermaker became keenly aware of the importance of the mass media in shaping people's worldviews (Wolf & Trager, 1971). To further explore this ideological force in modern culture, she cast her critical eye on the domestic film industry and did a year of fieldwork in Hollywood (1946–1947).

As Powdermaker was wrapping up her Hollywood research, several other anthropologists were launching other kinds of studies in large-scale societies. In 1950, Swiss anthropologist Alfred Métraux put together an international team of U.S., French, and Brazilian researchers to study contemporary race relations in the South American country, Brazil. The project, sponsored by the newly founded global institution UNESCO (United Nations Education, Science, and Culture Organization), was part of the UN's global campaign against racial prejudice and discrimination. Headquartered in Paris, Métraux selected Brazil as a research site primarily for comparative purposes. Like the United States, it was a former European colony with a large multi-ethnic population and a long history of black slavery. It had abolished slavery twenty-five years later than the United States but had made much more progress in terms of its race relations.

In contrast to the racially segregated United States, Brazil was believed to be an ideal example of harmonious, tolerant, and overall positive cross-racial relations. The research findings yielded unexpected results, showing that dark-skinned Brazilians of African descent did face systemic social and economic discrimination—albeit not in the political and legal form of racial segregation that pervaded the United States at the time (Prins & Krebs, 2007).

In 1956 and 1957, anthropologist Julian Steward left the United States to supervise an anthropological research team in developing countries such as Kenya, Nigeria, Peru, Mexico, Japan, Malaya, Indonesia, and Burma (now Myanmar). His goal was to study the comparative impact of industrialization and urbanization upon these different populations. Other anthropologists launched similar projects in other parts of the world.

Studying Peasant Communities

In the 1950s, as anthropologists widened their scope to consider the impact of complex state societies on the traditional indigenous groups central to early anthropological study, some researchers zeroed in on peasant communities. Peasants represent an important social category, standing midway between modern industrial society and traditional subsistence foragers, herders, farmers, and fishers. Part of larger, more complex societies, peasant communities exist worldwide, and peasants number in the many hundreds of millions.

Peasantry represents the largest social category of our species to date. Because peasant unrest over economic and social problems fuels political instability in many developing countries, anthropological studies of these rural populations in Latin America, Africa, Asia, and elsewhere are considered both significant and practical. In addition to improving policies aimed at social and economic development in rural communities, anthropological peasant studies may offer insights into how to deal with peasants resisting challenges to their traditional way of life. Such anthropological research may be useful in promoting

© Harald E.L. Prins

Figure 14.3 **A Voice for Peasants**
Peasant studies came to the fore during the 1950s as anthropologists began investigating rural peoples in state societies and the impact of capitalism on traditional small-scale communities. Here a Guaraní-speaking peasant leader addresses a crowd in front of the presidential palace in Paraguay's capital city of Asunción at a massive protest rally against land dispossession.

social justice by helping to solve, manage, or avoid social conflicts and political violence, including rebellions and guerrilla warfare or insurgencies (Figure 14.3).

Advocacy Anthropology

By the 1960s, European colonial powers had relinquished almost all of their overseas domains. Many anthropologists turned their attention to the newly independent countries in Africa and Asia, whereas others focused on South and Central America. However, as anti-Western sentiment and political upheaval seriously complicated fieldwork in many parts of the world, significant numbers of anthropologists investigated important issues of cultural change and conflict inside Europe and North America.

Many of these issues, which remain focal points to this day, involve immigrants and refugees coming from places where anthropologists have conducted research.

Some anthropologists have gone beyond studying such groups to playing a role in helping them adjust to their new circumstances—an example of applied anthropology. Others have become advocates for peasant communities, ethnic or religious minorities, or indigenous groups struggling to hold onto their ancestral lands, natural resources, and customary ways of life. Both focus on identifying, preventing, or solving problems and challenges in groups that form part of complex societies and whose circumstances and affairs are conditioned or even determined by powerful outside institutions or corporations over which they generally have little or no control.

One of the first anthropological research projects explicitly and publicly addressing the quest for social justice and cultural survival took place from 1948 to 1959 among the Meskwaki, or Fox Indians, on their reservation in the state of Iowa. Based on long-term fieldwork with this North American Indian community, anthropologist Sol Tax challenged government-sponsored applied anthropological research projects and proposed instead that researchers work directly with "disadvantaged, exploited, and oppressed communities [to help *them*] identify and solve their [*own*] problems" (Field, 2004, p. 476; see also Lurie, 1973).

Over the past few decades, anthropologists committed to social justice and human rights have become increasingly involved in efforts to assist indigenous groups, peasant communities, and ethnic minorities. Today, most anthropologists committed to community-based and politically involved research refer to their work as engaged anthropology or **advocacy anthropology**.

For example, Mexican anthropologist Rosalva Aída Hernández Castillo has practiced advocacy anthropology for two decades. Putting her journalism background to use, she has combined her academic work with print and broadcast media, as well as video, to promote women's rights in her homeland. Born and raised in Baja California, she earned her doctorate at Stanford University and returned to her parental homeland. Now a professor at the Center for Advanced Studies in Social Anthropology (CIESAS) in Mexico City, she has conducted fieldwork in Maya Indian communities in Chiapas near the Guatemalan border. Since the mid-1990s, this region has been the heartland of an indigenous revolutionary movement that effectively defends indigenous rights, promotes regional autonomy, and supports self-determination. Named after a Mexican revolutionary hero, these Zapatistas oppose neoliberalism (free-market capitalism) as pushed by business corporations, defended by the central government's bureaucracy, and made possible by military force. As noted by this feminist anthropologist, the Zapatista cause is also "the first military political movement in Latin America to claim women's rights as a fundamental part of its political agenda" (Hernández, 2016). Informed by her experiences with the Zapatistas as well as her work with

advocacy anthropology Research that is community based and politically involved.

Courtesy of Rosalva Aída Hernández Castillo

Figure 14.4 Advocacy Anthropologist Rosalva Aída Hernández Castillo
Through her research among the Maya in the Mexican-Guatemalan borderlands and her work
in various legal activist projects in southwestern Mexico, Rosalva Aída Hernández Castillo
incorporates indigenous perspectives into feminist theory. Here we see her at the VII Encounter
of the Continental Network of Indigenous Women of the Americas, held in Guatemala in
2015. (She is in the center, dressed in white, with her arm around another Network member.)
Collaborating with this Network since its creation in 1995, Hernández is considered one of the
group's *compañeras solidarias* ("solidary companions"). For the 2015 gathering, she was invited
to coordinate a workshop on indigenous law, community justice, and gender rights.

women prisoners, Hernández's feminist theorizing incorporates an indigenous perspective with a commitment to women's rights, battling gender discrimination, and fighting racism (Figure 14.4).

Studying Up

Given anthropology's mission to understand the human condition in its full cross-cultural range and complexity—not just in distant places or at the margins of our own societies—some scholars have called for ethnographic research in the centers of political and economic power in the world's dominant societies. This perspective is especially important for applied and advocacy anthropologists researching groups or communities embedded in larger and more complex processes of state-level politics and economics or even transnational levels of global institutions and multinational corporations. Of particular note in this effort is U.S. anthropologist Laura Nader. Coining the term *studying up*, she has called upon anthropologists to focus on Western elites, government bureaucracies, global corporations, philanthropic foundations, media empires, business clubs, and so on.

Studying up is easier said than done because it is a formidable challenge to do participant observation in such well-guarded circles. And when these elites are confronted with research projects or findings not to their liking, they

have the capacity and political power to stop or seriously obstruct the research or the dissemination of its results.

Globalization and Multi-Sited Ethnography

As noted in Chapter 1, the impact of globalization is everywhere. Distant localities are becoming linked in such a way that forces and activities occurring thousands of miles away are shaping local events and situations, and vice versa. Connected by modern transportation, world trade, finance capital, transnational labor pools, and information superhighways, even the most geographically remote communities have become increasingly interdependent. Indeed, all of humanity now exists in what we refer to in this text as a *globalscape*—a worldwide interconnected landscape with multiple intertwining and overlapping peoples and cultures on the move.

One consequence of globalization is the formation of *diasporic* populations (*diaspora* is a Greek word, originally meaning "scattering"), living and working far from their original homeland. Some diasporic groups feel uprooted and fragmented, but others are able to transcend vast distances and stay in touch with family and friends through communication technologies. With Internet access to news from their home towns and countries, combined with e-mail, text messaging, and a variety of social media

Courtesy of Catherine Besteman

Figure 14.5 Multi-Sited Ethnography
U.S. anthropologist Catherine Besteman began fieldwork with Bantu communities in southern Somalia's Jubba Valley in the late 1980s, just before the outbreak of the civil war that decimated the country and forced many into exile. Since 2003, thousands of Somali Bantu have relocated to Lewiston, Maine, which has become an additional site for Besteman's ongoing research. Some of her undergraduate students at nearby Colby College participate in her work with these refugees. In the photo on the left, Besteman (in orange blouse) is conducting interviews in the Somali village of Qardale. In the photo on the right, Besteman's students Elizabeth Powell and Nicole Mitchell are interviewing Iman Osman in his family's Lewiston apartment the year he graduated from high school. He and his family fled the war when he was just 4 years old; they lived in a refugee camp for a decade before finally coming to the United States.

platforms, geographically dispersed individuals spend more and more of their time in cyberspace (Appadurai, 1996; Oiarzabal & Reips, 2012). This electronically mediated environment enables people who are far from home to remain informed, to maintain their social networks, and even to hold onto a historical sense of ethnic identity that culturally distinguishes them from those with whom they share their daily routines in actual geographic space.

Globalization has given rise to **multi-sited ethnography**—the investigation and documentation of peoples and cultures embedded in the larger structures of a globalizing world, utilizing a range of methods in various locations of time and space. Researchers engaged in such mobile ethnography seek to capture the emerging global dimension by following individual actors, organizations, objects, images, stories, conflicts, and even pathogens as they move about in various interrelated transnational situations and locations (Marcus, 1995; Robben & Sluka, 2007). Refugee communities around the world also fall into this category (Figure 14.5).

One example of multi-sited ethnographic research on a diasporic ethnic group is a study on transnational Han Chinese identities by Chinese American anthropologist Andrea Louie. Louie's fieldwork carried her from San Francisco to Hong Kong to southern China—including her ancestral home in the Cantonese village Tiegang in Guangdong Province. Her paternal great-grandfather left the village in the 1840s, crossing the Pacific Ocean to work on railroad construction during the California Gold Rush. But other family members remained in their ancestral homeland. Here, Louie describes her research investigating Chinese identities from different and changing perspectives:

> My fieldwork on Chinese identities employed a type of mobile [ethnography] aimed at examining various parts of a "relationship" being forged anew across national boundaries that draws on metaphors of shared heritage and place.... I interviewed people in their homes and apartments; in cafes, culture centers, and McDonald's restaurants; and in rural Chinese villages and on jet planes, focusing on various moments and contexts of interaction within which multiple and often discrepant discourses of Chineseness are brought together. (Louie, 2004, pp. 8–9)

multi-sited ethnography The investigation and documentation of peoples and cultures embedded in the larger structures of a globalizing world, utilizing a range of methods in various locations of time and space.

Multi-sited ethnography has brought a greater interdisciplinary approach to fieldwork, including theoretical ideas and research methods from cultural studies, media studies, and mass communication. One example is the development of ethnographic studies of social networks, communicative practices, and other cultural expressions in cyberspace by means of digital visual and audio technologies. This **digital ethnography** is sometimes also referred to as *cyberethnography* or *netnography* (Murthy, 2011).

Even in the fast-changing, globalizing world of the 21st century, core ethnographic research methods developed over a century ago continue to be relevant and revealing. New technologies have been added to the anthropologist's toolkit, but the hallmarks of our discipline—holistic research through fieldwork with participant observation—is still a valued and productive tradition. Having presented a sweeping historical overview of shifting anthropological research challenges and strategies, we turn now to the topic of research methods.

Doing Ethnography

Every culture has underlying rules or standards that are rarely obvious. A major challenge to the anthropologist is to identify and analyze those rules. Fundamental to the effort is **ethnographic fieldwork**—extended on-location research to gather detailed and in-depth information on a society's customary ideas, values, and practices through participation in its collective social life.

Although the scope of cultural anthropology has expanded to include urban life in complex industrial and postindustrial societies, and even virtual communities in cyberspace, ethnographic methods developed for fieldwork in traditional small-scale societies continue to be central to anthropological research in all types of communities. The methodology still includes personal observation of and participation in the everyday activities of the community, along with interviews, mapping, collection of genealogical data, and recording of sounds and visual images. It all begins with selecting a research site and a research problem or question.

Site Selection and Research Question

Anthropologists usually work outside their own culture, society, or ethnic group, most often in a foreign country. This is because anthropological study within one's own society presents special problems, such as unsuspected biases that can result from private experiences and one's own social standing in the society. For this reason, anthropologists tend to begin their careers by first studying in other cultures. The more one learns of other cultures,

the more one gains a fresh and revealing perspective on one's own.

But wherever the site, research requires advance planning that usually includes obtaining funding and securing permission from the community to be studied (and, where mandated, permission from government officials as well). If possible, researchers make a preliminary trip to the site to make arrangements before moving there for more extended research.

After exploring the local conditions and circumstances, ethnographers have the opportunity to better define their specific research question or problem. For instance, what is the psychological impact of a new highway on members of a traditionally isolated farming community? Or how does the introduction of electronic media such as cell phones influence long-established gender relations in cultures with religious restrictions on social contact between men and women?

Preparatory Research

Before heading into the field, anthropologists do preparatory research. This includes delving into any existing written, visual, or audio information available about the people and place one has chosen to study. It may involve contacting and interviewing others who have some knowledge about or experience with the community, region, or country.

Because communication is key in ethnographic research, anthropologists need to learn the language used in the community selected for fieldwork. Many of the more than 6,000 languages currently spoken in the world have been recorded and written down, especially during the past century, so it is possible to learn some foreign languages prior to fieldwork. However, numerous native languages have not yet been written down. In such cases, researchers may be able to find someone who is minimally bilingual to help them gain some proficiency with the language. Another possibility is to first learn an already recorded and closely related language, which provides some elementary communication skills during the early phase of the actual fieldwork.

Importantly, anthropologists prepare for fieldwork by studying theoretical, historical, ethnographic, and other literature relevant to the proposed research. Having delved into the existing literature, they may then formulate a theoretical framework and research question to guide them in their fieldwork. Such was the case when U.S. anthropologist Napoleon Chagnon applied sociobiological theory to his study of violence within Yanomamö

digital ethnography An ethnographic study of social networks, communicative practices, and other cultural expressions in cyberspace by means of digital visual and audio technologies; also called *cyberethnography* or *netnography*.

ethnographic fieldwork Extended on-location research to gather detailed and in-depth information on a society's customary ideas, values, and practices through participation in its collective social life.

Indian communities in South America's tropical rainforest. Chagnon theorized that males with an aggressive reputation as killers were reproductively more successful than those without such a status (Chagnon, 1988a). Another U.S. anthropologist, Christopher Boehm, took a different theoretical approach in his research on blood revenge among Slavic mountain people in Montenegro. He framed his research question in terms of the ecological function of this violent tradition because it regulated relations between groups competing for survival in a harsh environment with scarce natural resources (Boehm, 1987).

Participant Observation: Ethnographic Tools and Aids

Once in the field, anthropologists rely on *participant observation*—a research method in which one learns about a group's behaviors and beliefs through social involvement and personal observation within the community, as well as interviews and discussion with individual members of the group over an extended stay in the community (Figure 14.6). This work requires an ability to socially and psychologically adapt to a community with a different way of life. Keen personal observation skills are also essential, skills that employ *all* the senses—sight, touch, smell, taste, and hearing—in order to perceive collective life in the other culture.

When participating in an unfamiliar culture, anthropologists are often helped by one or more generous individuals in the village or neighborhood. They may also be taken in by a family—or even adopted—and through participation in the daily routine of a household, they will gradually become familiar with the community's basic shared cultural features.

Anthropologists may also formally enlist the assistance of **key consultants**—members of the society being studied who provide information to help researchers understand the meaning of what they observe. (Early anthropologists referred to such individuals as *informants*.) These insiders help researchers unravel the mysteries of what at first is an unfamiliar, puzzling, and unpredictable world. To compensate local individuals for their help, fieldworkers may thank them for their time and expertise with goods, services, or cash.

Notebooks, pen/pencil, camera, and sound and video recorders are an anthropologist's most essential ethnographic tools in the field. Most also use laptop computers equipped with data processing programs. Typically,

Tara Mandala INC

Figure 14.6 Participant Observation
The hallmark research methodology for anthropologists is participant observation—illustrated by this photo of U.S. anthropologist Julia Jean (*center*), who is both observing *and* participating in a Hindu ritual at a temple for the goddess Kamakhya in northeastern India.

today's anthropological field kits also include GPS equipment, smartphones, and other handheld technological devices. And some researchers now incorporate small drones (flying robots) equipped with lightweight video cameras to collect data and document observations.

Researchers may focus on a particular cultural aspect or issue, but they will consider the culture as a whole for the sake of context. This holistic and integrative approach, a hallmark of anthropology, requires being tuned in to nearly countless details of daily life, both the ordinary and the extraordinary. By taking part in community life, anthropologists learn why and how events are organized and carried out. Through alert and sustained participation—carefully watching, questioning, listening, and analyzing over a period of time—they can usually identify, explain, and often even predict a group's behavior.

Data Gathering: The Ethnographer's Approach

Information collected by ethnographers falls into two main categories: quantitative and qualitative. **Quantitative data** consist of statistical or measurable information, such

---

key consultant A member of the society being studied who provides information that helps researchers understand the meaning of what they observe; early anthropologists referred to such an individual as an *informant*.

quantitative data Statistical or measurable information, such as demographic composition, the types and quantities of crops grown, or the ratio of spouses born and raised within or outside the community.

Courtesy of Jeffrey Snodgrass

Figure 14.7 Surveys in Cyberspace
U.S. anthropologist Jeffrey Snodgrass has been studying videogaming since 2008. Conducting participant observation research in and around the World of Warcraft (WoW), he has gathered information about this virtual community through interviewing and surveying its members. Snodgrass has been particularly fascinated by players' relationships to their WoW avatars, the in-game graphical representations of their characters. Via avatars, gamers can temporarily separate or even dissociate from their actual-world identities and enter WoW's fantasyscape. Here, Snodgrass (the pointy-eared Draenei shaman seated front left) and his virtual research team of graduate and undergraduate collaborators pose beneath WoW's Goblin Messiah.

as population density, demographic composition of people and animals, and the number and size of houses; the hours worked per day; the types and quantities of crops grown; the amount of carbohydrates or animal protein consumed per individual; the quantity of wood, dung, or other kinds of fuel used to cook food or heat dwellings; the number of children born out of wedlock; the ratio of spouses born and raised within or outside the community; and so on.

Qualitative data include nonstatistical information about features such as settlement patterns, natural resources, social networks of kinship relations, customary beliefs and practices, personal life histories, and so on. Often, these unquantifiable data are the most important part of ethnographic research because they capture the essence of a culture; this information provides us with deeper insights into the unique lives of different peoples, helping us understand what, why, and how they feel, think, and act in their own distinctive ways.

Taking Surveys

Unlike many other social scientists, anthropologists do not usually go into the field equipped with predetermined surveys or questionnaires. Those who use surveys usually do so after spending enough time on location to have gained the community's confidence and with the experience to compose a questionnaire with categories that are culturally relevant. Whether studying a community in geographic space or cyberspace, anthropologists who use surveys view them as one small part in a large research strategy that includes a considerable amount of qualitative data (Figure 14.7). They recognize that only by keeping an open mind while thoughtfully watching, listening, participating, and asking questions can they discover many aspects of a culture.

qualitative data Nonstatistical information such as personal life stories and customary beliefs and practices.

As fieldwork proceeds, anthropologists sort their complex impressions and observations into a meaningful whole, sometimes by formulating and testing limited or low-level hypotheses, but just as often by making use of imagination or intuition and following up on hunches. What is important is that the results are constantly checked for accuracy and consistency. If the parts fail to fit together in a way that is internally coherent, it may be that a mistake has been made and further inquiry is necessary.

Two studies of a village in Peru illustrate the problem of gathering data through surveys alone. A sociologist conducted one study by surveying the villagers with a questionnaire and concluded that people in the village invariably worked together on one another's privately owned plots of land. By contrast, a cultural anthropologist who lived in the village for over a year (including the brief period when the sociologist did his study) witnessed that particular practice of communal labor only once. The anthropologist's long-term participant observation revealed that although the idea of labor exchange relations was important to the people's sense of themselves, it was not a common economic practice (Chambers, 1995).

The point here is that questionnaires all too easily embody the concepts and categories of the researcher, usually an outsider, rather than those of the people being studied. Moreover, questionnaires tend to concentrate on what is measurable, answerable, and workable as a question, rather than probing the less obvious and more complex qualitative aspects of society or culture.

Finally, for a host of reasons—fear, ignorance, hostility, hope of reward—people may give false, incomplete, or biased information (Sanjek, 1990). Keeping culture-bound ideas, which are often embedded in standardized questionnaires, out of research methods is an important point in all ethnographic research.

Interviewing

Asking questions is fundamental to ethnographic fieldwork. Anthropologists pose questions in **informal interviews** (unstructured, open-ended conversations in everyday life) and in **formal interviews** (structured question-and-answer sessions carefully annotated as they occur and based on prepared questions). Informal interviews may be carried out at any time and in any place—on horseback, in a car or canoe, by a cooking fire, during ritual events, while walking through the community with a local inhabitant, and the list goes on. Such casual exchanges are essential, for it is often in these conversations that people share most freely. Moreover, the questions put forth in formal interviews typically grow out of cultural knowledge and insights gained during informal ones.

Getting people to open up is an art born of a genuine interest in both the information and the person who is sharing it. It requires dropping assumptions and cultivating an ability to *really* listen. It may require a willingness to be the "village idiot" by asking simple questions to which the answers seem obvious. Also, effective interviewers learn early on that numerous follow-up questions are vital given that first answers may mask truth rather than reveal it. Questions generally fall into one of two categories: *open-ended questions* (Can you tell me about your childhood?) and *closed questions* seeking specific pieces of information (Where and when were you born?).

Interviews are used to collect a vast range of cultural information: from life histories, genealogies, and myths to craft techniques and midwife practices to beliefs concerning everything from illness to food taboos. Genealogical information can be especially useful because it provides data about a range of social customs (such as cousin marriage), worldviews (such as ancestor worship), political relations (such as alliances), and economic arrangements (such as hunting or harvesting on clan-owned lands).

Researchers employ an **eliciting device**—an activity or object that encourages individuals to recall and share information. There are countless examples of eliciting devices: taking a walk with a local and asking about songs, legends, and place names linked to geographic features; sharing details about one's own family and neighborhood and inviting a telling in return; joining in a community activity and asking a local to explain the practice and why the participants are doing it; taking and sharing photographs of cultural objects or activities and asking locals to explain what they see in the pictures; presenting research findings to community members and documenting their responses.

Mapping

Many anthropologists have done fieldwork in remote places where there is little geographic documentation. Even if cartographers have mapped the region, standard maps seldom show geographic and spatial features that are culturally significant to the people living there. People inhabiting areas that form part of their ancestral homeland have a particular understanding of the area and their own names for local places. These native names may convey essential geographic information, describing the distinctive features of a locality such as its physical appearance, its specific dangers, or its precious resources.

Place names may derive from certain political realities such as headquarters, territorial boundaries, and so on. Others may make sense only in the cultural context of a local people's worldview as recounted in their myths, legends, songs, or other narrative traditions. Thus, to truly understand a place, some anthropologists make their own detailed geographic maps documenting culturally relevant features in the landscape inhabited by the people they

---

informal interview An unstructured, open-ended conversation in everyday life.

formal interview A structured question-and-answer session, carefully annotated as it occurs and based on prepared questions.

eliciting device An activity or object that encourages individuals to recall and share information.

study. In addition to mapping the local place names and geographic features, anthropologists may also map out information relevant to the local subsistence, such as animal migration routes, favorite fishing areas, and places where medicinal plants can be harvested or firewood can be cut.

Many anthropologists are involved in indigenous land use and occupancy studies for various reasons, including the documentation of traditional land claims. Researchers constructing individual map biographies may gather information from a variety of sources: local oral histories; early written descriptions of explorers, traders, missionaries, and other visitors; and data obtained from archaeological excavations.

One such ethnogeographic research project took place in northwestern Canada, during the planning stage of the building of the Alaska Highway natural gas pipeline. Because the line would cut directly though the lands of indigenous peoples, local community leaders and federal officials insisted that a study be conducted to determine how the new construction would affect native

inhabitants. Canadian anthropologist Hugh Brody, one of the researchers in this ethnogeographic study, explained:

> These maps are the key to the studies and their greatest contribution. Hunters, trappers, fishermen, and berry-pickers mapped out all the land they had ever used in their lifetimes, encircling hunting areas species by species, marking gathering location and camping sites—everything their life on the land had entailed that could be marked on a map. (Brody, 1981, p. 147)

Today, using global positioning system (GPS) technology, researchers can measure precise distances by triangulating the travel time of radio signals from various orbiting satellites. They can create maps that pinpoint human settlement locations and the layout of dwellings, gardens, public spaces, watering holes, pastures, surrounding mountains, rivers, lakes, seashores, islands, swamps, forests, deserts, and any other relevant feature in the regional environment (**Figure 14.8**).

Figure 14.8 **Collecting GPS Data**
For U.S. anthropologist Michael Heckenberger, doing fieldwork among the Kuikuro people of the upper Xingu River in the southern margins of the Amazon rainforest has become a collaborative undertaking. Together with other specialists on his research team, he has trained local tribespeople to help with the research project about their ancestral culture, which includes searching for the remains of ancient earthworks and mapping them. The photos above show trained local assistant Laquai Kuikuro collecting GPS data in a modern field of manioc—a dietary staple of indigenous Amazonian communities in Brazil—and later reviewing the downloaded data on a computer. On the left is a map showing GPS-charted indigenous earthworks in the upper Xingu region superimposed over a Landsat satellite image.

To store, edit, analyze, integrate, and display this geographically referenced spatial information, some anthropologists use cartographic digital technology or a geographic information system (GIS). A GIS makes it possible to map the geographic features and natural resources in a certain environment—and to link these data to ethnographic information about population density and distribution, social networks of kinship relations, seasonal patterns of land use, private or collective claims of ownership, travel routes, sources of water, and so on. With GIS, researchers can also integrate information about beliefs, myths, legends, songs, and other culturally relevant data associated with distinct locations. Moreover, they can create interactive inquiries for analysis of research data as well as natural and cultural resource management (Schoepfle, 2001).

Photographing and Filming

As already noted, during fieldwork, most anthropologists use cameras, as well as notepads, computers, or sound recording devices to document their observations. Photography has been instrumental in anthropological research for more than a century. For instance, in the early 1880s, Franz Boas took photographs during his first fieldwork among the Inuit in the Canadian Arctic. And just a few years after the invention of the moving picture camera in 1894, anthropologists began filming people in action—recording traditional dances and other ethnographic subjects of interest.

As film technology developed, anthropologists turned increasingly to visual media for a wide range of cross-cultural research purposes. Some employed still photography in community surveys and elicitation techniques. Others took film cameras into the field to document the disappearing world of traditional foragers, herders, and farmers surviving in remote places. A few focused their research on documenting traditional patterns of nonverbal communication such as body language and use of social space. Soon after the 1960 invention of the portable synchronous-sound camera, ethnographic filmmaking became increasingly important in producing a cross-cultural record of peoples all across the globe.

Since the digital revolution that began in the 1980s, there has been an explosive growth in visual media all across the world. It is not unusual for anthropologists to arrive in remote villages where at least a few native inhabitants take their own pictures or record their own stories and music. For researchers in the field, native-made audiovisual documents represent a wealth of precious cultural information. The Anthropologists of Note feature in this chapter details the long history of such equipment in anthropology.

Challenges of Ethnographic Fieldwork

Ethnographic fieldwork offers a range of opportunities to gain better and deeper insight into the community being studied, but it comes with a Pandora's box of challenges. As touched upon in Chapter 1, anthropologists in the field are likely to face physical, social, mental, political, and ethical challenges, all while having to remain fully engaged in work and social activities with the community. In the following paragraphs we offer details on some of the most common personal struggles anthropologists face in the field.

Social Acceptance

Having decided where to do ethnographic research and what to focus on, anthropologists embark on the journey to their field site. Typically moving into a community with a culture unlike their own, most experience **culture shock** (personal disorientation and anxiety) and loneliness at least during the initial stages of their work—work that requires them to establish social contacts with strangers who have little or no idea who they are, why they have come, or what they want from them. In short, visiting anthropologists are as much a mystery to those they intend to study as the group is to the researchers.

There is no sure way of predicting how one will be received, but it is certain that success in ethnographic fieldwork depends on mutual goodwill and the ability to develop friendships and other meaningful social relations. Anthropologists who are adopted into networks of kinship relations gain social access and certain rights—and assume social obligations associated with their new kinship status. These relationships can be deep and enduring, as illustrated by Smithsonian anthropologist William Crocker's description of his return to the Canela tribal community after a twelve-year absence. He had lived among these Amazonian Indians in Brazil off and on for a total of sixty-six months from the 1950s through the 1970s (**Figure 14.9**). When he stepped out of the single-motor missionary plane that had brought him back in 1991, he was quickly surrounded by Canela:

> Once on the ground, I groped for names and terms of address while shaking many hands. Soon my Canela mother, Tutkhwey (dove-woman), pulled me over to the shade of a plane's wing and pushed me down to a mat on the ground. She put both hands on my shoulders and, kneeling beside me, her head by mine, cried out words of mourning in a loud yodeling manner. Tears and phlegm dripped onto my shoulder and knees. According to a custom now abandoned by the younger women, she was crying for the loss of a grown daughter, Tsep-khwey (bat-woman), as well as for my return. (Crocker & Crocker, 2004, p. 1)

---

culture shock In fieldwork, the anthropologist's personal disorientation and anxiety, which may result in depression.

Figure 14.9 Social Acceptance in Fieldwork
U.S. anthropologist William Crocker did fieldwork among Canela Indians in Brazil over several decades. He still visits the community regularly. In this 1964 photograph, a Canela woman (M~i~i- kw'ej, or Alligator Woman) gives him a traditional haircut while other members of the community look on. She is the wife of his adoptive Canela "brother" and therefore a wife to Crocker in Canela kinship terms. Among the Canela, it is improper for a mother, sister, or daughter to cut a man's hair.

Since that reunion, Crocker has visited the Canela community every other year, always receiving a warm welcome and staying with locals. Although many anthropologists are successful in gaining social acceptance and even adoption status in communities where they do participant observation, they rarely go completely native and abandon their own homeland. Even after long stays in a community, and after learning to behave appropriately and communicate well, few become complete insiders.

Distrust and Political Tension

A particularly serious challenge in anthropological fieldwork is the possibility of getting caught in political rivalries and unwittingly used by factions within the community or being viewed with suspicion by government authorities who may interpret anthropologists' systematic inquiries as spying. For example, U.S. anthropologist June Nash has faced serious political and personal challenges doing fieldwork in various Latin American communities experiencing violent changes. As an outsider, she tried to avoid becoming embroiled in local conflicts but could not maintain her position as an impartial observer while researching a tin mining community in the Bolivian highlands. When the conflict between local miners and bosses controlling the armed forces became violent, Nash found herself in a revolutionary setting in which miners viewed her tape recorder as an instrument of espionage and suspected her of being a CIA agent (Nash, 1976).

All anthropologists face the overriding challenge of winning the trust that allows people to be themselves and share an unmasked version of their culture with a newcomer. Some do not succeed in meeting this challenge. So it was with U.S. anthropologist Lincoln Keiser in his difficult fieldwork in the remote town of Thull, situated in the mountains of northwestern Pakistan. Keiser ventured there to explore customary blood feuding among a Kohistani tribal community of 6,000 Muslims making their living by a mix of farming and herding in the rugged region. However, the people he had traveled so far to study did not want him there. As Keiser recounted, many of the fiercely independent and armed tribesmen in this area despised him as a foreign "infidel":

Throughout my stay in Thull, many people remained convinced I was a creature sent by the devil to harm the community.... [Doing fieldwork there] was a test I failed, for a *jirga* [political council] of my most vocal opponents ultimately forced me to leave Thull three months before I had planned.... Still, I learned from being hated. (Keiser, 1991, p. 103)

ANTHROPOLOGISTS OF NOTE

Margaret Mead (1901–1978) • Gregory Bateson (1904–1980)

From 1936 to 1938 **Margaret Mead** and **Gregory Bateson** did collaborative ethnographic fieldwork in Bali. Bateson, Mead's husband at the time, was a British anthropologist trained by Alfred C. Haddon, who led the 1898 Torres Strait expedition and is credited with making the first ethnographic film in the field. During their stay in Bali, Bateson took about 25,000 photographs and shot 22,000 feet of motion picture film, and in 1942 the couple coauthored the photographic ethnography *Balinese Character: A Photographic Analysis.*[a]

In 1938, after two years of fieldwork in Bali, Margaret Mead and Gregory Bateson began research in Papua New Guinea, where they staged this photograph of themselves to highlight the importance of cameras as part of the ethnographic toolkit. Note the camera on a tripod behind Mead and other cameras atop the desk.

Library of Congress, Prints and Photographs Division

That same year, Bateson worked as an anthropological film analyst studying German motion pictures. Soon Mead and a few other anthropologists became involved in thematic analysis of foreign fictional films. She later compiled a number of such visual anthropology studies in a coedited volume titled *The Study of Culture at a Distance.*[b]

Mead became a tireless promoter of the scholarly use of ethnographic photography and film. In 1960, the year the portable sync-sound film camera was invented, Mead was serving as president of the American Anthropology Association. In her presidential address at the association's annual gathering, she pointed out what she saw as shortcomings in the discipline and urged anthropologists to use cameras more effectively.[c] Chiding her colleagues for not fully utilizing new technological developments, she complained that anthropology had come "to depend on words, and words, and words."

Mead's legacy is commemorated in numerous venues, including the Margaret Mead Film Festival hosted annually since 1977 by the American Museum of Natural History in New York City. Thus, it was fitting that during the Margaret Mead Centennial celebrations in 2001 the American Anthropological Association endorsed a landmark visual media policy statement urging academic committees to consider ethnographic visuals—and not just ethnographic writings—when evaluating scholarly output of academics up for hire, promotion, and tenure.

[a] Bateson, G., & Mead, M. (1942). *Balinese character: A photographic analysis.* New York: New York Academy of Sciences.

[b] Mead, M., & Métraux, R. (Eds.). (1953). *The study of culture at a distance.* Chicago: University of Chicago Press.

[c] Mead, M. (1961, June). Anthropology among the sciences. *American Anthropologist* 63 (3), 475–482. Delivered as the presidential address at the annual meeting of the American Anthropological Association, November 18, 1960, Minneapolis.

Gender, Age, Ideology, Ethnicity, and Skin Color

The challenges of Keiser's fieldwork stemmed in part from his non-Muslim religious identity, marking him as an outsider in the local community. Gender, age, ethnicity, and skin color can also impact a researcher's access to a community. For instance, male ethnographers may face prohibitions or severe restrictions in interviewing women or observing certain women's activities. Similarly, a female researcher may not be welcomed into male communities with gender-segregation traditions. With respect to skin color, African American anthropologist Norris Brock Johnson encountered social obstacles while doing fieldwork in the American Midwest, but his dark skin helped him gain "admission to the world of black Caribbean shipwrights" on the island of Bequia, where he studied traditional boatmaking (Robben, 2007, p. 61; see also Johnson, 1984).

Physical Danger

Ethnographic fieldwork in exotic places can be an adventure, but sometimes it presents physical danger. Some anthropologists have died in the field due to accidents or illnesses—and a small handful have been killed (Embree, 1951; Price, 2011). An accident ended the life of U.S. anthropologist Michelle Rosaldo. As a 37-year-old mother and university professor, she returned to the Philippines for more fieldwork with the Ilongot. Trekking along a mountain trail on Luzon Island with her husband and fellow anthropologist, she slipped and fell to her death.

Figure 14.10 Dangerous Anthropology
Swedish anthropologist Anna Hedlund has done research in a range of politically tense and physically dangerous settings. Currently, she is investigating the culture of rebel groups in the DRC, focusing on how combatants define and legitimize violence. The work is based on extensive fieldwork in various military camps in South Kivu Province, eastern Congo. Here, we see her with combatants, pausing during a five-day trek to the rebel camp in the forest. Their faces have been blocked out to protect their identities.

Another tragic accident involved Richard Condon, part of an American and Russian research team funded by the U.S. National Science Foundation for an anthropological study of health, population growth, and socialization in Alaska and the Russian Far East. In the late summer of 1995, he and three colleagues, along with five Yup'ik Eskimos, were traveling along the Bering Strait when their *umiak* ("skin-boat") flipped. Apparently, a whale, which had been previously wounded by a party of seafaring Siberian Eskimo hunters, attacked their boat. All nine men perished in the ice-cold water (Wenzel & McCartney, 1996).

Swedish anthropologist Anna Hedlund faced danger of a different sort in recent years while researching rebel groups in the Democratic Republic of Congo (DRC) in Africa. Living among rebels and investigating how they define and legitimize violence, she was surrounded by political tension and conflict (Figure 14.10).

Subjectivity, Reflexivity, and Validation

Whether working near home or abroad, when endeavoring to identify the rules that underlie each culture, ethnographers must grapple with the very real challenge of bias or subjectivity—their own and that of members in the community being studied. Researchers are expected to constantly check their own personal or cultural biases and assumptions as they work—and to present these self-examinations along with their observations. This practice of critical self-reflection is known as *reflexivity*.

Because perceptions of reality may vary, an anthropologist must be careful in describing a culture. To do so accurately, the researcher needs to seek out and consider three kinds of data:

- The people's own understanding of their culture and the general rules they share: their ideal sense of the way their own society ought to be.
- The extent to which people believe they are observing those rules: how they think they really behave.
- The behavior that can be directly observed: what the anthropologist actually sees happening.

Clearly, the way people think they *should* behave, the way in which they think they *do* behave, and the way in which they *actually* behave may be different. By carefully examining and comparing these elements, anthropologists can draw up a set of rules that may explain the acceptable range of behavior within a culture.

Beyond the possibility of drawing false conclusions based on a group's ideal sense of itself, anthropologists run the risk of misinterpretation due to personal feelings and biases shaped by their own culture, as well as gender and age. It is important to recognize this challenge and make every effort to overcome it, for otherwise one may seriously misconstrue what one sees.

A case in point is the story of how male bias in the Polish culture in which Malinowski was raised caused him to ignore or miss significant factors in his pioneering study of the Trobrianders. Unlike today, when anthropologists receive special training before going into the field, Malinowski set out to do fieldwork in 1914 with little formal preparation. This chapter's Original Study, written by U.S. anthropologist Annette Weiner, who ventured to the same islands almost sixty years later, illustrates how gender can impact one's research findings—both in terms of the bias that may affect a researcher's outlook and in terms of what native consultants may feel comfortable sharing with a particular researcher.

ORIGINAL STUDY

The Importance of Trobriand Women BY ANNETTE B. WEINER

Walking into a village at the beginning of fieldwork is entering a world without cultural guideposts. The task of learning values that others live by is never easy. The rigors of fieldwork involve listening and watching, learning a new language of speech and actions, and most of all, letting go of one's own cultural assumptions in order to understand the meanings others give to work, power, death, family, and friends. During my fieldwork in the Trobriand Islands of Papua New Guinea, I wrestled doggedly with each of these problems—and with the added challenge that I was working in the footsteps of a celebrated anthropological ancestor, Bronislaw Kasper Malinowski....

In 1971, before my first trip to the Trobriands, I thought I understood many things about Trobriand customs and beliefs from having read Malinowski's exhaustive writings. Once there, however, I found that I had much more to discover. Finding significant differences in areas of importance, I gradually came to understand how he reached certain conclusions....

My most significant point of departure from Malinowski's analyses was the attention I gave to women's productive work. In my original research plans, women were not the central focus of study, but on the first day I took up residence in a village I was taken by them to watch a distribution of their own wealth—bundles of banana leaves and banana fiber skirts—which they exchanged with other women in commemoration of someone who had recently died. Watching that event forced me to take women's economic roles more seriously than I would have from reading Malinowski's studies.

Although Malinowski noted the high status of Trobriand women, he attributed their importance to the fact that Trobrianders reckon descent through women.... Yet he never considered that this significance was underwritten by women's own wealth because he did not systematically investigate the women's productive activities....

My taking seriously the importance of women's wealth not only brought women as the neglected half of society clearly into the ethnographic picture but also forced me to revise many of Malinowski's assumptions about Trobriand men.... For Malinowski, the basic relationships within a Trobriand family were guided by the matrilineal principle of "mother-right" and "father-love." A father was called "stranger" and had little authority over his own children. A woman's brother was the commanding figure and exercised control over his sister's sons....

In my study of Trobriand women and men, a different configuration of reckoning descent through the maternal line emerged. A Trobriand father is not a "stranger" in

Estate of Annette B. Weiner

In the Trobriand Islands, women's wealth consists of banana leaves and banana-fiber skirts, large quantities of which must be given away upon the death of a relative.

At the same time, this giving creates obligations on the part of a man's children toward him that last even beyond his death. Thus, the roles that men and their children play in each other's lives are worked out through extensive cycles of exchanges, which define the strength of their relationships to each other and eventually benefit the other members of both their matrilineages. Central to these exchanges are women and their wealth.

...Only recently have anthropologists begun to understand the importance of taking women's work seriously. The "women's point of view" was largely ignored in the study of gender roles because anthropologists generally perceived women as living in the shadows of men—occupying the private rather than the public sectors of society, rearing children rather than engaging in economic or political pursuits.

Malinowski's definition, nor is he a powerless figure. The father is one of the most important persons in his child's life, and remains so even after his child grows up and marries. He gives his child many opportunities to gain things from his matrilineage, thereby adding to the available resources that he or she can draw upon.

Adapted from Weiner, A. B. (1988). *The Trobrianders of Papua New Guinea* (pp. 4–7). New York: Holt, Rinehart & Winston. Reprinted by permission of Cengage Learning.

As the Original Study makes clear, determining the accuracy of anthropological descriptions and conclusions can be difficult. In the natural sciences, scientists can replicate observations and experiments to try to establish the reliability of other researchers' conclusions. Thus, scientists can see for themselves whether their colleagues have gotten it right. But validating ethnographic research is uniquely challenging because access to sites may be limited or barred altogether, due to a number of factors: insufficient funding, logistical difficulties in reaching the site, problems in obtaining permits, and changing cultural and environmental conditions. These factors mean that what could be observed in a certain context at a certain time cannot be observed at others. As a result, one researcher cannot easily confirm the reliability or completeness of another's account.

For this reason, anthropologists bear a heavy responsibility for factual reporting, including disclosing key issues related to their research: Why was a particular location selected as a research site and for which research objectives? What were the local conditions during fieldwork? Who provided the key information and major insights? How were data collected and recorded? Without such background information, it is difficult to judge the validity of the account and the soundness of the researcher's conclusions.

Completing an Ethnography

After collecting ethnographic information, the next challenge is to piece together all that has been gathered into a coherent narrative that accurately describes the culture. Traditionally, ethnographies are detailed written descriptions composed of chapters on topics such as the circumstances and place of fieldwork itself; historical background; the community or group today; its natural environment; settlement patterns; subsistence practices; networks of kinship relations and other forms of social organization; marriage and sexuality; economic exchanges; political institutions; myths, sacred beliefs, and ceremonies; and current developments. These may be illustrated with photographs and accompanied by maps, kinship diagrams, and figures showing social and political organizational structures, settlement layout, floor plans of dwellings, seasonal cycles, and so on.

Sometimes ethnographic research is documented not only in writing but also with sound recordings and on film. Visual records may be used for documentation and illustration as well as for analysis or as a means of gathering additional information in interviews. Moreover, footage shot for the sake of documentation and research

Figure 14.11 Anthropologist-Filmmaker Hu Tai-Li
An award-winning pioneer of ethnographic films in Taiwan, Tai-Li is a professor at National Chin-Hua University. She has directed and produced a half-dozen documentaries on a range of topics— including traditional rituals and music, development issues, and national and ethnic identity. Here she is filming the Maleveq ("Five-Year Worship") rituals in the village of Kulalao, southern Taiwan. During this ceremony, lasting several days, indigenous Paiwan people celebrate their alliance with tribal ancestors and deities. Traditional belief holds that ancestral spirits attend this gathering; villagers beseech their blessings, welcoming them with special songs, dances, and food.

Institute of Ethnology

may be edited into a documentary film. Not unlike a written ethnography, such a film is a structured whole composed of numerous selected sequences, visual montage, juxtaposition of sound and visual image, and narrative sequencing, all coherently edited into an accurate visual representation of the ethnographic subject (El Guindi, 2004) (Figure 14.11).

In recent years anthropologists have experimented with various digital media (Ginsburg, Abu-Lughod, & Larkin, 2009). The emergence of digital technologies has vastly enhanced the potential for anthropological research, interpretation, and presentation. Digital recording devices provide ethnographers with a wealth of material to analyze and utilize in building hypotheses. They also open the door to sharing findings in varied and interactive ways, including DVDs, online photo essays, podcasts, and video blogs.

Building Ethnological Theories

Largely descriptive in nature, ethnography provides the basic data needed for *ethnology*—the branch of cultural anthropology that makes cross-cultural comparisons and develops theories that explain why certain important

differences or similarities occur between groups. As noted in Chapter 1, the end product of quality anthropological research is a coherent statement about culture or human nature that provides an explanatory framework or **theory** for understanding the ideas and actions of the people being studied. As discussed in Chapter 1, theory is distinct from doctrine and dogma, which are assertions of opinions or beliefs formally handed down by an authority as indisputably true and accepted as a matter of faith.

Anthropologists do not claim that any one theory about culture is the absolute truth. Rather they judge or measure a theory's validity and soundness by varying degrees of probability; what is considered to be true is what is most probable. But although anthropologists are reluctant to make absolute statements about complex issues such as exactly how cultures function or change, they can and do provide fact-based evidence about whether assumptions have support or are unfounded. Therefore, a *theory*, contrary to widespread misuse of the term, is much more than mere speculation; it is a critically examined explanation of observed reality.

Always open to future challenges born of new evidence or insights, scientific theory depends on demonstrable, empirical evidence and repeated testing. So it is that, as our cross-cultural knowledge expands, the odds favor some anthropological theories over others. Old explanations or interpretations must sometimes be discarded as new theories based on better or more complete

---

theory A coherent statement that provides an explanatory framework for understanding; an explanation or interpretation supported by a reliable body of data.

evidence are shown to be more effective or probable. Last but not least, theories also guide anthropologists in formulating new research questions and help them decide what data to collect and how to give meaning to their data.

Ethnology and the Comparative Method

Theories in anthropology may be generated from world-wide cross-cultural or historical comparisons or even comparisons with other species. For instance, anthropologists may examine a global sample of societies in order to discover whether a hypothesis proposed to explain certain phenomena is supported by fact-based evidence. Of necessity, cross-cultural researchers depend upon evidence gathered by other scholars as well as their own findings.

A key resource that makes this possible is the Human Relations Area Files (HRAF), which is a vast collection of cross-indexed ethnographic, biocultural, and archaeological data catalogued by cultural characteristics and geographic location. This ever-growing data bank classifies more than 700 cultural characteristics and includes nearly 400 societies, past and present, from all around the world. Archived in about 300 libraries (on microfiche and/or online) and approaching a million pages of information, the HRAF facilitates comparative research on almost any cultural feature imaginable—warfare, subsistence practices, settlement patterns, marriage, rituals, and so on.

Among other things, anthropologists interested in finding explanations for certain social or cultural beliefs and practices can use the HRAF to test their hypotheses. For example, Peggy Reeves Sanday examined a sample of 156 societies drawn from the HRAF in an attempt to answer her comparative research questions concerning dominance and gender in different societies. Her study, published in 1981 (*Female Power and Male Dominance*), disproves the common misperception that women are universally subordinate to men, sheds light on the way men and women relate to each other, and ranks as a major landmark in the study of gender.

Cultural comparisons are not restricted to contemporary ethnographic data. Indeed, anthropologists frequently turn to archaeological or historical data to test hypotheses about cultural change. Cultural characteristics thought to be caused by certain specified conditions can be tested archaeologically by investigating similar situations where such conditions actually occurred. Also useful are data provided in *ethnohistories*, which are studies of cultures of the recent past through oral histories; accounts of explorers, missionaries, and traders; and analysis of records such as land titles, birth and death records, and other archival materials.

A Brief Overview of Anthropology's Theoretical Perspectives

In the previous chapter, we presented the barrel model of culture as a dynamic system of adaptation in which social structure, infrastructure, and superstructure intricately interact. Helping us to imagine culture as an integrated whole, this model allows us to think about something very complex by reducing it to a simplified scheme or basic design. Although most anthropologists generally conceptualize culture as holistic and integrative, they may have very different takes on the relative significance of different elements that make up the whole and exactly how they relate to one another.

Entire books have been written about each of anthropology's numerous theoretical perspectives. Here we offer a general overview to convey the scope of anthropological theories and their role in explaining and interpreting cultures.

Mentalist Perspective

When analyzing a culture, some argue that humans act primarily on the basis of their ideas, concepts, or symbolic representations. In their research and analysis, these anthropologists usually emphasize that to understand or explain why humans behave as they do, one must first get into other people's heads and try to understand how they imagine, think, feel, and speak about the world in which they live. Because of the primacy of the superstructure (ideas, values), this is known as an *idealist* or **mentalist perspective**.

Examples of mentalist perspectives include psychological and cognitive anthropology (culture and personality), ethnoscience, structuralism, and postmodernism, as well as symbolic and interpretive anthropology. For example, in *structuralism*, as formulated by French anthropologist Claude Lévi-Strauss, culture is analyzed as a product of the human brain's mental structure that makes us conceptualize our world and social reality in terms of binary opposites (such as life/death, day/night, hot/cold, male/female, friend/enemy, raw/cooked) and their mediations (through myth, kinship, law, and so forth).

Another mentalist perspective, *interpretive anthropology*, most famously associated with U.S. anthropologist Clifford Geertz, views humans primarily as "symbolizing, conceptualizing, and meaning-seeking" creatures (Geertz, 1973, p. 5). Geertz developed an artful ethnographic research strategy in which a culturally significant event or

mentalist perspective A theoretical approach stressing the primacy of superstructure in cultural research and analysis; also known as the *idealist perspective*.

social drama (for instance, a Balinese cockfight) is chosen for observation and analysis as a form of "deep play" that may provide essential cultural insights. Peeling back layer upon layer of socially constructed meanings, the anthropologist offers what Geertz calls a "thick description" of the event in a detailed ethnographic narrative.

Materialist Perspective

Many other anthropologists hold a theoretical perspective in which they stress explaining culture by first analyzing the material conditions that they see as determining people's lives. They may begin their research with an inventory of available natural resources for food and shelter, the number of mouths to feed and bodies to keep warm, the tools used in making a living, and so on. Anthropologists who highlight such environmental or economic factors in shaping cultures share a **materialist perspective**.

Examples of materialist theoretical approaches include Marxism, neo-evolutionism, cultural ecology, sociobiology, and cultural materialism. In *cultural ecology*, for instance, anthropologists focus primarily on the subsistence mechanisms in a culture that enable a group to successfully adapt to its natural environment. Building on cultural ecology, some anthropologists include considerations of political economy such as industrial production, capitalist markets, wage labor, and finance capital. A *political economy* perspective is closely associated with Marxist theory, which essentially explains major societal changes as the result of growing conflicts between opposing social classes, namely those who possess property and those who do not.

One result of widening the scope—combining cultural ecology and political economy to take into account the emerging world systems of international production and trade relations—is known as *political ecology*. Closely related is *cultural materialism*, a theoretical research strategy identified with Marvin Harris (1979). Placing primary emphasis on the role of environment, demography, technology, and economy in determining a culture's mental and social conditions, Harris argues that anthropologists can best explain ideas, values, and beliefs as adaptations to economic and environmental conditions (see the Biocultural Connection).

Other Theoretical Perspectives

Not all anthropological perspectives fall neatly into mentalist or materialist camps. For example, some give priority to social structure, focusing on this middle layer in our barrel model. Although it is difficult to pigeonhole

various perspectives in this group, theoretical explanations worked out by pioneering French social thinkers influenced the development of several *structural-functionalist* theories that focus on the underlying patterns or structures of social relationships, attributing functions to cultural institutions in terms of the contributions they make toward maintaining a group's social order.

Beyond these three general groups, there are various other anthropological approaches. Some stress the importance of identifying general patterns or even discovering laws. Early anthropologists believed that they could discover such laws by means of the theory of *unilinear cultural evolution* of universal human progress, beginning with what was then called "savagery," followed by "barbarism," and gradually making progress toward a condition of human perfection known as "high civilization" (Carneiro, 2003).

Although anthropologists have long abandoned such sweeping generalizations as unscientific and ethnocentric, some continued to search for universal laws in the general development of human cultures by focusing on technological development as measured in the growing capacity for energy capture per capita of the population. This theoretical perspective is sometimes called *neo-evolutionism*. Others seek to explain recurring patterns in human social behavior in terms of laws of natural selection by focusing on possible relationships with human genetics, a theoretical perspective identified with *sociobiology*. Yet others stress that broad generalizations are impossible because each culture is distinct and can only be understood as resulting from unique historical processes and circumstances. Some even go a step further and focus on in-depth description and analysis of personal life histories of individual members in a group in order to reveal the work of a culture.

Beyond these cultural historical approaches, there are other theoretical perspectives that do not aim for laws or generalizations to explain culture. Theoretical perspectives that reject measuring and evaluating different cultures by means of some sort of universal standard, and that stress that cultures can only be explained or interpreted in their own unique terms, are associated with the important anthropological principle known as *cultural relativism*, discussed in the previous chapter.

Ethical Responsibilities in Anthropological Research

As explained in this chapter, anthropologists obtain information about different peoples and their cultures through long-term, full-immersion fieldwork based on personal observation of and participation in the everyday activities of the community. They are usually befriended and sometimes even adopted, gradually becoming familiar with the local social structures and cultural features and even with

---

materialist perspective A theoretical approach stressing the primacy of infrastructure (material conditions) in cultural research and analysis.

Pig Lovers and Pig Haters BY MARVIN HARRIS

In the Old Testament of the Bible, the Israelite's God (Yahweh) denounced the pig as an unclean beast that pollutes if tasted or touched. Later, Allah conveyed the same basic message to his prophet Muhammad. Among millions of Jews and Muslims today, the pig remains an abomination, even though it can convert grains and tubers into high-grade fats and protein more efficiently than any other animal.

What prompted condemnation of an animal whose meat is relished by the greater part of humanity? For centuries, the most popular explanation was that the pig wallows in its own urine and eats excrement. But linking this to religious abhorrence leads to inconsistencies. Cows kept in a confined space also splash about in their own urine and feces.

These inconsistencies were recognized in the 12th century by Maimonides, a widely respected Jewish philosopher and physician in Egypt, who said God condemned swine as a public health measure because pork had "a bad and damaging effect upon the body." The mid-1800s discovery that eating undercooked pork caused trichinosis appeared to verify Maimonides's reasoning. Reform-minded Jews then renounced the taboo, convinced that if well-cooked pork did not endanger public health, eating it would not offend God.

Scholars have suggested this taboo stemmed from the idea that the animal was once considered divine—but this explanation falls short since sheep, goats, and cows were also once worshiped in the Middle East, and their meat is enjoyed by all religious groups in the region.

I think the real explanation for this religious condemnation lies in the fact that pig farming threatened the integrity of the basic cultural and natural ecosystems of the Middle East. Until their conquest of the Jordan Valley in Palestine over 3,000 years ago, the Israelites were nomadic herders, living almost entirely from sheep, goats, and cattle. Like all pastoralists, they maintained close relationships with sedentary farmers who held the oases and the great rivers. With this mixed farming and pastoral complex, the pork prohibition constituted a sound ecological strategy. The pastoralists could not raise pigs in their arid habitats, and among the semi-sedentary farming populations pigs were more of a threat than an asset.

The basic reason for this is that the world zones of pastoral nomadism correspond to unforested plains and hills that are too arid for rainfall agriculture and that cannot easily be irrigated. The domestic animals best adapted to these zones are ruminants (including cattle, sheep, and goats), which can digest grass, leaves, and other cellulose foods more effectively than other mammals.

The pig, however, is primarily a creature of forests and shaded riverbanks. Although it is omnivorous, its best weight gain is from foods low in cellulose (nuts, fruits, tubers, and especially grains), making it a direct competitor of man. It cannot subsist on grass alone and is ill-adapted to the hot, dry climate of the grasslands, mountains, and deserts in the Middle East. To compensate for its lack of protective hair and an inability to sweat, the pig must dampen its skin with external moisture. It prefers to do this by wallowing in fresh clean mud, but will cover its skin with its own urine and feces if nothing else if available. So there is some truth to the theory that the religious uncleanliness of the pig rests upon actual physical dirtiness.

Among the ancient mixed farming and pastoralist communities of the Middle East, domestic animals were valued primarily as sources of milk, cheese, hides, dung, fiber, and traction for plowing. Goats, sheep, and cattle provided all of this, plus an occasional supplement of lean meat. From the beginning, therefore, pork must have been a luxury food, esteemed for its succulent, tender, and fatty qualities.

Between 4,000 and 9,000 years ago, the human population in the Middle East increased sixty-fold. Extensive deforestation accompanied this rise, largely due to damage caused by sheep and goat herds. Shade and water, the natural conditions appropriate for raising pigs, became ever more scarce, and pork became even more of a luxury.

The Middle East is the wrong place to raise pigs, but pork remains a luscious treat. People find it difficult to resist such temptations on their own. Hence Yahweh and Allah were heard to say that swine were unclean—unfit to eat or touch. In short, it was ecologically maladaptive to try to raise pigs in substantial numbers, and small-scale production would only increase the temptation. Better then, to prohibit the consumption of pork entirely.

Biocultural Question

Consider a taboo you follow and come up with an explanation for it other than the conventional one that most people accept.

Adapted from Harris, M. (1989). *Cows, pigs, wars, and witches: The riddles of culture* (pp. 35–60). New York: Vintage Books/Random House.

highly personal or politically sensitive details known only to trusted insiders.

Because the community is usually part of a larger and more powerful complex society, anthropological knowledge about how the locals live, what they own, what motivates them, and how they are organized has the potential to make the community vulnerable to exploitation and manipulation. In this context, it is good to be reminded of the ancient Latin saying *scientia potentia est* ("knowledge is power"). In other words, anthropological knowledge may have far-reaching, and possibly negative, consequences for the peoples being studied.

Are there any rules that may guide anthropologists in their ethical decision making and help them judge right from wrong? This important issue is addressed in the code of ethics of the American Anthropological Association (discussed in Chapter 1). First formalized in 1971 and modified in its current form in 1998, this document outlines the various ethical responsibilities and moral obligations of anthropologists, including this central principle: "Anthropological researchers must do everything in their power to ensure that their research does not harm the safety, dignity, or privacy of the people with whom they work, conduct research, or perform other professional activities."

The first step in this endeavor is to communicate in advance the nature, purpose, and potential impact of the planned study to individuals who provide information—and to obtain their informed consent or formal recorded agreement to participate in the research. But protecting the community one studies requires more than that; it demands constant vigilance and alertness. There are some situations in which this is particularly challenging—including working for a global business corporation, international bank, or government agency, such as the foreign service, police, or military (American Anthropological Association, 2007; González, 2009; McFate, 2007). This challenge came to the fore again when the U.S. government recruited social scientists, including anthropologists, to assist the military in understanding the complexities of the "human terrain" in armed conflict environments such as Afghanistan and Iraq (Figure 14.12).

Because anthropologists generally disapprove of politicizing ethnographic information and are committed to the ideal of "do no harm," the idea of militarizing anthropology in arenas of violent conflict has sparked intense debate. It may not be possible to fully anticipate all the cross-cultural and long-term consequences—uses and abuses—of one's research findings. Navigating this ethical gray area is often difficult, but it is each anthropologist's responsibility to be aware of moral responsibilities and to take every possible precaution to ensure that one's research does not jeopardize the well-being of the people being studied.

Figure 14.12 Militarizing Anthropology
Embedded in U.S. Army units, social scientists, including anthropologists, have conducted sociocultural assessments as part of the "human terrain system" (HTS). Designed to improve the military's ability to understand the complexities of the human terrain (civilian population) as it applied to operations in Iraq and Afghanistan, HTS was part of a counterinsurgency strategy against regional insurgents from 2006 through 2014. Anthropological involvement in the U.S. government's struggle for hearts and minds in war zones has been controversial since the mid-1960s. Here we see U.S. HTS team member Ted Callahan talking to local residents about a tribal dispute in Paktya Province, Afghanistan.

CHAPTER CHECKLIST

What was the worldwide social context in which anthropology emerged as a discipline?

✓ Anthropology emerged during the heyday of colonialism (1870s–1930s). Europeans focused on the study of traditional peoples in overseas colonies they controlled, whereas North Americans focused primarily on the indigenous communities in their own countries.

✓ Expecting that indigenous cultures would disappear through the impositions of colonialism, early anthropologists engaged in salvage ethnography (documenting endangered cultures); this is now known as urgent anthropology. In the 1930s, anthropologists began studying culture contact—how traditional cultures change when coming in contact with expanding capitalist societies. In the United States, this has become known as acculturation.

✓ Applied anthropology—using anthropological knowledge and methods to solve practical problems in communities—came to the fore in the 1930s as dominant societies tried to understand traditional indigenous cultures in order to control them more effectively.

How have ethnographic research approaches changed and expanded since the discipline began?

✓ As a result of World War II and the Cold War era following, some anthropologists began studies of cultures at a distance, developing national character studies through investigating film, literature, and newspapers.

✓ Anthropologists also began broadening their focus, including turning their attention to modern state societies and investigating in their own countries, in settings ranging from factories to farming communities to suburban neighborhoods. For example, Powdermaker's research on racism in the South in the 1930s and her investigation of the Hollywood film industry, as well as Métraux's international team studying contemporary race relations in Brazil, typify a new understanding of the role of anthropology.

How have anthropologists attempted to address the negative effects of massive cultural change imposed on less powerful groups by elite cultures?

✓ In the 1950s anthropologists began studying peasants to understand the impact of complex state societies on traditional indigenous groups.

✓ Recognizing that their knowledge could be used to help people in ways defined by the people themselves, some anthropologists took up advocacy anthropology—research that is community based and politically involved.

✓ Some anthropologists, such as Laura Nader, have urged *studying up*—ethnographic research in the world's centers of political and economic power—to reveal how elites function in maintaining their positions.

How do anthropologists conduct their ethnographic research today?

✓ Multi-sited ethnography investigates and documents peoples and cultures embedded in the larger structures of a globalizing world. Ethnography, a detailed description of a particular culture, relies upon fieldwork—extended on-location research to gather detailed and in-depth information on a society's customary ideas, values, and practices through participation in its collective social life.

✓ Participant observation is learning about a group's behaviors and beliefs through social involvement and personal observation with the community, as well as interviews and discussions with individual members of the group over an extended stay in the community. Key consultants (previously called informants) are individuals in the society being studied who provide information that helps researchers understand what they observe.

✓ Ethnographers gather two types of data: Quantitative data consist of population density; qualitative data describe features such as social networks of kinship relations, customary beliefs and practices, and personal life histories.

✓ Interviewing can be either informal (unstructured, open-ended conversations in everyday life) or formal (structured question/answer sessions). Ethnographic mapping goes beyond standard mapmaking to show geographic and spatial features that are culturally significant to the people living there, such as place names and stories about locations.

✓ Most anthropologists use cameras as well as notepads, computers, or sound recording devices to document their observations. Today's anthropologists routinely carry digital recording equipment to the field and invite and train local members of the community to help with recording.

What challenges do ethnographers face?

✓ Culture shock and not being socially accepted by the society are common ethnographic difficulties. A major step toward being accepted and gaining access to information is being adopted into a network of kinship relations.

✓ Anthropologists must avoid getting involved in political rivalries and unwittingly used by factions within the community.

✓ An ethnographer's age, ideology, ethnicity, or skin color may block access to a community's individuals or ideas.

✓ Ethnographers may also be in physical danger through illness, accident, and occasional hostility.

✓ Ethnographers grapple with the challenge of bias or subjectivity—their own and that of members of the community being challenged.

✓ Validating ethnographic research is uniquely challenging because subsequent access to sites may be limited or barred altogether.

What is involved in producing an ethnographic study?

✓ Traditionally, ethnographies are written narratives, illustrated with photographs and accompanied by maps, kinship diagrams, and figures showing social and political organizational structures, settlement layout, seasonal cycles, and so on.

✓ More and more often today, ethnographic research is documented not only in writing but also with sound recordings and on film.

What is involved in doing ethnology?

✓ Ethnography provides the basic data needed for ethnology—the branch of cultural anthropology that makes cross-cultural comparisons and develops theories that explain why certain important differences or similarities occur between groups. Theories—coherent statements providing explanations for these differences or similarities—are developed through ethnology.

✓ Ethnology relies on the comparative method. Theories in anthropology may be generated from worldwide cross-cultural or historical comparisons or even comparisons with other species.

✓ The Human Relations Area Files is a vast collection of cross-indexed ethnographic, biocultural, and archaeological data catalogued by cultural characteristics and geographic location.

What are the key theoretical perspectives in anthropology?

✓ The two broadest categories of anthropological theory are mentalist and materialist.

✓ The mentalist perspective stresses the primacy of superstructure in cultural research and analysis.

✓ The materialist perspective stresses the primacy of infrastructure (material conditions) in cultural research and analysis.

What are the ethical responsibilities in anthropological research?

✓ The ethical code of the American Anthropological Association outlines the various ethical responsibilities and moral obligations of anthropologists.

✓ The central principle of the AAA ethics code is to ensure that anthropological research does not negatively impact the people being studied.

QUESTIONS FOR REFLECTION

1. Taking on the challenge of describing and interpreting human cultures, anthropologists have long relied on ethnographic fieldwork, including participant observation, as depicted in this chapter's opening photograph. What makes this research method uniquely challenging and effective? Of what use might the findings be for meeting the unique challenges of our globalizing world?

2. Early anthropologists engaged in salvage ethnography (urgent anthropology) to create a reliable record of indigenous cultures once widely expected to vanish. Although many indigenous communities did lose customary practices due to acculturation, descendants of those cultures can now turn to anthropological records to revitalize their ancestral ways of life. Do you think this is a good thing? Why or why not?

3. If you were invited to "study up," on which cultural group would you focus? How would you go about getting access to that group for participant observation, and what serious obstacles might you encounter?

4. In light of professional ethics, what moral dilemmas might anthropologists face in choosing to advise a government in exploring or implementing a nonviolent solution to a military conflict? How is military anthropology different from other forms of applied anthropology, such as working for the Foreign Service, the World Bank, the Roman Catholic Church, or an international business corporation such as IBM and Intel?

DIGGING INTO ANTHROPOLOGY

Your Own Multi-Sited Community

The 21st century is marked by rapid world change driven by digital technological innovations that are transforming the way we experience time and space, how we communicate, where we work, how we inform and entertain ourselves, where we travel, and how we pay for almost all that we do or need. Many of us are in touch with distant relatives and friends, some of whom are on the move for reasons of labor, leisure, or as refugees escaping from danger or poverty. Digging into your own "multi-sited" social network, mark the geographic locations of about three dozen relatives, friends, and acquaintances on a map. Then select six individuals in that network and divide them into three groups: two with whom you share your residence; two with whom you interact at school, work, or for leisure; and two with whom you exchange texts and pictures but rarely if ever see in person. Next, make note of your own daily routine (the what, when, where of meals, work, transportation and movement, and so on). Then, based on that list, use your everyday technology to dig into the daily routine of the six people in your network. Record and compare the information you have gathered, and draw your own conclusion about the similarities and differences in the daily lives of people in your own multi-sited community.

Pietro Scozzari/Age fotostock/Alamy

CHALLENGE ISSUE

As social creatures dependent upon one another for survival, we humans face the challenge of processing and sharing large amounts of information about countless things connected to our well-being in a multiplicity of situations. We do this with a variety of distinctive gestures, sounds, touches, and body postures. Our most sophisticated means of communication is through language—a foundation stone of every human culture. As shown in this photo of a busy street in Chinatown, an ethnic enclave in Thailand's capital city of Bangkok, success in international trade and tourism often depends on multilingual communication. To attract buyers, local merchants advertise their goods and services in three languages, each with a distinctive script: Thai, English, and Chinese. For more than 400 years, traders venturing overseas from China's coastal cities have formed bustling commercial centers in densely populated urban ghettos known as Chinatowns. Such sites can be found in major cities on every continent, from Amsterdam, Jakarta, and Johannesburg, to Lima, Melbourne, Mumbai, Nagasaki, San Francisco, and Toronto. These are just a few important cities in China's expanding global trading empire.

Language and Communication

The human ability to communicate through language rests firmly on our biological makeup. We are "programmed" for language, be it through sounds or gestures. (Sign languages, such as American Sign Language or ASL, are fully developed languages in their own right.) Beyond the cries of babies, which are not learned but which do communicate, humans must learn their language. So it is that children from anywhere in the world readily acquire the language of their culture.

Language is a system of communication using symbolic sounds, gestures, or marks that are put together according to certain rules, resulting in meanings that are intelligible to all who share that language. As discussed in a previous chapter, these sounds, gestures, and marks are *symbols*—signs that are arbitrarily linked to something else and represent it in a meaningful way. For example, the word *crying* is a symbol, a combination of sounds to which we assign the meaning of a particular action and which we can use to communicate that meaning, whether or not anyone around us is actually crying.

A **signal**, unlike a culturally learned symbol, or meaningful sign, is an instinctive sound or gesture that has a natural or self-evident meaning. A scream, a sigh, and a cough, for example, are sound signals that convey some kind of emotional or physical state. Throughout the animal kingdom, species communicate essential information by means of signals.

Over the past few decades, researchers aiming to understand the biological basis, social use, and evolutionary development of language have investigated a fascinating array of animal communication systems, including dolphin whistles, whale songs, elephant rumbles, bee dances, and orangutan gestures. Some have studied language acquisition aptitude among apes by teaching them to communicate using ASL or lexigrams (symbols) on keyboard devices. As noted in Chapter 4, their research makes it clear that although great ape species cannot literally speak, they can develop language skills to the level of a 2- to 3-year-old human child.

language A system of communication using symbolic sounds, gestures, or marks that are put together according to certain rules, resulting in meanings that are intelligible to all who share that language.

signal An instinctive sound or gesture that has a natural or self-evident meaning.

In this chapter you will learn to

- Define language and distinguish between sign and symbol.

- Specify the three branches of linguistic anthropology.

- Observe cross-cultural differences in nonverbal means of communication.

- Trace the emergence of language, speech, and writing.

- Assess the close relationship between culture and language.

- Discuss the significance of literacy and telecommunication in today's world.

A remarkable example of the many scientific efforts under way in this area is the work being done with Chantek, an orangutan who has learned some 150 gestures, many of which he puts together in innovative ways. Featured in the Original Study, his story illustrates the creative process of language development and the capacity of a nonhuman primate to recognize symbols (see also Cartmill & Byrne, 2010).

ORIGINAL STUDY

Can Chantek Talk in Codes? *BY H. LYN WHITE MILES*

My foster son is a confused adolescent gang member who sometimes finds himself in trouble. On one occasion, he was locked up and tried to escape—not to do any real harm but to have some fun. When I arrived to see what had happened, Chantek told me he was thirsty and angrily mentioned the "key man" who could set him free. In a few hesitant words, he recounted how he got "out" and how he "broke" some things. While fixing his gaze on the door, he asked, "Where are the keys?" When I explained that I didn't have them, he leaned on one arm, looked warily around, gestured toward the door, and whispered, "You—*secret* open?" He was asking me to assist in his second "escape" for the day.

Chantek (*left*) is now an adult male orangutan, as evidenced by his size and large cheek pads. Here we see him with Dumadi, an infant in his group at Zoo Atlanta.

My unusual foster son is an orangutan, Chantek, who belongs to the *Pongo pygmaeus* and not the *Homo sapiens* "gang." He is an "enculturated orangutan" who for some time has played a key role in my primatology research on great ape language and cognition. During our time together at the University of Tennessee, Chattanooga, Chantek lived freely with me—not only learning sign language but also taking trips to the mall, parks, and a nearby lake. When in recent years he had to be moved to a nearby zoo, he encountered restrictions that he did not understand, and he quickly named the zookeeper "key man." Thus, his brief escape to forage for "cheese-meat-breads" (cheeseburgers).

Chantek acquired many symbolic processes of human language during his time at the university where he was surrounded by anthropology students using Orangutan Sign Language (OSL), a pidgin gestural communication based on American Sign Language.[a] His vocabulary included names for people, places, foods, actions, objects, animals, colors, pronouns, locations, attributes ("good," "hurt"), and emphasis ("more," "time-to-do"). His language ability was similar to the use of language by 2- to 3-year-old human children.[b] Building on his 150-sign vocabulary, Chantek also invented terms, such as "Dave-missing-finger" for an injured worker, "tomato-toothpaste" for ketchup, and "eye-drink" for contact lens solution. He even nicknamed himself "Tek" by touching his hand to his opposite shoulder, rather than the more cumbersome cheek-pad touch for "Chantek."

He created more complex meanings by combining his signs in new sequences such as asking me to secretly open the door—an association of words I had never used with him. He nuanced his communications with subtle modulations of meaning and could dissect the elements of his signs. In almost metaphorical ways, he signed "dog" for pictures of dogs, barking noises on the radio, and even strange orangutans on TV whom he called "orange dogs." He signed "break" before he broke and shared crackers and after he dismantled his toilet. He signed "bad" to himself before he grabbed a cat, when he bit into a radish, and when he sadly inspected a dead bird.

Chantek could play imitative games and also illustrated some of the functions of language such as displaced reference by talking about keys that were not present. He showed code switching by utilizing a different dialect, style, or register through whispering "secret" and making his signs very small in a tiny space hidden by his hairy long arms. We also used code switching when Chantek shifted from his intimate informal language with me to more formal communication when the keeper arrived, and Chantek signed he was "sorry," but with less than convincing articulation.

Chantek is a code switcher in another sense as well because he is a member of a small group of intelligent nonhumans who are "cultural hybrids" or "dual-cultured," meaning that he is a member of one species raised by another. His life journey has involved finding his way between two different worlds—his own orangutan gestural communication, leaf and stick tools, and navigation in his environment versus the world of human culture, technology, and language, as he learns to shade his meanings to fit the situation, play tic-tac-toe and computer games, and create stone tools and found art assemblage and jewelry.[c]

Significantly, Chantek engaged in deception by attempting his escape in the first place and by subtly lying about what had really happened. This phenomenon has been called the benchmark of language because it requires symbolically creating or assuming an alternate reality and "theory of mind." I learned that Chantek told at least three lies a week including signing "dirty" to go to the bathroom only to play with the knobs on the washing machine, or distracting my attention with words about dangerous "big cats" while he deceptively reached into my pocket for treats. Chantek even stole and pretended to swallow a pencil eraser and then lied by opening his mouth, signing "eat."

Early language research with apes focused on vocabulary lists and acquisition rates just to "prove" that apes could acquire some human symbols. The contest seemed to be whether human language was unique—and the answer always had to preserve our *Homo*-centric superiority. My anthropological work with Chantek has had the opportunity to focus on the development, functional use, and evolutionary significance of both natural ape and human communication, culture, and cognition. The issue is now more about how both apes and humans use communication and cultural traditions to meet our needs, to varying degrees. My anthropological approach looked at the development of communication in cultural context and explored how Chantek and I created a communication code together in what Andrew Lock called "the guided re-invention of language."[d] Analyzing my findings with those of earlier developmental studies of the cognitive and linguistic skills of nonhuman primates, I discovered that Chantek was far less imitative and more original in his communication because his human companions interrupted him less and allowed his inventive use of language more.

Chantek may live into his 50s or 60s, so there is still much more he can show us about the mind, culture, and language ability of orangutans. Given my own North American indigenous roots, I see his dual-cultured existence in terms of the Coast Salish tribal concept of "where different waters meet and are transformed." Chantek said this best by calling himself "orangutan person"—neither human nor natural ape but benefiting from the cultures of both. In fact, the Great Ape Project has proposed that apes might be legal persons who should have limited human rights.

However, in his zoo environment, administrators have had difficulty in doing code switching of their own. Among other things, they have discouraged Chantek's use of sign language, perhaps out of misguided efforts to restore him to a natural orangutan or fear that he will complain about the food or publicly sign "Chantek want go home." My vision is the creation of a Communication and Culture Center where intelligent and sentient animals like Chantek will have greater agency and learning opportunities than are currently provided and can explore their dual-cultured natures. Imagine enculturated apes making tools, communicating with us on the Internet, engaging in meaningful work, and inventing their own culture based on symbols. If we were to *really* listen to Chantek, what would he tell us?

Written expressly for this text, 2012.

---

[a] Miles, H. L. W. (1990). The cognitive foundations for reference in a signing orangutan. In S. T. Parker & K. R. Gibson (Eds.), *"Language" and intelligence in monkeys and apes: Comparative developmental perspectives* (pp. 511–539). Cambridge, UK: Cambridge University Press.

[b] Miles, H. L. (1999). Symbolic communication with and by great apes. In S. T. Parker, R. Mitchell, & H. Miles (Eds.), *The mentality of gorillas and orangutans: Comparative perspectives* (pp. 197–210). Cambridge, UK: Cambridge University Press.

[c] Ibid.

[d] Lock, A. (1980). *The guided reinvention of language.* New York: Academic Press.

We need to acquire more knowledge about the various systems of animal communication before we will know their implications for our understanding of the nature and evolution of languages. Meanwhile, even as debate continues over how human and animal communication relate to each other, we cannot dismiss communication among nonhuman species as a set of simple instinctive reflexes or fixed action patterns (Cartmill & Byrne, 2010; Gentry et al., 2009; McCarthy, Jensvold, & Fouts, 2013).

Although language studies such as the one involving Chantek reveal much about primate cognition, the fact remains that human culture is ultimately dependent on an elaborate system of communication far more complex than that of any other species—including our fellow primates. The reason for this is the sheer amount of knowledge that must be learned by each person from other individuals in order to fully participate in society, where almost everything is based on socially learned behavior. Learning can and does take place in the absence of language by way of observation and imitation, guided by a limited number of meaningful signs or symbols. However, all known human cultures are so rich in content that they require communication systems that not only can give precise labels to various classes of phenomena but also permit people to think and talk about their own and others' experiences and expectations—past, present, and future.

The central and most highly developed human system of communication is language. Knowledge of the workings of language, then, is essential to a full understanding of what culture is about and how it operates.

Linguistic Research and the Nature of Language

Any human language—Chinese, English, Swahili, or whatever—is a means of transmitting information and sharing with others both collective and individual experiences. It is a system that enables us to translate our concerns, beliefs, and perceptions into symbols that can be understood and interpreted by others.

In spoken language, this is done by taking sounds—no language uses more than about fifty—and developing rules for putting them together in meaningful ways. Sign languages do the same, not with sound but by shaping and moving hands and other parts of the body and with facial expressions, including mouthing. The vast array of languages in the world—some 6,000 or so distinctive ones—may well astound us by their complexity and great differences, yet language experts have found that each is fundamentally organized in similar ways.

The roots of **linguistics**—the systematic study of all aspects of language—trace back to the works of ancient language specialists in South Asia more than 2,000 years ago. The age of European exploration and expansion, from the 1400s into the 1900s, set the stage for a great leap forward in the scientific study of languages. Explorers, traders, missionaries, and other travelers accumulated information about a huge diversity of languages from all around the world. An estimated 12,000 languages still existed when they began their inquiries.

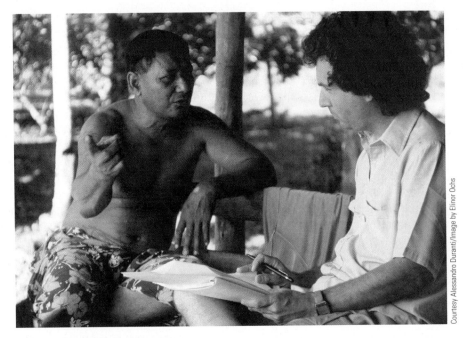

Figure 15.1 Linguistic Research in Samoa
Author of numerous studies in linguistic anthropology, Alessandro Duranti of the University of California, Los Angeles, began his research on Samoan language and culture about thirty-five years ago in Falefa village on Upolu Island. One of nine islands collectively inhabited by about 250,000 Samoans sharing the same language, Upolu was first settled about 3,000 years ago by seafarers who established villages on hundreds of tropical islands scattered throughout the Central Pacific and collectively known as Polynesia. Samoan is one of about forty closely related Polynesian languages, which together form a small branch of the Oceanic language family: 450 languages spoken by 2 million people inhabiting about 25,000 islands widely scattered throughout the Pacific. Duranti, an Italian-born U.S. anthropologist, is shown here as a young linguist working with Salesa Asiata on a translation of a recorded conversation to learn more about speaking in social interaction and as a cultural practice.

Linguists in the past 150 years, including anthropologists, made significant contributions in comparative research—discovering patterns, relationships, and systems in the sounds and structures of different languages and formulating laws and principles concerning language. While still collecting data, researchers have made considerable progress in discovering the reasoning process behind language construction, testing and working from new and improved theories (Figure 15.1). Today, the discipline of linguistics includes three main branches: descriptive linguistics, historical linguistics, and a third branch that focuses on language in relation to social and cultural settings.

Descriptive Linguistics

How can an anthropologist, a trader, a missionary, a diplomat, or any other outsider research a foreign language that has not yet been described and analyzed, or for which there are no readily available written materials? There are

linguistics The systematic study of all aspects of language.

hundreds of such undocumented languages in the world. Fortunately, effective methods have been developed to help with the task. Descriptive linguistics involves unraveling a language by recording, describing, and analyzing all of its features. It is a painstaking, but ultimately rewarding process in that it provides deeper understanding of a language—its structure, its unique linguistic repertoire (figures of speech, word plays, and so on), and its relationship to other languages.

The process of unlocking the underlying rules of a spoken language requires a trained ear and a thorough understanding of how multiple different speech sounds are produced. Without such know-how, it is extremely difficult to write out or make intelligent use of any data concerning a particular language. To satisfy this preliminary requirement, most people need special training in phonetics, discussed next.

Phonology

To describe and analyze any language, one needs first an inventory of all its distinctive sounds. The systematic identification and description of the distinctive sounds in a language is known as **phonetics**. Rooted in the Greek word *phone* (meaning "sound"), phonetics is basic to **phonology**, the study of language sounds.

Some of the sounds used in other languages may seem very much like those of the researcher's own speech pattern, but others may be unfamiliar. For example, the *th* sound common in English does not exist in the German language and is difficult for most German speakers to pronounce, just as the *r* sound used in numerous languages is tough for Chinese speakers. And the unique "click" sounds used in Bushman languages in southern Africa are difficult for speakers of just about every other language.

While collecting speech sounds or utterances, the linguist works to isolate the **phoneme**—the smallest unit of sound that makes a difference in meaning but has no meaning by itself. Linguists carry out this analysis through a process called the *minimal-pair test*. They try to find two short words that appear to be exactly alike except for one sound, such as *bit* and *pit* in English. If the substitution of *b* for *p* in this minimal pair makes a difference in meaning, as it does in English, then those two sounds have been identified as distinct phonemes of the language and will require two different symbols to record.

If, however, linguists find two different pronunciations (as when "butter" is pronounced "budder") and then find no difference in their meaning for native speakers, the sounds represented will be considered variants of the same phoneme. In such cases, for economy of representation only one of the two symbols will be used to record that sound wherever it is found.

As this example suggests, linguists distinguish many more phonemes (44) in English speech than the 26 letters used in the English alphabet. To transcribe different languages, which include many sounds foreign to English, linguists have developed the International Phonetic Alphabet (IPA): 107 letters, 52 diacritics (marks that change the sound value of the letter to which they are added), and 4 prosodic marks (designating rhythm, stress, and intonation). Beyond this linguistic standard, speech pathologists have developed additional letters and notations, enabling them to transcribe a range of less common sounds.

Morphology, Syntax, and Grammar

While making and studying an inventory of distinctive sounds, linguists also look at **morphology**, the study of the patterns or rules of word formation in a language (including rules concerning verb tense, pluralization, and compound words). They do this by marking out specific sounds and sound combinations that seem to have meaning. The smallest unit of sound that carries meaning in a language is a **morpheme**.

A morpheme is distinct from a phoneme, which can change a word but which has no meaning by itself. For example, a linguist studying English in a North American farming community would soon learn that *cow* is a morpheme—a meaningful combination of the phonemes *c*, *o*, and *w*. Pointing to two of these animals, the linguist would elicit the word *cows* from local speakers. This would reveal yet another morpheme—the *s*—which can be added to the original morpheme to indicate plural.

The next step in unraveling a language is to identify its **syntax**—the patterns or rules by which morphemes are arranged into phrases and sentences. The **grammar** of the language will ultimately consist of all observations about its morphemes and syntax.

One of the strengths of modern descriptive linguistics is the objectivity of its methods. For example, English-speaking anthropologists who specialize in this will not approach a language with the idea that it must have nouns, verbs, prepositions, or any other of the form classes identifiable in English. This allows for unanticipated discoveries. For instance, unlike many other languages, English does not distinguish between feminine and masculine nouns.

---

phonetics The systematic identification and description of distinctive speech sounds in a language.

phonology The study of language sounds.

phoneme The smallest unit of sound that makes a difference in meaning in a language but has no meaning by itself.

morphology The study of the patterns or rules of word formation in a language, including the guidelines for verb tense, pluralization, and compound words.

morpheme The smallest unit of sound that carries a meaning in language. It is distinct from a phoneme, which can alter meaning but has no meaning by itself.

syntax The patterns or rules by which words are arranged into phrases and sentences.

grammar The entire formal structure of a language, including morphology and syntax.

English speakers use the definite article *the* in front of any noun, whereas Spanish varies with gender and numbers, requiring four types of such definite articles: *la* (singular feminine), *el* (singular masculine), *las* (plural feminine), and *los* (plural masculine)—as in *las casas* (the houses) and *los jardines* (the gardens).

German speakers go one step further, utilizing three gendered articles in singular, but only one in plural: *die* (singular feminine), *der* (singular masculine), *das* (singular neuter), and *die* (plural, regardless of gender). For cultural historical reasons, Germans consider the house neuter, so they say *das Haus*, but they concur with Spaniards that the garden is masculine. Some nouns, however, reverse gender in German–Spanish translation: the feminine sun (*die Sonne*) switches genders into a masculine *el sol*, and the masculine moon (*der Mond*) turns into a feminine *la luna*. However, these language gender issues are not relevant everywhere. In the Andean highlands in South America, Quechua-speaking Indians are not concerned with whether nouns are gendered or neutral, for their language has no definite articles at all.

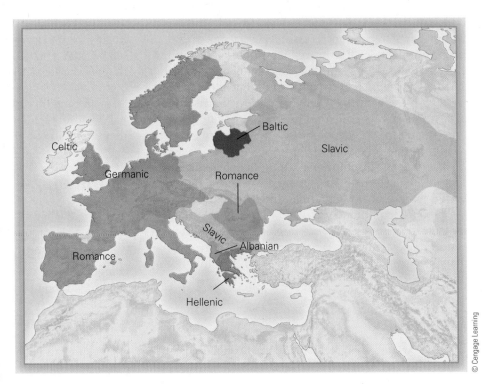

Figure 15.2 **Indo-European Language Subgroups in Europe**
Not all languages spoken in Europe are part of the Indo-European family. For example, Basque—an isolated language also known as Euskara—is still spoken in the French–Spanish borderland. Moreover, languages spoken by Hungarians, Estonians, Finns, Komi (in northeast Russia), and Sámi (in northern Scandinavia) belong to the Uralic language family.

© Cengage Learning

Historical Linguistics

All spoken languages change in the course of generations, and many are now defunct. In addition to deciphering "dead" languages that are no longer spoken, historical linguists investigate relationships between earlier and later forms of the same language, study older languages to track the processes of change into modern ones, and examine interrelationships among older languages. For example, they attempt to sort out the development of Latin (spoken almost 1,500 years ago in southern Europe) into the Romance languages of Italian, Spanish, Portuguese, French, and Romanian by identifying natural shifts in the original language and tracking modifications brought on by centuries of direct contact with Germanic-speaking invaders from northern Europe.

language family A group of languages descended from a single ancestral language.

linguistic divergence The development of different languages from a single ancestral language.

When focusing on long-term processes of change, historical linguists depend on written records of languages. They have achieved considerable success in working out the relationships among different languages, and these are reflected in classification schemes. For example, English is one of approximately 140 languages classified in the larger Indo-European language family (Figure 15.2). A **language family** is a group of languages descended from a single ancestral language. This family is subdivided into some eleven subgroups (Germanic, Romance, and so on), indicating that there has been a long period (6,000 years or so) of **linguistic divergence** from an ancient unified language (reconstructed as Proto-Indo-European) into separate "daughter" languages. English is one of several languages in the Germanic subgroup (Figure 15.3), all of which are more closely related to one another than they are to the languages of any other subgroup of the Indo-European family.

Despite the differences between them, the languages of one subgroup share certain features when compared to those of another. As an illustration, the word for father in the Germanic languages always starts with an *f* or closely related *v* sound: Dutch *vader,* German *Vater,* Gothic *Fadar.* Among the Romance languages, by contrast, the comparable word always starts with a *p*: French *père,* Spanish and Italian *padre*—all derived from the Latin *pater.* The original Indo-European word for father was *p'tēr,* so in this case,

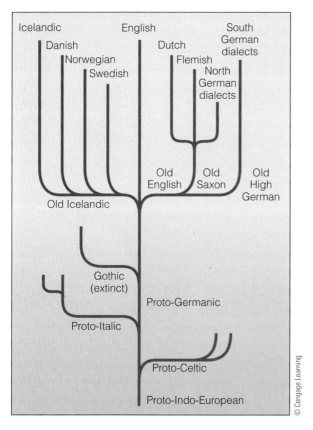

Figure 15.3 The English Language Family Tree
English is one of a group of languages in the Germanic subgroup of the Indo-European family. This diagram shows its relationship to languages in the same subgroup. The root is an ancestral language originally spoken by early farmers and herders who spread north and west over Europe, bringing with them both their customs and their language.

the Romance languages have retained the earlier pronunciation, whereas the Germanic languages have diverged.

Historical linguists are not limited to the faraway past, for even modern languages are constantly transforming—adding new words, dropping others, or changing meaning. Studying them in their specific cultural context can help us understand the processes of change that may have led to linguistic divergence in the past.

Processes of Linguistic Divergence

One force for change is selective borrowing between languages. This is evident in the many French words present in the English language—and in the growing number of English words cropping up in languages all around the world due to globalization. Technological breakthroughs resulting in new equipment and products also prompt linguistic shifts. For instance, the electronic revolution that brought us radio, television, computers, and mobile phones has created entirely new vocabularies. Internet use has widened the meaning of a host of already existing English words—from *hacking* and *surfing* to *spam* and *troll*. Entirely new words such as *phishing* and *vlogging* have been coined, leading to the creation of Internet dictionaries such as netlingo.com and webopedia.com.

There is also a tendency for any group within a larger society to create its own unique vocabulary, whether it is a street gang, sorority, religious group, or military platoon. By changing the meaning of existing words or inventing new ones, members of the in-group can communicate with fellow members while effectively excluding outsiders who may be within hearing range. Increasing professional specialization also contributes to coining new words and greatly expanding vocabularies.

Language Loss and Revival

Perhaps the most powerful force for linguistic change is the domination of one society over another. Such controls persist today in many parts of the world, such as Taiwan's indigenous peoples being governed by Mandarin-speaking Chinese or Tarascan Indians by Spanish-speaking Mexicans. In many cases, foreign political control has resulted in linguistic erosion or even complete disappearance, sometimes leaving only a faint trace in old, indigenous names for geographic features such as hills and rivers.

Over the last 500 years, about half of the world's 12,000 or so languages have become extinct as a direct result of warfare, epidemics, and forced assimilation brought on by colonial powers and other aggressive outsiders. As we discussed in Chapter 1, other than the dominant languages today, very few people speak the remaining 6,000 languages, and these languages are losing speakers rapidly due to globalization. Half have fewer than 10,000 speakers each, and about half of those are spoken by less than 1,000 each. Put another way, half of the world's languages are spoken by less than 2 percent of the world's population (Lewis et al, 2015; see also Crystal, 2002).

In North America, only 150 of the original 300 indigenous languages still exist, and many of these surviving tongues are moving toward extinction at an alarming rate. Thousands of indigenous languages elsewhere in the world are also threatened. For example, fewer than ten people still speak N|uu, a "click" language traditionally spoken in South Africa's Kalahari Desert. N|uu is the only surviving language of the !Ui branch of the Tuu language family (previously called Southern Khoisan) (Figure 15.4).

Anthropologists predict that the number of languages spoken in the world today will be cut in half by the year 2100, in large part because children born

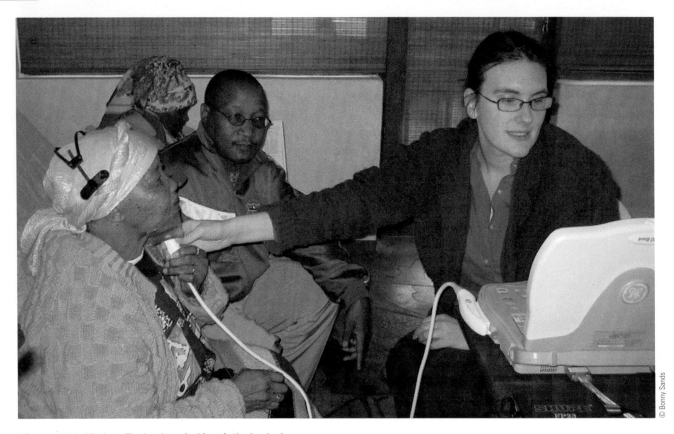

© Bonny Sands

Figure 15.4 Modern Technology in Linguistic Analysis
Several linguistic anthropologists are collaborating on field research with speakers of
endangered Khoisan "click" languages such as N|uu in southern Africa. Using a portable
ultrasound-imaging machine, they can capture the tongue movements of the click consonants.
Here, U.S. linguist Johanna Brugman holds an ultrasound probe under the chin of one of the
ten remaining N|uu speakers, Ouma Katrina Esau, who is helping to document how click sounds
are made. Clicks are produced by creating suction within a cavity formed between the front
and back parts of the tongue—except in the case of bilabial clicks in which the cavity is made
between the lips and the back of the tongue. N|uu is one of only three languages remaining in
the world that use bilabial clicks as consonants. The vertical bar in the word *N|uu* indicates a
click sound.

into ethnic minority groups no longer use the ancestral
language when they go to school, migrate to cities, join
the larger workforce, and are exposed to printed and
electronic media. The printing press, radio, satellite television, Internet, and text messaging are driving the need
for a shared language, and increasingly that is English.
In the past 500 years, this language—originally spoken
by about 2.5 million people living only in part of the
British Isles in northwestern Europe—has spread around
the world. Today, some 400 million people (5.5 percent
of the global population) claim English as their native
tongue. About 1.5 billion others (nearly 20 percent
of humanity) speak it as a second or foreign language
(Crystal, 2012).

Although a shared language allows people from different ethnic backgrounds to communicate, there is the risk
that a global spread of one language may contribute to the
disappearance of others. And with the extinction of each
language, we lose "hundreds of generations of traditional
knowledge encoded in these ancestral tongues"—a vast
repository of knowledge about the natural world, plants,
animals, ecosystems, and cultural traditions (Living
Tongues, 2015).

Sometimes, in reaction to a real or perceived threat of
cultural dominance by powerful foreign societies, ethnic
groups and even entire countries may seek to maintain or
reclaim their unique identity by purging their vocabularies of "foreign" terms. Emerging as a significant force for
linguistic change, such **linguistic nationalism** is particularly characteristic of the former colonial countries of
Africa and Asia today. It is not limited to those countries,
however, as one can see by periodic French attempts to

linguistic nationalism The attempt by ethnic groups and even countries
to proclaim independence by purging their language of foreign terms.

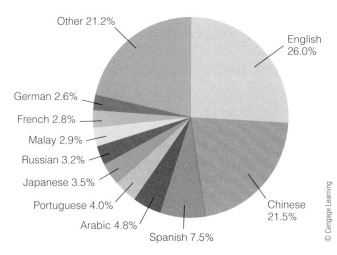

Figure 15.5 Language Use on the Internet
Although the world's digital divide is narrowing, with new languages being added to Internet operating systems at an accelerated rate, the divide is still dramatic. As illustrated here, over 80 percent of today's 2.8 billion Internet users are native speakers of just 10 of the world's 6,000 languages. Among the fastest-growing Internet language groups today are Arabic, Malay, and Portuguese (also spoken in Brazil). (Figures shown in the pie chart are rounded.)
Based on Internet World Stats: Usage and Population Statistics. (2015, June 30). Internet world users by language. http://www.internetworldstats .com/stats7.htm

purge their language of Americanisms (such as *le hamburger*) and government approval for other terms (such as *couriel* instead of *e-mail*).

A key issue in language preservation efforts today is the impact of electronic media, such as the Internet, where content still exists in relatively few languages, and more than 80 percent of Internet users are native speakers of just 10 of the world's 6,000 languages (Figure 15.5). Some Internet giants (Mozilla and Google) are translating their operating systems, in some cases using volunteer native speakers to come up with culture-specific words for English terms such as *cookie, mouse, crash*, and *windows*. For Fulah speakers in West Africa, *crash* became *hookii* (a cow falling over but not dying). For Mexico's Zapotec speakers, most of whom live in windowless houses, computer windows became *eyes* ("Cookies, caches and cows," 2014).

A prime means by which powerful groups assert their dominance over ethnic minorities living within their borders is to suppress their languages. Challenging this, minorities are actively involved in language revitalization. For many, efforts to counter the threat of linguistic extinction or to resurrect already extinct languages are part of a larger struggle to maintain their sense of cultural identity and dignity. Among numerous examples of this is Manx, a Celtic language historically spoken on the Isle of Man in southwestern England. Although its last native speaker died in 1974, Manx is now the subject of a successful language revival endeavor. Similar efforts are under way in a number of North American Indian communities,

including the work of anthropologist S. Neyooxet Greymorning, a Southern Arapaho, who has developed ways to revive indigenous languages, including his own. He tells his story in the Anthropology Applied feature.

Language in Its Social and Cultural Settings

Language is not simply a matter of combining sounds according to certain rules to come up with meaningful utterances. Individuals communicate with one another constantly—in households, in the street, on the job, and so on. People often vary in the ways they perform speech based on social context and cultural factors such as gender, age, class, and ethnicity. Moreover, what people choose to speak about, whisper, or keep silent about reflects what is socially important or culturally meaningful in their community. For that reason, linguistic anthropologists also focus on the actual use of language in relation to its various distinctive social and cultural settings. This third branch of linguistic study falls into two categories: sociolinguistics and ethnolinguistics.

Sociolinguistics

Sociolinguistics, the study of the relationship between language and society, examines how social categories—such as age, gender, ethnicity, religion, occupation, and class—influence the use and significance of distinctive styles of speech. We examine two of the major influences on language next: gender and social dialect.

Language and Gender

As a major factor in personal and social identity, gender is often reflected in language use, so it is not surprising that numerous thought-provoking sociolinguistic topics fall under the category of gender. These include research on **gendered speech**—distinct male and female speech patterns, which vary across social and cultural settings. One of the first in-depth studies in this genre explored the relationship of gender and power to explain why North American women exhibit less decisive speech styles than men. A subsequent wave of related scholarly work has produced new insights about language as a social speech "performance" in both private and public settings (Lakoff, 2004).

---

sociolinguistics The study of the relationship between language and society through examining how social categories—such as age, gender, ethnicity, religion, occupation, and class—influence the use and significance of distinctive styles of speech.

gendered speech Distinct male and female speech patterns that vary across social and cultural settings.

ANTHROPOLOGY APPLIED

When Bambi Spoke Arapaho: Preserving Indigenous Languages

By S. Neyooxet Greymorning

In life, there are experiences later recognized as defining moments. For me, a moment like that happened in my second year of college when some mysterious individual stood over me and asked, "What are you doing to help your people?" I remember getting up, going to the library, and walking along the stacks. Trailing my fingers over books, I pulled one out. It was about the overall status of American Indian languages in the United States. I opened it, looked up Arapaho, and read that it was among the healthiest native languages. Comforted by this, it didn't occur to me that a rapidly dwindling number of young Arapaho speakers was signaling the demise of my ancestral tongue. Years later when I told tribal elder Francis Brown about this, he said, "The elders called your name."

When I went on to graduate school and studied anthropology, I felt driven to take almost every linguistic class available. Soon, I understood that to lose a language is to lose aspects of how a people make sense of themselves and the world they live in and the values that culturally and psychologically bind a people together shaping their identity. I decided to spend the summer on the Wind River Reservation in central Wyoming putting together an Arapaho dictionary. Then I learned that Dr. Zdeněk Salzmann, a Czech anthropologist who did linguistic work with the Arapaho, had the same idea. I called him, and he suggested we work together.

As a graduate student I dedicated myself to gaining the knowledge, skills, and experience that could contribute to revitalizing languages. Upon completing my doctorate in 1992, I was invited to direct a language and culture program on the Wind River Reservation where Arapaho language instruction had been introduced within the public school system in the late 1970s. By 1993, although Arapaho was taught from kindergarten to high school, my assessment revealed students were able to say only a few basic phrases and vocabulary words having to do with food, animals, colors, and numbers—nothing near fluency and the goal of keeping Arapaho alive.

Recognizing the need for a different approach, I began laying the groundwork to

Greymorning speaking about language revitalization.

Gendered speech research also includes the study of distinct male and female syntax exhibited in various languages around the world, such as the Lakota language, still spoken at the Pine Ridge and Rosebud Indian reservations in South Dakota. When a Lakota woman asks someone, "How are you?" she says, "Tonikt*hkahe*?" But when her brother poses the same question, he says, "Tonikt*ukahwo*?" (**Figure 15.6**). As explained by Michael Two Horses, "Our language is gender-specific in the area of commands, queries, and a couple of other things" (personal communication, April 2003).

Social Dialects

Sociolinguists are also interested in **dialect**—the varying form of a language that reflects a particular region, occupation, or social class and that is similar enough to be mutually intelligible. Technically, all dialects are languages—there is nothing partial or sublinguistic about them—and the point at which two different dialects become distinctly different languages is roughly the point at which speakers of one are almost totally unable to communicate with speakers of the other.

However, the distinction between language and dialect is not always objective and can be a political issue. Such is the case in China, the world's most populous country with just over 1.4 billion inhabitants, almost all of whom speak Chinese. In fact, there are many Chinese languages, each consisting of many regional dialects. For instance, people in Shanghai actually use a dialect of Wu Chinese spoken in the eastern region, whereas natives of Guangdong (Canton) speak a dialect of Yuehai, the major language of southwestern China. Migrants from the northern parts of the country, where numerous dialects of Mandarin Chinese are traditionally spoken, understand almost nothing of Wu or Yuehai because these Chinese languages are foreign to them. For this reason, almost all Chinese nationals today learn Standard Chinese, the country's official language, historically developed as a lingua franca based on a Mandarin dialect traditionally spoken in the country's capital city, Beijing.

---

dialect The varying form of a language that reflects a particular region, occupation, or social class and that is similar enough to be mutually intelligible.

establish one of the first full-day language immersion preschools on a reservation: Hinono'eitiino'oowu'—the Arapaho Language Lodge. The aim was for language "providers" to speak only Arapaho and use a multifaceted approach that included not only word and phrase acquisition, but also response exercises, visual association, and interaction with videos and audio cassettes of songs.

I contacted Disney Studios and convinced them to allow us to translate *Bambi* into Arapaho as a learning aid.[a] *Bambi* seemed like a good choice because it echoed traditional stories in which animals speak, it was a story that most children on the reservation knew, and as the story unfolds Bambi uses simple childlike language as he learns to talk.

However, even a multifaceted approach that included Bambi speaking Arapaho was not turning the tide of language demise, so I began to think through the challenges with increased focus. From 1996 to 2002, I gradually developed a new approach, Accelerated Second Language Acquisition (ASLA©™). During 2003, using my children as language learners, I tested and honed

ASLA into a workable methodology that helps retune the brain so people learn to visualize the language rather than continually translate back and forth in their minds between the language they know and the one they're learning.

To encourage language teachers on the reservation to adopt this approach, I modeled teaching Arapaho through ASLA at the University of Montana with remarkable results. Beyond efforts to help preserve Arapaho, I'm regularly asked to give ASLA workshops for others who are committed to indigenous language revitalization. To date, I have had contact with over 1,200 individual language instructors from more than 60 different communities in the United States, Canada, and Australia, representing over 40 different languages.[b]

The challenge of preserving languages is daunting. But something my uncle told me during a boyhood visit with him encourages me to be counted among those who keep trying. He woke me at dawn and took me to a pond. There was no wind, and the water was like glass. After instructing me to pick up a small stone, he said, "Now drop

it in the pond and tell me what you see." Releasing the stone, I watched it make ever-widening circles on the water. "I want you to always remember," said my uncle, "that nothing is so small that it can't put something larger than itself into motion."

Written expressly for this text, 2010.

---

[a] See Greymorning, S. N. (2001). Reflections on the Arapaho Language Project or, when Bambi spoke Arapaho and other tales of Arapaho language revitalization efforts. In K. Hale & L. Hinton, *The green book of language revitalization in practice* (pp. 287–297). New York: Academic.

[b] "Accelerated Second Language Acquisition training held." (2015, August 21). *Red Lake Nation News.* http://www.redlakenationnews. com/story/2015/08/21/news/accelerated-second-language-acquisition-training-held/38464.html (retrieved November 18, 2015); for video examples of students of ASLA speaking Arapaho, plus written comments from language instructors and students about ASLA, go to Strengthening Indigenous Languages and Cultures (SILC): www.nsilc.org.

Figure 15.6 Gendered Speech Makers of the feature film *Dances With Wolves* aimed for cultural authenticity by casting Native American actors and hiring a female language coach to teach Lakota to those who did not know how to speak it. However, the lessons did not include the gendered speech aspect of Lakota—the fact that females and males follow different rules of syntax. So, when Lakota speakers saw the film, and heard actors portraying Lakota warriors speaking like women, they snickered and then howled with laughter.

© Orion Pictures Corporation/Everett Collection

Figure 15.7 Linguistic Relativity
Aymara Indians living in the highlands of Bolivia and Peru in South America depend on the potato as their major source of food. Their language has over 200 words for this vegetable, reflecting the many varieties they traditionally grow and the many different ways they preserve and prepare it. This is an example of linguistic relativity.

Linguistic boundaries are not only geographic or territorial; they may also indicate or reflect social class, economic status, political rank, or ethnic identity. In many societies where different dialects are spoken, individuals often become skilled at switching back and forth between them, depending on the situation in which they are speaking. Without being conscious of it, we all do the same thing when we switch from formality to informality in our speech, depending upon where we are and to whom we are talking. The process of changing from one language mode to another as the situation demands, whether from one language to another or from one dialect of a language to another, is known as **code switching**.

code switching The practice of changing from one mode of speech to another as the situation demands, whether from one language to another or from one dialect of a language to another.

ethnolinguistics A branch of linguistics that studies the relationships between language and culture and how they mutually influence and inform each other.

Ethnolinguistics

The study of the relationships between language and culture, and how they mutually influence and inform each other, is the domain of **ethnolinguistics**. In this type of research, anthropologists may investigate how a language reflects the culturally significant aspects of a people's traditional natural environment. For example, Aymara Indians living in the Bolivian highlands depend on the potato as their major source of food, and their language has over 200 words for this vegetable, reflecting the many varieties they traditionally grow and the many different ways that they preserve and prepare it (Figure 15.7). Similarly, many people in the United States today possess a rich vocabulary allowing them to precisely distinguish between many different types of cars, categorized by model, year, and manufacturer.

Another example concerns cultural categories of color: Languages have different ways of dividing and naming the range of light in the electromagnetic spectrum visible to the naked human eye. In modern English we speak of black, red, orange, yellow, green, blue, indigo, violet, and white, as well as "invisible" colors such as ultraviolet and infrared. Other languages mark out different groupings on this continuum of hues. For instance, Indians in Mexico's northwestern mountains speaking Tarahumara have just one word for both green and blue—*siyoname*.

The idea that the words and grammar of a language are directly linked to culture and affect how speakers of the language perceive and think about the world is termed **linguistic relativity**. This theoretical concept is associated with the pioneering ethnolinguistic research carried out by anthropologist Edward Sapir and his student Benjamin Whorf during the 1930s. Focusing on the interplay of language, thought, and culture, their research resulted in what is now known as the *Sapir-Whorf hypothesis*: the idea that each language provides particular grooves of linguistic expression that predispose speakers of that language to perceive the world in a certain way.

Whorf gained many of these insights while translating English into Hopi, a North American Indian language still spoken in Arizona. Doing this work, he discovered that Hopi differs from English not only in vocabulary but also in terms of its grammatical categories such as nouns and verbs. For instance, Hopi use numbers for counting and measuring things that have physical existence, but they do not apply numbers in the same way to abstractions like time. They would have no problem translating an English sentence such as, "I see fifteen sheep grazing on three acres of grassland," but an equally simple sentence such as "Three weeks ago, I enjoyed my fifteen minutes of fame" would require a much more complex translation into Hopi.

It is also of note that Hopi verbs express tenses differently than English verbs. Rather than marking past, present, and future, with *-ed*, *-ing*, or *will*, Hopi requires additional words to indicate if an event is completed, is still ongoing, or is expected to take place. So instead of saying, "Three strangers stayed for fifteen days in our village," a Hopi would say something like, "We remember three strangers stay in our village until the sixteenth day."

In addition, Hopi verbs do not express tense by their forms. Unlike English verbs that change form to indicate past, present, and future, Hopi verbs distinguish between a statement of fact (if the speaker actually witnesses a certain event), a statement of expectation, and a statement that expresses regularity. For instance, when you ask an English-speaking athlete "Do you run?" he may answer yes, when in fact he may at that moment be sitting in an armchair watching TV. A Hopi athlete asked the same question in his own language might respond no, because in Hopi the statement of fact "he runs" translates as *wari* ("running occurs"), whereas the statement that expresses regularity—"he runs," such as on the track team—translates as *wari-kngwe* ("running occurs characteristically").

This shows that the Hopi language structures thinking and behavior with a focus on the present—on getting ready and carrying out what needs to be done right now. Based on his research on the Hopi language and culture, Whorf developed his important theoretical insight "that the structure of the language one habitually uses influences the manner in which one understands his environment. The picture of the universe shifts from tongue to tongue" (Carroll, 1956, p. vi).

In the 1990s linguistic anthropologists devised new research strategies to actually test Sapir and Whorf's original hypothesis. One study found that speakers of Swedish and Finnish (neighboring peoples who speak radically different languages) working at similar jobs in similar regions under similar laws and regulations showed significantly different rates of on-the-job accidents (Lucy, 1997). The rates were substantially lower among the Swedish speakers. What emerges from comparison of the two languages is that Swedish (one of the Indo-European languages) emphasizes information about movement in three-dimensional space. Finnish (a Ural-Altaic language unrelated to Indo-European languages) emphasizes more static relations among coherent temporal entities. As a consequence, it seems that Finns organized the workplace in a way that favored the individual person over the temporal organization in the overall production process. This in turn led to frequent production disruptions, haste, and (ultimately) accidents. If language does mirror cultural reality, it would follow that changes in a culture will sooner or later be reflected in changes in the language (Wolff & Holmes, 2011). We see this, for example, with respect to public recognition of alternative sexual orientations or gender expressions in English-speaking North America where the term *LGBTI* (initials standing for lesbian, gay, bisexual, transgender, and intersex) has become common.

Language Versatility

In most societies throughout the world, it is not unusual for individuals to be fluent in two, three, or more languages. They succeed in this in large part because they experience training in multiple languages as children.

In some regions where groups speaking different languages coexist and interact, people often understand one another but may choose not to speak the other's language. Such is the case in the borderlands of northern Bolivia and southern Peru where Quechua-speaking and Aymara-speaking Indians are neighbors. When an Aymara farmer speaks to a Quechua herder in Aymara, the Quechua will reply in Quechua, and vice versa, each knowing that the other understands both languages even if speaking just one. The ability to comprehend two languages but express oneself in only one is known as *receptive* or *passive bilingualism*.

linguistic relativity The idea that language to some extent shapes the way in which people perceive and think about the world.

In our globalized world, being bilingual or multilingual may open doors of communication not only for trade but for work, diplomacy, art, and friendship. Ironically, reluctance to learn another language prevails in the United States despite the fact that the majority language in the Americas is not English but Spanish; Spanish is not only the majority language of the hemisphere, but also, in the United States today it is spoken by nearly 40 million people in their homes. Notably, the number and percentage of U.S. residents speaking a language other than English at home increased from 11 percent (23 million) in 1980 to 21 percent (63 million) in 2014 (Geller, 2015).

Figure 15.8 Nonverbal Communication
Humans convey far more information through nonverbal means, such as voice tone and body language, than through speaking. In this photo, the sorrow of Kashmiri women in Panjran mourning the violent death of a fellow villager is obvious. Killed in a gun battle, he was a journalism student who had recently joined a Muslim rebel group fighting against Indian troops controlling Kashmir, a Muslim majority state in the Himalayas. These women show their grief during the funeral procession.

Beyond Words: The Gesture–Call System

As efficient as they are at naming and talking about ideas, actions, and things, all languages are to some degree inadequate at communicating certain kinds of information that people need to know in order to fully understand what is being said. For this reason, human speech is always embedded within a *gesture–call system,* similar to the type we see exhibited by nonhuman primates.

The various sounds and gestures of this system serve to "key" speech, providing listeners with the appropriate frame for interpreting what a speaker is saying. Messages about human emotions and intentions are effectively communicated by this gesture–call system: Is the speaker happy, sad, mad, enthusiastic, tired, or in some other emotional state? Is he or she requesting information, denying something, reporting factually, or lying? Very little of this information is conveyed by spoken language alone. Research shows that humans convey far more information through nonverbal means (tone of voice, body language)

than through verbal means in their interactions and communications with each other (Poyatos, 2002).

Nonverbal Communication

The **gesture** component of the gesture–call system consists of facial expressions and body postures and motions that convey intended as well as subconscious messages. The study of such nonverbal signals is known as **kinesics**.

Humanity's repertoire of body language is enormous. This is evident if you consider just one aspect of it: the fact that a human being has about fifty facial muscles and is thereby capable of making more than 7,000 facial expressions! Thus, it should not be surprising to hear that at least 60 percent of our total communication takes place nonverbally (Figure 15.8).

Often, gestural messages complement spoken messages—for instance, nodding the head while affirming something verbally, raising eyebrows when asking a question, or using hands and fingers to illustrate or emphasize what is being talked about. However, nonverbal signals are sometimes at odds with verbal ones, and they have the power to override or undercut them. For example, a person may say the words "I love you" a thousand times to another, but if it is not true, the nonverbal signals will likely communicate that falseness.

Cross-cultural studies in this field show that there are many similarities around the world in such basic facial expressions as smiling, laughing, crying, and displaying

gesture A facial expression and body posture and motion that convey an intended as well as a subconscious message.

kinesics The study of nonverbal signals in body language including facial expressions and bodily postures and motions.

VISUAL COUNTERPOINT

Dechen Choekhor Mahvihara

AP Images/Gil Yohanan

Figure 15.9 Social Space Across Cultures
Cultures around the world have noticeably different attitudes concerning social space—how far or close individuals stand or sit from each other, and also how low or high they may be positioned to indicate rank difference. The photo on the left shows His Eminence the 9th Kyabje Drukpa Choegon Rinpoche (the spiritual head of the Dechen Choekhor lineage in the Red Hat sect) reaching down to bestow "empowerment" on a young priest in a ceremony attended by fellow Buddhist monks at the Tsechu Monastery in Tibet, China. In the photo on the right, we see Turkey's ambassador in the office of Israel's deputy foreign minister, who symbolically humiliated this Muslim dignitary by seating him on a low couch. This ignited a diplomatic crisis reported around the world. In contrast, the elevated seating position of the Buddhist leader is not only culturally prescribed, but accepted and expected by his followers.

shock or anger. The smirks, frowns, and gasps that we have inherited from our primate ancestry require little learning and are harder to fake than conventional or socially obtained gestures that members of a group share, albeit not always consciously so.

Routine greetings are also similar around the world. Balinese, Italians, and Bushmen, for example, all smile and nod, and if the individuals are especially friendly, they will raise their eyebrows for a fraction of a second. By doing so, they signal a readiness for contact. The Japanese, however, suppress the eyebrow flash, regarding it as indecent. This example illustrates that there are important cross-cultural differences as well as similarities.

Another example can be found in gestural expressions for yes and no. In North America, one nods the head down then up for yes or shakes it left and right for no. The people of Sri Lanka also nod to answer yes to a factual question, but if asked to do something, a slow sideways movement of the head means yes. In Greece, the nodded head means yes, but no is indicated by jerking the head back so as to lift the face, usually with the eyes closed and the eyebrows raised.

Another aspect of body language has to do with social space: how people position themselves physically in relation to others. **Proxemics**, the cross-cultural study of social

space, came to the fore through the work of anthropologist Edward Hall, who coined the term (Hall, 1963, 1990). Hall's research on nonverbal communication showed that people from different cultures have different frameworks for defining and organizing social space—the personal space they establish around their bodies, as well as the macrolevel sensibilities that shape cultural expectations about how streets, neighborhoods, and cities should be arranged.

Among other things, Hall's investigation of personal space revealed that every culture has distinctive standards for distance in social interaction. For example, when two colleagues enculturated in the same society stand and talk together in an office, both will probably move in accordance to the same cultural standard of "appropriate" distance. Not surprisingly, the potential for nonverbal miscommunication is substantial when people from different cultural backgrounds meet. Further, social space can also involve different levels of relative height. In stratified societies, where people are hierarchically divided, high-ranked individuals may place themselves on an elevated platform, symbolically expressing their superior status (Figure 15.9).

proxemics The cross-cultural study of people's perception and use of social space.

Hall identified the range of cultural variation in four categories of proxemically relevant social spaces: intimate (0 to .45 meter or 18 inches), personal-casual (.45 to 1.2 meters or 1.5 to 4 feet), social-consultive (1.2 to 3.6 meters or 4 to 12 feet), and public distance (3.6 meters or 12 feet, and beyond). Hall warned that different cultural definitions of socially accepted use of space within these categories can lead to serious miscommunication and misunderstanding in cross-cultural settings (Hall, 1990). His research has been fundamental for the present-day training of international businesspeople, diplomats, and others involved in intercultural work.

Paralanguage

The second component of the gesture–call system is **paralanguage**—specific voice effects that accompany speech and contribute to communication. These include vocalizations such as giggling, groaning, or sighing, as well as voice qualities such as volume, intensity, pitch, and tempo.

The importance of paralanguage is suggested by the comment, "It's not so much *what* was said as *how* it was said." Whispering or shouting can make a big difference in meaning, even though the uttered words would be the same when written down. Minor differences in pitch, tempo, and phrasing may seem less obvious, but they still impact how words are perceived. Studies show, for example, that even subliminal messages communicated below the threshold of conscious perception by seemingly minor differences in phrasing, tempo, length of answers, and the like are far more important in courtroom proceedings than even the most perceptive trial lawyer may have realized. Among other things, *how* a witness gives testimony alters the reception it gets from jurors and influences the witness's credibility (O'Barr & Conley, 1993).

Communication has changed radically with the rise of e-mail, text messaging, and Twitter. These technologies resemble the spontaneity and speed of face-to-face communication but lack the body signals and voice qualifiers that nuance what is being said (and hint at how it is being received). Studies show that the intended tone of e-mail messages is perceived correctly only 56 percent of the time. Misunderstood messages can quickly create problems and hostility. Because the risk of miscommunication with these technologies abounds, despite use of emoticons and emojis that represent the writer's mood or attitude, certain sensitive exchanges are better made in person (Kruger et al., 2005).

paralanguage The voice effects that accompany language and convey meaning, including vocalizations such as giggling, groaning, or sighing, as well as voice qualities such as pitch and tempo.

tonal language A language in which the sound pitch of a spoken word is an essential part of its pronunciation and meaning.

whistled speech An exchange of whistled words using a phonetic emulation of the sounds produced in spoken voice.

Tonal Languages

There is enormous diversity in the ways languages are spoken. In addition to hundreds of vowels and consonants, sounds can be divided into tones—rises and falls in pitch that play a key role in distinguishing one word from another. About 70 percent of the world's languages are a **tonal language** in which the various distinctive sound pitches of spoken words are not only an essential part of their pronunciation but are also key to their meaning.

Worldwide, at least one-third of the population speaks a tonal language, including many in Africa, Central America, and East Asia. For example, Mandarin Chinese has four contrasting tones: flat, rising, falling, and falling then rising. These tones are used to distinguish among normally stressed syllables that are otherwise identical. So, depending on intonation, *ba* can mean "to uproot," "to hold," "eight," or "a harrow" (farm tool) (Catford, 1988). Yuehai, the Chinese language spoken in Guangdong (Canton) and Hong Kong, uses six contrasting tones, and some Chinese languages have as many as nine.

In nontonal languages such as English, tone can be used to convey an attitude or to change a statement into a question. But tone alone does not change the meaning of individual words as it does in Mandarin, where careless use of tones with the syllable *ma* could cause one to call someone's mother a horse!

Talking Drums and Whistled Speech

Even a very loud human voice has its natural limits beyond which our ears cannot pick up the sound. Of course, sounds carry farther in some environments than in others. For example, shouts across a lake or canyon are more easily heard than those passing through a thick forest.

Until the telecommunication inventions of the 19th century, acoustic space was limited by natural factors. Yet, long ago people found ways to expand their acoustic range, sounding information far beyond their loudest vocal reach. One example is the *talking drum*. Widespread among tonal-speaking peoples in West Africa, these large drums can transmit coded information that can be heard from as far away as 12 kilometers (7½ miles).

Another traditional telecommunication system used to expand acoustic space is **whistled speech**, or whistled language—an exchange of whistled words using a phonetic emulation of the sounds produced in spoken voice (Meyer, 2008; Meyer & Gautheron, 2006; Meyer, Meunier, & Dentel, 2007). Whistling sounds are generated by blowing, producing air vibrations at the mouth's aperture; the faster the air stream, the higher the noise.

Whistled speech can be more effective across greater distances than shouted talk because it occurs at a higher pitch or frequency range. Although whistled speech tends to be an abridged form of everyday spoken language, its vocabulary can be considerable. For instance, the whistled form of Spanish known as Silbo, traditionally used on the island of La Gomera off the northwest coast of Africa, includes some 2,000 whistled words.

Although its precise origins are not known, whistled speech still occurs in more than thirty languages around the world. It is found most often in communities that speak tonal languages, such as the Yupik-speaking Eskimos of St. Lawrence Island, who may have developed whistled speech to aid them when kayaking through dense fog or hunting in snowfields (Figure 15.10). Like the talking drum, it is an endangered tradition—disappearing in part because the communities where the practice once thrived are no longer isolated or because the ancestral lifeways are vanishing or already gone. Moreover, the ever-expanding reach of mobile phones and other electronic telecommunication technologies have contributed to its demise (Meyer & Gautheron, 2006).

© Rolex/Jacques Belat

Figure 15.10 Whistled Speech
Occurring in about thirty languages around the world, whistled speech allows community members to exchange essential information in an abridged form of everyday spoken language. Here we see Elaine Kingeekuk, a Siberian Yupik speaker from St. Lawrence Island, Alaska, demonstrating whistled speech. A retired schoolteacher, she assists French linguist Julien Meyer in documenting her whistled language.

The Origins of Language

Cultures all around the world have sacred stories or myths addressing the age-old question of the origins of human language. Anthropologists collecting these stories have often found that cultural groups tend to locate the place of origin in their own ancestral homelands and believe that the first humans also spoke their language.

For example, ancient Israelites believed that it was Yahweh, the divine creator, who had given them Hebrew, the original tongue spoken in paradise. Later, when humans began building the Tower of Babel to signify their own power and to link earth and heaven, Yahweh intervened. He created a confusion of tongues so that people could no longer understand one another, and he scattered them all across the face of the earth, leaving the massive tower unfinished (Figure 15.11).

Early scientific efforts to explain the origin of language suffered from a lack of solid data. Today, there is more scientific evidence, including genetic information, to work with—better knowledge of primate brains, new studies of primate communication, more information on the development of linguistic competence in children, more human fossils that can be used to tentatively reconstruct what ancient brains and vocal tracts were like, and a better understanding of the lifeways of early human ancestors. We still cannot conclusively prove how, when, and where human language first developed, but we can now theorize reasonably on the basis of more and better information.

The archaeological fossil and genetic records suggest that the archaic humans known as Neandertals (an extinct species living during the Ice Age in western Eurasia) had the neurological and anatomical features necessary for speech (D'Anastasio et al., 2013). No skulls of the recently discovered Denisovan hominins have been found, but genetic analysis of a small finger-bone fragment and two molars suggests that these archaic humans ranging in Asia were close enough to Neandertals— their western "cousins" at the time—that they, too, shared that capacity (Dediu & Levinson, 2013).

Because human language is embedded within a gesture–call system of a type that we share with nonhuman primates (especially great apes), anthropologists have gained considerable insight into human language by observing the communication systems of fellow primates (Roberts, Roberts, & Vick, 2014), including Chantek profiled earlier in this chapter. Like humans, apes are capable of referring to events removed in time and space, a phenomenon known as **displacement** and one of the

displacement A term referring to things and events removed in time and space.

Iraq/Mesopotamia: Tower of Babel by Bruegel the Younger, 17th century/Pictures from History/Bridgeman Images

Figure 15.11 The Tower of Babel
Described in the first book of the Bible, the Tower of Babel symbolizes an ancient myth about the origins of language diversity. According to this story, a united people speaking one language set out to build a tower to signify their power and link earth to heaven. Angered by their pride, their god Yahweh stopped the effort by confusing their languages and scattering them across the globe.

spoken language took place, all would agree that spoken languages are at least as old as the species *Homo sapiens*.

From Speech to Writing

When anthropology developed as an academic discipline well over a century ago, it concentrated on small traditional communities that relied primarily on personal interaction and oral communication for survival. Cultures that depend on talking and listening often have rich traditions of storytelling and speechmaking, which play a central role in education, conflict resolution, political decision making, spiritual or supernatural practices, and many other aspects of life.

Traditional orators (from the Latin *orare*, "to speak")

distinctive features of human language (Fouts & Waters, 2001; Lyn et al., 2014).

Because there is continuity between gestural and spoken language, the latter could have emerged from the former through increasing emphasis on finely controlled movements of the mouth and throat. The soft tissues of the vocal tract related to speech are not preserved in the fossil record. But as outlined in this chapter's Biocultural Connection, a comparison of the vocal anatomy of chimps and humans allows paleoanthropologists to identify the anatomical differences responsible for human speech that appeared over the course of human evolution.

There are obvious advantages to spoken over gestural language for a species increasingly dependent on tool use for survival. To talk with your hands, you must stop whatever else you are doing with them; speech does not interfere with that. Other benefits include being able to talk in the dark, past solid objects, or among speakers whose attention is diverted. Although we do not know precisely when the changeover to

are usually trained from the time they are young. They often enhance their extraordinary memorization skills through rhyme, rhythm, and melody. Orators may also employ special objects to help them remember—notched sticks, knotted strings, bands embroidered with shells, and so forth. Traditional Iroquois Indian orators often performed their formal speeches with *wampum belts* made of hemp string with white and bluish-purple shell beads woven into distinctive patterns symbolizing important messages or agreements, including treaties with other nations.

Thousands of languages, past and present, have existed only in spoken form, but many others have been documented in visual graphic symbols of some sort. Over time, simplified pictures of things (pictographs) and ideas (ideographs) evolved into more stylized symbolic forms.

Although different peoples invented a variety of graphic styles, anthropologists distinguish an actual **writing system** as a set of visible or tactile signs used to represent units of language in a systematic way. Symbols carved into 8,600-year-old tortoise shells recently found in western China may represent the world's earliest evidence of elementary writing (Li et al., 2003).

writing system A set of visible or tactile signs used to represent units of language in a systematic way.

The Biology of Human Speech

Although other primates have shown some capacity for language (a socially agreed-upon code of communication), actual speech is unique to humans; this ability is linked to humans' distinct anatomical development of the vocal organs.

Of key importance are the positions of the human larynx (voice box) and the epiglottis. The larynx, situated in the respiratory tract between the pharynx (throat) and trachea (windpipe), contains the vocal cords. The epiglottis is the structure that separates the esophagus, or food pipe, from the windpipe as food passes from the mouth to the stomach. (See the figure for comparative diagrams of the anatomy of this region in apes and humans.)

As humans mature and develop the neurological and muscular coordination for speech, the larynx and epiglottis shift to a downward position. The human tongue bends at the back of the throat and is attached to the pharynx, the region of the throat where the food tract and airway share a common path. Sound occurs as air exhaled from the lungs passes over the vocal cords and causes them to vibrate.

Through continuous interactive movements of the tongue, pharynx, lips, and teeth, as well as nasal passages, the sounds are alternately modified to produce speech—the uniquely patterned sounds of a particular language. Based on longstanding socially learned patterns of speech, different languages stress certain distinctive types of sounds as significant and ignore others. For instance, languages belonging to the Iroquoian family—such as Mohawk, Seneca, and Cherokee—are among the few in the world that have no bilabial stops (*b* and *p* sounds). They also lack the labio-dental spirants (*f* and *v* sounds), leaving the bilabial nasal *m* sound as the only consonant requiring lip articulation.

It takes many years of practice for people to master the muscular movements needed to produce the precise sounds of any particular language. But no human can produce the finely controlled speech sounds without a lowered position of the larynx and epiglottis.

Biocultural Question

The human capacity for speech allows us to say and understand many thousands of words. Because macaws and other parrots also learn many words, do they have speech? And if so, do they actually think?

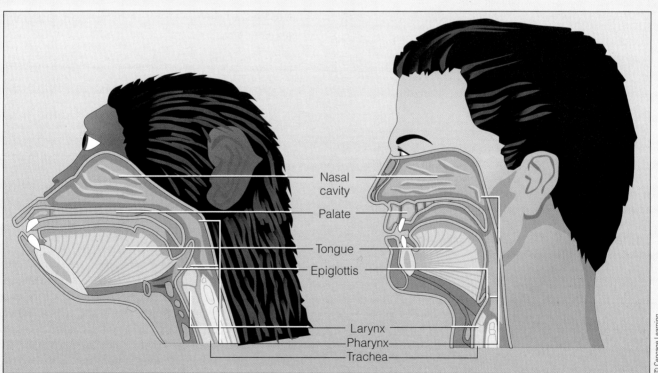

Nasal cavity
Palate
Tongue
Epiglottis
Larynx
Pharynx
Trachea

© Cengage Learning

A comparison of human and ape vocal organs.

Fine Art Premium/Corbis

Figure 15.12 The Rosetta Stone
This polished granite-like stele, inscribed with a royal decree in three scripts, was placed in an Egyptian temple over 2,200 years ago. The upper text is in ancient Egyptian hieroglyphs, the middle portion is in Late Egyptian cursive script, and the lowest is in ancient Greek. Rediscovered in 1799 by a French soldier in a military expedition to Egypt, and captured by the British two years later, this text provided the key to deciphering Egyptian hieroglyphs. It has been on display in the British Museum in London since 1802.

A fully developed early writing system is Egyptian hieroglyphics, developed some 5,000 years ago and in use for about 3,500 years (Figure 15.12). Another very old system is *cuneiform*, an arrangement of wedge-shaped imprints developed primarily in Mesopotamia (southern Iraq), which lasted nearly as long. Cuneiform writing

stands out among other early forms in that it led to the first phonetic writing system—that is, an **alphabet** or series of symbols representing the sounds of a language—ultimately spawning a wide array of alphabetic writing. A written character (*grapheme*) or **letter** is the smallest unit of a writing system, comparable to a phoneme in spoken language. About two millennia after the Mesopotamian and Egyptian writing systems were established, others began to appear, developing independently in distant locations around the world.

Most of the letters used in modern alphabets (including the English alphabet) derive from a writing system invented by Semitic-speaking peoples in the eastern Mediterranean who selectively adopted a number of Egyptian hieroglyphs. About 2,800 years ago, suiting distinctive sounds in their tongue, this system was modified by their Greek neighbors. The word *alphabet* comes from the first two letters in the Greek writing system, *alpha* and *beta*. When Latin-speaking Romans expanded their empire throughout much of Europe, northern Africa, and western Asia, they used a modified Greek alphabet. From the 15th century onward, as European nations grew their trade networks and built colonial empires, the Latin alphabet spread far and wide, making it possible to mechanically reproduce writings in any human language. Although other writing systems—such as Arabic, Chinese, Cyrillic, and Devanāgari—are used by perhaps half of literate humanity, digital media continue to expand the use of the Latin alphabet as a global writing system.

Literacy and Modern Telecommunication

Thousands of years have passed since literacy first emerged, yet today one in five adults—775 million people—cannot read and write. Two-thirds of them are women, with rural women topping the list. (For example, about a third of India's more than 1.2 billion inhabitants cannot read and write.) Worldwide, 75 million children remain out of school, and millions more young people leave school without a level of literacy adequate for productive participation in their societies (UNESCO Institute for Statistics, 2014).

Although many people in the world still rely on others to write and read for them, the global telecommunication revolution has reached the most remote villagers on earth. The demand for mobile phones is high, even among the poor in rural backlands and urban slums—and they make long-distance communication possible without literacy (Figure 15.13).

In today's fast-changing globalizing world where 90 percent of all humans live within mobile coverage, mobile phones are more than a means of communication.

alphabet A series of symbols representing the sounds of a language arranged in a traditional order.
letter A written character or grapheme.

Daniel Irungu/Epa/Corbis

Figure 15.13 Telecommunications and Mobile Banking
The telecommunication revolution is reaching even the most remote places on earth thanks to satellite phones and cell phone towers powered by fossil fuel, the sun, or the wind. Among the conveniences it offers is mobile banking, which has revolutionized how people in Kenya send and receive cash. They do it through M-Pesa (M stands for "mobile," and Pesa means "money" in Swahili). Although a majority of Kenyans do not have a bank account, eight in ten have access to a cell phone. About 85,000 M-Pesa kiosks, like the one pictured here, are scattered across the country, similar to a grid of ATMs. Users can deposit cash at a kiosk and then text it to someone who can pick it up at another kiosk. This has improved commerce and brought basic necessities to poorer areas.

They have become survival tools, with nearly 3.8 billion mobile cellular users worldwide at the start of 2016—more than half the human population. On the move and surrounded by strangers, people use their mobiles to get and give information, to send and receive money, to express their individuality, and to stay in touch—tweeting instead of whistling to avoid feeling lost in the global jungle (GSMA Intelligence, 2016).

CHAPTER CHECKLIST

What is language, and does the term apply only to humans?

✓ Language is a system of communication using sounds, gestures, or marks put together according to a set of rules. Through language, people are able to share experiences, concerns, and beliefs.

✓ Researchers aiming to understand the biological basis, social use, and evolutionary development of language have investigated the communication systems of an array of animal species. Some have studied language acquisition aptitude among great apes by teaching them to communicate using ASL or lexigrams on keyboard devices. Findings show that although great apes cannot literally speak, they can develop language skills to the level of a 2- to 3-year-old human child.

What are the areas of linguistic anthropology?

✓ The three branches of language study in anthropology are descriptive linguistics, historical linguistics, and language in relation to social and cultural settings.

✓ Descriptive linguists mark out and explain the features of a language at a particular time in its history. Their work includes phonology (the study of language sound patterns) and the investigation of grammar—all rules concerning morphemes (the smallest units of meaningful combinations of sounds) and syntax (the principles according to which phrases and sentences are built).

✓ Historical linguists investigate relationships between earlier and later forms of the same language—including identifying the forces behind the changes that have taken place in languages in the course of linguistic divergence. Their work provides a means of roughly dating certain migrations, invasions, and cross-cultural interactions.

✓ Sociolinguists and ethnolinguists study languages in relation to social and cultural settings. Sociolinguists study the relationship between language and society, examining how social categories (such as age, gender, ethnicity, religion, occupation, and class) influence the use and significance of distinctive styles of speech. Ethnolinguists study the dynamic relationship between language and culture and how they mutually influence and inform each other.

How have languages evolved through time, and why have so many disappeared?

✓ All languages change—borrowing terms from other languages or inventing new words for new technologies or social realities. A major cause of language change is the domination of one society over another, which over the last 500 years has led to the disappearance of about half the world's 12,000 languages. Linguistic nationalism and language revitalization have emerged in reaction to language loss and to the domination of the English language.

✓ Many languages have become extinct as a direct result of warfare, epidemics, and forced assimilation brought on by colonial powers and other aggressive outsiders. Other

than the dominant languages in the world today, very few people speak the remaining languages, and many of them are losing speakers rapidly due to globalization.

✓ A social dialect is the language of a group of people within a larger one, all of whom may speak more or less the same language.

Is language more than words?

✓ Human language is embedded in a gesture–call system inherited from our primate ancestors that serves to "key" speech, providing the appropriate frame for interpreting linguistic form. The gesture component consists of facial expressions and body postures and motions that convey intended as well as subconscious messages. Kinesics is the study of such body language. Proxemics is the study of how people perceive and use space. The call component of the gesture–call system is represented by paralanguage, consisting of various voice qualities such as pitch and tempo and vocalizations such as giggling or sighing.

✓ About 70 percent of the world's languages are tonal, in which the musical pitch of spoken words is an essential part of their pronunciation and meaning.

✓ Long before modern telecommunication systems, people found ways to expand their acoustic range—including using talking drums and whistled speech.

What are the origins of spoken and written language, and how do modern telecommunication systems impact literacy around the world?

✓ Worldwide, cultures have sacred stories or myths about the origin of human languages. Language experts agree that spoken languages are at least as old as the species *Homo sapiens*.

✓ The first writing systems—Egyptian hieroglyphics and cuneiform—developed about 5,000 years ago. Symbols carved into 8,600-year-old tortoise shells found in western China may represent the world's earliest evidence of elementary writing.

✓ The global telecom industry reaches into the most remote corners of the world, not only transforming how people communicate, but also with whom and about what.

QUESTIONS FOR REFLECTION

1. Taking a second look at this chapter's opening photo, imagine yourself in a foreign city that has signs in three different languages—none of them your own.

In what ways do you feel prepared or unprepared to meet the challenge of communicating effectively in our increasingly globalized world?

2. Over the last 500 years, half of the world's 12,000 languages vanished. It is now estimated that about 30 languages per year will become extinct during the current century. What might the consequences of this be over time?

3. Applying the principle of linguistic relativity to your own language, consider how your language may have shaped your perceptions of objective reality. How might your sense of time be different if you grew up speaking Hopi?

4. Because much of our communication is nonverbal, how effective do you think text message codes like OJ (only joking), XD (excited), VSF (very sad face), or G (grin) are in digital communication when e-mailing or texting? Have your digital messages ever been misunderstood? If so, what do you think was at the root of the miscommunication, and how was it resolved?

DIGGING INTO ANTHROPOLOGY

Body Talk

Millions of people around the world communicate cross-culturally on a regular basis, both verbally and nonverbally. When making personal contact, we send and receive information with our clothes, bodies, facial expressions, hand gestures, and even leg positions. Likewise, we create "invisible bubbles" within our social space, marking personal boundaries. We are rarely aware of the fact that most of our body language and use of social space are culturally encoded. For that reason, there is ample opportunity for miscommunication in cross-cultural encounters. Dig into the relationship between language and culture, observing six randomly selected individuals from at least two different cultural backgrounds or ethnicities. Make note of their facial expressions, hand gestures, and leg positions and determine the boundaries of their intimate, personal, and public distances. You could try an anthropological experiment in kinesics and proxemics: Engaging with several unsuspecting friends or relatives, alter your own body language, reset your bubble boundaries, and note their confusion or misinterpretation. Write up an analysis and description of your social communication experiment.

Dean Conger/Encyclopedia/Corbis

CHALLENGE ISSUE

Every society faces the challenge of humanizing its children, teaching them the values, social codes, and skills that enable them to become contributing members in the community. Most traditional communities raise children in ways that condition them for their future social status as adult men and women—making sure they have the appropriate clothes and other culturally significant features and skills indicative of their group and gender. This photo, taken at the winter camp of a Khanty reindeer herding family in northwestern Siberia, shows mothers and their fur-clad children on a reindeer sled in front of a portable rawhide home. Underneath their warm outerwear, everyone likely is dressed in brightly colored clothing embroidered by Khanty women with designs passed down through generations. In Khanty culture, infants are believed to be reincarnated ancestors who, like all children still without teeth, can talk with shamans. In a special naming ceremony, a child magically reveals his or her identity to a clairvoyant female elder who divines which ancestor the infant embodies to determine the child's name (Balzer, 1981). Today, there are nearly 30,000 Khanty, organized in male-dominated clans. Some groups primarily depend on fishing, hunting, and fur trapping, while others are nomadic reindeer breeders, as pictured here. They speak a language related to Hungarian, but most also know Russian because their subarctic homeland was annexed centuries ago. Remote but not isolated, local families continue their traditions despite being connected to the wider world with electricity, radios, and televisions.

Social Identity, Personality, and Gender

In 1690 English philosopher John Locke presented the *tabula rasa* ("blank slate") theory in his book *An Essay Concerning Human Understanding*. This notion holds that humans are born with minds that are as empty of information as a blank slate, and what they become in life is written on "the slate" by their life experiences. The implication is that at birth all individuals are basically the same in their potential for character development and that their adult personalities are exclusively the products of their postnatal experiences, which differ from culture to culture.

Locke's idea offered high hopes for the all-embracing impact of intellectual and moral instruction on a child's character formation. However, we now know that it missed the mark, for it did not take into consideration any potential genetic contributions to human behavior. Based on human genetic research, anthropologists now recognize that an identifiable portion of our behavior is genetically influenced (Harpending & Cochran, 2002). This means that humans are born with a particular set of inherited tendencies that help mark out their adult personality. Although this genetic inheritance sets certain broad potentials and limitations, an individual's cultural environment, gender, social status, and unique life experiences, particularly in the early childhood years, also play a significant role in personality formation.

Because different cultures structure the birthing, raising, and education of children in different ways, these practices and their effects on adult personalities are important subjects of anthropological inquiry. Such cross-cultural studies gave rise to the specialization of psychological anthropology and are the subjects of this chapter.

In this chapter you will learn to

- Assess the cultural forces that shape personality and social identity.

- Explain how cultures are learned and passed on to new generations.

- Discuss gender from a cross-cultural perspective.

- Illustrate the cultural relativity of normality and abnormality.

- Identify culturally specific mental disorders.

Enculturation: The Self and Social Identity

From the moment of birth, a person faces multiple survival challenges. Obviously, newborns cannot take care of their own biological needs. Only in myths and romantic fantasies do we encounter stories about children successfully coming of age alone in the wilderness or accomplishing this feat having been raised by animals in the wild. Millions of children around the world have been fascinated by stories about Tarzan and the apes or the jungle boy Mowgli and the wolves. Moreover, young and old alike have been captivated by newspaper hoaxes about "wild" children, such as reports of a 10-year-old boy found running among gazelles in the Syrian Desert in 1946.

Fanciful imaginings aside, human children are biologically ill equipped to survive without culture. This point has been driven home by several documented cases about feral children (*feral* comes from *fera*, which is Latin for "wild animal") who grew up deprived of human contact. None of them had a happy ending. For instance, there was nothing romantic about the girl Kamala, supposedly rescued from a wolf den in India in 1920: According to the rector of the local orphanage who took her in, she moved about on all fours, howled instead of spoke, and bit people who tried to feed her.

Because culture is socially constructed and learned rather than biologically inherited, all societies must somehow ensure that culture is adequately transmitted from one generation to the next—a process we have already defined as *enculturation*. Because each group lives by a particular set of cultural rules, children must learn the behavioral rules of their society in order to survive. Much of that learning takes place in the first few years when children learn how to feel, think, speak, and ultimately act like adults who successfully embody being Kikuyu, Lakota, Russian, Tibetan, or whatever ethnic or national group into which they are born.

The primary agents of early enculturation in all societies are members of the infant's household, especially the child's mother. (Various cultural factors influence the child even before birth through what a pregnant mother eats, drinks, and inhales, as well as the sounds, rhythms, and activity patterns of her everyday life.) Who the other members are depends on how households are organized in each particular society.

As a young person grows up, others outside the household increasingly participate in the enculturation process. These usually include neighbors, other relatives, and certainly the individual's peers. In some complex societies with a greater division of labor, professionals are brought into the process to provide formal instruction. In many societies children are allowed to learn through observation and participation, at their own speed.

self-awareness The ability to identify oneself as an individual, to reflect on oneself, and to evaluate oneself.

Self-Awareness

Enculturation begins with the development of **self-awareness**—the ability to identify oneself as an individual creature, to reflect on oneself, and to evaluate oneself (Figure 16.1). Humans do not have this cognitive ability at birth, even though it is essential for their successful social functioning. It is self-awareness that permits one to take social responsibility for one's conduct, to learn how to react to others, and to assume a variety of roles in society. An important aspect of self-awareness is the attachment of positive value to one's self. This helps motivate young individuals to conform to their culture's expectations, generally to their advantage.

Self-awareness does not come all at once. Developmental psychologists have found that self and non-self are not clearly distinguished until a child is about 2 or 3 years of age (Rochat, 2001; 2010). Self-awareness develops in concert with neuromotor development, which is known to proceed at a slower rate in infants from industrial societies

Figure 16.1 Self-Awareness
Recognizing herself in the mirror, this child has taken a major step in developing the self-awareness necessary to understand that she is a distinct individual. Mirror recognition typically happens around the age of 20 months, but that varies across cultures.

VIEW STOCK RF/AGE Fotostock

than in infants in many, perhaps even most, small-scale farming or foraging communities. The reasons for this slower rate are not yet clear, although the amount of human contact and stimulation that infants receive seems to play an important role.

In the majority of the world's societies, infants routinely sleep with their parents, or at least their mothers. Also, they are carried or held most other times, usually in an upright position, often in the company of other people and amid various activities. Always in close proximity, the mother typically responds to a cry or "fuss" within seconds, usually offering the infant her breast.

This steady stream of stimuli is significant, for studies show that stimulation plays a key role in the hardwiring of the brain; it is necessary for development of the neural circuitry. Notably, the longer children are breast-fed, the better their overall health, the higher they will score on cognitive tests, and the lower the risk of obesity, allergies, and attention deficit hyperactivity disorder (Dettwyler, 1997; World Health Organization, 2015a). Because our biological heritage as primates has programmed us to develop in response to social stimuli, it is not surprising that self-awareness and a variety of other beneficial qualities develop more rapidly in response to close contact with other humans.

Social Identity Through Personal Naming

Personal names are important devices for self-definition in all cultures. It is through naming that a social group acknowledges a child's birthright and establishes its social identity. Among the many cultural rules that exist in each society, those having to do with naming are unique because they individualize a person and at the same time identify one as a group member. Names often express and represent multiple aspects of group identity—ethnic, gender, religious, political, or even rank, class, or caste. Without a name, an individual is anonymous, has no social identity. For this reason, many cultures consider name selection to be an important issue and mark the naming of a child with a special event or ritual known as a **naming ceremony**.

Naming Practices Across Cultures

Worldwide, there are countless approaches to naming. For example, Aymara Indians in the Bolivian highland village of Laymi do not consider an infant truly human until they have given the child a name—and naming does not happen until the child begins to speak the Aymara language, typically around the age of 2. Once the child shows the ability to speak like a human, he or she is considered fit to be recognized as such with a proper name. The naming ceremony marks the toddler's social transition from a state of nature to culture and consequently to full acceptance into the Laymi community.

Unlike the Aymara, Icelanders name babies at birth. Following ancient custom, Icelandic infants receive their father's personal given name as their last name. The suffix *sen* is added to a boy's name and *dottir* to a girl's name. Thus, a brother and sister whose father is named Sven Olafsen would have the last names Svensen and Svensdottir, respectively.

Although such *patronyms* are common in Iceland, sometimes the mother's first name is chosen for her child's surname. Such *matronyms* (surnames based on mother's names) may be preferred for a boy or girl whose mother remains unmarried, is divorced, or simply prefers her own name identifying family status. Thus, a sister and a brother whose mother is named Eva would have the last names Evasdottir and Evason. Matronymic traditions occur in several other parts of the world, including the Indonesian island of Sumatra, homeland of the Minangkabau. In this ethnic group of several million people, children are members of their mother's clan, inheriting her family name.

Among the Netsilik Inuit in Arctic Canada, a mother experiencing a difficult delivery would call out the names of deceased people of admirable character. The name being called at the moment of birth is thought to enter the infant's body and help the delivery, and the child would bear that name thereafter. Inuit parents may also name their children for deceased relatives in the belief that the spiritual identification will help shape their character (Balikci, 1970).

It is common in numerous cultures for a person to receive a name soon after birth and then acquire new names during subsequent life phases. Navajo Indians from the southwestern United States name a child at birth, but traditionalists often give the baby an additional ancestral clan name soon after the child laughs for the first time. Among the Navajo, laughter is seen as the earliest expression of human language, a positive and joyful signal that life as a social being has started. Thus, it is an occasion for celebration, and the person who prompted that very first laugh invites family and close friends to a First Laugh Ceremony. At the gathering, the party sponsor places rock salt in the baby's hand and helps slide the salt all over the little one's body. Representing tears—of both laughter and sadness—the salt is said to provide strength and protection, leading to a long, happy life. Then the ancestral name is given.

In many cultures, a firstborn child's naming ceremony also marks a change in the parents' social status. This is reflected in what is known as *teknonymy* (from *teknon*, the Greek word for "child"), in which someone assumes an honorific name, usually derived from the oldest son, in place of (or alongside) his or her own given name. In Arab societies, such an honorific is known as *kunya*. For example, a young man who names his firstborn son Ishaq becomes known as Abu Ishaq ("Father of Isaac"), whereas his wife may assume the name Umm Ishaq ("Mother of Isaac"). Teknonymy occurs in societies in which only close relatives are permitted to address someone by their other personal name. If outsiders or inferiors do so, it may be

naming ceremony A special event or ritual to mark the naming of a child.

regarded as inappropriate or disrespectful. Such a taboo exists among the Tuareg of the Sahara Desert in northern Africa, for example, where the honorific name is preferred over the personal name (Figure 16.2).

Naming and Identity Politics

Because names symbolically express and represent an individual's cultural self, they may gain particular significance in personal and collective identity politics. For instance, when an ethnic group or nation falls under the control of a more powerful and expanding neighboring group, its members may be forced to assimilate and give up their cultural identity. One early indicator may be that families belonging to the subjugated or overwhelmed group decide to abandon their own ancestral naming traditions. Such was the case when Russia expanded its empire into Siberia and colonized the Turkic-speaking Xakas. Within a few generations, most Xakas had Russian names (Harrison, 2002).

Name-change stories are also common among immigrants hoping to avoid racial discrimination or ethnic stigmatization. For instance, it was not uncommon for Jewish immigrants and their U.S.-born children trying to succeed in the entertainment industry to Americanize their names: Comedian Joan Molinsky became Joan Rivers and fashion designer Ralph Lifshitz became Ralph Lauren.

In identity politics, naming can also be a resistance strategy by a minority group asserting its cultural pride or even rights of self-determination against a dominant society. For instance, in the United States, African Americans with inherited Christian names that were imposed upon their enslaved ancestors have, in growing numbers, rejected those names. Many have also abandoned the faith tradition represented by those names to become members of the Nation of Islam (Black Muslims). An enduring example of this is champion boxer Cassius Clay, who converted to Islam in the mid-1960s. Like others, he rejected his "slave name" and adopted the name Muhammad Ali.

Brent Stirton/ Getty Images

Figure 16.2 Tuareg Naming Ceremony
Tuareg women gather around bowls of noodles for a newborn's naming ceremony inside a tented home typical of those long used by these Sahara Desert nomads in northern Niger. For this special occasion, the women have smeared their hands and faces with indigo. Traditionally, Tuareg children are named on the eighth day after birth, and relatives come from near and far to participate and celebrate the arrival of a new member in their clan. The father and other male relatives gather outside for a Muslim religious ceremony, led by a *marabout*. This holy man offers a prayer and then ritually cuts the throat of a ram slaughtered for the feast. At that moment, the father publicly reveals his child's name, usually one taken from the Quran.

Self and the Behavioral Environment

The development of self-awareness requires basic orientations that structure the psychological fields in which the self acts. These include object orientation, spatial orientation, temporal orientation, and normative orientation.

Every individual must learn about a world of objects other than the self. Through this *object orientation*, each culture singles out for attention certain environmental features, while ignoring others or lumping them together into broad categories. A culture also explains the perceived environment. This is important, for a cultural explanation of one's surroundings imposes order and provides the individual with a sense of direction needed to act meaningfully and effectively. Behind this lies a powerful psychological drive to reduce uncertainty. When confronted with ambiguity, people invariably strive to clarify and give structure to the situation; they do this in ways that their particular culture deems appropriate. Thus, our observations and explanations of the universe are largely culturally constructed and mediated symbolically through language. In short, we perceive reality through a cultural lens.

The behavioral environment in which the self acts also involves *spatial orientation*, or the ability to get from one object or place to another. Names and significant features of places are important references for spatial orientation. Directing someone to the nearest bus stop, maneuvering through airports, or traveling through deep underground networks in subway tunnels are examples of highly complex cognitive tasks based on spatial orientation and memory. So is a Yupik Eskimo hunter's ability to kayak or sled long distances across vast Arctic water, ice, or snow—determining the route by means of a mental map, gauging his location by the position of the sun in daytime, the stars at night, and even by the winds and smell of the air. Technological

revolutions in the 20th century have led to the invention of a newly created media environment, where we learn to orient ourselves in cyberspace. Without our spatial orientations, whether in natural or virtual reality, navigating through daily life would be impossible (**Figure 16.3**).

Temporal orientation, which gives people a sense of their place in time, is also part of the behavioral environment. Connecting past actions with those of the present and future provides a sense of self-continuity. This is the function of a calendar. Derived from the Latin word *kalendae*, which originally referred to a public announcement at the first day of a new month, or moon, such a chart gives people a framework for organizing their days, weeks, months, and even years.

A final aspect of the behavioral environment is the *normative orientation*. Moral values, ideals, and principles, which are cultural in origin, are as much a part of the individual's behavioral environment as are trees, rivers, and mountains. Without them people would have nothing by which to gauge their own actions or those of others. Normative orientation includes, but is not limited to, standards that indicate what ranges of behavior are acceptable for males, females, and whichever additional gender roles exist in a particular society.

Culture and Personality

In the process of enculturation, each individual is introduced to a society's natural and human-made environment along with a collective body of ideas about the self and others. The result is a kind of internalized cultural *master plan* of the cosmos by means of which the individual learns to feel, think, and act as a social being. It is each person's particular guide on how to run the maze

Figure 16.3 Spatial Orientation
Traditionally, each culture provides its members with a comprehensive design for living. This includes spatial orientation needed to act and move safely within their environment. Born and raised in the Arctic, Inuit and other Eskimos find many meaningful reference points in a region that appears endlessly empty and monotonous to outsiders. Without spatial orientation, one would soon be lost and likely perish.

Alinari Archives/Getty Images

of life. When we speak of someone's **personality**—the distinctive way a person thinks, feels, and behaves—we are generalizing about that person's internalized cultural master plan over time. Thus, personalities are products of enculturation, as experienced by individuals, each with his or her distinctive genetic makeup.

Derived from the Latin word *persona,* meaning "mask," the term *personality* relates to the idea of learning to play one's role on the stage of daily life based on the cultural master plan that has historically organized and directed the community in which an individual is raised. Gradually, the mask begins to shape that person until there is little sense of the mask as something superimposed. Instead, it feels natural, as if one were born with it. The individual has successfully internalized the culture.

A Cross-Cultural Perspective on Gender and Personality

Although *what* one learns is important to personality development, most anthropologists assume that *how* one learns is no less important. Along with psychological theorists, anthropologists view childhood experiences as strongly influencing adult personality, and they are most interested in analyses that seek to shed light on the particular cultural differences in shaping personality.

U.S. anthropologist Margaret Mead pioneered the cross-cultural study of sex and gender in relationship to personality. (As discussed in an earlier chapter, sex is biologically determined, while gender is socially constructed.) In the early 1930s she studied three ethnic groups in Papua New Guinea—the Arapesh, the Mundugamor, and the Tchambuli. Her comparative research suggested that whatever biological differences exist between men and women, they are extremely malleable. In short, she concluded, biology is not destiny. She found that among the Arapesh, relations between men and women were expected to be equal, with both genders exhibiting what most Westerners traditionally consider feminine traits (cooperative, nurturing, and gentle). Mead also discovered gender equality among the Mundugamor (now generally called Biwat); however, in that community both genders displayed supposedly masculine traits (individualistic, assertive, volatile, aggressive). Among the Tchambuli (now called Chambri), however, she found that women dominated men (Mead, 1963).

More recent anthropological research suggests that some of Mead's interpretations of gender roles were incorrect—for instance, Chambri women neither dominate Chambri men nor vice versa. Yet, overall her research generated new insights into the human condition, showing that male dominance is not genetically fixed in our human "nature." Instead, it is socially constructed in the context of particular cultural adaptations, and

consequently alternative gender arrangements can be created. (The Anthropologist of Note feature in this chapter profiles Mead's mentor, colleague, and close friend Ruth Benedict, who did pathbreaking research on personality as a cultural construct.) Although biological influence in male–female behavior cannot be ruled out, it has nonetheless become clear that each culture provides different opportunities and has different expectations for ideal or acceptable behavior (Errington & Gewertz, 2001).

Case Study: Childrearing and Gender among the Ju/'hoansi

To understand the importance of childrearing practices for the development of gender-related personality characteristics, consider the Ju/'hoansi Bushmen, native to the Kalahari Desert in southern Africa. Traditionally subsisting as nomadic hunter-gatherers (foragers), in the latter 20th century many Ju/'hoansi were forced to settle down—tending small herds of goats, planting gardens for their livelihood, and engaging in occasional wage labor on white-owned farms (Wyckoff-Baird, 1996).

Ju/'hoansi who traditionally forage for a living emphasize equality and disapprove of dominance and aggressiveness in either gender. Ideally, males are as mild-mannered as females, and females are as energetic and self-reliant as males. By contrast, among the Ju/'hoansi who have recently settled in permanent villages, males and females exhibit personality characteristics resembling those historically thought of as masculine and feminine in many agrarian, pastoral, or industrial societies.

Among the food foragers, a child receives extensive personal care from his or her mother during the first few years of life, because the space between births is typically four to five years. When women go to collect wild plant foods in the bush, however, they may leave the children in the care of their fathers or other community adults, one-third to one-half of whom are in camp on any given day. Because these caretakers include men as well as women, children are as habituated to the male presence as to the female one (**Figure 16.4**). Among these foragers, no one grows up to respect or fear male authority any more than female authority. In fact, instead of being punished by either parent, a child who misbehaves will simply be carried away and introduced to some other more agreeable activity.

Children of both sexes spend much of their time in playgroups that include boys and girls of widely different

Figure 16.4 Ju/'hoansi Parenting
In traditional Ju/'hoansi society, fathers as well as mothers show great indulgence to children. Children are as habituated to male caretakers as to female ones, and they do not fear or respect male authority any more than female authority.

ages. Older children, boys as well as girls, keep an eye out for the younger ones. In short, Ju/'hoansi children in traditional foraging groups have few experiences that set one gender apart from the other.

The situation is very different for Ju/'hoansi who have been forced to abandon their traditional foraging life and who now reside in permanent settlements. Women spend much of their time at home preparing food, doing other domestic chores, and tending the children. Men, meanwhile, spend many hours outside the household growing crops, raising animals, or doing wage labor. As a result, children are less habituated to their presence. This remoteness of the men, coupled with their more extensive knowledge of the outside world and their access to money, tends to strengthen male influence in the household.

Within these village households, gender typecasting begins early. As soon as girls are old enough, they are expected to attend to many of the needs of their younger siblings, thereby allowing their mothers more time to deal with other domestic tasks. This shapes and limits the behavior of girls, who cannot range as widely or explore as freely as they could without little brothers and sisters in tow. Boys, by contrast, have little to do with babies and toddlers, and when they are assigned work, it generally takes them away from the household. Thus, the space that village girls occupy becomes restricted, and they are trained in behaviors that promote passivity and nurturance, whereas village boys begin to learn the distant, controlling roles they will later play as adult men.

When comparing childrearing traditions in different cultures, we find that a group's economic organization and the social relations in its subsistence practices impact the way a child is brought up, and this, in turn, affects the adult personality. Cross-cultural comparisons also show that there are alternative practices for raising children, which means that changing the societal conditions in which one's children grow up can alter significantly the way men and women act and interact. With this in mind, we turn to a brief discussion of different childrearing practices.

Three Childrearing Patterns

Just before Margaret Mead's pioneering comparative research on gender, psychological anthropologists carried out a significant and wide-ranging series of cross-cultural studies on the effects of childrearing on personality. Among other things, their work showed that it is possible to identify three general patterns of childrearing. These patterns stem from practices that, regardless of the reason for their existence, have the effect of emphasizing dependence on the one hand and independence on the other. For convenience, we will call these *dependence training*, *independence training*, and *interdependence training* (Whiting & Child, 1953).

Dependence Training

Dependence training socializes children to think of themselves in terms of the larger whole. Its effect is to create community members whose idea of selfhood transcends individualism, promoting compliance in the performance of assigned tasks and keeping individuals within the group. This pattern is typically associated with extended families, which consist of several husband, wife, children units within the same household. Dependence training is most likely to be found in societies with an economy based on subsistence farming but also in foraging societies where several family groups may live together for at least part of the year.

Big extended families are important because they provide the labor force necessary to till the soil, tend whatever flocks are kept, and carry out other part-time economic pursuits considered necessary for existence. But built into these large families are potentially disruptive tensions. For example, important family decisions must be collectively accepted and followed. In addition, the in-marrying spouses—husbands and wives who come from other groups—must conform themselves to the group's will, something that may not be easy for them.

Dependence training helps to keep these potential problems under control and involves both supportive and corrective aspects. On the supportive side, parents

dependence training Childrearing practices that foster compliance in the performance of assigned tasks and dependence on the domestic group, rather than reliance on oneself.

Ruth Fulton Benedict (1887–1947)

Ruth Fulton Benedict came late to anthropology. After her graduation from Vassar College, she taught high school English, published poetry, and tried her hand at social work. At age 31, she began studying anthropology, first at the New School for Social Research in New York City and then at Columbia University. Having earned her doctorate under Franz Boas, she joined his department. One of her first students was Margaret Mead.

As Benedict herself once said, the main purpose of anthropology is "to make the world safe for human differences." In anthropology, she developed the idea that culture is a collective projection of the personality of those who create it. In her most famous book, *Patterns of Culture* (1934), she compared the cultures of three peoples—the Kwakiutl Indians of the coastal Pacific in Canada, the Zuni Indians of the Arizona desert in the United States, and the Melanesians of Dobu Island off the southern shore of Papua New Guinea. She held that each was comparable to a great work of art, with an internal coherence and consistency of its own.

Seeing the Kwakiutl as egocentric, individualistic, and ecstatic in their rituals, she labeled their cultural configuration "Dionysian" (named after the Greek god of wine and noisy feasting). The Zuni—whom she saw as living by the golden mean, wanting no part of excess or disruptive psychological states and distrusting of individualism—she characterized as "Apollonian" (named after the Greek god of poetry who exemplified beauty). The Dobuans, whom she saw as fearful and hate-filled, with a culture of supernatural powers, she characterized as "paranoid."

Another theme in Benedict's work *Patterns of Culture* is that deviance should be understood as a conflict between an individual's

Ruth Benedict is known for her pioneering work on personality as a cultural construct.

The Granger Collection, New York

personality and the norms of the culture to which the person belongs. Still in print today, *Patterns* has sold close to 2 million copies in a dozen languages. It had great influence on Mead during her cross-cultural gender studies among the Papuas in New Guinea.

Although *Patterns of Culture* still enjoys popularity in some circles, anthropologists have long since abandoned its approach as impressionistic. To compound the problem, Benedict's characterizations of cultures are misleading. For example, the supposedly Apollonian Zunis indulge in such seemingly Dionysian practices as sword swallowing and walking over hot coals, and the use of value-laden terms such as *paranoid* prejudices others against the culture so labeled. Nonetheless, Benedict's book did have an enormous and valuable influence on the field because it focused attention on the relationship between culture and personality and popularized the reality of cultural variation.

are easygoing, and mothers yield to the desires of their young, particularly in the form of breast-feeding, which is provided on demand, continues for several years, and reinforces the idea that the family is the main agent in providing for children's needs. Also on the supportive side, at a relatively young age children are assigned a number of child-care and domestic tasks, all of which make significant and obvious contributions to the family's welfare. Thus, children learn early on that it is normal for family members to share and actively help one another.

On the corrective side, adults actively discourage selfish or aggressive behavior. Moreover, they tend to be insistent on overall obedience, which commonly inclines the individual toward being subordinate to the group. This combination of encouragement and discouragement in the socialization process teaches individuals to put the group's needs above their own—to be obedient, supportive, noncompetitive, and generally responsible, to stay within the fold and not do anything potentially disruptive. A person's

very definition of self in such cultures comes from the individual being a part of a larger social whole rather than from his or her individual existence.

Independence Training

Independence training fosters individual self-reliance and personal achievement. It is typically associated with societies in which a basic social unit consisting of parent(s) and offspring primarily must fend for itself. Independence training is particularly characteristic of trading, industrial, and postindustrial societies where self-sufficiency and individual personal achievement are important traits for success, if not survival—especially for men and increasingly for women.

This childrearing pattern also involves both encouragement and discouragement. On the negative side, a schedule, more than demand, dictates infant feeding. In North America, as noted previously, babies are rarely nursed for more than a year. Many parents resort to an artificial nipple (pacifier) to satisfy the baby's sucking instincts—typically doing so to calm the child rather than to provide the infant with a way to strengthen and train coordination in the muscles used for feeding and speech.

independence training Childrearing practices that foster independence, self-reliance, and personal achievement.

White middle-class parents in North America, for example, are comparatively quick to start feeding infants baby food and even try to get them to feed themselves. Many are delighted if they can prop their infants up in the crib or playpen so that they can hold their own bottles. Moreover, as soon after birth as possible, children are commonly given their own private space, away from their parents. Collective responsibility is not pushed upon children; they are not usually given significant domestic tasks until later in childhood; and these are often carried out for personal benefit (such as to earn an allowance to spend as they wish) rather than as contributions to the family's welfare.

Displays of individual will, assertiveness, and even aggression are tolerated to a greater degree than in cultures where dependence training is the rule. In schools, and even in the family, competition and winning are emphasized. Schools in the United States, for example, devote considerable resources to competitive sports. Competition is fostered within the classroom as well—overtly through practices such as spelling bees and awards and covertly through customs such as grading on a curve. In addition, there are various popularity contests, such as crowning a prom queen and king or holding an election to choose the classmate who is "best looking" or "most likely to succeed." Thus, no matter how many certificates or trophies are handed out for simply participating in sports and other competitive events, by the time individuals have grown up in U.S. society, they have received a clear message: Life is about winning or losing, and losing is equal to failure (Turnbull, 1983a).

In sum, independence training is culturally adaptive in societies that emphasize individual achievement and expect members to look out for their own interests. Its socialization patterns and cultural values and expectations are increasingly prevalent throughout the world as a result of globalism, resulting in a splintering of traditional communities.

Interdependence Training

An intermediary type in patterns of childrearing, representing features of both dependence and independence training, also exists. Known as *interdependence training*, this has been observed among the Beng, a group of about 20,000 Mande-speaking farmers living in villages in the tropical woodlands of Côte d'Ivoire, West Africa. Each family forms a large household, which includes the spirits of deceased ancestors. These spirits, known as *wru*, spend nights with their living relatives but depart at dawn for their invisible spirit village called *wrugbe*.

Believing in reincarnation, the Beng look upon infants not as new creatures but as reincarnated spirit ancestors gradually emerging from *wrugbe* back into everyday life. For this reason, Beng babies are embraced as profoundly spiritual beings who at first are only tentatively attached to life on earth. Their cries are interpreted as a longing for something from *wrugbe*, and good parents do everything within their power to make earthly life so comfortable and appealing that the babies will not be tempted to return there. This includes extensive grooming of the little ones to help attract additional care and love from relatives and neighbors (**Figure 16.5**).

Held much of the day by an array of caregivers and breast-fed by other women in addition to the biological mother, Beng babies develop a broad variety of social ties and emotional attachments and appear generally free of stranger anxiety. Also, because they are thought to be living partly in the spirit world, these tiny "old souls" are allowed to determine their own sleeping and nursing schedules. The Beng cultural concept of an infant as reincarnated ancestor or some other deceased relative influences how he or she is cared for by parents and others in

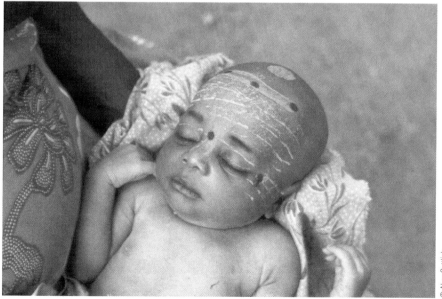

Figure 16.5 Beng Baby in Côte d'Ivoire, West Africa
Beng people see babies as reincarnated ancestors with strong ties to the spirit world. To make sure these tiny "old souls" are not tempted to return to their *wrugbe*, or spirit village, they do everything possible to make earthly life appealing to them. This includes beautifying the child, as shown here, to help attract care from relatives and neighbors.

the community. Because a newborn embodies someone who may already have lived a long life, the infant is accorded a high level of agency, and this influences the child's particular personality formation.

Having studied childrearing practices among these West African farmers, U.S. anthropologist Alma Gottlieb concludes that in Beng communities the social goal is to promote *interdependence* rather than independence, in contrast to what is the normal practice in most North American families today. In sum, Beng babies are made to feel constantly cherished by as many people as possible, learning early on that individual security comes through the intertwining of lives, collectively sharing joys and burdens (Gottlieb, 1998, 2004a, 2004b, 2006).

Figure 16.6 *Waiteri*: **Heroic Male Identity**
Yanomami Indians living in the Amazon rainforest of Venezuela show off as *waiteri* in a public performance befitting the traditional warrior ideal in their culture.

Group Personality

Clearly, there is a complex relationship between culture and personality, with customary practices and other aspects of culture systemically influencing personality development. Anthropologists have considered whether whole societies might be analyzed in terms of particular personality types and whether it would be possible to conduct such a study on group personality without falling into the trap of stereotyping. The answer is a qualified yes, especially with respect to traditional communities. The larger and more complex a society becomes, the greater its range in different personalities. In an abstract way, we may speak of a generalized cultural personality for a society, so long as we do not expect to find a uniformity of personalities within that society.

Modal Personality

Any productive approach to the problem of group personality must recognize that each individual is unique to a degree in both genetic inheritance and life experiences, and it must leave room for a range of different personality types in any society. In addition, personality traits that may be regarded as appropriate in men may not be so regarded in women, and vice versa. Given these qualifiers, we may focus our attention on the **modal personality**, defined as those character traits that occur with the highest frequency in a social group and are therefore the most representative of its culture. Modal personality is a statistical

concept rather than the personality of an average person in a particular society. As such, modal personalities of different groups can be identified and compared.

Take, for example, Yanomami Indians who subsist on hunting, gathering, and cultivating food gardens in the tropical forests of Venezuela in South America. Commonly, Yanomami males strive to conform to a masculine ideal in their culture that they call *waiteri*: being courageous, ferocious, humorous, and generous, all wrapped up into heroic male identity (Chagnon, 1990; Ramos, 1987). Yet, there are men in their villages who are quiet and who have less combative personalities. It is all too easy for an outsider to overlook these individuals when other, more "typical" Yanomami are in the front row, pushing and demanding attention (Figure 16.6).

National Character

Not that long ago, Italy's tourism minister publicly commented on "typical characteristics" of Germans, referring to them as "hyper-nationalistic blonds" and "beer-drinking slobs" holding "noisy burping contests" on Italy's beaches ("Italy–Germany verbal war hots up," 2003). Outraged (and proud of his country's excellent beer), Germany's chancellor canceled his planned vacation to Italy and demanded an official apology. While many Germans may actually think of Italians as dark-eyed, hot-blooded spaghetti eaters, saying so in public might cause an uproar.

Unflattering stereotypes about groups of foreigners are deeply rooted in cultural traditions everywhere. For instance, many Japanese generally regard Koreans as stingy, crude, and aggressive, whereas many Koreans believe that

modal personality Character traits that occur with the highest frequency in a social group and are therefore the most representative of its culture.

Nora Stribrna/Reuters/Corbis

Figure 16.7 Core Values
The collectively shared core values of North Korean culture promote the integration of the individual into a larger group, as we see in this view of the Arirang Mass Games in Pyongyang with over 150,000 gymnasts and performers taking part in 2013. Graphics in the background are made by kids holding colored pieces of cardboard.

Japanese are cold and arrogant. Similarly, you may have in mind some image, perhaps not well defined, of the "typical" Scott, Turk, or Mexican. And U.S. citizens traveling abroad may be insulted that others think of Americans as loud, brash, and arrogant Yankees. Although these are simply stereotypes, we might ask if these beliefs have any basis in fact. In reality, does such a thing as *national character* exist?

Early in the discipline's history, some anthropologists thought that the answer might be yes. However, it was quickly determined that national character studies were flawed, mainly because they made generalizations based on limited data, relatively small samples of informants, and questionable assumptions about developmental psychology. Furthermore, nations organized as states are far more variegated and complex than traditional small-scale societies, and as such defy such simple generalizations.

Core Values

An alternative approach to national character—one that allows for the fact that not all personalities in a group will conform to cultural ideals—is that of Chinese American anthropologist Francis Hsu (1983). His **core value** approach focused on the values especially promoted in a particular culture and their related personality traits.

Hsu suggested that the Chinese traditionally value kin ties and cooperation above all else. To them, mutual dependence is the very essence of personal relationships and has been for thousands of years. Compliance and subordination of one's will to that of family and kin transcend all else, whereas self-reliance is neither promoted nor a source of pride. In totalitarian states such as North Korea, however, subordination is not to one's family but to the nation ruled by an authoritarian leader demanding complete submission of the all-powerful state's subjects. In such societies, core values include obedience, conformity, and repression of individuality, publicly expressed by collective participation in state-sponsored public spectacles such as parades and mass rallies (**Figure 16.7**).

core value A value especially promoted by a particular culture.

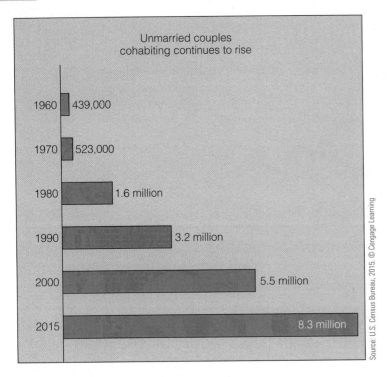

Source: U.S. Census Bureau, 2015. © Cengage Learning

Figure 16.8 Cohabitation Rate in the United States
The number of unmarried opposite-sex couples cohabiting in the United States continues to rise. These couples now make up 12 percent of all opposite-sex U.S. couples, married and unmarried.

Perhaps the core value held in highest esteem by most North Americans of European descent is rugged individualism—traditionally for men but for women as well today. Each individual is supposed to be able to achieve anything he or she likes, given a willingness to work hard enough.

To the degree that it motivates individuals to work hard and to go where the jobs are, this individualism fits well with the demands of a global market economy. Whereas individuals in many traditional societies are firmly bound into a larger group to which they have lifelong obligations, most urban North Americans and western Europeans live isolated from relatives other than their young children and spouse—and even the commitment to marriage and childrearing has lessened (Figure 16.8). Growing numbers of people in western Europe, North America, and other industrial or postindustrial societies choose singlehood or cohabitation over marriage. Among those who do wed, many do so later in life, often prompted by the birth of a child. This individualism is also indicated by high divorce rates—more than 40 percent in the United States (Morello, 2011; Natadecha-Sponsal, 1993; Noack, 2001).

Alternative Gender Models

As touched on earlier, the gender roles assigned to each sex vary from culture to culture and have an impact on personality formation. But what if the sex of an individual is not self-evident, as revealed in this chapter's Original Study? Written when its U.S. author was an undergraduate student of philosophy, this narrative offers a compelling personal account of the emotional difficulties associated with intersexuality and gender ambiguity.

ORIGINAL STUDY

The Blessed Curse BY R. K. WILLIAMSON

One morning not so long ago, a child was born. This birth, however, was no occasion for the customary celebration. Something was wrong: something very grave, very serious, very sinister. This child was born between sexes, an "intersexed" child. From the day of its birth, this child would be caught in a series of struggles involving virtually every aspect of its life. Things that required little thought under "ordinary" circumstances were, in this instance, extraordinarily difficult. Simple questions now had an air of complexity: "What is it, a girl or a boy?" "What do we name it?" "How shall we raise it?" "Who (or what) is to blame for this?"

A Foot in Both Worlds

The child referred to in the introductory paragraph is myself. As the great-granddaughter of a Cherokee woman, I was exposed to the Native American view of people who were born intersexed, and those who exhibited transgendered characteristics. This view sees such individuals in a very positive and affirming light. Yet my immediate family (mother, father, and brothers) were firmly fixed in a negative Christian Euramerican point of view. As a result, I was presented with two different and conflicting views of myself. This resulted in a lot of confusion within me about what I was, how I came to be born the way I was, and what my intersexuality meant in terms of my spirituality as well as my place in society.

I remember, even as a small child, getting mixed messages about my worth as a human being. My grandmother, in keeping with Native American ways, would tell me stories about my birth. She would tell me how she knew when I was born that I had a special place in life, given to me by God, the Great Spirit, and that I had been given "a great strength that girls never have, yet a gentle tenderness that boys never know" and that I was "too pretty and beautiful to be a boy only and too strong to be a girl only." She rejoiced at this "special gift" and taught me that it meant that the Great Spirit had "something important for me to do in this life." I remember how good I felt inside when she told me these things and how I soberly contemplated, even at the young age of 5, that I must be diligent and try to learn and carry out the purpose designed just for me by the Great Spirit.

My parents, however, were so repulsed by my intersexuality that they would never speak of it directly. They would just refer to it as "the work of Satan." To them, I was not at all blessed with a "special gift" from some "Great Spirit," but was "cursed and given over to the Devil" by God. My father treated me with contempt, and my mother wavered between contempt and distant indifference. I was taken from one charismatic church to another in order to have the "demon of mixed sex" cast out of me. At some of these "deliverance" services I was even given a napkin to cough out the demon into!

In the end, no demon ever popped out of me. Still I grew up believing that there was something inherent within me that caused God to hate me, that my intersexuality was a punishment for this something, a mark of condemnation.

Whenever I stayed at my grandmother's house, my fears would be allayed, for she would once again remind me that I was fortunate to have been given this special gift. She was distraught that my parents were treating me

cruelly and pleaded with them to let me live with her, but they would not let me stay at her home permanently. Nevertheless, they did let me spend a significant portion of my childhood with her. Had it not been for that, I might not have been able to survive the tremendous trials that awaited me in my walk through life.

A Personal Resolution

For me, the resolution to the dual message I was receiving was slow in coming, largely due to the fear and self-hatred instilled in me by Christianity. Eventually, though, the spirit wins out. I came to adopt my grandmother's teaching about my intersexuality. Through therapy, and a new, loving home environment, I was able to shed the constant fear of eternal punishment I felt for something I had no control over. After all, I did not create myself.

Because of my own experience, and drawing on the teaching of my grandmother, I am now able to see myself as a wondrous creation of the Great Spirit—but not only me. All creation is wondrous. There is a purpose for everyone in the gender spectrum. Each person's spirit is unique in her or his or her-his own way. It is only by living true to the nature that was bestowed upon us by the Great Spirit, in my view, that we are able to be at peace with ourselves and be in harmony with our neighbor. This, to me, is the Great Meaning and the Great Purpose.

Adapted from Williamson, R. K. (1995). The blessed curse: Spirituality and sexual difference as viewed by Euramerican and Native American cultures. *The College News 18* (4). Reprinted with permission of the author.

Intersexuality

The biological facts of human nature are not always as clear-cut as most people assume. At the level of chromosomes, biological sex is determined according to whether a person's 23rd chromosomal set is XX (female) or XY (male). Some of the genes on these chromosomes control sexual development. This standard biological package does not apply to all humans; some are **intersexual**—a person who is born with reproductive organs, genitalia, and/or sex chromosomes that are not exclusively male or female. These individuals do not fit neatly into a binary gender standard (see Chase, 1998; Dreger, 1998; Fausto-Sterling, 1993).

For example, some people are born with only one X chromosome instead of the usual two. A person with this chromosomal complex, known as Turner syndrome, develops female external genitalia but has nonfunctional ovaries and is therefore infertile. Other individuals are born with the XY sex chromosomes of a male but have an abnormality on the X chromosome that affects the body's sensitivity to androgens (male hormones). This is known as *androgen insensitivity syndrome* (AIS). An adult XY person with

complete AIS appears fully female with a normal clitoris, labia, and breasts. Internally, these individuals possess testes (up in the abdomen, rather than in their usual descended position in the scrotal sack), but they are otherwise born without a complete set of either male or female internal genital organs. They generally possess a short, blind-ended vagina.

Intersexed individuals have both testicular and ovarian tissue. They may have separate ovaries and testes, but more commonly they have *ovotestes*—gonads containing both types of tissue. About 60 percent of intersexed people possess XX (female) sex chromosomes, and the remainder may have XY or a mosaic (a mixture). Their external genitalia may be ambiguous or female, and they may have a uterus or (more commonly) a hemi-uterus (half-uterus) (Fausto-Sterling, 2012).

U.S. biologist Anne Fausto-Sterling, a specialist in biology and gender, notes that the concept of intersexuality is rooted in an idealized biological world in which our species

intersexual A person born with reproductive organs, genitalia, and/or sex chromosomes that are not exclusively male or female.

is perfectly divided into two kinds. She explains that our culture glosses over the fact that some women have facial hair while some men do not, and some women have deep voices while some men have high-pitched squeaky ones. Further, if we investigate closer, there is little sexual dimorphism at the biological level: The chromosomes, hormones, internal sex structures, gonads, and genitalia are much more varied than commonly believed (Fausto-Sterling, 2012).

Intersexuality may be unusual but it is not uncommon. About 1 percent of all humans are intersexed in some (not necessarily visible) way—almost 75 million people worldwide (Blackless et al., 2000). In other words, there are three times more intersexuals than Australians. Until recently, it was rarely discussed publicly in many societies. Since the mid-1900s, individuals with financial means in technologically advanced parts of the world have had the option of reconstructive surgery and hormonal treatments to alter such conditions. Many parents who can afford this option have chosen it when faced with raising a visibly intersexed child in a culture intolerant of such minorities. However, there is a growing movement to put off such irreversible procedures until the child becomes old enough to make the choice.

Obviously, a society's attitude toward these individuals can impact their personality—their fundamental sense of self and how they express it. Today, a growing number of people consider themselves gender neutral and wish to live that way. Evidence of this includes gender-neutral housing and unisex bathrooms offered on many university campuses to accommodate students who do not fall neatly into male or female categories (Fausto-Sterling, 2012; Kantrowitz, 2010).

Moreover, for languages that use gender-specific pronouns, gender-neutral terms are now popularly and officially used. For example, in 2015 the official dictionary of the Swedish language introduced the gender-neutral pronoun *hen*, adding it to the options of *han* ("he") and *hon* ("she") ("Sweden adds gender-neutral pronoun to dictionary," 2015). And across the United States, a growing number of colleges and universities give students the option of specifying a preferred gender pronoun (PGP), such as *ze* to replace *she* or *he* (Leff, 2014; Scelfo, 2015).

Transgender

When mapping the sexual landscape, anthropologists report that "gender bending" exists in many cultures all around the world, playing a significant role in shaping behaviors and personalities. For example, dozens of indigenous communities in the Great Plains and the southwestern United States traditionally created social space for alternatively gendered individuals in their communities. Such a person today is commonly identified as **transgender**—someone who identifies with or expresses a gender identity that differs from the one that matches the person's sex at birth.

The Lakota of the northern Plains had a third-gender category of culturally accepted transgendered males who dressed as women and were thought to possess both male and female spirits. They called (and still call) these third-gender individuals *winkte*, applying the term to a male "who wants to be a woman." Thought to have special curing powers, *winktes* traditionally enjoyed considerable prestige in their communities. Among the neighboring Cheyenne, such a person was called *hemanah*, literally meaning "half-man, half-woman" (Medicine, 1994). The preferred term among most North American Indians today is *two-spirits* (Jacobs, 1994).

Such third-gender individuals are well known in Samoa, where males who take on the identity of females are referred to as *fa'afafines* ("the female way"). Becoming a *fa'afafine* is an accepted option for boys who prefer to dance, cook, clean house, and care for children and the elderly. In large families, it is not unusual to find two or three boys being raised as girls to take on domestic roles in their households (Holmes, 2000).

Transgenders cannot be simply lumped together as homosexuals. For example, the Tagalog-speaking people in the Philippines use the word *bakla* to refer to a man who views himself "as a male with a female heart." These individuals cross-dress on a daily basis, often becoming more "feminine" than Philippine women in their use of heavy makeup, in the clothing they wear, and in the way they walk. Like the Samoan *fa'afafines*, they are generally not sexually attracted to other *bakla* but are drawn to heterosexual men instead. In contrast, 1976 U.S. Olympic gold medalist Bruce Jenner, who transitioned to Caitlyn Jenner in 2015 after fathering six children in three marriages, is still attracted to women—and does not identify as lesbian (Corriston, 2015) (Figure 16.9).

Another example is found among the Bugis, a Muslim ethnic group inhabiting Sulawesi Island in Indonesia and numbering more than 6 million. The Bugis acknowledge five genders: *oroané* (masculine male), *makunrai* (feminine female), *calabai* (feminine male), *calalai* (masculine female), and *bissu* (neither male nor female) (Davies, 2007). Representing and embodying all genders, *bissu* are traditionally high-ranking celibate intersexuals. Their name derives from the Bugis term for "clean" (*bessi*), and as such they serve as shamans, mediating between the human world and the spirit world, inhabited by *dewata* (genderless spirits or gods). As one high-ranking Bugis, Angkong Petta Rala, explained in an interview, "*Bissu* do not bleed, do not have breasts, and do not menstruate, therefore they are *clean* or *holy*" (Umar, 2008, pp. 7–8).

In addition, worldwide there are people who are gender variants: permanent or incidental transvestites (cross-dressers) without being homosexuals. Clearly, the cross-cultural sex and gender scheme is complex; the late 19th-century "homosexuality" and "heterosexuality" labels are inadequate to cover the full range of sex and gender diversity (Schilt & Westbrook, 2009).

transgender A person who identifies with or expresses a gender identity that differs from the one that matches the person's sex at birth.

AP Images

Alo Ceballos/GC Images/Getty Images

Figure 16.9 Celebrated as an all-American hero, Bruce Jenner was one of the world's greatest athletes. After being crowned champion in the 1975 Pan American Games, he competed in the 1976 Olympic Games, winning the gold medal in the decathlon (comprised of ten track and field events, including running, pole vaulting, javelin throwing, and long jumping, as shown here). Forty years later, he announced on television that he was "transitioning" from male to female and taking the new name Caitlyn. Typically, transitioning involves reassignment surgery and sex reassignment therapy, which may include hormone replacement therapy.

Castration

In addition to people who are intersexed or alternatively gendered, throughout history many boys and adult men have been subjected to neutering—crushing, cutting, or otherwise damaging their testicles. Commonly known as *castration*, this is an ancient and widespread cultural practice to transform someone's sexual status and thereby one's social identity.

Males sentenced as sex offenders in the United States and a growing number of European countries may request or be forced to undergo chemical castration, limiting or destroying their sex drive, not only as punishment but also as corrective treatment. Historically, archaeological evidence from ancient Egypt, Iraq, Iran, and China suggests that castrating war captives may have begun several thousand years ago. Boys captured during war or slave-raiding expeditions were often castrated before being sold and shipped off to serve in foreign households, including royal courts. Some castrated men were selected to manage a ruler's harem, the women's quarters in a wealthy lord's household. In Europe, they became known as *eunuchs* (Greek for "guardian of the bed"). Eunuchs could rise to high status as priests and administrators, and some were even appointed to serve as military commanders as happened in the great Persian, Byzantine, and Chinese empires.

In parts of Europe, from the 1500s until late 1800s, a cultural institution of musical eunuchs existed. Historically known as *castrati*, they participated in operas and in

Figure 16.10 *Hijra* **Performers**
These elegantly dressed street performers are eunuchs, part of a broad alternative gender category in India known as *hijras*, which includes intersexuals, transgenders, and castrated males. The exact number of castrated males in India is unknown, but estimates range from 500,000 to 1 million. On the occasion pictured here, thousands of *hijras* from across the country gathered in the remote northern town of Rath—300 kilometers (185 miles) south of Lucknow, the capital of Uttar Pradesh state—for a convention to chart their collective agenda, including a more active role in politics.

what seems normal and acceptable (if not always popular) in one society might be considered abnormal and unacceptable—ridiculous, shameful, and sometimes even criminal—in another. For instance, according to a recent global report, state-sponsored homophobia (the irrational fear of humans with same-sex preferences) thrives in many countries, fueling aggressive intolerance. Worldwide, 78 out of 193 countries have laws criminalizing same-sex sexual acts between consenting adults. Most of these countries punish individuals found guilty with imprisonment, although five countries (Iran, Mauritania, Saudi Arabia, Sudan, Yemen—plus parts of Nigeria and Somalia) punish them with the death penalty (Itaborahy & Zhu, 2014). Yet, as discussed earlier in this text, most countries do not have such laws, and a growing number have passed legislation legalizing same-sex marriage.

The complexity, variability, and acceptability or unacceptability of sex and gender schemes across cultures is an important piece of the human puzzle—one that prods us to rethink social codes and the range of forces that shape personality as well as each society's definition of *normal* overall.

Roman Catholic Church choirs, singing the female parts. Castrated before they reached puberty so as to retain their high voices, these selected boys were often orphans or came from poor families. Without functioning testes to produce male sex hormones, physical development into manhood is aborted, so deeper voices—as well as body hair, semen production, and other usual male attributes—were not part of a castrati's biology.

One of the few places where there are still a substantial number of eunuchs—at least 500,000—is India. There, along with intersexuals and transgenders, they are known as *hijras*. Traditionally, *hijras* performed at important occasions such as births and marriages, but today many make a living, at least in part, as street performers (Figure 16.10). Collectively, these alternatively gendered individuals who are "neither man nor woman" are thought to number about 6 million in India alone (Nanda, 1999).

The Social Context of Sexual and Gender Identity

The cultural standards that define normal behavior for any society are determined by that society itself. Thus,

Normal and Abnormal Personality in Social Context

The boundaries that distinguish the normal from the abnormal vary across cultures and time, as do the standards of what is socially acceptable. In many cultures, individuals may stand out as "different" without being considered "abnormal" in the strictest sense of the word—and without suffering social rejection, ridicule, censure, condemnation, imprisonment, or some other penalty. Moreover, some cultures not only tolerate or accept a much wider range of diversity than others, but they may actually accord special status to the deviant or eccentric as unique, extraordinary, even sacred, as illustrated by the following example.

Sadhus: Holy Men in Hindu Culture

In India and Nepal, ascetic Hindu monks known as *sadhus* provide an ethnographic example of a culture in which abnormal individuals are socially accepted and even honored.

Also, these individuals illustrate the degree to which one's social identity and sense of personal self are cultural constructs. Surrendering all social, material, and sexual attachments to normal human pleasures and delights, *sadhus* dedicate themselves to achieving spiritual union with the divine or universal soul. Practicing intense meditation and yoga, they strive for liberation from the physical limits of the individual mortal self, including the cycle of life and death.

When a young Hindu man in India or Nepal decides to become a *sadhu*, he must transform his personal identity, change his sense of self, and leave his place in the social order. Detaching himself from the pursuit of earthly pleasures (*kama*) and power and wealth (*artha*), he makes a radical break with his family and friends and abandons the moral principles and rules of conduct prescribed for his caste (*dharma*). Symbolically expressing his death as a typical Hindu, he participates in his own funeral ceremony, followed by a ritual rebirth. As a born-again, he acquires a new identity as a *sadhu* and is initiated into a sect of religious mystics.

The life of the *sadhu* demands extraordinary concentration and near superhuman effort, as can be seen when they assume the most extreme yoga postures. It is a life of suffering that may even include self-torture as a form of extreme penance. On a regular basis they apply ashes to their body, face, and long, matted hair. Some pierce their tongue or cheeks with a long iron rod, stab a knife through their arm or leg, or stick their head into a small hole in the ground for hours on end. Naked or near naked ("sky-clad"), they spend most of their time around cremation grounds. One subsect, known as Aghori, drink and eat from bowls made from human skulls as a daily reminder of human mortality (Figure 16.11).

Most Hindus revere and sometimes even fear *sadhus*. Sightings are not rare because an estimated 5 million

Figure 16.11 *Sadhu* **Holy Man**
This Shaivite *sadhu* of the Aghori subsect drinks from a bowl made out of a human skull, symbolizing human mortality. He is a strict follower of the Hindu god Shiva, whose image can be seen behind him.

A Cross-Cultural Perspective on Psychosomatic Symptoms and Mental Health

Biomedicine, the dominant medical system of European and North American cultures, sometimes identifies physical ailments experienced by individuals as *psychosomatic*—a term derived from *psyche* ("mind") and *soma* ("body"). These ailments (also known as conversion disorders) can be serious and painful, but because a precise physiological cause cannot be identified through scientific methods, the illness is viewed as something rooted in mental or emotional causes—and thus on some level not quite real.

Each culture possesses its own historically developed ideas about health, illness, and associated healing practices. Although biomedicine is based in modern Western traditions of science, it is also steeped in the cultural beliefs and practices of the societies within which it operates. Fundamentally informed by a dualistic mind–body model, biomedicine represents the human body as a complex machine with parts that can be manipulated by experts. This approach has resulted in spectacular treatments, such as antibiotics that have eradicated certain infectious diseases.

Today, the remarkable breakthroughs of biomedicine are spreading rapidly throughout the world, and people from cultures with different healing systems are moving into countries where biomedicine dominates. This makes treating illnesses defined by biomedicine as psychosomatic disorders all the more difficult.

Indicative of our biocultural complexity, psychological factors such as emotional stress, worry, and anxiety may stem from cultural contexts and result in increased physiological agitation like irregular heart pounding or palpitations, heightened blood pressure, headaches, stomach and intestinal problems, muscle pains and tensions, rashes, appetite loss, insomnia, fatigue, and a range of other troubles. Indeed, when individuals are unable to deal successfully with stressful situations in daily life and do not get the opportunity for adequate mental rest and relaxation, their natural immune systems may weaken, increasing their chances of getting a cold or some other illness. For people forced to adapt to a quickly changing way of life in their own country or immigrants adjusting to a foreign culture, these pressures may result in a range of disorders that are difficult to explain from the perspective of biomedicine.

Medical and psychological approaches developed in European and North American societies are often unsuccessful in dealing with these problems, for a number of reasons. For one, the various immigrant ethnic groups have different concepts of mind and body than do medical practitioners trained in Western medicine. Among many Caribbean peoples, for example, a widely held belief is that spiritual forces are active in the world and that they influence human identity and behavior. For someone with what a biomedical physician would label a psychosomatic problem, it is normal to seek help from a local *curandero* or *curandera* ("folk healer"), *a santiguadora* ("herbalist"), or even a *santero* (a Santería priest) rather than a medical doctor or psychiatrist. Not only does the client not understand the symbols of Western psychiatry, but a psychiatric visit is often too expensive and may imply that the person is *loco*.

More and more, however, anthropologists have become increasingly involved in cross-cultural medical mediation, challenging negative biases and correcting misinformation about non-Western indigenous perceptions of mind–body connections. The inclusion of culturally appropriate healing approaches has gained acceptance among the Western medical and psychological establishment in Europe, North America, and many other parts of the world.

Biocultural Question

Given the cross-cultural differences in concepts of reality, mind and matter, and spirit and body, should authorities in a pluralistic society apply uniform standards to faith healers as to medical doctors?

---

sadhus live in India and Nepal (Heitzman & Wordem, 2006; Kelly, 2006). Of course, if one of these bearded, long-haired, and nearly naked Hindu monks decided to practice his extreme yoga exercises and other sacred devotions in China, Europe, or North America, most onlookers would consider such a person to be severely mentally disturbed.

Mental Disorders Across Time and Cultures

As the Hindu mystic monks in South Asia illustrate, no matter how extreme or bizarre certain behaviors might seem in a particular place and time, the abnormal is not always socially rejected. Moreover, the standards that define normal behavior may shift over time. For example, the American Psychiatric Association declassified homosexuality as a mental disorder in 1973. Other major mental health organizations followed, including the World Health Organization in 1990 (Herek, 2015).

Just as social attitudes concerning a wide range of both psychological and physical differences change over time within a society, they also vary across cultures—as described in this chapter's Biocultural Connection.

Cultural Relativity and Abnormality

As the example of the *sadhus* in India and Nepal illustrates, what people interpret as abnormal is behavior that deviates from a culturally determined standard of what is normal. The behavior of *sadhus* is deviant but still acceptable in this culture because they occupy a unique position in society that is publicly recognized as spiritual extremists leading an extraordinary way of life. Generally, however, abnormal or deviant behavior is unacceptable, as indicated by the labels identifying such individuals: "crazy," "deranged" or "insane." The stigma of these labels also indicates intolerance for mental illness, whether true or not. Beyond cultural variation and unequal standards, abnormality may be the result of an individual experiencing delusions.

Does this suggest that normalcy is a meaningless concept when applied to personality? Within the context of a particular culture, the concept of normal personality is quite significant. Irving Hallowell, a major figure in the development of psychological anthropology, ironically observed that it is normal to share the delusions traditionally accepted by one's society. A person's state of mind may be so delusional that in medical or psychological terms that individual may be diagnosed as psychotic.

Interestingly, certain types of psychoses are more prevalent in some cultures than others and may not occur in some societies at all. This does not mean that genetic or biochemical factors are irrelevant, but it does suggest that cultural factors play a role. If severe enough, culturally induced conflicts can produce psychosis and also determine its particular form.

Ethnic Psychoses or Culture-Bound Syndromes

An *ethnic psychosis*, or **culture-bound syndrome**, is a mental disorder specific to a particular cultural group (Simons & Hughes, 1985). A historical example is *windigo psychosis*, limited to northern Algonquian-speaking groups such as the Cree and Ojibwa. In their traditional belief systems, these Indians recognized the existence of cannibalistic monsters called windigos. Individuals afflicted by the psychosis developed the delusion that, falling under the control of these monsters, they were themselves transformed into windigos, with a craving for human flesh. As this happened, the psychotic individuals perceived people around them turning into edible animals—fat beavers, for instance. Although there are no known instances where sufferers of windigo psychosis actually devoured humans, they were acutely afraid of doing so, and people around them feared that they might.

Windigo psychosis may seem different from clinical cases of paranoid schizophrenia found in European and North American cultures, but a closer look suggests otherwise. Psychotic individuals draw upon whatever imagery and symbolism their culture has to offer. For instance, the delusions of Irish schizophrenics may draw upon the images and symbols of Irish Catholicism and feature Virgin and Savior motifs. In short, the underlying biomedical structure of the mental disorder may be the same in all cases, but its expression is culturally specific.

A Western example of a culture-bound syndrome is *hysteria*, expressed by fainting spells, choking fits, and even seizures and blindness. Identified in industrializing societies of 19th-century Europe and North America, this disorder was particularly associated with young urban women in well-to-do social circles. In fact, the term invented for this "nervous disease" is derived from the Greek word meaning "uterus." Not only has the diagnosis of this disorder declined in the course of the 20th century, but the term itself was banished from the medical nomenclature (Gordon, 2000).

In recent decades, we have seen the rise of two related culture-bound syndromes associated with consumer capitalism: *bulimia nervosa* and *anorexia nervosa*. Both are characterized by a distorted body image and an obsessive desire to be thin. Bulimia involves frequent binge eating followed by various means of purging, including vomiting. Anorexia is evidenced in self-starvation that may result in death. Bulimia and anorexia are primarily diagnosed in female adolescents who reside in a culture that exalts thinness, even as fast food and leisure snacking are more prevalent. With the globalization of consumer society's fat–thin contradiction, its associated psychological eating disorders are also crossing borders. In the past decade, Brazil, China, India, and Japan have come close to being on a par with the United States in deaths related to psychological eating disorders (Dutta, 2015; Littlewood, 2004).

Personal Identity and Mental Health in Globalizing Society

Anthropologists view childrearing, gender issues, social identity, and emotional and mental health issues in their cultural context; this perspective recognizes that each individual's unique personality, feelings of happiness or unhappiness, and overall sense of health are shaped or influenced by the particular culture within which the person is born and raised to function as a valued member of the community. With the spread of modern consumer culture and its associated psychological disorders, people all around the world face sometimes bewildering challenges hurled at them by the forces of globalization. These forces impact how people raise their children, how their personalities are influenced, and how they maintain their individual and collective social, psychological, and mental health.

Over the last several decades, medical and psychological anthropologists have made valuable contributions to improving healthcare, not only in so-called developing countries far away, but also in their own societies. However, far too often mental health practices prevailing in Europe and North America remain ethnocentric when theorizing and treating psychological disorders—a problem reinforced by a reductionist biomedical mindset that

culture-bound syndrome A mental disorder specific to a particular cultural group; also known as ethnic psychosis.

largely ignores the role of cultural factors in the cause, expression, course, and outcome of mental disorders. Furthermore, commercial pressures on the healthcare establishment favor bioscience and pharmacotherapy, with drug companies providing quick and often inexpensive fixes for the problem (Luhrmann, 2001).

Informed by cultural relativist views on what is considered normal and what is considered deviant, anthropological perspectives on identity, mental health, and psychiatric disorders are especially useful in pluralistic societies where people from different ethnic groups, each with a distinctive culture, coexist and interact. Intensified by globalization, this multi-ethnic convergence drives home the need for a medical pluralism providing multiple healing modalities suited for the cultural dynamics of the 21st century.

CHAPTER CHECKLIST

What is enculturation, and how does it shape a person's personality and identity?

✓ Enculturation, the process by which individuals become members of their society, begins soon after birth. Its first agents are the members of an individual's household, and then it involves other members of society. An individual must have self-awareness before enculturation can proceed.

✓ A child's birthright and social identity are established through personal naming, a universal practice with numerous cross-cultural variations. A name is an important device for self-definition—without one, an individual has no identity, no self. Many cultures mark the naming of a child with a special ceremony.

✓ For self-awareness to emerge and function, four basic orientations are necessary to structure the behavioral environment in which the self acts: object orientation (learning about a world of objects other than the self), spatial orientation, temporal orientation, and normative orientation (an understanding of the values, ideals, and standards that constitute the behavioral environment).

How do childrearing practices and concepts of sex and gender influence a person's behavior, personality, and identity?

✓ Each culture presents different opportunities and expectations concerning gender and ideal or acceptable male–female behavior. In some cultures, male–female relations are based on equal status, with both genders expected to behave similarly. In others, male–female relations are based on inequality and are marked by different standards of expected behavior.

✓ Through cross-cultural studies psychological anthropologists have established the interrelation of personality, childrearing practices, and other aspects of culture.

✓ Dependence training, usually associated with traditional farming societies, stresses compliance in the performance of assigned tasks and dependence on the domestic group, rather than reliance on oneself. Independence training—typical of societies characterized by small, independent families—prizes self-reliance, independent behavior, and personal achievement. Interdependence training, practiced among the Beng of West Africa, teaches children that individual security comes through the intertwining of lives. Some anthropologists contend that childrearing practices derive from a society's need to produce particular kinds of adult personalities.

What are alternative gender models, and how are they viewed cross-culturally?

✓ Intersexuals—individuals born with reproductive organs, genitalia, and/or sex chromosomes that are not exclusively male or female—do not fit neatly into either a male or female biological standard or into a binary gender standard.

✓ Numerous cultures have created social space for intersexual as well as transgender individuals—physically male or female people who cross over or occupy an alternative social position in the binary male–female gender construction.

What determines cultural norms, and is there such a thing as group personality or national character?

✓ Early on, anthropologists tried to determine whether it was possible to delineate a group personality without stereotyping. Each culture chooses, from the vast array of possibilities, those traits that it sees as normative or ideal. Individuals who conform to these traits are rewarded; the rest are not.

✓ National character studies looked for basic personality traits shared by the majority of people of modern countries. Researchers have attempted to determine the childrearing practices and education that shape such a group personality. However, many anthropologists believe national character theories are based on unscientific and overly generalized data; others focus on the core values promoted in particular societies.

✓ What is defined as normal behavior in any culture is determined by the culture itself; what may be acceptable or even admirable in one may not be so regarded in another. Abnormality involves developing personality traits not accepted by a culture.

Does culture play a role in a person's mental health?

✓ Culturally induced conflicts can produce psychological disturbance and can determine the form of the disturbance. Similarly, mental disorders that have a biological cause, like schizophrenia, will be expressed by symptoms specific to the culture of the afflicted individual. Culture-bound syndromes, or ethnic psychoses, are mental disorders specific to a particular ethnic group.

✓ Multi-ethnic convergence, intensified by globalization, drives home the need for a medical pluralism providing multiple healing modalities suited for the cultural dynamics of the 21st century.

QUESTIONS FOR REFLECTION

1. Considering the cultural significance of naming ceremonies in so many societies, including among the Khanty profiled in the Challenge Issue, what do you think motivated your parents when they named you? Does that have any influence on your sense of self?

2. Do you think that the type of childhood training you received shaped your personality? If so, would you continue that approach with your own children?

3. About 70 million people in today's world are intersexed, and only a very small fraction of them have access to reconstructive sexual surgery. What do you think of societies that have created cultural space for alternative gender options beyond the strictly male or female categories?

4. Do you know someone in your family, neighborhood, or school who is "abnormal"? What is the basis for that judgment, and do you think everyone shares that opinion? Can you imagine that personal habits you consider normal would be viewed as deviant in the past or in another country?

DIGGING INTO ANTHROPOLOGY

Gender Across Generations

Our sex is biologically determined, but gender is a cultural construct so its associated behaviors are culturally variable and historically malleable. Most cultures distinguish minimally between two genders, but many recognize a third—and some a fourth or even a fifth gender. Explore the range of culturally prescribed and socially acceptable male–female behaviors in your own social environment. By observing and interviewing individuals from three generations, find out how males and females in your own circle of friends, relatives, and neighbors define femininity (characteristics of the ideal woman) and masculinity (characteristics of the ideal man). Beforehand, formulate questions that will open the door to responses that may indicate a gender differentiation more complex than the stereotypical male–female contrast.

CHALLENGE ISSUE

Facing the challenge of getting food, fuel, shelter, and other necessities, humans must hunt, gather, produce, or otherwise obtain the means to satisfy such needs. During the span of human existence, this has been accomplished in a range of highly contrasting natural environments by means of various biological and cultural adaptations. Inventing or borrowing technologies, humans have developed distinctive subsistence arrangements to feed their families. Thus, we find foragers in Australia's desert, fishers on Alaska's seacoast, manioc planters in Brazil's rainforest, goat herders in Iran's mountains, steel-mill laborers in South Korea, computer techs in India's cities, and poultry farmers in rural Alabama. All human activities impact their environments, some radically transforming the landscape. Here we see Chinese farmers practicing wet-rice cultivation on the mountainous slopes in Guangxi Province. They have carved out terraces to capture rainwater, prevent soil erosion, and increase food production.

Patterns of Subsistence

All living beings must satisfy certain basic needs to stay alive—including food, water, and shelter. Moreover, because these needs must be met on an ongoing basis, no creature could long survive if its relations with the environment were random and chaotic. People have a huge advantage over other animals in this regard. We have developed advanced levels of culture.

Thanks to culture, if the rains do not come and the hot sun turns grassland into desert, we know how to pump water from deep wells to irrigate pastures and feed our grazing animals. Conversely, if too much rain turns our pastures into marshlands, we have ways to drain flooded fields. To guard against famine, we have devised methods to preserve food and place it in safe storage. And if our stomachs are incapable of digesting a particular food, we have learned that cooking can make it edible.

Despite such cultural knowhow, we are still subject to the basic pressures that face all living creatures, and it is important to understand human survival from this point of view. The crucial concept that underlies such a perspective is adaptation.

Adaptation

As discussed earlier in this book, *adaptation* is the process organisms undergo to achieve a beneficial adjustment to a particular environment. What makes human adaptation unique among all other species is our capacity to produce and reproduce culture, enabling us to creatively adapt to an extraordinary range of radically different environments. The biological underpinnings of this capacity include complex brains and a long period of growth and development.

How humans adjust to the burdens and opportunities presented in daily life is the basic concern of all cultures. As defined in a previous chapter, a people's *cultural adaptation* consists of a complex of ideas, activities, and technologies that enable them to survive and even thrive; in turn, that adaptation impacts their environment.

In this chapter you will learn to

- Recognize the relationship between cultural adaptation and long-term cultural change.

- Distinguish between the different food-collecting and food-producing systems developed around the world over the course of about 200,000 years.

- Analyze the interrelationship of natural environment, technology, and social organization in cultures as systems of adaptation.

- Assess the significance of the Neolithic revolution in the context of cultural evolution.

- Explain the process of parallel evolution in contrast to convergent evolution.

- Critically discuss mass food production in the age of globalization.

Through their distinctive cultures, different human groups have managed to adapt to a hugely diverse range of natural environments—from Arctic snowfields to Polynesian coral islands, from the Arabian Desert to the Amazon rainforest. Notably, adaptation occurs not only when humans make changes in their natural environment but also when they are biologically changed by that environment, as illustrated in this chapter's Biocultural Connection.

Adaptation, Environment, and Ecosystem

Human beings, like other organisms, survive as members of a population within a natural *environment*—a defined space with limited resources that presents certain possibilities and limitations. People might just as easily farm as fish, but we do not expect to find farmers in Siberia's frozen tundra or fishermen in the middle of North Africa's Sahara Desert. Anthropologists have adopted the ecologists' concept of **ecosystem**, defined as a system, or functioning whole, composed of both the natural environment and all the organisms living within it. Involving both organisms and their environment, the process of adaptation establishes an ever-shifting balance between the needs of a population and the potential of its environment. Populations must have the flexibility to cope with variability and change within their ecosystem in order to sustain themselves over the long run.

Case Study: The Tsembaga

The Tsembaga people of Papua New Guinea are one of countless examples of populations adapting to fluctuations in their ecosystems by means of culture. The Tsembaga are one of about twenty local groups of Maring speakers who support themselves chiefly through sweet potatoes grown by women in food gardens cultivated with digging sticks or hoes (Rappaport, 1969). These Papuas also raise pigs, which fulfill important functions in the community. Devouring almost anything edible, pigs keep the village free of garbage and even human excrement; moreover, they serve as status symbols for their male owners. Rarely slaughtered, pigs are reserved primarily for large feasts when allies are needed to help fight in periodic warfare against rival groups competing for scarce land. At such times they are sacrificed to ancestral spirits, and their meat is ritually consumed by everyone at the great pig feast.

Hostilities are periodically fueled by ecological pressures in which pigs play a significant role. Valued for sanitizing the village and protected as prestige animals, pig populations multiply quickly, and in time great numbers of them raid the food gardens. Threatening the food supplies of the Tsembaga, they become a serious problem.

The need to expand food cultivation in order to feed the prestigious but pesky pigs puts a strain on the land best suited for farming. Male-owned pigs rooting for the sweet potatoes greatly irritate the women working in the food gardens. The growing tension in the ecosystem results in periodic fighting between the Tsembaga and rival neighbors.

Armed hostilities usually end after several weeks, followed by a pig feast ritual. For this event, the Tsembaga butcher and roast almost all of their pigs and feast heartily on them with invited allies. By means of this feast, the male Tsembaga hosts gain prestige and eliminate a major source of irritation and complaint in their families and between neighbors. Moreover, feasting on animal protein leaves everyone well fed and physically strengthened. Even without hostilities over scarce land, such large pig feasts have been held whenever the pig population has become unmanageable—every five to ten years, depending on the groups' success in growing crops and raising animals. Thus, the cycle of fighting and feasting keeps the ecosystemic balance among humans, animals, crops, and land.

Adaptation and Culture Areas

From early on, anthropologists recognized that ethnic groups living within the same broad habitat often share certain cultural traits. These similarities reflect the fundamental relationship between their comparable natural environments, available resources, and subsistence practices, as well as the contact and exchange with neighboring populations.

Classifying groups according to their cultural traits, anthropologists have mapped out geographic regions in which a number of societies have similar ways of life. Such a region, or **culture area**, often corresponds to an ecological expanse. In sub-Arctic North America, for example, migratory caribou herds graze across the vast tundra. For dozens of different groups that have made this area their home, these animals provide a major source of food as well as material for shelter and clothing. Adapting to more or less the same ecological resources in this sub-Arctic landscape, these groups have developed similar

---

ecosystem A system, or a functioning whole, composed of both the natural environment and all the organisms living within it.

culture area A geographic region in which a number of societies follow similar patterns of life.

Surviving in the Andes: Aymara Adaptation to High Altitude

However adaptable we are as a species through our diverse cultures, some natural environments pose such extreme climatic challenges that the human body must make physical adaptations to successfully survive. The central Andean highlands of Bolivia offer an interesting example of complex biocultural interaction, where a biologically adapted human body type has emerged due to natural selection.

Known as the *altiplano*, this high plateau has an average elevation of 4,000 meters (13,000 feet). Many thousands of years ago, small groups of human foragers in the warm lowlands climbed up the mountain slopes in search of game and other food. The higher they moved, the harder it became to breathe due to decreasing molecular concentration, or partial pressure, of oxygen in the inspired air. However, upon reaching the cold and treeless highlands, they found herds of llamas and hardy food plants, including potatoes—reasons to stay. Eventually (about 4,000 years ago) their descendants domesticated both the llamas and the potatoes and developed a new way of life as high-altitude agropastoralists.

The llamas provided meat and hides, as well as milk and wool. And the potatoes, a rich source of carbohydrates, became their staple food. Over the course of many centuries, the Aymara selectively cultivated more than 200 varieties of these tubers on small family-owned tracts of land. They boiled them fresh for immediate consumption and also freeze-dried and preserved them as *chuño*, which is the Aymara's major source of nutrition to this day.

Still surviving as highland subsistence farmers and herders, these Aymara Indians have adapted culturally and biologically to the cold and harsh conditions of Bolivia's altiplano. They live and go about their work at extremely high altitudes (up to 4,800 meters or 15,600 feet), in which partial pressure of oxygen in the air is far lower than that to which most humans are biologically accustomed.

Aymara Indians, who survive as farmers and herders, move across the altiplano (high plateau) in Bolivia with their llamas.

Experiencing a marked *hypoxia* (insufficient oxygenation of the blood), a person's normal physiological response to being active at such heights is quick and heavy breathing. Most outsiders visiting the altiplano typically need several days to acclimatize to these conditions. Going too high too quickly can cause *soroche* ("mountain sickness"), with physiological problems such as pulmonary hypertension, increased heart rates, shortness of breath, headaches, fever, lethargy, and nausea. These symptoms usually disappear when one becomes fully acclimated, but most people will still be quickly exhausted by otherwise normal physical exercise.

For the Aymara Indians whose ancestors have inhabited the altiplano for many thousands of years, the situation is different. Through generations of natural selection, their bodies have become biologically adapted to the low oxygen levels.[a] Short-legged and barrel-chested, their small bodies have an unusually large thoracic volume compared to their tropical lowland neighbors and most other humans. Remarkably,

their expanded heart and lungs possess about 30 percent greater pulmonary diffusing capacity to oxygenate blood.

In short, the distinctly broad chests of the Aymara Indians are biological evidence of their adaptation to the low-oxygen atmosphere of a natural habitat in which they survive as high-altitude agropastoralists.

Biocultural Question

If a group of Aymara Indians abandons their high-altitude homeland in the Bolivian altiplano and settles for a new life in the coastal lowlands, will their descendants still living in this low-altitude environment a dozen generations later have smaller chests?

---

[a] For more information, see Baker, P. (Ed.). (1978). *The biology of high altitude peoples.* London: Cambridge University Press; Rupert, J. L., & Hochachka, P. W. (2001). The evidence for hereditary factors contributing to high altitude adaptation in Andean natives: A review. *High Altitude Medicine & Biology 2* (2), 235–256.

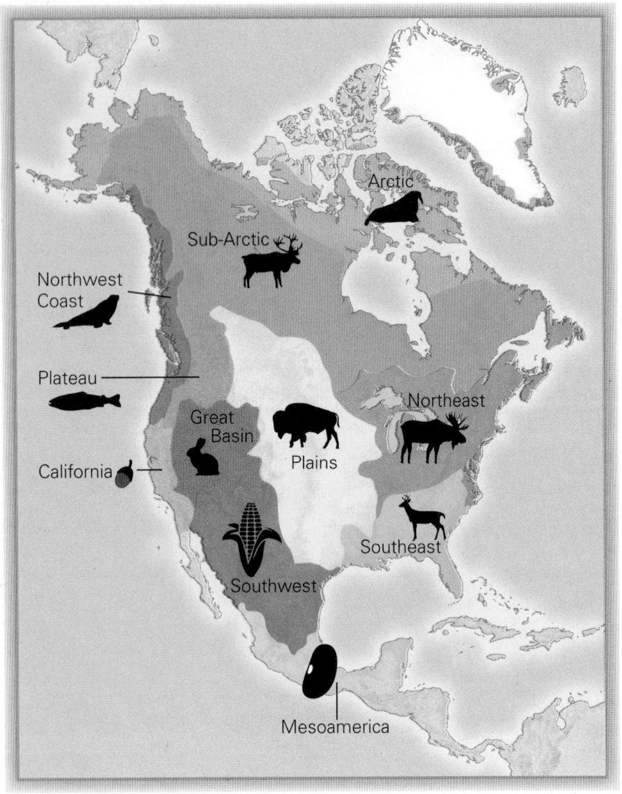

Figure 17.1 Culture Areas
This map shows the major indigenous culture areas in North and Central America, highlighting a key traditional food source for each. Native cultures within each area were similar.

subsistence technologies and practices over the course of generations. Although they speak very different languages, they share a similar way of life, and thus all these different caribou-hunting groups, each with their own particular cultural identity, form part of the same culture area (Figure 17.1).

Modes of Subsistence

Human societies all around the world have developed cultural infrastructures compatible with the natural resources they have available to them and within the limitations of their various habitats. Each mode of subsistence involves resources and the technology required to effectively capture and utilize them, as well as the kinds of work arrangements that are developed to best suit a society's needs. In the next few pages, we will discuss the major types of cultural infrastructure, beginning with the oldest and most universal mode of subsistence: food foraging.

food foraging A mode of subsistence involving some combination of hunting, fishing, and gathering of wild plant foods.

Food-Foraging Societies

Before the domestication of food plants and animals, all people sustained themselves through **food foraging**, a mode of subsistence involving some combination of hunting, fishing, and gathering wild plant foods (roots, bulbs, leaves, seeds, nuts, fruits, honey, and so forth). When food foragers had the earth to themselves, they had their pick of the best environments. But gradually, areas with rich soils and ample supplies of water were appropriated by farming societies and more recently by industrial and postindustrial societies in which machines largely replaced human labor, hand tools, and animal power. One after the other, small foraging communities were edged out of their traditional habitats by expanding food-producing societies.

Today, only about 200,000 people (less than 0.003 percent of the world population of well over 7 billion) still subsist mainly as traditional foragers—hunting, fishing, and gathering. They are found only in the world's most marginal areas (frozen Arctic tundra, deserts, and inaccessible forests) and typically lead a migratory existence that makes it impractical to accumulate many material possessions. Because foraging cultures have nearly disappeared in areas having a natural abundance of food and fuel resources, anthropologists are necessarily cautious about generalizing about the ancient human past based on in-depth studies of still-existing foraging groups that have adapted to more marginal habitats.

Present-day people who subsist by hunting, fishing, and wild plant collection are seldom or never completely isolated. In fact, many groups historically participate in trade networks involving non-foragers, meeting the demand for commodities such as furs, hides, feathers, ivory, pearls, fish, nuts, and honey within larger trading networks. Like everyone else, most food foragers are now part of a larger system with social, economic, and political relations extending far beyond regional, national, or even continental boundaries (Figure 17.2).

Characteristics of Food-Foraging Societies

Among the few remaining food-foraging societies, there are some common features: mobility, small group size, flexible division of labor by gender, food sharing, egalitarianism, communal property, and rarity of warfare.

Mobility

Food foragers move as needed within a circumscribed region that is their home range to tap into naturally available food sources. Some groups, such as the Ju/'hoansi in the Kalahari Desert of southern Africa who depend on the reliable and highly drought-resistant mongongo nut, may keep to fairly fixed annual routes and cover only a

Figure 17.2 Remote but Not Isolated Peoples of the Kalahari Desert
Human groups (including food foragers) do not exist in isolation except occasionally—and even then not for long. The bicycle this Bushman of southern Africa is riding is indicative of his links with the wider world, just as the wild *tsama* melons (watermelons), bow, and quiver of arrows speak of his traditional hunter-gatherer life. For 2,000 years, Bushmen have been interacting regularly with neighboring farmers and pastoralists. Moreover, food foragers have supplied much of the commodities desired by the rest of the world, such as the elephant ivory used for keyboards on pianos so widely sought in 19th-century North America.

© Anthony Bannister; Gallo Images Corbis

restricted territory. Others, such as the traditional Shoshone in the western highlands of North America, had to cover a wider territory, their course determined by the local availability of the erratically productive pine nut.

A crucial factor in this mobility is availability of water. The distance between the food supply and the water must not be so great that more energy is required to fetch water than can be obtained from the food.

Small Group Size

Another characteristic of the food-foraging adaptation is the small size of local groups, typically fewer than a hundred people. No completely satisfactory explanation for this has been offered, but both ecological and social factors are involved. Among the ecological factors is the **carrying capacity** of the land—the number of people that the available resources can support at a given level of food-getting techniques. This requires adjusting to seasonal and long-term changes in resource availability. Carrying capacity involves not only the immediate presence of food and water but also the tools and work necessary to secure them, as well as short- and long-term fluctuations in their availability.

In addition to seasonal or local adjustments, food foragers must make long-term adjustments to resources. Food-foraging populations usually stabilize at numbers well below the carrying capacity of their land. In fact, the home ranges of most food foragers can support from three to five times as many people as they typically do. In the long run, it may be more adaptive for a group to keep its numbers low rather than to expand indefinitely and risk disaster by a sudden and unexpected natural reduction in food resources. The population density of foraging groups surviving in marginal environments today rarely exceeds one person per square mile—a very low density.

How food-foraging peoples regulate population size relates to two things: how much body fat they accumulate and how they care for their children. Ovulation requires a certain minimum of body fat. The *menarche* (a girl's first menstruation) in hunting and gathering societies surviving in areas with relatively few natural resources, such as the Kalahari Desert in southwestern Africa, generally begins about 5 years later than in most agricultural or industrial societies. For example, the mean age for menarche among !Kung Bushmen is 16.6 years, and the mean age of !Kung mothers bearing their first child is 21.4 years (Howell, 2010). Once a child is born, the mother nurses the child several times each hour, even at night, and this continues over a period of four or five years. The constant stimulation of the mother's nipples suppresses the level of hormones that promote ovulation, making conception less likely (Konner & Worthman, 1980; Small, 1997). Continuing to nurse for several years, women give birth only at widely spaced intervals. Thus, the total number of offspring remains low, effectively maintaining a stable and sustainable population size (Figure 17.3).

Flexible Division of Labor by Gender

Division of labor, present in all human societies, is probably as old as human culture. Among food foragers, the hunting and butchering of large game as well as the processing of hard or tough raw materials are almost universally male occupations. By contrast, women's work in foraging societies usually focuses on collecting and processing a variety of plant foods, as well as other domestic chores that can

carrying capacity The number of people that the available resources can support at a given level of food-getting techniques.

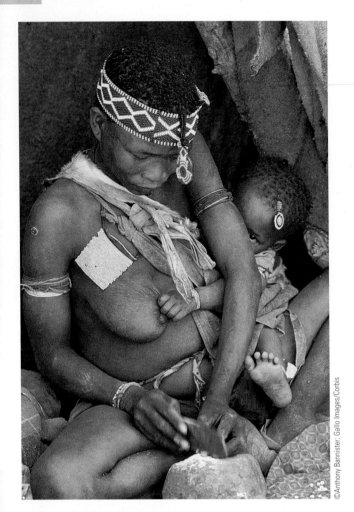

©Anthony Bannister; Gallo Images/Corbis

Figure 17.3 Natural Birth Control
Frequent nursing of children over four or five years acts to suppress ovulation among food foragers such as the Ju/'hoansi. As a consequence, women give birth to relatively few offspring at widely spaced intervals.

be fit to the demands of breast-feeding and that are more compatible with pregnancy and childbirth.

Among food foragers today, the work of women is no less arduous than that of men. For example, Ju/'hoansi women may walk 12 miles a day to gather food, two or three times a week. They are carrying not only their children but also, on the return home, between 15 and 33 pounds of food. Still, they do not have to travel quite as far as do men on the hunt, and their work is usually less dangerous. Also, their tasks require less rapid mobility, do not need complete and undivided attention, and are readily resumed after interruption.

All of this is compatible with those biological differences that remain between the sexes. Certainly, women who are pregnant or who have infants to nurse cannot travel long distances in pursuit of game as easily as men can.

But, saying that differing gender roles among food foragers is compatible with the biological differences between men and women is *not* saying that these roles are biologically

determined. In fact, the division of labor by gender is often far less rigid among food foragers than it is in most other types of society. Thus, Ju/'hoansi males, when the occasion demands, willingly and without embarrassment gather wild plant foods, build huts, and collect water, even though all are regarded as women's work. Likewise, in coastal Algonquian societies, women traditionally took an active part in harvesting fish and shellfish such as clams and oysters.

Although women in foraging societies commonly spend some time each day gathering wild foods, men rarely hunt on a daily basis (Figure 17.4). The amount of energy expended in hunting, especially in hot climates, is often greater than the energy return from the kill. Too much time spent searching out game might actually be counterproductive. Energy itself is derived primarily from plant carbohydrates, and it is usually the female gatherers who bring in the bulk of the calories. A certain amount of meat in the diet, though, guarantees high-quality protein that is less easily obtained from plant sources because meat contains exactly the right balance of all the amino acids (the building blocks of protein) the human body requires. No one plant food does this, and in order to get by without meat people must hit on exactly the right combination of plants to provide the essential amino acids in the correct proportions.

Food Sharing

Another key feature of human social organization associated with food foraging is the sharing of food. Among the Ju/'hoansi, women have control over the food they collect and can share it with whomever they choose. Men, by contrast, are constrained by rules that specify how much meat is to be distributed and to whom. For the individual hunter, meat sharing is really a way of storing it for the future: His generosity, obligatory though it might be, gives him a claim on the future kills of other hunters. As a cultural trait, food sharing has the obvious survival value of distributing resources needed for subsistence.

Egalitarian Social Relations

A key characteristic of the food-foraging society is its egalitarianism. Because foragers are usually highly mobile and lack animal or mechanical transportation, they must be able to travel without many encumbrances, especially on food-getting expeditions. By necessity, the material goods they carry with them are limited to the bare essentials, which include implements for hunting, gathering, fishing, building, and cooking. (For example, the average weight of an individual's personal belongings among the Ju/'hoansi is just under 25 pounds.) In this context, it makes little sense for them to accumulate luxuries or surplus goods, and the fact that no one owns significantly more than another helps to limit status differences.

It is important to realize that discrepancy in social standing by itself does not constitute inequality, a point that is easily misunderstood especially when relations between men and women are concerned. In most traditional

VISUAL COUNTERPOINT

Figure 17.4 Gender and Labor
Although food foragers such as the Ju/'hoansi Bushmen in southern Africa have a flexible division of labor, men usually do the hunting, whereas women prepare food. Both men and women gather wild foods such as ostrich eggs and edible plants—fruits, nuts, and tubers. Here, Ju/'hoansi men return from a successful porcupine hunt, and women prepare a 3-pound ostrich egg omelet (equivalent to about two dozen chicken eggs). Traditionally, once the bird's large, hard shell has been emptied, it serves as a very useful water container. If it shatters, pieces are fashioned into jewelry.

food-foraging societies, women did not and do not defer to men. To be sure, women may be excluded from some rituals in which men participate, but the reverse is also true. Moreover, women control the fruits of their labor, not the men. Nor do women sacrifice their autonomy even in societies in which male hunting, rather than female gathering, brings in the bulk of the food.

Communal Property

Food foragers make no attempt to accumulate surplus foodstuffs, often an important source of status in agrarian societies. This does not mean that they live constantly on the verge of starvation because their environment is their natural storehouse. Except in the coldest climates (where a surplus must be set aside to see people through the long, lean winter season) or in times of acute ecological disaster, some food can almost always be found in a group's territory. Because food resources are typically shared and distributed equally throughout the group, no one achieves the wealth or status that hoarding might produce. In such a society, having more than others is a sign of deviance rather than a desirable characteristic.

The food forager's concept of territory contributes as much to social equality as it does to the equal distribution of resources. Most groups have home ranges within which access to resources is open to all members. What is available to one is available to all. If a Mbuti Pygmy hunter living in the forests of Central Africa discovers a honey tree, he has first rights; but when he has taken his share, others have a turn. No individual within the community privately owns the tree; the system is first come, first served.

Rarity of Warfare

Although much has been written on the theoretical importance of hunting for shaping the supposedly competitive and aggressive nature of the human species, most anthropologists are unconvinced by these arguments. To be sure, warlike behavior on the part of food-foraging peoples is known, but such behavior is a relatively recent phenomenon in response to pressure from expansionist states. In the absence of such pressures, food-foraging peoples are remarkably nonaggressive and place more emphasis on peacefulness and cooperation than they do on violent competition.

How Technology Impacts Cultural Adaptations among Foragers

Like habitat, technology plays an important role in shaping the characteristics of the foraging life. Just as the availability of water, game animals, and other seasonal resources influence the movement, population size, and division of labor by gender among food-foraging groups, so too do different hunting technologies and techniques play a part in determining movement, as well as population size and division of labor by gender.

Consider, for example, the Mbuti Pygmies in the Ituri forest of the Democratic Republic of Congo in Central Africa. All Mbuti bands hunt elephants with spears. However, for other game some of the bands use bows, and others use large nets. Those equipped with nets have a cooperative division of labor in which men, women, and children collaborate in driving antelope and other game into the nets for the kill. Usually, this involves very long hours and movement over great distances as participants surround the animals and beat the woods noisily to chase the game in one direction toward the great nets. Because this sort of "beat-hunt" requires the cooperation of up to thirty families, those using this method have relatively large camps.

Among Mbuti bow hunters, on the other hand, only men go after the game. These archers tend to stay closer to the village for shorter periods of time and live in smaller groups, typically of no more than six families. Although there is no significant difference in overall population density between net- and bow-hunting areas, archers generally harvest a greater diversity of animal species, including monkeys (Bailey & Aunger, 1989; Terashima, 1983).

Food-Producing Societies

Habitat and technology do not tell the whole story of how we humans feed ourselves. After the emergence of tool-making, which enabled humans to consume significant amounts of meat as well as plant foods, the next truly momentous event in human history was the domestication of plants and animals. Over time, this achievement transformed cultural systems, with humans developing new economic arrangements, social structures, and ideological patterns based on plant cultivation, breeding and raising animals, or a mixture of both.

The transition from food foraging to food production first took place about 10,000 years ago in Southwest Asia (the Fertile Crescent, including the Jordan River Valley and neighboring regions in the Middle East). This was the beginning of the **Neolithic** or New Stone Age (from the Greek *neo* meaning "new" and *lith* meaning "stone") in which people possessed stone-based technologies and depended on domesticated plants, animals, or both. Within the next few thousand years, similar early transitions to agricultural economies took place independently in other parts of the world where human groups began to raise and (later) alter wild cereal plants such as wheat, maize (corn), and rice; legumes such as beans; gourds such as squash; and tubers such as potatoes. Doing the same with a number of wild animal species ranging in their hunting territories, people began to domesticate goats, sheep, pigs, cattle, and llamas (Figure 17.5).

Because these activities radically changed almost every aspect of cultural systems, anthropologists use the term **Neolithic revolution**. As humans became increasingly dependent on domesticated crops, they mostly gave up their mobile way of life and settled down to till the soil, sow, weed, protect, harvest, and safely store their crops. No longer on the move, they could build more permanent dwellings and began to make pottery for storage of water, food, and so on.

Just why this change came about is one of the important questions in anthropology. Because food production requires more work than food foraging, is more monotonous, and is often a less secure means of subsistence, it is unlikely that people became food producers voluntarily.

Initially, it appears that food production arose as a largely unintended byproduct of existing food management practices. Among many examples, we may consider the Paiute Indians, whose desert habitat in the western highlands of North America includes some oasis-like marshlands. These foragers discovered how to irrigate wild crops in their otherwise very dry homeland, thus increasing the quantity of wild seeds and bulbs to be harvested. Although their ecological intervention was very limited, it allowed them to settle down for longer periods in greater numbers than otherwise would have been possible.

Unlike the Paiute, who stopped just short of a Neolithic revolution, other groups elsewhere in the world continued to transform their landscapes in ways that favored the appearance of new varieties of particular plants and animals, which came to take on increasing importance for people's subsistence. Although probably at first accidental, food production became a matter of necessity as population growth outstripped people's ability to sustain themselves through food foraging. For them, food production became a subsistence option of last resort.

Neolithic The New Stone Age; a prehistoric period beginning about 10,000 years ago in which peoples possessed stone-based technologies and depended on domesticated plants and/or animals for subsistence.

Neolithic revolution The domestication of plants and animals by peoples with stone-based technologies beginning about 10,000 years ago and leading to radical transformations in cultural systems; sometimes referred to as the *Neolithic transition*.

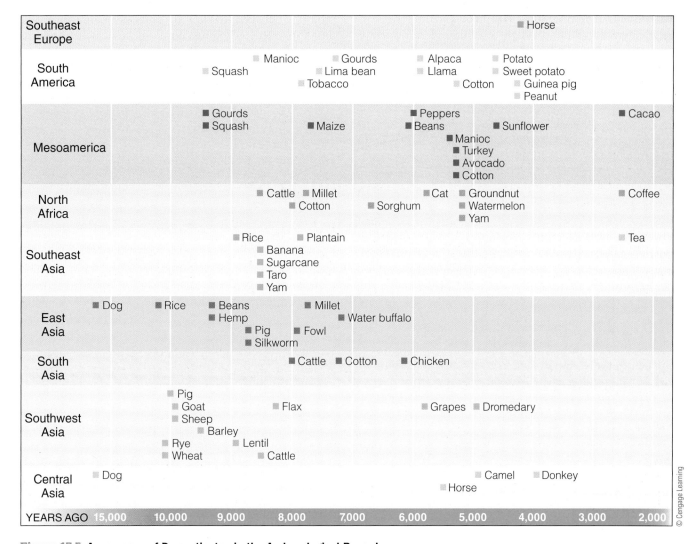

Figure 17.5 **Appearance of Domesticates in the Archaeological Record**

Producing Food in Gardens: Horticulture

With the advent of plant domestication, some societies took up **horticulture** (from the Latin *hortus,* meaning "garden") in which small communities of gardeners cultivate crops with simple hand tools, using neither irrigation nor plow. Typically, horticulturists cultivate several varieties of food plants together in small, hand-cleared food gardens. Because they do not usually fertilize the soil, they use a given garden plot for only a few years before abandoning it in favor of a new one. Often, horticulturists grow enough food for their subsistence, and occasionally they produce a modest surplus that can be used for other purposes such as inter-village feasts and exchange. Although their major food supplies may come from their gardens, many horticulturists will also fish, hunt game, and collect wild plant foods when need and opportunity arise.

One of the most widespread forms of horticulture, especially in the tropics, is **slash-and-burn cultivation**, or *swidden farming,* in which the natural vegetation is cut, the slash is subsequently burned, and crops are then planted among the ashes. This is an ecologically sophisticated and sustainable way of raising food, especially in the tropics, when carried out under the right conditions: low population densities and adequate amounts of land. It mimics the diversity of the natural ecosystem, growing several different crops in the same field. Mixed together, the crops are less vulnerable to pests and plant diseases than a single crop.

Not only is the system ecologically sound, but it is far more energy efficient than modern farming methods used in developed countries like the United States,

horticulture The cultivation of crops in food gardens, carried out with simple hand tools such as digging sticks and hoes.

slash-and-burn cultivation An extensive form of horticulture in which the natural vegetation is cut, the slash is subsequently burned, and crops are then planted among the ashes; also known as *swidden farming.*

where natural resources such as land and fuel are still relatively cheap and abundant, and many farms operate with financial support in the form of government subsidies or tax breaks. Although high-tech farming requires more energy input than it yields, slash-and-burn farming produces between 10 and 20 units of energy for every unit expended. A good example of how such a tropical food-gardening system works is provided by the Mekranoti Kayapo Indians of Brazil's Amazon forest, profiled in the Original Study.

ORIGINAL STUDY

Gardens of the Mekranoti Kayapo BY DENNIS WERNER

To plant a garden, Mekranoti men clear the forest and burn the debris. Then, in the ashes, men and women plant sweet potatoes, manioc, bananas, corn, pumpkins, papaya, sugar cane, pineapple, cotton, tobacco, and annatto, whose seeds yield achiote, the red dye used for painting ornaments and people's bodies. Because the Mekranoti don't bother with weeding, the forest gradually invades the garden. After the second year, only manioc, sweet potatoes, and bananas remain. And after three years or so there is usually nothing left but bananas. Except for a few tree species that require hundreds of years to grow, the area will look like the original forest twenty-five to thirty years later.

This gardening technique, known as slash-and-burn, is one of the most common in the world. At one time critics condemned it as wasteful and ecologically destructive, but today we know that, especially in the humid tropics, it may be one of the best gardening methods possible.

Continuous high temperatures encourage the growth of the microorganisms that cause rot, so organic matter quickly breaks down into simple minerals. The heavy rains dissolve these valuable nutrients and carry them deep into the soils, out of the reach of plants. The tropical forest maintains its richness because the heavy foliage shades the earth, cooling it and inhibiting the growth of the decomposers. A good deal of the rain is captured by leaves before ever reaching the ground.

When a tree falls in the forest and begins to rot, other plants quickly absorb the nutrients that are released. In contrast, with open-field agriculture, the sun heats the earth, the decomposers multiply, and the rains quickly leach the soils of their nutrients. In a few years a lush forest, if cleared for open one-crop agriculture, can be transformed into a barren wasteland.

A few months after the Mekranoti plant banana and papaya, these trees shade the soil, just as the larger forest trees do. The mixing of different kinds of plants in the same area means that minerals can be absorbed as soon as they are released; corn picks up nutrients very fast, whereas manioc is slow. Also, the small and temporary clearings mean that the forest can quickly reinvade its lost territory.

Because decomposers need moisture as well as warmth, the long Mekranoti dry season could alter this whole picture of soil ecology. But soil samples from recently burned Mekranoti fields and the adjacent forest floor showed that, as in most of the humid tropics, the high fertility of the Indians' garden plots comes from the trees that are burned there, not from the soil, as in temperate climates.

Getting a good burn is a tricky operation. Perhaps for this reason the more experienced and knowledgeable members of the community oversee its timing. If done too early, the rains will leach out the minerals in the ash before planting time. If too late, the debris will be too wet to burn properly. Then, insects and weeds that could plague the plants will not die and few minerals will be released into the soil. If the winds are too weak, the burn will not cover the entire plot. If they are too strong, the fire can get out of hand.

Shortly after burning the plots and clearing some of the charred debris, people begin the long job of planting, which takes up all of September and lasts into October. In the center of the circular garden plot the women dig holes and throw in a few pieces of sweet potatoes. After covering the tubers with dirt, they usually ask a male to stomp on the mound and make a ritual noise resembling a Bronx cheer—magic to ensure a large crop. Forming a large ring around the sweet potatoes, the Indians thrust pieces of manioc stems into the ground, one after the other. Once grown, these stems form a dense barrier around the sweet potato patch. Outside of the manioc ring, women plant yams, cotton, sugar cane, and annatto. An outermost circle of banana stalks and papaya trees is sowed by simply throwing the seeds on the ground, whereas corn, pumpkins, watermelons, and pineapple are planted throughout the garden; rapid growers, they are harvested long before the manioc matures.

When I lived with the Mekranoti, Western agronomists—accustomed to single-crop fields and a harvest that happens all at once—knew very little about slash-and-burn crop cultivation. Curious about the productivity of Mekranoti horticulture, I began measuring off areas of gardens to count how many manioc plants, ears of corn, or pumpkins were found there. The women thought it strange to see me struggling through the tangle of plants to measure off areas, 10 meters by 10 meters, placing string along the borders, and then counting what was inside. Sometimes I asked a woman to dig up all of the sweet potatoes within the marked-off area. My requests were bizarre, but they cooperated, holding on to the ends of the measuring tapes or sending their children to help. For some plants, like bananas, I simply counted the number of clumps of stalks in the garden, and the number of banana bunches I could see growing in various clumps. By watching how long it took the bananas to grow, from the time I could see them until they were harvested, I could calculate a garden's total banana yield per year.

Combining the time allocation data with the garden productivities, I got an idea of how hard the Mekranoti need to work to survive. The data showed that for every hour of gardening one Mekranoti adult produces almost 18,000 kilocalories of food. (As a basis for comparison, people in the United States consume approximately 3,000 kilocalories of food per day.) As insurance against bad years, and in case they receive visitors from other villages, they grow far more produce than they need. But even so, they don't need to work very hard to survive. A look at the average amount of time adults spend on different tasks every week shows just how easygoing life in horticultural societies can be:

8.5 hours	Gardening
6.0 hours	Hunting
1.5 hours	Fishing
1.0 hour	Gathering wild foods
33.5 hours	All other jobs

Altogether, the Mekranoti need to work less than 51 hours a week, and this includes getting to and from work, cooking, repairing broken tools, and all of the other things we normally don't count as part of our work week.

Adapted from Werner, D. (1990). *Amazon journey* (pp. 105–112). Englewood Cliffs, NJ: Prentice-Hall.

Producing Food on Farms: Agriculture

In contrast to horticulture, **agriculture** (from the Latin *agri*, meaning "field") is growing food plants like grains, tubers, fruits, and vegetables in soil prepared and maintained for crop production. This more intensive food production involves using technologies other than hand tools, such as plows, fertilizers, and/or irrigation. Historically, agriculture often relied on humans or draft animals for plowing and transport; it now often depends on fuel-powered tractors and trucks to produce food on larger plots of land. But the ingenuity of some early agriculturalists is illustrated in this chapter's Anthropology Applied feature, highlighting an ecologically sound mountain terracing and irrigation system established 1,000 years ago.

Among agriculturists, surplus crop cultivation is generally substantial—providing food not only for their own needs but also for those of various full-time specialists and nonproducing consumers. This surplus may be traded or sold for cash, or it may be coerced out of the farmers through taxes, rent, or tribute (forced gifts acknowledging submission or protection) paid to landowners or other dominant groups. The landowners and specialists—such as traders, carpenters, blacksmiths, sculptors, basketmakers, and stonecutters—typically reside in substantial towns or cities, where political power is centralized in the hands of a socially elite class. Dominated by more powerful groups and markets, much of what the farmers do is governed by political and economic forces over which they have little control.

Early food producers have developed several major crop complexes: two adapted to dry uplands and two to tropical wetlands. In the dry uplands of Southwest Asia, for example, farmers time their agricultural activities with the rhythm of the changing seasons, cultivating wheat, barley, oat, flax, rye, and millet. In the tropical wetlands of Southeast Asia, rice and tubers such as yams and taro are cultivated. In the Americas, people have adapted to natural environments similar to those of Africa and Eurasia but have cultivated their own indigenous plants: Typically, maize, beans, squash, and potatoes are grown in drier areas, whereas manioc is extensively grown in the tropical wetlands.

Characteristics of Crop-Producing Societies

One of the most significant correlates of crop cultivation is the development of fixed settlements, in which farming families reside together near their cultivated fields. The task of food production lends itself to a different kind of social organization. Because the hard work of some members of the group can provide food for all, others become free to devote their time to inventing and manufacturing the equipment needed for a new sedentary way of life. Tools for digging and harvesting, pottery for storage and cooking,

agriculture Intensive crop cultivation, employing plows, fertilizers, and/or irrigation.

Agricultural Development and the Anthropologist

Indigenous peoples have often impressed anthropologists with their traditional practices, which display both ingenuity and knowledge. Beyond the profession of anthropology, people, especially Westerners, have adopted the popular notion that indigenous groups invariably live in some sort of blissful oneness with the environment. But this was never the message of anthropologists, who know that traditional peoples are only human and, as such, are capable of making mistakes. Just as we have much to learn from their successes, so too can we learn from their failures.

Archaeologist Ann Kendall is doing just this in the Patacancha Valley in the Andes Mountains of southern Peru. Kendall is director and founder of the Cusichaca Trust, near Oxford, England, a rural development organization that revives ancient farming practices. In the late 1980s, after working for ten years on archaeological excavations and rural development projects, she invited botanist Alex Chepstow-Lusty of Cambridge University to investigate climatic change and paleoecological data. His findings, along with Kendall's, provided evidence of intensive farming in the Patacancha Valley, beginning about 4,000 years ago. The research showed that over time, widespread clearing to establish and maintain farm

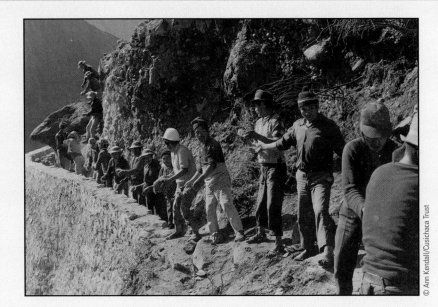

Mountain terracing in Peru has counteracted erosion and provided irrigation for farmland.

plots, coupled with minimal terracing of the hillsides, had resulted in tremendous soil loss through erosion. By 1,900 years ago, soil degradation and a cooling climate had led to a dramatic reduction in farming. Then, about 1,000 years ago, farming was revived, this time with soil-sparing techniques.

Kendall's investigations have documented intensive irrigated-terrace construction over two periods of occupation, including Inca development of the area. It was a sophisticated system, devised to counteract erosion and achieve maximum agricultural production.[a] The effort required workers to haul load after load of soil up from the valley floor. In addition, they planted alder trees to stabilize the soil and to provide both firewood and building materials.

So successful was this farming system by Inca times that the number of people living in the valley quadrupled to some 4,000, about the same as it is now. However, yet another reversal of fortune occurred when the Spanish took over Peru, and the terraces and trees here and elsewhere were allowed to deteriorate.

Armed with these research findings and information and insights gathered through interviews and meetings with locals, the

Cusichaca Trust supported the restoration of the terraces and 5.8 kilometers (3.6 miles) of canal. The effort relied on local labor working with traditional methods and materials—clay (with a cactus mix to keep it moist), stone, and soil. Local families have replanted 160 hectares of the renovated pre-conquest terraces with maize, potatoes, and wheat, and the plots are up to ten times more productive than they were.

Among other related accomplishments, twenty-one water systems have been installed, which reach more than 800 large families, and a traditional concept of home-based gardens has been adapted to introduce European-style vegetable gardens to improve diet and health and to facilitate market gardening. Since 1997, these projects have been under an independent local rural development organization known as ADESA. The Cusichaca Trust has continued its pioneering work in areas of extreme poverty in Peru farther to the north, such as Apurímac and Ayacucho, using tried and tested traditional technology in the restoration of ancient canal and terrace systems.[b]

---

[a] For background information, see Krajick, K. (1998, July 17). Greenfarming by the Incas? *Science 281* (5375), 322.

[b] See www.cusichaca.org.

Figure 17.6 **Transhumance, Pyrénées-Atlantiques, France**
At spring's end, a farmer living in the mountain valleys of southwestern France leads his cattle to high-altitude summer pastures. Since herds are often left to graze in open rangeland, most farmers put a bell on the lead cow in order to track the animals. In many rural French communities, spring and autumn moves are marked by a festival that includes parading herds through town. The event is all the greater in the fall when the animals return fattened and with calves.

Christian Goupi/AGE Fotostock

clothing made of woven textiles, and housing made of stone, wood, or sun-dried bricks all come out of the new settled living conditions and the altered division of labor.

The transition from foraging to food production also brought important changes in social structure. At first, social relations were egalitarian and hardly different from those that prevailed among food foragers. As settlements grew, however, and large numbers of people had to share important resources such as land and water, a greater division of labor developed, and society became more complex in organization.

Mixed Farming: Crop Growing and Animal Breeding

As noted previously, indigenous food-producing cultures in the western hemisphere depended primarily on growing domesticated indigenous crops such as manioc, corn, and beans. With some exceptions—including the Aymara and Quechua, who traditionally also keep llamas and alpacas in their high-altitude homeland in the Andes Mountains of South America (see the Biocultural Connection)—American Indians obtained sufficient meat, fat, leather, and wool from wild game.

In contrast, Eurasian and African food-producing peoples often do not have an opportunity to obtain enough vitally important animal proteins from wild game, fish, or fowl. Many have developed a mixed subsistence strategy that combines crop cultivation with raising animals for food, labor, or trade. Depending on cultural traditions, ecological circumstances, and animal habits, some species are kept in barns or fenced-off fields, whereas others may range freely in and around the settlement or

designated pastures, albeit under supervision, branded or otherwise marked by their owners as private property.

Likewise, many ancient agricultural communities adapted to mountainous environments from the Alps to the Himalayas have traditionally herded livestock (cows, sheep, horses, and so on) in high summer pastures, leaving their narrow lowland valleys for alternative use—farming grains, keeping orchards, and growing vegetables and hay to feed animals in the winter season. After the crop harvest, before the weather turns cold and snow covers the higher pastures, those who left the village to tend the herds bring the animals back to the valley and settle in for the winter season.

Figure 17.6 illustrates a contemporary instance of this "vertical" seasonal movement of herders and their livestock between high-altitude summer pastures and lowland valleys; this is an example of *transhumance* (*trans* means "across"; *humus* means "earth") (Cole & Wolf, 1999; see also Jones, 2005). In contrast to transhumance, in which a number of men from the village annually move with their herds to seasonal pastures while other community members remain home in the settlement, there are also cultures in which the entire community migrates with the herds to their alternate grazing grounds—as described in the next section.

Herding Grazing Animals: Pastoralism

One of the more striking examples of human adaptation to the environment is **pastoralism**—breeding and managing large herds of domesticated herbivores (grazing and

pastoralism The breeding and managing of migratory herds of domesticated grazing animals, such as goats, sheep, cattle, llamas, and camels.

browsing animals), such as goats, sheep, cattle, horses, llamas, or camels. Unlike the forms of animal husbandry discussed previously, pastoralism is a specialized way of life centered on breeding and herding animals.

Dependent on livestock for daily survival, families in pastoral cultures own herds of grazing animals whose need for food and drink determines their everyday routines. When a dozen or more herding families join together, their collective herds may number in the thousands and sometimes even a few hundred thousand. Unlike crop cultivators who need to remain close to their fields, pastoral peoples do not usually establish permanent settlements because they must follow or lead their large herds to new pastures on a regular basis. Like their herds, most pastoralists must be mobile and have adjusted their way of life accordingly.

In environments that are too dry, cold, steep, or rocky for farming, nomadic pastoralism is an effective way of living, far more so than sheep or cattle ranching. One example of an environment that fits this description is the vast, arid grassland region that stretches eastward from North Africa through the Arabian Desert, across the plateau of Iran and into Turkestan and Mongolia. Today, in Africa and Asia alone, more than 21 million people are pastoralists, still migrating with their herds. These nomadic groups regard movement as a natural part of life.

Case Study: Bakhtiari Herders

Counted among the world's pastoral groups are the Bakhtiari, a fiercely independent people with a way of life uniquely adapted to the seasonal fluctuations of the unforgiving Zagros Mountains of western Iran (Barth, 1962; Coon, 1958; Salzman, 1967). For many thousands of years, Bakhtiari life has revolved around the seasonal migrations needed to provide good grazing lands for herds of goats and fat-tailed sheep—hazardous journeys as long as 300 kilometers (185 miles), over mountains as high as 3,700 meters (about 12,000 feet), and through deep chasms and churning watercourses.

Each fall, before the harsh winter comes to the mountains, these nomads load their tents and other belongings on donkeys and drive their flocks down to the warm plains that border western Iraq. Here the grazing land is excellent and well watered during the winter months. In the spring, when the low-lying pastures dry up, they return to the mountain valleys, where a new crop of grass is sprouting. For this trek, they split into five groups, each composed of some 5,000 individuals and 50,000 animals.

The return trip north is especially dangerous because the mountain snows are melting, and the gorges are full of turbulent, ice-cold water rushing down from the mountain peaks. This long trek is further burdened by the newborn spring lambs and goat kids. Where the watercourses are not very deep, the nomads ford them. The Bakhtiari cross deep channels, including one river that is a half-mile wide, with the help of inflatable goatskin rafts, on which they place infants and elderly or infirm family members, as well as lambs and kids. Men swim alongside the rafts, pushing them through the icy water. If they work from dawn to dusk, the nomads can get all of the people and animals across the river in five days. Dozens of animals drown each day.

In the mountain passes, where a biting wind numbs the skin and brings tears to the eyes, the Bakhtiari trek a rugged slippery trail. Climbing the steep escarpments is dangerous, and often the stronger men must carry their children and the baby goats on their shoulders as they make their way over the ice and snow to the lush mountain valley that is their destination.

The journey is familiar but not predictable. It can take weeks because the flocks travel slowly and need constant attention. Men and older boys walk the route, driving the sheep and goats as they go. Women and children usually ride atop mules and donkeys, along with the tents and other equipment (Figure 17.7).

Reaching their destination, the Bakhtiari set up tents—traditionally cloth shelters woven by the women. The tents are a fine example of adaptation to a changing environment. Made of black goat-hair, they retain heat and repel water during the winter and keep out heat during the summer. These portable homes are easy to erect, take down, and transport. Inside, the furnishings are sparse and functional, but also artful. Heavy felt pads or elaborate wool rugs, also woven by the women, cover the ground, and stacks of blankets, goatskin containers, copper utensils, clay jugs, and bags of grain are pressed against the inside walls of the tent.

Central to Bakhtiari subsistence, sheep and goats provide milk, cheese, butter, meat, hides, and wool. Women and girls spend considerable time spinning wool into yarn—sometimes doing so while riding atop donkeys on the less difficult parts of their migration. They use the yarn to make not only rugs and tents, but also clothing, storage bags, and other essentials. With men owning and controlling the animals, which are of primary importance in Bakhtiari life, women generally have less economic and political power than their fathers, brothers, or husbands, but they are not without influence.

The Bakhtiari live in the political state of Iran but have their own traditional system of justice, including laws and a penal code. Tribal leaders or *khans* (men who are elected or who inherit their office) govern the Bakhtiari. Most Bakhtiari *khans* grew wealthy when oil was discovered in their homeland around the start of the 20th century, and many of them are well educated, having attended Iranian or foreign universities.

© S. Eran Images and Stories

Figure 17.7 Bakhtiari Pastoralists
In the Zagros Mountains region of Iran, pastoral nomads follow seasonal pastures. Migrating vast distances with their pack donkeys and mules, they lead huge herds of goats and sheep over rugged terrain that includes perilously steep, snowy passes and fast ice-cold rivers.

Despite this, and although some of them own houses in cities, the *khans* spend much of their lives among their people in the mountains. The predominance of males in both economic and political affairs is common among pastoral nomads; theirs is very much a man's world. That said, elderly Bakhtiari women eventually may gain a good deal of power. And some women of all ages today are gaining a measure of economic control by selling their beautiful handmade rugs to traders, which brings in cash to their households.

Although pastoral nomads like the Bakhtiari depend on their herds to meet their basic daily needs, they also trade surplus animals, leather, and wool (plus various crafts such as woven rugs) with farmers or merchants. In exchange they receive crops and valued commodities such as flour, dried fruit, spices, tea, metal knives, pots and kettles, cotton or linen textiles, guns, and (more recently) lightweight plastic containers, sheets, and so on. In other words, there are many ties that connect them to surrounding agricultural and industrial societies.

Intensive Agriculture: Urbanization and Peasantry

With the intensification of agriculture, some farming settlements grew into towns and even cities (**Figure 17.8**).

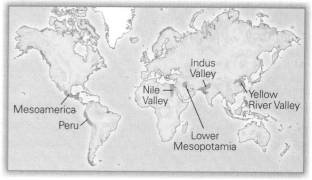

© Cengage Learning

Figure 17.8 Locations of Major Early Civilizations
The indigenous civilizations of the western hemisphere developed wholly independently of those in Africa and Eurasia. Chinese civilizations may have developed independently of those that arose early in Mesopotamia, the Nile Valley, and the Indus Valley.

With urbanization came greater complexity—labor specialization, the formation of elite groups, public management, taxation, and policing. For food and fuel, urbanized populations depended on what was produced or foraged in surrounding areas. Thus, the urban ruling class sought to widen its territorial power and political control over rural populations.

Once a powerful group managed to dominate a community of farmers, it also imposed its rules, forcing them to work harder and obliging them to make payments in farm produce or labor services as fees for land use and protection or as acknowledgment of submission. Burdened by taxes to feed those repressing them, these farmers were left with little for their own families and lost their independence. Subjected to an ever-more dominant group, they became a **peasant** class. These small-scale producers of crops or livestock live on land that they own or rent in exchange for labor, crops, or money and are usually exploited by more powerful groups in a complex society (Wolf, 1966).

This is the situation in many parts of the world today. No matter how hard they work, peasants typically possess too little land of their own to go beyond meeting the most basic needs of their families. Unable to produce enough of a surplus to sell for cash, they rarely have capital to buy the laborsaving equipment that could increase their production. Most peasants remain stuck in poverty, struggling to make ends meet. Meanwhile, big landowners and wealthy merchants have the means to expand their holdings and to invest in new machinery that leads to increased productivity and profitability.

Industrial Food Production

Until about 200 years ago, human societies worldwide had developed cultural infrastructures based on foraging, horticulture, agriculture, or pastoralism. This changed with the invention of the steam engine in England, which brought about an industrial revolution that quickly spread to other parts of the globe. Replacing animal and human labor, as well as hand tools, new machines (first powered by steam, then by biofuels—coal, gas, oil) boosted factory production and mass transportation. Throughout the 1800s and 1900s, this resulted in a large-scale **industrial society**. Technological inventions utilizing electricity and (since the 1940s) nuclear energy brought about more dramatic changes in social and economic organization on a worldwide scale.

Modern industrial technologies have transformed food production. In contrast to traditional farms and plantations, which historically depended on human labor (often forced) and on animal power in many places,

modern agriculture depends on newly invented laborsaving devices such as tractors, combines, milking machines, and so on. With large machines plowing, seeding, weeding, mowing, and harvesting crops, the need for farmhands and other rural workers is sharply diminished. This has also happened with livestock—in particular, hogs, cattle, and poultry.

We can define **industrial food production** as large-scale businesses involved in mass food production, processing, and marketing that primarily rely on laborsaving machines. It has had far-reaching economic, social, and political consequences, not all of which are readily recognized as related and intertwined. Today, large food-producing corporations own enormous tracts of land on which they mass produce tons of mechanically harvested crops or raise huge numbers of meat animals. Crops and animals alike are harvested, processed, packed, and shipped with ever-greater efficiency to supermarkets to feed largely urban masses. Profits are considerable, especially for corporate owners and shareholders.

Although meat, poultry, and other agricultural products are relatively cheap and thus affordable, industrial food production by agribusiness has often been a disaster for millions of peasants and small farmers. Even medium-sized farms growing corn, wheat, or potatoes or raising cows, hogs, and chickens can rarely compete without government subsidies. For that reason, the number of family-owned farms in western Europe and North America has dramatically declined in the past few decades. This process has led to huge drops in many rural populations, decimating many farming communities.

For the family farms that have managed to survive, there is seldom enough income to cover the costs of a large household, including education, healthcare, farm and household insurance, and taxes. This situation forces individuals to seek money-earning opportunities elsewhere, often far away. Ironically, some hire on as cheap wage laborers in poultry- or meat-packing plants where working conditions are distasteful and often dangerous.

Maximizing profits, agribusinesses are constantly streamlining food production and seeking ways to reduce labor costs by trimming the number of workers, minimizing employee benefits, and driving down wages. The largest of these have gone global in a push for market expansion beyond regional or even national boundaries.

Today, the United States is the world's largest producer of chicken meat—some 36 billion pounds annually. On average, each American consumes 85 pounds of chicken a year, but much of the country's production is exported. The $55 billion U.S. poultry business exports billions of tons of chicken annually to dozens of countries around the world. Over 900,000 tons go to Russia (mostly legs—more than a billion of them). Another 400,000 tons go to China, comprised primarily of some 1.2 billion chicken feet (see the

peasant A small-scale producer of crops or livestock living on land that is self-owned or rented in exchange for labor, crops, or money; often exploited by more powerful groups in a complex society.

industrial society A society in which human labor, hand tools, and animal power are largely replaced by machines, with an economy primarily based on big factories.

industrial food production Large-scale businesses involved in mass food production, processing, and marketing, which primarily rely on laborsaving machines.

Figure 17.9 Chicken Harvester
Chickens ready for butchering are usually grabbed by their feet, stuffed in crates, and trucked off to the slaughterhouse. But some farmers use mechanical harvesters. Moving through a chicken barn, a harvester can pick up about 200 birds in 30 seconds. Once full, it places the birds in holding containers. From there, the chickens are mechanically transferred to a packing unit, which automatically counts them and places them into drawers that are stacked, loaded onto a truck, and transported to a processing plant. There the chickens are mass killed, cut up, and packaged.

© Anglia Autoflow Ltd.

Globalscape feature). Large-scale chicken farms, with enclosed "chicken houses" big enough to hold about 23,000 birds, are located primarily in the southern United States where there is ready access to corn and soy feed (Figure 17.9). The country's biggest processing plant, located in Mississippi, slaughters about 2.5 million chickens per week.

The industrial food production and global marketing complex, involving a network of interlinked distribution centers, is made possible by an electronic-digital revolution that began in the late 20th century. Increasingly, the economies of countries all around the world are based on the research and development of knowledge and technologies, as well as on providing information, services, and finance capital on a global scale.

Adaptation in Cultural Evolution

Human groups adapt to their environments by means of their cultures. These environments are not always stable; they may change and often do, primarily as a consequence of human activity in the ecosystem. Moreover, people may migrate to a very different environment, requiring an adaptive change. The result is that cultures may slowly develop into a different type over the course of time; they *evolve*. This is called **cultural evolution**. The process is sometimes confused with the idea of **progress**—the notion that humans are moving forward to a better, more advanced stage in their development toward perfection.

Yet not all changes turn out to be positive in the long run, nor do they improve conditions for every member of a society even in the short run. Notably, people in urban industrial societies are not more highly developed than those who depend on farming, herding, or food foraging.

A long-term perspective is required to detect cultural evolution because the adaptive changes in the cultural system occur over the course of generations. When a new technology or different natural resource changes a society's economic base, its social organization may be adjusted, and that, in turn, may alter its collective worldview, even spiritual ideas and practices. A good example of this is the Comanche, whose known prehistory begins in the highlands of southern Idaho (Wallace & Hoebel, 1952). Living in that harsh, arid region, these North American Indians traditionally subsisted on wild plants, small animals, and occasionally larger game. Their simple material equipment was limited to what they (and their dogs) could carry or pull, and their groups were restricted in size. The shaman, who was a combination of healer and spiritual guide, wielded whatever social power the group allowed.

At some point in their past, many centuries ago, the Comanche moved east onto the Great Plains, attracted by enormous bison herds. As much larger groups could be supported by the new and plentiful food supply, the

cultural evolution Cultural change over time—not to be confused with progress.

progress In anthropology, a relative concept signifying that a society or country is moving forward to a better, more advanced stage in its cultural development toward greater perfection.

Chicken Out: Bush's Legs or Phoenix Talons?

Every evening in Moscow, Russians can be found enjoying a traditional dinner that may begin with *borscht* (beet soup) and *smetana* (sour cream), followed by a main course of *kotleta po-kievski* (boneless fried chicken breast). But, if the budget is a bit tight, dinner might be *nozhki busha* (chicken legs), baked, fried, or roasted—served with cabbage and potatoes.

Foreign visitors may recognize the breast entrée as chicken Kiev but may be baffled to learn that the specialty *nozhki busha* translates as "Bush's legs." That is because these big meaty legs are imported from the United States and first appeared on Russian menus when the Soviet Union collapsed in 1991, during George H. W. Bush's presidency (1989–1993). At the time, the Russian economy was dismal, and few people could afford beef or pork. Even chicken legs were too expensive for ordinary Russians. To help the transition to a capitalist democracy, the U.S. government promoted the advantages of free markets and global trade. What better propaganda than cheap chicken—especially because the American preference for white meat resulted in a surplus of the dark-meat legs. And so it was that the U.S. poultry industry entered the Russian market. Today, Russia imports more U.S. chicken than it produces on its own farms, especially legs—over a billion!

What happens with a typical 6-pound broiler chicken butchered by a Mexican immigrant working for minimum wage in a Mississippi poultry plant? As we have seen, its legs are served up in Moscow, and its breasts end up on U.S. dining tables or on the menus of international airlines. And the rest of the bird? One of its frozen wings goes into a giant container shipped to Korea; the other to West Africa. The offal (neck, heart, liver, and guts) is transported to Jamaica, where it is boiled and dished up in soup. The excess fat gets converted into biodiesel fuel at an experimental refinery in Texas. And what about its cute yellow feet? They are exported to Shanghai, deep fried, stewed, and served up as a delicacy called *fèngzhuâ*, or Phoenix talons, last seen being nibbled on by a visiting New York banker.

Global Twister

What happens to the feathers?

The Buffalo Hunt, c.1832 (coloured engraving), Catlin, George (1794–1872)/Bibliotheque Nationale, Paris, France/ Giraudon/The Bridgeman Art Library

Figure 17.10 **The Bison Hunt**
This 1832 colored engraving of a Comanche bison hunt is by artist George Catlin (1796–1872). Plains Indians such as the Comanche, Cheyenne, and Lakota developed similar cultures because they had to adapt to similar environmental conditions.

Comanche needed a more complex political organization. Eventually, they acquired horses and guns from European and neighboring Indian traders. This enhanced their hunting capabilities significantly and led to the emergence of powerful hunting chiefs (Figure 17.10).

To increase the number of horses, the Comanche became raiders, and their hunting chiefs evolved into war chiefs. The once materially unburdened and peaceful hunter-gatherers of the dry highlands became wealthy, and raiding became a way of life. In the late 18th and early 19th centuries, they dominated the southern Plains (now primarily Texas and Oklahoma). In moving from one regional environment to another and in adopting a new technology, the Comanche were able to take advantage of existing cultural capabilities to thrive in their new situation.

Types of Cultural Evolution

Sometimes societies that slowly develop independently of one another find similar solutions to similar problems. For example, the Cheyenne Indians originally lived in the woodlands of the Great Lakes region where they cultivated corn and gathered wild rice, which fostered a distinct set of social, political, and religious practices. Then their better-armed eastern neighbors pushed them west into the Great Plains, where they adapted to a new ecosystem within a few generations. They gave up their food gardens and became horse-riding bison hunters. By adapting to life on the Great Plains, they slowly developed a culture resembling that of the Comanche, even though the cultural historical backgrounds of the two groups differed significantly. This is an example of **convergent evolution**—the development of similar cultural adaptations to similar environmental conditions by different peoples with different ancestral cultures.

Another type of cultural evolution is **parallel evolution**, in which similar cultural adaptations to

convergent evolution In cultural evolution, the development of similar cultural adaptations to similar environmental conditions by different peoples with different ancestral cultures.

parallel evolution In cultural evolution, the development of similar cultural adaptations to similar environmental conditions by peoples whose ancestral cultures were already somewhat alike.

similar environmental conditions are achieved by peoples whose ancestral cultures were already somewhat alike. For example, the development of farming in Mexico and Southwest Asia took place independently, as people in both regions, whose lifeways were already comparable, became dependent on a narrow range of plant foods that required human intervention for their protection and reproductive success. Both developed intensive forms of agriculture, built large cities, and created complex social and political organizations.

As the following example illustrates, human groups do not always make the necessary adaptive changes. This can lead to disastrous results, including the deaths of countless people (and other creatures) and the destruction of the natural environment.

Case Study: The Environmental Collapse of Easter Island

Among the many examples of catastrophic environmental destruction is Easter Island in the southern Pacific, first settled about 800 years ago by Polynesian seafarers. Other Polynesians referred to this remote 163-square-kilometer (63-square-mile) island as Rapa Nui, and its inhabitants became known as Rapanui.

When the Rapanui arrived, 75 percent of the island was densely forested, primarily with jubaea palms. Clearing the woods for food gardens of taros, yams, and sweet potatoes, the Rapanui also raised domesticated chickens, hunted wild birds, fished the ocean, and gathered nuts, fruits, and seeds. They prospered, producing surpluses, growing dramatically in number; and they formed into a few dozen clans under a paramount chief, a sacred king.

Trees, felled for fuel and to build homes and fishing canoes, were also used as rollers for transporting huge stone statues, which became an extraordinary hallmark of Rapanui culture (Figure 17.11). However, over time, success turned to failure—evidently due to a collapse of the fragile ecosystem brought about by a combination of natural and cultural factors (Alfonso-Durruty, 2012).

Rats, which had come to the island with the Polynesian settlers, contributed to the demise. Feasting on palm seeds and reproducing rapidly, the rat population soared and hindered the reseeding of the slow-growing trees. By the mid-1600s, the palm forests had disappeared, done in by rats and human deforestation. As the forests disappeared, rich topsoil eroded, other indigenous and endemic plants became extinct, crop yields diminished, springs dried up, and flocks of migrant birds stopped coming to the island to roost. Moreover, from about 1600 to 1640, El Niño—a warming of water surface temperatures—decreased biomass production, diminishing fish and other marine resources (Stenseth & Voje, 2009).

All of this led to periodic famine and chronic warfare between Rapanui rival factions. With their nearest neighbors over 2,500 kilometers (1,500 miles) to their west,

Figure 17.11 Stone Heads, Easter Island
Few places have caused as much speculation as this tiny volcanic island, also known by the indigenous name of Rapa Nui. Isolated in the middle of the southern Pacific Ocean, it is one of the most remote and remarkable places on earth. Nearly 900 colossal stone statues, known as *moai*, punctuate the landscape. Towering up to 20 meters (65 feet), they were made by the Rapanui people—Polynesian seafarers who settled there about 800 years ago. After generations of prosperity and population growth, the Rapanui faced an environmental collapse.

they were truly an isolated people who had nowhere to go. By the time Dutch seafarers arrived on Rapa Nui in 1722 (the name "Easter Island" was given by the Dutch explorers who landed there on Easter Sunday), its population had dropped from about 15,000 to 3,000. During the next two centuries, other foreigners added to the Rapanui's problems, bringing diseases and other miseries. These additional stressors nearly eliminated the Rapanui from their treeless island, now covered by grass and volcanic rock (Métraux, 1957; Mieth & Bork, 2010).

Environmental destruction on a much more massive scale has occurred in many other parts of the world, especially in the course of the 20th century, ruining the lives of millions. Considering such collapses of ecosystems, we must avoid falling into the ethnocentric trap of equating change with progress or with seeing all change as adaptive.

Population Growth and the Limits of Progress

New subsistence strategies developed over the past few centuries using technological inventions to more effectively harness energy are commonly valued as progress. Yet, as discussed in this chapter, not all innovations turn out to be positive in the long run, nor do they improve the quality of life for every member of a society even in the short run.

A few thousand generations ago, our anatomically modern human ancestors emerged in Africa. Reproducing successfully, they multiplied a thousand times between 100,000 and 10,000 years ago, when there may have been as many as 5 million *Homo sapiens*. Having migrated from Africa into Eurasia, Australia, and the Americas, they continued to increase in numbers, reaching a worldwide total of more than 250 million about 2,000 years ago. This incremental population growth accelerated, reaching 1 billion in the mid-1800s. In the mid-1980s, the global population stood at 5 billion, and today that number is nearly 7.5 billion.

From their earliest days, humans have not only invented or adopted new technologies in their quest for subsistence, but also migrated, ultimately occupying every continent on earth. Adjusting as they went, each of these migrating groups developed their own cultural repertoire of ideas and practices to secure food, fuel, and safety for themselves and their offspring. Measured in terms of population growth, geographic expansion, and technological know-how, *Homo sapiens* has been enormously successful in adapting itself to a wide range of different natural environments and developing the means required to satisfy its needs. As long as the collective needs of a population remain within its means, the group can be said to enjoy a degree of relative abundance or affluence. However, when the needs of a group exceed the available means, the group will face shortages or scarcity.

Because abundance and shortage are based on the relationship between means and needs, affluence and scarcity are relative concepts. And for that reason, anthropologists tend to be cautious about the uncritical use of the term *progress* as applied to economic development. Although there is no question that millions of people do enjoy a life of health and abundance, perhaps more so than their own ancestors, a few billion must work harder and longer hours to put food on the table. And according to the World Bank, more than a billion people worldwide still live in extreme poverty, and many more experience hunger and die too young. For them, the notion of human progress does not match their reality.

CHAPTER CHECKLIST

What are adaptation, cultural adaptation, ecosystem, and culture areas?

✓ Adaptation is the process organisms undergo to achieve a beneficial adjustment to a particular environment. The environment is a defined space with limited resources that presents certain possibilities and limitations.

✓ Adaptation occurs not only when humans make changes in their natural environment but also when they are biologically changed by that environment.

✓ Cultural adaptation is the complex of ideas, activities, and technologies that enable people to survive in a certain environment and in turn impacts the environment.

✓ An ecosystem is a functioning whole composed of the natural environment and all the organisms living in it.

✓ Culture areas are geographic regions in which a number of societies have similar ways of life. Such regions often correspond to ecological regions.

What are the major subsistence strategies and the characteristics of the societies that practice them?

✓ Food foraging, the oldest and most universal mode of subsistence, requires people to relocate according to changing food sources. Its characteristics include mobility, small group size, flexible male/female labor division, food sharing, egalitarianism, communal property, and rarity of warfare.

✓ The shift from food foraging to food production, known as the Neolithic revolution, began about 10,000 years ago. It involved the domestication of plants and animals.

✓ Horticulture, the cultivation of crops in gardens using simple hand tools, includes slash-and-burn cultivation in which the natural vegetation is cut, the slash is burned, and crops are planted among the ashes.

✓ Agriculture, a more complex activity, involves growing crops on farms with irrigation, fertilizers, and animal-powered plows. Food production led to fixed settlements, new technologies, and altered division of labor.

✓ Mixed farming involves crop growing and animal breeding; it may occur in mountainous environments where farmers practice transhumance, moving their livestock between high-altitude summer pastures and lowland valleys.

✓ Pastoralism relies on breeding and managing large herds of domesticated herbivores, such as cattle, sheep, and goats. Pastoralists are usually nomadic, moving as needed to provide animals with pasture and water.

✓ Intensive agriculture led to urbanization and peasantry. Farm settlements grew into towns and cities, and social complexity expanded to include labor specialization, elite classes, public management, taxation, and policing.

✓ Industrial food production features large-scale businesses involved in mass food production, processing, and marketing, and relying on laborsaving machines. It is rooted in the industrial revolution, which began in the late 1700s with the invention of the steam engine. Machines replaced human labor, animal power, and hand tools, leading to massive cultural change in many societies.

✓ Today's industrial food production and global marketing complex, involving a network of interlinked distribution centers, are made possible by an electronic-digital revolution that began in the late 20th century.

What is cultural evolution?

✓ Cultural evolution, the changing of cultures over time, should not be confused with the idea of progress—the notion that humans are moving forward to a better, more advanced stage in their development toward perfection.

✓ Convergent evolution is the development of similar cultural adaptations to similar environmental conditions by different peoples with different ancestral cultures. Parallel evolution is the same phenomenon, but it emerges with peoples whose ancestral cultures were already similar.

✓ Human groups do not always make the necessary adaptive changes, and this can devastate populations and the natural environment. Easter Island is a tragic example of catastrophic environmental destruction.

QUESTIONS FOR REFLECTION

1. In capturing essential natural resources, humans often modify their environments. Have you seen any examples of landscapes radically transformed for economic reasons, as shown in the terraced mountains of China in the Challenge Issue? Who do you think benefits or loses the most?

2. What was so radical about the domestication of plants and animals that led to it being referred to as the Neolithic *revolution*? Can you think of any equally radical changes in subsistence practices going on in the world today?

3. Consider the ideas of change and "progress" in light of the agricultural development project described in the Anthropology Applied feature. Come up with your own definition of progress that goes beyond the standard idea of technological and material advancement.

4. Technological development in industrial societies often results in highly productive machines effectively replacing animal and human workers. Think of a useful mechanical device and consider its benefits and costs, not only to you but also to others.

DIGGING INTO ANTHROPOLOGY

Global Dining

When shopping for groceries in a supermarket, try to imagine the great chain of human hands involved in getting the food, drinks, herbs, and spices from all corners of the world to your table. Make a list of all the things you have bought and consumed in one week. Then determine the place or origin of each on a map and trace the likely routes by which these commodities entered your store and ultimately ended up inside you. Some food for thought: You are an embodiment of globalization.

Arvind Garg/Encyclopedia/Corbis

CHALLENGE ISSUE

All humans face the challenge of securing resources needed for immediate and long-term survival. Whatever we lack, we may seek to get through aid, gifts, exchange, or trade. In modern market economies, people can exchange almost anything of value without actually meeting in person. But the market in traditional agricultural and pastoral societies is a geographic location where people personally meet to exchange commodities on designated days. In such economic transactions, humans forge and affirm social networks that play a key role in the search for safety and well-being. Here we see an open market at the plaza in front of the 400-year-old Christian church in Chichicastenango, an ancient Maya K'iche Indian city in the highlands of Guatemala. On Thursdays and Sundays, vendors and buyers gather here to peddle and purchase everything from tools, pots, and woven textiles to chickens, vegetables, spices, and medicinal plants.

Economic Systems

An **economic system** is an organized arrangement for producing, distributing, and consuming goods. In pursuing a particular means of subsistence, people necessarily produce, distribute, and consume things, so our discussion of subsistence patterns in the previous chapter obviously involved economic matters. Yet economic systems encompass much more than we have covered so far.

Economic Anthropology

Although anthropologists have adopted theories and concepts from economists, theoretical principles derived from the study of capitalist market economies have limited applicability to economic systems in societies that are not industrialized and where people do not produce and exchange goods for private profit. This is because, in these non-state societies, the economic sphere of behavior is not separate from the social, political, and religious spheres and thus is not completely free to follow its own purely economic logic.

Economic behavior and institutions can be analyzed in strictly economic terms, but doing so ignores various noneconomic considerations that impact the way things are in real life. To explain how the wants and demands of a given society are balanced against the supply of goods and services available, anthropologists take into account an all-encompassing variable: culture. This was well illustrated by U.S. anthropologist Annette Weiner in her study of yam production among the Trobriand Islanders, who inhabit a group of coral islands that lie in the southern Pacific Ocean off the eastern tip of New Guinea (Weiner, 1988).

Case Study: The Yam Complex in Trobriand Culture

Trobriand men spend a great deal of their time and energy raising yams—not for themselves or their own households, but to give to others, normally their sisters and married daughters. However, the purpose of cultivating these starchy edible roots is not to provision the households that receive them, because most of what

economic system An organized arrangement for producing, distributing, and consuming goods.

In this chapter you will learn to

- Explain why the anthropological variable of culture is important in understanding noncapitalist economies.

- Distinguish various economic arrangements for producing, distributing, and consuming goods.

- Compare forms of gift exchange, redistribution, and trade.

- Analyze how leveling mechanisms actually work in different cultures.

- Describe the role of money in market economies.

- Summarize the impact of global markets on local communities.

people eat they grow for themselves in gardens where they plant taro, sweet potatoes, tapioca, greens, beans, and squash, as well as breadfruit and banana trees. The reason a man gives yams to a woman is to show his support for her husband and to enhance his own influence.

Once received by the woman, the gift yams are loaded into her husband's yam house, symbolizing his worth as a man of power and influence in his community. He may use some of these yams to purchase a variety of things, including shell armbands, necklaces, and earrings, as well as betel nuts, pigs, chickens, and locally produced goods such as wooden bowls, combs, floor mats, lime pots, and even magic spells (Figure 18.1). But some yams will

be used to fulfill social obligations. For instance, a man is expected to present yams to the relatives of his daughter's husband when she marries and again when a member of the husband's family dies.

A man who aspires to high status and power is expected to show his personal worth by organizing a yam competition, during which he gives away huge quantities of yams to invited guests. In Weiner's words: "A yam house, then, is like a bank account; when full, a man is wealthy and powerful. Until yams are cooked or they rot, they may circulate as limited currency. That is why, once harvested, the usage of yams for daily food is avoided as much as possible" (Weiner, 1988, p. 86).

By giving yams to his sister or daughter, a man not only expresses his confidence in the woman's husband, but also makes the latter indebted to him. The recipient rewards the gardener and his helpers by throwing a feast, at which they are fed cooked yams, taro, and—what everyone especially looks forward to—ample pieces of pork. But this in no way pays off the debt, which can be repaid only in women's wealth: bundles of banana leaves and skirts made of the same material dyed red.

Banana leaf bundles are of no utilitarian value, but extensive labor is invested in their production, and large quantities of them, along with skirts, are regarded as essential for paying off all the members of other family groups who were close to a recently deceased relative in life and who assisted with the funeral. Also, the wealth and vitality of the dead person's family group are measured by the quality and quantity of the bundles and skirts so distributed.

Because a man has received yams from his wife's brother, he is obligated to provide his wife with yams to purchase the necessary bundles and skirts, beyond those she has produced, to help with payments following the death of a member of her family. Deaths can occur at any time, so a man must have yams available for his wife when she needs them. This anticipated need, and the fact that she may require all of his yams, act as an effective check on a man's wealth.

Trobriand Islanders, like people everywhere, assign meanings to objects that make those objects worth far more than their cost in labor or materials. Yams, for example, establish long-term relationships that lead to other advantages, such as access to land, protection, assistance, and other kinds of wealth.

Figure 18.1 A Trobriand Yam Storage House
Trobriand Island men devote a great deal of time and energy to raising yams—not for themselves but to give to others. Here we see Chief Tokesawaga sitting beside prestige yams in his village on Kiriwina—one of the Trobriand Islands in Papua New Guinea. Yams, stored in special yam houses, symbolize wealth, and having a full yam house indicates the owner's prosperity and prestige. Another prestige item visible in this photo is the shell armband the chief is wearing, described later in this chapter.

Banana leaf bundles and skirts, for their part, are symbolic of the political status of families and of their immortality. In their distribution, which is related to death rituals, we see how men in Trobriand society are ultimately dependent on women and their valuables. Looked at in terms of modern capitalist economics, these activities appear meaningless, but viewed in terms of traditional Trobriand values and concerns, they make a great deal of sense. Thus, yam exchanges are as much social and political transactions as they are economic ones.

Production and Its Resources

In every society, traditional customs and social rules determine the kinds of work done, who does the work, attitudes toward the work, how it is accomplished, and who controls the resources necessary to produce desired goods, knowledge, and services. The primary resources in any culture are raw materials, technology, and labor power. The rules directing access to these resources are embedded in a people's culture and determine the way the economy operates within any given natural environment.

Land and Water Resources

Human societies regulate allocation of valuable natural resources—especially land and water. Food foragers must determine who will hunt game and gather plants in their home range and where these activities take place. Groups that rely on fishing or growing crops need to make similar decisions concerning who will carry out which task on which stretch of water or land. Farmers must have some means of determining title to land and access to water supplies for irrigation. Pastoralists require a system that determines rights to watering places and grazing land, as well as the right of access to land where they move their herds.

In capitalist societies, a system of private ownership of land and rights to natural resources generally prevails. Although elaborate laws have been enacted to regulate the buying, owning, and selling of land and water resources, if individuals wish to reallocate valuable forests or farmland to some other purpose, for instance, they generally can.

In traditional nonindustrial societies, land is often controlled by kinship groups such as the family or band rather than by individuals. For example, among the Ju/'hoansi of the Kalahari Desert, each band of ten to thirty people lives on roughly 650 square kilometers (250 square miles) of land, which they consider to be their territory—their own country. These territories are not defined by boundaries (property lines separating neighboring units of land)

Anthony Bannister/Gallo Images/Documentary Value/Corbis

Figure 18.2 Core Features as Territory Markers
Food foragers, like the Ju/'hoansi of the Kalahari Desert in southern Africa, define their territories on the basis of core features such as waterholes. Here women gather water into empty ostrich eggshells.

but in terms of waterholes that are located within them (Figure 18.2). The land is said to be owned by those who have lived the longest in the band, usually a group of brothers and sisters or cousins. Their concept of landholding, however, is not something easily translated into modern Western terms of private ownership. Within Ju/'hoansi traditional worldview, no part of their homeland can be sold for money or traded away for goods. Outsiders must ask permission to enter the territory, but denying the request would be unthinkable.

© Cengage Learning

The practice of defining territories on the basis of *core features*—waterholes, waterways (as among Indians of the northeastern United States), unique sites where ancestral spirits are thought to dwell (as among the Aborigines in Australia), or something else—is typical of food foragers. Territorial boundaries are not always precisely defined, and to avoid friction foragers may designate part of their territory as a buffer zone between them and their neighbors. The adaptive value of such a "no man's land" is obvious: The size of band territories, as well as the size of the bands, can adjust to keep in balance with availability of resources in any given place. Such adjustment would be more difficult under a system of individual ownership of clearly bounded land.

Among some African and Asian rural societies, a *tributary* system of land ownership still prevails. Historically, this system was common in many parts of the world, including numerous European countries before the rise of capitalism. All land is said to belong to the king, *khan*, maharaja, emir, or head chief, who allocates it to various subchiefs, who in turn distribute it to family groups. Then the family group leaders assign individual plots to each farmer. These men owe allegiance to the subchiefs (or nobles) and to the head chief (or king). The people who work the land must pay *tribute* (obligatory gift or contribution, like rent or taxes in a cash economy) in the form of products or special services, such as fighting for the king when necessary.

Using the land does not signify ownership; rather, the right to use it is a kind of lease. And as long as the land is kept in use, rights to such use will pass to the user's heirs. When an individual no longer uses the allocated land, it reverts to the head of the large family group, who reallocates it to some other group member. The important operative principle here is that the system extends the individual's right to use land for an indefinite period, but the land is not "owned" outright. This serves to maintain the integrity of valuable farmland as such, preventing its loss through subdivision and conversion to other uses.

Technology Resources

All societies have some means of creating and allocating tools that are used to produce goods, as well as traditions for passing them on to succeeding generations. A society's **technology**—the number and types of tools employed, combined with knowledge about how to make and use them—is directly related to the lifeways of its members. Food foragers and pastoral nomads who are frequently on the move are apt to have fewer and more portable tools than more settled peoples such as sedentary farmers.

Food foragers make and use a variety of tools, many ingenious in their effectiveness. Some of these they make for their individual use, but codes of generosity are such that a person may not refuse to give or loan what is requested.

technology Tools and other material equipment, together with the knowledge of how to make and use them.

Tools may be given or loaned to others in exchange for the products resulting from their use. For example, a Ju/'hoansi who gives his arrows to another hunter has a right to a share of any animals the hunter kills. Game is considered to belong to the man whose arrow killed it, even when he is not present on the hunt. In this context, it makes little sense for them to accumulate luxuries or surplus goods, and the fact that no one owns significantly more than another helps to limit status differences.

Among horticulturalists, the axe, digging stick, hoe, and containers are important tools. The person who makes a tool has first rights to it, but when he or she is not using it, any family member may ask to use it, and the request is rarely denied. Refusal would cause people to treat the tool owner with scorn for this singular lack of concern for others. If a relative helps raise the crop traded for a particular tool, that relative becomes part owner of the implement, and it may not be traded or given away without his or her permission.

In permanently settled agricultural communities, tools and other productive goods are more complex, heavier, and costlier to make. In such settings, individual ownership tends to be more absolute, as are the conditions under which people may borrow and use such equipment. It is easy to replace a knife lost by a relative during palm cultivation but much more difficult to replace an iron plow or a diesel-fueled harvesting machine. Rights to the ownership of complex tools are more rigidly applied; generally, the person who has manufactured or purchased such equipment is considered the sole owner, and this person decides who may use it and under which conditions, including compensation.

Labor Resources and Patterns

In addition to raw materials and technology, labor is a key resource in any economic system. A look around the world reveals many different labor patterns, but there is almost always a basic division of labor by gender and by age.

Division of Labor by Gender

Anthropologists have studied extensively the social division of labor by gender across cultures. Whether men or women do a particular job varies from group to group, but typically work has been and often continues to be divided into the tasks of either one or the other. For example, the practices most widely regarded as women's work have tended to be those that can be carried out near home and that are easily resumed after interruption. The tasks historically regarded as men's work have tended to be those requiring physical strength, rapid mobilization of high bursts of energy, frequent travel at some distance from home, and assumption of high levels of risk and danger.

However, there are many exceptions to these generalizations, as in societies where women regularly carry burdensome loads or put in long hours of hard work cultivating crops in the fields (**Figure 18.3**). In many societies,

Figure 18.3 Women's Work?
These Hmong women in Vietnam are carrying heavy firewood, even though this work may be considered inappropriate for women in some cultures. For villagers living in the rural areas of developing countries all around the world, firewood is used as a source of energy for preparing meals—and women are usually the ones who collect and haul it.

women perform almost three-fourths of all work in the food gardens, farm fields, and households but lack ownership or control over the products of their labor.

Instead of looking for biological factors to explain the social division of labor, a more useful strategy is to examine the kinds of work that men and women do in the context of specific societies to see how they relate to other cultural and historical factors. Researchers find a continuum of patterns, ranging from flexible integration of men and women to rigid segregation by gender (Sanday, 1981).

The *flexible/integrated pattern* is seen most often among food foragers (as well as in communities in which crops are traditionally cultivated primarily for family consumption). In such societies, men and women perform up to 35 percent of activities with approximately equal participation, and tasks deemed especially appropriate for one gender may be performed by the other without loss

of face, as the situation warrants. Where these practices prevail, boys and girls grow up in much the same way, learn to value cooperation over competition, and become equally habituated to adult men and women, who interact with one another on a relatively equal basis.

Societies following a *segregated pattern* define almost all work as either masculine or feminine, so men and women rarely engage in joint efforts of any kind. In such societies, it is inconceivable that someone would even think of doing something considered the work of the opposite sex. This pattern is frequently seen in pastoral nomadic, intensive agricultural, and industrial societies, where men's work keeps them outside the home for much of the time. Typically, men in such societies are expected to be tough, aggressive, and competitive—and this often involves assertions of male superiority, and hence authority, over women. Male dominance is associated with fierce rivalry for scarce resources. Historically, escalating aggression within and between societies has often upset egalitarian gender relations.

In the third pattern of labor division by gender, sometimes called the *dual sex configuration,* men and women carry out their work separately, as in societies segregated by gender, but the relationship between them is one of balanced complementarity rather than inequality. Although each gender manages its own affairs, the interests of both men and women are represented at all levels. Thus, as in integrated societies, neither gender exerts dominance over the other. The pattern may be seen among certain American Indian peoples with economies based upon subsistence farming, as well as among several West African kingdoms.

In postindustrial societies, the division of labor by gender becomes blurred and even irrelevant, resembling the flexible/integrated pattern of traditional foragers just described. Although gender preferences and discrimination in the workplace exist in societies making the economic transition, cultural ideas that are more fitting for agricultural or industrial societies predictably change in due time, adjusting to postindustrial challenges and opportunities.

Division of Labor by Age

Division of labor according to age is also typical of human societies. Among the Ju/'hoansi, for example, children are not expected to contribute significantly to subsistence until they reach their late teens. Until they possess adult levels of strength and endurance, many "bush" foods are tough for them to gather. So youngsters contribute primarily by taking care of their littlest siblings while grownups deal with subsistence needs.

Although elderly Ju/'hoansi will usually do some foraging for themselves, they are not expected to contribute much food. By virtue of their advanced age, they have memories of customary practices and events that happened far in the past. Thus, they are repositories of accumulated wisdom and are able to suggest solutions to problems younger adults have never faced. Considered useful for their knowledge, they are far from being unproductive members of society.

In some food-foraging societies, women do continue to make a significant contribution to provisioning in their later years. For example, among the Hadza of East Africa, the input of older women is critical to their daughters when they have new infants to nurse. The energy costs of lactation, along with the tasks of holding, carrying, and nursing an infant, all diminish the mother's foraging efficiency. Those most immediately affected by this are a woman's weaned children not yet old enough to forage effectively for themselves—but everyone's needs are met thanks to the additional foraging efforts of grandmothers (Hawkes, O'Connell, & Blurton Jones, 1997).

In many traditional farming societies, children as well as older people may make a greater contribution to the economy in terms of work and responsibility than is common in industrial or postindustrial societies. In most peasant communities around the world, children not only look after their younger brothers and sisters but also help with housework, in the barn, or in the fields. By age 7 or so, boys begin to help out, weed the fields, bring in crops, care for small animals, or catch some fish and small game. By that same age, girls begin helping with housework—preparing food, fetching wood and water, sweeping, selling goods at local markets, and so forth (Vogt, 1990).

Notably, there is no universal age standard when a young person is ready to transition out of childhood and is prepared to assume the rights and obligations of an adult. In fact, childhood is a historically changing social construct that varies across cultures. In some cultures it ends as early as age 12, in others as late as 21. It is also noteworthy that not every culture clearly distinguishes work or labor from other activities.

The problem of "child labor" across the globe has been internationally evaluated in terms of violation of human rights. Many wealthy capitalist societies in western Europe and North America long ago passed laws officially prohibiting institutionalized child labor. However, they still import vast quantities of goods available at bargain prices because they are made by poorly paid children—items ranging from rugs and carpets to clothing, toys, and soccer balls (Doherty, 2012). In 1990, almost all the member states of the United Nations agreed to define a child as a person under the age of 18, unless the age of majority is attained earlier under a state's own domestic legislation (United Nations Human Rights, 2015).

Notwithstanding national or international efforts to define childhood and regulate labor conforming to government bureaucratic standards, minors under 18 perform wage labor in many industrial societies, where poor and often large families count on every possible contribution to the household. In these societies, economic necessity may easily lead to the exploitation of minors as cheap labor on farms, in mines, and in factories. Child labor has become a matter of increasing concern as large capitalist corporations rely more and more on the low-cost production of food and goods in the world's poorer countries. Today, 168 million children (ages 5 to 17) are trapped in

Figure 18.4 Child Labor in India
Many of the soccer balls that children play with in the United States and Europe are handstitched by children in India, most working in factories under brutal conditions for pennies a day. After past scandals about soccer ball factories using child labor, many companies started adding labels stating that the balls were not made with child labor—but those labels are often sewn on the balls by children as young as 6 years old.

child labor, almost all in developing economies where their families depend on the extra income they bring home (Figure 18.4). More than half (85 million) are working in hazardous environments (International Labour Organization, 2015).

Cooperative Labor

Cooperative work groups can be found everywhere—in both foraging and food-producing societies and in industrial societies. Often, if the effort involves the whole community, a festive spirit infuses the work.

For example, in many rural parts of sub-Saharan Africa, work parties begin with the display of a pot of beer to be consumed after the tasks have been finished. Home-brewed from millet, their major cereal crop, the beer is not really payment for the work; indeed, the labor involved is worth far more than the beer consumed. Rather, drinking the low-alcohol but highly nutritious beverage together is more of a symbolic activity to celebrate the spirit of friendship and mutual support. Recompense comes as

Figure 18.5 Task Specialization: Mining Salt in Ethiopia
Scorching hot and dry, the Danakil Depression in northeastern Africa lies some 370 feet below sea level—the remains of what was once part of the Red Sea—with enormous salt flats. Afar nomads come here periodically to quarry this rock salt. Using camels, they haul the heavy slabs to the interior highlands for trade.

individuals sooner or later participate in work parties for others. In areas all around the world, farmers traditionally help one another during harvest and haying seasons, often sharing major pieces of equipment.

In most human societies, the basic unit within which work takes place is the household. Traditionally—and still in many parts of the world—it is both a unit of production and consumption, where work as well as meals and domestic comfort are shared. In industrial societies these two economic spheres are now usually separated. This development is the result, in part, of task specialization.

Task Specialization

In contemporary industrial and postindustrial societies, there is a great diversity of specialized tasks to be performed, and individuals cannot begin to know all the tasks customarily seen as fitting for their age and gender. However, although specialization continues to increase, modern technologies make gender-based labor divisions less relevant. By contrast, in small-scale foraging and traditional crop-cultivating societies, in which division of labor typically occurs along lines of age and gender, each person has knowledge and competence in all aspects of work appropriate to his or her age and gender. Yet, even in these nonindustrial societies there is a measure of specialization.

An example of task specialization can be found among the Afar people of the Danakil Depression in the borderlands of Eritrea and Ethiopia, one of the lowest and hottest places on earth. The desolate landscape features

sulfur fields, smoking fissures, volcanic tremors, and vast salt plains. Since ancient times, groups of Afar men have mined the salt, hacking blocks from the plain's crust. The work is backbreaking, all the more so with temperatures soaring to 140 degrees Fahrenheit.

Along with the physical strength required for such work under the most trying conditions, successful mining demands specialized planning and organization skills for getting to and from the worksite. Pack camels have to be fed in advance because importing sufficient fodder for them interferes with their ability to carry the salt (Figure 18.5). Food and water, packed by Afar women at the desert's edge, must be carried in for the miners, typically numbering thirty to forty per group. Travel is arranged for nighttime to avoid the scorching sun (Haile, 1966; O'Mahoney, 1970).

In the past few decades, we have seen the emergence of new forms of task specialization in an international division of labor and in response to global markets of supply and demand. Many of these specializations are

Global Ecotourism and Local Indigenous Culture in Bolivia
By Amanda Stronza

We traveled in a small fleet of motorized canoes. As the sun dipped behind the trees one steamy afternoon in April 2002, we turned the last few bends of the Tuichi River and arrived at our destination, the Chalalán Ecolodge of northern Bolivia. Our group included eighteen indigenous leaders from various parts of the Amazon rainforest, a handful of regional tour operators, conservationists, environmental journalists, and me—an applied anthropologist studying the effects of ecotourism on local livelihoods, cultural traditions, and resource use. We had been navigating for nine hours through lowland rainforest to visit one of the first indigenous, community-run ecotourism lodges in the world.

As we wended our way, combing the riverbanks for caimans, capybaras, tapirs, and jaguars, our conversations meandered too. Mostly, the indigenous leaders shared stories of how ecotourism had affected their own forests and communities. They spoke of tourists who brought both opportunities and conflicts, and of their own efforts to balance conservation and development. They compared notes on wildlife in their regions, the kinds of visitors they had attracted, the profits they'd earned, the new skills they had gained, and the challenges they were facing as they sought to protect their lands and

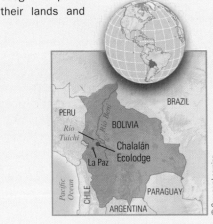

cultural traditions while also engaging with the global tourism industry.

Having studied ecotourism in the Amazon since 1993, I felt honored to be on board participating in these discussions. With support from the Critical Ecosystem Partnership Fund, I had the opportunity that year—the International Year of Ecotourism [2002]—to assemble leaders from three indigenous ecotourism projects in South America. All three were partnerships between local communities and private tour companies or nongovernmental organizations. For example, the lodge we were visiting, Chalalán, came about through a partnership between the Quechua-Tacana community of San José de Uchupiamonas, Bolivia, and two global organizations: Conservation International and the Inter-American Development Bank. Much of the $1,450,000 invested in Chalalán went toward preparing community members to assume full ownership and management of the lodge within five years. After a successful transfer in 2001, the lodge now belonged to San José's 600-member Quechua-Tacana community.

The indigenous leaders who gathered for this trip had keen, firsthand knowledge about the costs and benefits ecotourism can bring. They were former hunters, now leading tourists as birding and wildlife guides; small farmers and artisans making traditional handicrafts to sell to visitors; river-savvy fishermen supplementing their incomes by driving tour boats; and local leaders whose intimate knowledge of their communities helped them manage their own tour companies. Among them was Chalalán's general manager Guido Mamani, who recounted the benefits Chalalán had brought to the Tacana of San José. "Ten years ago," he recalled, "people were leaving San José because there were few ways to make a living. Today, they are returning because of pride in the success of Chalalán. Now, they see opportunity here."

As a result of their renewed pride in their mix of Quechua and Tacana histories, the community has begun hosting tourists for cultural tours in San José. "We want to give tourists presentations about the community and our customs," Mamani explained, "including our legends, dances, traditional music, the coca leaves, the traditional meals. We want to show our culture through special walks focusing on medicinal and other useful plants."

Mamani and the other indigenous ecotourism leaders characterized the success of their lodges in three ways: economic, social, and environmental. Chalalán, for example, counted its economic success in terms of employment and new income. It directly employs eighteen to twenty-four people at a time, and additional families supply farm produce and native fruits to the lodge. With artisans selling handicrafts to tourists, the community has gained regional fame for its wooden carved masks. The social benefits of Chalalán include new resources for education, healthcare, and communication. With their profits from tourism, the community built a school, a clinic, and a potable water system. They also purchased an antenna, solar panels, and a satellite dish to connect with the world from their remote forests along the Tuichi River.

Beyond these sorts of material improvements, ecotourism has catalyzed symbolic changes for the people of San José. "We have new solidarity in our cultural traditions," one woman noted, "and now we want to show who we are to the outside world." These experiences of Chalalán and similar projects suggest that ecotourism may be more than just a conservation and development idea—it may also be a source of pride, empowerment, and strengthened cultural identity among indigenous peoples.

Written expressly for this text, 2011.

linked to tourism, now one of the world's largest industries. Estimates vary, but in 2015 this ever-growing industry employed nearly 280 million people and contributed more than $7.6 trillion to the global economy—nearly 10 percent of the total value of goods and services produced worldwide (World Travel & Tourism Council, 2015). Some communities that still hold onto a natural habitat with a wealth of plant and animal life are able to tap into a specialized niche known as *ecotourism*, as detailed in this chapter's Anthropology Applied feature.

Distribution and Exchange

In societies without a money economy, the rewards for labor are usually direct. The workers in a family group consume what they harvest, eat what the hunter or gatherer brings home, and use the tools they themselves make. But even where no formal medium of exchange such as money exists, some distribution of goods takes place. Anthropologists often classify the cultural systems of distributing material goods into three modes: reciprocity, redistribution, and market exchange.

Reciprocity

Reciprocity refers to the exchange of goods and services, of roughly equal value, between two parties. This may involve gift giving. Notably, individuals or groups in most

© Stan Washburn/Anthro-Photo

Figure 18.6 **Generalized Reciprocity among the Ju/'hoansi**
These Ju/'hoansi men are cutting up meat that will be shared by others in the camp. Food distribution practices of such food foragers are an example of generalized reciprocity.

cultures like to think that the main point of the transaction is the gifted object itself, yet what actually matters are the social ties that are created or reinforced between givers and receivers. Because reciprocity is about a relationship between the self and others, gift giving is seldom really selfless. The overriding, if unconscious, motive is to fulfill social obligations associated with establishing or reaffirming relationships. Moreover, gift giving without expecting or desiring a counter gift may bring prestige, enhancing someone's social status, as discussed later in this chapter.

Cultural traditions dictate the specific manner and occasion of exchange. For example, when indigenous hunters in Australia kill a kangaroo, the meat is divided among the hunters' families and other relatives. Each person in the camp gets a particular share, the size depending on the nature of the person's kinship tie to the hunters. Such obligatory sharing of food reinforces community bonds and ensures that everyone eats. By giving away part of a kill, the hunters get social credit for a similar amount of food in the future.

Reciprocity falls into several categories. The Australian food distribution example just noted constitutes an example of **generalized reciprocity**—exchange in which the value of what is given is not calculated, nor is the time of repayment specified (Figure 18.6). Gift giving, in the unselfish sense, also falls into this category. So, too, does the act of a kindhearted soul who stops to help a stranded motorist or someone else in distress and refuses payment with the admonition: "Pay it forward" or "Pass it on to the next person in need."

Most generalized reciprocity, however, occurs among close kin or people who otherwise have very close ties with one another. Within such circles of intimacy, people give to others when they have the means and can count on receiving from others in time of need. Typically, participants will not consider such exchanges in economic terms but will couch them explicitly in terms of family and friendship social relations.

Exchanges that occur within a group of relatives or between friends generally take the form of generalized or balanced reciprocity. In **balanced reciprocity**, the giving and receiving, as well as the time involved, are quite specific: Someone has a direct obligation to reciprocate promptly in equal value in order for the social relationship to continue. Examples of balanced reciprocity in contemporary North American society include customary practices such as hosting a baby shower for young friends expecting their first child, giving presents at birthdays and various other culturally prescribed special occasions, and buying drinks when it is one's turn at a gathering of friends and associates.

---

reciprocity The exchange of goods and services, of approximately equal value, between two parties.

generalized reciprocity A mode of exchange in which the value of the gift is not calculated, nor is the time of repayment specified.

balanced reciprocity A mode of exchange in which the giving and the receiving are specific as to the value of the goods or services and the time of their delivery.

Giving, receiving, and sharing as so far described constitute a form of social security or insurance. A family contributes to others when they have the means and can count on receiving from others in time of need.

Negative reciprocity is a third form of exchange, in which the aim is to get something for as little as possible. The parties involved have opposing interests and are not usually closely related; they may be strangers or even enemies. They are people with whom exchanges are often neither fair nor balanced, and they are not expected to be. This type of reciprocity may involve hard bargaining, manipulation, or outright cheating. An extreme form of negative reciprocity is to take something by force, while realizing that one's victim may seek compensation or retribution for losses.

Trade and Barter

Trade refers to a transaction in which two or more people are involved in an exchange of something—a quantity of food, fuel, clothing, jewelry, animals, or money, for example—for something else of equal value. In such a transaction, the value of the trade goods can be fixed by previous agreements or negotiated on the spot by the trading partners.

When there is no money involved and the parties negotiate a direct exchange of one trade good for another, the transaction is considered a *barter*. In barter, arguing about the price and terms of the deal may well be in the form of negative reciprocity, with each party aiming to get the better end of the deal. Relative value is calculated, and despite an outward show of indifference, sharp dealing is generally the rule, when compared to the more balanced nature of exchanges within a group.

One interesting mechanism for facilitating exchange between potentially adversarial groups is **silent trade** in which no verbal communication takes place. In fact, it may involve no actual face-to-face contact at all. Such cases have often characterized the dealings between food-foraging peoples and their food-producing neighbors—such as the Mbuti Pygmy of Congo's Ituri forest, who trade bushmeat for plantains and other crops grown by Bantu villagers on small farms. It works like this: People from the forest leave trade goods in a clearing, then retreat and wait. Agriculturalists come to the spot, survey the goods, leave what they think is a fair exchange of their own wares, and then leave. The forest people return, and if satisfied with the offer, take it with them. If not, they leave it untouched, signifying that they expect more. In this way, for 2,000 or so years, foragers have supplied various commodities in demand to a wider economy (Turnbull, 1961; Wilkie & Curran, 1993).

Silent trade may occur due to lack of a common language. A more probable explanation is that it helps control situations of distrust and potential conflict—maintaining peace by preventing direct contact. Another possibility that does not exclude the others is that it makes exchange possible when problems of status might make verbal communication unthinkable. In any event, silent trade provides for the exchange of goods between groups despite potential barriers.

Kula Ring: Gift Giving and Trading in the South Pacific

Balanced reciprocity can take more complicated forms, whereby mutual gift giving serves to facilitate social interaction, smoothing relations between traders wanting to do business. One classic ethnographic example of balanced reciprocity between trading partners seeking to be friends and do business at the same time is the **Kula ring** in the southwestern Pacific Ocean. First described by Polish anthropologist Bronislaw Malinowski, the Kula ring involves thousands of seafarers going to great lengths to establish and maintain good trade relations. This centuries-old ceremonial exchange system continues to this day (Malinowski, 1961; Weiner, 1988).

Kula participants are men of influence who travel to islands within the Trobriand ring to exchange prestige items—red shell necklaces (*soulava*), which are circulated around the ring of islands in a clockwise direction, and white shell armbands (*mwali*), which are carried in the opposite direction (**Figure 18.7**). Each man in the Kula is

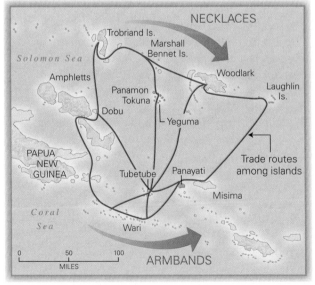

Figure 18.7 Kula Ring
The ceremonial gift exchanges of shell necklaces and armbands in the Kula ring encourage trade and barter throughout the Melanesian islands.

---

negative reciprocity A mode of exchange in which the aim is to get something for as little as possible. Neither fair nor balanced, it may involve hard bargaining, manipulation, outright cheating, or theft.

silent trade A mode of exchange of goods between mutually distrusting ethnic groups so as to avoid direct personal contact.

Kula ring A mode of balanced reciprocity that reinforces trade and social relations among the seafaring Melanesians who inhabit a large ring of islands in the southwestern Pacific Ocean.

Figure 18.8 Kula Boat
In Melanesia, men of influence paddle and sail within a large ring of islands in the southwestern
Pacific off the eastern coast of Papua New Guinea to participate in the ceremonial trading of
Kula shells, which eases trade relations and builds personal prestige.

linked to partners on the islands that neighbor his own. To a partner residing on an island in the clockwise direction, he offers a *soulava* and receives in return a *mwali*. He makes the reverse exchange of a *mwali* for a *soulava* to a partner living in the counterclockwise direction. Each of these trade partners eventually passes on the object to a Kula partner farther along the chain of islands.

Soulava and *mwali* are ranked according to their size, their color, how finely they are polished, and their particular histories. Some of them are so famous that they create a sensation when they appear in a village.

Traditionally, men make their Kula journeys in elaborately carved dugout canoes, sailing and paddling these boats, which are 6 to 7.5 meters (20 to 25 feet) long, across open waters to shores some 100 kilometers (about 60 miles) or more away (Figure 18.8). The adventure is often dangerous and may take men away from their homes for several weeks, sometimes even months. Although men on Kula voyages may use the opportunity to trade for practical goods, acquiring such items is not always the reason for these voyages—nor is Kula exchange a necessary part of regular trade expeditions.

Perhaps the best way to view the Kula is as an indigenous insurance policy in an economy fraught with danger and uncertainty. It establishes and reinforces social partnerships among traders doing business on distant shores, ensuring a welcome reception from people who have similar vested interests. This ceremonial exchange network does more than simply enhance the trade of

foods and other goods essential for survival. Melanesians participating in the Kula ring have no doubt that their social position has to do with the company they keep, the circles in which they move. They derive their social prestige from the reputations of their partners and the valuables that they circulate. By giving and receiving armbands and necklaces that accumulate the histories of their travels and the names of those who have possessed them, men proclaim their individual fame and talent, gaining considerable influence for themselves in the process.

Like other forms of currency, *soulava* and *mwali* must flow from hand to hand; once they stop flowing, they may lose their value. A man who takes these valuables out of their interisland circuit invites criticism. Not only might he lose prestige or social capital as a man of influence, but he might become a target of sorcery for unraveling the cultural fabric that holds the islands together as a functioning social and economic order.

As this example from the South Pacific illustrates, the potential tension between trading partners may be resolved or lessened by participation in a ritual of balanced reciprocity. As an elaborate complex of ceremony, political relationships, economic exchange, travel, magic, and social integration, the Kula ring illustrates the inseparability of economic matters from the rest of culture. Although perhaps difficult to recognize, this is just as true in modern industrial societies as it is in traditional Trobriand society—as is evident when heads of state engage in ceremonial gift exchanges at official visits.

Redistribution

Redistribution is a form of exchange in which goods flow into a central place where they are sorted, counted, and reallocated. In societies with a sufficient surplus to support some sort of government, goods in the form of gifts, taxes, *tribute* (obligatory contributions or gifts such as crops, goods, and services), and the spoils of war are gathered into storehouses controlled by a chief or some other leader. From there they are handed out again. The leadership has three motives in redistributing this income: The first is to gain or maintain a position of power through a display of wealth and generosity; the second is to assure those who support the leadership an adequate standard of living by providing them with desired goods; and the third is to establish alliances with leaders of other groups by hosting them at lavish parties and giving them valuable goods.

The redistribution system of the ancient Inca empire in the Andean highlands of South America was one of the most efficient the world has ever known, both in the collection of tribute and in its methods of administrative control (Mason, 1957). Administrators kept inventories of resources and a census of the population, which at its peak reached 6 million. Each craft specialist had to produce a specific quota of goods from materials supplied by overseers. Required labor was used for some agricultural and mining work. Unpaid labor was also used in a program of public works that included a remarkable system of roads and bridges throughout the mountainous terrain, aqueducts that guaranteed a supply of water, temples for worship, and storehouses that held surplus food for times of famine.

Overseers kept careful account of income and expenditures. A central administration, regulated by the Inca emperor and his relatives, had the responsibility for ensuring that production was maintained and that commodities were distributed. Holding power over this command economy, the ruling elite lived in great luxury, but sufficient goods were redistributed to the common people to make sure that no one would be left in dire need or face the indignity of pauperism.

Taxes imposed by the central governments of countries all around the world today are one form of redistribution—required payments typically based on a percentage of one's income and property value. Typically, a portion of the taxes goes toward supporting the government itself whereas the rest is redistributed either in cash (such as welfare payments and government loans or subsidies to businesses) or in the form of services (such as military defense, law enforcement, food and drug inspection, education, highway and bridge construction, and the like).

Spending Wealth to Gain Prestige

In societies where people devote most of their time to subsistence activities, gradations of wealth are small, kept that way through various cultural mechanisms and systems of reciprocity that serve to spread quite fairly what little wealth exists.

It is a different situation in ranked societies where substantial surpluses are produced and the gap between the have-nots and the have-lots can be considerable. In these societies, the social prestige that comes from showy displays—known as **conspicuous consumption**—is a strong motivator for the distribution of wealth. In industrial and postindustrial societies, excessive efforts to impress others with one's wealth or status play a prominent role. The display of symbolic prestige items particular to these societies—designer clothes, expensive jewelry, mansions, luxury cars, private planes—fits neatly into an economy based on consumer wants.

A form of conspicuous consumption also occurs in some crop-cultivating and foraging societies. Various American Indian groups living along the Northwest Coast—including the Tlingit, Haida, and Kwakwaka'wakw (Kwakiutl)—illustrate this through potlatches. A **potlatch** is a ceremonial event in which a village chief publicly gives away stockpiled food and other goods that signify wealth (Figure 18.9). The term comes from the Chinook Indian word *patshatl*, which means "gift."

Traditionally, a chief whose village had built up enough surplus to host such a feast for other villages in the region would give away large piles of sea otter furs, dried salmon, blankets, and other valuables while making boastful speeches about his generosity, greatness, and glorious ancestors. While other chiefs became indebted to him, he reaped the glory of successful and generous leadership and saw his prestige rise. In the future, his own village might face shortages, and he would find himself on the receiving end of a potlatch. Should that happen, he would have to listen to the self-serving and pompous speeches of rival chiefs. Obliged to receive, he would temporarily lose prestige and status.

In extreme displays of wealth, chiefs even destroyed some of their precious possessions. This occurred with some frequency in the second half of the 19th century, after European contact triggered a process of cultural change that included new trade wealth. Outsiders might view such grandiose displays as wasteful to the extreme. However, these extravagant giveaway ceremonies have played an ecologically adaptive role in a coastal region where villages alternately faced periods of scarcity and abundance and relied upon alliances and trade relations with one another for long-term survival. The potlatch

redistribution A mode of exchange in which goods flow into a central place, where they are sorted, counted, and reallocated.

conspicuous consumption A showy display of wealth for social prestige.

potlatch On the Northwest Coast of North America, an indigenous ceremonial event in which a village chief publicly gives away stockpiled food and other goods that signify wealth.

AP Images/Daily Sitka Sentinel/James Poulson

Figure 18.9 **Potlatch Today**
Among Native Americans living along the Northwest Coast of North America, one gains prestige
by giving away valuables at the potlatch feast. Here we see Tlingit clan members dressed in
traditional Chilkat and Raven's Tail robes during a recent potlatch in Sitka, Alaska.

provided a ceremonial opportunity to strategically redistribute surplus food and goods among allied villages in response to periodic fluctuations in fortune.

A strategy that features this sort of accumulation of surplus goods for the express purpose of displaying wealth and giving it away to raise one's status is known as a **prestige economy**. In contrast to conspicuous consumption in industrial and postindustrial societies, the emphasis is not on amassing goods that then become unavailable to others. Instead, it is on gaining wealth in order to give it away for the sake of prestige and status.

Leveling Mechanisms

The potlatch is an example of a **leveling mechanism**—a cultural obligation compelling prosperous members of a community to give away goods, host public feasts, provide free service, or otherwise demonstrate generosity so that no person permanently accumulates significantly more wealth than anyone else. With leveling mechanisms at work, greater wealth brings greater social pressure to spend and give generously. In exchange for such demonstrated altruism, a person not only increases his or her

social standing in the community, but may also keep disruptive envy at bay.

Underscoring the value of collective well-being over individual self-interest, leveling mechanisms are important for the long-term survival of traditional communities. The potlatch is just one example of many cultural varieties of leveling mechanism. By pressuring members into sharing their wealth in their own community rather than hoarding it or privately investing it elsewhere, leveling mechanisms do more than keep resources in circulation. They also reduce social tensions among relatives, neighbors, and others in the community, promoting a collective sense of togetherness. An added practical benefit is that they ensure that necessary services within the society are performed.

prestige economy The creation of a surplus for the express purpose of displaying wealth and giving it away to raise one's status.

leveling mechanism A cultural obligation compelling prosperous members of a community to give away goods, host public feasts, provide free service, or otherwise demonstrate generosity so that no person permanently accumulates significantly more wealth than anyone else.

VISUAL COUNTERPOINT

Figure 18.10 Going to Market
Global capitalism and its economy of scale is evident in these photos that convey part of the story of how tea travels from vast plantations, such as this one in Assam, northeast India, to grocery stores and specialty shops around the world. Typically, tea is handpicked into baskets or bags. Much of it ends up on mammoth container ships, including the world's largest ship, pictured here. Able to carry 19,100 containers, China's *CSCL Globe* is 400 meters (437 yards) long and 54 meters (59 yards) wide—about the dimensions of four football fields. Globally, tea exports surpass 1.8 million tons, earning close to $6 billion.

Market Exchange and the Marketplace

Typically, until well into the 20th century, **market exchange**—the buying and selling of goods and services, with prices generally determined by rules of supply and demand—was carried out in specific localities or *marketplaces*. Simply put, in market exchange, the greater the demand and/or the lower the supply, the higher the price. This is still the case in much of the nonindustrial world and even in numerous centuries-old European and Asian towns and cities. In food-producing societies, marketplaces overseen by a centralized political authority provide the opportunity for food producers and craftspeople in the surrounding rural territories to exchange some of their crops, livestock, and products for needed commodities (trade goods) manufactured in factories or in the workshops of craft specialists, who usually live in towns and cities. Thus, markets require some sort of complex division of labor as well as centralized political organization.

The traditional market is local, specific, and contained—like the one in Guatemala pictured at the beginning of this chapter. Prices are typically set on the basis of face-to-face bargaining rather than by unseen forces

wholly removed from the transaction itself. Notably, sales do not necessarily involve money; instead, goods may be directly exchanged through some form of barter.

In industrializing and industrial societies, many market transactions still take place in a specific identifiable location—including international trade fairs such as the mammoth fair held twice a year in Guangzhou (Canton), southern China's oldest trading port city. In the fall of 2014, more than 24,000 Chinese enterprises participated in the 116th Canton Fair along with 1,300 international chains (including WalMart, Carrefour, and Home Depot) and 551 companies from 45 foreign countries. Combined, they offered some 150,000 products and generated over $29 billion in sales among more than 186,000 buyers from more than 200 countries (PR Newswire, 2014).

One of the most widely traded global commodities is tea (*Camellia sinensis*), dried leaves from a plant cultivated in China for more than 4,500 years. In the 1600s, soon after this drink found its way to Europe, tea export surged as prime cargo in merchant ships sailing across the oceans in search of markets. Today, annual world tea production is about 5 million tons, most of which is still grown on large plantations in China (1.9 million tons). Since the late 1700s, tea has also been commercially grown in India, where production has reached about 1.2 million tons. Globally, tea exports surpass 1.8 million tons, earning close to $6 billion. Typically, it is handpicked, placed in baskets or bags, and shipped overseas in huge cargo vessels (**Figure 18.10**).

---

market exchange The buying and selling of goods and services, with prices set by rules of supply and demand.

In the global economy, and especially since the launching of the World Wide Web some twenty-five years ago, it is increasingly common for people living in technologically wired parts of the world to buy and sell everything from cattle to cars without ever being in the same city, let alone the same space. For example, think of the U.S.-based e-commerce company Amazon (154,000 employees and a customer base of more than 30 million people) and the Chinese online retail firm Alibaba (with 35,000 employees and featuring nearly a billion products) where all buying and selling occur in cyberspace, transcending international boundaries in a flash.

The faceless market exchanges that take place in the global capitalist system stand in stark contrast to experiences in the traditional marketplaces of precapitalist and nonindustrial societies. Traditional "real space" markets echo the excitement of a fair. They are colorful places where interactions happen amid a host of sights, sounds, and smells that awaken the senses. Typically, vendors and often their family members produced the goods they are selling, thereby personalizing the transactions. Dancers and musicians may perform, and feasting and fighting usually mark the end of the day. In these markets social relationships and personal interactions are key elements, and noneconomic activities may overshadow economic ones. In short, such markets are gathering places where people renew friendships, see relatives, gossip, and keep up with the world, while procuring needed goods they cannot produce for themselves (Plattner, 1989).

Money as a Means of Exchange

Although there are marketplaces without money of any sort, money does facilitate trade. **Money** may be defined as something used to make payments for other goods and services as well as to measure their value. Its critical attributes are durability, transportability, divisibility, recognizability, and interchangeability. Items that have been used as money in various societies include salt, shells, precious stones, special beads, livestock, and valuable metals, such as iron, copper, silver, and gold. As described in this chapter's Biocultural Connection, cacao beans were also used as money—and more.

About 5,000 years ago, merchants and others in Mesopotamia (a vast area between the Tigris and Euphrates rivers, encompassing much of present-day Iraq and neighboring border areas) began using pieces of precious metal such as silver in their transactions. Once they agreed on the value of these pieces as a means of exchange (money), more complex commercial

developments followed. As the means of exchange was standardized in terms of value, it became easier to accumulate, lend, or borrow money for specified amounts and periods of time against payment of interest. Gradually, some merchants began to do business with money itself, and they became bankers.

As the use of money became widespread, the metal units were adapted to long-term use, easy storage, and long-distance transportation. In many cultures, such pieces of iron, copper, or silver were cast as miniature models of especially valuable implements like sword blades, axes, or spades. But, some 2,600 years ago in the ancient kingdom of Lydia (southwestern Turkey), they were molded into small, flat discs conforming to different sizes and weights (Davies, 2005). Over the next few centuries, metal coins were also standardized in terms of the metal's purity and value, such as 100 units of copper equals 10 units of silver equals 1 unit of gold.

By about 2,000 years ago, the commercial use of such coins was spreading throughout much of Europe and becoming increasingly common in parts of Asia and Africa, especially along trade routes and in urban centers. Thus, money set into motion radical economic changes in many traditional societies and introduced what has been called *merchant capitalism* in many parts of the world (Wolf, 1982).

Local Economies and Global Capitalism

Imposing market production schemes on other societies and ignoring cultural differences can have unintended negative economic consequences, especially in this era of globalization. For example, it has led prosperous countries to impose inappropriate development schemes in parts of the world that they regard as economically underdeveloped. Typically, these schemes focus on increasing the target country's gross national product through large-scale production that all too often boosts the well-being of a few but results in poverty, poor health, discontent, and a host of other ills for many others.

Among many examples of this scenario is the global production of soy, which has increased greatly in many parts of the world. Of particular note is Paraguay, where big landowners, in cooperation with large agribusinesses (most of which are owned by neighboring

money A means of exchange used to make payments for other goods and services as well as to measure their value.

Cacao: The Love Bean in the Money Tree

Several thousand years ago Indians in the tropical lowlands of southern Mexico discovered how to produce a hot brew from ground, roasted beans. They collected these beans from melon-shaped fruit pods growing in trees identified by today's scientists as *Theobroma cacao*. By adding honey, vanilla, and some flowers for flavoring, they produced a beverage that made them feel good, and they believed that these beans were gifts from their gods.

Soon, cacao beans became part of long-distance trade networks and appeared in the Mexican highlands, where the Aztec elite adopted this drink brewed from *cacahuatl*, calling it "chocolatl." In fact, these beans were so highly valued that Aztecs also used them as money. When Spanish invaders conquered Guatemala and Mexico in the 1520s, they adopted the region's practice of using cacao beans as currency inside their new colony. They also embraced the custom of drinking chocolate, which they introduced to Europe, where it became a luxury drink as well as a medicine.[a]

Over the next 500 years, chocolate developed into a $14 billion global business, with the United States as the top importer of cacao beans or cacao products. Women buy 75 percent of the chocolate products, and on Valentine's Day more than $1 billion worth of chocolate is sold.

What is it about chocolate that makes it a natural aphrodisiac? Other than carbohydrates, minerals, and vitamins, it contains about 300 chemicals, including some with mood-altering effects. For instance, cacao beans contain several chemical components that trigger feelings of pleasure in the human brain. In addition to tryptophan, which increases serotonin levels, chocolate also contains phenylethylamine, an amphetamine-like substance that stimulates the body's own dopamine and has slight antidepressant effects. Chocolate contains anandamide (*anan* means "bliss" in Sanskrit), a messenger molecule that triggers the brain's pleasure center. Also naturally produced in the brain, anandamide's mood-enhancing effect is the same as that obtained from marijuana leaves. Finally, chocolate also contains a mild stimulant called theobromine ("food of god"), which stimulates the brain's production of natural opiates, reducing pain and increasing feelings of satisfaction and even euphoria.

These chemicals help explain why the last Aztec ruler Montezuma drank so much chocolate. A Spanish eyewitness, who visited his royal palace in the Aztec capital in 1519, later reported that Montezuma's servants sometimes brought their powerful lord

> in cups of pure gold a drink made from the cocoa-plant, which they said he took before visiting his wives. . . . I saw them bring in a good fifty large jugs of this chocolate, all frothed up, of which he would drink a little. They always served it with great reverence.[b]

Biocultural Question

Viewed as a divine gift by Mexican Indians, chocolate stimulates our brain's pleasure center. Why would women buy this natural love drug in much greater quantities than men?

Florian Kopp/Alamy

On average, each cacao tree produces about 30 pods a year, and each pod contains 30 cacao beans (seeds). It takes about 450 beans to make 1 pound of chocolate. Here we see the harvest of the cacao pods.

[a] For an excellent cultural history of chocolate, see Coe, S. D., & Coe, M. D. (1996). *The true history of chocolate*. New York: Thames & Hudston; Grivetti, L. E. (2005). *From aphrodisiac to health food: A cultural history of chocolate*. *Karger Gazette* (68). Basel, Switzerland: S. Karger.

[b] del Castillo, B. D. (1963). *The conquest of New Spain* (pp. 226–227) (translation and introduction by J. M. Cohen). New York: Penguin.

Raveendran/AFP/Getty Images

Figure 18.11 Protesting Genetically Modified Crops
In 2013, U.S. legislators failed to pass a bill making it compulsory to label genetically modified (GM) food, prompting a flurry of protests against the American multinational agrochemical and agricultural biotechnology corporation Monsanto in fifty countries that year. Protests within the United States and around the world continue. Here we see farmers from across India who have traveled to their country's capital city New Delhi. Wearing garlands of *brinjals* (eggplants or aubergines), they demanded that the government ban GM crops, claiming that they endanger public health. Protests such as these form part of worldwide actions by rural peoples threatened by powerful capitalist corporations profiting from agribusinesses that produce genetically engineered food crops.

Brazilians), produce genetically modified seeds, developed and marketed by foreign companies, especially the U.S.-based multinational corporation Monsanto. Although these landowners and agribusinesses possess just 1 percent of the total number of Paraguayan farms, they own almost 80 percent of the country's agricultural land. Exporting the soy, they make hefty profits because production costs are low, and international demand is high for soy-based cattle feed and biofuel. Similar stories can be found in developing countries around the world (Figure 18.11).

Hundreds of thousands of poor Paraguayans—small farmers, landless peasants, rural laborers, and their families—are victimized by such large-scale production. Traditionally growing much of their own food (plus a bit extra for the local market) on small plots, many of them have been edged out and forced to work for hunger wages or to migrate to cities, or even abroad, in order to survive. Those who stay in rural areas face malnutrition and other hardships because they lack enough fertile land to feed their families and do not earn enough to buy basic foodstuffs (Fogel & Riquelme, 2005).

Because every culture is an integrated system (as illustrated by the barrel model presented in the chapter on culture), a shift in the infrastructure, or economic base, impacts interlinked elements of the society's

Rosita Worl

Alaskan anthropologist **Rosita Worl,** whose Tlingit names are Yeidiklats'akw and Kaa hani, belongs to the Thunderbird Clan from the ancient village of Klukwan in southeastern Alaska. During her growing-up years by the Chilkat River, elders taught her to speak loudly so her words could be heard above the sound of crashing water. And her mother, a cannery union organizer, took her along to meetings.

As a university student, Worl led a public protest for the first time—successfully challenging a development scheme in Juneau detrimental to local Tlingit. When she decided to pursue her anthropology doctorate at Harvard, she did so with a strong sense of purpose: "You have to be analytical about your culture," she says. "At one time, before coming into contact with other societies, we were just able to live our culture, but now we have to be able to keep it intact while integrating it into modern institutions. We have to be able to communicate our cultural values to others and understand how those modern institutions impact those values."

Worl's graduate studies included fieldwork among the Inupiat of Alaska's North Slope region—research that resulted in her becoming a spokesperson at state, national, and international levels

David Sheakley, Sealaska Heritage Institute

Tlingit anthropologist Rosita Worl is president of the Sealaska Heritage Institute and a board member of the Alaska Federation of Natives.

for the protection of whaling practices and the indigenous subsistence lifestyle. For over three decades now, she has fought to safeguard traditional rights to natural resources essential for survival, for current and future generations, including her own children and grandchildren.

A recognized leader in sustainable, culturally informed economic development, Worl has held several major positions at the Sealaska Corporation, a large Native-owned business enterprise with almost 18,000 shareholders primarily of Tlingit and neighboring Haida and Tsimshian descent. Created under the 1971 Alaska Native Claims Settlement Act, Sealaska is now the largest private landholder in southeastern Alaska. Its subsidiaries collectively employ over a thousand people and include timber harvesting, marketing of wood products, land and forest resource management, construction, and information technology. Putting the holistic perspective and analytical tools of anthropology into practice, Worl has spearheaded efforts to incorporate the cultural values of southeast Alaska Natives into Sealaska—including shareholding opportunities for employees.

Currently, Worl serves as president of Sealaska Heritage Institute, a Native nonprofit organization that seeks to perpetuate and enhance Tlingit, Haida, and Tsimshian cultures, including language preservation and revitalization. Also on the faculty of the University of Alaska, Southeast, she has written extensively about indigenous Alaska for academic and general audiences. She founded the journal *Alaska Native News* to educate Native Alaskans on a range of issues and is deeply involved in the implementation of the 1990 Native American Graves Protection and Repatriation Act.

Sought for her knowledge and expertise, Worl has served on the board of directors of the Smithsonian Institution's National Museum of the American Indian, as well as Cultural Survival, Inc. She has earned many honors for her work, including the American Anthropological Association's Solon T. Kimball Award for Public and Applied Anthropology, received in 2008 in recognition of her exemplary career in applying anthropology to public life in Alaska and beyond.

social structure and superstructure. As the ethnographic examples of the potlatch and the Kula ring show, economic activities in traditional cultures are intricately intertwined with social and political relations and may even involve spiritual elements. Agribusinesses and other large-scale economic operations or development schemes that do not take such structural complexities into consideration may have unforeseen harmful consequences for a society.

Fortunately, there is now a growing awareness on the part of development officials that future projects are unlikely to achieve sustainable success without the kind of expertise that anthropologists can bring to bear. And, in some parts of the world anthropologists with indigenous roots are leading the way in shaping development agendas that build on rather than destroy tradition—as related in this chapter's Anthropologist of Note about Rosita Worl, a Tlingit from Juneau, Alaska.

Informal Economy and the Escape from State Bureaucracy

Powerful business corporations promote their profit-making agendas through slogans such as "free trade," "free markets," and "free enterprise." But the commercial success of such enterprises, foreign or domestic, does not come without a price, and all too often that price is paid by still-surviving indigenous foragers, small farmers, herders, fishermen, local artisans such as weavers and carpenters, and so on. From their viewpoint, such slogans of freedom have the ring of "savage capitalism," a term now commonly used in Latin America to describe a world order in which the powerless are often condemned to poverty and misery.

Many of these powerful corporations are successful, at least in part because they manage to avoid the taxes imposed on smaller businesses. The same is often true for the wealthy, who have special access to loopholes and other opportunities to reduce or eliminate taxes that others are obliged to pay. Some of those less privileged, though, have found creative ways to avoid paying taxes and to "beat the system." The system, in this case, refers to the managing bureaucracy in a state-organized society politically controlled by an elected or appointed governing elite.

State bureaucracies seek to manage and control economic activities for regulation and taxation purposes. However, they do not always succeed in these efforts for a variety of reasons: insufficient government resources; underpaid, unskilled, or unmotivated inspectors and administrators; and a culture of corruption. In state-organized societies where large numbers of people habitually avoid bureaucratic regulators seeking to monitor and tax their activities, there is a separate, undocumented economic system known as the **informal economy**—a network of producing and circulating marketable commodities, labor, and services that for various reasons escapes government control (enumeration, regulation, or other types of public monitoring or auditing).

This informal sector may encompass a range of activities: house cleaning, child care, gardening, repair or construction work, making and selling alcoholic beverages, street peddling, money lending, begging, prostitution, gambling, drug dealing, pickpocketing, and labor by illegal foreign workers, to mention just a few.

These off-the-books activities, including fraud and trade in stolen or smuggled goods on the black market, are certainly not new but generally have been dismissed by economists as of marginal importance. Yet, in many countries of the world, the informal economy is, in fact, more important than the formal economy and may involve more than half the labor force and up to 40 percent of a country's gross national product (GNP). In many places, large numbers of under- and unemployed people, who have only limited access to the formal economic sector, "improvise," getting by on scant resources. Meanwhile, more affluent members of society may dodge various regulations in order to maximize returns or to vent their frustrations at their perceived loss of self-determination in the face of increasing government regulation.

Many adult men and women from poor regions in the world seek cash-earning opportunities abroad when they cannot find a paying job within their own country. For multiple reasons such as visa requirements, most laborers who cross international borders legally get temporary work permits as "guest workers" but are not immigrants in that foreign country.

North Africa and Southwest Asia are cheap foreign labor reservoirs for the wealthy industrialized countries of western Europe, whereas Latin America and the Caribbean provide workers for the United States, which draws more migrant laborers than any other country in the world. These workers often send *remittances* (a portion of their earnings) to their families back in their home village or town abroad. In 2015, the World Bank reported that $436 billion in remittances flowed to developing countries in the previous year. The top recipients of officially recorded remittances that year were India ($70 billion), China ($64 billion), the Philippines ($28 billion), and Mexico ($25 billion) (World Bank, 2015a).

For a very poor country such as Jamaica, the total annual inflow of remittances (nearly $2.3 billion in 2014) comprises about 15 percent of that Caribbean island's income. Over a quarter of Jamaicans receive remittances from relatives working abroad, and the average value of such cash transfers for a typical Jamaican household is higher than the average per capita gross domestic product (GDP) in that island nation. For a specific example, see this chapter's Globalscape.

Now that globalization is connecting national, regional, and local markets in which natural resources, commodities, and human labor are bought and sold, people everywhere in the world face new economic opportunities and confront new challenges. Not only are natural environments more quickly and radically transformed by means of new powerful technologies, but long-established subsistence practices, economic arrangements, social organizations, and associated ideas, beliefs, and values are also under enormous pressure.

---

informal economy A network of producing and circulating marketable commodities, labor, and services that for various reasons escapes government control.

GLOBALSCAPE

How Much for a Red Delicious?

Each fall, several hundred Jamaicans migrate to Maine for the apple harvest.[a] While plucking the trees with speed and skill, they listen to reggae music that reminds them of home. Calling each other "brother," they go by nicknames like "Rasta." Most are poor peasants from mountain villages in the Caribbean where they grow yams. But their villages do not produce enough to feed their families, so they go elsewhere to earn cash.

Before leaving Jamaica, they must cut their dreadlocks and shave their beards. Screened and contracted by a labor recruiter in Kingston, they receive a temporary foreign farm worker visa from the U.S. embassy and then fly to Miami. Traveling northward by bus, many work on tobacco farms en route to Maine's orchards (and in Florida's sugarcane fields on the way home). Earning the minimum hourly wage as regulated by the federal H-2A program for "temporary agricultural workers," they work seven days a week, up to ten hours daily. Orchard owners value these foreigners because they are twice as productive as local pickers. Moreover, handpicked apples graded "extra fancy" earn farmers eight times the price of apples destined for processing.

While in the United States, the Jamaicans remain quite isolated, trying to save as much as they can so they can send more money home. Just before leaving the country, most of them buy goods to take home as gifts or to resell for profit—from shoes and clothing to electronics and refrigerators.

Throughout most of the 1900s, rural labor conditions for seasonal migrant workers in the United States were likened to indentured service (causing some critics to call the federal

H-2A program "rent-a-slave"). Nonetheless, many Jamaicans endured the hardships, pursuing harvesting work as an opportunity to escape from the dismal poverty on their Caribbean island.

Notably, conditions began to improve in the 1990s after the U.S. Department of Labor established the Adverse Effect Wage Rate, requiring agricultural employers to pay nonimmigrant agricultural workers a wage that would not adversely affect the employment opportunities of U.S. workers. This significantly increased the hourly wages of foreign farmhands. However, like minimum wage standards for U.S. citizens, these increases have not kept up with inflation—and do not change the fact that migrant laborers must exercise extreme frugality and spend long months away from home in order to support their families.[b]

Global Twister

When you take a big bite from your next apple, think of the Jamaican laborers who might have picked it. What do you think is "fair value"?

---

[a] See Rathke, L. (1989). To Maine for apples. *Salt Magazine* 9 (4), 24–47; see also, Knothe, A. (2014, June 15). Seasonal workers in H2A guest worker program vital to central Mass. orchards. *Telegram.com*. http://www.telegram.com/article/20140615 /NEWS/306159974 (retrieved December 18, 2015)

[b] U.S. Department of Labor. (2015). Wage and hour division (WHD): History of federal minimum wage rates under the Fair Labor Standards Act, 1938–2009. *U.S. Dept. of Labor*. http://www.dol .gov/whd/minwage/chart.htm (retrieved December 18, 2015)

CHAPTER CHECKLIST

What is an economic system, relative to subsistence?

✓ An economic system is an organized arrangement for producing, distributing, and consuming goods. Each society allocates natural resources (especially land, water, and fuel), technology, and labor according to its own priorities.

✓ In food-foraging societies, core features of the region may mark a group's territory. This provides flexibility because the size of a group and its territories can be adjusted according to the availability of resources in any particular place.

✓ The technology of a people (the tools they use and knowledge about them) is related to their mode of subsistence. All societies have some means of creating and allocating the tools used to produce goods.

✓ Labor is a major productive resource, and the allotment of work is commonly governed by rules according to gender and age. Cross-culturally, only a few broad generalizations apply to the kinds of work performed by men and women.

✓ A more productive strategy is to examine the types of work that men and women do in the context of specific societies to see how it relates to other cultural and historical factors.

✓ The cooperation of many people working together is a typical feature of both nonindustrial and industrial societies. Task specialization is important even in societies with very simple technologies.

How are goods distributed?

✓ The processes of distribution may be distinguished as reciprocity, redistribution, and market exchange.

✓ Reciprocity, the exchange of goods and services of roughly equal value, comes in three forms: generalized (in which the value is not calculated, nor the time of repayment specified); balanced (in which one has an obligation to reciprocate promptly); and negative (in which the aim is to get something for as little as possible).

✓ A classic ethnographic example of balanced reciprocity between trading partners seeking to maintain social ties while also doing business is the Kula ring among islanders of the southwestern Pacific Ocean. The Kula ring involves both balanced reciprocity and sharp trading.

✓ Trade is a transaction in which two or more people are involved in an exchange of something for something else of equal value. Such exchanges have elements of reciprocity but involve a greater calculation of the relative value of goods exchanged.

✓ Barter is a form of trade in which no money is involved, and the parties negotiate a direct exchange of one trade good for another. It may well be in the form of negative reciprocity, as each party aims to get the better end of the deal.

✓ Redistribution requires a strong, centralized political organization. A government assesses a tax or tribute on each citizen to support its activities, leaders, and religious elite and then redistributes the rest, usually in the form of public services. The system of tax collection and delivery of government services and subsidies in the United States is a form of redistribution.

✓ Conspicuous consumption, or display for social prestige, is a motivating force in societies that produce a surplus of goods. The prestige comes from publicly giving away one's valuables, as in the potlatch ceremony, which is also an example of a leveling mechanism.

What is market exchange, and where is the marketplace?

✓ In nonindustrial societies, the marketplace is usually a specific site where people exchange produce, livestock, and material items they have made. It also functions as a place to socialize and get news.

✓ Although market exchanges may take place through bartering and other forms of reciprocity, money (something used to make payments for goods and services as well as to measure their value) makes market exchange more efficient.

✓ In state-organized societies with market economies, the informal sector—composed of economic activities set up to avoid official scrutiny and regulation—may be more important than the formal sector. The informal economy includes remittances (earnings) that migrant laborers working abroad send to their families back in their home village or town.

How does global capitalism impact local economies?

✓ When powerful countries impose market production schemes on other societies, the impact can be negative—as in the global production of soy in Paraguay where big landowners in cooperation with large agribusinesses have edged out small farmers and landless peasants.

✓ Increasingly, development officials are utilizing the expertise that anthropologists provide in planning their projects.

QUESTIONS FOR REFLECTION

1. Imagine a global banking crisis in which the capitalist economy based on money, interest, and credit has collapsed. How long do you think it would take for a market to develop like the one in the highlands of Guatemala, shown in the chapter opening photograph? Which goods do you think would have exchange value in your culture, and what would you do to get those goods in fair trade?

2. Consider the differences between the three varieties of reciprocity. What role does each play in your own experience as a member of a family, local community, and wider society?

3. As the potlatch ceremony shows, prestige may be gained by giving away wealth. Does such a prestige-building mechanism exist in your own society? If so, how does it work?

4. Economic relations in traditional cultures are usually wrapped up in social, political, and even spiritual issues. Can you think of any examples in your own society in which the economic sphere is inextricably intertwined with other structures in the cultural system?

DIGGING INTO ANTHROPOLOGY

Luxury Foods and Hunger Wages

When shopping for groceries in a supermarket, think of this chapter's Biocultural Connection and the Visual Counterpoint and try to imagine the great chain of human hands involved in getting something as simple as a package of tea, a box of chocolate, or a pound of coffee to your grocery store. Track down the country of origin for one of those luxury items, along with the location of the plantation and the name of the company or person who owns it. Next, identify the laborers working on that plantation—their ethnicity and gender, as well as their wages and health conditions. How are the leaves or beans packed and warehoused prior to being shipped overseas? From which seaport or airport is your selected commodity shipped? Where is it shipped to, and how is it transported to your store? Compare the store price per ounce and calculate how much it cost to produce, buy, transport, and sell, in order to determine the percentage of profit made. Finally, after having enjoyed the delicious treat, take time to imagine where an ambitious entrepreneur might try to squeeze more profits from this business.

SAM PANTHAKY/AFP/Getty Images

CHALLENGE ISSUE

Worldwide, humans face the challenge of managing sexual relations and forging social alliances essential to the survival of individuals and their offspring. Adapting to particular natural environments and distinct economic and political challenges, each group establishes its own social arrangements in terms of childrearing tasks, gender relations, household and family structures, and residence patterns. Because marriage and family play a fundamental role in any society, wedding rituals are especially significant. Whether private or public, sacred or secular, weddings reveal, confirm, and underscore important cultural values. Symbolically rich, they usually feature certain speech rituals, plus prescribed apparel, postures and gestures, food and drink, and songs and dances passed down through generations. Here we see a Muslim bride in Gujarat, western India, surrounded by female relatives and friends on the eve before her wedding. Their hands are beautifully decorated with traditional designs created with dye made from the crushed leaves of the tropical henna tree. Known as *mehndi*, this temporary body art is an age-old custom among Muslims and Hindus in parts of southern Asia, as well as northern Africa. Often the groom's name is hidden within elegant designs of flowers and vines that symbolize love, fertility, and protection. A bride's *mehndi* evening, traditionally held at her parents' home, is a lively female-only gathering with special food, singing, and lovemaking instructions, along with hand painting.

Sex, Marriage, and Family

Unlike individuals raised in traditional Muslim families, such as the bride featured in this chapter's opening photo, young people in the Trobriand Islands of the South Pacific traditionally enjoy great sexual freedom. By age 7 or 8, children begin playing erotic games and imitating adult seductive attitudes. Within another four or five years, they start pursuing sexual partners in earnest—experimenting erotically with a variety of individuals.

© Cengage Learning

Because attracting sexual partners ranks high among young Trobrianders, they spend a great deal of time beautifying themselves (Figure 19.1). Their daily conversations are loaded with sexual hints, and they employ magical spells as well as small gifts to entice a prospective sex partner to the beach at night or to the house in which boys sleep apart from their parents. Because girls also sleep apart from their parents, young people have considerable freedom in arranging their erotic explorations. Boys and girls play this game as equals, with neither having an advantage over the other (Weiner, 1988).

By the time Trobrianders are in their mid-teens, meetings between lovers may take up most of the night, and love affairs are apt to last for several months. Ultimately, a young islander begins to meet the same partner again and again, rejecting the advances of others. When the couple is ready, they appear together one morning outside the young man's house as a way of announcing their intention to marry.

Until the latter part of the 20th century, the Trobriand attitude toward adolescent sexuality was in marked contrast to that of most Western cultures in Europe and North America, where individuals were not supposed to have sexual

In this chapter you will learn to

- Discuss how different cultures regulate sexual relations.

- Distinguish several marriage forms and understand their determinants and functions.

- Contrast family and household forms across cultures.

- Explain a range of marital residence patterns.

- Weigh the impact of globalization and reproductive technology on marriage and family.

Figure 19.1 Sex Appeal among the Trobrianders
To attract lovers, young Trobriand women and men must look as attractive and seductive as possible. This young woman's father has given her face painting and adornments to enhance her beauty.

relations before or outside of marriage. Since then, practices in much of the modern industrialized world have converged toward those of the Trobrianders, even though the traditional ideal of premarital sexual abstinence has not been abandoned entirely and is upheld in many traditional Christian, Muslim, and similarly conservative families.

Regulation of Sexual Relations

In the absence of effective birth control, the usual outcome of sexual activity between fertile individuals of the opposite sex is that, sooner or later, the woman becomes pregnant. Given the intricate array of social responsibilities involved in rearing the children that are born of sexual relations—and the potential for conflict resulting

from unregulated sexual activity—it is not surprising that all societies have cultural rules that seek to regulate those relations. However, those rules vary considerably across cultures.

For instance, in some societies, sexual intercourse during pregnancy is taboo, whereas in others it is looked upon positively as something that promotes the growth of the fetus. And although some cultures sharply condemn same-sex acts or relations, many others are indifferent and do not even have a special term to distinguish homosexuality as significant in its own right.

In several cultures same-sex acts are not only accepted but prescribed. Such is the case in some Papua societies in New Guinea, for example, where certain male-to-male sexual acts are part of initiation rituals required of all boys to become respected adult men (Kirkpatrick, 2000). In those cultures, people traditionally see the transmission of semen from sexually mature males to younger boys, through oral sex, as vital for building up the strength needed to protect against the supposedly debilitating effects of adult heterosexual intercourse (Herdt, 1993).

Despite longstanding culture-based opposition to homosexuality in many areas of the world, this sexual orientation exists within the wider range of human sexual relations, emotional attractions, and social identities, and it is far from uncommon (Figure 19.2). Across the globe, the expression of homosexuality ranges from lifelong loving relationships to casual sexual encounters, and from being fully open to being utterly private and secretive.

During the past few decades, public denigration and condemnation of homosexuality have diminished dramatically in numerous countries, and same-sex relationships have become a publicly accepted part of the cosmopolitan lifestyle in metropolitan centers from Amsterdam to Paris and Rio de Janeiro to San Francisco. As recently as 2009, India decriminalized homosexuality, followed by several other countries, including Lebanon in 2014 and Mozambique in 2015. Clearly, the social rules and cultural meanings of all sexual behavior are subject to great variability—not only across cultures but also across time.

Marriage and the Regulation of Sexual Relations

In much of the world, the traditional ideal was (and in many communities still is) for individuals to establish a family through marriage, by which one also gains an exclusive right of sexual access to another person. The main purpose of sexual intercourse was not just erotic pleasure but reproduction. Recognizing the potential risks of

© Hideo Haga/Haga/The Image Works

Figure 19.2 Expressions of Same-Sex Affection

Although same-sex relationships have existed for thousands of years and are permitted in many parts of the world, homosexuals in sexually restrictive societies are shamed and shunned, and may be beaten, flogged, banished, imprisoned, or even murdered. Even in societies that have become less restrictive, public displays of same-sex affection (between men in particular) are often looked upon as distasteful or even disgusting. One widespread exception is the sports arena where athletes freely hug each other, and may even pat each other on the behind or leap into each other's arms without bringing their sexual orientation into question. Attitudes are shifting all around the globe, however, as evident in this photo of two just-wed Argentinean men kissing after receiving their official marriage license on November 16, 2009—the first in Latin America. This Buenos Aires couple sought a license not only because they love each other, but also because they wanted the shared health insurance policy, inheritance rights, and other privileges married couples in their country traditionally enjoy.

unregulated sexual relations, including unplanned pregnancies by a man other than the lawful husband, these societies have often criminalized extramarital affairs as adultery. Reinforcing public awareness of the moral rules, authorities past and present have turned sexual transgressions such as adultery into a public spectacle of shame, torture, or even death.

Among European Christian colonists in 17th- and 18th-century New England, for example, a woman's participation in adultery was a serious crime. Although it did not lead to stoning, as was custom among ancient Israelites, women so accused were shunned by the community and could be imprisoned. Such restrictions remain (or are sometimes reinstated) in those traditional societies in northern Africa and western Asia where age-old Shariah law regulates social behavior in strict accordance with Muslim fundamentalist standards of morality.

For example, in a Taliban-controlled village in northern Afghanistan, conservative *mullahs* (priests) found a young couple guilty of adultery, proclaiming it an

offense prohibited by God. Buried waist-deep in holes outside the village, the 23-year-old married woman and her 28-year-old lover were stoned to death in the summer of 2010, a brutal spectacle attended by hundreds of villagers and filmed on a mobile phone (Amnesty International, 2010). Turning legal transgressions into a public display, authorities reinforce awareness of the rules of social conduct, even if a sentence is ultimately dropped or changed.

A side effect of such restrictions on sexual behavior is that they may limit the spread of sexually transmitted diseases (Gray, 2004; UNAIDS, 2014). Yet most cultures do not sharply regulate an individual's sexual practices. Indeed, a majority of cultures are considered sexually permissive or semi-permissive (the former having few or no restrictions on sexual experimentation before marriage, the latter allowing some experimentation but less openly). A minority of known societies—about 15 percent—have rules requiring that sexual involvement take place only within marriage.

Marriage as a Universal Institution

This brings us to an anthropological definition of **marriage**—a culturally sanctioned union between two or more people that establishes certain rights and obligations between the people, between them and their children, and between them and their in-laws. Such marriage rights and obligations most often include, but are not limited to, sex, labor, property, childrearing, exchange, and status. Thus defined, marriage is universal. Notably, our definition of *marriage* refers to "people" rather than "a man and a woman" because in some countries same-sex marriages are socially acceptable and allowed by law, even though opposite-sex marriages are far more common. We will return to this point later in the chapter.

In many cultures, marriage is considered the central and most important social institution. In such cultures, people will spend considerable time and energy on maintaining marriage as an institution. They may do so in various ways, including highlighting the ritual moment when the wedding takes place, festively memorializing the event at designated times such as anniversaries, and making it difficult to divorce.

In some societies, however, marriage is a relatively marginal institution and is not considered central to the establishment and maintenance of family life and society. For instance, marriage has lost much of its traditional significance in wealthy northwestern European nations, in part due to changes in the political economy, more balanced gender relations, and shared public benefits of these capitalist welfare states. And historically, marriage has been of marginal significance for the Nayar in southwestern India, profiled in the following passage.

Sexual and Marriage Practices among the Nayar

Situated in the Indian state of Kerala, the Nayar are a landowning warrior caste; kinsmen related in the female line make up corporations that traditionally hold their estates. These blood relatives live together in a large household, with the eldest male serving as manager.

Like Trobriand Islanders, the Nayar are a sexually permissive culture. A classic anthropological study describes three transactions related to traditional Nayar

sexual and marriage practices, many of which have changed since the mid-1900s (Fuller, 1976; Goodenough, 1970; Gough, 1959). The first, occurring shortly before a girl experiences her first menstruation, involves a ceremony that joins her with a "ritual husband." This union does not necessarily involve sexual relations and lasts only a few days. Neither individual has any further obligation, but when the girl becomes a woman, she and her children typically participate in ritual mourning for the man when he dies. This temporary union establishes the girl as an adult ready for motherhood and eligible for sexual activity with men approved by her household.

The second transaction takes place when a young Nayar woman enters into a continuing sexual liaison with a man approved by her family. This is a formal relationship that requires the man to present her with gifts three times each year until the relationship is terminated. In return, the man can spend nights with her. Despite ongoing sexual privileges, however, this "visiting husband" has no economic obligations to her, nor is her home regarded as his home. In fact, she may have the same arrangement with more than one man at the same time. Regardless of the number of men with whom she is involved, this second transaction, the Nayar version of marriage, clearly specifies who has sexual rights to whom and includes rules that deter conflicts between the men.

If a Nayar woman becomes pregnant, one of the men with whom she has a relationship (who may or may not be the biological father) must formally acknowledge paternity by presenting gifts to the woman and the midwife. This establishes the child's birthrights—as does birth registration in Western societies. Once a man has ritually acknowledged fatherhood by gift giving, he may continue to take interest in the child, but he has no further obligations. Support and education for the child are the responsibility of the mother and her brothers, with whom she and her offspring live.

Indeed, unlike most other cultural groups in the world, the traditional Nayar household includes only the mother, her children, and her other biological or blood relatives, technically known as **consanguineal kin**. It does not include any of the "husbands" or other people related through marriage—known as **affinal kin**. In other words, sisters and their offspring all live together with their brothers and their mother and her brothers. Historically, this arrangement addressed the need for security in a cultural group in which warfare was common.

---

marriage A culturally sanctioned union between two or more people that establishes certain rights and obligations between the people, between them and their children, and between them and their in-laws. Such marriage rights and obligations most often include, but are not limited to, sex, labor, property, childrearing, exchange, and status.

consanguineal kin Biologically related relatives, commonly referred to as blood relatives.

affinal kin People related through marriage.

Among the Nayar, sexual relations are forbidden between consanguineal relatives and thus are permitted only with individuals who live in other households. This brings us to another human universal: the incest taboo.

Incest Taboo

Just as marriage in its various forms is found in all cultures, so is the **incest taboo**—the prohibition of sexual contact between certain close relatives. But what is defined as "close" is not the same in all cultures. Moreover, such definitions may be subject to change over time. Although the scope and details of the taboo vary across cultures and time, almost all societies past and present strongly forbid sexual relations at least between parents and children and nearly always between siblings. In some societies the taboo extends to other close relatives, such as cousins, and even to some relatives linked through marriage.

Anthropologists have long been fascinated by the incest taboo and have proposed several explanations for its cross-cultural existence and variation. The simplest explanation is that our species has an "instinctive" repulsion for incest. Although research shows that primates tend to avoid having sex with close relatives, particularly when there are alternative mating partners, this explanation falls short given violations of the incest taboo (Wolf & Durham, 2004). In the United States, for instance, it is reported that about 9 percent of children under 18 years of age have experienced incestuous relations (U.S. Dept. of Health and Human Services, 2015; Whelehan, 1985).

Historically, some scholars argued that the incest taboo prevents the harmful genetic effects of inbreeding. Although this is so, it is also true that, as with domestic animals, inbreeding can increase desired characteristics as well as detrimental ones. Furthermore, undesirable effects will show up sooner than without inbreeding, so whatever genes are responsible for them are quickly eliminated from the population. That said, a preference for a more genetically different mate does tend to maintain a higher level of genetic diversity within a population, and in evolution this variation works to a species' advantage. Without genetic diversity a species is less likely to successfully adapt biologically to environmental change.

The inbreeding or biological avoidance theory can be challenged on several fronts. For example, there are historical exceptions to the incest taboo, such as a requirement that the ruler of the Inca empire in ancient Peru be married to his own (half) sister. Sharing the same father, both siblings belonged to the political dynasty that derived its sacred right to rule the empire from Inti, its ancestral Sun God. And by virtue of this royal lineage's godly origin, their children could claim the same sacred political status as their human/divine father and mother. Ancient emperors in Egypt also practiced such religiously prescribed incest based on a similar claim to divine royal

status. In addition, detailed census records made in Egypt about 2,000 years ago show that brother–sister marriages were not uncommon among ordinary members of the farming class, and we have no evidence for linking this cultural practice to any biological imperatives (Leavitt, 2013).

Coming at the question from a nonbiological perspective, some anthropologists have put forth the idea that the incest taboo exists as a cultural means to preserve the stability and integrity of the family, which is essential to maintaining social order. Sexual relations between members other than a husband and wife would introduce competition within the family, destroying the harmony of a social unit fundamental to societal order. Others have theorized that the taboo, by prohibiting sexual relations and marriage between close relatives, promotes establishing family ties and forming alliances with other social groups.

Endogamy and Exogamy

Whatever its cause, the utility of the incest taboo can be seen by examining its effects on social structure. Closely related to prohibitions against incest are cultural rules against **endogamy** (from Greek *endon*, "within," and *gamos*, "marriage"), or marriage within a particular group of individuals (cousins and in-laws, for example). If the group is defined as one's immediate family alone, then societies generally prohibit or at least discourage endogamy, thereby promoting **exogamy** (from Greek *exo*, "outside," and *gamos*, "marriage") or marriage outside the group. Yet, a society that practices exogamy at one level may practice endogamy at another. Among the Trobriand Islanders, for example, individuals have to marry outside their own clan and lineage (exogamy). However, because eligible sex partners are to be found within one's own community, village endogamy is commonly practiced.

Since the early 20th century, restrictions on marriages involving close kin have increased in Europe and other parts of the world. Because of this, worldwide migrations by peoples from countries in which such marriages remain customary may lead to cross-cultural problems (Figure 19.3). British anthropologist Adam Kuper recently discussed this issue based on research with Muslim immigrant families from Pakistan. According to Kuper,

> In Pakistan, and in the Pakistani diaspora, a preference is commonly expressed for marriage within the extended family or *birādarī*. . . . Perhaps unexpectedly, the rate of cousin marriage among Pakistani immigrants to Britain is higher than the

incest taboo The prohibition of sexual relations between closely related individuals.
endogamy Marriage within a particular group or category of individuals.
exogamy Marriage outside a particular group or category of individuals.

© PJR Travel/Alamy Stock Photo

Figure 19.3 Cousin Marriage
Large numbers of Muslim immigrant families are settling in western Europe. Many hail not only from Pakistan but also from former French and British colonies in Asia and Africa where cousin marriage is common. Here we see such a traditional family, conforming to Shariah (Islamic sacred law), relaxing in the heart of London.

rate in rural Pakistan. And the rate of cousin marriage is particularly high among younger British Pakistanis. Around a third of the marriages of the immigrant generation were with first cousins, but well over half the marriages of the British-born generation are with first cousins. This is a consequence of British immigration regulations. . . . It is very difficult to enter Britain unless one is married to a British citizen. In most cousin marriages, one partner immigrates to Britain from Pakistan. Alison Shaw found that 90 per cent of the first-cousin marriages in her sample of British Pakistanis in Oxford involved one spouse who came directly from Pakistan. . . . (Kuper, 2008, p. 731)

Kuper notes that although health risks to offspring of such close-kin marriages are "rather low" and generally "within the limits of acceptability," research by geneticists does indicate that "the risk of birth defects or infant mortality is roughly doubled for the children of first cousins." However, he adds, in western Europe this debate is not just about medical risks, but also about immigration and cultural friction: "Father's brother's daughter marriage is taken to be a defining feature of Islamic culture, and it is blamed not only for overloading the health service but also for resistance to integration and cultural stagnation. It is also associated with patriarchy, the suppression of women, and forced marriages" (Kuper, 2008, p. 731).

In the United States, where twenty-five states ban first-cousin marriage and six restrict it, there is a general assumption nationwide that these laws are rooted in genetics (Ottenheimer, 1996). (See a discussion of U.S. marriage prohibitions in the Biocultural Connection.)

Early anthropologists suggested that many human groups long ago recognized certain advantages of exogamy as an effective means of creating long-lasting bonds of friendship. French anthropologist Claude Lévi-Strauss (see the Anthropologist of Note) elaborated on this idea. He explained exogamy as an alliance system in which distinctive communities participate in an exchange of marriageable males and/or females. By extending the social network, potential enemies turn into relatives who may provide support in times of hardship or violent conflict.

Building on the theory advanced by Lévi-Strauss, other anthropologists have proposed that exogamy is an important means of creating and maintaining political alliances and promoting trade between groups, thereby ensuring mutual protection and access to needed goods and resources not otherwise available. Forging wider kinship networks, exogamy also functions to integrate distinct groups and thus potentially reduces violent conflict.

Distinction Between Marriage and Mating

In contrast to mating, which occurs when individuals join for purposes of sexual relations, marriage is a socially binding and culturally recognized relationship. Only marriage is backed by social, political, and ideological factors that regulate sexual relations as well as reproductive rights and obligations. Even among the previously discussed Nayar in India, for whom traditional marriage seems to involve little other than a sexual relationship, a woman's husband is legally obligated to provide her with gifts at specified intervals. Additionally, a Nayar woman may not legally have sex with a man to whom she is not married.

Thus, although mating occurs in nearly every other animal species, marriage is a cultural institution unique to humans. This is evident when we consider the various forms of marriage around the world.

Marriage Prohibitions in the United States

By Martin Ottenheimer

In the United States, every state has laws prohibiting the marriage of some relatives. Every state forbids parent–child and sibling marriages, but there is considerable variation in prohibitions concerning more distant relatives. For example, although twenty-five states ban marriage between first cousins, nineteen states and the District of Columbia allow it, and others permit it under certain conditions. Notably, the United States is the only country in the Western world that has prohibitions against first-cousin marriage.

Many people in the United States believe that laws forbidding marriage between family members exist because parents who are too close biologically run the risk of producing children with mental and physical defects. Convinced that first cousins fall within this "too close" category, they believe laws against first-cousin marriage were established to protect families from the effects of harmful genes.

There are two major problems with this belief: First, cousin prohibitions were enacted in the United States long before the discovery of the genetic mechanisms of disease. Second, genetic research has shown that offspring of first-cousin couples do not have any significantly greater risk of negative results than offspring of very distantly related parents.

Why, then, do some North Americans maintain this belief? To answer this question, it helps to know that laws against first-cousin marriage first appeared in the United States right after the mid-1800s when evolutionary models of human behavior became fashionable. In particular, a pre-Darwinian model that explained social evolution as dependent upon biological factors gained popularity. It supposed that "progress from savagery to civilization" was possible when humans ceased inbreeding. Cousin marriage was thought to be characteristic of savagery, the lowest form of human social life, and it was believed to inhibit the intellectual and social development of humans. It became associated with "primitive" behavior and dreaded as a threat to a civilized America.

Thus, a powerful myth emerged in American popular culture, which has since become embedded in law. That myth is held and defended to this day, sometimes with great emotion despite being based on a discredited social evolutionary theory and contradicted by the results of modern genetic research.

Recently, a group of geneticists published the results of a study of consanguineous unions, estimating that there is "about a 1.7–2.8% increased risk for congenital defects above the population background risk."[a] Not only is this a high estimate, it is also well within the bounds of the margin of statistical error. But even so, it is a lower risk than that associated with offspring from women over the age of 40—who are not forbidden by the government to marry or bear children.

Biocultural Question

What do you think is the underlying cultural logic that makes some societies traditionally forbid first cousins from marrying each other, whereas others, equally unfamiliar with genetics, accept or even prefer such marriages?

Written expressly for this text, 2005; revised and updated, 2011, 2015.

_____

[a]Bennett, R. L., et al. (2002, April). Genetic counseling and screening of consanguineous couples and their offspring: Recommendations of the National Society of Genetic Counselors. *Journal of Genetic Counseling 11* (2), 97–119.

Forms of Marriage

Within societies, and all the more so across cultures, we see contrasts in the constructs and contracts of marriage. Indeed, as is evident in the definition of marriage given previously, this institution comes in various forms—and these forms are distinct in terms of the number and gender of spouses involved.

Monogamy

Monogamy—marriage in which both partners have just one spouse—is the most common form of marriage worldwide. In North America and most of Europe, it is the only legally recognized form of marriage. In these places, not only are other forms prohibited, but systems of inheritance, whereby property and wealth are transferred from one generation to the next, are based on the institution of monogamous marriage. In some parts of the world where divorce rates are high and people who have been divorced remarry (including Europe and North America), an increasingly common form of marriage is **serial monogamy** whereby an individual marries a series of partners in succession.

_____

monogamy A marriage form in which both partners have just one spouse.

serial monogamy A marriage form in which an individual marries or lives with a series of partners in succession.

Claude Lévi-Strauss (1908–2009)

Claude Lévi-Strauss lived to be 100. When he died, he was the most celebrated anthropologist in the world. Born in Belgium, where his father briefly worked as a portrait painter, he grew up in Paris. As a boy during World War I, Claude lived with his grandfather, a rabbi of Versailles.

He studied law and philosophy at the Sorbonne, married a young anthropologist named Dina Dreyfus, and became a philosophy teacher. In 1935, the couple ventured across the ocean to Brazil's University of São Paulo, where his wife taught anthropology and he sociology. Influenced by 18th-century romantic philosopher Rousseau and fascinated by historical accounts of Brazilian Indians, he preferred ethnographic research and lectured on tribal social organization.

In 1937, he and Dina organized an expedition into the Amazon forest, visiting Bororo and other tribal villages and collecting artifacts for museums. In 1938, they made another journey and researched recently contacted Nambikwara Indians. Back in Paris together in 1939, their marriage dissolved. That same year, the Second World War erupted, and the French army mobilized its soldiers, including Lévi-Strauss.

A year after Nazi Germany conquered France in 1940, Lévi-Strauss escaped to New York City, where he became an anthropology professor at the New School for Social Research. Teaching courses on South American Indians during the war years, he befriended other European exiles, including the linguist Roman Jakobson, who pioneered the structural analysis of language.

After the war, Lévi-Strauss became French cultural consul in the United States, based in New York. Maintaining ties with the academic community, including anthropologist Margaret Mead, he completed his two-part doctoral thesis: "The Elementary Structures of Kinship" and "The Family and Social Life of the Nambikwara Indians." Theoretically influenced by Jakobson's structural linguistics, his thesis analyzed the logical structures underlying the social relations of kin-ordered societies.

Building on Marcel Mauss's 1925 study of gift exchange as a means to build or maintain a social relationship, he applied the concept of reciprocity to kinship, arguing that marriage is based on the exchange relationship between kin-groups of "wife-givers" and "wife-takers." Returning to France in late 1947, he became associate director of the ethnographic museum in Paris and successfully defended his thesis at the Sorbonne. His structural analysis was recognized as a pioneering study in kinship and marriage.

In 1949, Lévi-Strauss joined an international body of experts invited by UNESCO to discuss and define the "race concept," a disputed term associated with discrimination and genocide. Three years later, he authored *Race and History*, a book that became instrumental in UNESCO's worldwide campaign against racism and ethnocentrism. By then, he had become an anthropology professor at the École Pratique des Hautes Études in Paris. Continuing his prolific writing, he published *Tristes Tropiques* (1955). This memoir about his ethnographic adventures among Amazonian Indians won him international fame. His 1958 book, *Structural Anthropology*, also became a classic. It presented his theoretical perspective that the human mind produces logical structures, classifying reality in terms of binary oppositions (such as light–dark, good–evil, nature–culture, and male–female) and that all humans share a mental demand for order expressed in a drive toward classification.

In 1959, Lévi-Strauss became the chair of Social Anthropology at the Collège de France and founded his own institute there. Specializing in the comparative study of religion, he undertook a massive comparative study and structural analysis of myths, resulting in a series of instantaneously classic books. In 1973, he was elected to the centuries-old Académie Française, a prestigious institution with just forty members known as "immortals." Countless other honors from around the world followed.

Now, survived by his wife Monique and two sons, he lies in a small rural cemetery in Burgundy, near his old mansion, where he liked to reflect on the human condition.

French anthropologist Claude Lévi-Strauss in the Amazon rainforest in Brazil, c. 1936.

Apic/Hulton Archive/Getty Images

Polygamy

Monogamy is the most common marriage form worldwide, but it is not the preferred form in a majority of the world's cultures. That distinction goes to **polygamy** (one individual having multiple spouses) and specifically to **polygyny**, in which a man is married to more than one woman (*gyne* is Greek for "woman" and "wife"). Favored in about 80 to 85 percent of the world's cultures, polygyny is commonly practiced in parts of Asia and much of sub-Saharan Africa (Lloyd, 2005).

Although polygyny is the favored marriage form in these places, monogamy exceeds it, but for economic rather than moral or legal reasons. In many polygynous societies, in which a groom is usually expected to compensate a bride's family in cash or kind, a man must be fairly wealthy to be able to afford more than one wife. Multiple surveys of twenty-five sub-Saharan African countries where polygyny is common show that it declined by about half between the 1970s and

© AP Photo/Ben Curtis

Figure 19.4 **Polygyny**

Polygynous marriages are common in many parts of the world, including numerous African countries. Here we see a Senegalese businessman having dinner with his three wives and some of his children. Defying expectations that Western influences and urbanization would gradually do away with plural marriages, polygyny remains common among Muslims in Senegal and other parts of West Africa.

2001. There are many reasons for this dramatic decline, but one is due to families making an economic transition from traditional farming and herding to wage labor in cities. Nonetheless, polygyny remains highly significant in that part of the world, with an overall average of 25 percent of married women in such unions (Lloyd, 2005) (Figure 19.4).

Polygyny is particularly common in traditional food-producing societies that support themselves by herding grazing animals or growing crops and in which women do the bulk of cultivation. Under these conditions, women are valued both as workers and as child bearers. Where the labor of wives in polygynous households generates wealth and little support is required from husbands, the wives have a strong bargaining position within the household. Often, they have considerable freedom of movement and some economic independence through the sale of crafts or crops. Wealth-generating polygyny is found in its fullest elaboration in parts of sub-Saharan Africa and Southwest Asia, though it is known elsewhere as well (White, 1988).

In societies practicing wealth-generating polygyny, most men and women do enter into polygynous marriages, although some are able to do so earlier in life than others. This is made possible by a female-biased sex ratio and/or a mean age at marriage for females that is

significantly below that for males. In fact, this marriage pattern is frequently found in societies in which violence, including war, is common, and many young males die in battle. Their high combat mortality results in a population in which women outnumber men.

By contrast, in societies in which men are more heavily involved in productive work, generally only a small minority of marriages are polygynous. Under these circumstances, women are more dependent on men for support, so they are valued as child bearers more than for the work they do. This is commonly the case in pastoral nomadic societies in which men are the primary owners and tenders of livestock. This makes women especially vulnerable if they prove incapable of bearing children, which is one reason a man may seek another wife.

Another reason for a man to take on secondary wives is to demonstrate his high position in society. But where men do most of the productive work, they must work extremely hard to support more than one wife, and few actually do so. Usually, it is the exceptional hunter or male shaman ("medicine man") in a food-foraging society or a

polygamy A marriage form in which one individual has multiple spouses at the same time.

polygyny A marriage form in which a man is married to two or more women at the same time; a form of polygamy.

particularly wealthy man in a horticultural, agricultural, or pastoral society who is most apt to practice polygyny. When he does, it is usually of the *sororal* type, with the co-wives being sisters. Having lived their lives together before marriage, the sisters continue to do so with their husband, instead of occupying separate dwellings of their own.

Polygyny also occurs in a few places in Europe. For example, English laws concerning marriage changed in 1972 to accommodate immigrants who traditionally practiced polygyny. Since that time polygamous marriages have been legal in England for some specific religious minorities, including Muslims and Sephardic Jews. According to one family law specialist, the real impetus behind this law change was a growing concern that "destitute immigrant wives, abandoned by their husbands, [were] overburdening the welfare state" (Cretney, 2003, pp. 72–73).

About 100,000 people currently live in polygynous households in the United States. Of these, about 20,000 are Mormons belonging to the Fundamentalist Church of Jesus Christ of Latter-Day Saints, many of whom reside in the Utah–Arizona border towns of Hildale and Colorado City. They uphold a 19th-century Mormon doctrine that plural marriage brings exaltation in heaven—even though the practice was officially declared illegal in the United States in 1862 and was officially renounced in 1890 by the Church of Jesus Christ of Latter-Day Saints, the mainstream Mormon church headquartered in Salt Lake City.

The other 80,000 or so people in polygynous households in the United States are primarily immigrants (mostly Muslim) originating from Asian and African countries in which the practice is culturally embedded and legal. Polygynous households are also growing among Black Muslim orthodox households in several major U.S. cities (McDermott, 2011; Schilling, 2012). Ways in which laws prohibiting polygamy are circumvented include marriage of one spouse under civil law and others in religious ceremonies only. Individuals, usually males, may also marry additional spouses in different countries (Hagerty, 2008).

Despite its illegality and concerns that the practice can jeopardize the rights and well-being of women, regional law enforcement officials have adopted a "live and let live" attitude toward religious-based polygyny in their region. Women involved in the practice are sometimes outspoken in defending it. One woman—a lawyer and one of nine co-wives—expresses her attitude toward polygyny as follows:

> I see it as the ideal way for a woman to have a career and children. In our family, the women can help each other care for the children. Women in monogamous relationships don't have that luxury.

As I see it, if this lifestyle didn't already exist, it would have to be invented to accommodate career women. (Johnson, 1991, p. A22)

In some polygynous societies, if a man dies, leaving behind a wife and children, it is customary that one of his brothers marries the widowed sister-in-law. But this obligation does not preclude the brother having another wife then or in the future. This custom, called the *levirate* (from the Latin *levir,* which means "husband's brother"), provides security for the widow (and her children). A related polygynous tradition is the *sororate* (Latin *soror* means "sister"), in which a man has the right to marry a sister (usually younger) of his deceased wife. In some societies, the sororate also applies to a man who has married a woman who is unable to bear children. This practice entitles a man to a replacement wife from his in-laws. In societies that have the levirate and sororate—customary in many traditional foraging, farming, and herding cultures—the in-law relationship between the two families is maintained even after the spouse's death and secures an established alliance between two groups.

Although monogamy and polygyny are the most common forms of marriage in the world today, other forms do exist. **Polyandry**, the marriage of one woman to two or more men simultaneously, is practiced in only a few societies. The extreme rarity of polyandry could be due to longer life expectancy for women or to slightly lower female infant mortality, either of which might produce a society with a surplus of women.

Fewer than a dozen societies are known to have favored this form of marriage, but they involve people as widely separated from one another as the Marquesan Islanders of Polynesia and Tibetans in Asia (Figure 19.5). In Tibet, where inheritance is in the male line and arable land is limited, the practice of brothers sharing one wife (*fraternal polyandry*) keeps the land together by preventing it from being repeatedly subdivided among sons from one generation to the next. Unlike monogamy, it also holds down population growth, thereby avoiding increased pressures on resources. Finally, among Tibetans who practice a mixed economy of farming, herding, and trading in the Himalayas, fraternal polyandry provides the household with an adequate pool of male labor for all three subsistence activities (Levine & Silk, 1997).

Other Forms of Marriage

Notable among several other marriage forms is **group marriage**. Also known as *co-marriage,* this is a rare arrangement in which several men and women have sexual access to one another. Until a few decades ago, Inupiat Eskimos in northern Alaska, for instance, engaged in "spouse exchange" (*nuliaqatigiit*) between non-kin, with two conjugal husband–wife couples being united by shared sexual access. Highly institutionalized arrangements, these intimate

---

polyandry A marriage form in which a woman is married to two or more men at the same time; a form of polygamy.

group marriage A marriage form in which several men and women have sexual access to one another; also called *co-marriage.*

Figure 19.5 Polyandrous Marriage
Polyandry—marriage between one woman and two or more men—occurs in fewer than a dozen societies, including among the Nyinba people living in northwest Nepal's Nyinba Valley in the Humla district near Tibet. Pictured here, from right: the older husband Chhonchanab with first daughter Dralma, the wife Shilangma, the younger husband KaliBahadur, and the second daughter Tsering.

relationships implied ties of mutual aid and support across territorial boundaries and were expected to last throughout the lifetime of the participants (Chance, 1990). The ties between the couples were so strong that their children retained a sibling relationship to one another (Spencer, 1984).

There are also arrangements anthropologists categorize as **fictive marriage**—marriage by proxy to the symbols of someone not physically present in order to establish a social status for a spouse and heirs. One major reason for such a marriage is to control rights to property in the next generation. Various types of fictive marriages exist in different parts of the world. In the United States, for example, proxy marriage ceremonies accommodate physically separated partners, such as seafarers, prisoners, and military personnel deployed abroad.

In several traditional African societies—most famously among Nuer cattle herders of South Sudan—a woman may marry a man who has died without heirs. In such situations the deceased man's brother may become his stand-in, or proxy, and marry a woman on his behalf. As in the case of the marriage custom of the sororate discussed previously, the biological offspring will be considered as having been fathered by the dead man's spirit. Recognized as his legitimate children, they are his rightful heirs. Because

such spouses are absent in the flesh yet believed to exist in spirit form, anthropologists refer to these fictive unions as *ghost marriages* (Evans-Pritchard, 1951).

Choice of Spouse

The egalitarian ideal that individuals should be free to marry whomever they choose is an arrangement that, although common in much of Europe and the western hemisphere, certainly is not universally embraced. In many societies, marriage and the establishment of a family are considered far too important to be left to the desires of young people. The individual relationship of two people who are expected to spend their lives together and raise their children together is viewed as incidental to the more serious matter of allying two families through the marriage bond. Marriage involves a transfer of rights between families, including rights to property and rights over children, as well as sexual rights. Thus, marriages tend to be arranged for the economic and political advantage of the family unit.

fictive marriage A marriage form in which a proxy is used as a symbol of someone not physically present to establish the social status of a spouse and heirs.

Although arranged marriages are rare in North American society, they do occur. Among ethnic minorities, they may serve to preserve traditional values that people fear might otherwise be lost. Families of wealth and power may orchestrate such marriages by segregating their children in private schools and carefully steering them toward appropriate spouses. The Original Study illustrates how marriages may be arranged in cultures in which such traditional practices remain commonplace.

ORIGINAL STUDY

Arranging Marriage in India BY SERENA NANDA

© Cengage Learning

Six years after my first field trip to India, I returned to do research among the middle class in Bombay, a modern, sophisticated city. Planning to include a study of arranged marriages in my project, I thought I might even participate in arranging one myself. An opportunity presented itself almost immediately. A friend from my previous Indian trip was in the process of arranging for the marriage of her eldest son. Because my friend's family was eminently respectable and the boy himself personable, well educated, and nice looking, I was sure that by the end of my year's fieldwork, we would have found a match.

The basic rule seems to be that a family's reputation is most important. It is understood that matches would be arranged only within the same caste and general social class, although some crossing of subcastes is permissible if the class positions of the bride's and groom's families are similar. Although dowry is now prohibited by law in India, extensive gift exchanges took place with every marriage. Even when the boy's family does not "make demands," every girl's family nevertheless feels the obligation to give the traditional gifts—to the girl, to the boy, and to the boy's family. Particularly when the couple would be living in the joint family—that is, with the boy's parents and his married brothers and their families, as well as with unmarried siblings, which is still very common even among the urban, upper-middle class in India—the girl's parents are anxious to establish smooth relations between their family and that of the boy. Offering the proper gifts, even when not called "dowry," is often an important factor in influencing the relationship between the bride's and groom's families and perhaps, also, the treatment of the bride in her new home.

In a society where divorce is still a scandal and the divorce rate is exceedingly low, an arranged marriage is the beginning of a lifetime relationship not just between the bride and groom but between their families as well. Thus, although a girl's looks are important, her character is even more so because she is being judged as a prospective daughter-in-law as much as a prospective bride....

My friend is a highly esteemed wife, mother, and daughter-in-law. She is religious, soft-spoken, modest, and deferential. She rarely gossips and never quarrels, two qualities highly desirable in a woman. A family that has the reputation for gossip and conflict among its womenfolk will not find it easy to get good wives for their sons....

Originally from North India, my friend's family had lived for forty years in Bombay, where her husband owned a business. The family had delayed in seeking a match for their eldest son because he had been an air force pilot for several years, stationed in such remote places that it had seemed fruitless to try to find a girl who would be willing to accompany him. In their social class, a military career, despite its economic security, has little prestige and is considered a drawback in finding a suitable bride....

The son had recently left the military and joined his father's business. Because he was a college graduate, modern, and well traveled, from such a good family, and, I thought, quite handsome, it seemed to me that he, or rather his family, was in a position to pick and choose. I said as much to my friend. Although she agreed that there were many advantages on their side, she also said, "We must keep in mind that my son is both short and dark; these are drawbacks in finding the right match."...

An important source of contacts in trying to arrange her son's marriage was my friend's social club in Bombay. Many of the women had daughters of the right age, and some had already expressed an interest in my friend's son. I was most enthusiastic about the possibilities of one particular family who had five daughters, all of whom were pretty, demure, and well educated. Their mother had told my friend, "You can have your pick for your son, whichever one of my daughters appeals to you most." I saw a match in sight. "Surely," I said to my friend, "we will find one there. Let's go visit and make our choice." But my friend did not seem to share my enthusiasm.

When I kept pressing for an explanation of her reluctance, she admitted, "See, Serena, here is the problem. The family has so many daughters, how will they be able to provide nicely for any of them?...Because this is our eldest son, it's best if we marry him to a girl who is the only daughter, then the wedding will truly be a gala affair." I argued that surely the quality of the girls themselves made up for any deficiency in the elaborateness of the wedding. My friend admitted this point but still seemed reluctant to proceed.

Sophie Elbaz/Anzenberger/Redux

son or daughter, but we have spoiled the reputation of our family as well. And that will make it much harder for their brothers and sisters to get married. So we must be very careful."

What she said was true and I promised myself to be more patient. I had really hoped and expected that the match would be made before my year in India was up. But it was not to be. When I left India my friend seemed no further along in finding a suitable match for her son than when I had arrived.

Two years later, I returned to India and still my friend had not found a girl for her son. By this time, he was close to 30, and I think she was a little worried. Because she knew I had friends all over India, and I was going to be there for a year, she asked me to "help her in this work" and keep an eye out for someone suitable. . . .

It was almost at the end of my year's stay in India that I met a family with a marriageable daughter whom I felt might be a good possibility for my friend's son. . . . This new family had a successful business in a medium-sized city in central India and were from the same subcaste as my friend. The daughter was pretty and chic; in fact, she had studied fashion design in college. Her parents would not allow her to go off by herself to any of the major cities in India where she could make a career, but they had compromised with her wish to work by allowing her to run a small dress-making boutique from their home. In spite of her desire to have a career, the daughter was both modest and home-loving and had had a traditional, sheltered upbringing.

I mentioned the possibility of a match with my friend's son. The girl's parents were most interested. Although their daughter was not eager to marry just yet, the idea of living in Bombay—a sophisticated, extremely fashion-conscious city where she could continue her education in clothing design—was a great inducement. I gave the girl's father my friend's address.

Returning to Bombay on my way to New York, I told my friend of this newly discovered possibility. She seemed to feel there was potential but, in spite of my urging, would not make any moves herself. She rather preferred to wait for the girl's family to call upon them.

A year later I received a letter from my friend. The family had visited, and her daughter and their daughter had become very good friends. During that year, the two girls had frequently visited each other. I thought things looked promising.

Last week I received an invitation to a wedding: My friend's son and the girl were getting married. Because I had found the match, my presence was particularly requested at the wedding. I was thrilled. Success at last! As I prepared to leave for India, I began thinking, "Now, my friend's younger son, who do I know who has a nice girl for him . . . ?"

"Is there something else," I asked her, "some factor I have missed?" "Well," she finally said, "there is one other thing. They have one daughter already married and living in Bombay. The mother is always complaining to me that the girl's in-laws don't let her visit her own family often enough. So it makes me wonder, will she be that kind of mother who always wants her daughter at her own home? This will prevent the girl from adjusting to our house. It is not a good thing." And so, this family of five daughters was dropped as a possibility.

Somewhat disappointed, I nevertheless respected my friend's reasoning and geared up for the next prospect. This was also the daughter of a woman in my friend's social club. There was clear interest in this family and I could see why. The family's reputation was excellent; in fact, they came from a subcaste slightly higher than my friend's own. The girl, an only daughter, was pretty and well educated and had a brother studying in the United States. Yet, after expressing an interest to me in this family, all talk of them suddenly died down and the search began elsewhere.

"What happened to that girl as a prospect?" I asked one day. "You never mention her anymore. She is so pretty and so educated, what did you find wrong?"

"She is too educated. We've decided against it. My husband's father saw the girl on the bus the other day and thought her forward. A girl who 'roams about' the city by herself is not the girl for our family." My disappointment this time was even greater, as I thought the son would have liked the girl very much. . . . I learned that if the family of the girl has even a slightly higher social status than the family of the boy, the bride may think herself too good for them, and this too will cause problems. . . .

After one more candidate, who my friend decided was not attractive enough for her son, almost six months had passed, and I had become anxious. My friend laughed at my impatience: "You Americans want everything done so quickly. You get married quickly and then just as quickly get divorced. Here we take marriage more seriously. If a mistake is made we have not only ruined the life of our

Adapted from Nanda, S. (1992). Arranging a marriage in India. In P. R. De Vita (Ed.), *The naked anthropologist* (pp. 139–143). Belmont, CA: Wadsworth.

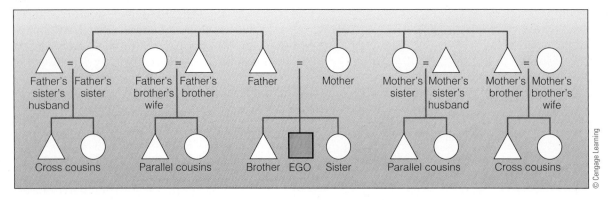

Figure 19.6 Kinship Relationships
Anthropologists use diagrams of this sort to illustrate kinship relationships. This one shows
the distinction between cross cousins and parallel cousins. In such diagrams, males are
always shown with triangles, females with circles, marital ties with an equal sign (=), sibling
relationships with a horizontal line, and parent–child relationships with a vertical line. Terms are
given from the perspective of the individual labeled EGO, who can be male or female.

Cousin Marriage

Cousin marriage is prohibited in some societies, but particular types of cousins are the preferred marriage partners
in others. Anthropologists distinguish between parallel
and cross cousins. A **parallel cousin** is the child of a
father's brother or a mother's sister (Figure 19.6). In some
societies, the preferred spouse for a man is his father's
brother's daughter (or, from the woman's point of view,
her father's brother's son). This is known as *patrilateral
parallel-cousin marriage.*

Although not obligatory, such marriages have been
favored historically among Arabs, the ancient Israelites,
and the ancient Greeks. In all of these societies male
dominance and descent are emphasized, but sons as well
as daughters may inherit property of value. Thus, when a
man marries his father's brother's daughter (or a woman
marries her father's brother's son), property is retained
within the single male line of descent. Generally, in these
societies the greater the property, the more this form of
parallel-cousin marriage is apt to occur.

A cross cousin is the child of a mother's brother or a
father's sister (see Figure 19.6). Some societies favor *ma-
trilateral cross-cousin marriage*—marriage of a man to his
mother's brother's daughter or a woman to her father's sister's son. This preference exists among food foragers (such
as the Aborigines of Australia) and some farming cultures
(including various peoples of southern India). Among
food foragers, who inherit relatively little in the way of
property, such marriages help establish and maintain ties
of solidarity between social groups. In agricultural societies, however, the transmission of property is an important
determinant. In societies that trace descent exclusively

in the female line, for instance, property and other important rights usually pass from a man to his sister's son;
under cross-cousin marriage, the sister's son is also the
man's daughter's husband.

For this reason, there is no single word for cousin in
many cultures. In Arabic, for example, there are eight different terms, distinguishing cousins not only by gender
but also by whether the person is related through his or
her mother's sister, mother's brother, father's brother, or
father's sister:

ibn al khāla	mother's sister's son
ibnat khāla	mother's sister's daughter
ibn khāl	mother's brother's son
ibnat khāl	mother's brother's daughter
ibn 'ama	father's sister's son
ibnat 'ama	father's sister's daughter
ibn 'am	father's brother's son
ibnat 'am	father's brother's daughter

Same-Sex Marriage

As noted earlier in this chapter, our cross-cultural definition
of marriage refers to a union between "people" rather than
between "a man and a woman" not only because it includes
polygamy but also because it includes marriages between
individuals of the same gender. Since the 1990s, "same-sex
marriages" are culturally acceptable and officially allowed
by law in a growing number of societies. This right to marriage affords same-sex spouses the same economic benefits
and rights as other married couples. These may range from
family health insurance to Social Security spousal benefits.

Marriages between individuals of the same gender may
provide a way of dealing with problems for which opposite-sex marriage offers no satisfactory solution. This is the
case with woman–woman marriage, a practice documented

parallel cousin The child of a father's brother or a mother's sister.
cross cousin The child of a mother's brother or a father's sister.

in about forty traditional cultures in sub-Saharan Africa (Green, 1998). However, where it does occur, it only involves a small minority of women who take the role of a female husband.

Woman–Woman Marriage among the Nandi

Details differ from one society to another, but woman–woman marriages among the Nandi of western Kenya may be taken as representative of such practices in Africa (Oboler, 1980). The Nandi are cattle herders who also do considerable farming. Control of most significant property and the primary means of production—livestock and land—is exclusively in the hands of men and may be transmitted only to their male heirs, usually their sons. Because polygyny is the preferred form of marriage, a man's property is normally divided equally among his wives for their sons to inherit. Within the household, each wife has her own home in which she lives with her children, but all are under the authority of the husband, who is a remote and aloof figure within the family. In such situations, the position of a woman who bears no sons is difficult; not only does she not help perpetuate her husband's male line—a major concern among the Nandi—but also she has no one to inherit the proper share of her husband's property.

To get around these problems, a woman of advanced age who bore no sons may become a female husband by marrying a young woman. The purpose of this arrangement is for the young wife to provide the male heirs her female husband could not. To accomplish this, the woman's wife enters into a sexual relationship with a man other than her female husband's male husband; usually it is one of his male relatives. No other obligations exist between this woman and her male sex partner, and her female husband is recognized as the social and legal father of any children born under these conditions.

In keeping with her role as female husband, this woman is expected to abandon her female gender identity and, ideally, dress and behave as a man. In practice, the ideal is not completely achieved, for the habits of a lifetime are difficult to reverse. Generally, it is in the context of domestic activities, which are most highly symbolic of female identity, that female husbands most completely assume a male identity.

The individuals in woman–woman marriages enjoy several advantages. By assuming male identity, a barren or sonless woman raises her status considerably and even

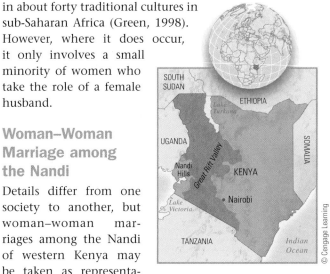

achieves near equality with men, who otherwise occupy a far more favored position in Nandi society than women. A woman who marries a female husband is usually one who is unable to make a good marriage, often because she (the female husband's wife) has lost face as a consequence of premarital pregnancy. By marrying a female husband, she too raises her status and also secures legitimacy for her children. Moreover, a female husband is usually less harsh and demanding, spends more time with her, and allows her a greater say in decision making than a male husband does. The one thing she may not do is engage in sexual activity with her marriage partner. In fact, female husbands are expected to abandon sexual activity altogether, including with their male husbands to whom they remain married even though the women now have their own wives.

Same-Sex Marriage Around the World Today

In contrast to woman–woman marriages among the Nandi are same-sex marriages that include sexual activity between partners. Over the past decades, the legal recognition of such unions has become a matter of vigorous debate in some parts of the world. Nearly twenty countries—including Argentina, Belgium, Brazil, Canada, Denmark, France, Iceland, Luxembourg, the Netherlands, New Zealand, Norway, Portugal, South Africa, Spain, Sweden, the United Kingdom, the United States, and Uruguay—have legalized same-sex marriage, and numerous other countries are moving toward doing so (**Figure 19.7**).

Despite these major shifts, the issue of same-sex marriage remains taboo, controversial, or unsettled in many parts of the world, with official policies sometimes swinging back and forth. This situation illustrates that cultures are dynamic and capable of change.

Marriage and Economic Exchange

Marriages in many human societies are formalized by some sort of economic exchange. This may take the form of a gift exchange known as **bridewealth** (sometimes called *bride-price*), which involves payments of money or valuable goods to a bride's parents or other close kin. This usually happens in patrilineal societies in which the bride will become a member of the household in which her husband grew up; this household will benefit from her labor as well as from the offspring she produces. Thus, her family must be compensated for their loss.

Bridewealth is not a simple buying and selling of women; rather, it can contribute to the bride's household

---

bridewealth The money or valuable goods paid by the groom or his family to the bride's family upon marriage; also called *bride-price.*

Figure 19.7 Same-Sex Marriage in the United States
Tory receives a celebratory kiss from her father alongside her new spouse, Monica, at their wedding in Connecticut, where same-sex marriage became legal in 2008.

© Marie Labbancz

(through purchases of furnishings, for example) or can help finance an elaborate and costly wedding celebration. It also enhances the stability of the marriage because it usually must be refunded if the couple separates. Other forms of compensation are an exchange of women between families—"My son will marry your daughter if your son will marry my daughter." Yet another is **bride service**, a period of time during which the (prospective) groom works for the bride's family (sometimes several years, as among ancient Israelites).

In a number of societies, especially those with an agriculturally based economy, women often bring a dowry with them at marriage. A **dowry** is a woman's share of parental property that, instead of passing to her upon her parents' deaths, is given to her at the time of her marriage (Figure 19.8). This does not mean that she retains control of this property after marriage. In some European and Asian countries, for example, a woman's property traditionally falls exclusively under her husband's control. Having benefited by what she has brought to the marriage, however, he is obligated to look out for her future well-being, including her security after his death. In North America today, a form of dowry persists with the custom of the bride's family paying the wedding expenses.

One of the functions of dowry is to ensure a woman's support in widowhood (or after divorce), an important consideration for societies in which men carry out the bulk of productive work and women are valued for their reproductive potential rather than for the work they do. In such societies, women incapable of bearing children are especially vulnerable, but the dowry they bring with them at marriage helps protect them against desertion. Another function of dowry is to reflect the economic status of the woman in societies in which differences in wealth are important. It also permits women, with the aid of their parents and kin, to compete through dowry for desirable (that is, wealthy) husbands.

Divorce

Like marriage, divorce in most societies is a matter of great concern to the couple's families because it impacts not only the individuals dissolving their marital relationship but also offspring, in-laws, other relatives, and sometimes entire communities. Indeed, divorce may have social, political, and economic consequences far beyond the breakup of a couple and their household.

Across cultures, divorce arrangements can be made for a variety of reasons and with varying degrees of difficulty. Among the Gusii farmers of western Kenya, for instance, sterility and impotence are grounds for a divorce. Among certain aboriginal peoples in northern Canada and

---

bride service A designated period of time when the groom works for the bride's family.

dowry A payment at the time of a woman's marriage that comes from her inheritance, made to either her or her husband.

Figure 19.8 Dowries in Traditional Rural Societies
A young Kyrgyz bride sits in front of colorful stacks of woven and richly embroidered blankets and other textiles that she brings into the new household as part of her *sep* (dowry). The *sep* also includes cutlery, dishes, clothes, pillows, wall hangings, and beautiful felt carpets. Notice the exquisitely carved and painted wooden dowry chest on the left, which indicates her parental family's high social status.

Chenchu foragers in central India, divorce is traditionally discouraged after children are born; couples usually are urged by their families to accept their differences. By contrast, in the southwestern United States, a traditional Hopi Indian woman in Arizona could divorce her husband at any time merely by placing his belongings outside the door to indicate he is no longer welcome. Among the most common reasons for divorce across cultures are infidelity, sterility, cruelty, and desertion (Betzig, 1989; Goodwin, 1999).

Although divorce rates may be high in various parts of the world, they have become so high in Western industrial and postindustrial societies that many worry about the future of what they view as traditional and familiar forms of marriage and the family. It is interesting to note that although divorce was next to impossible in Western societies between 1000 and 1800, in those centuries few marriages lasted more than about ten or twenty years, due to high mortality rates caused in part by inadequate healthcare and poor medical expertise (Stone, 2005). With increased longevity, separation by death has diminished and separation by legal action has grown. In the United States divorce rates have leveled off since peaking in the 1980s, but over 40 percent of marriages still do not survive (Morello, 2011).

Family and Household

Dependence on group living for survival is a basic human characteristic. We have inherited this from primate ancestors, although we have developed it in our own distinctly human way—through culture. However each culture defines what constitutes a family, this social unit forms the basic cooperative structure that ensures an individual's primary needs and provides the necessary care for children to develop as healthy and productive members of the group and thereby ensure its future.

Comparative historical and cross-cultural studies reveal a wide variety of family patterns, and these patterns may change over time. Thus, the definition of **family** is necessarily broad: two or more people related by blood, marriage, or adoption. The family may take many forms, ranging from a single parent with one or more children, to a married couple or polygamous spouses with offspring, to several generations of parents and their children.

family Two or more people related by blood, marriage, or adoption. The family may take many forms, ranging from a single parent with one or more children, to a married couple or polygamous spouses with or without offspring, to several generations of parents and their children.

Figure 19.9 Household Versus Family
Households can include many individuals not related to one another biologically or through marriage, as shown in this photo of nuns gathered together for a meal at the Sakyadhita Thilashin Nunnery School in Sagaing, near Mandalay, Myanmar.

© Melvyn Longhurst/Corbis

Family members may form a residential group or household, but not all households consist of family members. For purposes of cross-cultural comparison, anthropologists define the **household** as a domestic unit of one or more persons living in one residence. In the vast majority of human societies, most households are made up of families, but there are many other arrangements.

For instance, among the Mundurucu Indians—an indigenous ethnic group subsisting on hunting, fishing, and food gardens in the heart of Brazil's Amazon rainforest—married men and women are members of separate households, meeting periodically for sexual activity. At age 13, boys join their fathers in the men's house. Meanwhile, their sisters continue to live with their mothers and the younger boys in two or three houses grouped around the men's house. Thus, the men's house constitutes one household inhabited by adult males and their sexually mature sons, and the women's houses are inhabited by adult women and prepubescent boys and girls.

An array of other domestic arrangements can be found in other parts of the world, including situations in which co-residents of a household are not related biologically or by marriage—such as the service personnel in an elaborate royal household, apprentices in the household of craft specialists, or groups of children being raised by paired teams of adult male and female community members in an Israeli kibbutz (a collectively owned and operated agricultural settlement). So it is that *family* and *household* are not always synonymous (**Figure 19.9**).

Forms of the Family

To discuss the various forms families take in response to particular social, historical, and ecological circumstances, we must first distinguish between a **conjugal family** (in Latin *conjugere* means "to join together"), which is formed on the basis of marital ties, and a **consanguineal family** (based on the Latin word *consanguineus*, literally meaning "of the same blood"), which consists of related women, their brothers, and the women's offspring.

Consanguineal families are not common, but examples include the classic case of the Nayar described earlier in the chapter, as well as the Mosuo of southwestern China, and the Tory Islanders—a Roman Catholic, Gaelic-speaking fishing people living on a small island off the coast of Ireland. Typically, Tory Islanders are all close neighbors and do not marry until they are in their late 20s or early 30s. By then, commented one local woman,

> It's too late to break up arrangements that you have already known for a long time. . . . You know, I have my sisters and brothers to look after, why should I leave home to go live with a husband? After all, he's got his sisters and his brothers looking after him. (Fox, 1978, n.p.)

Notably, because the community numbers but a few hundred people, husbands and wives are within easy commuting distance of each other. According to a cross-cultural survey of family types in 192 cultures around the world, the

---

household A domestic unit of one or more persons living in one residence. Other than family members, a household may include nonrelatives, such as servants.

conjugal family A family established through marriage.

consanguineal family A family of blood relatives, consisting of related women, their brothers, and the women's offspring.

extended family is most common, present in nearly half of those cultures, compared to the nuclear family at 25 percent and the polygamous family at 22 percent (Winick, 1970).

The Nuclear Family

The most basic family unit is the **nuclear family**, made up of one or two parents and dependent offspring, which may include a stepparent, stepsiblings, and adopted children (Figure 19.10). Until recently, the term *nuclear family* referred only to the mother, father, and child(ren) unit—the family form that most North Americans, Europeans, and many others regard as the normal or natural nucleus of larger family units.

In the United States, traditional mother, father, child(ren) nuclear family households reached their highest frequency around 1950, when 60 percent of all households conformed to this model (Stacey, 1990). Today, such families make up about 20 percent of U.S. households, and the term *nuclear family* is used to cover the social reality of several types of small parent–child units, including single parents with children and same-sex couples with children (Babay, 2013; U.S. Census Bureau, 2012).

Industrialization and market capitalism have played a historical role in shaping the nuclear family most of us are familiar with today. One reason for this is that factories, mining and transportation companies, warehouses, shops, and other businesses generally pay individual wage earners only for the jobs they are hired to do. Whether these workers are single, married, divorced, or have siblings or children is really not a concern to the profit-seeking companies. Because jobs may come and go, individual wage earners must remain mobile to adapt to the labor markets. And because few wage earners have the financial resources to support large numbers of relatives without incomes of their own, industrial or postindustrial societies do not favor the continuance of larger extended families (discussed below), which are standard in most societies traditionally dependent on pastoral nomadism, agriculture, or horticulture.

Interestingly, the nuclear family is also likely to be prominent in traditional foraging societies such as that of the Eskimo people who live in the barren Arctic environments of eastern Siberia (Russia), Alaska, Greenland, and Canada (where Eskimos are known as Inuit). In the winter the traditional Inuit husband and wife, with their children, roam the vast Arctic Canadian snowscape in their quest for food. The husband hunts and makes shelters. The wife cooks, is responsible for the children, and makes the clothing and keeps it in good repair. One of a wife's traditional chores is to chew her husband's boots to soften the leather for the next day so that he can resume his quest for game. The wife and her children could not survive without the husband, and life for a man is unimaginable without a wife.

Similar to nuclear families in industrial societies, those living under especially harsh environmental conditions must be prepared to fend for themselves. Such isolation comes with its own set of challenges, including the difficulties of rearing children without multigenerational support and a lack of familial care for the elderly. Nonetheless, this form of family is well adapted to a mode of subsistence that requires a high degree of geographic mobility. For the Inuit in Canada, this mobility permits the hunt for food (Figure 19.11); for other North Americans, the hunt for jobs and improved social status require that the family unit be mobile.

The Extended Family

When two or more closely related nuclear families cluster together in a large domestic group, they form a unit known as the **extended family**. This larger family unit, common in traditional horticultural, agricultural, and pastoral societies around the world, typically consists of siblings with their spouses and offspring, and often their parents. All of these kin, some related by blood and some by marriage, live and work together for the common good and deal with outsiders as a single unit. Extended family households exist in many parts of the world—from the Maya of Central America and Mexico to Pashtun tribes in Afghanistan and neighboring Pakistan.

Because members of the younger generation bring their husbands or wives to live in the family, extended

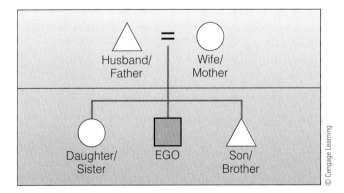

Figure 19.10 The Nuclear Family
This diagram shows the relationships in a traditional nuclear family, a form that is common but declining in North America and much of Europe.

nuclear family A group consisting of one or two parents and dependent offspring, which may include a stepparent, stepsiblings, and adopted children. Until recently this term referred only to the mother, father, and child(ren) unit.

extended family Two or more closely related nuclear families clustered together in a large domestic group.

Figure 19.11 Nuclear Families in the Canadian Arctic
Among Inuit people in Canada who still hunt for much of their food, nuclear families, such as the one shown here, are typical. Their isolation from other relatives is usually temporary. Much of the time they are found in groups of at least a few related families.

© Eastcott-Momatiuki/The Image Works

families have continuity through time. As older members die off, new members are born into the family. Extended families do involve particular challenges, however. Among these are difficulties that the in-marrying individual is likely to have in adjusting to the spouse's family.

Nontraditional Families and Nonfamily Households

In North America and parts of Europe, increasing numbers of people live in nonfamily households, either alone or with people who are not relatives. In fact, about one-third of households in the United States fall into this category (Figure 19.12). Many others live as members of what are often called *nontraditional families*.

Increasingly common are *cohabitation* households, made up of unmarried couples. Since 1960, such households have increased dramatically in number especially among young couples in their 20s and early 30s in North America and parts of Europe. In Norway, for example, over half of all live births now occur outside marriage. One reason for this is that Norwegian couples who have lived together for at least two years and who have children have many of the same rights and obligations as their married counterparts (Noack, 2001). For many, however, cohabitation represents a relatively short-term domestic arrangement because most cohabiting couples either marry or separate within two years (Forste, 2008).

Cohabitation breakup has contributed to the growing number of *single-parent* households—as have increases in divorce, sexual activity outside marriage, declining marriage rates among women of childbearing age, and the number of women preferring single motherhood. In the United States,

more than a third of all births occur outside of marriage (Stein & St. George, 2009). The proportion of U.S. single-parent households is still rising and now surpasses 13 percent, while the number comprised of married couples with children stands at about 25 percent. Although single-parent households account for about 13 percent of all U.S. households, they are home to about 30 percent of all children (under 18 years of age) in the country (U.S. Census Bureau, 2015).

In the vast majority of cases, a child in a single-parent household lives with the mother. Single-parent households headed by women are neither new nor restricted to industrial or postindustrial societies. They have been studied for a long time in Caribbean countries, where men historically have been exploited as a cheap source of labor for sugar, coffee, or banana plantations. In more recent decades, many of these men are now also working as temporary migrant laborers in foreign countries, primarily in the United States—often living in temporary households composed of fellow laborers.

Also significant today are the high numbers of *blended families*. These are families composed of a married couple together raising children from previous unions.

Residence Patterns

Anthropologists distinguish several residence patterns adopted by newly married couples across cultures. These arrangements are part of a cultural system's adaptation to ecological or labor market circumstances and various other factors.

Patrilocal residence is a pattern in which a married couple lives in the husband's father's place of residence. This arrangement is most often found in cultural situations where men play a predominant role in subsistence,

---

patrilocal residence A residence pattern in which a married couple lives in the husband's father's place of residence.

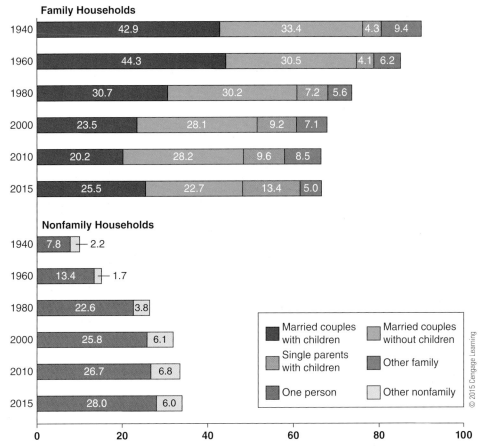

Percent Distribution of U.S. Households by Type, 1940–2015

Family Households

1940	42.9	33.4	4.3	9.4
1960	44.3	30.5	4.1	6.2
1980	30.7	30.2	7.2	5.6
2000	23.5	28.1	9.2	7.1
2010	20.2	28.2	9.6	8.5
2015	25.5	22.7	13.4	5.0

Nonfamily Households

1940	7.8	2.2
1960	13.4	1.7
1980	22.6	3.8
2000	25.8	6.1
2010	26.7	6.8
2015	28.0	6.0

Legend:
- Married couples with children
- Married couples without children
- Single parents with children
- Other family
- One person
- Other nonfamily

0   20   40   60   80   100

Figure 19.12 Household Change in the United States

A household comprises all the people who occupy a single housing unit—such as a family, a group of roommates, or an unmarried couple. Over the past 75 years, there have been dramatic changes in U.S. household structure. In 1940, married couples with children represented about 43 percent of all households, compared to married couples without children (33 percent), single-parent families (4 percent), and other types of family households (9 percent). Nonfamily households made up only 10 percent of households nationwide, and most of those were persons living alone. Today, only 25 percent of U.S. households are comprised of married couples with children, and the number of single-parent households now surpasses 13 percent (three-quarters of which are single-mother households). The number of people living alone now exceeds all of the other categories.

Note that percentages for subcategories may not sum to category totals due to rounding.

Sources: Jacobsen, Mather, & Dupuis, 2012; U.S. Census, 2015.

© 2015 Cengage Learning

particularly if they own property that can be accumulated; where polygyny is customary; where warfare is prominent enough to make cooperation among men especially important; and where an elaborate political organization exists in which men wield authority. These conditions are most often found together in societies that rely on animal husbandry and/or intensive agriculture for subsistence. Where patrilocal residence is customary, the bride often must move to a different band or community. In such cases, her parents' family is not only losing the services of a useful family member, but they are losing her potential offspring as well. Hence, usually there is some kind of compensation to her family, most commonly bridewealth.

Matrilocal residence, in which a married couple lives in the wife's mother's place of residence, is likely if cultural ecological circumstances make the role of the woman predominant for subsistence. It is found most often in horticultural societies where political organization is relatively uncentralized and cooperation among women is important. The Hopi Indians provide one example. Although Hopi men do the farming, the women control access to land and "own" the harvest. Men are not even allowed in the granaries. Under matrilocal residence, men usually do not move very far from the family in which they were raised, so they are available to help out there from time to time. Therefore, marriage usually does not involve compensation to the

groom's family. Less common, but also found in matrilineal societies, is *avunculocal residence*, in which the couple lives with the husband's mother's brother.

In **neolocal residence**, a married couple forms a household in a separate location. This occurs where the independence of the nuclear family is emphasized. In industrial societies such as the United States—where most economic activity occurs outside rather than inside the family and it is important for individuals to be able to move where jobs can be found—neolocal residence is better suited than any of the other patterns.

Also noteworthy is *ambilocal residence* (*ambi* in Latin means "both"). In this arrangement, the couple can join either the groom's or the bride's family, living wherever the resources are best or their presence is most needed or appreciated. This flexible pattern is particularly common among food-foraging peoples; if resources are scarce in the territory of the husband's family group, the couple may join the wife's relatives for more readily available food supplies in their domain.

matrilocal residence A residence pattern in which a married couple lives in the wife's mother's place of residence.

neolocal residence A residence pattern in which a married couple establishes its household in a location apart from either the husband's or the wife's relatives.

Marriage, Family, and Household in Our Technological and Globalized World

Large-scale immigration, modern technology, and multiple other factors in the emerging political economy of global capitalism also impact the cross-cultural mosaic of marriage, family, and household. For instance, electronic and digital communication by way of fiber-optic cables and satellites has transformed how individuals express sexual attraction and engage in romantic courtship.

Today, local, cross-cultural, and transnational love relations bloom via the Internet. Numerous online companies provide dating and matchmaking services, permitting individuals to post personal profiles and search for romantic partners or future spouses in a secured Internet setting. Such services also appeal to individuals in ethnic or religious diasporas seeking others with compatible personal, ethnic, or religious backgrounds. Indian matrimonial websites, for instance, are now also used for purposes of arranged marriages, allowing parents to upload a video profile of their child, screen potential suitors, and settle on the right match.

Social media also permit the pursuit of traditionally prohibited relationships through clandestine text messaging of forbidden desires and taboo intimacies—for example, across castes in India and between young unmarried men and women in traditional Muslim communities.

Figure 19.13 Factory Dormitory in China
Many of China's 260 million migrant laborers work in factories and live in dormitories such as this. Here we see workers eating lunch outside their dorm at a factory district in the southern Chinese city of Shenzhen in Guangdong Province.

Adoption and New Reproductive Technologies

Although it has not been uncommon for childless couples in many cultures throughout human history to adopt children, including orphans and even captives, today it is a transnational practice for adults from industrial and postindustrial countries to travel across the world in search of children to adopt, regardless of their ethnic heritage (see the Globalscape). Also increasingly common is open adoption, which makes it possible for a child to have a relationship with both the biological and the adoptive parents.

Among other contributing factors to today's diversity of families and households is **new reproductive technology (NRT)**, including various forms of *in vitro fertilization* (IVF) in which an egg is fertilized in a laboratory. The embryo is then transferred to the uterus to begin a pregnancy or is frozen for future use. In cases of IVF with a surrogate mother using donor egg and sperm, a newborn essentially has five parents: the birth parents who provided the egg and sperm, the surrogate mother who carried the baby, and the parents who will raise the baby.

Migrant Workforces

Also of note in terms of new residential patterns is the ever-growing number of households composed of temporary and migrant workers. Today, China has 260 million of them, mostly young people who have quit the peasant villages of their childhood and traveled to fast-growing cities to work in factories, shops, and restaurants. Some pile into apartments with friends or coworkers; others live in factory dormitories—new, single-generation households that stand in stark contrast to the multigenerational extended family households in which they were raised (Figure 19.13). Although many countries have passed legislation intended to provide migrants with protections concerning housing, as well as work conditions and pay

new reproductive technology An alternative means of reproduction, such as in vitro fertilization.

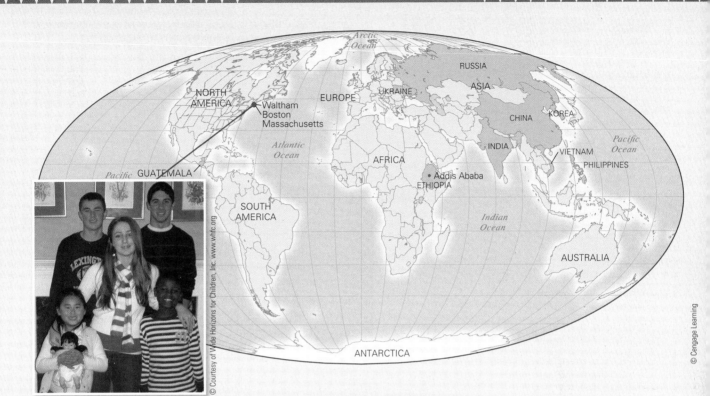

Transnational Child Exchange?

Settling into her seat for the flight to Boston, Kathryn cradled the sleepy head of her newly adopted son, Mesay. As the plane lifted away from African soil and presented a sweeping view of Ethiopia's capital, tears slid down her cheeks. Were the tears for Ethiopia's loss of a boy, a boy's loss of Ethiopia, or her profound joy for the gift of adoption?

Child exchange is a universal phenomenon, taking place across the world and throughout human history. Just as *marriage* and *kinship* mean different things in different cultures, so does *child exchange*, referred to in the English language as *adoption*. In some cultures, adoption is rare, whereas in others, such as in Polynesian communities in the Pacific Islands, it is very common. For instance, in a small village in Tahiti over 25 percent of children are raised by adoptive parents.

A cross-cultural understanding of adoption is vital now that child exchange has become part of the global flow—especially from poor countries in Africa, Latin America, Southeast Asia, and eastern Europe—to affluent countries in North America and western Europe. The global exchange of children initially involved war orphans after World War II. In recent decades, extreme poverty has become a major factor, as mothers confronting serious deprivation may feel forced to abandon, give away, or sometimes sell their children. Whether brokered by government or nongovernmental agencies, by for-profit or nonprofit enterprises, global child exchange has become a big business—legal and illegal, moral and amoral, joyful and sorrowful. This is especially true in poor countries where most workers earn less than a dollar a day, and a foreign adoption nets $12,000 to $35,000 in broker fees.

Since the early 1970s, about 500,000 foreign children have been adopted into families in the United States alone. A nearly equal number have ended up in other wealthy countries. The global flow to the United States peaked in 2004 when nearly 23,000 arrived—most from China (30 percent), Russia (25 percent), Guatemala (14 percent), and Korea (7 percent), with 5,500 flown in from other poor countries such as India, the Philippines, Ukraine, and Vietnam. Statistics vary and shift according to adoption rules.

Some countries have shut the door on foreign adoptions due to accusations of exporting or even selling children. Others restrict or prohibit it for religious reasons. Sudan, for example, forbids foreign adoption of Muslim children and automatically classifies religiously unidentified orphans as Muslim. A country that does not discriminate on the basis of religion is its neighbor Ethiopia, which has gained popularity as an infant-provider country. One of six U.S. agencies officially approved to do foreign adoptions from Ethiopia is Wide Horizons for Children in Waltham, Massachusetts, which has placed many Ethiopian children with U.S. families. Among them is Mesay (pictured in the family photo above), now settled into his new life with Kathryn, her husband, and their four other children, including a sister about his age, adopted from China as an infant.

Global Twister

How do you compare a European or North American woman who accepts a surrogate pregnancy fee of $115,000 to $150,000 to cover the costs of bearing a child for someone else to a Third World mother living in poverty, who decides to give up her child for adoption for a price?

(such as the 1983 Migrant and Seasonal Agricultural Worker Protection Act in the U.S.), the living situations for these workers are often miserable (Chang, 2005).

As the various ethnographic examples in this chapter illustrate, our species has invented a wide variety of marriage, family, and household forms, each in correspondence with related features in the social structure and conforming to the larger cultural system. In the face of new challenges, we explore and tinker in search of solutions, sometimes finding completely new forms and other times returning to time-tested patterns of more traditional varieties.

CHAPTER CHECKLIST

How do different cultures regulate sexual relations?

✓ Every society has rules and customs concerning sexual relations, marriage, household and family structures, and childrearing practices. These play important roles in establishing and maintaining the social alliances and continuity that help ensure a society's overall well-being.

✓ Most cultures are sexually permissive or semi-permissive and do not sharply regulate personal sexual practices. Others are restrictive, prohibiting all sexual activity outside of marriage. Of these, a few punish adultery by imprisonment, social exclusion, or even death, as traditionally prescribed by some religious laws.

✓ Incest taboos forbid marriage and sexual relations between certain close relatives. Such taboos are related to the practices of endogamy (marrying within a group) and exogamy (marrying outside a group).

What is marriage?

✓ Marriage is a culturally sanctioned union between two or more people that establishes certain rights and obligations between them, them and their children, and them and their in-laws.

✓ Marriage falls into several broad categories. Monogamy, having one spouse, is most common. Serial monogamy, in which a person marries a series of partners, is common among Europeans and North Americans.

✓ Polygamy (one individual having multiple spouses) comes in two forms: polygyny and polyandry. Although few marriages in a given society may be polygynous, it is a preferred form of marriage in the majority of the world's cultures.

✓ Because few communities have a surplus of men, polyandry (a woman having several husbands) is uncommon. Also rare is group marriage, in which several men and several women have sexual access to one another.

✓ In Western industrial and postindustrial countries, marriages are generally based on ideals of romantic love. In non-Western societies, economic considerations are of major concern in arranging marriages, and marriage serves to bind two families as allies.

✓ Preferred marriage partners in many societies are particular cross cousins (mother's brother's daughter if a man; father's sister's son if a woman) or, less commonly, parallel cousins on the paternal side (father's brother's son or daughter). Cross-cousin marriage is a means of maintaining and reinforcing solidarity between related groups.

✓ A growing number of societies support same-sex marriages. In some African cultures, traditional woman–woman marriages provide a socially approved way to deal with problems for which heterosexual marriages offer no satisfactory solution.

✓ In many cultures, marriages are formalized by economic exchange: Bridewealth is the payment of money or other valuables from the groom's to the bride's kin. Bride service occurs when the groom is expected to work for a period of time for the bride's family. A dowry is the payment of a woman's inheritance at the time of marriage to her or to her husband.

✓ Divorce is possible in all societies. Reasons and frequency vary, but the most common reasons across cultures are infidelity, sterility, cruelty, and desertion.

How do family and household differ, and what is the relationship between them?

✓ The family may take many forms, ranging from a single parent with one or more children, to a married couple or polygamous spouses with or without offspring, to several generations of parents and their children.

✓ A family is distinct from a household, which is a domestic unit of one or more people living in one residence. Other than family members, a household may include nonrelatives, such as servants. In the vast majority of human societies, most households are made up of families or parts of families, but there are many other household arrangements.

✓ The most basic domestic unit is the nuclear family—a group consisting of one or more parents and dependent offspring, which may include a stepparent, stepsiblings, and adopted children. Until recently, the term referred solely to the mother, father, and child(ren) unit.

✓ The nuclear family is common in the industrial and postindustrial countries of North America and Europe and also in societies living in harsh environments. It is well suited to the mobility required in food-foraging groups and in industrial societies where job changes are frequent.

✓ The extended family consists of several closely related nuclear families living and often working together in a single household.

What kinds of marital residence patterns exist across cultures?

✓ Three common residence patterns are patrilocal (married couples living in the locality of the husband's father's place of residence), matrilocal (living in the locality of the wife's mother's place of residence), and neolocal (living somewhere apart from the husband's or wife's parents).

✓ In North America and parts of Europe, increasing numbers of people live in nonfamily households, either alone or with nonrelatives. This includes unmarried cohabiting couples. Many others live in nontraditional families, including single-parent households and blended families.

How do globalization and technology impact marriage and family?

✓ New reproductive technologies, surrogacy, and international adoptions are adding additional dimensions to familial relationships.

✓ Another phenomenon changing the makeup of households and families worldwide is the ever-growing population of temporary and migrant workers.

QUESTIONS FOR REFLECTION

1. According to Hindu and Muslim tradition in South Asia and North Africa, a bride's *mehndi* evening is a lively female-only gathering with special food, singing, and lovemaking instructions, along with hand painting. Does your culture have similar gender-segregated pre-wedding events? If so, what is the purpose of such a celebration?

2. Members of traditional communities in countries where the state is either weak or absent depend on consanguineal and affinal relatives to help meet the basic challenges of survival. In such traditional societies, why would it be risky to choose marriage partners exclusively on the basis of romantic love? Can you imagine other factors playing a role if the long-term survival of your community is at stake?

3. Although most women in Europe and North America probably view polygyny as a marriage practice exclusively benefiting men, women in cultures where such marriages are traditional may stress more positive aspects of sharing a husband with several co-wives. Are there conditions under which you think polygyny could be considered relatively beneficial for women?

4. Many children in Europe and North America are raised in single-parent households. In contrast to the United States, where most children living with their unmarried mothers grow up in economically disadvantaged households, relatively few children raised by unmarried mothers in Norway face poverty. Why do you think that is?

DIGGING INTO ANTHROPOLOGY

Sex Rules?

Every culture has rules concerning sexual relationships. However, the rules vary across cultures and are not always sharply defined and applied. Digging into your own culture, make an inventory of six distinctive sets of sexual relationships you have observed in the media, noting the number of individuals involved, their age (including minors and seniors), their gender preference (including same sex and third gender), genetics (degree of family relation), marriage (including premarital, extramarital, postdivorce), and religion, racial, or ethnic identity (including interreligious, interethnic, interracial,

and international). Next, analyze how these relationships are viewed within your family and your wider community. Which are socially accepted, which are prohibited by law or faith, and what is the punishment for those who ignore or violate the rules? Formulate three questions about the social reasons and moral justifications for the prescriptions, prohibitions, and punishments in your community and present these questions to three people who are likely to have different opinions. Compare their answers, noting which answers are similar and which are not, and try to explain why. Conclude with a summary of your findings.

© Harald E. L. Prins

CHALLENGE ISSUE

All humans face the challenge of creating and maintaining a social network that reaches beyond close relatives or a single household to provide additional security and support. The most basic social network is arranged by kinship, often extending to more distantly related individuals claiming descent from the same ancestor. For many traditional peoples around the world, including Scottish highlanders, large kin-groups called *clans* have been important. There are several dozen Scottish clans, with members often sharing the same family name. Pictured here is the opening parade of the international Clan Grant summer games in Spey Valley, Scotland. Like members of other clans, the Grants publicly show their collective identity by wearing kilts and shawls with the distinct *tartan* (plaid) of their clan. Over several centuries, thousands of Scots were deported, fled, or emigrated from their homelands, settling overseas, especially in Australia, Canada, and the United States. Many, including people from the Grant clan, married into North American Indian tribes. Today, their widely scattered offspring can be found across the globe, including among Cherokee and Muskogee Indians. Aided by the Internet, many seek to reestablish social ties of shared descent, traveling long distances to clan gatherings to celebrate their cultural heritage with traditional dancing, piping, games, and food.

Kinship and Descent

All societies rely on some form of family and household organization to meet basic human needs: securing food, fuel, and shelter; protecting against danger; coordinating work; regulating sexual relations; and organizing childrearing. Although they may be efficient and flexible, family and household organizations may not be sufficient to handle all the challenges and opportunities people face. For example, members of one independent local group often need some means of interacting with people outside their immediate circle for defense against enemies or natural disasters such as floods. A wider circle may be necessary in forming a cooperative workforce for tasks that require more participants than close relatives alone can provide.

Humans have come up with many ways to widen their circles of societal interaction. One is through a formal political system, with personnel to make and enforce laws, keep the peace, allocate scarce resources, and coordinate other cultural functions. But the predominant way to organize in cultures that have not politically developed as state societies—especially foraging, crop-growing, and herding communities—is by means of **kinship**, a network of relatives into which individuals are born and married, and with whom they cooperate based on customarily prescribed rights and obligations. The more that individuals become enmeshed in larger networks, as happens in political states, the less they depend on kinship for survival. Still, as explained in this chapter, kinship remains fundamental in the organization of any society, past and present.

Descent Groups

A common way of organizing a society along kinship lines is by creating descent groups. Found in many societies, a **descent group** is any kin-group whose members share a direct line of descent from a real (historical) or fictional common ancestor. Members of such a group trace their shared connections back to an ancestor through a chain of

In this chapter you will learn to

- Explain how kinship is the basis of social organization in every culture.

- Apply kinship terminology as a cross-cultural code for analyzing social networks.

- Contrast cultures in which ancestry is traced through foremothers, forefathers, or both.

- Distinguish the characteristics of lineages and clans from those of kindreds.

- Identify three kinship terminology systems and the significance of their distinct classifications of close relatives for family attitudes and behavior.

- Interpret totemism as a cultural phenomenon.

- Discuss the significance of kinship in the contexts of adoption and new reproductive technologies.

---

kinship A network of relatives into which individuals are born and married, and with whom they cooperate based on customarily prescribed rights and obligations.

descent group Any kin-group whose members share a direct line of descent from a real (historical) or fictional common ancestor.

BIOCULTURAL CONNECTION

Maori Origins: Ancestral Genes and Mythical Canoes

Anthropologists have been fascinated to find that the oral traditions of Maori people in New Zealand fit quite well with scientific findings. New Zealand, an island country whose dramatic geography served as the setting for the *Lord of the Rings* film trilogy, lies in a remote corner of the Pacific Ocean about 1,900 kilometers (1,200 miles) southeast of Australia. Named by Dutch seafarers who landed on its shores in 1642, it was claimed by the British as a colony about 150 years later. Maori, the country's indigenous people, fought back but were outgunned, outnumbered, and forced to lay down their arms in the early 1870s. Today, nearly 600,000 of New Zealand's 4.1 million citizens claim some Maori ancestry.

Maori have an age-old legend about how they came to Aotearoa ("Land of the Long White Cloud"), their name for New Zealand: More than twenty-five generations ago, their Polynesian ancestors

arrived in a great fleet of sailing canoes from Hawaiki, their mythical homeland sometimes identified with Tahiti where the native language closely resembles their own. According to chants and genealogies passed down through the ages, this fleet consisted of at least seven (perhaps up to thirteen) seafaring canoes. Each of these large dugouts, estimated to weigh about 5 tons, had a single claw-shaped sail and carried 50 to 120 people, plus food supplies, plants, and animals.

As described by Maori anthropologist Te Rangi Hiroa (Peter Buck), the seafaring skills of these voyagers enabled them to navigate by currents, winds, and stars across vast ocean expanses.[a] Perhaps escaping warfare and tribute payments in Hawaiki, they probably made the five-week-long voyage around 1350, although there were earlier and later canoes as well.

Traditional Maori society is organized into about thirty different *iwis* ("tribes"), grouped into thirteen *wakas* ("canoes"), each with its own traditional territory. Today, prior to giving a formal talk, Maori still introduce themselves by identifying their *iwi*, their *waka*, and the major sacred places of their ancestral territory. Their genealogy connects them to their tribe's founding ancestor who was a crewmember or perhaps even a chief in one of the giant canoes mentioned in the legend of the Great Fleet.[b]

Maori oral traditions about their origins mesh with scientific data based on anthropological and more recent genetic research. Study by outsiders can be

controversial because Maori equate an individual's genes to his or her genealogy, which belongs to one's *iwi* or ancestral community. Considered sacred and entrusted to the tribal elders, genealogy is traditionally surrounded by *tapu* ("sacred prohibitions").[c] The Maori term for genealogy is *whakapapa* ("to set layer upon layer"), which is also a word for gene. This Maori term captures something of the original *genous*, the Greek word for "begetting offspring." Another Maori word for gene is *ira tangata* ("life spirit of mortals"), and for them, a gene has *mauri* (a "life force"). Given these spiritual associations, genetic investigations of Maori DNA could not proceed until the Maori themselves became actively involved in the research.

Together with other researchers, Maori geneticist Adele Whyte has examined sex-linked genetic markers, namely mitochondrial DNA in women and Y chromosomes in men.[d] She recently calculated that the number of Polynesian females required to found New Zealand's Maori population ranged between 170 and 230 women. If the original fleet sailing to Aotearoa consisted of seven large canoes, it probably carried a total of about 600 people (men, women, and children).

A comparison of the DNA of Maori with that of Polynesians across the Pacific Ocean and peoples from Southeast Asia reveals a genetic map of ancient Maori migration routes. Mitochondrial DNA, which is passed along virtually unchanged from mothers to their children, provides a genetic clock linking today's Polynesians

parent–child links. Typically, a set of culturally meaningful obligations and taboos helps hold the structured social group together.

Even when a society becomes politically organized as a state, elements of such kin-groups may continue. We see this with many traditional indigenous societies that have become part of larger state societies yet endure as distinctive ethnic groups. So it is with the Maori of New Zealand, featured in this chapter's Biocultural Connection. Retaining key elements of their traditional kinship

structure, they are still organized in about thirty large descent groups known as *iwi* ("tribe"), which form part of larger social and territorial units known as *waka* ("canoe").

Descent group membership must be sharply defined in order to operate effectively in a kin-ordered society. If membership is allowed to overlap, it is unclear where someone's primary loyalty belongs, especially when different descent groups have conflicting interests. Membership can be determined in a number of ways. The most common way is what anthropologists refer to as *unilineal descent*.

The canoes the ancient Maori used probably looked similar to this contemporary Maori sea canoe.

to southern Taiwan's indigenous coastal peoples, showing that female ancestors originally set out from that island off the southeastern coast of China about 6,000 years ago.[e] In the next few thousand years, they migrated by way of the Philippines and then hopped south and east from island to island. Adding to their gene pool in the course of later generations, Melanesian males from New Guinea and elsewhere joined the migrating bands before arriving in Aotearoa.

In short, Maori cultural traditions in New Zealand are generally substantiated by anthropological as well as molecular biological data.

Biocultural Question

Why do you think the Maori view genealogy as sacred and attach certain prohibitions to it?

_____

[a]Buck, P. H. (1938). *Vikings of the Pacific.* Chicago: University of Chicago Press.

[b]Hanson, A. (1989). The making of the Maori: Culture invention and its logic. *American Anthropologist 91* (4), 890–902.

[c]Mead, A. T. P. (1996). Genealogy, sacredness, and the commodities market. *Cultural Survival Quarterly 20* (2). https://www.culturalsurvival.org/ourpublications/csq/article/genealogy-sacredness-and-commodities-market (retrieved December 4, 2015)

[d]Whyte, A. L. H. (2005). Human evolution in Polynesia. *Human Biology 77* (2), 157–177.

[e]Wilford, J. N. (2008, January 18). Pacific Islanders' ancestry emerges in genetic study. *New York Times.* http://www.nytimes.com/2008/01/18/world/asia/18islands.html (retrieved December 4, 2015)

Unilineal Descent

Unilineal descent (sometimes called *unilateral descent*) establishes group membership based on descent traced exclusively through either the male *or* the female line of ancestry. Traditionally, unilineal descent groups are common in many parts of the world. Each newborn becomes part of a specific descent group, traced through the female line (**matrilineal descent**) or through the male line (**patrilineal descent**). In matrilineal societies females are culturally recognized as socially significant because they are considered responsible for the descent group's continued existence. In patrilineal societies, this

unilineal descent Descent traced exclusively through either the male or the female line of ancestry to establish group membership; sometimes called *unilateral descent*.

matrilineal descent Descent traced exclusively through the female line of ancestry to establish group membership.

patrilineal descent Descent traced exclusively through the male line of ancestry to establish group membership.

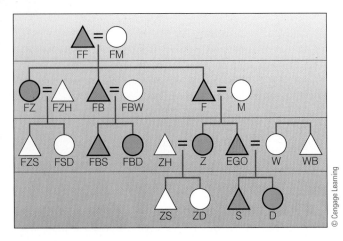

© Cengage Learning

Figure 20.1 **Tracing Patrilineal Descent**
Only the individuals symbolized by a blue circle or triangle are in the same descent group as EGO (the central person from whom the degree of each kinship relationship is traced). The abbreviation F stands for father, B for brother, H for husband, S for son, M for mother, Z for sister, W for wife, D for daughter. In English, the word *cousin* covers both FZS and FSD.

responsibility falls on the male members of the descent group, thereby enhancing their social importance.

The two major forms of a unilineal descent group are the lineage and the clan. A **lineage** is a unilineal kin-group descended from a common male or female ancestor or founder who lived four to six generations ago and in which relationships among members can be exactly stated in genealogical terms. A **clan** is an extended unilineal kin-group, often consisting of several lineages, whose members claim common descent from a remote ancestor, usually legendary or mythological.

Patrilineal Descent and Organization

Patrilineal descent is the more widespread of the two unilineal descent systems. Members of a patrilineal group trace their descent from a common male ancestor (Figure 20.1). Brothers and sisters belong to the descent group of their father's father, their father, their father's siblings, and their father's brother's children. A man's son and daughter also trace their descent back through his ancestor. In the typical patrilineal group, authority over the children rests with the father or his elder brother. A woman's children are born into her husband's descent group, while she remains part of her own father's descent group.

Patrilineal kinship organization is traditionally embedded in many cultures worldwide and often endures despite radical political and economic changes. So it is among the Han, China's ethnic majority. Even after the 1949 communist

revolution that radically changed Chinese society, remnants of the old patrilineal clan system persist—especially in China's rural areas and on the neighboring island of Taiwan.

Patrilineal Descent among Han Chinese

Over the past few millennia, the basic social unit for economic cooperation among the Han Chinese has been the large extended family, typically including aged parents and their sons, their sons' wives, and their sons' children. Historically, with *patrilocal* residence (defined in the previous chapter) being the norm, Han children have grown up in a

© Cengage Learning

household dominated by their father and his male relatives. Children have customarily maintained a respectful social distance from their fathers, who represent authority.

With brothers and their sons being part of the same household, a Han boy's paternal uncle is like a second father. He is treated with the same obedience and respect as the father, and his sons are like brothers. Thus, the Han distinguish between cousins who are children of one's father's brother (*tahng-shoong*) and cousins who are the offspring of one's father's sister, mother's sister, and mother's brother, who are lumped together as *beo-shoong*. (This practice remains evident in the Han language even among those who no longer live in traditional patrilocal households.) Traditionally, when extended families become too large and unwieldy, one or more sons establish separate households—but the tie to their household of birth remains strong.

Although family membership was and is important for each Han individual, the traditional primary social unit is the lineage, or in Han terms, the *tsu*. Each *tsu* is a corporate kin-group, a collective whose members trace their ancestry back about five generations exclusively through the male line to a common ancestor. A woman belongs to her father's *tsu*, but traditionally, for all practical purposes, she is absorbed by the *tsu* of her husband, with whom she lives after marriage.

The *tsu* can be counted on to help its members economically, and it functions as a legal body, passing judgment on misbehaving members. People affiliated with the same *tsu* come together on ceremonial occasions, including weddings, funerals, and rituals honoring their ancestors. Recently deceased ancestors, up to about three generations back, are given offerings of food and paper money on the anniversaries of their births and deaths, whereas more distant ancestors are collectively worshiped five times a year. Each *tsu* maintains its own shrine for storage of ancestral tablets on which the names of all members are recorded (Figure 20.2).

---

lineage A unilineal kin-group descended from a common ancestor or founder who lived four to six generations ago and in which relationships among members can be exactly stated in genealogical terms.

clan An extended unilineal kin-group, often consisting of several lineages, whose members claim common descent from a remote ancestor, usually legendary or mythological.

© Li jianhui/Panorama/The Image Works

Figure 20.2 An Ancestral Temple in Zhejiang Province, China
Among the Han, the ethnic majority in China, almost all ancestral temples, or clan houses, are dedicated to male forebears, reflecting the country's long-established patrilineal rules of descent and cultural values. Clan members affirm their place in the kin-group by making offerings to the ancestors in special temples such as the one pictured here, located in a family home.

Just as families periodically split up into new ones, larger descent groups periodically splinter along the lines of their main family branches. Causes for this include disputes among brothers over management of landholdings and suspicion of unfair division of profits. Even after such splits, a new *tsu* continues to recognize and honor its lineage tie to the old *tsu*. Thus, over many generations, a whole hierarchy of descent groups comes into being, with all persons having the same surname considering themselves to be members of a great patrilineal clan. With this comes the rule that individuals bearing the same clan surname cannot marry each other. This marriage rule is still widely practiced today.

Traditionally, owing obedience and respect to their fathers and older patrilineal relatives, Han children marry whomever their parents choose for them, and sons are required to care for their elderly parents and to fulfill ceremonial obligations to them after their death. In turn, inheritance passes from fathers to sons, with an extra share going to the eldest because he ordinarily makes the greatest contribution to the household.

Han women, by contrast, traditionally have no claims on their families' heritable property. Once married, a woman is in effect cast off by her own *tsu* in order to produce children for her husband's family and *tsu*. Yet, members of her birth *tsu* retain some interest in her after her departure. For example, her mother typically assists her in the birth of her children, and her brothers or some other male relative may intervene if her husband or other members of his family treat her badly.

Although *tsu* bonds have weakened in communist China, some of the obligations and attitudes of the traditional corporate kin-group persist there today, as well as on the island of Taiwan. At a minimum, contemporary Han Chinese maintain the traditions of children obeying and respecting their fathers and older patrilineal relatives.

As the Han example suggests, males dominate in a patrilineal society. No matter how needed and valued women may be, they find themselves in a challenging position. Far from resigning themselves to being subordinate, however, they actively work the system to their own advantage as best they can.

Matrilineal Descent and Organization

Matrilineal descent is traced exclusively through the female line (Figure 20.3). In a matrilineal system, brothers and sisters belong to the descent group of the mother, the mother's mother, the mother's siblings, and the mother's

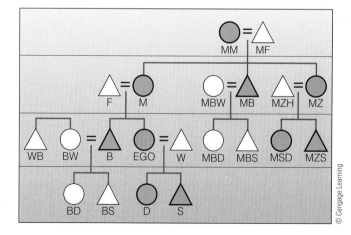

© Cengage Learning

Figure 20.3 Tracing Matrilineal Descent
This diagram can be compared with patrilineal descent in Figure 20.1. The two patterns are virtually mirror images. Note that a man cannot transmit descent to his own children.

Figure 20.4 Matrilineal Family among the Mosuo
Unlike the Han, the ethnic majority in China who are patrilineal, several ethnic minorities in southwestern China are matrilineal, including the Mosuo. The women in the Mosuo family shown here are blood relatives of one another, and the men are their brothers. Mosuo husbands live apart from their wives, in the households of their sisters.

sisters' children. Thus, a man's own children belong to his wife's descent group, not his.

In such arrangements, a woman may have considerable power but rarely exercises exclusive authority in her descent group. Typically, she shares power with her brothers, rather than husband. For example, among the Mosuo, one of several matrilineal ethnic minorities in southwestern China, women are heads of their households. They usually make the family's business decisions, and property passes through the female line of descent. Yet, political power in Mosuo communities tends to be in the hands of males (Mathieu, 2003) (Figure 20.4).

Matrilineal systems are usually found in horticultural societies in which women perform much of the work in the house and nearby food gardens. Matrilineal descent in part prevails because women's labor as crop cultivators is vital to the society. A major function of matrilineal systems is to provide continuous female solidarity within the female work group.

Though not true of all matrilineal systems, a common feature is the relative weakness of the social tie between wife and husband. A woman's husband lacks authority in the household they share. Instead, one of her brothers distributes goods, organizes work, settles disputes, supervises rituals, and administers inheritance and succession rules. Meanwhile, the husband fulfills the same role in his own sister's household. Furthermore, his sister's son rather

than his own son is the designated heir to his property and status. Thus, because sibling relations remain strong and marital ties are culturally less significant, divorce in unsatisfying marriages is more easily obtained in matrilineal than in patrilineal societies.

Matrilineal Descent among Hopi Indians

Among the Hopi Indians, a farming people whose ancestors have lived for many centuries in *pueblos* ("villages") in the desert lands of northeastern Arizona, society is divided into a number of clans based strictly on matrilineal descent (Connelly, 1979). At birth, a Hopi baby is assigned to his or her mother's clan. This affiliation is so important that, in a very real sense, a person has no social identity in the community apart from it. Two or more clans together constitute larger supra-clan units, which anthropologists refer to as *phratries* (discussed later in this chapter).

Phratries and clans are the major kinship units in Hopi culture, but the basic functional social units consist of lineages,

and there are several in each village. A senior woman (usually the eldest) heads each Hopi lineage, with her brother or mother's brother keeping the sacred "medicine bundle" (objects of spiritual power considered essential for peoples' well-being) and playing an active role in running lineage affairs. The senior woman may act as mediator to help resolve disputes among group members. Also, although her brother and mother's brother have the right to offer her advice and criticism, they are equally obligated to listen to what she has to say, and she does not yield her authority to them.

Most female authority, however, is exerted within the household, and here men clearly take second place. These households consist of the women of the matrilineage with their husbands, daughters, and unmarried sons, all of whom used to live in sets of adjacent rooms in single large buildings. Today, nuclear families often live (frequently with a maternal relative or two) in separate houses, but motorized vehicles enable related households to maintain close contact and cooperation as before.

Hopi lineages function as landholding corporations, allocating land for the support of member households. "Outsiders," the husbands of the women whose lineage owns the land, farm these lands, and the harvest belongs to these women. Thus, Hopi men spend their lives laboring for their wives' lineages, and in return they are given food and shelter.

Sons learn from their fathers how to farm, yet a man has no real authority over his son. When parents have difficulty with an unruly child, the mother's brother is called upon to mete out discipline. A man's loyalties are therefore divided between the households of his wife and his sisters. According to tradition, if a man is perceived as being an unsatisfactory husband, his wife merely has to place his personal belongings outside the door, and the marriage is over.

In addition to their economic and legal functions, matrilineages play a role in Hopi ceremonial activities. A lineage owns a special house where the "clan mother" stores and cares for the clan's religious paraphernalia. Together with her brother, the clan's "big uncle," the clan mother helps manage ceremonial activities.

Other Forms of Descent

Whatever form of descent predominates, the kin of both mother and father are important components of the social structure in all societies. Just because descent may be traced matrilineally, this does not mean that patrilineal relatives are necessarily unimportant. By way of example, among the matrilineal Trobriand Islanders in the southern Pacific, discussed in previous chapters, children belong to their mother's descent groups, yet fathers play an important role in their upbringing. Upon marriage, the bride and groom's paternal relatives contribute to the exchange of gifts, and throughout life a man may expect his paternal kin to help him improve his economic and political position in society. Eventually, sons may expect to inherit personal property from their fathers.

Across the globe, several other forms of descent have been developed in the course of cultural evolution. Among Samoan Islanders (and many other cultures in the Pacific as well as in Southeast Asia), for instance, a person traditionally has the option of affiliating with either the mother's or the father's descent group. Known as *ambilineal descent,* such a kin-ordered system provides a measure of flexibility. However, this flexibility also introduces a possibility of dispute and conflict as unilineal groups compete for members. This problem does not arise under *double descent,* or double unilineal descent, a rare system in which descent is matrilineal for some purposes and patrilineal for others.

Generally, where double descent is traced, the matrilineal and patrilineal groups take action in different spheres of society. For example, among the Yakö of eastern Nigeria, property is divided into both patrilineal and matrilineal possessions (Forde, 1968). The patrilineage owns perpetually productive resources, such as land, whereas the matrilineage owns consumable property, such as livestock. The legally weaker matriline is somewhat more important in religious matters than the patriline. Through double descent, a Yakö might inherit grazing lands from the father's patrilineal group and certain ritual privileges from the mother's matrilineal group.

Finally, when descent derives equally from the mother's and father's families, anthropologists use the term **bilateral descent**. In such a system individuals trace descent through both of their parents' ancestors. We recognize bilateral descent when individuals apply the same genealogical terms to identify similarly related individuals on both sides of the family. For instance, when they speak of a grandmother or grandfather, no indication is given as to whether these relatives are on the paternal or maternal side of the family.

Bilateral descent exists in various foraging cultures and is also common in many contemporary state societies with agricultural, industrial, or postindustrial economies. For example, although most people in Europe, Australia, and Latin America typically inherit their father's family name (indicative of a culture's history in which patrilineal descent is the norm), they usually consider themselves as much a member of their mother's as their father's family.

Descent Within the Larger Cultural System

There is a close relationship between the descent system and a cultural system's infrastructure. Generally, patrilineal descent predominates when male labor is considered of prime importance, as among herders and farmers. As already noted, matrilineal descent predominates mainly

---

bilateral descent Descent traced equally through father and mother's ancestors; associating each individual with blood relatives on both sides of the family.

in horticultural societies in which female work in food gardens is especially important. Numerous matrilineal societies are found in southern Asia, one of the world's earliest cradles of food production. They are also prominent in parts of indigenous North America, South America's tropical lowlands, and parts of Africa.

A lineage endures over generations because new members are continually born into it, replacing those who die. Its ongoing existence enables it to act like a corporation—owning property, organizing productive activities, distributing goods and labor power, assigning status, and regulating relations with other groups. As a repository of religious traditions, the descent group solidifies social cohesion. Ancestor worship, for example, is often a powerful force acting to enhance group solidarity. Thus, a lineage is a strong, effective base of social organization.

The descent group often endures in state-organized societies in which political institutions are ineffective or weakly developed. Such is the case in many countries of the world today, especially in remote mountainous or desert villages difficult to reach by state authorities. In those societies an individual has no legal or political status except as a lineage member. Citizenship is derived from lineage membership and legal status depends on it, so political powers are derived from it as well.

Because the ideas, values, and practices associated with traditional descent groups may be deeply embedded, such cultural patterns often endure in *diasporic communities* among immigrants who have relocated from their ancestral homelands and retain distinct identities as ethnic minority groups in their new host countries. In such situations, it is not uncommon for people to seek familiar, kin-ordered cultural solutions to challenges faced in unfamiliar state-organized settings. We see an example of this in the Original Study on honor killing among Turkish immigrants in the Netherlands.

Honor Killing in the Netherlands

ORIGINAL STUDY

BY CLEMENTINE VAN ECK

When I first told my anthropology professors I wanted to write my dissertation on honor killing among Turkish immigrants in the Netherlands, they told me no way. It was the mid-1990s, and everyone seemed to feel that writing negative things about struggling immigrants was discriminatory. Better to choose a subject that would help them deal with the challenges of settling in Dutch society, such as the problems they experienced as foreigners in school or at work. But I was quite determined to investigate this issue and finally found a professor who shared my interest—Dr. Anton Blok. He himself was specialized in Italian mafia,[a] so was quite used to violence of the cultural sort.

Before getting into some of the details of my research, I need to set the stage. Until the 1960s, the Netherlands was a relatively homogeneous society (despite its colonial past). The major differences among its people were not ethnic but religious, namely their distinct ties to Catholicism or Protestantism (of various kinds). The country's population makeup began to change dramatically after the economic boom of the 1960s created a need for cheap labor and led to an influx of migrants from poor areas in Mediterranean countries seeking wage-earning opportunities.

These newcomers came not as immigrants but as "guest laborers" (*gastarbeiders*) expected to return to their countries of origin, including Italy, Yugoslavia, Turkey, and Morocco. Although many did go back home, numerous others did not. In contrast to most of the guest workers from southern European nations, those from Turkey and Morocco are mainly Muslim. And unlike southern European workers who stayed on as immigrants and successfully assimilated into Dutch society, many of the Muslim newcomers formed isolated, diasporic communities.

During the past several decades, these communities have multiplied and rapidly expanded in size and are concentrated in certain areas of various cities. Today, the Turkish population in the Netherlands is about 450,000. Most of them have become Dutch citizens, but they maintain some key cultural features of their historical "honor-and-shame" traditions. And this is what is at stake when we are dealing with the problem of honor killing.

Anthropologists have identified honor-and-shame traditions in many parts of the world, especially in remote traditional herding and farming societies where the power of the political state is either absent or ineffective. People in such areas, my professor, Dr. Blok, explained,

cannot depend on stable centers of political control for the protection of life and patrimony. In the absence of effective state control, they have to rely on their own forces—on various forms of self-help. These conditions . . . put a premium on self-assertive qualities in men, involving the readiness and capacity to use physical force in order to guarantee the immunity of life and property, including women as the most precious and vulnerable part of the patrimony of men. The extremes of this sense of honour are reached when even merely glancing at a woman is felt as an affront, an incursion into a male domain, touching off a violent response.[b]

Beyond serving as a means of social control in isolated areas, honor-and-shame traditions may be used in situations where state mechanisms are alien to a certain group of people, as among some Turkish and Moroccan migrants in the Netherlands. Focusing on the latter, I tried to make sense of certain cultural practices that often baffle indigenous Dutch citizens accustomed to a highly organized bureaucratic state in which our personal security and justice are effectively managed by social workers, police, courts, and so on. Most of all, I wanted to understand honor killings.

Honor killings are murders in the form of a ritual, and they are carried out to purify tarnished honor—specifically honor having to do with something Turks refer to as *namus*. Both men and women possess *namus*. For women and girls *namus* means chastity, whereas for men it means having chaste family members. A man is therefore dependent for his *namus* on the conduct of the womenfolk in his family. This means in effect that women and girls must not have illicit contact with a member of the opposite sex and must avoid becoming the subject of gossip because gossip alone can impugn *namus*. The victim of an honor killing can be the girl or woman who tarnished her honor, or the man who did this to her (usually her boyfriend). The girl or woman is killed by her family members, the man is killed by the family of the girl/woman whose honor he has violated.

As I was wrapping up my PhD in 2000, Dutch society still did not seem quite ready to acknowledge the phenomenon of honor killing. That year a Kurdish boy whose parents were born in Turkey tried to shoot the boyfriend of his sister. Because the attempt took place in a high school and resulted in injury to several students and a teacher, authorities focused on the issue of school safety rather than on the cultural reasons behind the murder attempt.

A shift in government and public awareness of honor killing took place in 2004. That year three Muslim Turkish women were killed by their former husbands on the street. Coming in quick succession, one after the other, these murders did not escape the attention of government officials or the media. Finally, honor killing was on the national agenda. In November of that year I was appointed as cultural anthropologist at the Dutch police force in The Hague district and began working with law enforcers on honor killing cases there (and soon in other areas of the country).

On November 2, 2004, the day I gave an opening speech about honor killings to colleagues at my new job, a radical Muslim migrant from Morocco shot the famous Dutch author and film director Theo van Gogh, well known for his critical, often mocking, views on Islam. Although his murder was not an honor killing, it had key elements of that cleansing ritual: It occurred in a public place (on the street) in front of many people, the victim had to die (injury would not suffice), the killer used many shots (or knife thrusts), the killing was planned (it was not the product of a sudden outburst), and the killer had no remorse.

Let me tell you about a recent and quite typical case. On a Friday evening the local police in an eastern Dutch community called in the help of our police team. A 17-year-old Turkish girl had run away to the family home of her Dutch boyfriend, also 17. Her father, who had discovered that this boy had a police record, telephoned his parents and asked them to send the daughter home. The parents tried to calm him down and told him his daughter was safe at their house. But as he saw it, she was in the most dangerous place in the world, for she was with the boy she loved. This could only mean that her virginity was in jeopardy and therefore the *namus* of the whole family.

My colleagues and I concluded that the girl had to be taken out of her boyfriend's home that same night: The father knew the place, he did not want the boy as a son-in-law, and he believed his daughter was not mature enough to make a decision about something as important as marriage. ("Just having a boyfriend" was not allowed. You either marry or you do not have a boyfriend, at least not an obvious one.) Because of my honor killing research, I was well aware of similar situations that ended in honor killings. To leave the girl where she was would invite disaster.

After we persuaded the prosecutor that intervention was necessary, the girl was taken from her boyfriend's house and brought to a guarded shelter to prevent her from fleeing back to him the next day. This is anthropology-in-action. You cannot always just wait and see what will happen (although I admit that as a scholar this is very tempting); you have to take responsibility and take action if you are convinced that a human life is at stake.

When I took up the study of cultural anthropology, I did so just because it intrigued me. I never imagined that what I learned might become really useful. So, what I would like to say to anthropology students is: Never give up on an interesting subject. One day it might just matter that you have become an expert in that area. At this moment I am analyzing all kinds of threatening cases and drawing up genealogies of the families involved—all in the effort to deepen our understanding of and help prevent honor killings.

Written expressly for this text, 2011. Updated demographics 2016.

[a] Blok, A. (1974). *The mafia of a Sicilian village 1860–1960.* New York: Harper & Row.

[b] Blok, A. (1981). Rams and billy-goats: A key to the Mediterranean code of honour. *Man 16* (3), 427–440; see also Van Eck, C. (2003). *Purified by blood: Honour killings amongst Turks in the Netherlands.* Amsterdam: Amsterdam University Press.

Lineage Exogamy

A common characteristic of lineages is *exogamy*. As defined in the previous chapter, this means that lineage members must find their marriage partners in other lineages. One advantage of exogamy is that competition for desirable spouses within the group is reduced, promoting the group's internal cohesiveness. Lineage exogamy means that each marriage is more than a union between two individuals; it is also a new alliance between lineages. This helps to maintain them as components of larger social systems. Finally, lineage exogamy promotes open communication within a society, facilitating the diffusion of knowledge and exchange of goods and services from one lineage to another.

In contemporary North American Indian communities, kinship and descent still play an essential role in tribal membership—as illustrated in this chapter's Anthropology Applied.

From Lineage to Clan

In the course of time, as generation succeeds generation and new members are born into the lineage, the kingroup's membership may become too large to manage or may outgrow the lineage's resources. When this happens, as we have seen with the Chinese *tsu*, **fission** occurs; that is, the original lineage splits into new, smaller lineages. Usually, the members of the new lineages continue to recognize their original relationship to one another. The result of this process is the appearance of a larger kind of descent group: the clan.

As already noted, a *clan*—typically consisting of several lineages—is an extended unilineal descent group whose members claim common descent from a distant ancestor (usually legendary or mythological) but are unable to trace the precise genealogical links back to that ancestor. This stems from the great genealogical depth of the clan, whose founding ancestor lived so far in the past that the links must be assumed rather than known in detail. A clan differs from a lineage in another respect: It lacks the residential unity that is generally (although not always) characteristic of a lineage's core members.

As with the lineage, clan descent may be patrilineal, matrilineal, or ambilineal. Hopi Indians are an example of matrilineal clans (*matriclans*), whereas Han Chinese and Scottish highlanders pictured in this chapter's opening, provide examples of patrilineal clans (*patriclans*). Tracing descent exclusively through men from a founding paternal ancestor, Scottish highland clans are often identified with the prefix "Mac" or "Mc" (from an old

Celtic word meaning "son of"), such as MacDonald, McGregor, and Maclean.

Because clan membership is often dispersed rather than localized, it usually does not involve a shared holding of tangible property. Instead, it involves collective participation in ceremonial and political matters. Only on special occasions will the membership gather together for specific purposes.

However, clans may handle important integrative functions. Like lineages, they may regulate marriage through exogamy. Because of their dispersed membership, clans give individuals the right of entry into associated local groups no matter where they are. Members usually are expected to give protection and hospitality to others in the clan. Lacking the residential unity of lineages, clans frequently depend on symbols—of animals, plants, natural forces, colors, and special objects—to provide members with solidarity and a ready means of identification. These symbols, called *totems*, often are associated with the clan's mythical origin and reinforce for clan members an awareness of common descent.

The word *totem* comes from the Ojibwa American Indian word *ototeman*, meaning "he is a relative of mine." **Totemism** was defined by British anthropologist A. R. Radcliffe-Brown (1930) as a set of customary beliefs and practices "by which there is set up a special system of relations between the society and the plants, animals, and other natural objects that are important in the social life." For example, Aborigines in central Australia such as the Arunta traditionally believe that each clan descends from a mythological spirit animal.

Native Americans in northwest Canada such as the Tsimshian on the Pacific Coast also use totemic animals to designate their exogamous matrilineal clans but do not claim these creatures are mythological clan ancestors. Among these coastal Indians, individuals inherit their lineage affiliations from their mothers. As such, every Tsimshian forms part of a matrilineal "house group," a corporate kin-group known as a *waap* (the plural is *wuwaap*). Typically, each village consists of about twenty such houses, ranked according to importance. Each Tsimshian house group forms part of a larger exogamous matrilineal clan, of which there are four. And each matriclan is symbolically represented by an animal: Wolf, Eagle, Raven and Blackfish (Killer Whale). Carvings of these crest animals, along with several other animal and human images symbolically marking the mythology and history of the lineage and validating its claims and privileges, are displayed on monumental cedar *totem poles* in front of the large wooden dwellings inhabited by the *wuwaap* (Anderson, 2006) (Figure 20.5).

We can see a reductive variation of totemism in contemporary industrial and postindustrial societies in which sports teams are often given the names of such powerful wild animals as bears, lions, and wildcats. In the United States, this extends to the Democratic Party's donkey

---

fission In kinship studies, the splitting of a descent group into two or more new descent groups.

totemism The belief that people are related to particular animals, plants, or natural objects by virtue of descent from common ancestral spirits.

ANTHROPOLOGY APPLIED

Resolving a Native American Tribal Membership Dispute

By Harald E. L. Prins

In autumn 1998, I received a call from the tribal chief of the Aroostook Band of Micmacs (now also spelled Mi'kmaq) in northern Maine asking for help in resolving a bitter tribal membership dispute. The conflict centered on the fact that several hundred individuals had become tribal members without proper certification of their Mi'kmaq kinship status. Traditionalists in the community argued that their tribe's organization was being taken over by "non-Indians." With the formal status of so many members in question, the tribal administration could not properly determine who was entitled to benefit from the available health, housing, and education programs. After some hostile confrontations between the factions, tribal elders requested a formal inquiry into the membership controversy, and I was called in as a neutral party with a long history of working with the band.

My involvement as an advocacy anthropologist began in 1981 when this Mi'kmaq band first employed me, along with Bunny McBride, to help them achieve U.S. government recognition of their Indian status.

At the time, they formed a poor and landless community not yet officially recognized as a tribe. During that decade, we helped the band define its political strategies, which included petitioning for federal recognition of their Indian status; claiming their traditional rights to hunt, trap, and fish; and even demanding return of lost ancestral lands.

To generate popular support for the effort, I coproduced a film about the community ("Our Lives in Our Hands").[a] Most important, we gathered oral histories and detailed archival documentation to address kinship issues and other government criteria for tribal recognition. The latter included important genealogical records showing that most Mi'kmaq adults in the region were at least "half-blood" (having two of their grandparents officially recorded as Indians).

Based on this evidence, we effectively argued that the Aroostook Mi'kmaq could claim aboriginal title to lands in the region. Also, we were able to convince politicians in Washington, DC, to introduce a special bill to acknowledge their tribal status and settle their land claims. When formal hearings were held in 1990, I testified in the U.S. Senate as an expert witness for the band. The following year, the Aroostook Band of Micmacs Settlement Act became federal law. This made the band eligible for the financial assistance (health, housing, education, and child welfare) and economic development loans that are available to all federally recognized tribes in the United States. Moreover, the law provided the band with funding to buy a 5,000-acre territorial base in Maine.

Flush with federal funding and rapidly expanding its activities, the 500-member band became overwhelmed by complex bureaucratic regulations now governing their existence. Without formally established ground rules determining who could apply for tribal membership, and overlooking federally imposed regulations, hundreds of new names were rather casually added to its tribal rolls.

By 1997, the Aroostook band population had ballooned to almost 1,200 members, and Mi'kmaq traditionalists were questioning the legitimacy of many whose names had been added to the band roster. With mounting tension threatening to destroy the band, the tribal chief invited me to evaluate critically the membership claims of more than half the tribe. In early 1999, I reviewed the kinship records submitted by hundreds of individuals whose membership on the tribal rolls was in question. Several months later, I offered my final report to the Mi'kmaq community.

After traditional prayers, sweetgrass burning, drumming, and a traditional meal of salmon and moose, I formally presented my findings. Based on the official criteria, about 100 lineal descendants of the original members and just over 150 newcomers met the minimum required qualifications for membership; several hundred others would have to be removed from the tribal roster. After singing, drumming, and closing prayers, the Mi'kmaq gathering dispersed.

Today, two decades later, the band's membership has grown beyond 1,200, due to verified applications, as well as procreation. Faring well, it has purchased about 3,200 acres of land, including a small residential reservation near Presque Isle, now home to about 300 Mi'kmaq. Also located here are tribal administration offices, a health clinic, and a cultural center.

Written expressly for this text.

The Sanipass-Lafford family cluster in Chapman, Maine, represent a traditional Mi'kmaq residential kin-group. Such extended families typically include grandchildren and bilaterally related family members such as in-laws, uncles, and aunts. Taken from the Sanipass family album, this picture shows a handful of members in the mid-1980s: Marline Sanipass Morey with two of her nephews and uncles.

---

[a] "Our lives in our hands." (1986). DER documentary, produced by H. E. L. Prins & K. Carter. http://www.der.org/films/our-lives-in-our-hands.html (retrieved January 2, 2016)

Figure 20.5 Tshimshian People Raising a Totem Pole
The tradition of erecting totem poles to commemorate special events endures in several Native American communities in the Pacific Northwest. Carved from tall cedar trees, these spectacular monuments display a clan or lineage's ceremonial property and are prominently positioned as posts in the front of houses, as markers at gravesites, and at other places of significance. Often depicting legendary ancestors and mythological animals, the painted carvings symbolically represent a descent group's cultural status and associated privileges in the community. Noted carver David Boxley, a member of the Eagle clan, gifted this pole to the community.

and the Republican Party's elephant, and to the Elks, the Lions, and other fraternal and social organizations. These animal emblems, or *mascots*, however, do not involve the notion of biological descent and the strong sense of kinship that they symbolize for clans, nor are they linked with the traditional ritual observances associated with clan totems.

Phratry and Moiety

Two larger kinds of descent groups are the phratry and the moiety (Figure 20.6). A **phratry** (after the Greek word for "brotherhood") is a unilineal descent group composed of at least two clans that supposedly share a common ancestry, whether or not they really do. Like individuals in the clan, phratry members cannot trace precisely their descent links to a common ancestor, although they firmly believe such an ancestor existed.

If the entire society is divided into only two major descent groups, whether they are equivalent to clans or phratries, each group is called a **moiety** (after the French word *moitié,* for "half"). Members of the moiety believe themselves to share a common ancestor but cannot prove

it through definitive genealogical links. As a rule, the feelings of kinship among members of lineages and clans are stronger than those of members of phratries and moieties. This may be due to the much larger size and more diffuse nature of the latter groups.

Because feelings of kinship are often weaker between people from different clans, the moiety system is a cultural invention that keeps clan-based communities together by binding the clans into a social network of obligatory giving and receiving. By institutionalizing reciprocity between groups of clans, the moiety system joins together families who otherwise would not be sufficiently

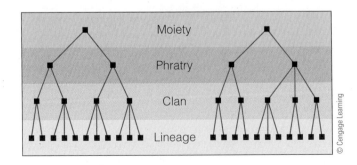

Figure 20.6 Descent Groups
This diagram shows the organizational hierarchy of the moiety, phratry, clan, and lineage. Each moiety is subdivided into phratries, each phratry is subdivided into clans, and each clan is subdivided into lineages.

---

phratry A unilineal descent group composed of at least two clans that supposedly share a common ancestry, whether or not they really do.

moiety A group, usually consisting of several clans, which results from a division of a society into two halves on the basis of descent.

invested in maintaining the commonwealth.

Like lineages and clans, phratries and moieties are often exogamous, and so are bound together by marriages between their members. And like clans, they provide members rights of access to other communities. In a community that does not include one's clan members, one's phratry members are still there to turn to for hospitality. Finally, moieties may perform reciprocal services for one another. Among them, individuals look to members of the opposite "half" in their community for the necessary mourning rituals when a member of their own moiety dies. Such interdependence between moieties serves to maintain the cohesion of the entire society.

The principle of institutionalized reciprocity between groups of matrilineal clans organized into two equal halves, or moieties, is beautifully illustrated in the circular settlement pattern of many traditional Indian villages in the tropical forests of South America's Amazon region (Figure 20.7). Dwellings located in half of the village are those of clans belonging to one exogamous moiety, and those on the opposite side are the dwellings of clans belonging to the other. Because their clans are often matrilineal, the institutionalized rules of reciprocity in this kin-ordered community traditionally require that a woman marry a man from a clan house on the opposite side of the village, who then moves into her ancestral clan house. Their son, however, will one day have to find a wife from his father's original moiety and will have to move to his father's mother's side of the village. In this way, the moiety system of institutionalized reciprocity functions like a social "zipper" between clans engaged in a repetitive cycle of exchange relations.

Figure 20.7 Village Life in Moieties
Many Amazonian Indians in South America's tropical woodlands traditionally live in circular villages socially divided into moieties. Here we see the Canela Indians' Escalvado village as it was in 1970. The village is 300 meters (165 feet) wide. The community's "upper" moiety meets in the western part. Nearly all of the 1,800 members of the Canela tribe reside in the village during festival seasons, but otherwise they are largely dispersed into their smaller, farm-centered circular villages. Behind the larger-circle village is a smaller abandoned village where part of the tribe lived before uniting under one chief. Missionaries built the landing strip that runs through it.

of extended family group known as the **kindred**—a grouping of blood relatives based on bilateral descent. The kindred is laterally rather than lineally organized—that is, it includes all relatives with whom **EGO** (the central person from whom the degree of each relationship is traced) shares at least one grandparent, great-grandparent, or even great-great-grandparent, on his or her father's *and* mother's side. Thus, depending on how many generations back one reckons, someone's kindred may include the entire direct-line offspring of his or her eight great-grandparents, or sometimes even sixteen great-great-grandparents (Figure 20.8).

In societies in which small domestic units (nuclear families or single-parent households) are of primary importance, bilateral kinship and kindred organization are likely to result. This can be seen in modern industrial

Bilateral Kinship and the Kindred

Important as patrilineal or matrilineal descent groups are in many cultures, such kin-groups do not exist in every society. In some, we encounter another type

kindred A grouping of blood relatives based on bilateral descent; includes all relatives with whom EGO shares at least one grandparent, great-grandparent, or even great-great-grandparent on his or her father's *and* mother's side.

EGO In kinship studies, the central person from whom the degree of each kinship relationship is traced.

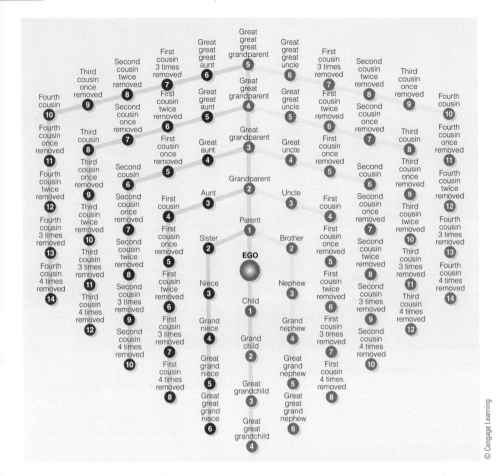

Figure 20.8 EGO and the Kindred
The kindred designates a person's exact degree of blood relatedness to other members of the family. This determines not only one's social obligations toward relatives, but also one's rights. For instance, when a wealthy widowed great-aunt without children dies without a will, specific surviving members of her kindred will be legally entitled to inherit from her.

(financial reparation for the loss of a murdered relative) is involved, such "next of kin" would be entitled to a share of it. In such societies, a trading or raiding party may be composed of a kindred, with the group coming together to perform a particular function, share in the results, and then disband. The kindred may also act as a ceremonial group for initiations and other rites of passage. Finally, kindreds may play a role in regulating marriage through exogamy.

Because kindreds are EGO-centered, each is unique, except among full siblings. Beyond being in the middle of one's own kindred, a person belongs to several kindreds centered on other individuals with memberships that overlap to various degrees. Thus, the social function of this system is that each person can turn to his or her own kindred for aid, or may be called upon by others, by virtue of being a member of their kindreds.

and postindustrial societies, in regions with emerging market economies, and in still-existing food-foraging societies across the globe.

Most Europeans and peoples of European descent in other parts of the world are familiar with the kindred; those who belong to it are simply referred to as "relatives." Typically, it includes those blood relatives on both sides of the family who are seen on important occasions, such as family weddings, reunions, and funerals. In Ireland, Puerto Rico, or the United States, for example, nearly everyone can identify the members of their kindred up to grandparents (or even great-grandparents) and to their first cousins, nephews, and nieces. Some can even identify second cousins in their kindred, but few can go beyond that.

In traditional societies with bilateral descent, kindreds play a significant role in a variety of situations. Kindred members ("next of kin") may be called upon to seek justice or revenge for harm done to someone in the group. They might raise bail, serve as witnesses, or help compensate a victim's family. If blood money

Kinship Terminology and Kinship Groups

The system of organizing people who are relatives into different kinds of groups—whether kindreds, lineages, or clans—influences how relatives are labeled. Kinship terminology systems vary considerably across cultures, reflecting the positions individuals occupy within their respective societies and helping to differentiate one relative from another. Distinguishing factors include gender, generational differences, or genealogical differences. In the various systems of kinship terminology, any one of these factors may be emphasized at the expense of others.

By looking at the terms a particular society uses for their relatives, an anthropologist can determine the structure of kin-groups, discern the most important relationships, and sometimes interpret the prevailing attitudes concerning various relationships. For instance, a number of languages use the same term to identify a brother and

Figure 20.9 Inuit Family in Greenland
The Inuit in Greenland are one of several large Eskimo groups inhabiting Arctic regions from Alaska to Canada, Greenland, and eastern Siberia. Although they speak different languages and dialects, they share a traditional way of life primarily based on hunting and fishing in which the nuclear family is the primary social unit. As such, their kinship terminology system specifically identifies EGO's mother, father, brother, and sister and lumps all other relatives into a few broad categories that do not distinguish the side of the family from which they derive. Here we see an Inuit family having a seal meat barbeque on an island near the village of Ilimanaq, Greenland.

a cousin, and others have a single word for cousin, niece, and nephew. Some cultures find it useful to distinguish the eldest brother from his younger brothers and have different words for them. And unlike English, many languages distinguish between an aunt who is a mother's sister and one who is a father's sister.

Regardless of the factors emphasized, all kinship terminologies accomplish two important tasks. First, they classify similar kinds of individuals into single specific categories; second, they separate different kinds of individuals into distinct categories. Generally, two or more kin are merged under the same term when the individuals have more or less the same rights and obligations with respect to the person referring to them as such. This is the case among most English-speaking North Americans, for instance, when someone refers to a mother's sister and a father's sister both as an aunt. As far as the speaker is concerned, both relatives possess a similar status.

Several different systems of kinship terminology result from the application of the previously discussed principles—including the Eskimo, Hawaiian, Iroquois, Crow, Omaha, Sudanese, Kariera, and Aranda systems,

each named after the ethnographic example first or best described by anthropologists. The last five of these systems are fascinating in their complexity and are found among only a few of the world's societies. However, to illustrate some of the basic principles involved, we will focus our attention on the first three systems.

The Eskimo System

The Eskimo system, which is comparatively rare among all the world's systems, is the one used by most contemporary Europeans, Australians, and North Americans. It is also used by a number of indigenous food-foraging peoples, including Arctic peoples such as the Inuit and other Eskimos—hence the name (Figure 20.9).

Sometimes referred to as the *lineal system,* the **Eskimo system** emphasizes the nuclear family by specifically

---

Eskimo system Kinship reckoning in which the nuclear family is emphasized by specifically identifying the mother, father, brother, and sister, while lumping together all other relatives into broad categories such as uncle, aunt, and cousin; also known as the *lineal system.*

© Uriel Sinai/Getty Images

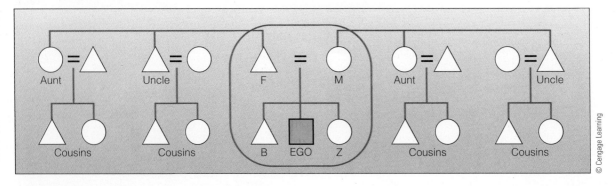

Figure 20.10 The Eskimo Kinship System
Kinship terminology in this system emphasizes the nuclear family (circled). EGO's father and mother are distinguished from EGO's aunts and uncles, and siblings are distinguished from cousins. However, no distinction is made between father's siblings and mother's siblings, nor between their offspring.

identifying mother, father, brother, and sister while lumping together all other relatives into a few large categories (Figure 20.10). For example, the father is distinguished from the father's brother (uncle), but the father's brother is not distinguished from the mother's brother (both are called uncle). The mother's sister and father's sister are treated similarly, both called aunt. In addition, all the sons and daughters of aunts and uncles are called cousin, thereby making a generational distinction but without indicating the side of the family to which they belong or even their gender.

Unlike other terminologies, the Eskimo system provides separate and distinct terms for nuclear family members. This is probably because the Eskimo system is generally found in bilateral societies where the dominant kin-group is the kindred, in which only immediate family members are important in day-to-day affairs. This is especially true of modern European and North American societies, in which many families are independent—living apart from and not directly involved with other relatives except on special occasions. Thus, these peoples generally distinguish between their closest kin (parents and siblings) but lump together other kin on both sides of the family (such as aunts, uncles, cousins).

The Hawaiian System

The **Hawaiian system** of kinship terminology, common (as its name implies) in Hawaii and other islands in the central Pacific Ocean but found elsewhere as well, is the least complex system in that it uses only a few terms. Also called the *generational system*, it refers to all relatives of the same generation and sex by the same term (Figure 20.11). For example, in one's parents' generation, the term used to refer to one's father is used as well for the father's brother and mother's brother. Similarly, one's mother, mother's sister, and father's sister are all grouped together under a single term. In EGO's generation, male and female cousins are distinguished by gender and are equated with brothers and sisters.

The Hawaiian system reflects the absence of strong unilineal descent, and members on both the father's and the mother's sides are viewed as more or less equal. The siblings of EGO's father and mother are all recognized as

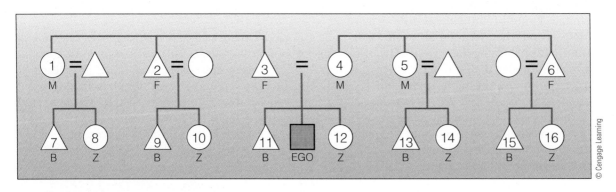

Figure 20.11 The Hawaiian Kinship System
In this kinship system the men numbered 2 and 6 are called by the same term as father (3); the women numbered 1 and 5 are called by the same term as mother (4). All cousins of EGO's own generation (7 through 16) are considered brothers (B) and sisters (Z).

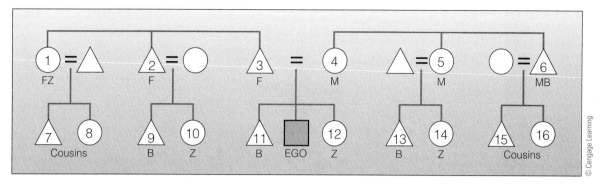

Figure 20.12 **The Iroquois Kinship System**
According to the Iroquois system of kinship terminology, EGO's father's brother (2) is called by the same term as the father (3); the mother's sister (5) is called by the same term as the mother (4); but the people numbered 1 and 6 are each referred to by a distinct term. Those people numbered 9 through 14 are all considered siblings, but 7, 8, 15, and 16 are considered cousins.

being similar relations and are merged under a single term appropriate for their gender. In like manner, the children belonging to the siblings of EGO's parents are related to EGO in the same way as are the brother and sister. Falling under the incest taboo, they are ruled out as potential marriage partners.

The Iroquois System

In the **Iroquois system** of kinship terminology, the father and father's brother are referred to by a single term, as are the mother and mother's sister; however, the father's sister and mother's brother are given separate terms (Figure 20.12). In one's own generation, brothers, sisters, and parallel cousins (offspring of parental siblings of the same sex—that is, the children of the mother's sister or father's brother) of the same sex are referred to by the same terms, which is logical enough considering that they are the offspring of people who are classified in the same category as EGO's actual mother and father. Cross cousins (offspring of parental siblings of opposite sex—that is, the children of the mother's brother or father's sister) are distinguished by terms that set them apart from all other kin. In fact, cross cousins are often preferred as spouses, for marriage to them reaffirms alliances between related lineages or clans.

Iroquois terminology, named for the Iroquois Indians of North America's woodlands, is in fact very widespread and is usually found with unilineal descent groups. It was, for example, the terminology in use until recently in rural Chinese society.

Making Relatives

Many societies may stress the biological in kinship, as the English term *blood relative* demonstrates, but what ultimately matters is the culturally defined social status of a person who is recognized as a relative, with all the specific rights and obligations that come with being a daughter, son, brother, or sister to someone else in that kin-group. That is what "being related" is all about and what gives it symbolic meaning with practical consequences. Each kin term marks out a specific set of rights and obligations for individuals socially identified by such a cultural label. In state societies governed by law, these rights may even be legally spelled out in detail.

Fictive Kin by Ritual Adoption

One example of making relatives of individuals who are not biologically related is adoption—as discussed in the previous chapter's Globalscape on the transnational adoption of children. Adoption is a longstanding and widespread cultural practice in many societies all around the world.

Historically, families and clans facing exceptional challenges to their survival sometimes went to war to obtain human captives from other societies—sometimes young men, but usually women and children. These captives would then be adopted. This occurred among Iroquois Indians in northeastern America. In the 17th and 18th centuries, they often incorporated specially selected war captives and other valued strangers, including European colonists, into their kin-groups in order to make up for population losses due to warfare and disease. As soon as these newcomers

Hawaiian system Kinship reckoning in which all relatives of the same sex and generation are referred to by the same term; also known as the *generational system*.

Iroquois system Kinship reckoning in which a father and father's brother are referred to by a single term, as are a mother and a mother's sister, but a father's sister and a mother's brother are given separate terms. Parallel cousins are classified with brothers and sisters, whereas cross cousins are classified separately but not equated with relatives of some other generation.

© Peter Turnley for Harper's/Corbis

Figure 20.13 Godparents at Baby's Baptism
In addition to being born into a family, people may gain relatives through adoption. Godparenting is a form of ritual adoption in which a person accepts certain lasting obligations toward someone else's child. Typically, it includes sponsoring the child's baptism ceremony, indicating a spiritual relationship. A variation of this institution is *compadrazgo*, or "coparenthood," especially common in Latin America. Here a Catholic priest in a small church in Bolivia is baptizing a baby in the company of the child's parents and godparents.

were ceremonially naturalized, they acquired essentially the same birthright status as those actually born into one of the families and were henceforth identified by the same kin term as the member being replaced.

Even today, in some traditional societies a type of ritual adoption might occur. For instance, especially in kin-ordered communities, the head of a clan or family may adopt an outsider, especially when such an individual is valued as a contributing member because of unique skills or contacts with the outside world.

Becoming a godparent is a form of ritual adoption traditionally practiced in many parts of Europe—and spreading to other parts of the world through European colonization or settlement. Generally, this involves the parent(s) of a newborn child inviting another adult, whether or not already a relative, to sponsor their child when he or she is baptized and formally named. This creates a spiritual relationship in which the godfather and godmother assume co-responsibility for the child's well-being (Figure 20.13).

One of the many variations of this institution is *compadrazgo*, or "coparenthood." Especially common in Latin America, *compadrazgo* involves a child's father and/or mother and godfather and/or godmother becoming linked to one another through the ritual of a Roman Catholic baptism; they thereby agree to certain mutual rights and obligations. In *compadrazgo*, the main emphasis is placed not on the child–godparent relationship but on the fictive kinship between the child's parents and the sponsor who becomes a ritual coparent, or *compadre*. Historically common in South Europe and Latin America, such quasi-kinship is

a pact for mutual support between the two *compadres*, co-parents, involved. Such a pact can be entered into between two *compadres* who are each other's equals in social and economic standing. Very often, however, it is formed between people, of whom one is wealthier, of higher social standing and more powerful politically than the other. (Wolf & Hansen, 1972, pp. 131–132)

Kinship and New Reproductive Technology

Advances in reproductive technology also pose new opportunities for kin-making. As defined in the previous chapter, *new reproductive technology* (NRT) is an alternative means of reproduction, such as in vitro fertilization. Since 1978, when the world's first test-tube baby was created, thousands of babies have been created outside the womb, without sexual intercourse—and all kinds of new technologies have become part of the reproductive repertoire.

These technologies have opened up a mind-boggling array of reproductive possibilities and social relations. For example, if a child is conceived from a donor egg, implanted in another woman's womb, to be raised by yet another woman, who is the child's mother? To complicate matters even further, the egg may have been fertilized by sperm from a donor not married to, or in a sexual relationship with, any of these women. Indeed, it has been suggested that about a dozen different modern kin-type categories are embraced in the concepts of mother and father in today's changing societies (Stone, 2005).

Clearly, new reproductive technology challenges previously held notions of parenthood and kinship. These techniques force us to rethink what being biologically related to others really means. Moreover, they drive home the point that the human capacity for securing relatives is not only impressive and ingenious but also fascinating.

CHAPTER CHECKLIST

What is kinship, and what role does it play in social organization?

✓ Kinship is a network of relatives into which individuals are born and married, and with whom they cooperate based on customarily prescribed rights and obligations.

✓ In nonindustrial societies, kin-groups commonly deal with challenges that families and households cannot handle alone—defense, resource allocation, cooperative labor. In larger and more complex societies, formal political systems take over many of these matters.

What is a descent group, and what are its various forms?

✓ A descent group is any kin-group whose members share a direct line of descent from a real (historical) or fictional common ancestor.

✓ Unilineal descent establishes kin-group membership exclusively through the male line (patrilineal) or female line (matrilineal). In all societies the kin of both mother and father are important elements in the social structure, regardless of how descent group membership is defined. However, unlike the patrilineal pattern, matrilineal descent does not automatically confer gender authority.

✓ There is a close relationship between a culture's infrastructure and its descent system. Generally, patrilineal descent predominates when male labor is considered of prime importance, as it is among pastoralists and agriculturalists. Matrilineal descent predominates mainly among horticulturalists where female subsistence work is vital.

✓ The two major forms of a unilineal descent group (patrilineal or matrilineal) are the lineage (a kin group descended from a common ancestor whose relationship to members can be exactly stated in genealogical terms) and the clan (an extended kin group, often consisting of several lineages, whose members claim common descent from a remote ancestor, usually legendary or mythological).

✓ Double descent (matrilineal for some purposes, patrilineal for others) is rare. Ambilineal descent provides a measure of flexibility in that an individual has the option of affiliating with either the mother's or father's descent group. Bilateral descent derives from both the mother's and father's families equally.

What role does descent play within the larger cultural system?

✓ Because lineages are commonly exogamous, sexual competition within the group is largely avoided, and marriage reinforces alliances between lineages. Lineage exogamy also serves to maintain open communication within a society and fosters the exchange of information between lineages.

✓ Unlike lineages, clan residence is usually dispersed. In the absence of residential unity, totems (symbols from nature that remind members of their common ancestry) often reinforce clan identification.

✓ A phratry is a unilineal descent group of two or more clans that supposedly share a common ancestry. When a society is divided into two halves, each half consisting of one or more clans, these two major descent groups are called moieties.

✓ In a bilateral descent system, individuals are affiliated equally with the mother's and father's families. Such a large group is socially impractical and is usually reduced to a small circle of paternal and maternal relatives called the kindred. A kindred is never the same for any two people except siblings. Bilateral kinship and kindred organization predominate in societies where nuclear families are common.

What does kinship terminology reveal about human relations?

✓ Kinship terminology varies across cultures and reveals the organizational structure of kinship groups, the importance of certain relationships, and prevailing attitudes about specific kin. Some languages use the same term to identify a brother and a cousin, suggesting that these kin are of equal importance to an individual. Kin merged under the same term have the same basic rights and obligations with respect to the person referring to them as such.

✓ The Eskimo system emphasizes the nuclear family and merges all other relatives in a given generation into a few large, generally undifferentiated categories.

✓ The Hawaiian system is the simplest system of kinship terminology, with all relatives of the same generation and gender referred to by the same term.

✓ In the Iroquois system, a single term is used for a father and his brother and another for a mother and her sister. Parallel cousins are equated with brothers and sisters but distinguished from cross cousins.

✓ Adoption and the practice of godparenting establish additional kin categories.

✓ New reproductive technologies separating conception from sexual intercourse and eggs from wombs challenge traditional notions of kinship and gender and create new social categories.

QUESTIONS FOR REFLECTION

1. Thousands of Scots and people of Scottish descent from across the globe travel annually to traditional events to gather together with their clans. Do you care about your own distant relatives or ancestors, and what will you pass on from your cultural heritage to the next generation?

2. People in modern industrial and postindustrial societies generally treasure ideas of personal freedom, individuality, and privacy as essential to their happiness. Considering the social functions of kinship relations in traditional non-state societies, why do you think that such ideas may be considered unsociable and even dangerously selfish?

3. In some North American Indian languages, the English word for loneliness is translated as "I have no relatives." What does that tell you about the importance of kinship in traditional cultures?

4. Today, many people use social media to stay in touch with relatives, friends, schoolmates, and colleagues. In your social media network, where are these individuals geographically located? How often do you see them in real space, and is your interaction with them different in person than online?

DIGGING INTO ANTHROPOLOGY

What's in a Name?

A culture's kinship terminology system offers a quick but crucially important insight into the group's social structure. This is especially true for traditional communities of foragers, herders, and farmers, but remains important in industrial and postindustrial societies in the age of globalization. By means of computers and mobile devices linked to the Internet, migrant workers, refugees, foreign students, members of diasporic communities, and others with relatives dispersed across the world stay involved in family affairs. Identify someone in your own family, neighborhood, or circle of friends whose consanguineal and/or affinal relatives do not all live in the same neighborhood, region, or even country. Interview that person ("EGO") with the purpose of mapping that individual's kin-group. Identify how EGO is related to each member and note why these other people are significant in EGO's life. Next, ask the informant for the kin terms he or she uses to distinguish these relatives from one another. Finally, match each of these kin terms with the kin types (such as mother's father's sister's son or brother's wife's daughter and so on). Finally, analyze the system and apply the relevant anthropological concepts as reviewed in this chapter.

Johannes Eisele/AFP/Getty Images

Beyond ties of kinship and household, people extend their social networks to cope with multiple challenges of human survival. They form groups based on shared identities, interests, or objectives, with memberships that may be compulsory or voluntary. Together, individuals interact, collaborate, and overcome obstacles. Collective action strengthens ties that bind and reduces tensions that divide. Playing games, including sports, has a similar effect. Athletes show off superior mental or physical skills within and between teams while revealing or acting out some of their culture's core values. Many sports have their origins in warfare, with rivals demonstrating skills and endurance. Here we see Afghan horsemen playing *buzkashi* ("goat-grabbing"). In this traditional game, sometimes up to 200 riders fiercely compete for possession of a headless body of a goat. Players from rival teams pick up and carry the carcass around a marker at one end of the field and then throw it into the scoring circle at the opposite end. Competing for glory and prize money on special holidays, all the players—and spectators—in this national sport are male, reflecting gender segregation in Afghan cultures.

Grouping by Gender, Age, Common Interest, and Social Status

Anthropologists have given considerable attention to kinship and marriage, which operate as organizing principles in all societies and are usually the prime basis of social order in stateless societies. Yet, because ties of kinship and household are not always sufficient to handle all the challenges of human survival, people also form groups based on gender, age, common interest, and social status.

Grouping by Gender

As shown in preceding chapters, division of labor along gender lines occurs in all human societies. In some cultures, many tasks that men and women undertake may be shared, or people may perform work normally assigned to another gender without much ado. In others, however, men and women are rigidly gender segregated in what they do. Such is the case in many maritime cultures, where seafarers aboard fishing, whaling, and freight ships are usually men. For instance, we find temporary all-male communities aboard ships of coastal Basque fishermen in Spain, Yupik Eskimo whalers in Alaska, and Swahili merchants sailing along the East African coast. These seafarers commonly leave their wives, mothers, and daughters behind in their homeports, sometimes for months at a time.

Clearly demarcated grouping by gender also occurs in many traditional food-gardening societies. For instance, among the Mundurucu Indians of Brazil's Amazon rainforest, men and women work, eat, and sleep separately. From age 13 onward, males live together in one large house, whereas women, girls, and preteen boys occupy several houses grouped around the men's house: Men associate with men, and women with women.

Figure 21.1 Sacred Trumpets of the Amazon
Gender-based groups are common among the Mundurucu and numerous other Amazonian Indian nations such as the Yawalapiti pictured here, who live on the Tuatuari River in Brazil's upper Xingu region. Gender issues are symbolically worked out in their mythologies and ceremonial dances. One common theme concerns ownership of the sacred trumpets, which represent spiritual power. The tribesmen zealously guard these trumpets, and only men are allowed to play them. Traditionally, women were even forbidden to see them.

Organized in patrilineal clans, the Mundurucu believe their guardian spirits dwell in sacred trumpets (*karökö*) made of hollow wooden cylinders. The spirits are thought to protect the community from harm and help secure plenty of game animals. Exclusively controlled by men, the trumpets are phallic in form and are a central feature of exclusive men's cults. As the repositories of male power, these trumpets are carefully guarded and hidden in a sacred hut next to the large men's house.

According to Mundurucu myth, gender roles were once reversed. Women ruled over men and controlled the trumpets, which symbolized female reproductive capacities and power. But because women could not hunt, they could not supply the meat demanded by the spirits inhabiting the trumpets. Ever since taking the trumpets from the women and keeping them secret, men have ritually established their dominance (Murphy, 1959) (Figure 21.1).

Grouping by Age

Like gender, grouping by age is based on human biology and as such is a cultural universal. All human societies recognize a number of life stages. Even in its most minimal form—marking distinctions among immature, mature, and older people—age classification is significant. The demarcation and duration of these stages vary across cultures, but each one provides distinctive social roles and comes with certain cultural features such as specific patterns of activity, attitudes, obligations, and prohibitions.

In contrast to many industrial and postindustrial societies where senior citizens are often isolated and looked down upon, old age in many traditional societies is a person's period of greatest respect (for women it may mean the first social equality with men). Rarely are the elderly shunted aside or abandoned. Even the Inuit of the Canadian Arctic, who are often cited as a migratory people who traditionally abandoned their old and infirm relatives, did so only in truly desperate circumstances, when the traveling group's physical survival was at stake. In all oral tradition societies, elders are the repositories of accumulated wisdom for their people. Recognized as such and no longer expected to carry out many subsistence activities, they play a major role in passing on cultural knowledge to their grandchildren.

In many cultures, the social position of an individual in a specific life stage is also marked by a distinctive outward appearance in terms of dress, hairstyle, body paint, tattoos, insignia, or some other symbolic distinction. Typically, these stages are designed to help the transition from one age to another, to teach needed skills, or to lend economic assistance. Often they are taken as the basis for the formation of organized groups.

Institutions of Age Grouping

An organized category of people with membership on the basis of age is known as an **age grade**. Entry into and transfer out of age grades may be accomplished

age grade An organized category of people based on age; every individual passes through a series of such categories over his or her lifetime.

individually, either by a biological distinction, such as puberty, or by a socially recognized status, such as marriage or childbirth.

Members of an age grade may have much in common—engaging in similar activities and sharing the same orientation and aspirations. In many cultures, a specific time is established for ritually moving from a younger to an older grade. Among many examples of this is the traditional Jewish ceremony of the *bar mitzvah* (a Hebrew term meaning "son of the commandment"), marking that a 13-year-old boy has reached the age of religious duty and responsibility. *Bat mitzvah* ("daughter of the commandment") is the term for the equivalent ritual for a girl.

Although members of senior groups commonly expect respect from and acknowledge certain responsibilities to their juniors, this does not necessarily mean that one grade is seen as better, or worse, or even more important than another. There can be standardized competition (opposition) between age grades, such as that traditionally between first-year and second-year students on college campuses.

In addition to age grades, some societies feature age sets (sometimes referred to as *age classes*). An **age set** is a formally established group of people born during a certain timespan who move together through the series of age-grade categories. Members of an age set usually remain closely associated throughout their lives. This is akin to but distinct from the broad and informal North American practice of identifying generation clusters composed of all individuals born within a particular time frame—such as baby boomers (1946–1960), gen-Xers (1961–1981), and the millennial or Internet generation (1982–2000) (year spans approximate).

The notion of an age set implies strong feelings of loyalty and mutual support. Because such groups may possess property, songs, shield designs, and rituals and are internally organized for collective decision making and leadership, age sets are distinct from simple age grades.

Age Grouping in East Africa

Although age is a criterion for group membership in many parts of the world, its most varied and elaborate use is found in several pastoral groups in East Africa, such as the Maasai, Samburu, and Tiriki in Kenya (Sangree, 1965). All of these groups have similar rituals that mark the transition from one age group to the next (Figure 21.2).

In Tiriki society, each boy born within a 15-year period joins a particular age set. Seven named age sets exist, but only one is open for membership at a time. When it closes, the next one opens. And so it continues until the passage of 105 years (7 times 15), when the first set's membership is gone due to death, and it opens once again to take in new recruits.

Members of Tiriki age sets remain together for life as they move through four successive age grades. Advancement in age grades occurs at 15-year intervals, coinciding

Nigel Pavitt/John Warburton-Lee Photography/Alamy

Figure 21.2 Maasai Warrior Age-Grade Ceremony
Like the Tiriki and some other pastoralists in East Africa, the Maasai form age sets—established groups of people born during a similar timespan who move together through the series of age-grade categories. The opening parade, shown here, of the elaborate *eunoto* ceremony begins the coming of age of *morans* ("warriors") for Maasai subclans of western Kenya. At the end of the ceremony, these men will be in the next age grade—junior adults—ready to marry and start families. Members of the same age set, they were initiated together into the Warrior age grade as teenagers. They spent their Warrior years raiding cattle (an old tradition that is now illegal but nonetheless still practiced) and protecting their community homes and animal enclosures (from wild animals and other cattle raiders). The *eunoto* ceremony includes a ritual in which mothers shave the heads of the Warriors, marking the end of many freedoms and the passage to manhood.

with the closing of the oldest age set and the opening of a new one.

Each age group has its own particular duties and responsibilities. Traditionally, the first age grade, the Warriors, served as guardians of the country, and members gained renown through fighting. Under British colonial rule, however, this traditional function largely fell by the wayside with the decline of intergroup raiding and warfare. Today, individual members of this age grade may find excitement and adventure by leaving their community for extended employment or study.

age set A formally established group of people born during a certain timespan who move together through the series of age-grade categories; sometimes called *age class*.

Figure 21.3 Common-Interest Associations
Among countless common-interest associations around the world is the Shriners, a secret fraternal order of middle-class males committed to "fun, fellowship, and service." Founded in the United States in 1870, the group was named after the Ancient Arabic Order of Nobles of the Mystic Shrine. Today, it is an international organization with 200 chapters across North and South America, Europe, and Southeast Asia.

© Todd Gipstein/Corbis

The next age grade, the Elder Warriors, had few specialized tasks in earlier days beyond learning skills they would need later on by assuming an increasing share of administrative activities. For example, they would chair the postfuneral gatherings held to settle property claims after someone's death. Traditionally, Elder Warriors also served as envoys between elders of different communities. Nowadays, they hold nearly all of the administrative and executive roles opened up by the creation and growth of a centralized Tiriki administrative bureaucracy.

Judicial Elders, the third age grade, traditionally handled most tasks connected with the administration and settlement of local disputes. Today, they still serve as the local judiciary body.

Members of the Ritual Elders, the senior age grade, used to preside over the priestly functions of ancestral shrine observances on the household level, at subclan meetings, at semiannual community appeals, and at rites of initiation into the various age grades. They also were credited with access to special magical powers. With the decline of ancestor worship over the past several decades,

many of these traditional functions have been lost, and no new ones have arisen to take their places. Nonetheless, Ritual Elders continue to hold the most important positions in the initiation ceremonies, and their power as sorcerers and expungers of witchcraft is still recognized.

Grouping by Common Interest

The rise of urban, industrialized societies in which individuals are often separated from their kin has led to a proliferation of **common-interest associations**— associations that result from an act of joining and are based on sharing particular activities, objectives, values, or beliefs (Figure 21.3). Some groups are rooted in common ethnic, religious, or regional background. Such associations help people meet a range of needs from companionship to safe work conditions to learning a new language and customs upon moving from one country to another.

Common-interest associations are also found in many traditional societies, and there is some evidence that they arose with the emergence of the first horticultural villages. Notably, associations in traditional societies may be just as

common-interest association An association that results from the act of joining, based on sharing particular activities, objectives, values, or beliefs, sometimes rooted in common ethnic, religious, or regional background.

VISUAL COUNTERPOINT

Figure 21.4 Induction of an Ashanti Chief in New York City
Today, about a quarter-million African-born immigrants live in New York City, and more come from
Ghana than from any other country on that continent. Many are part of Ghana's Ashanti ethnic
group and are members of the Asanteman Association of the USA and its New York branch. They
swear allegiance to their traditional king in Ghana (the Asantehene) and elect a local chief, who
carries the title of Asantefuohene. New York's newest Ashanti chief, formally addressed as Nana
Okokyeredom Owoahene Acheampong Tieku, works in the Bronx as an accountant and goes by the
name Michael. The king sent a high-ranking chief from Ghana for his 2012 swearing-in ceremony.

complex and highly organized as those found in industrialized countries.

Kinds of Common-Interest Associations

The variety of common-interest associations is astonishing. In the United States, they include sport, hobby,
and civic service clubs; religious and spiritual organizations; political parties; labor unions; environmental
organizations; urban gangs; private militias; immigrant
groups; academic organizations; women's and men's
clubs of all sorts—the list goes on and on. Their goals
may include the pursuit of friendship, recreation, and
the promotion of certain values, as well as governing,
seeking peace on a local or global scale, and defending
economic interests.

Some associations aim to preserve traditional songs,
history, language, moral beliefs, and other customs among
members of various ethnic minorities. So it is among
many immigrant groups from Africa who live in major
cities around the world, including in the United States.
Today, about 250,000 African-born immigrants live in the
New York metropolitan area.

The city's largest African group hails from Ghana, a
former British colony in West Africa. Using electronic

media, Ghanaians manage to maintain regular contact
with relatives, friends, and others back home. Many
of them are Ashanti, a large ethnic group historically
powerful as an independent nation politically organized
since the 1670s as a kingdom with a confederation of
thirty-seven paramount chiefdoms. Known as *Asanteman*,
this kingdom is governed to this day by a ruler who carries the royal title of Asantehene and resides in the royal
palace of his ancestors. His sacred power is symbolized by
the "golden stool," believed to have floated down from
heaven into the lap of his forefather and containing the
spirit-soul (*sunsum*) of the Ashanti nation. The current
king is a British-educated business professional with international executive experience.

For purposes of mutual support and to maintain their
cultural identity in the diaspora, Ashanti migrants in
New York City formed the Asanteman Association of the
USA in 1982, which now has numerous branches across
country. Members swear allegiance to their king in Ghana
and elect local chiefs in the cities where they now live
(Figure 21.4).

Jews, another ethnic minority group, sometimes establish a sense of traditional community by means of symbolic
geographic boundary markers. This chapter's Original
Study provides a detailed example of how Orthodox Jews
maintain their cultural identity, even within a modern city.

Todd Heisler/The New York Times/Redux

Dave Sanders/The New York Times/Redux

ORIGINAL STUDY

The Jewish *Eruv*: Symbolic Place in Public Space

BY SUSAN LEES

Cultural anthropologists are interested in how a geographic space becomes a culturally meaningful *place*—an area that we may think of as "our territory" or that we designate for one particular purpose or another, such as pasturing animals, playing sports, gardening, or worshiping. There are certain boundaries to such places. We may mark them off with lines or symbols not readily comprehensible to outsiders.

At times, different cultural groups may occupy the same geographic space, but each will see and divide it differently in terms that are meaningful only within their group. We see this on maps where international borders cut through traditional tribal or ethnic group territories. And we see it in various urban communities that may divide up their city spaces in ways perceptible only to themselves.

An example can be found among Orthodox Jews who ritually define the boundaries of their communities for the purpose of Sabbath observance: Once a week, on the seventh day religiously reserved for worship and obligatory rest, the area enclosed by the boundaries becomes, by definition, a single shared symbolic domain. This symbolically enclosed space is called an *eruv*, which means "combination" of the private spaces of the household and the public areas of the sidewalks, streets, and perhaps parks. On the Sabbath, these spaces are ritually converted into one big communal household.

The purpose of the *eruv* for Orthodox communities is to accommodate one of the many Sabbath prohibitions on religiously defined "work": the work of "carrying" objects from a private domain to a public one, or vice versa, or carrying objects for any distance in a public domain. On the Sabbath, if there is an *eruv*, observant Jews may carry within the entire *eruv* enclosure as if they were in their own homes. For instance, they are permitted to push a baby stroller or a wheelchair within the ritually enclosed neighborhood. This makes it possible for whole families—including small children and disabled individuals—to attend religious services in the synagogue or to socialize with one another and still be faithful to traditional law.

Historically, *eruv* boundaries were the walls of houses and courtyards and city walls within which communities were enclosed. But today, where there are no walls, communities sometimes erect thin strings or wires, or just use wires already there on utility poles (such as phone or electricity wires) to demarcate the boundaries. These are known to members of the community but usually are invisible to outsiders because they are part of the urban landscape.

I was first drawn to the subject of the *eruv* three decades ago, when I leafed through my mother's copy of the Code of Jewish Law still found in many American Jewish households. Much of this text concerns rules about observing the Sabbath.

As an anthropologist, I was intrigued by explanations given for certain practices because they heightened awareness of the uniqueness of Jewish identity in a world where temptations to assimilate with the larger, dominant culture were strong. The *eruv* captured my interest because it seemed to create, not just prohibit something. It transformed a group of diverse urban households into one common household, not just a community but a real "private" home. The symbolic "walls" around this collective domain were erected not to keep others out but to enclose its members and thus erase the actual walls of each individual household.

The ritual that creates an *eruv* requires that one member take a loaf of bread and make other members co-owners of that loaf; the symbolism of a household is shared ownership (not consumption) of this most symbolically meaningful food. The boundaries of the *eruv* "household" they co-inhabit must be contiguous, broken only by symbolic doorways through which they can pass as if through doorways of their individual homes. As long as the contiguity is maintained, they can extend the *eruv* to incorporate hundreds or even thousands of other houses. The majority of North American Jews who are members of religious congregations belong to Reform synagogues (the other major groups are Conservative and Orthodox), and American Reform Judaism officially abandoned the *eruv* as a Sabbath practice in 1846. When I first became interested in the subject, there were rather few *eruvin* anywhere.

But in the early 1970s, on the heels of the 1960s civil rights movement in the United States, a shift in Jewish identity issues occurred, and some younger generation

This map illustrates the *eruv* boundaries in Washington, DC—one of many symbolically enclosed spaces created by Orthodox Jews in cities around the world.

Jews began to turn to traditional practices that distinguished them from mainstream society and more assimilated Jews. It was in this context that a proliferation of new *eruvin* occurred in both urban and suburban contexts.

Most *eruvin* have been established without conflict, but a few have been highly controversial. In my research, I was interested to find that Jews are among the principal parties on both sides of *eruv* conflicts. Opponents of the *eruv* appear to fear the creation, or re-creation, of ghettos of inassimilable Jews who neither conform to nor respect the ideals of the dominant or mainstream culture—who appear "foreign" in appearance and practices. When Jewish religious leaders were first developing the laws of the *eruv* more than 2,000 years ago, this problem of how Jews could maintain a communal identity while living as a diasporic group (dispersed from their ancestral homeland) was among their primary concerns.

The *eruv* is one symbolic device to reinforce community as neighborhood—to establish a meaningful place for a distinct group in a diverse society. Neighborhood identities like these can be the basis for disputes about exclusivity, but they can also ease the maintenance of cultural traditions and humanize life in the city.

Written expressly for this text, 2008.

Men's and Women's Associations

In some societies women have not established formal common-interest associations to the extent that men have, either because women are restricted by their male-dominated culture or because women are absorbed on the domestic front with a host of activities compatible with childrearing. Moreover, some functions of men's associations—such as military combat duties—often are culturally defined as fit only for adult males or are repugnant to women. Still, as cross-cultural research makes clear, women often play important roles in associations of their own as well as in those in which men predominate. Notably, an ever-expanding feminist movement has directly or indirectly inspired and promoted the formation of professional organizations for women.

Women's rights organizations, consciousness-raising groups, and professional clubs are examples of some of the associations arising directly or indirectly out of feminist movements. These groups cover the entire range of association formation, from simple friendship and support groups to associations centered on politics, sports, the arts, spirituality, charity, and economic endeavors—on a national and even international scale. One example of a global female youth movement is the World Association of Girl Guides and Girl Scouts. Founded in England in 1928, this association supports young-female scouting organizations with a total membership of over 10 million girls and young women in 145 countries.

In some parts of the developing world—notably Africa—women's social clubs complement the men's. These clubs offer mutual support and spiritual counseling, as well as information on economic opportunities; they are also concerned with educating women and with charitable and wealth-generating activities. Increasingly, women's clubs are devoted to politics.

In rural areas all around the world, women's craft associations and cooperatives are increasingly common and economically productive. Many are enhanced through Internet marketing opportunities, which make it possible for the cooperatives to sell directly to buyers in far-off places, especially Western markets. Others take advantage of the ever-growing number of tourists looking for adventure in travel to remote areas (Figure 21.5).

© jdandrews/earthXplorer.com

Figure 21.5 Women's Weaving Cooperative in Peru
Established in a small Andean highland village about halfway between Písac and the ancient Inca royal capital Cuzco, this co-op is committed to spinning, dying, and weaving wool from llamas and alpacas as women here have done for many generations—completely by hand using only natural materials and dyes. Most of the men in Ccaccaccollo, Peru, work as carriers for tourists hiking the Inca Trail.

Figure 21.6 Constant Communication
High-speed wireless networks in affluent Japan, as in many other parts of the world, make it possible for people to continually tap into information and exchange messages and images by means of portable computers or, increasingly, web-enabled mobile telephones. For Japanese commuters, who spend hours staring at tiny screens on their mobiles while riding the world's most extensive network of subways and commuter trains, microblogging is especially popular.

A striking example on the economic front is the Self-Employed Women's Association (SEWA), headquartered in Ahmedabad, India. With close to 1.5 million members, it is the largest union of informal sector workers in the country. Working with more than 250 cooperatives and thousands of individual artisans and small-scale farmers from poor rural areas, SEWA has helped to establish support services vital to helping women achieve the goals of full employment and self-reliance—services in areas such as savings and credit, healthcare, child care, insurance, legal aid, capacity building, and communication. SEWA's Trade Facilitation Centre has grown into a global network aimed at making women's voices and contributions significant factors in world trade decisions.

Associations in the Digital Age

Despite the diversity and vitality of common-interest associations, nowadays people across the globe spend less time socializing with others in person. Instead, hundreds of millions spend their time with an ever-growing array of electronic and/or digital devices, communicating with others, entertaining themselves, and shopping.

Whether accessed by computer or mobile phone, social networking platforms—such as Facebook (with over 1.5 billion active users worldwide), Gmail (900 million), Instagram (400 million), Twitter (300 million), and China's WeChat (650 million)—enable individuals to

text message and exchange images with "friends" as they continually update their personal or other information (Statistica, 2016).

As noted in the chapter on language and communication, at the start of 2016 there were nearly 3.8 billion mobile phone users worldwide—more than half the human population. (Mobile cellular subscriptions were twice that number due to various factors, such as individuals purchasing multiple sim cards and having both private and business phones) (GSMA Intelligence, 2016). Notably, about 90 percent of the world's population is within mobile coverage (Figure 21.6) (Ericsson, 2016).

Social media tools are now also used by office managers, city mayors, law enforcers, physicians, and school principals for purposes of quick communication and have become instrumental in the functioning of many social groups. Importantly, in highly mobile societies and globally interconnected cultures, social media makes it possible to build and expand social networks regardless of geographic distance and across international boundaries.

Grouping by Social Status in Stratified Societies

Social stratification is a common and powerful structuring force in many of the world's societies. Basically, a **stratified society** is one in which people are hierarchically divided and ranked into social strata, or layers, and do not share equally in the basic resources that support income, status, and power. Members of the bottom

stratified society A society in which people are hierarchically divided and ranked into social strata, or layers, and do not share equally in the basic resources that support income, status, and power.

Anthropologists and Social Impact Assessment

Anthropologists frequently do a type of policy research called a *social impact assessment*, which entails collecting data about a community or neighborhood for planners of development projects. Such an assessment seeks to determine a project's effect by determining how and upon whom its impact will fall and whether the impact is likely to be positive or negative.

In the United States, any project requiring a federal permit or license or using federal funds by law must be preceded by a social impact assessment as part of the environmental review process. Examples of such projects include highway construction, urban renewal, water diversion schemes, and land reclamation. Often, such projects are sited so that their impact falls most heavily on neighborhoods or communities inhabited by people in low socioeconomic strata—sometimes because the projects are viewed as a way of improving the lives of poor people and sometimes because the poor people have less political power to block these proposals.

As an illustration of this kind of work, U.S. anthropologist Sue Ellen Jacobs was hired to do a social impact assessment of a water diversion project in New Mexico planned by the Bureau of Land Reclamation in cooperation with the Bureau of Indian Affairs. This project proposed construction of a diversion dam and an extensive canal system for irrigation on the Rio Grande. The project would affect twenty-two communities primarily inhabited by Hispanic Americans, as well as two Indian pueblos. Unemployment was high in the region, and the project was seen as a way to promote urbanization, which theoretically would be associated with industrial development and would also bring new land into production for intensive agriculture.

What the planners failed to take into account was that both the Hispanic and Indian populations were heavily committed to farming for household consumption (with some surpluses raised for the market), using a system of irrigation canals that had been established for 300 years. These canals are maintained by elected supervisors familiar with the communities and knowledgeable about water laws, ditch management, and sustainable crop production. Such individuals can resolve conflicts concerning water allocation and land use, among other issues. Under the proposed project, this system was to be given up in favor of one in which fewer people would control larger tracts of land and water allocation would be in the hands of a government technocrat. One of the strongest measures of local government would be lost.

Not surprisingly, Jacobs discovered widespread community opposition to this project, and her report helped convince Congress that any positive impact was far outweighed by negative effects. One of the major objections to the construction project was that it would obliterate the centuries-old irrigation system. Project planners had not recognized the antiquity and cultural significance of these traditional irrigation structures, referring to them as "temporary diversion structures." The fact that the old dams associated with the ditches were attached to local descent groups was simply not acknowledged in the government documents.

Beyond infringing on local control, the project threatened the community with a range of negative side effects: problems linked to population growth and relocation, a loss of fishing and other river-related resources, and new health hazards, including increased threat of drowning, insect breeding, and airborne dust.

Based in part on Van Willigen, J. (1986). *Applied anthropology* (p. 169). South Hadley, MA: Bergin & Garvey. See also Van Willigen, J. (2002). *Applied anthropology: An introduction.* Westport, CT: Bergin & Garvey.

---

strata ("have-nots") typically have fewer resources, lower prestige, and less power than those in top-ranked strata (the "have-lots"). In addition, they usually face greater or more oppressive restrictions and obligations and must work harder for far less material reward and social recognition.

In short, social stratification amounts to culturally institutionalized inequality. In the United States, certain ethnic (or racial) minorities—in particular Hispanic, African American, and American Indian groups—are among those who have been historically marginalized, posing a challenge for individuals born into these low-ranked strata to move up the social ladder. As profiled in this chapter's Anthropology Applied feature, their needs are often ignored in development efforts.

A stratified society stands in sharp contrast to an **egalitarian society**, in which everyone has about equal rank and power and about the same access to basic resources. In these societies, social values of communal sharing are culturally emphasized and approved; wealth hoarding and elitist pretensions are despised, belittled, or ridiculed. As we saw in earlier chapters, foraging societies are characteristically egalitarian, although there are some exceptions.

Social Class and Caste

A **social class** may be defined as a category of individuals in a stratified society who have equal or nearly equal prestige according to the system of evaluation. The

---

egalitarian society A society in which people have about the same rank and share equally in the basic resources that support income, status, and power.

social class A category of individuals in a stratified society who enjoy equal or nearly equal prestige according to the hierarchical system of evaluation.

qualification "nearly equal" is important because a certain amount of inequality may occur even within a given class. Class distinctions are not always clear-cut and obvious in societies that have a wide and continuous range of differential privileges.

A **caste** is a closed social class in a stratified society in which membership is determined by birth and fixed for life. The opposite of the principle that all humans are born equal, the caste system is based on the principle that humans are born and remain unequal until death. Castes are strongly endogamous, and offspring are automatically members of their parents' caste.

The Traditional Hindu Caste System

The classic ethnographic example of a caste system is the traditional Hindu caste system of India (also found in some other parts of Asia), which encompasses a complex hierarchy of closed social groups ranking from "ritual purity" at the top to "filth" at the bottom. Each of some 2,000 different castes considers itself as a distinct community higher or lower than other castes, although their particular ranking varies across geographic regions and over time.

The different castes are associated with specific occupations and customs, such as food habits and styles of dress, along with rituals involving notions of purity and pollution. Ritual pollution is the result of contact such as touching, accepting food from, or having sex with a member of a lower caste. To remain pure, traditional Hindus are taught to follow the ritual path of duty, or *dharma*, of the specific caste into which they are born, and to avoid everyone and everything considered taboo to their caste. For this reason, castes are always endogamous. Differences in caste rankings are traditionally justified by the religious doctrine of the transmigration of the soul, or *karma*—a belief that one's status in this life is determined by one's deeds in previous lifetimes.

All of these castes, or *jatis*, are organized into four ranked orders, or *varnas* (literally meaning "colors"), distinguished partly by occupation and ranked in order of descending religious status of purity (Figure 21.7). The religious foundation for this social hierarchy is found in a 2,000-year-old sacred text known as the Laws of Manu,

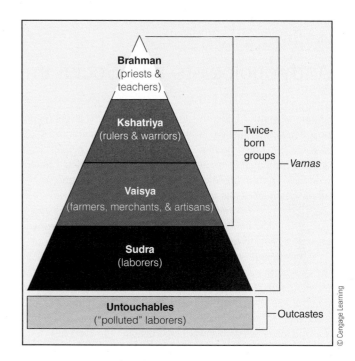

Figure 21.7 The Hindu Caste System
Hindu castes are organized into four "grades of being" called *varnas* ("colors") that determine what members are permitted to do, touch, or eat; where they live; how they dress; and whom they can marry. The highest-ranking order Brahman is associated with the color white, below which are Kshatriya (red) and Vaisya (brown). Below these three are Sudra (black), who make a living as laborers. Lower still are the "polluted" laborers, the Untouchables, who are charged with cleaning the streets and with the collection and disposal of garbage, animal carcasses, and sewage.

which traditional Hindus consider to be the highest authority on their cultural institutions. It defines the Brahmans as the purest and therefore highest *varna*.

As priests and teachers, Brahmans represent the world of religion and learning. Next comes the order of rulers and warriors, known as the Kshatriyas. Graded below them are the Vaisyas (farmers, merchants, and artisans) who are engaged in trade, cultivation, and skilled crafts. At the bottom are the Sudras (laborers), an order required to serve the other three *varnas*. Members born into these four *varnas* are believed to have been reincarnated from a morally correct earlier life in a lower-ranked order.

Falling outside the *varna* system is a fifth category of degraded individuals. These outcastes, known as Untouchables or as Dalits (a Sanskrit name meaning "crushed" or "suppressed"), are tasked with doing the dirty work in society—collecting garbage, removing animal carcasses, cleaning streets, and disposing of dung, sewage, and other refuse (Figure 21.8). Brahmans and members of other *varnas* avoid direct contact with Untouchables, believing that touching or accepting food from them would result in ritual pollution. Commonly associated with filth, outcastes constitute a large pool of cheap labor at the beck and call of those controlling economic and political affairs.

caste A closed social class in a stratified society in which membership is determined by birth and fixed for life.

Figure 21.8 Doing the Dirty Work
Cleaning sewers is a task that falls to Dalits (Untouchables) in India's traditional hierarchical caste system. They are also responsible for collecting and disposing of rubbish and animal dung, as well as removing human excrement from public toilets. Here we see a young Dalit man stepping out of the sewage drain he has been cleaning in New Delhi. Every day many thousands of Dalits all across India manually unplug the dirtiest sewers and drains without any safety equipment or protection. Injuries and serious health problems come with this work, claiming many lives.

India's national constitution of 1950 sought to abolish the caste system, but the traditional hierarchy remains deeply entrenched in Hindu culture and is still widespread throughout southern Asia. In what has been called India's hidden apartheid, entire villages in many Indian states remain completely segregated by caste.

Dalits represent about 15 percent of India's population—over 200 million people—and must endure social isolation, humiliation, and discrimination based exclusively on their birth status. Even their shadows are seen as polluting. They may not drink water from public wells or visit the same temples as the higher castes. Their children are still often made to sit at the back of classrooms, and in rural areas some are denied access to education altogether. More than 60 percent of all Dalits are illiterate. However, over the past half-century, Dalits, in concert with the lowest-ranking Sudra castes, have built a civil rights movement—described later in this chapter (Kanti, 2014; Thompson, 2014).

Other Stratified Systems

Similar caste-like situations exist elsewhere in the world. In several other South and Central American countries, for example, the wealthy upper class remains almost exclusively of European descent and rarely intermarries with people of American Indian or African descent.

Most European stratified societies were historically organized in closed social classes known as *estates*—ranked as clergy, nobility, and citizens—each with distinctive political rights (privileges). Titles and forms of address hierarchically identified these estates, and they were publicly distinguished by dress and codes of behavior. Not unlike the lowest castes in the Hindu caste system, a large underclass of millions of serfs ranked at the bottom of the European hierarchy. Prohibited from owning land or a business, *serfs* could not vote and did not enjoy the rights of free citizens. Often dirt poor, they worked on large farms and houses owned by the elite. Unlike slaves, they could not be traded as personal property of their masters, but they were restricted in their right to free movement and required their master's consent to marry.

Serfdom existed for many centuries in much of Europe. Russia was that continent's last country to abolish this system in 1861—just four years before slavery was abolished in the United States. It was several more decades before the slave system officially ended in Brazil, China, and other countries.

Historical Racial Segregation in South Africa and the United States

Other than social class, caste, and estate, the hierarchy in a stratified society may be based on ethnic origin or skin color. For instance, dark-skinned individuals culturally classified as colored or black may encounter social rules excluding them from certain jobs or neighborhoods and making it difficult if not impossible to befriend or marry someone with a lighter skin color. (As discussed earlier in our text, the terms *race*, *black*, and *white* are purely social constructions, with no basis in biology. For simplicity, we use them here without quotation marks.)

One of the best-known historical examples of a pluralistic country with social stratification based on the notion of race is South Africa. From 1948 to 1992, a minority of 4.5 million people of European descent sought to protect its power and "racial purity" by means of a repressive regime of racial segregation and discrimination against 25 million indigenous black Africans. Known as *apartheid* (an Afrikaans Dutch term meaning "segregation" or "separation"), this white superiority ideology officially relegated indigenous dark-skinned Africans to a low-ranking stratum. Similar to the Hindu caste system with its concepts of ritual purity and pollution, South African whites feared pollution of their purity through direct personal contact with blacks.

Until the mid-20th century, institutionalized racial segregation prevailed in the United States, where the country's ruling upper class was historically comprised exclusively of individuals of European (Caucasian or white) descent. For generations, it was against the law for whites to marry blacks or American Indians. Even after black slavery was abolished in the United States in 1865, such interracial mixing prohibitions remained in force in many states from Maine to Florida. Despite significant steps toward equality since enactment of civil rights laws in the 1960s, elements of officially prohibited race-based segregation and race-based discrimination persist (Boshara, 2003; Kennickell, 2003).

Indicators of Social Status

Social classes are manifested in various ways, including *symbolic indicators*. For example, in the United States certain activities and possessions are indicative of class: occupation (a garbage collector has a different class

status than a medical specialist); wealth (rich people are generally in a higher social class than poor people); dress ("white collar" versus "blue collar"); form of recreation (people in the upper class are expected to play golf rather than shoot pool down at the pool hall—but they can shoot pool at home or in a club); residential location (people in the upper class do not ordinarily live in slums); kind of car; and so on. Class rankings do not fully correlate with economic status or pay scales. The local garbage collector or unionized car-factory laborer typically make more money than an average college professor with a doctorate.

Symbolic indicators involve factors of lifestyle, but differences in life chances may also signal differences in class standing. Thus there is also a tendency for greater physical stature and better overall health among people of the upper class—the result of healthier diet and protection from serious illness in their growing-up years. This correlates with a lower infant mortality and longer life expectancy for the upper class. See the Biocultural Connection feature for a tragic description of such institutionalized racism.

Maintaining Stratification

In any system of stratification, those who dominate proclaim their supposedly superior status by means of a powerful ideology. Typically, they assert this ideology through intimidation or propaganda (in the form of gossip, media, religious doctrine, and so forth) that presents their position as normal, natural, divinely guided, or at least well deserved. With the aid of culturally institutionalized thought structures, religious and otherwise, those in power seek to justify their own privileges and hope that members of the lower classes will "know their place" and accept their subordinated status.

India's traditional caste system with its Hindu doctrines assigns people to a particular position in the social hierarchy. It carries the idea that if individuals faithfully perform the duties appropriate to their caste in this lifetime (*dharma*), then they can expect to be reborn into a higher caste in a future existence (*karma*). Thus, in the minds of orthodox Hindus, one's caste position is something earned rather than the accident of birth that it appears to be to outside observers.

In contrast, the principle of human equality is fundamental to the American worldview articulated in the U.S. Declaration of Independence, which declares "that all men are created equal [and] endowed by their Creator with certain unalienable Rights, that among these are Life, Liberty and the pursuit of Happiness." The founding principle prevails—despite this stratified society's history of racial and gender discrimination and its stark differences in wealth, status, and power.

African Burial Ground Project *BY MICHAEL BLAKEY*

In 1991, construction workers in lower Manhattan unearthed what turned out to be part of a 6-acre burial ground containing remains of an estimated 15,000 enslaved African captives brought to New York in the 17th and 18th centuries to build the city and provide the labor for its thriving economy. The discovery sparked controversy as the African American public held protests and prayer vigils to stop the part of a federal building project that nearly destroyed the site. In 1993, the site was designated a National Historic Landmark, which opened the door to researching and protecting the site.

© A. J. Giordano/Corbis SABA

The excavation site of the African Burial Ground in Lower Manhattan in New York City now features a distinctive memorial that commemorates this important historical archaeological project. Now a national monument, the site is managed by the National Park Service.

As a biological anthropologist and African American, I had a unique opportunity to work together with the descendant African American community to develop a plan that included both extensive biocultural research and the humane retention of the sacred nature of the site, ultimately through reburial and the creation of a fitting memorial. The research also involved archaeological and historical studies that used a broad African diasporic context for understanding the lifetime experiences of these people who were enslaved and buried in New York.

Studying a sample population of 419 individuals from the burial ground, our team used an exhaustive range of skeletal biological methods, producing a database containing more than 200,000 observations of genetics, morphology, age, sex, growth and development, muscle development, trauma, nutrition, and disease. The bones revealed an unmistakable link between biology and culture: physical wear and tear of an entire community brought on by the social institution of slavery.

We now know, based on this study, that life for Africans in colonial New York was characterized by poor nutrition, grueling physical labor that enlarged and often tore muscles, and death rates that were unusually high for 15- to 25-year-olds. Many of these young adults died soon after arriving on slaving ships. Few Africans lived past 40 years of age, and less than 2 percent lived beyond 55. Church records show strikingly different mortality trends for the Europeans of New York: About eight times as many English as Africans lived past 55 years of age, and mortality in adolescence and the early 20s was relatively low.

Skeletal research also showed that those Africans who died as children and were most likely to have been born in New York exhibited stunted and disrupted growth and exposure to high levels of lead pollution—unlike those who had been born in Africa (and were distinguishable because they had filed teeth). Fertility was very low among enslaved women in New York, and infant mortality was high. In these respects, this northern colonial city was very similar to South Carolina and the Caribbean to which its economy was tied—regions where conditions for African captives were among the harshest.

Individuals in this deeply troubling burial ground came from warring African states including Calibar, Asante, Benin, Dahomey, Congo, Madagascar, and many others—states that wrestled with the European demand for human slaves. They resisted their enslavement through rebellion, and they resisted their dehumanization by carefully burying their dead and preserving what they could of their cultures.

Biocultural Question

Although few question that slavery is an inhuman system of labor exploitation, was it economically rational for slave owners to mistreat their "human chattel," as indicated by the poor health, low fertility, and high mortality of African slaves in colonial New York?

Adapted from Blakey, M. (2003). *African Burial Ground Project.* Department of Anthropology, College of William & Mary. Revised and updated by the author. See also Blakey, M. (May, 2010). African Burial Ground Project: Paradigm for cooperation? *Museum International 62* (1–2), 61–68.

Figure 21.9 The Gulabi Gang
Sometimes referred to as "pink vigilantes," these poor rural women are part of a movement challenging their country's repressive status quo. Most of them are Dalits (Untouchables). Dressed in pink saris (*gulabi* means "pink" in Hindi), they demand justice by shaming and intimidating abusive men as well as corrupt officials who deny them equal access to water, farming supplies, and other resources.

Jonas Gratzer/Getty Images

Social Mobility

Most stratified societies offer at least some **social mobility**—an upward or downward change in one's social class position. The prospect of improving status and wealth helps to ease the strains inherent in any system of inequality.

Social mobility is most common in societies made up of independent nuclear families where individuals are closely tied to fewer people, especially when neolocal residence is the norm, and it is assumed that individuals will leave their family of birth when they become adults. In such social settings—through hard work, occupational success, opportune marriage, and dissociation from the lower-class family in which they grew up—individuals can more easily move up in status and rank.

In societies in which the extended family or lineage is the usual form, upward social mobility is more difficult because each individual is strongly tied to many relatives (both close and more distant); those climbing the social ladder are culturally obliged to leave none in the kin-group behind. In all likelihood, many relatives of the highly successful Côte d'Ivoire soccer players described in this chapter's Globalscape have collectively experienced upward mobility through their kinship ties to these newly wealthy athletes.

Societies that permit a great deal of upward and downward mobility are referred to as *open-class societies*—although the openness is apt to be less in practice than members hope or believe. In the United States, regardless of its ideology of human equality, most mobility involves

moving up or down only a notch; if this continues in a family over several generations, however, it may add up to a major change. Nonetheless, U.S. society makes much of the relatively rare examples of great upward mobility consistent with its cultural values (rags to riches) and tends to overlook the numerous cases of little or no upward (not to mention downward) mobility.

Caste societies exemplify *closed-class societies* because of their severe institutionalized limits on social mobility. Yet, even the Hindu caste system, with its guiding ideology that all social hierarchies within it are eternally fixed, has a degree of flexibility and mobility. Individuals may not move up or down the caste hierarchy, but whole groups can do so depending on claims they assert for higher ranking and on how well they can convince or manipulate others into acknowledging their claims.

During the past half-century, political activism has stirred among members of India's vast underclass of Dalits, now numbering about 250 million scattered all across this massive South Asian country of 1.2 billion people. A growing political force, Dalits are now organizing themselves on local, regional, and even national levels. Their movement for civil rights is facilitated by increased access to digital communication technology.

In recent years, Dalit women in many parts of India have joined hands with the intention of claiming social justice. Perhaps best known among them is a group in India's northern province of Uttar Pradesh who vigorously protest government discrimination and official corruption and strive to create opportunities for women. Dressed in vibrant pink saris and wielding traditional Indian fighting sticks known as *lathi*, they are the Gulabi ("Pink") Gang (Figure 21.9). They demand justice—shaming and intimidating abusive men and corrupt officials who deny

---

social mobility An upward or downward change in one's social class position in a stratified society.

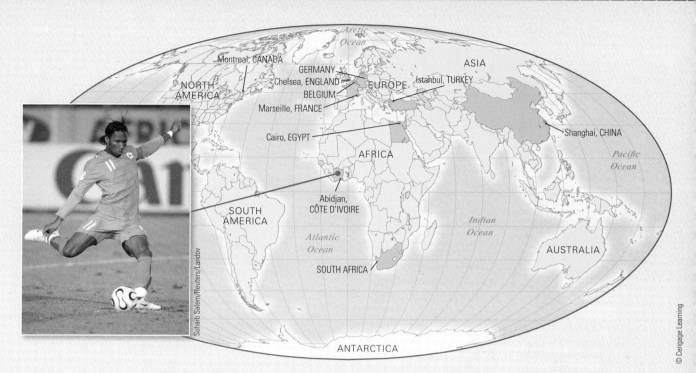

Suhaib Salem/Reuters/Landov

© Cengage Learning

Playing Football for Pay and Peace?

The world's most popular sport is football (called *soccer* in the United States), with countless amateur and professional clubs and associations on every continent. The game originated in the British Isles, where youth at schools and adults with money and leisure time competed for championships—a luxury out of reach for the working class.

This changed about 150 years ago, when tournaments turned into commercial spectacles with clubs earning revenues from ticket and advertising sales. Initially opposed by upper-class traditionalists defending the sport as a healthy and character-building activity for amateurs (*amator*, Latin for "lover"), the emergence of professional clubs made it possible for athletes from the British working class to play for pay.

Today, most professionals playing for the world's top football clubs are young millionaires such as Didier Drogba (pictured here), a striker best known for his years with England's champion club, Chelsea, and as captain of his own country's national team—the Côte d'Ivoire "Elephants." Born in Abidjan, the major city in this former French West African colony, Drogba is a southerner belonging to the Bete, one of the country's sixty-five ethnic groups. Recruited at an early age for a Belgian club, he was drafted by a French club in Marseille for $8 million. Chosen French Player of the Year in 2004, after just one season, he signed with England's champion team, Chelsea, for a record $42-million multi-year contract (not counting endorsements). In 2012, he left Chelsea and gave a year apiece to clubs in China and Turkey, only to return to Chelsea for another two years. In 2014, England's football fans voted him the club's best ever player. He holds Chelsea's record for goals made by a foreign player and is that team's fourth highest goal scorer of all time. In 2015, he made the move to Montreal Impact. His earnings over the years make him one of the world's highest paid footballers.

With the average Ivoirian earning less than $1,000 per year, it is not surprising that athletic talents like Drogba venture across the globe for fortune and fame. In fact, all members of the Côte d'Ivoire national football team normally play abroad, most for wealthy European clubs. Meanwhile, their home country has been wracked by a brutal civil war pitting southern ethnic groups against northern ones.

Ninety percent of Côte d'Ivoire's foreign exchange earnings come from cocoa beans. As a world-renowned sports star, Drogba began appearing in ads promoting the international sale of Ivoirian chocolate. He also began to promote peace: During the 2006 World Cup games in Germany, enthusiastically watched on television by millions of fellow Ivoirians back home, team captain Drogba and his teammates (representing both southern and northern Côte d'Ivoire) pleaded that the unity of the Elephants in the stadium should inspire fellow Ivoirians to settle their conflict and reunite as a country. In 2007, a peace agreement was signed after Drogba helped move the Elephants' African Cup of Nations qualifier match to the rebel stronghold of Bouaké, where warring leaders found themselves celebrating their national team together.

Fighting broke out again in early February 2011 over contested political elections. Soon thereafter, Drogba joined the Truth, Reconciliation, and Dialogue Commission as a representative—his eye still on the goal of bringing lasting peace to his home nation. In 2014, having captained the Côte d'Ivoire team for nine years and inspired his teammates in that year's World Cup, Drogba retired from the Elephants. He had scored 65 goals across 104 matches—more than double the scoring output of any other player in the national team's history.

Global Twister

How realistic is Drogba's idea that a national multi-ethnic soccer team can help unite his country's rival factions in a lasting way?

them equal access to water, farming supplies, and other resources. As one of these "pink vigilantes" puts it, "On my own I have no rights, but together, as the Gulabi Gang, we have power" (Dunbar, 2008).

The Dalit women's movement in India illustrates that even long-established and culturally entrenched hierarchical orders are not immune to challenge, reform, or revolution. Great disparities in wealth, power, and privilege persist and even grow in many parts of the world, but there are notable social changes in the opposite direction. In the course of the 19th century, slavery was abolished and declared illegal nearly everywhere in the world. And in the last century, civil rights, women's rights, and other human rights movements resulted in social and legal reforms, as well as changes in ideas and values regarding hierarchical social orders in many countries.

CHAPTER CHECKLIST

Beyond kinship, what kinds of groups do humans form and why?

✓ Because ties of kinship and household are not always sufficient to handle all the challenges of human survival, people also form groups based on gender, age, common interest, and social status.

✓ Grouping by gender separates men and women to varying degrees in different societies; in some they may be together much of the time, whereas in others they may spend much of their time apart, even to the extreme of eating and sleeping separately.

✓ Age grouping may augment or replace kinship grouping. An age grade is a category of people organized by age. Some societies also have age sets, which are composed of individuals who are initiated into an age grade at the same time and move together through a series of life stages.

✓ Common-interest associations are based on sharing particular activities, objectives, values, or beliefs. Linked to social change and urbanization, their roots may be found in the first horticultural villages.

✓ The Internet has lessened face-to-face interaction while opening up new forms of virtual communication through social media.

What is a stratified society, and what are the possibilities and limitations of upward and downward social mobility?

✓ A stratified society is divided into two or more categories of people who do not share equally in basic resources that support income, status, and power. Societies may be stratified by gender, age, social class, or caste.

✓ A social class is comprised of individuals who enjoy equal or nearly equal prestige according to a society's system of evaluation.

✓ A caste is a closed social class with membership determined by birth and fixed for life. A classic example is the traditional Hindu caste system of India. It encompasses a complex ranking of 2,000 castes associated with specific occupations and customs, and organized into four basic orders or *varnas*.

✓ The hierarchy in a stratified society may also be based on ethnic origin or notions of race. In South Africa, for example, people of European descent maintained power through apartheid—a repressive regime of racial segregation and discrimination against indigenous black Africans from 1948 to 1992. A racist regime also existed in the United States.

✓ Most stratified societies offer at least some social mobility—upward or downward change in one's social class position. Even in caste societies, which impose severe institutionalized limits on social mobility, there is some flexibility through group action, as seen in the Dalit movement in India.

✓ In contrast to a stratified society is an egalitarian one in which people have about the same rank and share equally in the basic resources that support income, status, and power.

QUESTIONS FOR REFLECTION

1. Soon after domesticating wild horses more than 5,000 years ago, tribesmen in Central Asia herded their flocks of sheep and goats on horseback. Highly mobile, they also launched swift surprise attacks on enemies. This tradition is reflected in *buzkashi*, Afghanistan's national sport. Which core values do you think are reflected or expressed in the sport most popular in your own country?

2. When young adults leave their parental home to go to college or find employment in a distant part of

the country, they face the challenge of establishing new social relationships—ones that are not based on kinship but on common interest. To which common-interest associations do you belong and why?

3. Do you think that members of an upper class or caste in a socially stratified system have a greater vested interest in the idea of law and order than those forced to exist on the bottom of such societies? Why or why not?

4. Slavery in the United States was officially abolished in 1865. Almost a century later, race-based segregation was officially outlawed in the United States, about the same time as caste-based discrimination of Untouchables was constitutionally outlawed in India. Do you think that these laws have ended discrimination against historically repressed groups? If not, what do you think is required to end social injustice?

DIGGING INTO ANTHROPOLOGY

Comfortable Connecting?

Choose a social media platform (such as Facebook, Twitter, Pinterest, LinkedIn, or Instagram) that you use regularly. Make a list of the ways you use it with relatives, friends, schoolmates, colleagues, or associates. Then make a list noting the geographic locations of the twenty individuals in your digital social network with whom you most often communicate. How often do you see them in real space, and is your interaction with them different in person than online? (If you don't use social media, find someone you know well who does and interview the person to find answers to these questions.) Analyze your findings, and draw some conclusions about how your social media self (or that of the interviewee) may be different from your face-to-face self.

Photo by United Nation Relief and Works Agency via Getty Images

Maintaining peace and order is a daily challenge in every society, especially when different ethnic and religious communities coexist under the same political umbrella. Pluralistic societies such as Switzerland, a republic with four national languages, have long enjoyed peace and prosperity. But others risk sectarian violence among factions divided by ethnicity, religion, language, or region. When the cultural fabric that keeps a society together is fragile or unravels, the state may fail, collapsing into conflict and chaos. Escaping the peril, refugees flee in search of safety, shelter, and food. Millions end up in camps, condemned to a hopeless existence. Such was the case with British-controlled Palestine in 1947 when the United Nations General Assembly passed a resolution for that territory to be partitioned between Jews and Arabs. It allowed for the formation of the Jewish state of Israel in 1948, but some 700,000 Muslims and Christians were forced into exile. Many Palestinians ended up in Yarmouk Camp on the outskirts of Syria's capital city of Damascus. Eventually, more than 160,000 sought refuge there, creating a ghetto in that 2-square-kilometer (500-acre) area. In this photograph, we see that neighborhood, which in 2013 came under siege in Syria's civil war. Most managed to flee, but 20,000 remained, stuck in a wasteland of despair. Those who fled are now among the 4 million Syrian refugees displaced throughout the Middle East, about half of whom have escaped to Jordan, Lebanon, Turkey, and beyond.

Politics, Power, War, and Peace

22

In all societies, from the largest to the smallest, people face the challenge of maintaining social order, securing safety, protecting property, and resolving conflicts. This involves mobilizing, contesting, and controlling power. All human relations entail a degree of **power**, which refers to the ability of individuals or groups to impose their will upon others and make them do things even against their own wants or wishes.

Ranging from persuasion to violence, power drives politics—a term that derives from the Greek word *polis*, referring to a self-governing "city." Many definitions have been proposed, but one of the most basic is that **politics** is the process determining who gets what, when, and how (Lasswell, 1990). In the political process, coalitions of individuals and groups defend or dispute an established economic, social, or ideological order as they negotiate or fight with rival factions and foreign neighbors. Political organization takes many forms, of which the *state* is just one.

Ironically, the political ties that facilitate human coexistence and cooperation also create the dynamics that may lead to social tension and sometimes to violent conflict within and between groups. We see this in a wide range of situations, from riots to rebellions to revolutions. Therefore, every society must have ways and means for resolving internal conflicts and preventing the breakdown of its social order. Moreover, each society must possess the capacity to deal with neighboring societies in peaceful or troubled times.

Today, state governments and international political coalitions play a central role in maintaining social order across the globe. Despite the predominance of state societies, there are many groups in which political organization consists of flexible and informal kinship systems. Between these two polarities of kin-ordered and state-organized political systems lies a world of variety.

> **power** The ability of individuals or groups to impose their will upon others and make them do things even against their own wants or wishes.
>
> **politics** The process determining who gets what, when, and how.

In this chapter you will learn to

- Analyze how the issue of power is crucially important in every society.

- Recognize the difference between authority and coercion.

- Distinguish and discuss types of political organization and leadership.

- Determine how politics, economics, and maintenance of (in)equality are linked.

- Contrast systems of justice and conflict resolution across cultures.

- Recognize major causes of violent conflict, past and present.

- Identify the role of ideology in justifying aggression versus nonviolent resistance.

- Evaluate the importance of diplomacy and treaties in restoring and maintaining peace.

Systems of Political Organization

The term **political organization** refers to the way power is accumulated, arranged, executed, and structurally embedded in society, whether in organizing a whale hunt, managing irrigated farmlands, collecting taxes, or raising a military force. In short, it is the means through which a society creates and maintains social order. It assumes a variety of forms among the peoples of the world, but anthropologists have simplified this complex subject by identifying four basic kinds of political systems: bands, tribes, chiefdoms, and states (**Figure 22.1**). The first two are uncentralized systems; the latter two are centralized.

Uncentralized Political Systems

Until recently, many non-Western peoples have had neither chiefs with established rights and duties nor any fixed form of government, as those who live in modern states understand the term. Instead, marriage and kinship have formed their principal means of social organization. The economies of these societies are primarily of a subsistence type, and populations are typically small.

Power in this egalitarian form of political organization is shared, with nobody exercising exclusive control over collective resources or public affairs. Important decisions are usually made in a collective manner by agreement among adults. Leaders do not have real power to force compliance with the society's customs or rules, but if individuals do not conform, they are likely to become

TYPES OF POLITICAL ORGANIZATION

The symbol → indicates that the attribute varies between less and more complex societies of that type.

	BAND	TRIBE	CHIEFDOM	STATE
MEMBERSHIP				
Number of people	Dozens and up	Hundreds and up	Thousands and up	Tens of thousands and up
Settlement pattern	Mobile	Mobile or fixed: 1 or more villages	Fixed: 2 or more villages	Fixed: Many villages and cities
Basis of relationships	Kin	Kin, descent groups	Kin, rank, and residence	Class and residence
Ethnicities and languages	1	1	1	1 or more
GOVERNMENT				
Decision making, leadership	Egalitarian	Egalitarian or Big Man	Centralized, hereditary	Centralized
Bureaucracy	None	None	None, or 1 or 2 levels	Many levels
Monopoly of force and information	No	No	No → Yes	Yes
Conflict resolution	Informal	Informal	Centralized	Laws, judges
Hierarchy of settlement	No	No	No → Paramount village or head town	Capital
ECONOMY				
Food production	No	No → Yes	Yes → Intensive	Intensive
Labor specialization	No	No	No → Yes	Yes
Exchanges	Reciprocal	Reciprocal	Redistributive (tribute)	Redistributive (taxes)
Control of land	Band	Descent group	Chief	Various
SOCIETY				
Stratified	No	No	Yes, ranked by kin	Yes, by class or caste
Slavery	No	No	Some, small-scale	Some, large-scale
Luxury goods for elite	No	No	Yes	Yes
Public architecture	No	No	No → Yes	Yes
Indigenous literacy	No	No	No → Some	Often

© Cengage Learning

Figure 22.1 Four Types of Political Systems
This figure outlines the four basic types of political systems: bands, tribes, chiefdoms, and states. Bands and tribes are uncentralized political organizations; chiefdoms and states are centralized.

targets of scorn and gossip—and may even be banished or killed.

Bands

The **band** is a relatively small and loosely organized kin-ordered group that inhabits a common territory and that may split periodically into smaller family groups that are politically and economically independent. Bands are found among food foragers and other small-scale migratory communities in which people organize into politically autonomous extended family groups that usually camp together as long as environmental and subsistence circumstances are favorable. Bands periodically break up into smaller groups to forage for food or visit other relatives. The band is the oldest form of political organization because all humans were once food foragers and remained so until the development of farming and pastoralism over the past 10,000 years.

Given their foraging mode of subsistence, band population densities are usually less than one person per square mile. Because bands are egalitarian and small, numbering at most a few hundred people, there is no real need for formal, centralized political systems. Everyone is related to—and knows on a personal basis—everyone else with whom dealings are required, so there is high value placed on getting along. Conflicts that do arise are usually settled informally through gossip, ridicule, direct negotiation, or mediation. When negotiation or mediation are used, the focus is on reaching a solution considered fair by all concerned parties, rather than on conforming to some abstract law or rule.

Decisions affecting a band are made with the participation of all its adult members, with an emphasis on achieving consensus—a collective agreement—rather than a simple majority. Individuals become leaders by virtue of their abilities and serve in that capacity only as long as they retain the confidence of the community. They have no real power to force people to abide by their decisions. A leader who tries to coerce quickly runs into resistance and loses followers.

An example of the informal nature of band leadership is found among the Ju/'hoansi Bushmen of the Kalahari Desert, mentioned in earlier chapters. Each Ju/'hoansi band is composed of a group of families that live together, linked through kinship ties to one another and to the headman (or, less often, headwoman). The head, called the *kxau*, or "owner," is the focal point for the band's claims on the waterholes in the territory through which it traditionally ranges as a migratory community (Figure 22.2). He or she does not personally own the waterholes and surrounding lands but symbolically represents the ancestral rights of band members to them. If the head leaves the area to live elsewhere, people turn to someone else to lead them.

Documentary Educational Resources

Figure 22.2 Band Leadership
Toma Tsamkxao was the headman of a Ju/'hoansi band. Lightly armed, he led his migratory community of hunters and gatherers in the Kalahari Desert. They ranged the region freely much as their ancestors did for almost 40,000 years. About half a century ago, outsiders imposed radical changes on Bushmen bands. Some, guided by wise leaders like Tsamkxao, survived the upheaval and now subsist on a mix of livestock and crop farming, crafts and tourism, and some traditional foraging.

When local resources are no longer adequate to sustain a band, the leader coordinates and leads the move, selecting the new campsite. Except for the privilege of having first choice of a spot for his or her own fire, the leader of the band has few unique rewards or duties. For example, a Ju/'hoansi head is not a judge and does not punish other band members. Troublemakers and wrongdoers are judged and held accountable by public opinion, usually expressed by gossip, which can play an important role in curbing socially unacceptable behavior.

Through gossip—talking behind someone's back and spreading rumors about behavior considered disruptive, shameful, or ridiculous—people accomplish several objectives while avoiding the potential disruption of open confrontation. First, gossip underscores and reinforces the cultural standards of those who abide by the unwritten rules of proper conduct. At the same time, the gossip discredits those who violate standards of socially acceptable

political organization The way power, as the capacity to do something, is accumulated, arranged, executed, and structurally embedded in society; the means through which a society creates and maintains social order and reduces social disorder.

band A relatively small and loosely organized kin-ordered group that inhabits a specific territory and that may split periodically into smaller extended family groups that are politically and economically independent.

behavior. Furthermore, because gossip can damage a person's reputation and is often fueled by hidden jealousy or a secret desire to retaliate against someone considered too accomplished or successful, it may function as a leveling mechanism to reduce a real or perceived threat of an individual becoming too dominant.

Another prime technique in small-scale societies for resolving disputes, or even avoiding them in the first place, is *fission*, meaning that anyone unable to get along with others of their group may feel pressured to split off and move to a different group in which existing kinship ties give them rights of entry.

Tribes

The second type of uncentralized authority system is the tribe. In anthropology, the term **tribe** refers to a wide range of kin-ordered groups that are politically integrated by some unifying factor and whose members share a common ancestry, identity, culture, language, and territory.

Typically, a tribe has an economy based on some form of crop cultivation or livestock raising. Tribes develop when a number of culturally related bands come together, peacefully settle disputes, participate in periodic visiting and communal feasting, and intermarry for purposes of economic exchange and/or collective self-defense against common enemies. For this reason, tribal membership is usually larger than band membership. Moreover, tribal population densities generally far exceed that of migratory bands and may be as high as 100 people per square kilometer (250 people per square mile). Greater population density introduces a new set of problems, as opportunities for bickering, begging, adultery, and theft increase markedly, especially among people living in permanent villages.

Each tribe consists of one or more self-supporting and self-governing local communities (including bands) that may then form alliances with others for various purposes. As in the band, political organization in the tribe is often informal and temporary. Whenever a situation arises requiring political integration of all or several groups within the tribe—perhaps for defense, to carry out a raid, to pool resources in times of scarcity, or to capitalize on a windfall that must be distributed quickly lest it spoil—groups come together to deal with the situation in a cooperative manner. When the problem is satisfactorily solved, each group then resumes autonomy.

In many tribal societies, the organizing unit and seat of political authority is the clan, composed of people who claim descent from a common ancestor. Within the clan, elders or headmen and/or headwomen regulate members' affairs and represent their clan in interactions with other clans. The elders of all the clans may form a council that

acts within the community or for the community in dealings with outsiders. Because clan members usually do not all live together in a single local community, clan organization facilitates joint action with members of related communities when necessary.

Leadership in tribal societies is relatively informal. The Big Man common in Melanesian cultures in the South Pacific illustrates this. Heading up localized descent groups or a territorial group, such a leader combines a measure of interest in his community's welfare with a great deal of cunning and calculation for his own personal gain. His power is personal, for the Big Man holds no political office in any formal sense, nor is he elected. His prestige as a political leader is the result of strategic acts that raise him above most other tribe members and attract loyal followers who benefit from or depend on his success.

The Kapauku in the west central highlands of New Guinea typify this form of political organization. Among them, the Big Man is called the *tonowi* ("rich one"). To achieve this status, one must be male, wealthy, generous, and eloquent. Physical bravery and an ability to deal with the supernatural are also common *tonowi* characteristics, but they are not essential (Figure 22.3).

A Kapauku Big Man functions as the headman of the village unit in a wide variety of situations within and beyond the community. He represents his group in dealing with outsiders and other villages and acts as negotiator and/or judge when disputes break out among his followers. As a *tonowi*, he acquires political power by giving loans. Villagers comply with his requests because they are in his debt (often interest free), and they do not want to have to repay their loans. Those who have not yet borrowed from him may wish to do so in the future, so they, too, want to keep his goodwill. A *tonowi* who refuses to lend money to fellow villagers may be shunned, ridiculed, and, in extreme cases, even killed by a group of warriors. Such unfavorable reactions ensure that individual economic wealth is dispersed throughout the community.

A Big Man gains further support from his relatives and from taking into his household young male apprentices who receive business training along with food and shelter. He also gives them a loan that enables them to marry when the apprenticeship ends. In return, they act as messengers and bodyguards. After leaving, they remain tied to the *tonowi* by bonds of affection and gratitude.

Because a Big Man's wealth comes from his success at breeding pigs (the focus of the entire Kapauku economy, as described in the chapter on patterns of subsistence), it is not uncommon for a *tonowi* to lose his fortune rapidly

---

tribe In anthropology, the term for a range of kin-ordered groups that are politically integrated by some unifying factor and whose members share a common ancestry, identity, culture, language, and territory.

Figure 22.3 Big Man from West Papua, New Guinea
Wearing his official regalia, the *tonowi* is recognizable among
fellow Kapauku and neighboring Papua highlanders as a man of
wealth and power.

George Holton/Science Source

due to poor management or simple bad luck with his pigs.
Thus, the Kapauku political structure shifts frequently: As
one man loses wealth and consequently power, another
gains it and becomes a *tonowi*. These changes prevent any
single Big Man from holding political power for too long.

Political Integration Beyond the Kin-Group

Age sets, age grades, and common-interest groups
are among the political integration mechanisms used
by tribal societies. Cutting across territorial and kin-
groupings, these organizations link members from different lineages and clans. For example, among the Tiriki
of East Africa (as discussed in the previous chapter), the
Warrior age grade guards the village and grazing lands,
whereas Judicial Elders resolve disputes. The oldest age
grade, the Ritual Elders, advise on matters involving the
well-being of all the Tiriki people. With the tribe's political affairs in the hands of the various age grades and
their officers, this type of organization enables the largely
independent kin-groups to solve conflicts and sometimes
avoid feuding between the lineages.

The Pashtun, a large ethnic group with tribes on both
sides of the border between Afghanistan and Pakistan,
provide another example of decentralized political organization. Periodically, groups of male elders, each representing
their kinfolk, gather to deal with collective challenges. In
such a political assembly, known as a *jirga*, these Pashtun
tribal leaders make joint decisions by consensus—from settling disputes, working out treaties, and resolving trade issues
to establishing law and order in their war-torn homelands.

Centralized Political Systems

When populations grow, individuals specialize, division
of labor increases, and surplus is exchanged in expanding
trade networks, political authority may become concentrated in a single individual (the chief) or in a body of
individuals (the state). In centralized systems such as chiefdoms and states, political organization relies more heavily
on institutionalized power, authority, and even coercion.

Chiefdoms

A **chiefdom** is a politically organized territory centrally
ruled by a chief heading a kin-based society with prestige
ranking and a redistributive economy. Rank in such a hierarchical political system is determined by the closeness
of one's relationship to the chief. The position of the chief
is usually for life and often hereditary. In patrilineal societies, the title passes from a man to his younger brother,
a son, or his sister's son, but it in some cultures it may
pass to widows, sisters, or daughters. Unlike the headman
or headwoman in bands and tribes, the leader of a chiefdom is generally a true authority figure with the power to
command, settle disputes, punish, and reward. This chief
serves to maintain peace and order within and between
allied communities.

Chiefdoms have a recognized hierarchy consisting of
leaders who control major and minor subdivisions. Such an
arrangement is a chain of command, linking leaders at every
level, with each owing personal loyalty to the chief. It serves
to bind groups in the heartland to the chief's headquarters,
whether it is a large tent, wood house, or stone hall.

Chiefs usually control the economic activities of those
who fall under their political rule. Typically, chiefdoms
involve redistributive systems, and the chief has control
over surplus goods and perhaps even over the community's labor force. Thus, the chief may demand a share of the
harvested crop from farmers, which may then be redistributed throughout the domain. Similarly, manpower may
be periodically drafted to form battle groups, build fortifications, dig irrigation works, or construct ceremonial sites.

The chief may also amass a great amount of personal
wealth and pass it on to offspring. Land, cattle, and luxury
goods produced by specialists can be collected by the

chiefdom A politically organized society in which several neighboring
communities inhabiting a territory are united under a single ruler.

Figure 22.4 Traditional Trial, Kpelle Tribal Village Court
A Kpelle chief in Liberia, West Africa, listens to a dispute in his district. Settling disputes is one of several ongoing traditional tasks that fall to paramount chiefs among Kpelle people.

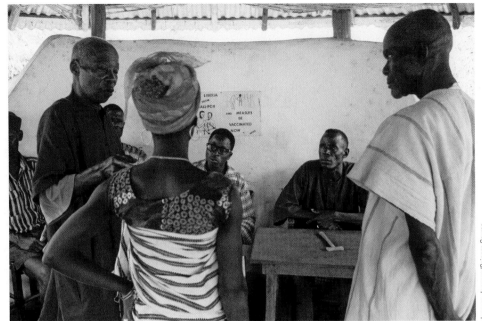

Jacques Jangoux/Science Source

chief and become part of the power base. Moreover, high-ranking families of the chiefdom may engage in the same practice and use their possessions as evidence of superior social status.

Traditionally, chiefdoms in all parts of the world have been unstable, with lesser chiefs trying to take power from higher-ranking chiefs or rival chiefs vying for supreme power as *paramount chiefs*. In precolonial Hawaii, for example, where war was the way to gain territory and maintain power, great chiefs set out to conquer each other in an effort to become paramount chief of all the islands. When one chief defeated another, the loser and all his nobles were dispossessed of property and were lucky if they escaped alive. The new paramount chief then appointed his own supporters to positions of political power.

The political distinction between a paramount chiefdom, princely state, or kingdom by whatever name cannot be sharply drawn. As an intermediary form of political organization between tribes and states, most chiefdoms, paramount chiefdoms, and kingdoms have disappeared in the course of time. However, many hundreds still exist in parts of Asia and Africa, for example—albeit no longer as politically independent or sovereign domains. In English, the title *paramount chief* is often equated with "king," a term also used to cover a range of indigenous royal titles such as *maharaja* (in Hindi), *emir* or *sultan* (in Arabic), and *fürst* (in Germanic Europe).

An example of this form of political organization may be seen among the Kpelle, the largest ethnic group in

Liberia, a pluralistic West African country inhabited by about thirty ethnic groups. Traditionally, the Kpelle are politically divided in several independent paramount chiefdoms, each comprising an alliance of smaller chiefdoms. In the 1800s, freed slaves from the United States colonized the country. Independent since 1847, and long dominated by their descendents, Liberia never became politically centralized. Paramount chiefs among the Kpelle and their neighbors retained political, administrative, and legal control of regional affairs as salaried state officials, mediating between the inhabitants in their districts (traditional chiefdoms) and Liberia's central government (Figure 22.4).

© Cengage Learning

States

The **state** is a political institution established to manage and defend a complex, socially stratified society occupying a defined territory. The most formal of political systems, it is organized and directed by a government that has the capacity and authority to manage and tax its subjects, make laws and maintain order, and use military force to defend or expand its territories. Two of the smallest states today measure less than 2.5 square kilometers (1 square mile), whereas the largest covers about 17 million square kilometers (6.6 million square miles).

state A political institution established to manage and defend a complex, socially stratified society occupying a defined territory.

Often states are ruled by coalitions of well-connected and wealthy individuals or groups that have accumulated and fought over power. Possessing the resources (including money, weapons, and manpower), these ruling elites exercise power through institutions, such as a government and its bureaucracy, which allow them to arrange and rearrange a society's social and economic order.

A large population in a state-organized society requires increased food production and wider distribution networks. Together, these lead to a transformation of the landscape by way of irrigation and terracing, carefully managed crop rotation cycles, intensive competition for clearly demarcated lands and roads, and enough farmers and other rural workers to support market systems and a specialized urban sector.

Under such conditions, corporate groups that stress exclusive membership multiply rapidly, ethnic differentiation and ethnocentrism become more pronounced, and the potential for social conflict increases dramatically. Given these circumstances, state institutions—which minimally involve a bureaucracy, a military, and (often) an official religion—provide the means for numerous and diverse groups to function together as an integrated whole.

An important aspect of the state is its delegation of authority to maintain order within and outside its borders. Police, foreign ministries, war ministries, and other bureaucracies function to control and punish disruptive acts of crime, dissension, and rebellion. By such agencies the state asserts authority impersonally and in a consistent, predictable manner.

States first began to emerge over 5,000 years ago. Often unstable, many have disappeared in the course of time, some temporarily and others forever. Some were annexed by other states, and others collapsed or fragmented into smaller political units. Although some present-day states are very old—such as Japan, which has endured as a state for almost 1,500 years—few are older than the United States, an independent country since 1783.

A key distinction to make at this point is between state and nation. A **nation** is a people who share a collective identity based on a common culture, language, territorial base, and history (Clay, 1996). Today, there are roughly 5,000 nations (including tribes and ethnic groups) throughout the world, many of which have existed since before recorded history. By contrast, there are almost 200 independent states in the world today, most of which did not exist before the end of World War II (1945).

As these numbers imply, nation and state do not always coincide, as they do, for example, in Iceland, Japan, and Swaziland. In fact, about 75 percent of the world's states are *pluralistic societies*, defined in an earlier chapter as societies in which two or more ethnic groups

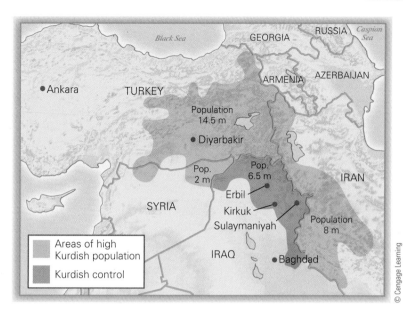

Figure 22.5 The Kurdish Nation Across State Borders
The Kurds—most of whom live in Turkey, Iran, Iraq, and Syria—are an example of a nation without a state. This map indicates their politically divided ancestral homeland (Kurdistan), where the majority of Kurds remain and notes their population in the adjoining states where their numbers are highest. Kurds also live outside the demarcated areas. About 60,000, mainly Yazidis, reside in Armenia and Azerbaijan. Many others are dispersed in a global diaspora: Some 750,000 have moved to Germany; 150,000 to France; 80,000 to Sweden; and 75,000 to Lebanon. Thousands more have migrated elsewhere in the world.

or nationalities are politically organized into one territorial state but maintain their cultural differences. Typically, smaller nations (including tribes) and other groups find themselves at the mercy of one or more powerful nations or ethnic groups gaining political control over the state.

Frequently facing discrimination or repression, some minority nations seek to improve their political position by seceding and founding an independent state. So it is with the Kurds, an Iranian-speaking Sunni Muslim nation whose ancestral homeland of about 200,000 square kilometers (77,000 square miles) has been subdivided among the modern states of Turkey, Syria, Iraq, and Iran. With a population of about 35 million, they are much more numerous than Australians, for example. In fact, the total population of the four Scandinavian countries—Denmark, Finland, Norway, and Sweden—is less than that of the Kurds. For decades, they have been fighting for their independence. As a result of the civil wars in Iraq and Syria, where the centralized power of the state has weakened, Kurds have gained political autonomy in regions internationally still considered part of these two failing states (**Figure 22.5** and **Figure 22.6**).

---

nation A people who share a collective identity based on a common culture, language, territorial base, and history.

© Eddie Gerald/Alamy Stock Photo

Figure 22.6 Kurdish Fighters Struggling for Independence
For decades, the Kurds have been fighting for political independence in their ancestral homeland. Here we see female guerrilla combatants of the PKK (Kurdistan Workers' Party) in the Qandil Mountains, near the Iranian border of northern Iraq.

Political Systems and the Question of Authority

Whatever a society's political system, it must find some way to obtain and retain the people's allegiance. In uncentralized systems, in which every adult participates in all decision making, loyalty and cooperation are freely given because each person is considered a part of the political system. However, as the group grows larger and the organization becomes more formal, the problem of obtaining and keeping public support becomes greater.

Centralized political systems may rely upon **coercion** as a means of social control, imposing obedience or submission by force or intimidation. This, however, can be risky because the large numbers of personnel needed to apply force may themselves become a political power. Also, the emphasis on force may create resentment and lessen cooperation. Thus, hardfisted regimes such as dictatorships are generally short-lived; most societies choose less extreme forms of social coercion. In the United States, this is reflected in the increasing emphasis placed on *cultural* controls, discussed later in this chapter. Laura Nader (see the Anthropologist of Note) is well known for

her anthropological research concerning issues of power, including cultural control.

Also basic to the political process is the concept of **authority**, claiming and exercising power as justified by law or custom of tradition. Unlike coercion, which imposes obedience or submission by force or intimidation, authority is based on the socially accepted rules, collective ideas, or codified laws binding people together as a society. Without these rules, ideologies, and laws, however different in each culture, political rule lacks *legitimacy* and will be interpreted and perhaps openly challenged as unjust and wrong, opening the door to forced removal.

In a *monarchy*—a state headed by a single ruler—political authority can be based on different sources of legitimacy, including divine will, birthright in a royal lineage, or an election held among free citizens or a wealthy upper class (nobles). In a *theocracy*—a state ruled by a priestly elite headed by a supreme priest claiming holy or even divine status—legitimacy is embedded in sacred doctrine. In an *aristocracy*, on the other hand, the ruling noble elite claims legitimacy traditionally rooted in a ritual mixture of high-status ancestry and class endogamy, military dominance, economic wealth, and ceremonial capital.

Finally, in a *democracy* rulers claim legitimacy based on the idea that they act as representatives of the free citizens who elected them into office with the mandate to act on the basis of collectively approved rules in the form of law. A democracy may have a king or queen as symbolic head. With an elected president as titular head, such a state is usually identified as a *republic*.

Politics and Religion

Frequently, religion legitimizes the political order and leadership. Religious beliefs may influence or provide authoritative approval to customary rules and laws. For instance, acts that people believe to be sinful, such as murder, are often illegal as well.

In both industrial and nonindustrial societies, belief in the supernatural is important and is reflected in people's political institutions. Politics and religion mesh in many countries, including the United States where the newly elected president takes the oath of office by swearing on a Bible, the holy book of Christianity. Other instances of the use of religion to legitimize political power in the

---

coercion Imposition of obedience or submission by force or intimidation.
authority Claiming and exercising power as justified by law or custom of tradition.

ANTHROPOLOGIST OF NOTE

Laura Nader (b. 1930)

Courtesy of Dr. Laura Nader

Laura Nader, a cultural anthropology professor at the University of California, Berkeley, specializes in law, dispute resolution, and controlling processes.

Laura Nader has stood out among her peers from the start of her career in 1960, when she became the first woman faculty member in the Anthropology Department at the University of California, Berkeley.

Nader and her three siblings grew up in Winsted, Connecticut, children of immigrants from Lebanon. As she recalls, "My dad left Lebanon for political reasons, and when he came to the land of the free, he took it seriously. So we were raised to believe that you should be involved in public issues."[a] They were also taught to question assumptions.

Both Nader and her younger brother Ralph have made careers of doing this. She is an anthropologist noted for her cross-cultural research on law, justice, and social control and their connection to power structures. He is a consumer advocate and former U.S. presidential candidate who is well known for being a watchdog on issues of public health and the safety and quality of life.

Laura Nader's undergraduate studies included a study-abroad year in Mexico. Later, while earning her doctorate in anthropology at Radcliffe College, she returned to Mexico to do fieldwork in a Zapotec Indian peasant village in the Sierra Madre Mountains of Oaxaca. Reflecting on this and subsequent research, she says,

In the 1950s, when I went to southern Mexico, I was studying how the Zapotec organize their lives, what they do with their problems, what they do when they go to court. And when I came back to this country, I started looking at American equivalents, at how Americans solve their consumer and service complaints.[b]

Nader's first decade of teaching at Berkeley coincided with the Vietnam War, an era when the campus was in a perpetual state of turmoil with students demonstrating for peace and civil rights. Becoming a scholar-activist, she called upon colleagues to "study up" and do research on the world's power elite. "The study of man," she wrote in 1972, "is confronted with an unprecedented situation: Never before have a few, by their actions and inactions, had the power of life and death over so many members of the species."[c]

To date, the results of Nader's own research have appeared in over a hundred publications. Among these are her numerous books, including *Naked Science: Anthropological Inquiry into Boundaries, Power, and Knowledge* (1996), *The Life of the Law: Anthropological Projects* (2002), *Plunder: When the Rule of Law Is illegal* (coauthored with Ugo Mattei, 2008), and *Culture and Dignity: Dialogues Between the Middle East and the West* (2013).

Playing a leading role in the development of the anthropology of law, Nader has taken on specialists in the fields of law, children's issues, nuclear energy, and science (including her own profession), critically questioning the basic assumptions ("central dogmas") under which these experts operate. She presses her students to do the same—to think critically, question authority, and break free from the "controlling processes" of the power elite. In 2000, Nader accepted one of the highest honors of the American Anthropological Association—an invitation to give the distinguished lecture at its annual gathering.

Today, at age 85, Nader still teaches at Berkeley. In a recent interview she said this about the discipline she has been committed to for so many years:

For me anthropology is the freest of scientific endeavors because it potentially does not stop at boundaries that interfere with the capacity of the mind for self-reflection. This is a moment for new syntheses in a world that is both interconnected and disconnected, on a planet where long term survival is at risk. Anthropologists should not shrink from the big questions. We have a large part to play.[d]

---

[a] "Conversation with Laura Nader." (2000, November). *California Monthly.*

[b] Ibid.

[c] Nader, L. (1972). Up the anthropologist: Perspectives gained from studying up. In D. Hymes (Ed.), *Reinventing anthropology* (p. 284). New York: Pantheon Books.

[d] De Lauri, A. (2013, December 18). Think like an anthropologist: A conversation with Laura Nader. *Allegra Lab.* http://allegralaboratory.net/think-like-an-anthropologist-a-conversation-with-laura-nader/ (retrieved January 4, 2016)

United States are the phrases "one nation, under God" in the Pledge of Allegiance, "In God We Trust" etched in coins, and "so help me God," which is routinely used in legal proceedings.

Religious legitimization of government is more clearly defined in Israel, which defines itself as a Jewish state.

There, two chief *rabbis* (Jewish priests) alternate as president of the country's Chief Rabbinate. Recognized as the supreme authority for Judaism in that country, it claims jurisdiction over many aspects of Jewish life and supervises rabbinical courts. Managed by the Ministry of Religious Services, the Chief Rabbinate court is part of

VISUAL COUNTERPOINT

Figure 22.7 Church and State in Iran and Great Britain
In contrast to countries such as the United States, where religion and state are constitutionally separated, countries such as Iran and Great Britain permit a much closer relationship between political and religious affairs. For instance, since 1989, a grand ayatollah named Ali Khamenei has held the title of Supreme Leader of the Islamic Republic of Iran, serving as the country's highest-ranking religious and political authority. In England, Queen Elizabeth is not only her country's nominal head of state but also the Supreme Governor of the Church of England, which entitles her to appoint the Anglican bishops in that state.

Israel's judicial system, and its verdicts are carried out and enforced by the police.

Another example of religious legitimization of government is seen in Kano in the savannahs of northern Nigeria, where the emir governs a traditional kingdom inhabited by the Hausa and Fulani ethnic groups. The emir rules by Shariah, a moral and legal code based on what traditional Muslims accept as God's infallible law. In an annual festival marking the end of the Muslim holy month of Ramadan, regional chiefs heading cavalry regiments showcase their horsemanship at a military parade in a public display of loyalty to their ruler.

Since 1979, when the Islamic revolution toppled the dictatorship of the *shah* ("emperor") in Iran, that country has been a theocratic republic, with a democratically elected president and parliament subordinate to the supreme religious authority of the most holy of all Shia Muslim holy men—the *grand ayatollah*. Numerous other examples in which political and religious institutions are intricately intertwined can be found across the globe (Figure 22.7).

Politics and Gender

Historically, irrespective of cultural configuration or type of political organization, women have held important positions of political leadership far less often than men. But there have been many significant exceptions, including some female chiefs heading American Indian chiefdoms in the Caribbean and southeastern United States. Traditionally, there were also female rulers of Polynesian chiefdoms and kingdoms in the Pacific, including Tonga, Samoa, and Hawaii. Moreover, there were numerous powerful queens heading monarchies and even empires in Asia, Africa, and Europe during the past few thousand years (Linnekin, 1990; Ralston & Thomas, 1987; Trocolli, 2006).

Perhaps the most notable example among historical female rulers was Queen Victoria, the long-reigning queen of England, Scotland, Wales, and Ireland. Also recognized as monarch in a host of colonies all over the world, Victoria even acquired the title Empress of India. Ruling the British empire for nearly sixty-four years

(1837–1901), she was perhaps the world's wealthiest and most powerful leader. In 2015, Victoria's great-great-granddaughter Queen Elizabeth II surpassed the duration of her reign. Crowned ruler of England and Scotland, Elizabeth is also the symbolic head of the Commonwealth, an intergovernmental organization of fifty-four independent states (almost all former British colonies), collectively promoting free trade, rule of law, human rights, and world peace.

High-profile female leadership is becoming more common, and in most contemporary societies women have gained the same political rights and opportunities as men. In recent years, a growing number of women have been elected as their country's presidents, chancellors, or prime ministers across the globe. Others lead political opposition parties, sometimes heading mass movements. Among the latter is Aung San Suu Kyi in Myanmar, profiled toward the end of this chapter.

Although there have been and continue to be many societies in which women have lower visibility in the political arena, that does not necessarily indicate that they lack power in political affairs. For example, among the six allied Iroquois Indian nations in northeastern America, only men were appointed to serve as high-ranking chiefs on the confederacy's grand council; however, they were completely beholden to women, for only their "clan mothers" could select candidates to this high political office. Moreover, women actively lobbied the men on the council, and the clan mothers had the right to depose a chief representing their clan whenever it suited them.

As for women having more visible roles in traditional societies, one example is the dual-gender government system of the Igbo in Nigeria, West Africa. Among the Igbo, each political unit traditionally had separate political institutions for men and women, so that both genders had an autonomous sphere of authority as well as an area of shared responsibility (Njoku, 1990; Okonjo,  1976). At the head of each political unit was a male *obi*, considered the head of government although he presided over only the male community, and a female *omu*, the acknowledged mother of the whole community but in practice concerned with the female section. Unlike a queen (though both she and the *obi* were crowned), the *omu* was neither the *obi*'s wife nor the previous *obi*'s daughter.

Just as the *obi* had a council of dignitaries to advise him and act as a check against any arbitrary exercise of power, a council of women served the *omu*. The duties of the *omu* and her advisors involved tasks such as establishing rules and regulations for the community market (marketing was a woman's activity) and hearing cases involving women brought to her from throughout the town or village. If such cases also involved men, then she and her council would cooperate with the *obi* and his council.

In the Igbo system, women managed their own affairs. They had the right to enforce their decisions and rules with sanctions similar to those employed by men, including strikes, boycotts, and "sitting on" someone, including a man:

> To "sit on" or "make war on" a man involved gathering at his compound, sometimes late at night, dancing, singing scurrilous songs which detailed the women's grievances against him and often called his manhood into question, banging on his hut with the pestles women used for pounding yams, and perhaps demolishing his hut or plastering it with mud and roughing him up a bit. A man might be sanctioned in this way for mistreating his wife, for violating the women's market rules, or for letting his cows eat the women's crops. The women would stay at his hut throughout the day, and late into the night if necessary, until he repented and promised to mend his ways. (Van Allen, 1997, p. 450)

Cultural Controls in Maintaining Order

Every society has **cultural controls**—means of ensuring that individuals or groups conduct themselves in ways that support the social order. We may distinguish between internal and external forms of cultural control.

Internalized Control

As discussed in an earlier chapter, individuals raised in a particular culture undergo a process of enculturation during which ideas, values, and associated structures of emotion are internalized, impacting their thoughts, feelings, and behavior. The internalization of cultural control leads to what we know as *self-control*—a person's capacity to manage his or her spontaneous feelings and to restrain impulsive behavior.

cultural control Control through beliefs and values deeply internalized in the minds of individuals.

Self-control may be motivated by ideas or emotions associated with positive cultural values such as self-denial for the common good. For example, many cultures honor traditions of charity, self-sacrifice, or other good deeds. Performed out of a desire to help those in need, such acts of kindness or generosity may spring from a spiritual or religious **worldview**—the collective body of ideas members of a culture generally share concerning the ultimate shape and substance of their reality.

Self-control may also be motivated by negative ideas and associated emotions such as shame, guilt, fear of bad luck or evil spirits, or terror of divine punishment—concepts that are culturally relative and variable. For example, Wape hunters in Papua New Guinea believe that their ancestral spirits roam the woods and will sabotage any hunter who has wronged them or their descendants by preventing him from finding game or hitting his mark. Like devout Christians who avoid sinning for fear of hell, Wape hunters avoid quarrels and maintain tranquility within the community for fear of supernatural punishment, even though no one in their village may be aware of their bad deed.

Externalized Control

Because internalized controls are not wholly sufficient even in bands and tribes, every society develops externalized **social controls**. One type of such control is known as a **sanction**—a social directive designed to encourage or coerce conformity to cultural standards of acceptable social behavior.

Sanctions may be positive or negative. Positive sanctions consist of incentives to conform, such as awards, titles, promotions, and other demonstrations of approval. Negative sanctions consist of threats such as ridiculing, humiliating, fining, flogging, banishing, jailing, and even killing for violating the standards.

Furthermore, sanctions may be formal or informal, depending on whether or not a customary law or legal statute is involved. In the United States, a man who goes shirtless to a church service may be subject to a variety of informal sanctions, ranging from disapproving glances from the clergy to the chuckling of other parishioners. If, however, he were to show up without any clothing at all, he would be subject to the formal negative sanction of arrest for indecent exposure. Only in the second instance

would he have been guilty of breaking the **law**—formal rules of conduct that, when violated, effectuate negative sanctions.

For sanctions to be effective, they must be applied consistently, and they must be generally known among members of the society. Even if some individuals are not convinced of the advantages of social conformity, they are still more likely to obey society's rules than to accept the consequences of not doing so.

Cultural Control: Witchcraft

In societies with or without centralized political systems, witchcraft sometimes functions as an agent of cultural control and involves both self-control and social controls. An individual will think twice before offending a neighbor if convinced that the neighbor could retaliate by resorting to black magic. Similarly, individuals may not wish to be accused of practicing witchcraft, and so they behave with greater circumspection (Figure 22.8).

Tied to adversity—bad harvests, sickness, death—accusations of sorcery or witchcraft ("black magic") are typically directed at low status or marginal persons. Often, older women and widows are targeted, especially in male-dominated villages in the rural backlands of rapidly changing societies. Charged with causing misfortune by casting evil spells, they are viewed a threats to the moral order.

Among the Azande of South Sudan, people who think they have been bewitched may consult an oracle, who, after performing the appropriate mystical rites, may establish or confirm the identity of the offending witch (Evans-Pritchard, 1937; Films Media Group, 1981). Confronted with this evidence, the witch will usually agree to cooperate in order to avoid any additional trouble. Should the victim die, the relatives of the deceased may choose to make magic against the witch, ultimately accepting the death of some villager as evidence of both guilt and the efficacy of their magic.

For the Azande, witchcraft provides not only a sanction against antisocial behavior but also a means of dealing with natural hostilities and death. No one wishes to be thought of as a witch, and surely no one wishes to be victimized by one. By institutionalizing their emotional responses, the Azande successfully maintain social order.

Today, witch hunts are on the rise in many parts of sub-Saharan Africa, but also in Papua New Guinea, northeast India, Nepal, and other parts of the world. In the past fifteen years, about 2,500 accused witches in India have been murdered—commonly being tortured into a confession and then being burned alive or butchered with knives, axes, or stones (McCoy, 2014; United Nations Human Rights, 2009).

---

worldview The collective body of ideas members of a culture generally share concerning the ultimate shape and substance of their reality.

social control External control through open coercion.

sanction An externalized social control designed to encourage conformity to social norms.

law Formal rules of conduct that, when violated, effectuate negative sanctions.

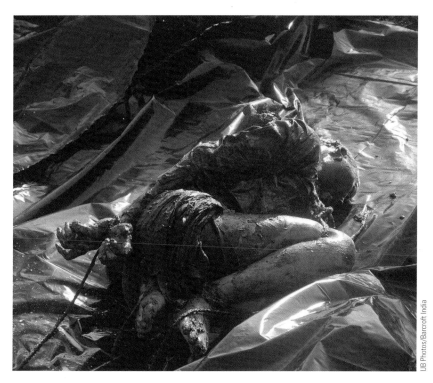

UB Photos/Barcroft India

Figure 22.8 Witch-Hunting in the 21st Century
In many parts of the world today—including regions in Africa, South Asia, and
Melanesia—people are accused of being witches. The targets can be men and even
children, but most often they are women, especially those who are widowed and
poor, or outspoken and seen as a threat to a male-dominated social order. Their
cases are remarkably similar: Sickness, death, or some other misfortune strikes their
community, and these individuals are blamed, punished, banished, driven to suicide,
or even killed. The woman pictured here, brutally murdered and buried in a rice paddy
field, was a victim of witch-hunting in India's state of Assam. Her tragic case is not
unusual. Every year since 1995, 150 to 200 women accused of witchcraft have been
killed in India. Beyond witch hunts prompted by escalating tension, marking women as
witches has become a common ploy to grab land, settle scores and grudges, or mete
out punishment for rejected sexual advances. Witch-hunters are rarely reported to
authorities, and of those who are, barely 2 percent are convicted (Sharma, 2012).

Holding Trials, Settling Disputes, and Punishing Crimes

State societies make a clear distinction between offenses
against an individual and those against the state. In non-
state societies such as bands and tribes, however, all
offenses are viewed as transgressions against individuals or
kin-groups (families, clans, and so on). Disputes between
individuals or kin-groups may seriously disrupt the social
order, especially in small communities where the dispu-
tants, though small in absolute numbers, may represent a
large percentage of the total population.

Among traditional Inuit bands in northern Canada, for
example, there is no effective domestic or economic unit
beyond the family. A dispute between
two people will interfere with the ability
of members of separate families to come
to one another's aid when necessary and
is consequently a matter of wider social
concern. By collectively evaluating the
situation and determining who is right
or wrong, community members focus
on restoring social harmony rather than
punishing offenders. Without binding
legal authority, they customarily settle a
dispute through a *song duel* in which the
individuals insult each other with songs
specially composed for the occasion. The
audience is the jury, and their applause
settles the conflict. If, however, social
harmony cannot be restored—and that is
the goal, rather than assigning and punishing guilt—one or the other disputant
may move to another band (**Figure 22.9**).

By contrast, in most modern state
societies someone who commits an offense against another person may become
subject to a series of complex legal proceedings. In criminal cases the primary
concern is to assign and punish guilt
rather than to help out the victim. The
offender will be arrested by the police;
tried before a judge and perhaps a jury;
and, depending on the severity of the
crime, may be fined, imprisoned, or even
executed. Rarely does the victim receive
restitution or compensation. Throughout
this chain of events, the accused party is
dealt with by police, judges, jurors, and
jailers, who typically have no personal ac-
quaintance whatsoever with the plaintiff
or the defendant. The judge's work is dif-
ficult and complex. In addition to sifting through evidence
presented in a courtroom trial, he or she must consider a
wide range of norms, values, and earlier rulings to arrive at
a decision that is considered just, not only by the disputing
parties but by the public and other judges as well.

In many chiefdoms, incorruptible supernatural, or at
least nonhuman, powers are thought to make judgments
through a *trial by ordeal*. For example, among the Kpelle
of Liberia discussed earlier in this chapter, when guilt is in
doubt, a licensed "ordeal operator" may apply a hot knife
to a suspect's leg. If the leg is burned, the suspect is guilty;
if not, innocence is assumed. But the operator does not
merely heat the knife and apply it. After massaging the
suspect's legs and determining the knife is hot enough,
the operator then strokes his own leg with it without being burned, demonstrating that the innocent will escape
injury. The knife is then applied to the suspect.

Flicker Alley LCC

Figure 22.9 Inuit Song Duel
Among Inuit of northern Canada, the traditional way of settling a dispute in the community is through a song duel, in which the individuals insult each other in songs composed for the occasion. The applause of onlookers determines the winner, and the affair is considered closed; no further action is expected.

Up to this point—consciously or unconsciously—the operator has read the suspect's nonverbal cues: gestures, the degree of muscular tension, amount of perspiration. From this the operator can judge whether the anxiety exhibited by the accused indicates probable guilt; in effect, a psychological stress evaluation has been made. As the knife is applied, it is manipulated to either burn or not burn the suspect, once this judgment has been made. The operator does this manipulation easily by controlling how long the knife is in the fire, as well as the pressure and angle at which it is pressed against the leg (Gibbs, 1983).

The use of the lie detector (polygraph) in the United States is a similar example of assessing guilt, although the guiding ideology is scientifically grounded rather than metaphysical. This machine is thought to establish objectively who is lying and who is not, but in reality the polygraph operator cannot just "read" the needles of the machine. He or she must judge whether they are registering a high level of anxiety brought on by the testing situation, as opposed to the stress of guilt. Thus, the polygraph operator has something in common with the Kpelle ordeal operator.

Punitive justice, such as flogging or jailing, may be the most common approach to justice in state societies, but it has not proven to be an effective way of changing criminal behavior. In North America over the past four decades, there has been significant movement away from the courts in favor of outside negotiation and mediation. For example, indigenous communities in Canada have successfully

urged their federal government to reform justice services to make them more consistent with indigenous values and traditions (Criminal Code of Canada, §718.2e). In particular, they have pressed for restorative justice techniques such as the Talking Circle. For this, parties involved in a conflict come together in a circle with equal opportunity to express their views—one at a time, free of interruption. Usually, a "talking stick" (or an eagle feather or some other symbolic object) is held by whoever is speaking to signal that she or he has the right to talk at that moment, and others have the responsibility to listen.

Violent Conflict and Warfare

Regulation of a society's internal affairs is an important function of any political system, but it is by no means the sole function. Another is the management of its external affairs—relations not just among different states but among different bands, lineages, clans, or whatever the largest autonomous political unit may be. And just as force, threatened or actual, may be used to maintain or restore order within a society, such powerful pressures are also used in the conduct of external affairs.

Humans have a grim track record when it comes to violence. Far more lethal than spontaneous and individual outbursts of aggression, organized violence in the form of war is responsible for enormous destruction of life and property. In the past 5,000 years or so, some 14,000 wars have been fought, resulting in many hundreds of millions of casualties. In the 20th century alone, an estimated 150 million people lost their lives due to human violence.

The scope of violent conflict is wide. It ranges from individual fights, local feuds, raids, and piracy (see the Globalscape), to rebellions, insurgencies, guerrilla attacks, and formally declared wars fought by professional armed forces.

Why War?

Different motives, strategic objectives, and political or moral justifications for war exist. Some societies engage in defensive wars only and avoid armed confrontations with others unless seriously threatened or actually attacked. Others initiate aggressive wars to pursue particular strategic goals, including material benefits in the form of precious resources such as oil, as well as territorial expansion or control over trade routes. Competition for scarce resources may turn violent and lead to war, but aggressive wars may also be waged for ideological reasons, such as spreading one's worldview or religion and defeating "evil" and "wrongdoers" elsewhere.

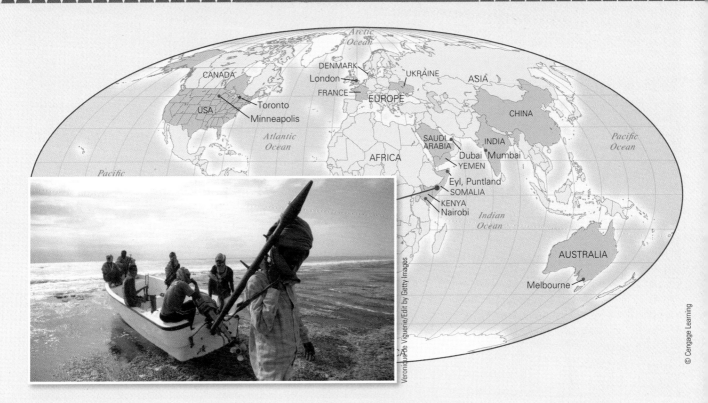

Veronique De Viguerie/Edit by Getty Images

© Cengage Learning

Pirate Pursuits in Puntland?

Abshir Boya, a towering Somali pirate, is active in the coastal waters off the Horn of Africa, which juts deep into the Arabian Sea. He lives in the old fishing port of Eyl in Puntland, an autonomous territory in Somalia. By 2009, Eyl had become a pirate haven, holding a dozen hijacked foreign ships and their multinational crews.

Like Boya, most of the few hundred other pirates based in Puntland are Darod clansmen pressed out of their traditional fisheries by foreign commercial fleets polluting their coasts and depleting their fish stocks. Since 1991, Somalia has been splintered by rebellions, clan rivalries, and armed foreign interventions. It no longer has a centralized power system maintaining law and order for its citizens, who survive on an average annual income of $600. With a national economy in tatters, Boya and his clansmen spied the wealth passing through the Arabian Sea and decided to grab a share.

Bankrolled by emigrated Somali investors living in cities such as Melbourne, Dubai, Nairobi, London, Toronto, and Minneapolis, pirate gangs are equipped with radios, cell phones, and GPS, plus semi-automatic pistols, assault rifles, and rocket-propelled grenade launchers, often bought in Yemen. Speeding across open sea in skiffs, they chase cargo ships, oil tankers, and cruise ships from around the world, including the United States, Canada, Denmark, France, Saudi Arabia, India, and China.

Some pirate captains have banked success, including Boya, who claims to have led over twenty-five hijackings. Ship owners pay huge ransoms—thirty-one of them in 2011, averaging $5 million each. Somali sea bandits—about a thousand in total—are obliged to pay their backers and share earnings with many poor relatives in their large clans. Notably, ransoms represented only about 2 percent of piracy costs for shippers in 2011. Insurance companies covering the ships took in $635 million, and private armed security forces earned $530 million. About thirty countries spent a total of $1.3 billion on military operations. These and numerous other antipiracy expenses totaled nearly $7 billion.[a]

At their peak of success in 2009, Somali pirates held dozens of captured ships and nearly a thousand seamen. By mid-2012, those numbers were down to about a dozen vessels and several hundred crew, due to an increase in foreign naval patrols and prosecutions. Earlier that year, the European Union toughened its antipiracy mandate to allow forces patrolling the Indian Ocean to attack bases in Somalia. Numerous Somali pirates have been killed or captured. Nonetheless, piracy continues; there is still no international consensus on how to handle it, so there are still ransoms to be claimed by the most daring pirates.[b] Although criminal prosecution of piracy in international waters is problematic due to jurisdiction questions, many pirates are now in jails in half a dozen foreign countries, including the United States.

Global Twister

What is justice for Somali fishermen pressed into piracy?

[a] Oceans Beyond Piracy: One Earth Future Foundation. (2015). *The economic cost of Somali piracy 2011*. http://oceansbeyondpiracy .org/publications/economic-cost-somali-piracy-2011 (retrieved December 9, 2015)

[b] Anyimadu, A. (2015, July 21). With Somali pirates, pay the ransom until there's a global consensus. *New York Times*. http://www .nytimes.com/roomfordebate/2013/08/07/when-ransoms-pay -for-terrorism/with-somali-pirates-pay-the-ransom-until-theres-global -consensus (retrieved January 1, 2016)

Medyan Dairieh/ZUMA Press/Corbis

Figure 22.10 Islamic State Militants

Fighters of the self-proclaimed Islamic State, also known as Daesh (the acronym of its Arabic name), have been waging a brutal *jihad* ("holy war") to expand Sunni Muslim fundamentalism across the globe. Declaring a worldwide *caliphate*, this fanatical militant group pledges allegiance to a leader who has claimed the ancient title of *caliph*—the divinely appointed successor to the prophet Muhammad. They enforce a radical interpretation of Shariah law drawn from the Quran, a copy of which is held up by the fighter on the right side of this photo. Another *jihadist* raises his right index finger in a symbolic gesture alluding to their belief in the oneness of God, while a third holds the group's black banner, a flag flown by the Prophet in Islamic tradition. Representing the Prophet's seal, the white circle encloses the Arabic text for "Muhammad is the prophet of God." This banner is a symbol in Islamic tradition announcing the advent of the Mahdi, a spiritual leader who will rule before the end of the world and triumph over injustice. The Islamic State now holds territory in large parts of Syria and Iraq and is expanding terrorist operations.

Religious and other ideological justifications for war are rooted in a society's worldview. They range from the Christian Crusades targeting Muslims in Palestine and surrounding Islamic territories about 700 to 900 years ago to the more recent brutal *jihad* ("holy war") waged by fanatic Islamic fundamentalists in North Africa and Southwest Asia. Militant extremists, such as ad-Dawlah al-Islāmīyah (abbreviated to Daesh), often direct this modern-day Islamic fundamentalism. Better known in the English-speaking part of the world as the Islamic State (IS), this radical splinter group of al-Qaeda based in Iraq and Syria aims to restore what it believes to be "pure" Islam. Toward that end, it seeks to expel so-called infidels (nonbelievers) from ancestral soil; to topple regimes that it thinks promote or tolerate religious "corruption"; and to destroy statues, shrines, and temples dedicated to what it sees as false gods (**Figure 22.10**).

Beyond such explanations for warfare, is there something in our genetic makeup that makes it inevitable?

Some argue that males of the human species are naturally aggressive. As evidence they point to aggressive group behavior exhibited by chimpanzees in Tanzania, where researchers observed one group systematically destroy another and take over their territory. And there is ample evidence that armed conflicts in the form of deadly feuds and raids between groups of fishers, hunters, herders, and food producers have been going on for thousands of years.

However, warfare among humans is not a universal phenomenon and not an unavoidable expression of genetic predisposition for violent behavior (see this chapter's Biocultural Connection). In fact, in various parts of the world there are societies that do not practice warfare as we know it. Examples include people as diverse as the Ju/'hoansi Bushmen and Pygmy peoples of southern Africa, the Arapesh of New Guinea, and the Jain of India, as well as the Amish of North America. Moreover, among societies that do practice warfare, levels of violence may differ dramatically.

BIOCULTURAL CONNECTION

Sex, Gender, and Human Violence

At the start of the 21st century, war and violence are no longer the strictly male domains that they were in many societies in the past. War has become embedded in civilian life in many parts of the world, and it impacts the daily lives of women and children. Moreover, women now serve in the military forces of several states, although their participation in combat is often limited. Some female soldiers in the United States argue that gender should not limit their participation in combat as they consider themselves as strong, capable, and well trained as their male counterparts. Others believe that biologically based sex differences make war a particularly male domain.

Scientists have long argued that males are more suited to combat because natural selection has made them on average larger and stronger than females. Darwin first proposed this idea, known as sexual selection, in the 19th century. At that time he theorized that physical specializations in animal species—such as horns, vibrant plumage, and, in the case of humans, intelligence and tool use—demonstrate selection acting upon males to aid in the competition for mates. In these scenarios, male reproductive success is thought to be optimized through a strategy of "spreading seed"—in other words, by being sexually active with as many females as possible.

Females, on the other hand, are considered gatekeepers who optimize their reproductive success through caring for individual offspring. According to this theory of sexual selection, in species where male–male competition is high, males

will be considerably larger than females, and aggression will serve males well. In monogamous species, males and females will be of similar sizes.

Primatologist Richard Wrangham has taken the idea of sexual selection even further. In his book *Demonic Males*, he explores the idea that both male aggression and patriarchy have an evolutionary basis. He states that humans, like our close cousin the chimpanzee, are "party gang" species characterized by strong bonds among groups of males who have dominion over an expandable territory. These features "suffice to account for natural selection's ugly legacy, the tendency to look for killing opportunities when hostile neighbors meet."[a] Violence, in turn, generates a male-dominated social order: "Patriarchy comes from biology in the sense that it emerges from men's temperaments out of their evolutionarily derived efforts to control women and at the same time have solidarity with fellow males in competition against outsiders."[b] Although Wrangham allows that evolutionary forces have shaped women as well, he suggests that females' evolutionary interests cannot be met without cooperation with males.

Feminist scholars have pointed out that these scientific models are gendered in that they incorporate the norms derived from the scientists' culture. Darwin's original model of sexual selection incorporated the Victorian gender norms of the passive female and active male. Primatologist Linda Fedigan suggests that in Darwinian models women evolved in

positive directions only by a coattails process whereby females were "pulled along" toward improved biological states by virtue of the progress of the genes they shared with males.[c] Wrangham's more recent *Demonic Males* theory is similarly shaped by culture. It incorporates the dominant world order (military states) and the gender norms (aggressive males) it values. In both cases, the putatively scientific theory has created a natural basis for a series of social conventions.

This does not mean that biological differences between the sexes cannot be studied in the natural world. Instead, scientists studying sex differences must be especially sensitive to how they may project cultural beliefs onto nature. Meanwhile, the attitudes of some women soldiers continue to challenge generalizations regarding "military specialization" by gender.

Biocultural Question

All across the world, males are far more likely to serve as warriors than females and, consequently, are far more likely to lose their lives on the battlefield. Do you think that there is any structural relationship between high male combat mortality rates and polgyny as the preferred marriage type in most traditional cultures?

[a] Wrangham, R., & Peterson, D. (1996). *Demonic males* (p. 168). Boston: Houghton Mifflin.
[b] Ibid., p. 125.
[c] Fedigan, L. M. (1986). The changing role of women in models of human evolution. *Annual Review of Anthropology 15*, 25–66.

Evolution of Warfare

We have ample reason to suppose that war—not to be confused with more limited forms of deadly violence such as raids—has become a problem only in the last 10,000 years, since the invention of food-production techniques and especially since the formation of centralized states 5,000 years ago. It has reached crisis proportions in the past 200 years, with the invention of modern weaponry and increased direction of violence against civilian populations.

About a century ago, tens of thousands of soldiers on the French-German frontline in World War I experienced chemical warfare for the first time in history. Although other poison gases had been used a few years earlier, troops in the trenches in 1917 were attacked by mustard gas—a chemical poison that causes blindness, large blisters on exposed skin, and (if inhaled) bleeding and blistering in the mouth, throat, and lungs. The development of weapons of mass destruction has been horrendously effective.

Today, the chemical, biological, and nuclear weapon arsenals stockpiled by many states are sufficient to wipe out all life on the planet, many times over. Because dangerous poisons, such as the anthrax bacterium or the nerve gas Sarin, are cheap and easy to produce, non-state groups, including terrorists, also seek to acquire to them, if only to threaten to use them against more powerful opponents.

The evolution of warfare continues to be driven by new inventions in military technology, with weapons becoming increasingly complex and effective—from machine guns, supersonic jet fighters, and atomic bombs to high-energy laser beams, pilotless drones, and computer viruses. Precision killing in modern warfare, however, is an illusion as casualties among civilians far outnumber the casualty rate of soldiers (Figure 22.11).

Ideologies of Aggression

Whatever may be possible in terms of military technology, it takes ideas and motivation to turn humans into killers, and that stems from culture. As noted earlier in this chapter, justifications for war are fixed in a society's worldview. It is said that war dehumanizes others—an ideological process that usually begins with degrading opponents to a lower status as barbaric, evil, ugly, worthless, or otherwise inferior. Having thus dehumanized their adversaries, humans conjure justifications for slaughter and pillage, often raping vanquished women, mutilating enemy bodies for trophies, and turning captives into slaves.

No matter how extreme and negative the emotions may be when confronting the enemy, warriors are usually physically and mentally trained for combat. In preparing and conditioning young men (and sometimes women)

Heather Ainsworth/The New York Times/Redux

Figure 22.11 Drone Pilot Operator
From his computer console at a military command post in New York State, this U.S. Attack Wing airman remotely operates a drone aircraft in support of U.S. ground troops battling enemies in tribal territories of Afghanistan and neighboring Pakistan. Equipped with Hellfire missiles, his drone surveys the terrain with powerful cameras beaming live video via satellite. Drones can be thought of as modern versions of dangerous spirits magically directed by invisible warlords. U.S. forces have used Predator drones since 1995, targeting enemies primarily in Muslim insurgencies across western Asia and North Africa. During that same period, the entertainment industry has provided opportunities for "child soldiers" across the globe to play telewarfare video games in arcades or at home.

for the battlefield, they are indoctrinated by an ideology justifying war, which may come wrapped in magic and other metaphysics. There are all too many examples of how religious and ideological justifications for war are entrenched in a society's worldview. So-called holy wars can flare up across the religious spectrum. The following example from East Africa provides a more detailed look.

Case Study: A Christian Holy War in Uganda

Once described as the pearl of Africa, Uganda is a pluralistic country with about 34 million inhabitants divided into more than a dozen ethnic groups, including the Acholi. During the colonial period, British missionaries converted a large majority of Ugandans to Christianity.

Since gaining independence in 1962, Uganda has suffered numerous regional insurgencies, civil wars, and interethnic clashes, resulting in death or displacement for millions. During the 1981–1986 Ugandan Bush War, Acholi soldiers fought with the losing faction, suffering huge losses and humiliation.

By 1986, many Acholi Christians believed the apocalypse described in the Bible's Book of Revelation was upon them. One such Acholi was Alice Auma, a 30-year-old woman who had been married and divorced twice for being barren. Alice found inspiration in the biblical promise of a "new earth" free of suffering and death. Through a vision she believed was divine, she learned that a holy messenger had chosen her as his spirit-medium. Sometimes this powerful spirit took possession of Alice. She named him *Lakwena*—the Acholi word for "apostle" or "messenger from God"—and claimed that he commanded the heavenly force of 144,000 redeemed men described in Revelation.

In 1986, spiritually empowered by Lakwena, Alice became a *nebi* (Acholi translation for a "biblical prophet"). At séances, she gave herself over to *malaika* (Swahili for "angels"), who filled her with power to heal people diagnosed as victims of evil spirits. Gaining a reputation as a witchdoctor, she became known as Alice Lakwena. Her patients included many Acholi soldiers who believed they were possessed by *cen*—the polluting spirits of killed enemies seeking revenge. To keep their soul and body clean, Alice ordered them to abstain from alcohol and sex.

Feeling divinely directed to liberate her homeland from evil and found a Christian theocracy based on the Ten Commandments, Alice recruited 8,000 Acholi and other northern warriors for a crusade to free Uganda from all enemies of God. She called her militant cult the Holy Spirit Mobile Force. In late 1987, supernaturally aided by Lakwena and his phantom army of 144,000, Alice led 7,000 of her warriors southward, aiming to capture Uganda's capital city, Kampala.

Filled with *malaika*, Alice's troops marched in cross-shaped battle formations, carrying Bibles and singing hymns. They had smeared their bodies with holy oil extracted from wild shea nuts, assured it would shield them from bullets. They were armed with rifles, plus magic sticks and stones blessed to explode when hurled at the enemy. In the first few battles, they scored victories when terrified government troops ran away. But 80 kilometers (50 miles) east of Kampala, the Holy Spirit Mobile Force was massacred, mowed down in a barrage of mortar attacks and machine-gun fire. Convinced that bullets could not pierce the purified, Alice interpreted this defeat as evidence that evil spirits had gained control over many in her own army. Abandoning the battlefield, she escaped into Kenya where she died in a refugee camp twenty years later.

Hundreds of Holy Spirit warriors who survived the ordeal joined other rebel groups, including the Lord's Resistance Army (LRA) formed by Joseph Kony, an Acholi witchdoctor. A former Roman Catholic altar boy related to Alice, Kony adopted some of her spiritual repertoire in founding a militant cult based on a mixture of indigenized Christian and Muslim beliefs and practices. After growing to a force of 4,000 warriors, his insurgency degenerated into a murderous campaign based on terror tactics. The LRA also kidnapped many thousands of children, indoctrinating them to become merciless fighters (Figure 22.12).

By 2006, LRA troops had dwindled to about 600, and the Uganda army had forced them across the border into the Democratic Republic of Congo. The rebels hid out in Garamba National Park—a vast wilderness inhabited by elephants, giraffes, hippos, rare white rhinoceroses, and many other animals.

Since then and despite peace talk efforts, Kony's soldiers continue to carry out periodic raids. For instance, in a June 2008 foray into South Sudan, they forcibly added some 1,000 new recruits, including hundreds of abducted children. In air and ground military offensives throughout the following six months, Ugandan soldiers attacked rebel camps in the Garamba forest, killing more than 150 LRA troops, capturing another 50 (including several low-level commanders), and rescuing many of the kidnapped children and other forced recruits. The LRA retaliated with killing raids, capturing replacement recruits, including more children.

In the past few years, nearly half a million people have fled their villages for fear of attack—not only in the

Figure 22.12 Young Acholi Soldier in the Lord's Resistance Army
After Alice Lakwena's crusade ended in a bloodbath, her relative Joseph Kony adopted some of her ideas, forming the Lord's Resistance Army (LRA). Unlike Alice, he often forced children into service. In 2006 he and his fighters, including the armed teenager pictured here, retreated into the Democratic Republic of Congo's vast Garamba National Park and staged raids from there. Wanted for war crimes and accused of being a demon, Kony remains in hiding.

Democratic Republic of Congo, but also in neighboring South Sudan and the Central African Republic. Kony, the rebel army's charismatic Christian cult leader, remains at large, still believing in his divinely guided insurgency (Allen, 2006; Behrend, 1999; Finnström, 2008).

Genocide

As these cross-cultural examples of violent conflict indicate, warfare often involves a complex dynamic of economic, political, and ideological interests. This is especially true when violence escalates into **genocide**—the physical extermination of one people by another, either as

genocide The physical extermination of one people by another, either as a deliberate act or as the accidental outcome of activities carried out by one people with little regard for their impact on others.

a deliberate act or as the accidental outcome of activities carried out by one people with little regard for their impact on others. All genocides contain eight recognizable stages: classification, symbolization, dehumanization, organization, polarization, preparation, extermination, and denial (Stanton, 1998).

The most widely known act of genocide in recent history was the attempt of the Nazis during World War II to wipe out European Jews and Roma (Gypsies) in the name of racial superiority and improvement of the human species. Reference to this mass extermination as the Holocaust—as if it were unique—tends to blind us to the fact that genocide is an age-old and ongoing phenomenon, with many examples from across the globe and throughout human history. Less known are the mass killings of some 1.5 million Armenians. Historically, this large ethnic group with its own language formed a kingdom in the West Asian highlands now divided between the republics of Armenia, Iran, and Turkey. As a Christian minority, Armenians were incorporated within the Ottoman empire for centuries but were targeted for extermination or deportation in 1915. Many of those who survived the subsequent massacres in what is now Turkey fled abroad, transforming "the Armenians into one of the world's largest diaspora peoples—estimated at up to 10 million people, more than three times [the Republic of] Armenia's population" (Herszenhorn, 2015).

Among numerous more contemporary examples of genocide, government-sponsored terrorism against indigenous communities in Guatemala reached its height in the 1980s, the same decade in which Saddam Hussein's government used poison gas against the Kurdish ethnic minority in northern Iraq. In 1994, Hutus in the African country of Rwanda slaughtered about 800,000 of their Tutsi neighbors (Human Rights Watch Report, 1999). Estimates vary, but during the 20th century, as many as 83 million people may have died of genocide (White, 2003). The horrors continue in the current century, particularly in Africa and Asia, but also in other parts of the world.

Armed Conflicts Today

Since the last decade of the 20th century, several dozen wars have raged around the globe. They occur not only *between* states but primarily *within* pluralistic countries where interethnic conflicts abound and/or where the political leadership and government bureaucracy are corrupt, ineffective, or without popular support. A contemporary example is Syria, noted in this chapter's opening page. The population of this West Asian country is about 60 percent Arabs, 10 percent Kurds, and 2 percent Turkmen—all Sunni Muslims. The Alawites and Ismaili sects represent a Shia Muslim minority of 16 percent, whereas the rest are Druse (2 percent) or belong to various Christian denominations (10 percent, down from 30 percent in the 1920s). An estimated 500,000 are Palestinian refugees, and another 2 million are Iraqis who fled fighting in their homeland. Since 2011 when the Syrian civil war erupted, about 250,000 inhabitants have been killed (40 percent of whom were women and children). More than 4 million Syrians are now refugees with many seeking a new life in northwestern Europe.

Foreign military intervention is a hallmark of many long-lasting wars in regions that are strategically important or that are rich in natural resources, including the Democratic Republic of Congo, a failed state in mineral-rich Africa. There, a violent war erupted in 1998 that ultimately involved eight neighboring countries and about twenty-five armed forces. Claiming the lives of nearly 6 million people and forcing millions more to flee their home villages, this gruesome war with mass murder and mass rape is known as Africa's World War. Beyond massacres, it led to large-scale destruction of roads, bridges, and buildings, dooming survivors to an insecure existence of daily hardship.

Notably, many armies around the world recruit children. Experts estimate that some 250,000 child soldiers, many as young as 12 years old, are participating in armed conflicts around the world, especially in Africa ("Child soldiers global report 2008," 2009; "5th report on children and armed conflict in the DR Congo," 2014; see also UN News Centre, 2014).

Beyond these wars there are numerous so-called low-intensity wars involving guerrilla organizations, rebel armies, resistance movements, terrorist cells, and a host of other armed groups engaged in violent conflict with official state-controlled armed forces. Every year, confrontations result in hundreds of hot spots and violent flash points, most of which are never reported in the world's major news media.

Peacemaking

Throughout history, people have tried to prevent conflicts from escalating into violence, just as they have endeavored to end existing violence and restore peaceful relations. Thus, diplomacy and nonviolent resistance are a vital part of this chapter's discussion.

Peace Through Diplomacy

Most societies have established diplomatic procedures to resolve conflicts, and some have been more successful than others at implementing them to maintain peace. Typically, politically organized groups designate high-ranking trusted individuals to discuss a mutually acceptable agreement to secure peace. Authorized as representatives acting on behalf of their tribal elders, chief, king, or other sovereign head, these people usually carry evidence of their official status and mission as envoys or diplomats.

A formally binding agreement between two or more groups that are independent and politically self-governing (such as tribes, chiefdoms, and states) is a contract known as a **treaty**. Determining issues of war and peace and influencing the survival and well-being of multitudes, treaty making is ritually concluded with a ceremonial performance.

In different cultures across the globe, a wide range of ceremonial artifacts have been used in diplomatic protocol—such as special shell-beaded belts (*wampum*) presented by Iroquois chiefs and long-stemmed tobacco pipes smoked by Lakota leaders and numerous other Plains Indian peoples. Thus equipped, delegates participate in formal rituals brokering terms of agreement, including mutually binding rules to prevent or end conflict and live in friendship and peace. These terms so negotiated may secure rights of access or claims to tracts of disputed land, water, other natural resources, safe passage across territorial boundaries for trade or pilgrimages to sacred sites, and a host of other issues setting rules to maintain order and avoid conflict. Today, many indigenous nations who could not resist more powerful states claiming political control or ownership over their ancestral lands are appealing to international organizations for support in their struggle against repression, respect for their human rights and cultural freedom, and restoration of their political rights of self-determination in their homeland.

Politics of Nonviolent Resistance

There are other options for resolving major political conflicts besides fighting with deadly weapons or international diplomacy. In 1947, India and Pakistan gained political independence from their British colonial overlords in part due to a nonviolent resistance movement led by Mohandas Gandhi.

Born into the Vaisya caste in Gujarat, in 1869, Gandhi was the son of a high-ranking district official. In 1888, he sailed to London, where he completed his law studies. Failing to establish himself as a lawyer in India, the 23-year-old accepted a position in Johannesburg, South Africa. There, like fellow dark-skinned Indians, he experienced racist discrimination.

Making a decision to fight colonial repression and injustice, Gandhi built a movement founded on the concept of *satyagraha*, which he conceived while serving as a legal advisor for Indian traders and laborers working in British South Africa in 1906. The term is based on the Sanskrit

---

treaty A contract or formally binding agreement between two or more groups that are independent and self-governing political groups such as tribes, chiefdoms, and states.

words *satya* ("truth"), implying love, and *agraha* ("firmness"). As he described it in 1908, applying *satyagraha* to the pursuit of truth required weaning one's opponent from the error of injustice:

> by patience and sympathy. . . . And patience
> means self-suffering. So the doctrine came to mean
> vindication of truth, not by infliction of suffering on
> the opponent, but on one's own self. . . . A satyagrahi
> enjoys a degree of freedom not possible for others,
> for he becomes a truly fearless person. Once his mind
> is rid of fear, he will never agree to be another's slave.
> (Gandhi, 1999, vol. 19, p. 220, & vol. 8, p. 151)

Returning to India in 1915, Gandhi mobilized the first of many mass protests against colonial injustices applying *satyagraha* as a "weapon of the strong" that "admits no violence under any circumstance" (Gandhi, 1999).

The journey toward independence was long and full of losses for Gandhi and his *satyagrahis*, but they emerged victorious in 1947. Tragically, six months later, as Gandhi strove to maintain peace between religious factions, a Hindu extremist assassinated the 79-year-old hero.

Gandhi's triumphant example lives on. Among the many current examples of nonviolent resistance is the National League for Democracy (NLD), a popular mass movement to end the military grip on power in Myanmar, formerly known as Burma. Its founder and leader, Aung San Suu Kyi, is an Oxford University-trained political leader raised in the Buddhist tradition like most of her followers. She is the daughter of a freedom fighter who led the country to its 1947 independence from British colonial rule.

In 1988 Suu Kyi founded the National League for Democracy (NLD) as a coordinating body for nonviolent resistance. Two years later, after winning a majority of the national votes and gaining 81 percent of the seats in the Myanmar Parliament, she was placed under house arrest and isolated from the public, as well as from her husband and two children. Refusing to compromise her principles and accept exile, she endured in solitude and periodically went on hunger strikes. She became one of the world's most prominent political prisoners and was awarded the Nobel Peace Prize and many other international honors for her courageous human rights activism.

In 2011, having been confined for fifteen of the previous twenty-one years and widowed, she finally regained her freedom and resumed her public role as head of the opposition movement. Six months later, the NLD Party won most of the vacant seats in the House of Representatives, with Suu Kyi taking her long-denied seat in Myanmar Parliament. In 2015, the NLD won an absolute majority in both houses of Parliament, fortifying the democratic influence of its founder and chairperson Suu Kyi (**Figure 22.13**).

Figure 22.13 Myanmar's New Parliament
Pro-democracy leader Aung San Suu Kyi attends the first day of a new parliament session in Naypyitaw, Myanmar, on February 1, 2016. Suu Kyi's National League for Democracy now holds a majority of seats after the party's landslide victory in the November 2015 election. The previous parliament was dominated by army-backed candidates, in a country that had spent nearly five decades under military rule.

William Ury: Dispute Resolution and the Anthropologist

In an era when disputes quickly escalate into violence, conflict management is of growing importance. A world leader in this profession is U.S. anthropologist William L. Ury, an independent negotiations specialist who has wide-ranging experience working out conflicts—from family feuds to boardroom battles to ethnic wars.

In his first year at graduate school, Ury began looking for ways to apply anthropology to practical problems, including conflicts of all dimensions. He wrote a paper about the role of anthropology in peacemaking and on a whim sent it to Roger Fisher, a law professor noted for his work in negotiation and world affairs. Fisher, in turn, invited the young graduate student to coauthor a kind of how-to book for international mediators. The book they researched and wrote together turned out to have a far wider audience because it presented basic principles of negotiation that could be applied to household spats, manager–employee conflicts, or international crises. Titled *Getting to Yes: Negotiating Agreement Without Giving In*, it sold millions of copies, was translated into twenty-one languages, and earned the nickname "the negotiator's bible."

While working on *Getting to Yes*, Ury and Fisher cofounded the Program on Negotiation (PON) at Harvard Law School, pulling together an interdisciplinary group of academics interested in new approaches to and applications of the negotiation process. Today, this applied research center is a multi-university consortium that trains mediators, businesspeople, and government officials in negotiation skills. It has four key goals: (1) design, implement, and evaluate better dispute resolution practices; (2) promote collaboration among practitioners and scholars; (3) develop education programs and materials for instruction in negotiation and dispute resolution; (4) increase public awareness and understanding of successful conflict resolution efforts.

In 1982, Ury earned his doctorate in anthropology from Harvard with a dissertation titled "Talk Out or Walk Out: The Role and Control of Conflict in a Kentucky Coal Mine." Afterward, he taught for several years while maintaining a leadership role at PON. In particular, he devoted himself to PON's Global Negotiation Initiative. With former U.S. president Jimmy Carter, he cofounded the International Negotiation Network, a nongovernmental body seeking to end civil wars around the world.

Utilizing a cross-cultural perspective sharpened through years of anthropological research, Ury has specialized in ethnic and secessionist disputes, including those between white and black South Africans, Serbs and Croats, Turks and Kurds, Catholics and Protestants in Northern Ireland, and Russians and Chechens in the former Soviet Union. The Russian Parliament awarded him a Distinguished Service Medal for his work on resolving ethnic conflicts.

Among the most effective tools in Ury's applied anthropology work are the books he continues to write on dispute resolution—from his 1993 *Getting Past No* to his 2007 title, *The Power of a Positive No*. His 1999 book, *Getting to Peace: Transforming Conflict at Home, at Work, and in the World*, he examines what he calls the "third side," which is the role that the surrounding community can play in preventing, resolving, and containing destructive conflict between two parties.[a] His books have been translated into more than thirty languages.

Like others in this field, Ury aims to create a culture of negotiation in a world where adversarial, win–lose attitudes are out of step with the increasingly interdependent relations among people.[b] In writing and action, he challenges entrenched ideas that violence and war are inevitable, offering convincing evidence that human beings have as much inherent potential for cooperation and coexistence as they do for violent conflict. Certain that violence is a choice, Ury says, "Conflict is not going to end, but violence can."[c]

---

[a] Pease, T. (2000, Spring). Taking the third side. *Andover Bulletin 93* (3), 24. Ury also covers this topic in his 2010 talk for the noted TED series: http://www.ted.com/talks/william_ury

[b] See Weber, L. (2015, January 23). Your own worst enemy in a negotiation? Look in the mirror. *Wall Street Journal*. http://blogs.wsj.com/atwork/2015/01/23/your-worst-enemy-in-a-negotiation-look-in-the-mirror/ (retrieved January 4, 2016); see also the Program on Negotiation website: http://www.pon.harvard.edu/

[c] Ury, W. L. (2002, Winter). A global immune system. *Andover Bulletin 95* (2).

Throughout the world, liberation, civil rights, and pro-democracy movements have successfully applied the politics of nonviolent action in their struggles against political repression, racist discrimination, and dictatorships (Sharp, 1973, 2010; Stolberg, 2011). And some anthropologists have made significant contributions in the arena of peaceful conflict resolution, as chronicled in this chapter's Anthropology Applied feature.

As the cross-cultural examples featured in this chapter show, the political challenges of maintaining order and resolving conflicts are complex, involving economic, political, and ideological factors. Military technology has led to the launching of ever-more effective killing machines operating in factories of death. The challenge of eliminating human violence has never been greater than it is in today's world—nor has the cost of *not* finding a way to do so. Throughout history and across the globe, individuals and groups have created, adopted, and applied ways to avoid and resolve conflicts by means of nonviolence. As we will see in the next chapter, the search for peace and harmony crosses political and chronological boundaries and is among the challenges humans engage through religion and spirituality.

CHAPTER CHECKLIST

What is power, and why is it a vital issue in every society?

✓ Power is the ability of individuals or groups to impose their will upon others and make them do things even against their own wants and wishes. Ranging from persuasion to violence, power drives politics—the process of determining who gets what, when, and how.

✓ A society's political organization establishes how power is accumulated, arranged, executed, and structurally embedded in that society.

What are the different types of political organization?

✓ Political organizations, which can be uncentralized or centralized, include bands, tribes, chiefdoms, and states.

✓ The band is a relatively small (a few hundred people at most) and loosely organized kin-ordered group that inhabits a specific territory and that may split into smaller extended family groups that are politically and economically independent.

✓ Typically, bands are found among food foragers and other nomadic societies where people organize into politically autonomous family groups. Political organization in bands is democratic, and informal control is exerted by public opinion in the form of gossip and ridicule.

✓ In anthropology, a tribe is a kin-ordered group politically integrated by a unifying factor and whose members share a common ancestry, identity, culture, language, and territory. With an economy usually based on crop cultivation or herding, the tribe's population is larger than that of the band. Political organization is transitory, and leaders have no coercive means of maintaining authority.

✓ In many tribal societies, the organizing political unit is the clan, comprised of people who consider themselves descended from a common ancestor. Another type of tribal leadership is the Big Man, who builds up his wealth and political power until he must be reckoned with as a leader.

✓ As societies grow and become more complex socially, politically, and economically, leadership becomes more centralized.

✓ A chiefdom is a politically organized society in which several neighboring communities inhabiting a territory are united under a chief who heads a ranked hierarchy of people.

✓ The most centralized political organization is the state—an institution established to manage and defend a complex, socially stratified society occupying a defined territory.

✓ States are inherently unstable and transitory and differ from nations, which are communities of people who share a collective identity based on a common culture, language, territorial base, and history.

How do political organizations establish authority?

✓ Authority—claiming and exercising power as justified by law or custom of tradition—is basic to the political process. Unlike coercion, which imposes obedience by force or intimidation, authority is based on the socially accepted rules or codified laws binding people together as a society.

✓ Most governments use some measure of ideology, including religion, to legitimize political power.

✓ Historically, far fewer women than men have held important positions of political leadership, but there have been significant exceptions. Today, high-profile female leadership is increasingly common.

How do political systems maintain social order and handle misconduct, crime, and conflict within a society?

✓ There are two kinds of cultural control. Internalized or self-control is comprised of deeply ingrained sentiments about what is proper and what is not. Externalized control includes sanctions or social directives designed to encourage or coerce conformity to cultural standards of acceptable behavior.

✓ Law is formal rules of conduct that, when violated, lead to negative sanctions. In centralized political systems, this authority rests with the government and court system, whereas uncentralized societies give this authority directly to the injured party.

✓ All societies use negotiation to settle individual disputes. In negotiation, the parties to the dispute reach an agreement themselves, with or without the help of a third party. Typically, in non-state societies, efforts to resolve disputes focus on restoring social harmony. Punitive justice (such as imprisonment) stands in contrast to restorative justice.

Why war and how did it evolve?

✓ Violent conflict—ranging from individual fights to local feuds to formally declared international wars fought by professional armed forces—may be waged over scarce resources, territorial expansion, or ideology.

✓ War, a rather recent phenomenon, became prominent as populations grew in the wake of the Neolithic revolution. In the past 5,000 years, humans have fought some 14,000 wars resulting in many hundreds of millions of casualties, yet war is not a universal phenomenon. Some societies engage in defensive wars only and try to avoid armed confrontations, and some societies do not practice warfare as we know it.

✓ New inventions in military technology have dramatically increased the complexity of warfare and the number of civilian casualties.

✓ Genocide is the physical extermination of one people by another.

What nonviolent approaches do humans use to resolve conflicts?

✓ Throughout history, people have used diplomacy to prevent conflicts from escalating into violence.

✓ Treaties are formally binding agreements between two or more groups that are independent and self-governing political groups such as tribes, chiefdoms, and states.

✓ In 1947, India and Pakistan gained political independence from their British colonial overlords in part due to a nonviolent resistance movement led by Mohandas Gandhi.

✓ A present-day example of nonviolent resistance is the popular mass movement to end the military grip on power in Myanmar led by Aung San Suu Kyi.

QUESTIONS FOR REFLECTION

1. In Syria, a pluralistic society with many ethnic and religious groups, a civil war has turned into sectarian violence with numerous factions and splinter groups fighting each other. Can you imagine your own country becoming a theocracy, dictatorship, or even a failed state? What does it take to maintain tolerance and peaceful order?

2. Do you think there is a relationship between a profitable arms industry, promoting military dominance, and the pursuit of war as a means of solving conflicts? If so, what is the role of an ideology that asserts national and/or religious righteousness?

3. When your own government commits its military to fight on foreign soil, on what basis does it seek to justify the decision to send soldiers into deadly combat against a declared enemy opponent?

4. Do you think nonviolent resistance is effective as a tactic challenging social or political injustice? Can you imagine a situation in which such protest is not only effective but would also be legitimate? If so, on what grounds?

DIGGING INTO ANTHROPOLOGY

Politics and Purses

In many countries, political power is concentrated in the hands of a wealthy elite owning or controlling large corporations. Assuming you live in a democracy, please select three politicians in your state, province, or district who have successfully run for high public office. Check newspapers, websites, and other sources of information about their election campaign financing, with a focus on major individual, corporate, or institutional donors. Contact each of these three elected officials and ask them, or their staffers, to explain what these donors expect to get in return for their support. Because actions speak louder than words, check which decisions were made that directly or indirectly favor these donors.

Josef Polleross/Getty Images

As self-reflecting beings, humans face the challenge of making sense of our place in the universe. We puzzle over truly big questions about time and space and wrestle with existential questions about our own fate, life, and death. For countless generations, our species has creatively engaged in such reflections on the unknown, the mysterious, the supernatural. We do this through our culture in sacred narratives and rituals—prayers, chants, dances, prostrations, burnings, and sacrificial offerings—the cornerstones of many religions. In the small Himalaya kingdom of Bhutan, where many people remain illiterate, Buddhist monks perform religious legends in theatrical dance while trumpets offer sacred sounds to the divine. Here we see the ceremonial Stag and Hounds dance, Shawo Shachi, in a centuries-old *dzong* or fortified monastery. The dog-masked dancer acts out an ancient legend about Guru Rinpoche. This supreme saint tamed bloodthirsty hunting dogs with songs and pacified their infuriated master, converting him to Buddhism. Subduing demonic forces, the saint bought harmony and happiness through sacred teachings and inspired many followers. The state religion in Bhutan is a branch of Tibetan Buddhism established by an ascetic monk in the late 12th century. Achieving living sainthood, this monk reincarnated many times in the course of centuries and founded a spiritual lineage of ruling priest-kings. By collectively commemorating him, present-day monks reinforce the beliefs and practices that support their nation's traditional power structure.

Spirituality, Religion, and Shamanism

23

Religions play an important role in determining cultural identity in many societies across the globe, sometimes overruling other major identity markers such as kinship, social class, and ethnicity or nationality. From an anthropological point of view, spirituality and religion are part of a cultural system's *superstructure,* earlier defined as the collective body of ideas, beliefs, and values by which members of a culture make sense of the world and their place in it. In contrast to theology or other disciplines, anthropology examines the entirety of shared concepts concerning the ultimate shape and substance of reality in terms of a people's *worldview*—the collective body of ideas members of a culture generally share concerning the ultimate shape and substance of their reality.

Notably, just 16 percent of the world's population is categorized as nonreligious. This broad label covers a range of worldviews—from atheism to secular humanism to individually held spiritual beliefs that do not fit any formally institutionalized religion. (Figure 23.1).

The superstructure of cultural systems is intricately connected with the infrastructure and social structure. Guided by our barrel model, we therefore expect adaptations in the superstructure when there are technological, economic, social, and/or political changes. Based on that principle, worldwide transformations in the ideological landscape are to be anticipated as an integral component of globalization. Reviewing world history for the past few thousand years, scholars recognize radical transformations in religious and spiritual beliefs and rituals everywhere. Taking the long view, we discover that, like political states discussed in the previous chapter, most religions we know today are, in fact, not that old. And even those that appear to be old are quite different from when they began.

In this chapter we offer a cross-cultural review and comparative historical perspective on a wide range of spiritual traditions and religions. We explain how societies have developed worldviews concerning the non-ordinary, mysterious, transcendental, or supernatural—cultural superstructures with particular repertoires of spiritual beliefs, ritual practices, and religious institutions, often considered sacred or holy.

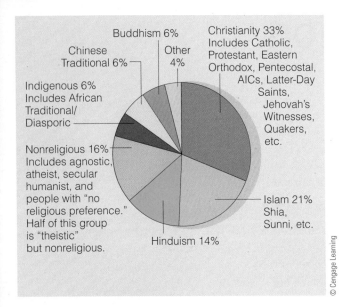

Figure 23.1 Major Religions of the World
This chart shows the world's major religions with percentages of their adherents. The total adds up to more than 100 percent due to rounding. Two have enormous followings: Christianity, with about 2.2 billion adherents (half of whom are Roman Catholic), and Islam, with over 1.5 billion (an overwhelming majority of whom are Sunni). Within both religions are numerous major and minor divisions, splits, and sects.

Sources: adherents.com; Pew Research Center, 2011.

Roles of Spirituality and Religion

Among people in all societies, particular spiritual or religious beliefs and practices fulfill individual and collective psychological and emotional needs. They reduce anxiety by providing an orderly view of the universe and answers to existential questions, including those concerning suffering and death. They provide a path by which people transcend the burdens of mortal existence and attain, if only momentarily, hope and relief.

Spiritual or religious beliefs and practices serve numerous cultural purposes. For instance, a religion held in common by a group of people reinforces community values and provides moral guidelines for personal conduct. It also offers narratives and rituals used to confirm a social hierarchy and legitimize political power; conversely, it may allow for narratives *countering* the divine claims of powerholders, even providing justifications and rituals to resist and challenge them. In addition, people may turn to religion or spirituality in the hope of reaching a specific goal, such as restoring health, securing a harvest, ending violence, or being rescued from danger (Figure 23.2).

Anthropologists recognize that not everyone believes in a supernatural force or entity, but they also agree that there is no known culture that does not provide some set

Figure 23.2 Bugi Sailors Praying, Indonesia
The Bugi of Sulawesi (Celebes) are famous for their oceangoing schooners. For generations, these Indonesian seafarers have plied the waters between Malaysia and Australia, transporting spices and other freight. Life at sea is risky—sudden storms, piracy, and other mishaps—and sailors pray for safety. This prayerful Bugi gathering in Jakarta on Java Island took place on a holiday ending Ramadan, the Islamic month of fasting. During that time Muslims refrain from eating, drinking liquids, smoking, and sexual activities, from sunrise to sunset. This taboo serves to purify thought and build restraint for Allah's sake.

of ideas about existence beyond ordinary and empirically verifiable reality—ideas concerning the supernatural or metaphysical. Because such ideas serve cultural purposes and fulfill emotional and psychological needs, it makes sense that spirituality and religions developed tens of thousands of years ago and occur across the globe.

In the wake of major technological inventions and new discoveries since the 1600s, European intellectuals predicted that magic, myth, and religion would be replaced by empirical research, proven facts, and scientific theories. Some even forecasted the end of religion altogether. But to date, and despite tremendous scientific achievements, that has not occurred. Confronted by radical cultural changes, and feeling threatened by upheaval, many turn to religion and spirituality in search of reassuring answers and hope.

Anthropological Approach to Spirituality and Religion

Worldwide, people are inspired and guided by strongly held ideas about the supernatural, putting into practice what they deeply believe to be true or right. It is not the responsibility of anthropologists to pass judgment on the metaphysical truth of any particular faith system, but it is our task to show how each embodies a number of revealing facts about humanity and the particular cultural superstructure within which these religious or spiritual beliefs are ideologically embedded.

Based on a cross-cultural and comparative historical perspective on worldviews, we define **religion** as an organized system of ideas about the spiritual sphere or the supernatural, along with associated ceremonial practices by which people try to interpret and/or influence aspects of the universe otherwise beyond their control. Similar to religion, **spirituality** is concerned with the sacred, as distinguished from ordinary reality, but it is often individual rather than collective and does not require a formal institution. Both indicate that many aspects of the human experience are thought to be beyond natural or scientific explanation.

Spirituality and/or religion continue to play a role in all known cultures. However, considerable variability exists globally (**Figure 23.3**). At one end of the anthropological spectrum are food-foraging peoples, who have limited technological ability and social division of labor to exploit or control their natural environment. Broadly speaking, they hold that nature is pregnant with the spiritual. Embedded and manifested in all aspects of their culture, spirituality permeates their daily activities—from food hunting or gathering to making fires, building homes, and conversations about life before or after death. It also mirrors and confirms the egalitarian nature of social relations in their societies, in that individuals do not

plead with high-ranking deities for aid the way members of stratified societies more typically do. Their holistic worldview is often referred to as *naturalistic*, an imprecise but workable term.

At the other end of our spectrum are state societies with commercial or industrial economies, sophisticated technologies, and social stratification based on a complex division of labor. There, high-ranking social groups typically seek to control and manage the construction of a society's worldview as an ideological means of legitimizing and reinforcing their vested interests in its hierarchical structure. Usually featuring a ranked order of supernatural beings—for instance, God and (in some religions) the angels, saints, or other holy figures—it simultaneously reflects and reinforces the stratified system in which it is embedded. In such societies, religious activities are usually reserved for designated locations, times, and occasions.

Religions provide a powerful ideology justifying inequality in a state society, but they may also inspire subordinated peoples to envision an alternative social order freeing them from exploitation, repression, and humiliation. Thus, religiously motivated social movements have challenged political establishments.

Myth and the Mapping of a Sacred Worldview

Because much remains beyond human capacity to actually observe and explain based on obvious or empirical evidence alone, people have creatively worked out narratives explaining the fundamentals of human existence—where we and everything in our world came from, why we are here, and where we are going. These narratives form part of a people's worldview or *cosmology*—their understanding of the universe, its form and workings. Falling into the category of **myth** (*mythos*, Greek for "word," "speech"), these stories play a fundamental role in religious and spiritual beliefs and practices. Myths are believed to be true, even sacred, by those subscribing to the particular worldview engendering such narratives.

Typically, a myth features supernatural forces or beings engaged in extraordinary or miraculous performances. It may offer a morality play, providing an ethical code

---

religion An organized system of ideas about the spiritual sphere or the supernatural, along with associated ceremonial practices by which people try to interpret and/or influence aspects of the universe otherwise beyond their control.

spirituality Concern with the sacred, as distinguished from material matters. In contrast to religion, spirituality is often individual rather than collective and does not require a distinctive format or traditional organization.

myth A sacred narrative that explains the fundamentals of human existence—where we and everything in our world came from, why we are here, and where we are going.

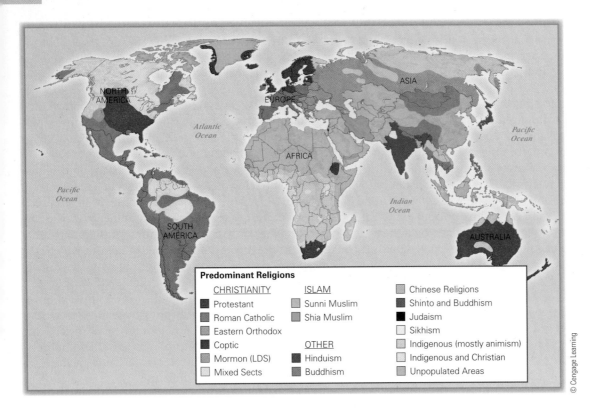

Figure 23.3 Global Distribution of Predominant Religions
This map depicts the global distribution of major religions, indicating where they predominate. In some areas, the mixture of different religions is such that no single faith is shared by most of that region's inhabitants. Not detailed enough to show pockets with significant numbers of a particular faith (such as Israel's 6 million Jews), it also omits many religions that are dispersed or eclipsed by others—including several worldwide ones such as Ahmadiyya (a Muslim sect, with 10 million adherents), Jehovah's Witnesses (a Christian sect with 7 million adherents), and Bahá'í (with 6 million adherents, emphasizing the spiritual unity of all mankind and recognizing divine messengers from various religions).

for its audience and guidelines for human behavior. For example, the Puranas (a body of religious texts, including cosmological myths, considered sacred by Buddhists and Hindus) are rich in such material. So are the Bible, Quran, and Torah, each held sacred in distinct but historically related religions originating in Southwest Asia. Whether orally transmitted in poems or stories, musically in songs, in dance motions, in pictures or sculptures, or in writing, these representations have been passed on from generation to generation and inform believers with a sacred map of the *cosmos*, or universe, and their place in it.

Supernatural Beings and Spiritual Forces

A hallmark of religion is belief in spiritual forces and supernatural beings. Attempting to control by religious means what cannot be controlled in other ways, humans turn to prayer, sacrifice, and other religious or

spiritual rituals. Their actions presuppose the existence of spiritual forces that can be tapped into, or supernatural beings interested in human affairs and available for aid. In many cultures, these supernatural forces or spiritual beings are associated with unique geographic locations valued as sacred sites—extraordinary rock formations, lakes, wells, waterfalls, mountains, and so forth. Supernatural beings can be divided into three categories: deities (gods and goddesses), ancestral spirits, and other sorts of spirit beings.

Gods and Goddesses

Not all religions *anthropomorphize* the divine, but many do. Symbolically constructing a divine order that mirrors a society's gender structure, many religions recognize male and female deities. Gods and goddesses, or divinities, are the great and more remote supernatural beings. Generally speaking, cultures that subordinate women to men attribute masculine gender to the more powerful gods or to a supreme deity. For instance, in traditional

Christian religions believers speak of God as a father who had a divine son born from a human mother, but they do not entertain thoughts of God as a mother or as a divine daughter. Such male-privileging religions developed in many societies traditionally based on the herding of animals or intensive agriculture with frequent warfare, and politics controlled by men.

Goddesses, by contrast, are likely to be prominent in societies where women play a significant role in the economy and enjoy relative equality with men. Such societies are most often those that depend on crop cultivation traditionally carried out solely or mostly by women. Typically, these may feature fertility and earth goddesses.

Some religions recognize deities represented as male–female combinations. For example, one of the Greek gods, also recognized in the Roman empire, was Hermaphroditus, the beautiful two-sexed son of Hermes (or Mercury) and Aphrodite (or Venus). Hindus recognize a similar third-gender divinity when they worship Ardhanarishvara ("the Lord who is half woman") (Figure 23.4).

If a religion recognizes only one supremely powerful divinity as creator and master of the universe, we speak of **monotheism**. If it acknowledges more than one divinity, each governing a particular domain, we label it **polytheism**. Gods and goddesses of ancient Greece illustrate the latter: Zeus ruled the sky, Poseidon the sea, and Hades the underworld and the dead. In addition to these three brothers, Greek mythology features a host of other deities, both male and female, each similarly concerned with specific aspects of life and the universe. Athena and Nike, for instance, were goddesses of war and victory, respectively. A **pantheon**, or a collective of gods and goddesses worshiped in a society, is common in many religions, today most famously in Hinduism.

Because states typically have grown through conquest, often their pantheons have expanded, with local deities of conquered peoples being incorporated into the official state pantheon. A frequent feature of pantheons is the presence of a supreme deity, who may be all but totally ignored by humans. Aztecs of the Mexican highlands, for instance, recognized a supreme duo to whom they paid little attention. Assuming this divine pair was unlikely to be interested in ordinary humans, they devoted themselves to lesser deities thought to be more directly concerned with human affairs.

Figure 23.4 Ardhanarishvara, a Dual-Gender Divinity
Some religions recognize deities as physically resembling human beings, males and females. Among the many gods in the Hindu tradition is one that embodies both genders at once. Pictured here is Ardhanarishvara—a composite androgynous form of the Hindu god Shiva and his consort Parvati. Having just one female breast, this divinity represents a synthesis of masculine and feminine energies of the universe.

Ancestral Spirits

Beliefs in ancestral spirits support the idea that human beings consist of intertwined components: body/matter (physical) and mind/soul (spiritual). This dualistic concept

monotheism The belief in only one supremely powerful divinity as creator and master of the universe.
polytheism The belief in multiple gods and/or goddesses.
pantheon A collective of gods and goddesses worshiped in a society.

carries with it the possibility of a spirit being freed from the body—through dream, trance, or death—and even having a separate existence. Frequently, where a belief in ancestral spirits exists, these nonphysical beings are seen as retaining an active interest and membership in society.

Beliefs in ancestral spirits are found in many parts of the world, especially among people having unilineal descent systems with their associated ancestor orientation. In several African cultures, the concept is highly elaborate, and people believe ancestral spirits behave much like humans; they are able to feel hot, cold, and pain and may even die a second death by drowning or burning. Because spirits sometimes participate in family and lineage events, seats will be provided for them, even though they are invisible. If spirits are annoyed, they may send sickness or death. Eventually, they are reborn as new members of their lineage, so adults need to observe infants closely to determine just who has been reborn. Such beliefs provide a strong sense of solidarity among members of the same kin-group through the generations.

Other Types of Supernatural Beings and Spiritual Forces

In cross-cultural research, anthropologists encounter a range of spiritual and religious beliefs or practices in addition to those in which people worship one or more gods and goddesses and revere ancestral spirits. They also find societies in which people believe in numerous other distinct spirit beings, including many varieties of a belief in an impersonal spirit power or supernatural force.

Animism

One of the most widespread concepts concerning supernatural beings is **animism**, a belief that nature is enlivened or energized by distinct personalized spirit beings separable from physical bodies or the material substance they inhabit. Spirits such as souls and ghosts are thought to dwell in humans, animals, and plants, as well as human-made artifacts and natural features such as stones, mountains, and wells; for animists, the world is filled with particular spirits. These beings are a highly diverse lot. Less remote than gods and goddesses, they may be benevolent, malevolent, or just plain neutral. Involved in people's daily affairs, they also may be awesome, terrifying, lovable, or mischievous. Because they may be pleased or irritated by human actions, people are obliged to be concerned about them.

Animism is typical of those who see themselves as being a part of nature rather than dominating or superior to it. This includes most food foragers and food gardeners, among others. Deities, if they are believed to exist at all in such societies, may be seen as having created the world and perhaps making it fit to live in; but in animism, spirits are the ones to beseech when ill, the ones to help or hinder the shaman, and the ones whom the ordinary hunter may meet when off in the wilderness.

Animatism

Although supernatural power is often thought of as being vested in spirit beings, it does not have to be. Such is the case with **animatism**—the belief that nature is enlivened or energized by an impersonal force or supernatural energy, which may make itself manifest in any special place, thing, or living creature. This basic concept, which probably developed well before the first transition from food foraging to food production 10,000 years ago, is still present in many societies around the world today. For example, in China it appears in the form of a concept known as *qi* (or *ch'i*), which may be translated as "vital energy." Inuit people in Arctic Canada think of this force in terms of a "cosmic breath-soul" they call *sila*. In northeastern America, Algonquian-speaking indigenous peoples refer to impersonal spirit power as *manitou*.

One of the best-studied examples of animatism can be found in the Pacific where Oceanic peoples inhabiting hundreds of islands share a concept they refer to as *mana*—the idea of a cosmic energy passing into and through everything. Affecting living and nonliving matter alike, *mana* is probably best defined as "supernaturally conferred potency" (Keesing, 1992, p. 236)—similar to "the force" in the *Star Wars* films. Traditional Maori, Tahitians, Tongans, and other Oceanic peoples typically attribute success—identified by actual achievements such as triumph in combat, bountiful harvest, and abundant fish or game—to *mana*. As far as they are concerned, belief in this supernatural force rests on pragmatic evidence.

Animism (a belief in distinct spirit beings) and animatism (which lacks particular substance or individual form) are often found in the same culture. This is the case among the Inuit, who believe in spirit beings known as *anirniit* as well as in the impersonal spirit power they call *sila* (Merkur, 1983) (Figure 23.5).

In many religious traditions, certain geographic places are thought to be spiritually significant or are held sacred for various reasons, including ideas here discussed in terms of animism and animatism. Typically, such sites are rivers, lakes, waterfalls, islands, forests, caves, and—especially—mountains. We revisit the topic of sacred sites later in the chapter.

---

animism The belief that nature is enlivened or energized by distinct personalized spirit beings separable from bodies.

animatism The belief that nature is enlivened or energized by an impersonal spiritual force or supernatural energy, which may make itself manifest in any special place, thing, or living creature.

H. Mark Weidman Photography/Alamy

Figure 23.5 Inuit Food Ritual
Inuit of Arctic Canada refer to spirit beings as *anirniit* (singular *anirniq*, meaning "breath") and
still obey certain taboos and perform rituals when killing game animals and dividing the meat.
This is to avoid offending the animal's spirit (which remains alive and may take revenge on
the hunter). Today, most Inuit are Christians, and their concept of *anirniq* is akin to "soul." But
traditional food rituals continue, including the fair distribution of meat from a whale hunt. In this
photo, an Inuit community follows tradition in collecting shares of beluga whale in the Arctic
village of Pangnirtung on Baffin Island.

Religious Specialists

Most cultures include individuals who guide others in
their spiritual search and ritual practices. Thought to
be inspired, enlightened, or even holy, they command
respect for their skills in contacting and influencing spiritual beings and manipulating or connecting to supernatural forces. Often, they display unique personality traits
that make them particularly well suited to perform these
tasks for which they have undergone special training.

Priests and Priestesses

In societies with resources to support a full-time religious
specialist, a **priest or priestess** will be authorized to
perform sacred rituals and mediate between fellow humans and supernatural powers, divine spirits, or deities. In
many societies, they are familiar figures known by official
titles such as *lama, kahuna, imam, priest, minister, rabbi,
swami,* or *copa pitào.* How they dress, what they eat, where
they live, and numerous other indicators may distinguish
them from others in society and symbolically indicate
their special status.

Reserving exclusive rights to exercise spiritual power,
groups of priests and/or priestesses bond together in an
effort to monopolize the means of sacred practice. This
includes controlling holy sites of worship, supervising
prescribed rituals, and maintaining possession of regalia,
relics, statues, images, texts, and other representations
of holiness. In so doing, they also create, promote, and
maintain the ideological sources needed to symbolically
construct the religious authority from which they derive
their legitimacy.

When deities are identified in masculine terms, it is
not surprising that the most important religious leadership positions are reserved for men. Such is the case
in Judaism and Islam, as well as the Roman Catholic
Church, the latter of which has always been headed by
a male pope and his all-male council, the College of
Cardinals.

priest or priestess A full-time religious specialist formally recognized
for his or her role in guiding the religious practices of others and for
contacting and influencing supernatural powers.

Change Your *Karma* and Change Your Sex?

By Hillary Crane

East China Sea

Shanghai

CHINA

HONG KONG

Taipei

TAIWAN

Taiwan Strait

South China Sea

Philippine Sea

© Cengage Learning

As Mahayana Buddhists, Taiwanese Chan (Zen) monastics believe that all humans are able to reach enlightenment and be released from reincarnation. But they believe it is easier for some because of the situation into which they are born—for example, if one is born in a country where Buddhism is practiced, in a family that teaches proper behavior, or with exceptional mental or physical gifts.

Chan monastics view contrasting human circumstances as the result of the *karma* accrued in previous lives. They believe certain behavior—such as diligently practicing Buddhism—improves *karma* and the chances of attaining spiritual goals in this lifetime or coming back in a better birth. Other behavior—such as killing a living being, eating meat, desiring or becoming attached to things or people—accrues bad *karma*.

One way *karma* manifests itself is in one's sex. Taiwanese Buddhists believe that being born female makes it harder to attain spiritual goals. This idea comes, in part, from the inferior status of women in Taiwan and the belief that their "complicated bodies" and monthly menstruation cycles can distract them. Moreover, they believe, women are more enmeshed in their families than men, and their emotional ties keep them focused on worldly rather than spiritual tasks.

Taiwanese Buddhists who decide to become monks and nuns must break from their families to enter a monastery. Because women are thought to be more attached to their families than are men, leaving home is seen as a particularly big step for nuns and a sign that they are more like men than most women. In fact, a nun's character is considered masculine, unlike the frightened, indecisive, and emotional traits usually associated with women in Taiwan. When they leave home nuns even stop referring to themselves as women and call one another *shixiong*

("*dharma* brother"). They use this linguistic change to signal that they identify themselves as men and to remind one another to behave like men, particularly like the monks at the temple.

Monastics also reduce their attachments to worldly things like music and food. Nuns usually emphasize forsaking food and eat as little as possible. Their appearance, already quite masculine because they shave their heads and wear loose, gray clothing, becomes even more so when they lose weight—particularly in their hips, breasts, and thighs. Also, after becoming monastics, they often experience a slowing or stopping of their menses. Although these physical changes can be attributed to change in diet and lifestyle, the nuns point to them as signs they are becoming men, making progress toward their spiritual goals, and improving their *karma*.

Biocultural Question

The Zen Buddhist ideal of enlightenment, realized when the soul is released from reincarnation, prescribes an extreme ascetic lifestyle for nuns that makes them physically incapable of biological reproduction. Do you think that their infertility allows these female monastics to emotionally adapt to a way of life that denies them motherhood?

Written expressly for this text, 2008.

Female religious specialists are likely to be found only in societies in which women are acknowledged to significantly contribute to the economy, and gods and goddesses are both recognized (Lehman, 2002). Also, all around the world women fully devoted to a religious life have formed their own gender-segregated institutions such as all-female convents headed by an abbess. Such nunneries not only exist in countries with longstanding Christian traditions, but were also founded in the Himalayas and many other Buddhist regions in southern and eastern Asia, including Taiwan, as described by U.S. anthropologist Hillary Crane in the Biocultural Connection.

Spiritual Lineages: Legitimizing Religious Leadership

As with political institutions discussed in the previous chapter, religious organizations are maintained by rules that define ideological boundaries, establish membership criteria, and regulate continuity of legitimate leadership in the faith community. And, like other institutions, religions have always been challenged by changes. Even in a highly stable cultural system, every generation must deal with natural transitions in the life cycle, including death of religious leaders. In many religions, spiritual leadership is thought to be vested in divine authority, representing or even embodying the divine itself. How do religions secure legitimate successors and avoid disruption and confusion?

Several major religions follow a principle of leadership in which divine authority is passed down from a spiritual founding figure, such as a prophet or saint, to a chain of successors who derive legitimacy as religious leaders from their status in such a lineage. Here identified as **spiritual lineage**, this principle has been worked out in numerous cross-cultural variations over the course of thousands of years. It not only applies to leadership of entire religions but to segmental divisions of religions, such as sects and orders.

Whereas kings in traditional political dynasties derive legitimacy from their ancestral blood lineage, religious leaders obtain it from their spiritual line of descent as specified in each particular religious tradition. The longer these lineages have existed, the greater their opportunities for building up a fund of symbolic capital—ideas and rituals, including sacred gestures, dances, songs, and texts. This fund also includes regalia, paintings, statues, and sacred architecture such as shrines, tombs, and temples, along with the land on which they stand. Thus, some religious leaders and their followers have accumulated a considerable amount of material wealth utilized in the exercise of religious authority, in addition to the immaterial holdings of traditional knowledge and sacred rituals.

Here, to illustrate the cross-cultural range of spiritual lineages, we distinguish four major forms. First, in some religions, spiritual leaders or high-ranking priests claim divine authority based on recognized biological descent from a common ancestor believed to have been a prophet, saint, or otherwise sacred, holy, or even divine being. Such is the case with *kohanim* (high-ranking Israelite priests) claiming patrilineal descent from the legendary high priest Aaron, believed to have lived about 3,500 years ago.

In other religions, leaders personally groom, train, and appoint a spiritual heir, a successor tasked with guarding and continuing the spiritual legacy of the order or sect as established by its founder. For example, a sect of Muslim mystics known as Sufi is widely dispersed across Asia and North Africa and historically divided into many dozens of orders or brotherhoods. A master teacher, known by an honorific title such as *sheikh*, heads each brotherhood. The sheikh derives his spiritual authority from his position in a *silsila* (Arabic, meaning "chain"), named after a founding saint who originally laid down a particular method of prayer and ritual practiced by followers seeking oneness with God (Abun-Nasr, 2007; Anjum, 2006).

A third form of legitimizing the authority of a religious leader is by election. In such cases, a group of leading elders comes together in a ritual gathering at a traditionally designated location and chooses one of their own to succeed the deceased leader. One of the best-known examples in world history is the election of a pope by a group of cardinals—"princes" of the Roman Catholic Church who

proclaim the new pope to be the divinely ordained spiritual heir of St. Peter, Vicar of Christ. Believed by 1.2 billion Christians to hold the sacred key to heaven, the pope is traditionally addressed as "Holy Father." The current Pope Francis is the 266th holder of this nearly 2,000-year-old religious office.

A fourth and final example of spiritual lineage is found in Tibetan Buddhism, divided into four major orders or schools. Each has its own monasteries, monks of various ranks from novice to lama, and a wealth of ancient texts, ritual practices, meditations, and other sacred knowledge passed on largely by oral tradition. Highest in rank among the monks are reincarnated saints. These are individuals who, fully emanating the divine Buddha spirit, achieved enlightenment during their lifetime; led by compassion, they chose to give up *nirvana* ("eternal bliss") after death to return to life on earth. To fulfill this role, such a saintly person must be recognized. Toward this end, a select group of high-ranking lamas guided by omens seeks out a newborn boy believed to be a *tulku* ("emanated incarnation") of a recently deceased saintly lama in their spiritual lineage. Once they find the little boy, they ritually induct and enthrone him and begin grooming him for his designated spiritual leadership position in the Buddhist order.

Of about 500 *tulku* lineages in Tibetan Buddhism, the most famous is the Dalai Lama ("teacher who is spiritually as deep as the ocean"). For centuries, this illustrious lineage has been the highest-ranking political and spiritual position among Tibetan Buddhists. Its origins trace back to a high-ranking monk named Gendun Drup (1391–1474), thought to have embodied the Buddha spirit of compassion. A few years after the death of the thirteenth Dalai Lama in 1933, high-ranking monks from his order identified a 2-year-old boy in a small farming village as his reincarnated "wisdom mind." Renaming him Tenzin Gyatso, they later enthroned the little *tulku* as His Holiness, the fourteenth Dalai Lama (Figure 23.6).

Shamans

Societies without religious professionals have existed far longer than those that have them. Although lacking full-time specialists, they have always included individuals considered capable of connecting with supernatural beings and forces—individuals such as shamans. That capacity, partially based on learned techniques, is also based on personality and particular emotional experiences that could be described as mystical. Supplied with spiritual knowledge in the form of a vision or some other extraordinary revelation, these individuals are believed to

---

spiritual lineage A principle of leadership in which divine authority is passed down from a spiritual founding figure, such as a prophet or saint, to a chain of successors.

Eyes Wide Open/Getty Images

Figure 23.6 Dalai Lama
Of the 500 or so lineages in Tibetan Buddhism, the most famous is the Dalai Lama. Here we see the fourteenth Dalai Lama, Tenzin Gyatso, conducting a teaching on "the essence of refined gold" at the main Tibetan temple in Dharamshala, India. Dharamshala is the center for the world's exiled Tibetans. Following the 1959 Tibetan uprising, the fourteenth Dalai Lama fled here, followed by an influx of Tibetan refugees.

be supernaturally empowered to heal the sick, change the weather, control the movements of animals, and foretell the future. As they perfect these and related skills, they may combine the role of a diviner and a healer, becoming a shaman.

Originally, the Tungus word *shaman* referred to a medical-religious specialist, or spiritual guide, among the Tungus people and other Siberian pastoral nomads with animist beliefs. By means of various techniques such as fasting, drumming, chanting, or dancing, as well as hallucinogenic mushrooms, these shamans enter into a trance. In this waking dream state, they experience

visions of an alternate reality inhabited by spirit beings such as guardian animal spirits who may assist with healing. Similar spiritual practices exist in many indigenous cultures outside Siberia, especially in the Americas. For that reason, the term *shaman* is frequently applied to a variety of part-time spiritual leaders, diviners, and traditional healers active in many other parts of the world (Kehoe, 2000).

Anthropologist Michael Harner (see Anthropologist of Note), a modern-day shamanic practitioner famous for his participant observation among Shuar (or Jívaro) Indian shamans in the Amazon rainforest, defines a **shaman** as someone who enters an altered state of consciousness "to contact and utilize an ordinarily hidden reality in order to acquire knowledge, power, and to help other persons. The shaman has at least one, and usually more, 'spirits' in his or her personal service" (Harner, 1980, p. 20).

Shamanic Experience

Someone may become a shaman by passing through stages of learning and practical experience, often involving psychological and emotional ordeals brought about by isolation, fasting, physical torture, sensory deprivation, and/or *hallucination* (Latin for "mental wandering"). Hallucinations may occur when one is in a trance state; they can come about spontaneously, but they can also be induced by drumming or consuming mind-altering drugs such as psychoactive vines or mushrooms.

Because shamanism is rooted in altered states of consciousness and the human nervous system universally produces these trance states, individuals experience similarly-structured visual, auditory, somatic (touch), olfactory (smell), and gustatory (taste) hallucinations. The widespread occurrence of shamanism and the remarkable similarities among shamanic traditions everywhere are consequences of this universal neurological inheritance. But the meanings ascribed to sensations experienced in altered states and made of their content are culturally determined; hence, despite their overall similarities, indigenous traditions typically vary in particular details.

Shamans can be contrasted with priests and priestesses in that the latter serve deities of the society. As agents of divine beings, priests and priestesses order believers what to think and do, whereas shamans may challenge or negotiate with the spirits. In return for services rendered, shamans may collect a fee—money, fresh meat, or some other valuable item. In some cases, shamans are rewarded by the prestige that comes as a result of a healing or some other extraordinary feat.

Shamanic Healing

Shamans are essentially spiritual go-betweens who act on behalf of a client, often to bring about healing or to foretell a future event. Typically, they enter a trance state, experience the sensation of traveling to the alternate world, and see and interact with spirit beings. Shamans may try

Michael J. Harner (b. 1929)

A world-renowned expert on shamanism, U.S. anthropologist **Michael Harner** studied at the University of California, Berkeley. Starting out in archaeology and collaborating with Alfred Kroeber on Mojave pottery research, he later switched to ethnography. Intrigued by the Jívaro, legendary for shrinking human heads, he ventured into eastern Ecuador's tropical forest in 1956, at age 27. For nearly a year, he lived among these Amazonian Indians, now better known as Shuar. They still subsisted on food gardens and by hunting and gathering; they fiercely guarded their freedom and launched raids on enemy tribes.

Holding an animistic worldview, the Shuar distinguish between what Harner has identified as ordinary and non-ordinary realities. They believe that supernatural forces govern daily life and that spirit beings can be perceived and engaged only by shamans capable of entering non-ordinary reality. They access this reality by drinking *natema*, a bitter brew made from a jungle vine known as *ayahuasca* ("vine of the soul"). As they told Harner, drinking this hallucinogenic potion, shamans enter an altered state of consciousness in which they perceive and engage what they believe are the "true" forces governing sickness and health, life and death.

Harner returned to the Upper Amazon in 1960 for more ethnographic fieldwork, this time among the Conibo in eastern Peru. Seeking greater insight on *ayahuasca's* psychological impact on the native cosmology, he drank the magic brew. Passing through the door of perception into the shamanic view of reality, he found himself in a world beyond his "wildest dreams": a supernatural landscape inhabited by spirit beings. Singing incredibly beautiful music, they began to carry his soul away and he felt he was dying. Coming out of this experience, and later ones with Conibo shamans, Harner realized that anthropologists had seriously underestimated the powerful influence hallucinogenic drugs traditionally have on Amazonian Indian ideologies and practices.

In 1963, Harner earned his doctorate at UC Berkeley, and the next year went back to Shuar country for additional shamanic experience. In 1966, having taught at UC Berkeley and served as associate director of the Lowie Museum of Anthropology, he became a visiting professor at Yale and Columbia University. In 1969, he did fieldwork among a neighboring Jivaroan-speaking tribe, the Achuara, and the following year joined the graduate faculty of the New School for Social Research in New York City. Over the next few years he published his monograph, *The Jívaro: People of the Sacred Waterfalls*, an edited volume titled *Hallucinogens and Shamanism*, and numerous academic articles.

Continuing cross-cultural research on shamanism, Harner became interested in drumming as an alternative means of achieving what he now identifies as SSC (shamanic state of consciousness). Learning and using this method of monotonous percussive sound ("sonic driving"), he began offering training workshops and published *The Way of the Shaman*, a groundbreaking book now translated into a dozen languages.

Collaborating with his wife, clinical psychologist Sandra Harner, in 1979 he started the Center for Shamanic Studies, now called the Foundation for Shamanic Studies, a nonprofit charitable and educational organization dedicated to the preservation, study, and transmission of shamanic knowledge. Its indigenous assistance program supports the survival of shamanic healing knowledge among such peoples as the Canadian Inuit, Scandinavian Sámi, and Tuvans of Central Asia and Siberia.

Since resigning from his university professorship in 1987, this anthropologist has been fully devoted to shamanic studies and healing practice, training others, including physicians, psychotherapists, and other healthcare professionals. The foundation's faculty assists him in this work.

In his most recent book, *Cave and Cosmos: Shamanic Encounters with Spirits and Heavens* (2013), Harner recounts and compares experiences of shamanic "ascension" and offers instructions on his core shamanism techniques.

© 2011 France Viana

Michael Harner—anthropologist, shaman, and founder of the Foundation for Shamanic Studies in Mill Valley, California.

to impose their will upon these spirits, an inherently dangerous contest, considering the superhuman powers that spirits are thought to possess.

An example of this can be seen in the trance dances of the Ju/'hoansi Bushmen of Africa's Kalahari Desert. Traditional Ju/'hoansi belief holds that illness and misfortune are caused by invisible arrows shot by spirits. Healers, who possess the powerful healing force called *n/um* (the Ju/'hoansi equivalent of *mana*), can remove the arrows. Some healers can activate *n/um* by solo singing or instrument playing, but more often this is accomplished through the healing ceremony or trance dance (Figure 23.7).

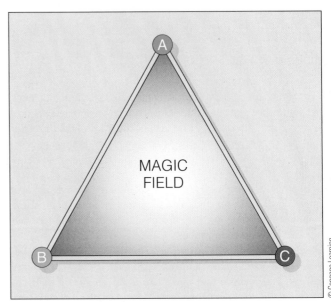

Figure 23.8 The Shamanic Complex
Shamanic healing takes place within a "magic field" created when the shaman (A) and patient (B), as well as their community (C), are all convinced that the shaman is a genuine healing master using appropriate techniques that are effective and beneficial. Similar psychological processes are involved in Western medical treatments.

Figure 23.7 Ju/'hoansi Shaman Healer and Helper in Trance Dance
Ju/'hoansi shamans may find their way into a trance by dancing around a fire to the pulsating sound of melodies sung by women. Eventually, sometimes after several hours, "the music, the strenuous dancing, the smoke, the heat of the fire, and the healers' intense concentration cause their *n/um* to heat up. When it comes to a boil, trance is achieved. At that moment, the *n/um* becomes available as a powerful healing force to serve the entire community. In trance, a healer lays hands on and ritually cures everyone sitting around the fire" (Shostak, 2000, pp. 259–260).

The precise effects of the shamanic treatment are not known, but its psychological and emotional impact is thought to contribute to the patient's recovery. From an anthropological perspective, shamanic healings can be understood by means of a three-cornered model: the *shamanic complex*, which is created by the interrelationship of the shaman, the patient, and the community to which both belong (Figure 23.8). For healing to occur, the shaman needs to be convinced of the effectiveness of his or her spiritual powers and techniques. Likewise, the patient must see the shaman as a genuine healing master using appropriate techniques. Finally, to complete this triangular "magic field," the community within which the shaman operates on the patient must view the healing ceremony and its practitioner as potentially effective and beneficial.

Shamanic healing ceremonies involve social-psychological dynamics also present in Western medical treatments. Consider, for example, the *placebo effect*—the beneficial result a patient experiences after a particular treatment, due to the person's expectations concerning the treatment rather than from the treatment itself. Notably, some people involved in contemporary biomedicine work collaboratively with practitioners of traditional belief systems toward the healing of various illnesses (Harner & Harner, 2000; Offiong, 1999).

Ritual Performances

A **ritual** is a culturally prescribed symbolic act or procedure designed to guide members of a community in an orderly way through personal and collective transitions. Relieving anxiety and tensions in crises, rituals provide symbolic means of reinforcing a group's social bonds. Not all of them concern the sacred (consider, for example, student graduation ceremonies in North America). But those that do are ideologically linked to beliefs in the supernatural, playing a crucial role as spirituality or religion in action. Anthropologists have classified several different types of ritual. Among these are rituals of purification, rites of passage, rites of intensification, and magical rituals, including witchcraft.

Rites of Purification: Taboo and Cleansing Ceremonies

In many religious and spiritual traditions, rituals have been developed to symbolically restore one's place in the cosmic order, removing "dirt," washing "impurity," and making "clean" in body, mind, and soul. In every society, people follow certain culturally prescribed rules about what is dirty or filthy, or whichever term symbolically represents pollution—rules that say what they cannot eat, drink, touch, talk, or even think about. For instance, many millions of Hindus eat pork but avoid beef because they regard the cow as a sacred animal. On the other hand, many millions of Muslims consume beef but avoid pork because in Islam swine is considered unclean. In this Muslims have something in common with Jews, who also avoid pork.

Culturally prescribed avoidances involving ritual prohibitions are known as **taboo**, a term derived from the Polynesian word *tabu* (or *tapu*). Among Pacific Islanders it refers to something that has supernatural power and is to be avoided. Especially applied to sacredness, blood and anything associated with sickness and death, taboos are taken very seriously. When a taboo is violated, believers expect supernatural punishment will follow. This penalty may come in magical form as misfortune—an unlucky accident, resulting in loss, sickness, or death. It is also possible that the taboo breaker will be punished by designated members in the community and may be ordered to undergo a purification ritual and make a sacrifice. Sometimes, the ultimate sacrifice is demanded, and the offender is executed.

When someone has violated a taboo, or is otherwise no longer "clean," in many cultures a **rite of purification** is used to establish or restore purity. These rites may involve one person, but many are group or community ceremonial affairs. As symbolic acts, purification rituals are filled with spiritual or religious meaning. They impact participants emotionally and psychologically (restoring a sense of inner peace and cosmic harmony), as well as socially, such as by establishing or restoring harmony within their family, community, or some other group.

A cross-cultural comparison of these spiritual or religious ceremonies shows that the four elements of water, air, fire, and earth have been used in a wide range of rituals for thousands of years all across the globe. For instance, cleansing by water is very common in many forms of baptism, hot steam is used in sweat lodges, and burning of fragrant organic matter (such as plant leaves or resins) is used in smoking and smudging ceremonies. The human body and mind may also be subjected to rituals of internal purification by means of prayer, meditation, chanting, fasting, or dancing (Figure 23.9).

Rites of Passage

A **rite of passage** is a ritual marking important ceremonial moment when members of a society move from one distinctive social stage in life to another, such as birth, marriage, and death. When crossing the boundary (*limen*) between such stages, people briefly cease to be part of the stage left behind and have not yet become integrated into the next. Like travelers passing through a border area between two countries not controlled by either of them, they are neither here nor there. Guiding people through such uncertain transit zones, rituals associated with changing social status unfold in three phases: *separation* (preliminary), *transition* (liminary), and *incorporation* (post-liminary).

Phase one is the ceremonial removal of the individual from everyday society, phase two is a period of ritual isolation, and phase three is the formal return and readmission back into society in his or her new status (Van Gennep, 1960). Because certain transitions in the human life cycle are crucially important to the individual as well as to the social order of the community, these rituals may involve a religious specialist, such as a priest or priestess.

This sequence of phases occurs in a great array of rites of passage all around the world—from wedding ceremonies marking the transition from single to married status to ceremonies identifying the transference of religious leadership in a spiritual lineage to a designated heir to ceremonies initiating new members into a distinctive group.

---

ritual A culturally prescribed symbolic act or procedure designed to guide members of a community in an orderly way through personal and collective transitions.

taboo Culturally prescribed avoidances involving ritual prohibitions, which, if not observed, lead to supernatural punishment.

rite of purification A symbolic act carried out by an individual or a group to establish or restore purity when someone has violated a taboo or is otherwise unclean.

rite of passage A ritual that marks an important ceremonial moment when members of a society move from one distinctive social stage in life to another, such as birth, marriage, and death. It features three phases: separation, transition, and incorporation.

K. M. Westerman/Documentary/Corbis

Figure 23.9 A Sufi *Sema* (Prayer Dance) in Aleppo, Syria
Sufism, a mystical Muslim movement that emerged a thousand years ago, emphasizes the surrender of individual ego and attachment to worldly things in order to be receptive to God's grace. Known as whirling dervishes, these Sufi dancers are part of the Mevlevi brotherhood, a spiritual lineage founded by the Persian Sufi master (*mawlana*) Jalal ad-Din ar-Rumi in the 13th century. According to Mevlevi tradition, during the *sema* the soul is freed from earthly ties and is able to jubilantly commune with the divine. (*Dervish* literally means "doorway" and is thought to be an entrance from the material world to the spiritual.) The felt hat represents personal ego's tombstone, and the wide skirt symbolizes its shroud.

For instance, when Maasai boys in East Africa's grasslands move into the Warrior age set; they are ritually removed from their families and circumcised, returning weeks later as armed young men with a distinctive hairstyle and dress.

Another example is the ritual preparation for womanhood experienced by Mende girls in West Africa. Soon after their first menstruation, they are separated from family and spend weeks in seclusion. Discarding their childhood clothes, they learn the moral and practical responsibilities of motherhood from senior women. Believing circumcision enhances a girl's reproductive potential, these elders are tasked with removing each girl's clitoris (considered a female version of a penis). A good deal of singing,

dancing, storytelling, and food accompany the ordeal and the training, which produces a strong sense of sisterhood. The girls emerge from their initiation as women in knowledgeable control of their sexuality, eligible for marriage and childbearing (MacCormack, 1977).

Rites of Intensification

A **rite of intensification** is a ritual held to reaffirm the ties that bind a group together when crisis threatens the social order. Whatever the precise nature of the crisis—a death in the family, an earthquake, an epidemic, or a terrorist attack—community rituals are organized to ease anxiety, prevent a breakdown, and orient individuals toward a restoration of collective well-being. A celebratory affirmation of the group's ideals and values reassures

rite of intensification A ritual that takes place during a crisis in the life of the group and serves to bind individuals together.

people that the upheaval is temporary and that normal life will continue.

Rites of intensification do not have to be limited to times of overt crisis. In regions where human activities change in accordance with seasonal climatic shifts, these rites may take the form of annual ceremonies. They are particularly common among horticultural and agricultural peoples. For example, solstice ceremonies are staged to correspond with the crucially important planting and harvesting seasons, ritually articulating traditional ideas about the role of the supernatural in the cyclical return of rain, the light and warmth of the sun, and other factors of nature vital to healthy and bountiful crops. A similar cultural linkage between the annual subsistence cycle and the ceremonial calendar with its rites of intensification can be found in societies based on seasonal fishing and herding or hunting of migratory animals.

Magical Rituals

People in many cultures believe that supernatural powers can be compelled to act in certain ways for good or evil purposes by recourse to specified formulas. In short, they believe in **magic** and carry out magical rituals. Such rituals are intended to ensure positive ends such as good crops, fertility of livestock, replenishment of hunted game, prevention of accidents, healing of illness, protection against injury, promise of victory, and the defeat of enemies, real or imagined. In traditional societies many of these rituals rely on *fetishes*—objects believed to possess magical powers (Figure 23.10).

Magical rituals are also popular in wealthy industrialized societies. Individuals commonly seek "good luck" when the outcome is in doubt or beyond one's influence—from lighting a votive candle for someone going through a hard time, to wearing lucky boxers on a hot date, to the curious gesturing baseball pitchers perform on the mound.

Anthropologists distinguish between two fundamental principles of magic. The first principle—that like produces like—is identified as **imitative magic** or *sympathetic magic*. In Myanmar in Southeast Asia, for example, a rejected and spiteful lover might engage a sorcerer to make an image of his would-be love. If this image were tossed into water, to the accompaniment of certain charms, it was expected that the girl would go mad and suffer a fate similar to that of her image.

The second principle is that of **contagious magic**—the idea that things or persons once in contact can influence each other after the contact is broken. The most common example of contagious magic is the permanent relationship between an individual and any part of his or her body, such as hair, fingernails, or teeth. For instance, the Basutos of Lesotho in southern Africa were careful to conceal their extracted teeth to make sure they did not fall into the hands of certain mythical beings who could harm the owners of the teeth by working magic on them.

© SSPL/The Image Works

Figure 23.10 **Congolese Fetish**

This 100-year-old carving from the Democratic Republic of Congo is a *nkondi*, with supernatural power coming in part from magic herbs hidden inside by a diviner. Such fetishes are traditionally used to identify wrongdoers, including thieves and witches responsible for mishaps, diseases, or death. A *nkondi* is activated by provocations (such as hammering nails into it) or invocations urging magic punishment of the suspects.

Related to this is the custom in Western societies of treasuring things that have been touched by special people. Such items range from a saint's relics to possessions of other admired or idolized individuals, from rock stars to sports heroes to spiritual gurus.

---

magic Specific formulas and actions used to compel supernatural powers to act in certain ways for good or evil purposes.

imitative magic Magic based on the principle that like produces like; sometimes called *sympathetic magic*.

contagious magic Magic based on the principle that things or persons once in contact can influence each other after the contact is broken.

Earl & Nazima Kowall/Corbis

AP Images/ANAT GIVON

Figure 23.11 Divination
The range of traditional divination techniques still practiced in many hundreds of cultures is very large. Several techniques have become popular far outside the regions where they originated, including "bone throwing." On the left, we see Ndebele women healers ("witchdoctors") known as *sangomas*, in Gemsbokspruit, Mpumalanga Province, South Africa, practicing this craft. In the other photo, a well-known *feng shui* master in Hong Kong is using his "24 mountains" compass to determine a building's energy (*ch'i* or *qi*) outside a client's apartment.

Divination: Omens and Oracles

Designed to access or influence supernatural powers, magical rituals have been developed to prepare for the uncertain future—for the unseen and for the not yet present. Fears of pending dangers—for example, storms, attacks, betrayals, diseases, and death—call for precautionary measures, such as what to avoid and where to go. How does one find and interpret the signs, or *omens*, foretelling the future? The answer, as developed in many cultures, is through **divination**, a magical ritual designed to discover what is unknowable by ordinary means, in particular signs predicting fate or destiny.

Various ancient methods of divination exist, including *geomancy* (from Greek, *geo* for "earth" and *manteia* for "divination"), a technique traditionally considered sacred and practiced by shamans, prophets, fortunetellers, or other oracles in communication with supernatural forces. Skilled to interpret omens, a diviner practicing geomancy may toss a handful of sand or pebbles, for example, and then analyze its random patterns, searching for information hidden to ordinary people. Other divination methods include decoding flame or smoke patterns in a fire, deciphering cloud formations

in the air, or interpreting colors, ripples, and whirls in water.

More widely known is the divination technique involving palm reading, perhaps most famously practiced by female Gypsy fortunetellers. So-called mediums are also popular. In the United States, for example, many people believe mediums can contact the spirits of dead relatives and pass on messages from beyond by means of an ancient ritual method known as *necromancy*.

Believed to possess knowledge hidden from ordinary people, diviners are feared in many cultures. However, they are also in high demand among those who believe in a diviner's capacity to predict the future and provide insightful consultation concerning an important or risky undertaking. One example of this is an ancient Chinese divination technique known as *feng shui*, literally translated as "wind-water." This method has gained popularity in North America, especially on the Pacific Coast where growing numbers of homebuilders and buyers hire *feng shui* consultants to help them design or redesign homes and offices to conform to the principle of *qi* or *ch'i* ("vital energy") (Figure 23.11).

In some religious traditions, including Islam and Christianity, fortunetelling and other divination rituals have long been viewed with suspicion, and in many places these practices have been prohibited. Especially when performed by individuals functioning in other religious or spiritual traditions believed to be false or worse, divination is condemned as evil magic, sorcery, or witchcraft.

divination A magical procedure or spiritual ritual designed to discern what is not knowable by ordinary means, such as foretelling the future by interpreting omens.

Witchcraft: Anxiety and Fears of Evil Magic

Magical rituals intended to cause misfortune or inflict harm are often referred to as sorcery or **witchcraft**—practices by individuals embodying evil spirit power or those collaborating with malevolent supernatural beings. In contrast to magic-working experts inclined to do good, these individuals inspire fear.

Fear of witches is especially prevalent during periods of uncertainty and transition. When mysterious illnesses, devastating droughts, accidental deaths, economic uncertainties, and other upheavals disturb the cultural order, confusion may result in a surge of suspicion and a focus on disliked, unsociable, isolated individuals. Especially in patrilineal or patrilocal communities, the accused is often an older woman, typically single or widowed and without children. Among matrilineal and matrilocal groups, however, people tend to think of witches as male. Not all individuals accused of "evil magic" are punished, tortured, or killed, but witchcraft accusations clearly function as a social control mechanism, horribly reinforcing the moral code.

Navajo Skin-Walkers

Beliefs in evil magic are widespread and take many forms. One interesting example comes from the Navajo, Native Americans historically surviving as sheepherders and small-scale irrigation farmers in the vast deserts of Arizona and New Mexico. The Navajo have a substantial repertoire of sacred rituals for healing victims of sorcery, all related to accusations of evil magic.

Among Navajos, who live in a residence group organized around a head woman, traditional belief holds that a person suffering from severe anxiety disorder, repetitive nightmares, or delusions is a victim of sorcery. The idea is that a ghost or some other evil spirit, traveling under cover of darkness, is responsible. And according to the Navajo, the suspect is a powerful sorcerer, almost always a man, probably someone who has killed a relative and committed incest.

These dangerous Navajo sorcerers, resembling the werewolf of European folklore and the Nagual in rural Mexico, are believed to be able to change themselves into animal form. Referred to as a *'ánt'įįhnii* ("skin-walker"), such a sorcerer stealthily goes to a secluded spot, such as a cave at night. There, he transforms into a coyote or wolf. Disguised in animal form, he emerges and runs fast toward his victim, bringing on *'ánt'į* ("the curse"). Having completed his accursed mission, the skin-walker swiftly returns to his hideaway, transforms again into human form, and slips back into his home before dawn (Kluckhohn, 1944; Selinger, 2007).

Sacred Sites: Saints, Shrines, and Miracles

Sacred sites are typically positioned in a transitional, or *liminary*, zone between the natural and supernatural, the secular and spiritual, earth and heaven. Reaching high into the sky, mountaintops are often considered to be magical places, shrouded in mystery. For instance, the Japanese view the snowcapped perfect volcanic cone of Mount Fuji ("Ever-Lasting Life") as a sacred place. Likewise, the Kikuyu view Mount Kenya as the earthly dwelling place of their creator god Ngai.

Some sites become sacred because they are places where ordinary human beings experienced something extraordinary—heard a divine voice or saw a guardian spirit, patron saint, or archangel. Often a site is declared sacred because believers associate it with a miracle-working mystic, saint, prophet, or other holy person. The tombs of such individuals often turn into shrines (*scrinium*, Latin for "round box" or "container," holding relics). For example, stories of miraculous events and special powers emanating from Muslim tombs are common wherever Sufism, a far-reaching mystical branch of Islam, is popular (Gladney, 2004).

Based on the principle of contagious magic, any material substance physically linked to a miraculous event or individual may itself become revered as holy or sacred. This may include bones, hair, or any other body part believed to have belonged to a saint, or something the person wore, possessed, or simply touched. All these things may be treasured as holy relics and safeguarded in a shrine, inspiring the faithful.

Burial sites of saints often gain such importance that people feel inspired to construct a very large shrine for the saint's entombment; termed a *mausoleum*, some of these are large enough for the interment of lesser saints and pious individuals desiring proximity to the sacred saint after death. However large or small, shrines are religious focal points for prayer, meditation, and sacrifice.

Pilgrimages: Devotion in Motion

Every year, many millions of devotees of many religions—including Buddhism, Christianity, Hinduism, Islam, and their many branches—walk, climb, or even crawl to a sacred or holy site. Whether it is a saint's tomb, a mountain, lake, river, waterfall, or some other particular place believed to be metaphysically significant, *pilgrims* (from Latin *peregrinus*, meaning "wanderer") travel there seeking enlightenment, proving their devotion, and/or hoping to experience a miracle.

witchcraft Magical rituals intended to cause misfortune or inflict harm.

A devotion in motion, a **pilgrimage** demands personal sacrifices from the travelers. Enjoying little comfort, pilgrims may suffer from hunger and thirst, heat and cold, pain and fear while on the road, sometimes for many days or even months. During their sacred journey, they participate in a religious drama, performing ritually prescribed acts such as prayers, chants, or prostrations. To identify their status as spiritually inspired travelers, some wear special clothes, shave their heads, and carry amulets.

One of the most challenging pilgrimages is the climb up the slopes of a mountain range in the Himalayas where Mount Kailash rises 6,700 meters (over 22,000 feet). Located in western Tibet, this black, snowcapped mountain stands out boldly in a dramatic landscape sacred to Hindus and Buddhists, as well as Jains and Bönpos. The latter, who practice an ancient Tibetan shamanic religion, refer to this hallowed mountain as Tisé ("Water Peak") because it is the source of four sacred rivers. For Hindus, it is the holy abode of Lord Shiva, the destroyer of ignorance and illusion and the divine source of yoga. Jains view Kailash as the sacred place where their divine cultural hero Rishabha ("Bull")—an incarnation of Lord Vishnu—first achieved full enlightenment. Finally, Tibetan Buddhists revere it as Gangs Rinpoche ("Snow Lord") and believe it to be the abode of Khorlo Demchok ("Circle of Bliss")—a wrathful deity who uses his power to destroy the three major obstacles to enlightenment: anger, greed, and ignorance.

For all four of these religious traditions, climbing to the summit of this holy mountain is taboo. So, pilgrims demonstrate their devotion by means of a ritual encirclement, or circumambulation—clockwise by Buddhists and Hindus, and in reverse by Jains and Bönpos. The rugged, 52-kilometer (32-mile) trek is seen as a sacred ritual that removes sins and brings good fortune. Each year thousands follow the ancient tradition of encircling the mountain on foot. The most devout pilgrims turn their circumambulation into a sacrificial ordeal: Prostrating their bodies full length, they extend their hands forward and make a mark on the ground with their fingers; then they rise, pray, crawl ahead on hands and knees to the mark, and then repeat the process again and again (Figure 23.12).

One of the world's largest pilgrimages is the *hajj*—a performance of piety now made by 1.8 million Muslims traveling to Mecca in Saudi Arabia each year from all across the globe. The largest contingent of *hajjis*—about 300,000 a year—comes from Indonesia. One of the five pillars of Islam, the *hajj* brings all of these pilgrims together for collective prayers and other sacred rituals at the Kaaba in Mecca, their religion's holiest site.

Christianity, originating in what was an eastern province of the Roman empire about 2,000 years ago, has created a sacred landscape dotted with dozens of major pilgrimage sites in Southwest Asia and Europe. As in other ancient religions, these sites are symbolically associated

Glogowski/laif/Redux

Figure 23.12 Pilgrimage to Mount Kailash in Tibet
Rising 6,700 meters (over 22,000 feet), this mountain has been sacred for many generations to Buddhists and Hindus, as well as Jains and Bönpos (followers of Tibet's indigenous religion, Bön). Every year a few thousand pilgrims make the tortuous 52-kilometer (32-mile) trek around it. Some of them crawl the entire distance.

with miracles and legendary holy men and women. For example, for nearly a millennium Christian pilgrims from all over Europe have made the long and difficult journey to Santiago de Compostela. Tens of thousands travel to this Spanish seaport each year—most by foot, some by bicycle, and a few on horseback like their medieval counterparts. About 180,000 pilgrims walk the final 100 kilometers (62 miles) to the old cathedral with the shrine containing the sacred remains of the apostle Saint James venerated as Santiago (Santo Iago) since the Middle Ages and recognized as the official patron saint of Spain. Many more Roman Catholics make pilgrimages to shrines devoted to Saint Mary, as described in the following section.

Female Saints: Divine Protection for the Weak

Many religions consider the divine to be primarily or exclusively masculine, as noted earlier. Ideologically

---

pilgrimage A devotion in motion; traveling, often on foot, to a sacred or holy site to reach for enlightenment, prove devotion, and/or experience a miracle.

reproducing the hierarchical social order dominated by men, this arrangement reflects the worldview of traditional cultures that revere male deities, prophets, and saints in officially sponsored cults and devotions. But religions are not monolithic, and some provide flexible spiritual space for alternatives. We see this in Christian cults devoted to female saints such as Mary, the virgin mother of Jesus Christ, the son of God.

More powerful than the pope in Rome, Mary has been loved and adored as a holy mother residing in heaven. Worldwide, Roman Catholic multitudes look up to her for divine protection. Like other Christian saints, she is thought to perform miracles and to be capable of physically manifesting herself at places and times of her choosing. Through the centuries, many believers claim to have witnessed such holy moments, some officially reporting the miracle. Typically, these believers are young members of the underclass—herders, peasants, or housemaids, for example. Beyond stories about the female saint manifesting herself to such low-status individuals, the discovery of sacred relics (such as a drowned or buried statue representing Mary) may also generate excitement and hope in difficult times.

As folk-based popular religious movements, Saint Mary cults not only developed across Europe, but also in Latin America, the Philippines, and other parts of the world historically colonized and dominated by Roman Catholics originating in Europe. The religious ideas and rituals of Catholicism changed many indigenous cultures—and were also changed by them. Of particular interest in this shifting religious landscape are Black Madonnas: brown or dark-colored clay or wooden statues, or painted images, representing the virgin mother.

A popular devotion involving a brown-skinned Saint Mary concerns the Virgin of Guadalupe. This Mexican cult originated in 1531, a decade after a Spanish army had conquered the Aztec Indian empire. That year, a recently converted Aztec Christian claimed that a holy woman miraculously appeared to him in a blaze of light at the foot of a hill—now part of Mexico City. Speaking in his native tongue and resembling an Aztec fertility goddess, the mysterious brown-skinned woman told him a shrine had to be built in her honor. Known as the Virgin of Guadalupe, she became the patron saint of Mexico. Today,

Figure 23.13 Virgin of Guadalupe Pilgrim, Mexico City
On December 9, 1531, Saint Mary appeared to Mexican Indian Juan Diego, a recent Christian convert, as he passed by Tepeyac Hill in what is now Mexico City. At the site of this encounter, the Basilica of Our Lady of Guadalupe was built with a shrine containing sacred evidence of this miraculous apparition. Pictured here are Christian pilgrims walking toward the shrine, which attracts more than 6 million devotees a year, making it one of the largest pilgrimage sites in the world.

most of the 6 million pilgrims who visit her shrine each year are indigenous or *mestizo* Mexicans (**Figure 23.13**).

Desecration: Ruining Sacred Sites

Although popular shrines are destinations for believers from near and far, they are also potential targets of **desecration**. By means of such ideologically inspired violation of a sacred site, enemies aim to inflict harm, if only symbolically, on people judged to have impure, false, or evil beliefs and ritual practices. Desecrations have occurred across the globe for thousands of years, as evidenced in archaeological sites and recorded in oral traditions or historical documents.

For example, during the Protestant Reformation in the 16th and 17th centuries, Christian Protestant iconoclasts campaigning against idolatry in northwestern Europe destroyed untold numbers of ancient Roman Catholic

desecration Ideologically inspired violation of a sacred site intended to inflict harm, if only symbolically, on people judged to have impure, false, or even evil beliefs and ritual practices.

statues and other treasures kept in sacred shrines. More recently, militant Muslim fundamentalists in North Africa and West Asia have blown up or bulldozed ancient statues of divinities and centuries-old religious shrines they denounce as objects of "false worship." Intolerance and destruction in the name of religion is not unique to Christian or Muslim puritans, as militant Hindus and others also engage in similar desecrations. Desecration can also be inspired by *anti*religious fervor, as occurred with China's Cultural Revolution in the 1960s, when masses of activists, swept up in state-sponsored zeal, went on a rampage destroying religious monuments, sculptures, carvings, and paintings, as well as a large number of age-old sacred shrines.

Cultural Dynamics in the Superstructure: Religious and Spiritual Change

New technologies, improved means of transportation, internationalization of production and labor markets, and worldwide movements of ideas and practices all contribute to challenging and even destabilizing long-established cultural systems and associated worldviews. Reacting to these challenges, people often turn to the supernatural to allay the anxiety of a world going awry. Some bundle or devise their own spiritual beliefs and rituals. Others form or join new spiritual movements.

Typically, these religious movements call for a radical return to traditional foundations prescribed in sacred texts and narrowly interpreted by conservative spiritual leaders. Examples include Islamic fundamentalism in countries such as Nigeria, Egypt, and Iran; Jewish fundamentalism in Israel and the United States; and Hindu fundamentalism in India. Christian fundamentalism is represented in the dramatic growth of evangelical denominations in the United States, Latin America, and sub-Saharan Africa.

With over 2,000 distinctive faiths, the U.S. religious landscape is highly diversified, and the country has given birth to many new religions, a few of which have gone global. Moreover, in the past few decades, Asian immigrant groups have greatly added to the religious diversification in North America as well as in Europe. In response, even global finance business is adapting to the changing ideological landscape, as illustrated in this chapter's Original Study on Shariah-compliant banking.

ORIGINAL STUDY

Sacred Law in Global Capitalism   *BY BILL MAURER*

I will never forget my introduction to Islamic banking. It happened at a 1998 conference when I happened into a darkened room where the founder of an Islamic investment firm was showing a clip from the old Hollywood classic movie, *It's a Wonderful Life*. On the screen, George Bailey, played by Jimmy Stewart, faces an anxious crowd of Bedford Falls citizens, who have rushed into his Building and Loan desperate to get their money. There is about to be a run on the bank.

One of the townspeople says he wants his money, *now*. George protests, "But you're thinking of this place all wrong—as if I had the money back in a safe. The money's not *here*. Why, your money's in Joe's house that's right next to yours, and in the Kennedy house . . . and in a hundred others. You're lending them the money to build and then they're gonna pay it back. . . . Now, we can get through this thing all right. We've got to stick together, though. We've got to have faith in each other." The people cry, "I've got doctor's bills to pay!" "Can't feed my kids on faith!"

Then Mary, George's newlywed bride, shouts from behind the counter, "I've got two thousand dollars!" and holds up a wad of bills. It is the money for their honeymoon. George chimes in, "This'll tide us over until the bank reopens tomorrow." He proceeds to disburse money based on people's stated needs ("Could I have $17.50?" one woman asks meekly) and guaranteed only by his trust in them.

Seconds before 6 o'clock, the last client leaves. George has just two dollars left. He, his Uncle Billy, and two cousins count down the seconds and then lock the doors. They have managed to stay in business for one more day. They place the two remaining dollars in a tray, and George offers a toast: "To Mama Dollar and to Papa Dollar, and if you want this old Building and Loan to stay in business you better have a family real quick." "I wish they were rabbits," says Cousin Tilly.

At this point in the film, the conference host paused the video and said, "This is the first *lariba* movie." A murmur went through the crowd. No one quite knew what he meant. Most of the audience was Muslim; this was a Christmas movie. What was our host trying to say?

I now know that *lariba* is Arabic for "no increase." The Quran invokes the term *riba* (increase) twenty times, and the term is often translated as interest or usury (excessive interest). Islamic banking and finance aim to avoid *riba* through profit-and-loss sharing, leasing, or other forms of equity- or asset-based financing.

Palani Mohan /The New York Times/Redux

Until the early 1990s, millions of Muslims throughout the world had few investment opportunities due to the ethics derived from Shariah law. Since then, hundreds of Islamic financial institutions have emerged in over fifty countries. Big U.S. and European banks, including Citibank, have also entered the Islamic banking business in order to tap into the rising oil wealth. Today, Shariah-compliant banks manage well over $750 billion globally. Here we see three Muslim women in Kuala Lumpur, Malaysia.

After that 1998 conference, I began my study of global Islamic banking, including the efforts of American Muslims to create a new kind of "Islamic" mortgage that enables devout Muslims to buy a home in accordance with Islam's prohibition of interest. Instead of financing a home purchase with interest-bearing debt, Islamic alternatives rely on either leasing contracts (a sort of rent-to-own arrangement where the bank owns the house and the purchaser buys out the bank's share over time) or a partnership arrangement (like a joint business venture). Rather than having debt and interest at the center of the mortgage, as in a conventional loan, the house itself and its fair market rental value are at the center. The purchaser buys

We are all aware of the recent global financial crisis, which led to the collapse of major corporations, the nationalization of big banks and car companies, massive unemployment, and unnerving insecurity for many people in the United States and around the world. One of the leading causes of the crisis was the marketing of debt to people who probably could not repay, and the packaging of those debts into complicated financial instruments that were supposed to curb risk but instead increased it.

What, you might ask, does anthropology have to contribute to the study of the financial markets, money, and the wider economy? Quite a lot, actually. Among other things, anthropologists have repeatedly demonstrated that economic decisions thought to be purely rational and self-interested are actually deeply embedded in social relationships, cultural values, and religious beliefs.

Take securitized debt instruments, for example—loans like mortgages, chopped up and rebundled together into salable commodities. When they started to go sour, many commentators blamed the instruments' complexity and called for a return to an economy based on real things instead of abstract tradable debt. However, we know from our research across the globe that peoples in different cultures do not always differentiate the real from the abstract in the same way. A person's reputation might be deemed more solid and real than a piece of gold. And a piece of gold has real value only because people agree to it as a convention.

out the bank's share over time. At the center is the asset—the real thing—not the debt.

Of course, there is no reason why a joint partnership to own a piece of property is any more "real" or less "abstract" than bundling together debt. It depends on one's point of view, and one's precommitments to certain values—prohibiting interest and sharing risk, for example, or distributing risk onto others. In Islamic finance, the former is seen as "Shariah compliant," or in accord with Islamic law; and the latter, as unjust because it offloads one's own share of risk onto others.

At the same time, Islamic mortgages often require relatively large down payments; this excludes poorer people from achieving the American dream of homeownership. So, we need to ask ourselves whether the virtues of adherence to the precepts of one's religion outweigh broader social goals of financial inclusion.

Global Islamic banking today owes much to the immigration of Middle Eastern and South Asian students and professionals to the United States and western Europe since the 1970s, and the consolidation of large U.S.–Muslim organizations. The oil boom in the Middle East during the 1970s, which sparked renewed interest in Islamic banking in many Muslim-majority countries, also encouraged the development of a loosely knit interconnected network of Muslim international businessmen, who, working for oil and chemical companies as well as financial firms, gained experience in Western regulatory and business environments.

Islamic home financing expanded greatly after the 2001 terrorist attack on New York's World Trade Center and the Pentagon; these attacks sent shockwaves through the capitalist world system dominated by Wall Street. First of all, Americans in general, Muslims included, took their money out of the stock market after the attack and started investing in real estate, buoyed by low interest rates and feeding the speculative real estate bubble. Second, Islamic mutual funds had been able to maintain their "Islamicity" in part by contributing a portion of their profits to charity in order to religiously "cleanse" the funds; however, as charities came under governmental suspicion for terrorist money laundering, many Muslims withdrew their investments from these funds. Third, home financing, American Muslims told me, is the cornerstone of the "American

dream," and they were eager to demonstrate their commitment to that dream.

People involved in Islamic banking and finance are continually engaged in an effort to define precisely what their field is. Is *riba* simply Arabic for "interest," or does *riba* refer only to "excessive interest" or usury? Does the prohibition say something about justice, or does it moralize about proper market relationships? Like any aspect of culture—economy included—Islamic banking is always a field of debate. And more debate, not less, may help us all to find just, peaceful, and profitable ways out of the various catastrophes we continually make for ourselves, as we create the abstractions and realities that mutually determine our lives together.

Written expressly for this text, 2010.

Revitalization Movements

No anthropological consideration of religion is complete without some mention of **revitalization movements**— movements for radical cultural reform in response to widespread social disruption and collective feelings of great stress and despair. As a deliberate effort to construct a more satisfying culture, revitalization movements aim to reform not just the religious sphere of activity but may also impact an entire cultural system.

Many such movements developed in indigenous societies where European colonial exploitation caused enormous upheaval. They also occurred in 16th-century Europe—as evidenced in the emergence of Puritans, Mennonites, and other Protestant groups when traditional societies faced radical transformations triggered by early capitalism and other forces. Likewise, revitalization movements emerged in response to the industrial revolution triggering similar radical transformations in agrarian societies in the 19th century. These occurred not only in Europe but also in the northeastern United States, where Mormonism, Jehovah's Witnesses, Seventh-Day Adventists, and others began as Christian revitalization movements.

Revitalization movements can be found in many religions. They are evident in the revival or introduction of traditional American Indian ceremonies such as the sweat lodge now common on many tribal reservations in North America, as well as the spectacular Sun Dance ceremony held each summer at various reservations in the Great Plains. Similar cultural revivals of "spiritual neo-traditions" are on the rise in many parts of the world, including Europe (Prins, 1994). Multitudes in northwestern

Europe, attracted to a naturalistic worldview, now also practice forms of "ecospiritualism" (Prins, 1996). Often this involves a revival of ancient pre-Christian traditions, such as Asatru in Scandinavia and Druidry in the British Isles. Seeking a sacred relationship with nature, adherents worship the earth, elements of the sky, and spirits they believe arise from sacred places like rivers and mountains (**Figure 23.14**).

Syncretic Religions

In Africa, during and following the period of foreign colonization and missionization, indigenous groups resisted or creatively revised Christian teachings and formed culturally appropriate religious movements. During the past century, thousands of indigenous Christian churches have been founded in Africa. These churches are often born of alternative theological interpretations and new divinely inspired revelations. They also originate from disapproval by foreign missionaries concerning the preservation of traditional beliefs and rituals culturally associated with animism, ancestor worship, and spirit possession, as well as kinship and marriage.

Today, the African continent is as religiously and spiritually diverse as ever. Although at least 40 percent of the population is Christian, and more than another 40 percent is Muslim, myriad African indigenous religions persist and are often merged with Christianity or Islam.

Syncretic Religions Across the Atlantic: Vodou in Haiti

In almost four centuries of trans-Atlantic slave trading, African captives—stolen from hundreds of towns and villages from Mauretania south to Angola and

---

revitalization movement A social movement for radical cultural reform in response to widespread social disruption and collective feelings of great stress and despair.

Figure 23.14 Stonehenge, Wiltshire County, England
In 2010, the neo-tradition of Druidry was officially recognized as a religion in Great Britain.
Stonehenge, a 4,500-year-old Neolithic site, is one of its sacred centers. With 10,000 followers,
modern Druidry is rooted in the pre-Christian tradition of the Celtic peoples indigenous to the
British Isles.

beyond—were shipped across the ocean to labor on cotton, sugar, coffee, and tobacco plantations from Virginia to Brazil. Ripped from family and community, individual slaves clung to some of their ancestral beliefs and knowledge of rituals.

Sharing a life of forced labor, slaves from different ethnic, linguistic, and religious backgrounds formed small communities, pooled remembered religious ideas and rituals, and creatively forged a spiritual repertoire of their own. Founded on a mix of Yoruba and other African beliefs and practices, their emerging religions also incorporated Christian features, including terminology from the languages of slave-owning colonists. In some cases, elements from a region's indigenous American cultures were also included.

Such creative blending of indigenous and foreign beliefs and practices into new cultural forms is known as **syncretism**. Especially after slavery was abolished in the course of the 1800s, these syncretic spiritual repertoires developed into Afro-Caribbean religions such as Vodou in Haiti and Santería in Cuba, which resemble Candomblé in Brazil. All of these religions are spreading as adherents freely migrate across borders (Fernández Olmos & Paravisini-Gebert, 2003).

The name *vodou* (or *voodoo*) means "divine spirit" in the language of the Fon, a large ethnic group in West Africa. Providing an escape from the indignities of poverty and hopelessness, Vodou was developed by former slaves.

Now mostly poor black peasants, they are nominal Roman Catholics who, like their African ancestors across the Atlantic, believe in spirit possession.

Vodou rituals center on the worship of what Haitians refer to as *loas*—also known in Creole as *saints*. This tradition is essentially based on a belief in a reciprocal relationship between the spirits of the living and those of the dead, representing multiple expressions of the divine. Vodou priests summon spirits of deceased ancestors and other relatives by drumming in a temple. Dancing to the beat, worshipers enter into trance. This is when a person's spirit temporarily vacates the human body, replaced by a *loa* from the spirit world who takes possession—the moment of divine grace (Figure 23.15).

Secularization and Religious Pluralism

Although Christianity in Europe is losing ground as a result of Islam's rise, a far more substantial decline is due to **secularization**. In this process of cultural change,

syncretism The creative blending of indigenous and foreign beliefs and practices into new cultural forms.

secularization A process of cultural change in which a population tends toward a nonreligious worldview, ignoring or rejecting institutionalized spiritual beliefs and rituals.

Steve Winter/National Geographic Stock

Figure 23.15 **Haitian Women in a Vodou Bathing Ritual**
In mid-July every year, thousands of Haitian pilgrims journey to a sacred waterfall in the mountains
north of Port-au-Prince, Haiti, in reverence to a Black Madonna known as Our Lady of Carmel.
This Marian devotion is ritually associated with a major *loa*, or Vodou spirit, named Erzulie Dantor,
who mysteriously appeared on a palm tree at this waterfall about 150 years ago. Since then, an
important devotional activity is bathing in this sacred water, a deeply spiritual experience in which
Vodou practitioners like these women enter a trance filled with divine grace.

a population tends toward a nonreligious worldview, ignoring or rejecting institutionalized spiritual beliefs and
rituals. Over the last few decades, growing numbers of
western Europeans have declared themselves to be without religion.

Secularization is especially noteworthy in a prosperous
capitalist country like Germany, which has been for many
centuries predominantly Lutheran and Roman Catholic.
Today, almost 40 percent of Germans identify themselves
as nonreligious, compared to a mere 4 percent forty
years ago. In contrast, religion is becoming *more* important in many parts of eastern Europe where atheism was
communist state ideology for several generations in the
20th century.

Secularization also takes place in other wealthy industrialized countries. In the United States, for example,
20 percent of all adults are religiously unaffiliated—and
the figure jumps to about 35 percent among adults

under 30. Their ranks include more than 13 million
self-described atheists and agnostics—nearly 6 percent of
the U.S. public (Pew Research Center, 2012). As in other
large countries, there are regional contrasts, with the secularization trend among New Englanders far outpacing
several areas in the southeastern United States, where 80
to 85 percent claim that religion plays an important role
in their lives.

As chronicled in this chapter, the quest for metaphysical explanations and revelations occurs everywhere in
countless ways—from massive religious gatherings to
the recurrent rise of new spiritual leaders and religious
movements, growing participation in pilgrimages and
spiritual healing ceremonies, and persistent efforts to
safeguard places that people have designated as sacred
sites. In this cross-cultural survey of religion and spirituality, we explored and contrasted numerous worldviews

with their symbolic constructs of the universe and our place in it. Clearly, religion and spirituality are not just about spiritual beliefs and rituals, however important these may be. They are also fundamental in the construction of social identities and motivate people to act in prescribed ways.

Performing religion or spirituality, individually or collectively, people not only express what they feel and think but also *who* they are. The need to find deeper meaning in life and to make sense of an increasingly complex, uncharted, confusing, and even frightening world drives humans to continue their explorations—religious and spiritual, as well as scientific. All of this makes the anthropological study of religion not only fascinating but crucial in our efforts to better understand our species in all its creative and destructive cultural capacity.

CHAPTER CHECKLIST

What are religion and spirituality, and what role do they play in a cultural system?

✓ Religion is an organized system of ideas about the spiritual sphere or the supernatural, and it is a key part of every culture's worldview. Like religion, spirituality is concerned with sacred matters, but it is often individual rather than collective and does not require a distinctive format or traditional organization.

✓ Among food-foraging peoples, religion is intertwined with everyday life. As societies become more complex, it may be restricted to particular occasions.

✓ Spiritual and religious beliefs and practices fulfill numerous psychological and emotional needs, such as reducing anxiety by providing an orderly view of the universe and answering existential questions.

✓ Myths are narratives that explain the fundamentals of human existence—where we and everything in our world came from, why we are here, and where we are going.

✓ A traditional religion reinforces group norms and provides moral sanctions for individual conduct. Its narratives and rituals confirm the existing social order, but it may also provide vehicles for challenging that order. People often turn to religion or spirituality in the hope of reaching a specific goal such as restoring health.

What types of supernatural beings and forces are included in the worldview of humans?

✓ Religion is characterized by a belief in supernatural beings and forces that can be appealed to for aid through prayer, sacrifice, and other rituals. Supernatural beings include major deities (gods and goddesses), ancestral spirits, and other sorts of spirit beings.

✓ Gods and goddesses are great but remote beings that control the universe. Whether people recognize gods, goddesses, or both has to do with

how men and women relate to each other in everyday life.

✓ Monotheism holds that there is one supreme divinity; polytheism acknowledges more than one deity.

✓ Belief in ancestral spirits is based on the dualistic idea that human beings consist of a body and a soul or vital spirit that continues to participate in human affairs after death.

✓ Animism, the belief that nature is enlivened by distinct personalized spirit beings separable from bodies, is common among peoples who see themselves as part of nature rather than superior to it.

✓ Animatism, often found alongside animism, is a belief that nature is enlivened by an impersonal spiritual force, which may make itself manifest in any special place, thing, or living creature.

What are the different types of religious specialists?

✓ Priests and priestesses are full-time religious specialists authorized to perform sacred rituals and mediate with supernatural powers on behalf of others.

✓ Priests and priestesses typically hold their position by way of spiritual lineage in which divine authority is passed down from a spiritual founder to a chain of successors.

✓ There are four major forms of spiritual lineage: biological descent, training and appointment by religious leaders, election, and recognition of a reincarnated saint.

✓ Shamans are individuals skilled at entering an altered state of consciousness to contact and utilize an ordinarily hidden reality in order to acquire knowledge and supernatural power to help other people.

What are religious rituals and rites, and what purposes do they serve?

✓ A religious ritual is a culturally symbolic act or procedure designed to guide members of a community in an orderly way through personal and collective transitions. It is religion in action—the means through which people relate to the supernatural.

✓ Rites of purification are rituals performed to establish or restore purity when someone has violated a taboo or is otherwise unclean.

✓ Rites of passage are rituals marking an important stage in an individual's life cycle, such as birth, marriage, and death. They feature three phases: separation, transition, and incorporation.

✓ Rites of intensification are rituals that ease anxiety and bind people together when they face a collective crisis or change. Such rituals may also be staged to mark seasonal changes and subsistence cycles.

What are magic, divination, and witchcraft?

✓ People in many cultures believe in magic: the idea that supernatural powers can be compelled to act in certain ways for good or evil purposes through specified formulas.

✓ Divination is a magical procedure or spiritual ritual designed to find out what is not knowable by ordinary means, particularly through signs foretelling fate or destiny.

✓ Witchcraft—magical ritual intended to cause misfortune or inflict harm and often referred to as sorcery—is believed to be practiced by people who embody evil spirit power or collaborate with malevolent supernatural beings.

✓ Belief in witchcraft is widespread, takes many forms, and is especially common during periods of uncertainty.

What are sacred sites and pilgrimages?

✓ Sacred sites may be places where ordinary people experienced something extraordinary or places associated with a holy person, or they may be exceptional natural places, especially mountaintops.

✓ A pilgrimage is a devotion in motion—a journey, often on foot, to a sacred site by individuals reaching for enlightenment, proving devotion, and/or hoping to experience a miracle. Among the largest pilgrimages is the *hajj* made by 1.8 million Muslims traveling to Mecca in Saudi Arabia each year from all around the world.

✓ Many pilgrimages center on cults of the Virgin Mary. These include Black Madonnas—dark-colored statues or painted images representing the virgin mother—such as the Virgin of Guadalupe whose shrine in Mexico City draws 6 million pilgrims a year.

✓ Sacred sites are potential targets of desecration— ideological violation of a sacred site aimed at harming, if only symbolically, people judged to have impure, false, or evil beliefs and ritual practices.

What are revitalization movements, and how are they connected to social upheaval?

✓ Revitalization movements arise when people seek radical cultural reform in response to widespread social disruption and collective feelings of anxiety and despair.

✓ Revitalization examples include Mormonism in the United States, ecospiritualism in many Western nations (such as the rise of Druidry in England), and the revival of traditional American Indian ceremonies.

✓ Syncretism, the creative blending of indigenous and foreign beliefs and practices into new cultural forms, can be found worldwide. It includes the practice of Vodou among former slaves in Haiti, which features elements of Roman Catholicism and traditional African beliefs such as spirit possession.

What is secularization?

✓ Secularization is a process of cultural change in which a population tends toward a nonreligious worldview, ignoring or rejecting institutionalized spiritual beliefs and rituals.

✓ Fairly common in wealthy countries, secularization has become especially prevalent in western Europe.

QUESTIONS FOR REFLECTION

1. For countless generations, humans have creatively reflected on the universe and their place in it. Often this is done through sacred rituals—culturally specific prayers, chants, prostrations, sacrificial offerings, or dances, such as the Buddhist Stag and Hounds dance in Bhutan, pictured at the start of this chapter. Are you personally familiar with a periodic reenactment or visual representation commemorating a significant historical event in a major religious tradition? How does that representation relate to your own existence? Does it have any meaning to you, your family, or others in your community?

2. People in every culture experience anxiety, fear, and social tension, and many attribute accidents, illnesses, or other misfortunes to evil magic practiced by malevolent individuals such as witches or sorcerers. Do you believe people really possess such supernatural powers to inflict harm?

3. Do the basic dynamics of the shamanic complex also apply to preachers or priests in modern churches and medical doctors working in modern hospitals? Can you think of some similarities among the shaman, preacher, and medical doctor in terms of their respective fields of operation?

4. Revitalization movements occur in reaction to the upheavals caused by rapid colonization and modernization. Do you think that the rise of religious fundamentalism among Christians, Muslims, Jews, and Hindus is a response to such upheavals? If yes, how so?

DIGGING INTO ANTHROPOLOGY

Going Through a Phase

In every society, people take part in ceremonies, each of which has its own particular rituals. Having read about various ritual practices in this chapter, select a rite of passage you have personally witnessed or participated in (such as college graduation, marriage, or funeral). Identify and briefly describe each of its three phases, and summarize why this social event requires the ceremonial staging of a cultural ritual.

Sue Cunningham Photographic/Alamy

Sue Cunningham Photographic/Alamy

CHALLENGE ISSUE

Humans in all cultures face the challenge of creatively articulating ideas and emotions concerning themselves and the world around them. Across the globe, people have developed art forms—musical, visual, verbal, movement, and so on—that symbolically express meanings and messages. Art is often personal but may also communicate, stimulate, and reinforce experiences and feelings of collective cultural identity. So it is with these Amazonian Indians in traditional ceremonial paint and dress—members of the Kayapo tribe inhabiting Brazil's Xingu River area. Their heads are crowned with colorful radiating feathers that represent the universe. Their faces and bodies are painted with black and red designs that convey strength—the black dye made of charcoal and *genipap* fruit juice, the red of crushed *urucu* seeds. And they carry age-old tribal weapons—clubs, spears, bows, and arrows. In this case, they armed and adorned themselves to stage a political protest in the streets of São Paulo, one of Brazil's major cities. With dance, song, oratory, and body ornamentation, they demonstrated against an $18.5 billion hydropower project, the third largest in the world. For two decades they tried to halt the building of a huge dam that threatens their health and way of life. Their artful protests attracted worldwide attention but failed to stop the massive project set to generate cheap electricity for millions.

The Arts

Humans in all cultures throughout time have expressed feelings and ideas about themselves and the world around them through **art**—the creative use of the human imagination to aesthetically interpret, express, and engage life, modifying experienced reality in the process. Art comes in many forms, including visual, verbal, musical, and motion—sometimes in combination and in an ever-expanding array of formats made possible by the continual emergence of new technologies. Most societies, past and present, have used art to symbolically express almost every part of their culture, including ideas about religion, kinship, ethnic identity, and death.

From an anthropological perspective, the photo that opens this chapter is far more than a curious image of traditionally painted, feathered, and armed Kayapo Indians in the Brazilian Amazon. It is an illustration of **performance art**—a creatively expressed promotion of ideas by artful means dramatically staged to challenge opinion and/or provoke purposeful action. In Kayapo culture, dancing combined with the singing of warrior chants is a traditional variation of this art form. Here we see the warriors in the modern city of Altamira protesting against a huge hydroelectric dam. Through this particular performance, staged as a public spectacle in an electronic media environment, they aimed to reach a global audience of millions and win widespread support for their political struggle (Conklin, 1997; Prins, 2002). Performance art is not always successful. Although demonstrations by Kayapo and neighboring tribes of the Xingu River drew international attention, the dam is now near completion. Soon it will flood 400 square kilometers (150 square miles) of tropical forest and destroy their habitat.

Despite daily evidence of political (and commercial) uses of art, most people living in the industrialized corners of the world think of the arts almost exclusively as an aesthetic pleasure for personal or shared enjoyment. From this "art for art's sake" perspective, art appears to be confined to a distinctive cultural domain, quite apart from political, economic, religious, and otherwise pragmatic or ideological activities.

art The creative use of the human imagination to aesthetically interpret, express, and engage life, modifying experienced reality in the process.

performance art A creatively expressed promotion of ideas by artful means dramatically staged to challenge opinion and/or provoke purposeful action.

In this chapter you will learn to

- Define art and examine how it is intertwined with other parts of a cultural system.

- Summarize anthropology's cross-cultural and comparative historical perspective on art.

- Identify different types of art, each with specific anthropological examples.

- Recognize how art expresses worldview and analyze its functions in the context of religion and shamanism.

- Explain and give examples of the relationship between art and cultural identity.

- Analyze how art has become a commodity in a market economy, and critically evaluate what that means in a globalized environment of rapid change.

But in most traditional cultures, art is so deeply embedded in various aspects of life that many of these cultures do not have a distinctive term for it.

For instance, commenting on beautiful ivory figurines carved by Aivilik Inuit (Eskimo hunters in Arctic Canada), U.S. anthropologist Edmund Carpenter observed:

No word meaning "art" occurs in Aivilik, nor does "artist."... Art to the Aivilik is an act, not an object; a ritual, not a possession.... They are more interested in the creative activity than in the product of that activity [and do not differentiate between] works of art and utilitarian objects: but the two are usually one. (Carpenter, 1959, n.p.)

This intricate link between art and other aspects of life is evident in the way art has been incorporated into everyday, functional objects—from utensils, pottery, and baskets used to serve, carry, or store food, to carpets and mats woven by nomadic herders to cover the ground inside their portable tent dwellings. Designs painted on or woven or carved into such objects typically express ideas, values, relationships, and objects that have meaning to an entire community (Figure 24.1).

Artful expression is as basic to human beings as talking and is by no means limited to a unique category of individuals specialized as artists. We see this in the way people in all cultures adorn their bodies in certain ways—and how, by doing so, make a statement about who they are, both as individuals and as members of society. Similarly, people in all cultures tell stories in which they express their values, hopes, and concerns and in the process reveal much about themselves and the nature of the world as they see it.

In short, all peoples engage in artistic expression in one way or another. And, they have been doing this in countless ways for more than 40,000 years—from painting animals on ancient rock walls to digital music jamming on iPhones.

Whether a particular work of art is intended to be appreciated purely for beauty or to serve some practical purpose, it requires the same special combination of symbolic representation of form and expression of feeling that constitute the creative imagination. Because human creativity and the ability to symbolize are universal, art is an important subject for anthropological study.

The Anthropological Study of Art

Anthropologists have found that art often reflects a society's collective ideas, values, and concerns. Indeed, through the cross-cultural study of art, we may discover much about different worldviews and religious beliefs, as well as political ideas, social values, kinship structures, economic relations, and historical memory.

In approaching art as a cultural phenomenon, anthropologists have the pleasant task of cataloguing, photographing,

Figure 24.1 Functional Art
Traditional bags artfully woven by Ayoreo Indian women are used to carry the food they hunt or gather (such as tortoises) in the Gran Chaco, their wilderness domain in the borderlands of Paraguay and Bolivia. The bags are made out of wild pineapple (*dajudie*) leaf fibers, which the women pull and twist into strong strands and then dye with natural pigments. Each weaves a pattern distinctive of their clan. The Ayoreo pictured here stayed remote from the modern world until 2004 when encroachment on their traditional territory forced them to make contact. They continue to make and use these bags, which can now also be seen hanging on museum walls and on the shoulders of fashionable women from New York to Paris.

recording, describing, and analyzing all possible forms of imaginative activity in any particular culture. An enormous variety of forms and modes of artistic expression exists in the world. Because people everywhere continue to create and develop in ever-new ways, there is no end to the interesting process of collecting and describing the world's ornaments, ceremonial masks, body decorations, clothing variations, blanket and rug designs, pottery and basket styles, monuments, architectural embellishments, legends, work songs, dances, and other art forms—many of them rich with religious symbolism.

To study and analyze art, anthropologists employ a combination of *aesthetic*, *narrative*, and *interpretive* approaches. The distinctions among these methods can be illustrated through a famous work of Western art, Leonardo da Vinci's painting *The Last Supper*, showing Jesus Christ and his apostles on their last night together before his arrest and crucifixion. A non-Christian viewing this late 15th-century mural in Italy will see thirteen people at a table, apparently enjoying a meal. Although one of the men clutches a bag of money and appears to have knocked over a dish of salt, nothing else in the scene seems out of the ordinary.

Aesthetically, our non-Christian observer may admire the way the composition fits the space available, how the attitudes of the men are depicted, and the means by which the artist conveys a sense of movement. As *narrative*, the painting may be seen as a record of customs, table manners, dress, and architecture. But to *interpret* this picture—to perceive its real meaning—the viewer must be aware that in Christian symbolic culture money traditionally represents the root of all evil, and spilling the salt suggests impending disaster. But even this is not enough; to fully understand this work of art, one must know something of the beliefs of Christianity. And if one wishes to understand renditions of the Last Supper made by artists in other corners of the world, it is necessary to bring insights about those cultures into the equation as well (Figure 24.2). In other words, moving to the interpretive level of studying

Figure 24.2 *The Last Supper* **by Marcos Zapata (c. 1710–1773)**
To interpret this painting, one must know about Christianity and the artist's cultural background. It depicts the final meal shared by a spiritual leader and his twelve followers the eve before his execution, an event commemorated by Christians for 2,000 years. For centuries, artists in many societies have imagined this event in paintings, often copying from others before them. This artist was an indigenous painter living in Cuzco, once capital of the Inca empire and long colonized by Spaniards. Baptized as a Christian, he was influenced by European imagery but made cultural adjustments so fellow Andean Indians coming to the church would understand its significance. Directly looking at us is St. Peter, showing his sacred key to heaven. At the center of the table sits Jesus, foretelling his death as a sacrifice, promising he will resurrect and return as the Messiah. However, instead of lamb, Zapata painted a roasted *cui* (*Cavia porcellus*) on the platter. Traditionally eaten by Andean highlanders, this domesticated guinea pig has long been used for sacrificial and divining purposes; it is a culturally relevant substitute for the sacrificial lamb, a traditional Israelite symbol representing their divine rescue from slavery in Egypt. He also substituted red wine with *chicha*, an indigenous beer made of fermented maize.

Courtesy of Erin Erkun

© 1996 The Rock Foundation. Courtesy of Edmund Carpenter

© Danita Delimont/Alamy Stock Photo

Hourglass

Hanging Limbs

Hocker

Figure 24.3 Kinship Symbolism in Art
In the figure at left, the top row shows the stylized human figures that are the basic bricks used in the construction of genealogical patterns. The bottom row shows how these basic figures are linked arm and leg with diagonally adjacent figures to depict descent. For thousands of years people all over the world have linked such figures together, creating the familiar geometric patterns that we see in countless art forms—from pottery to sculpture to weavings—patterns that informed eyes recognize as genealogical. Pictured in the figure on the right are traditional wooden shields with kinship designs made by Asmat people in West Papua.

art requires knowledge of the symbols and beliefs of the people responsible for the art (Lewis-Williams, 1990).

A good way to deepen our insight into the relationship between art and the rest of culture is to examine critically some of the generalizations that have already been made about specific art forms. Because it is impossible to cover all art forms in the space of a single chapter, we will concentrate on just a few—visual, verbal, and musical.

Visual Art

For many people, the first thing that springs to mind in connection with the word *art* is some sort of visual image, such as a painting. Created primarily for visual perception, **visual art** ranges from images rendered on various surfaces to sculptures and weavings made with an array of materials.

In many parts of the world, people have been making pictures in one way or another for a very long time— etching in bone; engraving in rock; carving and painting on wood, gourds, and clay pots; or painting on cave walls, textiles, animal hides, or even their own bodies. Some form of visual art is a part of every historically known human culture, and extraordinary examples have been found at prehistoric sites dating back more than 40,000 years.

Symbolism in Visual Art

As a type of symbolic expression, visual art may be representational (imitating closely the forms of nature) or abstract (drawing from natural forms but representing only their basic patterns or arrangements). In some of the American Indian art of the Northwest Coast, for example, animal figures may be so highly stylized as to be difficult for an outsider to identify. Although the art appears abstract, the artist has created it based on nature, even though he or she has exaggerated and deliberately transformed various shapes to express a particular feeling toward the animals. Because artists do these exaggerations and transformations according to the aesthetic principles of their Indian culture, their meanings are understood not just by the artist but by other members of the community as well.

This collective understanding of symbols is a hallmark in traditional art. Unlike modern Western art, which is judged in large part on its creative originality and the unique vision of an individual artist, traditional art is all about community and shared symbolism. Consider, for example, symbols related to kinship. As discussed in earlier chapters, small-scale traditional societies—hunter-gatherers, nomadic herders, slash-and-burn horticulturists—are profoundly interested in kinship relations. In such societies, kinship may be symbolically expressed in stylized motifs and colorful designs etched or painted on human skin, animal hides or bones, pottery, wood, rocks, or almost any other surface imaginable. To cultural outsiders these designs appear to be purely decorative, ornamental, or abstract, but they can actually be decoded in terms of genealogical iconography primarily illustrating social relations of marriage and descent (Prins, 1998; Schuster & Carpenter, 1996) (Figure 24.3).

Shared symbolism has also been fundamental to the traditional visual art of tattooing—although that is changing in some parts of the world, as discussed in this chapter's Original Study.

visual art Art created primarily for visual perception, ranging from etchings and paintings on various surfaces (including the human body) to sculptures and weavings made with an array of materials.

The Modern Tattoo Community BY MARGO DEMELLO

As an anthropology graduate student in the early 1990s, I had no idea what (or, more accurately, whom) to study for my field research. Working as an animal advocate, I had a house full of creatures to care for, which left me in no position for long-term travel to a far-off field site.

Then one of my professors suggested a topic that was literally under my nose—tattooing. I myself had several tattoos and spent quite a bit of time with other tattooed people, including my husband, who had just become a professional tattooist.

Early on in my research, I, along with my husband, strove to find a way to "join" what is known as the "tattoo community," finding that it was not as friendly and open as we had imagined it to be. As an anthropologist, I came to see that the sense of exclusion we felt reflected the fact that we were on the lower rungs of a highly stratified social group in which an artist's status is based on such features as class, geography, and professional and artistic credentials, and a "fan" might be judged on the type and extent of his or her tattoos, the artist(s) who created them, the level of media coverage achieved, and more. This awareness led to one of the major focuses of my work: how class and status increasingly came to define this once working-class art form.

Ultimately, I spent almost five years studying and writing about tattooing, finding my "community" wherever tattooed people talked about themselves and each other— within the pages of tattoo magazines and mainstream newspapers, on Internet newsgroups, and at tattoo-oriented events across the country. I spent countless hours in tattoo shops watching the artists work; I collected what I call "tattoo narratives," which are often elaborate, sometimes spiritual, stories that people tell about their tattoos; and I followed the careers of seminal artists. I even learned to tattoo a bit myself, placing a few particularly ugly images on my patient husband's body.

Tattoos are created by inserting ink or some other pigment through the epidermis (outer skin) into the dermis (the second layer of skin) through the use of needles. They may be beautiful as designs in and of themselves, but they can also express a multitude of meanings about the wearer and his or her place within the social group. Whether used in an overt punitive fashion (as in the tattooing of slaves or prisoners) or to mark clan or cult membership, religious or tribal affiliation, social status, or marital position, tattoos have historically been a social sign. They have long been one of the simplest ways of establishing humans as social beings. In fact, tattooing is one of the most persistent and universal forms of body art and may date back as far as the Upper Paleolithic era (10,000–40,000 years ago).

Tattoos as signs derive their communicative power from more than a simple sign-to-meaning correspondence: They also communicate through color, style, manner of execution, and location on the body. Traditionally inscribed on easily viewable parts of the body, tattoos were designed to be "read" by others and were part of a collectively understood system of inscription. However, for many middle-class North Americans today tattoos are more about private statement than public sign, and these individuals, especially women, tend to favor smaller tattoos in private spots.

The process by which tattooing has expanded in the United States from a working-class folk art into a more widespread and often refined aesthetic practice is related to a number of shifts in North American culture that occurred during the 1970s and 1980s. This time period saw the introduction of finely trained artists into tattooing, bringing with them radically different backgrounds and artistic sensibilities to draw from. More and more middle-class men and women began getting tattooed, attracted by the expanded artistic choices and the new, more spiritual context of body decoration.

Tattoos have been partially transformed into fine art by a process of redefinition and framing based on formal qualities (that is, the skill of the artist, the iconic content of the tattoo, the style in which the tattoo is executed, and so on) and ideological qualities (the discourses that surround "artistic" tattoos, discourses that point to some higher reality on which the tattoo is based). When it is judged that a tattoo has certain formal artistic qualities as well as expresses a higher, often spiritual, reality, then it is seen as art.

Although it may seem as though tattoos are not good candidates to be defined as art, due to their lack of permanence (the body, after all, ages and dies) and their seeming inability to be displayed within a gallery setting, modern tattoo art shows get around these problems by photographing tattoos and displaying them in a way that showcases the "art" and often minimizes the body. By both literally and figuratively "framing" tattoos in a museum or gallery setting, or within an art book, the tattoo is removed from its social function and remade into art.

The basic working-class American tattoo designs (such as "Mother" or "Donna" inscribed alongside a heart) have been relegated to the bottom rung of today's tattoo

Ulrich Doering / Alamy

Tattoo artist with a client at the international Southern Ink Xposure Tattoo Convention.

hierarchy in the United States. Such tattoos are now seen by middle-class artists and fans as too literal, too transparently obvious, and too grounded in everyday experience and social life to qualify as art.

The modern, artistic tattoos that have increasingly gained favor are less "readable" and no longer have an easily recognizable function. Often derived from foreign (or "exotic") cultures (such as Polynesia) and custom-drawn for the wearer, they tend to eliminate the social aspect in favor of the highly individualistic. Some are purely decorative, and those that are intended to signify meaning often do so only for the individual or those in his or her intimate circle.

Tattoos in the United States have traveled a long way from the tattoo of old: brought to North America by way of British Captain James Cook's 18th-century explorations of the Pacific, moving, over time, from a mark of affiliation to a highly individual statement of personal identity, losing and regaining function, meaning, and content along the way. In our increasingly global world, tattoo designs and motifs move swiftly and easily across cultural boundaries. As this happens, their original, communal meanings are often lost—but they are not meaningless. An animal crest tattoo traditionally worn by Indians on the northwest coast of North America to signify clan membership may now be worn by a non-Native in Boston as an artful, often private, sign of rebellion against Western "coat and tie" consumer culture.

Written expressly for this text, 2005.

Rock Art from Southern Africa

Rock art—paintings and engravings made on large rock surfaces—is one of the world's oldest art traditions, dating back at least 40,000 years. Bushmen in southern Africa practiced this art continually from 27,000 years ago (perhaps earlier) until the beginning of the 20th century when European colonization led to the demise of their societies. Their art depicted humans and animals in sophisticated ways, often in highly animated scenes. It also featured what appear to be abstract signs—dots, zigzags, nested curves, and the like. Until fairly recently, non-Bushmen were puzzled by the significance of these abstract features and by the fact that new pictures were often created directly over existing images.

These early ancestors of the Bushmen used charcoal and specularite (a variety of the mineral hematite) for the color black; silica, china clay, and gypsum for white; and

ferric oxide for red and reddish-brown hues—and mixed the colors with fat, blood, and perhaps water. They applied the paint with great skill—with lines and shading that elegantly captured the contours of the animals' bodies and details such as the twist of an eland's horns or the black line running along its back.

The art shows Bushmen hunting various animals—especially eland, a massive antelope they believed possessed supernatural powers (**Figure 24.4**). Often male hunters are outfitted with spears or bows, arrows, and quivers. Some scenes show hunting nets and fish traps. Women are also portrayed—identifiable by their sexual characteristics and their stone-weighted digging sticks.

Researchers, interpreting southern Africa's prehistoric rock art in light of ethnographic research among modern-day Bushmen communities, suggest certain designs relate to the shamanic trance dance. These often include fly whisks

Figure 24.4 Rock Art by Bushmen in Southern Africa Bushmen created rock paintings and engravings depicting animals they believed possessed great supernatural powers, especially the eland. Many of these renderings also featured trance dancing, sometimes showing shamans magically transforming into birds, appearing elongated and weightless as if in flight or water—imagery based on altered states of consciousness experienced in trance.

Prisma/Superstock

(used to extract invisible arrows of sickness) and designs of hand-clapping women surrounding dancing men whose bodies are bent forward in the distinctive posture caused by the cramping of abdominal muscles as they go into trance. The designs also show dancers' arms outstretched behind their backs, which present-day Bushmen do to catch more *n/um* (supernatural power).

For a more complete interpretation of trance-influenced art, anthropologists explore a possible linkage with altered states of consciousness. Brain research indicates that humans typically move through three stages when entering a trance. First, the nervous system generates images of luminous, pulsating, revolving, and constantly shifting geometric patterns known as *entoptic phenomena*. Usually, these include dots, zigzags, grids, filigrees, nested curves, and parallel lines, often in a spiral pattern. Next, the brain tries to make sense of these abstract forms. Here, cultural influences come into play, so a trancing tribesman in southern Africa's Kalahari region may construe a grid pattern as markings on the skin of a giraffe or nested curves as a honeycomb (honey is a delicacy in the region). A Canadian wheat farmer or Chinese shoemaker would construe the patterns in very different ways.

Finally, during the deepest trance stage, people tend to feel as if they are at one with their visions, passing into a rotating tunnel or vortex. Typically, the tunnel has lattice-like sides in which *iconic images* of animals, humans, and monsters appear, merging with the entoptic forms of the early trance stages. Trancing individuals usually see things that have high significance within their own culture. Thus, Bushmen often see the eland, which they believe carries supernatural powers for making rain. One of the things

shamans try to do in trance is to "capture" these envisioned elands for purposes of making rain.

All of this helps us understand why elands are so prominent in Bushmen rock art. Moreover, it reveals the significance of the zigzags, dots, grids, and so forth that are so often a part of the compositions. The interpretive approach makes clear, then, that the rock art of southern Africa is probably connected with the practices and beliefs of shamanism. After shamans came out of trance and reflected on their visions, they painted or engraved their recollections on the rock faces. A similar interpretive analysis is needed to fully understand the art of Huichol Indians living in Mexico, as profiled in this chapter's Biocultural Connection feature.

Verbal Art

Verbal art is creative word use on display that includes stories, myths, legends, tales, poetry, metaphor, rhyme, chants, rap, drama, cant, proverbs, jokes, puns, riddles, and tongue twisters.

Since the 19th century, when Europe's traditional rural cultures changed as a result of urbanization and modernization, the historical heritage of communities and regions has been at risk of being forgotten or otherwise lost. Alarmed about these vanishing traditions—including legends, songs, dances, dress, and crafts—people interested

verbal art Creative word use on display that includes stories, myths, legends, tales, poetry, metaphor, rhyme, chants, rap, drama, cant, proverbs, jokes, puns, riddles, and tongue twisters.

BIOCULTURAL CONNECTION

Peyote Art: Divine Visions among the Huichol

For generations, Huichol Indians living in Mexico's mountainous western Sierra Madre region have created art remarkable for its vibrant colors. They are especially noted for their spectacular beadwork and embroidery. Although many people far and wide appreciate the intricate beauty of Huichol art, most are probably unaware that the colorful designs express a religious worldview tied to the chemical substance of a sacred plant: a small cactus "button" known as peyote (*Lophophora williamsii*).[a]

Among the many Huichol gods and goddesses, all addressed in kinship terms, is Our Grandfather Fire. His principal spirit helper is Our Elder Brother Deer, a messenger between the gods and humans. Serving the Huichol as their spiritual guide, this divine deer is also the peyote cactus itself. Huichol Indians refer to peyote as *yawéi hikuri*, the "divine flesh of Elder Brother Deer." Guided by their shamans on a pilgrimage to harvest peyote, they "hunt" this "deer" in Wirikúta, the sacred desert highlands where their ancestor deities dwell. Having found and "shot" the first cactus button with an arrow, they gather many more, later to be consumed in fresh, dried, or liquid form.

Participating in a holy communion with the creator god, Huichol shamans consume peyote (the divine flesh) as a sacrament. Doing so, they enter into an ecstatic trance. With the help of peyote, their spiritual guide, they become hawks

or eagles soaring high in the sky. Having visions extending far across the world, they interact directly with their gods and seek advice on behalf of those who need help in dealing with illness and other misfortunes.

From a chemical point of view, peyote contains a psychotropic substance identified by scientists as an alkaloid. By consuming some of this toxic organic substance, the Huichol move into an altered state of consciousness. In this dreamlike psychological state, which is also profoundly emotional, they experience religiously inspired, brilliantly colored visions from their spirit world.

These are reflected in Huichol art, such as the piece pictured here in which a stylized peyote button and deer have been rendered in rainbow-hued beadwork by Huichol artist Olivia Carrillo, who lives in the peyote heartland of central Mexico. The sacred cactus, with its flower or star-like shape, is the most prominent symbolic design in Huichol art, beaded onto fabric and objects of all kinds or embroidered on clothing.

Huichol artist Olivia Carrillo makes peyote-inspired art in Real de Catorce, a town in the mountains of central Mexico. About an hour's horseback ride away from the Huichol sacred mountain Wirikúta, the town is located in the peyote heartland.

Biocultural Question

In Huichol Indian art we often find vibrantly colored peyote buttons, articulating shamanic visions induced by this psychotropic cactus. What was it that inspired traditional European artists to paint Christian holy men and women with a halo—a silver- or gold-colored ring around or above their heads?

[a] Schaeffer, S. B., & Furst, P. T. (Eds.). (1996). *People of the peyote: Huichol Indian history, religion, and survival*. Albuquerque: University of New Mexico Press.

---

in cultural preservation began collecting the unwritten popular stories (and other artistic traditions) of rural peoples. They coined the word **folklore** (*folk* refers to "ethnicity"; *lore* is "traditional knowledge") to distinguish between "folk art" shared by the community and the "fine art" collected by the elite.

Generally, the narratives that make up the verbal arts have been divided into several basic and recurring categories, including myth, legend, and tale.

Myth

As discussed in the previous chapter, the term **myth** comes from the Greek word *mythos*, meaning "speech" or "story." It is a narrative that explains the fundamentals of human existence—where we and everything in our world came from, why we are here, and where we are going. A myth provides a rationale for religious beliefs and practices and sets cultural standards for proper behavior.

---

folklore A term coined by 19th-century scholars studying the unwritten stories and other artistic traditions of rural peoples to distinguish between "folk art" and the "fine art" of the literate elite.

myth A sacred narrative that explains the fundamentals of human existence—where we and everything in our world came from, why we are here, and where we are going.

A typical creation or origin myth, traditional with the western Abenaki Indians of northwestern New England and southern Quebec, is as follows:

> In the beginning, *Tabaldak*, "The Owner," created all living things but one—the spirit being who was to accomplish the final transformation of the earth. *Tabaldak* made man and woman out of a piece of stone, but he didn't like the result, their hearts being cold and hard. So, he broke them up, and their remains today can be seen in the many stones that litter the landscape of the Abenaki homeland. Then *Tabaldak* tried again, this time using living wood, and from this came all later Abenakis. Like the trees from which the wood came, these people were rooted in the earth and could dance as gracefully as trees swaying in the wind.
>
> The one living thing not created by *Tabaldak* was *Odzihózo*, "He Makes Himself from Something." This transformer created himself out of dust, but he wasn't able to accomplish it all at once. At first, he managed only his head, body, and arms; the legs came later, growing slowly as legs do on a tadpole. Not waiting until his legs were grown, he set out to transform the shape of the earth. He dragged his body about with his hands, gouging channels that became the rivers. To make the mountains, he piled dirt up with his hands. Once his legs grew, *Odzihózo's* task was made easier; by merely extending his legs, he made the tributaries of the main stream. . . .
>
> The last work he made was Lake Champlain and liked it so well that he climbed onto a rock in Burlington Bay and changed himself into stone so he could sit there and enjoy his masterpiece through the ages. He is still there and he is still given offerings of tobacco as Abenakis pass this way. The Abenaki call the rock *Odzihózo*, since it is the Transformer himself. (Haviland & Power, 1994)

Such a myth, insofar as it is believed, accepted, and perpetuated in a culture, expresses part of a people's traditional worldview. This Abenaki myth accounts for the existence of rivers, mountains, lakes, and other features of the landscape (such as Odzihózo Rock pictured in Figure 24.5), as well as of humans and all other living things. It also sanctions particular attitudes and behaviors. The myth is a product of creative imagination and is a work of art, as well as potentially a religious statement.

Extrapolating from the details of this particular Abenaki myth, we may conclude that these Native Americans traditionally recognize having a close relationship with animals and plants, as well as rocks, rivers, and so on. Such ideas led them to show special respect to the animals they hunted in order to sustain their own lives. For example, before eating meat, they placed an offering of grease on the fire to thank Tabaldak.

A characteristic of myths, such as this one, is that they reduce the complex or unknown in terms of a basic story accepted as explanation in the community. Mythmaking

© Ray Brown

Figure 24.5 Odzihózo Rock, Lake Champlain, Burlington, Vermont
This small granite island is featured in the creation myth of the Abenaki Indians, the original inhabitants of the region. For untold generations, they have referred to it as Odzihózo after the mythical transformer who laid out the river channels and lake basins in northeastern North America.

is an extremely significant kind of human creativity, and studying the mythmaking process and its results can offer valuable insight into the way people perceive and think about their world.

Legend

A **legend** is a story about a memorable event or figure handed down by tradition and told as true but without actual historical evidence. Legends commonly consist of pseudo-historical narratives that account for the deeds of heroes, the movements of peoples, and the establishment of local customs, typically with a mixture of realism and the supernatural or extraordinary. As stories, they are not necessarily believed or disbelieved, but they usually serve to entertain as well as to instruct and to inspire or bolster pride in family, community, or nation. Legends all around the world tell us something about the cultures in which they are found.

A noteworthy example of a popular legend is that American Indians at Cape Cod welcomed the English Pilgrims who came to the "New World" seeking religious freedom—generously sharing their food and helping the newcomers survive their first winter. Gaining acceptance in the 19th century, this romantic first-arrival story is often told during Thanksgiving, an important national holiday in the United States. For Native Americans, it is a false representation of what actually happened almost 400 years ago—the beginning of a foreign invasion and violent dispossession of their ancestral homeland. Thus, many Native Americans do not celebrate Thanksgiving Day.

To a degree, in literate societies the function of legends has been taken over by history. The trouble is that history does not always tell people what they want to hear about themselves, or, conversely, it tells them things that they would prefer not to hear. By projecting their culture's hopes and expectations onto the record of the past, they seize upon and even exaggerate some past events while ignoring or giving scant attention to others. Although this often takes place unconsciously, so strong is the motivation to transform history into legend that states have even gone so far as to deliberately rewrite it.

An **epic** is a long, dramatic narrative, recounting the celebrated deeds of a historic or legendary hero, often sung or recited in poetic language. In parts of western and Central Africa, people hold remarkably elaborate and formalized recitations of extremely long legends, lasting several hours and even days. These long narratives have been described as veritable encyclopedias of a culture's most diverse aspects, with direct and indirect statements about history, institutions, relationships, values, and ideas. Epics are typically found in nonliterate societies with some form of state political organization; they serve to transmit and preserve a culture's legal and political precedents and practices.

Legends may incorporate mythological details, especially when they make an appeal to the supernatural, and are therefore not always clearly distinct from myth. Legends may also incorporate proverbs and incidental tales and thus be related to other forms of verbal art as well.

For the anthropologist, the secular and apparently realistic portions of legends, whether long or short, carry particular significance because of the clues they provide as to what constitutes a culture's approved or ideal ethical behavior. The subject matter of legends is essentially problem solving and mentoring, and the content is likely to include physical and psychological trials of many kinds. Certain questions may be answered explicitly or implicitly: In what circumstances, if any, does the culture permit homicide? What kinds of behavior are considered heroic or cowardly? Does the culture stress forgiveness over retaliation as an admirable trait?

Tale

A third type of creative narrative, the **tale**, is recognized as fiction that is for entertainment but may also draw a moral or teach a practical lesson. Consider this brief summary of a tale from Ghana in West Africa, known as "Father, Son, and Donkey" (**Figure 24.6**):

> A father and his son farmed their corn, sold it, and spent part of the profit on a donkey. When the hot season came, they harvested their yams and prepared to take them to storage, using their donkey. The father mounted the donkey and they all three proceeded on their way until they met some people. "What? You lazy man!" the people said to the father. "You let your young son walk barefoot on this hot ground while you ride on a donkey? For shame!" The father yielded his place to the son, and they proceeded until they came to an old woman. "What? You useless boy!" said the old woman. "You ride on the donkey and let your poor father walk barefoot on this hot ground? For shame!" The son dismounted, and both father and son walked on the road, leading the donkey behind them until they came to an old man. "What? You foolish people!" said the old man. "You have a donkey and you walk barefoot on the hot ground instead of riding?" And so it goes. Listen: When you are doing something and other people come along, just keep on doing what you like.

This is precisely the kind of tale that is of special interest in traditional folklore studies. It is an internationally popular "numbskull" tale. Versions of it have been recorded in India, Southwest Asia, southern and western Europe, and North America, as well as in West Africa. It is classified or catalogued as exhibiting a basic **motif** or story theme—father and son trying to please everyone—one of the many thousands that have been found to recur

---

legend A story about a memorable event or figure handed down by tradition and told as true but without historical evidence.

epic A long, dramatic narrative, recounting the celebrated deeds of a historic or legendary hero, often sung or recited in poetic language.

tale A creative narrative that is recognized as fiction for entertainment but may also draw a moral or teach a practical lesson.

Jon Sparks/Alamy

Figure 24.6 Father, Son, and Donkey
A Bedouin father and son wait for tourists to rent their donkey in Petra, Jordan. A scene such as this may bring to mind the internationally popular "Father, Son, and Donkey" tale. Told in different versions, this tale conveys a basic motif or story situation—father and son trying in vain to please everyone.

in tales around the world. Despite variations in detail, every version follows the same basic structure in the sequence of events, sometimes called the syntax of the tale: A peasant father and son work together, a beast of burden is purchased, the three set out on a short excursion, the father rides and is criticized, the son rides and is criticized, both walk and are criticized, and a conclusion is drawn.

Tales of this sort (not to mention myths and legends) that are found to have wide geographic distribution raise some questions: Where did they originate? Did the story arise only once and then pass from one culture to another (diffusion)? Or did the stories arise independently (independent invention) in response to like causes in similar settings, or perhaps as a consequence of inherited preferences and images deeply embedded in the evolutionary construction of the human brain? Or is it merely that there are logical limits to the structure of stories, so that, by coincidence, different cultures are bound to come up with similar motifs and syntax (Gould, 2000)?

The significance of tales for the anthropologist rests partly in this matter of their distribution. They provide evidence of either cultural contacts or cultural isolation and of limits of influence and cultural cohesion.

Anthropologists are interested, however, in more than these questions of distribution. Like legends, tales very often illustrate local solutions to universal human ethical problems, and in some sense they state a moral philosophy. Regardless of where the tale of the father,

the son, and the donkey originated, the fact that it is told in West Africa suggests that it states something valid for that culture. The tale's lesson of a necessary degree of self-confidence in the face of arbitrary social criticism is therefore something that can be found in the culture's values and beliefs.

Other Verbal Art

Myths, legends, and tales, prominent as they are in anthropological studies, in many cultures turn out to be no more important than many other verbal arts. In the culture of the Awlad 'Ali Bedouins of Egypt's western desert, for example, poetry is a lively and active verbal art, especially as a vehicle for personal expression and private communication. These Bedouins use two forms of poetry. One is the elaborately structured and heroic poems men chant or recite only on ceremonial occasions and in specific public contexts. The other is the *ghinnáwas* or "little songs" that punctuate everyday conversations, especially of women. Simple in structure, these deal with personal matters and feelings more appropriate to informal social situations, and older men regard them as the unimportant productions of women and youths (Figure 24.7).

Despite this official devaluation in the male-dominated Bedouin society, "little songs" play a vital part in people's daily lives. In these poems individuals are shielded from the consequences of making statements and expressing sentiments that contravene the moral system. Paradoxically, by sharing these "immoral" sentiments only with intimates and veiling them in impersonal traditional formulas, those who recite them demonstrate that they have a certain control, which actually enhances their moral standing. As is often true of folklore in general, the "little songs" of the Awlad 'Ali provide a culturally appropriate outlet for otherwise taboo thoughts or opinions (Abu-Lughod, 1986). The same is true for disaster jokes or comedic satire in numerous contemporary societies.

In all cultures the words of songs constitute a kind of poetry. Poetry and stories recited with gesture, movement, and props become drama. Drama combined with dance, music, and spectacle becomes a public celebration. The more we look at the individual arts, the clearer it becomes that they often are interrelated and interdependent. The verbal arts are, in fact, simply differing manifestations of the same creative imagination that produces music and the other arts.

Musical Art

Evidence of humans making music reaches far back in time. Archaeologists have found flutes and whistles (resembling today's recorders) made from the bones of mammoths and birds and dating back at least 42,000

---

motif An underlying theme around which a work of art is composed.

Figure 24.7 Bedouin Women Singing and Making Bread The *ghinnáwas* or "little songs" of the Awlad 'Ali Bedouins in Egypt punctuate conversations carried out while the people perform everyday chores. Through these songs, they can express what otherwise are taboo subjects.

© Anthro-Photo

years (Higham et al., 2012). And historically known food-foraging peoples were not without music. In the Kalahari Desert, for example, a Ju/'hoansi hunter off by himself would play a tune on his bow simply to help pass the time. (Long before anyone thought of beating swords into plowshares, some genius discovered that bows could be used not just to kill but to make music as well.) In northern New England, Abenaki shamans used cedar flutes to call game, lure enemies, and attract women. In addition, shamans would use a drum—over which two rawhide strings were stretched to produce a buzzing sound, representing singing—to allow communication with the spirit world.

The study of music in specific cultural settings, or **ethnomusicology**, began in the 19th century with the collection of folksongs and has developed into a specialized subfield of anthropological study. Ethnomusicologists look at music within its cultural context and from a comparative and relativistic perspective (Nettl, 2005). Early ethnomusicologists focused primarily on non-Western musical traditions in tribal cultures. Today, some also study folk music or music played and enjoyed in different ethnic communities within industrialized modern states.

Music is a form of communication that includes a nonverbal auditory component. The information it transmits is often abstract and emotional rather than concrete and objective, and different listeners experience it in a variety of ways. Such factors make it difficult to construct a definition that satisfies across cultures. Broadly speaking, **music** may be defined as an art form whose medium is sound and silence; a form of communication that includes a nonverbal auditory component with elements of tonality, rhythm, pitch, and timbre.

In general, human music is said to differ from natural sounds—the songs of birds, wolves, and whales, for example—by being almost everywhere perceived in terms of a repertoire of tones at fixed or regular intervals: in other words, a scale. Scale systems and their modifications make up what is known as *tonality* in music. These vary cross-culturally, so it is not surprising that something that sounds musical to one group of people may come across as noise to another.

Humans make closed systems out of a formless range of possible sounds by dividing the distance between a tone and its first overtone or sympathetic vibration (which always has exactly twice as many vibrations as the basic tone) into a series of measured steps. In the Western or European system, the distance between the basic tone and the first overtone is called the *octave*; it consists of seven steps—five whole tones and two semitones. The whole tones are further divided into semitones, collectively resulting in a twelve-tone musical scale. Interestingly, some birds pitch their songs to the same scale as Western music (Gray et al., 2001), perhaps influencing the way these people developed their scale.

One of the most common alternatives to the semitonal system is the *pentatonic* (five-tone) system, which divides the octave into five nearly equidistant tones. Such scales may be found all over the world, including in much European folk music. Arabic and Persian music have smaller units of a third of a tone with seventeen and

---

ethnomusicology The study of a society's music in terms of its cultural setting.

music Broadly speaking, an art form whose medium is sound and silence; a form of communication that includes a nonverbal auditory component with elements of tonality, pitch, rhythm, and timbre.

twenty-four steps in the octave. Even quartertone scales are used in large parts of South Asia, North Africa, and the Middle East with subtleties of shading that are nearly indistinguishable to most Western ears. Thus, even when Westerners can hear what sounds like melody and rhythm in these systems, for many the total result may sound peculiar or "out of tune."

Pitch is the quality of a sound governed by the rate of vibrations producing it—in other words, the degree of highness or lowness of a tone. *Timbre*, another element of music, is the characteristic quality of sound produced by a particular instrument or voice—also known as *tone color*. It is what distinguishes one musical sound from another, even when they have the same pitch and loudness. For example, a violin and a flute playing the same note equally loud have a different timbre.

Another organizing factor in music is *rhythm*. Involving tempo, stress, and measured repetition, it may be more important than tonality. One reason for this may be our constant exposure to natural pulses, such as our own heartbeat and patterns of breathing and walking. Even before we are born, we are exposed to our mother's heartbeat and to the rhythms of her movements, and as infants we experience rhythmic touching, petting, stroking, and rocking (Dissanayake, 2000).

The rhythms of traditional European music are most often measured into recurrent patterns of two, three, and four beats, with combinations of weak and strong beats to mark the division and form patterns. Non-European music is likely to move in patterns of five, seven, or eleven beats, with complex arrangements of internal beats and sometimes *polyrhythms*: one instrument or singer using a pattern of three beats, for example, whereas another uses a pattern of five or seven. Polyrhythms are frequent in the drum music of West Africa, which shows remarkable precision in the overlapping of rhythmic lines (**Figure 24.8**). Non-European music also may contain *shifting rhythms*: a pattern of three beats, for example, followed by a pattern of two or five beats with little or no regular recurrence or repetition of any one pattern, although the patterns are fixed and identifiable as units.

Melody involves both tonality and rhythm. It is a rhythmical succession of musical tones organized as a distinct phrase or sequence of phrases. The distinction between rhythm, melody, poetry, rhyming lyrics, and speech is not always clear-cut. This is the case, for example, with *rapping* (chanted or spoken word poetry performed to a beat). Moreover, while musical instruments often accompany vocalization, they may also be imitated, as is the case with *beatboxing* (vocal percussion, using mouth, voice, tongue, and lips mimicking sounds of drums, rattles, whistles, and so forth). Both rapping and beatboxing are popular forms of music associated with hip-hop culture now spread across the world, a diffusion aided by the Internet.

© Zale Seck

Figure 24.8 Senegalese Musician Zale Seck
Like so many other cultural elements, musical instruments and styles of playing and singing now circulate around the globe, as do the artists themselves. One such example is West African musician Saliou "Zale" Seck, known for his "funky crisscrossing rhythms." A member of the Lébou tribe, Zale was born in the old fishing town of Yoff, just north of Senegal's capital city of Dakar. He performs Wolof percussive music on a traditional skin-covered *djembe* (hand drum) and *sabar* (played with one hand and a stick). Coming from a long line of *griots* (oral historians-traditional storytellers), he transmits his people's memory through lyrics of love and humanity. Fluent in French (his country was a French colony for many years), Zale has toured Europe and played on radio and television in France. Zale has relocated to French-speaking Quebec in Canada to further pursue his musical career.

The Functions of Art

Beyond adding beauty and pleasure to life, art in all its many forms has countless functions—from social, economic, and political to emotional, religious, and psychological. For anthropologists and others seeking to understand cultures beyond their own, art offers insights into a society's worldview, giving clues about everything from sexuality and gender relations to religious beliefs, historical memory, political ideology, and perspectives on nature, both past and present.

Within a society, art may serve to display wealth, social status, religious affiliation, and political power. An example of this can be seen in the totem poles of American Indians living along the Northwest Coast. Carved from tall cedar trees, with stylized animal and human faces or bodies, these poles are a symbolic display of a family or clan's prestige and rank in their community's social hierarchy. Similarly, art is used to mark kinship ties, as seen in the colored patterns of Scottish tartans designed to identify clan affiliation. It can also affirm group solidarity and identity beyond local status or kinship lines, as evidenced in the stylized renderings of mascots for sports teams displayed in competitions. Likewise, art depicts national political emblems such as the dragon (Bhutan), bald eagle (United States), maple leaf (Canada), crescent moon (Maldives), and cedar tree (Lebanon) that typically appear on coins, flags, and government buildings.

Playing an important role in traditional manual labor, work songs have served (and in some places still do) to coordinate efforts in heavy or dangerous labor (such as weighing anchor and hoisting or reefing sails on ships), to synchronize axe or hammer strokes, and to pass time and relieve tedium (Figure 24.9). And music, as well as dance and other arts, may also be used, like magic, to "enchant"— to take advantage of the emotional or psychological predispositions of another person or group so as to cause them to perceive reality in a way favorable to the interests of the enchanter. Indeed, the arts may be used to manipulate a seemingly inexhaustible list of human emotions, including joy, grief, anger, gratitude, pride, jealousy, love, passion, and desire. Commercial marketing specialists are well aware

of this, which is why they routinely employ appealing music or seductive images in their advertising—as do promoters of political, ideological, charitable, or other causes.

As an activity or behavior that contributes to human well-being and that helps give shape and significance to life, art is often intricately intertwined with religion or spirituality. In fact, in elaborate ceremonies involving ornamentation, masks, costumes, songs, dances, and effigies, it is not easy to say precisely where art stops and religion begins. Often art is created to honor or beseech the aid of a god, patron saint, or guardian spirit (such as an angel, ancestor, or animal helper). Shamans drum to help create a trance state enabling them to enter the spirt world, Buddhist monks chant to focus their meditation. Christians sing hymns to praise God. Also, since ancient times, rituals and symbols concerning death have been infused with artistry—from evocative funereal music and beautiful sacred objects buried with a body to detailed mummy portraits in ancient Egypt. Today, in some parts of the world, artisans create coffins that are so creative that some find their way into museums as art (see the Globalscape feature).

Sometimes art is used to transmit culturally significant ideas about the origin or mysteries of the world, ancient struggles and victories, or remarkable ancestors, as in epic poems passed down from generation to generation. Myths, a verbal art form, may offer basic explanations about the world and set cultural standards for proper behavior. Other times art is employed to express political protest and influence events, as with *posters* or *graffiti* on buildings, marching songs in mass demonstrations, and a host of other public performances.

Figure 24.9 Laborers in Mali, West Africa, Working to the Beat of a Drum
The drumming helps to set the pace of work, unify the workforce, and relieve boredom.

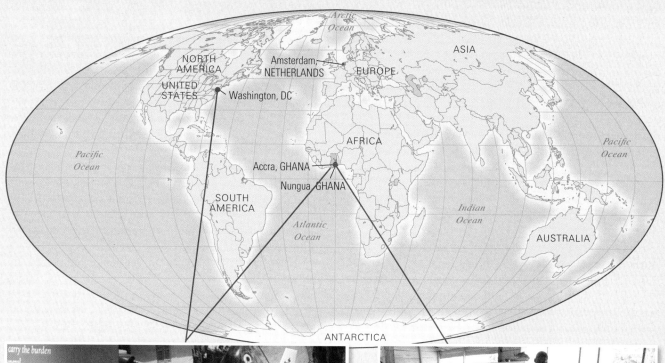

African Voices National Museum of Natural History, Smithsonian. Photography by Donald Hurlbert.

© Cengage Learning

© dpa picture alliance archive/Alamy Stock Photo

Do Coffins Fly?

In his workshop in Nungua, Ghana, master carpenter Paa Joe makes unique painted wooden coffins for clients in his Ga society and beyond. Some are spectacular, representing richly colored tropical fish or even luxury cars, such as Mercedes-Benz. Celebrating the life accomplishments of the deceased, these designer coffins show off the family's prominent status and wealth.

As a collective expression of culturally shared ideas about the afterlife, a Ga funeral ceremony reminds the mourners of important values embodied in the departed individual. Seeing the deceased off on a journey to the afterlife, Ga mourners call out praises to this person, and some may even pour schnapps on the coffin. Henceforth, the deceased will continue to be ritually honored as an ancestor by descendants.

The 747 jumbo jet coffin pictured here confers upon the deceased the prestige and mystique of air travel. Its colors, blue and white, are those of the KLM Royal Dutch Airline, a longtime provider of air service between this West African country and the rest of the world. Its creator, Paa Joe, began working at age 15 for his cousin Kane Quaye, a carpenter known for designer coffins. Later, Joe started his own workshop and soon began receiving orders from other parts of the world—not only from individuals but also from museums. Using wood, enamel paint, satin, and Christmas wrapping paper, Joe created this KLM airplane coffin in 1997 for the Smithsonian National Museum of Natural History in Washington, DC, where millions of visitors from all over the globe now admire this Ghanaian funereal ritual object.

Global Twister

When the Smithsonian Museum purchased one of Paa Joe's remarkable coffins for public display, did this West African ritual object transform into a work of art?

Based on script for the African Voices Exhibition at NMNH, Smithsonian, courtesy of Dr. Mari Jo Arnoldi.

Singers who use their art to stir awareness about social injustice, racism, political repression, or environmental threats may gain a following in some circles. They may also incur commercial boycotts, personal threats, or even imprisonment. There are many examples of this around the world. One comes from Russia, where the female punk rock protest group Pussy Riot began staging provocative performances in 2011, with feminist, lesbian, and other lyrical themes challenging the male-dominated political establishment in their homeland. Edited into music videos and uploaded on the Internet, their shows provoked authorities and prompted church leaders to denounce them as handmaidens of the devil. In 2012, three members of the band were arrested, convicted of delinquency "motivated by religious hatred," and served substantial jail time. Fearing the same fate, two others left the country.

Many minorities or marginalized groups have used music for purposes of self-identification—as a means of building group solidarity and distinguishing themselves from the dominant culture and sometimes as a channel for direct social and political commentary. Music gives basic human ideas a concrete form, made memorable and attractive through melody and rhythm. Whether a song's content is didactic, satiric, inspirational, celebratory, sacred, political, or militant, experiences and feelings that are hard to express in words alone are communicated in a symbolic and notable way that can be repeatedly performed and shared. This, in turn, shapes and gives meaning to the community.

In the United States there are numerous examples of marginalized social and ethnic groups sharing their collective emotions and expressing their pride, protest, or hopes through song. The clearest example may be African Americans, whose ancestors were captured and carried across the Atlantic Ocean to be sold as slaves. Out of their experience emerged spirituals and, ultimately, gospel, jazz, blues, rock and roll, hip-hop, and rap. These forms all found their way into U.S. mainstream culture and soon captivated audiences in many other parts of the world.

All across the globe, one can find musicians giving voice to social issues. In Australia, certain ceremonial songs of the Aborigines have taken on a new legal function, as they are being introduced into court as evidence of indigenous land ownership. These songs recount ancient adventures of mythic ancestors who lived in "Dreamtime" and created waterholes, mountains, valleys, and other significant features in the landscape. The ancestors' tracks are known as "songlines," and countless generations of Aborigines have been "singing up the country," passing on sacred ecological knowledge. This oral tradition helps Aborigines to claim extensive indigenous landownership, thus allowing them greater authority to use the land, as well as to negotiate and profit from the sale of natural resources (Koch, 2013).

Art, Globalization, and Cultural Survival

As members of a highly creative species, humans have developed and shared multiple art forms in the course of thousands of years, expressing personal or collective emotions, ideas, memories, hopes, or anything else important or entertaining. In this chapter, we have surveyed art traditions across time and cultures, suggesting the vast scope of creative expression. Artistic styles may have changed over the millenniums, yet there are remarkable correlations between ancient art and that of today. One of countless examples is art created in public spaces, such as 2,000-year-old petroglyphs painted on massive cliffs flanking riverways in China and contemporary graffiti painted on towering buildings flanking streets in urban centers around the globe (Figure 24.10).

Today, modern telecommunications technology facilitates a rapid and global spread of art forms, opens the door to global artistic collaborations, and makes it possible to share art in unprecedented ways across time and space. In this globalized age, indigenous peoples in remote corners of the world can market their artful creations online, and an Internet giant can create an international symphony orchestra: Responding to open auditions hosted by YouTube, musicians from all around the world posted videos of themselves playing Internet Symphony No. 1, *Eroica*, by Chinese composer Tan Dun. Winners traveled to New York City for a Carnegie Hall performance comprised of short live pieces plus a mashup of the video auditions.

Clearly, there is more to art than meets the eye or ear (not to mention the nose and tongue—consider how burning incense or tobacco is part of the artfulness of sacred ceremonies, and imagine the cross-cultural array of smells and tastes in the cooking arts). In fact, art is such a significant part of culture that many endangered indigenous groups around the world—those whose lifeways have been threatened first by colonialism and now by globalization—are using aesthetic expressions as part of a cultural survival strategy (see the Anthropology Applied feature).

Like the Kayapo Indian warriors in Brazil's Amazonian rainforest, protesting the environmental destruction as depicted in this chapter's opening photo, many have found that a traditional art form—a dance, a song, a dress, a basket, a carving, or anything that is distinctly beautiful and well made or performed—can serve as a powerful symbol that conveys the vital message: "We're still here, and we're still a culturally distinct people with our own particular beliefs and values."

Yet, globalization also poses some threats to traditional arts. For example, as discussed in the chapter on language and communication, globalization has fueled language loss. And as languages vanish, the particular myths and

Figure 24.10 **Ancient Rock Art and Modern Graffiti**
Human beings have creatively altered their visual space by painting, sculpting, or scratching all sorts of images conveying all sorts of messages—not all of which are approved or understood. What do these pictures or letters mean? We need to know something about the culture within which symbolic representations originate to decode meaning and message. This is also true for *graffiti*—an Italian word for scratches or scribbles. For thousands of years, people have scratched or painted drawings and inscriptions on walls in public spaces—cave walls, cliff walls, house walls, and almost any other flat surface. Graffiti may be made to intimidate or express anger or hate (as between rival gangs). Texts and images may also express beauty and share pleasure and good feelings. On the left we see a mural of a giant lizard crawling up the wall of an abandoned building in central Lisbon, Portugal, as photographed by Swedish visual anthropologist Christer Lindberg, who is interested in street art in urban landscapes. On the right we see ancient Chinese petroglyphs probably made more than 2,000 years ago on the face of Hua Mountain above the Zua River. Located in Guangxi near the Vietnamese border, these Huashan drawings feature about 1,600 human figures and animals, as well as circular symbols and drums, swords, and boats.

legends they conveyed are no longer told, and the songs they carried are no longer sung. There is also the risk that when art forms that have been traditionally embedded in a culture are commodified, they lose their deep meaning. Moreover, with the instant worldwide spread of newer art forms, such as mashups, traditional songs and dances may lose their appeal and be forgotten. In fact, throughout the world, the cultural heritage of thousands of communities remains at risk and a huge repertoire of traditional art—stories, songs, dances, costumes, paintings, sculptures, and so on—has already been lost, often without leaving a trace.

Bringing Back the Past

By Jennifer Sapiel Neptune

Near the turn of the 20th century, a young Penobscot woman sat for a photograph, wearing a very old and elaborately beaded ceremonial chief's collar. She was the daughter of Joseph and Elizabeth Nicola and the descendant of a long line of tribal leaders. Her name was Florence Nicola, and she would go on to live a long life, marry Leo Shay, raise a family, and be remembered as a fine basketmaker and dedicated advocate for our tribe. Her efforts brought increased educational opportunities, the right for Native people in the state of Maine to vote in state and federal elections, and the first bridge that would connect our small village of Indian Island in the Penobscot River to the mainland.

Now, over one hundred years later, the photograph has resurfaced and found its way back to her son, Charles Shay. Charles brought the photograph of his mother to our tribal historian who recognized the collar as one he had seen in the book *Penobscot Man* by Frank G. Speck, and he was then able to trace it to the collections of the Smithsonian Institution's Museum of the American Indian.

In the late part of the 19th century the idea of the "vanishing Indian" took hold in anthropology—leading to a specialized field known as "salvage ethnography," which sought to save traditional knowledge, life ways, and material culture. Collecting examples of material culture to be sold into museum collections had become a business for some—which was how the collar Florence wore in the photograph came to be purchased by George Heye sometime before 1905 and then joined the collections of the museum. I have always found it ironic that we as a people and culture did not vanish, but during this time many of our tribes' most precious material objects did.

As a teenager I spent a lot of time in the library at the University of Maine looking through photographs in books of Penobscot beadwork, appliqué ribbon work, basketry, and carvings that were now in

museums all over the world. I dreamed of being able to visit these objects, to study them up close, and to be able to find a way to bring them back into our world. It was for this reason that I went into anthropology, to learn how to research and write about my own culture. I started doing reproductions of the old beadwork designs, became a basketmaker, consulted on museum exhibitions, sold my own artwork, and worked with the Maine Indian Basketmakers Alliance promoting the work of basketmakers and artists from the four tribes in Maine.

In the spring of 2006 Charles showed me the photograph of his mother and asked me if I could make a reproduction of the collar for him.

As I worked on the collar, I was struck by how so much had changed since the late 18th century when the original collar was made. Back then the wool, silk ribbon, and beads its maker used had come by ship, horse, and foot from trade or treaty annuities; my materials were ordered over the Internet and came by UPS and FedEx. She worked by the light of the sun or fire; I worked mostly in the evenings with electric lights. Her world had northern forests still untouched by logging and filled with caribou and wolves; my world had airplanes, cars, and motorboats.

As I worked some more, I thought about what had stayed the same. We had lived and watched the sun rise and set on the same island our ancestors had for over 7,000 years. I wondered if we had stitched the same prayers into our work and if we used the same medicinal plants to soothe our aching hands and shoulders at the end of the day.

Penobscot artist and cultural anthropologist Jennifer Neptune hugs tribal elder Charles Shay after giving him the traditional collar he commissioned. Modeled after a collar owned by his ancestors and now in the Smithsonian Institution's National Museum of the American Indian, the piece took Neptune more than 300 hours to make.

Bangor Daily News/Bridget Brown

There are no words that can express how gratifying it was to hand over the finished collar to Charles—and to have played a part in returning to him, his family, and our tribe a part our history.

One hundred years ago when the collar left my community, anthropology seemed to be about taking objects, stories, and information away. As an anthropologist and artist I believe that I have a responsibility to use what I have learned to give back to my community. I have been so fortunate to be able to have spent time in museum collections visiting objects that most of my own people will never have the opportunity to see. What I learned from my time with the collar was that the objects that left still have a relationship with us today; they have a story that wants to be told, and they are waiting for someone to listen.

Written expressly for this text, 2011.

CHAPTER CHECKLIST

Why do anthropologists study art?

✓ Anthropologists have found that art often reflects a society's worldview.

✓ From myths, songs, dances, paintings, carvings, and other art forms, anthropologists may learn how a people imagine their reality and understand themselves and other beings around them.

✓ Through the cross-cultural study of art and creativity, we discover much about different worldviews, religious beliefs, political ideas, social values, kinship structures, economic relations, and historical memory.

What is art?

✓ Art is the creative use of the human imagination to aesthetically interpret, express, and engage life, modifying experienced reality in the process. It comes in many forms, including performance, visual, verbal, and musical.

✓ Performance art is a creatively expressed promotion of ideas by artful means dramatically staged to challenge opinion and/or provoke purposeful action.

✓ Visual art, created primarily for visual perception, ranges from etchings and paintings on various surfaces (including the human body) to sculptures and weavings made with an array of materials. Key approaches in analyzing visual art are aesthetic, narrative, and interpretive.

✓ Verbal art is creative word use on display that includes stories, myths, legends, tales, poetry, metaphor, rhyme, chants, rap, drama, cant, proverbs, jokes, puns, riddles, and tongue twisters.

How are myths, legends, and tales different from one another?

✓ A myth is a short story about how the cosmos came about, including the factors that are responsible for the way it is and the significant features of the worldview. An example is the Abenaki Indian creation story of Tabaldak and Odzihózo.

✓ A legend is a story about a memorable event or figure handed down by tradition and told as true but without historical evidence. A noteworthy example is the American Thanksgiving legend about English Pilgrims and American Indians.

✓ A tale is a creative narrative that is recognized as fiction for entertainment but may also draw a moral or teach a practical lesson. One example is the "Father, Son, and Donkey" story, told in different versions around the world.

What are music and ethnomusicology?

✓ Ethnomusicology, the study of a society's music in terms of its cultural setting, began in the 19th century with the collection of folksongs from non-Western musical traditions. Today, it includes music played in ethnic communities within industrialized modern states.

✓ Music is difficult to define in a way that satisfies across cultures. Broadly speaking, it as an art form whose medium is sound and silence or a form of communication that includes a nonverbal auditory component with elements of tonality, rhythm, pitch, and timbre.

What are the functions of art?

✓ Art in all its many forms has countless functions beyond providing aesthetic pleasure. Myths, for example, may offer basic explanations about the world and set cultural standards for proper behavior.

✓ The verbal arts generally transmit and preserve a culture's customs and values. Songs, too, may do this within the structures imposed by musical form.

✓ Any art form, to the degree that it is characteristic of a particular society, may contribute to the cohesiveness or solidarity of that society. Yet, art may also express political themes and be used to influence events and create social change.

✓ Often art is created for religious purposes, to honor or beseech the aid of a divine power, a sacred being, an ancestral spirit, or an animal spirit.

✓ Endangered indigenous groups whose lifeways have been threatened by colonialism and globalization use aesthetic expressions as part of a cultural survival strategy.

QUESTIONS FOR REFLECTION

1. In this chapter's opening photograph, you saw indigenous activists, colorfully painted and with feathered headdresses, participating in an important protest rally. If your livelihood was seriously threatened and you wanted to try to avoid violent confrontation, would you contemplate performance art as a means of political action? If so, how and by means of which art form?

2. Among the Maori in New Zealand, tattooing is a traditional form of skin art, and their tattoo designs

are typically based on cultural symbols understood by all members in the community. Are the tattoo designs in your culture based on traditional motifs that have a shared symbolic meaning?

3. Because kinship relations are important in small-scale traditional societies, these relationships are often symbolically represented in artistic designs and motifs. What are some of the major concerns in your society, and are these concerns reflected in any of your culture's art forms?

4. Many museums and private collectors in Europe and North America are interested in so-called tribal art, such as African statues or American Indian masks originally used in sacred rituals. Are there sacred objects such as paintings or carvings in your religion that might also be collected, bought, or sold as art?

DIGGING INTO ANTHROPOLOGY

A Heart for Art

All across the world, people creatively express ideas and feelings—including both joy and anger, hope and despair, dreams and fears. They do so through stories, songs, theater, paintings, dances, and other art forms. Keeping in mind the performance art of the Kayapo Indians pictured on this chapter's opening page, identify an art form publicly performed in your own community. Describe the artful performance, and note where, when, and why it is performed. Identify one of the performers (or someone closely involved), and find out about its creative origin, its guiding idea, and its purpose or message. Next contact at least four individuals (who differ in gender, age, and ethnicity, religion, or class) and ask what they think this art represents. Ask them what they think it means to the public and who ordered, permitted, paid for, or otherwise made this performance happen in a public space. Having gathered and organized this information, offer your own observation and opinion in a short essay on the role of public art in your community.

imageBROKER/Alamy

CHALLENGE ISSUE

Environmental, demographic, technological, and other changes challenge cultures to adjust at an ever-faster pace. Some peoples confront change on their own terms, welcoming new ideas, products, and practices as improvements. Often, however, outsiders introduce changes. These outsiders may be businesspeople backed by banks, eager to capitalize on economic opportunities, or governments striving to improve living standards and increase tax revenues. Such was the case when foreign capitalists introduced railways in India in the mid-1800s while Great Britain ruled and exploited that vast country as a cotton-producing colony. This occurred during the height of the industrial revolution, which began with the invention of the steam engine. Steam power was first harnessed to drive textile machines. Soon thereafter it led to the invention of steamboats and locomotives, revolutionizing transportation and radically reducing the cost of moving raw materials and commodities. Railways also provided passenger services, improving mobility of the labor force. Today, India has one of the world's largest railway networks, comprising almost 66,000 kilometers (41,000 miles) and carrying well over 8 billion passengers and more than 1 billion tons of freight annually. However, running this mass transportation network smoothly is a daily challenge, and there are many breakdowns and delays. Here we see passengers stranded at Allahabad Station in northern India, waiting for their delayed trains. Today, almost everyone knows what it is like to feel stranded when the modern technology we have come to depend upon breaks down—whether it is something as big as a train or small enough to fit in our hands.

Processes of Cultural Change

Anthropologists are interested not only in describing cultures and explaining how they are structured as systems of adaptation, but also in understanding why and how cultures change. Because systems generally work to maintain stability, cultures are often fairly steady and remain so unless there is a critical shift in one or more significant factors such as technology, demographics, markets, the natural environment—or in people's perceptions of the various conditions to which they are adapted.

Archaeological studies reveal how elements of a culture may persist for long periods. In Australia, for example, the cultures of indigenous inhabitants remained relatively consistent over many thousands of years because they successfully adapted to comparatively minor fluctuations in their social conditions and natural environments, making changes from time to time in tools, utensils, and other material support.

Although stability may be a striking feature of many traditional cultures, all cultures are capable of adapting to changing conditions—climatic, economic, political, or ideological. However, not all change is positive or adaptive, and not all cultures are equally well equipped for making the necessary adjustments in a timely fashion. In a stable society, change may occur gently and gradually, without altering in any fundamental way the culture's underlying structures. Sometimes, though, the pace of change increases dramatically. This is what happened during the industrial revolution, beginning with England, when its agriculture-based society transformed into a machine-based manufacturing society within a few generations beginning in the 1770s. Such changes may be disruptive to the point of destabilizing or even breaking down a cultural system. The modern world is full of such examples of radical changes, from the political-economic disintegration of the former Soviet Union and the dramatic capitalist transformation of communist China to the devastation by global corporations of indigenous communities inhabiting remote regions from the cold Arctic tundra to the hot Amazonian jungle.

In this chapter you will learn to

- Analyze why and how cultural systems change.

- Identify the key mechanisms of cultural change, providing examples.

- Explain the consequences of unequal power in culture contact.

- Compare directed and undirected change.

- Recognize and discuss reactions to repressive change.

- Assess the importance of self-determination in successful cultural change.

- Connect modernization ideology to international resource exploitation and global markets.

Cultural Change and the Relativity of Progress

The dynamic processes involved in cultural change are manifold, including accidental discoveries, deliberate inventions, and borrowing from other peoples who introduce or force new commodities, technologies, and practices. Change imposed upon one group by another continues in much of the world today as culture contact intensifies between societies unequal in power. Among those who have the power to drive and direct change in their favor, it is typically referred to as "progress," which literally translates as "to move forward"—that is, in a positive direction. But *progress* is a relative term because not everyone benefits from change. In fact, countless peoples (including traditional foraging, herding, and peasant communities in many parts of the world) have become the victims of state-sponsored or foreign-imposed economic development schemes, wreaking havoc on their communities.

In recent decades, growing numbers of anthropologists have focused on the historical impact of international market expansionism on rural and urban communities around the world, radically challenging, altering, or even destroying their traditional cultures. One of the first and most prominent among these scholars was Eric Wolf, an Austria-born U.S. anthropologist who personally experienced the global havoc and upheaval of the 20th century (see Anthropologist of Note).

Mechanisms of Change

Some of the major mechanisms involved in cultural change are innovation, diffusion, and cultural loss. These types of change are typically voluntary and are not imposed on a population by outside forces.

Innovation

A major factor in cultural change, innovation is any new idea, method, or device that gains widespread acceptance in society. **Primary innovation** is the creation, invention, or chance discovery of a completely new idea, method, or device. A **secondary innovation** is a deliberate application or modification of an existing idea, method, or device.

What makes people come up with, and accept, an innovation? The most obvious incentive is reflected in the age-old proverb "Necessity is the mother of invention." We see this in an early prehistoric example of a primary

innovation: the spear-thrower (also known as *atlatl*, its Aztec Indian name). Invented at least 15,000 years ago by big game hunters who needed more effective technology to ensure success and safety, this device made it possible to hurl a dart or javelin with much greater thrust. Using it increased a projectile's distance by 100 percent or more and delivered much more force upon impact. Thus equipped, a hunter boosted his kill range and gained competitive advantage. Much later examples of primary innovation are the bow and arrow, the wheel, the alphabet, the concept of zero, the telescope, and the steam engine (an 18th-century invention that launched the industrial revolution), to mention just a few major inventions.

Many innovations are the result of inventive designs and experimentation, but others come about through accidental discoveries. These may gain acceptance and spawn innovations within their particular cultural contexts. An innovation must be reasonably consistent with a society's needs, values, and goals in order to gain acceptance. Take, for instance, the invention of wheel-and-axle technology. About 1,500 years ago, indigenous peoples in Mesoamerica came up with the concept. But instead of building wagons to be pulled by trained dogs or human captives, they created wheeled animal figurines, most often representing dogs but also jaguars, monkeys, and other mammals, and left it at that. On the other side of the Atlantic, this same technology—discovered a few thousand years earlier—led to major secondary innovations resulting in a series of radical cultural changes in transportation technology, ultimately resulting in motorized vehicles such as cars, trains, and planes.

A culture's internal dynamics may encourage particular innovative tendencies, even as they may discourage or suppress others. Force of habit tends to obstruct ready acceptance of the new or unfamiliar because people typically stick with what they are used to rather than adopt something strange that requires adjustment on their part.

Obstacles to change are often ideologically embedded in religious traditions. Consider, for instance, early rejections of scientific insights about the earth's position in the universe. Polish mathematician and astronomer Nicolaus Copernicus discovered that the earth rotates around the sun and published his new *heliocentric* theory in 1534, just before he died. In the early 1600s, the Italian physicist and mathematician Galileo Galilei verified this controversial theory by means of a much-improved telescope. In 1633, not long after publishing and defending his findings, he was tried for heresy because his observational astronomy ran counter to the dogma of the Roman Catholic Church, which was firmly based on a *geocentric* worldview as revealed in sacred texts. Facing a death sentence, Galileo recanted and was condemned to life under house arrest. In 1758, after numerous additional scientific breakthroughs challenged Catholic dogma, heliocentric books were removed from the forbidden list of that powerful international institution.

primary innovation The creation, invention, or chance discovery of a completely new idea, method, or device.
secondary innovation The deliberate application or modification of an existing idea, method, or device.

ANTHROPOLOGIST OF NOTE

Eric R. Wolf (1923–1999)

Like the millions of peasants about whom he wrote, **Eric Wolf** personally experienced radical upheaval in his life due to powerful outside political forces. A war refugee in his teens, he survived the battlefields and mass murders of Nazi-occupied Europe. Driven by the inequities and atrocities he witnessed during World War II, he turned to anthropology to sort through issues of power. Viewing anthropology as the most scientific of the humanities and the most humane of the sciences, he became famous for his comparative historical studies on peasants, power, and the transforming impact of capitalism on traditional nations.

Wolf's life began in Austria shortly after the First World War. During that terrible conflict, his Austrian father had been a prisoner of war in Siberia, where he met Wolf's mother, a Russian exile. When peace returned, the couple married and settled in Vienna, where Eric was born in 1923. Growing up in Austria's capital and then (because of his father's job) in Sudetenland in what is now the Czech Republic, young Eric enjoyed a life of relative ease. He relished summers spent in the Alps among local peasants in exotic costumes, and he drank in his mother's tales about her father's adventures with Siberian nomads.

Life changed for Eric in 1938 when Adolf Hitler grabbed power in Germany, annexed Austria and Sudetenland, and threatened Jews like the Wolfs. Seeking security for their 15-year-old son, Eric's parents sent him to high school in England. In 1940, a year after World War II broke out, British authorities believed invasion was imminent and ordered aliens, including Eric, into an internment camp. There he met other refugees from Nazi-occupied Europe and had his first exposure to Marxist theories. Soon he left England for New York City and enrolled at Queens College, where Professor Hortense Powdermaker, a former student of Malinowski, introduced him to anthropology.

In 1943, the 20-year-old refugee enlisted in the U.S. Army's 10th Mountain Division. Fighting in the mountains of Tuscany, Italy, he won a Silver Star for combat bravery. At the war's end,

1994 Photograph by Michael Macdonald. EWLS (Eric Wolf's Last Student) and "staunch banner carrier for Wolfian anthropology" (Wolf 12/25/1998)

Born in Austria, Eric Wolf became a U.S. anthropologist famous for his pioneering research on peasant societies.

Wolf returned to New York City and studied anthropology under Julian Steward and Ruth Benedict at Columbia University. After earning his doctorate in 1951 based on fieldwork in Puerto Rico, he did extensive research on Mexican peasants.

In 1961, he became a professor at the University of Michigan. A prolific writer, Wolf gained tremendous recognition for his fourth book, *Peasant Wars of the Twentieth Century*, first published during the height of the Vietnam War. Protesting that war, he headed a newly founded ethics committee in the American Anthropological Association and helped expose counterinsurgency uses of anthropological research in Southeast Asia.

From 1971 onward, Wolf held a distinguished professorship at Lehman College of the City University of New York (CUNY), where his classes were filled with working-class students of all ethnic backgrounds, including many who took the anthropology courses he taught in Spanish. In addition, he taught at the Graduate Center (CUNY). Among his many publications is his award-winning book, *Europe and the People Without History* (1982). In 1990, he received a MacArthur "genius grant." In his final publications, he explored how ideas and power are connected through the medium of culture.

Diffusion

The spread of certain ideas, customs, or practices from one culture to another is known as **diffusion**. So common is cross-cultural borrowing that U.S. anthropologist Ralph Linton suggested that it accounts for as much as 90 percent of any culture's content.

People are creative about their borrowing, however, picking and choosing from multiple possibilities and sources. Usually, their selections are limited to those compatible with the existing culture. An example is the inclusion of bagpipes in the marching band of the Royal Bhutan Army. Traditionally played by Scottish Highland regiments when marching into combat and in official ceremonies, this musical instrument features one

double-reed pipe operated by finger stops and three drone pipes. All the pipes are sounded by air forced with the left arm from a leather bag kept filled by the player's breath. The bagpipe's drone sounds resemble those of Bhutan's traditional sacred trumpets played in ancient Buddhist religious ceremonies in this small Himalayan kingdom (Figure 25.1).

The extent of cultural borrowing can be surprising. Consider, for example, paper, the compass, and gunpowder. All three of these innovations were invented in China long before Europeans became aware of them about 700 years

diffusion The spread of certain ideas, customs, or practices from one culture to another.

Pedro Ugarte/AFP/Getty Images

Figure 25.1 Bagpipers, Royal Bhutan Army Marching Band
Unlike neighboring India, Bhutan remained independent from British colonial rule. This small Himalayan kingdom, known to the Bhutanese as Drukyul ("Land of the Dragons"), is generally averse to foreign cultural influences. However, the Drukpa ("Dragon People") have selectively embraced a few innovations, including the Scottish bagpipes, which found their way here via India during the colonial era. Wearing traditional dress, bagpipers in the Royal Army Band play imported instruments, producing a droning sound similar to age-old sacred trumpets played by Buddhist monks in this region. They and other Drukpa musicians lead the way for singing the national anthem Druk Tsendhen ("The Thunder Dragon Kingdom"), honoring the fifth traditional Druk Gyalpo ("Dragon King"), who serves as head of this Buddhist state.

ago. Accepting these foreign artifacts, Europeans and others analyzed and improved them where needed. Such is the case with the mixture of sulfur, charcoal, and potassium nitrate the Chinese used for fireworks and portable hand cannons. Soon after learning about it, Europeans, Koreans, and Arabs adopted and adapted this primitive artillery and gunpowder, triggering a revolution in traditional warfare from the 1300s onward. Two centuries later, Europeans introduced firearms to the Americas. Within decades, indigenous coastal groups began using them in their raids, transforming warfare as they had known it for generations.

America's indigenous peoples not only adopted weapons and other foreign trade goods, but also shared numerous inventions and discoveries their ancestors had made in the course of many centuries. Of special note is the range of domestic plants developed ("invented") by the

Indians—potatoes, beans, tomatoes, peanuts, avocados, manioc, chili peppers, squash, chocolate, sweet potatoes, and corn to name a few—all of which now furnish a major portion of the world's food supply. In fact, American Indians are recognized as primary contributors to the world's varied cuisine and credited with developing the largest array of nutritious foods (Weatherford, 1988).

Diffusion of a Global Staple Food: Maize

Particularly significant among the domesticated plants diffusing from the Americas is corn, also known as *maize* (derived from a Caribbean Indian word *maíz*). The English originally referred to this Native American cereal plant as "Indian corn." First cultivated by indigenous peoples in the Mexican highlands over 7,000 years ago, this food crop diffused to much of the rest of North, Central, and

Figure 25.2 Making Corn Mush in Italy
Having spread from the tropics of the Mexican highlands to much of the rest of North and South America, corn diffused rapidly to the rest of the world after Italian explorer Christopher Columbus first crossed the Atlantic in 1492. A long-time favorite dish in Italy is polenta (a thick mush made of cornmeal). Here we see it being made the traditional way: boiled in a big copper cauldron over a fire of hot coals and then spread out and cooled to firmness on a wooden or stone slab. In recent years, polenta has become a favored menu item in many chic U.S. restaurants.

© Hubert Stadler/Corbis

South America over the next few millennia. In 1493, the explorer Columbus returned from America to Spain with a sampling of maize. From Spain, it spread to neighboring countries in southern Europe (Figure 25.2). Portuguese traders then introduced this staple food to western Africa and South Asia; by the mid-1500s it had reached China.

Diffusing across the globe, maize has become one of the world's major staple foods and has been culturally incorporated under many different names. Today, a greater weight of maize is produced each year than rice, wheat, or any other grain—about 800 million tons, with over half of the global production taking place in the United States and China.

Currently, an enormous quantity of maize is grown for biomass fuel, such as ethanol, as an alternative to oil and other nonrenewable fossil fuels. Moreover, the production of genetically engineered maize (manipulated with herbicide or drought-resistant genes) has gained much ground, especially in the United States and many developing countries, but European farmers and a growing number of consumers condemn this practice.

Diffusion of a Global Measurement System: Metrics

Another remarkable example of diffusion—breaking through multiple language barriers and long-held local traditions—is the *metric* system used for measuring length, weight, capacity, currency, and temperature. Based on a classification in which standard units of measurement are multiplied or divided by 10 in order to produce larger or smaller units, this rational system has greatly simplified calculations.

A Dutch engineer first proposed the use of decimal fractions for measures, weights, and currency in everyday life. Three centuries later, in 1795, the French government adopted the metric system as its official system of measurement. Soon, this innovation was introduced to neighboring countries—standardizing a bewildering array of regional and local measurement systems on the European continent. It continued to spread, despite initial reluctance or even resistance in some countries, such as Great Britain. Since the early 1970s, that country and most of its former colonies have fully transitioned to metric. Today, at least officially, metrication is almost universal, with the exception of just three countries: Myanmar, Liberia, and the United States (Cardarelli, 2003; Vera, 2011).

Cultural Loss

Most often people look at cultural change as an accumulation of innovations. Frequently, however, the acceptance of a new innovation results in **cultural loss**—the abandonment of an existing practice or trait. For example, in ancient times chariots and carts were used widely in North Africa and Southwest Asia, but wheeled vehicles virtually disappeared from Morocco to Afghanistan about 1,500 years ago. Camels replaced them, not because of some reversion to the past but because camels used as pack animals worked better. The old roads from the Roman empire had deteriorated, and these sturdy animals traveled well with or without roads. Their endurance, longevity, and

---

cultural loss The abandonment of an existing practice or trait.

AP Images/Sayyid Azim

Figure 25.3 Camel Mobile Library
Providing books and reading materials to the Somali-speaking nomads in the remote Garissa and the Wajir areas in its northeastern districts, Kenya's National Library Association challenges the region's 85 percent illiteracy rate. The program consists of three teams, each with three male camels capable of traveling routes impassable even for 4-wheel drive vehicles. One camel is loaded with two boxes containing 200 books, one transports the library tent, and a third carries miscellaneous items needed for the program.

ability to ford rivers and traverse rough ground made pack camels admirably suited for the region. Plus, they were economical in terms of labor: A wagon required one man for every two draft animals, but a single person could manage up to six pack camels. To this day, in many remote and hot desert regions, camels are still the favored and most reliable form of transportation for many purposes (Figure 25.3).

Repressive Change

Innovation, diffusion, and cultural loss all may take place among peoples who are free to decide for themselves what changes they will or will not accept. Frequently, however, people are forced to make changes they would not willingly make, usually in the course of conquest and colonialism. A direct outcome in many cases is repressive change to a culture, which anthropologists call *acculturation*. The most radical form of repressive change is ethnocide.

acculturation The massive cultural change that occurs in a society when it experiences intensive firsthand contact with a more powerful society.

ethnocide The violent eradication of an ethnic group's collective cultural identity as a distinctive people; occurs when a dominant society deliberately sets out to destroy another society's cultural heritage.

Acculturation and Ethnocide

Acculturation is the massive cultural change that occurs in a society when it experiences intensive firsthand contact with a more powerful society. It always involves an element of force—either directly, as in conquests, or indirectly, as in the implicit or explicit threat that force will be used if people refuse to make the demanded changes (Figure 25.4).

In the course of culture contact, any number of things may happen. Merger or fusion occurs when two cultures lose their separate identities and form a single culture, as historically expressed by the *melting pot* ideology of English-speaking, Protestant Euramerican culture in the United States. Sometimes, though, one of the cultures loses its autonomy but retains its identity as a subculture in the form of a caste, class, or ethnic group. This is typical of conquest or slavery situations.

Acculturation may occur as a result of military conquest, political and economic expansion, or massive invasion and breaking up of cultural structures by dominant newcomers who know or care little about the traditional beliefs and practices of the people they seek to control. Under the sway of powerful outsiders—and unable to effectively resist imposed changes and obstructed in carrying out many of their own social, religious, and economic activities—subordinated groups are forced into new social and cultural practices that tend to isolate individuals and destroy the integrity of their traditional communities. In virtually all parts of the world today, people are faced with the tragedy of forced removal from their traditional homelands, as entire communities are uprooted to make way for hydroelectric projects, grazing lands for cattle, mining operations, or highway construction.

Ethnocide, the violent eradication of an ethnic group's collective cultural identity as a distinctive people, occurs when a dominant society deliberately sets out to destroy another society's cultural heritage. Such "culture death" may take place when a powerful nation aggressively expands its territorial control by annexing neighboring peoples and their territories, incorporating the conquered groups as subjects. A policy of ethnocide typically includes forbidding a subjugated nation's ancestral language, criminalizing their traditional customs, destroying their religion and demolishing sacred places and practices, breaking up their social organizations, and dispossessing or removing

© Harald E. L. Prins

Figure 25.4 Protesting Acculturation
Until a few decades ago, these Aché Indians survived as traditional hunters and gatherers in the deep tropical forest of eastern Paraguay. Not unlike the Ju/'hoansi of southern Africa, they were organized in small migratory bands and rarely had contact with outsiders. Armed with spears and bows and arrows, they could not defend their homeland against large numbers of foreign invaders equipped with chainsaws, bulldozers, and firearms. Massacres and foreign diseases, coupled with massive deforestation of their hunting territories, almost annihilated these people in the 1950s and 1960s. Since then, they have been exposed to intensive acculturation. Here we see the breakup of an Aché encampment in the middle of Asunción, Paraguay's capital city, where they lived during many weeks of protest against government policies.

the survivors from their homelands—in essence, stopping short of physical extermination while removing all traces of their unique culture.

Ethnocide may also take place when so many carriers of a culture die that those who manage to survive become refugees, living among peoples of different cultures. Examples of this may be seen in many parts of the world today.

Case Study: Ethnocide of the Yąnomami in Amazonia

During the past few centuries, many indigenous communities in North and South America have faced ethnocide. Even those living remotely in the vast tropical rainforests of the Amazon are endangered in their survival as their territories come within reach of timber, gold-mining, and oil-drilling companies.

Amazonian forests are being decimated, with an average annual loss of about 18,000 square kilometers (about 7,000 square miles) in Brazil alone. Roads are bulldozed to harvest valuable hardwood trees such as mahogany, *ipê*

("Brazilian walnut"), and *jatobá* ("Brazilian cherry"), which fetch high prices due to a growing international demand for luxury furniture, doors, decking, and floorings. Thanks to corruption and lack of oversight, much of this precious timber is illegally logged and laundered on a massive scale. Engaging in *ecocide* (environmental destruction), powerful entrepreneurs seeking to maximize profits push their labor crews deeper into the forest where they run into indigenous groups such as the Kayapo (mentioned in an earlier chapter). Hired killers have wiped out several communities of native peoples by targeting them from light planes with arsenic, dynamite, and machine guns.

Ethnocide is especially well documented for the Yąnomami Indians inhabiting the borderlands between Brazil and Venezuela. With a current population of about 24,000, these hunters and food gardeners occupy about 180,000 square kilometers (70,000 square miles). They reside in about 125 autonomous villages, each inhabited by 30 to 300 people living collectively in large circular dwellings known as *shabonos*. Until two generations ago, they were almost completely isolated from the outside world—although they did experience limited cultural change prior to first contact with foreign traders and Christian missionaries. Evidence for this was in their gardens, where they planted non-indigenous food crops—plantains and bananas, both originating in Africa—acquired through diffusion. This adoption increased gardening productivity, triggering population growth and, so it seems, more raids in intervillage conflicts.

Through trading and raiding, the Yąnomami also acquired iron tools, especially machetes and axes. Despite their fierce reputation, they soon became victims of repeated assaults by gold miners, cattle ranchers, and other foreigners seeking to capitalize on their natural resources. In the late 1960s, hundreds of Yąnomami died in a measles epidemic. Threats to their survival multiplied in the 1980s, when many thousands of Brazilian loggers and *garimpeiros* ("gold miners") invaded their lands, attacking villagers defending their territories. Miners also illegally crossed into Venezuela, spreading the violence. The Brazilian state, considering legalizing large-scale logging and mining in indigenous territories, stepped up its military presence in these borderlands, sending troops, building barracks, and expanding airstrips in the Yąnomami heartland. Huge stretches of forest were

torched to build mining camps. Dozens of planes flew in daily, transporting personnel, equipment, and fuel.

Miners, loggers, and soldiers lured Yąnomami women with commodities, infecting them with sexually transmitted diseases that spread quickly into the indigenous communities. On top of prostitution, the invaders introduced alcoholism. Processing the ore, miners also polluted the rivers with mercury, poisoning fish and other creatures, including the Yąnomami. Within the decade, 20 percent of the Yąnomami died, and 70 percent of their ancestral lands in Brazil were illegally expropriated.

A campaign against this ethnocide, led by the Committee for the Creation of Yąnomami Park and Survival International, forced the Brazilian government to protect indigenous territories and expel the miners. However, the destruction continued because *garimpeiros* crossed the border into Venezuela where they continued massacring Yąnomami men, women, and children.

In the mid-1990s, after years of pressure by the Inter-American Commission on Human Rights, Venezuelan state authorities finally agreed to protect the Yąnomami in the remote borderlands and to provide some basic healthcare to reduce alarming mortality rates. Like other Amazonian Indians, Yąnomami continue to struggle to survive as an indigenous people. They live in a climate of fear, with violent intimidation, physical threats, and occasional killings, aggravated by poor health, low life expectancy, and discrimination.

In such difficult times, spiritual leaders are especially important. Among these is Davi Kopenawa, a shaman from the Yąnomami village of Watoriketheri (Figure 25.5). He and other shamans—traditionally skilled in contacting

Figure 25.5 Yąnomami Shaman and Political Activist Davi Kopenawa
Traditionally, Yąnomami shamans such as Davi Kopenawa, seen here surrounded by women and children standing in front of their *shabono*, cure the sick by contacting the spirit world. Known as *shabori*, they apply their skills in negotiating extraordinary challenges with *hekura* ("dangerous spirits"). Today, those challenges include ethnocide and ecocide. Yąnomami rely on shamans such as Kopenawa to use their remarkable powers when negotiating with strangers representing powerful foreign institutions, corporations, and nongovernmental organizations in an effort to prevent further harm to their communities.

dangerous spirits in order to cure the sick and seek revenge against enemies—now confront the deadly forces of ethnocide and ecocide. Recognized as a spokesperson for the Yąnomami in Brazil, Kopenawa has gained an international reputation as a political activist. He uses his extraordinary powers in defense of his Amazonian homeland, negotiating with powerful foreign institutions, corporations, and nongovernmental organizations in a heroic effort to stop the relentless destruction of Brazil's indigenous peoples, cultures, and environment (Conklin, 2002; Kopenawa & Albert, 2010).

Directed Change

Although the process of acculturation often unfolds without planning, powerful elites may devise and enforce programs of cultural change, directing immigrant or subordinated groups into learning and accepting the dominant society's cultural beliefs and practices. So it was with the Ju/'hoansi of southern Africa, discussed in earlier chapters. Rounded up by government officials in the early 1960s, these Bushmen were confined to a reservation in Tsumkwe in Namibia where they could not possibly provide for their own needs. The government supplied them with rations, but these were insufficient to meet basic nutritional needs.

In poor health and prevented from developing meaningful alternatives to traditional activities, the Ju/'hoansi became embittered and depressed, and their death rate began to exceed the birthrate. Within the next few years, however, surviving Ju/'hoansi started to take matters into their own hands. They returned to waterholes in their traditional homeland, where, assisted by anthropologists and others concerned with their welfare,

they are trying to sustain themselves by raising livestock. Whether this will succeed remains to be seen because there are still many obstacles to overcome.

One byproduct of such dealings with indigenous peoples has been the growth of applied anthropology, which was originally focused on advising government programs of directed cultural change and solving practical problems through anthropological techniques and knowledge. Today, applied anthropologists are in growing demand in the field of international development because of their specialized knowledge of social structure, value systems, and the functional interrelatedness of cultures targeted for development.

Those working in this arena face a particular challenge: As anthropologists, they are bound to respect other peoples' dignity and cultural integrity, yet they are asked for advice on how to change certain aspects of those cultures. If the people themselves request the change, there is no difficulty, but typically the change is requested from outsiders. Supposedly, the proposed change is for the good of the targeted population, yet members of that community do not always see it that way. The extent to which applied anthropologists should advise outsiders about how to manipulate people to embrace the changes proposed for them is a serious ethical question, especially when it concerns people without the power to resist.

In direct response to such critical questions concerning the application and benefits of anthropological research, an alternative type of practical anthropology has emerged during the last half-century. Known by a variety of names—including action anthropology and committed, engaged, involved, and advocacy anthropology—this involves community-based research and action in collaboration and solidarity with indigenous societies, ethnic minorities, and other besieged or repressed groups.

There is some reason for optimism, but governments and other powerful institutions directly intervening in the affairs of different ethnic groups or foreign societies all too often fail to seek professional advice from anthropologists who possess relevant cross-cultural expertise and deeper insights. Such failures have contributed to a host of avoidable errors in planning and executing development programs in regions occupied by peoples whose survival is threatened and whose cultural heritage is endangered. In sum, the practical applications of anthropology are not only necessary but are vital to the survival of many threatened groups.

Reactions to Change

The reactions of indigenous peoples to the changes outsiders have thrust upon them have varied considerably. Some have responded by retreating to more remote areas but are running out of geographic options due to ever-advancing mining, deforestation, and agricultural operations. Others took up arms to fight back but were ultimately forced to surrender much of their ancestral land, after which they were reduced to an impoverished underclass in their own ancestral territories or were forced to relocate to areas with less economic value. Today, they continue to fight through nonviolent means to retain their identities as distinct peoples and seek to (re)gain control over natural resources.

Resisting **assimilation**, a process of cultural absorption of an ethnic minority by a dominant society, people

---

assimilation Cultural absorption of an ethnic minority by a dominant society.

often seek emotional comfort from **tradition**—customary ideas and practices passed on from generation to generation, which in a modernizing society may form an obstacle to new ways of doing things. Traditions play an important role in a cultural process identified as **accommodation**. In anthropology, this refers to an adaptation process by which a people modifies its traditional culture in response to pressures by a dominant society so as to preserve its distinctive ethnic identity and resist assimilation (Prins, 1996). In pursuit of such an accommodation strategy, ethnic groups may try to retain their distinctive identities by maintaining cultural boundaries such as holding onto traditional language, festive ceremonies, customary dress, ritual songs and dances, unique food, and so on. Later in this chapter we discuss two ethnographic examples of accommodation.

Syncretism

When people are able to hold on to some of their traditions in the face of powerful outside domination, the result may be *syncretism*—defined in an earlier chapter as the creative blending of indigenous and foreign beliefs or practices into new cultural forms. Not unlike hybrids in the animal or plant worlds, these new forms take shape in a dynamic process of cultural adaptation in which groups gradually negotiate a collective response to new challenges in their social environment. Vodou, practiced in Haiti and described in a previous chapter, is one of many examples of religious syncretism. But syncretism also occurs in other cultural domains, including art and fashion, architecture, marriage rituals, warfare, and even sports.

An intriguing illustration of syncretism can be found among the Trobriand Islanders of the southern Pacific. We touched on their cultural practices in earlier chapters, noting that yams are the staple of their subsistence, the wealth of their economy, and the core of their culture. After the yam crop is harvested, everyone celebrates. The major event in the traditional July and August harvest festivals is a *kayasa*, a ritual competition in which rival village chiefs show off their *kuvi*—colossal yams over 3.5 meters (12 feet) long. Centered on these huge tubers, the *kayasa* ceremony involves dancing and ritual fighting between neighboring communities. The chief hosting the event is always declared the winner.

When Trobrianders came under colonial rule, British administrators as well as Christian protestant missionaries and teachers took notice of the *kayasa* ceremony. They

found it scandalous for its erotic displays of "wild" dancing, accompanied by chanting and shouting—suggestive of sexual intercourse, body parts, and so on. A Methodist missionary set about "civilizing" these tropical islanders by teaching cricket at the mission school. He hoped this gentlemanly sport would replace Trobriand rivalry and fighting, encouraging proper bearing in dress, sportsmanship, and ultimately religion.

But that is not what happened. Although the Trobrianders took to the sport, they "rubbished" the British rules. Making cricket their own, they played in traditional battle dress and incorporated battle magic and erotic dancing into the game. They modified the British style of pitching, making it resemble the old Trobriand way of throwing a spear. And following the game, they held massive feasts, where wealth was displayed to enhance their prestige (**Figure 25.6**).

Cricket, in its altered form, serves traditional systems of prestige and exchange. Everyone associated with the sport displays exuberance and pride, and the players are as much concerned with conveying the full meaning of who they are as with scoring runs. From the sensual dressing in preparation for the game to the team chanting songs full of sexual metaphors to the erotic dancing between the innings, it is clear that each participant is playing for his own importance, for the fame of his team, and for the hundreds who watch the spirited spectacle.

Revitalization Movements

In contrast to cultural changes that are invited or initiated by peoples themselves, those that are imposed or experienced as disruptive may be resisted or rejected. Such a reaction may lead to a *reform movement* or take on a more extreme character as a *revitalization movement*. As noted in the chapter on religion and spirituality, such radical movements develop in response to widespread social disruption and collective feelings of anxiety and despair. Efforts to rekindle the fire, restore a sense of energy, and reclaim lost or abandoned cultural practices, these revitalization movements are often, but not always, religiously or spiritually based. Sometimes, they even take on an armed revolutionary character.

Anthropologists have identified a sequence common to the revitalization process. First is the normal state of society in which stress is not too great, and sufficient cultural means exist to satisfy needs. Next comes a phase of cultural upheaval, triggered by foreign invasion, domination, and exploitation, leading to growing frustration and stress brought about by cultural upheaval. A deepening of the crisis marks the third stage, in which normal means of resolving social and psychological tensions are inadequate or fail. The decline may trigger a radical response in the form of a collective effort to restore, or revitalize, the culture. During this phase, a prophet or some other spiritual leader inspired by supernatural visions or guidance

tradition Customary ideas and practices passed on from generation to generation, which in a modernizing society may form an obstacle to new ways of doing things.

accommodation In anthropology, refers to an adaptation process by which a people resists assimilation by modifying its traditional culture in response to pressures by a dominant society in order to preserve its distinctive ethnic identity.

Figure 25.6 Syncretism: Trobriand Cricket

Indigenous peoples have reacted to colonialism in many different ways. When British missionaries pressed Trobriand Islanders of Melanesia to celebrate their regular yam harvests with a game of "civilized" cricket rather than traditional "wild" erotic dances, Trobrianders responded by transforming the somewhat dull British sport into an exuberant event that featured sexual chants and dances between innings. This is an example of syncretism—the creative blending of indigenous and foreign beliefs and practices into new cultural forms.

© Wolfgang Kaehler/Corbis

attracts a following, leading to a cult and sometimes spiraling into a religious movement (Wallace, 1970).

Cargo Cults

One particular historical example of a revitalization movement is the **cargo cult**—a spiritual movement (especially common in Melanesia in the Southwest Pacific) in reaction to disruptive contact with Western capitalism; the cult promises resurrection of deceased relatives, destruction or enslavement of white foreigners, and the magical arrival of utopian riches.

Indigenous Melanesians referred to the white man's wealth as "cargo" (pidgin English for European trade goods transported by ships or airplanes). In times of great social stress, native prophets emerged, predicting that the time of suffering would come to an end and that a new paradise on earth would soon arrive. Their deceased ancestors would return to life, and the rich white man would magically disappear—swallowed by an earthquake or swept away by a huge wave. However, the valued Western trade goods would be left for the prophets and their cult followers, who performed rituals to hasten this supernatural redistribution of wealth (see Lindstrom, 1993; Worsley, 1957).

A Contemporary Indigenous Revitalization Movement: Qullasuyu

In contrast to Melanesia's cargo cults, which were intensive and passing, a revitalization movement may also gain political state support and change a society's cultural institutions. One example of this is under way in Bolivia, a pluralistic South American country where most citizens are of indigenous descent and still speak an ancestral home language other than Spanish. The two most common are Aymara and Quechua, spoken by people inhabiting what was historically known as Qullasuyu, the southeastern district of Tawantinsuyu (*Quechua* means "union of four districts"), the indigenous name for the ancient Inca empire.

Following the December 2005 election of Evo Morales, Bolivia's first indigenous president, the country's indigenous revitalization movement has enjoyed government support. The son of an Aymara Indian father and Quechua Indian mother, this socialist head of state was previously a militant peasant leader representing masses of migrant farmers growing coca in the subtropical lowlands. Since the 1980s, he had risen to prominence as an agrarian trade union leader promoting Indian farmers' rights. The day before his presidential inauguration in January 2006, his unique position as Bolivia's first indigenous president was publicly recognized at a special ceremony held at the famous archaeological site of Tiwanaku. Standing there, flanked by *amautas* ("spiritual leaders"), Morales was vested with the ancient royal title of *apu mallku* ("condor king") of Qullasuyu. Similar scenes marked inaugural ceremonies for his second and third terms as president.

Situated between La Paz and Lake Titicaca, Tiwanaku is unequaled in cultural significance as the ceremonial center of Bolivia's indigenous revitalization movement. Long

cargo cult A spiritual movement (especially noted in Melanesia) in reaction to disruptive contact with Western capitalism, promising resurrection of deceased relatives, destruction or enslavement of white foreigners, and the magical arrival of utopian riches.

Figure 25.7 Celebrating the Bolivian Indian New Year

For Bolivian Indians, participation in the Qullasuyu revitalization movement includes a return to precolonial indigenous beliefs and rituals, such as worshiping the sun as the supreme sky deity. In the Andean highlands of Bolivia, many Indians mark the New Year by participating in a neotraditional sunrise ceremony known in the Quechua language as the *Inti Raymi* ("Sun Feast"). Here we see a group of Quechua and Aymara Indians at Isla Inkawasi, a rocky outcrop in the middle of Salar de Uyuni, the world's largest salt flat at an elevation of 3,656 meters (11,995 feet). They gather there for the northern solstice at dawn in mid-June to receive the first rays of Tata Inti ("Father Sun").

Aizar Raldes/AFP/Getty Images

abandoned, its enormous temple complex with its large pyramid, Akapana, was the capital of an ancient civilization that endured for many centuries before mysteriously collapsing about a thousand years ago. Because its inhabitants left no written records, their language remains unknown, which means Aymara and Quechua peoples can share this archaeological site symbolically representing their proud cultural heritages. Vesting these ruins with political and spiritual meaning as a sacred monument, they feel inspired to reclaim indigenous autonomy and to reject the foreign culture imposed on them during almost 500 years of colonial domination and capitalist exploitation.

In 2007, pursuing his revitalization agenda, President Morales chose Tiwanaku for an official event celebrating the adoption of the United Nations Declaration for the Rights of Indigenous Peoples. Two years later, the seven-colored *wiphala* representing Qullasuyu became Bolivia's official co-flag. It now flies alongside the country's long-established red, yellow, and green national banner (Van Cott, 2008; Yates, 2011).

Beyond restoring, preserving, and protecting indigenous cultural sites, customs, and so on, the revitalization movement in Bolivia involves a reclamation of precolonial sacred rituals, such as the worship of indigenous earth and sky deities, in particular the sun and moon (Figure 25.7). Informed by an animistic worldview, the movement seeks to restore a more harmonious relationship among communities of

humans, animals, and plants, as well as the rest of the natural environment—recognizing all as part of one large ecosystem, a living Mother Earth, traditionally held sacred as Pachamama. Formalizing this, in 2010 Bolivia's Plurinational Legislative Assembly passed the *Ley de Derechos de la Madre Tierra* ("The Law of the Rights of Mother Earth"), granting all of nature equal rights to humans (Estado Plurinacional de Bolivia, 2010).

Rebellion and Revolution

When the scale of discontent within a society reaches a critical level, the possibilities are high for a violent reaction such as a rebellion or **insurgency**—organized armed resistance by a group of rebels to an established government or authority in power. For instance, there have been many peasant insurgencies around the world in the course of history. Historically, such uprisings are triggered by repressive regimes that impose new taxes on already struggling small farmers unable to feed their families under such levels of exploitation (Wolf, 1999b).

One recent example is the Zapatista Maya Indian insurgency in southern Mexico, which began in the mid-1990s and has not yet been resolved. This uprising involves thousands of poor Indian farmers whose livelihoods have been threatened by disruptive changes imposed on them; their human rights under the Mexican constitution have never been fully implemented (Figure 25.8).

In contrast to insurgencies, which have rather limited objectives, a **revolution**—a radical change in a society or culture—involves a more dramatic transformation.

insurgency An organized armed resistance or violent uprising to an established government or authority in power; also known as *rebellion*.

revolution Radical change in a society or culture. In the political arena, it involves the forced overthrow of the existing government and establishment of a completely new one.

Daniel Aguilar/Reuters/Corbis

Figure 25.8 Zapatista Revolutionary Movement
On New Year's Day 1994, when the North American Free Trade Agreement (NAFTA) went
into effect, 3,000 armed peasants belonging to the Zapatista revolutionary movement
invaded towns in southern Mexico. Mostly Maya Indians, they declared war on the Mexican
government, claiming that globalization was destroying their rural communities. Strong
Internet presence helped them build an international network of political support. Now
committed to nonviolent resistance to Mexican state control, Zapatistas have created
thirty-two self-governing municipalities grouped in five regional zones, called *caracoles*
("conch shells"), referring to Maya sacred cosmology as mythological upholders of the sky.
Here we see commanders of the Zapatista National Liberation Army during the closing
ceremony of an indigenous congress. Behind them is a banner that pays tribute to the
Zapatista's inspirational figure, Emiliano Zapata—one of Mexico's best-known peasant
revolutionaries.

Revolutions occur when the level of discontent in a society is very high. In the political arena, revolution involves the forced overthrow of the existing government and the establishment of a completely new one.

The question of why revolutions erupt, as well as why they frequently fail to live up to the expectations of the people initiating them, is uncertain. It is clear, however, that the colonial policies of countries such as Britain, France, Spain, Portugal, and the United States during the 19th and early 20th centuries have created a worldwide situation in which revolution is nearly inevitable. Despite the political independence most colonies have gained since World War II, powerful countries continue to exploit many of these "underdeveloped" countries for their natural resources and cheap labor, causing a deep resentment of rulers beholden to foreign powers. Further discontent has been caused as governing elites in newly independent states try to assert their control over peoples living within their boundaries. By virtue of a common ancestry, possession of distinct cultures, persistent occupation of their own territories, and traditions of self-determination, the peoples they aim to

control identify themselves as distinct nations and refuse to recognize the legitimacy of what they regard as a foreign government.

Thus, in many former colonies, large numbers of people have taken up arms to resist annexation and absorption by imposed state governments run by people of other nationalities. As they attempt to make their multi-ethnic states into unified countries, ruling elites of one nationality set about stripping the peoples of other nations within their states of their lands, resources, and particular cultural identities.

One of the most important facts of our time is that the vast majority of the distinct peoples of the world have never consented to rule by the governments of states within which they find themselves living (Nietschmann, 1987). In many newly emerging countries, such peoples feel they have no other option than to take up weapons in armed protest and fight.

Apart from rebellions against authoritarian regimes, such as in the Chinese, French, and Russian revolutions, many uprisings in modern times have been insurgencies against political rule imposed by foreign powers. Such resistance usually takes the form of national independence movements that wage campaigns of armed defiance against colonial or imperial dominance. The Mexican war of liberation against Spain in the early 1800s and the Algerian struggle for independence from France in the 1950s are relevant examples.

Of the hundreds of armed conflicts in the world today, almost all are in the economically poor countries of Africa, Asia, and Latin America, many of which were at one time under European colonial domination. Of these wars, most are between the state and one or more nations or ethnic groups within the state's borders. These groups are seeking to maintain or regain control of their personal lives, communities, lands, and resources in the face of what they regard as repression or subjugation by a foreign power.

Revolutions do not always accomplish what they set out to do. One of the stated goals of the 1949 Chinese communist revolution, for example, was to liberate women from the oppression of a strongly patriarchal society in which a woman owed lifelong obedience to a male relative—first her father, later her husband, and, after his death, her oldest son. Although changes were and continue to be made, the transformation overall has been frustrated by the cultural lens through which the revolutionaries viewed their work. A tradition of deeply rooted patriarchy extending back at least 2,200 years is not easily overcome and has influenced many of the decisions made by communist China's leaders since the revolution.

Despite the current rapid changes taking place in China's expanding urban areas, in many rural parts of the country a woman's life is still largely determined by her relationship to a man—be it her father, husband, or son—rather than by her own efforts or failures. Moreover, many rural women face official local policies that identify their primary roles as wives and mothers. When they do work outside the house, it is generally at jobs with low pay, low status, and no benefits (Figure 25.9). Women's no-wage home labor (and low-wage outside labor) have been essential to China's economic expansion, which relies on the allocation of labor by the heads of patrilineal households (Liu, 2007).

Facing obstacles that many rural Chinese women feel are insurmountable, more than 1 million of them attempt suicide each year—typically by swallowing pesticides or fertilizer. Of these, 150,000 die. Rural China is the only

Jim Xu/Getty Images

Figure 25.9 Rural Women Removing Chips from Computer Boards, Guiyu, China
Since the late 1980s, e-waste from developed countries has been imported to China and broken down at Guiyu. The city comprises 21 villages with 5,500 family workshops handling some 1.5 million tons of e-waste annually and being exposed to carcinogens. Many women are involved in this painstaking and unhealthy work. Here we see a woman heating up a computer board on a charcoal-fired steel surface to remove computer chips.

place on earth where the suicide rate for women is higher than it is for men (Hasija, 2011; Pearson et al., 2002).

The situation of rural women in China shows that the undermining of revolutionary goals, if it occurs, is not necessarily by political opponents. Rather, it may be a consequence of the revolutionaries' own traditional cultural background. In rural China, that includes patrilineal exogamy, patrilocality, and a patriarchal conservatism in which female labor is controlled by male heads of families. As long as these traditional views continue to hold sway, women will be seen as commodities.

Revolution is a relatively recent phenomenon, occurring only during the past 5,000 years or so. The reason is that rebellion requires a centralized political authority to rebel against, and states did not exist before 5,000 years ago. In kin-ordered societies organized as tribes and bands, without a centralized government, there could be no rebellion or political revolution.

Modernization

One of the most frequently used terms to describe social and cultural changes as they are occurring today is **modernization**. This is most clearly defined as an all-encompassing and global process of political and socioeconomic change, whereby developing societies acquire some of the cultural characteristics common to Western industrial societies.

Derived from the Latin word *modo* ("just now"), modernization literally refers to something "in the present time." The dominant idea behind this concept is that "becoming modern" is becoming like European, North American, and other wealthy industrial or postindustrial societies, with the clear implication that not to do so is to be stuck in the past—backward, inferior, and needing to be improved. It is unfortunate that the term *modernization* continues to be so widely used, but because it is, we need to recognize its problematic one-sidedness, even as we continue to use it.

The process of modernization may be best understood as consisting of five subprocesses, all interrelated and with no fixed order of appearance:

- *Technological development:* In the course of modernization, traditional knowledge and techniques give way to the application of scientific knowledge and techniques borrowed mainly from the industrialized West.
- *Agricultural development:* This is represented by a shift in emphasis from subsistence farming to commercial farming. Instead of raising crops and livestock for their own use, people turn with growing frequency to the production of cash crops, with increased reliance on a cash economy and on global markets for selling farm products and purchasing goods.
- *Urbanization:* This subprocess is marked particularly by population movements from rural settlements into cities.
- *Industrialization:* Here human and animal power become less important, and greater emphasis is placed on material

forms of energy—especially fossil fuels—to drive machines.
- *Telecommunication:* The fifth and most recent subprocess involves electronic and digital media processing and sharing of news, commodity prices, fashions, and entertainment, as well as political and religious opinions. Information is widely dispersed to a mass audience, far across national borders.

As modernization proceeds, other changes are likely to follow. In the political realm, political parties and some sort of electoral apparatus frequently appear, along with the development of an administrative bureaucracy. In formal education, institutional learning opportunities expand, literacy increases, and an indigenous educated elite develops. Many long-held rights and duties connected with kinship are altered, if not eliminated, especially when distant relatives are concerned. If social stratification is a factor, social mobility increases as ascribed status becomes less important and personal achievement counts for more.

Finally, as traditional beliefs and practices are undermined, formalized religion becomes less important in many areas of thought and behavior. As discussed in the chapter on religion, this may turn into a growing trend toward a nonreligious worldview with people ignoring or rejecting institutionalized spiritual beliefs and rituals. Known as *secularization*, this process is especially noteworthy in highly organized capitalist states like Germany, for many centuries predominantly Lutheran and Roman Catholic. Now, almost 40 percent of Germans identify themselves as nonreligious, an increase from less than 4 percent about forty years ago.

Secularization is also taking place in other western European countries, as well as in other parts of the world. However, in places in which the state is weak and unbridled, capitalism has dramatically increased insecurity among the exploited and impoverished masses, the opposite may result, with a reactionary trend toward a more spiritual or even religious worldview. This phenomenon is evident in many eastern European, Asian, and African countries—discussed in the chapter on religion.

Indigenous Accommodation to Modernization

A closer examination of traditional cultures that have felt the impact of modernization will help to illustrate some of the problems such cultures have encountered. Earlier in this chapter, we noted that ethnic groups, unable to resist changes but unwilling to surrender their distinctive cultural heritage and identity, may pursue a strategy of accommodation. Many have done so, but with variable success. Here we offer two ethnographic examples: the Sámi people living

modernization The process of political and socioeconomic change, whereby developing societies acquire some of the cultural characteristics of Western industrial societies.

in the Arctic and sub-Arctic tundra of northwest Russia and Scandinavia and the Shuar Indians of Ecuador.

Sámi Herders: The Snowmobile Revolution and Its Unintended Consequences

Until about half a century ago, Sámi reindeer herders in Scandinavia's Arctic tundra lived much like their ancestors, pursuing their livelihood through their traditional lifeways. In the 1960s, however, they purchased snowmobiles, expecting motorized transportation to make herding physically easier and economically more advantageous. But that is not what happened.

Given the high cost of buying, maintaining, and fueling the machines, Sámi herders faced a sharp rise in their need for money. To obtain cash, men began going outside their communities for wage labor more than just occasionally, as had previously been the case. Moreover, once snowmobiles were introduced, the familiar, prolonged, and largely peaceful relationship between herder and beast changed into a noisy, traumatic one. The humans that reindeer encountered came speeding out of the woods on noisy, smelly machines that invariably chased the animals, often for long distances. And instead of helping the reindeer in their winter food quest, aiding does with their calves, and protecting the herd from predators, the men appeared only periodically—either to slaughter or to castrate the animals (Figure 25.10).

The reindeer became wary of people, resulting in de-domestication, with reindeer scattering and running off to less accessible areas. In addition, snowmobile harassment seemed to adversely affect birthing and the survival of calves. For example, within a decade the average size of the family herd among the Sámi in Finland had dropped from fifty to twelve—a number that is not economically viable. The financial cost of mechanized herding and the decline in domesticated herd size have led many Sámi to abandon herding altogether (Pelto, 1973). Today, only about 10 percent of Sámi in Finland are full-time herders, and they vie with outside economic institutions such as forestry and tourism for access to and use of land (Williams, 2003). Their situation is echoed among the Sámi across Scandinavia (Wheelersburg, 1987).

Shuar Cattle Farmers: An Indigenous Experiment in Amazon's Tropical Forest

In contrast to the Sámi in northern Europe, the Shuar Indians of Ecuador's tropical forest deliberately avoided modernization until it was inevitable. Historically better known as Jívaro, these Amazonian Indians subsisted on hunting wild game and cultivating food gardens, periodically clearing small patches of forest by slash-and-burn. In 1964, threatened

Figure 25.10 Sámi Reindeer Herding
In the 1960s, Sámi reindeer herders in Scandinavia's Arctic tundra adopted newly invented snowmobiles, convinced that these machines would make traditional herding physically easier and economically more advantageous. As it turned out, the financial cost of mechanized herding and the decline in domesticated herd size caused many Sámi to abandon herding altogether.

with the loss of their land base as more and more Ecuadoran colonists intruded into their territory, leaders from the many, widely scattered Shuar communities came together and founded a fully independent ethnic organization—the Shuar Federation— to take control of their own future.

Recognized by Ecuador's government, the group is officially dedicated to promoting the social, economic, and cultural advancement of the growing Shuar population. Through their association, the Shuar took control of their own education, using their own language and mostly Shuar teachers; they established their own bilingual radio station and a bilingual newspaper; and they participated in coordinating their own economic development efforts with official government agencies. Perhaps most important, the alliance provided a means for dealing with the pressing problem of land control.

Ecuador's government categorized almost all tropical woodlands in the Upper Amazon as *tierra baldía* ("empty land") because, although indigenous people lived there in widely scattered communities, most of their ancestral hunting land remained undeveloped wilderness that lacked legal documentation of ownership. With many thousands of young *mestizo* (mixed Indian European ancestry) farmers in Ecuador's highland valleys unable to feed their growing families, officials encouraged them to resettle in the Oriente, the "Wild East" of Ecuador. In the 1960s, it comprised almost half of the country's territory, but only about 2.5 percent of its total population. Accordingly, roads and bridges were constructed, enabling *mestizos* to claim title to "free" land and also providing them with access to the national market and export. Further capitalizing on its "empty lands," the state began selling concessions to the foreign and domestic logging, oil, and mining companies extracting its natural resources.

Besieged by development, and without legally recognized title to their ancestral lands, the Shuar Federation attracted financial assistance and expert advice through foreign aid agencies and turned large tracts of woodland into pasture for cattle ranching. By the early 1970s, it had secured title to almost 1,000 square kilometers (39 square miles) of communal land and established a cattle herd of more than 15,000 head. Beyond supplementing the traditional Shuar diet of wild game and produce from slash-and-burn gardens, cattle provided them with something to sell—a means of earning cash to pay for commodities, healthcare, and so on.

Because Shuar turned to cattle primarily to secure legal title to their lands, it is not surprising that many switched to other income sources when alternatives opened up as a result of roads now connecting them to the rest of the country. In recent decades, many Shuar have largely

abandoned cattle grazing, even allowing a reforestation of pasturelands. Instead, now that their title is officially documented, they have turned to growing labor-intensive cash crops—not only fruits, plantain, and manioc, but also coffee and cacao for sale to urban consumers or for export (Rudel, Bates, & Machinguiashi, 2002).

The strategy of accommodation pursued by the Shuar shows that sometimes positive results can occur when indigenous peoples are free to determine their own destinies even in the face of intense outside pressures. Tragically, until recently, few have had that option. Nevertheless, like the Shuar, some groups have resourcefully resisted the outside forces of destruction arrayed against them. Some receive help from anthropologists, as discussed in this chapter's Anthropology Applied feature.

Globalization in the "Underdeveloped" World

Throughout the economically developing world—in Africa, Asia, Latin America, and elsewhere—whole countries are in the throes of radical political and economic change and overall cultural transformation. Inventions and major advances in industrial production, mass transportation, and communication and information technologies are transforming societies in Europe and North America as well. As discussed in Chapter 1, this worldwide process of accelerated modernization interconnecting all parts of the earth in one vast interrelated and all-encompassing system is known as *globalization*, evidenced in global movements of natural resources, trade goods, human labor, finance capital, information, and infectious diseases.

All around the globe we are witnessing the removal of economic activities—or at least their control—from family and community settings. In many societies, such modernization processes are now happening very fast, often without the necessary time to adjust. Changes that took generations to accomplish in Europe and North America are attempted within the span of a single generation in developing countries. In the process cultures frequently face unforeseen disruptions and a rapid erosion of dearly held values they had no intention of giving up. Anthropologists doing fieldwork in distant communities throughout the world witness how these traditional cultures have been impacted, and often destroyed, by powerful global forces.

Commonly, the burden of modernization in developing countries falls most heavily on women. For example, the commercialization of agriculture often involves land reforms that overlook or ignore women's traditional land rights. This reduces their control of and access to resources at the same time that mechanization of food production and processing drastically reduces their opportunities for employment. As a consequence, women are confined more and more to traditional domestic tasks, which are increasingly devalued as commercial production becomes the dominant concern.

Moreover, the domestic workload tends to increase because men are less available to help out; tasks such as

Development Anthropology and Dams

During much of his forty-year career in scholarly and applied work, Michael M. Horowitz served as president and executive director of the Institute for Development Anthropology (IDA) while holding the title of distinguished professor of anthropology at the State University of New York, Binghamton. His pioneering contributions to applied anthropology focused on achieving equitable economic growth, environmental sustainability, conflict resolution, and participatory government in the former colonial world.

After cofounding IDA in 1976, Horowitz became its principal leader. He has played a key role in bringing anthropology forward as an applied science in international development organizations such as the World Bank, the United Nations Fund for Women, and the U.S. Agency for International Development (USAID), as well as nongovernmental organizations (NGOs) such as Oxfam. He has mentored several generations of young scholars and professionals—paying particular attention to those from developing countries—encouraging the application of anthropology's comparative and holistic methodologies and theories to empower low-income majorities in the so-called underdeveloped world.

Horowitz's work with pastoralists and floodplain-dwellers has had substantial positive impact on the well-being of small producers and landholders in developing countries. A clear example of this is the impact of his work on the lives and livelihoods of people living downstream of a hydropower dam in West Africa. Beginning in the 1980s, he and his IDA team carried out rigorous anthropological research along the Senegal River. Their study showed that traditional, pre-dam, flood-recession farming yielded better results than irrigated agriculture and was better for the environment.

This finding influenced decisions made by these countries and affiliated NGOs

Visible from space, China's Three Gorges Dam is the world's largest and most powerful hydroelectric dam. With a length of about 2,300 meters (7,700 feet) and a height of 185 meters (330 feet), it controls the Yangtze, the world's third largest river. After fifteen years of construction with a price tag of $22 billion, it became operational in 2009. The dam was built to provide a clean energy alternative to coal and to control flooding along the Yangtze River. However, it has been controversial since its inception because it has flooded ancient archaeological and cultural sites, displacing more than 1.4 million people, and it has caused significant ecological changes, including risks of landslides that threaten some 4 million people. Unlike the dam described in this Anthropology Applied feature, not one social scientist was consulted in the planning and assessment phase of Three Gorges Dam.

to manage the system with a controlled release from the Manantali Dam in Mali in order to reproduce as nearly as possible the pre-dam flow system. Horowitz's long-term field research demonstrated that seasonal flooding would provide economic, environmental, and sociocultural benefits for nearly a million small producers.

The work carried out by Horowitz and his IDA colleagues on the Senegal River Basin Monitoring Activity (SRBMA) was a breakthrough in the concepts of resettlement and river management, and it continues to influence development policy, not only in Africa, but also in Southeast Asia. Recognizing Horowitz's contributions, the Society for Applied Anthropology presented him with the prestigious Bronislaw Malinowski Award in 2006.

Based in part on Young, W. C. (2000). Kimball Award winner. *Anthropology News* 41 (8), 29. See also Society for Applied Anthropology, 2006.

fuel gathering and water collection are made more difficult as common land and resources come to be privately owned and as woodlands are reserved for commercial exploitation. As well, the growing of nonfood crops for the world market—such as cotton and sisal or luxury crops such as tea, coffee, and cacao (the source of chocolate)—makes households vulnerable to wide price fluctuations. As a result, people cannot afford the high-quality diet that subsistence farming provided, and they become malnourished. In short, with modernization, women frequently

BIOCULTURAL CONNECTION

Studying the Emergence of New Diseases

Since the Neolithic, people have had to cope with a host of new diseases that began as a consequence of changes in human behavior. Over the past several decades, this has become a renewed source of concern following the resurgence of infectious diseases and the spread of a host of new and lethal diseases.[a]

More than thirty diseases new to medicine have emerged in the past thirty-five years. Perhaps the best known of these is AIDS, which has become a top killer among infectious diseases. Since 1981, almost 40 million people have died of AIDS, and today some 37 million people around the world are living with AIDS/HIV.[b] But there are others—like Ebola hemorrhagic fever, which causes victims to bleed to death, and other hemorrhagic fevers like dengue fever, Lassa fever, and hantavirus; invasive streptococcus A, which consumes the victims' flesh; Legionnaire's disease; and Lyme disease.

Although it is not clear what has sparked the appearance and spread of these new diseases, one theory is that some are the result of human activities. In particular, road construction and the intrusion of people into remote ecological settings, such as rainforests, along with worldwide shipping and airplane traffic, allow viruses and other infectious microbes to spread rapidly to large numbers of people. It is now generally accepted that the HIV virus responsible for AIDS transferred to humans from chimpanzees in the tropical forests of the Democratic Republic of Congo (DRC) as a consequence of hunting and butchering these animals for food. For the first thirty years, few people were affected; it was not until people began congregating in quickly growing cities like Kinshasa that conditions were ripe for an epidemic.

Most of the "new" viruses that have suddenly afflicted humans are in fact old ones present in animals—such as monkeys (monkey pox), rodents (hantavirus), deer (Lyme disease), and insects (West Nile virus). What is different is that something has enabled them to jump from their animal hosts to humans.

In the DRC, civil war created a situation in which villagers in the central part of the country were faced with starvation. Their response was to increase the hunting of animals, including monkeys, squirrels, and rats that carry a disease called monkey pox. Related to smallpox, the disease transfers easily to humans, resulting in the largest outbreak of this disease ever seen among humans. This outbreak has been even more serious because of an apparently new strain of the infection, enabling it to spread from person to person, instead of only from an animal host.[c]

Large-scale habitat disturbance is an obvious explanation for such disease transfers. In another part of the world, U.S. medical anthropologist Carol Jenkins (1945–2008) conducted early health-related research among various ethnic groups in Papua New Guinea (PNG) from 1982 to 1995. Aiming to understand the interplay between ecological disturbance and the emergence of new diseases, she tracked the health of local people in the wake of a massive logging operation. Her work provided valuable insights, such as clarifying how the disease organisms spread from animal hosts to humans.

Jenkins's research in PNG was unique because baseline health data on local people were gathered before the environment was disturbed. Researchers, many trained by Jenkins, continue to build on her studies.

The importance of such investigations is obvious: In a globalized world, as air travel allows diseases to spread worldwide, we need a fuller understanding of how pathogens interact with their hosts if we are to devise effective preventive and therapeutic strategies to deal with them.

Biocultural Question

Because new viruses and bacteria often spread rapidly, what do you think of government-funded research and development of killer diseases for purposes of biological warfare?

[a] Gibbons, A. (1993, August 6). Where are "new" diseases born? *Science 261* (5122), 680–681.

[b] "Global information and advice on HIV & AIDS." (2015). *AVERT.org*. www.avert.org (retrieved December 14, 2015)

[c] Cohen, J. (1997, July 18). Is an old virus up to new tricks? *Science 277* (5324), 312–313.

find themselves in an increasingly inferior position. As their workload increases, the value assigned to the work they do declines, as does their relative educational status, not to mention their health and nutrition.

Most anthropologists, based on their fieldwork experience, recognize that new roads, harbors, railways, and airstrips impact the earth's remaining wilderness—such as tropical forests, arid deserts, and Arctic tundra. These developments have costs. We opened this chapter with a photo of a train station in India. In that country, steel railways were first constructed to transport cotton to the seaport for shipment to the textile factories in Great Britain in the mid-1800s. Ships, trains, trucks, airplanes, and now also drones—as well as newspapers, magazines, radios, televisions, and cell phones—help bring about radical changes that local peoples often do not want and cannot stop because they are challenged to a degree that exceeds their coping capability. Meanwhile, powerful groups with interests in capitalizing on cheap natural and human resources wherever available justify their relentless expansion, arguing that modernization is both inevitable and good for everyone, in particular for "primitive" and "underdeveloped" peoples who ought to be given opportunities to prosper and become wealthy just like themselves. For a serious look at the consequences of these changes, see the Biocultural Connection feature.

This worldview overlooks the fact that the standard of living for the middle and upper classes in wealthy or industrialized countries is based on a consumption rate of nonrenewable resources whereby a small fraction of the world's population uses the vast majority of these natural resources. Unfortunately, despite rosy predictions about a better future, hundreds of millions of people in our world remain trapped in a wretched reality, struggling against poverty, hunger, poor health, and other dangers. In the next and final chapter of this book, we further explore the underlying structures and deeper causes of these problems and look at the role anthropology can and does play in helping to meet these challenges.

CHAPTER CHECKLIST

Why and how do cultural systems change?

✓ Stability may be a striking feature of many traditional cultures, but all cultures are capable of adapting to changing conditions—climatic, economic, political, or ideological.

✓ Dynamic processes involved in cultural change include accidental discoveries, deliberate inventions to solve some perceived problem, and borrowing from other peoples who introduce—or force—new commodities, technologies, and practices.

✓ *Progress* is a relative term that implies improvement as defined by the people who benefit from the changes.

What are the mechanisms of voluntary cultural change?

✓ Major mechanisms involved in voluntary cultural change are innovation, diffusion, and cultural loss.

✓ Innovation is any new idea, method, or device that gains widespread acceptance in society. A primary innovation is the creation, invention, or discovery of a new idea, method, or device. A secondary innovation is a deliberate application or modification of these innovations.

✓ A culture's internal dynamics may encourage certain innovative tendencies while discouraging others. Force of habit may obstruct the acceptance of an innovation.

✓ Diffusion, the spread of certain ideas, customs, or practices from one culture to another, may account for up to 90 percent of a culture's content. Many domestic food plants developed by American Indians spread around the world, including corn, also known as maize. Typically, people borrow only those cultural elements that are compatible with their own.

✓ Cultural loss involves the abandonment of some practice or trait.

What is repressive change?

✓ Frequently, one group forces changes upon another, usually in the course of conquest and colonialism.

✓ Acculturation is the massive cultural change that occurs in a society when it experiences intensive firsthand contact with a more powerful society. It may occur as a result of military conquest, political and economic expansion, or the substantial influx of dominant newcomers.

✓ Ethnocide is the violent eradication of an ethnic group's collective cultural identity as a distinctive people. It occurs when a dominant society deliberately sets out to destroy another society's cultural heritage. Among many examples is the experience of Yąnomami Indians of the Amazon forest in Brazil and Venezuela.

What is directed change?

✓ Although the process of acculturation often unfolds without planning, powerful elites may devise and enforce programs of cultural change, directing immigrant or subordinated groups into learning and accepting a dominant society's cultural beliefs and practices.

✓ Applied anthropology—the application of anthropological insights and methods to solving practical problems—arose as anthropologists sought to provide colonial administrators with a better understanding of native cultures, either to better control them or to avoid their serious disruption.

✓ An alternative type of practical anthropology emerged in the latter 20th century. Known by various names including action anthropology, it involves community-based research and action in collaboration with indigenous societies, ethnic minorities, and other besieged or repressed groups. A serious ethical issue for applied anthropologists is how far they should go in trying to change the ways of other peoples.

How do people react to repressive change?

✓ Some have retreated to inaccessible places in hopes of being left alone, whereas others have lapsed into apathy.

✓ Some, like the Trobriand Islanders, have reasserted their traditional culture's values by modifying foreign practices to conform to indigenous values, a phenomenon known as syncretism.

✓ If a culture's values are widely out of step with the reality of their daily lives, revitalization movements may arise.

✓ One example of a revitalization movement is the cargo cult (especially noted in Melanesia in the southwest Pacific) in reaction to disruptive contact with Western capitalism. A more recent example is the indigenous revitalization movement in Bolivia, led by the country's Aymara Indian president, Evo Morales.

✓ When the scale of discontent within a society is high, violent reaction such as rebellion or insurgency (organized armed resistance to the established government or authority in power) is likely. And if the level of dissatisfaction rises even higher, it may lead to revolution—a radical change in a society or culture. In the political arena, revolution refers to the forced overthrow of an existing government and the establishment of a new one.

What are modernization and self-determination?

✓ Modernization refers to an all-encompassing and global process of political and socioeconomic change, whereby developing societies acquire some of the cultural characteristics common to Western industrial societies.

✓ The process of modernization consists of five subprocesses: technological development, agricultural development, urbanization, industrialization, and telecommunication. Other changes follow in the areas of political organization, education, social organization, and religion. As traditional beliefs and practices are undermined, secularization may rise.

✓ Self-determination is deeply valued by traditional cultures feeling the impact of modernization and other cultural changes.

✓ Attempting to claim self-determination does not guarantee success. Sámi reindeer herders living in northern Scandinavia discovered this when they adopted snowmobiles and faced a dramatic decline in the size of their herds. In contrast, Shuar Indians in the Amazon who subsisted on wild game and forest gardens increased their social and economic security when they turned to raising cattle as a means of securing legal title to their lands.

QUESTIONS FOR REFLECTION

1. When societies are swept up in the processes of modernization—whether they involve changes in transportation, agriculture, industrialization, or telecommunication—all levels of their cultural systems are affected. How do you envision the long-term consequences of humanity's ever-expanding dependence on the conveniences offered by these changes?

2. Do you think that ecocide and ethnocide are inevitable in economic development and modernization processes across the globe? If so, why? If not, what makes you think so?

3. Globalization radically challenges most of us to adjust at an ever-faster pace within increasingly complex transnational settings. Do you feel that these changes are good for everyone?

4. When hearing or reading about insurgencies or violent uprisings in the news, have you ever wondered why people are willing to risk their lives to bring about change? What do you think accounts for that level of commitment?

DIGGING INTO ANTHROPOLOGY

Life Without Imports

In this chapter we discussed diffusion and the fact that as much as 90 percent of any culture's content is borrowed. Imagine a political revolution in which the new authorities prohibit the consumption of any imported goods and also make it a crime to see foreign movies, read foreign literature, or get news from foreign sources of information. Make an inventory of your own family's habits and identify how many things you eat, drink, wear, or use that are grown or produced in your own country. Next, compare that list with an inventory of similar items that were imported. Determine the ratio of domestic and foreign commodities and estimate the degree of cultural change.

Lou-Foto/Alamy

CHALLENGE ISSUE

For thousands of years, humans have met the challenges of survival by adapting to their natural environment and transforming it to fit their needs. They turned deserts, forests, swamps, and mountainsides into pastures, farmlands, and industrial centers, creating opportunities (and unanticipated challenges) for an ever-growing population. Since the start of the industrial revolution about two centuries ago, inaugurating what is now known as the Anthropocene, the human population has expanded from 1 billion to about 7.4 billion—more than half now living and working in urban areas. With the launching of telecommunication satellites in the 1950s—followed by the Internet in the 1960s, personal computers in the 1970s, and the World Wide Web in the 1990s—the digital revolution has accelerated the globalization process. Spinning webs of interconnectivity, people everywhere are adapting to new media environments. Using social media, a few billion humans weave in and out of cyberspace on a daily basis for work, news, entertainment, politics, and social networking. The population explosion and technological innovations radically impact all aspects of culture in societies across the globe—from infrastructure to social structure to worldview. In China, cyber cafés known as 网吧 (*wangba*) can be found in most cities. This is one of hundreds in Beijing, the capital city.

Global Challenges, Local Responses, and the Role of Anthropology

26

Today, billions of people take it for granted that they can slip into cyberspace and connect with others regardless of geographic distance thanks to electronic, fiber-optic, and digital telecommunication technology. Well over 1,300 operational satellites orbit the earth—revolving between about 160 and 35,786 kilometers (99 and 22,236 miles) above the ocean surface (Figure 26.1). About half of these are designated specifically for telecommunication, whereas others serve military, scientific, and weather forecasting purposes. Also included among these are about 50 global positioning satellites (GPS), orbiting at 16,000 kilometers (9,940 miles) above earth (Union of Concerned Scientists, 2015). Wireless telecommunication technology by means of mobile, mass-produced electronic equipment—from laptops to smartphones—fuels globalization in ways unimaginable to most people just three decades ago.

Because industrialization and globalization seem unstoppable, we are compelled to ask: Can the thousands of different societies that have existed for centuries, if not millennia, maintain their distinctive cultural identities and deal successfully with the multiple challenges hurled at them? Moreover, can our species successfully adapt to the dynamic global ecosystem of the **Anthropocene**—a geological epoch defined by massive environmental changes brought on by humans since the industrial revolution?

Cultural Revolutions: From *Terra Incognita* to Google Earth

Just five centuries ago, much of the earth was still unmapped *terra incognita*. That does not mean that people had no knowledge of foreign cultures: Long-distance migrations and journeys by traders, raiders, and pilgrims have been part of human history for millennia. But these explorations were not accurately documented

Anthropocene A geological epoch defined by massive environmental changes brought on by humans since the industrial revolution.

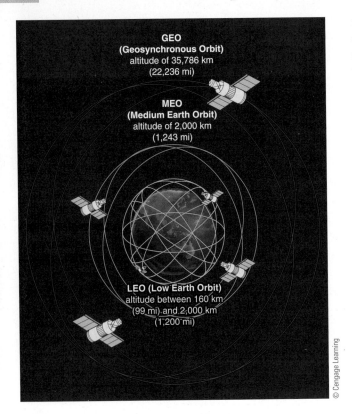

GEO
(Geosynchronous Orbit)
altitude of 35,786 km
(22,236 mi)

MEO
(Medium Earth Orbit)
altitude of 2,000 km
(1,243 mi)

LEO (Low Earth Orbit)
altitude between 160 km
(99 mi) and 2,000 km
(1,200 mi)

© Cengage Learning

Figure 26.1 How Crowded Is It Up There?
There are 1,300 operational satellites orbiting the earth—revolving between 160 and 35,786 kilometers (99 and 22,236 miles) above the ocean surface. About half of these are designated specifically for telecommunication, whereas others serve military, scientific, and weather forecasting purposes. Also included among these are about 50 global positioning satellites (GPS).

and summarized in a comprehensive format. And so it was that Norse voyages to Canada's northeast coast more than a thousand years ago and Chinese naval expeditions (equipped with compass) to eastern Africa in the early 1400s had little or no impact on our geographic understanding of the world.

This changed soon after Christopher Columbus first crossed the Atlantic Ocean in 1492 and Ferdinand Magellan's expedition completed the first circumnavigation of the globe in 1522. News of their discoveries of foreign lands, peoples, and natural resources spread quickly by means of the recently invented movable-type printing press. Geographic information improved, and cartographers began printing more accurate maps, leading to the publication of the first world atlas in 1570. Not long afterward, observational astronomy verified that the earth is not the center of the universe.

Just over two centuries ago, the invention of steam engines and other machinery launched the industrial revolution, with large-scale factory production and an expanding transportation network of steam-powered trains and ships. The invention of electrical generators and the incandescent lightbulb in the mid-1800s radically transformed patterns of human behavior within a few generations. The speed of change accelerated with the introduction of gasoline- or petrol-fueled internal combustion engines in the 1870s,

which led to automobiles, followed by airplanes a few decades later—part of the mass travel and transportation revolution of the 20th century. That period also brought major innovations in telecommunications technology—from print media to telegraph, camera, telephone, radio, television, communications satellites, and the Internet—making it possible to exchange more information with more people faster and over greater distances.

Of note in this fast process of radical cultural change is the discovery of nuclear fission in the late 1930s. During World War II (1939–1945), the United States developed enriched uranium, built the world's first nuclear reactor to breed plutonium, and produced the first nuclear weapons. In 1945, U.S. warplanes dropped atomic bombs on the citizens of Hiroshima and Nagasaki, forcing the Japanese enemy into unconditional surrender.

Today, more than thirty countries operate hundreds of nuclear power reactors generating heat and electricity. Of these, nine have stockpiled nuclear weapons, collectively owning an arsenal estimated at about 10,000 warheads capable of destroying human civilization many times over (Arms Control Association, 2015). Nuclear energy may have benefited many societies, but some accidents have been disastrous. All of these technological inventions have transformed our natural environments, the ways we humans live—and how we perceive our place and destiny in the universe. In 1969, American astronauts landed on the moon. Three years later, on an aborted lunar trip, they took the first full-view photo of earth (Figure 26.2). This image had a profound impact on humanity, igniting the environmental movement and the idea of "One Earth, One World."

NASA Johnson Space Center

Figure 26.2 First Full-View Photo of Earth
This famous "Blue Marble" shot represents the first photograph in which our planet is in full view. The crew took the picture on December 7, 1972, as *Apollo 17* left earth's orbit for the moon. With the sun at their backs, the crew had a perfectly lit view of the blue planet.

About a dozen years before this photograph was taken, the United States had secretly launched its first strategic reconnaissance satellite for photographic surveillance of the earth's surface. During the Cold War with Russia and its communist allies (1947–1989), technological improvements led to an eye-in-the-sky investigation system. Specializing in geospatial data visualization applications, a CIA-funded company created EarthViewer 3D in 2001. Three years later, Google, a U.S.-based megacorporation providing Internet-related products and services, acquired the technology that made this virtual globe, map, and geographic information program commercially available to the public.

Today, we inhabit a planet that is under constant surveillance from satellites relentlessly orbiting high above us. We now find it normal that we can download detailed photographs of almost any spot on earth—and that such images make it possible to track radical changes in our world's natural environments, from massive deforestation to garbage dumping, air pollution, and urbanization.

A Global Culture?

The ever-growing interconnectedness of our species—evident in the global flow of humans, their products, and their ideas made possible by modern mass transportation and telecommunications media—has resulted in many external similarities across cultures. This has spawned speculations that humanity's future will feature a single homogenous global culture.

Certainly, it is striking—the extent to which such items as Western-style fast food, soft drinks, clothing, music, and movies have spread to virtually all parts of the globe. Among many examples is the U.S.-based global corporation McDonald's—the world's largest fast-food chain. With 36,000 restaurants in more than 100 countries, McDonald's serves close to 70 million customers a day (McDonald's, 2015) (Figure 26.3). Famous for its Big Mac hamburger, it has become emblematic of what is often perceived as the homogenization of the world's different cultures in the age of globalization, sometimes referred to as the "McDonaldization" of societies (Ritzer, 1983).

Patrick Baz/AFP/Getty Images

Figure 26.3 **McDonald's, Riyadh, Saudi Arabia**
A U.S.-based company founded in 1955, McDonald's is the leading global food service retailer with more than 36,000 restaurants in more than 100 countries. Its Golden Arches have become an internationally recognized symbol for fast-service fries, chicken, hamburgers, salads, and milkshakes. Many of these restaurants are franchises owned and operated by local businesspeople who are members of the same society as most of their customers. Success depends not only on quality fast food and quick service, but also on respecting cultural food taboos. In India, home to nearly a billion Hindus who obey a taboo on beef, the Big Mac is made with lamb or chicken and is known as a Maharaja Mac. Beef burgers are not a problem in Saudi Arabia, where the first McDonald's franchise opened in 1993. Operated by Arab Muslims, there are now about 100 McDonald's in that nation, including this one in the capital city of Riyadh, where men and women are gender segregated in different lines and dining areas.

Yet, as we look at reactionary movements—including the rise of religious fundamentalism, nationalism, and ethnic identity politics around the world—the forecast of a single global culture appears unrealistic. If a single homogenous global culture is not in the making, what is?

Global Integration Processes

For more than a century now, integration processes have been pursued on a worldwide scale, albeit with mixed success. One of the first international organizations was the Red Cross, followed by the international Olympic Games (Figure 26.4). The need for global integration became all the more urgent in the wake of the Second World War, which ended with atomic bombs and resulted in the ruination of hundreds of cities and the deaths of 55 million people. Recognizing the urgency

of international cooperation, the world's most powerful states instituted the World Bank and the International Monetary Fund in 1944. To prevent perpetual war, they also formed the United Nations (UN) in 1945, soon followed by a number of global nongovernmental organizations (NGOs), such as the World Health Organization (WHO). Likewise, global humanitarian aid organizations formed, such as Amnesty International and Doctors Without Borders.

In addition, countries all around the world have developed mass tourism industries that connect people in other ways. Tourism is a $1.25 trillion industry in which more than 1 billion international tourists travel each year (United Nations World Tourism Organization, 2015).

Such global integration mechanisms connect people all around the world, and they play a constructive role in maintaining a world system. Notably, however, they do not produce a global transnational culture.

ZUMA Press, Inc./Alamy Stock Photo

Figure 26.4 2014 Winter Olympics, Sochi, Russia
The Olympics are unique among the many strands in today's global web. Inspired by the ancient Greek sporting event held at Olympia 2,000 years ago, the games have become a global spectacle, with thousands of athletes from all around the world competing in a different country every four years. In today's world—where powerful states have conquered and destroyed many smaller nations and tens of millions have been killed in warfare worldwide—this global sports gathering is a crucial ritual, celebrating international peace in a friendly rivalry for medals and prestige.

Pluralistic Societies and Multiculturalism

As described in the chapter on politics, ethnic groups or nations have organized as independent states for about 5,000 years. Many expanded—often by means of military conquest—and as republics, kingdoms, or empires engaged in nation-building projects, pressing subjects or allied peoples into cultural assimilation. Other neighboring ethnic groups joined together, confederating into one political union or territorial state. In such *pluralistic societies*, each member group maintains its distinctive language and cultural heritage.

Today, there are a number of other forms of political integration among neighboring ethnic groups, such as the twenty-eight member states that comprise the European Union. These countries achieved this unification despite the hindrances of linguistic differences, distinctive cultural traditions, bureaucratic red tape, and economic disparities.

One way of curbing divisive pressures inherent in pluralistic societies is to officially adopt a public policy of **multiculturalism** based on mutual respect and tolerance for cultural differences. In contrast to state policies of assimilation in which a dominant ethnic group uses its power to impose its own culture as the standard, policies of multiculturalism assert the value of different cultures coexisting within a country. They call upon citizens from all ethnic groups to accept the rights of others to freely express their views and values. An example of long-established multiculturalism may be seen in states such as Switzerland, where peoples speaking German, French, Italian, and Romansh coexist under the same government.

Cultural pluralism is more common than multiculturalism, but several multi-ethnic countries are reevaluating their cultural assimilation policies. One example is the United States, which now has over 120 different ethnic groups within its borders, in addition to hundreds of federally recognized American Indian groups. Another is Australia with over a hundred ethnic groups and eighty languages spoken within its territorial boundaries. Many European countries are engaged in similar public debates, as many millions of foreign immigrants have settled there during the past few decades.

Pluralistic Societies and Fragmentation

Pluralistic societies, in virtually all parts of the world, show a tendency to fragment, usually along major linguistic, religious, or ethno-nationalist divisions. Because of this trend, some predict a world in which ethnic groups will become increasingly nationalistic rather than united in response to globalization, each group stressing its unique cultural heritage and emphasizing differences with neighboring groups. This *devolution* inclination is evident in numerous nationalist movements today—including separatist movements of the Karen in Myanmar and the Kurds in Turkey, Syria, and Iraq. In Mexico, the Maya continue to seek greater political self-determination on their tribal territories. Similar movements by indigenous nations objecting to their subordinated status as *internal colonies* also occur in many other countries, including Canada and the United States.

When states with extensive territories lack adequate transportation and communication networks or major unifying cultural forces (such as a common religion or national language), it is more likely that separatist intentions will be realized. One recent example is the political breakup of the Soviet Union in 1991 into about a dozen independent republics—Russia, Armenia, Belarus, Estonia, Ukraine, Moldova, and Georgia, among others. Since then, some of these republics have fragmented even further. For example, in 2008, two of Georgia's ethnically distinct regions (South Ossetia and Abkhazia) officially split after years of separatist pressure. And in 2013, Ukraine's predominantly ethnic Russian Crimean Peninsula region broke away and was annexed by Russia.

Among examples from other corners of the world, Sudan in northeastern Africa officially split along an ethnic, religious, and geographic fault line in 2011, producing international recognition of the Republic of South Sudan as the 193rd member state of the United Nations. Since then, fierce fighting between two major ethnic groups there (the Dinka and the Nuer) indicates that there may be further territorial fragmentation.

Global Migrations: Migrants, Transnationals, and Refugees

Throughout history, challenges such as famine, poverty, and violent intimidation by dangerous neighbors have forced people to move—often scattering members of threatened ethnic groups. People also move for other reasons, including economic opportunity and political or religious freedom. Whether forced or free, **migration**—mobility in geographic space, involving temporary or permanent change in usual place of residence—has always had a significant effect on world social geography; it has contributed to cultural change and development, to the diffusion of ideas and innovations, and to the complex mixture of peoples and cultures found in the world today.

Internal migration occurs when people move within the boundaries of their country, shifting their usual residence

multiculturalism The public policy for managing cultural diversity in a multi-ethnic society, officially stressing mutual respect and tolerance for cultural differences within a country's borders.

migration Mobility in geographic space, involving temporary or permanent change in usual place of residence. Internal migration is movement within countries; external migration is movement to a foreign country.

from one region to another. Typically, migrants leave their farms, villages, and small towns in the rural backlands and move to cities to find greater economic opportunity, escape from poverty and starvation, and possibly avoid armed conflict in their home region. *External migration* is movement from one country to another. Such migration may be voluntary (people seeking better conditions and opportunities abroad), but all too often it may be involuntary. People who are taken as slaves or prisoners—or who have been driven from their homelands by war, political unrest, religious persecution, or environmental disasters— are involuntary migrants.

Every year, a few million people migrate to wealthy countries in search of wage labor and a better future for themselves and their offspring (Figure 26.5). Although most cross international borders as legal immigrants, seeking work permits and ultimately citizenship in their new homeland, many migrants are illegal and do not enjoy crucial rights and benefits. Migrants also include *transnationals,* people who earn their living in one country while remaining citizens of another.

Today, beyond the masses of people who migrate for work, some 60 million people are refugees or internally displaced persons (IDPs) who have fled their homes due to war. Refugees are those who flee to foreign countries while

IDPs seek shelter within their home countries. Most are struggling in makeshift camps where they cannot make a living. According to the United Nation's Refugee Agency, "Globally, one in every 122 humans is now either a refugee, internally displaced, or seeking asylum. If this were the population of a country, it would be the world's 24th biggest" (UNHCR, 2015b) (Figure 26.6).

Diasporas and Xenophobia

Over the past few decades, mass migration across international borders has dramatically impacted the ethnic composition of affluent societies in Australia, western Europe, and North America. For example, today, the number of foreign-born people residing in the United States is close to 42 million—about 13 percent of the total population. Just over half come from Latin America, including about 12 million from Mexico alone (Pew Research Center, 2015). As the largest and fastest-growing group of immigrants in the United States, Latino immigrants are settled primarily in California and Texas, where many form Spanish-speaking ethnic enclaves.

In addition, the United States is now home to over 25 million immigrants from Asian countries (such as China and India) and sub-Saharan African countries (such as Nigeria and Ethiopia). Over the past three decades,

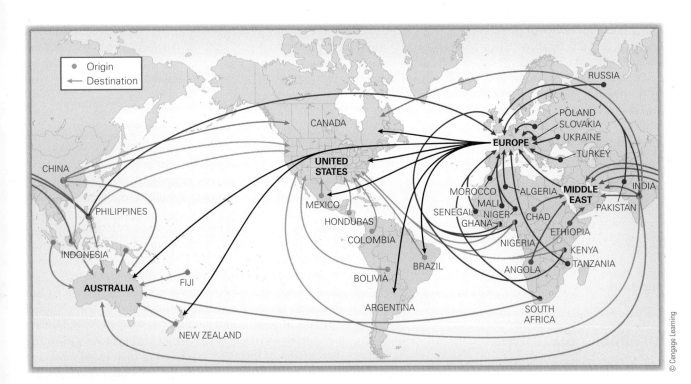

Figure 26.5 Migrating for Work

In our globalized world, tens of millions of people have moved across international borders for better income-earning opportunities. They include farm and meat plant laborers, cleaners, cab drivers, construction workers, servers in the tourism industry, as well as shopkeepers, nurses, doctors, engineers, and computer specialists. Not shown here is the international flow of refugees who are forced to flee to save their lives or preserve their freedom.

Figure 26.6 World's Largest Refugee Camp

In the African country of Somalia, extended drought and years of civil war have caused chronic famine and chased huge numbers of people out of the country. Some 350,000 are stuck in this vast camp complex in Dadaab, Kenya, near the Somalia border—and at times the numbers have swelled to nearly 500,000. It was established in 1991 to provide food and shelter for up to 90,000 refugees fleeing the war, but two decades of ongoing conflict and natural disasters in Somalia have generated a continuous flow of Somalis into the camp, requiring the creation of numerous extensions, including this one set up to shelter 5,000 people. Now housing almost five times the number for which it was originally built, the Dadaab camp is jammed, and resources are inadequate. Moreover, situated on a floodplain, it is inaccessible for extended periods during the rainy season, making the delivery of life-saving food, water, and healthcare unreliable.

the number of African immigrants self-identifying as "black" has rapidly increased from 65,000 to more than 1.1 million—and that figure continues to grow. Black immigrants from the Caribbean now number 1.7 million, but their rate of increase is slowing down. Collectively, these many millions of new immigrants contribute to the ever-changing multicultural fabric of U.S. society (Capps, McCabe, & Fix, 2011).

Meanwhile, on the other side of the Atlantic, almost 20 percent (about 12 million) of the people living in France today are foreign-born immigrants and their offspring, primarily originating from former colonial territories in West Africa and Southeast Asia. Islam is now the second-largest religion in France with about 6 million adherents.

About 3.5 million people of Turkish origin now reside in western Germany, not counting a few million other foreign-born immigrants and their offspring. Initially needed for cheap, unskilled labor, Turks were hired as "guest workers" in highly industrialized urban areas. Because most of them remained, the authorities instituted a family reunification policy, which resulted in hundreds of thousands of Turkish relatives entering the country. Even after several decades in Germany, many German Turks do not possess citizenship and have not become culturally integrated into German society. Turkish, spoken by Germany's largest ethnic minority, has become that country's second language. As a result of the Syrian civil war that began in 2012, about a million refugees from the West Asian conflict zone are also expected to settle in Germany, thus adding to the growing ethnic complexity of that country.

Confronted with millions of foreign immigrants, Europe's native-born or *autochthonous* (from the Greek *auto*, "self," and *khthon*, "soil") populations are currently wrestling with their national identities in a period of rapid change. With their concerns compounded by economic insecurity, social tensions are on the rise, and so are racism and ethnic intolerance, directed especially against foreign-born Muslims who do not assimilate.

In their *diaspora* (from the Greek *daspeirein*, "disperse"), migrants and refugees often face great challenges as poor newcomers to host societies. Moving into areas traditionally inhabited by other ethnic groups, they may face hostile opposition, especially when they compete for

Figure 26.7 Migrants on the Run
Bengali Muslims—newcomers to villages in India's northeast state of Assam—leave their homes following ethnic clashes with the indigenous Bodos in which many people were killed and dozens of homes were burned to the ground. Government troops sent to quell communal clashes over land rights were ordered to shoot suspected rioters on sight.

scarce resources, pose a threat to security, or are otherwise unwelcome as newcomers. As such, they may be targeted for a hate-mongering campaign. Such **xenophobia**—fear or hatred of strangers or anything foreign—is especially inflammatory in times of economic uncertainty when health and well-being are threatened and social tensions rise. Under such circumstances, space for intercultural tolerance narrows, social boundaries become more sharply defined, and ethnic differences are emphasized over human commonalities.

Sometimes, attitudes toward migrant laborers and recent immigrants grow so intensely negative that it does not take much to ignite brutal violence. Such outbreaks are all too common in many countries, including South Africa and India. In the summer of 2012, for example, xenophobia erupted into interethnic violence in Assam, northeast India, as the Bodos, an indigenous Buddhist mountain people, clashed with Bengali-speaking Muslim immigrants over scarce farmland. Within a few weeks, dozens of people from both sides had been killed, and many more were wounded. Nearly 400 settlements in disputed areas were abandoned, as about 400,000 Bengalis packed up what they could carry and fled. This population is now dispersed in 270 refugee camps (**Figure 26.7**).

Although migrants frequently experience hostility, hardship, disappointment, and sometimes failure in their

new countries, those who remain trapped in their troubled lands of origin often face worse challenges: malnutrition, hunger, chronic disease, and violence. For solace and support, many newcomers form or join communities of people who have come from the same part of the world. Also, modern transportation, telecommunication technology, and electronic cash transfers make it possible for *diasporic communities* all across the globe to interact with relatives and friends who have settled elsewhere, as well as with their country of origin. Today, most migrants reach across the miles to loved ones, sharing news as well as emotional and financial support. Worldwide, electronic transfers to developing countries total about $440 billion per year (World Bank, 2015a).

Migrants, Urbanization, and Slums

Most migrants are poor and begin their new lives in expanding urban areas. During the past fifty years, the world's urban population has more than tripled. Today, for the first time in world history, close to half of our species now resides in urban areas—over 3.5 billion people. Just two centuries ago, at the start of the industrial revolution, only about 3 percent of the world's population lived in cities.

Until 1950, the largest city in the world was London. Although briefly overtaken by New York, the current urban frontrunner has long been Tokyo, now counting 38 million inhabitants. In fact, the 10 largest cities in the world are all in Asia, except for New York (now dropped to 8th place). Cities have grown not only in size but also in number. Today, there are almost 500 cities with populations exceeding 1 million. Of these more than 25 are megacities, each with populations over 10 million. Urban areas are gaining about 67 million people per year—about 1.3 million every week. As the global population grows, the number of big cities will increase substantially, with the majority located in coastal areas of developing countries.

Historically, cities grow primarily as a result of migration by masses of people escaping rural poverty or seeking economic opportunity. Many of these migrants have little or no education, lack technical skills, and have just one way to earn a living: selling their labor power on the lowest rung of the economic ladder. Expectations crushed by harsh reality, and far away from their home regions, migrants often find themselves condemned

---

xenophobia Fear or hatred of strangers or anything foreign.

Figure 26.8 Slum in Manila
Half of the inhabitants of Manila, the capital of the Philippines, live in slums such as this.

to a life in squalor in crowded shantytowns or slums, with limited access to clean water, waste disposal, and electricity.

One of the main concentrations of urban poor on the planet today can be found in Lagos, Nigeria's commercial capital and now Africa's largest city. In just four decades, its population has exploded from less than 1.4 million in 1970 to perhaps 21 million today. Unable to manage the enormous influx of migrants and their offspring, the city now features huge overcrowded slums where two-thirds of the city's inhabitants reside. Lagos is not unique: Unplanned, makeshift, urban squatter settlements are burgeoning around the globe. For instance, about half of the 11 million inhabitants of Manila, capital of the Philippines, now live in slums (Figure 26.8).

Worldwide, about 1 billion people currently reside in slums, and the number is rapidly growing. About 60 percent of these slum-dwellers live in Asia, 20 percent in Africa, 13 percent in Latin America and the Caribbean, and only 6 percent in Europe. In sub-Saharan Africa, 72 percent of the urban population lives in slums—a higher proportion than anywhere else in the world (Birch & Wachter, 2011; United Nations Human Settlements Programme, 2003).

Structural Power in the Age of Globalization

How did our species manage to construct such a world—so interconnected and so unfairly arranged between millions of have-lots and billions of have-nots? Part of the explanation, most scholars will agree, lies in a new form of expansive international capitalism that has emerged since the mid-1900s. Operating under the banner of globalization, it builds on earlier cultural structures of worldwide trade networks, and it is the successor to a system of colonialism in which a handful of powerful, mainly European, capitalist states ruled and exploited foreign nations inhabiting distant territories.

Enormously complex and turbulent, globalization is a dynamically structured process in which individuals, business corporations, and political institutions actively rearrange and restructure the political and economic field to their own competitive advantage, vying for increasingly scarce natural resources, cheap labor, new commercial markets, and ever-larger profits. This restructuring occurs in a world-encompassing arena and requires a great deal of *power*. As earlier discussed in the chapter on politics,

Figure 26.9 Global Military Spending by Country

In 2014, world military spending reached nearly $1.78 trillion, with the United States accounting for more than 34 percent of the total. (Expenditures are rounded to the nearest billion.)

Source: Stockholm International Peace Research Institute, 2015.

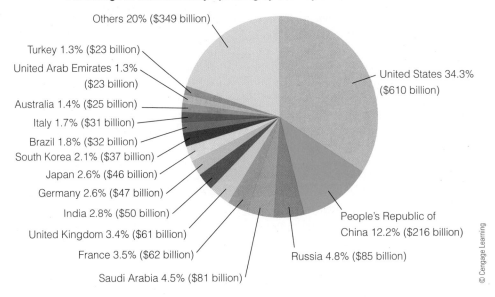

Percentage of Global Military Spending by Country in *Billions* of Dollars

- Others 20% ($349 billion)
- Turkey 1.3% ($23 billion)
- United Arab Emirates 1.3% ($23 billion)
- Australia 1.4% ($25 billion)
- Italy 1.7% ($31 billion)
- Brazil 1.8% ($32 billion)
- South Korea 2.1% ($37 billion)
- Japan 2.6% ($46 billion)
- Germany 2.6% ($47 billion)
- India 2.8% ($50 billion)
- United Kingdom 3.4% ($61 billion)
- France 3.5% ($62 billion)
- Saudi Arabia 4.5% ($81 billion)
- United States 34.3% ($610 billion)
- People's Republic of China 12.2% ($216 billion)
- Russia 4.8% ($85 billion)

© Cengage Learning

power refers to the ability of individuals or groups to impose their will upon others and make them do things even against their own wants or wishes.

Here we are concerned with **structural power**—macro-level power that manages or restructures political and economic relations within and among societies while simultaneously shaping or changing people's ideology (ideas, beliefs, and values) (Wolf, 1999a); it is a compound of hard power and soft power. In contrast to **hard power**, which *coerces* by military force and/or financial pressure, **soft power** coopts or manipulates, skillfully pressing people through attraction and persuasion to change their ideology (ideas, beliefs, and values). Propaganda is a form of soft power, although the exercise of ideological influence (the global struggle for hearts and minds) also operates through more subtle means, such as foreign aid, international diplomacy, news media, sports, entertainment, museum exhibits, and academic exchanges (Nye, 2002).

Military Hard Power

Today, the United States has more hard power at its disposal than any of its allies or rivals worldwide. It is the global leader in military expenditure, spending $610 billion in 2014, followed by China ($216 billion). As the world's still dominant superpower, the United States is responsible for about 34 percent of the $1.78 trillion spent on arms worldwide (Figure 26.9).

Worldwide, nine states have nuclear-weapon capability: China, France, Russia, the United Kingdom, and the United States, as well as Israel, India, Pakistan, and North Korea. Of these, Russia and the United States have by far the largest nuclear arsenals at their disposal. The United States possesses just over 4,700 operational warheads, compared to Russia's 4,500. In addition, these two countries have, respectively, 3,200 and 2,340 retired warheads that are still intact but awaiting dismantlement (Arms Control Association, 2015).

In addition to military might, hard power involves using finance capital as a political instrument of coercion or intimidation in the global structuring process, capable of forcing less powerful states to weaken the systems protecting their workers, natural resources, and local markets. The world's wealthiest and most powerful countries—including the United States, Russia, China, Japan, Germany, Britain, and France—have repeatedly threatened or actually used the levers of structural power to impose changes on a foreign political landscape by means of trade embargos, armed interventions, or full-scale invasions.

Home to more global corporations than any other country, the United States endeavors to protect its interests by investing in what it refers to as "free trade" as well as a "global security environment." However, through maneuvering toward this strategic objective, the nuclear-armed superpower often confronts opposition from (potentially) hostile rivals such as Russia and, increasingly, China, contesting its ambitions for worldwide supremacy. Numerous other countries, unable to afford expensive weapons systems or blocked from developing or acquiring them, have invested in biological or chemical weaponry. Still others, including relatively powerless political groups, have resorted to insurgencies, guerrilla tactics, or terrorism.

structural power Macro-level power that manages or restructures political and economic relations within and among societies while simultaneously shaping or changing people's ideology (ideas, beliefs, and values); a compound of hard power and soft power.

hard power Macro-level power that manages or restructures economic and political relations and coerces by military force and/or financial pressure.

soft power Macro-level power that coopts or manipulates, skillfully pressing people through attraction and persuasion to shape or change their ideology (ideas, beliefs, and values).

Economic Hard Power

Global corporations, rare before the latter half of the 20th century, now are a far-reaching economic and political force in the world. Modern-day business giants such as Shell, Toyota, and General Electric are actually clusters of several corporations joined by ties of common ownership and responsive to a common management strategy. Usually tightly controlled by a head office in one country, transnational megacorporations organize and integrate production across the international boundaries of different countries for interests formulated in corporate boardrooms, regardless of whether these are consistent with the interests of people in the countries in which they operate. Each of the world's top ten business giants currently generates annual revenues well over $200 billion, and four of them top the $400 billion mark (Fortune, 2015) (Figure 26.10).

So great is the power of large businesses operating all across the globe that they increasingly thwart the wishes of national governments or international organizations such as the United Nations and the International Court of Justice. Because megacorporations restrict information about their operations, it can be difficult for governments to make informed policy decisions. For example, regulating today's global pharmaceutical industry is all but impossible, not just because of complex cross-border business arrangements, but also because of fraud, including sales of counterfeit prescription drugs, some of which are harmful and even lethal. For example some 200,000 die annually due to fake and substandard malaria drugs alone (Goldacre, 2013; Moran, 2013).

Beyond this information problem, global corporations have repeatedly shown they can overrule foreign policy decisions. This raises the issue of whether the global arena should be controlled by immense powerful private

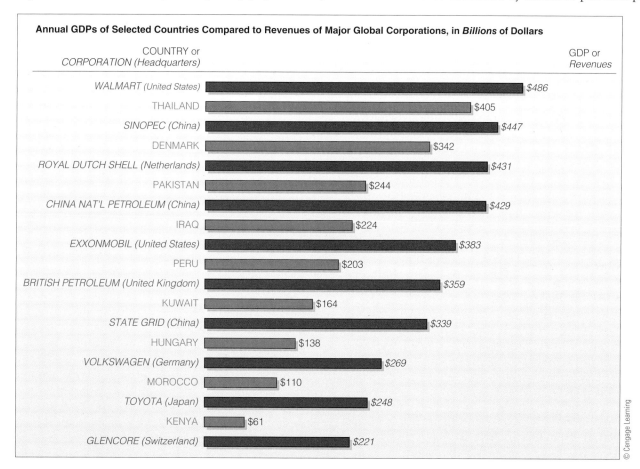

Annual GDPs of Selected Countries Compared to Revenues of Major Global Corporations, in *Billions* of Dollars

COUNTRY or CORPORATION (Headquarters)	GDP or Revenues
WALMART (United States)	$486
THAILAND	$405
SINOPEC (China)	$447
DENMARK	$342
ROYAL DUTCH SHELL (Netherlands)	$431
PAKISTAN	$244
CHINA NAT'L PETROLEUM (China)	$429
IRAQ	$224
EXXONMOBIL (United States)	$383
PERU	$203
BRITISH PETROLEUM (United Kingdom)	$359
KUWAIT	$164
STATE GRID (China)	$339
HUNGARY	$138
VOLKSWAGEN (Germany)	$269
MOROCCO	$110
TOYOTA (Japan)	$248
KENYA	$61
GLENCORE (Switzerland)	$221

© Cengage Learning

Figure 26.10 GDPs of Selected Countries and Revenues of Global Corporations
In today's consumer-driven world, it is not uncommon for the yearly revenues of large multinational corporations to equal and even exceed the total value of all goods and services produced within many countries per year, known as a country's gross domestic product (GDP). This graph shows the annual GDPs of selected countries alongside the annual revenues of leading global corporations. Notably, revenues of each of the top four corporations exceeded the GDPs of 162 of the world's 195 countries. Not shown here are the countries with the highest and lowest GDPs. Nearly half have GDPs under $20 billion, and 20 fall below $1 billion. Only 14 countries surpass $1 trillion, including the United States at more than $15 trillion, with China in second place at over $6 trillion. Note that GDP says nothing about the unequal distribution of wealth within a country.

Sources: Based on Fortune's "Global 500" list of corporate revenues (2015) and the World Bank, World Development Indicators (2016).

corporations interested only in financial profits. According to a study that diagrammed the interrelationships of more than 43,000 corporations, 147 companies control nearly 40 percent of the monetary value of all transnational corporations. Of the top 50 of these companies, most are involved in banking, financial services, and insurance (Ehrenberg, 2011; Vitali, Glattfelder, & Battiston, 2011).

With production, trading, and banking operations on a global scale, the breakdown in one part of the system may trigger a worldwide chain reaction of failures. This is what occurred with the global financial crisis in 2008, sparked by the bankruptcy of a handful of mismanaged Wall Street firms—a crisis with worldwide ramifications not yet resolved.

Globalization does more than create a worldwide arena in which megacorporations reap megaprofits. It also wreaks havoc in many traditional cultures, destroying their natural habitats and disrupting their long-established social organization.

Soft Power: A Global Media Environment

In addition to reliance on military and economic hard power in the global quest for dominance and profit, competing states and corporations utilize the ideological persuasion of soft power transmitted through information technology. One of the major tasks of soft power is to sell the general idea of globalization as something positive and progressive (as "freedom," "free trade," "free market") and to frame or brand anything that opposes capitalism in negative terms.

Global mass media corporations, for example, possess enormous soft power. They produce and distribute news and other information through transnational cable and satellite networks, as well as websites. These media giants not only report news but also select the visual imagery and determine what to stress or repress. By means of their tremendous soft power, these corporations influence public perception and action ("hearts and minds").

The far-reaching capabilities of modern electronic and digital technologies have led to the creation of a global media environment that plays a major role in how individuals and even societies view themselves and their place in the world. The global flow of information made possible by fiber-optic cables, cell towers, and communication satellites orbiting the earth is almost entirely digital-electronic, taking place in a new boundless cultural space that has been called a "global mediascape" (Appadurai, 1990).

In recent years, the power of corporations has become all the greater through media expansion. Over the past two decades, a global commercial media system has developed, dominated by a few megacorporations (such as Comcast, Disney, Facebook, and Google), most based in the United States. Control of television, Internet, and other media, as well as the advertising industry, gives global corporations enormous influence on the ideas and behavior of hundreds of millions of ordinary people across the world (Figure 26.11).

© Harald E. L. Prins

Figure 26.11 Global Branding
The poorest people in the world often wear clothing discarded by those who are better off—and people from all walks of life can be found wearing clothes with corporate logos, as demonstrated by this Maká Indian woman in Paraguay. The power wielded by big business (such as the Disney media corporation) is illustrated by the fact that corporations influence consumers to pay for clothing and countless other goods that advertise corporate products.

Owned and controlled by large corporations, social media are used for a vast range of purposes—from product advertising to evangelizing, from fund-raising to popular entertainment, from connecting with friends and family to rallying support for political action. But they are not free. For corporations, banks, and governments, social media tools are a means of harnessing soft power for purposes of influencing public opinion, moving capital, selling music, or gaining prestige. As such, these instruments can be (and are) manipulated for propaganda, public opinion making, government surveillance, personal data mining, and deception for political and military purposes. That brings us to the subject of structural violence.

Problems of Structural Violence

Structural power and its associated concepts of hard and soft power enable us to better understand the regional, national, as well as global arena in which local communities

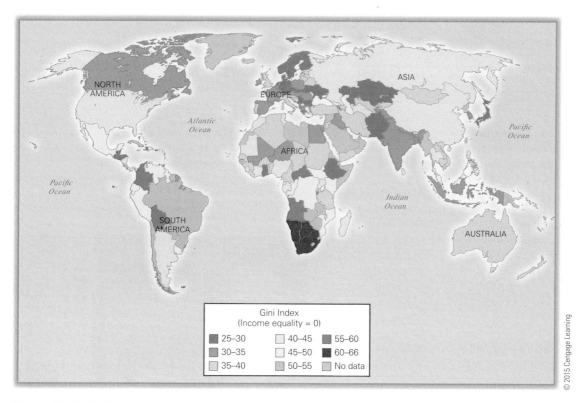

Figure 26.12 **Gini Income Equality Index**
The Gini index ranges from 0 to 100, with 0 corresponding to perfect equality (everyone has the same income) and 100 corresponding to perfect inequality (one person has all the income, and everyone else has zero income). Today China and the United States have similar income gaps (42.1 and 40.8, respectively), Norway has the smallest gap (25.8), and numerous countries in Africa and Latin America have the greatest income disparity with Gini ratings in the 50s or 60s.

throughout the world are now compelled to operate and the unequal distribution of wealth, health, and power in today's world. When structural power undermines the well-being of individuals or groups, we speak of **structural violence**—physical and/or psychological harm (including repression, environmental destruction, poverty, hunger, illness, and premature death) caused by impersonal, exploitative, and unjust social, political, and economic systems (Farmer, 1996).

Generally speaking, structural violence concerns the impersonal systemic violation of the human rights of individuals and communities to a healthy, peaceful, and dignified life. Human rights abuses are nothing new, but structural violence and its countless manifestations have intensified due to overpopulation, environmental destruction, and growing inequality in the Anthropocene.

Poverty

Earlier we mentioned the more than sevenfold increase of humans in just eight generations, leading to overpopulation problems, especially in parts of Asia and Africa. This problem is structurally linked to worldwide differences in wealth and health. In 1960, the average income for the twenty wealthiest countries in the world was fifteen times that of the twenty poorest countries. Today, it is about thirty times higher (World Bank, 2015b; see also Davies

et al., 2008). Notably, these broad-stroke figures fail to indicate that some of the world's poorest countries have a small number of very rich citizens and that some very wealthy countries include many poor inhabitants.

In fact, the income disparity between rich and poor *within* most countries has been widening in recent years—as evident in the *Gini income inequality index* annually posted by the United Nations. The Gini index ranges from 0 to 100, with 0 corresponding to perfect equality (everyone has the same income) and 100 corresponding to perfect inequality (one person has all the income, and everyone else has zero income). For example, in communist China, home to about 1.3 billion people, income disparity has skyrocketed to 42.1—even surpassing that of the world's leading capitalist country, the United States, where the gap has widened to 40.8. Income distribution is far more equal in most of Europe, and the smallest rich–poor gap in the world is in Norway (25.8). Countries with the greatest income inequality are clustered in southern Africa and Latin America where numerous countries have Gini ratings in the 50s or 60s (Figure 26.12).

structural violence Physical and/or psychological harm (including repression, environmental destruction, poverty, hunger, illness, and premature death) caused by impersonal, exploitative, and unjust social, political, and economic systems.

ANTHROPOLOGY APPLIED

Anthropologist S. Ann Dunham, Mother of a U.S. President

By Nancy I. Cooper

As our plane descended over the island of Java, the most spectacular sight of my life came into view: a full-blown eruption of Merapi volcano billowing clouds of ash straight up into the sky. On the lower slopes of this exploding "mountain of fire" (*gunung api*), hundreds of thousands of people would have to flee their homes and farms. My thoughts were with them—and with my friend Ann Dunham. She had researched and worked with rural people in this region as an applied anthropologist before her untimely death at age 52 in 1995. I had known her while doing my own research here on Indonesia's most populated island. I was returning to meet some of the people she had known.

Stanley Ann Dunham's life started out ordinary enough in an American working-class family from Kansas. They lived in several states before settling in the ethnically diverse state of Hawai'i. As a teen Ann thrived there, embracing the common humanity in cultural differences. At the University of Hawai'i in Honolulu, she met and

married an economics student from Kenya, East Africa. In 1961, she gave birth to his namesake, Barack Obama, Jr., who would grow up to be the forty-fourth president of the United States. The marriage was short-lived, and Ann became a single parent.

While studying anthropology, Ann met and married Lolo Soetoro, a geography student from Java. In 1967 she and her young son joined him in Jakarta, Indonesia's capital city. Befriending local boys, "Barry" happily roamed nearby fields among goats and water buffalo. Ann gave birth to daughter Maya and became interested in handmade crafts like basketry, ceramics, and leatherwork, trying her own hand at weaving and batik. This interest grew

into concern about the welfare of small enterprises embedded within larger, more powerful economic systems.

Soon, Ann began working as a consultant, hired by what became a long list of mostly foreign aid and economic

Ann Dunham turns the wheel of an agricultural machine in Pakistan in 1987.

Measured on a global scale, the chasm between have-lots and have-nots has reached stratospheric proportions (Oxfam, 2016; World Bank, 2015c):

- The 62 richest people on earth possess nearly $1.8 trillion—the same amount shared by 3.6 billion people at the bottom half of the world's income scale.
- Since 2000, the poorest half of the world's population has received just 1 percent of the total increase in global wealth, while half of that increase has gone to the top 1 percent.
- Nearly 10 percent of people in the world live on less than $1.90 a day.

These statistics represent a gross inequity that poses a radical challenge for achieving global security and well-being. The situation would be even worse without the efforts of individuals, organizations, and institutions dedicated to narrowing the insupportable gap between the world's wealthiest and poorest peoples. Among those was U.S. anthropologist Ann Dunham—the mother of the

forty-fourth president of the United States, Barack Obama. She is featured in this chapter's Anthropology Applied.

Hunger, Obesity, and Malnutrition

Today, over a quarter of the world's countries do not produce enough food to feed their populations, and they cannot afford to import what is needed. Worldwide, about 800 million people experience chronic hunger—about 1 out of 9 individuals. Each year, famine claims the lives of more than 3 million children ages 5 and under, and those who survive it often suffer physical and mental impairment (Food and Agriculture Organization of the United Nations, 2013; World Food Programme, 2015).

Many of the world's hungry are victims of structural violence. This is because the increasing rate of starvation is due not only to environmental calamities, but to human actions ranging from warfare to massive job cuts,

development organizations. At the Ford Foundation's Southeast Asia regional office in Jakarta, for example, she oversaw grants in the Women and Employment branch and collaborated on a study of rural women in the outlying islands of Indonesia. In the 1980s, as a cottage industries development consultant with the Agricultural Development Bank of Pakistan, she arranged credit for low-income handicraft castes in the Punjab, including blacksmiths.

Next, Ann became a research coordinator (funded by USAID and the World Bank) at Bank Rakyat Indonesia, helping implement a microcredit project for owners of small rural businesses. Today, this bank has one of the largest microfinance programs in the world, and microcredit is widely recognized as a significant means of lessening poverty. In between appointments, Ann returned to Hawai'i to settle her children in school and continue her own studies. She also did a brief stint with Women's World Banking based in New York City.

The data Ann and her research teams collected during these years, combined with her anthropological fieldwork, culminated in her 1992 doctoral dissertation on peasant blacksmithing, published by Duke University Press in 2009.[a] In both words and action, Ann argued against Western modernization theories that insisted that all developing economies must go through the same stages Western capitalist economies experienced in order to succeed in the global market environment. Recognizing the disturbing effects that rapid modernization often has on indigenous populations with colonial histories, she refuted such damaging notions and sought ways to solve the real challenges of emerging economies with sensitivity and analytical prowess.

Ann Dunham's contributions were formally recognized fifteen years after her death when she was awarded Indonesia's highest civilian honor. Accepting the prize on behalf of his mother from President Susilo Bambang Yudhoyono, President Obama said, "In honoring her, you honor the spirit that led her to travel into villages throughout the country."

I felt that spirit as I traveled through Java's limestone hills where we had worked years earlier. Word spread quickly through the village of Kajar that Ann's friend was visiting, and I was greeted warmly. I sat with the family of the late owner of the blacksmithing cooperative featured in Ann's book, swapping stories about her and looking at photos she had taken of them and fellow villagers. And I spent long hours visiting with blacksmiths as they hammered hot scrap metal into useful tools.

All too soon it was time to leave. Volcanic ash had shut down the airport where I had landed, so I left the region by rail. As the train pulled away from the station, images of blacksmithing and new friends danced in my head, along with renewed memories of an engaged anthropologist whose work changed people's lives for the better.

Written expressly for this text, 2011.

----

[a] Ann died before having an opportunity to revise her dissertation for publication, as she had planned; Alice G. Dewey, her advisor, and I, her fellow graduate student, carried it to completion at the request of Ann's daughter Maya.

growing poverty rates, and the collapse of local markets caused by foreign imports. For example, in several sub-Saharan African countries plagued by chronic civil strife, it has been almost impossible to raise and harvest crops because hordes of hungry refugees, roaming militias, and underpaid soldiers constantly raid the fields.

Beyond violent political, ethnic, or religious conflicts that uproot families from their traditional food sources, famine is fueled by a global food production and distribution system geared to satisfy the demands of the world's most powerful countries. For example, in Africa, Asia, and Latin America, millions of acres once devoted to subsistence farming have been given over to raising cash crops for export. This has enriched members of elite social classes in these parts of the world, while satisfying the appetites of people in developed countries for coffee, tea, chocolate, bananas, and beef. Small-scale farmers who used to till the land for their own food needs have been relocated—either to urban areas, where all too often there is no employment for them, or to areas ecologically unsuited for farming.

Ironically, although many millions are starving in some parts of the world, many millions of others are overeating—literally eating themselves to death. In fact, the number of overfed people now exceeds those who are underfed. According to the World Health Organization, nearly 2 billion adults, 18 years and older, are now overweight worldwide. Of these, about 600 million are obese but still often malnourished in that their diets lack certain nutrients (World Health Organization, 2015b) (Figure 26.13).

A key ingredient in obesity is the high sugar and fat content of mass-marketed foods. Thus, in Japan, where food habits differ significantly from those in the United States, obesity plagues just over 3 percent of the population, compared to the U.S. rate of 35 percent among adults and 17 percent among those ages 2 to 19. In fact, U.S. obesity figures have doubled over the past three decades, placing it at the top of the obesity chart among wealthy industrialized countries. Obesity rates differ between men and women, higher and lower income groups, and various ethnic groups. The highest U.S. rate is among African

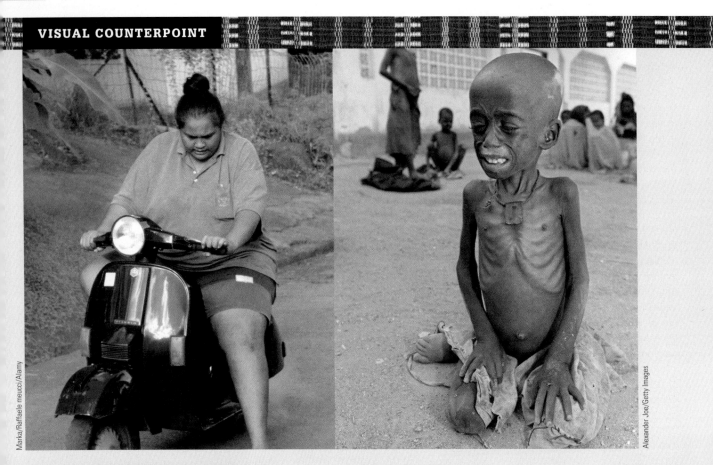

Marka/Raffaele meucci/Alamy

Alexander Joe/Getty Images

Figure 26.13 Structural Violence and Malnutrition
Today, some 800 million people in the world face chronic hunger. Meanwhile, nearly 2 billion adults, 18 years and older, are overweight. About 600 million in the latter category are obese but still malnourished because their diets lack certain essential nutrients. On the left is a woman on the South Pacific island of Nauru, where about 80 percent of the 14,000 inhabitants are classified as obese. Their small tropical paradise stripped bare by phosphate mining companies, these indigenous peoples have become dependent upon imported junk food. Many are now ill and dying from diabetes and other diseases historically uncommon among Oceanic peoples. On the right, we see a starving child in the African country of Somalia. Poverty (often compounded by political conflict) is the main cause of child hunger. Hundreds of millions of children in developing countries, especially in sub-Saharan Africa, do not get enough protein or calories and thereby are at high risk for stunted growth, illness, and early death.

American women, half of whom suffer from obesity (Centers for Disease Control and Prevention, 2015).

The problem has become a serious concern even in some developing countries, especially where people have switched to a diet based on processed or fast food. The highest rates of obesity in the world can now be found among island nations in the Pacific Ocean, such as Nauru, Fiji, Samoa, and Tonga. Nauru, formerly known as Pleasant Island, tops the list.

Pollution and Global Warming

Pollution is another key aspect of structural violence brought on by the world's most powerful countries, which are also the greatest producers and consumers of energy. Over the past 200 years, since the beginning of the Anthropocene, global cultural development has relied on burning increasing quantities of fossil fuels (coal, oil, and gas), with dire results: Massive deforestation and desertification—along with severe air, water, and soil pollution—now threaten all life on earth.

In addition, fossil fuel use has dramatically increased carbon dioxide levels, trapping more heat in the earth's atmosphere. Most atmospheric scientists believe that the efficiency of the atmosphere in retaining heat—the greenhouse effect—is being enhanced by increased carbon dioxide, methane, and other gases produced by industrial and agricultural activities. The result, global warming, threatens to dramatically alter climates in all parts of the world.

Rising temperatures are causing more and greater storms, droughts, and heat waves, devastating populations in vulnerable areas. And if the massive meltdown of Arctic ice continues, rising sea levels will inundate low coastal areas worldwide. Entire islands may soon disappear, including thousands of villages and even large cities. Experts also predict that global warming will lead to an expansion of the geographic ranges of tropical diseases and increase the incidence of respiratory illnesses due to additional smog caused by warmer temperatures. Also, they expect an increase in deaths due to heat waves, as witnessed in Europe (70,000 deaths in 2003), Russia (55,000 deaths in 2010), and India (2,500 deaths in 2015) (IPCC, 2014; Samenow, 2015).

Notably, the few wealthy countries (primarily in western Europe and North America) that reaped many economic benefits from early industrialization and global trade were responsible for about two-thirds of the atmospheric buildup of carbon dioxide (CO_2), the major cause of global warming. By contrast, all of Africa—a continent about the size of Canada, Europe, and the United States, combined—was responsible for about 3 percent of global CO_2 emissions in the past hundred years.

Tragically, millions of peasants, herders, fishermen, and other folk inhabiting the developing countries in Africa (as well as those in Asia and Latin America) find themselves paying for the progress enjoyed by societies that have reaped the benefits of industrialization for several generations. They now suffer from global-induced droughts and floods, but they lack the capital to effectively deal with them.

Today, global CO_2 emissions stand at about 35.5 billion metric tons per year. China has become the top emitter, mainly due to dramatic and rapid economic growth—and the fact that it is home to 20 percent of the world's population. There, since 2002, CO_2 emissions have jumped 150 percent to 10.3 billion metric tons (29 percent of the world total). In contrast, the United States, which comprises less than 5 percent of the global population, annually emits 5.3 billion metric tons (15 percent of the global total). The European Union is responsible for 10.5 percent of all emissions—3.7 billion metric tons. On average, each person in the world adds 4.5 metric tons of CO_2 a year to the atmosphere. However, this figure varies greatly across the globe—from less than 2 tons on the African continent to 7.3 in the European Union, 7.4 in China, and 16.6 in the United States (Olivier et al., 2014; Sivak & Shoettle, 2012) (Figure 26.14).

Energy Consumption Per Person, by country, 2009.

Figure 26.14 Global Energy Consumption
North Americans have long been among the world's highest energy consumers, contributing significantly to carbon dioxide (CO_2) emissions, the major cause of global warming. Today, their consumption rate is more than 8 times higher than the average in Africa. The United States alone accounts for 15 percent of CO_2 emissions worldwide. Other top emitters are the European Union (10.5 percent), India (6 percent), and Russia (5 percent). But all are topped by China, which in recent years has soared to 29 percent (Olivier et al., 2014). (These figures and this map do not take climate into account; for that, see Sivak & Schoettle, 2012.)

Environmental degradation has grown exponentially since the industrial revolution. Much of this ruin is caused by ever-increasing amounts of non-biodegradable waste and toxic emissions into the soil, water, and air. Until very recently, this pollution was officially tolerated for the sake of maximizing profits that primarily benefit select individuals, groups, and societies. Today, industries in many parts of the world are producing highly toxic waste at unprecedented rates. Pollutants such as various oxides of nitrogen or sulfur cause the development of acid precipitation, which damages soil, vegetation, and wildlife. Air pollution in the form of smog is often dangerous for human health.

Finding their way into the world's oceans, toxic substances also create hazards for seafood consumers. For instance, Canada's indigenous Inuit people face health problems related to eating fish and sea mammals that feed in waters contaminated by industrial chemical waste such as polychlorinated biphenyls (PCBs) (see the Biocultural Connection). Also of great concern are harmful chemicals in plastics used for water bottles, baby bottles, and can linings. Environmental poisoning affects peoples all across the globe.

Structural violence also manifests itself in the shifting of manufacturing and hazardous waste disposal from developed to developing countries. In the late 1980s, a tightening of environmental regulations in industrialized countries led to a dramatic rise in the cost of hazardous waste disposal. Seeking cheaper ways to get rid of the wastes, "toxic traders" began shipping hazardous waste to eastern Europe and especially to poor and underdeveloped countries in western Africa—thereby passing on the health risks of poisonous cargo to the world's poorest people (see the Globalscape).

Reactions to Globalization

No matter how effectively a dominant state or corporation combines its hard and soft power, globalization does run into opposition. Pockets of resistance exist within the wealthy industrial and postindustrial states as well as elsewhere in the world. This resistance may be manifested in the rise of traditionalism and revitalization movements—efforts to return to life as it was (or how people think it was) before the familiar order became unhinged and people became unsettled. Some of these reactionary movements may take the form of resurgent ethno-nationalism or religious fundamentalist movements. Others may find expression in alternative grassroots movements—from radical environmental groups to peace groups to the more recently formed ecotarian movement that focuses on selecting food based on the ecological impact of its production and transportation.

One striking case of a cultural reaction to globalization is the Taliban, a group of Muslim religious fundamentalists in Afghanistan. The *Taliban* (the Pashto word for

"students," specifically of Islam) helped to force the Russian army out of their country and end the subsequent civil war. Then, rising to power in the 1990s, they imposed a radical version of traditional Islamic law (Shariah) in an effort to create an Islamic republic based on strict religious values.

In the United States, there has been a similar, though less radical, reaction against modernity. "Born again" and other fundamentalist citizens seek to shape or transform not only their towns but also states and even the entire country by electing politicians committed to forging a national culture based on what they see as American patriotism, English-only legislation, and traditional Christian values (Harding, 2001).

Ethnic Minorities and Indigenous Peoples: Struggles for Human Rights

Throughout this book, we have discussed a wide range of cultures all across the globe: some very large, like the Han in China, others very small, like the Kapauku in West Papua, New Guinea. Many of our examples involve peoples who see themselves as members of distinct nations by virtue of their birth and their cultural and territorial heritage—nations over whom peoples of some other ethnic background have tried to assert political control. An estimated 5,000 such national groups exist in the world today, compared to just under 200 internationally recognized countries.

Nearly all indigenous groups are relatively small nations, but some have populations exceeding that of many countries. For instance, the Karen people of Myanmar number between 4.5 to 5 million, and the Kurds—living in Iraq, Turkey, Syria, and Iran—number about 35 million. Whatever their numbers, most ethnic minorities have suffered repression or discrimination by more powerful groups that have dispossessed them, or control and govern them. In the early 1970s, indigenous peoples began to organize self-determination movements, resisting cultural changes forced upon them and challenging violations of their human rights. Joining forces across international borders, many have joined the World Council of Indigenous Peoples founded in 1975.

In 2007, after many years of popular media campaigns, political lobbying, and diplomatic pressure by hundreds of indigenous leaders and other activists all around the globe, the UN General Assembly finally adopted the Declaration on the Rights of Indigenous Peoples (Figure 26.15). This foundational document in the global human rights struggle contains some 150 articles urging respect for indigenous cultural heritage, calling for official recognition of indigenous land titles and rights of self-determination, and demanding an end to all forms of oppression and discrimination as a principle of international law.

Toxic Breast Milk Threatens Arctic Culture

Asked to picture the Inuit people inhabiting the Arctic coasts of Canada, Greenland, and Labrador, you are likely to envision them dressed in fur parkas and moving across a pristine, snow-covered landscape on dogsleds—perhaps coming home from hunting seal, walrus, or whale.

Such imaginings are still true—except for the pristine part. Although Inuit live nearer to the North Pole than to any city, factory, or farm, they are not isolated from the pollutants of modern society. Chemicals originating in the cities and farms of North America, Europe, and Asia travel thousands of miles to Inuit territories via winds, rivers, and ocean currents. These toxins have a long life in the Arctic, breaking down very slowly due to icy temperatures and low sunlight. Ingested by zooplankton, the chemicals spread through the seafood chain as one species consumes another. The result is alarming levels of pesticides, mercury, and industrial chemicals in Arctic animals—and in the Inuit people who rely on fishing and hunting for food.

Of particular note are toxic chemicals known as PCBs (polychlorinated biphenyls),

used widely over several decades for numerous purposes, such as industrial lubricants, insulating materials, and paint stabilizers. Research shows a widespread presence of PCBs in the breast milk of women around the globe. But nowhere on earth is the concentration higher than among the Inuit—on average seven times that of nursing mothers in Canada's biggest cities.[a]

PCBs have been linked to a wide range of health problems—from liver damage to weakened immune systems to cancer. Studies of children exposed to PCBs in the womb and through breast milk show impaired learning and memory functions.

Beyond having a destructive impact on the health of humans (and other animal species), PCBs are impacting the economy, social organization, and psychological well-being of Arctic peoples. Nowhere is this truer than among the 450 Inuit living on Broughton Island, near Canada's Baffin Island. Here, word of skyrocketing PCB levels cost the community its valuable market for Arctic char fish. Other Inuit refer to them as "PCB people," and it is said that Inuit men now avoid marrying women from the island.[b]

Inuit people, who have no real alternatives for affordable food, soundly reject the suggestion that the answer to these problems is a change of diet. Abandoning the consumption of traditional seafood would destroy a 4,000-year-old culture based on hunting and fishing. Countless aspects of traditional Inuit culture—from worldview and social arrangements to vocabularies and myths—are linked to Arctic animals and the skills it takes to rely on them for food and so many other things. As one Inuit put it: "Our foods do more than nourish our bodies. They feed our souls. When I eat Inuit foods, I know who I am."[c]

The manufacture of PCBs is now banned in many Western countries (including the United States), and PCB levels are gradually declining worldwide. However, because of their persistence (and widespread presence in remnant industrial goods such as fluorescent lighting fixtures and electrical appliances), they are still the highest-concentration toxins in breast milk, even among mothers born after the ban.

Furthermore, even as PCBs decline, other commercial chemicals are finding their way northward. To date, about 200 hazardous compounds originating in industrialized regions have been detected in the bodies of Arctic peoples.[d] Global warming is fueling the problem, because as glaciers and snow melt, long-stored toxins are released.

Biocultural Question

Because corporations are able to profit from large-scale and long-distance commercial activities, we should not be surprised that their operations may also cause serious damage to fellow humans in remote natural environments. What do you think of the profiteering of structural violence?

[a] Colborn, T., Dumanoski, D., & Myers, J. P. (1997). *Our stolen future* (pp. 107–108). New York: Plume/Penguin.

[b] Arctic Monitoring Assessment Project (AMAP). (2003). *AMAP assessment 2002: Human health in the Arctic* (pp. xii–xiii, 22–23). Oslo: AMAP.

[c] Ingmar Egede, quoted in Cone, M. (2005). *Silent snow: The slow poisoning of the Arctic* (p. 1). New York: Grove.

[d] Johansen, B. E. (2002). The Inuit's struggle with dioxins and other organic pollutants. *American Indian Quarterly 26* (3), 479–490; Natural Resources Defense Council. (2005, March 25). Healthy milk, healthy baby: Chemical pollution and mother's milk. www.NRDC.org/breastmilk/ (retrieved December 16, 2015); Williams, F. (2005, January 9). Toxic breast milk? *New York Times Magazine.* http://www.nytimes.com/2005/01/09/magazine/toxic-breast-milk.html (retrieved December 16, 2015)

Can this Inuit woman trust her breast milk?

© Lee Thomas/Alamy Stock Photo

GLOBALSCAPE

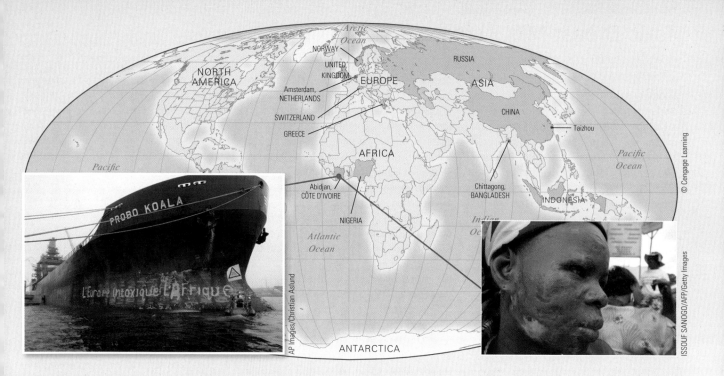

Probo Koala's Dirty Secrets?

One day in 2006, the *Probo Koala* unloaded a cargo of processed fuel in Nigeria, West Africa. Then the tanker sailed to Amsterdam where a Dutch treatment plant was to process its 400 tons of left-over toxic sludge. Navigating the oceans under the Panamanian flag, this ship's all-Russian crew served under a Greek captain. Managed and operated by a Greek maritime company, the ship's registered owner was based in Norway. For this journey, it was chartered by a Dutch subsidiary of Trafigura, a global multibillion-dollar company headquartered in Switzerland that specializes in transporting oil and mineral products.

When port authorities in Amsterdam discovered that the *Probo Koala*'s captain had underreported the poison levels in his cargo, the cost of treating the waste jumped to $600,000. Unwilling to pay the higher fee, the captain ordered his ship back to West Africa in search of a cheap place to dispose of the waste. Finding unscrupulous businessmen and corrupt officials in Côte d'Ivoire, he negotiated a dumping fee of about $18,000. Deposited in open-air waste pits on the edge of Abidjan (population 5 million), the substance gave off toxic gas that burned lungs and skin and caused severe headaches and vomiting—killing 17 people and injuring at least 30,000.

The *Probo Koala* forms part of a profitable global business network capitalizing on the more than 350 million tons of hazardous waste generated annually, primarily by industrial societies. Although most of this waste is now properly handled, some companies avoid environmental regulations and high treatment costs within Europe and North America, seeking cheap (possibly illegal) options, including dumping at sea. Many millions of tons of hazardous waste are transported across the oceans to underdeveloped countries.

In a 2009 out-of-court settlement, Trafigura agreed to pay a total of $43,000 to cover all claims. Many saw settlement as a slap on the hand that in no way matched the gravity of the crime. Convinced that Trafigura knew the toxicity and illegality of the dump, Greenpeace and Amnesty International carried out a three-year investigation on the incident. Released in the fall of 2012, the report calls for Trafigura to face a criminal trial in the United Kingdom and criticizes the lack of international regulations for preventing and dealing with toxic dumping activities.

Meanwhile, Trafigura has paid nearly $500 million in legal and reparation costs, but there are indications that the authorities in Côte d'Ivoire have failed to redistribute compensation to the victims of the dumping. Greenpeace and Amnesty International are calling for freedom from toxic waste dumping to be a human right, which would allow victims of large- and small-scale dumping to seek legal redress more easily, in national and international courts.[a]

In 2011, the *Probo Koala* was sold for scrap and headed toward the infamous ship-breaking beaches of Chittagong in Bangladesh. Hearing this—and aware of the dangers of dismantling the toxic ship there—environmentalists and labor rights organizations convinced the government of Bangladesh to turn the ship away. Renamed and re-sold, the ship operated between Indonesia and China, transporting ore until 2013 when she entered a ship-breaking yard in Taizhou, China.[b]

Global Twister

Although hazardous waste dumping by the *Probo Koala* resulted in the arrest of several African businessmen in Côte d'Ivoire, should the other participants in this global crime be judged and punished? If so, under which laws?

---

[a] Harvey, F. (2012, September 25). Trafigura lessons have not been learned, report warns. *The Guardian*. http://www.theguardian.com/environment/2012/sep/25/trafigura-lessons-toxic-waste-dumping (retrieved December 16, 2015)

[b] Des Bois, R. (2013, February 7). The end of the *Probo Koala*. http://www.robindesbois.org/english/probo_koala/the-end-of-the-probo-koala.html (retrieved December 15, 2015)

Niu Xiaole/Xinhua/Landov

Figure 26.15 Worldwide Indigenous Peoples Conference
In 1982 the United Nations Sub-Commission on the Promotion and Protection of Human Rights
established a Working Group on Indigenous Populations (WGIP). Eleven years later WGIP completed
a draft of the Declaration on the Rights of Indigenous Peoples, ratified in 2007. Here we see
delegates at the 2014 World Conference on Indigenous Peoples, held at UN headquarters in New
York. Many came in traditional dress, including the Trinidad and Tobago representative pictured here.

Anthropology's Role in Meeting the Challenges of Globalization

Globalization triggers worldwide changes, but different peoples and cultures are not necessarily changing in the same fashion or in the same direction. Worldwide, it places some individuals, groups, or regions in a favorable position to take advantage of new opportunities, but it confronts others with pain and no gain. As repeatedly noted in this textbook, globalization is a complex and dynamic process with a vast range of national, regional, and even local cultural reactions and adjustments.

Today, many of the cultures studied by the earliest anthropologists more than a century ago have changed profoundly in response to powerful outside influences and internal dynamics. Others have disappeared as a result of deadly epidemics, violent conflicts, acculturation, ethnocide, or genocide. All too often, the only detailed records we now possess of these altered and vanished cultures are those that some visiting anthropologist was able to document before it was too late.

But anthropologists do much more than try to preserve precious information about distinctive peoples and cultures, past and present. As chronicled in the pages of this book, they also attempt to explain why our bodies and cultures are similar or different, why and how they did or did not change. Moreover, they try to identify the particular knowledge and insights that each culture holds concerning the human condition—including contrasting views about the place of human beings in the world, how natural resources are used and treated, and how one relates to fellow humans and other species.

Paul Farmer (b. 1959)

U.S. medical anthropologist **Paul Farmer**—doctor, Harvard professor, world-renowned infectious disease specialist, and recipient of a MacArthur "genius grant"—grew up in a trailer park in Florida without running water.[a] Admitted to Duke University on scholarship, he majored in anthropology and labored alongside poor Haitian farm-workers in North Carolina's tobacco fields. After getting his BA in 1982, he spent a year in Haiti and found his life's calling: to diagnose and cure infectious diseases and transform healthcare on a global scale by focusing on the world's poorest communities. Returning to the United States, Farmer earned both an MD and a PhD in anthropology from Harvard in 1990.

While still a graduate student, Farmer returned frequently to Haiti and became increasingly involved in health issues in the area of Cange, a remote village in the destitute Central Plateau region. There, he formed a group called Zanmi Lasante (Haitian Kreyol for "Partners In Health"). A handful of other American activists joined

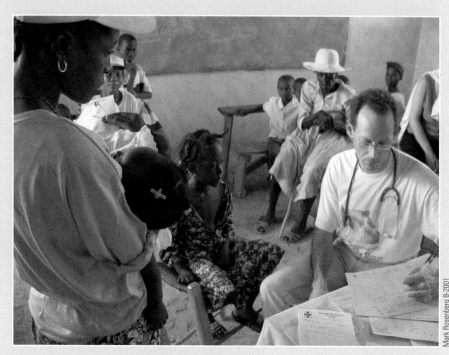

Medical anthropologist Paul Farmer with patients in Haiti.

him in the endeavor, including his fellow anthropologist and Harvard Medical School friend, Jim Yong Kim, who became president of the World Bank three decades later.

In 1985, the Zanmi Lasante group established a clinic with financial support from a Boston philanthropist. Two years later they founded the Boston-based Partners In Health (PIH) foundation to support their growing endeavor to help the poorest of the poor deal with infectious diseases, especially AIDS and tuberculosis.

The endeavor includes research (ethnographic as well as medical) needed to carry the work forward with a clear vision. As an applied anthropologist aiming to ease human suffering, Farmer bases his activism on holistic and interpretive ethnographic analysis that includes "a historical understanding of the large-scale social and economic structures in which affliction is embedded."[b] Issues of structural violence are fundamental in his research and practice. Noting that social and economic inequalities "have powerfully sculpted not only the [demographic] distribution of infectious diseases but also the course of health outcomes among the afflicted," he concludes, "inequality itself constitutes our modern plague."[c]

Since its founding, Zanmi Lasante has expanded its one-room clinic to a multiservice health complex that includes a primary school, an infirmary, a surgery wing, a training program for health outreach workers, a 104-bed hospital, a women's clinic, and a pediatric care facility. Moreover, it has pioneered the treatment of multidrug-resistant tuberculosis and HIV in Haiti. Partners In Health, now funded by a wide range of organizations, has

expanded its reach to include Lesotho, Malawi, and Rwanda in Africa, as well as Peru, Mexico, Russia, and the United States. The foundation's reach continues to grow, fueled by Farmer's passionate conviction that health is a human right.

In concert with his active and extensive work with PIH around the globe, Farmer is a professor of medical anthropology at Harvard University where he chairs the Department of Global Health and Social Medicine. He also maintains an active practice in infectious diseases and is chief of the Division of Social Medicine and Health Inequalities at Brigham and Women's Hospital in Boston. Among numerous honors, he has received the Margaret Mead Award from the American Anthropological Association and is the subject of the Pulitzer Prize–winning book by Tracy Kidder.

[a] This profile draws from numerous sources, including: Kidder, T. (2003). *Mountains beyond mountains: The quest of Dr. Paul Farmer, a man who would cure the world.* New York: Random House; Vine, D. (2013, May 23). *Tracing Paul Farmer's influence.* Washington, DC: American University, College of Arts & Sciences. http://www.american.edu/cas/news/paul-farmer-influence-in-anthropology.cfm (retrieved January 20, 2016)

[b] Farmer, P. (2004, June). An anthropology of structural violence. *Current Anthropology 45* (3), 305–325; see also Farmer, P. (1996). On suffering and structural violence: A view from below. *Daedalus 125* (1), 261–283.

[c] Farmer, P. (2001). *Infections and inequalities: The modern plagues* (p. 15). Berkeley: University of California Press.

And, importantly, there have always been anthropologists who reach beyond studying different cultures to assist besieged groups struggling to survive in today's rapidly changing world. In so doing, they put into practice their own knowledge about humankind—knowledge deepened through the comparative perspective of anthropology, which is cross-culturally, historically, and biologically informed. Counted among these applied anthropologists are Ann Dunham, profiled earlier in this chapter, and Paul Farmer, a world-renowned medical doctor, anthropologist, and human rights activist (see the Anthropologist of Note feature).

An interdisciplinary profession straddling the arts, sciences, and humanities, anthropology has a remarkable record of contributing important knowledge about our own species and all its stunning complexity and amazing variety. Anthropology's distinct holistic approach has helped to solve practical problems on local and global levels—and continues to do so today. More relevant than ever, it offers vital insight toward a cross-cultural understanding of globalization and its highly diverse local impact.

Most of the individuals drawn to this discipline are inspired by the old but still valid idea that anthropology must aim to live up to its longstanding ideal as the most liberating of the sciences. As stated by the famous anthropologist Margaret Mead, "Never doubt that a small group of committed people can change the world; indeed it is the only thing that ever has."

CHAPTER CHECKLIST

What does our world look like today?

✓ In the Anthropocene, beginning with the industrial revolution 200 years ago, modern technology has radically increased production, transportation, and communication worldwide, and the human population has grown to more than 7 billion—half living and working in urban areas.

✓ The growing interconnectedness of our species facilitated by modern mass transportation and telecommunications media has resulted in many external similarities across cultures, spawning speculation that humanity's future will feature a single homogenous global culture. This is sometimes referred to as the "McDonaldization" of societies.

✓ Beyond the worldwide flow of commodities and ideas (food, film, fashion, music, and so on), global integrative processes include NGOs, media, and sports, as well as humanitarian aid organizations.

✓ Anthropologists are skeptical that a global culture or political system is emerging; comparative historical and cross-cultural research shows the persistence of distinctive worldviews, and the tendency of large multi-ethnic states to come apart.

What are pluralistic societies and multiculturalism?

✓ In pluralistic societies two or more ethnic groups or nationalities are politically organized into one territorial state. Ethnic tension is common in such states and sometimes turns violent, which can lead to formal separation.

✓ To manage cultural diversity within such societies, some countries have adopted multiculturalism, which is an official public policy of mutual respect and tolerance for cultural differences.

✓ An example of long-established multiculturalism may be seen in states such as Switzerland, where people speaking German, French, Italian, and Romansh coexist under the same government.

Is fragmentation common in pluralistic societies?

✓ Pluralistic societies, in virtually all parts of the world, show a tendency to fragment, usually along major linguistic, religious, or ethno-nationalist divisions.

✓ Especially when state territories are extensive and lack adequate transportation and communication networks, as well as major unifying cultural forces such as a common religion or national language, separatist intentions may be realized.

✓ Throughout history, challenges such as famine, poverty, and violent threats by dangerous neighbors have forced people to move—often scattering members of an ethnic group.

✓ Migration—voluntary or involuntary—is temporary or permanent change from a usual place of residence. It may be internal (within the boundaries of one's country) or external (from one country to another).

✓ Every year several million people migrate to wealthy countries in search of wage labor and a better future. In addition 45 million refugees can be found in almost half of the world's countries.

✓ Migrants moving to areas traditionally inhabited by other ethnic groups may face xenophobia—fear or hatred of strangers.

✓ Most migrants begin their new lives in expanding urban areas. Today, 1 billion people live in slums.

What is structural power?

✓ Structural power refers to the macro-level power that manages or restructures political and economic relations within and among societies while simultaneously shaping or changing ideology (ideas, beliefs, and values). It has two components: hard power (which is coercive and is backed up by military force and/or financial pressure) and soft power (which coopts or manipulates through ideological persuasion).

✓ The most powerful country in the world today remains the United States, home to more global corporations than any other country and responsible for over 34 percent of the world's $1.78 trillion military expenditures.

✓ Cutting across international boundaries, global corporations are a powerful force for worldwide integration. Their power and wealth often exceed that of national governments.

✓ Competing states and corporations utilize the ideological persuasion of soft power (as transmitted through electronic and digital media, communication satellites, and other information technology) to sell the general idea of globalization as something positive and to frame or brand anything that opposes capitalism in negative terms.

✓ While providing megaprofits for large corporations, globalization often wreaks havoc in many traditional cultures and disrupts long-established social organization. This engenders worldwide resistance against superpower domination—and with that an emerging world system that is inherently unstable, vulnerable, and unpredictable.

How has the globalization of structural power led to an increase in structural violence?

✓ One result of globalization is the expansion and intensification of structural violence—physical and/or psychological harm (including repression, cultural and environmental destruction, poverty, hunger and obesity, illness, and premature death) caused by impersonal, exploitative, and unjust social, political, and economic systems.

✓ Reactions against the structural violence of globalization include the rise of traditionalism and revitalization movements—efforts to return to life as it was (or how people think it was) before the familiar order became unhinged and people became unsettled. These may take the form of resurgent ethno-nationalism or religious fundamentalist movements.

How might anthropological know-how help counter structural violence?

✓ Some dramatic changes in cultural values and motivations, as well as in social institutions and the types of technologies we employ, are required if humans are going to realize a sustainable future for generations to come. The shortsighted emphasis on consumerism and individual self-interest characteristic of the world's affluent countries needs to be abandoned in favor of a more balanced social and environmental ethic.

✓ Anthropologists have a contribution to make in bringing about this shift. They are well versed in the dangers of culture-bound thinking, and they bring a holistic biocultural and comparative historical perspective to the challenge of understanding and balancing the needs and desires of local communities in the age of globalization.

✓ Inspired by human rights ideals, there have always been "applied" anthropologists who reach beyond studying different cultures to assist besieged groups struggling to survive in today's rapidly changing world.

QUESTIONS FOR REFLECTION

1. Since the launching of the first satellites into orbit and the start of the Internet, the telecommunications revolution has changed how humans interact, work, entertain, and even make and maintain friendships. Can you imagine a world in which cyberspace and social media are supervised and censored by the government? How would you and your friends adjust to that new media environment? What steps would you take if you felt impelled to help prevent or reverse such control?

2. Reflecting on the human condition before and after the start of the Anthropocene epoch that began with the industrial revolution two centuries ago, how do the pre-Anthropocene challenges our species faced compare to those of today?

3. Considering the relationship between structural power and structural violence, does your own lifestyle—in terms of the clothing and food you buy, the transportation you use, and so on—reflect or have an effect on structural violence in the globalization process?

4. The World Health Organization, UNESCO, Oxfam, and Amnesty International are global institutions concerned with checking structural violence and human rights violations. Confronted with genocidal conflicts, famines, epidemics, and torture of political prisoners, activists in these organizations try to improve the human condition. Do you think an anthropological perspective might be of practical use in solving such worldwide problems? Can you think of an example?

DIGGING INTO ANTHROPOLOGY

How Are You Wired?

Since the late 20th century, our species has become "wired." Humans now communicate across great distances by means of an intercontinental network of fiber-optic lines and dozens of communications satellites that orbit the earth. This technology changes all cultures, including yours. With this in mind, select three individuals from different generations in your own family or community. Make a list of the telecommunications devices each of them uses. Do the same for yourself. Through interviews and observation, distinguish whether these devices are shared or individually used over the course of one random day. Note how often, how long, and for what purpose each is used and also whether the user was alone or among other people (besides yourself) when using the device(s). Finally, compare, analyze, and summarize your findings from this mini fieldwork.

Glossary

abduction Movement away from the midline of the body or away from the center of the hand or foot.

absolute or chronometric dating In archaeology and paleoanthropology, dating archaeological or fossil materials in units of absolute time using scientific properties such as rates of decay of radioactive elements.

acclimatization A long-term physiological adjustment made in order to attain equilibrium with a specific environmental stimulus.

accommodation In anthropology, refers to an adaptation process by which a people resists assimilation by modifying its traditional culture in response to pressures by a dominant society in order to preserve its distinctive ethnic identity.

acculturation The massive cultural change that occurs in a society when it experiences intensive firsthand contact with a more powerful society.

Acheulean tool tradition The prevalent style of the stone tools that are associated with *Homo erectus* remains; represented by the hand-axe.

action theory The theory that self-serving actions by forceful leaders play a role in civilization's emergence.

adaptation A series of beneficial adjustments to a particular environment.

adaptive radiation The rapid diversification of an evolving population as it adapts to a variety of available niches.

adduction Movement toward the midline of the body or toward the center of the hand or foot.

advocacy anthropology Research that is community based and politically involved.

affiliative Behaving in a manner that tends to promote social cohesion.

affinal kin People related through marriage.

age class A formally established group of people born during a certain timespan who move together through the series of age-grade categories; sometimes called *age set*.

age grade An organized category of people based on age; every individual passes through a series of such categories over his or her lifetime.

age set A formally established group of people born during a certain timespan who move together through the series of age-grade categories; sometimes called *age class*.

agriculture Intensive crop cultivation, employing plows, fertilizers, and/or irrigation.

allele An alternate form of a single gene.

Allen's rule The tendency for the bodies of mammals living in cold climates to have shorter appendages (arms and legs) than members of the same species living in warm climates.

alphabet A series of symbols representing the sounds of a language arranged in a traditional order.

altruism Concern for the welfare of others expressed as increased risk undertaken by individuals for the good of the group.

ambilocal residence A residence pattern in which a married couple may choose either matrilocal or patrilocal residence.

anagenesis A sustained directional shift in a population's average characteristics that leads to speciation.

analogous In biology, a term referring to structures of different organisms that are superficially similar due to similar function but that do not share a common developmental pathway or structure.

ancestral Characteristics appearing in a later species that also occurred in ancient populations.

animatism The belief that nature is enlivened or energized by an impersonal spiritual force or supernatural energy, which may make itself manifest in any special place, thing, or living creature.

animism The belief that nature is enlivened or energized by distinct personalized spirit beings separable from bodies.

Anthropocene A geological epoch defined by massive environmental changes brought on by humans since the industrial revolution.

anthropoid The suborder of primates that includes New World monkeys, Old World monkeys, and apes (including humans).

anthropology The study of humankind in all times and places.

applied anthropology The use of anthropological knowledge and methods to solve practical problems, often for a specific client.

arboreal Living in the trees.

arboreal hypothesis An explanation for primate evolution that proposes that life in the trees was responsible for enhanced visual acuity and manual dexterity in primates.

archaeology The study of cultures through the recovery and analysis of material remains and environmental data.

Archaic cultures The term used to refer to Mesolithic cultures in the Americas.

archaic *Homo sapiens* A loosely defined group within the genus *Homo* that "lumpers" assign to fossils with the combination of large brain size and ancestral features on the skull.

Ardipithecus One of the earliest genera of bipeds that lived in East Africa. *Ardipithecus* is actually divided into two species: the older, *A. kadabba,* which dates to between 5.2 and 5.8 million years ago, and the younger, *A. ramidus*, which dates to around 4.4 million years ago.

art The creative use of the human imagination to aesthetically interpret, express, and engage life, modifying experienced reality in the process.

artifact Any object fashioned or altered by humans.

assimilation Cultural absorption of an ethnic minority by a dominant society.

Aurignacian tradition Toolmaking tradition in Europe and western Asia at the beginning of the Upper Paleolithic.

Australopithecus The genus including several species of early bipeds from South Africa and East Africa living between about 1.1 and 4.3 million years ago, one of whom was directly ancestral to humans.

Australopithecus sediba A recently identified species of South African gracile australopithecine dated precisely to between 1.97 and 1.98 million years ago, with derived *Homo*-like characteristics in the hands and pelvis.

authority Claiming and exercising power as justified by law or custom of tradition.

balanced reciprocity A mode of exchange in which the giving and the receiving are specific as to the value of the goods or services and the time of their delivery.

band A relatively small and loosely organized kin-ordered group that inhabits a specific territory and that may split periodically into smaller extended family groups that are politically and economically independent.

Bergmann's rule The tendency for the bodies of mammals living in cold climates to be shorter and rounder than members of the same species living in warm climates.

bilateral descent Descent traced equally through father and mother's ancestors; associating each individual with blood relatives on both sides of the family.

binocular vision Vision with increased depth perception from two eyes set next to each other, allowing their visual fields to overlap.

bioarchaeology The archaeological study of human remains—bones, skulls, teeth, and sometimes hair, dried skin, or other tissue—to determine the influences of culture and environment on human biological variation.

biocultural An approach that focuses on the interaction of biology and culture.

biological anthropology The systematic study of humans as biological organisms; also known as *physical anthropology*.

bipedalism A special form of locomotion, distinguishing humans and their ancestors from the African great apes, in which the organism walks upright on two feet; also called *bipedality*.

blade technique A method of stone tool manufacture in which long, parallel-sided flakes are struck off the edges of a specially prepared core.

brachiation Moving from branch to branch using the arms, with the body hanging suspended below.

bride-price The money or valuable goods paid by the groom or his family to the bride's family upon marriage; also called *bridewealth*.

bride service A designated period of time when the groom works for the bride's family.

bridewealth The money or valuable goods paid by the groom or his family to the bride's family upon marriage; also called *bride-price*.

Bronze Age In the Old World, the period marked by the production of tools and ornaments of bronze; began about 5,000 years ago in China, the Mediterranean, and Southwest Asia, and about 500 years earlier in Southeast Asia.

burin A stone tool with chisel-like edges used for working bone, horn, antler, and ivory.

cargo cult A spiritual movement (especially noted in Melanesia) in reaction to disruptive contact with Western capitalism, promising resurrection of deceased relatives, destruction or enslavement of white foreigners, and the magical arrival of utopian riches.

carrying capacity The number of people that the available resources can support at a given level of food-getting techniques.

cartography The craft of making maps of remote regions.

caste A closed social class in a stratified society in which membership is determined by birth and fixed for life.

catarrhine The primate infraorder that includes Old World monkeys, apes, and humans.

chiefdom A politically organized society in which several neighboring communities inhabiting a territory are united under a single ruler.

chromosome In the cell nucleus, the structure visible during cellular division containing long strands of DNA combined with a protein.

chronometric or absolute dating In archaeology and paleoanthropology, dating archaeological or fossil materials in units of absolute time using scientific properties such as rates of decay of radioactive elements.

civilization In anthropology, a society in which large numbers of people live in cities, are socially stratified, and are governed by a ruling elite working through centrally organized political systems called states.

clade A taxonomic grouping that contains a single common ancestor and all of its descendants.

cladogenesis Speciation through a branching mechanism whereby an ancestral population gives rise to two or more descendant populations.

clan An extended unilineal kin-group, often consisting of several lineages, whose members claim common descent from a remote ancestor, usually legendary or mythological.

clavicle The collarbone connecting the sternum (breastbone) with the scapula (shoulder blade).

cline The gradual change in the frequency of an allele or trait over space.

code switching The practice of changing from one mode of speech to another as the situation demands, whether from one language to another or from one dialect of a language to another.

codon The three-base sequence of a gene that specifies a particular amino acid for inclusion in a protein.

coercion Imposition of obedience or submission by force or intimidation.

cognitive capacity A broad concept including intelligence, educability, concept formation, self-awareness, self-evaluation, attention span, sensitivity in discrimination, and creativity.

colonialism System by which a dominant society politically claims and controls a foreign territory primarily for purposes of settling and economic exploitation.

co-marriage A marriage form in which several men and women have sexual access to one another; also called *group marriage*.

common-interest association An association that results from the act of joining, based on sharing particular activities, objectives, values, or beliefs, sometimes rooted in common ethnic, religious, or regional background.

community In primatology, a unit of primate social organization composed of fifty or more individuals who collectively inhabit a large geographic area.

conjugal family A family established through marriage.

consanguineal family A family of blood relatives, consisting of related women, their brothers, and the women's offspring.

consanguineal kin Biologically related relatives, commonly referred to as blood relatives.

conspicuous consumption A showy display of wealth for social prestige.

contagious magic Magic based on the principle that things or persons once in contact can influence each other after the contact is broken.

continental drift According to the theory of plate tectonics, the movement of continents embedded in underlying plates on the earth's surface in relation to one another over the history of life on the planet.

convergent evolution In biological evolution, a process by which unrelated populations develop similarities to one another due to similar function rather than shared ancestry. In cultural evolution, the development of similar cultural adaptations to similar environmental conditions by different peoples with different ancestral cultures.

coprolite Fossilized excrement material providing evidence of the diet and health of past organisms.

core value A value especially promoted by a particular culture.

cranium The braincase of the skull.

Cro-Magnon A European people of the Upper Paleolithic after about 36,000 years ago.

cross cousin The child of a mother's brother or a father's sister.

cultural adaptation A complex of ideas, technologies, and activities that enables people to survive and even thrive in their environment.

cultural anthropology The study of patterns in human behavior, thought, and emotions, focusing on humans as culture-producing and culture-reproducing creatures. Also known as *social* or *sociocultural anthropology*.

cultural control Control through beliefs and values deeply internalized in the minds of individuals.

cultural evolution Cultural change over time—not to be confused with progress.

cultural loss The abandonment of an existing practice or trait.

cultural relativism The idea that one must suspend judgment of other people's practices in order to understand them in their own cultural terms.

cultural resource management A branch of archaeology concerned with survey and/or excavation of archaeological and historical remains that might be threatened by construction or development; also involved with policy surrounding protection of cultural resources.

culture A society's shared and socially transmitted ideas, values, and perceptions, which are used to make sense of experience and generate behavior and are reflected in that behavior.

culture area A geographic region in which a number of societies follow similar patterns of life.

culture-bound A perspective that produces theories about the world and reality that are based on the assumptions and values from the researcher's own culture.

culture-bound syndrome A mental disorder specific to a particular ethnic group; also known as *ethnic psychosis*.

culture shock In fieldwork, the anthropologist's personal disorientation and anxiety, which may result in depression.

cyberethnography An ethnographic study of social networks, communicative practices, and other cultural expressions in cyberspace by means of digital visual and audio technologies; also called *digital ethnography* and *netnography*.

datum point The starting point or reference for a grid system.

demographic A population characteristic such as the number of individuals of each age and sex.

dendrochronology In archaeology and paleoanthropology, a technique of chronometric dating based on the number of rings of growth found in tree trunks.

Denisovan A newly discovered group of archaic *Homo sapiens* from southern Siberia dated to between 30,000 and 50,000 years ago.

dental formula The number of each tooth type (incisors, canines, premolars, and molars) on one-half of each jaw. Unlike other mammals, primates possess equal numbers on their upper and lower jaws, making the dental formula for the species a single series of numbers.

dependence training Childrearing practices that foster compliance in the performance of assigned tasks and dependence on the domestic group, rather than reliance on oneself.

derived Characteristics appearing in a later species that did not occur in ancestral populations.

descent group Any kin-group whose members share a direct line of descent from a real (historical) or fictional common ancestor.

desecration Ideologically inspired violation of a sacred site intended to inflict harm, if only symbolically, on people judged to have impure, false, or even evil beliefs and ritual practices.

developmental adaptation A permanent phenotypic variation derived from interaction between genes and the environment during the period of growth and development.

dialect The varying form of a language that reflects a particular region, occupation, or social class and that is similar enough to be mutually intelligible.

diastema A space between the canines and other teeth allowing the large projecting canines to fit within the jaw.

diffusion The spread of certain ideas, customs, or practices from one culture to another.

digital ethnography An ethnographic study of social networks, communicative practices, and other cultural expressions in cyberspace by means of digital visual and audio technologies; also called *cyberethnography* or *netnography*.

disease A specific physical or biological abnormality.

displacement A term referring to things and events removed in time and space.

diurnal Active during the day and at rest at night.

divination A magical procedure or spiritual ritual designed to discern what is not knowable by ordinary means, such as foretelling the future by interpreting omens.

DNA (deoxyribonucleic acid) The genetic material consisting of a complex molecule whose base structure directs the synthesis of proteins.

doctrine An assertion of opinion or belief formally handed down by an authority as true and indisputable.

domestication An evolutionary process whereby humans modify, intentionally or unintentionally, the genetic makeup of a population of wild plants or animals, sometimes to the extent that members of the population cannot survive or cannot reproduce without human assistance.

dominance hierarchy An observed ranking system in primate societies, ordering individuals from high (alpha) to low standing corresponding to predictable behavioral interactions including domination.

dominant In genetics, a term to describe the ability of an allele for a trait to mask the presence of a recessive allele.

dowry A payment at the time of a woman's marriage that comes from her inheritance, made to either her or her husband.

ecofact The natural remains of plants and animals found in the archaeological record.

ecological niche A species' way of life considered in the full context of its environment including factors such as diet, activity, terrain, vegetation, predators, prey, and climate.

economic system An organized arrangement for producing, distributing, and consuming goods.

ecosystem A system, or a functioning whole, composed of both the natural environment and all the organisms living within it.

egalitarian society A society in which people have about the same rank and share equally in the basic resources that support income, status, and power.

EGO In kinship studies, the central person from whom the degree of each kinship relationship is traced.

eliciting device An activity or object that encourages individuals to recall and share information.

empirical An approach based on observations of the world rather than on intuition or faith.

enculturation The process by which a society's culture is passed on from one generation to the next and individuals become members of their society.

endemic The public health term for a disease that is widespread in a population.

endocast A cast of the inside of a skull; used to help determine the size and shape of the brain.

endogamy Marriage within a particular group or category of individuals.

entoptic phenomenon A vision of bright pulsating forms that is generated by the central nervous system and seen in states of trance.

enzyme A protein that initiates and directs chemical reactions.

epic A long, dramatic narrative, recounting the celebrated deeds of a historic or legendary hero, often sung or recited in poetic language.

epicanthic fold A fold of skin at the inner corner of the eye that covers the true corner of the eye; common in Asiatic populations.

epigenetics The study of changes in organisms that are caused by modification of gene function and expression rather than by modification of the DNA sequence.

Eskimo system Kinship reckoning in which the nuclear family is emphasized by specifically identifying the mother, father, brother, and sister, while lumping together all other relatives into broad categories such as uncle, aunt, and cousin; also known as the *lineal system*.

estrus In some primate females, the time of sexual receptivity during which ovulation is visibly displayed.

ethnic group People who collectively and publicly identify themselves as a distinct group based on shared cultural features such as common origin, language, customs, and traditional beliefs.

ethnicity The expression for the set of cultural ideas held by an ethnic group.

ethnic psychosis A mental disorder specific to a particular ethnic group; also known as *culture-bound syndrome.*

ethnocentrism The belief that the ways of one's own culture are the only proper ones.

ethnocide The violent eradication of an ethnic group's collective cultural identity as a distinctive people; occurs when a dominant society deliberately sets out to destroy another society's cultural heritage.

ethnographic fieldwork Extended on-location research to gather detailed and in-depth information on a society's customary ideas, values, and practices through participation in its collective social life.

ethnography A detailed description of a particular culture primarily based on fieldwork.

ethnolinguistics A branch of linguistics that studies the relationships between language and culture and how they mutually influence and inform each other.

ethnology The study and analysis of different cultures from a comparative or historical point of view, utilizing ethnographic accounts and developing anthropological theories that help explain why certain important differences or similarities occur among groups.

ethnomusicology The study of a society's music in terms of its cultural setting.

Eve hypothesis The theory that modern humans are all derived from one single population of archaic *Homo sapiens* who migrated out of Africa after 100,000 years ago, replacing all other archaic forms due to their superior cultural capabilities; also known as the *recent African origins hypothesis* or the *out of Africa hypothesis.*

evolution The changes in allele frequencies in populations; also known as *microevolution.*

evolutionary medicine An approach to human sickness and health combining principles of evolutionary theory and human evolutionary history.

exogamy Marriage outside a particular group or category of individuals.

experimental archaeology The recreation of ancient lifeways by modern paleoanthropologists and archaeologists in order to test hypotheses, interpretations, and assumptions about the past.

extended family Two or more closely related nuclear families clustered together into a large domestic group.

family Two or more people related by blood, marriage, or adoption. The family may take many forms, ranging from a single parent with one or more children, to a married couple or polygamous spouses with or without offspring, to several generations of parents and their children.

feature A nonportable element such as a hearth or a ditch or an architectural element such as a wall that is preserved in the archaeological record.

fictive marriage A marriage form in which a proxy is used as a symbol of someone not physically present to establish the social status of a spouse and heirs.

fieldwork The term anthropologists use for on-location research.

fission In kinship studies, the splitting of a descent group into two or more new descent groups.

flotation An archaeological technique employed to recover very tiny objects by immersion of soil samples in water to separate heavy from light particles.

fluorine dating In archaeology or paleoanthropology, a technique for relative dating based on the fact that the amount of fluorine in bones is proportional to their age.

folklore A term coined by 19th-century scholars studying the unwritten stories and other artistic traditions of rural peoples to distinguish between "folk art" and the "fine art" of the literate elite.

food foraging A mode of subsistence involving some combination of hunting, fishing, and gathering of wild plant foods.

foramen magnum A large opening in the skull; the spinal cord passes through this opening to connect to the brain.

forensic anthropology The examination of human biological and cultural remains for legal purposes.

formal interview A structured question-and-answer session, carefully annotated as it occurs and based on prepared questions.

fossil The mineralized remains of past life forms.

founder effect A particular form of genetic drift deriving from a small founding population not possessing all the alleles present in the original population.

gender The cultural elaborations and meanings assigned to the biological differentiation between the sexes.

gendered speech Distinct male and female speech patterns that vary across social and cultural settings.

gene The portion of a DNA molecule that directs the synthesis of specific proteins.

gene flow The introduction of alleles from the gene pool of one population into that of another.

gene pool All the genetic variants possessed by members of a population.

generalized reciprocity A mode of exchange in which the value of the gift is not calculated, nor is the time of repayment specified.

generational system Kinship reckoning in which all relatives of the same sex and generation are referred to by the same term; also known as the *Hawaiian system.*

genetic adaptation A discrete genetic change built into the allele frequency of a population or the microevolutionary change brought about by natural selection.

genetic code The set of rules by which codons (sequences of three bases) in genetic material specify amino acids in protein synthesis.

genetic drift The chance fluctuations of allele frequencies in the gene pool of a population.

genocide The physical extermination of one people by another, either as a deliberate act or as the accidental outcome of activities carried out by one people with little regard for their impact on others.

genome The complete structure sequence of DNA for a species.

genotype The alleles an individual possesses for a particular trait.

genus (genera) In the system of plant and animal classification, a group of like species.

gesture A facial expression and body posture and motion that convey an intended as well as a subconscious message.

globalization Worldwide interconnectedness, evidenced in rapid global movement of natural resources, trade goods, human labor, finance capital, information, and infectious diseases.

gracile australopithecine One member of the genus *Australopithecus* possessing a more lightly built chewing apparatus; probably had a diet that included more meat than that of the robust australopithecines; best represented by the South African species *A. africanus.*

grade A general level of biological organization seen among a group of species; useful for constructing evolutionary relationships.

grammar The entire formal structure of a language, including morphology and syntax.

grave goods Items such as utensils, figurines, and personal possessions, symbolically placed in the grave for the deceased person's use in the afterlife.

grid system A system for recording data in three dimensions from an archaeological excavation.

grooming The ritual cleaning of another animal's coat to remove parasites and other matter.

group marriage A marriage form in which several men and women have sexual access to one another; also called *co-marriage.*

haplorrhine The subdivision within the primate order based on shared genetic characteristics; includes tarsiers, New World monkeys, Old World monkeys, and apes (including humans).

hard power Macro-level power that manages or restructures economic and political relations and coerces by military force and/or financial pressure.

Hawaiian system Kinship reckoning in which all relatives of the same sex and generation are referred to by the same term; also known as the *generational system.*

health disparity A difference in the health status between the wealthy elite and the poor in stratified societies.

hemoglobin The protein that carries oxygen in red blood cells.

heterozygous A term referring to a chromosome pair that bears different alleles for a single gene.

historical archaeology The archaeological study of places for which written records exist.

holistic perspective A fundamental principle of anthropology: The various parts of human culture and biology must be viewed in the broadest possible context in order to understand their interconnections and interdependence.

homeotherm An animal that maintains a relatively constant body temperature despite environmental fluctuations.

home range The geographic area within which a group of primates usually moves.

hominid The African hominoid family that includes humans and their ancestors. Some scientists—recognizing the close relationship of humans, chimps, bonobos, and gorillas—use the term *hominid* to refer to all African hominoids. They then divide the hominid family into two subfamilies: the Paninae (chimps, bonobos, and gorillas) and the Homininae (humans and their ancestors).

hominin The taxonomic subfamily or tribe within the primates that includes humans and our ancestors.

hominoid The taxonomic superfamily within the Old World primates that includes gibbons, siamangs, orangutans, gorillas, chimpanzees, bonobos, and humans.

Homo The genus of bipeds that appeared about 2.5 million years ago, characterized by increased brain size compared to earlier bipeds. The genus is divided into various species based on features such as brain size, skull shape, and cultural capabilities.

Homo erectus "Upright human." A species within the genus *Homo* first appearing just after 2 million years ago in Africa and ultimately spreading throughout the Old World.

Homo habilis "Handy human." The first fossil members of the genus *Homo* appearing about 2.5 million years ago, with larger brains and smaller faces than australopithecines.

homologous In biology, a term referring to structures of two different organisms that arise in similar fashion and pass through similar stages during embryonic development, although they may have different functions.

homozygous A term referring to a chromosome pair that bears identical alleles for a single gene.

horticulture The cultivation of crops in food gardens, carried out with simple hand tools such as digging sticks and hoes.

household A domestic unit of one or more persons living in the same residence. Other than family members, a household may include nonrelatives, such as servants.

hunting response A cyclic expansion and contraction of the blood vessels of the limbs that balances releasing enough heat to prevent frostbite with maintaining heat in the body core.

hydraulic theory In archaeology, the theory that explains civilization's emergence as the result of the construction of elaborate irrigation systems, the functioning of which required full-time managers whose control blossomed into the first governing body and elite social class; also known as *irrigation theory*.

hypoglossal canal The opening in the skull that accommodates the tongue-controlling hypoglossal nerve.

hypothesis A tentative explanation of the relationships between certain phenomena.

hypoxia The reduced availability of oxygen in the atmosphere causing diminished oxygen at the cellular level.

idealist perspective A theoretical approach stressing the primacy of superstructure in cultural research and analysis; also known as the *mentalist perspective*.

illness The meanings and elaborations given to a particular physical state.

imitative magic Magic based on the principle that like produces like; sometimes called *sympathetic magic*.

incest taboo The prohibition of sexual relations between closely related individuals.

incorporation In a rite of passage, reincorporation of a temporarily removed individual into society in his or her new status.

independence training Childrearing practices that promote independence, self-reliance, and personal achievement.

industrial food production Large-scale businesses involved in mass food production, processing, and marketing, which primarily rely on laborsaving machines.

industrial society A society in which human labor, hand tools, and animal power are largely replaced by machines, with an economy primarily based on big factories.

informal economy A network of producing and circulating marketable commodities, labor, and services that for various reasons escape government control.

informal interview An unstructured, open-ended conversation in everyday life.

informant A member of the society being studied who provides information that helps researchers understand the meaning of what they observe. Early anthropologists referred to such an individual as a *key consultant*.

informed consent A formal recorded agreement between the subject and the researcher to participate in the research.

infrastructure The economic foundation of a society, including its subsistence practices and the tools and other material equipment used to make a living.

innovation Any new idea, method, or device that gains widespread acceptance in society.

insurgency An organized armed resistance or violent uprising to an established government or authority in power; also known as *rebellion*.

intersexual A person born with reproductive organs, genitalia, and/or sex chromosomes that are not exclusively male or female.

irrigation theory The theory that explains civilization's emergence as the result of the construction of elaborate irrigation systems, the functioning of which required full-time managers whose control blossomed into the first governing body and elite social class; also known as *hydraulic theory*.

Iroquois system Kinship reckoning in which a father and a father's brother are referred to by a single term, as are a mother and a mother's sister, but a father's sister and a mother's brother are given separate terms. Parallel cousins are classified with brothers and sisters, whereas cross cousins are classified separately but not equated with relatives of some other generation.

ischial callosity A hardened, nerveless pad on the buttocks that allows baboons and other primates to sit for long periods of time.

isotherm An animal whose body temperature rises or falls depending on the temperature of the surrounding environment.

karyotype The array of chromosomes found inside a single cell.

Kenyanthropus platyops A proposed genus and species of biped contemporaneous with early australopithecines; may not be a separate genus.

key consultant A member of the society being studied who provides information that helps researchers understand the meaning of what they observe. Early anthropologists referred to such an individual as an *informant*.

kindred A grouping of blood relatives based on bilateral descent; includes all relatives with whom EGO shares at least one grandparent, great-grandparent, or even great-great-grandparent on his or her father's *and* mother's side.

kinesics The study of nonverbal signals in body language including facial expressions and bodily postures and motions.

kinship A network of relatives into which individuals are born and married, and with whom they cooperate based on customarily prescribed rights and obligations.

k-selected Reproduction involving the production of relatively few offspring with high parental investment in each.

Kula ring A mode of balanced reciprocity that reinforces trade and social relations among the seafaring Melanesians who inhabit a large ring of islands in the southwestern Pacific Ocean.

lactase An enzyme in the small intestine that enables humans to assimilate lactose (milk sugar).

lactose A sugar that is the primary constituent of fresh milk.

language A system of communication using symbolic sounds, gestures, or marks that are put together according to certain rules, resulting in meanings that are intelligible to all who share that language.

language family A group of languages descended from a single ancestral language.

law Formal rules of conduct that, when violated, effectuate negative sanctions.

law of competitive exclusion When two closely related species compete for the same niche, one will out-compete the other, bringing about the latter's extinction.

law of independent assortment The Mendelian principle that genes controlling different traits are inherited independently of one another.

law of segregation The Mendelian principle that variants of genes for a particular trait retain their separate identities through the generations.

legend A story about a memorable event or figure handed down by tradition and told as true but without historical evidence.

legitimacy In politics, the right of political leaders to govern—to hold, use, and allocate power—based on the values a particular society embraces.

letter A written character or grapheme.

Levalloisian technique Toolmaking technique by which three or four long triangular flakes are detached from a specially prepared core; developed by members of the genus *Homo* transitional from *H. erectus* to *H. sapiens*.

leveling mechanism A cultural obligation compelling prosperous members of a community to give away goods, host public feasts, provide free service, or otherwise demonstrate generosity so that no person permanently accumulates significantly more wealth than anyone else.

lineage A unilineal kin-group descended from a common ancestor or founder who lived four to six generations ago and in which relationships among members can be exactly stated in genealogical terms.

lineal system Kinship reckoning in which the nuclear family is emphasized by specifically identifying the mother, father, brother, and sister, while lumping together all other relatives into broad categories such as uncle, aunt, and cousin; also known as the *Eskimo system*.

linguistic anthropology The study of human languages—looking at their structure, history, and relation to social and cultural contexts.

linguistic divergence The development of different languages from a single ancestral language.

linguistic nationalism The attempt by ethnic minorities and even countries to proclaim independence by purging their language of foreign terms.

linguistic relativity The idea that language to some extent shapes the way in which people perceive and think about the world.

linguistics The systematic study of all aspects of language.

Lomekwian tool tradition The earliest stone tools dated to 3.3 million years ago, discovered in 2015 in Kenya.

Lower Paleolithic The first part of the Old Stone Age beginning with the earliest Lomekwian tools spanning from about 200,000 or 250,000 years ago to 3.3 million years ago.

macroevolution Evolution above the species level or leading to the formation of new species.

magic Specific formulas and actions used to compel supernatural powers to act in certain ways for good or evil purposes.

mammal The class of vertebrate animals distinguished by bodies covered with hair or fur, self-regulating temperature, and in females, milk-producing mammary glands.

market exchange The buying and selling of goods and services, with prices set by rules of supply and demand.

marriage A culturally sanctioned union between two or more people that establishes certain rights and obligations between the people, between them and their children, and between them and their in-laws. Such marriage rights and obligations most often include, but are not limited to, sex, labor, property, childrearing, exchange, and status.

marrow The fatty nutritious tissue inside of long bones where blood cells are produced.

material culture The durable aspects of culture such as tools, structures, and art.

materialist perspective A theoretical approach stressing the primacy of infrastructure (material conditions) in cultural research and analysis.

matrilineal descent Descent traced exclusively through the female line of ancestry to establish group membership.

matrilocal residence A residence pattern in which a married couple lives in the wife's mother's place of residence.

mediation The settlement of a dispute through negotiation assisted by an unbiased third party.

medical anthropology A specialization in anthropology that brings theoretical and applied approaches from cultural and biological anthropology to the study of human health and disease.

medical pluralism The practice of multiple medical systems, each with its own techniques and beliefs, in a single society.

medical system A patterned set of ideas and practices relating to illness.

meiosis A kind of cell division that produces the sex cells, each of which has half the number of chromosomes found in other cells of the organism.

melanin A dark pigment produced in the outer layer of the skin that protects against damaging ultraviolet solar radiation.

menarche The first occurrence of menstruation in the human female.

menopause The cessation of menstruation cycles.

mentalist perspective A theoretical approach stressing the primacy of superstructure in cultural research and analysis; also known as the *idealist perspective*.

Mesoamerica The region extending from central Mexico to the northern regions of Central America.

Mesolithic The Middle Stone Age of Europe, Asia, and Africa beginning about 12,000 years ago.

metabolic rate The rate at which bodies burn energy (food) to function.

microevolution The changes in allele frequencies in populations; also known as *evolution*.

microlith A small blade of flint or similar stone, which when hafted (sometimes several of them) into a wooden handle would make a tool that was widespread in the Mesolithic.

midden A refuse or garbage disposal area in an archaeological site.

Middle Paleolithic The middle part of the Old Stone Age characterized by the development of the Mousterian tool tradition and the earlier Levalloisian techniques.

migration Mobility in geographic space, involving temporary or permanent change in usual place of residence. Internal migration is movement within countries; external migration is movement to a foreign country.

mitosis A kind of cell division that produces daughter cells that are genetic copies of the parent cell.

modal personality Character traits that occur with the highest frequency in a social group and are therefore the most representative of its culture.

modernization The process of political and socioeconomic change, whereby developing societies acquire some of the cultural characteristics of Western industrial societies.

moiety A group, usually consisting of several clans, which results from a division of a society into two halves on the basis of descent.

molecular anthropology The anthropological study of genes and genetic relationships, which contributes significantly to our understanding of human evolution, adaptation, and diversity.

molecular clock The technique that dates of divergences among related species can be calculated through an examination of the genetic mutations that have accrued since the divergence.

money A means of exchange used to make payments for other goods and services as well as to measure their value.

monogamous In primatology, mating for life with a single individual of the opposite sex.

monogamy A marriage form in which both partners have just one spouse.

monotheism The belief in only one supremely powerful divinity as creator and master of the universe.

morpheme The smallest unit of sound that carries a meaning in language. It is distinct from a phoneme, which can alter meaning but has no meaning by itself.

morphology The study of the patterns or rules of word formation in a language, including the guidelines for verb tense, pluralization, and compound words.

motif An underlying theme around which a work of art is composed.

Mousterian tool tradition The tool industry of the Neandertals and their contemporaries of Europe, Southwest Asia, and North Africa from 40,000 to 125,000 years ago.

multiculturalism The public policy for managing cultural diversity in a multi-ethnic society, officially stressing mutual respect and tolerance for cultural differences within a country's borders.

multiregional hypothesis The hypothesis that modern humans originated through a process of simultaneous local transition from *Homo erectus* to *Homo sapiens* throughout the inhabited world.

multi-sited ethnography The investigation and documentation of peoples and cultures embedded in the larger structures of a globalizing world, utilizing a range of methods in various locations of time and space.

music Broadly speaking, an art form whose medium is sound and silence; a form of communication that includes a nonverbal auditory component with elements of tonality, pitch, rhythm, and timbre.

mutation The chance alteration of genetic material that produces new variation.

myth A sacred narrative that explains the fundamentals of human existence—where we and everything in our world came from, why we are here, and where we are going.

NAGPRA The Native American Graves Protection and Repatriation Act, a federal law that outlines a process for the return of remains to related native peoples.

naming ceremony A special event or ritual to mark the naming of a child.

natal group The group or the community an animal has inhabited since birth.

nation A people who share a collective identity based on a common culture, language, territorial base, and history.

Natufian culture A Mesolithic culture from the lands that are now Israel, Lebanon, and western Syria, between about 10,200 and 12,500 years ago.

natural selection The evolutionary process through which factors in the environment exert pressure, favoring some individuals over others to produce the next generation.

Neandertal A distinct fossil group within the genus *Homo* inhabiting Europe and Southwest and Central Asia approximately 30,000 to 125,000 years ago; today's genetic evidence extends their range both forward and back in time.

negative reciprocity A mode of exchange in which the aim is to get something for as little as possible. Neither fair nor balanced, it may involve hard bargaining, manipulation, outright cheating, or theft.

negotiation The use of direct argument and compromise by the parties to a dispute to arrive voluntarily at a mutually satisfactory agreement.

Neolithic The New Stone Age; a prehistoric period beginning about 10,000 years ago in which peoples possessed stone-based technologies and depended on domesticated plants and/or animals for subsistence.

Neolithic revolution The domestication of plants and animals by peoples with stone-based technologies beginning about 10,000 years ago and leading to radical transformations in cultural systems; sometimes referred to as the *Neolithic transition*.

neolocal residence A residence pattern in which a married couple establishes its household in a location apart from either the husband's or the wife's relatives.

netnography An ethnographic study of social networks, communicative practices, and other cultural expressions in cyberspace by means of digital visual and audio technologies; also called *digital ethnography* and *cyberethnography*.

new reproductive technology (NRT) An alternative means of reproduction, such as in vitro fertilization.

nocturnal Active at night and at rest during the day.

notochord A rodlike structure of cartilage that, in vertebrates, is replaced by the vertebral column.

nuclear family A group consisting of one or two parents and dependent offspring, which may include a stepparent, stepsiblings, and adopted children. Until recently this term referred only to the mother, father, and child(ren) unit.

Oldowan tool tradition An early stone tool industry, beginning between 2.5 and 2.6 million years ago.

Old Stone Age A prehistoric period, characterized by the development of increasingly effective stone tool technologies, spanning from about 10,000 to 3.3 million years ago; also known as *Paleolithic*.

opposable Having the ability to bring the thumb or big toe in contact with the tips of the other digits on the same hand or foot in order to grasp objects.

out of Africa hypothesis The theory that modern humans are all derived from one single population of archaic *Homo sapiens* who migrated out of Africa after 100,000 years ago, replacing all other archaic forms due to their superior cultural capabilities; also known as the *recent African origins hypothesis* or the *Eve hypothesis*.

ovulation The moment when an egg released from an ovary into the womb is receptive for fertilization.

paleoanthropology The anthropological study of biological changes through time (evolution) to understand the origins and predecessors of the present human species.

Paleoindian The people who were the earliest inhabitants of North America.

palynology In archaeology and paleoanthropology, a technique of relative dating based on changes in fossil pollen over time.

pantheon A collective of gods and goddesses worshiped in a society.

paralanguage The voice effects that accompany language and convey meaning, including vocalizations such as giggling, groaning, or sighing, as well as voice qualities such as pitch and tempo.

parallel cousin The child of a father's brother or a mother's sister.

parallel evolution In cultural evolution, the development of similar cultural adaptations to similar environmental conditions by peoples whose ancestral cultures are already somewhat alike.

participant observation In ethnography, the technique of learning a people's culture through social participation and personal observation within the community being studied, as well as interviews and discussion with individual members of the group over an extended period of time.

pastoralism The breeding and managing of migratory herds of domesticated grazing animals, such as goats, sheep, cattle, llamas, and camels.

patrilineal descent Descent traced exclusively through the male line of ancestry to establish group membership.

patrilocal residence A residence pattern in which a married couple lives in the husband's father's place of residence.

peasant A small-scale producer of crops or livestock living on land that is self-owned or rented in exchange for labor, crops, or money; often exploited by more powerful groups in a complex society.

percussion method A technique of stone tool manufacture performed by striking the raw material with a hammerstone or by striking raw material against a stone anvil to remove flakes.

performance art A creatively expressed promotion of ideas by artful means dramatically staged to challenge opinion and/or provoke purposeful action.

personality The distinctive way a person thinks, feels, and behaves.

phenotype The observable characteristic of an organism that may or may not reflect a particular genotype due to the variable expression of dominant and recessive alleles.

phoneme The smallest unit of sound that makes a difference in meaning in a language but has no meaning by itself.

phonetics The systematic identification and description of distinctive speech sounds in a language.

phonology The study of language sounds.

phratry A unilineal descent group composed of at least two clans that supposedly share a common ancestry, whether or not they really do.

physical anthropology The systematic study of humans as biological organisms; also known as *biological anthropology.*

physiological adaptation A short-term physiological change in response to a specific environmental stimulus. An immediate short-term response is not very efficient and is gradually replaced by a longer-term response; see *acclimatization.*

pilgrimage A devotion in motion; traveling, often on foot, to a sacred or holy site to reach for enlightenment, prove devotion, and/or experience a miracle.

platyrrhine The primate infraorder that includes New World monkeys.

pluralistic society A complex society in which two or more ethnic groups or nationalities are politically organized into one territorial state but maintain their cultural differences.

political organization The way power, as the capacity to do something, is accumulated, arranged, executed, and structurally embedded in society; the means through which a society creates and maintains social order and reduces social disorder.

politics The process determining who gets what, when, and how.

polyandry A marriage form in which a woman is married to two or more men at the same time; a form of polygamy.

polygamy A marriage form in which one individual has multiple spouses at the same time.

polygenetic inheritance Two or more genes contributing to the phenotypic expression of a single characteristic.

polygyny A marriage form in which a man is married to two or more women at the same time; a form of polygamy.

polymerase chain reaction (PCR) A technique for amplifying or creating multiple copies of fragments of DNA so that it can be studied in the laboratory.

polymorphic A term to describe species with alternative forms (alleles) of particular genes.

polytheism The belief in multiple gods and/or goddesses.

polytypic A term to describe the expression of genetic variants in different frequencies in different populations of a species.

population In biology, a group of similar individuals that can and do interbreed.

postindustrial society A society with an economy based on research and development of new knowledge and technologies, as well as providing information, services, and finance capital on a global scale.

potassium-argon dating In archaeology and paleoanthropology, a technique of chronometric dating that measures the ratio of radioactive potassium to argon in volcanic debris associated with human remains.

potlatch On the Northwest Coast of North America, an indigenous ceremonial event in which a village chief publicly gives away stockpiled food and other goods that signify wealth.

power The ability of individuals or groups to impose their will upon others and make them do things even against their own wants or wishes.

preadapted Possessing characteristics that, by chance, are advantageous in future environmental conditions.

prehensile Having the ability to grasp.

prehistory A conventional term used to refer to the period of time before the appearance of written records.

pressure flaking A technique of stone tool manufacture in which a bone, antler, or wooden tool is used to press, rather than strike off, small flakes from a piece of flint or similar stone.

prestige economy The creation of a surplus for the express purpose of displaying wealth and giving it away to raise one's status.

priest or priestess A full-time religious specialist formally recognized for his or her role in guiding the religious practices of others and for contacting and influencing supernatural powers.

primary innovation The creation, invention, or chance discovery of a completely new idea, method, or device.

primate The group of mammals that includes lemurs, lorises, tarsiers, monkeys, apes, and humans.

primatology The study of living and fossil primates.

prion An infectious protein lacking any genetic material but capable of causing the reorganization and destruction of other proteins.

progress In anthropology, a relative concept signifying that a society or country is moving forward to a better, more advanced stage in its cultural development toward greater perfection.

projection In cartography, refers to the system of intersecting lines (of longitude and latitude) by which part or all of the globe is represented on a flat surface.

prosimian The suborder of primates that includes lemurs, lorises, and tarsiers.

proxemics The cross-cultural study of people's perception and use of space.

punctuated equilibrium A model of macroevolutionary change that suggests evolution occurs via long periods of stability or stasis punctuated by periods of rapid change.

qualitative data Nonstatistical information such as personal life stories and customary beliefs and practices.

quantitative data Statistical or measurable information, such as demographic composition, the types and quantities of crops grown, or the ratio of spouses born and raised within or outside the community.

race In biology, the taxonomic category of a subspecies that is not applicable to humans because the division of humans into discrete types does not represent the true nature of human biological variation. In some societies, race is an important social category.

racism A doctrine of superiority by which one group justifies the dehumanization and degradation of others based on their distinctive physical characteristics.

radiocarbon dating In archaeology and paleoanthropology, a technique of chronometric dating based on measuring the amount of radioactive carbon (^{14}C) left in organic materials found in archaeological sites.

rebellion Organized armed resistance to an established government or authority in power; also known as *insurgency.*

recent African origins hypothesis The hypothesis that modern humans are all derived from one single population of archaic *Homo sapiens* who migrated out of Africa after 100,000 years ago, replacing all other archaic forms due to their superior cultural capabilities; also known as the *Eve hypothesis* or the *out of Africa hypothesis.*

recessive In genetics, a term to describe an allele for a trait whose expression is masked by the presence of a dominant allele.

reciprocity The exchange of goods and services, of approximately equal value, between two parties.

reconciliation In primatology, a friendly reunion between former opponents not long after a conflict.

redistribution A mode of exchange in which goods flow into a central place, where they are sorted, counted, and reallocated.

relative dating In archaeology and paleoanthropology, designating an event, object, or fossil as being older or younger than another by noting the position in the earth, by measuring the amount of chemicals contained in fossil bones and artifacts, or by identifying its association with other plant, animal, or cultural remains.

religion An organized system of ideas about the spiritual sphere or the supernatural, along with associated ceremonial practices by which people try to interpret and/or influence aspects of the universe otherwise beyond their control.

reproductive success The production of fertile offspring by individual members of a population.

resistant strain A genetic variant of a specific bacterium that is not killed by antibiotics.

revitalization movement A social movement for radical cultural reform in response to widespread social disruption and collective feelings of great stress and despair.

revolution Radical change in a society or culture. In the political arena, it involves the forced overthrow of an existing government and establishment of a completely new one.

ribosome The structure in the cell where translation occurs.

rifting In geology, the process by which a rift, or a long narrow zone of faulting, results when two geologic plates separate.

rite of intensification A ritual that takes place during a crisis in the life of the group and serves to bind individuals together.

rite of passage A ritual that marks an important ceremonial moment when members of a society move from one distinctive social stage in life to another, such as birth, marriage, and death. It features three phases: separation, transition, and incorporation.

rite of purification A symbolic act carried out by an individual or a group to establish or restore purity when someone has violated a taboo or is otherwise unclean.

ritual A culturally prescribed symbolic act or procedure designed to guide members of a community in an orderly way through personal and collective transitions.

RNA (ribonucleic acid) Single-stranded molecules similar to DNA but with uracil substituted for the base thymine; transcribes and carries instructions from DNA within the nucleus to the ribosomes, where it directs protein synthesis. Some simple life forms contain RNA only.

robust australopithecine One member of the genus *Australopithecus*, living from 1 to 2.5 million years ago in East Africa and South Africa; known for the rugged nature of its chewing apparatus (large back teeth, large chewing muscles, and a bony ridge on the skull top to allow for these large muscles).

r-selected Reproduction involving the production of large numbers of offspring with relatively low parental investment in each.

sagittal crest A crest running from front to back on the top of the skull along the midline to provide a surface of bone for the attachment of the large temporal muscles for chewing.

Sahul The greater Australian landmass including Australia, New Guinea, and Tasmania. At times of maximum glaciation and low sea levels, these areas were continuous.

salvage ethnography Ethnographic research that documents endangered cultures; also known as *urgent anthropology*.

sanction An externalized social control designed to encourage conformity to social norms.

savannah Semi-arid plains environment as in East Africa.

scapula The shoulder blade.

secondary innovation The deliberate application or modification of an existing idea, method, or device.

secularization A process of cultural change in which a population tends toward a nonreligious worldview, ignoring or rejecting institutionalized spiritual beliefs and rituals.

secular trend A physical difference among related people from distinct generations that allows anthropologists to make inferences about environmental effects on growth and development.

self-awareness The ability to identify oneself as an individual, to reflect on oneself, and to evaluate oneself.

self-control A person's capacity to manage her or his spontaneous feelings, restraining impulsive behavior.

separation In a rite of passage, the temporary ritual removal of the individual from society.

serial monogamy A marriage form in which an individual marries or lives with a series of partners in succession.

seriation In archaeology and paleoanthropology, a technique for relative dating based on putting groups of objects into a sequence in relation to one another.

sexual dimorphism Within a single species, differences between males and females in the shape or size of a feature not directly related to reproduction, such as body size or canine tooth shape and size.

shaman A person who enters an altered state of consciousness to contact and utilize an ordinarily hidden reality in order to acquire knowledge, power, and to help others.

sickle-cell anemia An inherited form of anemia produced by a mutation in the hemoglobin protein that causes the red blood cells to assume a sickle shape.

signal An instinctive sound or gesture that has a natural or self-evident meaning.

silent trade A mode of exchange of goods between mutually distrusting ethnic groups so as to avoid direct personal contact.

sister chromatid One-half of the X shape of a chromosome visible after replication. Each half is a copy of the original chromosome.

slash-and-burn cultivation An extensive form of horticulture in which the natural vegetation is cut, the slash is subsequently burned, and crops are then planted among the ashes; also known as *swidden farming*.

social or sociocultural anthropology The study of patterns in human behavior, thought, and emotions, focusing on humans as culture-producing and culture-reproducing creatures. Also known as *cultural anthropology*.

social class A category of individuals in a stratified society who enjoy equal or nearly equal prestige according to the hierarchical system of evaluation.

social control External control through open coercion.

social mobility An upward or downward change in one's social class position in a stratified society.

social stratification The emergence of social classes—a series of ranked social categories according to characteristics such as wealth, occupation, or kin group.

social structure The rule-governed relationships—with all their rights and obligations—that hold members of a society together. This includes households, families, associations, and power relations, including politics.

society An organized group or groups of interdependent people who generally share a common territory, language, and culture and who act together for collective survival and well-being.

sociolinguistics The study of the relationship between language and society through examining how social categories—such as age, gender, ethnicity, religion, occupation, and class—influence the use and significance of distinctive styles of speech.

soft power Macro-level power that coopts or manipulates, skillfully pressing people through attraction and persuasion to shape or change their ideology (ideas, beliefs, and values).

soil mark A stain that shows up on the surface of recently plowed fields revealing an archaeological site.

speciation The process of forming new species.

species The smallest working unit in biological classificatory systems; reproductively isolated populations or groups of populations capable of interbreeding to produce fertile offspring.

spirituality Concern with the sacred, as distinguished from material matters. In contrast to religion, spirituality is often individual rather than collective and does not require a distinctive format or traditional organization.

spiritual lineage A principle of leadership in which divine authority is passed down from a spiritual founding figure, such as a prophet or saint, to a chain of successors.

stabilizing selection Natural selection acting to promote stability rather than change in a population's gene pool.

state A political institution established to manage and defend a complex, socially stratified society occupying a defined territory.

stereoscopic vision Complete three-dimensional vision, or depth perception, from binocular vision and nerve connections that run from each eye to both sides of the brain, allowing nerve cells to integrate the images derived from each eye.

stratified In archaeology, a term describing sites where the remains lie in layers, one upon another.

stratified society A society in which people are hierarchically divided and ranked into social strata, or layers, and do not share equally in the basic resources that support income, status, and power.

stratigraphy In archaeology and paleoanthropology, the most reliable method of relative dating by means of strata.

strepsirrhine The subdivision within the primate order based on shared genetic characteristics; includes lemurs and lorises.

structural power Macro-level power that manages or re-structures political and economic relations within and among societies while simultaneously shaping or changing people's ideology (ideas, beliefs, and values); a compound of hard power and soft power.

structural violence Physical and/or psychological harm (including repression, environmental destruction, poverty, hunger, illness, and premature death) caused by impersonal, exploitative, and unjust social, political, and economic systems.

subculture A distinctive set of ideas, values, and behavior patterns by which a group within a larger society operates, while still sharing common standards with that larger society.

Sunda The combined landmass of the contemporary islands of Java, Sumatra, Borneo, and Bali that was continuous with mainland Southeast Asia at times of low sea levels corresponding to maximum glaciation.

superstructure A society's shared sense of identity and worldview. The collective body of ideas, beliefs, and values by which members of a society make sense of the world—its shape, challenges, and opportunities—and understand their place in it. This includes religion and national ideology.

suspensory hanging apparatus The broad powerful shoulder joints and muscles found in all the hominoids, allowing these large-bodied primates to hang suspended below the tree branches.

swidden farming An extensive form of horticulture in which the natural vegetation is cut, the slash is subsequently burned, and crops are then planted among the ashes; also known as *slash-and-burn cultivation*.

symbol A sound, gesture, mark, or other sign that is arbitrarily linked to something else and represents it in a meaningful way.

sympathetic magic Magic based on the principle that like produces like; also known as *imitative magic*.

syncretism The creative blending of indigenous and foreign beliefs and practices into new cultural forms.

syntax The patterns or rules by which words are arranged into phrases and sentences.

taboo Culturally prescribed avoidances involving ritual prohibitions, which, if not observed, lead to supernatural punishment.

tale A creative narrative that is recognized as fiction for entertainment but may also draw a moral or teach a practical lesson.

taphonomy The study of how bones and other materials come to be preserved in the earth as fossils.

taxonomy The science of classification.

technology Tools and other material equipment, together with the knowledge of how to make and use them.

tertiary scavenger In a food chain, the third in line to get something from a carcass after a predator killed the prey.

theory A coherent statement that provides an explanatory framework for understanding; an explanation or interpretation supported by a reliable body of data.

thrifty genotype A human genotype that may permit the efficient storage of fat to draw on in times of food shortage and conservation of glucose and nitrogen.

tonal language A language in which the sound pitch of a spoken word is an essential part of its pronunciation and meaning.

tool An object used to facilitate some task or activity. Although toolmaking involves intentional modification of the material of which it is made, tool use may involve objects either modified for some particular purpose or completely unmodified.

totemism The belief that people are related to particular animals, plants, or natural objects by virtue of descent from common ancestral spirits.

tradition Customary ideas and practices passed on from generation to generation, which in a modernizing society may form an obstacle to new ways of doing things.

transcription The process of conversion of instructions from DNA into RNA.

transgender A person who identifies with or expresses a gender identity that differs from the one that matches the person's sex at birth.

transition In a rite of passage, temporary isolation of the individual following separation and prior to incorporation into society.

translation In genetics, the process of conversion of RNA instructions into proteins.

treaty A contract or formally binding agreement between two or more groups that are independent and self-governing political groups such as tribes, chiefdoms, and states.

tribe In anthropology, the term for a range of kin-ordered groups that are politically integrated by some unifying factor and whose members share a common ancestry, identity, culture, language, and territory.

unilineal descent Descent traced exclusively through either the male or the female line of ancestry to establish group membership; sometimes called *unilateral descent*.

Upper Paleolithic The last part (10,000 to 40,000 years ago) of the Old Stone Age, featuring tool industries characterized by long, slim blades and an explosion of creative symbolic forms.

urgent anthropology Ethnographic research that documents endangered cultures; also known as *salvage ethnography*.

vegeculture The cultivation of domesticated root crops such as yams, manioc, and taro together in a single field, generally by planting cuttings instead of seeds.

verbal art Creative word use on display that includes stories, myths, legends, tales, poetry, metaphor, rhyme, chants, rap, drama, cant, proverbs, jokes, puns, riddles, and tongue twisters.

vertebrate An animal with a backbone, including fish, amphibians, reptiles, birds, and mammals.

vertical clinging and leaping Using the back legs to propel oneself from a vertical branch while rotating 180 degrees, enabling one to land facing a second vertical branch.

visual art Art created primarily for visual perception, ranging from etchings and paintings on various surfaces (including the human body) to sculptures and weavings made with an array of materials.

visual predation hypothesis An explanation for primate evolution that proposes that hunting behavior in tree-dwelling primates was responsible for their enhanced visual acuity and manual dexterity.

whistled speech An exchange of whistled words using a phonetic emulation of the sounds produced in spoken voice.

witchcraft Magical rituals intended to cause misfortune or inflict harm.

worldview The collective body of ideas members of a culture generally share concerning the ultimate shape and substance of their reality.

writing system A set of visible or tactile signs used to represent units of language in a systematic way.

xenophobia Fear or hatred of strangers or anything foreign.

Bibliography

Abu-Lughod, L. (1986). *Veiled sentiments: Honor and poetry in a Bedouin society.* Berkeley: University of California Press.

Abun-Nasr, J. M. (2007). *Muslim communities of grace: The Sufi brotherhoods in Islamic religious life.* New York: Columbia University Press.

"Accelerated Second Language Acquisition training held." (2015, August 21). *Red Lake Nation News.* http://www .redlakenationnews.com/story/2015/08/21/news/accelerated -second-language-acquisition-training-held/38464.html (retrieved November 18, 2015)

Aguirre Beltrán, G. (1974). Applied anthropology in Mexico. *Human Organization 33* (1), 1–6.

Al-Azm, A., Al-Kuntar, S., & Daniels, B. I. (2014, September 2). ISIS' antiquities sideline. *New York Times.* http:// www.nytimes.com/2014/09/03/opinion/isis-antiquities -sideline.html?_r=0 (retrieved November 3, 2015)

Alemseged, Z., Spoor, F., Kimbel, W. H., Bobe, R., Geraads, D., Reed, D., & Wynn, J. G. (2006, September 21). A juvenile early hominin skeleton from Dikika, Ethiopia. *Nature 443* (21), 296–301.

Alfonso-Durraty, M. (2012). Personal communication.

Allen, J. S., & Cheer, S. M. (1996). The non-thrifty genotype. *Current Anthropology 37* (5), 831–842.

Allen, T. (2006). *Trial justice: The International Criminal Court and the Lord's Resistance Army.* London & New York: Zed Books/International African Institute.

Alvard, M. S., & Kuznar, L. (2001). Deferred harvests: The transition from hunting to animal husbandry. *American Anthropologist 103* (2), 295–311.

Amábile-Cuevas, C. F., & Chicurel, M. E. (1993). Horizontal gene transfer. *American Scientist 81* (4), 332–341.

Ambrose, S. H. (2001). Paleolithic technology and human evolution. *Science 291* (5509), 1748–1753.

American Anthropological Association. (1998). Statement on "race." http://www.americananthro.org/ConnectWithAAA /Content.aspx?ItemNumber=2583 (retrieved January 16, 2016)

American Anthropological Association. (2007, November 6). Executive board statement on the Human Terrain System Project. http://s3.amazonaws.com/rdcms-aaa/files/production /public/FileDownloads/pdfs/pdf/EB_Resolution_110807.pdf (retrieved November 17, 2015)

American Psychological Association. (2015). Ethnic and racial minorities & socioeconomic status. *APA.org.* http:// www.apa.org/pi/ses/resources/publications/factsheet-erm.aspx (retrieved November 6, 2015)

Amnesty International. (2010, August 16). Afghan couple stoned to death by Taleban. *Amnesty International.* https:// www.amnesty.ie/news/afghan-couple-stoned-death-taleban (retrieved December 2, 2015)

Ancestry.com. (2012, July). President Obama descends from Africa's first slave. *Ancestry.com.* http://blogs.ancestry.com /cm/2012/10/08/obama-related-to-americas-first-slave/ (retrieved November 6, 2015)

Anderson, M. S. (2006, June). *The Allied Tribes Tsimshian of north coastal British Columbia: Social organization, economy and trade.* PhD dissertation, University of British Columbia. http:// faculty.arts.ubc.ca/menzies/documents/anderson.pdf (retrieved December 7, 2015)

"A new beginning." (2015, April 29). African Wildlife Foundation. https://www.awf.org/blog/new-beginning (retrieved October 6, 2015)

Anjum, T. (2006). Sufism in history and its relationship with power. *Islamic Studies 45* (2), 221–268.

Anyimadu, A. (2015, July 21). With Somali pirates, pay the ransom until there's a global consensus. *New York Times.* http://www.nytimes.com/roomfordebate/2013/08/07 /when-ransoms-pay-for-terrorism/with-somali-pirates-pay-the -ransom-until-theres-global-consensus (retrieved January 1, 2016)

Appadurai, A. (1990). Disjuncture and difference in the global cultural economy. *Theory, Culture & Society 7,* 295–310.

Appadurai, A. (1996). *Modernity at large: Cultural dimensions of globalization.* Minneapolis: University of Minnesota Press.

Arctic Monitoring Assessment Project (AMAP). (2003). *AMAP assessment 2002: Human health in the Arctic* (pp. xii–xiii, 22–23). Oslo: AMAP.

Arms Control Association. (2015). Nuclear weapons: Who has what at a glance. *Fact Sheets & Briefs.* www.armscontrol .org/factsheets/Nuclearweaponswhohaswhat (retrieved December 15, 2015)

Arnold, F., Kishor, S., & Roy, T. K. (2002). Sex-selective abortions in India. *Population and Development Review 28* (4), 759–785.

Artists for World Peace. (2015). The International Peace Belt. http://www.artistsforworldpeace.org/the-international -peace-belt/ (retrieved October 20, 2015)

Asante, E. A. (2015, June 25). A naturally occurring variant of the human prion protein completely prevents prion disease. *Nature 522.* doi: 10.1038/NATURE14510

Atari: Game over: The long road here. (2014, November 20). Directed by Zak Penn. 66 min. Fuel Entertainment.

"Aunty Beryl Carmichael talks about the Dreaming." (2015). *The making of modern Australia.* http://www.abc.net.au /tv/makingaustralia/educationextras/episode-four/clip-three .htm

Aureli, F., & de Waal, F. B. M. (2000). *Natural conflict resolution.* Berkeley: University of California Press.

"AWF testifies on trafficking of Africa's great apes." (2014, October 20). African Wildlife Foundation. https:// www.awf.org/news/awf-testifies-trafficking-africas-great-apes (retrieved October 5, 2015)

Ayalon, D. (1999). *Eunuchs, caliphs, and sultans: A study in power relationships.* Jerusalem: Mangess Press.

Babay, E. (2013, November 26). Census: Big decline in nuclear family. *Philly.com.* http://www.philly.com/philly/news/How _American_families_are_changing.html (retrieved December 29, 2015)

Babiker, M. A., Umran, K. A., Shahri, A. A., Madan, M. A., & Islam, F. (1996). Unnecessary deprivation of common food items in glucose-6-phosphate dehydrogenase deficiency. *Annals of Saudi Medicine 16* (4), 462–463.

Bailey, R. C., & Aunger, R., Jr. (1989). Net hunters vs. archers: Variations in women's subsistence strategies in the Ituri forest. *Human Ecology 17* (3), 273–297.

Baker, P. (Ed.). (1978). *The biology of high altitude peoples*. London: Cambridge University Press.

Balikci, A. (1970). *The Netsilik Eskimo*. Garden City, NY: Natural History Press.

Balter, M. (1998). Why settle down? The mystery of communities. *Science* (5393) *282*, 1442–1444.

Balter, M. (1999). A long season puts Çatalhöyük in context. *Science 286* (5441), 890–891.

Balter, M. (2001a). Did plaster hold Neolithic society together? *Science 294* (5550), 2278–2281.

Balter, M. (2001b). In search of the first Europeans. *Science 291* (5507), 1722–1725.

Balzer, M. M. (1981). Rituals of gender identity: Markers of Siberian Khanty ethnicity, status, and belief. *American Anthropologist 83* (4), 850–867.

Barkai, R., & Liran, R. (2008). Midsummer sunset at Neolithic Jericho. *Time and Mind: The Journal of Archaeology, Consciousness, and Culture 1* (3), 273–284.

Barnard, A. (2015, August 24). ISIS speeds up destruction of antiquities in Syria. *New York Times*. http://www.nytimes.com/2015/08/25/world/isis-accelerates-destruction-of-antiquities-in-syria.html?_r=0 (retrieved November 3, 2015)

Barnouw, V. (1985). *Culture and personality* (4th ed.). Homewood, IL: Dorsey Press.

Barrett, L., Gaynor, D., Rendall, D., Mitchell, D., & Henzi, S. P. (2004). Habitual cave use and thermoregulation in chacma baboons (*Papio hamadryas ursinus*). *Journal of Human Evolution 46* (2), 215–222.

Barth, F. (1962). Nomadism in the mountain and plateau areas of South West Asia. *The problems of the arid zone* (pp. 341–355). Paris: UNESCO.

Bates, D. G. (2001). *Human adaptive strategies: Ecology, culture, and politics* (2nd ed.). Boston: Allen & Bacon.

Bates, I., Fenton, C., Gruber, J., Lalloo, D., Medina Lara, A., Squire, S. B., Theobald, S., Thomson, R., & Tolhurst, R. (2004, May). Vulnerability to malaria, tuberculosis, and HIV/AIDS infection and disease: Part I: Determinants operating at individual and household level. *Lancet Infectious Diseases 4* (5), 267–277.

Bateson, G., & Mead, M. (1942). *Balinese character: A photographic analysis*. New York: New York Academy of Sciences.

Behrend, H. (1999). *Alice Lakwena and the Holy Spirits: War in northern Uganda 1986–97*. Oxford, UK: James Currey.

Behringer, W. (2004). *Witches and witch-hunts: A global history*. Cambridge, UK: Polity Press.

Benedict, R. (1934). *Patterns of culture*. Boston: Houghton Mifflin.

Bennett, M. R., et al. (2009). Early hominin foot morphology based on 1.5-million-year-old footprints from Ileret, Kenya. *Science 323* (5918), 1197–1201.

Bennett, R. L., et al. (2002, April). Genetic counseling and screening of consanguineous couples and their offspring: Recommendations of the National Society of Genetic Counselors. *Journal of Genetic Counseling 11* (2), 97–119.

Berger, L. R., et al. (2015, September 10). *Homo naledi*, a new species of the genus *Homo* from the Dinaledi Chamber, South Africa. *eLife*. http://elifesciences.org/content/4/e09560 (retrieved November 5, 2015)

Bernard, H. R. (2006). *Research methods in anthropology: Qualitative and quantitative approaches* (4th ed.). Walnut Creek, CA: AltaMira Press.

Betzig, L. (1989, December). Causes of conjugal dissolution: A cross-cultural study. *Current Anthropology 30* (5), 654–676.

Birch, E. L., & Wachter, S. M. (Eds.). (2011). *Global urbanization*. Philadelphia: University of Pennsylvania Press.

Birdsell, J. H. (1977). The recalibration of a paradigm for the first peopling of Greater Australia. In J. Allen, J. Golson, & R. Jones (Eds.), *Sunda and Sahul: Prehistoric studies in Southeast Asia, Melanesia, and Australia* (pp. 113–167). New York: Academic Press.

Blackless, M., Charuvastra, A., Derryck, A., Fausto-Sterling, A., Lauzanne, K., & Lee, E. (2000). How sexually dimorphic are we? Review and synthesis. *American Journal of Human Biology 12* (2), 151–166.

Blakey, M. (2003). *African Burial Ground Project*. Department of Anthropology, College of William & Mary.

Blakey, M. (2010, May). African Burial Ground Project: Paradigm for cooperation? *Museum International 62* (1-2), 61–68.

Blok, A. (1974). *The mafia of a Sicilian village 1860–1960*. New York: Harper & Row.

Blok, A. (1981). Rams and billy-goats: A key to the Mediterranean code of honour. *Man 16* (3), 427–440.

Blom, A., Cipolleta, C., Brunsting, A. M. H., & Prins, H. T. (2004). Behavioral responses of gorillas to habituation in the Dzanga-Ndoki National Park, Central African Republic. *International Journal of Primatology 25* (1), 179–196.

Blumenbach, J. F. (1795). *On the natural variety of mankind*. Germany: University of Göttingen.

Boas, F. (1909, May 28). Race problems in America. *Science 29* (752), 839–849.

Bodley, J. H. (2007). *Anthropology and contemporary human problems* (5th ed.). Lanham, MD: AltaMira Press.

Bodley, J. H. (2008). *Victims of progress* (5th ed.). Lanham, MD: AltaMira Press.

Boehm, C. (1987). *Blood revenge*. Philadelphia: University of Pennsylvania Press.

Boehm, C. (2000). The evolution of moral communities. *School of American Research, 2000 Annual Report*, 7.

Bogucki, P. (1999). *The origins of human society*. Oxford, UK: Blackwell Press.

Bongaarts, J. (1998, October 16). Demographic consequences of declining fertility. *Science 182* (5388), 419–420.

Borrell, B. (2012, October 8). Forensic anthropologist uses DNA to solve real-life murder mysteries in Latin America. *Scientific American*. http://www.scientificamerican.com/article/qa-forensic-anthropologist-mercedes-doretti/ (retrieved July 1, 2015)

Boshara, R. (2003, January/February). Wealth inequality: The $6,000 solution. *Atlantic Monthly*. https://www.theatlantic.com/past/docs/issues/2003/01/boshara.htm (retrieved December 8, 2015)

Boškovic, A. (Ed.). (2009). *Other people's anthropologies: Ethnographic practice on the margins*. Oxford, UK: Berghahn Books.

Bourgois, P., & Schonberg, J. (2009). *Righteous dopefiend: Homeless, addiction, and poverty in urban America*. Berkeley: University of California Press.

Brace, C. L. (2000). *Evolution in an anthropological view*. Walnut Creek, CA: AltaMira Press.

Bradford, P. V., & Blume, H. (1992). *Ota Benga: The Pygmy in the zoo*. New York: St. Martin's Press.

Braudel, F. (1979). *The structures of everyday life: Civilization and capitalism 15th–18th century* (vol. 1, pp. 163–167). New York: Harper & Row.

Brettell, C. B., & Sargent, C. F. (Eds.). (2000). *Gender in cross-cultural perspective* (3rd ed.). Upper Saddle River, NJ: Prentice-Hall.

Brigham. C. C. (1923). *A study of American intelligence*. Princeton, NJ: Princeton University Press.

Brigham. C. C. (1930, March). Intelligence tests of immigrant groups. *Psychological Reviews 37* (2), 158–165.

Brody, H. (1981). *Maps and dreams: Indians and the British Columbia frontier*. New York: Pantheon.

Brunet, M., et al. (2002). A new hominid from the Upper Miocene of Chad, Central Africa. *Nature 418* (6894), 145–151.

Buck, P. H. (1938). *Vikings of the Pacific*. Chicago: University of Chicago Press.

Buckley, C. (2015, October 29). China ends one-child policy, allowing families two children. *New York Times*. http://www.nytimes.com/2015/10/30/world/asia/china-end-one-child-policy.html?_r=0 (retrieved December 3, 2015)

Capps, R., McCabe, K., & Fix, M. (2011, June). *Diverse streams: Black African migration to the United States*. Migration Policy Institute. http://www.migrationpolicy.org/research/new-streams-black-african-migration-united-states (retrieved December 15, 2015)

Caraher, W., Guins, R., Reinhard, A., Rothaus, R., & Weber, B. (2014, August 7). Why we dug Atari. *The Atlantic*. http://www.theatlantic.com/technology/archive/2014/08/why-we-dug-atari/375702/ (retrieved October 30, 2015)

Carbonell, E., et al. (2008). The first hominin of Europe. *Nature 452* (7186), 465–469.

Cardarelli, F. (2003). *Encyclopedia of scientific units, weights, and measures. Their SI equivalences and origins*. London: Springer.

Carneiro, R. L. (1970, August 21). A theory of the origin of the state. *Science 169* (3947), 733–738.

Carneiro, R. L. (2003). *Evolutionism in cultural anthropology: A critical history*. Boulder, CO: Westview Press.

Caroulis, J. (1996). Food for thought. *Pennsylvania Gazette 95* (3), 16.

Carpenter, E. S. (1959). *Eskimo*. Toronto: University of Toronto Press.

Carpenter, E. S. (1968). We wed ourselves to the mystery: A study of tribal art. *Explorations 22*, 66–74.

Carroll, J. B. (Ed.). (1956). *Language, thought and reality: Selected writings of Benjamin Lee Whorf*. Cambridge, MA: MIT Press.

Cartmill, E. A., & Byrne, R. W. (2010). Semantics of primate gestures: Intentional meanings of orangutan gestures. *Animal Cognition 13* (6), 793–804.

Cartmill, M. (1974). Rethinking primate origins. *Science 184* (4135), 436–443.

Cartmill, M. (1998). The gift of gab. *Discover 19* (11), 64.

Cashdan, E. (2008). Waist-to-hip ratio across cultures: Trade-offs between androgen- and estrogen-dependent traits. *Current Anthropology 49* (6), 1099–1107.

Catford, J. C. (1988). *A practical introduction to phonetics*. Oxford, UK: Clarendon Press.

CBS News/AP. (2015, June 15). California governor signs strict new vaccination law. *CBS News*. http://www.cbsnews.com/news/california-governor-signs-strict-new-vaccination-law/ (retrieved February 3, 2016)

Centers for Disease Control and Prevention. (2015). Overweight and obesity, data and statistics. *CDC.gov*. www.cdc.gov/obesity/data/index.html (retrieved December 16, 2015)

Chagnon, N. A. (1988a, February 26). Life histories, blood revenge, and warfare in a tribal population. *Science 239* (4843), 985–992.

Chagnon, N. A. (1988b). *Yanomamö: The fierce people* (3rd ed.). New York: Holt, Rinehart & Winston.

Chagnon, N. A. (1990). On Yanomamö violence: Reply to Albert. *Current Anthropology 31* (2), 49–53.

Chambers, R. (1995). *Rural development: Putting the last first*. Englewood Cliffs, NJ: Prentice-Hall.

Chan, J. W. C., & Vernon, P. E. (1988). Individual differences among the peoples of China. In J. W. Berry (Ed.), *Human abilities in cultural context* (pp. 340–357). Cambridge, UK: Cambridge University Press.

Chance, N. A. (1990). *The Iñupiat and Arctic Alaska: An ethnography of development*. New York: Harcourt.

Chang, L. T. (2005, June 8). A migrant worker sees rural home in a new light. *Wall Street Journal*. http://www.wsj.com/articles/SB111818776639053518 (retrieved December 3, 2015)

Chase, C. (1998). Hermaphrodites with attitude. *Gay and Lesbian Quarterly 4* (2), 189–211.

Chicurel, M. (2001). Can organisms speed their own evolution? *Science 292* (5523), 1824–1827.

"Child soldiers global report 2008." (2009). *Child Soldiers International*. http://www.child-soldiers.org/global_report_reader.php?id=97 (retrieved December 9, 2015)

Claeson, B. (1994). The privatization of justice: An ethnography of control. In L. Nader (Ed.), *Essays on controlling processes* (pp. 32–64). Kroeber Anthropological Society Papers (no. 77). Berkeley: University of California Press.

Clark, E. E. (1966). *Indian legends of the Pacific Northwest*. Berkeley: University of California Press.

Clark, G. A. (2002). Neandertal archaeology: Implications for our origins. *American Anthropologist 104* (1), 50–67.

Clarke, R. J., & Tobias, P. V. (1995). Sterkfontein member 2 foot bones of the oldest South African hominid. *Science 269* (5223), 521–524.

Clay, J. W. (1996). What's a nation? In W. A. Haviland & R. J. Gordon (Eds.), *Talking about people* (2nd ed., pp. 188–189). Mountain View, CA: Mayfield.

Coco, L. E. (1994). Silicone breast implants in America: A choice of the official breast? In L. Nader (Ed.), *Essays on controlling processes* (pp. 103–132). Kroeber Anthropological Society Papers (no. 77). Berkeley: University of California Press.

Coe, S. D., & Coe, M. D. (1996). *The true history of chocolate*. New York: Thames & Hudson.

Cohen, J. (1997, July 18). Is an old virus up to new tricks? *Science 277* (5324), 312–313.

Cohen, J. (2009). Out of Mexico? Scientists ponder swine flu's origin. *Science 324* (5928), 700–702.

Cohen, M. N., & Armelagos, G. J. (Eds.). (1984). *Paleopathology at the origins of agriculture*. Orlando: Academic Press.

Colborn, T., Dumanoski, D., & Myers, J. P. (1996). Hormonal sabotage. *Natural History 105* (3), 42–47.

Colborn, T., Dumanoski, D., & Myers, J. P. (1997). *Our stolen future*. New York: Plume/Penguin Books.

Cole, J. W., & Wolf, E. R. (1999). *The hidden frontier: Ecology and ethnicity in an alpine valley* (with a new introduction). Berkeley: University of California Press.

Collier, J., & Collier, M. (1986). *Visual anthropology: Photography as a research method*. Albuquerque: University of New Mexico Press.

Collins, B. (2005). *The trouble with poetry*. New York: Random House.

Conard, N. J. (2009). A female figurine from the basal Aurignacian deposits of Hohle Fels Cave in southwestern Germany. *Nature 459* (7244), 248–252.

Cone, M. (2005). *Silent snow: The slow poisoning of the Arctic*. New York: Grove Press.

Conklin, B. A. (1997). Body paint, feathers, and VCRs: Aesthetics and authenticity in Amazonian activism. *American Ethnologist 24* (4), 711–737.

Conklin, B. A. (2002). Shamans versus pirates in the Amazonian treasure chest. *American Anthropologist 104* (4), 1050–1061.

Conklin, H. C. (1955). Hanunóo color categories. *Southwestern Journal of Anthropology 11* (4), 339–344.

Connelly, J. C. (1979). Hopi social organization. In A. Ortiz (Ed.), *Handbook of North American Indians: Southwest* (vol. 9, pp. 539–553). Washington, DC: Smithsonian Institution.

"Conversation with Laura Nader." (2000, November). *California Monthly*.

"Cookies, caches and cows: Translating technological terms throws up some unusual challenges." (2014, September 27). Minority languages. *The Economist*. http://www.economist.com/news/international/21620221-translating-technological-terms-throws-up-some-peculiar-challenges-cookies-caches-and-cows (retrieved November 18, 2015)

Coon, C. S. (1958). *Caravan: The story of the Middle East*. New York: Holt, Rinehart & Winston.

Coon, C. S. (1962). *The origins of races*. New York: Knopf.

Copeland, S. R., Sponheimer, M., de Ruiter, D. J., Lee-Thorp, J. A., Codron, D., le Roux, P. J., Grimes, V., & Richards, M. P. (2011, June 2). Strontium isotope evidence for landscape use by early hominins. *Nature 474* (7349), 76–78.

Coppa, A., Bondioli, L., Cucina, A., Frayer, D. W., Jarrige, C., Jarrige, J.-F., Quivron, G., Rossi, M., Vidale, M., & Macchiarelli, R. (2006, April 6). Paleontology: Early Neolithic tradition of dentistry. *Nature 440* (7085), 755–756.

Corriston, M. (2015, April 24). Diane Sawyer asks Bruce Jenner: "Are you a lesbian?" *People*. http://www.people.com/article/bruce-jenner-interview-attracted-women (retrieved November 20, 2015)

Crane, H. (2001). *Men in spirit: The masculinization of Taiwanese Buddhist nuns*. PhD dissertation, Brown University.

Cretney, S. (2003). *Family law in the twentieth century: A history*. New York: Oxford University Press.

Criminal Code of Canada, § 718.2(e).

Crocker, W. A., & Crocker, J. (2004). *The Canela: Kinship, ritual, and sex in an Amazonian tribe*. Belmont, CA: Wadsworth.

Crutzen, P. J., & Stoermer, E. F. (2000, May). The "Anthropocene." *IGBP Newsletter May* (41), 17–18. http://www.igbp.net/download/18.316f18321323470177580001401/NL41.pdf (retrieved November 2, 2015)

Crystal, D. (2002). *Language death*. Cambridge, UK: Cambridge University Press.

Crystal, D. (2012, July 26). Is control of English shifting away from British and American native speakers? *ELT Weekly 4* (29). http://eltweekly.com/2012/07/vol-4-issue-29-david-crystal-is-control-of-english-shifting-away-from-british-and-american-native-speakers/ (retrieved November 18, 2015)

Culotta, E., & Koshland, D. E., Jr. (1994). DNA repair works its way to the top. *Science 266* (5193), 1926–1929.

D'Adesky, A.-C. (2004). *Moving mountains: The race to treat global AIDS.* New York: Verso.

D'Anastasio, R., et al. (2013). Micro-biomechanics of the Kebara 2 hyoid and its implications for speech in Neanderthals. *PLoS One 8* (12), e82261.

Darwin, C. (1859). *On the origin of species, by means of natural selection, or the preservation of favoured races in the struggle for life.* London: John Murray.

Darwin, C. (1871). *The descent of man, and selection in relation to sex.* New York: Random House (Modern Library).

Darwin, C. (1887). *Autobiography.* Reprinted in *The life and letters of Charles Darwin* (1902). F. Darwin (Ed.), London: John Murray.

Davies, E. (2013, January 31). Young bonobos offer comforting hugs and sex. *BBC Nature News.* http://www.bbc.co.uk/nature /21199540 (retrieved October 9, 2015)

Davies, G. (2005). *A history of money from the earliest times to present day* (3rd ed.). Cardiff, UK: University of Wales Press.

Davies, J. B., Sandström, S., Shorrocks, A., & Wolff, E. N. (2008, February). *The world distribution of household wealth.* United Nations University, Discussion Paper No. 2008/03. https://www.wider.unu.edu/sites/default/files/dp2008-03.pdf (retrieved December 16, 2015)

Davies, S. G. (2007). *Challenging gender norms: Five genders among the Bugis in Indonesia.* Belmont, CA: Thomson Wadsworth.

Dawkins, R. (1976). *The selfish gene.* Oxford, UK: Oxford University Press.

Deary, I. J. (2001). *Intelligence: A very short introduction.* Oxford, UK: Oxford University Press.

Dediu, D., & Levinson, S. C. (2013). On the antiquity of language: The reinterpretation of Neanderthal linguistic capacities and its consequences. *Frontiers in Psychology 4*, 397. http://journal.frontiersin.org/article/10.3389/fpsyg.2013.00397 /full (retrieved November 18, 2015)

Deetz, J. (1977). *In small things forgotten: The archaeology of early American life.* Garden City, NY: Doubleday/Anchor.

de la Torre, S., & Snowden, C. T. (2009). Dialects in pygmy marmosets? Population variation in call structure. *American Journal of Primatology 71* (5), 333–342.

De Lauri, A. (2013, December 18). Think like an anthropologist: A conversation with Laura Nader. *Allegra Lab.* http://allegralaboratory.net/think-like-an-anthropologist-a-conversation-with-laura-nader/ (retrieved January 4, 2016)

del Carmen Rodríguez Martínez, M., et al. (2006). Oldest writing in the New World. *Science 313* (5793), 1610–1614.

del Castillo, B. D. (1963). *The conquest of New Spain* (translation and introduction by J. M. Cohen). New York: Penguin Books.

DeMello, M. (2000). *Bodies of inscription: A cultural history of the modern tattoo community.* Durham, NC: Duke University Press.

Des Bois, R. (2013, February 7). The end of the *Probo Koala.* http://www.robindesbois.org/english/probo_koala/the-end-of -the-probo-koala.html (retrieved December 15, 2015)

DeSilva, J. M. (2009). Functional morphology of the ankle and the likelihood of climbing in early hominins. *Proceedings of the National Academy of Sciences USA 106* (16), 6567–6572.

Dettwyler, K. A. (1994). *Dancing skeletons: Life and death in West Africa.* Long Grove, IL: Waveland Press.

Dettwyler, K. A. (1997, October). When to wean. *Natural History 106* (9), 49.

de Waal, F. B. M. (2000). Primates—A natural heritage of conflict resolution. *Science 289* (5478), 586–590.

de Waal, F. B. M. (2001a). *The ape and the sushi master.* New York: Basic Books.

de Waal, F. B. M. (2001b). Sing the song of evolution. *Natural History 110* (8), 77.

de Waal, F. B. M. (2014). *The bonobo and the atheist: In search of humanism among the primates.* New York: Norton.

de Waal, F. B. M., Kano, T., & Parish, A. R. (1998). Commentary on C. B. Stanford's "Social behavior of chimpanzees and bonobos." *Current Anthropology 39* (4), 408, 413.

Diamond, J. (1997). *Guns, germs, and steel.* New York: Norton.

Diamond, J. (2005). *Collapse: How societies choose to fail or succeed.* New York: Viking/Penguin Books.

DiMaggio, E. N., et al. (2015). Late Pliocene fossiliferous sedimentary record and the environmental context of early *Homo* from Afar, Ethiopia. *Science 347* (6228), 1355–1359.

Dissanayake, E. (2000). Birth of the arts. *Natural History 109* (10), 84–91.

Doherty, B. (2012, September 22). Poor children made to stitch sports balls in sweatshops. *Sydney Morning Herald.* http://www.smh.com.au/national/poor-children-made -to-stitch-sports-balls-in-sweatshops-20120921-26c0z.html (retrieved November 30, 2015)

Dorit, R. (1997). Molecular evolution and scientific inquiry, misperceived. *American Scientist 85*, 475.

Douglas, M. (1966). *Purity and danger: An analysis of concepts of pollution and taboo.* London: Routledge & Kegan Paul.

Dreger, A. D. (1998, May/June). "Ambiguous sex"—or ambivalent medicine? Ethical issues in the treatment of intersexuality. *Hastings Center Report 28* (3), 24–35.

Duffy, T. P. (2013, August/September). The Great Hunger and the Celtic gene. *Irish America.* http://irishamerica. com/2013/08/the-great-hunger-and-the-celitc-gene/ (retrieved October 24, 2015)

Dunbar, P. (2008, January 19). The pink vigilantes: The Indian women fighting for women's rights. *Dailymail.com.* http:// www.dailymail.co.uk/news/article-509318/The-pink-vigilantes -The-Indian-women-fighting-womens-rights.html (retrieved December 8, 2015)

Dunham, S. A. (2009). *Surviving against the odds: Village industry in Indonesia.* Durham, NC: Duke University Press.

Durant, J. C. (2000, April 23). Everybody into the gene pool: A geneticist tracks the evolution of Darwinian theory through the discoveries of modern science. *New York Times Book Review,* 11–12.

Dutta, S. (2015, June 12). 11 countries with the highest rates of eating disorders in the world. *Insider Monkey.* http://www .insidermonkey.com/blog/11-countries-with-the-highest-rates -of-eating-disorders-in-the-world-353060/ (retrieved December 6, 2015)

Dye, C. L. (2013, April 7). Do we need God to be moral? *ABC News.* http://abcnews.go.com/Technology/god-moral/story? id=18898993 (retrieved October 9, 2015)

"Eating disorders (most recent) by country." (2004). *Nationmaster.com.* www.nationmaster.com/graph/mor_eat_dis -mortality-eating-disorders (retrieved August 1, 2012)

Eaton, S. B., Konner, M., & Shostak, M. (1988). Stone-agers in the fast lane: Chronic degenerative diseases in evolutionary perspective. *American Journal of Medicine 84* (4), 739–749.

Ehrenberg, R. (2011, September 24). Financial world dominated by a few deep pockets. *Science News 180* (7). https://www.sciencenews.org/article/financial-world -dominated-few-deep-pockets (retrieved December 16, 2015)

Ehrlich, P. R., & Ehrlich, A. H. (2008). *The dominant animal: Human evolution and the environment.* Washington, DC: Island Press.

Eichenseher, T. (2012, August 25). Gibbons and opera singers use the same voice tools. *National Geographic.* http://news .nationalgeographic.com/news/2012/08/120823-gibbon-song -opera-singer-helium-science-environment/ (retrieved October 27, 2015)

El Guindi, F. (2004). *Visual anthropology: Essential method and theory.* Walnut Creek, CA: AltaMira Press.

Ellison, P. T. (2003). *On fertile ground: A natural history of human reproduction.* Cambridge, MA: Harvard University Press.

Embree, J. F. (1951). Raymond Kennedy, 1906–50. *Far Eastern Quarterly 10* (2), 170–172.

Enerdata: Global Energy Statistical Yearbook. (2015). Total energy consumption. *Enerdata.* https://yearbook .enerdata.net/ (retrieved January 20, 2016)

Ericcson. (2016). Ericsson mobility report, November 2015. *Ericsson.com.* http://www.ericsson.com/mobility-report (retrieved January 5, 2016)

Erickson, C. L. (2001). Pre-Columbian fish farming in the Amazon. *Expedition 43* (3), 7–8.

Erickson, P. A., & Murphy, L. D. (2003). *A history of anthropological theory* (2nd ed.). Peterborough, Ontario: Broadview Press.

Errington, F. K., & Gewertz, D. B. (2001). *Cultural alternatives and a feminist anthropology: An analysis of culturally constructed gender interests in Papua New Guinea.* Cambridge, UK, & New York: Cambridge University Press.

Esber, G. S. (1987). Designing Apache houses with Apaches. In R. M. Wulff & S. J. Fiske (Eds.), *Anthropological praxis: Translating knowledge into action* (pp. 187–196). Boulder, CO: Westview Press.

Estado Plurinacional de Bolivia. (2010, November). *Anteproyecto de Ley de la Madre Tierra por las Organizaciones Sociales del Pacto de Unidad.* http://www.redunitas.org/NINA_Anteproyectode%20ley%20madre%20tierra.pdf (retrieved December 13, 2015)

Evans-Pritchard, E. E. (1937). *Witchcraft, oracles, and magic among the Azande.* London: Oxford University Press.

Evans-Pritchard, E. E. (1951). *Kinship and marriage among the Nuer.* New York: Oxford University Press.

Fagan, B. M. (1995). *People of the earth* (8th ed.). New York: HarperCollins.

Falk, D. (1990). Brain evolution in *Homo:* The "radiator" theory. *Behavioral and Brain Sciences 13* (2), 333–344.

Falk, D. (2004). *Braindance: New discoveries about human origins* (revised and expanded edition). Gainesville: University Press of Florida.

Farmer, P. (1996). On suffering and structural violence: A view from below. *Daedalus 125* (1), 261–283.

Farmer, P. (2001). *Infections and inequalities: The modern plagues.* Berkeley: University of California Press.

Farmer, P. (2004, June). An anthropology of structural violence. *Current Anthropology 45* (3), 305–325.

Fausto-Sterling, A. (1993, March/April). The five sexes: Why male and female are not enough. *The Sciences 33* (2), 20–24.

Fausto-Sterling, A. (2012). *Sex/gender: Biology in a social world.* New York: Routledge.

Fedigan, L. M. (1986). The changing role of women in models of human evolution. *Annual Review of Anthropology 15,* 25–66.

Fedigan, L. M. (1992). *Primate paradigms: Sex roles and social bonds.* Chicago: University of Chicago Press.

Fernández-Carriba, S., & Loeches, A. (2001). Fruit smearing by captive chimpanzees: A newly observed food-processing behavior. *Current Anthropology 42* (1), 143–147.

Fernández Olmos, M., & Paravisini-Gebert, L. (2003). *Creole religion of the Caribbean: An introduction from Vodou and Santería to Obeah and Espiritismo.* New York: New York University Press.

Ferrie, H. (1997). An interview with C. Loring Brace. *Current Anthropology 38* (5), 851–869.

Field, L. W. (2004). Beyond "applied" anthropology. In T. Biolsi (Ed.), *A companion to the anthropology of American Indians* (pp. 472–479). Oxford, UK: Blackwell Press.

"5th report on children and armed conflict in the DR Congo highlights progress and concerns for the protection of children." (2014, July 21). UN Office of the Special Representative of the Secretary-General for Children and Armed Conflict. https://childrenandarmedconflict.un.org/press-release/5th-report-on-caac-rdc/ (retrieved December 9, 2015)

Films Media Group. (1981). *Witchcraft among the Azande: Disappearing world.* ITV Global Entertainment Limit.

Finnström, S. (2008). *Living with bad surroundings: War, history, and everyday moments in northern Uganda.* Durham, NC: Duke University Press.

Fisher, R., & Ury, W. L. (1991). *Getting to yes: Negotiating agreement without giving in* (2nd ed.). Boston: Houghton Mifflin.

Flynn, J. R. (2012). *Are we getting smarter? Rising IQ in the 21st century.* New York: Cambridge University Press.

Fogel, R., & Riquelme, M. A. (2005). *Enclave sojero, merma de soberanía y pobreza.* Asuncion: Centro de Estudios Rurales Interdisciplinarios.

Folger, T. (1993). The naked and the bipedal. *Discover 14* (11), 34–35.

Food and Agriculture Organization of the United Nations. (2013, October 1). Global hunger down, but millions still chronically hungry. *FAO.org.* http://www.fao.org/news/story/en/item/198105/icode/ (retrieved December 16, 2015)

Forde, C. D. (1968). Double descent among the Yakö. In P. Bohannan & J. Middleton (Eds.), *Kinship and social organization* (pp. 179–191). Garden City, NY: Natural History Press.

Forste, R. (2008). Prelude to marriage, or alternative to marriage? A social demographic look at cohabitation in the U.S. Working paper. *Social Science Research Network.* http://papers.ssrn.com/sol3/papers.cfm?abstract_id=269172 (retrieved December 3, 2015)

Fortune. (2015). Global 500. *Fortune.com.* http://fortune.com/global500/ (retrieved December 15, 2015)

Fouts, R. S., & Waters, G. S. (2001). Chimpanzee sign language and Darwinian continuity: Evidence for a neurology continuity for language. *Neurological Research 23* (8), 787–794.

Fowke, K. R., Nagelkerke, N. J., Kimani, J., Simonsen, J. N., Anzala, A. O., Bwayo, J. J., MacDonald, K. S., Ngugi, E. N., & Plummer, F. A. (1996). Resistance to HIV-1 infection among persistently seronegative prostitutes in Nairobi, Kenya. *Lancet 348* (9038), 1347–1351.

Fox, R. (1978). *The Tory Islanders: A people of the Celtic fringe.* Cambridge, UK: Cambridge University Press.

Franzen, J. L., et al. (2009). Complete primate skeleton from the middle Eocene of Messel in Germany: Morphology and paleobiology. *PLoS One 4* (5), e5723.

Frisch, R. (2002). *Female fertility and the body fat connection.* Chicago: University of Chicago Press.

Fu, Q., et al. (2014, October 23). Genome sequence of a 45,000-year-old modern human from western Siberia. *Nature 514* (7523), 445–450.

Fuller, C. J. (1976). *The Nayars today.* Cambridge, UK: Cambridge University Press.

Gandhi, M. K. (Ed.). (1999). *The collected works of Mahatma Gandhi* (vols. 8 & 19). New Delhi: Publications Division, Government of India.

Gebo, D. L., Dagosto, D., Beard, K. C., & Tao, Q. (2001). Middle Eocene primate tarsals from China: Implications for haplorhine evolution. *American Journal of Physical Anthropology 116* (2), 83–107.

Geertz, C. (1973). *The interpretation of culture.* London: Hutchinson.

Geller, P. (2015, October 8). Arabic the fastest-growing language in the U.S. *Dr. Rich Swier.* http://drrichswier.com/2015/10/08/arabic-the-fastest-growing-language-in-the-u-s/ (retrieved December 15, 2015)

Gellin, B. G., Maibach E. W., & Marcuse E. K. (2000, November). Do parents understand immunizations? A national telephone survey. *Pediatrics 106* (5), 1097–1102.

Gentry, E., Breuer, T., Hobaiter, C., & Byrne, R. W. (2009, May). Gestural communication of the gorilla (*Gorilla gorilla*): Repertoire, intentionality and possible origins. *Animal Cognition 12* (3), 527–546.

Gero, J. M., & Conkey, M. W. (Eds.). (1991). *Engendered archaeology: Women and prehistory.* New York: Wiley-Blackwell.

Gibbons, A. (1993, August 6). Where are "new" diseases born? *Science 261* (5122), 680–681.

Gibbons, A. (2001a). The riddle of coexistence. *Science 291* (5509), 1725–1729.

Gibbons, A. (2001b). Studying humans—and their cousins and parasites. *Science 292* (5517), 627–629.

Gibbs, J. L., Jr. (1983). [Interview]. *Faces of culture: Program 18.* Fountain Valley, CA: Coast Telecourses.

Ginsburg, F. D., Abu-Lughod, L., & Larkin, B. (Eds.). (2009). *Media worlds: Anthropology on new terrain.* Berkeley: University of California Press.

Girl #4708. (2010, June 15). A collection of one. *Hello Korea! Adoptee repatriation adventure. Wordpress.com.* https://gyopo.wordpress.com/2010/06/16/a-collection-of-one/ (retrieved November 5, 2015)

Gladney, D. C. (2004). *Dislocating China: Muslims, minorities and other subaltern subjects.* London: Hurst.

"Global information and advice on HIV & AIDS." (2015). *AVERT.org.* www.avert.org (retrieved December 14, 2015)

Goldacre, B. (2013). *Bad pharma: How drug companies mislead doctors and harm patients.* New York: Faber & Faber.

Goldsmith, M. L. (2005). Habituating primates for field study: Ethical considerations for great apes. In T. Turner (Ed.), *Biological anthropology and ethics: From repatriation to genetic identity* (pp. 49–64). New York: SUNY Press.

Goldsmith, M. L., Glick, J., & Ngabirano, E. (2006). Gorillas living on the edge: Literally and figuratively. In N. E. Newton-Fisher, H. Notman, J. D. Paterson, & V. Reynolds (Eds.), *Primates of western Uganda* (pp. 405–422). New York: Springer.

González, R. J. (2009). *American counterinsurgency: Human science and the human terrain.* Chicago: University of Chicago Press.

Goodall, J. (1986). *The chimpanzees of Gombe: Patterns of behavior.* Cambridge, MA: Belknap Press.

Goodall, J. (1990). *Through a window: My thirty years with the chimpanzees of Gombe.* Boston: Houghton Mifflin.

Goodenough, W. H. (1970). *Description and comparison in cultural anthropology.* Chicago: Aldine.

Goodman, M., Baileym, W. J., Hayasaka, K., Stanhope, M. J., Slightom, J., & Czelusniak, J. (1994). Molecular evidence on primate phylogeny from DNA sequences. *American Journal of Physical Anthropology 94* (1), 3–24.

Goodwin, R. (1999). *Personal relationships across cultures.* New York: Routledge.

Gordon, R. (2000). *Eating disorders: Anatomy of a social epidemic* (2nd ed.). New York: Wiley-Blackwell.

Gordon, R., Lyons, H., & Lyons, A. (Eds.). (2010). *Fifty key anthropologists.* New York: Routledge.

Gottlieb, A. (1998, March). Do infants have religion? The spiritual lives of Beng babies. *American Anthropologist 100* (1), 122–135.

Gottlieb, A. (2004a). *The afterlife is where we come from: The culture of infancy in West Africa.* Chicago: University of Chicago Press.

Gottlieb, A. (2004b). Babies as ancestors, babies as spirits: The culture of infancy in West Africa. *Expedition 46* (3), 13–21.

Gottlieb, A. (2006). Non-Western approaches to spiritual development among infants and young children: A case study from West Africa. In E. C. Roehlkepartain, P. E. King, L. Wagener, & P. L. Benson (Eds.), *The handbook of spiritual development in childhood and adolescence* (pp. 150–162). Thousand Oaks, CA: Sage.

Gough, E. K. (1959). The Nayars and the definition of marriage. *Journal of the Royal Anthropological Institute of Great Britain and Ireland 89* (1), 23–34.

Gould, S. J. (1983). *Hen's teeth and horses' toes.* New York: Norton.

Gould, S. J. (1991a). *Bully for brontosaurus.* New York: Norton.

Gould, S. J. (1991b). *The flamingo's smile: Reflections in natural history.* New York: Norton.

Gould, S. J. (1994). The geometer of race. *Discover 15* (11), 65–69.

Gould, S. J. (2000). The narthex of San Marco and the pangenetic paradigm. *Natural History 109* (6), 29.

Grant, M. (1916). *The passing of the great race.* New York: Scribner's.

Grass, R. N., Heckel, R., Puddu, M., Paunescu, D., & Stark, W. J. (2015). Robust chemical preservation of digital information on DNA in silica with error-correcting codes. *Angewandte Chemie International Edition 54* (8), 2552–2555.

Gray, P. B. (2004, May). HIV and Islam: Is HIV prevalence lower among Muslims? *Social Science & Medicine 58* (9), 1751–1756.

Gray, P. M., Krause, B., Atema, J., Payne, R., Krumhansl, C., & Baptista, L. (2001). The music of nature and the nature of music. *Science 291* (5501), 52–54.

Green, B. (1998). The institution of woman-marriage in Africa: A cross-cultural analysis. *Ethnology 37* (4), 395–412.

Green, R. E., et al. (2010, May 7). A draft sequence of the Neandertal genome. *Science 328* (5979), 710–722.

Greymorning, S. N. (2001). Reflections on the Arapaho Language Project or, when Bambi spoke Arapaho and other tales of Arapaho language revitalization efforts. In L. Hinton & K. Hale (Eds.), *The green book of language revitalization in practice* (pp. 287–300). New York: Academic Press.

Grimm, D. (2015, April 20). Judge's ruling grants legal right to research chimps. *Science.* http://news.sciencemag.org/plants -animals/2015/04/judge-s-ruling-grants-legal-right-research -chimps (retrieved October 9, 2015)

Grivetti, L. E. (2005). *From aphrodisiac to health food: A cultural history of chocolate. Karger Gazette* (68). Basel, Switzerland: S. Karger.

"Group to trek through Cameroon's Dja Reserve." (2015, April 23). *The Outdoor Wire.* http://www .theoutdoorwire.com/story/142976853179bz8qvb05h (retrieved October 27, 2015)

GSMA Intelligence. (2016). Definitive data and analysis for the mobile industry. *GSMAintelligence.com.* https:// gsmaintelligence.com/ (retrieved January 5, 2016)

Guillette, E. A., Meza, M. M., Aquilar, M. G., Soto, A. D., & Garcia, I. E. (1998, June). An anthropological approach to the evaluation of preschool children exposed to pesticides in Mexico. *Environmental Health Perspectives 106* (6), 347–353.

Haber, M. (2015, April 3). Should grown men use emoji? *New York Times.* http://www.nytimes.com/2015/04/03/fashion /mens-style/should-grown-men-use-emoji.html?_r=0 (retrieved October 9, 2015)

Hagerty, B. B. (2008, May 29). Some Muslims in U.S. quietly engage in polygamy. *NPR.* http://www.npr.org/templates /story/story.php?storyId=90857818 (retrieved December 2, 2015)

Haglund, W. D., Conner, M., & Scott, D. D. (2001). The archaeology of contemporary mass graves. *Historical Archaeology 35* (1), 57–69.

Hahn, R. A. (1992). The state of federal health statistics on racial and ethnic groups. *Journal of the American Medical Association 267* (2), 268–271.

Haile, M. M. (1966). Salt mining in Enderta. *Journal of Ethiopian Studies 4* (2), 127–136.

Hale, B. (2012, August 6). A Q&A with Sue Savage-Rumbaugh. *Harper's Magazine.* http://harpers.org/blog/2012/08/a-qa-with -sue-savage-rumbaugh/ (retrieved October 9, 2015)

Hall, E. T. (1963). A system for the notation of proxemic behavior. *American Anthropologist 65*, 1003–1026.

Hall, E. T. (1990). *The hidden dimension.* New York: Anchor.

Hallowell, A. I. (1955). The self in its behavioral environment. In A. I. Hallowell (Ed.), *Culture and experience* (pp. 75–110). Philadelphia: University of Pennsylvania Press.

Hamilton, J. (2006, July 8). A voluble visit with two talking apes. National Public Radio. July 8, 2006. http://www.npr .org/2006/07/08/5503685/a-voluble-visit-with-two-talking -apes (retrieved October 9, 2015)

Handwerk, B. (2005, March 8). King Tut not murdered violently, CT scans show. *National Geographic News.* news .nationalgeographic.com/news/2005/03/0308_050308 _kingtutmurder.html (retrieved October 10, 2015)

Hanson, A. (1989). The making of the Maori: Culture invention and its logic. *American Anthropologist 91* (4), 890–902.

Harcourt-Smith, W. E. H., & Aiello, L. C. (2004). Fossils, feet and the evolution of human bipedal locomotion. *Journal of Anatomy 204* (5), 403–416.

Harding, S. F. (2001). *The book of Jerry Falwell: Fundamentalist language and politics.* Princeton, NJ: Princeton University Press.

Hare, B., Brown, M., Williamson, C., & Tomasello, M. (2002, November). The domestication of social cognition in dogs. *Science 298* (5598), 1634–1636.

Harmand, S., et al. (2015). 3.3-million-year-old stone tools from Lomekwi 3, West Turkana, Kenya. *Nature 521* (7552), 310–315.

Harner, M. J. (Ed.). (1973). *Hallucinogens and shamanism.* New York: Oxford University Press.

Harner, M. J. (1980). *The way of the shaman: A guide to power and healing.* San Francisco: Harper & Row.

Harner, M. J. (1984). *The Jívaro: People of the sacred waterfalls.* Berkeley: University of California Press.

Harner, M. J. (2013). *Cave and cosmos: Shamanic encounters with spirits and heavens.* Berkeley: North Atlantic Books.

Harner, M. J., & Harner, S. (2000). Core practices in the shamanic treatment of illness. *Shamanism 13* (1&2), 19–30.

Harpending, H., & Cochran, G. (2002). In our genes. *Proceedings of the National Academy of Sciences USA 99* (1), 10–12.

Harris, M. (1979). *Cultural materialism: The struggle for a science of culture.* New York: Random House.

Harris, M. (1989). *Cows, pigs, wars, and witches: The riddles of culture.* New York: Vintage/Random House.

Harrison, F. V. (2014, December 14). Reflections on the AAA die-in as a symbolic space of social death. *Savage Minds: Notes and Queries in Anthropology.* http://savageminds.org/2014 /12/12/reflections-on-the-aaa-die-in-as-a-symbolic-space-of -social-death/ (retrieved November 6, 2015)

Harrison, K. D. (2002). Naming practices and ethnic identity in Tuva. http://www.swarthmore.edu/SocSci/dharris2 /Harrison-CLS(corrected).pdf (retrieved November 19, 2015)

Hart, D. (2006, April 21). Humans as prey. *Chronicle of Higher Education.* http://chronicle.com/article/Humans-as-Prey/23846 (retrieved October 14, 2015)

Hart, D., & Sussman, R. W. (2005). *Man the hunted: Primates, predators, and human evolution.* Boulder, CO: Westview Press.

Harvey, F. (2012, September 25). Trafigura lessons have not been learned, report warns. *The Guardian.* http://www .theguardian.com/environment/2012/sep/25/trafigura-lessons -toxic-waste-dumping (retrieved December 16, 2015)

Hasija, N. (2011, September 26). Rising suicide rates among rural women in China. *Institute of Peace and Conflict Studies.* http:// www.ipcs.org/article/china/rising-suicide-rates-among-rural -women-in-china-3466.html (retrieved December 13, 2015)

Hasnain, M. (2005, October 27). Cultural approach to HIV/ AIDS harm reduction in Muslim countries. *Harm Reduction Journal 2,* 23.

Haviland, W. A. (2002). Settlement, society and demography at Tikal. In J. Sabloff (Ed.), *Tikal.* Santa Fe: School of American Research.

Haviland, W. A. (2014). *Excavations in residential areas of Tikal—Nonelite groups without shrines.* Tikal Report 20B. Philadelphia: University of Pennsylvania Museum of Archaeology and Anthropology.

Haviland, W. A., & Power, M. W. (1994). *The original Vermonters: Native inhabitants, past and present* (2nd ed.). Hanover, NH: University Press of New England.

Hawkes, K., O'Connell, J. F., & Blurton Jones, N. G. (1997). Hadza women's time allocation, offspring provisioning, and the evolution of long postmenopausal life spans. *Current Anthropology 38* (4), 551–577.

Hawks, J. (2009). Ankles of the australopithecines. *John Hawks Weblog.* http://johnhawks.net/weblog/reviews/early_hominids /anatomy/desilva-2009-chimpanzee-climbing-talus.html (retrieved October 11, 2015)

Hayne, J. (2015, August 31). 3D printing used to show ancient Irish spear butt actually part of musical instrument. *ABC News.* http://www.abc.net.au/news/2015-09-01/ancient -artefact-thought-to-be-a-weapon-sheds-light-on-music/6740352 (retrieved November 3, 2015)

Hays, B. (2015, January 9). Ape in Argentina granted human rights. *UPI.* http://www.upi.com/Science_News/2015/01/09 /Ape-in-Argentina-granted-human-rights/8321420835451/ (retrieved November 12, 2015)

Heitzman, J., & Wordem, R. L. (Eds.). (2006). *India: A country study* (sect. 2, 5th ed.). Washington, DC: Federal Research Division, Library of Congress.

Helman, C. B. (2007). *Culture, health, and illness: An introduction for health professionals.* New York: Butterworth Heinemann Medical.

Henshilwood, C. S., d'Errico, F., van Niekerk, K. L., Coquinot, Y., Jacobs, Z., Lauritzen, S.-E., Menu, M., & Garcia-Moreno. R. (2011). A 100,000-year-old ochre-processing workshop at Blombos Cave, South Africa. *Science 334* (6053), 219–222.

Herdt, G. H. (1993). Semen transactions in Sambia culture. In D. N. Suggs & A. W. Mirade (Eds.), *Culture and human sexuality* (pp. 298–327). Pacific Grove, CA: Brooks/Cole.

Herek, D. (2015). Facts about homosexuality and mental health. *University of California, Davis, Psychology Department.* http://psychology.ucdavis.edu/rainbow/html/facts_mental _health.html (retrieved November 20, 2015)

Hernández, R. A. (2016). Feminist activist research and intercultural dialogues. In J. C. Nash & H. C. Buechler (Eds.), *Ethnographic collaborations in Latin America: The effects of globalization.* New York: Palgrave Macmillan.

Herszenhorn, D. M. (2015, April 24). Armenia, on day of rain and sorrow, observes 100th anniversary of genocide. *New York Times.* http://www.nytimes.com/2015/04/25/world/europe /armenian-genocide-100th-anniversary.html?_r=2 (retrieved January 5, 2016)

Higham, T., Basell, L., Jacobi, R., Wood, R., Ramsey, C. B., & Conard, N. J. (2012). Testing models for the beginnings of the Aurignacian and the advent of figurative art and music: The radiocarbon chronology of Geißenklösterle. *Journal of Human Evolution 62* (6), 664–676.

Hillman, G., Hedges, R., Moore, A., Colledge, S., & Pettitt, P. (2001). New evidence of Late Glacial cereal cultivation at Abu Hureyra on the Eurphrates. *The Holocene 11* (4), 383–393.

Hitchcock, R. K., & Enghoff, M. (2004). *Capacity-building of first people of the Kalahari, Botswana: An evaluation.* Copenhagen: International Work Group for Indigenous Affairs.

Hodder, I. (2006). *The leopard's tale: Revealing the mysteries of Çatalhöyük.* New York: Thames & Hudson.

Holmes, L. D. (2000). "Paradise Bent" (film review). *American Anthropologist 102* (3), 604–605.

Horst, H., & Miller, D. (2006). *The cell phone: An anthropology of communication.* New York: Berg.

Howell, N. (2010). *Life histories of the Dobe !Kung: Food, fatness, and well-being over the lifespan.* Berkeley: University of California Press.

Hsu, F. L. K. (1983). *Rugged individualism reconsidered: Essays in psychological anthropology.* Knoxville: University of Tennessee Press.

Human Rights Watch Report. (1999, March). Genocide in Rwanda: Leave none to tell the tale. *Humanrights.org.* https:// www.hrw.org/reports/1999/rwanda/ (retrieved December 9, 2015)

Hymes, D. (1974). *Foundations in sociolinguistics: An ethnographic approach.* Philadelphia: University of Pennsylvania Press.

Imanishi, K. (2002). *The world of living things.* In P. J. Asquith (Ed.) and H. Kawakatsu, S. Yagi, & H. Takasaki (Trans.), *A Japanese view of nature.* New York: Routlege. (orig. 1941)

Inoue, S., & Matsuzawa, T. (2007). Working memory of numerals in chimpanzees. *Current Biology 17* (23), 1004–1005.

Institute of Medicine. (2006). *Sleep disorders and sleep deprivation: An unmet public health problem.* Washington, DC: National Academies Press.

International Labour Organization. (2015). World report on child labour 2015: Paving the way for decent work for young people. *International Labour Organization.* http://www .ilo.org/ipec/Informationresources/WCMS_358969/lang--en /index.htm (retrieved November 30, 2015)

International Union for Conservation of Nature (IUCN). (2015). Red list of threatened species, 2015. http:// www.iucnredlist.org/ (retrieved October 5, 2015)

Internet World Stats: Usage and Population Statistics. (2015. June 30). Internet world users by language. *InternetWorldStats.com.* http://www.internetworldstats.com /stats7.htm (retrieved November 18, 2015)

IPCC. (2014). *Climate change 2014: Synthesis report.* Contribution of Working Groups I, II, and III to the Fifth Assessment Report of the Intergovernmental Panel on Climate Change. Core Writing Team: R. K. Pachauri and L. A. Meyer (Eds.). Geneva: IPCC. http://ipcc.ch/report/ar5/syr/ (retrieved December 15, 2015)

Itaborahy, P. L., & Zhu, J. (2014). State-sponsored homophobia: A world survey of laws: Criminalisation, protection and recognition of same-sex love. Brussels: International Lesbian, Gay, Bisexual, Trans and Intersex Association. http://old.ilga.org/Statehomophobia/ILGA _SSHR_2014_Eng.pdf (retrieved November 20, 2015)

"Italy–Germany verbal war hots up." (2003, July 9). Reuters. *Deccan Herald.* http://archive.deccanherald.com /deccanherald/july09/f4.asp (retrieved November 20, 2015)

Jacobs, S. E. (1994). Native American two-spirits. *Anthropology Newsletter 35* (8), 7.

Jacobsen, L. A., Mather, M., & Dupuis, G. (2012). Household change in the United States. *PRB.org.* http://www.prb.org/Publications/Reports/2012/us-household -change.aspx (retrieved December 22, 2015)

Jacoby, R., & Glauberman, N. (Eds.). (1995). *The Bell Curve debate.* New York: Random House.

"Jailhouse nation: How to make America's penal system less punitive and more effective." (2015, July 20). How to make America's penal system less punitive and more effective. *The Economist, 415* (8943), 11.

Jane Goodall Institute. (2015). Early days. http://www .janegoodall.org/janes-story (retrieved October 3, 2015)

"Jane Goodall on why retirement isn't factoring in to her future plans." (2015, April 17). Jane Goodall interviewed by Ivan Semeniuk. *The Globe and Mail.* http:// www.theglobeandmail.com/news/news-video/video-jane -goodall-on-why-retirement-isnt-factoring-in-to-her-future -plans/article24004092/ (retrieved October 9, 2015)

Johansen, B. E. (2002). The Inuit's struggle with dioxins and other organic pollutants. *American Indian Quarterly 26* (3), 479–490.

Johnson, D. (1991, April 9). Polygamists emerge from secrecy, seeking not just peace but respect. *New York Times.*

http://www.nytimes.com/1991/04/09/us/polygamists-emerge-from-secrecy-seeking-not-just-peace-but-respect.html?pagewanted=all (retrieved December 2, 2015)

Johnson, N. B. (1984). Sex, color, and rites of passage in ethnographic research. *Human Organization 43* (2), 108–120.

Jones, M. (2015, January 14). Why a generation of adoptees is returning to South Korea. *New York Times Magazine.* http://www.nytimes.com/2015/01/18/magazine/why-a-generation-of-adoptees-is-returning-to-south-korea.html?_r=3 (retrieved November 5, 2015)

Jones, S. (2005). Transhumance re-examined. *Journal of the Royal Anthropological Institute 11* (4), 841–842.

Kanti, S. T. (2014, March). Human rights and Dalits in India: A sociological analysis. *International Research Journal of Social Sciences 3* (3), 36–40.

Kantrowitz, B. (2010, August 16). Life without gender? *Newsweek.* http://www.newsweek.com/life-without-gender-71847 (retrieved November 20, 2015)

Kaplan, M. (2007, May 31). Upright orangutans point way to walking: Tree dwellers can benefit from standing on two legs. *Nature.*http://www.nature.com/news/2007/070528/full/news070528-8.html (retrieved October 14, 2015)

Kaplan, M. (2008, August 5). Almost half of primate species face extinction. *Nature.* http://www.nature.com/news/2008/080805/full/news.2008.1013.html (retrieved October 7, 2015)

Karavanić, I., & Smith, F. H. (2000). More on the Neanderthal problem: The Vindija case. *Current Anthropology 41* (5), 838–840.

Kaw, E. (1993). Medicalization of racial features: Asian American women and cosmetic surgery. *Medical Anthropology Quarterly 7* (1), 74–89.

Kawakatsu, H. (1999). Imanishi's view of the world. *Journal of Japanese Trade and Industry 18* (2), 15.

Kay, R. F., Fleagle, J. G., & Simons, E. L. (1981). A revision of the Oligocene apes of the Fayum Province, Egypt. *American Journal of Physical Anthropology 55* (3), 293–322.

Keesing, R. M. (1992). Some problems in the study of Oceanic religion. *Anthropologica 34* (2), 231–246.

Kehoe, A. (2000). *Shamans and religion: An anthropological exploration in critical thinking.* Prospect Heights, IL: Waveland Press.

Keiser, L. (1991). *Friend by day, enemy by night: Organized vengeance in a Kohistani community.* Fort Worth: Holt, Rinehart & Winston.

Kelly, T. L. (2006). *Sadhus: The great renouncers.* Photography exhibit, Indigo Gallery, Naxal, Kathmandu, Nepal. https://asianart.com/exhibitions/sadhus/index.html (retrieved November 20, 2015)

Kennickell, A. B. (2003, November). *A rolling tide: Changes in the distribution of wealth in the U.S., 1989–2001.* http://www.federalreserve.gov/pubs/feds/2003/200324/200324pap.pdf (retrieved December 8, 2015)

Kibii, J. M., Churchill, S. E., Schmid, P. Carlson, K. J., Reed, N. D., de Ruiter, D. J., & Berger, L. R. (2011, September 9). A partial pelvis of *Australopithecus sediba. Science 333* (6048), 1407–1411.

Kidder, T. (2003). *Mountains beyond mountains: The quest of Dr. Paul Farmer, a man who would cure the world.* New York: Random House.

Kirkpatrick, R. C. (2000). The evolution of human homosexual behavior. *Current Anthropology 41* (3), 385–413.

Kitchen, A., Miyamoto, M. M., & Mulligan, C. J. (2008). A three-stage colonization model for the peopling of the Americas. *PLoS One 3* (2), e1596.

Kluckhohn, C. (1944). *Navajo witchcraft.* Boston: Beacon Press.

Knauft, B. (1991). Violence and sociality in human evolution. *Current Anthropology 32* (4), 391–409.

Knight, C., Studdert-Kennedy, M., & Hurford, J. (Eds.). (2000). *The evolutionary emergence of language: Social function and the origins of linguistic form.* Cambridge, UK: Cambridge University Press.

Knothe, A. (2014, June 15). Seasonal workers in H2A guest worker program vital to central Mass. orchards. *Telegram.com.* http://www.telegram.com/article/20140615/NEWS/306159974 (retrieved December 18, 2015)

Koch, G. (2013). We have the song so we have the land: Song and ceremony as proof of ownership in Aboriginal and Torres Strait Islander land claims. *AIATSIS Research Discussion Paper 33.*

http://aiatsis.gov.au/sites/default/files/products/discussion_paper/we-have-the-song-so-we-have-the-land.pdf (retrieved January 13, 2016)

Konner, M., & Worthman, C. (1980, February 15). Nursing frequency, gonadal function, and birth spacing among !Kung hunter-gatherers. *Science 207* (4432), 788–791.

Kopenawa, D., & Albert, B. (2010). *La chute du ciel: Paroles d'un chaman Yanomami.* Paris: Terre Humaine, Plon.

Krajick, K. (1998, July 17). Greenfarming by the Incas? *Science 281* (5375), 322.

Kraybill, D. B. (2001). *The riddle of Amish culture.* Baltimore: Johns Hopkins University Press.

Kruger, J., Epley, N., Parker, J., & Ng, Z.-W. (2005, December). Egocentrism over e-mail: Can we communicate as well as we think? *Journal of Personality and Social Psychology 89* (6), 925–936.

Kunzig, R. (1999). A tale of two obsessed archaeologists, one ancient city, and nagging doubts about whether science can ever hope to reveal the past. *Discover 20* (5), 84–92.

Kuper, A. (2008). Changing the subject—about cousin marriage, among other things. *Journal of the Royal Anthropological Institute 14* (4), 717–735.

LaFont, S. (Ed.). (2003). *Constructing sexualities: Readings in sexuality, gender, and culture.* Upper Saddle River, NJ: Prentice-Hall.

Lai, C. S. L., Fisher, S. E., Hurst, J. A., Vargha-Khadem, F., & Monaco, A. P. (2001). A forkhead-domain gene is mutated in a severe speech and language disorder. *Nature 413* (6855), 519–523.

Lakoff, R. T. (2004). *Language and woman's place: Text and commentaries.* M. Bucholtz (Ed.), revised and expanded edition. New York: Oxford University Press.

Lamichhaney, S., et al. (2015, February 19). Evolution of Darwin's finches and their beaks revealed by genome sequencing. *Nature 518* (7539), 371–375.

Lampl, M., Velhuis, J. D., & Johnson, M. L. (1992). Saltation and stasis: A model of human growth. *Science 258* (5083), 801–803.

Landau, M. (1991). *Narratives of human evolution.* New Haven, CT, and London: Yale University Press.

Larsen, C. S. (2003, August 5). Equality for the sexes in human evolution? Early hominid sexual dimorphism and implications for mating systems and social behaviour. *Proceedings of the National Academy of Sciences USA 100* (16), 9103–9104.

Lasswell, H. D. (1990). *Politics: Who gets what, when, how.* Gloucester, MA: Peter Smith.

Lawler, A. (2001, June 29). Writing gets a rewrite. *Science 292* (5526), 2418–2420.

Leach, E. (1982). *Social anthropology.* Glasgow: Fontana Paperbacks.

Leakey, M. G., Spoor, F., Brown, F. H., Gathogo, P. N., Kiare, C., Leakey, L. N., & McDougall, I. (2001). New hominin genus from eastern Africa shows diverse middle Pliocene lineages. *Nature 410* (6827), 433–440.

Leavitt, G. C. (2013). Tylor vs. Westermarck: Explaining the incest taboo. *Sociology Mind 3* (1), 45–51.

Lee, R. B., & Daly, R. H. (1999). *The Cambridge encyclopedia of hunters and gatherers.* New York: Cambridge University Press.

Leff, L. (2014, January 31). "Preferred" pronouns gain traction at US colleges. *Huffington Post.* http://www.huffingtonpost.com/2013/12/01/preferred-pronouns-colleges_n_4367970.html (retrieved November 20, 2015)

Lehman, E. C., Jr. (2002, Fall). Women's path into ministry: Six major studies. *Pulpit & Pew Research Reports* (entire issue) *1.* https://www.faithandleadership.com/programs/spe/resources/ppr/women.pdf (retrieved December 10, 2015)

Lestel, D. (1998). How chimpanzees have domesticated humans: Towards an anthropology of human–animal communication. *Anthropology Today 14* (3), 12–15.

Leth, P. M. (2007). The use of CT scanning in forensic autopsy. *Forensic Science, Medicine, and Pathology 3* (1), 65–69.

Levine, N. E., & Silk, J. B. (1997, June). Why polyandry fails: Sources of instability in polyandrous marriages. *Current Anthropology 38* (3), 375–398.

Levine, R. A. (2007). Ethnographic studies of childhood: A historical overview. *American Anthropologist 109* (2), 247–260.

Lévi-Strauss, C. (1952). *Race and history.* Paris: UNESCO.

Lévi-Strauss, C. (1955). *Tristes tropiques.* Paris: Librarie Plon.

Lévi-Strauss, C. (1963). The sorcerer and his magic. In *Structural anthropology.* New York: Basic Books. (orig. 1958)

Lewin, R. (1993). Paleolithic paint job. *Discover 14* (7), 64–70.

Lewis, M. P., Simons, G. F., & Fennig, C. D. (Eds.). (2015). *Ethnologue: Languages of the world* (18th ed.). Dallas: SIL International. www.ethnologue.com (retrieved January 25, 2016)

Lewis-Williams, J. D. (1990). *Discovering southern African rock art.* Cape Town & Johannesburg: David Philip.

Lewontin, R. C. (1972). The apportionment of human diversity. In T. Dobzhansky et al. (Eds.), *Evolutionary biology* (pp. 381–398). New York: Plenum Press.

Lewontin, R. C., Rose, S., & Kamin, L. J. (1984). *Not in our genes.* New York: Pantheon.

Li, X., Harbottle, G., Zhang, J., & Wang, C. (2003). The earliest writing? Sign use in the seventh millennium BC at Jiahu, Henan Province, China. *Antiquity 77* (295), 31–44.

Lindenbaum, S. (2013). *Kuru sorcery: Disease and danger in the New Guinea highlands* (rev. 2nd ed.). New York: Routledge.

Lindstrom, L. (1993). *Cargo cult: Strange stories of desire from Melanesia and beyond.* Honolulu: University of Hawaii Press.

Linnekin, J. (1990). *Sacred queens and women of consequence: Rank, gender, and colonialism in the Hawaiian Islands.* Ann Arbor: University of Michigan Press.

Littlewood, R. (2004). Commentary: Globalization, culture, body image, and eating disorders. *Culture, Medicine, and Psychiatry 28* (4), 597–602.

Liu, J. (2007). *Gender and work in urban China: Women workers of the unlucky generation.* London: Routledge.

Livi-Bacci, M. (2012). *A concise history of world population* (5th ed.). Hoboken, NJ: Wiley-Blackwell.

Living Tongues. (2015). http://livingtongues.org/ (retrieved November 18, 2015)

Lloyd, C. B. (Ed.). (2005). *Growing up global: The changing transitions to adulthood in developing countries.* Washington, DC: National Academies Press.

Lock, A. (1980). *The guided reinvention of language.* New York: Academic Press.

Lock, M. (2001). *Twice dead: Organ transplants and the reinvention of death.* Berkeley: University of California Press.

Locke, J. (1999). *An essay concerning human understanding.* Pennsylvania State University. ftp://ftp.dca.fee.unicamp.br/pub/docs/ia005/humanund.pdf (retrieved November 19, 2015) (orig. 1690)

Lougheed, K. (2012, August 23). Helium reveals gibbon's soprano skill: Ape uses operatic techniques to be heard across the forest. *Nature.* http://www.nature.com/news/helium-reveals-gibbon-s-soprano-skill-1.11257 (retrieved October 26, 2015)

Louie, A. (2004). *Chineseness across borders: Renegotiating Chinese identities in China and the United States.* Durham and London: Duke University Press.

Lovejoy, C. O. (1981, January 23). The origin of man. *Science 211* (4480), 341–350.

Lucy, J. A. (1997). Linguistic relativity. *Annual Review of Anthropology 26,* 291–312.

Luhrmann, T. M. (2001). *Of two minds: An anthropologist looks at American psychiatry.* New York: Vintage.

Lurie, N. O. (1973). Action anthropology and the American Indian. In *Anthropology and the American Indian: A symposium.* San Francisco: Indian Historical Press.

Lyn, H., Russell, J. L., Leavens, D. A., Bard, K. A., Boysen, S. T., Schaeffer, J. A., & Hopkins, W. D. (2014). Apes communicate about absent and displaced objects: Methodology matters. *Animal Cognition 17* (1), 85–94.

MacCormack, C. P. (1977, Autumn). Biological events and cultural control. *Signs 3* (1), 93–100.

Maggioncalda, A. N., & Sapolsky, R. M. (2009). Disturbing behaviors of the orangutan. *Scientific American Mind 20* (3), 14–19.

Mair, L. (1957). *An introduction to social anthropology.* London: Oxford University Press.

Malinowski, B. (1945). *The dynamics of culture change.* New Haven, CT: Yale University Press.

Malinowski, B. (1961). *Argonauts of the western Pacific.* New York: Dutton.

Mann, C. C. (2002). The real dirt on rainforest fertility. *Science 297* (5583), 920–923.

Mann, C. C. (2005). *1491: New revelations of the Americas before Columbus.* New York: Knopf.

"Manyara Ranch Primary School." (2015). African Wildlife Foundation. http://www.awf.org/projects/manyara-ranch-primary-school (retrieved October 6, 2015)

Marcus, G. E. (1995). Ethnography in/of the world system: The emergence of multi-sited ethnography. *Annual Review of Anthropology 24* (1), 95–117.

Marcus, J., & Flannery, K. V. (1996). *Zapotec civilization: How urban society evolved in Mexico's Oaxaca Valley.* New York: Thames & Hudson.

Marks, J. (2000, May 12). 98% alike (what our similarity to apes tells us about our understanding of genetics). *Chronicle of Higher Education,* B7.

Marks, J. (2008a). Caveat emptor: Genealogy for sale. *Newsletter of the ESRC Genomics Network 7,* 22–23.

Marks, J. (2008b). Race: Past, present, and future. In B. Koenig, S. Lee, & S. Richardson (Eds.), *Revisiting race in a genomic age* (pp. 21–38). New Brunswick, NJ: Rutgers University Press.

Marshack, A. (1989). Evolution of the human capacity: The symbolic evidence. *Yearbook of physical anthropology* (vol. 32, pp. 1–34). New York: Alan R. Liss.

Marshall, E. (2001). Pre-Clovis sites fight for acceptance. *Science 291* (5509), 1730–1732.

Martin, E. (1994). *Flexible bodies: Tracking immunity in American culture from the days of polio to the age of AIDS.* Boston: Beacon Press.

Martin, E. (1999). Flexible survivors. *Anthropology News 40* (6), 5–7.

Martin, E. (2009). *Bipolar expeditions: Mania and depression in American culture.* Princeton, NJ: Princeton University Press.

Martorell, R. (1988). Body size, adaptation, and function. *GDP,* 335–347.

Marx, P. (2015, March 23). About face. *New Yorker.* http://www.newyorker.com/magazine/2015/03/23/about-face (retrieved November 5, 2015)

Mason, J. A. (1957). *The ancient civilizations of Peru.* Baltimore: Penguin Books.

Mathieu, C. (2003). *A history and anthropological study of the ancient kingdoms of the Sino-Tibetan borderland—Naxi and Mosuo.* New York: Mellen.

Matory, W. E., Jr. (Ed.). (1998). *Ethnic considerations in facial aesthetic surgery.* Philadelphia: Lippincott-Raven.

Matsuzawa, T., & McGrew, W. C. (2008, July 22). Kinji Imanishi and 60 years of Japanese primatology. *Current Biology 18* (14), R587–R591.

Mattei, U., & Nader, L. (2008). *Plunder: When the rule of law is illegal.* Malden, MA: Blackwell.

Max Planck Institute for Evolutionary Anthropology. (2014, February 14). Public data set: Denisova genome. https://aws.amazon.com/datasets/denisova-genome/ (retrieved October 22, 2015)

McCarthy, M. S., Jensvold, M. L., & Fouts, D. H. (2013, May). Use of gesture sequences in captive chimpanzee (*Pan troglodytes*) play. *Animal Cognition 16* (3), 471–481.

McCaskill, C., Lucas, C., Bayley, R., & Hill, J. (2012). *The hidden treasure of Black ASL: Its history and structure* (with contributions from J. C. Hill, R. Dummet-King, P. Baldwin, & R. Hogue). Washington, DC: Gallaudet University Press.

McCoy, T. (2014, July 21). Thousands of women, accused of sorcery, tortured and executed in Indian witch hunts. *Washington Post.* https://www.washingtonpost.com/news/morning-mix/wp/2014/07/21/thousands-of-women-accused-of-sorcery-tortured-and-executed-in-indian-witch-hunts/ (retrieved December 9, 2015)

McDermott, L. (1996). Self-representation in Upper Paleolithic female figurines. *Current Anthropology 37* (2), 227–275.

McDermott, R. (2011, April 1). Polygamy: More common than you think. *Wall Street Journal.* http://www.wsj.com/articles/SB10001424052748703806304576234551596322690 (retrieved December 2, 2015)

McDonald's. (2015). Our company: An iconic brand, moving toward the future. http://www.aboutmcdonalds.com/mcd/our_company.html (retrieved December 15, 2015)

McElroy, A., & Townsend, P. K. (2003). *Medical anthropology in ecological perspective.* Boulder, CO: Westview Press.

McFate, M. (2007). *Role and effectiveness of socio-cultural knowledge for counterinsurgency.* Alexandria, VA: Institute for Defense Analysis.

McGrew, W. C. (2000). Dental care in chimps. *Science 288* (5472), 1747.

McHenry, H. M., & Jones, A. L. (2006). Hallucial convergence in early hominids. *Journal of Human Evolution 50* (5), 534–539.

McKenna, J. J., Ball, H. L., & Gettler, L. T. (2007). Mother–infant cosleeping, breastfeeding and sudden infant death syndrome: What biological anthropology has discovered about normal infant sleep and pediatric sleep medicine. *Yearbook of Physical Anthropology 50* (Suppl. 45), 133–161.

McKenna, J. J., & McDade, T. (2005, June). Why babies should never sleep alone: A review of the co-sleeping controversy in relation to SIDS, bedsharing, and breastfeeding. *Pediatric Respiratory Reviews 6* (2), 134–152.

Mead, A. T. P. (1996). Genealogy, sacredness, and the commodities market. *Cultural Survival Quarterly 20* (2). https://www.culturalsurvival.org/ourpublications/csq/article/genealogy-sacredness-and-commodities-market (retrieved December 4, 2015)

Mead, M. (1961, June). Anthropology among the sciences. *American Anthropologist 63* (3), 475–482.

Mead, M. (1963). *Sex and temperament in three primitive societies* (3rd ed.). New York: Morrow. (orig. 1935)

Mead, M., & Métraux, R. (Eds.). (1953). *The study of culture at a distance.* Chicago: University of Chicago Press.

Medicine, B. (1994). Gender. In M. B. Davis (Ed.), *Native America in the twentieth century.* New York: Garland.

"Mercedes Doretti: Forensic Anthropologist." (2007, January 28). *MacArthur Foundation.* http://www.macfound.org/fellows/820/ (retrieved July 1, 2015)

Mellars, P. (2009). Archaeology: Origins of the female image. *Nature 459* (7244), 176–177.

Merkur, D. (1983). Breath-soul and wind owner: The many and the one in Inuit religion. *American Indian Quarterly 7* (3), 23–39.

Métraux, A. (1957). *Easter Island: A stone-age civilization of the Pacific.* New York: Oxford University Press.

Meyer, J. (2008). Typology and acoustic strategies of whistled languages: Phonetic comparison and perceptual cues of whistled vowels. *Journal of the International Phonetic Association 38* (1), 69–94.

Meyer, J., & Gautheron, B. (2006). Whistled speech and whistled languages. In K. Brown (Ed.), *Encyclopedia of language & linguistics* (2nd ed., vol. 13, pp. 573–576). Oxford, UK: Elsevier.

Meyer, J., Meunier, F., & Dentel, L. (2007, August). Identification of natural whistled vowels by non-whistlers. *Interspeech 2007* (pp. 1593–1596). Antwerp, Belgium.

Meyer, M., et al. (2014, January 16). A mitochondrial genome sequence of a hominin from Sima de los Huesos. *Nature 505* (7483), 403–406.

Mieth, A., & Bork, H.-R. (2010, February). Humans, climate or introduced rats—which is to blame for the woodland destruction on prehistoric Rapa Nui (Easter Island)? *Journal of Archaeological Science 37* (2), 417–426.

Miles, H. L. (1999). Symbolic communication with and by great apes. In S. T. Parker, R. W, Mitchell, & H. L. Miles (Eds.), *The mentality of gorillas and orangutans: Comparative perspectives* (pp. 197–210). Cambridge, UK: Cambridge University Press.

Miles, H. L. W. (1990). The cognitive foundations for reference in a signing orangutan. In S. T. Parker & K. R. Gibson (Eds.), *"Language" and intelligence in monkeys and apes: Comparative developmental perspectives* (pp. 511–539). Cambridge, UK: Cambridge University Press.

Miles, H. L. W. (1993). Language and the orang-utan: The old "person" of the forest. In P. Cavalieri & P. Singer (Eds.), *The great ape project* (pp. 45–50). New York: St. Martin's Press.

Millon, R. (1973). The Teotihuacán map, part 1: Text, vol. 1. In *Urbanization at Teotihuacán, México.* Austin: University of Texas Press.

Mintz, S. W. (1985). *Sweetness and power: The place of sugar in modern history.* New York: Viking.

Mitchell, W. E. (1973, December). A new weapon stirs up old ghosts. *Natural History Magazine,* 77–84.

Montagu, A. (1998). *Man's most dangerous myth: The fallacy of race* (6th ed.). Lanham, MD: Rowman & Littlefield.

Moore, J. (1998). Commentary on C. B. Stanford's "Social behavior of chimps and bonobos." *Current Anthropology 39* (4), 412–413.

Moran, B. (2013, August 20). Cracking down on counterfeit drugs. *PBS NOVA Next.* http://www.pbs.org/wgbh/nova/next/body/uncovering-counterfeit-medicines/ (retrieved December 15, 2015)

Morello, C. (2011, May 18). Number of long-lasting marriages in U.S. has risen, Census Bureau reports. *Washington Post.* https://www.washingtonpost.com/local/number-of-long-lasting-marriages-in-us-has-risen-census-bureau-reports/2011/05/18/AFO8dW6G_story.html (retrieved November 20, 2015)

Muckle, R. (2014, September/October). Punk archaeology and excavating video games in New Mexico. *Anthropology News 55* (9-10), 4–5.

Murphy, R. F. (1959). Social structure and sex antagonism. *Southwestern Journal of Anthropology 15,* 89–98.

Murthy, D. (2011). Emergent digital ethnographic methods for social research. In S. N. Hesse-Biber (Ed.), *The handbook of emergent technologies in social research* (pp. 158–179). New York: Oxford University Press.

Mydans, S. (2001, August 12). He's not hairy, he's my brother. *New York Times.* www.nytimes.com/2001/08/12/weekinreview/ideas-trends-he-s-not-hairy-he-s-my-brother.html (retrieved October 9, 2015)

Nabhan, G. P. (2004). *Why some like it hot: Food, genes, and cultural diversity.* Washington, DC: Island Press.

Nader, L. (1972). Up the anthropologist: Perspectives gained from studying up. In D. Hymes (Ed.), *Reinventing anthropology* (pp. 284–311). New York: Pantheon Books.

Nader, L. (Ed.). (1996). *Naked science: Anthropological inquiry into boundaries, power, and knowledge.* New York: Routledge.

Nader, L. (1997). Controlling processes: Tracing the dynamics of power. *Current Anthropology 38* (5), 711–737.

Nader, L. (2002). *The life of the law: Anthropological projects.* Berkeley: University of California Press.

Nader, L. (2013). *Culture and dignity: Dialogues between the Middle East and the West.* Chichester, UK: Wiley-Blackwell.

Nanda, S. (1992). Arranging a marriage in India. In P. R. DeVita (Ed.), *The naked anthropologist* (pp. 139–143). Belmont, CA: Wadsworth.

Nanda, S. (1999). *Neither man nor woman: The hijras of India.* Belmont, CA: Wadsworth.

Nash, J. (1976). Ethnology in a revolutionary setting. In M. A. Rynkiewich & J. P. Spradley (Eds.), *Ethics and anthropology: Dilemmas in fieldwork.* New York: Wiley.

Natadecha-Sponsal, P. (1993). The young, the rich and the famous: Individualism as an American cultural value. In P. R. DeVita & J. D. Armstrong (Eds.), *Distant mirrors: America as a foreign culture* (pp. 46–53). Belmont, CA: Wadsworth.

Natural Resources Defense Council. (2005, March 25). Healthy milk, healthy baby: Chemical pollution and mother's milk. www.nrdc.org/breastmilk/ (retrieved December 16, 2015)

Nazzal, M. (2005). *Nauru: An environment destroyed and international law.* http://www.lawanddevelopment.org/docs/nauru.pdf (retrieved February 4, 2016)

Nekaris, K. A. I., Shepherd, C. R., Starr, C. R., & Nijman, V. (2010). Exploring cultural drivers for wildlife trade via an ethnoprimatological approach: A case study of slender and slow lorises (*Loris* and *Nycticebus*) in South and Southeast Asia. *American Journal of Primatology 71,* 1–10.

Nettle, B. (2005). *The study of ethnomusicology: Thirty-one issues and concepts.* Chicago: University of Illinois Press.

Nichols, J. (2008). Language spread rates as indicators of glacial-age peopling of the Americas. *Current Anthropology 49* (6), 1109–1117.

Nietschmann, B. (1987). The third world war. *Cultural Survival Quarterly 11* (3), 1–16.

Njoku, J. E. E. (1990). *The Igbos of Nigeria: Ancient rites, changes and survival* (African Studies, vol. 14). New York: Edwin Mellen Press.

Noack, T. (2001). Cohabitation in Norway: An accepted and gradually more regulated way of living. *International Journal of Law, Policy, and the Family 15* (1), 102–117.

Normile, D. (1998). Habitat seen as playing larger role in shaping behavior. *Science 279* (5356), 1454–1455.

Nunney, L. (1998). Are we selfish, are we nice, or are we nice because we are selfish? *Science 281* (5383), 1619–1621.

Nye, J. (2002). *The paradox of American power: Why the world's only superpower can't go it alone.* New York: Oxford University Press.

O'Barr, W. M., & Conley, J. M. (1993). When a juror watches a lawyer. In W. A. Haviland & R. J. Gordon (Eds.), *Talking about people* (2nd. ed., pp. 42–45). Mountain View, CA: Mayfield.

Oboler, R. S. (1980, January). Is the female husband a man? Woman/woman marriage among the Nandi of Kenya. *Ethnology 19* (1), 69–88.

O'Carroll, E. (2008, June 27). Spain to grant some human rights to apes. *Christian Science Monitor.* www.csmonitor.com /Environment/Bright-Green/2008/0627/spain-to-grant-some -human-rights-to-apes (retrieved October 9, 2015)

Oceans Beyond Piracy: One Earth Future Foundation. (2015). *The economic cost of Somali piracy 2011.* http:// oceansbeyondpiracy.org/publications/economic-cost-somali -piracy-2011 (retrieved December 9, 2015)

Offiong, D. A. (1999). Traditional healers in the Nigerian health care delivery system and the debate over integrating traditional and scientific medicine. *Anthropological Quarterly 72* (3), 118–130.

Okonjo, K. (1976). The dual-sex political system in operation: Igbo women and community politics in midwestern Nigeria. In N. Hafkin & E. Bay (Eds.), *Women in Africa.* Stanford, CA: Stanford University Press.

Oiarzabal, P. J., & Reips, U.-D. (2012). Migration and diaspora in the age of information and communication technologies. *Journal of Ethnic and Migration Studies 38* (9), 1333–1338.

Olivier, J. G. J., Janssens-Maenhout, G., Muntean, M., & Peters, J. A. H. W. (2014). *Trends in global CO_2 emissions: 2014 report.* The Hague: PBL Netherlands Environmental Assessment Agency. http://edgar.jrc.ec.europa.eu/news_docs /jrc-2014-trends-in-global-co2-emissions-2014-report-93171 .pdf (retrieved December 15, 2015)

O'Mahoney, K. (1970). The salt trail. *Journal of Ethiopian Studies 8* (2), 147–153.

Otte, M. (2000). On the suggested bone flute from Slovenia. *Current Anthropology 41* (2), 271–272.

Ottenheimer, M. (1996). *Forbidden relatives: The American myth of cousin marriage.* Champaign: University of Illinois Press.

"Our lives in our hands." (1986). DER documentary, produced by H. E. L. Prins & K. Carter. http://www.der.org /films/our-lives-in-our-hands.html (retrieved January 2, 2016)

Oxfam International. (2016). An economy for the 1%. *Oxfam.org.* https://www.oxfam.org/en/research/economy-1 (retrieved January 20, 2016)

Parés, J. M., Pérez-González, A, Weil, A. B., & Arsuaga, J. L. (2000). On the age of the hominid fossils at the Sima de los Huesos, Sierra de Atapuerca, Spain: Paleomagnetic evidence. *American Journal of Physical Anthropology 111* (4), 451–461.

"Patrick E. McGovern: Biomolecular Archaeology Project." (2015). *Penn Museum.* http://www.penn.museum /sites/biomoleculararchaeology/?page_id=143 (retrieved July 1, 2015)

Patterson, F. G. P., & Gordon, W. (2002). Twenty-seven years of Project Koko and Michael. In B. Galdikas, N. E. Briggs, L. K. Sheeran, G. L. Shapiro, & J. Goodall (Eds.), *All apes great and small: Chimpanzees, bonobos, and gorillas* (vol. 1, pp. 165–176). New York: Kluwer Academic.

Pearlman, J. (2015, November 6). University returns 40,000-year-old Mungo Man to Australia's Aborigines. *The Telegraph.* http://www.telegraph.co.uk/news/worldnews /australiaandthepacific/australia/11979442/University-returns -40000-year-old-Mungo-Man-to-Australias-Aborigines.html (retrieved November 21, 2015)

Pearson, V., Phillips, M. R., He, F., & Ji, H. (2002). Attempted suicide among young rural women in the People's Republic of China: Possibilities for prevention. *Suicide and Life-Threatening Behavior 32* (4), 359–369.

Pease, T. (2000, Spring). Taking the third side. *Andover Bulletin 93* (3), 24.

Pei, M. (2015, November 12). Calamity of China's one-child policy should never again be allowed anywhere. *Daily Nation.* http://www.nation.co.ke/oped/Opinion/Chinas-one-child -policy-should-never-be-allowed-anywhere/-/440808/2952622 /-/cihumjz/-/index.html (retrieved December 3, 2015)

Pelto, P. J. (1973). *The snowmobile revolution: Technology and social change in the Arctic.* Menlo Park, CA: Cummings.

Petersen, J. B., Neves, E. G, & Heckenberger, M. J. (2001). Gift from the past: *Terra preta* and prehistoric Amerindian occupation in Amazonia. In C. McEwan, C. Barreto, & E. G. Neves (Eds.), *Unknown Amazon: Culture in nature in ancient Brazil* (pp. 86–105). London: British Museum Press.

Pew Research Center, Forum on Religion & Public Life. (2011, January). The future of the global Muslim population: Projections for 2010–2030. *Pewforum.org.* http://www .pewforum.org/files/2011/01/FutureGlobalMuslimPopulation -WebPDF-Feb10.pdf (retrieved December 10, 2015)

Pew Research Center, Forum on Religion & Public Life. (2012, October 9). "Nones" on the rise. *Pewforum.org.* http:// www.pewforum.org/2012/10/09/nones-on-the-rise/ (retrieved December 10, 2015)

Pew Research Center, Hispanic Trends. (2015, September 28). Statistical portrait of the foreign-born population in the United States, 1960–2013. Authored by A. Brown & R. Stepler. *Pewhispanic.org.* http://www.pewhispanic.org/2015/09/28 /statistical-portrait-of-the-foreign-born-population-in-the -united-states-1960-2013-key-charts/ (retrieved December 25, 2015)

Piantadosi, C. A. (2003). *The biology of human survival: Life and death in extreme environments.* New York: Oxford University Press.

Pickering, T. R., Dirks, P. H. G. M., Jinnah, Z., de Ruiter, D. J., Churchill, S. E., Herries, A. I. R., Woodhead, J. D., Hellstrom, J. C., & Berger, L. R. (2011). *Australopithecus sediba* at 1.977 ma and implications for the origins of the genus *Homo. Science 333* (6048), 1421–1423.

Pickering, T. R., White, T. D., & Toth, N. (2000). Brief communication: Cutmarks on a Plio-Pleistocene hominid from Sterkfontein, South Africa. *American Journal of Physical Anthropology 111* (4), 579–584.

Pike, A. W. G., et al. (2012). U-series dating of Paleolithic art in 11 caves in Spain. *Science 336* (6087), 1409–1413.

Pink, S. (2001). *Doing visual ethnography: Images, media, and representation in research.* Thousand Oaks, CA: Sage.

Pinker, S. (1994). *The language instinct: How the mind creates language.* New York: William Morrow.

Plattner, S. (1989). Markets and market places. In S. Plattner (Ed.), *Economic anthropology.* Stanford, CA: Stanford University Press.

Pohl, M. E. D., Pope, K. O., & von Nagy, C. (2002). Olmec origins of Mesoamerican writing. *Science 298* (5600), 1984–1987.

Pollan, M. (2001). *The botany of desire: A plant's-eye view of the world.* New York: Random House.

Pollan, M. (2008). *In defense of food: An eater's manifesto.* New York: Penguin Books.

Pollock, N. J. (1995). Social fattening patterns in the Pacific— the positive side of obesity. A Nauru case study. In I. DeGarine & N. J. Pollock (Eds.), *Social aspects of obesity* (pp. 87–109). London: Routledge.

Population Media Center. (2015). PMC in Nigeria. *PopulationMediaCenter.org.* https://www.populationmedia.org /location/nigeria/ (retrieved November 10, 2015)

Pospisil, L. (1963). *The Kapauku Papuans of West New Guinea.* New York: Holt, Rinehart & Winston.

Powdermaker, H. (1939). *After freedom: A cultural study in the Deep South.* New York: Viking.

Poyatos, F. (2002). *Nonverbal communication across disciplines* (3 vols.). Amsterdam: John Benjamins.

Preston, D. (2015, March 2). Exclusive: Lost city discovered in the Honduran rain forest. *National Geographic.* http://news .nationalgeographic.com/2015/03/150302-honduras-lost-city -monkey-god-maya-ancient-archaeology/ (retrieved November 3, 2015)

Price, D. H. (2011). How the CIA and Pentagon harnessed anthropological research during the Second World War and Cold War with little critical notice. *Journal of Anthropological Research 67* (3), 333–356.

Prins, H. E. L. (1994). Neo-traditions in Native communities: Sweat lodge and Sun Dance among the Micmac today. In W. Cowan (Ed.), *Proceedings of the 25th Algonquian conference* (pp. 383–394). Ottawa: Carleton University Press.

Prins, H. E. L. (1996). *The Mi'kmaq: Resistance, accommodation, and cultural survival.* New York: Harcourt Brace.

Prins, H. E. L. (1998). Book review of Schuster, C., & Carpenter, E. *American Anthropologist 100* (3), 841.

Prins, H. E. L. (2002). Visual media and the primitivist perplex: Colonial fantasies and indigenous imagination in North America. In F. Ginsburg, L. Abu-Lughod, & B. Larkin (Eds.), *Media worlds: Anthropology on new terrain* (pp. 58–74). Berkeley: University of California Press.

Prins, H. E. L., & Krebs, E. (2007). Vers un monde sans mal: Alfred Métraux, un anthropologue à l'UNESCO (1946–1962). In *60 ans d'histoire de l'UNESCO: Actes du colloque international, Paris, 16–18 novembre 2005* (pp. 115–125). Paris: UNESCO.

Prins, H. E. L., & McBride, B. (2012). Upside down: Arctic realities & indigenous art (museum review essay). *American Anthropologist 114* (2), 359–364.

PR Newswire. (2014, December 7). The 116th Canton Fair—"Innovation keeps international buyers coming back for more." *PRNewswire.com.* http://www.prnewswire.com/news-releases/the-116th-canton-fair---innovation-keeps-international-buyers-coming-back-for-more-300005821.html (retrieved November 30, 2015)

Pruetz, J. D., & Bertolani, P. (2007, March 6). Savanna chimpanzees, *Pan troglodytes verus*, hunt with tools. *Current Biology 17* (5), 412–417.

Pruetz, J. D., Bertolani, P., Ontl, K. B., Lindshield, S., Shelley, M., & Wessling, E. G. (2015, April 15). New evidence on the tool-assisted hunting exhibited by chimpanzees (*Pan troglodytes verus*) in a savannah habitat at Fongoli, Sénégal. *Royal Society Open Science.* http://rsos.royalsocietypublishing.org/content/2/4/140507 (retrieved October 9, 2015)

Quinn, N. (2005). Universals of child rearing. *Anthropological Theory 5* (4), 477–516.

Radcliffe-Brown, A. R. (1930, October–December). The social organization of Australian tribes. *Oceana 1* (3), 322–341.

Raffaele, P. (2006, November). Speaking bonobo. *Smithsonian Magazine.* http://www.smithsonianmag.com/science-nature/speaking-bonobo-134931541/?no-ist=&page=1 (retrieved October 9, 2015)

Raghavan, M., et al. (2015, August 21). Genomic evidence for the Pleistocene and recent population history of Native Americans. *Science 349* (6250), aab3884.

Ralston, C., & Thomas, N. (Eds.). (1987). Sanctity and power: Gender in Polynesian history. *Journal of Pacific History* (special issue) *22* (3–4).

Ramos, A. R. (1987). Reflecting on the Yanomami: Ethnographic images and the pursuit of the exotic. *Current Anthropology 2* (3), 284–304.

Rapp, R. (1999). *Testing women, testing the fetus: The social impact of amniocentesis in America.* New York: Routledge.

Rappaport, R. A. (1969). Ritual regulation of environmental relations among a New Guinea people. In A. P. Vayda (Ed.), *Environment and cultural behavior* (pp. 181–201). Garden City, NY: Natural History Press.

Rasmussen, M., et al. (2011, October 7). An Aboriginal Australian genome reveals separate human dispersals into Asia, *Science 334* (6052), 94–98.

Rasmussen, M., et al. (2015, July 23). The ancestry and affiliations of Kennewick Man. *Nature 523* (7561), 455–458.

Rathje, W., & Murphy, C. (2001). *Rubbish!: The archaeology of garbage.* Tucson: University of Arizona Press.

Rathke, L. (1989). To Maine for apples. *Salt Magazine 9* (4), 24–47.

Recer, P. (1998, February 16). Apes shown to communicate in the wild. *Burlington Free Press,* 12A.

Reich, D., et al. (2010, December 23). Genetic history of an archaic hominin group from Denisova Cave in Siberia. *Nature 468* (7327), 1053–1060.

Reich, D., et al. (2012). Reconstructing Native American population history. *Nature 488* (7411), 370–374.

Relethford, J. H. (2001). Absence of regional affinities of Neandertal DNA with living humans does not reject multiregional evolution. *American Journal of Physical Anthropology 115* (1), 95–98.

Relethford, J. H., & Harpending, H. C. (1994). Craniometric variation, genetic theory, and modern human origins. *American Journal of Physical Anthropology 95* (3), 249–270.

Reynolds, V. (1994). Primates in the field, primates in the lab: Morality along the ape–human continuum. *Anthropology Today 10* (2), 3–5.

Ribeiro, G. L. (2009). Non-hegemonic globalizations: Alternative transnational processes and agents. *Anthropological Theory 9* (3), 297–329.

Ridley, M. (1999). *Genome: The autobiography of a species in 23 chapters.* New York: HarperCollins.

Rightmire, G. P. (1998). Evidence from facial morphology for similarity of Asian and African representatives of *Homo erectus. American Journal of Physical Anthropology 106* (1), 61–85.

Ritzer, G. (1983). The McDonaldization of society, *Journal of American Culture 6* (1), 100–107.

Robarge, D. (2014, December 15). From landfill to Smithsonian collections: "E.T. the Extraterrestrial" Atari 2600. *Smithsonian.* http://americanhistory.si.edu/blog/landfill-smithsonian-collections-et-extra-terrestrial-atari-2600-game (retrieved October 30, 2015)

Robben, A. C. G. M. (2007). Fieldwork identity: Introduction. In A. C. G. M. Robben & J. A. Sluka (Eds.), *Ethnographic fieldwork: An anthropological reader.* Malden, MA: Blackwell Press.

Robben, A. C. G. M., & Sluka, J. A. (Eds.). (2007). *Ethnographic fieldwork: An anthropological reader.* Malden, MA: Blackwell Press.

Roberts, A. I., Roberts, S. G. B., & Vick, S.-J. (2014, March). The repertoire and intentionality of gestural communication in wild chimpanzees. *Animal Cognition 17* (2), 317–336.

Rochat, P. (2001). Origins of self-concept. In G. Bremner & A. Fogel (Eds.), *Blackwell handbook of infant development* (pp. 191–212). Malden, MA: Blackwell Press.

Rochat, P. (2010). Emerging self-concept. In J. G. Bremner & T. D. Wachs (Eds.), *The Wiley-Blackwell handbook of infant development* (2nd ed., vol. 1, pp. 320–344). Malden, MA: Wiley-Blackwell.

Rogers, J. (1994). Levels of the genealogical hierarchy and the problem of hominoid phylogeny. *American Journal of Physical Anthropology 94* (1), 81–88.

Rosaldo, M. Z. (1980). *Knowledge and passion: Ilongot notions of self & social life* (Cambridge Studies in Cultural Systems). New York: Cambridge University Press.

Roscoe, W. (1991). *Zuni man-woman.* Albuquerque: University of New Mexico Press.

Rose, S. (2009, February 12). Darwin 200: Should scientists study race and IQ? NO: Science and society do not benefit. *Nature 457* (7231), 786–788.

Rudel, T. K., Bates, D., & Machinguiashi, R. (2002). Ecologically noble Amerindians? Cattle ranching and cash cropping among Shuar and colonists in Ecuador. *Latin American Research Review 37* (1), 144–159.

Rupert, J. L., & Hochachka, P. W. (2001). The evidence for hereditary factors contributing to high altitude adaptation in Andean natives: A review. *High Altitude Medicine & Biology 2* (2), 235–256.

Sacks, O. (1998). *Island of the colorblind.* New York: Knopf.

Sahlins, M. (1972). *Stone Age economics.* Chicago: Aldine.

Salzman, P. C. (1967, April). Political organization among nomadic peoples. *Proceedings of the American Philosophical Society 111* (2), 115–131.

Samenow, J. (2015, June 10). India's hellish heatwave, in hindsight. *Washington Post.* https://www.washingtonpost.com/news/capital-weather-gang/wp/2015/06/10/indias-hellish-heat-wave-in-hindsight/ (retrieved December 15, 2015)

Sanday, P. R. (1981). *Female power and male dominance: On the origins of sexual inequality.* Cambridge, UK: Cambridge University Press.

Sangree, W. H. (1965). The Bantu Tiriki of western Kenya. In J. L. Gibbs, Jr. (Ed.), *Peoples of Africa* (pp. 69–72). New York: Holt, Rinehart & Winston.

Sanjek, R. (1990). On ethnographic validity. In R. Sanjek (Ed.), *Field notes.* Ithaca, NY: Cornell University Press.

Sapolsky, R. (2002). *A primate's memoir: Love, death, and baboons in East Africa.* New York: Vintage.

Sarich, V. M., & Wilson, A. C. (1967). Immunological time scale for human evolution. *Science 158* (3805), 1200–1203.

Saturno, W. A., Stuart, D., Aveni, A. F., & Rossi, F. (2012, May 11). Ancient Maya astronomical tables from Xultan, Guatemala. *Science 336* (6082), 714–717.

Savage-Rumbaugh, S., & Lewin, R. (1994). *Kanzi: The ape at the brink of the human mind.* New York: Wiley.

Scally, A., et al. (2012). Insights into hominid evolution from the gorilla genome sequence. *Nature 483* (7388), 169–175.

Scelfo, J. (2015, February 3). A university recognizes a third gender: Neutral. *New York Times.* http://www.nytimes.com/2015/02/08/education/edlife/a-university-recognizes-a-third-gender-neutral (retrieved November 20, 1015)

Schaeffer, S. B., & Furst, P. T. (Eds.). (1996). *People of the peyote: Huichol Indian history, religion, and survival.* Albuquerque: University of New Mexico Press.

Scheper-Hughes, N. (2003, May 10). Keeping an eye on the global traffic in human organs. *Lancet 361* (9369), 1645–1648.

Schilling, C. (2012, August 20). Love, American style: Polygamy gets sizzle. *WorldNetDaily.* http://www.wnd.com/2012/08/love-american-style-polygamy-gets-sizzle/ (retrieved December 2, 2015)

Schilt, K., & Westbrook, L. (2009, August). Doing gender, doing heteronormativity: "Gender normals," transgender people, and the social maintenance of heterosexuality. *Gender & Society 23* (4), 440–464.

Schoepfle, M. (2001). Ethnographic Resources Inventory and the National Park Service. *Cultural Resource Management 24* (5), 7–8.

Schuster, C., & Carpenter, E. (1996). *Patterns that connect: Social symbolism in ancient and tribal art.* New York: Abrams.

Schuster, G., Smits, W., & Ullal, J. (2008). *Thinkers of the jungle: The orangutan report.* Potsdam, Germany: H. F. Ullmann.

Scully, T. (2008, June 25). Online anthropology draws protest from aboriginal group. *Nature 453* (7199), 1155.

Seiffert, E. R., Perry, J. M. G., Simons, E. L., & Boyer, D. M. (2009). Convergent evolution of anthropoid-like adaptations in Eocene adapiform primates. *Nature 461,* 1118–1121.

Selinger, B. (2007). The Navajo, psychosis, Lacan, and Derrida. *Texas Studies in Literature and Language 49* (1), 64–100.

Semenov, S. A. (1964). *Prehistoric technology.* New York: Barnes & Noble.

Senut, B., Pickford, M., Gommery, D., Mein, P., Cheboi, K., & Coppens, Y. (2001). First hominid from the Miocene (Lukeino Formation, Kenya). *C. R. Academy of Sciences, Paris 332* (2), 137–144.

Seyfarth, R. M., Cheney, D. L., & Marler, P. (1980a). Monkey responses to three different alarm calls: Evidence for predator classification and semantic communication. *Science 210* (4471), 801–803.

Seyfarth, R. M., Cheney, D. L., & Marler, P. (1980b). Vervet monkey alarm calls: Semantic communication in a free-ranging primate. *Animal Behavior 28* (4), 1070–1094.

Shabi, R. (2015, July 3). Looted in Syria—and sold in London: The British antiques shops dealing in artefacts smuggled by Isis. *The Guardian.* http://www.theguardian.com/world/2015/jul/03/antiquities-looted-by-isis-end-up-in-london-shops (retrieved November 3, 2015)

Sharma, N. (2012). Women and the stigma of witch-hunting. In S. Murtaza (Ed.), *Understanding women's issues—a feminist standpoint* (pp. 118–129). Germany: Lambert Academic Publishing.

Sharp, G. (1973). *The politics of nonviolent action.* Boston: Extending Horizons Books, Porter Sargent Publishers.

Sharp, G. (2010). *From dictatorship to democracy: A conceptual framework for liberation* (4th ed.). East Boston: Einstein Institution.

Sharpe, K., & Van Gelder, L. (2006). Evidence of cave marking by Paleolithic children. *Antiquity 80* (310), 937–947.

Sheets, P. D. (1993). Dawn of a New Stone Age in eye surgery. In R. J. Sharer & W. Ashmore (Eds.), *Archaeology: Discovering our past.* Palo Alto, CA: Mayfield.

Shook, J. R., et al. (Eds.). (2004). *Dictionary of modern American philosophers, 1860–1960.* Bristol, UK: Thoemmes Press.

Shostak, M. (2000). *Nisa: The life and words of a !Kung woman.* Cambridge, MA: Harvard University Press.

Shreeve, J. (1994). Terms of estrangement. *Discover 15* (11) http://discovermagazine.com/1994/nov/termsofestrangem445 (retrieved November 6, 2015)

Shreeve, J. (1995). *The Neandertal enigma: Solving the mystery of modern human origins.* New York: William Morrow.

Silverstein, J. (2012). Bonds beyond blood: DNA testing and refugee family resettlement. *Anthropology News 53* (4), 11.

Simons, R. C., & Hughes, C. C. (Eds.). (1985). *The culture-bound syndromes: Folk illnesses of psychiatric and anthropological interest.* New York: Springer.

Simpson, S. (1995, April). Whispers from the ice. *Alaska,* 23–28.

Simpson, S. W., Quade, J., Levin, N. E., Butler, R., Dupont-Nivet, G., Everett, M., & Semaw, S. (2008). A female *Homo erectus* pelvis from Gona, Ethiopia. *Science 322* (5904), 1089–1092.

Sivak, M., & Schoettle, B. (2012, July–August). Accounting for climate in ranking countries' carbon dioxide emissions. *American Scientist 100* (4), 278.

Skoglund, P., Mallick, S., Bortolini, M. C., Chennagiri, N., Hünemeier, T., Petzl-Erler, M. L., Salzano, F. M., Patterson, N., & Reich, D. (2015, September 3). Genetic evidence for two founding populations of the Americas. *Nature 525* (7567), 104–110.

Slocum, S. (1975). Woman the gatherer: Male bias in anthropology. In R. R. Reiter (Ed.), *Toward an anthropology of women.* New York: Monthly Review Press.

Sluka, J. A. (2007). Fieldwork relations and rapport: Introduction. In A. C. G. M. Robben & J. A. Sluka (Eds.), *Ethnographic fieldwork: An anthropological reader.* Malden, MA: Blackwell Press.

Small, M. F. (1997). Making connections. *American Scientist 85,* 502–504.

Smedley, A. (2007). *Race in North America: Origin and evolution of a worldview.* Boulder, CO: Westview Press.

Smith, W. W. (2009). *China's Tibet: Autonomy or assimilation?* Lanham, MD: Rowman & Littlefield.

Society for Applied Anthropology. (2006). Michael Horowitz: 2006 Bronislaw Malinowski Award recipient. *SFAA.net.* https://www.sfaa.net/index.php/about/prizes/distinguished-awards/malinowski-award/recipients/2006/ (retrieved January 16, 2016)

Songok, E. M., et al. (2012). Microarray analysis of HIV resistant female sex workers reveal a gene expression signature pattern reminiscent of a lowered immune activation state. *PLoS One 7* (1), e30048.

Spencer, R. F. (1984). North Alaska Coast Eskimo. In D. Damas (Ed.), *Arctic: Handbook of North American Indians* (vol. 5, pp. 320–337). Washington, DC: Smithsonian Institution Press.

Stacey, J. (1990). *Brave new families.* New York: Basic Books.

Stanton, G. H. (1998). The 8 stages of genocide. *Genocide Watch.* http://www.genocidewatch.org/aboutgenocide/8stagesofgenocide.html (retrieved November 6, 2015)

Statistica. (2016). Leading social networks worldwide as of November 2015, ranked by number of active users (in millions). *Statistica.com.* http://www.statista.com/statistics/272014/global-social-networks-ranked-by-number-of-users/ (retrieved January 5, 2016)

Stedman, H. H., Kozyak, B. W., Nelson, A., Thesier, D. M., Su, L. T., Low, D. W., Bridges, C. R., Shrager, J. B., Minugh-Purvis, N., & Mitchell, M. A. (2004, March 24). Myosin gene mutation correlates with anatomical changes in the human lineage. *Nature 428* (6981), 415–418.

Stein, A. D., & Lumey, L. H. (2000, August). The relationship between maternal and offspring birth weights after maternal prenatal famine exposure: The Dutch Famine Birth Cohort Study. *Human Biology 72* (4), 641–654.

Stein, R., & St. George, D. (2009, May 14). Unwed motherhood increases sharply in U.S., report shows. *Washington Post.* http://www.washingtonpost.com/wp-dyn/content/article/2009/05/13/AR2009051301628.html (retrieved December 3, 2015)

Stenseth, N. C., & Voje, K. L. (2009). Easter Island: Climate change might have contributed to past cultural and societal changes. *Climate Research 39,* 111–114.

Stern, M. J. (2015, July 31). Judge denies legal personhood to chimps—for now. *Slate.com.* www.slate.com/articles/news_and_politics/jurisprudence/2015/07/habeas_corpus_an_personhood_for_chimps_judge_barbara_jaffe_gives_liberty.html (retrieved October 9, 2015)

Stewart, F. A., & Pruetz, J. D. (2013). Do chimpanzee nests serve an anti-predatory function? *American Journal of Primatology 75* (6), 593–604.

Stockholm International Peace Research Institute. (2015, April 13). Trends in world military expenditure, 2014. Authored by S. Perlo-Freeman, A. Fleurant, W. D. Wezeman, & S. T. Wezeman. *SIPRI.org*. http://books.sipri.org/product _info?c_product_id=496# (retrieved December 15, 2015)

Stolberg, S. G. (2011, February 16). Shy U.S. intellectual created playbook used in a revolution. *New York Times*. http://www.nytimes.com/2011/02/17/world/middleeast/17sharp .html?_r=0 (retrieved December 9, 2015)

Stone, L. (2005). *Kinship and gender: An introduction* (3rd ed.). Boulder, CO: Westview Press.

Strengthening Indigenous Languages and Cultures (SILC). (2015). http://www.nsilc.org/ (retrieved November 18, 2015).

Strier, K. (1993, March). Menu for a monkey. *Natural History 102* (3), 42.

Strier, K. (2015, March 3). An interview with Karen Strier. *Anthropology TV 2014*. American Anthropological Association. http://www.youtube.com/watch?v=n4kQFqlE_jo (retrieved October 9, 2015)

Strum, S. C. (2010, February). The development of primate raiding: Implications for management and conservation. *International Journal of Primatology 31* (1), 133–156.

Strum, S., & Mitchell, W. (1987). Baboon models and muddles. In W. Kinsey (Ed.), *The evolution of human behavior: Primate models*. Albany: SUNY Press.

Suárez-Orozoco, M. M., Spindler, G., & Spindler, L. (1994). *The making of psychological anthropology, II*. Fort Worth: Harcourt Brace.

Suwa, G., Kono, R. T., Katoh, S., Asfaw, B., & Beyene, Y. (2007, August 23). A new species of great ape from the late Miocene epoch in Ethiopia. *Nature 448* (7156), 921–924.

"Sweden adds gender-neutral pronoun to dictionary." (2015, March 28). *The Guardian*. http://www.theguardian.com /world/2015/mar/24/sweden-adds-gender-neutral-pronoun-to -dictionary?CMP=share_btn_fb (retrieved November 20, 2015)

Sweeney, S. (2013, June 26). NIH director accepts recommendations to retire research chimpanzees. Jane Goodall Institute. http://www.janegoodall.org/media/news/nih-director -accepts-recommendations-retire-research-chimpanzees (retrieved October 9, 2015)

Tamm, E., et al. (2007, September 5). Beringian standstill and spread of Native American founders. *PLoS One 2* (9), e829.

Tanner, N., & Zihlman. A. (1976). Women in evolution. Part I: Innovation and selection in human origins. *Signs 1* (3), 585–608.

Tapper, M. (1999). *In the blood: Sickle-cell anemia and the politics of race*. Philadelphia: University of Pennsylvania Press.

Terashima, H. (1983). Mota and other hunting activities of the Mbuti archers: A socio-ecological study of subsistence technology. *African Studies Monograph (Kyoto) 3*, 71–85.

Thompson, C. (2014, August 12). Poverty for Hinduism's Dalit caste. *Borgen Magazine*. http://www.borgenmagazine.com /poverty-hinduisms-dalit-caste/ (retrieved December 8, 2015)

Thompson, K. (2012, July 30). Obama's purported link to early-American slave is latest twist in family tree. *Washington Post*. https://www.washingtonpost.com/politics/purported -obama-link-to-first-american-slave-is-latest-twist-in-presidents -family-tree/2012/07/30/gJQAYuG1KX_story.html (retrieved November 6, 2015)

Thorpe, S. K. S., Holder, R. L., & Crompton, R. H. (2007). Origin of human bipedalism as an adaptation for locomotion on flexible branches. *Science 316* (5829), 1328–1331.

Timmons, H., & Kumar, H. (2009, July 2). Indian court overturns gay sex ban. *New York Times*. http://www.nytimes .com/2009/07/03/world/asia/03india.html (retrieved December 28, 2015)

Toth, N., Schick, K. D., Savage-Rumbaugh, E. S., Sevcik, R. A., & Rumbaugh, D. M. (1993). Pan the tool-maker: Investigations in the stone tool-making and tool-using capabilities of a bonobo (*Pan paniscus*). *Journal of Archaeological Science 20* (1), 81–91.

Tracy, J. L., & Matsumoto, D. (2008). The spontaneous expression of pride and shame: Evidence for biologically innate nonverbal displays. *Proceedings of the National Academy of Sciences USA 105* (33), 11655–11660.

Trevathan, W., Smith, E. O., & McKenna, J. J. (Eds.). (1999). *Evolutionary medicine*. London: Oxford University Press.

Trifonov, V., Khiabanian, H., Greenbaum, B., & Rabadan, R. (2009, April 30). The origin of the recent swine influenza: A (H1N1) virus infecting humans. *Eurosurveillance 14* (17). http://www.eurosurveillance.org/ViewArticle. aspx?ArticleId=19193 (retrieved October 26, 2015)

Trocolli, R. (2006). *Elite status and gender: Women leaders in chiefdom societies of the southeastern U.S.* PhD dissertation, University of University of Florida.

Trouillot, M. R. (1996). Culture, color, and politics in Haiti. In S. Gregory & R. Sanjek (Eds.), *Race*. New Brunswick, NJ: Rutgers University Press.

Tsai, S.-S. H. (1996). *The eunuchs in the Ming dynasty*. Albany: SUNY Press.

Turnbull, C. M. (1961). *The forest people*. New York: Simon & Schuster.

Turnbull, C. M. (1983a). *The human cycle*. New York: Simon & Schuster.

Turnbull, C. M. (1983b). *Mbuti Pygmies: Change and adaptation*. New York: Holt, Rinehart & Winston.

"20 years of IGCP: Lessons learned in mountain gorilla conservation." (2011). International Gorilla Conservation Programme. http://www.igcp.org/wp-content/themes/igcp /docs/pdf/IGCPLessonsLearned_English_web.pdf (retrieved October 27, 2015)

Tylor, E. B. (1871). *Primitive culture: Researches into the development of mythology, philosophy, religion, language, art and customs*. London: Murray.

Umar, U. (2008). *Dancing with spirits: Negotiating bissu subjectivity through Adat*. Department of Religious Studies, University of Colorado, Boulder. Ann Arbor, MI: ProQuest.

UNAIDS. (2014). AIDS info, 2014. *UNAIDS.org*. http://aidsinfo .unaids.org/ (retrieved December 2, 2015)

UN Environment Programme. (2015). *Global waste management outlook*. https://www.iswa.org/fileadmin/galleries /Publications/ISWA_Reports/GWMO_summary_web.pdf (retrieved November 10, 2015)

UNESCO Institute for Statistics. (2014). The official source of literacy data. http://www.uis.unesco.org/literacy/Pages /default.aspx (retrieved November 19, 2015)

UNHCR: The UN Refugee Agency. (2015a). Myanmar. *UNHCR.org*. http://www.unhcr.org/pages/49e4877d6.html (retrieved September 29, 2015)

UNHCR: The UN Refugee Agency. (2015b, June 18). Worldwide displacement hits all-time high as war and persecution increase. *UNHCR.org*. http://www.unhcr. org/558193896.html (retrieved December 15, 2015)

Union of Concerned Scientists. (2015, September 1). UCS satellite database. *UCSusa.org*. http://www.ucsusa.org/nuclear -weapons/space-weapons/satellite-database#.Vpz4M1mgymY (retrieved January 20 2016)

United Nations. (1948). *The universal declaration of human rights*. http://www.un.org/en/universal-declaration-human -rights/index.html (retrieved February 5, 2016)

United Nations. (2008, March). United Nations declaration on the rights of indigenous peoples. *UN.org*. http://www.un.org /esa/socdev/unpfii/documents/DRIPS_en.pdf (retrieved December 19, 2015)

United Nations Human Rights. (2009). Witches in the 21st century. *United Nations Office for the High Commissioner for Human Rights*. http://www.ohchr.org/EN/NEWSEVENTS/Pages /Witches21stCentury.aspx (retrieved December 9, 2105)

United Nations Human Rights. (2015). Convention on the rights of the child. *United Nations Office for the High Commissioner for Human Rights*. http://www.ohchr.org/en/professionalinterest /pages/crc.aspx (retrieved November 30, 2015)

United Nations Human Settlements Programme. (2003). *The challenge of slums: Global report on human settlement, 2003*. London: Earthscan Publications.

United Nations World Tourism Organization. (2015). UNWTO Annual Report 2014. http://www2.unwto.org /annualreport2014 (retrieved December 15, 2015)

UN News Centre. (2014, October 29). South Sudan: UN officials welcome launch of campaign to end use of child soldiers. *UN.org*. http://www.un.org/apps/news/story.asp?NewsID=49194# .VmimM2SrTJM (retrieved December 9, 2015)

Ury, W. L. (1982). *Talk out or walk out: The role and control of conflict in a Kentucky coal mine*. PhD dissertation, Harvard University Press.

Ury, W. L. (1993). *Getting past no: Negotiating your way from confrontation.* New York: Bantam.

Ury, W. L. (1999). *Getting to peace: Transforming conflict at home, at work, and in the world.* New York: Viking.

Ury, W. L. (2002, Winter). A global immune system. *Andover Bulletin 95* (2).

Ury, W. L. (2007). *The power of a positive no.* New York: Bantam.

Ury, W. L. (2010, October). The walk from "no" to "yes." *TED Talks.* http://www.ted.com/talks/william_ury (retrieved December 9, 2015)

U.S. Census Bureau. (2012). America's family and living arrangements: 2012. *Census.gov.* https://www.census.gov/hhes/families/data/cps2012.html (retrieved December 29, 2015)

U.S. Census Bureau. (2013). Table C2. Household relationship and living arrangements of children under 18 years, by age and sex: 2013. *Census.gov.* https://www.census.gov/hhes/families/data/cps2013C.html (retrieved November 20, 2015)

U.S. Census Bureau. (2015). Families and living arrangements. *Census.gov.* http://www.census.gov/hhes/families/data/cps2015H.html (retrieved December 22, 2015)

U.S. Department of Health and Human Services. (2015). Child maltreatment. *Children's Bureau.* http://www.acf.hhs.gov/programs/cb/research-data-technology/statistics-research/child-maltreatment (retrieved December 2, 2015)

U.S. Department of Labor. (2015). Wage and hour division (WHD): History of federal minimum wage rates under the Fair Labor Standards Act, 1938–2009. *Dol.gov.* http://www.dol.gov/whd/minwage/chart.htm (retrieved December 18, 2015)

Van Allen, J. (1997). Sitting on a man: Colonialism and the lost political institutions of Igbo women. In R. Grinker & C. Steiner (Eds.), *Perspectives on Africa.* Boston: Blackwell Press.

Van Cott, D. L. (2008). *Radical democracy in the Andes.* Cambridge, UK: Cambridge University Press.

Van Eck, C. (2003). *Purified by blood: Honour killings amongst Turks in the Netherlands.* Amsterdam: Amsterdam University Press.

Van Gennep, A. (1960). *The rites of passage.* Translated by M. Vizedom & G. L. Caffee. Chicago: University of Chicago Press. (orig. 1909)

Van Willigen, J. (1986). *Applied anthropology.* South Hadley, MA: Bergin & Garvey.

Van Willigen, J. (2002). *Applied anthropology: An introduction.* Westport, CT: Bergin & Garvey.

Vera, H. (2011). *The social life of measures: Metrication in the United States and Mexico, 1789–2004.* PhD dissertation, Sociology and Historical Studies, New School for Social Research.

Vidya, R. (2002). Karnataka's unabating kidney trade. *Frontline.* http://www.frontline.in/static/html/fl1907/19070610.htm (retrieved February 5, 2016)

Villmoare, B., Kimbel, W. H., Seyoum, C., Campisano, C. J., DiMaggio, E. N., Rowan, J., Braun, D. R., Arrowsmith, A. R., & Reed, K. E. (2016, March 20). Early *Homo* from 2.8 ma from Ledi-Geraru, Afar, Ethiopia. *Science 347* (6228), 1352–1355.

Vine, D. (2013, May 23). *Tracing Paul Farmer's influence.* Washington, DC: American University, College of Arts & Sciences. http://www.american.edu/cas/news/paul-farmer-influence-in-anthropology.cfm (retrieved January 20, 2016)

Vitali, S., Glattfelder, J. B., & Battiston, S. (2011, October 26). The network of global corporate control. *PloS One 6* (10), e25995.

Vogt, E. Z. (1990). *The Zinacantecos of Mexico: A modern Maya way of life* (2nd ed.). Fort Worth: Holt, Rinehart & Winston.

Wakefield, A. J., et al. (1998). RETRACTED: Ileal-lymphoid-nodular hyperplasia, non-specific colitis, and pervasive developmental disorder in children. *Lancet 351* (9103), 637–641.

Wallace, A. F. C. (1970). *Culture and personality* (2nd ed.). New York: Random House.

Wallace, E., & Hoebel, E. A. (1952). *The Comanches.* Norman: University of Oklahoma Press.

Washington, H. (2006). *Medical apartheid: The dark history of medical experimentation on black Americans from colonial times to the present.* New York: Anchor.

Watson, J. D. (1968). *The double helix: A personal account of the discovery and structure of DNA.* New York: Atheneum.

Weatherford, J. (1988). *Indian givers: How the Indians of the Americas transformed the world.* New York: Ballantine.

Weaver, T. (2002). Gonzalo Aguirre Beltrán: Applied anthropology and indigenous policy. In *The dynamics of applied anthropology in the twentieth century: The Malinowski award papers* (pp. 34–37). Oklahoma City: Society for Applied Anthropology.

Weber, L. (2015, January 23). Your own worst enemy in a negotiation? Look in the mirror. *Wall Street Journal.* http://blogs.wsj.com/atwork/2015/01/23/your-worst-enemy-in-a-negotiation-look-in-the-mirror/ (retrieved January 4, 2016)

Weiner, A. B. (1988). *The Trobrianders of Papua New Guinea.* New York: Holt, Rinehart & Winston.

Wenzel, G. W., & McCartney, A. P. (1996, September). Richard Guy Condon (1952–1995). *Arctic 49* (3), 319–320.

Werner, D. (1990). *Amazon journey.* Englewood Cliffs, NJ: Prentice-Hall.

Wheeler, P. (1993). Human ancestors walked tall, stayed cool. *Natural History 102* (8), 65–66.

Wheelersburg, R. P. (1987). New transportation technology among Swedish Sámi reindeer herders. *Arctic Anthropology 24* (2), 99–116.

Whelehan, P. (1985). Book review: "Incest: A biosocial view." *American Anthropologist 87* (3), 677–678.

White, D. R. (1988). Rethinking polygyny: Co-wives, codes, and cultural systems. *Current Anthropology 29* (4), 529–572.

White, M. (2003, March 25). *Historical atlas of the twentieth century.* http://users.erols.com/mwhite28/20centry.htm (retrieved November 6, 2015)

White, T. (2003). Early hominids—diversity or distortion? *Science 299* (5615), 1994–1997.

White, T. D., Asfaw, B., Beyene, Y., Haile-Selassie, Y., Lovejoy, C. O., Suwa, G., & Woldegabriel, G. (2009, October). *Ardipithecus ramidus* and the paleobiology of early hominoids. *Science 326* (5949), 64, 75–86.

White, T. D. Asfaw, B., DeGusta, D., Gilbert, H., Richards, G. D., Suwa, G., & Howell, F. C. (2003). Pleistocene *Homo sapiens* from the Middle Awash, Ethiopia. *Nature 423* (6941), 742–747.

Whiting, J. W. M., & Child, I. L. (1953). *Child training and personality: A cross-cultural study.* New Haven, CT: Yale University Press.

Whorf, B. L. (1946). The Hopi language, Toreva dialect. In C. Osgood (Ed.), *Linguistic structures of native America* (pp. 158–183). New York: Viking Fund.

Whyte, A. L. H. (2005). Human evolution in Polynesia. *Human Biology 77* (2), 157–177.

"Why the stories are told: Told by Aunty Beryl Carmichael." (2015). http://tom33.global2.vic.edu.au/literacy/ (retrieved November 22, 2015)

Wiley, A. S. (2004). *An ecology of high-altitude infancy: A biocultural perspective.* Cambridge, UK: Cambridge University Press.

Wilford, J. N. (2008, January 18). Pacific Islanders' ancestry emerges in genetic study. *New York Times.* http://www.nytimes.com/2008/01/18/world/asia/18islands.html (retrieved December 4, 2015)

Wilkie, D. S., & Curran, B. (1993). Historical trends in forager and farmer exchange in the Ituri rainforest of northeastern Zaire. *Human Ecology 21* (4), 389–417.

Williams, F. (2005, January 9). Toxic breast milk? *New York Times Magazine.* http://www.nytimes.com/2005/01/09/magazine/toxic-breast-milk.html (retrieved December 16, 2015)

Williams, S. (2003). Tradition and change in the sub-Arctic: Sámi reindeer herding in the modern era. *Scandinavian Studies 75* (2), 228–256.

Williamson, R. K. (1995). The blessed curse: Spirituality and sexual difference as viewed by Euramerican and Native American cultures. *The College News 18* (4).

Wilson, A. C., & Sarich, V. M. (1969). A molecular time scale for human evolution. *Proceedings of the National Academy of Sciences USA 63* (4), 1088–1093.

Winick, C. (Ed.). (1970). *Dictionary of anthropology.* Totowa, NJ: Littlefield, Adams.

Wolf, A. P., & Durham, W. H. (Eds.). (2004). *Inbreeding, incest, and the incest taboo: The state of knowledge at the turn of the century.* Stanford, CA: Stanford University Press.

Wolf, E. R. (1966). *Peasants.* Englewood Cliffs, NJ: Prentice-Hall.

Wolf, E. R. (1982). *Europe and the people without history.* Berkeley: University of California Press.

Wolf, E. R. (1999a). *Envisioning power: Ideologies of dominance and crisis.* Berkeley: University of California Press.

Wolf, E. R. (1999b). *Peasant wars of the twentieth century* (2nd ed.). Norman: University of Oklahoma Press.

Wolf, E. R., & Hansen, E. C. (1972). *The human condition in Latin America.* New York: Oxford University Press.

Wolf, E. R., & Trager, G. I. (1971). Hortense Powdermaker: 1900–1970. *American Anthropologist 73* (3), 783–787.

Wolff, P., & Holmes, K. J. (2011, May/June). Linguistic relativity. *WIRE's Cognitive Science 2* (3), 253–265.

Wolpoff, M., & Caspari, R. (1997). *Race and human evolution.* New York: Simon & Schuster.

Woodford, M. H., Butynski, T. M., & Karesh W. B. (2002). Habituating the great apes: The disease risks. *Oryx 36* (2), 153–160.

Woodward, A. S. (1948). *The earliest Englishman.* London: Watts & Co.

World Bank. (2015a, April 13). Migration and remittances briefs. *WorldBank.org.* http://econ.worldbank.org/WBSITE /EXTERNAL/EXTDEC/EXTDECPROSPECTS/0,,contentM DK:21125572~pagePK:64165401~piPK:64165026~theSit ePK:476883,00.html (retrieved December 1, 2015)

World Bank. (2015b). Poverty and equity data. *WorldBank.org.* http://povertydata.worldbank.org/poverty/home/ (retrieved December 15, 2015)

World Bank. (2015c). Global monitoring report. *WorldBank .org.* http://www.worldbank.org/en/publication/global -monitoring-report (retrieved January 20, 2016)

World Bank, World Development Indicators. (2016). GDP at market prices (current US$). *Worldbank.org.* http:// data.worldbank.org/indicator/NY.GDP.MKTP.CD (retrieved January 20, 2016)

World Food Programme. (2015). Hunger statistics. *Wfp.org.* http://www.wfp.org/hunger/stats (retrieved January 20, 2016)

World Health Organization, Preamble to the Constitution. (1948). WHO definition of health. *World Health Organization.* http://www.who.int/about/definition/en /print.html (retrieved November 11, 2015)

World Health Organization. (2014, September). Children: Reducing mortality. Fact sheet no. 178. *World Health Organization.* http://www.who.int/mediacentre/factsheets /fs178/en/ (retrieved November 11, 2015)

World Health Organization. (2015a). Global strategy for infant and young child feeding. *World Health Organization.* http://www.who.int/nutrition/topics/global_strategy/en/ (retrieved November 19, 2015)

World Health Organization. (2015b, January). Obesity and overweight. Fact sheet no. 311. *WHO.int.* http://www.who.int /mediacentre/factsheets/fs311/en/ (retrieved January 20, 2016)

World Travel & Tourism Council. (2015). Benchmarking 2015. www.wttc.org (retrieved November 30, 2015)

World Watch Institute. (2015). Vision for a sustainable world. *Worldwatch.org.* www.worldwatch.org (retrieved December 20, 2015)

Worsley, P. (1957). *The trumpet shall sound: A study of "cargo" cults in Melanesia.* London: Macgibbon & Kee.

Worthman, C. M. (1999). Evolutionary perspectives on the onset of puberty. In W. R. Trevathan, E. O. Smith, & J. J. McKenna (Eds.), *Evolutionary medicine* (pp. 135–163). New York: Oxford University Press.

Wrangham, R., & Peterson, D. (1996). *Demonic males.* Boston: Houghton Mifflin.

Wu, X., & Poirier, F. E. (1995). *Human evolution in China.* New York: Oxford University Press.

Wyckoff-Baird, B. (1996, Summer). Indicators from Ju/'hoan Bushmen in Namibia. *Cultural Survival.* http://www .culturalsurvival.org/ourpublications/csq/article/indicators -juhoan-bushmen-namibia (retrieved November 19, 2015)

Yates, D. (2011). *Archaeological practice and political change: Transitions and transformations in the use of the past in nationalist, neoliberal and indigenous Bolivia.* PhD dissertation, Department of Archaeology, Cambridge, UK: University of Cambridge.

Yehuda, R., & Bierer, L. M. (2008). Transgenerational transmission of cortisol and PTSD. *Progress in Brain Research 167*, 121–135.

Yehuda, R., Daskalakis, N., Bierer, L., Bader, H., Klengel, T., Holsober, F., & Binder, E. (2015). Holocaust exposure induced intergenerational effects on FKBP5 methylation. *Biological Psychiatry.* doi: 10.1016/j.biopsych .2015.08.005 (retrieved November 10, 2015)

Young, W. C. (2000). Kimball award winner. *Anthropology News 41* (8), 29.

Yuhas, A. (2015, March 11). Archaeologists condemn *National Geographic* over claims of Honduran "lost cities." *The Guardian.* http://www.theguardian.com/world/2015/mar/11 /honduras-lost-cities-open-letter-national-geographic-report (retrieved November 3, 2015)

Zeder, M. A., & Hesse, B. (2000, March 24). The initial domestication of goats (*Capra hircus*) in the Zagros Mountains 10,000 years ago. *Science 287* (5461), 2254–2257.

Zilhão, J. (2000). Fate of the Neandertals. *Archaeology 53* (4), 24–31.

Index

Note: Italic page numbers indicate charts, figures, and maps.